Nineteenth-Century Literature Criticism

Guide to Gale Literary Criticism Series

For criticism on	Consult these Gale series
Authors now living or who died after December 31, 1999	*CONTEMPORARY LITERARY CRITICISM (CLC)*
Authors who died between 1900 and 1999	*TWENTIETH-CENTURY LITERARY CRITICISM (TCLC)*
Authors who died between 1800 and 1899	*NINETEENTH-CENTURY LITERATURE CRITICISM (NCLC)*
Authors who died between 1400 and 1799	*LITERATURE CRITICISM FROM 1400 TO 1800 (LC)* *SHAKESPEAREAN CRITICISM (SC)*
Authors who died before 1400	*CLASSICAL AND MEDIEVAL LITERATURE CRITICISM (CMLC)*
Authors of books for children and young adults	*CHILDREN'S LITERATURE REVIEW (CLR)*
Dramatists	*DRAMA CRITICISM (DC)*
Poets	*POETRY CRITICISM (PC)*
Short story writers	*SHORT STORY CRITICISM (SSC)*
Literary topics and movements	*HARLEM RENAISSANCE: A GALE CRITICAL COMPANION (HR)* *THE BEAT GENERATION: A GALE CRITICAL COMPANION (BG)* *FEMINISM IN LITERATURE: A GALE CRITICAL COMPANION (FL)* *GOTHIC LITERATURE: A GALE CRITICAL COMPANION (GL)*
Asian American writers of the last two hundred years	*ASIAN AMERICAN LITERATURE (AAL)*
Black writers of the past two hundred years	*BLACK LITERATURE CRITICISM (BLC)* *BLACK LITERATURE CRITICISM SUPPLEMENT (BLCS)* *BLACK LITERATURE CRITICISM: CLASSIC AND EMERGING AUTHORS SINCE 1950 (BLC-2)*
Hispanic writers of the late nineteenth and twentieth centuries	*HISPANIC LITERATURE CRITICISM (HLC)* *HISPANIC LITERATURE CRITICISM SUPPLEMENT (HLCS)*
Native North American writers and orators of the eighteenth, nineteenth, and twentieth centuries	*NATIVE NORTH AMERICAN LITERATURE (NNAL)*
Major authors from the Renaissance to the present	*WORLD LITERATURE CRITICISM, 1500 TO THE PRESENT (WLC)* *WORLD LITERATURE CRITICISM SUPPLEMENT (WLCS)*

ISSN 0732-1864

Volume 218

Nineteenth-Century Literature Criticism

Criticism of the
Works of Novelists, Philosophers, and Other
Creative Writers Who Died between 1800
and 1899, from the First Published Critical
Appraisals to Current Evaluations

Kathy D. Darrow
Project Editor

GALE
CENGAGE Learning·

Detroit • New York • San Francisco • New Haven, Conn • Waterville, Maine • London

Nineteenth-Century Literature Criticism, Vol. 218

Project Editor: Kathy D. Darrow

Editorial: Dana Barnes, Elizabeth Cranston, Kristen Dorsch, Jeffrey W. Hunter, Jelena O. Krstović, Michelle Lee, Thomas J. Schoenberg, Lawrence J. Trudeau

Data Capture: Katrina D. Coach, Gwen Tucker

Rights and Acquisitions: Jacqueline Flowers, Barb McNeil, Timothy Sisler

Composition and Electronic Capture: Gary Oudersluys

Manufacturing: Cynde Lentz

Product Manager: Janet Witalec

For product information and technology assistance, contact us at
Gale Customer Support, 1-800-877-4253.
For permission to use material from this text or product,
submit all requests online at **www.cengage.com/permissions.**
Further permissions questions can be emailed to
permissionrequest@cengage.com

Gale
27500 Drake Rd.
Farmington Hills, MI, 48331-3535

LIBRARY OF CONGRESS CATALOG CARD NUMBER 84-643008

ISBN-13: 978-1-4144-3852-8
ISBN-10: 1-4144-3852-4

ISSN 0732-1864

Printed in the United States of America
1 2 3 4 5 6 7 13 12 11 10 09

Contents

Preface vii

Acknowledgments xi

Literary Criticism Series Advisory Board xiii

Preface

Since its inception in 1981, *Nineteenth-Century Literature Criticism* (*NCLC*) has been a valuable resource for students and librarians seeking critical commentary on writers of this transitional period in world history. Designated an "Outstanding Reference Source" by the American Library Association with the publication of is first volume, *NCLC* has since been purchased by over 6,000 school, public, and university libraries. The series has covered more than 500 authors representing 38 nationalities and over 28,000 titles. No other reference source has surveyed the critical reaction to nineteenth-century authors and literature as thoroughly as *NCLC*.

Scope of the Series

NCLC is designed to introduce students and advanced readers to the authors of the nineteenth century and to the most significant interpretations of these authors' works. The great poets, novelists, short story writers, playwrights, and philosophers of this period are frequently studied in high school and college literature courses. By organizing and reprinting commentary written on these authors, *NCLC* helps students develop valuable insight into literary history, promotes a better understanding of the texts, and sparks ideas for papers and assignments. Each entry in *NCLC* presents a comprehensive survey of an author's career or an individual work of literature and provides the user with a multiplicity of interpretations and assessments. Such variety allows students to pursue their own interests; furthermore, it fosters an awareness that literature is dynamic and responsive to many different opinions.

Every fourth volume of *NCLC* is devoted to literary topics that cannot be covered under the author approach used in the rest of the series. Such topics include literary movements, prominent themes in nineteenth-century literature, literary reaction to political and historical events, significant eras in literary history, prominent literary anniversaries, and the literatures of cultures that are often overlooked by English-speaking readers.

NCLC continues the survey of criticism of world literature begun by Gale's *Contemporary Literary Criticism* (*CLC*) and *Twentieth-Century Literary Criticism* (*TCLC*).

Organization of the Book

An *NCLC* entry consists of the following elements:

- The **Author Heading** cites the name under which the author most commonly wrote, followed by birth and death dates. Also located here are any name variations under which an author wrote, including transliterated forms for authors whose native languages use nonroman alphabets. If the author wrote consistently under a pseudonym, the pseudonym will be listed in the author heading and the author's actual name given in parenthesis on the first line of the biographical and critical information. Uncertain birth or death dates are indicated by question marks. Single-work entries are preceded by a heading that consists of the most common form of the title in English translation (if applicable) and the original date of composition.

- The **Introduction** contains background information that introduces the reader to the author, work, or topic that is the subject of the entry.

- The list of **Principal Works** is ordered chronologically by date of first publication and lists the most important works by the author. The genre and publication date of each work is given. In the case of foreign authors whose works have been translated into English, the list will focus primarily on twentieth-century translations, selecting those works most commonly considered the best by critics. Unless otherwise indicated, dramas are dated by first performance, not first publication. Lists of **Representative Works** by different authors appear with topic entries.

- Reprinted **Criticism** is arranged chronologically in each entry to provide a useful perspective on changes in critical evaluation over time. The critic's name and the date of composition or publication of the critical work are given at the beginning of each piece of criticism. Unsigned criticism is preceded by the title of the source in which it appeared. All titles by the author featured in the text are printed in boldface type. Footnotes are reprinted at the end of each essay or excerpt. In the case of excerpted criticism, only those footnotes that pertain to the excerpted texts are included. Criticism in topic entries is arranged chronologically under a variety of subheadings to facilitate the study of different aspects of the topic.

- A complete **Bibliographical Citation** of the original essay or book precedes each piece of criticism.

- Critical essays are prefaced by brief **Annotations** explicating each piece.

- An annotated bibliography of **Further Reading** appears at the end of each entry and suggests resources for additional study. In some cases, significant essays for which the editors could not obtain reprint rights are included here. Boxed material following the further reading list provides references to other biographical and critical sources on the author in series published by Gale.

Indexes

Each volume of *NCLC* contains a **Cumulative Author Index** listing all authors who have appeared in a wide variety of reference sources published by Gale, including *NCLC*. A complete list of these sources is found facing the first page of the Author Index. The index also includes birth and death dates and cross references between pseudonyms and actual names.

A **Cumulative Nationality Index** lists all authors featured in *NCLC* by nationality, followed by the number of the *NCLC* volume in which their entry appears.

A **Cumulative Topic Index** lists the literary themes and topics treated in the series as well as in *Classical and Medieval Literature Criticism, Literature Criticism from 1400 to 1800, Twentieth-Century Literary Criticism,* and the *Contemporary Literary Criticism* Yearbook, which was discontinued in 1998.

An alphabetical **Title Index** accompanies each volume of *NCLC*, with the exception of the Topics volumes. Listings of titles by authors covered in the given volume are followed by the author's name and the corresponding page numbers where the titles are discussed. English translations of foreign titles and variations of titles are cross-referenced to the title under which a work was originally published. Titles of novels, dramas, nonfiction books, and poetry, short story, or essay collections are printed in italics, while individual poems, short stories, and essays are printed in roman type within quotation marks.

In response to numerous suggestions from librarians, Gale also produces an annual paperbound edition of the *NCLC* cumulative title index. This annual cumulation, which alphabetically lists all titles reviewed in the series, is available to all customers. Additional copies of this index are available upon request. Librarians and patrons will welcome this separate index; it saves shelf space, is easy to use, and is recyclable upon receipt of the next edition.

Citing *Nineteenth-Century Literature Criticism*

When citing criticism reprinted in the Literary Criticism Series, students should provide complete bibliographic information so that the cited essay can be located in the original print or electronic source. Students who quote directly from reprinted criticism may use any accepted bibliographic format, such as University of Chicago Press style or Modern Language Association style.

The examples below follow recommendations for preparing a bibliography set forth in *The Chicago Manual of Style*, 14th ed. (Chicago: The University of Chicago Press, 1993); the first example pertains to material drawn from periodicals, the second to material reprinted from books:

Franklin, J. Jeffrey. "The Victorian Discourse of Gambling: Speculations on *Middlemarch* and *The Duke's Children.*" *ELH* 61, no. 4 (winter 1994): 899-921. Reprinted in *Nineteenth-Century Literature Criticism.* Vol. 168, edited by Jessica Bomarito and Russel Whitaker, 39-51. Detroit: Thomson Gale, 2006.

Frank, Joseph. "*The Gambler*: A Study in Ethnopsychology." In *Freedom and Responsibility in Russian Literature: Essays in Honor of Robert Louis Jackson,* edited by Elizabeth Cheresh Allen and Gary Saul Morson, 69-85. Evanston, Ill.: Northwestern University Press, 1995. Reprinted in *Nineteenth-Century Literature Criticism.* Vol. 168, edited by Jessica Bomarito and Russel Whitaker, 75-84. Detroit: Thomson Gale, 2006.

The examples below follow recommendations for preparing a works cited list set forth in the *MLA Handbook for Writers of Research Papers,* 6th ed. (New York: The Modern Language Association of America, 2003); the first example pertains to material drawn from periodicals, the second to material reprinted from books:

Franklin, J. Jeffrey. "The Victorian Discourse of Gambling: Speculations on *Middlemarch* and *The Duke's Children.*" *ELH* 61.4 (winter 1994): 899-921. Reprinted in *Nineteenth-Century Literature Criticism.* Eds. Jessica Bomarito and Russel Whitaker. Vol. 168. Detroit: Thomson Gale, 2006. 39-51.

Frank, Joseph. "*The Gambler*: A Study in Ethnopsychology." *Freedom and Responsibility in Russian Literature: Essays in Honor of Robert Louis Jackson.* Eds. Elizabeth Cheresh Allen and Gary Saul Morson. Evanston, Ill.: Northwestern University Press, 1995. 69-85. Reprinted in *Nineteenth-Century Literature Criticism.* Eds. Jessica Bomarito and Russel Whitaker. Vol. 168. Detroit: Thomson Gale, 2006. 75-84.

Suggestions are Welcome

Readers who wish to suggest new features, topics, or authors to appear in future volumes, or who have other suggestions or comments are cordially invited to call, write, or fax the Associate Product Manager:

Product Manager, Literary Criticism Series
Gale
27500 Drake Road
Farmington Hills, MI 48331-3535
1-800-347-4253 (GALE)
Fax: 248-699-8884

Acknowledgments

The editors wish to thank the copyright holders of the criticism included in this volume and the permissions managers of many book and magazine publishing companies for assisting us in securing reproduction rights. Following is a list of the copyright holders who have granted us permission to reproduce material in this volume of *NCLC*. Every effort has been made to trace copyright, but if omissions have been made, please let us know.

COPYRIGHTED MATERIAL IN *NCLC*, VOLUME 218, WAS REPRODUCED FROM THE FOLLOWING PERIODICALS:

American Literature, v. 71, December, 1999. Copyright © 1999 Duke University Press. All rights reserved. Used by permission of the publisher.—*American Quarterly,* v. 48, September, 1996. Copyright © 1996 The Johns Hopkins University Press. Reproduced by permission.—*American Transcendental Quarterly,* v. 22, June, 2008. Copyright © 2008 by The University of Rhode Island. Reproduced by permission.—*boundary 2,* v. 25, spring, 1998. Copyright © 1998 Duke University Press. All rights reserved. Used by permission of the publisher.—*Children's Literature,* v. 36, 2008. Copyright © 2008 The Johns Hopkins University Press. Reproduced by permission.—*College Literature,* v. 32, winter, 2005. Copyright © 2005 by West Chester University. Reproduced by permission.—*French Historical Studies,* v. 17, spring, 1992. Copyright © 1992 by the Society for French Historical Studies. All rights reserved. Used by permission of the publisher.—*Frontiers: A Journal of Women Studies,* v. 19, 1998. Copyright © 1998 by Frontiers Editorial Collective. Reproduced by permission of the University of Nebraska Press.—*Journal of the History of Ideas,* v. 57, October, 1996. Copyright © 1996 by Journal of the History of Ideas, Inc. Reprinted by permission of the University of Pennsylvania Press.—*New Literary History,* v. 26, spring, 1995. Copyright © 1995 The Johns Hopkins University Press. Reproduced by permission.—*Nineteenth-Century Literature,* v. 60, December, 2005. Copyright © 2006 by The Regents of the University of California. Reproduced by permission.—*Rhetoric Society Quarterly,* v. 13, winter, 1983. Copyright © 1983, Rhetoric Society of America. Republished with permission of Rhetoric Society Quarterly, conveyed through Copyright Clearance Center, Inc.—*Studies in English Literature, 1500-1900,* v. 4, autumn, 1964; v. 13, autumn, 1973 Copyright © 1964, 1973 William Marsh Rice University. Both reproduced by permission.—*Texas Studies in Literature and Language,* v. 41, fall, 1999 for "Sentimental Discourse and the Bisexual Erotics of *Work*" by Gregory Eiselein. Copyright © 1999 by the University of Texas Press. All rights reserved. Reproduced by permission of the publisher and the author.—*Victorian Poetry,* January 1963, for "Dover Revisited: The Wordsworthian Matrix in the Poetry of Matthew Arnold" by U. C. Knoepflmacher. Copyright 1963 by West Virginia University. Reproduced by permission of the author.

COPYRIGHTED MATERIAL IN *NCLC*, VOLUME 218, WAS REPRODUCED FROM THE FOLLOWING BOOKS:

Allott, Miriam. From "Matthew Arnold: 'All One and Continuous,'" in *The Victorian Experience: The Poets.* Edited by Richard A. Levine. Ohio University Press, 1982. Reproduced by permission.—Anderson, Amanda. From *The Powers of Distance: Cosmopolitanism and the Cultivation of Detachment.* Princeton University Press, 2001. Copyright © 2001 by Princeton University Press. Reprinted by permission of Princeton University Press.—Blair, Kirstie. From *Victorian Poetry and the Culture of the Heart.* Clarendon Press, 2006. Copyright © 2006 Kirstie Blair. All rights reserved. Reproduced by permission of Oxford University Press.—Campbell, Kate. From "Matthew Arnold and Publicity: A Modern Critic as Journalist," in *Journalism, Literature and Modernity: From Hazlitt to Modernism.* Edited by Kate Campbell. Edinburgh University Press, 2000. Copyright © Kate Campbell. Reproduced by permission. www.euppublishing.com—Herzen, Alexandre. From *From the Other Shore, and The Russian People and Socialism.* Translated by Richard Wollheim. Weidenfeld and Nicolson, a division of The Orion Publishing Group, London, 1956. Reproduced by permission.—Hewlett, H. G. From "The Poems of Mr. Matthew Arnold," in *Matthew Arnold: The Poetry: The Critical Heritage.* Edited by Carl Dawson. Routledge & Kegan Paul, 1973. Copyright © 1973 Carl Dawson. Reproduced by permission of the publisher and the author.—Madden, William A. From *Matthew Arnold: A Study of the Aesthetic Temperament in Victorian England.* Indiana University Press, 1967. Copyright © 1967 by Indiana University Press. All rights reserved. Reproduced by permission.—Marks, Emerson R. From *Taming the Chaos: English Poetic Diction Theory Since the Renaissance.* Wayne State University Press, 1998. Copyright © 1998 by Wayne State University Press. All rights reserved. Reproduced with permission of the Wayne State University Press and the author.—Muller, Jerry Z. From *The Mind and the Market: Capitalism in Mod-

Gale Literature Product Advisory Board

The members of the Gale Literature Product Advisory Board—reference librarians from public and academic library systems—represent a cross-section of our customer base and offer a variety of informed perspectives on both the presentation and content of our literature products. Advisory board members assess and define such quality issues as the relevance, currency, and usefulness of the author coverage, critical content, and literary topics included in our series; evaluate the layout, presentation, and general quality of our printed volumes; provide feedback on the criteria used for selecting authors and topics covered in our series; provide suggestions for potential enhancements to our series; identify any gaps in our coverage of authors or literary topics, recommending authors or topics for inclusion; analyze the appropriateness of our content and presentation for various user audiences, such as high school students, undergraduates, graduate students, librarians, and educators; and offer feedback on any proposed changes/enhancements to our series. We wish to thank the following advisors for their advice throughout the year.

Louisa May Alcott
1832-1888

American novelist and short story, sketch, fairy tale, and letter writer.

The following entry presents an overview of Alcott's life and works. For discussion of the novel *Little Women* (1868-69), see *NCLC*, Volume 83; for additional discussion of Alcott's complete career, see *NCLC*, Volumes 6 and 58.

INTRODUCTION

Louisa May Alcott is among the most celebrated authors of nineteenth-century American literature. Her classic, *Little Women; or, Meg, Jo, Beth and Amy* (1868-69), is considered a landmark work of juvenile fiction and was one of the first novels to portray adolescent characters in a complex and realistic fashion. Over the years *Little Women* has influenced a wide range of women authors and intellectuals, most famously Simone de Beauvoir; in *Memoirs of a Dutiful Daughter* (1959), de Beauvoir claimed to have been first inspired to write by the character of Jo March. Alcott eventually wrote several sequels to the novel, the most prominent among them *Little Men: Life at Plumfield with Jo's Boys* (1871). In the twentieth century *Little Women* inspired several film and stage adaptations. Although best known as the author of novels for children and young adults, Alcott also produced works in a number of other genres over the course of her prolific career. *Hospital Sketches* (1863), based on personal correspondence, reflects Alcott's sensitive eye for human suffering, as well as her passion for progressive causes. Indeed, during her later career Alcott used her fame to become an outspoken public advocate for a variety of important issues, central among them the woman suffrage movement. While most commentators consider Alcott to be predominantly a children's author, feminist scholars and critics in recent decades have begun to evaluate her broader influence on modern ideas concerning female identity, traditional gender roles, and the relationship between literature and political/social reform.

BIOGRAPHICAL INFORMATION

Alcott was born in Germantown, Pennsylvania, on November 29, 1832, and spent most of her childhood in Boston and Concord, Massachusetts. Her father, Amos Bronson Alcott, was a respected educator, philosopher, and author and was a central figure in the transcendentalist movement; Alcott's mother, Abigail May Alcott, was descended from a prominent Boston family. The second of four girls, Alcott demonstrated a willful, independent spirit at a young age, as well as a lively imagination and intelligence. Alcott began writing during her early years, coauthoring short plays with her older sister, Anna, which they performed for family and friends.

By most biographical accounts, the Alcott household provided a nurturing, warm atmosphere, and Alcott's parents placed a high premium on intellectual achievement and moral virtue. Alcott and her sisters were educated at home by their father; their school days were characterized by a blend of formal learning, household chores, and imaginative play. Although Bronson Alcott's pedagogy was unorthodox, he held his daughters to fairly rigid standards; at her father's insistence Alcott began keeping a journal as a young girl, and she read widely. Alcott benefited from her interactions with her father's friends and acquaintances, among them Ralph Waldo Emerson, Henry David Thoreau, and Margaret Fuller, who helped broaden the precocious young girl's knowledge of literature, philosophy, and the natural sciences. Throughout these years, Alcott's parents also educated their daughters on a range of progressive social issues, particularly abolitionism and woman suffrage. These early experiences with causes of social justice made an indelible mark on Alcott's political ideals, and she remained committed to the reform movement throughout her life.

While they held a respectable place in Concord society, the Alcott family was far from ordinary, largely because of Bronson Alcott's revolutionary and uncompromising political ideals. His vehement eschewal of money and conventional employment often placed his family in financial peril, and much of Alcott's youth was defined by instability and economic hardship. The family's difficulties reached a low point in 1843, when Bronson Alcott attempted to establish a utopian community called Fruitlands in the central Massachusetts town of Harvard. The community failed to survive its first year, instilling in Alcott a profound skepticism toward her father's principles. Decades later, Alcott reflected on her experiences at Fruitlands in the satirical short story "Transcendental Wild Oats," published in the *Independent* on December 18, 1873.

As her family's financial situation became increasingly precarious, Alcott began taking odd jobs as a means of contributing money to the household, working for brief periods as a teacher, a private tutor, and a household servant. In her late teens she also began writing, selling her first poem to *Peterson's Magazine* in 1851. Her first book, the fairy tale collection *Flower Fables,* appeared in 1855. Over the next several years Alcott also authored a series of sensational short stories, which she published serially under the pseudonym A. M. Barnard. These stories quickly gained popularity and earned Alcott some much-needed income; her authorship of the works remained unknown during her lifetime, however, and wasn't established among scholars until the twentieth century. Alcott's younger sister, Elizabeth, died of scarlet fever in 1858; that same year her older sister, Anna, married.

In 1862, during the Civil War, Alcott moved to Washington, D.C., where she worked as a nurse in a hospital for Union soldiers. During this time she wrote frequent letters to her parents that later became the basis of *Hospital Sketches.* While working at the hospital Alcott contracted typhoid fever; the disease left her bedridden for several months and ultimately led to serious health problems that plagued her for the rest of her life. In 1864, a year after the publication of *Hospital Sketches,* Alcott produced two new works of fiction: *The Rose Family: A Fairy Tale* and the story collection *On Picket Duty, and Other Tales.* Her first novel, *Moods,* was also published in 1864. While *Moods* proved popular among readers, it elicited harsh criticism from reviewers, who regarded the novel's depiction of a couple's troubled marriage as immoral. Shortly after the novel came out, Alcott traveled to Europe, returning to the United States in 1866. Throughout this period, she regularly published her short fiction in magazines.

In 1867 Alcott took on the editorship of the children's magazine *Merry's Museum*; she also became the magazine's principle contributor. Around this time Thomas Niles, an editor at the Boston publisher Roberts Brothers, suggested that Alcott try her hand at writing a novel for girls. She began the project the following spring, drawing inspiration from her own family and her childhood in Concord. The result of her efforts, *Little Women; or, Meg, Jo, Beth and Amy,* was published in two volumes in 1868 and 1869. The novel caused an immediate sensation among both readers and critics, establishing Alcott as one of America's preeminent novelists. A new novel, *An Old-Fashioned Girl,* was published in two installments in *Merry's Museum* in 1870; the following year *Little Men: Life at Plumfield with Jo's Boys,* a sequel to *Little Women,* was published

Launched to nationwide fame by the success of her *Little Women* novels, Alcott produced a voluminous body of novels, story collections, and other works over the remaining decade and a half of her life. In 1872 she published the first two volumes of her popular *Aunt Jo's Scrap-Bag* collection; four more volumes of the series would appear between 1874 and 1882. During the first half of the 1870s, the original second volume of *Little Women* was republished in three separate editions, each time with a different title: *Little Women Wedded* (1872), *Little Women Married* (1873), and *Nice Wives* (1875). Other notable works from Alcott's later career include *Eight Cousins; or, The Aunt-Hill* (1875) and *Rose in Bloom* (1876), which chronicle the life of a young heiress, Rose Campbell; *Sparkles for Bright Eyes* (1879); and *Jack and Jill: A Village Story* (1880). In 1882, Alcott published a revised edition of her novel *Moods,* and a story collection, *Spinning-Wheel Stories,* appeared in 1884. Alcott completed *Jo's Boys, and How They Turned Out,* a sequel to *Little Men,* in 1886. Although none of these works achieved the popularity of *Little Women,* they continued to appeal to large audiences, and Alcott remained among the nation's most recognizable, and beloved, fiction authors until her death.

Alcott died in Roxbury, Massachusetts, on March 6, 1888, two days after the death of her father. She was buried in the Sleepy Hollow Cemetery in Concord. A new edition of *Little Women,* titled *Little Women and Good Wives,* was published posthumously in 1895.

MAJOR WORKS

Alcott remains most famous for *Little Women.* Semi-autobiographical in nature, the novel was based largely on Alcott's experiences growing up in Concord; indeed, the book's central characters, the March girls, are modeled closely after Alcott and her own sisters. In the nineteenth century most reviewers and readers hailed the work for its perceptive characterizations of adolescent girls, as well as for its tacit reinforcement of traditional values concerning marriage and domesticity. Many modern scholars, however, have identified a central tension in the novel between the idealized expectations imposed on the March sisters as they enter adulthood and the headstrong, almost defiant individuality of their childhood selves. In her first sequel to the novel, *Little Men: Life at Plumfield with Jo's Boys,* Alcott explored many of the themes introduced in *Little Women*: the book chronicles the coming of age of a group of boys and girls attending an unorthodox school. The work is particularly noteworthy for its depictions of progressive educational methods, and it is generally considered to be a testament to the lasting influence of Bronson Alcott's pedagogy on his daughter's intellectual life. *Eight Cousins; or, The Aunt-Hill* portrays the social and psychological education of a young orphan living with her wealthy aunts in Boston, a story that is continued in *Rose in Bloom.*

Though she found popular success as an author of juvenile fiction, Alcott's other works reflect a wider breadth of insight and sensibility. *Hospital Sketches* is noteworthy for its highly objective, dispassionate prose style, as well as for its sardonic wit. Late in her career, Alcott published "Transcendental Wild Oats," a story inspired by her father's failed efforts to launch the utopian community at Fruitlands. The work is valuable both as an illustration of Alcott's talent for satire and as a historical document outlining some of the principal tenets of political idealism in mid-nineteenth-century American society. In addition to her writings in mainstream genres, during her early career Alcott also authored a number of sensational thrillers. These pseudonymous works were later rediscovered by prominent Alcott scholar Madeleine B. Stern and have been published in various editions since the late twentieth century, notably in *Behind a Mask: The Unknown Thrillers of Louisa May Alcott* (1975).

CRITICAL RECEPTION

During her lifetime Alcott was among the most popular novelists in the United States. Critical responses to her early works, particularly *Hospital Sketches* and *Moods*, were generally very positive. Some commentators, on the other hand, expressed serious reservations about her ability to write realistic fiction. Reviewing *Moods* for the July 1865 issue of the *North American Review* (vol. 101, no. 208), Henry James discussed what he perceived to be an unusual tension underlying the work between "the author's ignorance of human nature, and her self-confidence in spite of this ignorance." Though James criticized Alcott for attempting to write about subjects she didn't understand, he also lauded the "beauty and vigor" of her imagination and described her talent as "above the average." Responses to *Little Women* were almost universally favorable. A reviewer for the *New Eclectic Magazine* (vol. 4; January 1869) particularly praised Alcott's depictions of the March sisters, calling them "noble girls" with a "perfect simplicity and freedom" in their interactions with boys and men. Many commentators were as intrigued by the novel as a social phenomenon as they were by its literary merit. In the April 1869 edition of the *Southern Review,* one critic responded to the work's publication by asserting that it was an "unmistakable sign of returning health in the taste of the juvenile American, that simple stories like this are in such demand." Writing in the July 1869 issue of the *Galaxy,* another reviewer (alluding to the widespread appeal of Alcott's work among readers) acknowledged that the novel's characters had already become "bosom friends to hundreds of other little women" across the country.

Many twentieth-century scholars and critics, while acknowledging the enduring appeal of Alcott's writings among readers, have come to regard her fiction as sentimental and moralistic. While some commentators, notably G. K. Chesterton, welcomed the ethical underpinnings of Alcott's work, others found her approach to moral issues simplistic and devoid of real substance. Critiquing *Little Women* in her essay "Miss Alcott's New England," published in *Modes and Morals* (1920), Katharine Fuller Gerould complained that she had not encountered a work "so blatantly full of morality" while simultaneously "so empty of religion." Other critics, notably Elizabeth Vincent, contended that Alcott's novel actually exerted a negative impact on young girls. In her essay "Subversive Miss Alcott," published in the *New Republic* on October 22, 1924, Vincent called the work a "pernicious influence," particularly in the manner in which it pandered to the "natural depraved taste for moralizing" typical of little girls; Vincent concluded her critique by calling on readers to censor the book in order to protect their daughters against the "subversions of the past." By the mid-twentieth century, however, most critics had begun to shift their focus away from questions of morality in Alcott's writings, assessing instead her place within the broader framework of nineteenth-century domestic fiction. In the decades following World War II, Madeleine B. Stern, a rare book dealer who developed a lifelong passion for Alcott's work, authored several landmark studies dedicated to the author's career; Stern's most influential critical writings are included in the essay collection *Louisa May Alcott: From Blood and Thunder to Hearth and Home* (1998). Important criticism from the early twenty-first century includes Stephanie Foote's "Resentful *Little Women*: Gender and Class Feeling in Louisa May Alcott," which examines Alcott's depictions of female emotion in the novel; and Sara Hackenberg's "Plots and Counterplots: The Defense of Sensational Fiction in Louisa May Alcott's 'Behind a Mask,'" which analyzes themes of female self-determination and creative freedom in Alcott's pseudonymously published thrillers.

PRINCIPAL WORKS

Flower Fables (fairy tales) 1855
Hospital Sketches (sketches) 1863
Moods (novel) 1864
On Picket Duty, and Other Tales (short stories) 1864
The Rose Family: A Fairy Tale (fairy tale) 1864
Morning-Glories, and Other Stories (short stories) 1867
The Mysterious Key, and What It Opened (novel) 1867
Little Women; or, Meg, Jo, Beth and Amy. 2 vols. (novel) 1868-69; volume two republished as *Little Women Wedded,* 1872; as *Little Women Married,* 1873; and as *Nice Wives,* 1875; both volumes republished as *Little Women and Good Wives,* 1895; volume one republished as *Little Women: Four Funny Sisters,* 1991

An Old-Fashioned Girl (novel) 1870

Little Men: Life at Plumfield with Jo's Boys (novel) 1871

Aunt Jo's Scrap-Bag. 6 vols. (short stories) 1872-82

Work: A Story of Experience (novel) 1873; published in journal *Christian Union*

"Transcendental Wild Oats" (short story) 1873; published in journal *The Independent*

Eight Cousins; or, The Aunt-Hill (novel) 1875

Rose in Bloom (novel) 1876

Sparkles for Bright Eyes (novel) 1879

Jack and Jill: A Village Story (novel) 1880

Spinning-Wheel Stories (short stories) 1884

Jo's Boys, and How They Turned Out (novel) 1886

Louisa May Alcott: Her Life, Letters, and Journals (letters and journals) 1889

Behind a Mask: The Unknown Thrillers of Louisa May Alcott (novellas) 1975

The Girlhood Diary of Louisa May Alcott, 1843-1846: Writings of a Young Author (diary) 2001

CRITICISM

Beverly Lyon Clark (essay date spring 1995)

SOURCE: Clark, Beverly Lyon. "Domesticating the School Story, Regendering a Genre: Alcott's *Little Men.*" *New Literary History* 26, no. 2 (spring 1995): 323-42.

[*In the following essay, Clark analyzes Alcott's deconstruction of conventional gender codes in the novel* Little Men. *Clark argues that, in domesticating certain elements of the schoolboy novel, Alcott effectively reinvents the traditional symbolic and narrative underpinnings of the genre.*]

One of the signs that children's literature is gaining respectability is the increasing attention paid to Louisa May Alcott in prestigious venues, as feminists negotiate between an early love for her work and subsequent misgivings. Since 1990, articles on Alcott have appeared in *Signs, American Literature,* and *New Literary History.* In the latter, Catharine R. Stimpson explores her passionate admiration for **Little Women** in the framework of theorizing the paracanon, works that (some) people love, the children's canon becoming the adults' paracanon (in a move that simultaneously creates space for children's literature and reinscribes it as subordinate).[1] So far, however, very little attention has been paid to **Little Men: Life at Plumfield with Jo's Boys** (1871), where Alcott has shifted her focus from family to school—shifted to a setting where a greater measure of

rebelliousness was possible, certainly not altogether out of the question. Furthermore, in writing this school story, and in crossing both genders and generations, Alcott destabilized the conventional codes—deconstructing and regendering, even re-generating, the genre.

The norms for the genre had been established in 1857 by Thomas Hughes's *Tom Brown's Schooldays,* the norms for what is too often considered "the" school story—to the extent that divergent stories, both earlier and later ones, have been rendered invisible.[2] In a canonical story, set at a British boys' public school, we would see the arrival of an ordinary good-natured boy, his awe of the older boys, and the larks and scrapes of his early years; we would see him rise through the ranks to the sixth form and become a creature of awe himself. We would witness our hero's prowess at rugby or cricket, perhaps his valiant attempt to defeat the school bully, perhaps his suffering a wrongful accusation but staunchly bearing the blame. Competition (sports, the fight with the bully) is thus balanced against peer solidarity (sports, not telling tales). Other commentators have underscored the connection of these stories with the imperial project[3] but not the gender connection—how the exclusion of females undergirds the genre.

For the canonical school story emerges when society separates "public" from "private," "public" schooling from "private" family. The school story symbolically carves out a realm where a boy could move from a private to a more public arena.[4] And it does so by eliminating females. Excluding mothers and girls—boys were even chary of admitting that they had sisters—lent the boys authority, an authority enacted in, for instance, the code against telling tales to adults.

These late-nineteenth-, early-twentieth-century stories were written mostly by men. One of the three books on the genre, Isabel Quigly's *The Heirs of Tom Brown,* devotes only one short chapter to girls' books and mentions hardly any women authors of boys' school stories. The other two critics give even shorter shrift to women authors—these men are, like schoolboys, chary of admitting to sisters. Yet a woman writing about boys is especially well positioned to illuminate the dialectics of the genre and to explore its positioning with respect to gender—and with respect to generations.

As a woman writing across gender (writing about males) and across generations (writing about children), Alcott can probe the instabilities of these two bifurcating, socially constructed categories, especially in a genre as gender marked as the school story (and age marked too, like all children's literature). Her work becomes a site for mediating conflicting codes and ideologies—here the ideologies associated with adulthood and childhood as they intersect with those of gender and, in passing, those of class.

When women write a boys' school story they may, for instance, tentatively adopt an accepted code, such as the schoolboy code against talebearing. But perhaps not having fully internalized the code, they at times proceed to contradict it, or are at pains to justify and contextualize it, or maybe (if they are Alcott) transform it. These activities are much less likely—indeed I have found virtually no evidence of them—in writers for whom the code seems second nature, men who once lived the code. Furthermore, like other women who have written boys' school stories—including Mary Martha Sherwood, Harriet Martineau, Ellen (Mrs. Henry) Wood, Angela Thirkell, Iris Murdoch—Alcott works at the interface of family and school more than any male writers of boys' school stories do.

Alcott's stance toward the established genre can be gauged in part by her redaction of the woman writer's "apology" for writing about boys. Two decades earlier the British E. J. May was simply self-deprecating: she excused her failure "to particularize the subjects for examination" by noting that her "classical and mathematical ignorance might cause mistakes more amusing to the erudite reader than pleasant to the author."[5] Alcott is less abject: "Cricket and football the boys had, of course—but after the stirring accounts of these games in the immortal 'Tom Brown at Rugby,' no feeble female pen may venture to do more than respectfully allude to them."[6] The ironic tone here hints that it's not so much Alcott's own feebleness that needs excuse as the emphasis on sports in an influential work like Hughes's. Where May apologized for leaving out something that no school-story author bothered including anyway—details about examinations—Alcott boldly announces her omission of a major ingredient of the canonical story, the blow-by-blow account of an athletic competition. Alcott also adopts a characteristic U.S. stance of resistance to Hughes, an anxiety to differentiate Tom Bailey from Tom Brown—a resistance emblematized by what amounts to her misquotation of the British title (the book appeared in the United States variously as *Tom Brown's Schooldays, School Days at Rugby,* and *Tom Brown at Rugby*).

Overall, Alcott's stance is complex—in part because, although she writes a story of a (mostly) boys' school, it is not necessarily a boys' story. For *Little Men* is the sequel to a classic girls' story, portraying the further adventures of an adult Jo March—and Alcott even manages to infiltrate a couple of girls into the school. Alcott is thereby enabled to evade the essentializing of male and female, making possible a new gender dialectic, illuminating what had been repressed in the canonical story, illuminating the denial of the feminine.

As a sequel the book simultaneously yields precedence to the family story it follows and also replaces the earlier story (much as it takes precedence over and is replaced by the final story in the March family series, *Jo's Boys* [1886], where the school is less salient). The position of *Little Men* as a sequel, or rather as a middle term in a series, has contributed to its relative obscurity. So too has its being a school story by a woman. Yet as a woman, an American woman, and a woman writing after Hughes had defined the form and stance of the school story (stabilizing the genre, clarifying what one could take an oppositional stance to—in one of those confrontations with what has gone before "by which culture institutionalizes itself, making tractable and even serviceable the sheer fluidity of historical process"[7]), and further as a daughter of the educational pioneer Bronson Alcott, Alcott is well positioned to dissect the values of the school story. She writes as a nineteenth-century woman, committed to nurturance and domesticity, even at school—as we will see in discussions of the relationship between family and school and of the portrayal of characters. She writes, further, as a nineteenth-century adult, committed to the authority of adults but willing to attempt to empower children, as long as they remain subject to adult moral authority.

Central to her endeavor is her dialectical synthesis of family and school. More than any other school-story writer, Alcott makes the home a school, the school a home.[8] To the newly-arrived Nat, Plumfield "seemed more like a great family than a school" (*LM* [*Little Men*] 42), headed by Mother and Father Bhaer (Jo March Bhaer and her husband Professor Bhaer). An important ingredient of this family atmosphere is the small size of the establishment: only twelve boys at first. And even this small number includes literal members of the family—the Bhaers' two sons, their three nephews—further integrating school and family.

This conflation of family and school enables Alcott to merge the two terms of the domestic feminism she espoused, a nineteenth-century feminism that focused on the family as the key to reforming society, "expanding the home to include the world, making everyone equally responsible for human nurturance."[9] As Mrs. Jo eventually exclaims, "Dear me, if men and women would only trust, understand, and help one another as my children do, what a capital place the world would be!" and her eyes "grew absent, as if she was looking at a new and charming state of society in which people lived as happily and innocently as her flock at Plumfield" (*LM* 370). As Jane Tompkins claims for *Uncle Tom's Cabin,* so does Alcott in effect claim "the power to work in, and change, the world."[10] In this respect Alcott's boys' school story differs from girls' school stories. Girls' stories may stress the congruence between family and school but not that between school and the world beyond. In part the emphasis on family counters the possibility that a girl might find some independence at school. But also girls were never supposed to enter that world beyond but to cycle back to the family—or a family—after school. As Nina Auerbach has said, "no girl can experience the effortless transition whereby the holy wars of school become those of adult reality, as they do in Tom Brown's tribute to his friend East."[11]

Nor, in **Little Men,** is influencing the world through the family possible without complexity or ambiguity. Opening up Plumfield to poor children, to domesticate them—taking in the likes of Nat and Dan—was at odds with a desire to protect the family, the school, from the world outside.[12] Likewise, the attempt to enlarge women's sphere, to domesticate the world, could be tinged with anxiety over the consequent dangers to women and also over the implicit denial of a more independent mode for women. Further, the maternal role that Mrs. Jo here adopts is one constructed by a patriarchal society—is not perhaps sufficiently revolutionary.[13] Finally, one way in which school can empower children is by distancing them from the only authority they have hitherto known, that of the family—so if school and family are conflated, it can be more difficult for a child to triangulate to his or her own authority.

Still, the conflation does enable Alcott to question the traditional mores of boys' schooling—to introduce the ethic of a girls' school to a boys' school, to introduce nurturing and domestic morality to the academic and athletic. Mrs. Jo may show some preference for "manly boys" instead of girlish ones, yet this school teaches boys "not to be ashamed of showing their emotions" nor of "own[ing] their loyalty to womankind" (**LM** 60, 226, 228). In keeping with the gender oxymoron she is addressed by—the "Mrs." feminine, the "Jo(e)" then masculine—she urges the crossing of gender attributes.

It's significant further that both Mrs. Jo and Mr. Bhaer are active in the running of the school, marrying the moral and the academic. He teaches academic lessons; she instills moral values—in this "odd school" where the important lessons are moral ones, where "self-knowledge, self-help, and self-control" are, in accordance with "Professor Bhaer's opinion," more important than Latin and Greek (**LM** 28). Whether it's a matter of welcoming the newcomer Nat, finding occupations for Daisy when the boys won't play with her, helping naughty Nan to adjust, remedying the disaster of Daisy's pretend ball, welcoming back the prodigal Dan and then finding outlets for his restlessness, rounding up lost children after a huckleberry expedition, telling stories around the fireside, preparing for Thanksgiving festivities, or, more generally, throwing in a timely comment to help a perplexed child, Mrs. Jo remains central to both school and book. Rarely are scenes set in Mr. Bhaer's domain, the classroom, and he has much less of an extracurricular presence than she does.

Still, even if she is the primary purveyor of moral values, his "opinion" seems to guide the school. As for her

ideas, some "were so droll it was impossible to help laughing at them, though usually they were quite sensible, and he was glad to carry them out" (**LM** 112). He laughs, then follows her suggestion; eventually he may even praise her for her droll idea of coeducation. Alcott thus displays some anxiety about women's ideas, but she also shows the workings of women's influence in the nineteenth century, the laughter a lightning rod that makes it possible nevertheless to accept Jo's idea. In fact, despite her attentiveness to Mr. Bhaer's "opinions," Jo would seem to be the dominant influence in the school. By making the adult Jo central, Alcott is able to incorporate female views in a male world, or perhaps to integrate private and public, reproduction and production, feminine and masculine, so as to transform the latter terms.[14]

Her portrayal of a central female character as the author's proxy makes Alcott's work different from all other boys' school stories I have located. Men who wrote boys' school stories seem not to have troubled themselves greatly about female characters; usually there aren't any. But women authors too seem to have had trouble imagining women in responsible positions in boys' schools, even when they devote a little attention to a headmaster's wife, as nineteenth-century authors Mary Martha Sherwood and Mary R. Baldwin do. **Little Men,** however, gives prominence to a responsible woman. In a sense, it is reminiscent of the occasional girls' school story by a man—in particular, early-nineteenth-century stories by Charles Lamb and George Mogridge—where a responsible adult of the same sex as the author may interact with children of the opposite sex. Yet in neither is the man central to the school. Rather, the character seems to be a displaced embodiment of the author's anxiety about writing a girls' story, his pathway into the story. No woman writing about boys' schools seems to have felt the need to include a comparable figure. Until Alcott, that is—and she transforms the character into the guiding spirit of the school, thereby transforming both school and story.

* * *

Not only is Mrs. Jo key to Alcott's regendering of the school story but so is the portrayal of other characters. For one thing, the school's clientele is expanded to include girls: the tomboy Nan arrives, and Daisy's role is redefined so that she seems not just to be keeping her twin Demi company but to be part of the school. Even Bess, Amy and Laurie's daughter, is temporarily added.[15] The girls' lessons may not be identical with the boys': the former learn to ply a needle. But they also, like the boys, learn to ply their wits.

Nan, in particular, attempts to push beyond traditional gender roles: she "clamored fiercely to be allowed to do everything that the boys did" (**LM** 255). She may need to be curbed, to "learn self-control, and be ready to use her freedom before she asked for it," yet Jo has the foresight to see a future for Nan not just within the home, nor even, given the girl's "intense love and pity for the weak and suffering," in nursing, but as "a capital doctor" (*LM* 256). The domestication of school is thus not constraining but empowering. And this empowering is quite different from that of the communities of women in Alcott's *Little Women* (early in the book) and *Work* (at the end). For Nan is to succeed in a public career as a doctor—and she evades domesticity to do so, never marrying. The domestication of a boys' school has thus redefined domesticity, repositioned it, expanding its reach while simultaneously enabling at least one young woman to escape it. In no other boys' school story is a feminine principle—and principal—so much in ascendance.[16]

In many ways, Nan is a later incarnation of the Jo March of *Little Women*. Like Jo, Nan provides a middle ground for diverging tendencies: as a tomboy, both feminine and masculine; as a newcomer, like other focal characters Nat and Dan, but one who quickly becomes an insider (her social class is not in question, as theirs is); even in terms of the letters of her name, mediating between Nat and Dan.

Yet Nan is not at the emotional heart of the work, nor, for all that she is the guiding spirit, is Mrs. Jo. Instead, the character who generates the most affect, the character through whom Alcott attempts to grapple with what remains most compelling and elusive, is the wild and difficult-to-tame Dan.[17] In providing the greatest challenge to Mrs. Jo's domesticating influence, this boy of the streets tests the limits of Alcott's domestic feminism. This boy whose looks are frequently mixed— "half-bold, half-sullen"; "half-resolute, half-reckless"; "half-fierce, half-imploring" (*LM* 91, 245, 247)[18]—this boundary case for whom Alcott lacks adequate categories shows the difficulty of crossing a gender barrier and also a class one, the difficulty of transgressing the former highlighted by the superposition of the latter. Dan is, in effect, a "problem" that marks "the limits of ideological certainly," threatening "to expose the artificiality of the binary logic" that separates genders[19]—and also Alcott's logic of cross-gendering transgression. Alcott wants Dan to rhyme with Nan, but he doesn't, not fully.

The only way Alcott can tame Dan sufficiently to integrate him into the world of the school, even temporarily, is to lame him. Curiously, a number of the boys at Plumfield are handicapped. One has a hump; another is feebleminded; another stutters. In part these disabilities allow Alcott to show how the school helps those whom the rest of society has failed to. Yet the handicaps have also helped to domesticate the boys, partly unman them if you will, to make them ripe for Jo's domestic influence.

As for Dan, at first he starts fights; he worries the cow in a pretend bullfight; his introduction of drinking, gambling, swearing, and smoking precipitates a dangerous fire.[20] Sent away, he wanders back to Plumfield and, having hurt his foot, is discovered before he disappears again. In the ensuing weeks of convalescence he is slowly "tamed by pain and patience" (*LM* 179). Yet Dan is not sufficiently invalided to be permanently tamed—he never becomes, in either *Little Men* or the subsequent *Jo's Boys,* a full member of the society in and around Plumfield—even an additional spell of invalidism in the sequel doesn't fit him to marry Bess. On some level, perhaps, he escapes from Jo's and Alcott's authority, succeeds in triangulating to his own.

In fact, like Nan, Dan escapes from the web of domesticity—he too never marries. Yet he escapes not to some pinnacle of success but rather because he doesn't fit in, is not a suitable mate for Bess—or rather because Alcott, like Jo, doesn't quite know what to make of him. Like Bertha in *Jane Eyre*, like Christophine in *Wide Sargasso Sea*, characters whose discursive grounding Gayatri Chakravorty Spivak explores, he remains tangential, unassimilated,[21] in his case marginalized by class.

Alcott's attempt to tame through laming echoes a trope common in girls' fiction of the time, such as Susan Coolidge's *What Katy Did* (1872) and Alcott's own *Jack and Jill* (1880): tomboys are tamed, learn to become little women, by enduring long periods, sometimes years, as invalids. Even Nan receives a dose of such confinement: after she loses herself and little Rob on a huckleberry expedition, she is tied to a sofa with a rope. Unlike the other invalided tomboys, though, Nan is confined for only hours, and the overt purpose is not so much to teach her to live with constriction but to learn to value her freedom: "a few hours of confinement taught Nan how precious it was" (*LM* 215-16). Of course the point is for her to learn to internalize constraint, but what the narrator emphasizes is the value of freedom.

Dan is thus perhaps treated like a tomboy, or like Jane Eyre's Mr. Rochester—another way in which Alcott incorporates some of the modes of girls and women into this story of boys.[22] Earlier women writers of school stories, like Martineau and Elizabeth Sandham, were able to lead boys to the paths of righteousness only by laming them. Martineau's Hugh crushes a foot when he falls off a wall, crushes it so badly that it has to be amputated.[23] After this accident that seems to preclude the traveling he had always dreamed of—he cannot now become a soldier or sailor—he learns forbearance and fortitude. And he is finally rewarded by finding a way to join the civil service and hence traveling to India after all.

It's appropriate, then, that one of the ways that Mrs. Jo helps Dan to beguile his days of convalescence—he too is lamed when trying to cross a wall, a metaphor, in his case, for his and Alcott's (lame) attempts to cross a class barrier—is by giving him Martineau's *Crofton Boys,* a "charming little book" that soon interested him even though he "did not love to read" (*LM* 172). The book is of course meant to teach Dan the use he should make of adversity. Yet also, as one of two predecessor school stories explicitly named in the novel, it shows Alcott acknowledging not just the canonical school story but the women's tradition that preceded Hughes. And the lack of irony in the reference to Martineau's book, unlike the apologia for not providing stirring Hughesian accounts of cricket and football, suggests that Alcott finds it preferable to locate herself in this other tradition.

So too with another reference to a school story, one "written years ago by a dear old lady" (*LM* 339), a story that Mrs. Jo retells to her school—no longer does she rely on her own powers of invention, as she had when she secretly wrote sensation stories in *Little Women*. The story is about a schoolboy who admits to extracting the fruit from some tarts and is later believed guilty of stealing a knife from a peddler—until the peddler returns to say he had simply misplaced the knife. Thus does Jo reflect on incidents in the life of Plumfield, in particular an incident of theft, working in moral reflections for the boys to meditate on: not, for instance, to "'hit a fellow when he is down,' as they say" (*LM* 342). But she herself has also in effect stolen the story, likewise the cliché that she sets off in quotation marks. Thus does Alcott underscore the extent to which she borrows from other sources in *Little Men,* including a tradition of school stories by "dear old ladies."

* * *

These borrowings from other adult authorities, other adults who addressed children, are part of Alcott's cross-generational project. For she is not just crossing genders and gendered literary traditions but also working across generations, an adult writing of and for children. As Jacqueline Rose points out, children's literature is always written across this gap, this rupture between the writer and the addressee, this rupture through which we adults attempt to regulate our relationship with language as well, associating the child, as we do, with the origins of language.[24]

Alcott's generational crossing in *Little Men* is particularly salient, for not only does she include an adult proxy but this proxy has herself crossed generations since *Little Women*. Not only does the relationship between Jo and her young people become a map of the relationship between Alcott and her child readers, but so does the relationship between Jo and her earlier tex-

tual self. The point of origin is no longer *Pilgrim's Progress,* as it was in *Little Women,* where Jo encountered her Apollyon and Meg dallied with Vanity Fair, but rather a book by a woman: *Little Women.* And in this self-referential process Alcott maps the younger generation onto the older, the characters of *Little Men* onto the characters of *Little Women.* Nan and Dan, in particular, are versions of Jo, both playing out Jo's urges to escape domesticity, both succeeding in ways that Jo did not.

In fact, this complex give and take between books blurs the generational focus, rather like the genre dialectic between school and family stories—and it blurs the focus more than in any contemporary boys' school story. Is this a story about children, or do we still have a strong interest in this latter-day Jo March? Or rather, does the author continue identifying with Jo, inviting the reader to do so too? Alcott is, in effect, playing out the implications of the double audience, both children and adults, to which children's literature is addressed,[25] Jo thus functioning as proxy not just for Alcott but for adult (and adult-identified) readers. And the mapping of one generation onto another prevents either from gaining priority.

Yet another kind of generational mapping figures in the book's genesis as well. For much as Maria Edgeworth honors her father's ideas in her classic collection of children's stories, *The Parent's Assistant* (1796), *Little Men* in many ways honors Bronson Alcott's philosophy of education. Both women seem to have been enabled to write of boys in part because of their relationships with their fathers. Edgeworth drew directly on her father's experiences as well as on his philosophical approach.[26] Alcott, though not particularly critical of her father's philosophy of education, does implicitly criticize the realization of some of his ideas. For Plumfield can be seen as a commentary on Bronson's failed attempt to achieve utopia at Fruitlands (see *HH* [*A Hunger for Home*] 166).

Like Bronson, Jo keeps careful records of each pupil, but she discusses them in private rather than in public, and the fictional Plumfield makes more use of peer pressure than Bronson's Temple School did (see *HH* 29, 186). Alcott further derived from her father such ideas as the stress on physical exercise, on not cramming the mind too much, on valuing the spiritual, on opposing corporal punishment, even on being open to coeducation—though the daughter seems to have been more enthusiastic about this last than the father was.[27] Thus Alcott charts her own way, her father's views helping to distance her from traditional ones, yet she also differentiates her own views from her father's.

Alcott even indulges, in *Little Men,* in a kind of generational inversion—perhaps an indirect way of responding to her father. When Nat has trouble giving up his habit of lying, Mr. Bhaer tells of his similar difficulties as a child and how his grandmother cured him—by snipping the end of his tongue. Mr. Bhaer's approach, however, is to get Nat to strike his elder with a ferule, rather than vice versa, a measure that apparently works. Thus does Mr. Bhaer invert the approach of an earlier generation, inverting the direction of punitive action—and by granting agency to the child, Alcott starts to question traditional sources of authority.

For Alcott does not assume that adults are the only sources of knowledge: as Jo notes, "half the science of teaching is knowing how much children do for one another, and when to mix them" (*LM* 114). That becomes her justification for her experiment in coeducation. Mr. Bhaer even avers that the children "teach us quite as much as we teach them" (*LM* 222). Though Mrs. Jo quickly circumscribes this teaching, limiting it to teaching the adults about child-rearing: "They never guess how many hints they give us as to the best way of managing them" (*LM* 222). In short, where canonical boys' school stories tended to pay lip service to the authority of adults yet actually acceded to schoolboys' priorities—such as sports[28]—Alcott pays lip service to the authority of children while nonetheless steering them toward the views of adult authorities. Mrs. Jo's moral presence dominates, even if she governs more by suasion than with a switch.

And she governs by emphasizing cooperation (with peers, with adults) over competition. That too is part of her cross-generational project, likewise one of the ways her work differs from that of canonical writers. I've already noted her disclaimer with respect to cricket and football and stirring accounts thereof. She doesn't altogether deny her schoolboys the competition provided by sports; she simply forbears including accounts of them.

Nor does she translate competition into the classroom, as other women authors of boys' stories have done, women like the American Mary Densel. Although Densel's *Tel Tyler at School* (1872) is, like Alcott's, part of a series, it stays with the first generation of children, simply branching out to a different sibling. There is then less compulsion to adopt the adult perspective, or to complicate the child's: Densel sticks closer to the Hughesian model. There is some discussion of baseball, for instance, when Tel first arrives at his military academy, even if we never witness a practice nor wait breathlessly for the outcome of a game.[29] More importantly, Densel devotes considerable attention to a declamation competition. The eponymous Tel eventually succeeds in winning it, only to question his reasons for wanting to win and then to disavow competition—selflessly supporting another boy's election to sergeant. This self-sacrifice is not in vain, however, for Tel goes on to win the school's highest prize, for "conduct, schol-

arship, and military standing."[30] Densel complexly endorses and disavows competition—ultimately, it seems, endorsing it.

Alcott, however, opts not to include any such competitions—not baseball, not declamation, not the good conduct prize. The closest analogue is Composition Day, when the pupils recite compositions based on natural history, telling about sponges and cats and dragonflies. In doing so they reinforce our sense of their characters, rather like the storytelling game of Rigmarole in *Little Women*. But also we can see the humor in—and feel superior to[31]—their efforts. Nan has written an essay on the sponge, with special attention to its use as a repository for ether held "to people's noses when they have teeth out": "*I* shall do this when I am bigger, and give ether to the sick, so they will go to sleep and not feel me cut off their legs and arms" (*LM* 288, Alcott's italics). The boy with a hunchback tells of his observations of dragonflies, especially how they burst out of their old skins—and thereby suggests, "to the minds of the elder listeners," how Dick would some day, "leaving his poor little body behind him, find a new and lovely shape in a fairer world than this" (*LM* 295). Composition Day is, in short, an occasion for fun, for revealing character, for teaching the reader how to read character allegorically—and for replicating Alcott's own activity as author. It is not an occasion for competition and conflict.

Alcott likewise avoids conflict between children and adults—likewise blurs the generational dialectic—in her treatment of the code against talebearing. Again she provides new perspectives, though her elaborate displacements of the trope are also evasive. In the canonical story, boys wouldn't dream of bearing tales about other boys to their teachers; they carefully draw the line between boys and masters. Before *Tom Brown*, though, and also afterwards in girls' school stories and in American boys' school stories, talebearing is treated with less consistency—setting into relief the contradictions that permeate the trope, contradictions between loyalty to peers and loyalty to adults and the religious and moral authority that the latter represent.

In *Little Men* Alcott sets up a conventional test of the talebearing ethic: the wrongful accusation. Nat is accused of stealing some money. He knew where it had been left and has a dubious background as a street musician, together with a lingering propensity for lying. He steadfastly denies guilt and accepts punishment, but not to protect someone else, as would be the case in the canonical school story. Instead he is himself protected by a more recent newcomer with an even more dubious background: Dan claims to be guilty. Only by inverting the significance of the phrase, making it an expression of peer solidarity rather than a violation of it, can Dan be said to tell a tale—he tells a lie. Just as Alcott subtly redefines the terms of the classic ingredient of the British school story, the wrongful accusation: she displaces the supreme sign of friendship from not telling the truth to (unspeakably un-British[32]) telling a lie. Furthermore, she gets Dan to insert himself into Nat's position not just by taking the blame but by using Nat's characteristic tool of lying. Still, as in other school stories, Dan is eventually cleared—after he saves the real culprit's life and the boy duly repents (this latter a plot move reminiscent of pre-Hughesian stories). Overall, Alcott redefines the grounds of the conventional, resituating it, implicitly questioning its provenance—only to capitulate to a standard ending, the improbable self-revelation of the culprit. At the same time, since there's no tale for Nat to tell, she could be said to evade the issue of talebearing—she protects her boys, as Mrs. Jo does, making it impossible for them to tell tales.

The plotting of Nat's wrongful accusation does, however, bring the boy to the verge of a more straightforward adumbration of the trope. Though this literal embodiment of talebearing is yet another displacement—it remains only potential, never actualized. When a schoolmate named Ned belittles the self-accused Dan, Nat hotly retorts, "I don't want to tell tales, but, by George! I will, if you don't let Dan alone" (*LM* 237). Whereupon Dan appears and tosses the boy in a brook—thereby abrogating the need for Nat to seek a reprisal by telling tales, and again evading the conflict between talebearing and loyalty to peers.

At the same time, in the same scene, Alcott redefines what it means to be a sneak. For when Nat threatens to tell, Ned jeers, "Then you'll be a sneak" (*LM* 237)—using "sneak" as nineteenth-century schoolboys generally did, to refer to someone who tells tales. Dan subsequently retorts, "You are a sneak yourself to badger Nat round the corner" (*LM* 237)—out of sight of Mr. Bhaer, who has forbidden the boys to tax Nat about the theft. Thus Dan reinstates an older meaning of "sneak," referring generally to anyone who acts in a clandestine manner. He trips Ned up verbally as well as physically, enabling Alcott to submerge talebearing, subordinate it, reorient it.

Another reference to telling tales in **Little Men** is more metaphoric—or perhaps more literal. When the visiting Mr. Laurie proposes to make a museum for the boys' natural history collections and, "with a merry look in his eyes," itemizes the inconvenient doorbugs, dead bats, and wasps' nests that Mrs. Jo has been stumbling over, it's clear to the boys "that someone told tales out of school, else how could he know of the existence of these inconvenient treasures" (*LM* 179-80). Quite literally, the tales have been told out of school—someone, presumably Jo, has been talking to Laurie. This literalization of the trope neutralizes the baggage of its customary significance, the conflict in loyalty for which it

is a nexus, as does the ascription to an adult authority of telling "tales out of school."[33] If a child's telling on another has by now become negative in school stories,[34] something that at least requires an apologetic excuse, what does it mean for an adult authority to tell tales— someone who is not bound by the strictures of the code, has in fact been the "other" that the code excludes? True, this adult is guilty of violating the code, but in a context where it is made to seem applicable to her, not just to schoolchildren. Alcott reorients the schoolchild code against talebearing, making light of it, as if telling tales is not just benign but even rather jolly. She reappropriates the trope for her own moral economy—using it to connect adults and schoolchildren rather than to demarcate their separation.[35]

* * *

Alcott further connects adult and child, male and female, further advocates cooperation over conflict, through her deployment of discursive registers. Her discursive field is not a playing or battle field but a horticultural one. Canonical school stories bolstered competition through the metaphorical subtext of war. In describing the Doctor's sermon in *Tom Brown's Schooldays*, Hughes stresses how this headmaster enlists his boys in a moral "battle-field ordained from of old," explaining "how that battle was to be fought; and stood there before them their fellow-soldier and captain of their band."[36] Girls' stories, and also other stories that emphasize an adult perspective, tend instead to describe the students as plants to be nurtured. In Sarah Fielding's *The Governess* (1749), the first novel for children and the first school story, we learn that most of the girls "had in them the Seeds of Good-will to each other, altho' those Seeds were choaked and over-run with the Weeds of Envy and Pride."[37] Or if garden imagery appears in a more canonical story like *Stalky & Co.* (1899)—a housemaster "lurched out with some hazy impression that he had sown good seed on poor ground"[38]—we can be certain that its application is undermined, Stalky and his friends sure to outflank any such attempt at moral cultivation.

So it's not surprising, given the traditions that Alcott prefers to draw on, to find that in **Little Men** she mutes the discourse of war and cultivates that of gardening. On the rare occasions when the word "battle" appears it's likely to be distanced through miniaturization and humor—little Rob gets "the best of the battle" with some squirrels over nuts (*LM* 312). Or the hired hand Silas may tell of a war experience, yet he emphasizes not the fighting but his devotion to his horse (who seemed in fact the more bellicose of the two) and how he and a Confederate soldier, both wounded, "helped one another like brothers" (*LM* 336). If, during the Civil War, fiction sometimes symbolically enacted the national rift by portraying two antagonistic brothers, one in blue and the other in gray (Alcott's version of such a story, **"The Brothers"** [1863], later titled **"My Contraband,"** makes the brothers black and white and thus grapples more directly with race than others do[39]), then in the following decade Alcott offers a vignette that symbolically heals the nation's wounds, making enemies into brothers, domesticating the nation as she has domesticated the school. Or alternatively, if in *Little Women* the Civil War makes possible a community of women by taking away the father (much as wars generally seem to have empowered women, opened doors to nontraditional activity for both Scarlett O'Haras and Rosie the Riveters), then in a postbellum world Alcott attempts to enlarge her community to include men—and to domesticate them.

Or to cultivate them. For *Little Men* is pervaded by the discourse of agriculture. The most extended example is Professor Bhaer's self-conscious allegory about "a great and wise gardener," some of whose undergardeners "did their duty and earned the rich wages he gave them; but others neglected their parts and let them run to waste, which displeased him much" (*LM* 43). Each member of the school then goes on to pledge what moral virtues he or she will cultivate. And much as the male-generated allegory of *Pilgrim's Progress* provides a moral and discursive framework for *Little Women,* so does this putatively male-generated allegory in *Little Men,* finally culminating—during the harvest celebration of Thanksgiving—in "the bouquet of laughing young faces" that surround Jo and the Professor, love having "taken root and blossomed beautifully in all the little gardens" (*LM* 372).

Yet in this bouquet that closes the book, "the professor and his wife were taken prisoner by many arms" (*LM* 372). Jo makes her last textual appearance not as Mrs. Jo, nor even as Mother Bhaer, but simply as the professor's wife. And imprisonment intrudes in this paragraph of love and flowers, an eruption of the effects of armed battle. Even Alcott's domestication of the school story cannot repress all traces of the canonical, as it hints not just at the joys but at the perils of domestication.

Another subtext that runs through the book and subverts the canonical is that of wages and payment. Alcott's intention is to encourage these boys who will have to work for their livings to start being independent: to keep hens whose eggs they sell to the Bhaers, likewise vegetables they've grown, to sell worms to one another or the fruits of their carpentry. Such endorsement of the bourgeois would be unthinkable for the British public-school boys of canonical stories, for whom having a family in trade was even worse than having a sister. In the United States, however, the myth of the self-made man made class boundaries seem more permeable. Alcott is, in effect, encouraging her boys to become Ben Franklins. Yet her vision remains eigh-

teenth century, preindustrial, as Jean Fagan Yellin has noted in another context.[40] The closest Alcott comes to acknowledging misgivings is in her portrayal of Jack, the most despicable boy, a sharp dealer like his Yankee trader of an uncle: hyper-acquisitive, Jack turns out to be the thief that Nat had been accused of being. Or rather he marks the cleavage between what John G. Cawelti has described as two strands of the myth of the self-made man: one, middle class and Protestant, stressed industry, frugality, honesty, and piety, leading to "a respectable competence in this world and eternal salvation in the world to come"; the other, emphasizing getting ahead, stressed initiative, aggressiveness, and competitiveness.[41] Jack reveals the slippage of the former into the latter, a slippage that, Alcott feels, must be sharply dealt with.

Whether Alcott is trying to appeal to the interests she envisions her readers as having, or is trying to steer them into what she sees as worthy versions of the self-made, or is simply spoken by the discourse of emergent industrialism that prevailed at the time, the language of the marketplace permeates *Little Men.*[42] Not only do boys get others to do tasks for them by offering payment (one gets others to collect grasshoppers for a prank and then "pays" them with peppermints) but one boy "pays" another for morally uplifting talk by sharing his knowledge of natural history, boys "pay" Dan for his sufferings when accused of theft by pooling their resources and buying him a microscope, and Jo is confident that the "wages" Dan needs for service are simply love and confidence. Even in his garden allegory Professor Bhaer speaks of earning "rich wages." So even though there is some attention to giving instead of paying—the punishment that Jack suffers is to give away his possessions (yet even here giving becomes punishment)—the discourse of the marketplace starts invading the spiritual economy that Alcott is attempting to endorse. Jack's giving away of his worldly goods, for instance, is described in terms of "buy[ing] up a little integrity, even at a high price, and secur[ing] the respect of his playmates, though it was not a salable article" (*LM* 273). The monetary language—"buy up," "high price," "secure," "salable"—is presumably translating Jack's favorite trope into spiritual coin. Yet the humorous breeziness of the sentence, its patness as it addresses the moral and the spiritual, starts unraveling the sentiment: the language shows that we can make a calculus of the spirit that attends to profit and loss. In her attempt to enter Jack's perspective, Alcott sullies—or reveals the contradictions underlying—her own. She may, through her mercantile discourse, subvert the class privilege underlying canonical stories, but she also subverts her own moral import. Like other writers in the second half of the nineteenth century, writers attempting to interpret an industrializing society through the lens of traditional religious views, she "tended to confuse economic success and moral merit" (*AS*

[*Apostles of the Self-Made Man*] 53). Or rather she hints at the workings of the Protestant ethic, the mutual implication of Protestantism and capitalism.

* * *

All together, Alcott domesticates the school story through reworking tropes and resituating the school, thereby regendering a genre. Her reworking carries a conscious gender valence: she is a woman reworking the boys' school story by writing about a woman central to a (mostly) boys' school. And in doing so she excavates the femininity suppressed by canonical stories. In bringing together family and school, school and world, Alcott voices tensions and conflicts and contradictions: between British and United States schools, the latter more likely to be coeducational; between British and United States literary traditions, the latter anxious to differentiate itself from the *Tom Brown* strand of boys' story; between, perhaps, "real" (United States) schools and an established genre. Alcott may be writing about her own experiences as a girl at school, about her father's as the creator of the experimental Temple School, about the experiences of her nieces and nephews. Yet, less committed to the systems espoused by the writers of the canonical school story—to their gender, to the system of the genre, to the educational system, to Britain, to the imperialism that the educational system buttressed, to the military discourse undergirding and implicated in all the rest—she felt less need to bury their contradictions.

In crossing generations, too, Alcott unearths hidden truths. At the end of the book, in a chapter devoted to thanksgiving and Thanksgiving, young Demi gives a history of the holiday that situates the moment and the book more truly than he knows: "The Pilgrims killed all the Indians, and got rich; and hung the witches, and were very good" (*LM* 358). Alcott here points to truths that elude the consciousnesses of her adult personae, points to how her forefathers had erected barriers: racial barriers that enabled them to get rich, gender barriers that enabled them to feel righteous. Yet at the same time women and Indians, wealth and goodness, are curiously confounded—the leveling "and"'s implicitly equate the terms. In **Little Men** as a whole, she similarly crosses the barriers of generations and genders, even of wealth and goodness—though race eludes her. Yet still in regendering and re-generating the genre of the school story—attending to what it marginalized—she reveals the process whereby it displaced and suppressed contradictions even as it pretended not to. Her regendering regenerates the genre.

Notes

1. Catharine R. Stimpson, "Reading for Love: Canons, Paracanons, and Whistling Jo March," *New Literary History,* 21 (1990), 957-76.

2. My emphasis on Hughes as origin, here and subsequently, misrepresents the complexity of the origins of the genre. Yet it's a misrepresentation that is not just convenient, given the scope of this essay; it also mimics the misrepresentations of previous literary critics and historians—it reproduces the established narrative of the genre's history. For the fullest histories see Isabel Quigly, *The Heirs of Tom Brown: The English School Story* (London, 1982); Peter William Musgrave, *From Brown to Bunter: The Life and Death of the School Story* (London, 1985); and Jeffrey Richards, *Happiest Days: The Public Schools in English Fiction* (Manchester, 1988).

3. See, for example, Quigly, *The Heirs of Tom Brown,* pp. 3ff.; John Raymond de Symons Honey, *Tom Brown's Universe: The Development of the English Public School in the Nineteenth Century* (New York, 1977), p. 225.

4. For a review of the rhetorical uses and limitations of the concept of separate spheres, specifically addressing United States history, see Linda K. Kerber, "Separate Spheres, Female Worlds, Woman's Place: The Rhetoric of Women's History," *Journal of American History,* 75 (1988), 9-39. My use of the terms here is provisional.

5. Emily J. May, *Louis' School Days: A Story for Boys* (1850; rpt. New York, 1851), p. 114.

6. Louisa May Alcott, *Little Men: Life at Plumfield with Jo's Boys* (1871; rpt. New York, 1947), p. 135; hereafter cited in text as *LM.*

7. Michael McKeon, *The Origins of the English Novel, 1600-1740* (Baltimore, 1987), p. 88.

8. William Blackburn is the one other critic who has commented on this conjunction—in "'Moral Pap for the Young'? A New Look at Louisa May Alcott's *Little Men,*" *Proceedings of the Seventh Annual Conference of the Children's Literature Association,* ed. Priscilla A. Ord (New Rochelle, 1982), p. 100—yet he does not go on to discuss the implications of this conjunction.

9. Sarah Elbert, *A Hunger for Home: Louisa May Alcott and* Little Women (Philadelphia, 1984), p. 166; hereafter cited in text as *HH.* Alcott herself may have supported women's suffrage, but she constantly subordinated her rights as an individual to her duties as a family member—her writing a way of supporting her family, at the same time that it extolled devotion to the family.

10. Jane Tompkins, *Sensational Designs: The Cultural Work of American Fiction, 1790-1860* (New York, 1985), p. 130.

11. Nina Auerbach, *Communities of Women: An Idea in Fiction* (Cambridge, Mass., 1978), p. 172.

12. See Charles Strickland, *Victorian Domesticity: Families in the Life and Art of Louisa May Alcott* (University, Ala., 1985), p. 152.

13. As Linda Zwinger suggests, "Sentimentalizing the mother is always already a patriarchal ploy" (*Daughters, Fathers, and the Novel: The Sentimental Romance of Heterosexuality* [Madison, Wis., 1991], p. 64). Where, in short, can we find a mother tongue that does not speak the Law of the Father? Alcott's writing here is not particularly traversed by a Kristevan semiotic and hence may simply reinscribe the patriarchal.

14. For a discussion of the "genderized complementarity" embodied in Jo and her husband at Plumfield Academy, one that enabled attention to the processes of both production and reproduction, to both reason and emotion, see Susan Laird, "The Ideal of the Educated Teacher—'Reclaiming a Conversation' with Louisa May Alcott," *Curriculum Inquiry,* 21 (1991), 282-88.

15. Though her addition, in particular, would seem if anything to sharpen gender distinctions: her refined femininity may inspire the boys to behave more politely, but it's by appealing "to the chivalrous instinct in them as something to love, admire, and protect with a tender sort of reverence," and Nan, in turn, is inspired to toil over the feminine activity of sewing "for love of Bess" (*LM,* pp. 228, 224).

16. The only other author to approach such a stance, certainly the only one in the nineteenth century, is the British economist and author Harriet Martineau. Martineau's *Crofton Boys* (1841) validates the feminine in part by providing a favorable role for the central character's sister and in part by suitably contextualizing schoolboy belittlement of girls.

17. Other critics often focus on him too: see Linda Black, "Louisa May Alcott's 'Huckleberry Finn,'" *Mark Twain Journal,* 21, no. 2 (Summer 1982), 15-17; Abigail Ann Hamblen, "The Divided World of Louisa May Alcott," in *Webs and Wardrobes: Humanist and Religious World Views in Children's Literature,* ed. Joseph O'Beirne Milner and Lucy Floyd Morcock Milner (Lanham, Md., 1987), pp. 57-64; Elizabeth Keyser, "Women and Girls in Louisa May Alcott's *Jo's Boys,*" *International Journal of Women's Studies,* 6 (1983), 465-69; Ruth K. MacDonald, *Louisa May Alcott* (Boston, 1983), pp. 35-36.

18. He likewise generates mixed looks in others, making Jo "half-merry, half-reproachful" (*LM,* p. 159).

19. Mary Poovey, *Uneven Developments: The Ideological Work of Gender in Mid-Victorian England* (Chicago, 1988), p. 12.

20. A similar dangerous fire appears in Alcott's adult novel *Work* (1873): there the fire, caused by the heroine's staying up late to read, functions primarily as a reminder of "the searing dangers of books to women" (Beverly Lyon Clark, "A Portrait of the Artist as a Little Woman," *Children's Literature,* 17 [1989], 82). Yet there is something to be said for books, there is something to be said for their attractiveness—for Alcott is after all writing books herself, and books that flirt with the dangerously fictive, for all that she attempts to emphasize the "truthfulness" of her books for children. The fire in *Little Men* is likewise meant as a reminder of searing dangers—as perhaps is the other significant fire in the book, the one to the Kittymouse, where Demi Brooke gets his sister Daisy and little Rob and Teddy to "sackerryfice" their favorite toys, this latter fire perhaps hinting at the dangers of self-sacrifice. But these fires too hint at attractions, the attractiveness of Dan's misdemeanors, the attractiveness of sacrifice to others.

21. Gayatri Chakravorty Spivak, "Three Women's Texts and a Critique of Imperialism," *Critical Inquiry,* 12 (1985), 243-61; rpt. in *The Feminist Reader: Essays in Gender and the Politics of Literary Criticism,* ed. Catherine Belsey and Jane Moore (New York, 1989), p. 186. Subsequently in *Jo's Boys* Dan becomes an instrument of an overtly imperial project when—a New World echo of Bronte's St. John Rivers—he undertakes missionary work among the Indians. And thus is race even more tangential than class in *Little Men.* All of the boys at Plumfield are white (crossing racial boundaries here would not be altogether unthinkable for Alcott, since her father had once admitted a black child to his Temple School, though the upshot of that action underscores the difficulty of imagining a viable interracial school: admitting this child was the final straw that caused the school to fail). And the Bhaers' black cook figures very little in the text—this black cook called Asia, one race conflated with the appurtenances of another. Alcott tended to ignore race in her children's literature.

22. For discussion of nineteenth-century attitudes toward tomboyism see Sharon O'Brien, "Tomboyism and Adolescent Conflict: Three Nineteenth-Century Case Studies," in *Woman's Being, Woman's Place: Female Identity and Vocation in American History,* ed. Mary Kelley (Boston, 1979), pp. 351-72. For discussion of "the blinding, maiming, or blighting motif" that appears in *Jane Eyre* and other novels when women write of men, see Elaine Showalter, *A Literature of Their Own: British Women Novelists from Brontë to Lessing* (Princeton, 1977), p. 150.

23. In what has been called a symbolic castration—see Diana Postlethwaite, "Mothering and Mesmerism in the Life of Harriet Martineau," *Signs,* 14 (1989), 599. Postlethwaite sees Hugh's disability as simultaneously a punishment for his aspirations, a metaphor for Martineau's gender handicap, and an agent of growth. The book thus provides "a vision of a male world transformed by the female sensibilities of suffering and sympathy" (601).

24. Jacqueline Rose, *The Case of Peter Pan or the Impossibility of Children's Fiction* (London, 1984), pp. 2ff., 8, 138-39.

25. See Zohar Shavit, in *Poetics of Children's Literature* (Athens, Ga., 1986), for the most extended discussion of the double audience.

26. To the extent that a favorite crux in Edgeworth criticism has been the degree to which Richard Lovell Edgeworth was responsible for inspiring and shaping his daughter's work, for good or ill—see, for example, Marilyn Butler, *Maria Edgeworth: A Literary Biography* (Oxford, 1972), pp. 6ff.

27. See MacDonald, *Louisa May Alcott,* pp. 31-34; see also Abigail Ann Hamblen, "Louisa May Alcott and the 'Revolution' in Education," *Journal of General Education,* 22 (1970), 81-92.

28. Although Tom increasingly adopts his headmaster's views, in the second half of *Tom Brown's Schooldays,* Hughes accommodates the child's perspective by attributing to the headmaster some of Tom's ideas of what a Rugby education is for: especially sports. Hughes's real-life headmaster, Thomas Arnold, had given priority to religious principles, gentlemanly conduct, and intellectual pursuits; he encouraged exercise simply as a means to stay healthy. Still, Arnold was sensitive to the child's point of view, even if he gave priority to an adult moral perspective. Further, subsequent attitudes toward sports, later in the century, reflect a complex interplay between boys and masters. Masters and headmasters may have initiated the emphasis on games in the 1850s, as a way of disciplining the boys' unruliness, yet they were building on the boys' preferences. The late-nineteenth-century mania for games in British public schools was both a pandering to boys' interests and a way of disciplining their energy—and also an admission that complete control was impossible. See J. A. Mangan, *Athleticism in the Victorian and Edwardian Public School: The Emergence and Consolidation of an Educational Ideology* (Cambridge, 1981), pp. 16ff.

29. Rather, we learn that his skill at it throws him in with an undesirable lot of boys—thus perhaps does Densel metonymically put down the *Tom Brown* type of story, by putting down athletes.

30. Mary Densel, *Tel Tyler at School* (New York, 1872), p. 184.

31. On this particular occasion it's only the younger pupils who recite, the ones most likely to be "quaint," the reader thereby invited to collude in condescending spectatorship, watching from an adult perspective.

32. See, for example, Gillian Avery, *Childhood's Pattern: A Study of the Heroes and Heroines of Children's Fiction, 1770-1950* (London, 1975), p. 141.

33. A phrase that continues to have more resonance in Britain than in the United States. The *OED* ([*Oxford English Dictionary,*] 1971) cites its appearance as early as 1546.

34. Alcott's first reference to telling tales draws on this strand of associations, when she introduces the minor character Ned, who, "without being at all bad, was just the sort of fellow who could very easily be led astray." She buttresses this statement by alluding to two standard school-story tropes: Ned "was apt to bully the small boys" and was "a little given to taletelling" (*LM,* p. 24). Yet even here she subverts the stereotypical, since a tendency toward either bullying or taletelling would brand a boy, usually irredeemably, in a canonical school story. But Ned, we have just been told, is not "at all bad." Perhaps she also subverts the expected when, as the story unfolds, we see what a minor role he plays: in a canonical story the bully or telltale would be the focus of negative affect.

35. Although adults in canonical stories often go along with the code, they do so by respecting boys who follow it, not by acting on it themselves.

36. Thomas Hughes, *Tom Brown's Schooldays* (1857; rpt. New York, 1968), p. 118.

37. Sarah Fielding, *The Governess; or, Little Female Academy* (1749; rpt. New York, 1987), p. 11.

38. Rudyard Kipling, *Stalky & Co.* (1899; rpt. London, 1987), p. 73.

39. See Kathleen Diffley, "Where My Heart Is Turning Ever: Civil War Stories and National Stability from Fort Sumter to the Centennial," *American Literary History,* 2 (1990), 649-53.

40. Jean Fagan Yellin, "From *Success* to *Experience*: Louisa May Alcott's *Work,*" *Massachusetts Review,* 21 (1980), 527-39.

41. John G. Cawelti, *Apostles of the Self-Made Man* (Chicago, 1965), pp. 4-5; hereafter cited in text as *AS.*

42. In a way that does not occur in *Little Women.* If such discourse was prevalent at the time, it prevailed in masculine rather than feminine contexts.

Elizabeth Young (essay date September 1996)

SOURCE: Young, Elizabeth. "A Wound of One's Own: Louisa May Alcott's Civil War Fiction." *American Quarterly* 48, no. 3 (September 1996): 439-74.

[*In the following excerpt, Young considers the relationship between feminine and national modes of identity in Alcott's fiction. Young identifies a process of feminization, both of the male body and of American society, in Alcott's Civil War writings.*]

As recent feminist scholarship on Louisa May Alcott suggests, the sunny public reputation of this writer was sharply at odds with her ongoing private struggles against the constraints of Victorian gender norms, the intellectual world of midcentury Concord, Massachusetts, and the obligations of an eccentric family. These conflicts pervade her fiction, from her best-known novel, *Little Women,* which implicitly maps a fierce and uneven struggle for female independence, to her recently reprinted sensational thrillers of the 1860s, which offer openly rebellious accounts of female defiance in plots involving deception, adultery, murder, and drug addiction. In bringing an "alternative Alcott" into view, however, critics have paid less attention to what was a central event in Alcott's life, as it was in nineteenth-century America: the Civil War.[1]

In 1862, at the age of thirty, Louisa May Alcott went to work as a nurse in a Union Army hospital in Georgetown. She was there for only a few weeks before contracting typhoid fever, yet the experience affected her for the rest of her life. The mercury prescribed for her cure permanently ruined her health, causing chronic pain and significantly contributing to her death at age fifty-six. So, too, did Alcott's exposure to the war profoundly influence her work, beginning with *Hospital Sketches,* the first-person account of the experiences of one Tribulation Periwinkle, a nurse for the Union Army. The book's six chapters chart her decision to work as a war nurse, her journey from Boston to Washington, her daily activities as a nurse, her impressions of Washington while forced to convalesce, and her comments on life in a wartime hospital. Thinly fictionalized, the origins of the text lay in a series of letters Alcott wrote to her family about her own experiences, which she then adapted into a set of sketches appearing in four installments in the spring of 1863 in the Boston abolitionist newspaper *The Commonwealth. Hospital Sketches* helped to launch her career as a professional author, while the war years and their aftermath were her most important period of literary development.[2]

At the center of the *Hospital Sketches* is the chapter entitled "A Night," whose tone is far more serious than the rest of the volume and whose narrative, the most sustained subplot of the text, focuses on the death of a soldier named John. Modeled on a dying Virginia blacksmith nursed by Alcott, John at first seems an unremarkable model of heroic masculinity in wartime. A figure of "broad chest and muscular limbs," he is described approvingly by the narrator as "so genuine a man."[3] Yet Alcott's characterization subtly redefines the masculinity of the mortally injured soldier. To begin with, although John is only a year younger than Periwinkle, his masculinity is strangely childlike: "Although the manliest man among my forty, he said, 'Yes, ma'am', like a little boy" (41). Further, what makes Periwinkle praise John as the "manliest man" is not only his boyishness but his *womanliness*: his smile is "as sweet as any woman's" (39), and when he says goodbye to his favorite companion, "They kissed each other, tenderly as women" (44). This image is in turn part of an implicit narrative of romance between the two men, who have "a David and Jonathan sort of friendship" (38). When John dies, the other man is accorded the status of mourning spouse: "Presently, the Jonathan who so loved this comely David, came creeping from his bed for a last look and word" (44). Taken together, these descriptions of John effect two related transformations of the language of military masculinity. In terms of sexuality, they articulate the homosociality of the battlefield in implicitly homoerotic terms. Alcott's language is akin to Walt Whitman's famously homoerotic paeans to the dying men whom he knew while serving as a Union Army nurse: "Many a soldier's loving arms about this neck have cross'd and rested, / Many a soldier's kiss dwells on these bearded lips."[4] In terms of gender, however, Alcott diverges from Whitman, for she locates homoerotic masculinity within a framework of femininity, such that love between men is described in female terms ("tenderly as women") and soldiers behave like affectionate little women. "Sweet," "comely," and "tender," John is as much heroine as hero, not unlike Stowe's Uncle Tom, who functions, as Elizabeth Ammons has argued, as "the supreme heroine" of *Uncle Tom's Cabin*.[5] In Alcott's metaphorical translation of female traits into male bodies, the best man in the wake of battle behaves like a woman.

At the same time, in an apparent reversal of this feminization, Alcott also suggests that the best woman for the hospital is surprisingly like a man. The hyperbolically feminine name Tribulation Periwinkle would seem to suggest that the nurse is quintessentially female. Specifically, the nurse is a maternal figure, and throughout *Hospital Sketches,* maternal imagery abounds, from Periwinkle's first assumption of "as matronly an aspect as a spinster could assume" (21) to her general feeling of "a motherly affection for them all" (32). Yet such maternal femininity is unstable, for it has the status of adopted performance, rather than innate identity, throughout the text. One of Alcott's first tasks is to bathe injured soldiers, an activity that precipitates a tentative impersonation of motherhood:

> [T]o scrub some dozen lords of creation at a moment's notice, was really—really—. . . . I drowned my scruples in my washbowl, clutched my soap manfully, and . . . made a dab at the first dirty specimen I saw. . . . I took heart and scrubbed away like any tidy parent . . . Some of them took the performance like sleepy children . . . others looked grimly scandalized, and several of the roughest colored like bashful girls.
>
> (23-24)

The tone of this passage—like much in the opening chapters of *Hospital Sketches*—is lighthearted, but its theme is more serious, as Alcott attempts to navigate the shock of her encounter with male bodies through metaphor. Initially unrepresentable ("really—really—"), the moment is negotiated by a series of gender crossovers, whereby soldiers are "like bashful girls" and Periwinkle acts "manfully." The infantilization of men is here, as in the depiction of John, preliminary to a renegotiation of gender: men become "sleepy children" on the way to becoming "bashful girls." Meanwhile, the role of mother—"like any tidy parent"—is precisely enshrined as *role,* its identity as constructed as the gender and generation of soldiers.

Elsewhere in the text, Periwinkle intermittently abandons this performance of maternity. Though she leaves for Washington "as if going on a bridal tour" (6), she more closely resembles a soldier on his tour of duty. Requesting a nursing position at the start, she declares, "I've enlisted!" (4), and she describes her teary farewell to her family in masculine terms: "I maintain that the soldier who cries when his mother says 'Good bye,' is the boy to fight best" (6). Such passages, as Jane Schultz notes, offer "an act of mimesis [in which] Trib aligns herself with male consciousness."[6] Periwinkle's allegiances are to masculinity, as she later declares explicitly: "I have a fellow feeling for lads, and always owed Fate a grudge because I wasn't a lord of creation instead of a lady" (68). Rather than incarnating an innate femininity, then, Periwinkle's nursing seems less a form of mothering than a means of soldiering.

More lad than lady in her approach to war, Periwinkle is also more soldier than nurse in her experience of military service. Arising only six weeks after her arrival in hospital, Periwinkle's illness might seem to signal a failure of strength, linking femininity and illness in pathologizing combination.[7] Yet *Hospital Sketches* defines female illness differently, implicitly equating the female nurse who falls ill with fever with the male soldier delirious from his war injuries. Immediately following the death of John, the first words of the next chapter transfer the question of the soldier's ill health to

Periwinkle herself, as a doctor informs her, "My dear girl, we shall have you sick in your bed, unless you keep yourself warm and quiet" (47). Shortly after, her weak lungs force her to convalesce; like soldiers, she too has "a painful consciousness of my pleura, and a realizing sense of bones in the human frame" (55). What links Periwinkle's suffering most directly to those of soldiers, however, is its psychic register. When her illness worsens, she finds that "Hours began to get confused; people looked odd; queer faces haunted the room, and the nights were one long fight with weariness and pain" (60). Such symptoms strongly echo those of the men hospitalized alongside John, such as a New Jersey soldier "crazed by the horrors" of the war:

> [H]is mind had suffered more than his body; some string of that delicate machine was over strained, and, for days, he had been reliving, in imagination, the scenes he could not forget, till his distress broke out in incoherent ravings, pitiful to hear. . . . [A]n incessant stream of defiant shouts, whispered warnings, and broken laments, poured from his lips . . .
>
> (35-36)

Periwinkle's "odd" people, "queer" faces, and "confused" hours reprise such nighttime hallucinations. If the origins of her illness diverge from those of soldiers, its effects converge with theirs in the domain of the psyche.

Periwinkle's symptoms seem closest to those of the Civil War soldier whose wounds, deracinated from their physical origins, now reside wholly in the psyche: the amputee. As Periwinkle describes it, the amputee is a "poor soul" who, after his surgery, "comes to himself, sick, faint, and wandering; full of strange pains and confused visions, of disagreeable sensations and sights" (69). This description is part of an ongoing emphasis upon dismemberment in the text. When Periwinkle first arrives at the hospital, for example, she focuses on the "legless, armless" wounded (22) and her initiation into hospital life involves witnessing the "irrepressible tremor of [the] tortured bodies" of patients awaiting amputation without ether (29); later, at the moment of John's death, "there was no sound in the room but the drip of water, from a stump or two" (44). During Periwinkle's own convalescence, she sits sewing at her window and watches convalescents "going in parties to be fitted to artificial limbs" (55). Finally, she notes that while nurses are not "obliged to witness amputations," she herself "witnessed several operations; for the height of my ambition was to go to the front after a battle, and . . . the sooner I inured myself to trying sights, the more useful I should be" (69-70). Throughout the text, Periwinkle seems irresistibly drawn to the "trying sight" of the amputee, whose sufferings not only structure her work as a nurse but engage her experiences as a patient.

A focus upon amputation is inevitable in any account of Civil War nursing, since it was the strategy most readily available to doctors coping with bullet wounds and infection. In linking the physical sufferings of the amputee with his mental condition, moreover, Alcott follows contemporary medical writers systematically exploring such neurological phenomena as "the phantom limb," most famously the Civil War doctor and novelist Silas Weir Mitchell.[8] Alcott's account is distinctive, however, in that she not only relocates injury from bodies to minds, but also implicitly connects the gender of the amputee with that of the nurse. In the metaphorical resonance between the "confused visions" of the amputee and Periwinkle, the narrative provides the nurse with the closest possible access to a form of injury from which, as a civilian, she is definitionally denied. Amputation, that which typically makes the soldier less than a man, is here used symbolically to make the nurse something more—or at least something other—than a woman. Even as she metaphorically feminizes the male soldier, Alcott also offers a metonymic displacement of war injury from bodies to minds and from men to women. In Alcott's Civil War hospital, the line of demarcation between the sexes is as much under pressure as the integrity of body and psyche.

* * *

What is at stake in these multiple forms of cross-gender identification, in which men act like women and women like men? In **Hospital Sketches,** I first want to argue, such metaphoric crossovers are intimately linked to Alcott's own psychic conflicts as woman and as writer and to the larger self-divisions of nineteenth-century female subjectivity to which her writings testify. Daughter of educator and reformer Bronson Alcott, raised in the heady intellectual milieu of midcentury Concord, Louisa May Alcott was encouraged in her literary aspirations to a degree unusual in Victorian America. Yet that encouragement was qualified in a variety of ways. Since Bronson and Abba May Alcott strictly monitored their four daughters' development, Louisa's work had to satisfy strict parental standards of philosophical value and moral worth; further, since Bronson was chronically insolvent, her writing had to bring financial rewards to support the family. The larger intellectual world of Concord in which the Alcotts circulated added to this sense of constraint. "To have had Mr. Emerson for an intellectual god all one's life," she once remarked in conversation to a friend, "is to be invested with a chain armor of propriety."[9]

Despite the innovations of her upbringing, in short, Louisa May Alcott came of age in a culture whose moral and familial constraints compounded, rather than undercut, the propriety demanded by Victorian gender ideology. It is no surprise that by age twelve, she registers the "chain armor of propriety" in her journal as a homiletic discourse on the necessities of self-denial: "What are the most valuable kinds of self-denial? Ap-

petite, temper. How is self-denial of temper known? If I control my temper, I am respectful and gentle, and every one sees it. What is the result of this self-denial? Every one loves me, and I am happy."[10] Faithfully copied from her daily lessons, these comments were almost certainly read by her parents; Bronson had been observing Louisa closely since her infancy, while Abba wrote in the same journal entry, "I often peep into your diary, hoping to see some record of more happy days."[11] Even Alcott's private exercise of self-discipline was open to surveillance, in a pedagogy of self-control monitored both internally and externally. Her coming-of-age accords closely with what Richard Brodhead, following Foucault, has termed the "disciplinary intimacy" characteristic of antebellum America, whereby self-imposed restraint lovingly taught by the family, rather than corporal punishment harshly imposed by an external authority, became the privileged mode for disciplining the self. For all the joyful eccentricities of Alcott's early life, she was governed by a self-regulating pedagogy that rewrote the implicitly male credo of Emersonian self-reliance as female self-denial.[12]

In this narrative of female identity as psychic self-regulation, Alcott's work provides insight into the possibilities, metaphoric as well as literal, afforded women by the onset of the Civil War. Alcott's private writings make clear an identification with masculinity that long predated but was energized by the war. At fourteen, for example, she wrote in her journal: "I was born with a boy's spirit under my bib and tucker. *I can't wait* [for a time] when I *can work*"; and at twenty-eight she echoed in a letter, "I was born with a boys nature & always had more sympathy for & interest in them than in girls, & have fought my fight for nearly fifteen [years] with a boys spirit under my 'bib & tucker' & a boys wrath when I got 'floored,' so I'm not preaching like a prim spinster but freeing my mind like one of 'our fellows.'"[13] In these quotations, a woman who speaks assertively is immediately suspect—"preaching like a prim spinster"—while maleness, by contrast, signifies a way of working and speaking freely, as much a style as an identity. Long before the war begins, Alcott identifies agency with masculinity, in a culture in which the only way to imagine being a person is to envision being a man.

When war arrives, it offers Alcott a particular psychic charge, since it increases the value of masculine freedom by framing it as patriotic duty. "War declared with the South," she writes in her journal, "I've often longed to see a war, and now I have my wish. I long to be a man; but as I can't fight, I will content myself with working for those who can."[14] At a turning point in her own life, she declares, "Thirty years old. Decided to go to Washington as a nurse. . . . Help needed, and I love nursing, and *must* let out my pent-up energy in some new way. . . . So I set forth . . . feeling as if I was the son of the house going to war."[15] Metaphorically turning from thirty-year-old "prim spinster" to "son of the house," Alcott grows up in wartime by growing down to her favorite state, that of boyhood. The war, in short, marks Alcott's coming-of-age as a man.[16]

Tribulation Periwinkle's soldier persona in *Hospital Sketches,* then, is first of all a matter of masculine agency. The text's cross-gender identifications serve as part of Alcott's ongoing linkage, at once literal and metaphorical, between war and female self-representation. What Alcott's private writings further suggest is the figurative importance of civil war to female identity, for they effect what Margaret Higonnet has called a "metaphoric transfer of civil war from an external, political realm to inner conflict over sexual choice and the proper gender roles."[17] Together, Alcott's private writings and *Hospital Sketches* chart a war that is civil in two senses of the term: both a battle against feminine civility and a painfully unresolved conflict within the borders of her own psyche.

We may begin to chart the connection between external Civil War and internal civil war in her texts by tracing the path of one of her favorite adjectives, "topsy-turvy." In a letter to her father on the occasion of their shared birthday, Alcott writes:

> I was a crass crying brown baby. . . . I fell with a crash into girlhood & continued . . . tumbling from one year to another till strengthened by such violent exercise the topsy-turvy girl shot up into a topsy-turvy woman who now twenty three years after sits big brown & brave. . . .[18]

Here is Concord at the start of the war:

> [T]he town is in a high state of topsy-turvyness . . . when quiet Concord does get stirred up it is a sight to behold. . . . Are you going to have a dab at the saucy Southerners? I long to fly at some body & free my mind on several points. . . .[19]

And here is Alcott's home life as she prepares to leave for Washington:

> Father [is] keeping his topsy-turvy family in order. . . . I am getting ready to go to Washington as an army nurse . . . if I was only a boy I'd march off tomorrow.[20]

In these quotations, the rhetoric of masculine identification forms part of a general language of inversion, one in which both the private Alcott and the public sphere constitute worlds turned upside down. "Topsy-turvy" moves from an ambiguous index of Alcott's own rebelliousness to an approbatory gloss upon the freeing dislocations caused by Civil War. Together, these passages posit civil war as a condition of unruliness in which nation ("those saucy Southerners"), town ("stirred up" Concord), and family (not "in order") are so disrupted that they mirror Alcott's own chronic rebelliousness.

These passages also suggest the racial dimensions of Alcott's topsy-turvyness. Raised in a fervently abolitionist family that regularly met with antislavery leaders and played host to John Brown's family, Alcott associated the war with the end of slavery and longed to "go South & help the blacks as I am no longer allowed to nurse the whites. The former seems the greater work."[21] Apart from these explicit antislavery politics, her letters also reveal an implicit metaphorical identification between herself as a disorderly woman and free African Americans. In an abolitionist culture saturated with *Uncle Tom's Cabin*—one of Alcott's favorite books—"Topsy" may also signal Stowe's unruly and intractable African American character. Like Topsy, topsy-turvy Louisa is a "brown baby" who "crash[ed] into girlhood."[22] Topsy-turvy is also the name of a two-headed doll common to this era, whose conjoined black and white torsos, as Karen Sánchez-Eppler has argued, suggest the intimate connections between black and white female bodies in nineteenth-century American culture.[23] Overturned, the white doll's skirts reveal a black doll in racist "pickaninny" caricature. Alcott's writings offer a particular psychic appropriation of such duality, whereby the fantasy of unruly blackness serves as the inverted counterpart to the constraints of white femininity.

Alcott's topsy-turvyness implicitly involves inversions of sexuality as well as gender and race. She declared in an interview, for example, that "I am more than half-persuaded that I am a man's soul, put by some freak of nature into a woman's body . . . because I have fallen in love in my life with so many pretty girls, and never once the least bit with any man."[24] Bringing together masculine identification with female object-choice, this passage is startlingly proleptic of the sexological language of the "invert," only just beginning to emerge by the end of Alcott's lifetime, which pathologized the lesbian as a "man's soul trapped in a woman's body."[25] Such codifications were prescriptive rather than descriptive, and Alcott's biographers provide little conclusive evidence about whether she was lesbian. But her comment suggests at minimum her swerve away from the accoutrements of heterosexuality—husband, children, household—which normatively accompanied Victorian womanhood. Thirty and still unmarried when she went to Washington, Alcott was topsy-turvy—or, to use another of her favorite adjectives, "queer"—by virtue of being a permanent spinster as well as a "boyish" girl.[26]

Hospital Sketches dramatizes the carnivalesque pleasures of such inversions, making topsy-turvyness into a symbolic condition of the Civil War. As Periwinkle leaves for Washington, Alcott adopts her characteristic phrase to describe "topsy-turvy Trib" (6). Periwinkle's journey relocates inversion from psychic to social domains. On the train, she watches as "the boys threw up their caps and cut capers as we passed" (18); when she arrives, she observes that "Pennsylvania Avenue . . . made me feel as if I'd crossed the water and landed somewhere in Carnival time" (18). As Mary Cappello notes, Alcott's descriptions of Washington are awash in accounts of pigs, dirt, and other boundary-dissolving expressions of the carnivalesque.[27] Her fictional name for the hospital, Hurly-burly House, is a synonym for inversion, and she herself fosters in her patients "the jolliest state of mind their condition allowed" (32). Such inversions are ongoing, for when the men return to the battlefield, "the rooms fall into an indescribable state of topsy-turvyness" (68). A disorderly psyche writ large, Hurly-burly House offers a symbolic extension of, as well as a literal outlet for, Alcott's own rebellions against normative femininity.

Hospital Sketches also adapts the racial dynamics of Alcott's private writings to the political setting of the Civil War. The convergence between private and public forms of carnival emerges most vividly in a scene that takes place on New Year's Eve, a traditionally celebratory time and in this case (31 December 1862) the night before the enactment of the Emancipation Proclamation. At this crucial moment, Nurse Periwinkle is sick in bed, but not too sick to register a connection between herself and a group of African American men outside her window:

> As the bells rung midnight, I electrified my room-mate by dancing out of bed, throwing up the window, and flapping my handkerchief, with a feeble cheer, in answer to the shout of a group of colored men in the street below. All night they tooted and trampled, fired crackers, sung 'Glory, Hallelujah. . . .'
>
> (59)

Literally on the eve of racial freedom, this moment is also a proclamation of emancipation for Alcott herself, combining the freedom of singing African American men with her own dancing and "flapping." In Alcott's metaphorical appropriation of racial difference, both she and the men below become slaves free from masters. Like other forms of cross-race contact, such as, the moment reveals as much about whiteness as about blackness.[28] In *Hospital Sketches,* African American characters form a site of psychic release for Alcott, a screen on which she can project her own unruly desires while safely displacing them elsewhere.

If *Hospital Sketches* resituates Alcott's internal revolt on a national stage, so too does it give new metaphoric resonance to an ongoing vocabulary of madness. In the New Year's Eve moment as elsewhere in her writings, she is never so much herself as when she is sick, an equation that predates the war but takes on new meaning from it. "I was so excited I pitched about like a mad woman," Alcott writes in an 1856 letter after attending an abolitionist speech.[29] Six years later, she notes in her first journal account of her nursing experience, "Am brought home nearly dead and have a fever," to which she later added, "which I enjoy very much, at least the crazy part."[30] In this addendum, the delirium caused by typhoid fever, like the earlier excitement of being a "mad woman," serves a liberatory function, as a rare psychic respite from self-abnegation. Alcott's second journal account of her illness elaborates "the crazy part" more fully:

> A mob at Baltimore breaking down the door to get me; being hung for a witch, burned, stoned & otherwise maltreated were some of my fancies. Also being tempted to join Dr W. & two of the nurses in worshipping the Devil. Also tending millions of sick men who never died or got well.[31]

These images contrast the horrors of daily nursing, a Sisyphean exercise in frustration, with the temptations of Devil worship and the lure of the witch—that quintessential emblem of unruly femininity. In this realization of topsy-turvyness as the dream work of the unconscious, Alcott transforms the activity of nursing into a full internal revolt against feminine civility.

In *Hospital Sketches,* the illness of the soldier-nurse extends the journal's language of hallucination to its metaphorical limits. In fictionalizing the same trajectory from "motherliness" to madness, *Hospital Sketches* masculinizes Periwinkle's fever, aligning it so closely with the illness of male soldiers that the sufferings of John and his fellow soldiers seem to serve as direct preparation for her own delirium. As *Hospital Sketches* crafts a new home, Hurly-burly House, for Alcott's domestic unrest, so too does the text translate her antebellum war fervor into actual war fever. In this translation, her illness gains new value, masculinized as battle service rather than essentialized as female hysteria. While *Hospital Sketches* grants new narrative power to this hallucination, however, it also curtails that power, as the suffering daughter is awakened from fever by the arrival of her father to fetch her safely home: "[W]hen he said, 'Come home,' I answered, 'Yes, father'; and so ended my career as an army nurse" (60).

Yet if the narrative of *Hospital Sketches* records the self-censoring victory of civility over the topsy-turvy inversions of war, the existence of the text itself points in a different direction: toward the war's productive effect upon her self-representation as an author. In a letter to a friend, for example, she declares that "*Hospital Sketches* still continues a great joke to me, & a sort of perpetual surprise-party, for to this day I cannot see why people like a few extracts from topsy-turvy letters written on inverted tin kettles."[32] The imagery of authorship in this passage is, once again, that of inversion. Such language suggests that Alcott's construction of authorship, like her representation of illness and madness, bears an intimate relation to the rhetoric of civil war.

As with her self-conceptions as "son of the house" and "mad woman," Alcott's representation of writing as rebellion predates her war experience. Throughout her journals and letters, Alcott describes the experience of writing as that of being in a "vortex" which frees her from regular duty, as in this 1860 letter to her sister:

> You ask what I am writing. Well, two books half done, nine stories simmering, and stacks of fairy stories moulding on the shelf. I can't do much, as I have no time to get into a real good vortex. It unfits me for work, worries Ma to see me look pale, eat nothing, and ply by night. These extinguishers keep genius from burning as I could wish. . . .[33]

The feverish implications of such "burning" efforts emerge more clearly in a journal entry about a stint of writing which "was very pleasant and queer while it lasted; but after three weeks of it I found that my mind was too rampant for my body, as my head was dizzy, legs shaky, and no sleep would come."[34] Here, writing is akin to a bout of illness, in which both mind and body are disordered and the former overwhelms the latter. With her mind "too rampant" for her body, Alcott constructs writing as a case of topsy-turvy brain fever. This is also the symptomatic presentation of Periwinkle's illness, but *Hospital Sketches* implicitly recasts the meaning of authorship by aligning writing fever with war fever. In her account of Periwinkle's dizzy head and shaky legs, Alcott implicitly legitimates the act of writing by conjoining personal literary desires with the patriotism of the suffering nurse.

Alcott's letters authorize writing through the metaphor of soldiering in another way, by linking her literary works to the bodily scars of male soldiers in battle. Such scars are constitutionally—in both senses of the term—denied to her; as John Limon notes, "as a daughter, she cannot assume the compensatory postures of wounded literary sons."[35] Denied a literal way to construct such scars for herself, however, Alcott finds a literary one. Apologizing to her friend Alfred Whitman for a delay in writing, she narrates:

> My only excuse is I've been to Washington a nursin in the army, got typhoid fever & came bundling home to rave, & ramp, & get my head shaved & almost retire into the tombs in consequence, not to mention picking up again, & appearing before the eyes of my grateful country in a wig & no particular flesh on my bones, also the writing some Hospital Sketches & when folks said put em in a book, doing the same & being drove wild with proof, & printers, & such matters . . .[36]

This passage characteristically unites different forms of mental disorder in a humorous tone, combining the "rave" of typhoid fever with the "wild" pressures of publication. Yet one moment more seriously brings the effects of wartime service back to Alcott's body: "get my head shaved & almost retire into the tombs in con-

sequence." One of the many physical effects of her typhoid fever, Alcott's baldness is a striking metaphor for the impact of the war upon her: a symbol for self-exposure, it specifically makes visible her skewed relation to conventional femininity. In a letter to a woman friend, she remarked, "I would advise all *young* ladies of thirty to shave their brows, pass a few months in the deepest seclusion & then find themselves back in their teens, as far as appearance goes."[37]

In *Hospital Sketches,* this wry image of teenage self-scrutiny undergoes an important transformation. In the story of Tribulation Periwinkle's illness, Alcott makes baldness manly, since it is metaphorically akin to the language of male war injury: "I take some satisfaction in the thought that, if I could not lay my head on the altar of my country, I have [laid] my hair" (61). If Alcott is a soldier returning from Washington, then her hair is her own amputated limb. Appearing, like a wounded soldier, before the eyes of a "grateful country," she wears a wig as a temporary prosthesis for the missing part. Once the "son of the house" off to war, she is now "back in her teens" with the battle scar of baldness.

The imagery of the wig is, in turn, intimately linked to her writing, since it serves as a crowning metaphor for the gender ambiguities of *Hospital Sketches* itself. Hair and head are extensions of one another, as she notes in her journal: "Felt badly about losing my one beauty. Never mind, it might have been my head & a wig outside is better than a loss of wits inside."[38] In the parallel between wig and wits, Alcott's fake hair is a physical covering for the outside of her head as her writing is a textual cover for its inside. In both cases, the covering aims at the creation of an appropriate appearance—the dutiful daughter, the "motherly" nurse—only to show up askew. Turning the woman nurse into the author-soldier, Alcott writes a book in which a brief, metaphoric departure from femininity has the hallucinatory yet profound impact of a fever dream. As the literary embodiment of her psychic scars, *Hospital Sketches* ultimately offers the promise of masculine agency as woman's phantom limb.

In aligning her fever with that of the soldier, then, Alcott provides a commentary upon the transformative importance of the Civil War for one nineteenth-century American woman writer. Of the two cross-gender images underpinning *Hospital Sketches*—the masculinized nurse and the feminized soldier—the former is particularly significant in relation to Alcott's self-representation as woman writer, for it constitutes an ingenious point of access to the language of masculine agency. From inversion and illness to madness and writing, Alcott's various languages of rebellion gather metaphorical as well as literal force from her relation to the Civil War. In this context, her metaphoric battle scars constitute a strategic redefinition of female subjectivity, one that reframes female inadequacy as male wounding. Femininity is here aligned with weakness and suffering, but that suffering is coded masculine; women live within the domestic sphere, but that sphere is redefined and honored as that of a convalescent "veteran." Most importantly, female authorship is newly validated as political duty and battle legacy. To put it another way, Alcott's war writings suggest that in a nineteenth-century culture that defined female subjectivity as scarring self-denial, femininity might inevitably be a wound, but at least the terms of such wounding could be altered and valorized. Alcott, I suggest, rewrites the woman writer's quest for a room of one's own into the double-edged desire—at once rebellious and self-regulating—for a wound of one's own.

* * *

In *Hospital Sketches,* I have argued thus far, the Civil War functions as a metaphor for Alcott's struggles as ambivalent Concord daughter and as emerging woman writer. Yet we can also trace this metaphorical relation between warring body politic and topsy-turvy individual body in reverse. For if the Civil War is symbolically linked to Alcott's own psyche, so too does her representation of individual bodies intervene in contemporary constructions of embodied nationhood. Rereading *Hospital Sketches,* we can see how Alcott develops her second image of cross-gendered identification: the feminized soldier. The complement to the figure of the masculinized nurse, the feminized soldier serves as a point of departure for Alcott's allegorical reinventions of the nation at war and in peace.

To understand these reinventions, we must first move from the intimate literary domain of Alcott's journals to the public sphere of national political discourse in the 1860s, and from the body of the individual male soldier to that of the nation as a whole. In the Civil War, politicians and writers adapted the well-established trope of the body politic in a variety of ways, representing the division of the nation in a complex rhetorical network of corporeal fractures and familial divorces. One prominent strategy of Northern politicians was to describe the fractured Union as an injured body, a strategy that served to naturalize at least three sets of Northern political needs. Most immediately, the language of injury served to condemn secession. As Boston minister Henry W. Bellows wrote in a popular 1863 pamphlet, "[T]his is a time of desperate war—when a desperate enemy is stabbing at the heart of the nation, the capital, and clutching at the nation's throat, the Mississippi river."[39] Promoting the integrity of the Union, such images also played a powerful role in what George Fredrickson has termed the "inner civil war" among Northern intellectuals. For Bellows as for other northerners, metaphors of an imperiled national body supported an authoritarian approach to reestablishing a democratic nation. Wendell

Phillips, for example, argued strenuously for a strong Northern government in "The War for the Union" (1863) by avowing that "The use of surgeons is, that when lancets are needed somebody may know how to use them, and save life. . . . [T]he Government may safely be trusted, in a great emergency, with despotic power, without fear of harm, or of wrecking the state."[40] Finally, in the abolitionist Northern rhetoric of the body politic, the most profound national disease was not national disunion or Northern disloyalty but slavery. Often represented as a cancer within the body politic, slavery metaphorically required amputation for the survival of the nation. As Lincoln declared, "[T]he moment came when I felt slavery must die that the nation might live!"[41]

As these examples suggest, the image of the injured body politic had its necessary complement in the figure of the government as a judiciously knife-wielding surgeon. Bellows suggested the full affective reach of the role of the surgeon-amputator: "[T]he nation is in a struggle of life and death, and the Government is the physician alone responsible for applying the remedies for its recovery."[42] The privileged actor in this drama was its principal surgeon, Lincoln, who also served as a metaphorical incorporation of the nation itself; as Bellows declares: "The head of a nation *is* a sacred person, representing, for the time he holds his office, the most valuable and solemn rights and duties of a people."[43] In an extension of the tradition of "the king's two bodies," Lincoln's synecdochic power took a final turn in the wake of his assassination, when he became not only the nation's sacred leader, but also its most heroic patient-martyr. The body politic, its limbs gangrenous from slavery and fractured by secession, would finally be cured not by the Godlike surgery of Lincoln but by his Christlike sacrifice.[44]

In these contexts, we can return to Alcott's *Hospital Sketches,* for in Alcott's implicitly symbolic narrative as in the explicitly metaphorical prose of Bellows, Phillips, and Lincoln, the suffering of the male body can be read as the crisis of a nation wracked by civil war. In *Hospital Sketches,* the body of the soldier is as radically disarticulated as that of the nation, as in the case of a wounded man who speaks jocularly of his lost limbs: "Lord! What a scramble there'll be for arms and legs, when we old boys come out of our graves, on the Judgment Day: wonder if we shall get our own again? If we do, my leg will have to tramp from Fredericksburg, my arm from here, I suppose, and meet my body, wherever it may be" (25). While this passage comically maps male appendages onto geographic regions, the sufferings of the martyred John may be interpreted more seriously as a metaphorical gloss upon the ailing union: "For hours he suffered dumbly, without a moment's respite, or a moment's murmuring; his limbs grew cold, his face damp, his lips white, and, again and again, he tore the covering off his breast, as if the lightest weight added to his agony" (44). If this focus on injury is, as I argued above, a displaced account of Alcott's internal conflicts about gender, we can also see it as part of the inner civil war among northerners writing about the nation. In Alcott's allegorical narrative as in the political rhetoric of Bellows and Lincoln, bodies signify as nations and the agonies of individual suffering echo the political exigencies of civil war.

The 1869 edition of the text, *Hospital Sketches and Camp and Fireside Stories,* provides further hints of the iconographic significance of John's suffering. Reprinting the entirety of the original *Hospital Sketches* as well as eight short stories (four of them about the war), this edition also included two illustrations. The frontispiece for the volume is a representation of John's suffering, captioned "The manliest man among my forty" and featuring Periwinkle with John. Behind these two figures are two illustrations on the wall: Abraham Lincoln, over whose head is the caption "In God We Trust," and a map of the reunified USA. Juxtaposed, these images effect a series of metonymic connections from Periwinkle to John, from John to the sanctified Lincoln ("In God We Trust"), and from Lincoln to the body politic ("USA," which only became a singular noun—that is, a unified body—as a result of the war). Lincoln is the key figure in this tableau, since his symbolic power is a synecdoche for the nation, while his assassination echoes the martyred death of John. This linkage between feminized soldier and fallen president capitalizes on a feminizing strand of cultural mythology already in place for Lincoln: in the words of contemporaries, he was a man "of almost child-like sweetness" and a type of "womanly tenderness," while William Herndon described him going to market wearing a shawl, children in tow, like a motherly housewife.[45] For Alcott, Lincoln's femininity is a valuable trait, tempering masculine authority with the compassion—and feminized martyrdom—of Christ himself. Read as a midwar text, then, John's story indirectly links soldier and nation; read as a retrospective text upon the war, his story more explicitly unites his martyrdom with that of the feminized Lincoln and Christ. Firmly located in a pantheon of feminized male heroes, John carries allegorical weight that extends from soldier to savior to nation.

If Alcott shares with political commentators a rhetoric of national injury, however, she differs from them in her account of cure. *Hospital Sketches* provides a narrative of national embodiment in which male leadership is disorderly at every level: in the operating room of the surgeon-amputator, in the larger social institution of the hospital, and in the national government itself. In this critique, the language of inversion that we have already examined is of central importance, but its valences are reversed. Rather than providing a liberatory discourse for white female subjectivity, topsy-turvyness now appears dystopically as a failure of nationhood.

Most obviously, *Hospital Sketches* has harsh words for surgeons. In particular, Periwinkle objects to one Doctor P., a doctor who has "a somewhat trying habit of regarding a man and his wound as separate institutions" (70), and who

> seemed to regard a dilapidated body very much as I should have regarded a damaged garment; and, turning up his cuffs, [began] cutting, sawing, patching and piecing, with the enthusiasm of an accomplished surgical seamstress. . . . The more intricate the wound, the better he liked it. A poor private, with both legs off, and shot through the lungs, possessed more attractions for him than a dozen generals, slightly scratched . . . and had any one appeared in small pieces, requesting to be put together again, he would have considered it a special dispensation.
>
> (29)

Here is another gender crossover, but one played for grotesquerie: described in domestic imagery as "an accomplished surgical seamstress," Dr. P. is criticized for his equation of bodies with damaged garments. Similarly, his preference for the private over the general is an index of his fanatical interest in dismembered bodies, rather than a praiseworthy inversion of social hierarchy. "In a state of bliss over a complicated amputation," Dr. P. "works away, with his head upside down" (52). Dr. P's sense of responsibility is "upside down" along with his head, in an account that offers an inverted burlesque of the sacred surgeon-healer described by Bellows and embodied by Lincoln.

If medical authority in *Hospital Sketches* appears grossly inadequate to the demands of the injured bodies in its care, hospital administration fares no better. At Hurly-burly House,

> disorder, discomfort, bad management, and no visible head, reduced things to a condition which I despair of describing. The circumlocution fashion prevailed, forms and fusses tormented our souls, and unnecessary strictness in one place was counterbalanced by unpardonable laxity in another.
>
> (51)

This passage offers a veritable frenzy of institutional inversion: disorder, imbalance, circumlocution, and an unbalanced bodily economy in which there is "no visible head." Like the nation sick from war and slavery, the hospital is a poorly regulated body that cannot survive its injuries. "Hurly-burly House," Periwinkle declares without regret at the end, "has ceased to exist as a hospital; so let it rest, with all its sins upon its head" (73).

Finally, the national government is similarly uncontrolled, as Periwinkle discovers when she visits the Senate, "hoping to hear and see if this large machine was run any better than some small ones I knew of":

> I was too late, and found the Speaker's chair occupied by a colored gentleman of ten; while two others were . . . having a hot debate on the cornball question, as they gathered the waste paper strewn about the floor into bags; and several white members played leap-frog over the desks, a much wholesomer relaxation than some of the older Senators indulge in, I fancy.
>
> (53)

In the "large machine" as in the "small ones," the language of unruliness runs riot: waste covers the floor and "leap-frog" is the game of the day. This passage is written for comic effect, but the coherence of its imagery with Alcott's account of hospital administration is revealing. In this version of the "world turned upside down," body and body politic alike suffer from their leaders, who range from sadistic surgeon to absent hospital "head" to "colored gentleman of ten." Alcott's inclusion of this last character alerts us once again to the salience of racial imagery to her representation of inversion. The ten-year old "colored gentleman" represents another incarnation of Topsy, but now in a pejorative mode. When such a character is in "the Speaker's Chair" of Congress, the result is chaos rather than carnival.

What, then, would Periwinkle—and Alcott—prefer instead? *Hospital Sketches* offers a few glimpses of a very different kind of hospital: at the start, for example, members of Periwinkle's family merrily invent roles for themselves in a "model hospital" upon hearing that she is to be a nurse (4); later, Periwinkle marvels at the impeccable administration of Armory House, the hospital to which she had originally planned to go and which she visits during her convalescence. In an ideal hospital, Periwinkle would be in charge, not only caring for male soldiers but intervening in race relations in the hospital. The only other illustration in *Hospital Sketches* glosses a revealing moment in the text, when Periwinkle rebukes a white nurse from Virginia who refuses to pick up a black child in the kitchen. Seizing the child, Periwinkle lectures the white nurse on abolitionism; the caption for the accompanying image reads "one hand stirred gruel for sick America, and the other hugged baby Africa" (59). If the frontispiece to *Hospital Sketches* puts Periwinkle in the picture, this illustration situates her as a white leader literally highlighted against a black background. The image suggests a fantasy of white female authority in which Periwinkle leads both "sick America" and "baby Africa."[46]

Periwinkle cannot realize this racially hierarchical gender fantasy within the confines of Hurly-burly House, where male leadership still holds sway. In a headless hospital where nurses can only be foot soldiers, Periwinkle must remain silent in the face of hospital mismanagement: "I feel like a boiling tea-kettle, with the lid ready to fly off and damage somebody" (51). In relation to Dr. P., this language of self-policing is even more overt, as she assumes a divided attitude of external masochism and internal sadism: "I obeyed [Dr. P.], cherishing the while a strong desire to insinuate a few of his own disagreeable knives and scissors into him, and see how he liked it. A very disrespectable and ridiculous fancy" (71).[47]

In *Hospital Sketches,* Alcott suggests that as a female citizen in a male republic, she has no choice but to be patient with surgeons. In her subsequent Civil War fiction, however, she gets to play doctor, offering several related versions of a revitalized body politic. Consistently engaging the imagery of Civil War feminization, these texts—which include **"My Contraband"** (1863; also called **"The Brothers"**), **"A Hospital Christmas"** (1864), *Little Women* (1868-69), *Work* (1873), and *Jo's Boys* (1886)—gradually shift in emphasis from a focus on male injury to one on female healing. In particular, Alcott's most famous novel, *Little Women,* may be understood as continuing the narrative of national recovery that *Hospital Sketches* only begins to imagine. *Little Women* offers Alcott's first full-scale version of a reconstructed body politic, one that is effectively controlled by female virtues, even—or especially—when evacuated of female bodies.

Its first half set during the Civil War, *Little Women* is a war novel, though it is seldom defined by critics as such.[48] In particular, the story of the March sisters, like Alcott's earlier writing, interprets war through the figure of the suffering Civil War soldier. There are at least three injured soldiers in *Little Women,* beginning with the patriarch of the March family, a chaplain in the Union Army who falls dangerously ill and recovers at a hospital in Washington. Yet Mr. March is a peripheral character in the narrative, and his war service is presented in terms of its distance from the rest of the family. Far more visible and important to the narrative is Beth, whose illness dominates the novel twice, from her initial bout with scarlet fever to her lingering death twenty-two chapters and several years later. Beth's illness is linked with the female domestic sphere—she contracts scarlet fever from tending a sick baby—but its representation is invested with the narrative energy Alcott had previously given to the wounds of soldiers, and her symptoms are akin to those of the feverish patients of *Hospital Sketches*: "[S]he did not know the familiar faces round her, but addressed them by wrong names, and called imploringly for her mother."[49] Her death is described in the terms of Christian martyrdom Alcott had previously used for the soldier-hero John: "[T]he natural rebellion over, the old peace returned" (415) and "in the dark hour before the dawn, on the bosom where she had drawn her first breath, she quietly drew her last" (419). As with John, her death is available for an allegorical reading, particularly as it coincides with the end of "rebellion" and the return of "old peace." In Beth's illness, Alcott combines the conventions of the war novel with the narrative frame of domestic fiction, translating the pathos of the dying male soldier into that of the dying little sister.[50]

But there is still another injured military figure in the text. Jo March, the novel's heroine, is also its regretful soldier-manqué: "I can't get over my disappointment in not being a boy, and it's worse than ever now, for I'm dying to go and fight with papa" (3), she declares at the outset, and shortly thereafter she laments, "Don't I wish I could go as a drummer, a *vivan*—what's its name? or a nurse, so I could be near him and help him" (8). These adjunct military roles—drummer, nurse, and "vivandiere," or provider of goods and support—are unavailable to her, but she gets her chance to participate in the war metaphorically, when she has her hair cut off for the cause: "I felt queer when I saw the dear old hair laid out on the table, and felt only the short, rough ends on my head. It almost seemed as if I'd an arm or a leg off" (163). This is haircutting as amputation, in a reprise of Periwinkle's earlier alignment between a woman giving up her hair and a soldier losing a limb in battle. The moment further reroutes the representation of male injury in the novel, moving not only from sick fathers to sick daughters, but also from dying daughters to live ones. From her initial focus on the soldier as a feminized man, Alcott has come full circle to the model of soldier as masculinized woman.

Like the novel's truest soldier, its ablest surgeon-leader is a woman. Marmee is Beth's most valued nurse, but more importantly, she is the household's best manager, teaching her daughters practical lessons in domestic economy and moral lessons about "the sweetness of self-denial and self-control" (82). Unlike the administrators of Hurly-burly House, Marmee is able to bring order out of chaos, as when, after the girls have made themselves irritable during a week of leisure, she gently lectures them on the value of industry: "Work is wholesome, and there is plenty for everyone; it keeps us from *ennui* and mischief. . . . I am quite satisfied with the experiment, and fancy that we shall not have to repeat it; only don't go to the other extreme, and delve like slaves" (117-18). While Marmee's words offer harsh lessons in individual female self-abnegation, they also articulate a more utopian social vision of a self-regulating body politic. Neither a topsy-turvy Hurly-burly House nor a national world relying on "slaves," the all-female March household of the first half of the novel provides an exemplary model for the wartime nation, its metaphoric frame now shifted from the locus of the body to that of the household. As Kathleen Diffley has shown, Alcott is one of many writers narrating the

political reconstruction of "the house divided" through literary plots.[51] The national domestic scene is the domestic household writ large, or as Lincoln himself had declared in a speech in the campaign of 1860, "If the Republican party of this nation shall ever have the national house entrusted to its keeping, it will be the duty of that party to attend to all the affairs of national housekeeping."[52]

Set during the postwar years, the second half of *Little Women* provides an exhaustive inventory of the types of national "housekeeping" that may emerge after the Civil War is over. If Marmee is the incumbent president of the March republic, then her daughters are her successors, and the households they establish constitute Alcott's allegorical experiments in domestic order for the nation recovering from domestic war. Meg, the first to marry, is too insular in her concerns, and too dependent on John Brooke, to interest Alcott as a symbol of political authority. Her domesticity competes with the public sphere, as when her husband attempts to read the newspaper. "Demi's colic got into the shipping list, and Daisy's fall affected the price of stocks,—for Mrs. Brooke was only interested in domestic news" (389). If Meg is too "domestic," Amy is too foreign, both in her European travels and in her marriage to the wealthy Laurie, which establishes her as an aristocrat rather than a truly democratic American. Neither Meg nor Amy can fulfill the mandate whereby "In America," as the narrator remarks, "girls early sign a declaration of independence, and enjoy their freedom with republican zest" (388).

In this equation of the American girl with American government, it is Jo, of course, who is the trust representative of "republican zest"—a legacy of both the earlier "declaration of independence" and the more recently completed Civil War. Jo offers the best hope for leading postwar America, as exemplified in the household of boys she establishes in the novel's final chapter, after marrying Professor Bhaer: "Think what luxury; Plumfield my own, and a wilderness of boys to enjoy it with me!" (483). Ending with a celebration of Marmee's sixtieth birthday, the novel consolidates its election of Jo as new leader, surrounding her with surrogate boys as well as her own two sons, "tumbling on the grass beside her" (490). Ensconced at Plumfield, Jo has now assumed her mother's role. With her own topsy-turvyness displaced onto the "topsy-turvy heads" of boys (483) and the "tumbling" of her own sons, she will govern Alcott's reconstructed America.

What kind of body politic does Alcott construct in Plumfield? Plumfield brings to fruition Nurse Periwinkle's hope for a better-managed Hurly-burly House, since Plumfield is a hospital for the male psyche, centered on a therapeutic search for "the good spot which exists in the heart of the naughtiest, sauciest, most tantalizing little ragamuffin" (485). The key to this world is its home-like status, its domestic construction as an extended family over which Jo holds moral sway. Turning from patient to doctor, Jo fulfills the thwarted legacy of Tribulation Periwinkle. Like Periwinkle, Jo voices a desire for masculine authority: "I'm the man of the family now papa is away" (5). Unlike Periwinkle, Jo gets the opportunity to exercise this desire in her own realm of social power; she combines the compassion of Nurse P. with the authority of Dr. P. Now called Mother Bhaer, Jo redefines the leader as matriarch. Motherhood is, however, reconceived as a strategy rather than an identity; it is significant, for example, that Jo takes on the position of metaphorical mother to the boys of Plumfield before she has her own sons. This is, then, a postwar world in which hospital has become home, health is moral rather than physical, and leadership consists of mothering as well as doctoring the nation.

In this world, moreover, feminization takes on a new meaning, at once less visible and more fundamental than in *Hospital Sketches.* Unlike John of *Hospital Sketches,* the boys of Plumfield seem unambiguously male. Yet feminization is essential to Plumfield, since the moral lessons that Jo will teach her boys are ones that she herself has learned in the household of little women with her sisters and Marmee. These little men are feminized into adulthood, not so much by their literal exposure to the authoritative Mother Bhaer as by their psychic imitation of female self-control. The teaching of self-control that is Plumfield's ultimate goal— "the most rampant ragamuffin was conquered in the end" (485)—makes Jo's boys into self-regulating subjects: that is, psychic little women. As Brodhead notes, Plumfield offers the "disciplinary intimacy" of Alcott's childhood writ large, as a "founding mythology or privileged system of truth."[53] Self-mastery is now conceived from the perspective of parent rather than child and community rather than individual—conceived, in short, as a pedagogic mode for national regeneration. By the end of *Little Women,* Alcott is training the male citizenry of the postwar nation by making a country of little women.

This process will continue in the book's sequel, *Little Men* (1871) and in Alcott's last novel, *Jo's Boys* (1886). *Little Men* is virtually obsessed with the inculcation of male self-discipline as supervised by women; as Mother Bhaer remarks, "[O]ne of my favorite fancies is to look at my family as a small world, to watch the progress of my little men, and, lately, to see how well the influence of my little women works upon them."[54] *Jo's Boys* registers the symbolic importance of the Civil War to this "small world," transposing a series of Civil War metaphors to the new context of the fight for suffrage; one of the novel's many allusions to the Union cause, for example, frames the struggle for women's rights as "the battle cry of freedom."[55] *Hospital Sketches* had hinted at the battle for suffrage, with Tribulation Periwinkle

declaring as she leaves for Washington, "I'm a woman's rights woman" (9). Twenty-five years later, Alcott develops this hint into a significant feature of her Plumfield world, with a new heroine, Nan, who is fittingly both a doctor—Alcott's icon of leadership—and a feminist. The Civil War has come into a new era, its metaphorical connotations of battle now explicitly enlisted in support of feminism.[56]

For Alcott, then, feminization encompasses a variety of imaginative possibilities whereby traditional gender boundaries are breached in the service of the nation. Feminization for Alcott involves a radical reworking of the relation between men and women, such that men not only come under the influence of women, but also introject the disciplinary mode of self-mastery that characterizes the female psyche. Women, meanwhile, take on increasingly central roles within the body politic, but their social authority derives more from the deliberate deployment of conventionally female behaviors such as mothering than it does from an essentialized femininity. At its broadest reaches, feminization becomes feminism, metaphorically updated into a civil war over suffrage. Turning boys and girls alike into little women, feminization transforms the nation into a body healed from slavery and a household restored from the disorder of war. In a sustained contribution to the political and literary culture of postwar America, Alcott reconstructs the body politic in the shape of a woman.

Notes

1. For useful reassessments of Alcott's career, see Sarah Elbert, *A Hunger for Home: Louisa May Alcott's Place in American Culture* (New Brunswick, N.J., 1977); Elaine Showalter, Introduction to *Alternative Alcott* (New Brunswick, N.J., 1988); Madeleine Stern, Introduction to *Louisa May Alcott: Selected Fiction* (Boston, 1990); and Daniel Shealy, Madeleine B. Stern, and Joel Myerson, eds., *Critical Essays on Louisa May Alcott* (Boston, 1984). For critical discussions of Alcott's thrillers, see Judith Fetterley, "Impersonating *Little Women*: The Radicalism of Alcott's 'Behind a Mask,'" *Women's Studies* 10 (1983): 1-14; and Elizabeth Keyser, *Whispers in the Dark: The Fiction of Louisa May Alcott* (Knoxville, Tenn., 1993).

2. In addition to *Hospital Sketches,* in the 1860s Alcott published the novels *Moods* and *Little Women* and more than fifty short works of fiction and journalism, including war stories, gothic thrillers, fantasy tales, and essays on contemporary political issues. On Alcott's career in the 1860s, see Richard H. Brodhead, *Cultures of Letters: Scenes of Reading and Writing in Nineteenth-Century America* (Chicago, 1993), 69-106. Alcott is anthologized as a Civil War writer in [Louis P.] Ma-

sur, [ed.,] *"The Real War"* [*The Real War Will Never Get in the Books: Selections from Writers During the Civil War* (New York, 1993)], 19-37. Discussions of *Hospital Sketches* may be found in Elbert, *A Hunger for Home,* 164-68; Bessie Z. Jones, Introduction to *Hospital Sketches,* by Louisa May Alcott (Cambridge, Mass., 1960), vii-xliv; Stern, Introduction to *Critical Essays* [*Critical Essays on Louisa May Alcott*], 25-40; and esp. Mary Cappello, *"'Looking About Me With All My Eyes': Censored Viewing, Carnival, and Louisa May Alcott's *Hospital Sketches,"* *Arizona Quarterly* 50 (autumn 1994): 59-88, and Jane E. Schultz, "Embattled Care: Narrative Authority in Louisa May Alcott's *Hospital Sketches,"* *Legacy* 9 (fall 1992): 104-18.

3. Alcott, *Hospital Sketches,* in *Alternative Alcott,* 43, 46. All subsequent quotations are taken from this edition and included parenthetically in the text.

4. Walt Whitman, "The Wound-Dresser," in *Walt Whitman: Complete Poetry and Collected Prose,* ed. Justin Kaplan (New York, 1982), 445. For discussion of the homoerotics of Whitman's poetry, see Michael Moon, *Disseminating Whitman: Revision and Corporeality in "Leaves of Grass"* (Cambridge, Mass., 1991), 171-222, and Betsy Erkkila and Jay Grossman, eds., *Breaking Bounds: Whitman and American Cultural Studies* (New York, 1996).

5. Elizabeth Ammons, "Heroines in *Uncle Tom's Cabin,*" in *Critical Essays on Harriet Beecher Stowe,* ed. Elizabeth Ammons (Boston, 1990), 159. For a recent critique of this argument, see Cynthia Griffin Wolff, "'Masculinity' in *Uncle Tom's Cabin,*" *American Quarterly* 47 (Dec. 1995): 595-618.

6. Schultz, "Embattled Care," 106.

7. See Diane Price Herndl, *Invalid Women: Figuring Feminine Illness in American Fiction and Culture, 1840-1940* (Chapel Hill, N.C., 1993).

8. For discussion of Union Army nurses, see Kristie Ross, "Arranging a Doll's House: Refined Women as Union Nurses," in *Divided Houses* [*: Gender and the American Civil War,* eds. Catherine Clinton and Nina Silber (New York, 1990),], 97-113; Jane E. Schultz, "The Inhospitable Hospital: Gender and Professionalism in Civil War Medicine," *Signs* 17 (winter 1992): 363-92; and Ann Douglas Wood, "The War Within a War: Women Nurses in the Union Army," *Civil War History* 18 (Sept. 1972): 197-212. On amputation in the war, see Stewart Brooks, *Civil War Medicine* (Springfield, Ill., 1972): 90-105; on the Civil War experience of

S. Weir Mitchell, see Debra Journet, "Phantom Limbs and 'Body-Ego': S. Weir Mitchell's 'George Dedlo,'" *Mosaic* 23 (winter 1990): 87-99.

9. LaSalle Corbell Pickett, *Reminiscences of People I Have Known,* in Stern, ed., *Critical Essays,* 42.

10. Louisa May Alcott, journal entry, Jan. 1845, in *The Journals of Louisa May Alcott,* eds. Joel Myerson, Daniel Shealy, and Madeleine Stern (Boston, 1989), 56.

11. Jan. 1845, *Journals* [*The Journals of Louisa May Alcott*], 55.

12. See Brodhead, *Cultures of Letters;* "disciplinary intimacy" is first defined on 17-18. Alcott was literally a daughter of this movement, since her father helped to disseminate its principles, and her biography as a whole offers, as Brodhead argues, "a major historical exhibit of a real child . . . being brought up on this culturally sponsored plan" (73).

13. Journal entry, Oct. 1856, *Journals,* 79; letter to Alfred Whitman, 2 Mar. 1860, in Alcott, *The Selected Letters of Louisa May Alcott,* eds. Joel Myerson, Daniel Shealy, and Madeleine Stern (Boston, 1987), 51-52.

14. Journal entry, Apr. 1861, *Journals,* 105.

15. Journal entries, Nov. 1862 and Dec. 1862, *Journals,* 110.

16. For some women, this identification with masculinity was not only psychological; at least four hundred women cross-dressed as soldiers in the war. For overviews of women who cross-dressed as Civil War soldiers, see Richard Hall, *Patriots in Disguise: Women Warriors of the Civil War* (New York, 1993), and C. Kay Larson, "Bonny Yank and Ginny Reb," *Minerva* 8 (spring 1990): 33-48. For an analysis of one such soldier, see Elizabeth Young, "Confederate Counterfeit: The Case of the Cross-Dressed Civil War Soldier," in *Passing and the Fictions of Identity,* ed. Elaine K. Ginsberg (Durham, N.C., 1996), 181-217.

17. Margaret Higonnet, "Civil Wars and Sexual Territories," in *Arms and the Woman: War, Gender, and Literary Representation,* eds. Helen M. Cooper, Adrienne Auslander Munich, and Susan Merrill Squier (Chapel Hill, N.C., 1989), 87.

18. Letter to Amos Bronson Alcott, 28 Nov. 1855, *Letters* [*The Selected Letters of Louisa May Alcott*], 14.

19. Letter to Alfred Whitman, 19 May 1861, *Letters,* 64-65.

20. Letter to Mrs. Joseph Chatfield Alcox, early Dec. 1862, *Letters,* 80.

21. Letter to Thomas Wentworth Higginson, 12 Nov. 1863, *Letters,* 96. For an account of the work of women abolitionists in this period, see Wendy Hamand Venet, *Neither Ballots Nor Bullets: Women Abolitionists and the Civil War* (Charlottesville, Va., 1991).

22. Alcott had included *Uncle Tom's Cabin* in an 1852 list of the "best" novels, "books I like" (*Journals,* 67-68). Elbert discusses Alcott's lifelong admiration for the novel in *A Hunger for Home,* 104, 147-48, 213.

23. Karen Sánchez-Eppler, *Touching Liberty: Abolition, Feminism, and the Politics of the Body* (Berkeley, Calif., 1993), 133-41. On the widespread influence of Stowe's Topsy, see Thomas F. Gossett, Uncle Tom's Cabin *and American Culture* (Dallas, Tex., 1985), 132-37, 379-81.

24. Interview with Louise Chandler Moulton, in *Our Famous Women* (Hartford, Conn., 1884), 49; quoted and discussed in Showalter, *Alternative Alcott,* xx.

25. The first American usages of "inversion" were in the 1880s. For discussion of the development of this language, see George Chauncey, Jr., "From Sexual Inversion to Homosexuality: Medicine and the Changing Conceptualization of Female Deviance," *Salmagundi* 58-59 (1982-1983): 114-46.

26. For another discussion of Alcott's sexuality, see Michael Warner, "Written on the Bodice: Louisa May Alcott Unbound," *Village Voice Literary Supplement* 133 (Mar. 1995): 10-11.

27. Cappello, "'Looking About Me With All My Eyes,'" esp. 60.

28. On the complexities of minstrelsy, see Eric Lott, *Love and Theft: Blackface Minstrelsy and the American Working Class* (New York, 1993). See also Toni Morrison, *Playing in the Dark: Whiteness and the Literary Imagination* (Cambridge, Mass., 1993), and Shelley Fisher Fishkin, "Interrogating 'Whiteness,' Complicating 'Blackness': Remapping American Culture," *American Quarterly* 47 (Sept. 1995): 428-66.

29. Letter to Anna Alcott, 6 Nov. 1856, *Letters,* 22. Alcott's full description of this event suggests its sexual connotations: "I was so excited I pitched about like a mad woman, shouted, waved, hung onto fences, rushed thro crowds, & swarmed about in a state [of] rapterous insanity till it was all over & then I went home hoarse and worn out."

30. Journal entry, Notes and Memoranda section for 1862, *Journals,* 111, 112. Alcott apparently added "which I enjoy very much, at least the crazy part" at a later date. This brief description was followed by a more extensive account of her Washington experience in the journal entry for Jan. 1863, 113-17.

31. Journal entry, Jan. 1863, [*Journals,*] 117. The full passage contains many other evocative images, including Alcott's marriage to a handsome "Spaniard" who "was mother, I suspect." For analyses of these dreams, see Elbert, *A Hunger for Home,* 156-58; Martha Saxton, *Louisa May* (Boston, 1977), 257-58; and Showalter, *Alternative Alcott,* xix-xx.

32. Letter to Mary Elizabeth Waterman, 6 Nov. 1863, *Letters,* 95.

33. Letter to Anna Alcott Pratt, ca. Aug. 1860, *Letters,* 59.

34. Journal entry, Feb. 1861, *Journals,* 104.

35. John Limon, *Writing After War: American War Fiction from Realism to Postmodernism* (New York, 1994), 188.

36. Letter to Alfred Whitman, Sept. 1863, *Letters,* 91-92.

37. Letter to Mary Elizabeth Waterman, 6 Nov. 1863, *Letters,* 95.

38. Journal entry, Feb. 1863, *Journals,* 117.

39. Henry W. Bellows, "Unconditional Loyalty," in *Union Pamphlets of the Civil War,* vol. 1, ed. Frank Freidel (Cambridge, Mass., 1967), 1:515.

40. Wendell Phillips, "The War for the Union; A Lecture," in *Union Pamphlets of the Civil War,* 1:312.

41. Lincoln's comment is recounted by F. B. Carpenter in *Six Months at the White House* (1866), 76, and quoted in James McPherson, "How Lincoln Won the War with Metaphors," in *Abraham Lincoln and the Second American Revolution* (New York, 1990), 107. On the "inner civil war," see George Fredrickson, *The Inner Civil War: Northern Intellectuals and the Crisis of the Union* (New York, 1965), esp. 53-78. On Civil War uses of the trope of the body politic, see Timothy Sweet, *Traces of War: Poetry, Photography, and the Crisis of the Union* (Baltimore, Md., 1990), 16-24.

42. Bellows, "Unconditional Loyalty," 514.

43. Ibid., 513.

44. For discussion of Lincoln as a sacrificial body, see Michael Rogin, "The King's Two Bodies: Lincoln, Wilson, Nixon, and Presidential Sacrifice," in *Ronald Reagan, the Movie, and Other Episodes in Political Demonology* (Berkeley, Calif., 1987), 81-114.

45. George Forgie, *Patricide in the House Divided* (New York, 1979), 255.

46. For analysis of race in *Hospital Sketches,* see Cappello, "'Looking About Me With All My Eyes.'" Discussions of race in other works by Alcott include Abigail Hemblen, "Louisa May Alcott and the Racial Question," in *Critical Essays,* 50-64; and Mary Dougherty, "Contraband Desire," Session on "National Alcott," Modern Language Association convention, Chicago, 30 Dec. 1995.

47. For discussion of the array of conflicts between nurses and doctors in Civil War hospitals, see Schultz, "Inhospitable Hospital."

48. Notable exceptions are Limon, *Writing After War,* 183-88; and Judith Fetterley, "*Little Women*: Alcott's Civil War," *Feminist Studies* 5 (1979): 369-83. For an overview of the extensive critical commentary on *Little Women,* see Ann B. Murphy, "The Borders of Ethical, Erotic, and Artistic Possibilities in *Little Women,*" *Signs* 15 (spring 1990): 562-85; for discussion of readers' responses to the text, see Barbara Sicherman, "Reading *Little Women*: The Many Lives of a Text," in *U.S. History as Women's History,* eds. Linda Kerber, Alice Kessler-Harris, and Kathryn Kish Sklar (Chapel Hill, N.C., 1995), 245-66.

49. Louisa May Alcott, *Little Women,* ed. Elaine Showalter (New York, 1989), 183. All subsequent quotations are taken from this edition and cited parenthetically in the text.

50. For discussion of Mr. March, see James D. Wallace, "Where the Absent Father Went: Alcott's *Work,*" in *Refiguring the Father: New Feminist Readers of Patriarchy,* eds. Patricia Yaeger and Beth Kowaleski-Wallace (Carbondale, Ill., 1989), 259-74; and Lynda Zwinger, *Daughters, Fathers, and the Novel: The Sentimental Romance of Heterosexuality* (Madison, Wisc., 1991), 46-75. For discussion of Beth in relation to the Civil War, see Limon, *Writing After War,* 185.

51. Kathleen Diffley, *Where My Heart is Turning Ever: Civil War Stories and Constitutional Reform, 1861-1876* (Athens, Ga., 1992); see esp. the analysis of Alcott's "My Contraband," 34-39.

52. "Speech at New Haven, Connecticut," in Abraham Lincoln, *Speeches and Writings, 1859-1865,* ed. Don E. Fehrenbacher (New York, 1989), 132. For discussion of Northern images of Reconstruction, see Nina Silber, *The Romance of Reunion: Northerners and the South, 1965-1900* (Chapel Hill, N.C., 1993).

53. Brodhead, *Cultures of Letters,* 71. For other discussions of Plumfield, see Nina Auerbach, *Communities of Women: An Idea in Fiction* (Cambridge, Mass., 1978), 70-73; and Elbert, *A Hunger for Home,* 231-36.

54. Louisa May Alcott, *Little Men* (1871; Boston, 1994), 329.

55. Louisa May Alcott, *Jo's Boys* (1886; Boston, 1994), 91.

56. Alcott's fullest expression of explicitly feminist politics is in the novel *Work* (1873), which also situates the emergence of a female body politic in the wake of the death of a Civil War soldier. For discussion of *Work* as a Civil War text, see Higonnet, "Civil Wars and Sexual Territories," 87-89; for an analysis of the novel's politics, see Glenn Hendler, "The Limits of Sympathy: Louisa May Alcott and the Sentimental Novel," *ALH* [*American Literary History*] 3 (winter 1991): 685-706.

Linda Grasso (essay date 1998)

SOURCE: Grasso, Linda. "Louisa May Alcott's 'Magic Inkstand': *Little Women,* Feminism, and the Myth of Regeneration." *Frontiers: A Journal of Women Studies* 19, no. 1 (1998): 177-92.

[*In the following essay, Grasso contrasts Alcott's* Little Women *with the 1994 film adaptation of the novel. Grasso suggests that many of the novel's thematic complexities—in particular the underlying tension between representations of domesticity and revolt—are ignored in the film version.*]

> I'd have a stable full of Arabian steeds, rooms piled with books, and I'd write out of a magic inkstand, so that my works should be as famous as Laurie's music. I want to do something splendid before I go into my castle,—something heroic, or wonderful,—that won't be forgotten after I'm dead. I don't know what, but I am on the watch for it, and mean to astonish you all, some day. I think I shall write books, and get rich and famous; that would suit me, so that is *my* favorite dream.
>
> —Louisa May Alcott, *Little Women*

> The story of a family of four girls seen in their crucial adolescent years, [*Little Women*] has survived the successive waves of both American feminism and anti-feminism, able in some mysterious way to assume a protective coloration that blends with the prevailing ideological winds, emerging fresh, whole—and different—for the next generation of women.
>
> —Madelon Bedell, from the introduction to a 1983 reprint of *Little Women*

> I tried to write the film as I imagined [Louisa May Alcott] would have written it today, freed of the cultural restraints of the time she lived in.
>
> —Robin Swicord, commenting on her 1994 screenplay for *Little Women*

The most recent film adaptation of Louisa May Alcott's **Little Women** proves, once again, that the fantasy of regeneration is an enduring American concept. In the same way that Phillis Wheatley, J. Hector St. John de Crèvecoeur, and Benjamin Franklin mythologize the notion that self, community, and economic status can be regenerated in a newly independent America, the creators of the latest Hollywood version of *Little Women* mythologize the notion that Louisa May Alcott's nineteenth-century vision, experience, and sensibility can be regenerated in a newly liberated 1990s.[1] In this latest reincarnation of what Madelon Bedell identifies as "*the* American female myth," windows are a resonant symbol of historical connection.[2] At the same time that the audience is invited to look into the March family's honey-hued windows where silhouettes of animated young women fret and frolic, we are also invited to look into the windows of our own time where we are shown how much feminism has accomplished.

To white, middle-class female viewers who fervently want to believe that they have experienced the same regeneration they see on the screen, the view is exhilarating. "Freed of cultural restraints," Alcott's little white women no longer live in a world in which "duties and desires [are] desperately antagonistic";[3] they are no longer hampered by lack of professional opportunities, inspiring mentors, or suitable lovers; they are no longer subject to crippling proscriptions of appropriate feminine behavior. Because they are free to "embrace their liberty" in the truest Emersonian sense, the newly regenerated Meg, Jo, Beth, and Amy, like the newly regenerated viewers, no longer need a political movement called feminism.

The film's opening montage of a resplendent snow-covered New England landscape is an apt metaphor for the way in which Louisa May Alcott's vision and experience are regenerated for late twentieth-century popular culture consumption: The pristine loveliness of the white snow covers the sullied and sordid muddiness that feminist scholars have been painstakingly excavating for the last thirty years.[4] In their quest to remake *Little Women* into a mainstream feminist fantasy, the filmmakers take several artistic liberties, all of which glamorize less than glamorous historical realities. To begin with, the film's distortion of how Alcott came to write *Little Women* perpetuates the myth that "writing from the heart" is a sanctified literary practice that exists outside market forces. In actuality, the opposite is true. Alcott wrote *Little Women* because an enterprising publisher wanted to capitalize on the untapped market for young, female readers. After two requests, she grudgingly accepted the assignment because it promised the most lucrative reward, but, as her journal entries make clear, she was far from enthusiastic about the project: "Mr. N wants a *girls' story,* and I begin *Little Women.* Marmee, Anna, and May all approve my plan. So I plod away, though I don't enjoy this sort of thing.

Never liked girls or knew many, except my sisters; but our queer plays and experiences may prove interesting, though I doubt it."[5]

By keeping this history shrouded, the film sanitizes the economic realities that shaped nineteenth-century women writers' careers. It also privileges a male-centered, class-based conception of literary value that victimized Alcott as well as many of her female contemporaries. As Richard Brodhead has recently argued, when Alcott was exiled from the "new world of high letters" that was redefining standards of literary excellence in post-Civil War America, "she shut down a level of ambition" to which she had previously aspired.[6] The film's suggestion that James T. Fields, one of high culture's most influential gatekeepers, recognized the value of *Little Women* and published it without delay promulgates the fantasy that Alcott was warmly welcomed into masculine high culture and remains enshrined there in the 1990s. In reality, it was Fields who advised Alcott "to stick to [her] teaching," because she could not write.[7]

The film's excision of the most troubling features of Alcott's life and text is another example of the way in which the filmmakers apply a protective veneer over the rough edges of historical reality. The representation of the March family's moral reform fervor is a case in point. While the film celebrates the Alcott's abolitionist high-mindedness—"Why the March's haven't bought silk in years; they have views on slavery"—implying that they, and not the frivolous, aristocratic Moffats, are moral exemplars, it conveniently ignores the anti-Irish sentiment in Alcott's work. Indeed, it is significant that Alcott's racism emerges in one of the episodes to which the filmmakers refer, yet its presence is ignored. In the novel, when Amy's authoritarian male teacher commands her to throw away the "oh, so plump and juicy" limes that are then "exulted over by the little Irish children, who were their sworn foes," Alcott not only figures frustrated desire as food denied; she also conveys the ultimate indignity of class infraction: The lower-class Irish, who "shout from the street," get to "feast" on what the white, middle-class girls rightfully deserve. As Alcott describes it, "This—this was too much; all flashed indignant or appealing glances at the inexorable Davis [the teacher for whom 'manners, morals, feelings, and examples were not considered of any particular importance'], and one passionate lime lover burst into tears."[8]

Alcott's representation of the Irish as the "Africanist presence" in *Little Women* is not surprising given her allegiance to a reform ethos that advocated the institutionalization of white, middle-class values and practices as the key to social reconstruction.[9] The ethnocentric attitudes of Alcott's mother, Abby, perfectly illustrate the racialist and class biases that influenced reformers' views of the people they hoped to remake in their own image. Because Abby identified with what she perceived to be the dignified forbearance of black people's suffering, she found blacks "far more interesting than the God-invoking Irish." Because she believed black people responded to poverty in the same way she did, she considered them redeemable. On the other hand, she sees the "God-invoking Irish" as the literal embodiment of social disorder. Not only do they have the potential to "infest" America with their undesirable religious beliefs and corrupted ethics, "like mice . . . they have come over to take cupboard, tub, and all." Their behavior also breaches the fundamental tenets of middle-class decorum: They "choke with benedictions or crush you with curses."[10] By refusing to confront this less-than-honorable side of the Alcott legacy, the filmmakers promulgate the fantasy that white, middle-class feminist icons never embraced racist beliefs or engaged in racist practices.

The film's most egregious distortion, however, is its heady eradication of all the tensions, conflicts, ambiguities, and paradoxes that feminist literary scholars now recognize as the paradigmatic encapsulation of the white, middle-class, nineteenth-century writing woman's dilemma. Riddled throughout *Little Women,* as well as the text of Alcott's life, are tensions between self-sacrifice and self-fulfillment, social responsibility and personal gratification, allegiance to family and desire for autonomy, yearning for ambition and retreat into disparaging self-effacement. Perhaps the greatest tension of all was Alcott's conflicted feelings about the intense anger she expressed behind the mask of a pseudonym in lurid "blood and thunder tales." This conflict is poignantly dramatized in *Little Women* when Jo fears that by writing "thrilling tales" she was "unconsciously . . . beginning to desecrate some of the womanliest attributes of a woman's character." These misgivings, coupled with Professor Bhaer's censure, lead her to "[stuff] the whole bundle into her stove, nearly setting the chimney afire with the blaze." This scene vividly renders Alcott's tortuous predicament. In order to adhere to middle-class codes of gendered respectability, she must relinquish her primary source of income as well as her primary mode of self-expression. When Jo destroys her sensation stories, she symbolically destroys her anger and independence.[11]

Alcott's inability to resolve these conflicts, and the ways in which they affect her imaginative vision and conception of herself as a writer, have been the subject of much feminist analysis. Judith Fetterley's argument that the Civil War is "an obvious metaphor" for the conflict between *Little Women*'s overt message of domestic capitulation and its covert message of feminist revolt is a classic example. More recently, Elizabeth Young has proposed that because Alcott's "primary weapon of national transformation—female discipline—all too easily rebounds upon women themselves" her

conception of womanhood is both liberating and inhibiting. While Alcott imagines that "the sufferings of the nation may be resolved through recourse to a fictional world of little women, . . . the woman writer must continue to encode and concede her own anger and ambition."[12]

The film acknowledges none of these conflicts and complexities. Jo never promises to take the place of her dying sister—the "household saint"—nor does she suffer pangs of conscience when she "[finds] her promise very hard to keep." Expressing anger is not an issue: Neither she nor Marmee practice "the art of holding [their] tongue[s]."[13] When it is time to be "paired off," Jo finds a lover who assures her he does not want to be her teacher; his humble and respectful criticism, not to mention his influential connections, make it possible for her to become a respectably published writer. The film conveniently jettisons any allusions to Professor Bhaer's censorious role. In the novel, Alcott imagines him as the embodiment of "conscience"—the gendered, white middle-class ethos that demands the repression of female desire—who is "satisfied" when he knows "that [Jo] had given up writing." Thus, in Alcott's imagination, Professor Bhaer's "lessons in love" are the primary cause of Jo's "internal revolutions."[14] In the film, none of these "internal revolutions" are visible. The only conflicts Jo endures are imposed from the outside world; she is never subject to inner turmoil. In the film's greatest bastardization of all, the strident, unrepentantly angry, regenerated Jo is now also stunningly beautiful.

This glamorized, prettified, regeneration of Alcott's feminist legacy proved to be enormously appealing to late twentieth-century critics. When the film was released by Columbia Pictures in December of 1994, it was promoted as cheerful, sweet-tempered, holiday entertainment. In the words of one critic, the film was "a perfect gift for the entire family."[15] Reviewed in countless newspapers and magazines, from the most mainstream *Time* and *Newsweek* to the most specialized *Air Force Times* and *Army Times,* it was deemed a smashing success. In the *New York Times,* Janet Maslin hailed this adaptation of "one of the most seductively nostalgic novels any child ever discovers" as "the loveliest *Little Women* ever on screen."[16] In the *New Yorker,* Terrence Rafferty praised its "graceful and mysteriously affecting" power, noting that Gillian Armstrong "has filmed *Little Women* as if it were the story of a culture coming of age."[17] In *Newsweek,* David Ansen proclaimed that "this lovely, lived-in *Little Women*" was a "handcrafted valentine" that allowed "Alcott's sense, sensibility and sentiment [to] find new life" in the most unlikely of times.[18]

Ansen was right. The film's release initiated a veritable Alcott renaissance in the popular press. There were reconsiderations of Alcott's legacy and its relevance in the 1990s; commentaries about previous film versions of *Little Women* and the ways in which each inscribe a particular set of cultural values at different historical moments; and assessments of how and why a new "female-driven" movie trend is emerging in Hollywood. Yet, these articles are about more than the film, its creators, and its stars. What lurks between the lines is a discourse about the definition and value of feminism, for in every review and article feminism is either implicitly or explicitly evoked. What becomes evident then is that the reception of the 1994 film version of *Little Women* is an opportune source for analyzing how feminism is being interpreted in the mainstream media.

George Lipsitz reminds us that popular culture forms never have one set of meanings, nor do they ever serve a singular political agenda. On the contrary, at the same time that they "create conditions of possibility [by] expand[ing] the present [and] informing it with memories of the past and hopes for the future, . . . they also engender accommodation with prevailing power realities, separating art from life, and internalizing the dominant culture's norms and values as necessary and inevitable."[19] By enabling a discourse about feminism to emerge, the latest regeneration of *Little Women* in film has certainly created "conditions of possibility" in a culture that still believes male visions and experiences are the norm. The film has subverted this equation by foregrounding women's experiences and paying tribute to the power of sisterhood; it has introduced—or in some cases reintroduced—Alcott as a writer worthy of attention; and it has created a context in which issues such as gender disparity can be meaningfully broached. Yet, at the same time that the remake of the film and its reception have made feminism visible, they have also delimited and constrained it by circumscribing what it means. In the film and the discourse it has engendered, Alcott, *Little Women,* and feminism are stripped of a complex and nuanced history. This has serious political consequences, for when an interpretation of feminism that is bereft of history and political radicalism is disseminated through popular culture mediums, it assists the passage of laws and policies that maintain race and gender hierarchies.

Nowhere is this more apparent than in the way in which the film evokes a nostalgic longing for a mythical, white-centered world in which women lovingly inhabit the interiors of intimate, warm houses rather than intrude upon the prerogatives of the masculine marketplace. As Elizabeth Francis has observed:

> The film is nostalgic for the home as a woman-centered world. . . . Unlike Alcott's novel, the film's emphasis on domesticity can function only as nostalgia, both for viewers having read *Little Women* and, more dangerously, nostalgia for the seemingly simple, womanly times in the mid-nineteenth-century home when there was more meaning, more feeling, more of everything we seem to have forgotten or lost.[20]

In her trenchant analysis of the ways in which poor, single mothers have become contemporary culture's version of the "folk devil," Ruth Sidel notes that political leaders frequently invoke notions of an idealized past to support their claims that society's greatest ills are caused by the breakdown of "family values."[21] Functioning as nostalgia, the film appeals to right-wing ideologues who see these "family values" in the mythical, golden-era past depicted on the screen.

The film's historically eclipsed view of feminism is equally damaging. The "enchantingly pretty" nineteenth century that the filmmakers create is a world in which gender consciousness and social practices have been magically transformed.[22] In this feminist utopia, self-fulfillment replaces self-sacrifice as the paramount virtue; the value of education and physical fitness are taken for granted; self-worth based on intelligence, not physical appearance, is continuously stressed; and the pursuit of ambition is rewarded. By injecting late twentieth-century feminist values into a nineteenth century arena, the filmmakers imply that nineteenth-century women never had to identify gender oppression or struggle against it. Thus the film suggests that feminist activism requires no effort and that it has no history or context. It is not dangerous, time-consuming, or difficult; it has no origins or breakages because it has always existed. It is as if enlightened mothers have instructed willingly receptive daughters in late twentieth-century feminist tenets, no matter what century they inhabited.[23]

The film's representation of Marmee as a feminist icon is especially problematic in this regard. Given that Susan Sarandon's presence signifies feminist rebelliousness, it is clear that the filmmakers wanted to transform Marmee from a "stout, motherly lady, with a 'can-I-help-you' look about her which was truly delightful" into a feminist mentor.[24] Yet, once again, such a simplistic reversal bowdlerizes the complexity of Alcott's vision. In *Little Women,* Marmee is far from an unambivalent figure. Although she speaks in the cadences of nineteenth-century domestic manuals and plays a major role in Jo's gender socialization, it is she who suggests that Jo turn to writing when she is in the depths of despair. As Ann B. Murphy points out, "Much of *Little Women*'s power derives from its exploration of the previously repressed, complex mother-daughter relationship, without portraying that bond as either idealized perfection or pernicious destruction."[25] It is this ambivalent role of the mother as both nurturer of female creativity and enforcer of patriarchal dictates that the film expunges.

Moreover, by turning Marmee into an ardent feminist, the filmmakers ironically reverse Alcott's vision of her. As Abby Alcott's most recent biographer, Cynthia H. Barton, has recently noted, "Marmee in Louisa's *Little Women* was a distillation of all that was good and generous and gentle in her mother and in their family life, a loving tribute, but only half the story."[26] The other half of the story, which Barton attempts to tell, is that of a perpetually hardworking, overburdened, angry woman who was frequently depressed, ill, and pregnant. The tolls that Abby Alcott's "long, hard, romantic married years" exacted on her mental and physical health did not escape her daughter's notice. Soon after her mother died, Alcott wrote in her journal: "Life was hard for her, and no one understood all she had to bear but we, her children."[27] Although Alcott originally intended to pay tribute to her mother by writing her biography, she found the task too emotionally draining. In time, she, her father, and other family heirs destroyed the evidence of Abby Alcott's tortured discontent because they feared it would damage the family's reputation.[28] By transforming Marmee into a stalwart, feminist matriarch who feels no turmoil, conflict, or ambivalence about her familial role, the film continues to censor Abby Alcott's life story.

This leveling of history has serious political ramifications. Like the discourse about feminist progress, it conveys the message that gender liberation has been accomplished, and thus that there is no need for social transformation. When these perceptions are translated into laws and social policies, as we have recently seen, they become pernicious indeed. The dismantling of affirmative action programs in the University of California system, for example, is premised on the notion that race and gender discrimination are anachronisms. Equally significant, the leveling of feminist history participates in the *public* erasure of a vitally charged nineteenth-century women's history because it renders that history invisible. Nowhere is this more evident than in the way in which reviewers repeatedly used stereotypes associated with quaint sentimentalism to characterize the film. Female-gendered code words and images such as "magical," "charming," "lovely," "enchanting," "literary sugar rush," "artfully sewn doily," and "hand-crafted valentine" are the antithesis of civic-minded political involvement. Indeed, in the public imagination, these words and images connote a golden-era past in which all the women are white, all the houses are in New England, and everyone cherishes the institution of marriage as a sacred foundation of civilization. These connotations belittle the legacy of nineteenth-century women's activism by robbing it of its multiracial anger and political savvy. They are the popular culture equivalents of references to Harriet Beecher Stowe as a "Crusader in Crinoline," or characterizations of the mid-nineteenth century as the "flush" and "fervid" "feminine fifties."[29]

The film thwarts Alcott's artistic and political vision in much the same way that the discourse it generated thwarts the legacy of nineteenth-century women's activism. "I tried to write the film as I imagined [Alcott] would have written it today, freed of the cultural restraints of the time she lived in," screenwriter Robin Swicord has declared.[30] Yet if Swicord had truly attempted to do this, she would have imagined a different destiny for Jo. When writing *Little Women,* Alcott was constrained by the demands of her publisher and audience to write a "conventional girl's story" that concluded in marriage. Alcott, however, did not want Jo, her alter ego, to succumb to the myth of heterosexual romance. Instead, she wanted Jo to "[remain] a literary spinster." Although she finally did capitulate to the "young ladies [who] wrote . . . clamorously demanding that [Jo] should marry Laurie, or somebody," she engaged in her own mischievous form of subversion while doing so. "Out of perversity [I] went & made a funny match for her," she informs one of her correspondents.[31]

One hundred and twenty-six years later, Gillian Armstrong, Denise Di Novi and Robin Swicord, the female trio who made *Little Women,* are still constrained by a culture that prohibits depictions of women outside heterosexual relationships, motherhood, and family. But unlike Alcott, they do not resist "out of perversity" by imagining an alternative destiny for Jo. Thus, rather than freeing Alcott's vision from "cultural restraints," Swicord, Armstrong, and Di Novi continue to imprison it. Rather than celebrating Alcott the feminist, Swicord, Armstrong, and Di Novi betray Alcott the visionary, for even in the "enlightened" 1990s they still cannot invent a new plot or "write beyond the ending" of heterosexual romance.[32] Alcott would have been disappointed.[33]

She also would have been outraged at the way in which her regenerated legacy was being used to foster pernicious fictions about the state of late twentieth-century feminism. The same month that *Little Women* opened, *Glamour* reported in its Gnotes column actor Eric Stoltz's quip, "I don't have much of a role in *Little Women.* I'm the token penis."[34] This comment and *Glamour*'s reporting of it are emblematic of the discourse the film generated: Feminism has accomplished such a profound social transformation that women now have as much power, or, in this case, even more power, than men. The notion of progress, of gender "evolution," is pervasive. "Feminism is now able to be less strident because we've actually made some gains and can relax a bit," Armstrong declares.[35] A *New York Times* article about the proliferation of woman-centered films reinforces this view. We learn, for example, that while only a few short years ago there were no women running studios, now there are several. This means, of course, that women in the 1990s have the money and clout to promote the making of films that speak to their own gendered interests, and the films that they and their enlightened male colleagues promote offer models of contemporary womanhood.[36] According to *Vogue* writer

Mary Gaitskill, "In today's movie parlance 'strong woman' tends to mean a babe with a gun. It definitely means a woman who knows how to get angry, to get sexy, and who, goddamnit, knows what time it is."[37]

Because "strong women" have rectified the imbalance of power in society, the discourse implies, feminism is now obsolete. It is no longer necessary to use divisive terms such as "feminist"; now we can all be nonpartisan humanists working in harmony. Armstrong, Di Novi, and Swicord give voice to these ideas in several published interviews. Kristine McKenna reports, for example, that the three women "groan in unison at the mention of 'feminism'" and that "Armstrong has a particular aversion to the label, as it's something she's been trying to transcend since 1979 when her debut picture, *My Brilliant Career,* led to her being branded as a maker of women's films." Because "feminism" has "come to be such a terrible turn-off," Armstrong is "reluctant to say the word out loud." Because collective gender identification robs the artist of individuality, Armstrong believes "true equality" will never be achieved "until people drop the label 'woman' before 'director.'" Women have different directing styles, Armstrong argues, "because we're all different human beings, not because we're women or men."[38] Feminism is no longer relevant, this logic implies, because gender difference is no longer a salient feature of social life. In essence then, feminism is presented as a destructive force that interferes with artistic integrity, disrupts social harmony, and impedes the quest for "true equality." Severed from context and history, feminism limits, distorts, and confuses; it blocks rather than promotes women's advancement.

Yet, at the same time Di Novi and Armstrong disassociate themselves from "terrible turn-off" feminism, they also invent their own historically inaccurate, depoliticized version. To these women, feminism has a very limited and finite history, and it means women no longer have to resist marriage, motherhood, and men. Producer Di Novi, for example, effectively erases the history of feminism's longevity by speaking as if feminism originated in the 1960s. It is possible to see how feminism has "evolved," she suggests, if we compare the difference between the endings of *My Brilliant Career* and *Little Women.* Whereas in *My Brilliant Career* the heroine rejects marriage in order to pursue her writing career, in *Little Women* the heroine welcomes marriage as well as a career. According to Di Novi, this difference demonstrates how "[*Little Women*] is grounded in an evolved kind of feminism," a feminism that is "more humanist and inclusive," a "feminism that's able to embrace men and motherhood in a way 60s feminism couldn't."[39] In addition to the assumption that no previous social movement for women's freedoms, rights, and equality had existed prior to the 1960s, Di Novi's statement betrays an extreme discomfort with a combative, confrontational feminism whose political project envisions the radical restructuring of society. Feminism of the 1960s is not "humanist" because it dared to de-center the premise that women's lives were defined by men and motherhood.

Armstrong's and Di Novi's notions of a "humanist" feminism help us to understand why their version of feminism is repeatedly yoked to women's familial roles. "Feminism is [not] about refusing to marry and have children," Armstrong asserts. What is especially progressive about *Little Women,* Di Novi believes, is Alcott's representation of an egalitarian marriage: "One of the things I love about the relationship between Jo and Professor Bhaer is that it begins in friendship and develops from there. Those are the marriages that work and we rarely see them in movies."[40] This heterosexually centered view of feminism is unproblematically accepted by critics and reviewers as well. What makes Armstrong's film version of *Little Women* "a true 1990's invention," Anne Hollander suggests, is that it "is the only one to reward Jo's forceful independence with a really sexy, intelligent lover who also won't interfere with her work."[41]

Hence feminism never threatens heterosexual relations or the institutions of marriage and motherhood. On the contrary, feminism is about loving men, accepting them as partners at home and in the workplace, and assuring them that their anxieties are misguided. "There are still terrible fears about 'feminism,'" Armstrong reports:

> You wouldn't believe the number of male journalists who ask me questions like, "So you make these women's films—I assume you'd prefer to have a woman cinematographer?" I tell them I'm not a separatist and I love men—in fact, I'm married to one! Feminism has had irreparable amounts of bad press that has led men to assume it's about women rejecting men. Consequently, we worry about this being portrayed as a feminist film—of course it is that, but there are many other things in it as well.[42]

Armstrong's political vision is animated by the desire to ameliorate society's fears about radical feminism. By promoting a version of feminism in which women's concerns are replaced by men's, she assures the public that feminism in the 1990s need not challenge male hegemony. This point is underscored when she notes that while she "is pleased" that *Little Women* will introduce young girls to "Louisa May Alcott's thoughts on very intimate parts of a woman's life—adolescence and finding first love," she'd "be even more pleased if men discover there's something there for them too."[43]

The 1994 regeneration of *Little Women* circumscribes the meaning of feminism at the same time that it makes a benign, depoliticized version of it visible. Eradicating contradictions about female power and artistry that are fundamental features of Alcott's novel, the film suggests that these contradictions are nonexistent. Swicord believes that *Little Women* is a "recognition of the female spirit," and she hopes that the film will "inspire a new generation of young girls" to realize that they can "go out and make the dream come true, band together and survive just fine."[44] Yet, in Swicord's vision, the "female spirit" and the "dream" are still integrally related to the myth of heterosexual romance. As Caryn James points out, the "sentimental courtship" between Jo and Professor Bhaer "is an extreme perversion of the novel," but it is this "fairy tale romance" that makes the movie "appealing."[45] In the most general sense, the "fairy tale romance" that the film encodes is that women can be beautiful, intelligent, artistic, sister-loving individuals who no longer need to forfeit marriage. This message, that little white women in the liberated 1990s can find ultimate fulfillment in familial roles, suggests that feminism cannot exist outside family relationships; it must be contained within socially and legally approved heterosexual arrangements. Such a message buttresses ideologies about the "naturalness" of heterosexual coupling and patriarchal family structures, and it is these ideologies that are now being translated into pernicious social policies such as "the defense of marriage act" and "welfare reform."

More than anything else, this analysis suggests that there is no collective memory of a complex and nuanced feminist legacy, except for the one that is created and reproduced in the academy. Indeed, the schism between popular culture versions of feminism and academic feminism is troublingly stark. An article titled "Does *Little Women* Belittle Women?," which appeared in the January 1995 issue of *Vogue,* is a striking illustration of this divide. In this hip, sharp-tongued polemic, Mary Gaitskill finds it hard to understand why "feminist-leaning filmmakers would see a goody-goody story as an inspiration to women."[46] To her, the newly released *Little Women* is nothing but a lesson in psychological and sexual regulation. Gaitskill's article is noteworthy for two reasons. First, progress ideology is one of its underlying themes, and, second, the erasure of a collective memory of feminist history and Alcott scholarship are prominent features. Gaitskill argues her position without any apparent knowledge that a well-documented debate about the very issues she is addressing has existed for years. Ann B. Murphy succinctly summarizes the two dichotomous positions when she poses the following questions: "Is *Little Women* adolescent, sentimental, and repressive, an instrument for teaching girls how to become 'little,' domesticated, and silent? [Or] is the novel subversive, matriarchal, and implicitly revolutionary, fostering discontent with the very model of female domesticity it purports to admire?"[47] Her response is that there are no "rigid" answers. Like other feminist critics, she emphasizes the complexity of the novel's irresolvable tensions:

[*Little Women*] is passionately memorable for young girls because it warns of the dangers that lie ahead—domestic incarceration, narcissistic objectification, sacrificial goodness, and the enforced silencing of voice, eroticism, and anger—and partly because it offers an alternative vision of adulthood-in-community, of female subjectivity, and above all of female oedipal narrative, restoring the lost, maternal presence in our lives.[48]

Because Gaitskill is unaware of this scholarship, her own thinking is formed in a vacuum, and her essay is presented as if no one has pondered such questions before her.

The ultimate irony, however, is that the title of Gaitskill's essay was the same one used for a 1973 *New York Times* article that argues the reverse position. In that article, when the author compares the 1970 BBC adaptation of *Little Women,* which was then showing on television, to the standard representations of "women as a gaggle of witless wonders endowed with the intelligence, independence, and emotional maturity of retarded guppies," she concludes that *Little Women* "takes on the force of a feminist tract."[49] Writing twenty-two years after second-wave feminism created a context in which both the 1973 article and her own could be published, Gaitskill leads us to believe that gender liberation has been achieved. Writing twenty-two years after feminist scholarship has radically altered an understanding of Louisa May Alcott and *Little Women,* Gaitskill leads us to believe that this work does not exist. Given these implications, what becomes evident is that the mythical portrayal of feminist progress in popular culture is predicated upon the erasure of feminist history in the academy.

Notes

1. There is no consensus about the number of times *Little Women* has been made into film. According to Kristine McKenna, Armstrong's version is the "sixth attempt to bring *Little Women* to the screen" (Kristine McKenna, "Not So *Little Women*," *Los Angeles Times,* December 27, 1994, F13). Gloria T. Delmar suggests, however, that if one counts silent films, Hollywood releases, television movies, and cartoons, the 1994 version is the eighth time *Little Women* has been adapted to the screen. If productions that use themes and characters from *Little Women* but translate them into late twentieth-century contexts, such as the movie *Foxes* and the television situation comedy *Facts of Life* (which ran from 1979 through 1988), are added, then the 1994 version is the tenth adaptation. See the section on film adaptations in *Louisa May Alcott and* Little Women*: Biography, Critique, Publications, Poems, Songs and Contemporary Relevance* (Jefferson, N.C.: McFarland & Co., Inc., 1990), 178-88. Determining the exact number of versions

is less significant than the fact that there is a film adaptation for every decade of the twentieth century, with the exception of the 1920s and 1960s.

2. Madelon Bedell believes that *Little Women* "may be *the* American female myth, its subject the primordial one of the passage from childhood, from girl to woman" (Madelon Bedell, introduction to *Little Women* [New York: Modern Library, 1983], xi). Elaine Showalter concurs. In *Sister's Choice: Tradition and Change in American Women's Writing* (Oxford: Clarendon Press, 1991), she begins a discussion of *Little Women* by echoing Bedell's claim: "In the eyes of many readers and critics, Louisa May Alcott's *Little Women* (1868) is '*the* American female myth,' and Alcott's heroine Jo March has become the most influential figure of the independent and creative American woman" (42).

3. In "Psyche's Art" (1868), Louisa May Alcott describes the frustrations of a woman artist who cannot work free from domestic intrusion: "Sculpture and sewing, calls and crayons, Ruskin and receipt-books, didn't work well together, and poor Psyche found duties and desires desperately antagonistic." Reprinted in *Alternative Alcott,* ed. and introd. Elaine Showalter (New Brunswick, N. J.: Rutgers University Press, 1988), 215.

4. Although Leona Rostenberg and Madeleine Stern uncovered Louisa May Alcott's anonymous and pseudonymous "blood and thunder tales" in the early 1940s, it has only been within the last few decades that Alcott's life, legacy, and career have undergone radical reevaluation. In addition to the publication of several editions of the thrillers, as well as other revalued texts, there is now a growing body of scholarship on all aspects of Alcott's work. See, for example, Elaine Showalter's introduction to *Alternative Alcott*; Sarah Elbert, *A Hunger for Home: Louisa May Alcott's Place in American Culture* (New Brunswick, N. J.: Rutgers University Press, 1987); and Elizabeth Young, "A Wound of One's Own: Louisa May Alcott's Civil War Fiction," *American Quarterly* 48:3 (1996): 439-74. Rostenberg and Stern describe their discovery of Alcott's "double life" in *Old Books, Rare Friends: Two Literary Sleuths and Their Shared Passion* (New York: Doubleday, 1997), 116-31.

5. *The Journals of Louisa May Alcott,* ed. Joel Myerson, Daniel Shealy, and Madeleine B. Stern (Boston: Little, Brown and Co., 1989), 165-66.

6. Richard H. Brodhead, *Culture of Letters: Scenes of Reading and Writing in Nineteenth-Century America* (Chicago: University of Chicago Press, 1993), 87-88.

7. Alcott, *Journals [The Journals of Louisa May Alcott]* (1862): "I went back to my writing, which pays much better, though Mr F[ields]. did say, 'Stick to your teaching; you can't write.' I said, 'I won't teach; and I can write, and I'll prove it'" (109).

8. Louisa May Alcott, *Little Women,* introd. Elaine Showalter (1868; reprint, New York: Penguin Books, 1989), 68, 67.

9. In *Playing in the Dark: Whiteness and the Literary Imagination* (Cambridge: Harvard University Press, 1992), Toni Morrison argues that locating the "Africanist presence" in literary texts elucidates the ways in which white writers have historically used the "racial other" to displace fears, define self, and imagine all aspects of the human condition—including what it means to be independent, powerful, and free.

10. Abby Alcott's racialist sentiments are recorded in reports of her work with the poor. Excerpts from these reports are quoted in Cynthia H. Barton, *Transcendental Wife: The Life of Abigail May Alcott* (New York: University Press of America, 1996), 151.

11. Alcott, *Little Women,* 349, 356.

12. Judith Fetterley, "*Little Women*: Alcott's Civil War," *Feminist Studies* 5: 2 (1979): 369-83; and Young, "A Wound of One's Own," 441, 470.

13. Alcott, *Little Women,* 414, 432, 297.

14. Alcott, *Little Women,* 356-57, 468, 357.

15. Bob Thomas, *Associated Press,* excerpted in a two-page advertisement in the *New York Times,* January 15, 1995, 2; 8-9.

16. Janet Maslin, "Gold Standard for Girlhood All Across America," *New York Times,* December 21, 1994, B1-2.

17. Terrence Rafferty, "American Gothic," *The New Yorker,* January 9, 1995, 83-84.

18. David Ansen, "Natural Born Kindness," *Newsweek,* January 9, 1995, 57.

19. George Lipsitz, *Time Passages: Collective Memory and American Popular Culture* (Minneapolis: University of Minnesota Press, 1990), 16.

20. Elizabeth Francis, "Review of *Little Women*," *The Journal of American History* 82:3 (1995): 1312-13. Francis's generous reading of the film is significantly different from my own.

21. Ruth Sidel, *Keeping Women and Children Last: America's War on the Poor* (New York: Penguin Books, 1996).

22. Janet Maslin, "Gold Standard" ["The Gold Standard for Girlhood All Across America"].

23. In direct opposition to Maslin who proclaims that "Ms. Armstrong reinvents *Little Women* for present-day audiences without ever forgetting it's a story with a past" ("Gold Standard," B1), Caryn James believes the film "strains to make the 19th century novel relevant today" by "clumsily" injecting references to racism and sexism "without historical context" ("Amy Had Golden Curls; Jo Had A Rat. Who Would You Rather Be?" *New York Times,* December 25, 1994, 7, 17). It is significant that James's view is informed by historical knowledge of both Alcott and the period in which she lived.

24. Alcott, *Little Women,* 7.

25. Ann B. Murphy, "The Borders of Ethical, Erotic, and Artistic Possibilities in *Little Women*," *Signs* 3:15 (1990): 575.

26. Barton, *Transcendental Wife,* 51.

27. Ednah D. Cheney, *Louisa May Alcott,* introd. Ann Douglas (1889; reprint, New York: Chelsea House, 1980), 344; and Alcott, *Journals,* 206.

28. Barton, *Transcendental Wife,* 30, 52, 64; Cheney, *Louisa May Alcott,* 332, 344; *The Selected Letters of Louisa May Alcott,* ed. Joel Myerson, Daniel Shealy, and Madeleine B. Stern (Boston: Little, Brown and Co., 1987), xxxv; and Madeleine B. Stern, *Louisa May Alcott: A Biography* (New York: Random House, 1996), 266.

29. Forest Wilson, *Crusader in Crinoline: The Life of Harriet Beecher Stowe* (Philadelphia: J. B. Lippincott, 1941); and Fred Lewis Pattee, *The Feminine Fifties* (New York: D. Appleton-Century Co., 1940). For examples of how feminist literary scholars have analyzed the insidious biases in these characterizations, see Judith Fetterley, introduction to *Provisions: A Reader from Nineteenth-Century American Women* (Bloomington: Indiana University Press, 1985), 1-40; Susan K. Harris, *Nineteenth-Century American Women's Novels: Interpretative Strategies* (Cambridge: Cambridge University Press, 1990); and Jane Tompkins, *Sensational Designs: The Cultural Work of American Fiction, 1790-1860* (New York: Oxford University Press, 1985).

30. Quoted in McKenna, "Not So *Little Women*," F13.

31. Alcott, *Selected Letters* [*The Selected Letters of Louisa May Alcott*], 125.

32. Carolyn Heilbrun, *Writing a Woman's Life* (New York: Norton, 1988); and Rachel Blau DuPlessis, *Writing Beyond the Ending: Narrative Strategies of Twentieth-Century Women Writers* (Bloomington: Indiana University Press, 1985).

33. James also speculates about Alcott's reaction: "Louisa May Alcott, in her heavenly 'somewhere else,' may be tearing out her hair in grief at this latest version of her story. Or maybe not. Perhaps this is her revenge. Finally Jo is pretty and marries the handsome man in the room next door. He even knows the word 'Transcendentalist.' Finally, Jo is more like Amy" ("Amy Had Golden Curls" ["Amy Had Golden Curls; Jo Had a Rat"], 17).

34. "Gnotes: Seen Heard, Noted and Quoted," *Glamour,* January 1995, 123.

35. Quoted in McKenna, "Not So *Little Women*," F14.

36. Laurie Halpern Benenson, "Women's Ensemble Films Come of Age (Again)," *New York Times,* December 18, 1994, 36.

37. Mary Gaitskill, "Does *Little Women* Belittle Women?" *Vogue,* January 1995, 36+.

38. Quoted in McKenna, "Not So *Little Women*," F1, F14; and Mary Hardesty, "The Brilliant Career of Gillian Armstrong," *DGA* [*Directors Guild of America*] *Magazine,* September 1995, <http://www.dga.org/magazine/v20-4/vol20-4.html> (July 30, 1997).

39. Quoted in McKenna, "Not So *Little Women*," F13-14.

40. Quoted in McKenna, "Not So *Little Women*," F13-14.

41. Anne Hollander, "Portraying *Little Women* Through the Ages," *New York Times,* January 15, 1995, 11+.

42. Quoted in McKenna, "Not So *Little Women*," F14.

43. Quoted in McKenna, "Not So *Little Women*," F14.

44. Quoted in Gaitskill, "Does *Little Women* Belittle Women?" 38.

45. James, "Amy Had Golden Curls," 17.

46. Gaitskill, "Does *Little Women* Belittle Women?" 44.

47. Murphy, "The Borders of Ethical" ["The Borders of Ethical, Erotic, and Artistic Possibilities in *Little Women*"], 564-65.

48. Murphy, "The Borders of Ethical," 584.

49. Stephanie Harrington, "Does *Little Women* Belittle Women?" *New York Times,* June 10, 1973, 19+. Reprinted in *Critical Essays on Louisa May Alcott,* ed. Madeleine B. Stern (Boston: G. K. Hall & Co., 1984), 110-12.

Gregory Eiselein (essay date fall 1999)

SOURCE: Eiselein, Gregory. "Sentimental Discourse and the Bisexual Erotics of *Work*." *Texas Studies in Literature and Language* 41, no. 3 (fall 1999): 203-35.

[*In the following essay, Eiselein examines Alcott's eroticization of sentimentality in the novel.*]

THE EROTICS OF SENTIMENTAL FORMS

A feminist re-evaluation of sentimentalism began two decades ago with some now-famous polemics about the politics of sentimental forms. Ann Douglas's *The Feminization of American Culture* saw the "triumph of the 'feminizing' sentimental forces" as the "continuation of male hegemony in different guises." Jane Tompkins's *Sensational Designs* argued conversely that the sentimental was an expression of women's power in the antebellum United States.[1] Recently, the debate has been complicated and recast. Those studying nineteenth-century sentimentality are now likely to begin, as I do, with the assumption that no specific political position inheres in the sentimental. As Lauren Berlant puts it, "female sentimental discourse is a mode of abstraction that has no a priori political implications for the power of women or other marginalized groups." Instead of imagining the sentimental as either profeminist or antifeminist, culturally deadening bathos or culturally salvific pathos, critics have begun mapping the complex, unstable, and contingent relationships of power that connect sentimental forms to the social world. Critics now talk about the sentimental as "labile," manifold, complex, volatile.[2] What I would like to add to this discussion of the complexities, dialogics, and instabilities of sentimental discourses is an examination of the political work of sentimental representations of sexuality.

I begin by looking at the sometimes fluid erotics of sentimental forms, particularly sentimentalism's blurring of identification into desire. In the following two sections I use this discussion of the sentimental to examine and contrast antifeminist discourse of the 1870s with Louisa May Alcott's *Work* (1873).[3] Appealing to readers' identifications and fears, antifeminist discourse represented wage-earning women and their feminist supporters as unattractive, unfulfilled, and unnatural. Taking a much different stand, Alcott's *Work* championed the value of working women to society and "the real dignity of labor," as one reviewer put it. The book's overtly feminist content prompted nineteenth-century reviewers to consider it "a contribution to the literature of the 'labor question' and the 'woman question'" but "nothing as a work of art." Recent critics have called the novel polemical and didactic. I would like to suggest, however, that something more subtle than polemic happens in *Work*, something more erotic than polemic. Like the leaders of the women's movement, Alcott did glorify work and made herself "busy . . . proving 'Woman's Right to Labor.'"[4] Alcott's defense of work also eroticized work. Alcott countered antifeminist imagery and forwarded a feminist, prolabor position by using sentimental discourses to eroticize the representation of women workers and the romantic-erotic possibilities opened up by work.

Critics have tended to ignore or dismiss the erotic dimensions of nineteenth-century sentimentalism. In *Hard Facts,* for example, Philip Fisher sees sexual desire and sentimental emotional investments as explicitly opposed to each other.[5] While such a view does resemble the middle-class Victorian idealizing and desexualizing of children, the family, and the always already sexualized figure of the mother, the notion that sentimentalism somehow avoids the erotic is not tenable. Michel Foucault argues famously that Victorians were hardly reticent but were in fact garrulous on the subject of sex. What historians imagined as a Victorian censorship of sex, Foucault sees as "an apparatus for producing an ever greater quantity of discourse about sex." These discourses tended to spiritualize erotic unions, eroticize purity, value self-control in sexual practices, and privilege the home as the site for the manufacture of sexual identities.[6]

The representation of sexuality in sentimental discourse was, in any case, ambivalent, complex, and contradictory. In *The Royal Path of Life,* a domestic advice handbook from the 1870s, for example, T. L. Haines and L. W. Yaggy describe the figure of the mother with the following stylized and sexualized sentimental language:

> Woman's charms are certainly many and powerful. The expanding rose, just bursting into beauty, has an irresistible bewitchingness;—the blooming bride, led triumphantly to the hymeneal altar, awakens admiration and interest, and the blush of her cheek fills with delight;—but the charm of maternity is more sublime than all these. . . . Mother! ecstatic sound so twined round our hearts that they must cease to throb ere we forget it! 'tis our first love.[7]

The passage pulsates and palpitates with the sentimental diction of romantic love and eroticism: first love, throbbing hearts, ecstasy, sublimity, pleasure in looking and being looked at, beauty, charms, awakenings, blushings, expandings, bloomings. This chapter on mothers represents them as figures for identification or chaste reverence, but it also eroticizes mothers and women in general, figuring them as sentimental-erotic clichés like the "expanding rose" and "the blooming bride." The authors insist these sexualized figures naturally attract attention because of their powerful charms and "irresistible bewitchingness." As she blushes "with delight," the bride "awakens admiration and interest," though Haines and Yaggy are unclear about who is admiring and who is interested, who is identifying and who desiring, and why. Amid this sexualized effusion, readers learn that "the charm of maternity is more sublime than all these." The invocation of the sublime tends to obfuscate any precise idea about what the attraction of maternity is. Readers might see the passage as a contrast between the highly erotic (pre-sexual) pre-mothers and the "sublime," exalted, pure, spiritual (but already sexual) mother herself. Readers might also conclude that the mother's attractiveness is so great, so superior to the adolescent girl's or bride's, that the authors have lost their ability to describe such allures. These two interpretations, the first emphasizing purity and the second sexuality, are not, however, mutually exclusive in sentimental discourse, but rather dialectically allied, mutually dependent on the other. As Joy S. Kasson points out, the sexuality of nineteenth-century sentimental forms usually held "contradictory meanings"—"eroticism indulged and denied, passion and passionlessness, power and powerlessness."[8]

Although some critics have begun to examine the sexuality of sentimental forms (especially incest and what we would call heterosexuality[9]), most studies of sentimentalism continue to foreground identification and sympathy in opposition to sexual desire, as Fisher does.[10] Identification and desire cannot, however, always be so neatly separated from each other. Eve Sedgwick identifies sentimentality itself (and, by way of her deconstructive logic, antisentimentality and resentimentality) with an erotic discourse capable of "symbolizing slippages between identification and desire." Sedgwick's *Epistemology of the Closet* along with James Creech's *Closet Writing/Gay Reading* have highlighted the need for an examination of sentimentalism's connections to nonheterosexual desire and to the blurring of the identification/desire binary.[11] Generally speaking, nineteenth-century sentimental forms seem to complicate the identification/desire distinction in two ways: (1) Sentimentalism *represents* slippages between identifications and sexual desires in its portrayal of characters' emotional lives; (2) It *facilitates* similar slippages in readers' emotional lives by encouraging vicarious responses to texts.

Sentimentalism's blurring of identification and desire begins with its focus on interior affective states and its privileging of affective interiority. Sentimental writers tell us a lot about characters' emotional investments, revealing elaborate emotional worlds with complex relations among various feelings, including overlappings of identifications and desires. In Rose Terry Cooke's "My Visitation" (1858), for example, the female narrator talks about "falling passionately in love with Eleanor Wyse" (16).[12] The narrator describes their relationship in terms of erotic passion: she admires Eleanor's physical beauty (particularly her eyes, figure, mouth, and lips) and feels a "blind, irrational, all-enduring devotion" (16) to her. Her love for Eleanor is masochistic, an erotic groveling wish to be used by Eleanor:

> I, still blind, adored her more. She found in me a receptivity that suited her, and a useful power of patient endurance. Her will made me a potent instrument. What she wanted she must have, and her want was my law. No time, no pains, no patience were wanting in me to fulfill her ends. I served her truly.
>
> (18)

The narrator's masochistic adoration, which she calls "fervor," produces a kind of identification, which she calls "respect," whereby the narrator attempts to become like her beloved, to follow her beloved's "noble theories" (17). When the narrator says, "I was glad to be clay as long as she was queen and deity" (17), her figurative language highlights the sadomasochistic erotics of their relationship: the narrator is the base clay to be walked upon, and Eleanor is all-powerful, a queen, a deity. But these metaphors also emphasize the narrator's malleable, clay-like subjectivity, which is to be molded into an image of Eleanor. The narrator points out that "even in my deepest humiliation before her sublime theories and superhuman ideals I unconsciously grew better myself. A capacity for worship implies much, and results in much" (18). While this masochistic worship of Eleanor leads the narrator to her desired humiliation, it also provides her unconsciously with opportunities for "much" self-growth, for identificatory transformation.

Unfortunately, but perhaps not unexpectedly, Eleanor betrays the narrator. Filled with sorrow, the narrator finds comfort in the arms of Herman Van Alstyne, Eleanor's rebuffed former beau. While enthralled with Eleanor, the narrator and Herman identify with each other and establish a friendship on the basis of mutually discovered similarities: "Never did I perceive a charm in the landscape that he had not noticed before or simultaneously with me; the same felicity of diction or of thought in what we read struck us as with one stroke; we liked the same people, read the same books" (22). But she has no romantic feelings for him: "I could not marry him—for I had but the lesser part of a heart to give any man. I loved a woman too well to love or to marry" (22). Following Eleanor's betrayal, however, she comes to appreciate his looks and integrity (28) and falls in love with him: "I [was] drawn toward Herman by the strongest tie that can bind one heart to another. . . . it pleased God that I should live to receive my heart's desire; what began in gratitude ended in love" (28). What began as identification ends as connubial bliss and the fulfillment of her "heart's desire." The narrator's "desire" always includes an element of identification, just as it takes women and men as its objects. When Eleanor dies and the narrator grows exhausted with grief, she takes pleasure in submitting to Herman's consolation: "I obeyed. . . . quiet, but languid, I laid my head upon his breast, and, held by the firm grasp of his arm, I rested, and he consoled me; a deep and vital draught of peace slaked my soul's feverish thirst" (29). She has transformed Herman into the focus for her masochistic desire. Yet when she falls asleep on Christmas Eve, Eleanor's ghost visits to beg forgiveness. As the narrator bestows her pardon ("Eleanor! Yes love, darling! yes, forever" [31]), she realizes joyously, ecstatically that "Herman and Eleanor both loved me" (31).

Another way in which sentimentalism shades identification into desire is through the vicarious relations it offers readers. Sentimental discourse entices readers to identify themselves with the characters' emotions and experiences. Still, as many sentimental writers (like Alcott) must have realized, neither the author nor society can precisely control the ways readers vicariously respond to a story. Some reader-response examinations of sentimentalism have suggested that readers' identifications do not always follow the most prescribed or strictly gendered paths. Barbara Sicherman, for example, has shown that young female readers of a book like *Little Women* loved it not so much for its lessons in self-control, but for its literary, ambitious, boyish, and adventurous heroine (Jo March) whom they wanted to emulate.[13] *Little Women* is interesting in this context because it offers so many opportunities for not only cross-sex/same-sex gender identifications but also same-sex/cross-sex desires (often via vicarious identifications with Jo's desires). There are heteroerotic aspects to Jo's relationship with Laurie, the boy with the girl's name; indeed, Alcott's refusal to bring Jo and Laurie together has created dissatisfaction among readers for generations. Jo marries the father-like Professor Bhaer, and they have children. Yet Jo also expresses homoerotic feelings for women, especially members of her family: she "just wish[es] [she] could marry Meg," says she's "in love with" Meg, and tells Marmee that "Mothers are the *best* lovers in the world."[14]

In other words, sentimentalism does not exactly resist the erotic. Sentimentalism's erotics, like its politics, are not necessarily fixed. Blurring the distinction between identification and desire, sentimental erotics can be bisexual, polymorphous, shifting. In *Work,* as I demonstrate in the final section of this essay, Alcott takes advantage of the fluidity and complexity of sentimental discourse to eroticize images of workers and the cross-sex/same-sex desires made possible by work. She uses sentimental discourse to create a bisexual erotics of work—"bisexual" in the ordinary sense of denoting romantic or sexual attraction to both sexes, but also in Maria Pramaggiore's sense of "an ambiguous and often undecidable location where identification meets desire." In her essay calling for "a more nuanced approach to the issue of identification, in terms of spectators' and

characters' multiple sexual and identificatory investments," Pramaggiore associates "bisexual" desire with a refusal to choose between sexual desire and identification.[15] While *Work* offers vicarious pleasures, it does not always fix the readers' vicarious relation to the text as either identification or desire. The novel allows readers to refuse to choose between identification and desire; it facilitates eroticized identification. Furthermore, as if to model eroticized identification for readers, *Work* represents its characters' emotional or loving investments in a way that troubles the identification/desire distinction.

WAGE-EARNING WOMEN AND THE CULTURAL POLITICS OF ANTIFEMINISM

Sentimental representations of romantic love between women, as in "My Visitation," were not uncommon in nineteenth-century American culture. Images of romantic, physically affectionate relationships among women, sometimes called "sentimental friendship," regularly appeared in nineteenth-century writing.[16] Historians often discuss these relationships in terms of romantic friendships and ideas about separate spheres. Beginning with Carroll Smith-Rosenberg's "The Female World of Love and Ritual: Relations between Women in Nineteenth-Century America" (1975), scholarship about these relationships has generated controversy. Some scholars have called these relationships "lesbian," a designation that seems valid from a twentieth-century point of view, even though the idea of "lesbian" as a specific kind of sexual identity is anachronistic in a nineteenth-century context. Other historians—while acknowledging that sentimental friendships did include romance, professions of adoration and infatuation, and indeed physical contact—have refused the suggestion that "sexuality" played a role in these relationships. Recent historical scholarship on women's relationships in the nineteenth century has recommended avoiding both historical anachronism and denials of same-sex sexuality. Our twentieth-century taxonomy of sexual identities is not the best place to begin historical understanding of these relationships, yet it seems clear that sentimental friendships nourished not only romantic affections but also sexual desires and practices.[17]

Wage labor was also a critical factor in the historical construction of these same-sex relationships. During and after the Civil War, as their husbands, brothers, sons, uncles, and fathers went off to fight (hundreds of thousands never returning), women were taking up new kinds of work and entering the paid labor force in larger numbers than ever before. Between 1865 and 1890 the number of wage-earning women tripled. By 1870 women held one-fourth of all nonfarm jobs, and more than 350,000 women worked as industrial manual laborers. By 1876, 10 percent of Boston's population were wage-earning women, and wage-earning women were usually unmarried. During the nineteenth century the number of never-married women steadily increased, and these single women needed income-producing jobs to support themselves. Usually they had to take low-paying, unrewarding jobs: 70 percent of wage-earning women worked as domestic servants, and four-fifths of the remaining 30 percent took low-wage "sweat-shop" jobs in the garment industry.[18] Despite less than adequate employment opportunities, women's entrance into the wage-labor force gave them the chance to live independently and to interact with other women in settings not overseen by the family. This independence in turn facilitated the development of new kinds of erotic, domestic, and romantic relationships between women. In other words, it was not only the homosociality of separate spheres and romantic friendships but also working and living apart from the heterosexual family that enabled and sustained women's domestic, sexual, and loving companionships with other women.[19]

The relationships enabled by the entry of more women into the economic public sphere became the subject of numerous realist and sentimental novels in the post-Civil War era. Novels like Elizabeth Stuart Phelps's *The Silent Partner* (1871), Beverly Ellison Warner's *Troubled Waters* (1885), and Alcott's **Work** critique the injustices suffered by women workers, celebrate cooperative and loving relationships among women, and reveal how wage labor has the potential to offer women new kinds of personal, economic, and political power. Women living and working apart from the heterosexual family were also targets of anxiety and ridicule in novels like Henry James's *The Bostonians* (1886) and Mark Twain and Charles Dudley Warner's *The Gilded Age* (1873). In all of these novels, profeminist and antifeminist, women's sexuality and the sexual dangers faced by working women are recurrent themes.[20]

The expansion of women's presence outside the home led to the construction of alliances between working-class women and middle-class feminists. The well-known exploitation and fraudulent mistreatment of women in the paid labor force helped persuade middle-class feminists to establish protective associations for working women. Organizations like the Working Women's Protective Union and the Working Women's Association championed working-class causes and endeavored to establish cross-class feminist alliances, though their mission was often hampered by bourgeois misunderstanding of wage labor and the lives of the working class and working poor.[21] These alliances—along with the proliferating representations of the sexual dangers faced by working women and the sheer increase in the numbers of women living and working apart from the heterosexual family—generated anxiety and even intense antifeminist hostility toward working women and feminists in postbellum American society.

While gaining support and expanding its social and political power in the 1870s, the women's rights movement also met fierce opposition on numerous fronts. This was an era of derisive, sometimes vicious, antifeminist backlash as well as progressive feminist activism. Although it often relied on stock elements from sentimental discourse, antifeminism was just as often cynical or antisentimental in its attempt to thwart identifications and desires across class and gender boundaries. A typical feature of antifeminist discourse was *ad hominem* invective. A writer for *The Ladies' Repository* illustrated a standard attack by quoting a particularly strident bit of antifeminist diatribe:

> I had read frequent accounts of this body as "a concentration of all that was vulgar, coarse, and masculine, disaffected old maids, fault-finding widows, childless married women, who had rushed together to vent their spleen upon the world, to exasperate each other, to court notoriety, and to unburden themselves of the gall of bitterness."[22]

Although the author distanced herself from this antifeminist tirade, *The Ladies' Repository* did not in general. In an 1871 article Olive Raymond explained the women's movement failure:

> These noisy aspirants for political power are constantly furnishing the gravest and most powerful arguments against the cause they loudly and zealously defend. Witness the divisions, jealousies, and artful maneuvering, and listen to the vituperation, and bitter warfare in their own camp! Imagine all this on a larger scale, and we have a more hideous picture even than the masculine political world presents.[23]

While purporting to offer an objective analysis of the inadequacies of the women's movement (its tactical errors, its infighting, its lack of rhetorical savvy), this essay's primary function was to delegitimate feminism by representing its advocates as loud, bitchy, vain, "hideous." Mainstream antifeminism in the 1870s, much like contemporary antifeminism, attempted to impede or frustrate growing support for the women's movement by representing those associated with the movement as unattractive, disagreeable, repulsive.

Antifeminist discourse also discouraged vicarious allegiances to wage-earning female characters by associating them with corruption, crime, and sexual wrongdoing. In Susan F. Cooper's "Two of My Lady-Loves" (1872), for example, the story's two working women—Rosabella, who is "a factory girl," and Adelina, who works in a "dollar-store"—suffer differing but predictably pitiful fates. At the story's end, Hiram Jenks tells the narrator the sad news:

> "Adelina ran away last spring with Smith's son. He has had a couple of other wives already. They are keeping a saloon in Kansas." "Ay, ay. Sorry to hear it. I hope Rosabella has done better?" "Rosabella, Sir, has gone to the bad."[24]

No one explains how Rosabella went bad because (in 1872) there is no need. Rosabella has become a "fallen woman." Middle-class readers no doubt worried that this might be the fate of some working women. Yet the consistency with which images of working-class women as sexually "fallen" appear and reappear suggests that readers also expected it.

These representations of working women's sexualities generated considerable apprehension. Discourse about the "white slave trade," for instance, as Rosalyn Baxandall and Linda Gordon have explained, "captured anxieties about young women entering large cities in search of work and the possibilities of a sex life unsupervised by family and community."[25] Yet American culture not only portrayed women as vulnerable to sexual threat, as in Cooper's story or "white slave trade" discourse, it also imagined women as the sexual threat. In "The Stitching Girls" (1869), a poem from the *Lynn Transcript,* seamstresses appear as sexually alluring and dangerous:

> The stitching girls, the witching girls
> The jaunty, dainty, stitching girls
> With Cupid's dart they pierce the heart—
> The pleasing, teasing stitching girls. . . .
> They break your heart and then depart
> The naughty, haughty stitching girls.[26]

These young working women are not merely "naughty" and "witching," they also wield the dangerously phallic "Cupid's dart" as effortlessly as they might stitching needles. The representation of women's sexuality functions here to make the young women seem threatening, just as it turns men into the innocent victims.

The most common antifeminist attacks on working women were claims about women's "nature" and women's "sphere" and the censure of those who transgressed their "proper" gender roles. Women who played sports were called "ridiculous" and "contemptible" "Amazons," just as women who took an interest in politics were seen as "frantic," "wild for woman's rights," and "[d]esirous of coarse notoriety." "Effeminate Men and Masculine Women" (1872) offered a bold disparagement of the woman "whose ambition it is to fling herself into the active fray of life as one of the bold and eager fighters, instead of standing to the side as the care-taker and solacer of those who must fight." Women who behaved in ways considered masculine or aggressive were vulnerable to charges of deviance and criminality. Antifeminist literature regarded "masculine" women who wanted a wage-earning job outside the home as foolish or misguided. These texts insisted that women's incapacity for certain kinds of work was inherent, innate, biological. Thus, a typical antifeminist response to women's rights was the claim that inequality between the sexes stemmed from "the very foundation of their natures" and that "nearly all through Nature the female animal is subordinate to the male."[27]

Antifeminist discourse also worked to discredit desires that might persuade women to join the movement or to long for what feminists sought—legal rights, education, jobs, and the vote. In 1870 *Appletons' Journal* printed Henry Abbey's poem, "Wear and Want," accompanied by two engravings.[28] The poem presents two adjacent, contrasting tableaux—one in which a "beautiful" middle-class woman, "sighing for lack of wear," sits in her warm, lovely house and another in which a poor, hungry, barely clothed "mother stood, holding her dying child" in the midst of a cold winter storm. In its portrayal of these two women, the poem puns on the words "want" and "wear." Both women want wear. The poor woman lacks but desperately needs (wants) some clothing (wear) as well as some food and shelter, while the affluent woman yearns for (wants) something to do or some way to use her abilities (wear). The poem does not use the contrast to point out disturbing economic injustice or urge middle-class action to help poor women who must work to support themselves. Instead, the poem censures the affluent woman in the engraving for being restless and dissatisfied:

> Our sin is as sharp as a serpent's tooth,
>   When we pine for things that we do not need.
> Shame, shame to the heart and its wicked pride,
> That, having much, is unsatisfied.

The poem represents bourgeois women who "pine for things we do not need" (like, say, an education or a job to relieve the tedium of domestic life) as shameful, wicked, ungrateful. Sighs from dissatisfied women with nice homes are, when compared to the wants of the working poor, shameful. The picture of the woman wearing tattered clothes is part of this admonishment to bourgeois women to give up their yearnings. Encouraging a disidentification with women outside the home, the downward comparison reminds middle-class women that life could be worse, that they would much rather stay comfortably at home than suffer the cold cruelties of life outside the domestic sphere. Thus, the poem's title might have been "Wear *or* Want," a stern warning to middle-class women that they have two options: join the ranks of bourgeois women who sit at home weary with boredom or join the working poor worn down by poverty.

While shaming bourgeois women's desire to look outside the home for work, Abbey's poem and the engravings also make poor working women seem pretty awful—miserable, pathetic, ugly, as unattractive as suffrists, though entitled to more pity than suffrists. Abbey's portrayal of the poor woman is full of sentimental pathos: she is "freezing and weak, in the merciless street" and "holding her dying child." Readers are supposed to regard her with pity, just as they are supposed to withhold pity from the dissatisfied middle-class woman for whom "No song would be trilled for the gloom of her brow, / If pity were voiced like a bird on a bough." Still, the poem and the engravings do not ask readers to do anything about poor working women. They just remind the middle classes that poverty is worse than boredom. The attitude toward poor women is revulsion, and that is what enables it to work as a warning.

These antifeminist representations sought their interventions via the identifications and desires of readers. Antifeminist discourse portrayed working women and their supporters as sexually and martially undesirable, unattractive, sexually impure, sexually threatening, unnatural, even repulsive. It tried to delegitimate the aspirations of women wanting work and a life apart from the heteronormative home, just as it fostered disidentification with these women by suggesting that their wishes and desires were morally wrong, dangerous, and unnatural. To discourage actual political attachments and allegiances among women, antifeminism attempted to thwart vicarious attachments and allegiances.

THE BISEXUAL EROTICS AND POLITICS OF *WORK*

For the most part, **Work** did not respond directly to antifeminism or propose new feminist ideas. Real social change for women, Alcott realized, would entail more than championing a prolabor cause and nay-saying antifeminist attacks. Social change must also involve an appeal to or transformation of the desires, identifications, and ideals of individuals in the society. Understanding this at some level, antifeminists generated images of working women and feminists as undesirable and unfulfilled. Alcott countered this antifeminist imagery by eroticizing work. Using sentimentalism's complex and unstable symbolizations of pleasure, desire, and identification, Alcott's novel tinctures the representation of work with bisexual eroticism, an erotics that reveals how identifications and desires travel routes that are not always monosexual. **Work** represents women workers as desirable and desiring, and it envisions multiple romantic-erotic possibilities for women in the workplace. Along the way, **Work** illustrates that despite the antifeminist obstacles that limit women's opportunities and desires, women and their desires are the solution to the sexual-political barriers that keep women from working and coming together.

In contrast to the disagreeable images of women workers in antifeminist discourse, Alcott portrays workers as desiring and desirable—sympathetically appealing but also intellectually and sexually attractive. For example, in the final chapter, as Christie delivers a speech at a feminist meeting, Alcott emphasizes not Christie's words or ideas, but the working women's response to Christie. The women identify with her ("The women felt that this speaker was one of them" [333]), and her address exudes "a spirit of companionship that uplifted

their despondent hearts" (333). Christie's identification with these women and their identification with her inspires solidarity. Still, this identification is not separable from physical attraction. Christie speaks because she "felt a steadily increasing sympathy for all, and a strong desire to bring the helpers and the helped into truer relations with each other" (331).[29] The "faces of the workwomen touched her heart" (331), just as Christie's beauty moves the women. They are drawn to Christie because they see her as "this figure with health on the cheeks, hope in the eyes, courage on the lips, and the ardor of a wide benevolence warming the whole countenance . . . full of unconscious dignity and beauty, an example to comfort, touch, and inspire them" (333). As they look at Christie's "cheeks," "eyes," "lips," "face," and "figure" and admire her "beauty," they are drawn to her passion, her "ardor," as well as her "hope" and "courage"—more abstract qualities which are nonetheless embodied in her "eyes" and "lips." Besides Christie and these "work-women," there are other desirable and desiring working women throughout the novel. Christie herself is infatuated with Rachel, a coworker. Christie's rival, the working-class Kitty, is also described in terms of her sexual beauty (226). A detailed look at two examples, Christie and Lucy in chapter three, should reveal how and why Alcott eroticizes images of working women.

When Christie leaves her job as a servant to try her luck in the theater, she meets Lucy, "a gay little lass" (30), an actress described as "pretty" (30) and "comely" (38). Lucy "initiat[es] her into the mysteries of the [theater]" (34), flirtatiously coaxing Christie into becoming an actress: "'Don't be prim, now, but say yes, like a trump, as you are,' added Lucy, waving a pink satin train temptingly before her friend" (32). When Christie gets a role opposite St. George—a sexy young man who has "'heavenly eyes,' 'distracting legs,' and a 'melting voice'" (42)—Lucy grows jealous, even though Christie's romance with St. George is strictly an onstage one. Christie makes an effort to prove her affection and gratitude, but "she fail[s] to win Lucy back" (41). Thinkers from Freud to Sedgwick and Garber have suggested that jealousy can function as a defense against or mask for other passions, including homoerotic attachment to a rival.[30] And jealousy among other emotions is what structures a triangulated bisexual relationship among Lucy, Christie, and St. George. Christie and St. George's relationship is a theatrical, simulated hetero-courtship, while Lucy's relationship to St. George is marked by active anaclitic desire—Lucy wants to have St. George. Lucy and Christie's bond entails both desire and identification, homoerotic affection and homosocial/heterosexual rivalry over St. George, the male love object. The bisexual triangle eroticizes all three characters, including both working women.

Alcott repeats this bisexual triangle pattern in a melodrama within the novel, Charles Reade and Tom Taylor's *Masks and Faces.* In the play, St. George plays the husband (Vane), Lucy the betrayed wife (Mabel), and Christie the other woman (Peg). While watching Lucy as Mabel and hearing "real love and longing thrill her trembling words with sudden power and passion" as Mabel prays for "her rival to give her back her husband's heart" (44-45), Christie realizes that this love triangle has deeply distressed Lucy, just as it has worn out Christie, who wants to set things right. Before Christie can *say* anything to Lucy, however, an on-stage accident provides Christie with the chance to *demonstrate* her love and devotion to Lucy—and sentimentalism always prefers sincere demonstrations of love to mere professions. As a mechanical prop falls to the stage floor, Christie springs forward to save Lucy from the crash. The near fatal disaster leaves "poor Peg [Christie] lying mute and pallid in Mabel's [Lucy's] arms" (45), which is where Christie has wanted to be since the beginning of Lucy's delusional jealousy. *Masks and Faces* functions as a fictional simulation of what is happening in the novel's (fictional) plot and as another instance of triangulated desire in the novel's pattern of triangulated desire. By including this sentimental drama within the novel, Alcott not only draws attention to her own redeployment of sentimentalism's falseness/ sincerity (masks/faces) binary, but she also makes explicit her own use and sentimental melodrama's use of a triangulated bisexual erotics.

It was not, of course, unusual to find erotic actresses in nineteenth-century popular culture. Representations of these working women titillated various nineteenth-century audiences, but they also generated uncertainty and anxiety. Images hinting at the sexuality of working women were reminders that some unmarried working women could escape the family's and community's oversight of their sexual lives. Like "The jaunty, dainty stitching girls," actresses were represented as a sexually enticing and probably dangerous class of working women. *The Women of New York* (1869) described actresses as "remarkable beauties" and "jealous, hypersensitive creatures" who use "loose language" and have "a morbid love of applause." It expressed concern about "a new brood of [actresses], generally of unusual physical beauty, but not always of the highest sense of decorum," who "depend upon their personal attractions for an engagement, and are less loth than the older and more deserving actresses to exhibit themselves on the street."[31] The *to-be-looked-at-ness* of these female figures, to use Laura Mulvey's formation, could make them erotically pleasing to some (but also, therefore, menacing to others who might see such images as a source of competition for sexual attention) and also sexually threatening to some male viewers (a reminder of sexual difference and the implied threat of castration).[32]

One response to this threatening uncertainty was moralizing. In an 1872 article on theater history, for example, the Reverend J. W. Carhart noted a direct connection between allowing women to act and "extremely lax morals," and he criticized all performers for "their looseness on the subject of marriage" and "lavish promiscuousness."[33] Another typical response to the anxiety produced by the threatening-erotic images of actresses was objectification—the transformation of the female figure into a vapid object of sexual desire. The New York Book Company used such an icon, an alluring chorus girl (a type of actress) with exposed cleavage and bare legs, to grab the attention of browsers. Alcott's erotic working women are fascinating in this context precisely because they do not play the role of sexual object, but insist on the role of sexual agent. Lucy and Christie behave as sexual agents, desiring and choosing, while St. George is simply a sexual object, known mostly for his "heavenly eyes" and "distracting legs" (42). During the on-stage disaster, Alcott emphasizes St. George's object-like status: as Christie heroically saves Lucy and Lucy holds Christie in her arms afterwards, "Vane [the character St. George plays] wrung his hands" (45) in a passive and emotional gesture appropriate to an erotic object.

In other words, Alcott not only makes her images of working women attractive and desirable, she also makes them vehicles for identification. In response to the antifeminist claim that feminist and working women are undesirable and unsatisfied, Alcott presents characters like Lucy and Christie as not only desirable but also desiring and empowered. Such characters tend to dedifferentiate identification and desire in the reader's vicarious relationship to the novel. Does the reader identify with and want to be like the actress? Does the reader imagine that she (or he) wants to have the passionate and sexy actress? Does the reader want to be like the actress because the audience or the other characters desire her? Does the reader identify with her because through this identification the reader can vicariously experience desire for St. George and his distracting legs and gorgeous eyes? Questions like these and their resistance to fixed answers suggest that *Work*'s sentimentality operates at least partially as a bisexual erotics that permits readers to explore the erotic possibilities of identification.

Alcott also answers antifeminist polemics by highlighting the occasions for romantic relationships opened up by work. Alcott's representation of these relationships is sentimental, and she depicts these relationships as bisexual: in the sense that Christie feels erotic attraction to women and men, and in the sense that Christie's erotic attraction seems constituted out of desires and identifications. The greatest pleasure that work promises wage-earning women, according to the novel, is a partial release from economic patriarchy. *Work* recalls the sentimental formula in which the heroine follows her heart in searching for true love. Yet the novel also departs from a related sentimental tradition wherein true love and other sentimental attachments are, as Eva Cherniavsky puts it, "governed by the logic of economic dependencies."[34] Mrs. Wilkins warns Christie against "goin' to marry for a livin'," saying "I'd rather one of my girls should grub the wust kind all their days than do that" (252-53). Mrs. Wilkins believes wage-earning work, no matter how bad, is the way women avoid marriages of economic dependency, and Christie ultimately agrees. Despite opportunities to marry into economic security, Christie declines Joe Butterfield's marriage proposal and twice refuses Philip Fletcher, and instead falls in love with Rachel and David. As a working woman, Christie can choose lovers according to her own sexual desires, according to erotic not economic need. "Happy women," Helen Carrol calls working women, specifically actresses, like Christie, "they can love as they like!" (79). Although she does love as she likes, not until a third of the way through the novel does Christie find romantic true love. However, the course of this true love is neither smooth nor straight. It is bifurcated and must happen around, through, and because of her primary passion for work. Christie's first true love is Rachel whom she meets working in the city as a seamstress. Her second love is David whom she meets working in the country as a gardener. Only after this pair of job-romances and a few more triangulated rivalries can Christie find a bisexual arrangement that brings vocational and romantic happiness. This bisexual triangle is the result of a surprising coincidence, what Garber might call "the paradoxical 'accident' of a perfect design."[35]

When she takes a sewing job, Christie finds among the other working women "one, and one only, who attracted her" (103). Rachel's "black dress, peculiar face, and silent ways attracted Christie," and Rachel in turn "watched her with covert interest, stealing quick, shy glances at her as she sat musing over her work" (103). When the two women make eye contact, the confident and pursuing Christie smiles, and the demure Rachel blushes: "Rachel only colored, kept her eyes fixed on her work, and was more reserved than ever" (103). Christie is drawn to Rachel's beauty; she imagines Rachel as "one who had known some great sorrow" and looks admiringly upon her "bright, abundant hair," "youthfully red, soft lips" with their "mournful droop," as well as her "eyes" full of "indescribable expression," eyes that Christie thinks are "[s]trangely haunting" (103). Despite Christie's obvious interest, Rachel remains unresponsive. Still, the undaunted Christie believes that Rachel's "eyes" belie her true feelings and that her "fugitive glances betrayed the longing of a lonely heart" (104). Because "her own heart was very solitary" (104), Christie actively begins to court this timid, melancholy beauty. As the novel explains:

> She wooed this shy, cold girl as patiently and as gently as a lover might, determined to win her confidence, because all others had failed to do it. Sometimes she left a flower in Rachel's basket, always smiled and nodded as she entered, and often stopped to admire the work of

her tasteful fingers. It was impossible to resist such friendly overtures, and slowly Rachel's coldness melted; into the beseeching eyes came a look of gratitude.

(104)

To describe this relationship, Alcott uses the sentimental discourse of romantic love. The novel presents Christie as the sincere pursuer and Rachel as the timid pursued, and it provides a detailed, sensuous description of the beloved being wooed (103). Several uncertainties—coy glances, blushing, the hesitation of the pursued, the mysterious emotion that the beloved carries within her—intensify and eroticize the courtship. As in sentimental literary tradition, Alcott emphasizes interior affective states: although she attempts to hide her feelings, Rachel's blushing, expressive eyes and glimpses at Christie reveal loneliness, emotional turmoil, and indeed a reciprocal interest in Christie. The diction describing the courtship is sentimental, especially the mention of "the longing of a lonely heart" and the numerous other references to the heart. Alcott recalls a cardinal theme of sentimentalism by emphasizing the sincerity of Rachel's affection for Christie; indeed, Rachel masks her true feelings only because her "longing" for Christie is so deep and genuine: "the longing of [Rachel's] lonely heart . . . dared not yield itself to the genial companionship so freely offered it" (104). This suspicious reserve is unwarranted, however, because Christie's feelings *are* sincere. Christie admires Rachel's uniqueness, woos her slowly and gently, and leaves her tokens of unfeigned affection (the flowers, which are so important to the erotic-romantic discourse in this novel).

As these passages indicate, an important dimension to Christie and Rachel's relationship is their identification with each other, identifications that Alcott highlights through the novel by accentuating the similarities between them. Both are young working women, and both are "different from the others" (103) who work in the shop. While the others chat endlessly about "[d]ress, gossip, and wages" (103), neither Christie nor Rachel take interest in these conversations. The similarity Alcott most emphasizes is the mutual loneliness and the longings that loneliness generates. Still, identification is hardly the only bond in this relationship. Eventually, Rachel lets herself be won over by Christie's assiduous affection, and to Christie's eager "Then I may love you?" (105), Rachel responds with a clear "Yes" (105). The novel then describes how "Christie kissed her warmly, whisked away the tear, and began to paint the delights in store for them in her most enthusiastic way, being much elated with her victory; while Rachel listened with a newly kindled light in her lovely eyes" (105). As the kissing and elating over "her victory" suggests, Christie plays a pursuing, dominant role in this love affair. Christie "lavish[es] the affection of her generous nature on a creature sadder and more solitary than herself," explaining to Rachel, "I must love somebody and 'love them hard'" and "I know you need some one to look after you, and I love dearly to take care of people" (105). Rachel's desire, on the other hand, is passive anaclitic—she wants Christie to want her. Because of her mysterious past, Rachel cannot yet accept Christie's offer of "the whole of her heart" and "the larger half of her little room," that is, Christie's proposal that they live together and "be so cosy evenings with our books and work" (105). Still, as an expression of her passive anaclitic desire for the hard-loving Christie, Rachel pleads, "love me, dear, and some day I'll show you all my heart" (105).

Christie's desire for/identification with Rachel make sense in relation to Christie's desire for, identification with, and idealization of her own parents. As in many sentimental texts, the parents are dead; and, because of this loss, they play an all the more powerful role in the imaginary order of the heroine's desires and identifications. Christie, the novel tells us, has inherited "[h]er father's old books" and "his refined tastes," which have left her dissatisfied with the usual options available to young women in her rural community, the prospect of "becom[ing] a farmer's household drudge" (13). Emulating her poor but educated father, Christie seeks a romance with a poor but proud and desirable working woman. Just as powerful as this emulation of her father's active anaclitic desire (*to have* someone like her mother) is Christie's identification with her mother, her wish *to be like* her mother. She considers her mother's life "a beautiful example" (11), she's determined to "do the same" (10), and she thinks of her mother as being "so like herself" (12). Thus, when Christie meets Rachel—a woman who resembles Christie's idealization of her mother, a woman who works to support herself, who craves independence, and who loves without regard to wealth—Christie falls for her in part because she wants to be like her. Christie's desire for Rachel is complex, a merging of identification with desire: her love for Rachel is both active anaclitic (emulating her father's example and identifying with his desire, Christie *wants to have* this peculiar and independent working woman) and active narcissistic (she *wants to be like* Rachel because Rachel resembles her mother's "beautiful example").

In the narration of Rachel and Christie's amour, the most clearly sensual and erotic relationship in the novel, Alcott sews details of their romance into and around descriptions of work, so that romance and work become one piece. Although she is not fond of sewing, pledging early in the novel to turn to it only as a last resort (17), Christie stays at the sewing shop because of Rachel: Christie "[m]ost assuredly" would have left Mrs. King's for better, healthier job prospects "had not one slender tie held her till it grew into a bond so strong she could not break it" (103). To emphasize Christie's delight with the relationship, Alcott figures her heroine as cheerful and efficient workplace appliance: Christie "was rapidly becoming a sort of sewing-machine when life was brightened for her by the finding of a friend" (103). When eagerly describing for Rachel the romantic-domestic bliss they could have living together, Christie's description includes not only "cosy evenings" and "books" (a metonymy for her father's psychic-sexual legacy) but also "work" (a metonymy for her mother's psychic-sexual legacy). Alcott's sentimental response to antifeminism presents the joys of same-sex romance as another incentive for women to enter the wage-earning world, the world of "working girls." Work not only offers women dignity and independence, it also offers them the chance to find true love.

After Miss Cotton discovers that Rachel is a "fallen" woman and fires her, Christie and Rachel separate: "Christie, remembering only that they were two loving women, alone in a world of sin and sorrow, took Rachel into her arms, kissed and cried over her with sisterly affection, and watched her prayerfully, as she went away" (112). Alcott's narration of the sweet and sorrowful parting is erotic (kisses and embraces of "two loving women"), sentimental (tears), and religious (prayers). The breakup depresses Christie who cannot imagine living without Rachel: "It is not always want, insanity, or sin that drives women to desperate deaths; often it is a dreadful loneliness of heart" (118). At the moment Christie is poised to throw herself into the river, Rachel returns to rescue her. "Christie's heart was thrilled" (126), and Rachel begins talking about a home, which Christie hopes is with Rachel. But Rachel has no plans to stay and takes Christie to Mrs. Wilkins's home, where Christie learns "A Cure for Despair" (chapter 8). The cure is work.

Later, in the gardens at Mrs. Sterling's place, work facilitates Christie's romance with her second true love, David. As they work alongside each other, the workplace becomes the context for the development of their love. In the gardens Christie and David communicate with the language of flowers, an erotic discourse.[36] Christie initially expresses irritation with David, saying "he won't seem to care for anything but watching over his mother, reading his old books, and making flowers bloom double when they ought to be single" (194). This language of double flowers is loaded with double meanings. In the nineteenth-century language of flowers, double flowers are emblems of romantic-erotic union. The double flowers also suggest David's and Christie's doubly gendered identities.[37] Christie maintains a steadfast defense of single flowers and her own singleness, however, because she is unwilling to give up her right to work. She tells David how she sees herself as one of those "who are compelled to be fellow workers with men" (207). Wanting to begin their relationship on the basis of an identification as "fellow workers," Christie downplays gender differences. Indeed, Christie prefers to relate to David as if she were a man, as his "younger brother" (208). Not at all put off by her wish for masculine brotherliness, David responds with an enthusiastic "I wish you were!" (208). David likes her identification with men and her longing to interact with men as self-supporting equals.

Their relationship does not develop into a romance, however, until both experience the pains and pleasures of triangulated bisexual relationships. When Kitty returns to the Sterlings', Christie and Kitty meet for the first time. The attractive and flirty Kitty loves to avoid work and talk about marriage and lovers. "[B]eing a born flirt [who] tried all her powers on David, veiled under guileless girlishness," Kitty uses a "thousand little coquetries" to entice David into discussions about "heart affairs" (229). Kitty's presence unhinges Christie, who begins to suffer "constant pin-pricks of jealousy" (228), and eventually Christie leaves her job at the Sterlings'. Although Christie's rivalry with Kitty is the primary cause of the chronic, agonizing jealousy that Christie feels, this rivalry is complicated by Christie's identification with and attraction to Kitty. Despite important differences between Kitty and Christie, both are working-class, both have left repressive domestic situations, both have refused to stay at home to marry a local boy, both have experienced exploitation as working women, and both desire David (a shared erotic object). Alcott even uses "Kitty" as one of Christie's nicknames (6). The similarities between them suggest that Christie would not have great difficulty seeing aspects of her own life and identity (or Rachel's) in Kitty's experience. Moreover, Christie finds Kitty attractive or, at least, "very pretty" (229), even as she dislikes her attitude toward work and loathes her as a rival. Christie's jealous belief that David desires Kitty is delusional—in Freudian terms, a projection of and defense against her own desire for Kitty. Although Christie's attraction to Kitty has no existence separate from the rivalry over David, Christie's relationship with Kitty is more than a competition for a man—it's also a relationship (like most rivalries) charged with identification, projection, and desire.

David suffers the pain of jealousy when Philip Fletcher reappears to renew his romantic interest in Christie. David's jealousy causes him to become more verbal and engaged than usual, just as it prompts him to look at and desire Christie more than ever. In the final moments of a gathering hosted by Mr. Power, David gazes on "the reflection of her face in the long mirror" (247). The novel tells us that "She seemed a new Christie to David, in that excited mood" (248). The mood here is erotic jealousy, and both seem possessed by it. This jealousy is the sign of mutual erotic attraction, and the desire builds as each attempts to restrain it. Although his eyes are "fixed, yet full of fire," revealing that he is "a man intent on subduing some strong impulse," David "relapse[s] into his accustomed quietude" (249). Christie practices denial: "'It was the wonderful music that excited him: that was all,' thought Christie" (249).

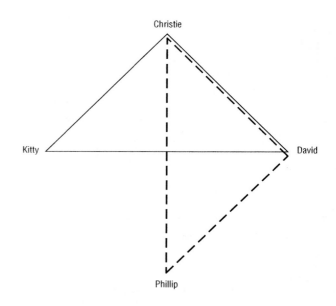

Figure 1. *Erotic triangles in* Work.

These two interlocking erotic triangles, Christie-David-Kitty and David-Christie-Philip (Figure 1), produce the jealousy that is the sign and cause of the others' desire, but these two triangles also paralyze the progress of Christie and David's romance. Thinking that David loves Kitty, Christie flees the Sterlings' place. Thinking wrongly that Christie plans to marry Fletcher, David continues his celibate ways. The irresolution of the love plot brought on by the appearance of the *faux* rivals and the interlocking erotic triangles is structurally related to the novel's deliberations on the "labor question" and the "woman question." The dilemma that the novel sets out to mediate is the opposition of women and work (the cultural prohibitions that discourage and prevent women from pursuing wage-earning vocations). If the opposition of women and work is entered as the initial binary into a Greimasian semiotic square,[38] which then produces each term's "contradictory," four terms emerge: women, work, not-women (or men), not-work (Figure 2).

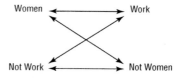

Figure 2. *"Women" and "Work" in a Greimasian square.*

On a certain structural level, these conceptual oppositions could be said to generate the novel's ideological field as well as its conflicts and plot. The terms work and not-women are embodied in the novel's most industrious male character, David, just as the opposition between not-women and not-work is mediated by Philip—the wealthy bachelor who has no need to work. "Lazy little Kitty" (234) unites not-work and women. The synthesis of the two major terms, women and work, is attempted by the protagonist herself, Christie; and it is through Christie that Alcott attempts to mediate the cultural opposition of women and work. The completed schema (Figure 3) and its congruence with the interlocking triangles (Figure 4) reveal the structural significance of these erotic relationships to the primary social-ideological contradiction the novel attempts to resolve. The paralysis in the love plot produced by the interlocking erotic triangles coincides with the irresolution of the contradiction between women and work. The threat that Christie would become "Mr. Fletcher's wife" (258) as her next occupation opens the possibility that Christie might never mediate this contradiction, that she could become a "wife" excluded from wage-earning labor. This irresolution dominates the middle of *Work*—until Rachel's return.

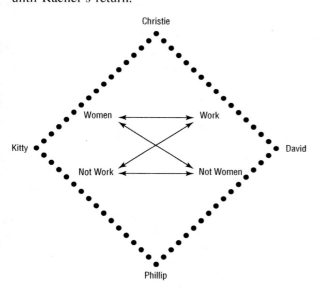

Figure 3. *Characters' relationships to "Women" and "Work."*

Christie remains "haunted" (262) by the thought that David might marry Kitty. Thus, when David prepares to tell Christie his "happy news," she expects him to announce his engagement to Kitty. Instead, he produces a picture that Christie examines, asking "Is it my Rachel?" (264). David's response is a resounding, "It is *my* Letty!" (264). Thinking that Letty is the name of David's lost lover, Christie's reaction is pain-filled amazement:

> Christie seemed to hear in it the death knell of her faith in him. The picture fell from the hands she put up, as if to ward off some heavy blow, and her voice was sharp with reproachful anguish, as she cried:

"O David, David, anything but that!"

(264-65)

Where does this anguished, stupefied horror come from? Why would news of Letty's return cause Christie to lose "faith in him"? Certainly, news that David's heart would forever belong to a rival would pain Christie. On the other hand, Christie has prepared herself for the news that Kitty and David would marry. She is braced to hear she has lost David. Moreover, Christie has always respected (if not accurately understood) David's mournful attachment to "his lost Letty" (262). Christie could more easily approve of his marriage to his first true love than to Kitty, whom Christie misrecognizes as a substitute for Letty within David's life ("she reminds him of his lost Letty, and so he thinks he loves her" [262], Christie thinks to herself). Perhaps, then, Christie's anguish is about the loss of Rachel; the horror springs from her realization that "my Rachel" has returned not to love her, but David. This interpretation of Christie's reaction accounts for her loss of faith in David in a way the first interpretation cannot. She would not consider him untrue if he were simply being faithful to his first beloved, but she might lose "her faith in him" if she thought he would betray her by taking Rachel, *her* first love, *her* lost beloved. A still better reading of Christie's response acknowledges that her horrified anguish is the product of a (mis)perceived double loss. In thinking that David and Rachel would marry, Christie believes that she has lost both of her true loves and that, in a doubling of the painful irony, they have been taken from her by her beloveds.

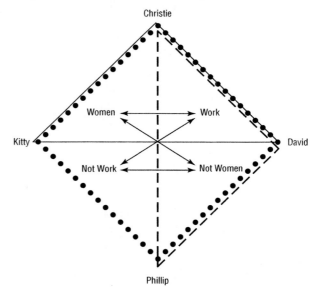

Figure 4. *Congruence of erotic triangles with Greimasian square.*

Eventually, Christie learns that Letty/Rachel is actually David's lost sister. As they delight in her return and "the happy fact that Rachel and Letty were one" (268), David and Christie begin to open up to each other. After months of jealousy and denial, they admit their love for one another and decide to marry. What is significant about the resolution of this love plot is that the paralyzing pair of interlocking erotic triangles is replaced not by a heterosexual dyad (husband and wife) but by a bisexual triangle (David-Christie-Rachel/Letty). Rachel/Letty is not only the catalyst that allows David and Christie to overcome the jealousies that paralyze them into romantic inaction, she is also the long-lost beloved who completes Christie's bisexual triangle, the crucial third who brings the three together. Thus, what Christie had initially thought was a double loss turns out to be a double gain—a situation that Alcott emphasizes two or three times. David's marriage proposal to Christie includes an announcement (enticement) that "Letty longs for you" (273). Christie realizes, "Now I've not only got you [David] but Letty also" (272), just as David recognizes, "there is no need to choose between us" (273), between Letty and Christie. The chapter ends with Christie's declaration that "'double flowers' *are* loveliest and best" (274). In this context, the double flowers accrue still more meaning. They signify Christie's re-union(s) with David *and* Rachel, her desires for David *and* Rachel, her identifications with David *and* Rachel, her love for a man *and* a woman, her bisexuality.

Just as the paralysis in the love plot coincides with the threat to Christie's ability to mediate the terms women and work, the resolution of the love plot into a "perfect" bisexual trio reinaugurates Christie's attempts to unite these concerns. Following Letty's return, David and Christie enlist for Civil War duty. Although he wonders at first whether she ought to go, she insists, "You *will* let me do it, and in return I will marry you" (281). She conditions their marriage on her right to work as a nurse. Refusing to wear "bridal white" (293), the sign of her sexual purity and availability to only him, Christie "will be married in [her] uniform as David is" (292), the sign of her identification with him and their new work. The day they are married becomes the day they are both "mustered in" to service. Although most nineteenth-century women, even feminists, thought married women should work only in cases of extreme economic exigency,[39] Christie refuses to accept the conventional social opposition between work and marriage for women and heads to war after the wedding.

Likewise, in the remaining chapters, the novel refuses to see widowhood, motherhood, an inheritance, or disagreements between working women and middle-class women as reasons to stop striving toward a uniting of women and work. As Christie enters widowhood, for example, David from his deathbed urges her, "Don't mourn, dear heart, but work" (315). When their child is born, Christie plans "to teach her to labor heartily and

see no degradation in it" (323). When she collects an inheritance from Uncle Enos, she puts aside portions for Ruth, Letty, and Mrs. Sterling, and uses the rest to expand "David's work" (328) providing refuge and work (in the gardens) for working women. In the final chapter, Christie aims to bring together women and work by attempting to unite different classes of women on the issue of work and by serving as a voice for women workers. *Work* ends with a scene in which Christie leads a group of women to dedicate themselves to the women's movement:

> With an impulsive gesture Christie stretched her hands to the friends about her, and with one accord they laid theirs on hers, a loving league of sisters, old and young, black and white, rich and poor, each ready to do her part to hasten the coming of the happy end.
>
> (343)

This scene, in its representation of empathetic connections across race, class, and generational boundaries, is a good example of Alcott's use of sentimentalism. In a scene about women's political solidarity, Alcott strengthens its appeal by emphasizing spontaneous affection (Christie's "impulsive gesture" to hold hands), intimacy ("with one accord they laid theirs on hers"), love (the women are described as "a loving league of sisters"), and perhaps even *jouissance* (the wished for "coming of the happy end"). The bonding here is emotional, but also intimate and physical. The women make their boundary-crossing connections because of shared aims and shared work (each has "to do her part" for the cause); and the work here is figured as the path to future satisfaction. In this passage marked by boundary-crossing identifications and desires among women, Alcott uses sentimentalism to create a pleasing contrast to images of feminists as "disaffected old maids, fault-finding widows, childless married women, who had rushed together to vent their spleen upon the world." Moreover, this last chapter represents Christie doing precisely the cultural work that Alcott intends for the novel—a mediation of the opposition of women and work.

My purpose in examining Alcott's mediation of women and work via a bisexual erotics of work has not been to amplify, as in Garber's *Vice Versa*, our realization that bisexuality is everywhere. Instead, I have indicated what representations of bisexuality could do politically and highlighted the way a conventional stylistic mode, sentimentalism, treated nonheterosexual desire. Rather than reinforcing conventional gender divisions of nineteenth-century American society, sentimental discourse, as it take shapes in *Work,* actually challenges the antifeminist insistence on rigid gender-labor roles by eroticizing women workers, feminists, and work itself as the occasion for bisexual desire. That sentimental discourses could accommodate the representation of work as a site for the play of sexual desire outside compulsory heterosexuality and patriarchal marriage exemplifies Foucault's observations about "the tactical polyvalence of discourses." Alcott's deployment of sentimental discourse is then a kind of rejoinder to the critical denigration of sentimentalism for its moral rigidity, aesthetic feebleness, and political naiveté. This essay has also complicated claims that Alcott's writing is polemical or didactic. While *Work* is a political novel, its political means are not aggressively disputatious or narrowly instructive. Like many Victorian Americans, Alcott knew readers took up novels for pleasure. For *Work* to persuade or critique, it would have to please. *Work*'s bisexually erotic images of women and work are distinct examples of the way Alcott came to use enjoyment, pleasure, identification, and desire as vital factors within a sentimental political rhetoric.[40]

Notes

1. Ann Douglas, *The Feminization of American Culture* (1977; New York: Anchor Press, 1988), 13; Jane Tompkins, *Sensational Designs: The Cultural Work of American Fiction, 1790-1860* (New York: Oxford University Press, 1985).

2. Lauren Berlant, "The Female Woman: Fanny Fern and the Form of Sentiment," in *The Culture of Sentiment: Race, Gender, and Sentimentality in Nineteenth-Century America,* ed. Shirley Samuels (New York: Oxford University Press, 1992), 270. Lynn Wardley describes the sentimental as "labile" in "Relic, Fetish, Femmage: The Aesthetics of Sentiment in the Wake of Stowe" (Samuels, ed., *Culture of Sentiment,* 220). In *Mixed Feelings: Feminism, Mass Culture, and Victorian Sensationalism* (New Brunswick: Rutgers University Press, 1992), Ann Cvetkovich points out that the sentimental has "a double function," like sensationalism: it both registers and displaces affect (100). Stephanie A. Smith's attention to maternal figures likewise reveals a complexity within the sentimental as she illustrates how "sentimental representations screen, reveal, substitute for, and bear problematic inscriptions" (*Conceived by Liberty: Maternal Figures and Nineteenth-Century American Literature* [Ithaca: Cornell University Press, 1994], 41).

3. Louisa May Alcott, *Work: A Story of Experience,* ed. Joy S. Kasson (New York: Penguin, 1994). References to *Work* are noted parenthetically in the text.

4. "*Work,*" *The Literary World* (July 1873): 19; "Recent Novels," *The Nation* (31 July 1873): 73; Alcott to Lucy Stone, 1 October 1873, in *Selected Letters of Louisa May Alcott,* ed. Joel Myerson and Daniel Shealy (Boston: Little Brown, 1987), 178. Critics who see work as "polemical" or "didactic" include Elizabeth Langland, "Female Stories of Experience: Alcott's *Little Women* in Light of *Work,*" in *The Voyage In: Fictions of Female Development,* ed. Elizabeth Abel, Marianne Hirsch, and Elizabeth Langland (Hanover: University Press of New England, 1983), 117; Sarah Elbert, *A Hunger for Home: Louisa May Alcott's Place in American Culture* (New Brunswick: Rutgers University Press, 1987), 248; and Susan K. Harris, *19th-Century American Women's Novels: Interpretative Strategies* (Cambridge: Cambridge University Press, 1990), 171-96. *Work* is a political novel, but attention to the political or "polemical" aspects of the book has led some critics, like Langland, for instance, to overlook the novel's eroticism. Comparing *Work* to the male *Bildungsroman,* Langland says "the protagonist, Christie Devon, is denied the sexual affairs of the male *Bildungsheld*" (114). I find such observations puzzling because while Christie's adventures are different from those in a male *Bildungsroman,* Christie's romantic life and sexual desires are central not only to the form and plot but also the politics of the novel.

5. Philip Fisher, *Hard Facts: Setting and Form in the American Novel* (New York: Oxford University Press, 1985), 102. Criticism on nineteenth-century sentimentality has long insisted that sentimental art forms evade the treatment of sexuality and passion. A well-known version of this argument appears in Leslie A. Fiedler, *Love and Death in the American Novel* (New York: Criterion Books, 1960), 254-369. I should note that Fiedler disparages sentimental writing for its evasion of the erotic, while Fisher seems to admire sentimentalism for the same reason.

6. Michel Foucault, *The History of Sexuality, Volume I: An Introduction,* trans. Robert Hurley (1978; New York: Vintage, 1990), 23. See John D'Emilio and Estelle B. Freedman, *Intimate Matters: A History of Sexuality in America* (New York: Harper & Row, 1988), 55-85; and T. Walter Herbert, *Dearest Beloved: The Hawthornes and the Making of the Middle-Class Family* (Berkeley: University of California Press, 1993), 138-48.

7. T. L. Haines and L. W. Yaggy, *The Royal Path of Life: or, Aims and Aids to Success and Happiness* (Chicago: Western Publishing House, 1876), 30.

8. Joy S. Kasson, "Narratives of the Female Body: The Greek Slave," in Samuels, ed., *Culture of Sentiment,* 190. For more on maternal figures in sentimental discourse, see Smith; also Eva Cherniavsky, *That Pale Mother Rising: Sentimental Discourse and the Imitation of Motherhood in 19th-Century America* (Bloomington: Indiana University Press, 1995).

9. A growing body of criticism is exploring incestuous heterosexual desire in sentimental discourse. In *Daughters, Fathers, and the Novel: The Sentimental Romance of Heterosexuality* (Madison: University of Wisconsin Press, 1991), for example, Lynda Zwinger argues that sentimentalism plays a key role in the production of heterosexual desire: "the sentimentalized representation of woman as a desiring daughter and of the father as innocent of any but culturally sanctioned designs upon her . . . ground the system of cultural constructs and prescriptions that we have learned to think of as heterosexual desire" (7). See also Karen Sánchez-Eppler, "Temperance in the Bed of a Child: Incest and Social Order in Nineteenth-Century America," *American Quarterly* 47 (1995): 1-33.

10. See, for instance, Joanne Dobson, "Reclaiming Sentimental Literature," *American Literature* 69 (1997): 267, 286n19.

11. Eve Kosofsky Sedgwick, *Epistemology of the Closet* (Berkeley: University of California Press, 1990), 159; James Creech, *Closet Writing/Gay Reading: The Case of Melville's* Pierre (Chicago: University of Chicago Press, 1993), 44-51. For more on the indissociability of desire and identification, see Diana Fuss, *Identification Papers* (New York: Routledge, 1995).

12. Rose Terry Cooke, "My Visitation," in *"How Celia Changed Her Mind" and Selected Stories,* ed. Elizabeth Ammons (New Brunswick: Rutgers University Press, 1986), 14-31.

13. See Barbara Sicherman, "Reading and Ambition: M. Carey Thomas and Female Heroism," *American Quarterly* 45 (1993): 73-103; and "Reading *Little Women*: The Many Lives of a Text," in *U.S. History as Women's History: New Feminist Essays,* ed. Linda K. Kerber, Alice Kessler-Harris, and Kathryn Kish Sklar (Chapel Hill: University of North Carolina Press, 1995), 245-66.

14. Louisa May Alcott, *Little Women* (Boston: Roberts Brothers, 1868-69; New York: Penguin, 1989), 203, 170, 437.

15. Maria Pramaggiore, "Straddling the Screen: Bisexual Spectatorship and Contemporary Narrative Film," *RePresenting Bisexualities: Subjects and Cultures of Fluid Desire,* ed. Donald E. Hall and Maria Pramaggiore (New York: New York University Press, 1996), 292, 293n3.

16. On "sentimental friendship," see Dinah Mulock Craik's *A Woman's Thoughts about Women* (1858), quoted in Sara M. Putzell-Korab, "Passion between Women in the Victorian Novel," *Sexuality and Victorian Literature,* ed. Don Richard Cox (Knoxville: University of Tennessee Press, 1984),

182. For representative portrayals of intimate relationships between women in nineteenth-century American fiction, see Margaret J. M. Sweat, *Ethel's Love-Life* (New York: Rudd & Carleton, 1859), esp. 75-93; Louisa M. Alcott, *An Old-Fashioned Girl* (Boston: Roberts Brothers, 1870; Akron and New York: Saalfield Publishing Company, 1928), 273-92; Louisa May Alcott, *Diana and Persis,* ed. Sarah Elbert (New York: Arno, 1978); Henry James, *The Bostonians* (1886; Harmondsworth: Penguin, 1966); and Susan Koppelman, ed., *Two Friends and Other Nineteenth-Century Lesbian Stories by American Women Writers* (New York: Penguin, 1994).

17. The classic studies are Carroll Smith-Rosenberg, "The Female World of Love and Ritual: Relations between Women in Nineteenth-Century America," *Signs* 1 (1975): 1-29; and Lillian Faderman, *Surpassing the Love of Men: Romantic Friendship and Love between Women from the Renaissance to the Present* (New York: William Morrow, 1981), 147-253. For an overview of the issues in the historiographical controversy, see Leila J. Rupp, "'Imagine My Surprise': Women's Relationships in Historical Perspective," *Frontiers* 5 (1981): 61-70. A superb introduction to nineteenth-century same-sex intimacy can be found in D'Emilio and Freedman, *Intimate Matters,* 121-30.

18. Rosalyn Baxandall and Linda Gordon, eds., *America's Working Women: A Documentary History, 1600 to the Present,* rev. ed. (New York: Norton, 1995), 84; William Leach, *True Love and Perfect Union: The Feminist Reform of Sex and Society* (New York: Basic Books, 1980), 163, 165; Carl N. Degler, *At Odds: Women and the Family in America from the Revolution to the Present* (New York: Oxford University Press, 1980), 152. See also Alice Kessler-Harris, *Out to Work: A History of Wage-Earning Women in the United States* (New York: Oxford University Press, 1982), 45-141.

19. Recently, historians and literary critics have begun to contextualize nineteenth-century homosexual relationships (usually men's relationships) in terms of the industrial revolution, the rise of capitalism, and the expansion of wage-labor. In *By the Sweat of the Brow: Literature and Labor in Antebellum America* (Chicago: University of Chicago Press, 1993), for example, Nicholas Bromell examines the connections that Melville's *Redburn* (1849) makes between work and male homosexual love (77). Alcott's novel suggests, as I will show, that work offers a similar possibility for women who love women. See D'Emilio and Freedman, *Intimate Matters,* 129. See also John D'Emilio, "Capitalism and Gay Identity," *The Lesbian and Gay*

Studies Reader, ed. Henry Abelove, Michèle Aina Barale, and David M. Halperin (New York and London: Routledge, 1993), 467-76.

20. For more on the representation of the sexual threat associated with working women in nineteenth-century American fiction, see Barbara Bardes and Suzanne Gossett, *Declarations of Independence: Women and Political Power in Nineteenth-Century American Fiction* (New Brunswick: Rutgers University Press, 1990), esp. 100-129.

21. Ellen Carol DuBois, *Feminism and Suffrage: The Emergence of an Independent Women's Movement in America, 1848-1869* (Ithaca: Cornell University Press, 1978), 138-53; Leach, *True Love and Perfect Union,* 163-67, 180-89; Kessler-Harris, *Out to Work,* 75-107.

22. Meta Lander, "The Woman Movement," *The Ladies' Repository* (June 1870): 383.

23. Olive Raymond, "Woman and Work," *The Ladies' Repository* (July 1871): 14.

24. Susan F. Cooper, "Two of My Lady-Loves," *Harpers New Monthly Magazine* (June 1872): 132, 133.

25. Baxandall and Gordon, *America's Working Women,* 115.

26. "The Stitching Girls," *Lynn Transcript* (26 June 1869), in Mary H. Blewett, *We Will Rise in Our Might: Workingwomen's Voices from Nineteenth-Century New England* (Ithaca: Cornell University Press, 1991), 93-94.

27. "Table-Talk," *Appletons' Journal* (22 January 1870): 109; "Effeminate Men and Masculine Women," *The Ladies' Repository* (August 1872): 301; "Table-Talk," *Appletons' Journal* (19 August 1871): 218. See George Chauncey Jr., "From Sexual Inversion to Homosexuality: Medicine and the Changing Conceptualization of Female Deviance," *Salmagundi* 58-59 (Fall 1982-Winter 1983): 114-46; and Carroll Smith-Rosenberg, *Disorderly Conduct: Visions of Gender in Victorian America* (New York: Knopf, 1985), 245-96.

28. Henry Abbey, "Wear and Want," *Appletons' Journal* (19 February 1870): 212-13.

29. For a different perspective on sympathetic identification in *Work,* see Glenn Hendler, "The Limits of Sympathy: Louisa May Alcott and the Sentimental Novel," *American Literary History* 3 (1991): 685-706.

30. See Sigmund Freud, "Some Neurotic Symptoms in Jealousy, Paranoia and Homosexuality" (1922), in *Standard Edition of the Complete Psychological Works of Sigmund Freud,* trans. and ed. James

Strachey, 24 vols. (London: Hogarth Press, 1953-74), 18:225-30; Eve Kosofsky Sedgwick, *Between Men: English Literature and Male Homosocial Desire* (New York: Columbia University Press, 1985); and Marjorie Garber, *Vice Versa: Bisexuality and the Eroticism of Everyday Life* (New York: Simon & Schuster, 1995), 443-55.

31. George Ellington, *The Women of New York* (New York: New York Book Co., 1869), 524, 526, 527.

32. See Laura Mulvey, "Visual Pleasure and Narrative Cinema," *Screen* 16 (1975): 6-18.

33. Rev. J. W. Carhart, "The Theater and Religion," *Ladies' Repository* (December 1872): 429, 433.

34. Cherniavsky, *That Pale Mother Rising,* 36.

35. Garber, *Vice Versa,* 528.

36. See James D. Wallace, "Where the Absent Father Went: Alcott's *Work,*" in *Refiguring the Father: New Feminist Readings of Patriarchy,* ed. Patricia Yaeger and Beth Kowaleski-Wallace (Carbondale and Edwardsville: Southern Illinois University Press, 1989), 266.

37. See Elizabeth Lennox Keyser, *Whispers in the Dark: The Fiction of Louisa May Alcott* (Knoxville: University of Tennessee Press, 1993), 113.

38. See A. J. Greimas and F. Rastier, "The Interaction of Semiotic Constraints," *Yale French Studies* 41 (1968): 86-105.

39. See Baxandall and Gordon, *America's Working Women,* 102.

40. Foucault, *History of Sexuality,* 100. For an example of Victorian awareness of the place of pleasure in readers' selections of books, see "What the People Read," *The Literary World* (March 1874): 153-54.

Gustavus Stadler (essay date December 1999)

SOURCE: Stadler, Gustavus. "Louisa May Alcott's Queer Geniuses." *American Literature* 71, no. 4 (December 1999): 657-77.

[*In the following essay, Stadler characterizes the ties between sexuality, gender, and literary genius in Alcott's fiction.*]

In 1870, at the close of a decade in which the *Atlantic Monthly* had consolidated its position as arbiter of literary value in the Northeast while excising a number of female authors from its list of contributors, James Russell Lowell, the magazine's editor from 1857 to 1861, published a book containing an essay on the genius of Jean-Jacques Rousseau. Lowell's essay is remarkable for its apparent contradiction of the gender politics embedded in the *Atlantic*'s recent editorial decisions, since it describes a model of genius that is curiously bisexual, in Freud's sense. As the essay's title, "Rousseau and the Sentimentalists," makes quite clear, one issue Lowell was negotiating was the relationship between genius and sentiment, between literary production and the unruly but necessary forces of affect—forces that, then as now, were customarily associated in bourgeois culture with femininity. In the penultimate sentence of his essay Lowell maps the subjectivity of genius by impersonating it, gendering it, and sexualizing it: "If, as some fanciful physiologists have assumed, there be a masculine and feminine lobe of the brain, it would seem that in men of sentimental turn the masculine half fell in love with and made an idol of the other, obeying and admiring all the pretty whims of this *folle du logis*."[1] Throughout much of the essay, Lowell has been attempting to defend the value of genius despite its imputed narcissism. He continues to do so here, specifically by shaping the genius's interiority as a heterosexual courtship, a wooing of the feminine lobe by the masculine. Yet this model quickly slides from a relation of "half love" into one of identification and mimesis, of imitating the "pretty whims" of the "*folle du logis*"—none other than the madwoman in the attic. Lowell then closes the essay by noting the possible weakness inherent in the necessary presence of femininity within the genius, a threat that Rousseau has been genius enough (or not genius enough?) to contain. Lowell leaves us quite uncertain whether this imitative femininity is merely the occupational hazard or the inevitable occupation of the genius (to borrow a J. L. Austin witticism).

Lowell's gender-bending essay was written two years after Alcott published her best-known work, *Little Women,* and several more years after the *Atlantic* had largely ceased to solicit work from Alcott and other female authors such as Harriet Stowe, Rebecca Harding Davis, and Gail Hamilton. Nonetheless, the shiftiness of gender and sexual categories that Lowell identifies with genius in "Rousseau and Sentiment" also marks the term's frequent appearances in Alcott's fiction. In *Little Women,* for example, while Jo is verbally sparring with the lovesick Laurie in a game loosely resembling "Truth or Dare," she is asked by the young man what her greatest desire is. Jo replies sassily and sharply, "Genius. Do you think you can give it to me?"[2] Jo is flirting here, but she is also explicitly substituting "genius" for the boy-sister named Laurie, who is as contradictorily gendered as Jo herself, though a more world-bound object of desire.

It is particularly fascinating to see manifestations of such contradictions in the work of Alcott, an author conventionally assumed to write within a wholly female literary domain. While continually representing genius as a subject position she herself cannot occupy, from which she cannot speak, Alcott repeatedly portrays the figure of genius as oddly productive for those intimate with it but apparently excluded from its mantle. For Alcott, genius was a persistent if ungraspable preoccupation; the assurance in *Little Women* that Alcott stand-in Jo March "did not think herself a genius by any means" (265) only sets the stage for later Alcott efforts such as the unfinished novel *Diana and Persis,* a narrative rumination on balancing domestic responsibilities with artistic talent and passions, and perhaps for the apparently never-developed idea for a book titled simply *Genius.*[3]

This essay argues that while the category of genius has continually been used by cultural arbiters to homogenize notions of cultural value, it has also permitted extremely insightful exploration of the contradictions and complications of gendering authorial production. Viewed this way, genius is a productive entry point for expanding our understanding of midcentury U.S. literature across gender lines and cultural levels. Most importantly, I think, the concept of genius may help us to add nuance to the heavily gendered grid through which we read and teach much of this work. For one of the most notable aspects of nineteenth-century definitions of genius is how *queer* they are: that is to say, how frequently they attempt to contain gendered qualities that would otherwise be seen as highly contradictory, how they eroticize—often without regard to normatively gendered patterns of eroticism—experiences of reading and writing. In the figure of *the* genius, nineteenth-century writers create a subject position whose oddness and peculiarity seem to challenge the standards of normativity even as they help to perpetuate the normative's sense of its cultural self-worth.

This queer perspective allows us to reposition the category of genius in American literary studies. Nina Baym's exhaustively researched *Novels, Readers, and Reviewers* finds that among female fiction writers at midcentury, "only three were discussed in American magazines as though they were eligible to be thought of as examples of genius: George Sand, Harriet Beecher Stowe, and Charlotte Brontë."[4] While *domesticity* and *sentimentalism* have served as categories under which the bulk of women's midcentury writing has been classified, *genius* has often been seen as the high cultural term applicable to the alternative to this work, the locus from which Nathaniel Hawthorne indicted the "damned mob of scribbling women." Critics of the right, left, and center have worked to perpetuate this division, forming a great tradition of American literary geniuses patterned on F. R. Leavis's or carving out a space for women writers and readers in which the patriarchal standards of genius do not apply.

If we think of the gendered opposition between genius and sentiment as an organizing paradigm of nineteenth-century literary production and reception, it is remarkable, though perhaps inevitable, how much the two terms travel across the binary divide that separates them. One often finds, for example, female sentimental writers such as Fanny Fern and Alcott ruminating almost obsessively on the nature of literary genius, or male literary "geniuses" like Henry James returning again and again to questions of sentiment and affect. We can observe the flexibility of these terms in other writers as well: Washington Irving, Edgar Allan Poe, Margaret Fuller, Nathaniel Willis, Elizabeth Stoddard, and Lowell, among others, spring to mind. This fluidity suggests that genius was not simply a male attribute in nineteenth-century literary culture; it was, rather, an aspirational norm that in its ambiguous imbrication with sentimentality served as a contested site for discourses of gender, authorship, and literary value.

There are some real advantages in focusing on nineteenth-century literary production as an array of practices within which flexible and relational models of genius and sentiment circulated. By foregrounding the porousness of the boundary between seemingly opposed ideological territories—"separate spheres," for example, or high cultural production and low—this approach prevents us from reifying and polarizing literary practices along gender lines. Moreover, in adopting this perspective a variety of polygendered investments in the writing and reading process suddenly come into view—investments through which we can probe and further detail our understanding of eroticisms, of patterns of identification, and of pedagogical relations in nineteenth-century American literature.

* * *

Given her milieu's general distaste for and disinterest in *naming* female figures as geniuses, Alcott tended to frame her writings on the topic relationally, often describing in her private writings her awe before such revered ancestors and contemporaries as Goethe and Emerson. One model for such a relation was provided by Margaret Fuller's friendship with Emerson, another by the acolyte-child Mignon in Goethe's *Wilhelm Meister.* Fuller and Mignon both inhabited gender in an exceptional manner, but they did so in ways quite different from one another. Perhaps equally important for Alcott was a textual relationship indirectly introduced to her by Emerson: the correspondence between the German authors Bettina von Arnim and Goethe as portrayed in von Arnim's epistolary novel, *Goethe's Correspondence with a Child.* Published in 1835 and first translated into English by the author two years later, von Arnim's book was discovered by a fifteen-year-old Alcott during a visit to Emerson's library. The text, which was highly popular in the United States, represents the rapturous

state, for von Arnim, of being a reader of Goethe more than it reflects on the content of his writings or on the young woman's relationship with the older man. It uses von Arnim's contact with the writer and his books only as the starting point for fanciful flights of narrative, memoir, and aesthetic philosophy. Von Arnim's claim that the correspondence took place when she was twelve (she was actually twenty-two) only added to the outlandish impression the book made, especially on American and English readers, at least some of whom were suspicious about the letters' authenticity. Also adding to the sensationalism surrounding the book was the apparently accurate story that von Arnim had learned English solely to translate the book and had succeeded in doing so in a remarkably brief period of time.[5]

Von Arnim seems a particularly fruitful model for the structure of genius we find in Alcott, particularly because of the erotically charged devotion portrayed in her book on Goethe and her later book on the poet Günderode, which Margaret Fuller translated into English in 1842. Both books blend the genres of collected letters, memoir, novel, and essay; both are also presented as having been inspired by a state of rapture or possession engendered by the more well-known, more conventionally authorial figure. Both *Günderode* and *Goethe's Correspondence with a Child*—which also include rapturous letters to Günderode and to Goethe's mother—seem to disconnect von Arnim's entire relation to genius from heterosexuality or cross-sex fertility. Christina Zwarg has argued that Emerson and Fuller's relationship was modeled largely on von Arnim's *Günderode,* and that Fuller derived from the correspondence "a complete confusion and ultimate displacement of familiar gender roles as well as some traditional genre considerations."[6] Von Arnim's book or books may well have offered Alcott, too, a template for imagining a sexually charged pairing that rearranged traditional gender and erotic roles and produced literary writing.

* * *

In the atmosphere in which Alcott wrote, as she was simultaneously becoming tremendously famous and being further distanced from the elite center of American literary life, the notion of genius was coming to embody larger debates about the role and value of sentiment in literary writing. In the Lowell essay cited earlier, Rousseau is characterized as a genius of sentiment, which Lowell defines as "emotion ripened by a slow ferment of the mind and qualified to an agreeable temperance by that taste which is the conscience of polite society." Yet Lowell's model poses problems both for himself and for the emerging school of social realists epitomized by William Dean Howells, who would eventually take control of the *Atlantic.* While Lowell is generally sympathetic to sentiment as a component of literary production, he notes through the example of

Rousseau the danger of becoming what he calls a "sentimentalist." The sentimentalist evades the regulation of "taste" and inevitably slides into decadence and dissipation: "the sentimentalist always insists on taking his emotion neat, and, as his sense gradually deadens to the stimulus, increases his dose till he ends in a kind of moral deliquium. At first the debaucher, he becomes at last the victim of his sensations."[7] For Howells, too, the term genius carries connotations of moral decadence (as he wrote in 1886 in an editor's column devoted to Goethe) and degrades the realist argument that literary excellence can more readily be achieved by application and the rigorous study of human life than by any innate gift of the senses.[8]

In examining Alcott's writings, I am particularly interested in Lowell's use of the phrase "victim of his sensations" to describe his exemplary figure of genius, Rousseau. The victim, the martyr, the consumptive: in these figures the discourses of romanticism and the literary phenomenon we have come to define as American women's sentimentalism meet. The inevitable dissipation that produces Rousseau's genius is paralleled by the consumptive decline of the sentimental heroine, who also suffers from a disease of the sensations; both instances of decline result in textual production and resolution. It is on this queer turf, in which famous literary men become madwomen and dying girls enable women to become public authors, that the discourse of genius holds the most promise for disrupting and diversifying the assumptions about gender and sexuality that undergird our understanding of nineteenth-century American literature.

The remainder of this essay looks at models of genius in two texts by Alcott, *Little Women* and the 1866 sensation novella "The Freak of a Genius." Juxtaposed, these texts demonstrate how richly same-sex attraction and cross-gender identification and mimesis inform Alcott's conception of literary production. They point to genius as less a kind of secular divine than a nexus for currents of queerness deeply embedded in the social and literary environs of New England in the latter half of the nineteenth century.

* * *

Productive sites of disjuncture emerge most centrally in *Little Women* in the implicit association of the consumptive genius John Keats with the consumptive sentimental heroine Beth March. But constructing a lens through which to examine genius in *Little Women* requires a study of the dynamics of genius in **"The Freak of a Genius,"** a long magazine story Alcott published across two numbers of *Frank Leslie's Illustrated Newspaper* in 1866, two years before the appearance of her best-known book. Alcott rewrote the tale of genius, with its frailty and its seductiveness, twelve years later

in *A Modern Mephistopheles,* but the earlier version is, I believe, more illuminating with regard to Alcott's use of genius to scrutinize polarities of gender during the period when men such as Lowell were beginning to institutionalize highbrow literature.

"Freak" ["The Freak of a Genius"] concerns the relationship between two men, Kent and St. George, who have entered into what seems to be a productive partnership for both. Kent is a poet, and St. George wants to be one. St. George is younger, much better looking, and much more charming in public situations, but he is unable to make himself write again after the failure of his first book of poetry. The two make a "bargain" that is almost immediately an open secret in the narrative, although the "actual" revelation doesn't come until well into the middle of the story: Kent will write his brilliant poems and St. George will act as their author in public, enjoying the homage of a largely female public that the older man finds embarrassing and stultifying. At the most basic level, Alcott seems to be identifying across gender with the figure of Kent. She was famously reticent about embracing the public aspect of the writing life; she also saw herself as much like Kent physically, frumpy and unattractive. St. George becomes in this reading a fantasized prosthetic body with which to battle the rigors of the public sphere, to endure being read in public. The structure here suggests that Alcott, like Lowell, conceptualizes genius as being made up of two halves: a feminine half (St. George) and a masculine half (Kent) that relies on the mimetic capabilities of the feminine half. As we will see, St. George's feminized mimetic faculties are given the edge of madness that Lowell described as a necessary component of genius. Alcott's apparent identification with Kent suggests that her model of authorship finds a generative eroticism in the hermeneutic practices set in motion by the suspect category of genius.

The female public's romance with St. George is mirrored by Kent's erotic attraction to the younger man, whose theatrical grace contrasts with the older poet's blunt awkwardness. The story suggests that Kent's affection is returned, and the attraction between the men is presented in a coy but perfectly clear manner:

> [said Kent:] "There was but one blemish in your first [book], the critics said. The poet wrote of love, yet it was evident he had never felt it."
>
> "I'm not so sure of that," murmured the boy, with a sidelong glance at his companion.[9]

Since the book referred to here was actually authored by Kent but publicly claimed by St. George, the "sidelong glance" can refer both to Kent's presumed desire for the young man and St. George's reciprocal desire for the older one.[10] Part of St. George's appeal is that he simply looks the part of a genius, an appearance described in the text in terms of feminine beauty: "large white lids hid [his] eyes, and long lashes rested on his cheeks as smoothly rounded as a girl's" (431). These are the charms the "bargain" brings to Kent, who tells St. George near the beginning, "I do not find that I have paid too high a price for affection" (432). Yet Kent's use of commercial language here, as well as his assumption of a position parallel to that of the girls who swoon over St. George at parties, has an implicitly feminizing effect on the older man.

The queer desires flourish here amid and through the phantom presence of cross-sex erotics, represented both by the female readers' attraction to St. George and by the effort Kent makes, toward the story's beginning, to provide St. George with a female partner so as to "understand the passion of which he writes" (431). In order to create the appearance that his public self has "felt" love, Kent urges St. George to wed a woman, and he takes the young man to a party filled with female admirers. Kent has preselected his neighbors, the sisters Margaret and May, as the most eligible candidates. Margaret, while more intelligent, is also more skeptical of St. George's apparent success. Echoing a line of thought commonly expressed in one strain of the contemporary discourse on genius, she sees the public signs of genius as also potential markers of danger; at the party at which St. George meets the women, she remarks on genius's vulnerability to "indolence" and "neglect."[11] At this point we observe a remarkable transformation in St. George: "St. George's eyes fell like a bashful girl's; he colored, and sat silent for a moment; then as Kent moved away he rose, turned the chair and sat down near Margaret with such an altered air that May shrunk back with sudden timidity, for the boy had vanished, and the man appeared" (436). St. George acts to allay Margaret's doubts by moving rapidly across gender roles, a theatrical deployment of the gender duplicity accorded literary genius. His performance apparently quells temporarily Margaret's doubts—doubts inevitably raised, it would seem, by the mention of "genius."

But the narrative maintains a sense of suspicion. Kent moves away upon St. George's blush, but only to take up a position as covert spectator: "Kent stood a little apart, apparently intent on a portfolio of rare engravings, but May fancied he listened as attentively as herself, for she detected an occasional flash of the eye, curl of the lip, or involuntary gesture of the head, which betrayed him though he uttered not a word" (436). In other words, Kent watching St. George speaking on genius—and speaking *to* the posited danger of genius's emptiness—becomes (through May) a spectacle for the reader. The visibility and theatricality of the two men's secret comes into greater prominence when St. George burns in shame; he subsequently inflames Kent's interest by giving a performance of genius—a performance that, by making Kent a detached but desiring spectator,

identifies the older man with the giddy young women who fawn over the young poet.

It is important to note that the erotic component of this relationship arises as a result of the aura of suspicion, not despite it. It is produced directly *by* the suspicion that genius is empty, a mere screen that shields amoral behavior and disguises a core of shallowness. What **"The Freak of a Genius"** does, then, as it makes an open secret of St. George's performatively successful but "empty" genius, is create a drama *around,* rather than *of,* the search for proof. That is, there is no actual mystery plot culminating in St. George's exposure as a fraud; rather, the tale maps the patterns of demand and desire for such information that inevitably surround the attribution of genius. In this sense, the story dramatizes an epistemology of genius. This epistemology, built on a hermeneutics of suspicion, parallels contemporary discourses of information seeking and confession incitement associated with consolidating modern notions of sexual identity.[12]

Margaret's suspicions are correct. St. George is indolent and neglectful, or at least lazy and dissipated. He is also party to an erotic attachment, his continuing relationship with Kent, that undermines his interest in heterosexual marriage. St. George does finally marry May, the demure sister, but the marriage leaves both unhappy. St. George spends the bulk of his time engaging in behaviors that have been historically coded as will-shattering, decadent, "addictive," and "queer": frequenting French bohemia, gambling, drinking.[13] His character traits lend credence to the suspicion that he is the eponymous "Freak" of the story. The power of the story's economy of secrecy is most highly dramatized when Margaret deduces the secret of the bargain between the two men and St. George directly drowns himself.

Kent, of course, remains, unrecognized as an author until after St. George's death and Margaret's revelation. Yet **"The Freak of a Genius"** is not a simple morality tale in which St. George's deviance is punished and Kent's good will finally given its due. For the posthumous presence of St. George, of St. George-as-performative-genius, remains peculiarly productive of literary activity. Not only does the young non-poet's penchant for self-destruction construct the story's narrative, but it has a lasting effect on the older man that the text specifically associates with public authorship, with effects on an audience. When Kent finds St. George's body in the Paris Morgue, the story hyperbolizes the spectacularity of the tragedy and emphasizes its legacy for the older man:

> Cold and pale as a beautiful statue he lay under the scanty covering allowed the dead in that sad place. A stream of water flowed continually over the rounded limbs, pale face, and drenched hair, and above him

hung the plain suit he had worn. Before the grating stood a curious throng, admiring, criticising, pitying "the young man, so charming, so romantic, so pathetic," and at the door, surrounded by sympathizing men and women, leaned Kent, bowed down with a speechless, tearless sorrow, which left its traces on him all his life.

(488)

Even in death, St. George's erotic, public efficacy lives on. He remains a spectacle; he remains a public figure in front of a "curious throng." At the Morgue, he is not a corpse but a statue, a monument. Moreover, his supposed lack of substance is marked here not as absence but as the vital power of nakedness (in the sexy image of water flowing over "rounded limbs, pale face, and drenched hair"), which is contrasted with the "plain suit" hanging nearby. His spectacular force is not to be repressed by the countering force of the narrative's move toward closure; although he has drowned, he will float.[14]

This irrepressible power—and its impression on an audience—is for Alcott the working model of writing, as the final paragraphs of the story make clear. Among the mass gazing at St. George's corpse stands Kent, for whom the spectacle becomes another kind of monument; through his "sorrow," he incorporates St. George's "traces" and soon turns them into traces on paper. He embarks on his own successful, openly public writing career. He marries Margaret, settles into a home with her and May, and writes the story of his life:

> Long after, when the young poet was forgotten by all but the faithful three, when Kent was a happy man with children on his knee and a noble wife beside him, when May had put off her widow's weeds and found comfort in Albany's affections, another and an entirely different book appeared, to take the public by storm, give the author a late-won but enduring fame, and stamp his long silence as "THE FREAK OF A GENIUS."

(488)

The tale thus maps writing, the establishment of a writing career, and the formation of domestic heterosexuality as results of the process of mourning and incorporating a lost same-sex erotic bond.[15] The freak here is no longer St. George's identity but Kent's act in concealing his authorship, the "bargain"/bond itself, now formally written (the text's capital letters draw attention to their printed status), now, in fact, the story we hold in our hands and activate into literariness as we read. Over the course of the tale, the significance of the word *freak* has evolved, designating first St. George, then the deal Kent strikes with St. George, and finally the act of composing a piece of public writing and the composition itself. It is a freak of genius that it can perform in this polyvalent way. It encompasses the act of reading and consuming St. George, his own consumption by tragedy, and the writing of that story of consumption.

* * *

Perhaps the most memorable mention of genius in all of Alcott's texts comes in the chapter of *Little Women* entitled "Literary Lessons," which begins by portraying Jo March working furiously on her first novel in the garret of the March home. During Jo's retreats to the garret, "the family . . . kept their distance, merely popping in their heads semi-occasionally, to ask, with interest, 'Does genius burn, Jo?'" (265). The phrasing of the question plays upon the etymology of the term *genius*, which, as Christine Battersby has shown, is derived from the Latin word for male fertility, a property that in the West was associated with the heat of the male body until at least the Enlightenment era.[16] The family's words also allude to ideals of domesticity, in which a flaming hearth and a lamp in the dark night serve as symbols of middle-class content and security.[17] The family's question and the novel's portrayal of Jo's writing as a struggle taking place amid daily domestic activities evoke the difficulties of Alcott's life as a writer in Concord. Given Bronson Alcott's philosophical opposition to taking money for work, Alcott was responsible for keeping the family home fires burning, as well as for keeping her own and her father's genius burning.[18] She lived among the famed intellectuals of Concord—Emerson, Thoreau, Hawthorne, and her father—and coped with the pleasures and pressures of such an environment.[19] Her use of the term *burning*, then, works to cross the gendered discourses of intellectual and domestic labor at both a personal and cultural level. Importantly, the term also plays upon a genealogy of female same-sex eroticism that goes back to Sappho's frequent use of the term and was brought up-to-date by Alcott-idol Charlotte Brontë's embodiment of the erotics of female homosocial environments in *Jane Eyre*'s Helen Burns.[20] With genius granted this specifically erotic valence and positioned as an external force, when the members of the March family approach the garret to ask whether genius burns, they are asking whether Jo's great desire burns within her—and whether she has yet been sufficiently possessed by the force of genius to generate her writing, a formulation of literary production that immediately recalls the relationship between Kent and St. George in **"The Freak of a Genius."**

In its model of authorship, **Little Women** constructs an ambiguous relationship between activity and passivity similar to that seen in the relationship between Kent and St. George. Although Kent is in one sense the passive partner (transfixed by the spectacle of St. George's beauty and theatricality), he is also active in his role as the "real" writer. Similarly, Jo March writes after falling into a state of possession, what she (and Alcott in her journals) calls a "vortex": "Every few weeks she would shut herself up in her room, put on her scribbling suit, and 'fall into a vortex,' as she expressed it, writing away at her novel with all her heart and soul, for till that was finished she could find no peace" (265). Alcott used similar language to describe the process she went through eight years earlier while writing her first adult novel, *Moods*: "Genius burned so fiercely that for four weeks I wrote all day and planned nearly all night, being quite possessed by my work."[21] The later parts of *Little Women* feature other scenes in which Jo is subject to vortex-like swoons; in one prominent example she attends a party at which she faints on hearing the "world being picked to pieces" in a discussion of philosophy among intellectual "celebrities" whom she admires, leaving her "with a sense of being turned adrift in time and space, like a young balloon out on a holiday" (352).

Though the association of genius with burning is an old one, *Little Women* is particularly adept in its play with the ideological content of burning as domestic hearth versus burning as genius authorship and with the word's grammatical doubleness. Burning is used repeatedly in the novel both intransitively (burning as display) and transitively (burning as it effects a change in something or someone). During the preparations for the society party that Meg and Jo attend toward the beginning of the novel, for example, Jo trumps Meg's complaint about not having a silk dress to wear by lamenting, "Yours is as good as new, but I forgot the burn and the tear in mine; whatever shall I do? The burn shows horridly, and I can't take any out" (23). The burn's potential to embarrass the girls at the party associates burning with blushes and the dangers of display. But the scene also reminds us that fires—such as the one that burned the dress when Jo stood too close to it—also burn transitively. The hearth is an active, potentially dangerous, performative agent; it is not simply a reflection of domestic sanctity. Moreover, in Alcott's literary world, a hairdo, a dress, or a schoolhouse can ignite at the blink of an eye, and manuscripts and printed matter seem doomed to the irresistible attractions of fireplaces. Faces continually burn in shame, in love, in anger. Finally, Jo March, sitting in her garret in her ink-stained pinafore, her cap's "cheerful red bow . . . a beacon to the inquiring eyes of her family" (265), faces a perpetual battle to ignite her writing process, to make genius burn.[22]

One of the most compelling representations of the dynamics of burning in *Little Women* comes in the opening scene, as the novel introduces Beth, the shy, blushing March sister. Amid the talk of Christmas, Beth recalls a scene from Christmas past:

> "I used to be so frightened when it was my turn to sit in the big chair with a crown on, and see you all come marching round to give the presents, with a kiss. I liked the things and the kisses, but it was dreadful to

have you sit looking at me while I opened the bundles," said Beth, who was toasting her face and the bread for tea, at the same time.

(5)

The passage illustrates the pathetic fallacy, for the interior burning of a childhood memory is mirrored by the external burning both of Beth's face and the toast she is charring. This is a moment of shame inspired by memory's internal force as well as by the exterior force of display ("it was dreadful to have you sit looking at me"), a moment of confrontation with the external world. Indeed, the shame itself is similarly double, for it both reflects and performs the intensifying of sisterly bonds. This intensification also calls into question whether Beth's embarrassment is from within: doesn't it come as much from without, from the circle of sisters mirroring the memory? Meanwhile, as with any blush, Beth's face both burns and is burned: the affect registers on the cusp between transitivity and intransitivity and makes Beth both active and passive.[23] In her essay "Queer Performativity," Eve Kosofsky Sedgwick describes shame as "the affect which mantles the threshold between introversion and extroversion, between absorption and theatricality."[24] Throughout the novel Beth's role seems to be to embody this powerful union of the apparently opposed forces of display and reticence, passivity and action, a mode Sedgwick has associated with a genealogy of queer performance practices.

Burning Beth, beginning a long period of physical decline after an unfortunate charity visit to the consumptive child of a German immigrant family, soon refines her role in Jo's life, increasingly becoming an external source of inspiration, or perhaps we should say ignition, for Jo's writing. That is to say, Beth and Jo become a genius-pair resembling Alcott and Emerson, Fuller and Emerson, Bettina von Arnim and Goethe, or Kent and St. George. Here, as in **"The Freak of a Genius,"** a same-sex relationship is given ostensibly masculine-feminine dynamics and the act of publication is associated with the masculine figure's (Jo's) melancholic, imitative reaction to the feminine figure's (Beth's) death.

Beth's drawn-out death from consumption has been read by several critics as the turning point in the novel, the point at which Jo is domesticated as a bourgeois female by the sacrifice of the novel's perfectly mortal heroine, its own version of Stowe's Little Eva or Dickens's Little Nell. Richard Brodhead, for example, has commented on the "deep conservatism" of this aspect of the narrative.[25] Viewing Beth's death through the model of the genius-pair, however, generates a quite different reading. Like Kent, the older poet who is so deeply impressed by the crowd watching the naked dead body of his protégé, Jo and Alcott find the power of the publicly celebrated figure both seductive and productive, generative of both writing and the embrace of public authorship. Not only does Beth encourage Jo's efforts throughout the novel with exhortations like, "You're a regular Shakespeare, Jo!" but it is finally the force of Beth's illness that leads Jo to send the manuscript of her novel out to be published. While she has already begun to publish sensation stories anonymously, Jo obsesses and hesitates over her novel because it will be the first of her works to appear under her own name. As various members of the family debate possible changes in the book's narrative, Beth intervenes:

> "I should like to see it printed *soon*," was all Beth said, and smiled in saying it; but there was an unconscious emphasis on the last word, and a wistful look in the eyes that never lost their childlike candor, which chilled Jo's heart, for a minute, with a foreboding fear, and decided her to make her little venture "soon."
>
> (270)

In a sense, Beth is the one writing here; her dying is enabling the book to take material shape, to become "printed."[26] After this scene Jo does send the book off. The "foreboding fear," the "chill" in Jo's heart, and most of all the mourning that Beth's consumption already allows produce the first published work in which Jo identifies herself as the author. The chill, the fear, and the mourning write Jo's name across the book and put it out into the world.[27] Alcott thus portrays the force of sister Beth and the mass-cultural trope of the grievable sentimental heroine as the main impetus behind Jo's open publishing.

Upon the publication of Jo's novel, both the scale and wild unpredictability of the reviews throw the young novelist into "a state of bewilderment, from which it took some time to recover." One reviewer calls it "one of the best American novels written in years," while another denounces it as "a dangerous book" (271). But Jo deprecates the trauma of the experience, claiming, "Not being a genius, like Keats, it won't kill me" (272). Jo is alluding here to the legend, popular on both sides of the Atlantic, that Keats's terminal illness had been brought on by harsh reviews of his poem "Endymion."[28] Yet I think Alcott is writing with some irony here, the most obvious aspect of which is that someone *is* killed, very soon: Beth. Both Beth and Keats die of that provocatively named disease, consumption, and both succumb to their sickness soon after an act of literary publishing. In this hybridization of the tragic sentimental heroine and the tragic romantic genius, Alcott finds a model of authorship in which "consumption" becomes productive, becomes the position of authorship.

Christine Battersby has identified and historicized this aspect of genius-as-effect as central to late-eighteenth-century/early romantic concepts of genius that were in-

timately linked with the necessary presence, in theories of the sublime, of a spectator who is overpowered by artistic force.[29] Alcott's and Lowell's writings display the persistence of this idea into the late nineteenth century. The object of the force of genius is a public or—as we saw with Kent—an individual whose affective response mirrors the public's seduction. The sentimental legend of Keats might also be linked to this older model of genius. By drawing attention away from Keats's poetry and toward a poet whose life was so short that he produced relatively little, the model seems to suggest that the force of genius depends more on the writer's constructed persona than on his or her writings.

Alcott may have learned about Keats in discussions among Brook Farm denizens, whose attention to the poet is reflected in several numbers of the community's publication, the *Harbinger*. Moreover, 1848 saw the publication to numerous and largely favorable reviews of R. M. Milnes's *Life, Letters, and Literary Remains of John Keats . . . Complete in One Volume*.[30] Keats's friend Joseph Severn, who attended the poet at his deathbed, wrote in a front-page essay in the April 1863 *Atlantic Monthly*, "It is a singular pleasure to the few personal friends of Keats in England (who may still have to defend him against the old and worn-out slanders) that in America he has always had a solid fame, independent of the old English prejudices."[31] Yet it seems likely that much of Alcott's knowledge of Keats, and perhaps that of many American readers, came through Lowell's writings. And Lowell, even while writing about Keats's verse, participated in the tendency to read Keats's person; in fact, Lowell baldly states in a long essay entitled "Keats," "There are few poets whose works contain slighter hints of their personal history than those of Keats; yet there are, perhaps, even fewer whose real lives, or rather the conditions upon which they lived, are more clearly traceable in what they have written."[32] Writing about Keats's person, though, inevitably meant writing about his illness, which led Lowell and a host of other critics to write about his body. What Lowell called Keats's fine "sensibility," another writer described as his "feminine delicacy"; both reflected the impression that "[h]is spirit seemed too ethereal for earth . . . his sense of beauty was a disease."[33] In "Keats," Lowell provides an extended discussion of the poet's physicality and its role in his lasting reputation:

> We are not without experience of natures so purely intellectual that their bodies had no more concern in their mental doings and sufferings than a house has with the good or ill fortunes of its occupant. But poets are not built upon this plan, and especially poets like Keats, in whom the moral seems to have so perfectly interfused the physical man, that you might almost say he could

feel sorrow with his hands, so truly did his body, like that of Donne's Mistress Boulstred, think and remember and forebode.[34]

Once again, an ostensibly male genius's gift is associated with femininity, represented here by the figure of Mistress Boulstred. Lowell writes that Keats suffered from the disease of feeling too much, and that therefore "his health was injured by the failure of his book" (229). Keats thus resembles Lowell's Rousseau or Alcott's St. George in being a "victim of his own sensations," although the sensations Keats experienced were morally far less unkempt.

Lowell's use here of the house as a metaphor for the bodies of "purely intellectual" natures, impervious (unlike Keats's) to emotion, is surprising given the extent to which figurations of Keats resemble those of the sentimental heroines of domestic fiction both in their femininity and their shuttling between tropes of disembodiment (ethereality) and embodiment (blushing, susceptibility to illness). But Lowell's interest lay in establishing an American tradition of high literary writing, a project reflected in his role in excising Alcott, Stowe, Rebecca Harding Davis, and other women writers from the list of *Atlantic* contributors by the 1870s; he would hardly be likely to align Keats with phenomenally popular characters such as *Uncle Tom Cabin*'s Little Eva. Instead, it is Alcott who develops in full the lines of confluence between female and male sentiment, between the sentimentalism of Eva and the sentimentalism of Rousseau. Stories such as **"The Freak of a Genius,"** which involves the highly eroticized relationship of a male writer and his male muse, illustrate the generic and gendered flexibility of genius as a trope for authorship, a flexibility made possible by Alcott's mobilization of the queer formations of gender inherent in nineteenth-century models of genius and by her exploitation of the ease with which the heroic burning of a male poet may remind us of shy Beth's burning face of shame—and eventually of her burning out from consumption and leaving a book behind.

* * *

The literary productivity of genius need not be exclusively associated with a list of proto-modernist figures; we might learn much more about gender and cultural value if we examine the term as it is appropriated and redefined within a variety of authorial spheres. Particular attention ought to be paid to the manner in which genius as relationality questions the gendering and eroticization of literary production and consumption. Genius has traditionally been seen as a term deployed to organize literary discourse from a position outside the social realm, as a kind of secular divine. Yet works by Alcott and others, read in a deeper cultural context than that in which they are often placed, illustrate especially effectively how much the concept of genius is embedded in the social as a term that embodies a host of cultural anxieties about gender, consumption, production, and sexuality. It requires more energy to ignore its volatility than to study it.

Notes

1. James Russell Lowell, "Rousseau and the Sentimentalists," in *Among My Books* (Boston: Fields, Osgood, 1870), 379-80.

2. Louisa May Alcott, *Little Women* (Harmondsworth: Penguin Books, 1989), 131. Further quotations from this novel will be cited parenthetically in the text.

3. The four extant chapters of *Diana and Persis,* which was based on Alcott sister May's experience as a painter in Europe and given up upon May's death, are reprinted in *The Alternative Alcott,* ed. Elaine Showalter (New Brunswick, N.J.: Rutgers Univ. Press, 1988). Around the time Alcott mentions *Genius,* she was also exploring the possibility of writing a novel based on her father's life; it is unclear to me whether these two projects were one and the same.

4. Nina Baym, *Novels, Readers, and Reviewers* (Ithaca, N.Y.: Cornell Univ. Press, 1984), 255.

5. The best source for information on the publication history of von Arnim's *Goethe's Correspondence with a Child* is Hildegard Platzer Collins and Philip Allison Shelley, "The Reception in England and America of Bettina von Arnim's *Goethe's Correspondence with a Child,*" in *Anglo-German and American-German Crosscurrents,* ed. Philip Allison Shelley and Arthur O. Lewis Jr. (Chapel Hill: Univ. of North Carolina Press, 1962).

6. Christina Zwarg, *Feminist Conversations: Fuller, Emerson, and the Play of Reading* (Ithaca, N.Y.: Cornell Univ. Press, 1995), 89.

7. Lowell, "Rousseau and the Sentimentalists," 366.

8. William Dean Howells, "Editor's Study," *Harper's,* June 1886, 154.

9. Louisa May Alcott, "The Freak of a Genius," in *Behind the Mask: Complete Thrillers,* ed. Madeline Stern (Boston: Northeastern University Press, 1993), 431. Further quotations from this story are from this edition and will be cited parenthetically in the text.

10. It is fascinating to note the remarkable similarity between this story and Henry James's "The Lesson of the Master," another narrative of suspicion

centering on a genius figure that traces a man's initiation into authorship despite his apparent betrayal by his former genius-icon. In that tale the empty genius is also named St. George, although he is the older and more staid of the two writers who are the story's principal characters.

11. The names Alcott uses for the women are both provocative. *May,* the name given to the vapid younger sister, is of course the real name of Amy March, the youngest Alcott girl. The source of Margaret's name may be *Faust,* which would further suggest the phantom presence of Goethe; it also seems likely that Alcott is here alluding to Margaret Fuller as well. Alcott would also give the name Margaret to her older sister, Anna, in *Little Women.*

12. I am, of course, referring to the historical trends that Michel Foucault describes in critiquing the "repressive hypothesis" in his *History of Sexuality, Vol. I: An Introduction,* trans. Alan Sheridan (New York: Vintage, 1980), Part I, *passim.*

13. On the coarticulation of nonnormative sexualities and "addictive" behaviors, see Eve Sedgwick, "Epidemics of the Will," in her *Tendencies* (Durham, N.C.: Duke Univ. Press, 1993).

14. This image of a queer corpse brought to the surface of a body of water recalls the final appearance of Count Fosco in Wilkie Collins's *The Woman in White.* On this moment, see D. A. Miller, *The Novel and the Police* (Berkeley and Los Angeles: Univ. of California Press, 1984), 188-89.

15. Judith Butler has usefully examined Freud's developmental narrative to remap heterosexuality as formed along these lines; see her *Gender Trouble: Feminism and the Subversion of Identity* (New York: Routledge, 1990), 57-66.

16. See Christine Battersby, *Gender and Genius: Toward a Feminist Aesthetics* (London: Women's Press, 1989), 28-34. Battersby sees a line of inheritance for this idea and its philosophical implications for creativity running from Aristotle to Schopenhauer.

17. See Margaret Hindle Hazen and Robert Hazen, *Keepers of the Flame: The Role of Fire in American Culture 1775-1925* (Princeton: Princeton Univ. Press, 1992), 18-64.

18. Biographies of Alcott include Madeline Stern, *Louisa May Alcott* (Norman: Univ. of Oklahoma Press, 1950); Madelon Bedell, *The Alcotts: Biography of a Family* (New York: Clarkson Potter, 1980); and Martha Saxton, *Louisa May: A Modern Biography of Louisa May Alcott* (Boston: Houghton Mifflin, 1977).

19. One model especially relevant to the trope of the suspicious, perhaps empty genius may well have been Alcott's father Bronson. Renowned for his radicalism and his frequent obtuseness, Bronson sparked Ralph Waldo Emerson to write, "Yet could I see plainly that I conversed with the most extraordinary man and the highest genius of the time," a judgment Emerson modified radically years later when he wrote, "This noble genius discredits genius to me. I do not want any more such persons to exist" (*Selections from Ralph Waldo Emerson,* ed. Stephen Whicher [Boston: Houghton Mifflin, 1957], 125, 130).

20. On Sappho, see Page DuBois, *Sappho is Burning* (Chicago: Univ. of Chicago Press, 1995). I thank Joe Russo for initially pointing me toward Byron's reference to "Burning Sappho."

21. *The Journals of Louisa May Alcott,* ed. Joel Myerson, Daniel Shealy, and Madeleine Stern (Athens: Univ. of Georgia Press, 1997), 99.

22. Examples of burning in the March/Plumfield novels are so numerous as almost to require no mention, but I cannot resist noting two of the most striking in *Little Men*: the sacrifice-ritual involving the burning of favorite toys for the "Naughty Kitty-Mouse" and the near burning down of the Plumfield schoolhouse by Jo's wild stand-in Dan.

23. For a compelling analysis of the blush in the nineteenth-century novel, see Mary Ann O'Farrell, *Telling Complexions: The Nineteenth-Century English Novel and the Blush* (Durham, N.C.: Duke Univ. Press, 1997).

24. Eve Kosofsky Sedgwick, "Queer Performativity: Henry James's *The Art of the Novel,*" *GLQ* [: A Journal of Lesbian and Gay Studies] 1 (November 1993): 6. The terms *absorption* and *theatricality* are the focus of Michael Fried's study of eighteenth-century French painting, *Absorption and Theatricality: Painting and Beholder in the Age of Diderot* (Chicago: Univ. of Chicago Press, 1980).

25. Richard Brodhead, *Cultures of Letters: Scenes of Writing and Instruction in Nineteenth-Century America* (Chicago: Univ. of Chicago Press, 1993), 91.

26. Jo's initial venture into sensation fiction, in a contest arranged by the "Spread Eagle" storypaper, is also conceived on Beth's behalf. Jo enters the contest with the aim of using the prize money to send the ailing Beth to a seaside resort. She wins

and overcomes Beth's deprecations of the idea of spending the money on a vacation: "Ah, but you shall go, I've set my heart on it; that's what I tried for, and that's why I succeeded. I never get on when I think of myself alone, so it will help me to work for you, don't you see?" (268-69). After a spell of sensation writing, Jo finishes her manuscript and reaffirms her claim to "never get on" when she thinks of herself alone by submitting the work to the family for advice and criticism.

27. We might also remind ourselves of the association in Alcott's mind between her sister Elizabeth and her master/muse Emerson, who developed a particularly intimate relationship with the youngest Alcott in the last months of her life and who served as a pall-bearer at her funeral.

28. Compare Edgar Allan Poe, *Marginalia* (Charlottesville: Univ. Press of Virginia, 1981), 81: "Keats died of a criticism."

29. Battersby, *Gender and Genius,* 75. Battersby's primary examples are from German romanticism, including the *Sturm und Drang* movement; she also notes that "[i]n Germany the . . . rapture over genius became so extreme that the decades between 1770 and 1790 have been labelled '*die Geniezeit*' ('The Age of Genius')."

30. On the importance of Milnes's biography in establishing Keats's American reputation, see Hyder Edward Rollins, *Keats's Reputation in America to 1848* (Cambridge: Harvard Univ. Press, 1946), 94-101.

31. Joseph Severn, "On the Vicissitudes of Keats's Fame," *Atlantic Monthly,* April 1863, 26.

32. James Russell Lowell, "Keats," *Lowell's Works I: Literary Essays* (Boston: Houghton Mifflin, 1898), 218.

33. Quoted without attribution in Rollins, *Keats's Reputation,* 80. See also Leon Chai, *The Romantic Foundations of the American Renaissance* (Ithaca, N.Y.: Cornell Univ. Press, 1987).

34. Lowell, "Keats," 229.

Stephanie Foote (essay date winter 2005)

SOURCE: Foote, Stephanie. "Resentful *Little Women*: Gender and Class Feeling in Louisa May Alcott." *College Literature* 32, no. 1 (winter 2005): 63-85.

[*In the following essay, Foote interprets the tension between positive and negative forms of emotion in Alcott's novel. In Foote's reading, the novel presents the* insularity of family and domesticity, as embodied in the March sisters, as an antidote to the class resentment and gender inequality that characterize society in general.]

In one of the most dramatic and emotionally charged scenes in Louisa May Alcott's 1868 novel *Little Women,* Amy retaliates against her sister Jo for a perceived slight. Jo refuses to let Amy accompany her on a rare outing to the theater, and Amy, resenting her exclusion, burns the only copy of Jo's hand-written collection of original stories. The manuscript of "half-a-dozen" fairy tales is the result of "the loving work of several years" (**1993** [*Little Women and Good Wives*], 68) and for Jo its destruction is catastrophic.[1] For their part, Jo's mother and sisters understand the significance of "Amy's bonfire," but they cannot quite understand the intensity of Jo's response. Jo's vow that she will never forgive Amy forcefully expresses her sense of injustice and injury, but it also disrupts the "sweet home-peace" of all of their lives (68). Despite some anxiety over Jo's behavior, the March family does not speak of the "great trouble" of Jo's anger, trusting that Jo's own "generous nature" will eventually dissolve "her resentment" (68).

Up to this point, the novel has paid close attention to Jo's ambition to be a writer, as well as to Amy's myriad personal faults, and it's therefore surprising that the novel spends almost no narrative effort to affirm that Jo has indeed been wronged. Even though the novel believes that her work is valuable and that Amy has done a terrible thing in destroying it, it is less interested in the objective justice of Jo's feelings than it is in the subjective way that she handles her anger. Accordingly, Amy's destruction of Jo's manuscript and Jo's subsequent rage are the prelude to an even more dramatic incident. Jo, unable to forgive Amy, fails to keep a close eye on her sister when Amy tags along to go skating, even though Jo knows that some of the ice is still too thin to skate over. Amy does indeed fall through thin ice into the freezing water, and after her melodramatic rescue, Jo is overcome by an access of self-recrimination. She tells her mother: "It seems as if I could do anything when I'm in a passion; I get so savage, I could hurt anyone and enjoy it. I'm afraid I *shall* do something dreadful some day and spoil my life and make everybody hate me" (Alcott **1993,** 71). Her confession elicits a famous and much-critiqued response from her mother that she too is angry nearly every day. Yet Jo's mother, unlike her quick-tempered daughter, is no longer tormented by her anger. She has learned to repress her anger, and she consoles Jo by telling her that the events of the day will help Jo school herself in a similar lesson of repression. The chapter closes with a weakened Amy and a chastened Jo "wordlessly" embracing in the newly restored "home-peace"; the drama of Jo's lost stories is all but forgotten, even by Jo, for the remainder of the novel.

But what, in the logic of the novel, is Jo to feel about her sister's destructive act? What is the reader to make of the absence of anything that we might call the recognition of injustice, either by Jo's family, or by the narrator? Why, that is to say, is Jo's *critical* response to her injury unrecognized unless it can be read as an *emotional* response? Why does her family rely on Jo's "generous" emotions, the very source of her trouble, to save her from her own anger? How, in other words, does the narrative incorporate and make use of negative and destructive emotions? The novel appears to mend Jo and Amy's contretemps quite neatly, yet its answers to the questions that underwrite such episodes of anger and recrimination are evasive at best. For example, while it is true that Amy's skating accident prompts Jo to say that she fears she will do something terrible, it is also true that Amy has already gotten into a "passion" in which she enjoyed hurting Jo, and in which she did something genuinely dreadful. But it is Jo, not Amy, who has run the risk of "making everybody hate" her, and it is Amy, not Jo, who is the final victim in this scenario.

I open with this anecdote for two reasons. First, it frames the incident that has received perhaps the most elaboration from feminist critics interested in the lessons that **Little Women** teaches to its readers and to its characters about gender, anger, and repression. Yet it is significant that this rich scene is almost never critiqued in its entirety; the events leading up to Jo and her mother's discussion of anger and repression are generally ignored. As I shall suggest, we miss something when we ignore such scenes in order to focus on how the novel seems to tell its readers that women must not have, much less act on, negative emotions. Specifically, we lose the opportunity to inquire into the novel's larger figuration of the *productivity* of negative emotional responses, responses that include but are not limited to anger, resentment, and self-recrimination, in order to understand its construction of a particular kind of "little woman."

Feminist critics have discussed the ways that sentimental or women's novels from the mid nineteenth century elevate female characters' positive emotional responses—sympathy, for example, or compassion—as antidotes to the harshness of the external social world. They have argued that such textual counterings of the demands of the competitive public sphere let women's fiction construct the home as a refuge from that world, as well as helping to imagine the possibilities for human interaction that might be considered more ethical because more familial. I would like to open up this general inquiry into emotion and affect in women's fiction by looking at the ways that destructive or dangerous emotions are figured in an enduringly popular text that appears to be devoted to a sentimental strategy of understanding the world. I shall argue that emotions like anger, resentment or envy signal that the home, rather than being the refuge from the social, or the template for a better version of the social, is a testing ground for the pressures of the outside world, especially for the pressures of an always-evolving regime of class and status distinctions.

I shall concentrate especially on selected moments in the text (selected, for there are many such moments) in which the March girls, who live something of an insular life in their rambling home, are confronted and addressed by the dense social and economic world of their surrounding community. Although the novel tends to present scenes in which facsimiles of the world are assimilated into the March household—the girls create their own post office, their own newspaper, and stage their own private theatricals, for example—they nonetheless participate with other people in more public spaces. They go to house parties, they have jobs, and they attend school. They find, though, that their contact with the greater world emphasizes their material poverty, and they often find themselves involved in scenes of social humiliation that provoke them to feel a sort of objectless resentment intimately related to their gender but also to their somewhat uncertain class status. Bluntly, gender and class are inseparable as we look at the kinds of negative feelings that the novel discusses. This lesson may seem too obvious—gender and class, after all, are now part of an established mantra of subject positions—but it bears repeating. Literary critics are skilled at understanding gender and class as historical positions, yet they are less skilled at seeing that they are also affective positions, and that affect and emotion themselves are historically produced and historically specific.[2]

Class is not merely about how much money one has, it is more finely about the kinds of feelings subjects experience as dangerous or natural or powerful. Class and status, as Pierre Bourdieu tells us, are matters of feeling, not merely matters of objective economic measurement. Not simply about social effects, class and status are also always about emotional affect, for class and status, although deeply structural, are first experienced as deeply personal. Class and status are therefore narrated as dispositions toward one's place in the world, as competitive relationships with others, even if those others are members of one's own family. This last is particularly salient in the world of women's fiction, for the kinds of distinctions produced by social competition are often narratively at odds with the palliative function of the sentimental home, and with the figuration of women as private, emotional centers who keep the world of economic distinction at bay.[3] A complex balance of social desire and a naturalized belief in taste and personal values, class and status play themselves out locally through a series of difficult negotiations with one's "real" and one's desired position next to others.

My analysis, I should say at the outset, is not meant to reveal the "real" logic of the novel by demonstrating that all along it has been about class and not gender. Although much of my argument will show that *Little Women* is replete with scenes of various kinds of emotional crises centered on dissonant understandings of class and status, I focus on such negative scenes to look at what *Little Women* shows us about how negative emotions in fact actively produce the specific forms of gender the book elaborates. It should be obvious that my concentration on gender's relationship to class is indebted to early feminist work on *Little Women,* for it is that work that first understood the novel as expressing historically complex ideas about gender. Feminist discussions of *Little Women,* generated in part by a desire to recover forgotten women's writing more generally, changed the parameters of literary history and made it possible to look at Alcott's text (which had not been forgotten, but which had certainly been critically ignored) as an important critique of the domestic sphere and women's place within it. Within the very broad parameters of an emerging feminist field of literary criticism, even otherwise dissimilar feminist readings shared, to a lesser or greater degree, a tendency to examine *Little Women* as an elucidation of the painful lessons of repression. Alcott's novel, in this reading, finally tells its readers that women must learn to repress or redirect their anger, even if their anger is, in the world of the novel, just and reasonable.[4]

It is hard to overestimate the debt contemporary criticism of the novel owes to such feminist analyses. Readings of *Little Women*'s lessons about gender have informed evaluations of its critical position in nineteenth-century American literature, most specifically in recent attempts to reevaluate its relationship to established genres. Does the novel index the invention of a genre of didactic literature for young girls? Does it demonstrate the thorough imbrication of children's literature with contemporary conversations about romantic love, personal morality, familial duty, and civic participation? Even more recently, critics have begun to illuminate the role of Alcott and her work in a mid-century world that extended changing possibilities for social mobility to women. Such critical work attends carefully to Alcott's figuration of the world of commodities, and to her meditations on the author's status as celebrity in a literary-historical market in which authors themselves were understood as commodities. In this reading, within a professionalizing literary marketplace, authors make a variety of highly constrained choices about their potential position in an increasingly stratified world of popular and elite audiences. The venues in which they published (and the unavailability of other venues), the speed with which they wrote, their attention to questions of audience all become markers by which to imagine the literary field as one in which social distinctions were performed and enacted.[5]

In an example of this kind of criticism, Richard Brodhead points out that the "domestic value system" in *Little Women* is unimaginable unless critics attend to its relationship to a complex social base. "By 1868" he writes, "the middle-class audience no longer needs to differentiate itself from the household economic order it was once imperfectly separated from but now needs to deploy its tools of self-definition against another threatening adjacency—the emerging leisure class world of the post-bellum years" (1993 [*Cultures of Letters*], 95). In this argument, Louisa May Alcott occupies a position as author that simultaneously acknowledges the class and status stratifications of the world of publication even as she finds a mode of writing that can imaginatively preserve the boundaries between the home and the market.

Little Women may indeed attempt to stabilize proper gender relations in a narrative that more or less invokes the increasingly market-driven world that Louisa May Alcott learned to negotiate. But it does so not just by preserving the distinction between markets and homes, but by recognizing, as critic Peter Stoneley (1999) ["'The Fashionable World Displayed'"] has argued, that the two are worrisomely prone to mixing. In my argument, it is only by paying close attention to the affective components of class and gender—components that are hard to name and classify, and therefore hard to legislate in either conventional juridical or conventional emotional terms—that we can redirect our attention away from the question of whether *Little Women* needs to sequester the idea of "the home" and focus more broadly on how structuring and structured class distinctions are first experienced as affective in the vocabulary of the gendered domestic sphere. Although it has been, as not a few critics have suggested, very difficult to track the emergence of "the middle class," we might use this novel to see how that broad identity becomes an especially powerful subject position when it is internalized in the register of the personal rather than understood as a structural or social problem.[6] Women, already excluded from the growth of a professionalized white collar identity historians have described as one of the effects of the emergent middle class in the mid-to-late nineteenth century, are especially sensitive barometers of the injuries that accompany the emergence of middle class styles and sensibilities. Limited in terms of their economic production but increasingly the target of advertisers seeking to solicit new forms of consumption, middle-class women become the guardians of the difference between economic class and social status, and they do so by knowing which feelings to have about which kinds of people. *Little Women,* rich in scenes of envy, desire, and ambition, lingers over moments of class shame and humiliation, using the home not as an escape from the potential social injuries of the public but as a stage on which the March girls can rehearse proper ways of behaving and proper ways of feeling.

Yet for that very reason *Little Women* must inevitably blur the boundaries between what kinds of distinctions should be made and where.

In the next part of this essay, I shall look at selected moments in which the lessons the girls learn in their home as well as within the larger social world about their status and class are first understood through profoundly negative emotions. Within these lessons, an appropriately classed and gendered little woman takes shape as she learns to read the world in a critically emotional vocabulary that will protect her from perceived slights as well as allow her to maintain a sense of social distinction that appears completely natural because it is based on an equally "natural" affective reading of the world.

II

Little Women has proven a remarkably enduring novel. Often reprinted and filmed, it tells the story of the four March girls who are living with their mother. During the first half of the novel (originally published as a free-standing novel also called *Little Women*), the girls' father is away from home, serving as chaplain to Union troops during the Civil War. Virtually the only masculine influence with which the girls come into contact is that of their neighbors, the Laurences. In the Laurence household are the elder Mr. Laurence, his grandson Laurie, and Laurie's tutor John Brooke. In the second half of the novel, originally published as a sequel to *Little Women,* the March girls are married off, one by one, in a procession only occasionally broken up by Jo's trip to New York, Amy's stay in Europe, and Beth's melodramatic death. Each of the two sections of the novel was very successful, enabling Louisa May Alcott to help her own family financially, and enjoy the social and economic benefits of a successful authorial career.[7]

The narrative of *Little Women* brings success and contentment to the surviving members of the March family, and by the end of the novel, Jo, Amy and Meg are happily married and are laboring in the fields best suited to the strengths as well as the weaknesses of their personalities. The novel may end well, but at its beginning, the young March girls struggle continually with a sense of dissatisfaction and unhappiness. The novel, for example, opens with a scene of resentment and injury. On Christmas Eve, the March girls, awaiting the return of their mother, lament their poverty. After Meg and Jo grumble over it, their youngest sister, Amy remarks with "an injured sniff" that it isn't "fair for some girls to have plenty of pretty things, and other girls nothing at all" (Alcott **1993,** 3). Here, a vague sense of class injury and gender injury are entwined; for Amy it isn't just that there isn't enough money, it's that there isn't enough money to be *like other girls.*

The social exclusion Amy feels is attached to a more general scene of economic decline. The March family

inhabits an ambiguous class position in the novel. The text suggests that the family was once wealthy; indeed it is one of the ongoing trials of at least two of the daughters to reconcile themselves to their economic fall. Amy, for example, "had a plaintive way of saying, 'When papa was rich we did so-and-so,' which was very touching" (Alcott **1993,** 37), and Meg finds her poverty especially onerous "because she could remember a time when home was beautiful, life full of ease and pleasure, and want of any kind unknown." She "seldom complained, but a sense of injustice made her feel bitter toward every one sometimes" (34). The Marches do have wealthy friends and relatives, and they occupy a social position that is strikingly incommensurate with their economic position; in the chapter "Calls," for example, Amy and Jo appear to be calling socially upon the King family, for whom the novel has earlier indicated Meg works as a governess. A similar tension between their social and economic status is foregrounded in the first chapter when we learn that Mrs. March, in whose absence the girls complain about their poverty, is out helping a less fortunate family.[8]

The tension between their economic and their social status is also schematized in the relationship of their house to that of their neighbors, the fantastically wealthy Laurence family.

> The garden separated the Marches' house from that of Mr. Laurence. Both stood in a suburb of the city, which was still country-like, with groves and lawns, large gardens and quiet streets. A low hedge parted the two estates. On one side was an old brown house, looking rather bare and shabby, robbed of the vines that in summer covered its walls, and the flowers which then surrounded it. On the other side was a stately stone mansion, plainly betokening every sort of comfort and luxury, from the big coach-house and well-kept grounds to the conservatory and the glimpses of lovely things one caught between the rich curtains.
>
> (Alcott **1993,** 42)

The domestic identity of the Marches—the warmth of their home, the innocent and wholesome quality of their company, the general nurturing qualities of Mrs. March—combined with the fact that all of the girls work suggests that the instability of legible class identity is crucial to the novel's understanding of gender, as well as to its understanding of why the girls feel injured. Each of the adult March girls works, either as a way of bringing in an income or as a way of saving expenses (two work outside the home, one works at home, and the other goes to school), but it is entirely unclear how they are understood or understand themselves as laborers as well as participants in a social world seemingly quite economically remote from them. Readers know that they were once rich and are now poor, but also know that the Marches socialize with the rich and patronize the poor. Richard Brodhead has argued that the novel enacts the "adjacency" of the middle classes to the upper classes, but what is interesting is how this adjacency also works to initialize an increasingly obvious tension in the novel between economic class and gender expectations.[9]

Although the text indicates that the Marches have not been long lived in their "bare and shabby" house, having moved from an undisclosed neighborhood, what is noteworthy is the lesson about the relationship between status and gender their shabby house helps to teach. While clearly the poorer house, the Marches have the more attractive home. It is decorated by "nature"; in the spring, the flowers that loving hands have planted ornament it, and an equally loving family lives in it. The mansion, on the other hand, is cold—"no motherly face ever smiled at the windows, and few people went in and out" (Alcott **1993,** 42). This language privileges the social value of the Marches, even as it privileges the economic value of the Laurences because it invokes gender values to compensate for economic values. Eventually, the opposition between the social value of the Marches and the economic value of the Laurences is erased, and the families "interchanged kindnesses without stopping to think which was the greater" (53). The Laurence and the March families draw more closely together—by the end, the two families have been united by marriage—because the March family supplies the lone child of the mansion with a home, but it is also noteworthy that the Laurence house supplies the March girls a kind of homelike public sphere. The Laurences share with the Marches their conservatory of flowers and their access to music and musical instruments, their European friends and their seemingly endless stories about traveling and living abroad. The process of visiting that household is for Beth much like roaming out into the world at large; it inspires within her the same fear and anxiety that she might feel were she to go unaccompanied to a marketplace. Protected by a familial or home-like relationship, the March girls can use the Laurence household as a kind of training ground for social behavior.

Yet if the novel allows the social proximity of the Laurence and the March household to enact a kind of colloquial equality between the two families, it does not imagine that this proximity will transform how others see the difference in status between the two families. Indeed, one of the first serious episodes of status dissonance—an episode created from equal parts of class desire and a sense of class injury—centers on how others perceive the ambitions and limitations of the March family. Meg, who is on a "vacation" from her workaday life with the Moffats, a family of greater wealth and prominence, finds that the lessons she has learned at home are insufficient to protect her from the distinctions others will make between her family and their own. Mrs. March worries that there is some danger that

Meg will come back from her visit to her wealthy friends "more discontented than she went" but she trusts that Meg will understand how to respond correctly to the differences between herself and her friends. At the Moffats, Meg is introduced to class distinctions that she readily understands and internalizes, and as with so many of the incidents of social conflict in this novel, she is overtaken by a host of negative emotions that center on the different kinds of value accorded to different social actors.

> The Moffats were very fashionable, and simple Meg was rather daunted, at first, by the splendour of the house and the elegance of its occupants. But they were kindly people, in spite of the frivolous life they led, and soon put their guest at her ease. Perhaps Meg felt, without understanding why, that they were not particularly cultivated or intelligent people, and that all their gilding could not quite conceal the ordinary material of which they were made.
>
> (Alcott **1993,** 76)

But even as Meg feels without understanding that the Moffats are not a particularly distinguished or cultivated family, she falls prey to a half-understood feeling of injury and resentment.

> The more she saw of Annie Moffat's pretty things, the more she envied her, and sighed to be rich. Home now looked bare and dismal as she thought of it, work grew harder than ever, and she felt that she was a very destitute and much injured girl.
>
> (Alcott **1993,** 77)

Although she sees that the other girls feel sorry for her, she proudly wears her own "dowdy" clothes at her hosts' first formal event. At the second ball the family gives, Meg becomes ashamed of the fact that she has only one good dancing gown, and lets the family dress her up. While she is circulating around the dance floor, she overhears a group of women discussing her mother's "plans" for the March girls' marriage to socially prominent men, including the Laurence heir, and is again ashamed, this time to have been the subject of such a vulgarly economic discussion. Even though she is ashamed, she "discovered that there is a charm about fine clothes which attracts a certain class of people, and secures their respect" (Alcott **1993,** 82), and revels in the distinction that she feels is her natural right even if it is procured by use of artifice. Laurie, who attends the second ball, finds the newly made-up Meg, now called Daisy by her hosts, to be a somewhat alarming example of elegant young womanhood, and he cannot approve of her behavior or appearance. It is perhaps his appearance as judge that first points up the ways in which her negative emotions must eventually resolve themselves in a domestic vocabulary already shot through with social distinctions, for Meg feels as much shame that her family's friend will report her to her mother as she feels anxiety that her mother may be trying to marry her to her "brother."

When Meg returns home and confesses her shortcomings and her behavior, Mrs. March says of the Moffats that they are "worldly, ill-bred, and full of these vulgar ideas about young people. I am more sorry than I can express for the mischief this visit may have done you" (Alcott **1993**, 87). She then advises Meg to "know and value the praise which is worth having, and to excite the admiration of excellent people by being modest as well as pretty" (87). But what has truly disturbed Meg is that the gossip about her mother's plans to marry her to Laurie "had opened a new world" and "much disturbed the peace of the old one, in which, till now, she had lived as happily as a child. Her innocent friendship with Laurie was spoiled" (79). The disruption of the home peace the novel prizes is dependent on exposing, in other words, the fact that there have always been inequalities and distinctions within the shared idyll of the March-Laurence household. Meg's friendship with Laurie is spoiled because it is revealed to have been founded on a social inequality that might be erased in the future through a socially ambitious marriage rather than through a fantasy that the two households are essentially the same in the first place.

What then does the novel do with the conflicted emotions of anger, shame, and injury that this incident inspires in Meg and Mrs. March? In order to restore peace to Meg, Mrs. March relies on a vocabulary of sentiment and family that dispenses with the idea that her daughters ought to marry money, but that also conflates the value of money with more conventional affective values.

> I am ambitious for you, but not to have you make a dash in the world—marry rich men merely because they are rich, or have splendid houses, which are not homes because love is wanting. Money is a needful and precious thing—and, when well used, a noble thing—but I never want you to think it is the first or only prize to strive for.
>
> (Alcott **1993**, 88)

Her argument is an indirect indictment of the Moffats, who do not have the ability to see the ways in which money might be valued by people of real distinction—people in other words, whose sense of their worth is not based on how much money they have but in how they understand the meaning of money in a "home" where love is not wanting. Indeed, commenting on the burgeoning flirtation between Meg and Mr. Brooke, Mrs. March says:

> Money is a good and useful thing . . . and I hope my girls will never feel the need of it too bitterly, nor be tempted by too much. I should like to know that John was firmly established in some good business, which gave him an income large enough to keep free from debt and make Meg comfortable. I'm not ambitious for a splendid fortune, a fashionable position, or a great

name for my girls. If rank and money come with love and virtue, also, I should accept them gratefully, and enjoy your good fortune.

> (Alcott **1993**, 179)

Mrs. March's practical idea about the use of money may, as Peter Stoneley has pointed out, testify to the novel's pragmatic insistence on the increasing inescapability of signs of social class, like particular kinds and styles of clothing, to signify personal worth. But it also testifies to the sublime belief that money is not intrinsically important because class—or rather classiness, as we now understand that term—is a personal quality. In other words, John Brooke ought not be a pauper, but he need not have a fortune because Meg is *already* in enjoyment of a way of reading distinction that her mother believes is a natural part of their family's existence.[10]

Meg is an object lesson in the management of negative emotion, for she is an object lesson in how the novel reads scenes of class and gender anxiety in a narrative of family life that has already understood the management of negative emotion as one of its tasks. Indeed, Meg, the most conventional of the novel's characters, is the first to leave her family and the first to join another. Her marriage begins the second half of *Little Women,* and when the novel discusses her, it is always in terms of her negotiation of the emotional difficulties of being a young wife and mother. It is no accident that she fully realizes that she will marry John Brooke immediately after her wealthy Aunt has protested that John is not a member of the proper social class. Meg, having previously enjoyed the power of her gender to cause emotional injury to John, decides to marry him in the face of her possible disinheritance. In other words, she responds to the threat of financial injury by relinquishing her potential to cause injury in the field of gender. Similarly, the episode in which Meg is "for the first time in her married life . . . afraid of her husband" because she has overspent her clothing allowance results in her muttered explanation that she is "tired of being poor" (Alcott **1993**, 351, 352). But the chapter, and the domestic episode itself, ends when Meg has made financial amends, "swallowing her pride" to sell dress material to her wealthy friend, an act that narratively and structurally seems to result in "the deepest experience of a woman's life"—pregnancy. At this moment, Meg's injury over being poor is not just displaced, it is structurally compensated by her ascension into the final season of the life of a good woman.

Meg's life, the most obviously domestic, might be the most complete and finished example of the novel's logic of the interchanges between inchoate, often negative feelings about class and gender, but it only forecasts the more problematic lessons of this logic.[11] *Little Women* is often read not as the story of Meg, but as the story of the boyish, independent, and rebellious Jo. Historically,

Jo has been the idol of girl readers, and biographies of Louisa May Alcott assert that Jo was also the favorite of her creator, who identified in herself the traits she had given to her character. But there is another way to tell the story of **Little Women,** and that is as the story of Amy, who is, after all is said and done, triumphant in the arenas of class and gender ambition.

The first half of the novel is largely critical of Amy, who is often the butt of narrative ridicule and the object of familial counsel on account of her personal affectations and her grandiose desires for social advancement. Spoiled, petted, and ignorant, Amy is initially the sign of how easily a woman's desire for airs and graces might become at turns comic or tragic.[12] In her investment in her own gender—her love of clothes and her own beauty—Amy is Jo's antithesis. Jo's disinvestment in her gender role is perhaps her most pronounced personal characteristic, and it is certainly the characteristic that has most persuaded her fans that she, rather than any of her sisters, is the most compelling site of readerly identification. Jo's irritation at the constraints of nineteenth-century gender roles ranges from her irritation that she can't fight in the Union army to her annoyance that she will have to wear gloves and pin up her hair every day.

Jo, scorning social convention, and Amy, happily enslaved by it, are at odds for nearly the entire first half of the novel. But while the narrator generally (although, as we have seen, not always) generates sympathy for Jo at the expense of Amy during their many contretemps in the first half of the novel, the second half tells a different story by privileging Amy, often at Jo's expense. While Jo's gender rebellion during her youth defined her personality, and made her attractive to her friends and family, it makes her a most unhappy young woman, misunderstood and often lonely as her two surviving sisters make successful entrances into the social world. Amy, on the other hand, after having sedulously tended her airs and affectations, grows into a young woman who pleases effortlessly and who reaps all manner of material rewards. Jo suffers, and Amy prospers, and their different fates are instructive for an analysis of how different kinds of responses to the social—critical and emotional—are privileged as the girls become little women.

In the course of the narrative, Beth dies, Meg marries and has twins, Amy sails to Europe, and Jo signs on as a governess for the children of a boarding house keeper in New York. Jo and Amy, who leave for parts unknown, end up in their respective situations in part by undergoing a test of their gender and class skills. Importantly, the test is at the hands of the wider world; it is not, as have been many of their earliest tests, administered at the hands of their own family, but as I shall show, the skills the two girls must demonstrate have been practiced within the domestic sphere.

In the chapter "Calls," Amy persuades Jo to accompany her in repaying a series of social calls to their friends and acquaintances. Jo accedes with good humor if not good grace, and relies on Amy to instruct her how to dress and act in each situation. Eager to please herself, and extract some fun out of what she considers an onerous chore, Jo exaggerates or parodies Amy's instructions for behavior at each of the homes they visit, imitating all of the possible styles of affected or ritualized social behavior. Amy, on the other hand, is universally pleasing. When Jo tells Amy that she doesn't want to make any calls, Amy responds practically that "it's a debt we owe society, and there's no one to pay it but you and me" (Alcott **1993,** 256), later telling Jo that "women should learn to be agreeable, particularly poor ones; for they have no other way of repaying the kindnesses they receive" (263). Amy's argument to Jo is that gender conformity helps to compensate for uncertain class position. In her logic, everyone must observe the conventions of social class, but those persons whose position in their "proper" class is suspect must observe them with especial care. Amy's logic of social debt is perfectly in accordance with an earlier instance of her activity outside the home. In "Amy's Valley of Humiliation," she is sent to the front of her class for sneaking in contraband items for her classmates to enjoy. Borrowing money from her sister because she is "dreadfully in debt" (59) she can finally treat her classmates to the forbidden pickled limes, whose exchanges are the key to attracting various social attentions from Amy's classmates. She explains to Meg, "They treat by turns; and I've had ever so many but haven't returned them, and I ought, for they are debts of honour, you know" (59).

The "debts of honour" that Amy feels so keenly as a child are narratively equivalent to the social debts she feels as an adult. Indeed, the two situations are parallel in a great many narrative details, except while Amy is punished as a schoolgirl, she is rewarded as an adult. During her punishment at school, she is overcome by a "bitter sense of wrong" (Alcott **1993,** 62), and during the family consultation about the events, her mother tells her that she doesn't "think the girls you associate with are doing you any good" (63), charging much of the blame for Amy's punishment to Amy's account. It is her desire to imitate and join the girls whose favors she has been attempting to repay that has caused her humiliation. Amy protests her mother's reading, saying that she wants to be "elegant," and to have fine manners and ladylike graces, but Mrs. March responds, "These things are always seen and felt in a person's manner and conversation if modestly used; but it is not necessary to display them" (64).

Amy, imitative to the last, learns her mother's lesson well. As her advice to Meg also demonstrated, Mrs. March's interest is in trying to relocate the source of class distinction to the proper performance of gender. It may not be necessary to display one's ambitions directly, for in the end, they will be "seen" as well as felt when they are properly cultivated. Certainly, if the novel is enacting a drama of how class is not just personalized, but gendered as a personal attribute, the focus on how they appear to others is crucial to the girls.

Thus, when Amy repays her debts during her social calls, she is rewarded beyond her wildest dreams. She is invited to sail to Europe with her aunt Carroll and her cousin Flo. The trip, which will be bankrolled by her aunt March, is the direct result of Amy's tactful response to a question about patronage, a condition she serenely tells them does "not trouble me when it is well meant" (Alcott **1993**, 265). To a similarly phrased inquiry, Jo responds, "I don't like favors; they oppress and make me feel like a slave; I'd rather do everything for myself and be perfectly independent" (265). Jo, who has behaved with the same characteristics that have amused her own family for so many years, finds that she is misread as a "cold" girl, and is exempted from the possibility of joining another family in order to rise in the world. Amy, willing to put herself in debt to her relatives now as in the past when she wore her cousin's hand-me-down clothes, wins a trip to Europe. Jo, staunchly independent, falls into despair. But part of what has happened in this section is that the text has reversed the valences of its characterization. Jo's independence has resulted in exclusion, not freedom, and Amy's social manipulation has resulted in recognition.

At the close of the chapter, Amy repeats the desires she has expressed so often throughout the novel. "You laugh at me when I say I want to be a lady, but I mean a true gentlewoman in mind and manners, and I try to do it as far as I know how. I can't explain exactly, but I want to be above the little meannesses and follies and faults that spoil so many women" (Alcott **1993**, 274). Indeed, she becomes a true gentlewoman by the end of the text, proved by her refusal of a merely mercenary marriage alliance (for which she is rewarded by becoming the fabulously wealthy Mrs. Theodore Laurence). Of her probable marriage to a wealthy Englishman, Amy writes to her family: "I may be mercenary, but I hate poverty, and don't mean to bear it a minute longer than I can help. One of us *must* marry well; Meg didn't, Jo won't, Beth can't yet, so I shall, and make everything cosy all round. I wouldn't marry a man I hated or despised" (284). Amy's decision not to marry this young man surprises even herself, but her decision to marry her family's closest friend most pointedly demonstrates the novel's endorsement of Amy rather than Jo.[13] When Meg begins to think of marrying John Brooke, Jo passionately tells her mother that she wishes she could marry Meg herself and "keep her in the family." Amy's union to Theodore Laurence not only works to keep her family together, it works to raise them in the world. Indeed,

Amy and her husband become the benefactors of the Marches, and of people *like* the Marches.

One of the ways to see the development of a home that is the source of felt or emotional responses to distinction is to look at two scenes that describe Amy's values in relationship to Laurie's. In the first, Amy, having encountered Laurie in Europe, finds that he has abandoned himself to laziness in the name of a broken heart. She chides him, telling him that she cannot bear his company because he is squandering his gifts and is tiresome and unambitious. After she scolds him, Laurie has a kind of awakening; taking her words to heart, he regains some of his former energy and direction. He also, therefore, makes himself a suitable mate for Amy, for what she has done in scolding him is to assert, as her own mother has before her, the sovereign power to legislate behavior through sentiment; to transform a vague sense of injustice into a critical emotion and to therefore address and assimilate it into a more domestically valuable position. Asserting her mastery over Laurie's wounded and negative feelings, Amy becomes eligible to have a family of her own, to construct a world in which desire, feeling, and injury can be converted into something more emotionally productive.

The second scene that reveals Amy's values happens after Amy and Laurie have married and have moved back to the house next to the Marches. With no artistic career as a necessity, and no need to become a working girl, Amy concurs with Laurie in his plan that they become patrons of occupants of the ambiguous class position the March girls once occupied. Laurie says to Amy:

> There's one sort of poverty that I particularly like to help. Out-and-out beggars get taken care of, but poor gentlefolks fare badly, because they won't ask, and people don't dare to offer charity; yet there are a thousand ways of helping them, if one only knows how to do it so delicately that it does not offend. I must say, I like to serve a decayed gentleman better than a blarneying beggar; I suppose it's wrong, but I do, though it is harder.
>
> (Alcott **1993**, 408)

Amy concurs, adding:

> [A]nd there's another class who can't ask, and who suffer in silence. I know something of it, for I belonged to it before you made a princess of me, as the king does the beggar-maid in the old story. Ambitious girls have a hard time, Laurie, and often have to see youth, health, and precious opportunities go by, just for want of a little help at the right minute. People have been very kind to me; and whenever I see girls struggling along, as we used to do, I want to put out my hand and help them, as I was helped.
>
> (Alcott **1993**, 409)

While we certainly might read this section to say that Amy—or the novel—recognizes the injustice of economic privation for the socially ambitious, it is also telling that it is only those persons who already feel entitled to recognition who are deemed worthy of financial help. Indeed, Amy's social triumph is completed in this circuit. Laurie tells his new wife, "though I trembled for you at one time, I was not disappointed, for the daughter was true to the mother's teaching. I told mamma so yesterday, and she looked as glad and grateful as if I'd given her a cheque for a million" (Alcott **1993**, 407).

As Amy is rewarded for her reading of the interdependence of class and status, a reading she facilitates by transforming her bumptious social airs into more mannered expressions of ladylikeness, Jo is punished for her inability to turn her irritation at the social world into a critical strategy that can help her enter it on her own terms. While Amy is away, Jo makes a study of resentment—or rather, she becomes a study of resentment and failed aspiration. After Amy's departure for Europe, and after Beth's death, Jo throws herself into the work of the household, trying to take Beth's place for the sake of her family.

Many critics have made incisive arguments about the transformation of Jo's rebelliousness, and the text's domestication of her character. But what is of especial interest to me is the way the domestication of Jo is deeply implicated in the lessons of class that she slowly comes to engage with not just emotionally—angrily, or resentfully, or yearningly—but critically. Jo—in certain ways a deeply democratic heroine in the sense of her character's belief in the value of social equality and personal independence, beliefs she advances in the very chapter "Calls" in which her aspirations will be trampled when she spends her time talking to a solidly middle-class youth instead of to a wealthy family—learns lessons about the proper social circulation of even the most democratic of women.

Her stay in New York provides some of the richest fodder for an examination of her domestication. In New York she has left home, in New York she becomes a professional author, and in New York she meets Professor Bhaer, the unlikely character who will become her husband. But in my argument, it is in New York that she is schooled in class distinctions and it is here that she learns to internalize and naturalize class and status distinctions *as if they were* natural distinctions. She therefore learns the lesson that Amy and Meg learn in the domestic sphere only when she leaves home, but it is only by learning them that she becomes ready to return home.

It is important to remember that Jo's tenure at Mrs. Kirke's boarding house is dependent on Mrs. Kirke's status as a gentlewoman. She is a trusted family friend, and she will treat Jo as she would a daughter. Jo moves from one family to another, from one domestic space to another. Although Jo's stay in New York is decidedly non-urban, since it takes place in the confines of the boarding house, it introduces her to some constitutively urban phenomenon—the pleasures of misrecognition, of unregulated association with persons not like herself, and of being at home in an anonymous and impersonal print sphere.

Although Jo goes to New York in part to escape an uncomfortable, impending romance with her neighbor Laurie, she also tells her mother that while she is there she will be able to "see and hear new things, get new ideas, and . . . bring home quantities of material for my rubbish [her writing]" (Alcott **1993**, 294). Her mission to gather new sensations for her writing is balanced by the fact that much of the new material she gathers finds its way into a conventionally domestic form—the letter to her family. Many of her letters tell her family about the life of the boarding house, in which Jo is something of a puzzle to her fellow boarders. She reports a conversation in which two young men pass judgement upon her, saying "handsome head, but no style" (300). Her own response is a mixture of outrage and exasperation. "A governess is as good as a clerk," she writes, finishing up by saying, "I hate ordinary people!" (300). Her letters are as she says herself, very "Bhaery," and detail her growing friendship with the Professor, a friendship, it is important to note, that takes place under the rubric of fair "bargains"—worker to worker. But what she does not report in the letters is the progress of her own writing.

The narrator details Jo's growing independence as a writer, as well as her growing success in placing her stories. Much has been made of the fact that Jo places her stories in an attempt to help her sister Beth by saving enough money to bring her to the mountains or the shore, and that her previous publications have been likewise motivated by a desire to provide for her family. But the conditions under which Jo places her stories are not only domestic. Jo is hired because a previous "hack"—a stranger to her—has left for a higher paying position. Stepping into a paying job as a "scribbler" or a "hack," Jo joins the working classes, delivering her stories on deadline, and filling her "emaciated" purse, Jo,

> Searched newspapers for accidents, incidents, and crimes; she excited the suspicions of public librarians by asking for works on poisons; she studied faces in the street, and characters, good, bad, and indifferent, all about her; she delved in the dust of ancient times for facts or fictions so old that they were as good as new, and introduced herself to folly, sin, and misery, as well as her limited opportunities allowed. She thought she was prospering finely; but unconsciously she was beginning to desecrate some of the womanliest attributes of a woman's character. She was living in bad society; and imaginary though it was, its influence affected her,

for she was feeding heart and fancy on dangerous and
unsubstantial food, and was fast brushing the innocent
bloom from her nature by a premature acquaintance
with the darker side of life.

(Alcott **1993,** 311)

The search for information—for experience that will
sell—means not only that Jo is betraying or sullying
her "womanly" attributes, but more specifically, that
she is sullying them by keeping bad company, by living
in "bad society." It is her circulation in bad society that
brings her to the attention of Professor Bhaer, who responds to her argument that "many respectable people
make an honest living out of what are called sensation
stories" by telling her that "if the respectable people
knew what harm they did, they would not feel that the
living *was* honest" (Alcott **1993,** 316).

By conflating the circulation of Jo and Jo's stories, Professor Bhaer reminds Jo that she has a moral obligation
to do things "she was [not] ashamed to own" at home
(Alcott **1993,** 316). His attempt to remove Jo from dangerous circulation among the masses is not only a romantic or a moral rescue, it is a class intervention
couched in standard phrases of morality. He is himself
a powerful example of what it means to labor in obscurity, to forego mere fame or repute, and he effectively
stops Jo from laboring in an infamous obscurity in order to profit from stories of ill-repute. But more importantly, he severs Jo from labor that has put her, however
tentatively, in the wrong society, and therefore, in the
wrong class. Class is a moral orientation toward the
world, and it is therefore inextricably tied to gender and
its "natural" relationship to the moral. The distinctions
to which Jo must adhere are also the distinctions that as
a woman she is uniquely able to make for others, and it
is Professor Bhaer's argument that Jo injures others
when she attempts to join the working class rather than
remaining in the class of good women. In this reading,
Jo's reconciliation to domesticity comes when she discovers that she is the site of an emotional reading by
someone else, as well being, as an author, the potential
site for the exercise of dangerously negative emotions.

Predictably, if is the negative emotion of shame that
first alerts Jo to how much she values Professor Bhaer,
it is Professor Bhaer's discovery of an unpublished
poem about her positive emotional attachment to her
family that inspires him to ask her to marry him. "I
read that, and I think to myself, She has a sorrow, she
is lonely, she would find comfort in true love" he tells
Jo, and although the narrative argues that she "would
never learn to be proper" because she kisses him in
public, it also argues that her writing and her sorrow
and her anger have found their appropriate redress in
the transformative domestic world of the "household
light and warmth and peace" that she next enters (Alcott
1993, 427).

III

Little Women shows us that class was an increasingly
important area of concern in the mid nineteenth century,
and it shows us also, that class was an already fractured
and multiply determined idea, encompassing ideas of
status, family name and honor, intellectual and community repute, as well as more conventional economic
markers. I have argued that in this novel, the characters
endure a series of mortifying confrontations with their
own social inadequacies, and that they therefore experience astonishingly negative emotions ranging from anger to shame to resentment to injury. Yet the novel is
not about negative emotions; rather it is a novel that re-
solves negative emotions without always repressing
them. It understands the domestic as a way to transform
such negative emotions by understanding the home as a
place where social distinctions can be learned, practiced, and reconfigured as "natural" distinctions. While
the characters' conflicts with the external world often
occur in the field of a newly emerging class system,
they are also understood from the perspective of the
family, which governs its members by standards that
cannot fully recognize nor redress serious emotional responses to injustice because it is already paradoxically
saturated with them.

As Jo's own writing shows us, the nineteenth-century
sentimental story provided a vocabulary for romantic
desire, but such a rhetoric rarely infuses the scenes of
the girls' courtships or marriages. Amy and Laurie agree
to marry while they are rowing together, a proposal that
comes at the expense of Laurie's more romantic visions, and only after Amy has given her beloved a round
scolding about his aristocratic laziness and his inability
to be either useful or industrious; Meg and John's wedding day proceeds most untraditionally, with Meg helping John put up the wedding decorations and giving her
first kiss as a married woman to her mother; Jo and
Professor Bhaer have a most unromantic declaration of
their feelings in a pouring rain storm. The key terms of
desire in the novel are reserved not for romance but for
the world of social and class ambition, yet in the end,
class ambition and the drive for social recognition have
been largely displaced, if not eliminated.

In the final pages of the novel, the remaining March
girls and their families gather at Plumfield, Jo's school
for wayward boys. As they sit at their mother's feet,
they recollect their "Castles in the Air," referring to a
similar gathering at which Meg once confessed her desire for a wealthy husband, Amy for artistic fame, and
Jo for literary success. Though they have each only
achieved a portion of their desires, they profess themselves content with lives in which their worldly ambitions have been subsumed by domestic concerns. Their
mother ratifies their happiness by spreading her arms as
if to encompass the entire extended family, saying "Oh,

my girls, however long you may live, I never can wish you a greater happiness than this!" (Alcott **1993,** 437).

But if the ending of novel seems to extort from its female characters a loyalty to the domestic ideal that must always appear to have somehow failed their former, more ambitious selves, it also tells us, paradoxically, that only by recreating the family can the injuries produced by structural or economic inequalities be transcended. Wendy Brown argues that liberalism's failure to adequately incorporate gender in its social and political analyses is most fully felt in the schizophrenia attending definitions of the home and the family. Women, charged with overcoming market constraints, are figured *in* the home and *by* the home as "non-civil" subjects. But the March girls, whose relationships to their families are everywhere implicated in markets, class ambition, social distinctions, and wage-earning, find that their ambitions for fame and renown, for fortune and comfort, for gentility as well as for freedom, can all be accommodated in the middle-class households that, in the world of the novel, are not only the sources, but the balms for their wounded and negative emotions.

Notes

1. The emotional genealogy behind feminist critics' rediscovery of this novel is beyond the scope of this essay, but it is nonetheless salient to my discussion, for *Little Women* is currently enjoying a renaissance among literary historians. Catharine Stimpson, for example, uses *Little Women* as an example of a paracanonical text. *Little Women,* she argues, is paracanonical because it measures "the gap between love and power" for its readers (1990, 967). Stimpson's argument relies on the idea that a text's ability to generate an emotional response is important in its own right. Indeed, she tells us that her earlier emotional responses are *critical* responses phrased in a language now unfamiliar or historically illegible to literary-critical discourse. The ability to generate sustained emotional responses across audiences is what signals that a text might be paracanonical, for the paracanonical names a category of texts that provides a way to access and assess an historiography of readers and their affective/critical relationship to literary discourse. "Texts," Stimpson tells us, "are paracanonical if some people have loved and do love them" (958). Stimpson's formulation is especially useful in this case because *Little Women* is not just a novel that elicits unofficial criticism by way of feelings; it is a novel that, as I shall show, is very much *about* the historically specific relationship between feelings and understanding.

2. *Little Women*'s inversion of conventional sentimental versions of the home and the marketplace might be usefully mapped onto its inversion of conventional gender roles as well. Although I shall not discuss this in this essay, it is worth noting how distinctly Mr. and Mrs. March split the labor of the household in the second half of the book. Mrs. March is often sent out into the world while Mr. March remains in the house as counselor and guide for his troubled daughters and friends. He, like a sentimental mother, is immune from the pressures of the working world, whereas Mrs. March, whose struggle against anger is in fact a struggle against her resentment at being continually impoverished by her dreamy spouse, is charged with the work of keeping her family sound, fed, and healthy.

3. See, for example Fetterley (1979) and Gaard (1991).

4. See for example Baym (1978) and Vallone (1995).

5. See for example Brodhead (1993), especially chapter 3, "Starting Out in the 1860s: Alcott, Authorship, and the Postbellum Literary Field," Stadler (1999), and Stoneley (1999).

6. For an excellent study of the difficulties attending the term "middle class," see Blumin (1989), especially chapter one, "The Elusive Middle Class."

7. The similarities between Alcott's own family history and the plot of *Little Women* have been extensively chronicled elsewhere. See Brodhead (1993), as well as the Alcott journals (Myerson, et. al. 1989).

8. Mother, known as Marmee, gives her daughters an object lesson in class and gender desire when she gives them a vacation. Meg and Jo work outside the home, despite "the unsatisfied desires of pleasure-loving youth" and find the demands of their other families (Meg is a governess, Jo a companion to her wealthy aunt) tiresome (Alcott 1993, 33). In the chapter "Experiments," the girls try a life of leisure, and they actually end up doing the difficult work of servants as well as the labor of ladies of leisure. Meg and Jo at first "wonder . . . why servants ever talked about hard work" (99), but soon discover how difficult it is to be a good housekeeper. At the end of their experiment, they throw an impromptu dinner party, which they prepare largely without the help of their servant. Unable to pull the dinner together, they end up serving an unpalatable mess to a notorious gossip who carries the tale of their failure to the rest of their friends. Although it is remembered as an amusing episode, the girls' failure to be good hostesses as well as to be good housekeepers results in public humiliation.

9. Peter Stoneley asserts that one of Alcott's favored themes is her distaste for economic display for its

own sake, arguing that such display is a symptom of a new ordering of classes that for Alcott sought to obscure an individual's finer qualities. Making qualities of fineness personal, though, relies on a notion of class that is not contrary to the world of social status as approved worth, but on a notion of class that recognizes and worries the potential injustice of such a conflation.

10. The March's gentle "birthright" is one of the reasons they can be friends with their wealthier neighbors, the Laurences. The senior Mr. Laurence knew Mrs. March's father, and gives his stamp of approval to the rest of the family based on what he knows of their good breeding.

11. This is not to say that Meg's pregnancy inoculates her against the sense of class injury she has experienced all the way through the novel. When Amy returns from Europe, for example, Meg is immediately conscious of the difference between their clothes, and then transforms her personal resentment into a vicarious experience of class triumph over the friend to whom she has been forced to sell her own dress material. "Meg became conscious that her own dress hadn't a Parisian air, that young Mrs. Moffat would be entirely eclipsed by young Mrs. Laurence, and that 'her ladyship' was altogether a most elegant and graceful woman" (Alcott 1993, 398). Additionally, the novel takes up Meg's domestic resentment when she feels neglected by her husband, who she feels is working too much and neglecting his family—she "felt injured because she did not know that she wanted him without being told" (346). She addresses John's neglect by dressing up and asking to be taken out, a lesson that the proper stabilization of class and gender require a certain amount of labor and display.

12. Amy's life provides a staggering number of scenes of social humiliation, partially because she is the character most invested in social advancement. She is humiliated at school when she tries to compete with her wealthier schoolmates by bringing in pickled limes. She is humiliated when she tries to throw an "elegant" lunch for the girls with whom she takes drawing lessons. She is pushed aside at a charity fair by being told she is not socially prominent enough to occupy the best booth. Any one of these scenes might be read as inspiring emotional responses that produce later class distinctions, but more important for this essay is how the novel charts Amy's rise next to Jo's decline.

13. Amy's admiration for the British and for inherited titles is not new in the book. While they are making their calls, Amy settles down at one household to talk to the Tudors: "Mr. Tudor's uncle had mar-

ried an English lady who was third cousin to a living lord, and Amy regarded the whole family with great respect; for, in spite of her American birth and breeding, she possessed that reverence for titles which haunts the best of us—that unacknowledged loyalty to the early faith in kings . . ." (Alcott 1993, 262).

Works Cited

Alcott, Louisa May. 1993. *Little Women and Good Wives*. Ed. Ann Thwaite. London: Everyman.

Baym, Nina. 1978. *Women's Fiction: A Guide to Novels By and About Women in America, 1820-1870*. Ithaca: Cornell University Press.

Blumin, Stuart. 1989. *The Emergence of the Middle Class: Social Experience in the American City, 1760-1900*. Cambridge: Cambridge University Press.

Bourdieu, Pierre. 1984. *Distinction: A Social Critique of the Judgement of Taste*. Cambridge: Harvard University Press.

Brodhead, Richard. 1993. *Cultures of Letters: Scenes of Reading and Writing in Nineteenth-Century America*. Chicago: University of Chicago Press.

Brown, Wendy. 1995. *States of Injury: Power and Freedom in Late Modernity*. Princeton: Princeton University Press.

Fetterley, Judith. 1979. "*Little Women*: Alcott's Civil War." *Feminist Studies* 5:2: 369-83.

Gaard, Greta. 1991. "'Self-Denial Was All the Fashion': Repressing Anger in *Little Women*." *Papers on Language and Literature: A Journal for Scholars and Critics of Language and Literature* 27:1: 3-19.

Myerson, Joel, Daniel Shealy, and Madeleine Stern, eds. 1989. *The Journals of Louisa May Alcott*. Boston: Little, Brown and Co.

Stadler, Gustave. 1999. "Louisa May Alcott's Queer Geniuses." *American Literature* 71:4: 657-677.

Stimpson, Catherine R. 1990. "Reading for Love: Canons, Paracanons, and Whistling Jo March." *New Literary History*: 21.4: 957-76.

Stoneley, Peter. 1999. "'The Fashionable World Displayed': Alcott and Social Power." *Studies In American Fiction* 27:1: 21-36.

Thwaite, Ann, ed. 1993. *Little Women and Good Wives*, by Louisa May Alcott. London: Everyman.

Vallone, Lynne. 1995. *Disciplines of Virtue: Girls' Culture in the Eighteenth and Nineteenth Centuries*. New Haven: Yale University Press.

Jennifer Doyle (essay date December 2005)

SOURCE: Doyle, Jennifer. "Jo March's Love Poems." *Nineteenth-Century Literature, Special Issue: Lesbian Aesthetics, Aestheticizing Lesbianism* 60, no. 3 (December 2005): 375-402.

[*In the following essay, Doyle studies representations of female identity in Alcott's* Little Women. *Doyle notes a central tension in the work between the outward trajectory of its characters' lives and its underlying social message.*]

When I teach Louisa May Alcott's **Little Women** (1868-69), I often begin with the following question: How has this novel, so firmly in place as a story about turning unruly girls into good little women (into "good wives," according to the title for the second half of the book, in which the girls either die or get married), managed nevertheless to have enjoyed a long career as a workable handbook on how to be a tomboy, a woman writer, a feminist intellectual, a dyke?[1] What do we make of the hold of Alcott's novel on women like Simone de Beauvoir (who wrote short stories in order to be more like Jo March) or the members of the lesbian theater-troupe Split Britches, who staged a play about it?[2] M. Carey Thomas, for example, actually began her childhood diary as Jo ("PRIVATE JOURNAL KEPT BY JO MARCH—COMMENCED JUNE 20, 1870").[3] She went on to cofound Bryn Mawr College and shepherd a generation of girls into exactly the kind of future unimaginable in Alcott's novel.

As **Little Women** opens, Jo March slouches through her world complaining that she wants to be a boy:

> I hate to think I've got to grow up and be Miss March, and wear long gowns, and look as prim as a China-aster. It's bad enough to be a girl, any-way, when I like boy's games, and work, and manners. I can't get over my disappointment in not being a boy, and it's worse than ever now, for I'm dying to go and fight with papa, and I can only stay at home and knit like a poky old woman.[4]

Jo heroically cuts off her hair in order to sell it and raise money for her father (who is off fighting in the Civil War) and asserts that if she cannot have her sisters, no one can ("I just wish I could marry Meg myself" [p. 203]). But by the end of the book, this same character morphs into a paragon of feminine self-denial and restraint. As she mourns the death of her beloved sister Beth, Jo begins to adopt the characteristics of a good little woman, sweeping the floors of the house, putting the needs and desires of others before her own. The most obvious romantic partner for her, the effeminate neighbor Laurie, is married off to another sister, and Jo ends up, at the end of the novel, marrying a much older, patriarchal man named Professor Bhaer.

She never really gets to be the writer that she sets out to become; instead, she opens up a school for little boys, presumably nursing them into the kind of life that is not quite possible for the girls in her world.

Why is it, in spite of the fact that the novel famously imagines for young women a choice between marriage or death (an uninhabitable choice between submission and disappearance), that reading **Little Women** is nevertheless cited by generations of women as a key moment in their own self-production, *not* as "good wives" but as, in Adrienne Rich's words, "*marriage resist[ers]*"?[5] It is a fine example of a novel that seems to say one thing (in asking its women characters to give up their romantic attachments to women), and does another (by offering women readers a manual on how to maintain them). The novel's social impact, in other words, is completely at odds with the trajectory of its plot. Here we may add the question that always confronts the nineteenth-century student of works like **Little Women** (e.g., Herman Melville's *Moby-Dick* [1851] and Walt Whitman's *Leaves of Grass* [1855]), whose stories are not complete without an accounting of their importance to gay readers, even given their historical origin before the modern articulation of gay identity as such: can there really be lesbian characters in **Little Women** if, for the woman who wrote it and for the first audience to read it, lesbian identity did not exist? How should we think about the history of its authorship, and about the history of its readership?[6]

All too often, an under-examined commitment to historical period backs us into corners in which we wring our hands over who can be called what, and when—who is a lesbian, in what period, and how? The long life of Jo March as not only a prototype for the lesbian feminist intellectual, but also as, in fact, a *legibly* lesbian character, renders such wrangling over historical precision unconvincing as a response to the question of how a queer novel works on readers (now and then) across time. The novel demands a more creative approach to the subject of timing and identity formation. Judith Halberstam uses the term "queer temporality" to signal the thematization and formal exploration of timing in gay literature responding to the AIDS epidemic (e.g., Michael Cunningham's *The Hours* [1998]). She proposes that we look at queer subcultural practices as a similar resistance to "family time," to the "reproductive time," as, in a sense, radical extensions of adolescence. Family time, along with "the time of inheritance," "connects the family to the historical past of the nation, and glances ahead to connect the family to the future of both familial and national stability."[7] Queer temporality, she argues (drawing on Eve Kosofsky Sedgwick and Michel Foucault), can also be a way of refuting the evolutionary logic of a historicism that imagines the past as "the logic for the present, and [in which] the future represents the fruition of this logic."[8]

Like much queer fiction, *Little Women* raises the question of how gay and lesbian readers get from here to there (from the page to the world) and from then to now (from the time of its authorship to the time of its reading), and back again.

The dissonance between *Little Women*'s plot and *Little Women*'s effects is a great case study for the limits of reading the latter through the former. And, I would like to argue here, it indicates the necessity of flexible, creative, and, ultimately, dialectical models of reading to queer literary studies—ones that might refuse the relentlessly temporal logic of plot and, in doing so, attend both to the politics of form and to the novel's particularly lesbian effects.

Dialectical criticism allows us (or pushes us) to consider what queer studies might be besides the representation and production of identities. Fredric Jameson, for example, describes the difference between non-dialectical and dialectical criticism as a matter of degrees of sophistication, in which dialectical criticism is able to respond not only to the question posed by a text but also to the assumptions that underwrite that question. Jameson writes:

> faced with obscure poetry, the naïve reader attempts at once to *interpret,* to resolve the immediate difficulties back into the transparency of rational thought; whereas for a dialectically trained reader, it is the obscurity itself which is the object of his reading, and its specific quality and structure which he attempts to define and to compare with other forms of verbal opacity. Thus our thought no longer takes official problems at face value, but walks behind the screen to assess the very origin of the subject-object relationship in the first place.[9]

There are several ways in which a statement like this is compelling in a queer context. First, it allows for a mode of analysis, of writing, about the representation of sexuality that might dilate around something other than the sexual identities of the characters of a fictional narrative—around something other than plot analysis and symbolic decoding. (And so, for example, one might write about the problem of *knowing* sexual identity itself, as does Eve Kosofsky Sedgwick, or of the relationship between desire, paranoia, and the novel, as does D. A. Miller.)[10] Jameson's statement also speaks to the sense that it might be interesting to think about where and how sexuality and desire "happen" in literature *besides* the articulation/production of sexual identities. It rhymes, too, with Foucault's suspicion of the production of sex as the great secret of everything, and with the position of the critic who must then figure out how to write against the pressure of the repressive hypothesis (which, with its diagnostic drive, is decidedly not dialectical).[11]

Alcott's most popular narrative is particularly ripe for a dialectical reading because critics tend to take the transparency of this novel for granted. If the density of a modernist work (for example) forces the question of opacity itself to the critical foreground, then the apparent sincerity of sentimental writing should force us to question the nature of this textual transparency. *Little Women* lingered for decades in the very *un*literary category of children's literature—and even today, most of the scholarship on Alcott's writing is closer to (if not explicitly identified with) new historicism than to the critical modes associated with formal textual analysis, such as psychoanalytic theory or deconstruction. In general, scholars have used the story of this novel—meaning not only the story it tells, but also the story of its production—as a way to access the lived contradictions of nineteenth-century domestic culture (a culture that, on the one hand, was defined by an ethos of self-denial and restraint, and, on the other hand, produced the foundations for lesbian identity and culture itself). As a result, much of the criticism on Alcott is grounded in either new historicist or biographical criticism (or in some combination thereof).[12]

Most feminist readings of *Little Women* begin with a gesture toward the contradictory effects of reading the novel, and nearly all of them wrestle with the novel's strained conclusion.[13] Kathryn Kent writes that when it comes to addressing sexuality in the novel, the issue is represented in Alcott scholarship as a tension between the "overt" and "covert" messages of the novel. From some critical perspectives (e.g., that of Judith Fetterley) the possibilities of romantic and sexual love between women is the novel's covert "secret message," hidden behind the surface of a story in which that homosexuality is unthinkable.[14] This reading, Kent argues, underrepresents the degree to which the homoerotics of the novel are actually "there in full view" (*Making Girls into Women,* p. 50). The problem, she argues, is that such readings not only produce a closet for Jo that does not exist within the novel (and that may not have existed as such for Alcott and her readers), but they also flatten out the lesbian possibilities woven into sentimental and domestic structures themselves. Kent argues, for example, that the imitative and pedagogic process of making Jo into a "little woman," in which she absorbs aspects of the women around her (Marmee, Beth), has a profound relationship to lesbian erotics in especially its emphasis on the homoerotics of the pedagogic mise-en-scène.[15]

In her important work on Alcott, Kent weaves a reading of the narrative of Jo's development across Alcott's writing into a larger story about the emergence of the modern lesbian subject from sentimental and domestic culture (in which the disciplinary mise-en-scène of school plays a major part, as the space in which gender identity becomes something one can learn—and, in becoming something acquired, is denaturalized). Kent thus approaches the novel both as a historical artifact and as a social agent in and of itself. As a consequence, this combined perspective on the novel places it at the heart of lesbian subject formation in the United States without reading that aspect of the novel's life as somehow contradictory with the story it tells. My own interest in *Little Women* is an extension of this project into an exploration of the politics of the novel's form—in particular, into an exploration of how the novel itself teaches us to read, as we are asked to read poems written by the fictional author, Jo March.

* * *

Since I first reread *Little Women* as an adult, I have been fascinated by the poems that Jo March writes in the novel—poems that we, as readers, get to see. I have been particularly intrigued by Jo's writing, because the writing process itself is represented as so intense, as a "fall into a vortex" (*Little Women,* p. 265) of oblivion to the world and passion for it.[16] Two of these poems appear in Book Two. As is well known within the lore of Alcott studies, the novel we know today is not exactly the novel that Alcott set out to write. The original text as commissioned by her publishers, who wanted a story for girls, ended with Meg's marriage, Jo's acceptance of her sister's departure into matrimony, and Jo's reluctant movement toward the adaptation of the upright posture and good behavior of womanhood. At the end of Book One, Jo's queer friendship with her similarly oddly gendered counterpart (the effeminate and infinitely affable Laurie) is still intact, and still ambiguous. Her ambitions as a writer are also in place.

Little Women was so popular, however, that readers begged Alcott's publisher for more—and, in particular, they asked for the matrimonial resolution of Jo and Laurie's relationship. In an 1869 letter Alcott writes: "Jo should have remained a literary spinster but so many enthusiastic young ladies wrote to me clamourously demanding that she should marry Laurie, *or* somebody, that I didn't dare to refuse & out of perversity went & made a funny match for her."[17] So Alcott, in a sequel cynically titled "Good Wives," pairs her heroine off with Professor Bhaer—an older, fatherly figure rendered in the novel as virtually sexless.[18]

Critics have often explored the subject of Jo's desire to be a writer, especially her struggle to sell her writing without compromising her literary ambitions (a struggle that mirrors Alcott's own story and is traditionally read as the best explanation for the novel's appeal to unruly women). Yet few critics have made more than passing mention of the writing that actually appears within the narrative framework of the book, or even of Alcott's writing itself. Scholars have proved reluctant to comment on these matters because, as mentioned above, Alcott's work tends to favor critical models grounded in historical and cultural questions over text-based analysis, and also perhaps because the scenes in the novel that describe the writing process are so much more engaging than the stilted poems that appear as their product later in the novel. Ann Murphy observes that many Alcott scholars steer clear of this novel altogether: "the text of *Little Women* remains something of a tarbaby, a sticky, sentimental, entrapping experience or place rather than a knowable object—and thus a fitting emblem of its own subversive content, which resists women's objectification and seeks a new vision of women's subjectivity and space" ("Borders of Ethical, Erotic, and Artistic Possibilities in *Little Women,*" pp. 563-64).[19] Murphy's remarks—which suggest that the book works metonymically as a stand-in for the body and, in particular, as a stand-in for an unruly female body—asks us to consider the "objectness" of the narrative (and the way in which this narrative seems to resist certain kinds of attention) as an allegory for the objectness of women. Where for Murphy the novel's feminism lies ultimately in the way in which its main character resists becoming a sexual object (by, for example, marrying not out of passion but out of a shared intellectual and professional interest), I suggest that the opposite is true. Insofar as we are encouraged to think of a novel as a thing, the body as an object, and reading as an intersubjective process (as something that happens between female bodies), we are also, with *Little Women,* given access to a distinctly homoerotic, and feminist, possibility—one that allows us to think outside the box, as it were.

* * *

Jo's poems are introduced directly into the novel, set off on the page for us to read in their entirety, as poetry. It is important that the poems are not represented to us as she writes them—they occur in the novel at exactly the moment they are read by a character in the story. The two poems that appear in "Good Wives"—**"My Beth"** and **"In the Garret"**—describe Jo's love and affection for her sisters and offer some of the most overt expressions of romantic love between women in the novel. Both poems are elegies written around Beth's death (one before and one after). We see the poems as they are held in the hands of a reader (first Beth and then Jo herself), and they appear as plot devices that move Jo toward womanhood—meaning, here, marriage. **"In the Garret"** is the last example of Jo's writing, and it is the only published work by the fictional author that we read.

Jo's poems escape notice because the literary status of such writing is bizarre: poems in novels work almost like parenthetical writing—the reader may feel as though she has permission to skip over the poem, especially in a novel whose textual transparency works against the grain of poetry. When reading a poem by Emily Dickinson, for example, we linger over a rhyme, a break, a repetition of sound and image, but when reading Alcott's prose we almost never stop to consider the textual opacity of her writing—even when the narrative is interrupted by a poem. In the case of **"In the Garret,"** the poem becomes more a prop within a scene than a continuation of the narrative. In general we do not expect such writing to tell us what is happening; more nearly, we expect such writing to repeat what is happening around the poem, to mirror the story in which it appears. They are breaks, thresholds, boundaries around which the story pauses—and if we pause with it, then the narrative loses its grip.

Our encounters with Jo's poems are staged during pivotal moments of the novel—the frame is so laden with drama that one may feel a particular license to ignore their content in favor of the resolution of the plot. This is to say that in this novel Jo's literary rendition of her attachment to her sisters (and to Beth, in particular) is set at odds with narrative development. The form that contains it (literally, the novel) becomes the very thing that produces the movement away from lesbian attachment. The representation of lesbian attachment in *Little Women,* then, is a formal problem.

"My Beth," for example, takes place in "The Valley of the Shadow," the chapter in which Beth, the best and most pure sister of all the March girls, dies. Beth's death, perhaps the most-remembered sequence in the novel, initiates the plot's resolution, setting into motion Jo's own marriage. By this point Jo has been nothing less than absolutely devoted to this particular sister, in part for all of the ways in which Beth's success in being the perfect girl marks off (but also enables) the disaster of Jo's own attempts to assimilate to that category. Jo pens this poem while keeping watch over her ailing sister, and Beth sees the poem after Jo has fallen asleep in a chair next to her bed. Beth looks among her books for "something to make her forget the mortal weariness that was almost as hard to bear as pain," and finds the poem: "a little paper scribbled over, in Jo's hand. The name caught her eye, and the blurred look of the lines made her sure that tears had fallen on it" (*Little Women,* p. 416). As Beth reads the poem, it is through her eyes that we, as readers, gain access to the text:

"MY BETH"

> Sitting patient in the shadow
>   Till the blessed light shall come,
> A serene and saintly presence
>   Sanctifies our troubled home.
> Earthly joys, and hopes, and sorrows,
>   Break like ripples on the strand
> Of the deep and solemn river
>   Where her willing feet now stand.
>
> Oh, my sister, passing from me,
>   Out of human care and strife,
> Leave me, as a gift, those virtues
>   Which have beautified your life.

> Dear, bequeath me that great patience
>   Which has power to sustain
> A cheerful, uncomplaining spirit
>   In its prison-house of pain.
>
> Give me, for I need it sorely,
>   Of that courage, wise and sweet,
> Which has made the path of duty
>   Green beneath your willing feet.
> Give me that unselfish nature,
>   That with charity devine [*sic*]
> Can pardon wrong for love's dear sake—
>   Meek heart, forgive me mine!
>
> Thus our parting daily loseth
>   Something of its bitter pain,
> And while learning this hard lesson,
>   My great loss becomes my gain.
> For the touch of grief will render
>   My wild nature more serene,
> Give to life new aspirations—
>   A new trust in the unseen.
>
> Henceforth, safe across the river,
>   I shall see forever more
> A beloved, household spirit
>   Waiting for me on the shore.
> Hope and faith, born of my sorrow,
>   Guardian angels shall become,
> And the sister gone before me,
>   By their hands shall lead me home.

> (*Little Women,* pp. 417-18)

As I have suggested above, we must think of this poem in at least three ways: first, as a piece of writing represented within the novel and as an agent within the plot; second, as a literary work in and of itself (a poem); and third, as a narrative break, a diversion *from* the plot's trajectory. By staging Beth reading Jo's poem, Alcott allegorically links the reader *of* a novel to a reader *in* the novel. She invites us to think about how the novel structurally anticipates its own consumption, and to imagine the relationship between reader and book as one that both produces and contains prohibited desire.

Jo's biggest problem in *Little Women* is the difficulty she has with being womanly. Much of the story's pathos is generated by her attempt to reconcile her drive, passion, and ambition with the social and familial demand that she be a good girl. In this rather amazing statement, Jo asks her sister to "bequeath . . . that great patience / Which has power to sustain / A cheerful, uncomplaining spirit / In its prison-house of pain." In Jo's poem, that "unselfish nature" passes to Jo through the process of mourning. The femininity that Jo fails to acquire out of identification, she acquires out of loss and desire. Grief, at the loss of the sister that she could neither be nor have, will make a woman out of her. Reading the poem brings "a look of inexpressible comfort to Beth's face, for her one regret had been that she had done so little; and this seemed to assure her that her life had not been useless—that her death would not bring the despair she feared" (*Little Women,* p. 418). Mere paragraphs after reading Jo's poetic promise, Beth dies—fulfilling a particularly lesbian literary destiny as she willingly becomes the dematerialized object of her sister's desire. Roberta Trites writes:

> Transforming Beth into a ghost frees Alcott to explore the subtleties of homoeroticism without alarming any Victorian censors. After this point in the text, Beth exists for Jo only as a disembodied memory, but one which she can fondle and caress without censure. Beth dies not to uphold the passivity of the Cult of True Womanhood [as is often assumed in feminist readings of the book], but to veil the lesbianism fueling the novel.
>
> ("Queer Performances," pp. 149-50)[20]

By writing Beth's body out of the novel, Alcott, in other words, gives Jo a different kind of access to the pleasures of her attachment to her sister. Beth's death thus, in Trites's view, both creates a closet for Jo and enables the expression of lesbian attachment as a form of haunting. But when we think about this series of events—the reading of the poem, Beth's death, Jo's mourning—less through the logic of character development, and more through the presence of the reader, we can begin to see Beth's death somewhat differently. In these lines Jo, on the one hand, maps out a path to successful mourning, in which she might incorporate and absorb her loss and, presumably, move on; and, on the other hand, she promises to love her sister "forever," identifies with and inhabits Beth's "prison-house of pain," and vows to wait patiently (like a lover) for the moment when they might be reunited.

"My Beth" is an odd elegy. Written as it is while Beth is not only living and breathing, but right next to Jo, the poem conjures a loss for the near future, and indeed makes that loss possible. The staging of the encounter with this poem gestures toward one of the signatures of romantic expressions of prohibited desire. Writing of elegiac expressions of love between men, George E. Haggerty explains that the expression of such desire is, in these elegiac forms, "realized at the moment of its impossibility." He continues: "If this love can be expressed only at the moment of loss, then it threatens to become loss itself. While at first this fact may seem paralyzing and limiting in the ways that a homophobic culture might wish, the elegy tradition sometimes manages . . . to articulate same-sex desire in terms that refuse to be confined by the bedside or the grave."[21] In *Little Women* Alcott seems to suggest that one way of responding to a world that at every turn wills you to fit into a story in which you do not belong is to write (or read) yourself (or the object of your desire) out of it.

Sure enough, as "My Beth" predicts, grief does gradually soften Jo:

> Brooms and dishcloths never could be as distasteful as they once had been, for Beth had presided over both; and something of her housewifely spirit seemed to lin-

ger round the little mop and the old brush, that was never thrown away. As she used them, Jo found herself humming the songs Beth used to hum, imitating Beth's orderly ways, and giving the little touches here and there that kept everything fresh and cosy.

> (*Little Women,* p. 434)

In a way, Jo becomes a ghost herself—taking on so many different aspects of her sister that she, too, starts to evaporate from the story. Jo in fact methodically rehearses the processes that Judith Butler describes in her writing on desire, loss, and psychic identification. Consider the harmony between the order of events (in which Jo imagines Beth's death, conjures up the experience of loss, and incorporates Beth's best qualities into herself) and Judith Butler's argument for the primacy of imitation, of mimesis to the formation of desire and identity. Butler writes:

> In Freud's view, . . . incorporation—a kind of psychic miming—is a response to, and refusal of, *loss*. Gender as the site of such psychic mimes is thus constituted by the variously gendered Others who have been loved and lost, where the loss is suspended through a melancholic and imaginary incorporation (and preservation) of those Others into the psyche.[22]

In which case, in reading the novel, we would privilege Beth's death as the cause of Jo's feminization. But, Butler continues, other psychoanalytic theorists have argued that identification may not be initiated by loss, but rather by mimesis, fantasy, or representation:

> Over and against this account of psychic mimesis by way of incorporation and melancholy, the theory of primary mimetism argues an even stronger position in favor of the non-self-identity of the psychic subject. Mimetism is not motivated by a drama of loss and wishful recovery, but appears to precede and constitute desire . . . itself; in this sense, mimetism would be prior to the possibility of loss and the disappointments of love.
>
> ("Imitation and Gender Subordination," p. 26)

Identity, as theorized here, is contingent and intersubjective—identity is not a position but a process that unfolds between people. In *Little Women* it is not exactly loss that enables the poetic expression of homoerotic attachment, but rather a fantasy about loss.[23] Beth's death first appears in the novel as a representation, as a poem. Jo's writing performatively enacts the disappearance of Beth's body from the story, but only at the moment it is read—Beth's death is an effect of *reading* Jo's poem.[24]

After Beth dies, Jo, at the urging of her mother, returns to her desk to write—and pens her most successful story yet (although, of course, we never see it). Jo explains: "If there *is* anything good or true in what I write, it isn't mine; I owe it all to you and mother, and to Beth" (*Little Women,* p. 436). It is in this chapter, "All Alone," that Alcott represents Jo's coltish spirit as domesticated—Jo yields up her attachments to the women in her family almost completely (in a statement, though, that paradoxically reaffirms her homoerotic attachments): "Mothers are the *best* lovers in the world; but, I don't mind . . . that I'd like to try all kinds" (p. 437). Soon after she makes this confession, Jo retreats upstairs: "Up in the garret, where Jo's unquiet wanderings ended, stood four little wooden chests in a row, each marked with its owner's name, and each filled with relics of the childhood and girlhood ended now for all" (pp. 438-39). At this point we come to a textual wormhole: while in the attic Jo pens a poem, **"In the Garret,"** which we see only later in "Under the Umbrella," the penultimate chapter.

Toward the very end of the novel Jo comes to realize that she actually loves Professor Bhaer. He visits, things go well and not so well, and, just when she thinks it is all over, he reappears. They confess their affections for each other, and Jo asks him: "Now tell me what brought you, at last, just when I most wanted you?" "This," he replies, taking "a little worn paper out of his waistcoat pocket." Jo unfolds the paper and recognizes "one of her own contributions to a paper that paid for poetry, which accounted for her sending it an occasional attempt." Bhaer explains: "I found it by chance; I knew it by the names and the initials, and in it there was one little verse that seemed to call me. Read and find him" (p. 476). At this point the poem is, so to speak, reprinted in the narrative, and we read it over Jo's shoulder.

"In the Garret" (pp. 476-79) is quite long—six stanzas of sixteen lines—and it is plodding: an introduction and a conclusion frame four stanzas. Here we get a portrait of Jo "in the garret," taking a kind of sentimental inventory as she reviews the contents of each March girl's hope chest. The poem opens:

"In the Garret"

Four little chests all in a row,
    Dim with dust, and worn by time,
All fashioned and filled, long ago,
    By children now in their prime.
Four little keys hung side by side,
    With faded ribbons, brave and gay,
When fastened there with childish pride,
    Long ago, on a rainy day.
Four little names, one on each lid,
    Carved out by a boyish hand,
And underneath there lieth hid
    Histories of the happy band
Once playing here, and pausing oft
    To hear the sweet refrain,
That came and went on the roof aloft,
    In the falling summer rain.

From here the author describes each of the hope chests, in often overtly erotic language:

'Meg' on the first lid, smooth and fair,
    I look in with loving eyes,
For folded there, with well-known care,
    A goodly gathering lies—
The record of a peaceful life,
    Gifts to gentle child and girl,
A bridal gown, lines to a wife,
    A tiny shoe, a baby curl.
No toys in this first chest remain,
    For all are carried away,
In their old age, to join again
    In another small Meg's play.
Ah, happy mother! well I know
    You hear like a sweet refrain,
Lullabies ever soft and low,
    In the falling summer rain.

'Jo' on the next lid, scratched and worn,
    And within a motley store
Of headless dolls, of school-books torn,
    Birds and beasts that speak no more.
Spoils brought home from the fairy ground
    Only trod by youthful feet,
Dreams of a future never found,
    Memories of a past still sweet;
Half-writ poems, stories wild,
    April letters, warm and cold,
Diaries of a wilful child,
    Hints of a woman early old;
A woman in a lonely home,
    Hearing like a sad refrain,—
'Be worthy love, and love will come,'
    In the falling summer rain.

Presumably, it is in the last two lines of this stanza that Professor Bhaer imagines himself ("Be worthy love, and love will come," etc.). But clearly, what makes Jo "early old" and her home "lonely" is the loss described in the following lines:

My 'Beth!' the dust is always swept
    From the lid that bears your name,
As if by loving eyes that wept,
    By careful hands that often came.
Death canonized for us one saint,
    Ever less human than divine,
And still we lay, with tender plaint,
    Relics in this household shrine.

The silver bell, so seldom rung,
    The little cap which last she wore,
The fair, dead Catherine that hung
    By angels borne above her door;
The songs she sang, without lament,
    In her prison-house of pain,
Forever are they sweetly blent
    With the falling summer rain.

Amy, typically, provides relief:

Upon the last lid's polished field—
    Legend now both fair and true—
A gallant knight bears on his shield,
    'Amy,' in letters gold and blue.
Within the snoods that bound her hair,

Slippers that have danced their last,
Faded flowers laid by with care,
Fans whose airy toils are past—
Gay valentines all ardent flames,
Trifles that have borne their part
In girlish hopes, and fears, and shames.
The record of a maiden heart,
Now learning fairer, truer spells,
Hearing, like a blithe refrain,
The silver sound of bridal bells
In the falling summer rain.

The sequence of sisterly boxes is introduced by an erotic vocabulary of boxes, locks, and keys—of a "boyish hand" carving into wood the names of a "happy band" of four girls and then exploring what lies underneath each lid. All of this is suspended in the ungainly rhyme of "hand" and "band"—which sets up my own first misreading of the poem, as written with Jo's "happy hand." This hand wanders over each chest, feeling "Meg" "smooth and fair," "Jo" "scratched and worn," Beth, from whom "the dust is always swept," and so on. The speaker explores the hope chests "with loving eyes," and with "loving eyes that wept" and "careful hands that often came" she catalogs and caresses the details of each girl's movement through the novel.

The poem wraps up with an oedipal scene in which the girls' chests are imagined finally lined up for "the Father's sight," in an afterlife in which they are reunited:

Four little chests all in a row,
Dim with dust, and worn by time,
Four women, taught by weal and woe,
To love and labor in their prime.
Four sisters, parted for an hour,—
None lost, one only gone before,
Made by love's immortal power,
Nearest and dearest evermore.
Oh, when these hidden stores of ours
Lie open to the Father's sight,
May they be rich in golden hours,—
Deeds that show fairer for the light.
Lives whose brave music long shall ring
Like a spirit-stirring strain,
Souls that shall gladly soar and sing
In the long sunshine, after rain.

It is signed, simply, "J. M." We can assume that Professor Bhaer reads himself into the end of the "Jo" stanza or perhaps, somewhat more disturbingly, in the concluding stanza ("Oh, when these hidden stores of ours / Lie open to the Father's sight"). Bhaer imagines that the poem is ultimately about the poet's desire for him. But when we read the poem itself, we see that there is room for other arguments about what the poem's narrator really wants. The loss described by the stanza devoted to "Jo" might just as easily be read as the death described in the stanza that follows—Beth as dead, but also Beth (or women more generally) as prohibited. And we can certainly read Jo's stanza as a description

of how her world is forcibly limited by her "oddity." "Be worthy love" is a direct echo of the promise that she made to keep her sister in her heart "forever more" in **"My Beth"** (*Little Women,* p. 418). This interpretation is borne out by the intense homoerotics of **"In the Garret,"** which lands Jo in the attic (projecting backward into the novel to the process of mourning Beth) caressing "four little chests," each a synecdoche for a sister.

As if confirming our urge to see Professor Bhaer as misreading Jo's writing, Jo disavows the poem: "It's very bad poetry. . . . I never thought it would go where it could tell tales" (*Little Women,* p. 479). Jo then tears the poem up into little pieces, at which point Bhaer asserts, rather alarmingly: "Let it go,—it has done its duty,—and I will haf a fresh one when I read all the brown book in which she keeps her little secrets" (p. 479). He takes her hand in his, and they agree to marry.

In the case of each of Jo March's poems, we have an interesting repetition: staged, for our reading, are scenes of reading, in which what is being read are the desires (and the writing) of one of the novel's characters. Further, we as readers witness a character reading themselves into the poem—imagining themselves, in fact, as the textual subject, as what the speaker in the poem wants most. Both actions identify with the poet's description of an absence. Each poem elaborates a hole that the reader imagines she or he might either become (Beth) or replace (Bhaer).

I have taken the time to sketch out the dynamics of these scenes because they indicate how intensely Alcott's novel foregrounds the act of reading itself as the mise-en-scène of desire, as the primary space in which Jo, as a literary subject, is constituted—but also, finally, as the space in which Alcott presents to us not Jo's desire to be a writer but Jo's desire to have a reader.

* * *

Around the poems **"My Beth"** and **"In the Garret"** *Little Women* imagines a girl split—at once both author and reader. Jo writes not only for an audience but also for the single, specific reader of the novel—the act of writing is the projection of the self into a space of desire that is, one hopes, already there, waiting. (We might here recall the early setting of Jo's queer romance with Laurie, in which, as she enjoys the company of her sisters, she makes sure to leave the room's curtains open, knowing that Laurie is watching.)[25] This desire for recognition is triangulated (and constituted) through the body of the novel's reader, who is allegorically worked into each of these poetical encounters.[26] Perhaps this is why as a girl M. Carey Thomas approached her diary as Jo March, and why Simone de Beauvoir felt that she had to write short stories in order to be like Jo—not only because they identified with the unruly tomboy but also, more precisely, because they wanted Jo's audience.

As it constitutes the scene of reading as an encounter between author, reader (internal), and reader (external), the novel anticipates Teresa de Lauretis's axiom that "it takes two women, not one, to make a lesbian";[27] this aspect of *Little Women* suggests that if we consider the audience (as is already implied by de Lauretis's work), then it may, in fact, take at least three. De Lauretis proposes "it takes two" in her reading of Sheila McLaughlin's 1987 film *She Must Be Seeing Things,* which is also centered on an author-surrogate named Jo. In this film Jo's lover, Agatha, while in the course of making a film, reads Jo's diary and imagines that Jo has another lover. In her analysis of this film and of its difference from other, more conventional lesbian films (such as Donna Deitch's *Desert Hearts* [1985]), de Lauretis revises the thematization of the problem of lesbian visibility in cinema in order to consider a lesbian film that is less preoccupied with putting lesbians on screen than it is with the complexity of representing lesbian desire.

The women of *She Must Be Seeing Things* are literally represented as "seeing things" (Jo, as she makes films; Agatha in her imagination, as she imagines that Jo is cheating on her). De Lauretis argues: "so far as dominant culture is concerned, both might as well be 'seeing things,' that is, imagining them. For indeed some of the things Jo sees through her film—women desiring women, and a film that inscribes that desire in its narrative through an articulation of the system of the look—such things do not exist in dominant representations in our culture" ("Film and the Visible," pp. 228-29). For de Lauretis, what makes this film interesting is not so much its content, but rather how that content is framed and how that frame is rendered visible to the spectator. She explains:

> the originality of McLaughlin's film, in my opinion, consists precisely in its foregrounding of that frame of reference, making *it* visible, and at the same time shifting it, moving it aside, as it were, enough to let us see through the gap, the contradiction; enough to create a space for questioning not only what *they* see but also what *we* see in the film; enough to let us see ourselves seeing, and with what eyes.
>
> ("Film and the Visible," p. 255)

What makes *She Must Be Seeing Things* interesting as a lesbian text is that it foregrounds women seeing, and seeing each other. In doing so, it allows for a representation of the density of vision and for a form of visual intimacy and exchange that is both complex and unpredictable. "This is a film about two women who share a common fantasy, a lesbian fantasy, and," De Lauretis continues, citing psychoanalytic theories of fantasy and

subject formation, "if 'the origin of the subject [her]self' is located 'in the field of fantasy,' then this very fantasy, which they share, constitutes them as a lesbian subject" ("Film and the Visible," p. 232).[28]

Similarly, as it mirrors the act of reading within the narrative framework and hitches the pivotal marital moment to a patriarch's misguided and deeply self-serving act of interpretation, *Little Women* cultivates an awareness of the unevenness, the unpredictability of the act of reading—and of the formative powers of interpretation. What becomes increasingly visible as we shift our attention from narrative arc to poetical detail is the particularly uneasy relationship of form and content, as it relates to lesbian desire in a narrative environment in which female development seems synonymous with a subjective disappearance into a marital haze. Alcott's rendition of the difficulty of inhabiting narrative forms through the oddity of Jo's poems echoes a poem by Emily Dickinson, another writer famous for falling into vortexes in her attic:

> They shut me up in Prose—
> As when a little Girl
> They put me in the Closet—
> Because they liked me "still"—
>
> Still! Could themself have peeped—
> And seen my Brain—go round—
> They might as wise have lodged a Bird
> For Treason—in the Pound—
>
> Himself has but to will
> And easy as a Star
> Abolish his Captivity—
> And laugh—No more have I—[29]

How we read Jo March's poetry has everything to do with how sympathetic we are to the narrative arc of *Little Women.* It is not enough to decode the poems, to read back into them the narrative development of the novel in which they appear (for example, to see in **"My Beth"** a prediction of the action of the following chapters), since this is exactly the kind of circular logic that Fredric Jameson decries as naive reading. This type of interpretation, in the end, provides an overly neat diagnosis of the character and the novel (as, for example, closeted), a reading that is not much less limiting than the seemingly happy resolution of Jo's old maidenhood.

A poem in a novel is a little like Dickinson's bird in the pound—it is similarly disobliged to respect the boundaries of that form. *This* is how the novel teaches us to read: even if the March girls are framed by a marital story, it remains the case that we, as readers, are not bound by the same contract that binds the characters in the novel to marital resolution. Catherine R. Stimpson writes:

> Generations of female readers, lucky enough to have books, have maneuvered themselves around Alcott's most obviously constrictive maneuvers. They have con-

tinued to tutor themselves in unfeminine will through choosing which parts of *Little Women* and which Jo they will imitate, or, at the very least, find enchanting. Recidivists of reading, they return again and again to the far naughtier beginning and middle of the narrative. . . . For a female reader, then, much of the joy of *Little Women* exists because one part of the text encourages rebellion. When the novel falls into parts, she can choose which part to love.[30]

As these readers fall into a poem (to invoke Roland Barthes), they confound "the *moral unity* that society demands of every human product."[31]

And so it is not only Jo's mannishness that makes her a lesbian character, and not simply her desire for a girl—or even the narrative of the closet that the novel, on one level, offers us. Instead, it is our desire, as readers, for Jo's desire, and our willingness to get stuck—to forget the end, and the name of the man Jo marries, and to remember that she cut her hair off, that she slouches and swaggers, that she cannot sit still, and that she wants to marry her sisters. What makes *Little Women* a lesbian novel is the degree to which it works up an awareness of the problem of telling a story about making a girl into a lesbian. The reader of this story must have a different, more imaginative, kind of attention.

Little Women is perhaps more influenced by John Bunyan's *Pilgrim's Progress* (1678)—the book from which Alcott draws the novel's epigraph—than we have been willing to admit. For where that manual for good Christian behavior instructs its readers in the saintly way, *Little Women* encourages its readers to wander off the path. Alcott prefaces her novel with these words, adapted from Bunyan's work: "Go then, my little Book, and show to all / . . . / What thou dost keep close shut up in thy breast; / . . . / Tell them of Mercy . . . / . . . / Yea, let young damsels learn of her to prize / The world which is to come . . ." (*Little Women*, p. xxxv). While from one perspective (the same one that sees Jo off to marriage) the "world which is to come" is the afterlife awaiting good Christian girls, from another perspective that world is our own, the time and the place of *Little Women*'s readers—women like Simone de Beauvoir, M. Carey Thomas, and the members of Split Britches, a world populated, in other words, by the women that the novel seems to be waiting for.

The poems **"My Beth"** and **"In the Garret"** perform a dual function: they mark those points in the plot where Jo March's story turns away from homoerotic attachment and toward heterosexuality, and at the same time they exceed their function within the plot (as elegies, as signposts) in order to become queer details that carry the novel's lesbian possibilities to the reader—to that reader already reading against the grain.[32] Jo March's poems wire the novel's ideological conflicts into the book's formal structure. They mark off the distance in the novel between what the novel itself says and what it does, even in the tension between the poems' melancholic, anti-domestic function and their aggressively sentimental and regimented structure.

Homosexual desire therefore emerges in *Little Women* as a distinctly *literary* possibility—as a potential immanent to the gap between one reading practice and another. Lesbian attachment adheres to a writing and reading practice whose force lies outside the boundaries of the novel's plot, but, importantly, not outside the domain of the possible. Lesbian desire is produced as, and through, over-reading, through an aggressive interpretation—a reading for the thing that you cannot get if, as Judith Halberstam implies, "family time" is the only time by which you read the novel—for, in such a story, all the reader sees are sisters. (The only time I have ever encountered overt homophobia in teaching a course on literature and sexuality has been in resistance to reading this novel queerly, and that homophobia presented itself as a self-righteous horror of incest.) Lesbian reading produces the thing that no one actually *in* the novel seems to get—except, perhaps, Beth, and in her case that moment of understanding is the event that triggers her evaporation from the narrative in a crisis that we might reconsider as less a dead end than an escape hatch. (At the very least, her death allows Beth to become more than a sister to Jo, and creates a hole that the reader might imagine herself as filling.)

In an essay on form and content in literature, Monique Wittig asserts:

> Any important literary work is like the Trojan Horse at the time it is produced. Any work with a new form operates as a war machine, because its design and its goal is to pulverize the old forms and formal conventions. . . . And the stranger it appears, nonconforming, unassimilable, the longer it will take for the Trojan Horse to be accepted. Eventually it is adopted, and, even if slowly, it will eventually work like a mine. It will sap and blast out the ground where it was planted. The old literary forms, which everybody was used to, will eventually appear to be outdated, inefficient, and incapable of transformation.[33]

As Wittig tells the story, the Trojan Horse is first met with suspicion—as strange and unfamiliar. Eventually it wins over an audience that, in taking in this new form, unknowingly sets into motion the destruction of old narrative forms and the circulation of new ideas. While Alcott's novel is an entirely different kind of Trojan Horse than that which Wittig images (one almost immediately embraced by its readers, one whose external form is instantly recognizable), it nonetheless fulfills its mission. A novel ahead of its time that formally layers one possibility inside another, *Little Women* is a war machine in petticoats: a book about the right girl in the wrong story.

Notes

1. For a comprehensive discussion of Alcott's importance to the articulation of lesbian identity in American literature, see Kathryn R. Kent, *Making Girls into Women: American Women's Writing and the Rise of Lesbian Identity* (Durham, N.C.: Duke Univ. Press, 2003), pp. 43-104.

2. In her autobiography, *Memoirs of a Dutiful Daughter,* Simone de Beauvoir names *Little Women* as the "one book" in which, through Jo, she "had caught a glimpse of [her] future self" (see Simone de Beauvoir, *Memoirs of a Dutiful Daughter,* trans. James Kirkup [Cleveland: World Publishing Co., 1959], p. 94). For the text of the play *Little Women,* see *Split Britches: Lesbian Practice/Feminist Performance,* ed. Sue-Ellen Case (London and New York: Routledge, 1996), pp. 119-48.

3. See M. Carey Thomas, *The Making of a Feminist: Early Journals and Letters of M. Carey Thomas,* ed. Marjorie Housepian Dobkin (Kent, Ohio: Kent State Univ. Press, 1979), p. 38. Thomas made only a few entries in 1870. On 1 January 1871 she tried again, making the following promise: "JOURNAL KEPT BY JO MARCH, COMMENCED JAN. 1 WITH THE FIXED DETERMINATION NOT TO LET IT DROP BUT CONTINUE IT UNTIL JAN. 1872. AIM TO BE A WORTHY MEMBER OF THE S.S.S. MOTTO: 'PRIMUS LUDUS, SUPREMUS LUDUS, SEMPER LUDUS'"; the Latin translates roughly as: "Fun first, last, and always" (*Making of a Feminist,* p. 46).

4. Louisa May Alcott, *Little Women,* ed. Elaine Showalter (New York: Viking Penguin, 1989), p. 3. Further references are to this edition and appear in the text.

5. See Adrienne Rich, "Compulsory Heterosexuality and Lesbian Existence," *Signs,* 5 (1980), 649.

6. James Creech explores similar questions around Melville's *Pierre* (1852) and *Billy Budd* (first published 1920). See Creech, *Closet Writing/Gay Reading: The Case of Melville's "Pierre"* (Chicago: Univ. of Chicago Press, 1993), especially "Textual Cruising," pp. 93-155. See also Richard Dyer, "Believing in Fairies: The Author and The Homosexual," in *Inside/Out: Lesbian Theories, Gay Theories,* ed. Diana Fuss (New York and London: Routledge, 1991), pp. 185-201. In this essay Dyer explores this issue—how much sexual identity matters, and how to teach queer texts while respecting the fluidity and complexity of identity—in relation to film.

7. See Judith Halberstam, *In a Queer Time and Place: Transgender Bodies, Subcultural Lives* (New York: New York Univ. Press, 2005), p. 5.

8. See Halberstam, *In a Queer Time and Place,* pp. 10-11. Halberstam arrives at her formulation of queer temporality in part by working through two studies: Michel Foucault, *The History of Sexuality, Volume 1: An Introduction,* trans. Robert Hurley (New York: Vintage, 1978); and Stephen M. Barber and David L. Clark, "Queer Moments: The Performative Temporalities of Eve Kosofsky Sedgwick," in *Regarding Sedgwick: Essays on Queer Culture and Critical Theory,* ed. Barber and Clark (New York and London: Routledge, 2002), pp. 1-53.

9. Fredric Jameson, *Marxism and Form: Twentieth-Century Dialectical Theories of Literature* (Princeton: Princeton Univ. Press, 1971), p. 341.

10. See Sedgwick, *Epistemology of the Closet* (Berkeley and Los Angeles: Univ. of California Press, 1990); and Miller, *The Novel and the Police* (Berkeley and Los Angeles: Univ. of California Press, 1988).

11. Jameson in fact holds up Foucault as an exemplary dialectical historian (see *Marxism and Form,* p. 320).

12. For a particularly strong example of new historical approaches to Alcott, see Glenn Hendler, "The Limits of Sympathy: Louisa May Alcott and the Sentimental Novel," *American Literary History,* 3 (1991), 685-706. Kathryn Kent's work on Alcott in *Making Girls into Women* also borrows from new historicism; other examples include Elizabeth Young, *Disarming the Nation: Women's Writing and the American Civil War* (Chicago: Univ. of Chicago Press, 1999); and Karen Halttunen, "The Domestic Drama of Louisa May Alcott," *Feminist Studies,* 10 (1984), 250. Psychoanalytic approaches to literature do figure in Alcott criticism, but not as a way to explore the poetics of her writing (as is the case for Lacanian readings of literary figures such as Henry James)—these approaches to Alcott's writing focus instead on narrative and character development, on the development of Alcott herself as a writer, and on the relevance of these subjects to feminist criticism. For one of the most interesting examples of this approach, see Ann B. Murphy, "The Borders of Ethical, Erotic, and Artistic Possibilities in *Little Women,*" *Signs,* 15 (1990), 562-85. Kent and Murphy both offer cogent overviews of Alcott criticism. For a thorough bibliography of Alcott criticism, see Beverly Lyon Clark and Linnea Hendrickson, "Selected Bibliography of Alcott Biography and Criticism," in Little Women *and the Feminist Imagination: Criticism, Controversy, Personal Essays,* ed. Janice M. Alberghene and Beverly Lyon Clark (New York: Garland Publishing, 1999), pp. 381-420.

13. Barbara Sicherman and Elaine Showalter both take up the appeal of the novel to feminists: see Sicherman, "Reading *Little Women*: The Many Lives of a Text," in *U.S. History as Women's History: New Feminist Essays,* ed. Linda K. Kerber, Alice Kessler-Harris, and Kathryn Kish Sklar (Chapel Hill: Univ. of North Carolina Press, 1995), pp. 245-66, 414-24; and Showalter, "*Little Women*: The American Female Myth," in her *Sister's Choice: Tradition and Change in American Women's Writing: The Clarendon Lectures, 1989* (Oxford: Clarendon Press, 1991), pp. 42-64, 183-85.

14. See Fetterley, "*Little Women*: Alcott's Civil War," *Feminist Studies,* 5 (1979), 369-83; rpt. in Little Women *and the Feminist Imagination,* pp. 27-62.

15. Glenn Hendler, in "The Limits of Sympathy," also takes up Alcott's interest in imitation and theatricality (though not with an eye toward the homoerotics of such passages).

16. Gustavus Stadler explores the intensity and erotics of Alcott's representation of the writing process (see Stadler, "Louisa May Alcott's Queer Geniuses," *American Literature,* 71 [1999], 657-77).

17. Louisa May Alcott, letter to Elizabeth Powell, 20 March 1869, in *The Selected Letters of Louisa May Alcott,* ed. Joel Myerson and Daniel Shealy, assoc. ed. Madeleine B. Stern (Boston: Little, Brown, and Co., 1987), p. 125. Roberta Seelinger Trites cites this letter in her "'Queer Performances': Lesbian Politics in *Little Women,*" in Little Women *and the Feminist Imagination,* p. 141. Trites's essay offers one of the most cogent overviews of feminist responses (phobic and progressive) to lesbianism in Alcott's writing, as well as a thorough review of the lesbian plots and themes in *Little Women.*

18. This title for "Book Two" was given by Alcott's publishers in England.

19. Ann Murphy, "The Borders of Ethical, Erotic and Artistic Possibilities in *Little Women,*" pp. 563-64. In this essay Murphy offers a cogent summary and analysis of debates about the book's feminism (as well as a reading of the novel itself).

20. Trites sketches the harmony between this moment in the novel and Terry Castle's writing on haunting and lesbian desire in the novel (see "Queer Performances," pp. 148-50).

21. George E. Haggerty, "Love and Loss: An Elegy," *GLQ* [*: A Journal of Lesbian and Gay Studies*], 10 (2004), 387.

22. Judith Butler, "Imitation and Gender Insubordination," in *Inside Out: Lesbian Theories/Gay Theories,* p. 26. Butler famously expands on these issues in her *Gender Trouble: Feminism and the Subversion of Identity* (New York and London: Routledge, 1990).

23. Judith Butler also explores this issue in her "The Force of Fantasy: Feminism, Mapplethorpe, and Discursive Excess," *differences,* 2, no. 2 (1990), 105-25.

24. In his work on genius, writing, and Alcott, Gustavus Stadler explores the intimacy of the association between Beth and writing—it is around Beth's consumption that Jo, in fact, publishes her first novel, under her own name. Stadler writes: "Not only does Beth encourage Jo's efforts throughout the novel with exhortations like, 'You're a regular Shakespeare, Jo!' but it is finally the force of Beth's illness that leads Jo to send the manuscript of her novel out to be published" ("Louisa May Alcott's Queer Geniuses," p. 671). Stadler quotes Beth pleading with her sister: "I should so like to see it printed *soon*" (see *Little Women,* p. 270).

25. I thank Alex Wescott for pointing out the importance of this scene, in which Jo promises to Laurie: "We'll never draw that curtain any more, and I give you leave to look as much as you like" (*Little Women,* p. 50).

26. Here we have an inversion of what Michael Fried calls an *allegorie réel* in painting—in which an artist represents for the spectator aspects of the work's production, often mirroring the act of painting in order to place the spectator into an analogous relation to the canvas. In the case of *Little Women,* however, it is not the act of writing but the act of reading that is mirrored for a reading public. See Michael Fried, *Manet's Modernism; or, The Face of Painting in the 1860s* (Chicago: Univ. of Chicago Press, 1996).

27. See Teresa de Lauretis, "Film and the Visible," in *How Do I Look?: Queer Film and Video,* ed. Bad Object-Choices (Seattle: Bay Press, 1991), p. 232.

28. Here de Lauretis works through Jean Laplanche and Jean-Bertrand Pontalis's theory of fantasy and subject formation. See Jean Laplanche and J.-B. Pontalis, "Fantasy and the Origins of Sexuality" (1964), in *Formations of Fantasy,* ed. Victor Burgin, James Donald, and Cora Kaplan (London and New York: Methuen, 1986), pp. 5-34.

29. Emily Dickinson, poem 613 (c. 1862), in *The Complete Poems of Emily Dickinson,* ed. Thomas H. Johnson (Boston: Little, Brown, and Co., 1960), p. 302.

30. Stimpson, "Reading for Love, Canons, Paracanons, and Whistling Jo March," *New Literary History,* 21 (1990), 969-70.

31. Roland Barthes, *The Pleasure of the Text,* trans. Richard Miller (New York: Hill and Wang, 1975), p. 31. Stimpson cites this passage in "Reading for Love," p. 970.

32. And just as the odd relationship of the poems to the narrative framework within which they appear allegorizes the angled relationship of reader to text, so too they formally embody the methodological shift "from text to the drama between text and reader" that defines much feminist criticism—and that defines especially feminist criticism about this novel as it has struggled to reconcile the story with its audience. See Stimpson, "Reading for Love," p. 962.

33. Monique Wittig, "The Trojan Horse" (1984), rpt. in her *The Straight Mind and Other Essays* (Boston: Beacon Press, 1992), pp. 68-69.

Sara Hackenberg (essay date June 2008)

SOURCE: Hackenberg, Sara. "Plots and Counterplots: The Defense of Sensational Fiction in Louisa May Alcott's 'Behind a Mask.'" *American Transcendental Quarterly* 22, no. 2 (June 2008): 435-51.

[*In the following essay, Hackenberg addresses themes of female empowerment, social reform, and cultural progress in Alcott's 1866 novella "Behind a Mask." Hackenberg contends that the work's sensational style reflects the author's preoccupation with the transformative power of female creativity.*]

Louisa May Alcott is now well known for having led a sensationally double literary life: the author of the demure **Little Women** was also the author—anonymously and pseudonymously—of such thrillers as **"A Marble Woman; or, The Mysterious Model," "V. V.: or, Plots and Counterplots,"** and **"Behind a Mask; or, A Woman's Power."** Of all of Alcott's many potboilers, her four-part novella **"Behind a Mask"** has received perhaps the most contemporary critical attention. Madeline Stern and other critics have pronounced **"Behind a Mask"** Alcott's "most extraordinary" story; Elaine Showalter has hailed the tale as the "most skillful" of the lot; and, since the story's twentieth-century republication, a number of persuasive and contrasting positions have been taken regarding the motivations, limitations, and powers of the story's remarkable heroine, Jean Muir.[1]

Jean Muir captures critical attention largely for her entertaining and protean abilities to operate behind an extraordinary variety of masks. She initially appears in **"Behind a Mask"** as a sweet, wan nineteen-year-old Scottish governess who, newly arrived at her post in the sylvan English countryside with the titled Coventry family, proves well able to delight her employers with her graceful attentions and abilities. By the end of the first chapter of the story, however, the reader discovers a radically different view of the governess. Alone in her room, as she takes off makeup and false hair, Jean's "mobile features settled into their natural expression, weary, hard, bitter," and she is revealed to be "a haggard, worn, and moody woman of thirty at least" rather than the guileless ingénue she initially seems (12). As this opening transformation suggests, Jean is a consummate master of disguise with a troubled past. She is also an impressive master-observer who uses the details she discerns in her new environment to both play to the patrician family she serves and to skillfully "play" them, manipulating them to achieve her own ends. As Jean beguiles both the widowed Mrs. Coventry and her young charge Bella, she also effortlessly enthralls the family's two sons, Ned and Gerald. Her many poses—noble but destitute orphan, world traveler, horse-tamer, accomplished nurse, wronged victim, humble servant, romantic heroine, and, in an evening of *tableaux vivants* entertainment, alternately a damsel in distress and the Virgin Queen—drive both sons to distraction, and they fall madly in love with her (the younger, Ned, even attempting fratricide in a moment of desperate jealousy). Jean's rousing of the Coventry men, however, does not stop with the two brothers; she also works her artful charms on the family's wealthy, unmarried uncle, Sir John Coventry, who lives in the great manor house nearby. Sir John, as captivated as the rest by the accomplished actress, becomes Jean's final conquest. By the time the two duped brothers come to their senses and discover the scandalous history of the "real" Jean, it is simply too late. In the closing scene of the story, Jean triumphantly reveals to the family her ultimate metamorphosis: no longer a lowly governess, she has become the proud, newly-married Lady Coventry.

Most critics of **"Behind a Mask"** attend closely to the tale's radical gender and class dynamics: the way Alcott overtly aligns operating behind a mask with female power; the way Jean's many masquerades serve to expose readers to the idea that "natural" womanly tendencies to nurture, or to be modestly self-effacing, might simply *be* acts; the way working-girl Jean is well able to manipulate her powerful, moneyed employers and inexorably achieve her class-aspirant goals. Many critics also note, however, that Jean's final transformation into the role of wife to Lord Coventry potentially problematizes the story's radical message. For while Jean's assumption of the title "Lady Coventry" does help destabilize certain class biases such as the idea of aristocratic birth-privilege (an idea most of the other characters in the tale unthinkingly endorse), her marriage to Sir John also places her squarely in the position of sanctioning the hierarchical class entitlement that her earlier actions worked to critique. Additionally, the fact that the governess's ultimate ambition, despite all her formidable powers of artistry and perception, is to "trick" a man into marriage serves to affirm the idea that a woman's highest achievement—the goal towards which she should direct all her powers—is her marital status. Moreover, readers are explicitly assured at least three times in the tale that Jean, after her marriage, will permanently change her delightfully devious ways and spend the rest of her life as a true domestic angel, quietly and selflessly serving her lord: an uneasy ending for a story that has, up to the end, exposed angelic, domestic female behavior to be a diabolically manipulative, self-interested performance.[2]

With Jean's final unsettling transformation in mind, I propose a reading of **"Behind a Mask"** that, among other things, can allow for a smoother reconciliation of the story's end with the substance of its whole. Keeping in sight the ways in which gender and class operate in the tale, I consider how the story can be read as a complicated and allegorical meditation on storytelling itself. If we attend not just to the tale's depiction of a powerful female character (an extraordinary actress engaged in class and gender warfare) but also to the story's powerful, if masked, commentary on the influences, pleasures, and uses of different kinds of fiction, we discover another important facet of Alcott's radical politics. Jean Muir can be seen both as a psychologically complex character and as a kind of metafictional allegory: her sensationally "masked" character, as she enters and stirs up the Coventry household, can be seen to figure the new, sensational fictions that were infiltrating, disturbing, and titillating households of all stripes in 1860s America and England.

Alcott herself, at the time of composing **"Behind a Mask,"** was acutely aware of the powers, pleasures, and perils of writing sensational fiction. One of the pleasures of such literary production was certainly pecuniary: in 1863, she was delighted to earn a cool hundred-dollar prize for her story **"Pauline's Passion and Punishment,"** and throughout the 1860s her experiments with sensational fiction provided significant financial support for both herself and her family. Yet her engagement with such stories extended beyond fiscal rewards into an enthusiasm for and pleasure in the genre itself: she once told an interviewer that her "natural ambition" was "for the lurid style"; she observed in a journal entry how much she "enjoy[ed] romancing to suit [her]self"; she entertained the idea that such writing could be "good drill for fancy and language"; and the exultant verve and swagger with which she spun out her many "blood and thunder" tales is undeniable.[3]

As much, however, as Alcott might have enjoyed both concocting and earning from her exciting and "lurid" inventions, she also clearly acknowledged such fiction's dangerously risqué and déclassé status. As with most of her sensational thrillers, she carefully wrote **"Behind a Mask"** under a pseudonym while she simultaneously worked on the more "respectable" fiction to which she put her real name. Given that **"Behind a Mask"** was published just two years before *Little Women* catapulted the name Louisa May Alcott into a kind of wholesome household word, it is tempting to read the story the way Stern persuasively has, as a kind of dark literary watershed for Alcott: a tempestuous fictional purging of "many of the elements"—frustrations, difficulties, hardships—"that had gone into the life of its author"; a "gothic *roman à clef*" in which "the future author of *Little Women* sits for a dark but revealing portrait" (xvii-xviii). I suggest, however, that we might find in **"Behind a Mask"** not just a reflection of Alcott's own particular, complicated psyche, but also a compelling celebration of the complicated psychological effects sensation fiction might have on its writers and readers more generally. At the heart of the story's class and gender politics we find an allegorized battle of the books: one in which the "sensation" genre, a fictional mode largely seen as working-class and predominantly disparaged by critics of the time, serves to reinvigorate and significantly transform the "establishment" from within as it simultaneously works to energize its readers and empower its writers. **"Behind a Mask"** can be read as a parable that dramatizes the controversial emergence of sensation fiction on the mid-century literary scene and, in the end, champions its rather disreputable but seductively powerful arrival.

My allegorical reading of **"Behind a Mask,"** therefore, positions the story as a defense of sensational fiction. This defense begins with the story's opening lines, in which the old order—the "high culture" establishment—is succinctly exposed as smugly complacent, enervated, and rather useless. The first paragraphs of the tale present the reader with a concise summation of some of the stereotypical foibles of the entitled class: we meet a self-centered "peevish" hypochondriac (Mrs. Coventry); a languid, indolent young man (Gerald Coventry); and an offensively haughty and dismissive young woman (Lucia, the cousin and intended wife of Gerald) (3). All except the youngest Coventry sibling, Bella, are dismayed by the thought of the disruption (or "infliction," as Gerald puts it) of the new presence, in the form of Bella's governess, about to enter their family circle (3). Bella, however, who as a young, impressionable girl is the family member who would be associated most immediately with enthusiasm for distracting new sensations, professes only eagerness for Jean's imminent arrival, declaring "I've no doubt we shall be glad to have her, it's so dull here just now" (3-4).

Bella's optimistic anticipation of new excitement is soon rewarded: Jean's dramatic appearance swiftly disrupts the family discussion. Because Gerald, in his careless indolence, neglected to order a carriage for her,

Jean has been forced to walk to the house with all her belongings. Upon arriving, she pauses theatrically on the threshold before entering the room where the family waits. As she looks in on them, "cast[ing] a keen glance that impressed them curiously" before dropping her eyes and bowing to the family, the stage is set: this governess, like her almost-namesake Jane Eyre, will be a cogent observer of the domestic scene. Unlike Jane Eyre, however, who as a governess remains a quietly unobtrusive observing presence, Jean shortly proves to be both a canny observer *and* a fully active instigator of the story's unfolding events. Not willing, like Jane, to primarily pose as the recording agent of the story, a chronicler whose actions are largely reactions to the tale's turns of events, Jean is unmistakably a skilled and practiced actor who, from the moment she enters the Coventry household, blatantly seizes control of the narrative. As Lucia perceptively notes towards the end of the story, Jean's "art is wonderful": it is so ingenious that Lucia "cannot explain or detect it" except to sit by and powerlessly observe "the working of events which her hand seems to guide" (87).

While Lucia's assessment of Jean's artful powers comes late in the tale, we can see Jean's masterful abilities to set a plot in motion clearly demonstrated in the story's opening chapter. This chapter (as Alcott's choice of "Jean Muir" for her governess's name might immediately suggest) refers closely to Brontë's famous rags-to-riches novel: Christine Doyle and others have noted the many parallels between the opening scene of **"Behind a Mask"** and *Jane Eyre*, from Gerald's echo of Blanche Ingram's "aversion to the whole tribe" of governesses to Jean's physical echo of Jane as a "pale-faced girl in her plain black dress" with "irregular, but very expressive features" (3, 6). Alcott, however, both repeats and significantly revises Brontë's text in her story's opening. Unlike Jean Muir, Jane Eyre does eventually find herself collected from the train station in a carriage, and when she arrives at Thornfield Hall she is immediately and respectfully attended to by Mrs. Fairfax, who leads her to the fire, orders ample food and drink, and allows her to retire to her bedroom in short order. Jean, conversely, not only has to walk from the train station, but her fatigued arrival is greeted with no rest or refreshment; rather, she is promptly "catechized" as to her instructional abilities and then asked to put them into instant practice (5). In short, Jean must immediately perform for her employers, and the impressive alacrity with which she responds to this demand shows just how able she is to seize control of and substantially modify the operating story.[4]

Jean's first performance both disarms and charms her audience. Upon informing Mrs. Coventry that she is indeed "fitted to teach music, French, and drawing," she demonstrates her musical abilities, and the power of her playing utterly ensnares the family's attention. "Miss Muir," Alcott writes, "played like one who loved music and was perfect mistress of her art"; she "charmed them all by the magic of [the] spell" of her playing, so that "even indolent Gerald sat up to listen, and Lucia put down her needle, while Ned watched the slender white fingers as they flew, and wondered at the strength and skill which they possessed" (6-7). At the close of this spellbinding performance, Bella immediately "pleads" for another. Jean's obliging song is not only as potent as her playing, but it also brings the family to tears, being "so sweet, so sad, that the girl's eyes filled, and Mrs. Coventry looked for one of her many pocket-handkerchiefs" (7). However, Jean soon cuts her engrossing song abruptly short by staging a third performance, in which she melodramatically compels the family to attend to their inconsiderate neglect of her wellbeing. Like a proper romantic heroine, she suddenly and dramatically falls into a fainting fit mid-song, and as she lies "before the startled listeners, as white and rigid as if struck with death," the family springs into action: Ned, Bella, Lucia, Mrs. Coventry, and finally even Gerald, who in doing so demonstrates a new "unwonted energy," all leap to the governess's aid (7). Even as Gerald clearly recognizes Jean's collapse as a constructed performance—"Scene first, very well done," he whispers to Lucia (a comment Jean both hears and openly acknowledges, replying "Thanks. The last scene shall be still better.")—he finds himself experiencing a brand "new sensation, indefinable, yet strong" as for "the first time in his life" he "looked abashed" at his insolent words and indolent inaction (7).

With these three opening performances, Jean sets a counterplot in motion that quickly takes over the story: this will not be a tale, as the initial setup seems to suggest, about a family that endures the presence of an interloping governess, but rather a story about a family that finds itself in continual, fascinated reaction to the intriguing performances of a new teacher. Jean's performances clearly demonstrated the rather pedagogical nature of her machinations: she acts both to achieve her own ends *and* to teach this family new, important lessons in ways that reflect and extend her extremely competent work as governess to Bella. Jean realizes her transformative work on herself and on the Coventry family, moreover, as much through her considerable skills at storytelling as through her abilities at acting. Although Jean's status as a mesmerizing performer remains a central and crucial element of the story, it is also clear that under the governess's powerful mask lurk the figures of both an actress *and* a writer. From her initial pronouncement that she is a nineteen-year-old orphan to her invention of an aristocratic mother, we find Jean's masquerades most often effected simply through the stories she tells. Her skills at weaving plots, creating suspense, and telling tales work to fashion her into a surrogate for the sensational fiction writer. Indeed, Lucia observes that Jean's power lies more in her abilities at master-plotting than in her skill at dissembling: Jean's *hand,* according to Lucia, is the force guiding the events of the story. Jean's "slender white fingers," which Ned so admires initially for their "strength and skill," will, as the story progresses, essentially re-write each character in ways that alter them forever.

The first chapters of **"Behind a Mask"** move conspicuously between Jean's manipulation of the poetics of theater to those of story-weaving. After the fainting fit in the first chapter, for instance, Gerald not only notes Jean's facility with scene-making, but also likens her explicitly to a romantic, mysterious tale. As her performances make him suspect that she might be "at the bottom" of the "mystery" of his friend Sydney, the son of the family she previously served, who has "not been himself lately," Gerald accordingly decides to try to find out more of the story, remarking "I rather like romances in real life, if they are not too long, or difficult to read" (9). He does in fact continually attempt to "read" Jean, a task she alternatively furthers and foils in ways designed both to pique and maintain his attention. At one point, when Gerald wonders, *sotto voce,* why Jean "didn't keep Sydney after she had caught him," she magically appears at his side to provide another piece of the story, murmuring "because she had the utmost contempt for a titled fool" (10). A little later, however, Jean deliberately leaves Gerald in unsatisfied narrative suspense in a move that clearly mimics the actual cliff-hanging structure of the serial format taken by **"Behind a Mask"** and many other sensational tales. The morning of her first day with the Coventry family finds Jean entertaining Lucia, Ned, and Bella at breakfast with her stories:

> Soon she put off her sad, meek air and entertained them with gay anecdotes of her life in Paris, her travels in Russia when governess in Prince Jermadoff's family, and all manner of witty stories that kept them interested and merry long after the meal was over. In the middle of an absorbing adventure, Coventry came in, nodded lazily, lifted his brows, as if surprised at seeing the governess there, and began his breakfast as if the ennui of another day had already taken possession of him. Miss Muir stopped short, and no entreaties could induce her to go on.
>
> (18)

Jean, like a good serialist, assures them all that "another time I will finish it, if you like," and Gerald, in spite of himself, finds he is hooked: "As he entered, he had caught a part of the story which Miss Muir had been telling, and it had excited his curiosity so much that he found himself wondering what the end could be and wishing that he might hear it" (18, 20). This instance not only underlines Jean's narrative prowess, but it also highlights her inimitable style: when Gerald attempts to fill in some of the narrative gaps by asking Lucia and

Ned for a repetition of Jean's tale, Ned replies "that is impossible," for Jean's "accent and manner are half the charm" (19).

Jean's narrative style and her talent for weaving suspenseful and sensational stories serve admirably to charm everyone around her. Indeed, "the very servants liked her," and unlike the plight of the common governess, who, as Alcott's narrator notes, is often "a forlorn creature hovering between superiors and inferiors," Jean swiftly becomes "the life of the house" (25). As a "romance" waiting to be read, a force that finds itself deploying, often in serial installments, myriad "absorbing adventures," and a presence that captures the interest of both masters and servants alike, Jean functions not only as a compelling "writer" of sorts but also as an embodiment of the sensation story itself—a widely popular mode of fiction in the 1860s that regularly infiltrated both upstairs and downstairs domestic spaces. Moreover, like the sensation story, Jean regularly triggers noticeable changes in those with whom she interacts. Her stories and performances "seemed to produce a change in everyone, though no one could have explained how or why" (25). When Jean is viewed as a sensational text, her effect of discernibly altering her audience can be seen as a realization of contemporary critics' concerns about the titillating nature of the sensation tale. The sensation story was named as such not just for its dramatic and sensational revelations, but also for the literal, physical changes—such as accelerated heartbeats, rapid breathing, and goosebumps—that it could provoke in readers. And certainly Jean is, like the sensation story, notable for both the physical and emotional sensations she creates. Her initial effect on Gerald, for instance, of causing him to feel "a new sensation, indefinable, yet strong," is repeated numerous times throughout the story: as he attempts to "read" her, her unexpected comments regularly leave him "looking as if he had received another sensation" and her very presence elicits a variety of intense bodily reactions, from striking him "dumb" to "electrify[ing]" him (10, 31, 45). Simply touching Jean's hands causes Gerald to experience a reaction that reads as much like a response to a sensational text as it does a symptom of attraction: "his heart beat quicker, his breath grew unequal, and a thousand fancies danced through his brain" (39). From the initial "excitement" she causes in the family to the "mortal fear" she sparks at the end, there is no situation in which Jean does not make a distinct physical and emotional impact on those around her (102).

That the sensation story could produce such marked physical reactions in readers, of course, was a central reason that the genre was considered to be risqué and disreputable. Ann Cvetkovich reminds us that some critics regarded such fictionally-inspired bodily sensations with deep suspicion, considering them addictive and dangerously able to provoke further unruly "appetites" and "cravings" for excitements (20). Cvetkovich observes that many critics feared that the sensation story's powerful physiological effects could reduce "its readers to the condition of animals who are driven by instincts," and she notes one critic's response to the genre's popularity was to deem it "a virus spreading in all directions" (14, 20). The sensation story seemed especially dangerous precisely *because* of its ability to provoke altered states, both physical and emotional: an ability some critics feared could lead to an entropic devolution or to a social disease that threatened both individual bodies and the culture as a whole.

In defiance of critical fears about the deleterious effects of such exciting physical sensations, Jean's "electrifying" presence turns out to be, on the whole, positive and empowering for the Coventrys. She not only continually provides comfort, pleasure, and engrossing entertainment for the family, but she also repeatedly spurs those around her into productive action. Her performances, plots, and manipulations, in fact, significantly work to transform her audience into more responsible and more fully-realized adults. Her stories are, at root, generative: they turn most members of her primary audience into storytellers themselves and they prompt revealing, life-changing moments of personal introspection. Moreover, Alcott seems to gesture allegorically not just towards critical anxiety about the stimulating effects of sensation fiction in general, but also to critical worries about the specifically gendered dynamics of such fiction. Some critics regarded sensation stories, notable for being created as often (if not oftener) by women as by men, as productions that threatened both to potentially feminize or emasculate readers and, more broadly, to destabilize gendered boundaries. As if Alcott is both soothing fears about the generally sexiness of sensation fiction and also working to quell specific anxieties about its gendered effects on readers, Jean's storytelling serves not only to empower herself but also to markedly "make a man" of Ned and Gerald, as, simultaneously, she substantially reinvigorates the boys' older, gout-suffering uncle (37). Jean emerges from **"Behind a Mask"** as an embodiment of a popular sensation text that, rather than working as a dangerous opiate that lulls its readers into an escapist stupor while reinforcing negative or entropic changes, instead serves to make readers "rather wider awake than usual" and more capable of energetic, creative, productive action than ever before (22).

We see some of the earliest and overall most pronounced generative effects of Jean's sensational "text" in its impact on Gerald, the heir presumptive of the Coventry establishment. Despite his indolence, Gerald suddenly finds himself in the story's opening being spurred by Jean's presence into narrative creativity as he begins to speculate about Jean's relationship to his friend Sydney. As Jean's various dramatic actions—

lively storytelling; rich singing; writing mysterious letters and then tearing them up; acting multiple roles in an evening of *tableaux vivants*—continue to leave Gerald "amazed," he finds his new "unwonted energy" steadily increasing (28-29). Jean entertains Gerald (he notes several times how her "piquant character" was powerfully able to "lighten his ennui" [41]) at the same time as she significantly reveals him to himself. At the end of the first installment of the story, she sharply calls his attention to his brother's welfare when Gerald begins to blame Jean for "allowing" Ned to fall in love with her (31). Responding to Gerald's complaint, Jean highlights the older brother's own neglected responsibilities for his sibling, especially his indolence in helping Ned attain an adult occupation. She asserts:

> If the 'romantic boy' had been allowed to lead the life of a man, as he longed to do, he would have had no time to lose his heart to the first sorrowful girl whom he pitied. Mr. Coventry, the fault is yours. Do not blame your brother, but generously own your mistake and retrieve it in the speediest, kindest manner.
>
> (31)

Jean's criticism of the Coventry heir provided the sensational cliffhanger on which the first installment of the story originally ended. The second installment opens with Gerald's startled reaction:

> For an instant Gerald sat dumb. Never since his father died had anyone reproved him; seldom in his life had he been blamed. It was a new experience, and the very novelty added to the effect. He saw his fault, regretted it, and admired the brave sincerity of the girl in telling him of it. But he did not know how to deal with the case, and was forced to confess not only past negligence but present incapacity.
>
> (31)

The "effect" of Jean's words not only provides Gerald with yet another new sensation but also echoes and extends the words of his late father in a way that reveals to young Coventry his own faults and limits. Jean's supplanting of the dead patriarch's voice, along with her re-telling of Ned's story, ultimately spurs Gerald to new and better actions. The second installment of the story sees Gerald quickly setting Ned up at last in an adult job by getting him a military commission. By the start of the third installment, Gerald himself follows suit, fully stepping into his own adult work as he attempts to take over his father's responsibilities on the estate. Declaring that he will finally start to "attend to things as a master should," he concludes that his "ambition" is "to be all that [his] father was" (69). Jean's most profound "sensational" effect on Gerald is to cause him to announce that he has, in "earnest" and "with a will," decided to start "going to work" for the first time in his life (69).

While Jean's positive, life-changing impact is perhaps most glaringly seen in Gerald's transformation, the other Coventry family siblings find themselves also beginning to exhibit, under the "magic of [Jean's] spell," new creativity and newly adult character traits. Bella, like Gerald, responds to Jean's stories and actions by demonstrating a writerly invention, declaring that Jean's provocative presence has caused her to have "imagined such a nice little romance about her" that Bella explicitly plans to articulate (21). Younger brother Ned, as he falls in love with the captivating governess, also finds himself a newly active reader/writer: as Jean "reads a fascinating novel in the most fascinating style," Gerald notes that "Ned makes himself the hero, Miss Muir the heroine, and lives the love scene with . . . ardor" (26-27). Later, Ned's newly awakened abilities at engaged reading spur his pursuit of other types of knowledge, such as can be seen in the "detective" work he performs that results in his discovery of the letters revealing Jean's scandalous past (103). Both the sensations of passion and of chagrin that Jean provokes in Ned finally serve to leave him far more "self-possessed" than ever before; her effect on him explicitly makes "a man of him" in the end (96).

Even elderly Sir John finds himself responding creatively and self-beneficially to Jean's manipulations. At first, like Bella, Gerald, and Ned, Sir John succumbs to the lure of suspense and takes to narrative invention, "puzzl[ing] his brains with conjectures" about Jean's mysterious past while remaining "quite unconscious that she intended he should do so" (24). Later, Sir John finds himself newly invigorated not just by his active musings about Jean but also by Jean's careful re-writing of his character: under her stimulating influence, the ailing peer becomes a romantic, chivalrous, and courtly knight errant. From the moment Jean meets him and coyly pretends not to know who he is, shyly admitting as if to a stranger that she has "heard so many beautiful and noble things" about Sir John that she not only "respect[s]" but "love[s]" him for his "virtue and bravery," Sir John, like Ned and Gerald, becomes a new man. While Jean can certainly be seen as a serial conqueror of men (Alcott in fact literally paces her story's serial installments such that in the first one Ned swoons for Jean, the second sees Gerald succumbing to her charms, and the third finds Sir John offering the governess her third marriage proposal of the tale), she also can be seen as serially plotting to create these men anew, transforming them into better, more vigorous, and more appealing characters.

Jean's predominantly positive, transformative, and strengthening effects on those around her form the core of Alcott's defense of sensational fiction in **"Behind a Mask."** Sensational storytelling, as Jean performs it, does important social work: it not only awakens individuals to newly energetic activity, but it also inspires readers to solve problems creatively and encourages them to embrace important responsibilities. Alcott's defense of the sensational story, however, also extends beyond this core to other potentially more ambiguous aspects of the tale. From Jean's rather vindictive desire to "humble" the Coventry family and wreak "revenge" on Gerald and Lucia, to the governess's final assumption of the role of Lady Coventry, Alcott sustains her playful, allegorical celebration of sensational fiction (98-99). Jean's vengeance and marriage refocus Alcott's defense, as the story turns from the effects of sensation fiction on individual readers towards an exploration of the potential positive impact sensation fiction might have on the literary establishment as a whole.

Despite the many positive, productive changes Jean inspires in individual members of the Coventry family, which together have the effect of strengthening the family unit, she is also at times a distinctly dangerous and potentially destructive force. Indeed, her dangerous and vindictive side surfaces strongly in her relationship with Gerald, a character who also clearly demonstrates her positive, generative impact. Jean not only awakens Gerald, transforming him from indolent boy to ardent, hardworking man, but she also repeatedly endangers his life and prospects. Over the course of the narrative, she triggers Ned's dramatic attempt at fratricide, her marriage to Sir John potentially disinherits Gerald, and the acute shame she visits on both Gerald and Lucia possibly destroys forever any union between them. However, Jean's destructive effects are in every case balanced by her redemptive energies. After Ned stabs Gerald because of Jean, for instance, she responds by single-handedly saving Gerald's life. Her various "punishments" of Gerald are, like the changes she wreaks on the family members in general, part of her work of unmaking and remaking the family anew, just as she unmakes and remakes the plot of the narrative. In the end, we can see Jean's "revenge" on Gerald and Lucia as part of the story's larger project of re-imagining the established order as more healthy, more responsible, more democratic, and less hypocritical than it first appears to be.

Jean's project of reinvigorating the family while simultaneously seeking to dismantle some of its unthinking entitlements and hypocrisies becomes clear in the fourth and final installment of the story, which largely consists of a series of letters Jean wrote to a supposed "accomplice," a friend named Hortense, about her experiences serving the Coventrys (97). In three startlingly candid letters, Jean re-plots the narrative yet again, weaving another version of the three serial installments that readers have already encountered of the story and explicitly exposing many of her machinations, strategies, and goals. Her first letter contains suppressed ire at her initial treatment by the family, as she confidently declares that she can and will destroy some of their aristocratic arrogance: she will work to "humble them all" and make them "atone" for their patronizing insolence and overweening self-importance (98). The second letter details how well she has been able to manipulate every member of the family, while the third specifically addresses her vengeance toward Gerald's "falseness" and Lucia's "pride." In this last letter, Jean makes clear her disdain at both Gerald's inconstancy and Lucia's "Vashti"-like refusal to perform or act on her powers (99). Jean's epistolary exultation in her own creative, narrative prowess—"I laugh at the farce and enjoy it," she gloats—highlights her goal of shaming Gerald and Lucia. "I only wait," she declares, "to turn and reject this lover [Gerald] who has proved himself false to brother, mistress, and his own conscience." Noting that her successful seduction of Gerald causes Lucia to suffer "the sharpest pain a proud woman can endure," Jean delights in the idea that her plan of rejecting Gerald will further intensify Lucia's pain: she "will feel another pang when I tell her that I scorn her recreant lover, and give him back to her, to deal with as she will" (101).

Jean's implacable desire to shame Gerald and Lucia—a desire attained, as upon hearing the contents of the letters, Gerald "flushed scarlet with shame and anger" and Lucia wept "as if the pang had been sharper than even Jean foresaw" (101-02)—might at first seem antithetical to Alcott's project of defending and celebrating sensational fiction. However, it is possible to see in Gerald and Lucia's punishment another example of the social work the sensation narrative might do by exposing cultural inequities and double standards. Although Jean styles herself at the end of her first letter "Lady Tartuffe," she emerges more as a Molière than a version of his fictional hypocritical servant, for her punishment of Gerald and Lucia serves to expose their own forms of hypocrisy rather than present Jean's performances in a negative light. Throughout the story, Jean's effect on Gerald is consistently both generative *and* critical: she both wakes Gerald up and exposes ways in which his aristocratic entitlement—his indolence, his callous rejection of Lucia, his reneging on his promise to Ned that he would leave Jean alone—makes him act dishonorably and even cruelly. Similarly, her punishment of Lucia works to expose the hypocritical double standards that women in the ruling classes of the nineteenth century were continually forced to navigate, and that, indeed, Jean repeatedly uses to her own advantage. Her performances reveal, again and again, that the mandate for maidenly chastity *demands* some art; she gleefully exploits the nineteenth-century paradox that "good" women were expected to be passive, modest, and self-effacing while at the same time their primary "job" was to display themselves and manipulate circumstances to attract a husband. Lucia's steadfast refusal to acknowledge this bind, and her refusal to acknowledge, as Jean does, that a "mask" is a central component of a woman's power, leaves her both open to Jean's scorn and, finally, hoist by her own petard when she sees Jean captivate Gerald. One can only hypothesize that, had Lucia been willing to abandon the pose of haughty "hand-some iceberg" or "fair icicle" and display some active writerly invention, plotting to revise the world around her instead of suffering through the machinations of others, she and Jean might have shared a sisterly relationship rather than an antagonistic rivalry (98-99).

As "Lady Tartuffe," Jean rails against the hypocrisy of the ruling classes, whose aristocratic privilege relies on both birth position as an indicator of social value and an impossible double standard for women. While Jean's punishment of Gerald exposes the brutishness of patriarchal power, her punishment of Lucia exposes not only the truth that women must perform to uphold social ideals, but also the idea that women should begin to use their performances to help themselves; that they in fact must act for themselves to gain power; that refusing to plot, play, or enter the fray perpetuates disempowerment and is finally detrimental to the culture as a whole. This idea further intensifies with several other "roles" Jean adopts in the course of the story, most notably the three poses she strikes during an evening of *tableaux vivants*. During this evening of theatrical play, which occurs in the exact center of the novella, Jean's masquerades each serve to underline the power and heroism in women's plotting as they also add new layers of complexity to Jean's embodiment of sensational narrative.

Jean's first *tableau* reveals a scene from the apocryphal biblical "Book of Judith." Striking a pose of triumphant, vindictive courage just after the act of beheading Holofernes, Jean-as-Judith is both almost unrecognizable and also closer to her own "truth" than in any other scene (51). In her second pose, which she performs with Gerald, Jean appears as a young Roundhead maiden in star-crossed love with a fugitive Cavalier. For the third *tableau* Jean is transformed yet again into a regal Queen Bess. Each of these three poses, read in the context of the allegorical defense **"Behind a Mask"** mounts, provides an illustration of the themes of the allegory as a whole: the precariousness of the established order, the heroic and transformative power of women's plotting, and the culturally beneficial ascendancy of the apocryphal or illegitimate. The first *tableau* presents a popular but explicitly non-canonical text that celebrates the heroism of a seductive woman's successful plan to save her people: the biblical story of Judith, despite being marginalized by the official religious canon, was widely known and deeply influential.[5] The second *tableau* depicts one of the most unstable times in the British monarchy, with Jean's character functioning both as a preserver *and* modifier of the existing order: as the Cavalier's lover, she plots to save her young Royalist, but as a Roundhead maiden, she joins the Parliamentarian movement that eventually led to the Cromwellian Republic. In the final *tableau,* Jean embodies a monarch famous both for being declared illegitimate and for "re-making" her country anew by ushering in the prosperous "golden age" of the English Renaissance.

Jean's various *tableaux* poses highlight her ability, first glimpsed in Gerald's recognition of his father's voice and authority in Jean's critique of his behavior, to simultaneously inhabit both the margins *and* the center of power. As Judith, she embodies a powerful but marginal or illegitimate narrative that relates the story of a culture's redemption and preservation; Judith sensationally casts a seductive, "fallen" woman as a culture hero. Jean's three poses, in fact, each echo her own character's role in **"Behind a Mask"** of a woman who uses her ability to plot and counterplot in order to save herself and her culture, or of a marginal figure who usurps the voice of the establishment and who finally becomes an integral component of the establishment. Indeed, along these lines, Jean's final metamorphosis into Lady Coventry is the final flourish of the story's allegorical work to defend the marginalized sensational narrative and to celebrate its authority and legitimacy. When we read **"Behind a Mask"** as a parable illustrating the positive effects of sensational fiction and the ways in which it can reinvigorate, renew, or "save" a moribund power, Jean's final act of marrying Sir John can be seen as an optimistic anticipation of the embrace of the sensational text by the establishment. Under the allegorical defense the story suggests, its potentially problematic ending vision of a maverick, powerful, marginal woman acquiescing to patriarchal ideals in exchange for a new social position can be recast into a more positive and playful literary suggestion: if we marry "dangerous" working-class sensation fiction to the established literary status quo, we will change both, irrevocably, for the better. Indeed, while Jean's letters (the final instance of her prowess as a storyteller, her ability to seize control of the narrative, and her inventive, continual writing and re-writing of the story) cause Mrs. Coventry to exclaim that she is "mortally afraid of this creature" and to wildly react "as if Jean Muir would burst in to annihilate the whole family," such terrified fears remain only a rather amusing holdover from a character who has, under Jean's influence, been rapidly abandoning her enervated and hypochondriac state (102). Rather than "annihilate" the old order, Jean's presence in **"Behind a Mask"** serves to transform and invigorate it.

Even in Alcott's most famous work, **Little Women,** sensational fiction functions as a materially and spiritually transformative, strengthening force. Despite the novel's ostensible echo of Mrs. Coventry's fears that writerly sensations—or sensational plots—are dangerously "inflammable," the writing of such fiction notably invigorates Jo March, the novel's most compelling heroine (346). Jo finds that writing such fiction both provides her family with needed income *and* importantly boosts her sense of accomplishment: she notes at one point

that "it was *so* pleasant to find that she had learned to do something, though it was only to write a sensation story" and she delights in the ways that "she began to feel herself a power in the house, for by the magic of a pen, her 'rubbish' turned into comforts for them all" as "*The Duke's Daughter* paid the butcher's bill, *A Phantom Hand* put down a new carpet, and the *Curse of the Coventrys* proved the blessing of the Marches in the way of groceries and gowns" (263-64). In the end, Jo's experience with writing sensational stories not only provides her significant material benefit but also allows her to design her own life positively: despite her eventual decision to cease writing such "rubbishy" stories, "while her pen lay idle, [Jo] was learning other lessons . . . and laying a foundation for the *sensation story of her own life*" (348, my italics). Instead of merely existing as "inflammable nonsense," then, these stories can be celebrated for centrally and positively contributing to the complex unfolding of women's "own lives."

Jean Muir can be seen as an allegorical predecessor of Jo: a character whose life indeed functions like and as a "sensation story." Through the pointed imagery in **"Behind a Mask"** that casts Jean as both sensational fiction writer and sensational text, Alcott constructs a powerful defense for sensational, thrilling narratives. **"Behind a Mask"** illustrates ways in which sensational plotting does powerful social work as it galvanizes individual creativity and energy, encourages new heights of productivity, exposes social hypocrisy, and works as a democratizing force. The image of sensational fiction embodied by Jean Muir is, in the end, not one of revolution but rather of reform. Alcott defends sensational fiction in **"Behind a Mask"** by figuring it as a delicious and necessary tonic: it will not destroy the canon but rather change it for the better; it can, in the end, help to save a culture.

Notes

1. See Madeline Stern's "Introduction" to *Behind a Mask: The Unknown Thrillers of Louisa May Alcott* (xvii) and Elaine Showalter's "Introduction" to *Alternative Alcott* (xxix). "Behind a Mask," one of over thirty sensational stories written by Alcott, was originally serialized in four parts in *The Flag of Our Union* between October 13 and November 3, 1866. Stern's 1975 *Behind a Mask* edition made the story newly available to twentieth-century readers; since then, the story has been reprinted numerous times in both print and electronic versions.

2. See Judith Fetterley for a reading of the story's feminist project of exposing the "cultural constructs of 'femininity' and 'little womanhood'" as "roles women must play" (2); Fetterley also observes that the tale "asserts that there is no honest way for a woman to make a living" and suggests

that, at the end, Jean's radically successful impersonations transform her into "the culture's ultimate monster" (2, 12). See also Mary Elliott's assertion that Jean Muir is a both "profoundly subversive" character and one who "takes what she must to survive" (300, 308). More recently, Theresa Strouth Gaul notes the "interpretive dilemma" posed by the end of the tale, and, though she resists such a reading, acknowledges the persuasive interpretation of Jean's marriage to Sir John—her final "inculcation into the privileged class system which has previously victimized her"—as "the ultimate indicator of her containment at the hands of patriarchy" (848, 845). Christine Butterworth-McDermott and Cheri Louise Ross likewise grapple with the story's alternating messages about "dangerous, independent . . . actresses who use their abilities to subvert the patriarchal order" and a "patriarchal society" which "in effect, forces women to live duplicitous lives because of the necessity of finding a husband to provide economic security" (Ross 913).

3. Stern and Christine Doyle, among many others, have noted Alcott's enthusiastic journal and interview observations about sensational fiction, as well as her designation of such stories as "blood and thunder" tales (Stern vii, xix, xxvi; Doyle 50-51).

4. Gerald's disparaging comment echoes Blanche Ingram in *Jane Eyre* when Blanche declares, referring to governesses: "I have just one word to say about the whole tribe; they are a nuisance" (151); also, in *Jane Eyre,* much is made of the "irregularity" of Jane's face, as well as its expressive nature (137). However, where Jane seeks to "see without being seen" (141) Jean most desires *to* be seen; her plotting is executed through her many performances and stories as well as her continual bewitching display of herself.

5. Mary Chapman argues that Jean's version of Judith is based on a popular nineteenth-century painting that recasts the story as a narrative of rape and revenge; this argument helps demonstrate how very well-known and culturally pervasive the apocryphal story of Judith was in the nineteenth century.

Works Cited

Alcott, Louisa M. "Behind a Mask: or, A Woman's Power." 1866. Rpt. in *Behind A Mask: The Unknown Thrillers of Louisa May Alcott.* Ed. Madeline Stern. New York: William Morrow, 1995.

———. *Little Women.* 1868. New York: Barnes & Noble Classics, 2004.

Brontë, Charlotte. *Jane Eyre.* 1847. Rpt. in *Jane Eyre: A Norton Critical Edition.* Ed. Richard J. Dunn. New York: Norton, 2001.

Butterworth-McDermott, Christine. "Behind a Mask of Beauty: Alcott's Beast in Disguise." *American Transcendental Quarterly* 18.1 (2004): 25-48.

Chapman, Mary. "'Living Pictures': Women and Tableaux Vivants in Nineteenth-Century American Fiction and Culture." *Wide Angle* 18.3 (1996): 22-52.

Cvetkovich, Ann. *Mixed Feelings: Feminism, Mass Culture, and Victorian Sensationalism.* New Brunswick, NJ: Rutgers U P, 1992.

Doyle, Christine. *Louisa May Alcott and Charlotte Brontë: Transatlantic Translations.* Knoxville, TN: U of Tennessee P, 2000.

Elliott, Mary. "Outperforming Femininity: Public Conduct and Private Enterprise in Louise May Alcott's 'Behind a Mask.'" *American Transcendental Quarterly* 8.4. (1994): 299-310.

Fetterley, Judith. "Impersonating *Little Women*: The Radicalism of Alcott's 'Behind a Mask.'" *Women's Studies: An Interdisciplinary Journal* 10:1. (1983): 1-14.

Gaul, Theresa Strouth. "Trance-Formations: Mesmerism and 'A Woman's Power' in Louisa May Alcott's 'Behind a Mask.'" *Women's Studies: An Interdisciplinary Journal* 32.7 (2003): 835-51.

Ross, Cheri Louise. "Louisa May Alcott's (Con)Temporary Periodical Fiction: The Thrillers Live On." *Journal of Popular Culture* 38.5 (2005): 911-23.

Showalter, Elaine. Introduction. *Alternative Alcott.* New Brunswick, NJ: Rutgers U P, 1988. ix-xliii.

Stern, Madeleine. Introduction. *Behind a Mask: The Unknown Thrillers of Louisa May Alcott.* New York: William Morrow, 1995. vii-xxxiii.

Lorinda B. Cohoon (essay date 2008)

SOURCE: Cohoon, Lorinda B. "'A Highly Satisfactory Chinaman': Orientalism and American Girlhood in Louisa May Alcott's *Eight Cousins*." *Children's Literature* 36 (2008): 49-71.

[*In the following essay, Cohoon explores themes of cultural assimilation and gender in Alcott's* Eight Cousins.]

Discussing her grandniece Rose in Louisa May Alcott's ***Eight Cousins*** (1875), Aunt Plenty declares to her nephew Alec, "I, for one, freely confess that I don't know what to do with her any more than if she was one of those strange, outlandish birds you used to bring home from foreign parts" (41). In its linking of "out-landish birds" and little girls and in juxtapositions that contrast Rose with objects from foreign lands and men from China, *Eight Cousins* registers Alcott's polyvalent and frequently duplicitous positions on cultural issues of women's rights and American attitudes toward immigrants. Both women and immigrants are "othered," in part because both are disenfranchised and less powerful than the white men who are able to vote, choose representatives, and occupy political positions.

Alcott's text also internalizes national responses both to increased immigration from China and also to the growing practice of American imperialism. During the last three decades of the nineteenth century, the United States made moves to gain economic and political control in China, the Philippines, and other areas of the South Pacific. Through a discussion of how "orientalism" operates in children's texts that focus on life in the United States, this essay investigates how depictions of Rose's encounters with foreign objects and others condition her to understand herself as both exoticized and superior. Both *Eight Cousins* and its sequel *Rose in Bloom* (1876) show female citizenship as a complex negotiation between partial assimilation and defiance of convention. By linking Rose with Chinese immigrants, Alcott's texts explore how the process of balancing individual desires and cultural requirements applies to the transition from girlhood to womanhood and the move from cultural other to assimilated citizen.[1]

By contextualizing the ways in which the orientalist and orientalizing positions of superiority function in *Eight Cousins,* modern critics can gain further insight into how Rose is constructed as both other and othering as she grows to womanhood within the Campbell family. The *Oxford English Dictionary Online* defines empire as "supreme and extensive political dominion," and while Rose is depicted as "outlandish" and the men from China are portrayed as "queer guest[s]" who are set apart from those born in New England, certainly the Campbell family struggles to make Rose a part of its "extensive" dominion (41, 79). In "Self, Other, and Other Self," Roderick McGillis provides a definition of "imperialist forces" and discusses how forces of empire function in children's literature: "'imperialist forces' are all those institutional powers (Ideological State Apparatuses) that either subtly or openly attempt to fashion the way we think and behave. These forces invade all facets of our experience, from our billboards to the rest of our media, including our children's books. Their design is to maintain conditions of power and authority" (216). McGillis goes on to note that stories for children often contain complex othering movements: "Even when the stories of one culture do not refer to other cultures, they implicitly maintain the fiction of one culture's superiority to another, one people's superiority to another people. Or do they? Might it not be

possible to argue that a culture's stories inevitably must present that very culture as 'other'?" (216). *Eight Cousins* is set in New England, and most of the interactions take place between characters who are members of the same family, yet this text explores how belonging to a family depends on submitting to its ways and customs—its culture.

ORIENTALISM IN CHILDREN'S LITERATURE

Orientalism highlights the superiority of the self through a variety of strategies. Alcott's text uses several orientalizing techniques, including repeating words like "outlandish," "queer," or "curious" to draw contrasts between the normative or ordinary self and the other. Additional strategies include exoticizing and eroticizing the other. In a study of how such comparisons can reinforce cultural hegemony, Edward Said writes: "Orientalism depends for its strategy on this flexible *positional* superiority, which puts the Westerner in a whole series of possible relationships with the Orient without ever losing him the relative upper hand" (*Orientalism* 7). These "possible relationships" do not refuse to admit a connection between the other and the self, but the "*positional* superiority" that the discourse emphasizes serves to keep the other from achieving equality while keeping the white Western self in a position of power. In repeated explorations of Rose's self, Alcott's text describes Rose as positionally superior both to other girls in her community and to those others whom she encounters. Uncle Alec strives to strengthen her "positional superiority" by taking steps to make her a strong girl and an exemplary specimen of a Campbell. As Rose's identity is being restructured so that she can become a viable contributor to the family and an exemplary model of girlhood, her physical and spiritual states are carefully regulated by her uncle. At several points, Alcott's story links Rose's girlhood to China, sometimes focusing on leisure activities of rummaging and exploring her family's collections of Chinese artifacts, and at other times on education and the ways citizenship and national identity are conveyed through social interactions, dress, and behavior. Young readers, positioned to identify with Rose, are then aligned with her positional superiority.

The connections between a text written for children about domestic issues of home and family, and concerns associated with American policies on immigration, trade relations with Asia, and expansion of territories in Asia and the Caribbean, might at first seem tenuous. However, scholars focusing on postcolonial politics and culture have argued that recognition of empire in ostensibly domestic texts is essential to an understanding of its influence on all aspects of culture. In a discussion of Jane Austen's references to empire in *Mansfield Park,* Said writes about how art and literature can be linked to politics that use depictions of orientalism to maintain superiority or to establish grounds for imperialist conquest. He argues that such references should be read as "not neutral (any more than class and gender are neutral) but as politically charged, beseeching the attention and elucidation its considerable proportions require" (*Culture and Imperialism* 93).

Following Said, I argue that it is critical to explore the non-neutrality of orientalizing perspectives in children's literature, and to consider their function in texts such as *Eight Cousins* which are often read as representations of the lives of white, middle-class girls and the private, domestic sphere. Amy Kaplan points out in "Manifest Domesticity" that "the development of domestic discourse in America is contemporaneous with the discourse of Manifest Destiny" (583). She notes that discussion encouraging the domestication of the foreign other was used to promote a careful regulation of "the threat of foreignness within the boundaries of the home" (589). Domestic texts like *Eight Cousins,* then, reference how national politics and domestic culture merge in discussions of how to "build" healthy women who will make healthy homes and nations. Reading Alcott's text with an awareness of the non-neutrality of references to China can offer ways to identify, challenge, and decenter the orientalist perspectives that Alcott's text both promotes and critiques.

The rhetoric of Alcott's depiction of Rose, with its emphasis on her exotic status and her place and usefulness to the Campbell family, can be compared to disenfranchising policies and rhetoric used by American and Chinese diplomats and politicians in the years preceding the Chinese Exclusion Acts. The presence of scenes depicting U.S. relations with China in texts provided to children indicates that stereotypes and negative images of China were widely circulated in the years that preceded their official institutionalization, when the first anti-Chinese immigration acts were passed in 1882 to limit the number of Chinese immigrants entering the United States. Scholars of immigration history and culture argue that nineteenth-century amendments to the Constitution worked to prevent recent immigrants from gaining citizenship rights even as they granted rights of citizenship to African Americans.[2] Examinations of how China and its citizens were presented to middle-class American readers of children's literature can provide twenty-first-century scholars with insight into how attitudes toward Chinese immigration and Chinese American citizenships were reinforced.[3]

During the 1870s, the United States was interested in China as a potential marketplace for exported goods, and also as a source of inexpensive labor for large-scale projects. In the aftermath of the Civil War, as Howard Zinn notes in *A People's History of the United States,* the "industrial and political elites of the North and South" used marginalized, working-class, and immigrant populations to support the economic growth and stability of those with power:

> They would do it with the aid of, and at the expense of, black labor, white labor, Chinese labor, European immigrant labor, female labor, rewarding them differently by race, sex, national origin, and social class, in such a way as to create separate levels of oppression, a skillful terracing to stabilize the pyramid of wealth.
>
> (247)

In the 1870s, then, the stability of the elite was built upon the oppression of racialized others. During these decades, the United States' relationship with China was heavily weighted to favor its own interests, and well-established views of American superiority made it easy to subsequently close the doors to Chinese immigrants and to limit imports that advanced China's economic interests.[4] Boston had a long history of trade with China, a relationship solidified in 1844 by Caleb Cushing's establishment of a treaty that gave American citizens the protection of U.S. law when they traveled in China. Boston, associated with the independence of the United States, also has one of the nation's oldest Chinatowns, so it is significant that *Eight Cousins* takes place just outside of that city, with the Campbell family import/export business based in its ports.

Exotic Objects and Exotic Rose

Eight Cousins demonstrates Alcott's familiarity with the attitudes of Western and American superiority that shaped the import/export industries of the port city of Boston. In "Between 'Crockery-dom' and Barnum," Ronald and Mary Saracino Zboray discuss Boston's Chinese Museum exhibition (1845-47), arguing that the China trade made Chinese culture part of the everyday objects Bostonians used in their homes.[5] China and objects from China appear throughout *Eight Cousins,* particularly in episodes that focus on defining Rose's identity through comparisons with foreign objects and people. The Campbells' ancestral home becomes the warehouse that "stores" Rose; the text's emphasis on the material goods the family has gathered through its business contributes to the feeling that Rose, as a newly orphaned child who has been left with "no home but . . . with her great aunts," is another collected object (1). Just as Rose is described as an "outlandish bird," the house is described as "odd," "mysterious," and full of "curiosities": "it was a capital old mansion, and was full of all manner of odd nooks, charming rooms, and mysterious passages. Windows broke out in unexpected places, little balconies overhung the garden most romantically, and there was a long upper hall full of curiosities from all parts of the world; for the Campbells had been sea-captains for generations" (2). As the only girl among the seven boy cousins, and as a "delicate" body that must be cared for and coaxed into "blossom," Rose is depicted as just as exotic as the objects the Campbells collect (294, 295).

The links between Rose and valuable objects are emphasized when the exotic artifacts of the Campbells' journeys are used in an attempt to divert her from her grief over her father's death: "Aunt Plenty had even allowed Rose to rummage in her great china closet,—a spicy retreat, rich in all the 'goodies' that children love; but Rose seemed to care little for these toothsome temptations" (2). Rose's lack of interest in the "goodies"— the material goods that have been acquired through her family's business concerns with China—is seen as a symptom of her fragility and a sign that she needs a change in how she is being raised. The text's references to "curiosities," "rummaging," and "spicy" goods from China connect the family's experiment with Rose to the goods they have imported and collected from foreign lands (2, 33, 37, 46, 50, 55). If Rose cannot appreciate the Campbell family's treasures and business acumen, then the wealth and power she will inherit at adulthood might never be used to maintain its shipping empire. Rose's ennui, her lack of engagement with her family's history and business, and her "differentness" can be read as a form of what Anne Anlin Cheng describes as "racial melancholia," or a "model of identity" that "affects both dominant white culture and racial others; indeed, racial melancholia describes the dynamics that constitute their mutual definition through exclusion" (xi). In both *Eight Cousins* and *Rose in Bloom,* Rose constructs herself in response to outsiders who are not like her; these encounters help her to organize an identity that becomes relatively stable by the end of *Rose in Bloom,* but only by throwing off the initial melancholia that afflicts her.

Details that reference China pervade the first episodes. When Rose hears Phebe, her aunts' maid, sing for the first time, she looks for birds in the china closet, but only sees the kissing swallows on her aunts' Canton china (4). The text links the breakable, precious china to the beautiful and unusual sounds she hears. Rose then hides in the china closet to prepare herself to face her cousins for the first time (11). She is allowed access to this protected space because she herself is considered fragile; in the closet, her body, like the china, is both protected and exoticized. Even the typically New England spaces of church and school admit and contain the exotic; cousin Will draws "sailors and Chinamen" on the cuffs of his shirt during church services (36). In this scene, and later in the text, the exotic is used to make church and school more engaging. Simultaneously, the "sailors and Chinamen" on his cuffs connect Will to the positions of agent and explorer, since the drawings are like tattoos that an explorer might bring home, while Rose's appearance in the china closet aligns her with the valuable and fragile objects, designed to be preserved and collected. As the story unfolds, her relationship to the foreign objects and people slowly changes.

Exposure to exotic goods and scenes becomes a significant part of Rose's new life. Her uncle's idea that new experiences will infuse Rose with a strength she lacks can be compared to the U.S.'s argument that participating in imperialist conquest will improve the robustness of the nation.[6] Significantly, however, the discourses of empire used in Alcott's text differ from those used in nineteenth-century commentaries about expanding the reach of American empire, which tended to focus on imperialism's benefits for white men. Alcott's emphasis on a strong girlhood, and Rose's various resistances to her family's control of her even as she submits to their projects, provide insights into how imperialism operates. In *Culture and Imperialism,* Edward Said notes that "[n]ever was it the case that the imperial encounter pitted an active Western intruder against a supine or inert non-Western native; there was *always* some form of active resistance, and in the overwhelming majority of cases, the resistance finally won out" (xii). Alcott's text records resistances and submissions to empire, especially in discussions of Rose's rebellions against her new regimen and later in scenes that discuss the immigrants from China who work in the Campbells' shipping business. While Rose refuses to enjoy her aunts' collections, she submits, reluctantly at first, and then eagerly, to the strategies for education and upbringing offered to her by her uncle and cousins; these strategies both set her apart as "exotic," in need of the "wisest, tenderest care" at the same time that they attempt to make her a more central part of the family as a "lovely and a noble woman" (294).

When her Uncle Alec, who is also a physician, discusses his plans with Rose, he explains how he has mined the East for "curiosities" that he hopes will help him to build a healthy relationship with his new charge: "Knowing that I was coming home to find a ready-made daughter, I picked up all sorts of odd and pretty trifles along the way, hoping she would be able to find something she liked among them all. Early to-morrow we'll have a grand rummage" (33). Like Native Americans who were given trinkets by explorers of the Americas, Rose is offered "odd and pretty trifles" in exchange for her full cooperation with Uncle Alec's system of healthy education.[7] Rose's uncle loosens the tight belts she wears, and insists that she eat "parritch" or oatmeal for breakfast in order to become a "true Scotchwoman" and as "well and strong" as her cousins (34).[8] Each change in Rose's routine is accompanied by promises of gifts that are associated with her uncle's trips to India and China. When she is coaxed with these "odd trifles," Rose submits readily to methods that her aunts and neighbors find unconventional.

Rose's "blooming" can be understood as a rejuvenation that occurs through encounters with "exotic" cultures, people, and objects (293). In effect, the descriptions of these encounters work as ethnographic accounts that infuse Rose with a sense of belonging, despite her orphan state. Writing about the rejuvenation effect, Christopher Douglas explains: "the ethnographic legacy in contemporary minority writing continues to produce the ambivalent effect of inscribing minorities into the national fabric but simultaneously rendering their cultural citizenship status questionable. Through this uncertainty, white cultural citizenship is rejuvenated and made coherent again" (119).[9] Although Douglas's theory of rejuvenation focuses on contemporary minority writing, the "ambivalent effect" he describes applies to nineteenth-century women's writing because they occupied a marginalized "cultural citizenship status" (119).[10] When contrasted with positions occupied by Phebe, her family's servant, and Fun See and Wang Lo, men who have recently arrived from China, Rose's citizenship moves toward coherence. Through her responses to her uncle's girl-raising strategies, Rose negotiates means of accepting and resisting the Campbell family's conquest of her body and her inheritance to carve out a viable citizenship for herself.

Rose as Outsider and Insider

Uncle Alec works to change Rose's languid routine, treating her ennui with "doses" of activities designed to stimulate her mind and body (32). He also introduces new dietary restrictions, and with each supposedly healthful change, Rose's willingness to try out the new doses is tied to proving herself a good member of the Campbell family. Much of Rose's fragility is blamed on the multiple and competing programs for health and education she has been prescribed by her aunts before her uncle returns. Alec comments on Aunt Myra's conviction that Rose is near death: "We will show her how to make constitutions and turn pale-faced little ghosts into rosy, hearty girls" (28). Rose's encounters with other cultures and methods of education turn her into a "rosy, hearty girl" (28). While the comment about "how to make constitutions" obviously refers to physical health, it also suggests the United States' Constitution—indeed, the body and the nation are frequently connected in late nineteenth- and early twentieth-century discourses about national identity, a phenomenon David Palumbo-Liu notes in *Asian/American*.[11] *Eight Cousins* was produced on the eve of the centennial of 1776, and in its exploration of the making of a constitution for Rose, this 1870s text registers a concern with the nation's beginnings and the qualities that make American children American. Uncle Alec, then, becomes a "founding father" for Rose, writing new laws to bring her from unhealthy childhood into blooming womanhood.

Some of Uncle Alec's laws indicate that he sees Rose as having the potential to develop agency. He compares her to a craft that must have a captain: "I intend to try a course of uncles now, and see how that suits your con-

stitution. I'm going to have you all to myself, and no one is to give a word of advice unless I ask it. There is no other way to keep order aboard, and I am captain of this little craft, for a time at least" (30). As "captain," Uncle Alec insists on having the final authority over Rose, drawing the comparison between Rose and a ship—isolated from other nations and borders, yet freely able to move between them and connect them. The emphasis on firm rule and on keeping order connects to the kinds of authority colonizing officials were encouraged to establish in both British and U.S. colonies. Rose becomes, in effect, a vehicle, a ship engaged with tasks of establishing control over a variety of spaces and peoples. Unwilling to keep Rose displayed in a china cabinet, Uncle Alec sees her agency and ability to move and capitalize on or profitably use encounters with the other. With his help, she can become an agent who profits from the extent of the family's empire if she is carefully captained. His phrase "for a time" suggests that she, too, will move from being a ship to becoming her own captain. Even while she is being captained by her uncle, the metaphor of Rose as ship signals a movement to make her part of her family, her community, and her nation: while a ship has access to different lands and materials, it encounters these for pragmatic and economic gain. Furthermore, being registered to one country, ships are always nationally identified, routinely and exhaustively, in ports; they are ejected if they cannot be identified as having a taxable origin. Uncle Alec's "course," then, identifies Rose as belonging to him, and he moves her through a series of encounters with foreign objects and peoples with the goal of helping Rose to locate healthy, useful goals for herself that will solidify her place (and her usefulness) within the family.

Rose moves toward insider status through her participation in a carefully designed program that combines physical activity and education. In the "Satisfactory Chinaman" episode, Uncle Alec takes Rose to see shipping warehouses owned by the family, and he introduces Rose to two men from China. Her uncle asks her if she would like to go to China, and she asks whether it is "rather a long voyage?" (76). Her uncle says: "Steer around the Point into the harbor, and I'll give you a glimpse of China in twenty minutes or so" (76). Uncle Alec claims authority over both Rose and China by suggesting that he can "give a glimpse of China" if she will just follow his steering orders (76). At the same time, the suggestion that he can offer Rose access to an entire nation by condensing its history, resources, and culture into the goods available on a ship provides an example of the positional superiority that characterizes orientalism.

When they move closer to a bay "full of shipping," Rose's uncle explains: "Uncle Mac has a ship just in from Hong Kong, and I thought you would like to go and see it" (77). When she realizes where her uncle is planning to take her, Rose responds with enthusiasm: "I dearly love to go poking about in the warehouses with Uncle Mac; everything is so curious and new to me; and I'm specially interested in China because you have been there" (77). Rose's "poking about" is a small-scale version of imperialist exploration and conquest, and the ship serves as a microcosm of China—safe, selected, profitable, and controlled by American shipping magnates. While Rose visits the ship, whatever is other to her she describes as "curious and new," whether or not it is curious at all to the people from whose lands these goods have been exported (77). The dose of the "curious and new" is supposed to be good for her, make her stronger, less self-involved and self-indulgent. Rose must complete her doses to convince her uncle that she is moving toward the kind of young womanhood that will help her contribute to her family, region, and nation.

In Alcott's narrative, the men from China experience acceptance into American society through their "usefulness" to white middle-class citizens. In her Uncle Mac's warehouse, Rose can take whatever she finds appealing and can reject what is least useful or interesting. The judgments based on "usefulness" and "satisfaction" are applied both to the goods and to the men whom Rose meets in her uncle's warehouse. Adjectives used repeatedly to describe Rose's "trip to China" include "odd," "curious," and "queer," all evaluative terms that use an orientalist perspective to construct the norm (77, 79). Rose's uncle says, "now steer toward the wharf where the big ship with the queer flag is. That's the 'Rajah,' and we will go aboard if we can" (77). The name of the ship, "Rajah," points to an interest in India as well as China as a source for profit. As Rose approaches the docked vessel, the extent of its strangeness is emphasized, and this exposure to a new culture or experience seems to be a large part of the dose that Rose's uncle feels will contribute both to her health and her education: "In among the ships they went, by the wharves where the water was green and still, and queer barnacles grew on the slippery piles. Odd smells saluted her nose, and odd sights met her eyes, but Rose liked it all, and played she was really landing in Hong Kong when they glided up to the steps in the shadow of the tall 'Rajah'" (77). As her orientalizing "play" at "really landing in Hong Kong" continues, Rose is described as having "the satisfaction of poking her inquisitive little nose into every available corner, at the risk of being crushed, lost, or drowned" (78).[12] This excursion provides just one example of how Alec ignites and then satisfies Rose's desires for exploration and for "rummaging" within the carefully controlled environment of the ship that serves as a representative nation.

Uncle Alec tells Rose the details of the "Trip to China" and lets her know his expectations: "I'll show you two

genuine Chinamen who have just arrived. You will like to welcome Whang Lo and Fun See, I'm sure" (77). This indicates that he expects her to experiment with the role a captain plays in making visitors welcome to a ship. Rose, however, states that she wants to be the nonspeaking passive viewer rather than the captain/agent with speaking authority: "Don't ask me to speak to them, uncle; I shall be sure to laugh at the odd names and the pig-tails and the slanting eyes. Please let me just trot round after you; I like that best" (77). She says she might be afraid, but she develops what her uncle considers to be a positive interest in the men. She is drawn out in part by her appreciation for the goods and materials they offer, and also by their display of "delightfully Chinese" qualities (79).

At the meeting, Rose is disappointed by one of the men from China but pleased by the other, in proportion to how well they fit into her notions of what Chinese men should look like:

> Mr. Whang Lo was an elderly gentlemen in American costume, with his pig-tail neatly wound round his head. He spoke English, and was talking busily with Uncle Mac in the most commonplace way—so Rose considered *him* a failure. But Fun See was delightfully Chinese from his junk-like shoes to the button on his pagoda hat; for he had got himself up in style, and was a mass of silk jackets and slouchy trousers. He was short and fat, and waddled comically; his eyes were very "slanting," as Rose said; his queue [pigtail] was long, so were his nails; his yellow face was plump and shiny, and he was altogether a highly satisfactory Chinaman.
>
> (78-79)

In Alcott's texts, the word "satisfaction" is sometimes used in connection with tasks that have been completed in the proper and expected way. It is also a word that implies desires (whether erotic, physical, emotional) that have been fulfilled.[13] Rose's desire to be satisfied by the sight of a "Chinaman" suggests the complexity of obtaining the profit and health that Alec wants Rose to gain from this trip to China.

Significantly, Rose responds to the degree of assimilation she detects in the Chinese men by looking for heterogeneity rather than homogeneity. In this scene, Rose finds that one of the men will provide her with the healthy dose of the "curious and new" that she (and her uncle) seek at the warehouse. Whang Lo seems too "American" to satisfy Rose, who reads his adoption of Western dress as a signal that he is not a "true" Chinaman, in much the same way that her uncle has read Rose's dislike of "parritch"—a Scots-inflected form of the word "porridge"—as non-Scottish (and by implication non-Campbell) behavior (34). In scenes that are similar to Rose's evaluation of Whang Lo, Alec assesses the satisfactoriness of Rose's display of Campbell characteristics as she responds to his doses of the "curious and new." When Rose says, "I should like to see the world, but not in such a small, untidy, smelly place as this. We should go in a yacht all clean and comfortable; Charlie says that is the proper way," he answers, "You are not a true Campbell if you don't like the smell of tar and salt-water, nor Charlie either with his luxurious yacht" (78). Subsequently, Rose works to prove herself a "true Campbell" and to assimilate by following her uncle's plans. Repeated comments about the characteristics of true members of the family and true citizens of the culture are complicated by Rose's assessment of the satisfactoriness of the two men from China.

Whang Lo, in Rose's view, is "a failure" as a representative of China (79). Rose's response to Whang Lo suggests that his degree of assimilation is uninteresting, perhaps because it makes him too much like the uncles she is required to obey. Her dissatisfaction is exclusionary and seems fueled by a refusal to appreciate Whang Lo's ability to fully participate in her uncle's world. Like the policies that excluded the Chinese, many aspects of American culture excluded girls from participation, and in this single scene, Rose's encounter with the men from China draws attention both to her own exclusion and her participation in exclusion. With her disapproval of Whang Lo, Rose claims inclusion at his expense, and the scene highlights her growing understanding of how exclusion works and demonstrates one of the problematic ways that she can overcome her own outsider status.

ASSIMILATION AND DRESSING THE NATIONAL BODY

Rose can be read as a model nation and body whose age and potential reflect the youthfulness of the United States. After claiming Rose for himself, Alec proceeds to mitigate perceived internal and external threats to her body by testing how she responds to varieties of exposure to foreign, exoticized objects and people. Simultaneously, Alec's methods of raising Rose, including his choices about how he dresses her, make neighbors and family members perceive Rose herself as other. Just as she is disappointed with Mr. Whang Lo's physical appearance, Rose's body and dress frequently dissatisfy her uncle—when she first meets him, she wears her belts too tight, and she also wants to wear dresses that discourage the kind of active life he wishes her to have. He expands her belts, eventually replacing them with sashes, and asks her to take deep breaths to expand her waist: "when you have filled this out we will go on enlarging it till your waist is more like that of Hebe, goddess of health, and less like that of a fashion-plate,—the ugliest thing imaginable" (52-53). Alec focuses on Rose's girl-ness and molds her into a more androgynous American body by de-emphasizing her waist and

hips and providing her with clothes that allow her to run and skate.

Although her uncle does not tell her anything about women and girls from China, before meeting Whang Lo and Fun See, Rose worries about them being dissatisfied with her dress and body. She wonders if her American feet are too large to seem dainty to men from China. She assumes that all women from China have naturally small feet, and her uncle, who presumably has more familiarity with Chinese cultures, does not tell her about the history of foot binding and the class distinctions that have caused small feet to be seen as beautiful. Uncle Alec's silence about the pain and restriction associated with foot binding and his simultaneous interest in fashion reform for American girls reflect his conflicting impulses both to captain Rose and to give her agency. The relatively nongendered clothes outfit Rose to eventually become a captain of her ship even while they signal her uncle's control over her. Uncle Alec is intent on offering Rose freedom and agency through careful control of her dress; her Aunt Myra worries that Alec will dress Rose in "a Bloomer" and says that she "cannot bear" to see her "sacrificed to [Alec's] wild ideas of health" (212). Myra knows that people do talk and laugh about dress, especially clothes that are viewed as unusual or unfashionable, and the responses that are made to Fun See's dress reveal that clothes do mark insiders and outsiders.

In its description of Fun See's body and dress, the text constructs him as an object to be gazed upon for amusement. Rose promises her uncle that she will be kind, but the text describes her as noticing only his difference from everything that is familiar: "Rose . . . had not the least idea how to entertain the queer guest, who looked as if he had walked out of one of the rice paper landscapes on the wall, and sat nodding at her so like a toy Mandarin that she could hardly keep sober" (79). Rose compares Fun See with a toy and also with an image of a Chinese man who appears on a teapot that he unpacks from a box and gives to her: "it was made in the likeness of a plump little Chinaman. His hat was the cover, his queue the handle, and his pipe the nose. It stood upon feet in shoes turned up at the toes, and the smile on the fat, sleepy face was so like that on Fun's when he displayed the teapot, that Rose couldn't help laughing, which pleased him much" (80). Rose's laughter pleases Fun See, but she is laughing at him and at the ways in which the "fat, sleepy" image on the teapot compares to his embodiment of Chinese masculinity.

The description of Fun See's body and Rose's thoughts about him reveal how the text itself distances Rose from Fun See, positing her behavior and embodiment as ordinary and normal and his as other. The description positions Fun See as subservient—his goal is to entertain Rose, and it is his objectification that makes her laugh. His body and anatomy become trivialized receptacles designed to offer her pleasure—in the likeness Rose sees on the teapot, Fun See's head is hollowed out to bear her tea. When he is associated with a tool used to serve tea, a task linked to the feminine domestic sphere in Rose's world, Fun See is placed in a position of objectified subservience.

In addition to functioning as a means of objectification, the language used to describe Fun See highlights his difference from Americans, and this characterization compares to other depictions of the Chinese in literature, which, as Dominika Ferens notes, often signify the "un-American, unromantic, unheroic, undesirable, effeminate, and low-class" ("Winnifred Eaton/Onoto Watanna" 38). In the scene that follows the tea-set description, Rose assumes that Fun See has gone to fetch her food that she would rather not eat: "Tumbling off his seat, he waddled away as fast as his petticoats permitted, leaving Rose hoping that he had not gone to get a roasted rat, a stewed puppy, or any other foreign mess which civility would oblige her to eat" (80). Here, Fun See's "petticoats" connect his dress to women's clothing, indicating his distance from Rose's definitions of masculinity and Americanness. While Fun See's dress satisfies Rose through its contrast with the familiar, there is a sense of horror transferred onto the grotesque spectacle of the food Rose imagines she will have to eat to prove herself civil. Although clearly played for laughs, this scene has an undercurrent of violence with its image of stewed puppies. A sign of both culture and sustenance that can link people or keep them apart, the imagined food underscores the divisions between the Chinaman and Rose, who herself only begins to inhabit a position of normality and belonging by placing herself in a position of superiority in relation to Fun See.

Fun See returns not with a rat, but with a fan, an accessory that Rose can wear and carry as a memento of her encounter with China. The fan is described in detail, and Rose uses her knowledge of Western European theories of art to evaluate the fan's decoration as "peculiar": "Of course, there was no perspective whatever, which only gave it a peculiar charm to Rose, for in one place a lovely lady, with blue knitting-needles in her hair, sat directly upon the spire of a stately pagoda. In another charming view a brook appeared to flow in at the front door of a stout gentleman's house, and out at his chimney. In a third a zigzag wall went up into the sky like a flash of lightning, and a bird with two tails was apparently brooding over a fisherman whose boat was just going aground upon the moon" (81). Rose enjoys the fan for its otherness, but she disapproves of and disproves its logic as a world to be taken seriously. Her response delegitimizes the world that is depicted in much the same way that she refuses to recognize Fun

See as an agent or as anything other than an object. We see here how Rose has moved from being othered to clearly placing the other in its orientalized, subservient, and secondary position. Examining the fan allows Rose to gain a new sense of perspective, reorienting her to see her experiences as less marginal. Next to Fun See, Rose's life, living as an orphan with her bachelor uncle, appears closer to the norms of her own region.

SOCIAL SUPERIORITY AND ASSIMILATION THROUGH EXCLUSION

The Campbells are constructed as superior to other citizenship models of the neighborhood: Annabel Bliss, the prim little neighbor girl; the members of the working class such as Phebe, the young servant who cleans for Aunt Peace and Aunt Plenty; and the immigrants from China her uncle invites her to meet. In an appendix on "Model Minority Discourse and the Course of Healing," David Palumbo-Liu writes about popular twentieth-century Asian American novels that explore issues of assimilation, illness, and self. Palumbo-Liu sees these texts as addressing the ways that Asian American ethnic identity has been constructed: "in model minority discourse we find the instantiation of a collective psychic identification that constructs a very specific concept of the negotiation between social trauma and private health, assigning the ways that minority subjects are to 'mature' through achieving a specifically prescribed understanding of their place in the national community" (398). It might be said, then, that *Eight Cousins* does seem to explore "[courses] of healing" for those, like Rose and Fun See, who do not immediately fit into the dominant culture.[14] Palumbo-Liu points out that in "model minority discourse and self-affirmative action, the route to happiness (that is, health) follows the path of a specific *bildung* that reinforces dominant notions of subjectivity" (398). As Rose assimilates into "dominant notions of subjectivity," she draws from lessons she learns in her encounters with the other to heal and stabilize her position within her family, as she does in the Fun See episode. The Campbell family depends on Rose to improve her health so that she can contribute to its ongoing superiority.

The discursive moves that connect the superiority of the Campbells to the treatment of China as orientalized other correspond to numerous works of literature for both children and adults depicting China and other Asian cultures.[15] Late twentieth-century studies of attitudes toward China show how the orientalizing texts that began to be produced during the 1870s contributed specifically to the oppression of Chinese immigrants.[16] K. Scott Wong, for example, writes about the "yellow peril" industry: "the Chinese in America were confronted with an organized campaign to defame them in prose and in illustrations. Thus, the anti-Chinese movement was an early example of what is now often called a 'culture war'" ("Cultural Defenders" ["Cultural Defenders and Brokers"] 3). As Wong notes, the "yellow peril" literature, produced in many forms, contributed to anti-Chinese legislation, which emerged during the nineteenth century and continued to be developed and changed during the twentieth.

In subtle and not so subtle ways, *Eight Cousins* participates in the culture war to prevent recent immigrants from participating as equals in the dominant culture.[17] For example, when Uncle Alec explains Fun See's reasons for coming to the United States, he encourages Rose to be kind out of pity for his lack of education and youth (he is in his late teens): "Uncle Alec told her that Fun See had come out to be educated, and could only speak a little pigeon English; so she must be kind to the poor fellow, for he was only a lad, though he looked nearly as old as Mr. Whang Lo" (79). Although Rose complains that she is not given the respect she feels is due her age (thirteen when *Eight Cousins* begins), she is willing to treat Fun See like a young boy. His newness to the United States and his relative youth contribute to his construction in this text as infantile and ignorant. It is partly because Alec considers Fun See a "lad" in the process of becoming a man that he is deemed a suitable companion for Rose, a girl in the process of becoming a woman; in *Rose in Bloom,* Fun See courts and marries one of Rose's neighbors, Annabel Bliss, but this romance serves as comic relief for the more serious romances of Rose and Phebe.

In an interview, Maxine Hong Kingston discusses her response to Fun See's infantilized and comic representation: "I was reading all of Louisa May Alcott. In her book, there's a white girl, and I suppose it's sort of daring, but she marries a Chinese guy. He has a long pigtail. He's fat, short, weird. He was mainly a character of fun and so stereotyped, although I suppose it was accurate—by that time they hadn't cut off their pigtails yet. Up to that time, I had identified with all those little women, then I saw this guy, and I thought, 'My God, that's who I'm supposed to be—this little "Chinaman" guy.' It ejected me out of literature" (qtd. in Li 125).[18] In "Sui Sin Far and the Chinese American Canon," Wenxin Li discusses Kingston's response to Fun See and notes that the stereotype that is most problematic is not the pigtail, but the "fat, short, weird" image of Fun See. Li asks the question, "What kind of impact would [Sui Sin Far's] courageous, kind, and credible Chinese men have had on the formation of young Maxine Hong Kingston's ethnic consciousness?" (125). What kind of lasting influence did Fun See's image have on nineteenth-century white girl readers, who unlike Kingston, may have continued to complacently identify with the little white women without question or concern?

The number of laws and the complexity of arenas for enacting injustice against Chinese immigrants reveal the significance of Chinese Americans' roles in defining citizenship in the United States. Writing about categories of Asian citizenship, Lisa Lowe notes the connection between these categories and national identity:

> The figure of the Asian immigrant has served as a "screen," a phantasmatic site, on which the nation projects a series of condensed, complicated anxieties regarding external and internal threats to the mutable coherence of the national body: the invading multitude, the lascivious seductress, the servile yet treacherous domestic, the automaton whose inhuman efficiency will supersede American ingenuity. Indeed, it is precisely the unfixed liminality of the Asian immigrant—geographically, linguistically, and racially at odds with the context of the "national"—that has given rise to the necessity of endlessly fixing and repeating such stereotypes.
>
> (18)

While *Eight Cousins* and *Rose in Bloom* do not contain the specific stereotypes of the automaton, the treacherous domestic, and the seductress that Lowe mentions, the descriptions of the men from China combine these images. The two Chinese men Rose meets are both on display for her to observe as exotic objects. Fun See is excessively servile and childlike although he is reaching his older teen years; his gifts and costume "seduce" Rose, who, prior to the visit, had claimed she would watch the men from a distance. Whang Lo, although not an automaton, is described as dedicated to his work, efficient, and skilled at adapting to Western customs and dress.

The Chinese Exclusion Acts were promoted with rhetorical strategies that actively constructed the Chinese as diseased and weak outsiders with a culture and a history that could never be made to fit into Enlightenment models of individual progress.[19] By the end of *Eight Cousins,* Fun See has made changes in his dress and language that move him toward assimilation into Western culture: "He was in American costume now, with a cropped head, and spoke remarkably good English after six months at school; but, for all that, his yellow face and beady eyes made a curious contrast to the blond Campbells all about him. Will called him the 'Typhoon,' meaning Tycoon, and the name stuck to him, to his great disgust" (237). In this scene, the cousins mark Fun See's difference from them, despite the changes in his clothing and costume, by giving him a nickname that uses mistranslation or mispronunciation of a word associated with a wealthy person (tycoon) and replaces it with a word connected with the unpredictable danger of a storm. When Fun See is in his traditional costumes, he satisfies and diverts Rose, but when he changes his costume to Western dress, he offers the cousins "a vent for their merriment" (237). While it is unclear whether the cousins mispronounce "tycoon" as a way of belittling Fun See's "remarkably good English" or as a reference to a kind of storm that might occur on a voyage to China, the name indicates that both Fun See's lack of assimilation and his subsequent conformance to Western dress provide the Campbells with the means of excluding him from insider status in their clan.

Throughout *Eight Cousins* and *Rose in Bloom,* Rose's struggle involves establishing her citizenship within the family and also her place in the world beyond the comfort and security of the Campbells' wealth. As Rose becomes less "strange" and "outlandish" and more of a member of the Campbell clan, she must take an interest in the family's pursuits and this includes establishing her belonging by cultivating an interest in the other (*Eight Cousins* 41). At the end of Alcott's "Trip to China" episode, Fun See bows to Rose and Dr. Alec as they take their leave with "'three bendings and the nine knockings,' as they salute the Emperor, or 'Son of Heaven,'" (82). Rose is delighted at being equated with the Emperor, and does not question the subservience that Fun See shows. For her, these displays add to her feeling that she has "really been to China" (82). Although most of Rose's time has been spent receiving gifts, she agrees with her uncle that the excursion was "not a bad way to study geography" (82).

Rose happily accepts the generosity of Fun See and Whang Lo: "Mr. Whang Lo had given her a Chinese umbrella; Uncle Alec had got some lanterns to light up her balcony; the great fan lay in her lap, and the tea-set reposed at her feet" (82).[20] Indeed, Rose's geography lesson has taught her about the acquisition and expansion based geography of empire, and in her summary she chooses to foreground tea, which, through the teapot scene, the text has linked to Fun See's embodiment: "I have collected some useful information about China, which you may like, especially the teas. The best are Lapsing Souchong, Assam Pekoe, rare Ankoe, Flowery Pekoe. . . . Shanghai is on the Woosung River. Hong Kong means 'Island of sweet waters.' Singapore is 'Lion's Town.' 'Chops' are the boats they live in; and they drink tea out of little saucers. Principal productions are porcelain, tea, cinnamon, shawls, tin, tamarinds, and opium. They have beautiful temples and queer gods; and in Canton is the Dwelling of the Holy Pigs, fourteen of them, very big, and all blind" (94-95). The dose that her uncle has given her helps her to realize just how profitable and pleasurable her family's interest in the import/export business is.

In *Rose in Bloom,* the orientalist discourse that characterizes Fun See's representation complicates ongoing comments on Rose's "oddities"—she is aligned with

him, but also continually described as superior to Fun See and Annabel Bliss, the woman he marries. Both Rose's and Fun See's choices change as they grow up, and they both eventually consent to occupying more stable, assimilated places in their local and national communities. This second text in Alcott's series emphasizes choices that are available to those who are not in the dominant patriarchal positions. Both Annabel's right to happiness with Fun See and Fun See's right to choose Annabel as an object of desire are questioned (*Rose in Bloom* 188, 190). All of these projects challenge the white middle-class status quo and provide examples of the difficulties of making choices that defy or flaunt convention as one secures an insider position. By the end of the text, Rose and Fun See have assimilated in some ways and resisted convention in others; Rose's secure position within her own family is made to seem more desirable through its contrast with Fun See's provisional, always humorous, assimilation through his marriage to Annabel. One of the costs of the assimilation process is that Rose and Fun See cannot be too closely connected; despite similarities in their experiences, her belonging is demonstrated in part through her difference from him.

DIRECTIONS FOR STUDIES OF ORIENTALISM IN CHILDREN'S LITERATURE

Alcott's use of China in her story about a young girl finding health and securing a stable position within a family indicates that women writers actively displaced fears and misgivings their culture had about women's rights onto those whom their governments and familial cultures clearly characterized as outsiders. While Alcott's text does not describe the men from China as dangerous, diseased, or dishonest (three common descriptions used in the age of exclusion), their depictions serve to highlight the Campbells' customs as the superior norm. This text foregrounds examples of otherness to show Rose's progress in the family's project of making her a true Campbell and a girl with the strength to "bloom" and thus complete the duties of womanhood, which the text describes as "earnest purposes that make life beautiful and sacred" (326).

As Alcott's text articulates the difficulties of assimilation and negotiating a balance between self-construction and being constructed and controlled by others, readers of *Eight Cousins* are positioned to think of China as crowded and to understand its citizens as subservient and entertainingly unable to communicate in English.[21] Even while Rose is aligned at times with the men from China, she is also described as coming to see herself as belonging to her family and community and also as superior, comfortable with subservience from Fun See and deserving of the luxuries he offers her.[22] These orientalizing discourses privilege the West and Rose's Americanness and allow readers to move from attitudes of curiosity about foreign others, embedded in an interested superiority, to an acceptance of the kinds of oppressive policies that kept the Exclusion Acts in place well into the twentieth century. These policies have been powerful enough to continue to influence constructions of both Chinese and Chinese American identities into the present day. Orientalizing representations of China occur in children's texts like *Eight Cousins* that have played an important part in histories of American children's literature; ongoing studies can begin to challenge children's literature's resistances to and continued participation in these orientalizing perspectives.

Notes

1. I see citizenship as connected to but distinct from national identity, since citizenship is linked to participation in the decisions relating to how a family, community, or nation is governed. Will Kymlicka and Wayne Norman suggest that citizenship is a concept that "seems to integrate the demands of justice and community membership" (352).

2. Moon-Ho Jung made this argument in a presentation at the 2004 American Studies Association Conference in a paper titled "Outlawing 'Coolies': On Race in the Age of Emancipation." He published his paper in the September 2005 issue of *American Quarterly*. See also Najia Aarim-Heriot's *Chinese Immigrants, African Americans, and Racial Anxiety in the United States, 1848-82*.

3. Dominika Ferens points out that the use of the other to reinforce whiteness accounted for the popularity of narratives about Asians in the United States in the late nineteenth century. See *Edith and Winnifred Eaton* (11).

4. In "The Seduction of Origins," David Shih points out that "Official and unofficial anti-Chinese sentiment arose in the United States around 1849, soon after the Chinese arrived in California in large numbers" (54).

5. See "Canton Is Not Boston" by Teemu Ruskola. The Zborays note that the Chinese Museum printed over fifty thousand copies of its catalog, which described in detail the items displayed in the exhibition. Copies of this catalog might well have been available to Alcott when she was growing up.

6. See Zinn's discussion of Theodore Roosevelt's statements on the healthiness of war and expansionism (290-313).

7. Zinn opens his *People's History of the United States* by citing Columbus's use of "glass beads and hawks' bells" in opening trade with the Arawaks: "With fifty men we could subjugate them all and make them do whatever we want" (1).

8. *Eight Cousins* focuses on the importance of the Scottish heritage of the Campbell family. I will discuss the connections between this heritage and Rose's Americanness in a subsequent article.

9. See also David Palumbo-Liu's discussion of "Model Minority Discourse and the Course of Healing" in *Asian/American* (419-66).

10. Gloria Heyung Chun notes the need to decenter and challenge old constructions of east and west that have been used to structure commentaries on Chinese American identities (15).

11. See especially "(Re)Building the National Body," in which Palumbo-Liu notes that beginning in 1871, there were ongoing efforts to "legitimize [the United States'] powers to exclude and expel" (23). Many arguments were based on eugenics theories that suggested immigrant bodies would enfeeble the nation.

12. K. Scott Wong writes about depictions of American Chinatowns in "Chinatown: Conflicting Images, Contested Terrain" as sites of "negation and definition" (4). The Chinatown depictions, Wong notes, portray a "community that was forever foreign" (4). At the same time, "these images perversely helped define what American communities 'ought' to be like" (4). Similarly, Rose's "trip to China" helps her to see what she is not, and solidifies her sense of belonging to the Campbell clan.

13. For example, when *Little Women*'s Amy is in Europe, her feelings about letters from Laurie are described using the word "satisfactory": "His letters were such a comfort—for the home letters were very irregular, and were not half so satisfactory as his when they did come" (332).

14. The term "model-minority discourse" is a twentieth-century concept, but Palumbo-Liu's discussion of illness and assimilation provides useful insights into the movements toward belonging made by Rose and Fun See.

15. David Shih explains that "nineteenth-century labor interests 'produced' the Chinaman as an economic foe of white labor and the Chinese woman as a detriment to white decency" (54).

16. In their introduction to the *Lion and the Unicorn* issue focused on Asian American Children's Literature, Dolores de Manuel and Rocío G. Davis point out that "the complex representations of Asians in American literature show a movement

from misrepresentation through stereotyping to representations with more basis in reality, more multi-faceted and inclusive" (vii).

17. Several books on China that would have been available in the 1870s are discussed by Dominika Ferens in *Edith and Winnifred Eaton*. W. H. Medhurst's *China: Its State and Prospects* was published in Boston in 1838, J. G. Wood's *The Uncivilized Races* was published in the U.S. in 1870, and Reverend Justus Doolittle's *Social Life of the Chinese* became available in 1864.

18. I am indebted to one of the readers of this article for suggesting this connection.

19. See Wong's discussion of how the United States chooses "homogeneity and racial superiority over pluralism" with the passing of the Chinese Exclusion Acts ("Cultural Defenders" 9).

20. The tea-set reposes here, and since Rose has connected the tea-pot to Fun See, this scene also figures him as subservient, resting at her feet.

21. K. Scott Wong discusses how the Chinese elite worked to challenge representations of Chinese by publishing in popular magazines for adults: "By offering alternative representations of themselves and by answering some of the charges levied against them, these writers hoped that attacks against the Chinese would lessen, that immigration legislation would be liberalized, and that the Chinese would eventually find acceptance in the American polity" ("Cultural Defenders" 3-4). One area for further research would be to examine alternative representations written for children.

22. See, for example, the scene in which Rose plays at being an "Eastern princess" (62) and the final scene, when Uncle Alec explains that Rose "needs the wisest, tenderest care to keep a very ardent little soul from wearing out a finely organized little body" (294).

Works Cited

Aarim-Heriot, Najia. *Chinese Immigrants, African Americans, and Racial Anxiety in the United States, 1848-82.* Urbana: U of Illinois P, 2003.

Alcott, Louisa May. *Eight Cousins.* New York: Penguin, 1995.

———. *Little Women.* Ed. Anne K. Phillips and Gregory Eiselein. Norton Critical Edition. New York: Norton, 2004.

———. *Rose in Bloom.* New York: Penguin, 1995.

Chan, Sucheng. *Entry Denied: Exclusion and the Chinese Community in America, 1882-1943.* Philadelphia: Temple UP, 1991.

Cheng, Anne Anlin. *The Melancholy of Race.* Oxford: Oxford UP, 2000.

Chun, Gloria Heyung. *Of Orphans and Warriors: Inventing Chinese American Culture and Identity.* New Brunswick, NJ: Rutgers, 2000.

De Manuel, Dolores, and Rocío G. Davis. Editors' introduction. *Asian American Children's Literature.* Ed. De Manuel and Davis. Spec. issue of *The Lion and the Unicorn* 30.2 (2006): v-xv.

Douglas, Christopher. "Reading Ethnography: The Cold War Social Science of Jade Snow Wong's *Fifth Chinese Daughter* and *Brown v. Board of Education.*" Zhou and Najmi, 101-24.

"Empire." *Oxford English Dictionary Online.* 2000. Oxford English Dictionary. *<http://www.dictionary.oed.com//.*

Ferens, Dominika. *Edith and Winnifred Eaton: Chinatown Missions and Japanese Romance.* Urbana: U of Illinois P, 2002.

———. "Winnifred Eaton/Onoto Watanna: Establishing Ethnographic Authority." Zhou and Najmi, 30-47.

Jung, Moon-Ho. "Outlawing 'Coolies': On Race in the Age of Emancipation." American Studies Association Conference. Atlanta, Georgia. 13 November 2004.

———. "Outlawing 'Coolies': Race, Nation, and Empire in the Age of Emancipation." *American Quarterly* 57.3 (2005): 677-701.

Kaplan, Amy. "Manifest Domesticity." *American Literature* 70.3 (1998): 581-606.

Kymlicka, Will, and Wayne Norman. "Return of the Citizen: A Survey of Recent Work on Citizenship Theory." *Ethics* 104 (1994): 352-81.

Li, Wenxin. "Sui Sin Far and the Chinese American Canon: Toward a Post-Gender Wars Discourse." *MELUS* 29.3/4 (2004): 121-31.

Lowe, Lisa. *Immigrant Acts: On Asian American Cultural Politics.* Durham: Duke UP, 1996.

McGillis, Roderick. "Self, Other, and Other Self: Recognizing the Other in Children's Literature." *The Lion and the Unicorn* 21.2 (1997): 215-19.

Palumbo-Liu, David. *Asian/American: Historical Crossings of a Racial Frontier.* Champaign: U of Illinois P, 1999.

Ruskola, Teemu. "Canton Is Not Boston: The Invention of American Imperial Sovereignty." *American Quarterly* 57.3 (2005): 859-84.

Said, Edward. *Culture and Imperialism.* New York: Vintage, 1993.

———. *Orientalism.* London: Routledge and Kegan Paul, 1978.

Shih, David. "The Seduction of Origins: Sui Sin Far and the Race for Tradition." Zhou and Najmi, 48-76.

Wong, K. Scott. "Chinatown: Conflicting Images, Contested Terrain." *MELUS* 20.1 (1995): 3-15.

———. "Cultural Defenders and Brokers: Chinese Responses to the Anti-Chinese Movement." *Claiming America: Constructing Chinese American Identities During the Exclusion Era.* Ed. K. Scott Wong and Sucheng Chan. Philadelphia: Temple UP, 1998. 3-40.

Wong, K. Scott, and Sucheng Chan. *Claiming America: Constructing Chinese American Identities During the Exclusion Era.* Philadelphia: Temple UP, 1998.

Zboray, Ronald, and Mary Saracino Zboray. "Between 'Crockery-dom' and Barnum: Boston's Chinese Museum." *American Quarterly* 56.2 (2004): 271-307.

Zhou, Xiaojing, [and Samina Namji.] *Form and Transformation in Asian American Literature.* Seattle: U of Washington P, 2005.

Zinn, Howard. *A People's History of the United States.* New York: Harper, 1980.

FURTHER READING

Bibliographies

Eiselein, Gregory, and Anne K. Phillips, eds. *The Louisa May Alcott Encyclopedia.* Westport, Conn.: Greenwood Press, 2001, 418 p.

Includes a comprehensive survey of biographical and critical writings devoted to Alcott's life and career.

Payne, Alma. *Louisa May Alcott: A Reference Guide.* Boston: G. K. Hall & Company, 1980, 87 p.

Contains an overview of critical studies dedicated to Alcott's body of work.

Biographies

Anthony, Katherine. *Louisa May Alcott.* New York: Alfred A. Knopf, 1938, 315 p.

Considers the impact of Alcott's formative years on her literary career, focusing in particular on her family's moral standards.

Matteson, John. *Eden's Outcasts: The Story of Louisa May Alcott and Her Father.* New York: W. W. Norton, 2007, 497 p.

Examines the influence of Alcott's father, Bronson Alcott, on his daughter's intellectual and artistic development.

Saxton, Martha. *Louisa May: A Modern Biography of Louisa May Alcott.* Boston: Houghton Mifflin, 1977, 428 p.

Puts forward a psychoanalytical perspective on Alcott's life and writings while analyzing her career within the framework of nineteenth-century American society and culture.

Stern, Madeleine B. *Louisa May Alcott: A Biography.* Boston: Northeastern University Press, 1999, 422 p.

Comprises an authoritative and in-depth account of Alcott's life and career.

Criticism

Berman, Ruth. "'Spirituous Consolation': Alcott's Jokes on Drinking and Religion." *Children's Literature in Education* 39, no. 3 (September 2008): 169-85.

Evaluates Alcott's satirical attitude toward traditional morality and social mores in her *Hospital Sketches.*

Delamar, Gloria T. *Louisa May Alcott and Little Women: Biography, Critique, Publications, Poems, Songs and Contemporary Relevance.* Jefferson, N.C.: McFarland, 1990, 350 p.

Concentrates on Alcott's work as a poet and songwriter.

Eiselein, Gregory. *The Sketches of Louisa May Alcott.* Edited by Gregory Eiselein, New York: Ironweed Press, 2001, 283 p.

Contains an introductory essay analyzing elements of autobiography in Alcott's fiction.

———. "Contradictions in Louisa May Alcott's *Little Men.*" *New England Quarterly* 78, no. 1 (March 2005): 3-25.

Appraises the work's contradictory elements within the larger inconsistencies of nineteenth-century American society.

Elbert, Sarah, ed. *Louisa May Alcott on Race, Sex, and Slavery.* Boston: Northeastern University Press, 1997, 101 p.

Presents a range of critical perspectives on Alcott's attitudes toward race and gender.

Hirschhorn, Norbert, and Ian A. Greaves. "Louisa May Alcott, Her Mysterious Illness." *Perspectives in Biology and Medicine* 50, no. 2 (2007): 243-59.

Reexamines questions surrounding the alleged mercury poisoning that led to Alcott's death.

Stern, Madeleine B., ed. *Critical Essays on Louisa May Alcott.* Boston: G. K. Hall & Company, 1984, 295 p.

Consists of an array of critical studies on Alcott's body of work.

―――. *The Feminist Alcott: Stories of a Woman's Power.* Boston: Northeastern University Press, 1996, 288 p.

Includes an introduction exploring themes of gender identity and sexual power in Alcott's sensational fiction.

―――. *Louisa May Alcott: From Blood and Thunder to Hearth and Home.* Boston: Northeastern University Press, 1998, 274 p.

Collects a variety of Stern's critical essays on Alcott's work.

―――, ed. *Louisa May Alcott: Signature of Reform.* Boston: Northeastern University Press, 2002, 226 p.

Contains a critical introduction examining the relationship between Alcott's writings and the social reform movements of the nineteenth century.

Strickland, Charles. *Victorian Domesticity, Families in the Life and Art of Louisa May Alcott.* Tuscaloosa: University of Alabama Press, 1985, 198 p.

Addresses themes of domesticity and family in Alcott's fiction.

Williams, Susan S. "Revising Romance: Louisa May Alcott, Hawthorne, and the Civil War." In *Reclaiming Authorship, Literary Women in America, 1850-1900,* pp. 97-123. Philadelphia: University of Pennsylvania Press, 2006.

Discusses the underlying tension between Alcott's domestic fiction and her pseudonymously published thrillers.

Additional coverage of Alcott's life and career is contained in the following sources published by Gale: *American Writers Supplement,* **Vol. 1;** *Authors and Artists for Young Adults,* **Vol. 20;** *Beacham's Encyclopedia of Popular Fiction: Biography & Resources,* **Vol. 1;** *Beacham's Guide to Literature for Young Adults,* **Vol. 2;** *Children's Literature Review,* **Vols. 1, 38, 109;** *Concise Dictionary of American Literary Biography, 1865-1917; Dictionary of Literary Biography,* **Vols. 1, 42, 79, 223, 239, 242;** *Dictionary of Literary Biography Documentary Series,* **Vol. 14;** *DISCovering Authors; DISCovering Authors: British Edition; DISCovering Authors: Canadian Edition; DISCovering Authors Modules: Most-studied Authors* **and** *Novelists; DISCovering Authors 3.0; Feminism in Literature: A Gale Critical Companion,* **Ed. 1:2;** *Feminist Writers; Junior DISCovering Authors; Literature and Its Times,* **Vol. 2;** *Literature Resource Center; Major Authors and Illustrators for Children and Young Adults,* **Eds. 1, 2;** *Nineteenth-Century Literature Criticism,* **Vols. 6, 58, 83;** *Novels for Students,* **Vol. 12;** *Reference Guide to American Literature,* **Ed. 4;** *St. James Guide to Young Adult Writers; Short Story Criticism,* **Vols. 27, 98;** *Something About the Author,* **Vol. 100;** *Twayne's United States Authors; World Literature Criticism,* **Vol. 1;** *Writers for Children; Writers for Young Adults;* **and** *Yesterday's Authors of Books for Children,* **Vol. 1.**

Matthew Arnold
1822-1888

English poet, critic, essayist, letter writer, lecturer, and dramatist.

The following entry presents an overview of Arnold's life and works. For discussion of the essay *Culture and Anarchy: An Essay in Political and Social Criticism* (1869), see *NCLC,* Volume 126. For additional discussion of Arnold's complete career, see *NCLC,* Volumes 6, 29, and 89.

INTRODUCTION

Matthew Arnold is best known for giving voice to prominent Victorian concerns regarding aesthetics, social justice, and religious doubt. At a time when many in Great Britain felt a smug superiority about national accomplishments, Arnold was an outspoken critic of numerous aspects of British life, including education, religious institutions, and culture. Famous for his love for language, Arnold popularized certain familiar phrases, including "sweetness and light" (which he borrowed from Jonathan Swift), and playfully but pointedly redefining such terms as "barbarians," which he used to refer to the British aristocracy.

Arnold occupies a unique place among the so-called Victorian sages, acclaimed for his poetry as well as his prose. In his own writings, Arnold acknowledged Cardinal John Henry Newman, Johann Wolfgang von Goethe, William Wordsworth, and the French literary critic Charles Augustin Sainte-Beuve as the four thinkers he believed had most impacted his work. Subsequent scholars have also noted his debt to the German poet Heinrich Heine. Although Arnold's poetry is not as well known today as that of Alfred Lord Tennyson or Robert Browning, he was a respected poet in his day. He continues to enjoy a reputation for many of his poetic works, among them "Dover Beach" and "Stanzas from the Grande Chartreuse," which speak to the crises of the Victorian world. Such prose texts as "The Function of Criticism at the Present Time" (1864) and *Culture and Anarchy* (1869) continue to be read as valuable accounts of Victorian culture and thought.

Although Arnold had a reputation as a serious man of letters, those close to him knew him for his wit and sense of humor. He was a member of the famous London Athenaeum Club and a regular contributor to the periodicals of his day, where his works frequently inspired heated debate.

BIOGRAPHICAL INFORMATION

Born in 1822 in Laleham, Middlesex, England, Arnold grew up in a household focused on education. His father, Thomas Arnold, came to public attention as the reform-minded headmaster of Rugby School, one of England's oldest boys' boarding schools. Although Arnold was not a stand-out scholar, he developed a flair for writing at an early age. As a student at Rugby, he won a prize for his poem *Alaric at Rome* (1840). He also befriended Arthur Hugh Clough, his father's prized pupil. Arnold's family spent their summers in England's Lake District, where they were friendly with renowned poets William Wordsworth and Robert Southey. The landscape of the area would later play a role in Arnold's poetry, just as it had in the works of his famous predecessors.

Despite a reputation as a carefree and often rebellious student, Arnold won a prestigious scholarship to Balliol College, Oxford. He remained a free spirit at Oxford, flouting convention and often abandoning his studies for other pursuits. These Oxford experiences helped to shape his adult poetry. His bond with Arthur Hugh Clough grew during this time, and both were deeply affected by the unexpected death of Arnold's father in 1842. The two friends encouraged each other in the pursuit of poetry, a mutual interest. Arnold's poetic efforts were rewarded when he won the Newdigate Prize for his poem *Cromwell* (1843). He graduated with a second-class honors degree from Oxford in 1844.

After leaving Oxford, Arnold spent a year teaching at Rugby before being elected to a one-year fellowship at Oxford. At the end of the fellowship, Arnold became a private secretary to Lord Landsdowne. Landsdowne later arranged for him to take a position as an inspector of schools in 1851. Arnold would retain this job for thirty-five years. The salary allowed him to start a family, and he married Frances Lucy Wightman in June the same year. The couple had six children. Arnold's wife had a keen interest in his writing and often reviewed his work.

In 1857 Arnold returned to Oxford as a professor of poetry, a situation that required him to give three lectures a year and paid very little. He became the first scholar there to deliver his addresses in English rather than in the traditional Latin, and many of the lectures were later published. This position, which he held for ten years, changed Arnold's focus from poetry to criticism. Throughout his career, Arnold advocated a liberal education for all children. In 1859 he traveled to France, Switzerland, and Holland at the request of the Education Commission. There he studied the countries' educational systems, publishing his observations in *The Popular Education of France, with Notices of That of Holland and Switzerland* (1861).

In 1883 Arnold was invited by Andrew Carnegie to visit the United States. He spent six months there with his wife and one of his daughters and made a second trip in 1886. The same year, his declining health led him to resign his position as an inspector of schools; the resignation was made possible by a pension conferred on him by Prime Minister William Gladstone in 1883. In 1888 Arnold's experiences in the United States provided the basis for a series of lectures on "Life in America," later published under the title *Civilization in the United States: First and Last Impressions of America.* On April 15, 1888, not long after the publication of this essay, Arnold died of heart failure while running to catch a train. He was buried at Laleham-on-Thames, the place of his birth.

MAJOR WORKS

Arnold published his first collection of poetry, *The Strayed Reveller,* under the pseudonym A., in 1849. The collection was not well received, nor was its immediate successor, *Empedocles on Etna, and Other Poems* (1852). The title poem of the latter volume, written in two acts, depicts the final thoughts of the philosopher Empedocles before he throws himself into a volcano because he has outlived his era. Arnold first attained a degree of success with the 1853 volume *Poems,* which contains works from the earlier volumes minus "Empedocles on Etna" and with the addition of "The Scholar Gipsy" and "Sohrab and Rustum," two of his most commonly recognized works today. Taken together, these poems explore what Arnold describes in "The Scholar Gipsy" as "this strange disease of modern life"—lack of direction, religious doubt, and decaying social structures. *Poems* is known as much for its preface as for the verses it contains. The preface is Arnold's first significant work of literary criticism, and it provides an early articulation of his theory of poetry. Relying heavily on Aristotle, Arnold argues that poetry must not only be accurate but must also "infuse delight." It was because "Empedocles on Etna" failed to meet this second criterion, Arnold tells us, that it was excised from the volume. Arnold followed this work with *Poems: Second Series* (1855), which includes "Balder Dead," a

poem inspired by the Norse sagas. Arnold's last major poetical work, *New Poems,* was published in 1867; among its contents are "Thyrsis," an elegy to Arnold's friend Clough, who had died in 1861, and "Rugby Chapel," which honors the memory of Arnold's father.

While Arnold saw in literature, and especially in poetry, the opportunity to fill the void left by a national crisis of faith, he soon found himself unable to bridge that gulf through verse. After taking on the poetry professorship at Oxford, Arnold's focus turned to criticism. His Oxford lectures on Homer were published as *On Translating Homer* (1861) and *Last Words on Translating Homer* (1862). These works promote what Arnold terms the "grand style" and emphasize the importance of disinterestedness, or the ability to approach a topic from a detached and unemotional standpoint, as a trait of good criticism. In 1865 Arnold published *Essays in Criticism,* which includes "The Function of Criticism at the Present Time" and which brought the author a new level of public attention. In these essays Arnold argued that existing British criticism failed because of its inability to escape the bonds of politics and interest. The proper role of criticism, he wrote, is "simply to know the best that is known and thought in the world, and by in its turn making this known, to create a current of true and fresh ideas." With his emphasis on breaking through to new ideas, Arnold worked to elevate criticism to an art form in its own right.

Culture and Anarchy, one of Arnold's most frequently studied texts, grew out of his lectures and includes his responses to the public's reactions to them. In the essay, he takes the British people to task for their complacency and lack of "sweetness and light," and he advocates for the cultivation of a culture marked by the critical spirit, disinterestedness, and a willingness to question tradition and authority. It also famously divides the British populace into three categories: Barbarians (the aristocracy), Philistines (the middle classes), and the Populace (the lower classes). The essay introduces the governing distinction between Hebraism (an outlook associated with obedience) and Hellenism (an outlook associated with culture and criticism).

The publication of *St. Paul and Protestantism, with an Essay on Puritanism and the Church of England* (1870) evidenced a new shift in Arnold's concerns, this time toward questions of religion. Though some critics have felt that he dismissed religion, these texts call for religious unity and attempt to preserve a space for the church in an age of science. *Literature and Dogma* (1873) espouses Arnold's belief that the Bible ought to be considered a remarkable work of literature rather than a piece of dogma subject to historical scrutiny. The essay caused great debate, and Arnold addressed his critics in *God and the Bible: A Review of Objections to* Literature and Dogma (1875). After publishing *Last Es-*

says on Church and Religion in 1877, Arnold moved away from religion as a topic for his writing.

Arnold's final works include essays on a variety of literary and social issues. *Essays in Criticism: Second Series* (1888), a volume that Arnold assembled prior to his death and that was published posthumously, includes famous essays on such authors as Wordsworth and Milton. In it, Arnold makes his final statement about the value of poetry in the modern world. The volume is often considered one of his finest works of criticism.

CRITICAL RECEPTION

Arnold had an often tumultuous relationship with the literary critics of his day. His works of social and literary criticism inspired almost unprecedented discussion in the periodical press, and he himself was a frequent participant in these debates. Many of his works make direct reference to claims raised against him by his critics. We know from his 1853 preface to *Poems,* for example, that Arnold had been taken to task for treating outdated subject matter in such poems as "Empedocles on Etna"; and "The Function of Criticism at the Present Time" makes plain that his lectures on Homer had been censured for giving too much weight to the importance of criticism. *Culture and Anarchy* and *God and the Bible* were developed almost entirely in reaction to critics.

While Arnold's contemporaries often questioned his ideas, they largely respected his talents. Writing in 1887, Richard Holt Hutton attempted to reconcile his disdain for Arnold's writings on religion with his belief that Arnold was "the greatest of our elegiac poets" (*Essays on Some of the Modern Guides of English Thought in Matters of Faith,* 1887). Similarly, Frederic Harrison suggested that while Arnold's system of ideas tended to be "the narrowest and most capricious system that can be invented," he "has more general insight into the intellectual world of our age, and he sees into it more deeply and more surely than any other contemporary poet" (*Tennyson, Ruskin, Mill and Other Literary Estimates,* 1896).

Today Arnold enjoys a reputation as one of the most prominent of the Victorian poets, eclipsed only by Alfred Tennyson and Robert Browning. Stylistically, however, Arnold's poetry is often seen as simplistic, favoring plot over attention to meter. Contemporary scholars have tended to focus on it as an expression of the Victorian zeitgeist, a term Arnold used frequently in his own work. Among those poems such criticism has treated are "Dover Beach," which claims that the world "Hath really neither joy, nor love, nor light, / Nor certitude, not peace, nor help for pain"; and "Stanzas from the Grande Chartreuse," with its worry that the Victori-

ans are "Wandering between two worlds, one dead, / The other powerless to be born." The "dead" world has traditionally been read as the idealized world of the Romantic poets, and scholars have often attempted to ascertain the relationship between Arnold's poetry and that of Wordsworth. Arnold's essay "Wordsworth" (published in *Essays in Criticism: Second Series*) makes clear that he had a great admiration for Wordsworth, and, like his predecessor, he drew heavily on imagery from nature and childhood in his poetry. As current scholarship has noted, however, the realities of the Victorian world caused Arnold to move away from the idealism of romanticism. In "'The Moon Lies Fair': The Poetry of Matthew Arnold," Herbert Coursen Jr. explores Arnold's attempts to return to a Wordsworthian moment that was no longer attainable; William Madden describes Arnold's poetry as "post-Wordsworthian" (*Matthew Arnold: A Study of the Aesthetic Temperament,* 1967); and noted Victorian scholar U. C. Knoepflmacher examines Arnold's ironic use of Wordsworthian scenes and imagery in his critiques of Romantic philosophy ("Dover Revisited: The Wordsworthian Matrix in the Poetry of Matthew Arnold," 1973).

In his introduction to *The Essential Arnold* (1993), Clinton Machann asserts that "Arnold's status as the pre-eminent literary and literary-social critic of the [Victorian] era seems secure." As a general trend, Arnold is often admired for his lofty responses to his age and for his inventive prose but is criticized for what is frequently perceived as a lack of concrete content behind such catchphrases as "sweetness and light," "culture," and the "grand style." Critics have often pointed to Arnold's tendency to gloss over counterevidence in the texts from which he quoted as an indication of haphazard scholarship. Critical treatments of Arnold's prose texts have developed in several veins. Scholars with particular interests in specific topics, including Victorian education or theology, have naturally gravitated toward Arnold's writings on those subjects and have produced a large body of secondary criticism. Interest in issues of class, for example, has drawn scholars to Arnold's extensive critique of the "Philistine" middle classes in *Culture and Anarchy,* while writers interested in education have examined Arnold's career as a school inspector and his endorsement of European models of instruction in *The Popular Education of France, with Notices of That of Holland and Switzerland.* Although his writings on religion have been treated with less frequency in recent years, they were a common topic in Arnold criticism through the 1960s. The growth of studies on race and ethnicity in literature has led to renewed interest in Arnold's treatment of British identity and his work on Celtic language and literature. Daniel G. Williams, a scholar of Welsh literature, argues in *Ethnicity and Culture from Arnold to Du Bois* (2006) that Arnold's vision for British culture worked to actively subsume differences under the banner of "culture"—advocating, for example, the eradication of Welsh as a living language.

PRINCIPAL WORKS

Alaric at Rome: A Prize Poem (poem) 1840

Cromwell: A Prize Poem (poem) 1843

The Strayed Reveller, and Other Poems [as A.] (poetry) 1849

Empedocles on Etna, and Other Poems [as A.] (poetry) 1852

*Poems: A New Edition (poetry) 1853

†Poems: Second Series (poetry) 1855

Merope: A Tragedy (verse drama) 1858

England and the Italian Question (essay) 1859

On Translating Homer: Three Lectures Given at Oxford (lectures) 1861

The Popular Education of France, with Notices of That of Holland and Switzerland (essay) 1861

On Translating Homer: Last Words: A Lecture Given at Oxford (lecture) 1862

Heinrich Heine (essay) 1863

‡Essays in Criticism (criticism) 1865

§New Poems (poetry) 1867

On the Study of Celtic Literature (lectures) 1867

Culture and Anarchy: An Essay in Political and Social Criticism (criticism) 1869

St. Paul and Protestantism, with an Essay on Puritanism and the Church of England (essays) 1870

Friendship's Garland: Being the Conversations, Letters, and Opinions of the Late Arminius, Baron von Thunder-Ten-Tronckh (letters) 1871

Literature and Dogma: An Essay Towards a Better Apprehension of the Bible (essay) 1873

God and the Bible: A Review of Objections to Literature and Dogma (essay) 1875

Last Essays on Church and Religion (essays) 1877

Mixed Essays (essays) 1879

Irish Essays and Others (essays) 1882

Discourses in America (lectures) 1885

Civilization in the United States: First and Last Impressions of America (essay) 1888

Essays in Criticism: Second Series (criticism) 1888

Letters of Matthew Arnold, 1848-1888. 2 vols. (letters) 1895

Matthew Arnold's Notebooks (notebooks) 1902

The Works of Matthew Arnold. 15 vols. (criticism, essays, lectures, poetry, and letters) 1903-04

The Letters of Matthew Arnold to Arthur Hugh Clough (letters) 1932

The Poetical Works of Matthew Arnold (poetry) 1950

The Complete Prose Works of Matthew Arnold. 11 vols. (criticism, lectures, and essays) 1960-77

*This work contains the poems "The Scholar Gipsy" and "Sohrab and Rustum."

†This work contains the poem "Balder Dead."

‡This work contains the essay "The Function of Criticism at the Present Time," which was originally delivered as a lecture at Oxford in 1864.

§This work contains the poems "Stanzas from the Grande Chartreuse" (first published in *Fraser's Magazine* in 1855), "Dover Beach," and "Thyrsis."

CRITICISM

H. G. Hewlett (review date 1874)

SOURCE: Hewlett, H. G. "The Poems of Mr. Matthew Arnold." *Contemporary Review* 24 (September 1874): 539-67.

[*In the following review, Hewlett, a contemporary of Arnold's, situates Arnold's poetry within the British poetic tradition. Hewlett proposes a schema for classifying Arnold's works, offers readings of several poems, and concludes with a call for Arnold to turn his attention back to poetry.*]

Throughout the course of history analysis and synthesis have been observed to advance by alternate strides, the one accumulating Science, the other erecting Art. Equally alternate in its operations must be the activity of that mind which unites the opposite powers whereof Art and Science are the outcome. To be inspired and self-restrained, fervid and sceptical, at one and the same time, is an obvious impossibility; but to pass through these phases at successive periods, to reflect in the critical mood of to-day upon the passionate mood of yesterday, is an experience sufficiently familiar. To balance these moods skilfully, however, giving both free play, without suffering either to encroach upon the other's province, and correct the estimates of the visionary faculty without chilling its enthusiasm, is perhaps among the rarest of gifts. What is easier and more common is to keep the provinces entirely distinct, by not turning the critical faculty inward, but reserving its skill to dissect the productions of others. In this narrow sense, indeed, every poet must be more or less of a critic. Involuntarily, if not consciously, he criticizes what has been already achieved, and measures his own performance thereby. Attempts, therefore, to draw a strict line of demarcation between the poetical and critical functions, and represent their antagonism as internecine, are as futile as they are unjust, and only recoil upon the mischief-makers. The poet of our time who has avowed his high contempt of criticism, in a tone that curiously resembles the outcry of wounded irritability, asserts himself in the same breath the most unsparing critic of his fellow-craftsmen.[1] The only justification of the assumption that the two spheres are necessarily hostile, lies in a distinction which the development of intellectual action has long since deprived of significance. It may be worth while to recal and insist upon it, if the era of decadence through which other literatures have had to pass should ever befal our own, and the rules by which the poet has been critically discovered to work be adopted as substitutes for his intuition. But this danger is happily as yet remote, and meanwhile we may be confident that by those rare seers, to whom the stereoscope and the microscope are equally familiar, their several uses are not likely to be confounded.

The number of our illustrious writers who have been at the same time poets and critics is not yet large. Milton, Dryden, Pope, Wordsworth, Shelley, Byron, and Mrs. Browning, in the first rank; Sidney, Cowley, Prior, Young, Goldsmith, Cowper, Coleridge, Landor, and Scott, in the second rank, are nearly all that can be named among the dead. Of these the majority have been critics only of their fellows, and refrained from any systematic course of self-scrutiny. Wordsworth, Shelley, Byron, and Mrs. Browning, are eminent exceptions, being all intensely self-conscious; but the process of submitting the successive moods of their own minds to revision is comparatively rare with the three first. With Mrs. Browning it is frequent, but her thought is little more than transfigured emotion. Among living poets, Mr. Tennyson has devoted two masterpieces, "The Two Voices" and "In Memoriam," to the task of critical introspection, but they reflect only a single facet of his many-sided genius. In one remarkable poem, "Christmas-eve and Easter-day," and an occasional prologue or epilogue, Mr. Browning may be supposed to make his own mind the subject of analysis, but the personal element in his writings is infinitesimal as compared with the dramatic. The poet next in order, who has carried to its fullest extent the tendency which his forerunners and contemporaries have but indicated, and made it his special distinction at once to give rein to imaginative impulse and maintain the restraint of critical supervision, is Mr. Matthew Arnold. If his poetical are less widely known than his prose writings, they have already a recognized place in modern literature. They are free from certain blemishes and mannerisms which impair the value of his essays to those who most highly esteem them. The ironic humour that therein enlivens his gravest mood, and by which he has achieved the well-nigh impossible feat of making theology an entertaining study, is the only mental trait conspicuouly absent from his poetry; but the loss is atoned for by the discovery of other merits for which those who know him only as a prose-writer would never give him credit. Such differences as exist are manifestly superficial, and do not preclude a fundamental similarity. It is reasonable to interpret one transcript of a writer's mind by an-

other. In studying the poems we have found such acquaintance as we possess with the essays of service as an explanatory aid, and shall scarcely err in attempting to trace a continuity of thought and purpose between the two.

Twenty, or even fifteen, years ago, Mr. Arnold might have been claimed as a partizan by the Neo-Pagan school of thinkers. Not only were his poems imbued with the purest classical spirit, but the elaborate prefaces, in which he laid down the principles that had governed their composition, betrayed his hostility to current modes of thought and feeling, and indifference to the moral and spiritual forces most actively working in modern society, under phrases of vague and sweeping condemnation, suggestive of a deeper aversion and a loftier disdain than they were perhaps intended to convey. In the preface to his collected poems ([*Poems,*] 1853) he gives his reasons for rejecting the theory of modern criticism and the practice of modern art as radically unsound. Far from being "exhausted," as the critic contends, the past furnishes grander subjects for the poet than can ever be found in the present; its actions are greater, its personages nobler, its situations more intense. Far from the poet's ambition being worthy who depicts the condition of his own mind in a representative history, "no great poetical work has ever been produced with such an aim." "Faust," the work "of the greatest poet of modern time," is defective as a poem on that account. The highest art is objective; its noblest aim is to depict great actions. In neglect of the principles by which the Greeks were actuated, the weakness of modern art consists. For all sound intellectual guidance, "in the confusion of the present time," we are referred to them. By the close study of their models a young writer "will deliver himself from the jargon of modern criticism, and escape the danger of producing poetical works conceived in the spirit of the passing time, and which partake of its transitoriness." But they are not guides to us in Art alone. "Their commerce with the ancients appears to me to produce in those who constantly practice it a steadying and composing effect upon their judgment, not of literary works only, but of men and events in general." Those who have addicted themselves to such studies cannot accept the critic's invitation to find subjects for art in their own age. "They are told that it is an era of progress, an age commissioned to carry out the great ideas of industrial development and social amelioration. They reply that with all this they can do nothing; that the elements they need for the exercise of their art are great actions, calculated powerfully and delightfully to affect what is permanent in the human soul; that so far as the present can supply such actions they will gladly make use of them but that an age wanting in moral grandeur can with difficulty supply such, and an age of spiritual discomfort with difficulty be powerfully and delightfully affected by them." His own poems have been composed under this conviction. "In the sincere endeavour to learn and prac- tise, amid the bewildered confusion of our times, what is sound and true in poetical art, I seemed to myself to find the only sure guidance, the only solid footing among the ancients." In conformity with one of their principles, that "Art is dedicated to joy," and that the representation of situations "where the sufferer finds no vent in action" defeats this end by arousing painful emotions, he excludes from the collection his poem of **"Empedocles on Etna."** In the preface to the second edition (1854) Mr. Arnold justifies the spirit of these observations against the comments they had provoked, by a more distinct assertion of his convictions. We are to study the classic writers of antiquity, because "they can help to cure us of what is, it seems to me, the great vice of our intellect, manifesting itself in our incredible vagaries in literature, in art, in religion, in morals, namely, that it is *fantastic,* and wants *sanity.* Sanity, that is the great virtue of the ancient literature; the want of that is the great defect of the modern, in spite of all its variety and power." In the preface to *Merope* (1858) the writer refers to his principles as unchanged, and will not waste argument on critics who demand from a poet nothing but a representation of mental suffering. The animating motives of this attempt to reproduce the forms of Greek tragedy have been "a passion for the great Masters, and an effort to study them without fan- cifulness."

That absorbed in these studies and impressed with these convictions, Mr. Arnold should ever have become inter- ested in the subjective processes of modern thought, should have set himself to investigate the sources of current beliefs, and appear in the character of a theo- logical reformer, was the last development that might have been expected for his career. The phrase, however, that he has somewhere quoted from Cicero, may be fitly applied to himself—"Nemo doctus unquam muta- tionem consilii inconstantiam dixit esse." His prose writings, so far as we are acquainted with them, do not enable us to trace the steps by which this change has been effected. There is a wide gap to be filled, and all we can see is that it has not been bridged over sud- denly. In his *Essays in Criticism,* collected in 1865, the germs of his later essays are visible. There is an antici- pation of *Culture and Anarchy* in **"The Function of Criticism,"** of *Literature and Dogma* in **"Marcus Au- relius."** This last essay is a confession of the limitations by which the highest ethics of antiquity are circum- scribed; that on "Pagan and mediæval religious senti- ment" is a repudiation of the doctrines most distasteful to Christian feeling. In their tone these essays are al- most antithetical to the prefaces from which we have quoted. The reprobation, indeed, of much that modern society cherishes in its habits of thought and practice is as stern as ever, and the wisdom of the old world is still held up for our admiration and example; but the cen- sure and advice are no longer offered by a "spectator ab

extra," an alien who disdainfully comments on a polity in which he has no concern. They proceed from one among ourselves, who is qualified to censure us by rea- son of his close sympathy, to advise us by reason of his superior knowledge. In place of the narrowness which would restrict poetic art to objectivity, and condemn as sterile all ages that could not offer great actions for its themes, we find an avowal of belief that "the grand power of poetry is its interpretative power: that it inter- prets in two ways—by expressing with magical felicity the physiognomy and movement of the outward world, and . . . expressing with inspired conviction the ideas and laws of the inward world of man's moral and spiri- tual nature"—a catholic yet discriminating appreciation of poetic temperaments so dissimilar as those of Shakes- peare, Goethe, Wordsworth, Coleridge, Shelley, Keats, and Maurice de Guérin. The same insight that Mr. Ar- nold brings to bear upon the diversities of the poetic temperament penetrates still deeper. His intimate appre- hension of such characters as Marcus Aurelius, St. Fran- cis, Spinoza, Joubert, Heine, and Eugénie de Guérin, which embrace within their range the polar and tropical regions of the human soul—moral severity and sweet- ness, intellectual refinement and extravagance, religious ardour and sensibility—affords a guarantee of judicial impartiality, with which the partizans of every school, theological or secular, ought to feel satisfied. Himself no longer an extremist, but anxious, as he tells us, "to try and approach Truth on one side after another, not to strive nor cry, not to persist in pressing forward on any one side with violence and self-will," he assumes, for the first time in this volume, the position of arbiter be- tween the World and the Church, the armies of Reason and Progress on the one hand, of Faith and Conserva- tism on the other.

His latest and most notable efforts have proceeded still further in the direction of conciliation. In *Culture and Anarchy* (1869), he has urged the duty of cultivating the totality of human nature as a remedy for the private and public mischiefs incurred by the independent devel- opment of its several provinces,[2] pointing out the spe- cial need among ourselves of retrenching the excess of "Hebraism," and supplying the deficiency of "Helle- nism"—of correcting, that is, a narrow and exclusive attachment to the ethical principles and religious senti- ments inherited from Moses, David, Christ, and Paul, by a broad and comprehensive grasp of the rational principles and æsthetic ideas inherited from Plato, Aris- totle, Sophocles, and Phidias. That by thus fortifying the motives and means of right-doing by the motives and means of right-thinking, there would be set up in each individual, and in the State collectively, a standard of perfection or "best self," having for its object "to make reason and the will of God prevail," is the main drift of the essay. *St. Paul and Protestantism* expands this view by showing that the "best self" of which orga- nized Hebraism stands most in need is the "sweet reasonableness" of Christ, and by clearing away the chief misconceptions which have given rise to schism, seeks to promote harmony in the bosom of the Protestant Church. *Literature and Dogma* gives the same view its most important development by aiming a blow at the misconceptions which interpose a barrier to the reconciliation of Science and Religion. Abandoning the metaphysical abstractions and literary figments of theology as unsubstantial and unverifiable, the writer falls back upon the simplest elements of moral conseiousness and experience as a verifiable basis of belief. That while for Science God may be most adequately conceived as the "stream of tendency whereby all things fulfil the law of their being," for Religion, that is, "morality heightened by emotion," He may be most adequately conceived as "the Eternal Power, not ourselves, which makes for righteousness;" that the apprehension of this by Judaism constituted its historic vitality; and that the substantial benefit conferred by Jesus was to restore and perpetuate the failing intuition of this, by means of "a method of inwardness and a secret of self-renouncement," which have surpassed other rules of conduct in ensuring what it is the aim of all to attain, spiritual peace and joy—are the leading propositions here maintained.

Reconciliation is usually the product of a late stage of mental growth. It can never be attempted with better hope of success than by one who has served under the banners of both the parties between which he seeks to mediate, and has passed from the scene of conflict without losing his sympathy with either. Alike by the associations of his birth and training, and the natural bent of his genius, Mr. Arnold is exceptionally qualified for the task which he has undertaken. From both sides he is entitled to a respectful hearing, as the son of a man whose acumen and erudition were not less esteemed among "Hellenizers," than his moral nobleness and spiritual energy were held in veneration among "Hebraizers"— veneration which he did not forfeit by the concessions he had the courage to make in the direction of rational theology. That Mr. Arnold's training under such a father was imbued with the spirit of Hebraism, might be taken for granted had he not himself referred to it.[3] What his intellectual training was he sufficiently indicates by his ironic allusion to his "having been brought up at Oxford in the bad old times when we were stuffed with Greek and Aristotle."[4] The coincidence of such influences in early life is common to so many minds, that of itself it would confer no special advantage for the work of conciliation. We infer from the study of Mr. Arnold's poems, that he has acquired this advantage by having undergone the change just described, by a transfer of allegiance from one hostile banner to the other, and retirement from the strife into neutral ground without loss of sympathy with either combatant. The order in which his mind underwent this change, however, seems to have been the converse of that which he has since recommended us to follow. These poetic records of his progress show that Hellenism was at first the paramount influence; Hebraism being temporarily in abeyance, but gradually reasserting itself after a period of sceptical transition, which terminated in the ultimate vindication by each of its due share of authority. Speaking roughly, and with due latitude in the matter of dates, we may consider the Poems of his youth and the Prefaces of 1853-4 as on the same intellectual plane; the Poems of his early manhood as filling up the gap between the Prefaces and the Essays of 1865; the Poems of his maturity as explaining and justifying the tone of wise discernment and balanced conviction that characterizes his later Essays.

The interpretation thus put upon the poems will not be clear to readers who are content to accept them in their existing arrangement, and it is therefore necessary to revert to their original form and order. It must be obvious, however, that where we are dealing with successive transcripts of moods no rigorous limitation of dates can possibly be applicable. The least experienced in mental travail know how perpetually the lines of thought traverse and intermingle, how of two ideas, the one discarded yesterday may be the one accepted to-morrow, that the glimmer of light quickly obscured by mists may be the prevision of a revelation which finally commands assent. No other excuse is needed for freely extracting from these volumes any evidence of persistence, change, anticipation, relapse, or recurrence of idea that they may record, without carefully observing the consistency of the dates involved. Reserving for distinct consideration such as are obviously miscellaneous, we may tentatively group the poems into three divisions, corresponding with the periods of one-sidedness, transition, and equilibrium above noted. Each of these groups demands separate notice.

No one has more frankly admitted than Mr. Arnold in his later essays that Hellenism has its faulty side, "a side of moral weakness and of relaxation or insensibility of the moral fibre."[5] Nor from his present standpoint, probably, would he hesitate to endorse Mr. Gladstone's opinion that it was based upon a "principle of the sufficiency of this our human earthly life, without any capital regard to what is before us in futurity, or what is above and around us in the unseen world."[6] At a time, however, when the influence of Hellenism was paramount, no such apprehension of its deficiencies could be reasonably expected of him; and we cannot be surprised to find them reflected in the poems then composed. **"The Strayed Reveller"** is a vivid presentment of the splendid dream-world which intoxication with the cup of Circean pleasure has the power of creating. How momentary the enchantment, how hideous the waking, the author of the original myth did not neglect to show; but of that side of the picture there is no trace in Mr. Arnold's transcript. It cannot be said to be needed, because like all his poems this is intrinsically pure. For the pollutions of the old world, which, to some Neo-Pagan artists seem to constitute its chief attractions, he has never shown the faintest relish. His silence, nevertheless, must be taken to imply that he was sensible of no defect in the conception. The poem ends as it began with the passionate cry of the Reveller for a fresh draught of delirious delight:—

> Faster, faster,
> O Circe, Goddess,
> Let the wild, thronging train
> The bright procession
> Of eddying forms
> Sweep through my soul!

"Empedocles on Etna" (now happily restored to the collected works) is an elaborate attempt to portray in dramatic contrast the three leading types of Hellenic character—the thoughtful, brooding intellect that found expression in philosophy; the sensuous, joyous imagination that embodied itself in art; the credulous, matter-of-fact stamp of minds that made up the public with which philosophers and artists had to deal. Mr. Arnold's idea of Empedocles represents him as a teacher who has outlived not only his popularity, but his self-confidence, a thinker weary of the fruitless search after causes, dissatisfied with every explanation of the Universe that can be proposed, and though able to see for others, like his simple follower Pausanias, the wisdom of acquiescence in the inevitable, and that the moderate expectations thus dictated ensure sufficient happiness for man's life, is unable to apply the lesson to himself, and seeks refuge from despair in suicide. Full of pathetic majesty is the soliloquy of the troubled spirit as it braces up its strength for death. The retrospect of its bright youthful ambitions only deepens the sense of present gloom. Nor is the doubtful anticipation of the future more consoling, for Death may not be annihilation:—

> But mind—but thought—
> If these have been the master part of us;
> Where will they find their parent element? . . .
> But we shall still be in them, and they in us, . . .
> And they will be our lords, as they are now;
> And keep us prisoners of our consciousness,
> And never let us clasp and feel the All
> But through their forms, and modes, and stifling
>   veils; . . .
> And we shall feel the agony of thirst,
> The ineffable longing for the life of life
> Baffled for ever; and still thought and mind
> Will hurry us with them on their homeless
>   march;. . . .
> And then we shall unwillingly return
> Back to this meadow of calamity,
> This uncongenial place, this human life!
> And in our individual human state
> Go through the sad probation all again,
> To see if we will poise our life at last,

> To see if we will now at last be true
> To our own only true deep-buried selves,
> Being one with which, we are one with the whole
>   world.

His solitary gleam of comfort is that though he has

> Lived in wrath and gloom,
> Fierce, disputations, ever at war with man,
> Far from my own soul, far from warmth and light,

he has "not grown easy in these bonds," he has

> Loved no darkness, . . .
> Allowed no fear.

In the sense that it hath been granted him

> Not to die wholly, not to be all enslaved,

"the numbing cloud mounts off" his soul, and he breathes freely. In that moment, lest "the mists of despondency" should again envelope it, he takes the plunge.

Finely contrasted with this agony of morbid self-consciousness is the healthy, æsthetic serenity of Callicles, the young harp-player, whose love of natural beauty, and pity for the wounded spirit of Empedocles, have induced him to linger in one of the mountain-valleys within earshot, and minister the healing influence of music and song. A picture of the calm life which he desires for the sufferer is thus shadowed forth in his rendering of a Theban legend:—

> Far, far from here,
> The Adriatic breaks in a warm bay
> Among the green Illyrian hills! and there
> The sunshine in the happy glens is fair,
> And by the sea, and in the brakes
> The grass is cool, the sea-side air
> Buoyant and fresh, the mountain-flowers
> As virginal and sweet as ours.
> And there, they say, two bright and aged snakes,
> Who once were Cadmus and Harmonia,
> Bask in the glens, or on the warm sea-shore
> In breathless quiet, after all their ills;
> Nor do they see their country, nor the place
> Where the Sphinx lived among the frowning hills,
> Nor the unhappy palace of their race,
> Nor Thebes, nor the Ismenus, any more.

The verses assigned to Callicles illustrate in the most favourable aspect the writer's power of transmuting into English the manner of Greek lyrical poetry. Though not to be compared with the marvellous choric song in "The Lotos-Eaters," or even with some of the choruses in "Atalanta in Calydon," their gracious music must be confessed too exceptional with Mr. Arnold. His later attempts (in *Merope*) to represent accentually the choric rhythm of Greek tragedy are far less satisfactory, but these are avowedly experiments, made in default of finding English measures that produce the same effect; and criticism is frankly deprecated by the admission that "where the ear is guided solely by its own feeling there is a continual risk of failure and of offence." To an ordinary ear, we think, lyrical effect is best conveyed by regularity of metre and rhyme, as *e.g.,* in the concluding verses sung by Callicles in honour of the Muses:—

> Whose praise do they mention?
>   Of what is it told?
> What will be for ever,
>   What was from of old.
> First hymn they the Father
>   Of all things;—and then
> The rest of immortals,
>   The action of men.
> The day in his hotness,
>   The strife with the palm;
> The night in her silence,
>   The stars in their calm.

Some passages are strikingly graphic, especially such as paint the strange contrasts of volcanic scenery. Callicles thus describes his resting-place:—

> For 'tis the last
> Of all the woody, high, well-water'd dells
> On Etna; and the beam
> Of noon is broken there by chestnut boughs
> Down its steep verdant sides; the air
> Is freshened by the leaping stream, which throws
> Eternal showers of spray on the moss'd roots
> Of trees, and veins of turf, and long dark shoots
> Of ivy plants, and fragrant hanging bells
> Of hyacinths, and on late anemones
> That muffle its wet banks; but glade,
> And stream, and sward, and chestnut trees,
> End here. Etna beyond, in the broad glare
> Of the hot noon, without a shade,
> Slope behind slope, up to the peak, lies bare;
> The peak, round which the white clouds play.

The scene from the edge of the crater is still more vividly portrayed, as Empedocles gazes by night over the

> Sea of cloud
> That heaves its white and billowy vapours up
> To moat this isle of ashes from the world,
> . . . And that other fainter sea, far down,
> O'er whose lit floor a road of moon-beams leads
> To Etna's Liparëan sister-fires,
> And the long dusky line of Italy.

Though the direct intrusion of his personality is precluded by the dramatic form, the choice of theme and method of handling are commonly sufficient to mark a dramatist's sympathy. As respects the theme, we have Mr. Arnold's admission that to one situated as Empedocles, "modern problems have presented themselves; we hear already the doubts, we witness the discouragement of Hamlet and Faust" (Preface of 1853). The poem is temporarily excluded from his collected works, on the ground that its exhibition of unrelieved mental suffering is too painful, and a protest entered against the view that to attempt a representation of the state of one's own mind is a worthy poetic aim. This would not of itself amount to a confession that in the thoughts and feelings thus depicted the writer had been reflecting his own scepticism; but such a construction may be reasonably put upon it when we find him giving personal expression to similar thoughts and feelings in poems composed at the same time. We shall presently have to speak of the latter as a separate group, but any one may discover this similarity for himself who, after reading the soliloquies of Empedocles, compares the tone of **"A Summer-Night," "Self-Deception,"** and **"The Scholar-Gipsy."** The persistence with which Mr. Arnold contrasts "the disinterested objectivity" of Callicles with the subjective anguish of the philosopher may be taken to indicate his consolatory faith in the remedial virtues of Art. In **"Memorial Verses,"** another poem of this period, we find Goethe singled out for admiration because he prescribed the same panacea for the ills of his own time. To a mind dominated by the influence of Hellenism, no other conclusion could so fitly suggest itself.

"Mycerinus," though not belonging to the first group by its subject, strictly belongs to it in treatment. The legend told by Herodotus of the Egyptian King who, in the midst of his just and pure reign, was warned by an oracle that he had but six years to live, is here expanded into an impressive and painful picture. The spectacle of a man who, deeming long life to be the reward of just deeds, arraigns the Gods for withholding it, admonishes his subjects to pursue vice instead of virtue, if they would avoid his fate, and devotes his remaining years to a continous revel, is one which perhaps no one but a Neo-Pagan artist, an imitator "not to the manner born," prone to exaggerate the defects as well as the merits of his idol, would select as a congenial theme. If Mr. Arnold is right in his view that the highest aim of Greek tragedy was to produce "a sentiment of sublime acquiescence in the course of fate, and in the dispensations of human life,"⁷ Æschylus and Sophocles would no doubt have forborne the subject. A distinctively Christian artist might choose it to deduce a moral from it; an artist of complete culture might suffer it to point its own moral. Mr. Arnold does neither the one nor the other, but goes out of his way to thrust in a suggestion that throws no light on the positive darkness at which it is directed, and serves to obscure the true significance of the story. "It may be," he says, "that the eye of Mycerinus on his joyless feast"

> Dwelt with mere outward seeming, he within
> Took measure of his soul, and knew its strength;
> And by that silent knowledge, day by day,
> Was calm'd, ennobled, comforted, sustained.

That motives can safely be detached from conduct, an heroic spirit consist with an ignoble life, is a tenet which the author of **Literature and Dogma** would assuredly refuse to sanction. Apart from its ethical flaw, the poem is a fine one, statuesque in conception, lofty in diction, and solemn in rhythm. The writer's adherence to the Greek "principle," to which Mr. Gladstone has referred, has been maintained, it need hardly be said, at the expense of historical fidelity; no doctrines being more deeply-rooted in Egyptian belief than those which are here ignored.

"Sohrab and Rustum" and **"Balder Dead,"** narrative poems drawn respectively from Persian tradition and Scandinavian mythology, both belong to the first group in virtue of their Homeric treatment. We do not doubt that the author has done wisely to disregard as accidental the national peculiarities of the literatures that have furnished his themes, and obtain the advantage of following the world's greatest epical model by assuming all conceptions of an heroic age to be essentially similar. The simple flow of the narrative, unbroken by reflection, the breadth and ease of handling, the unrestrained expression of emotion, the diffuseness of the imagery drawn from natural objects, and the skilful use and repetition of sonorous names, remind one continually of Homer. The Eastern legend takes precedence of the Northern myth in right of its human interest, admitting a larger infusion of the pathos in which Mr. Arnold excels. It turns upon the fortunes of Sohrab, the unknown son of the great Persian warrior Rustum, who, in hope of winning a proud acknowledgment from his father, joined the hostile Tartar tribes, among whom he has attained high distinction, and, on the eve of a great battle, obtains leave from their general to challenge a Persian warrior to single combat. The challenge is accepted by Rustum, who fights in disguise. He and his son encounter on the sands beside the Oxus, each unknown to the other, but the former stirred by deep pity for the daring boy who rushes on death, the latter agitated by strange yearnings towards the majestic warrior who answers to his ideal of father. Rustum, believing that he has no son, repels Sohrab's eager appeal to disclose his name with a taunt that admits of but one rejoinder. The father is at first worsted, and once at the mercy of his son. In the second onset, carried away by excitement, he shouts his battle-cry—"Rustum!"—as he hurls his spear. The name puts Sohrab off his guard, and he falls mortally wounded. A threat extorted from his agony that Rustum will avenge him, brings about the recognition he has so long sought. To prove his parentage, he bares his arm imprinted with the seal which Rustum had given to his mother:—

> Rustum gazed, and gazed, and stood
> Speechless; and then he utter'd one sharp cry:
> 'O boy—*thy father!*' and his voice choked there.
> And then a dark cloud pass'd before his eyes,
> And his head swam, and he sank down to earth.
> But Sohrab crawl'd to where he lay, and cast
> His arms about his neck, and kiss'd his lips,

> And with fond, faltering fingers stroked his cheeks,
> Trying to call him back to life; and life
> Came back to Rustum, and he oped his eyes,
> And they stood wide with horror, and he seized
> In both his hands the dust which lay around,
> And threw it on his head, and smirch'd his hair,
> His hair, and face, and beard, and glittering arms;
> And strong convulsive groanings shook his breast,
> And his sobs choked him; and he clutch'd his sword
> To draw it, and for ever let life out:
> But Sohrab saw his thought, and held his hands.

The death of the son in his father's arms, amid the awestruck silence of the hosts as night falls, is told with simple solemnity. Not the least impressive touch of art is the recurring reference to the presence of the great river beside which the tragedy is enacted, that contrasts the calm dignity of its course with the unseemly turbulence of human passions, its unexhausted permanence with their transience and decay. The poet's faithfulness to his method of Greek conception is again shown in his treatment of death:—

> Unwillingly the spirit fled away,
> Regretting the warm mansion which it left,
> And youth, and bloom, and this delightful world.

The farewells of the dying son and the bereaved father contain nothing that betokens their conviction or desire of aught beyond the grave.

If Mr. Arnold fails to move his readers to equal interest in **"Balder Dead,"** the subject rather than himself may be responsible. The delineation of beings so anomalous as the Gods of Scandinavian mythology is attended with difficulties that Art can scarcely hope to overcome, the sense of which has a tendency to restrain one's sympathy. Those who are not thus repelled by the subject will find the treatment throughout in admirable keeping, and some of the descriptive passages singularly pictorial.

The special aptitude of Mr. Arnold's genius, in its early phases of development, for dealing with themes drawn from Hellenic or cognate sources, is attested by the inadequacy of his attempts in other directions. His **"Tristram and Isolt,"** a half-dramatic, half-narrative version of one of the most vivid and passionate stories in the Arthurian cycle of legends, is curiously tame and cold; its highest effects being attained in some graceful touches of sentiment and faithful landscape-painting. An unavoidable comparison with the superlative art of the master to whom the Arthurian cycle is consecrated might be thought to explain his failure in this instance, if it were not equally conspicuous in his treatment of a mediæval subject, such as **"The Church of Brou."** For genuine sympathy with a conception of post-Pagan or distinctively Christian art, he seems at this period to have been constitutionally indisposed, the spiritual conviction upon which such sympathy should be based being as yet wanting. The evidence of this deficiency must be mainly negative, but positive confirmation could scarcely be stronger than the language of the fine sonnet composed during the revolutionary crisis of 1848-9, when the springs of so many earnest natures were sounded to their depths:—

> Who props, thou ask'st, in these bad days, my mind?
> He much, the old man, who, clearest-shul'd of men,
> Saw the Wide Prospect, and the Asian Fen,
> And Tmolus Hill, and Smyrna bay, though blind.
> Much he, whose friendship I not long since won,
> That halting slave, who in Nicopolis
> Taught Arrian, when Vespasian's brutal son
> Clear'd Rome of what most shamed him. But be his
> My special thanks, whose even-balanced soul,
> From first youth tested up to extreme old age.
> Business could not make dull, nor passion wild;
> Who saw life steadily, and saw it whole;
> The mellow glory of the Attic stage.
> Singer of sweet Colonus and its child.

One has only to compare this confession with that put forth in the stanzas of "In Memoriam," written at the same period:—

> And all is well, though faith and form
>   Be sundered in the night of fear, &c.

to appreciate the difference as respects a basis of moral confidence between the "Hellenic" and the "Hebrew" spirit.

No tenets could better harmonize with a belief in the essential objectivity of Art than those of the Stoics, the most practical and least subjective of the schools. But it was the historic destiny of Stoicism to fall before Scepticism, and a modern adherent could expect no otherwise for himself. Mr. Arnold had scarcely announced a sense of security in his fortress than it seemed to be shaken. Doubts as to the all-sufficiency of Greek art and Stoical ethics to sustain a soul in the "bad times" of social anarchy obtrude themselves in the contemporary sonnets addressed to a Republican friend. They deprecate, indeed, all rash attempts to forestal the Divine determination of events, and preach the wisdom of patience as the only remedy for existing evils, but betray a feeling that is appreciably warmer than the due temperature of philosophic apathy:—

> If sadness at the long heart-wasting show,
> Wherein earth's great ones are disquieted;
> If thoughts, not idle, while before me flow,
> The armies of the homeless and unfed—
> If these are yours, if this is what you are,
> Then am I yours, and what you feel I share.

In **"Resignation,"** another poem of the same period, studiously calm as is the tenor of its individual counsels—

> Be passionate hopes not ill resigned,
> For quiet and a fearless mind; . . .

> For they, believe me, who await
> No gifts from chance have conquered Fate—

the surface is ever and anon disturbed by the welling-forth of emotional sympathy. It may be discerned in the description of the Gipsies, for whom—

> Time's busy touch,
> While it mends little troubles much; . . .
> They must live still; and yet, God knows,
> Crowded and keen the country grows!

and yet more clearly in the closing lines, which remind those who prefer an "intemperate prayer" to Fate,

> For movement, for an ampler sphere,

how many there are who suffer dumbly:—

> Not milder is the general lot,
> Because our spirits have forgot
> In action's dizzying eddy hurled,
> The something that infects the world.

In such passages as these there are indications, however faint, that "Hebraism," though still in abeyance, was troubling the writer's spirit. They inaugurate a period of transition which brought to a close his exclusive subservience to Hellenic influences. The first step taken in that direction was the abandonment of his cherished aversion to subjective poetry. His extravagant protests against it in theory continued long after he had assented to the practice, and were probably due to the consciousness of his own bias for what he deemed a fatal weakness. Nothing operates upon a strenuous nature more effectually, perhaps, than such a consciousness as an inducement to over-act the tyrant. But the soul holds on its course in supreme unconcern for all theories and prepossessions whatsoever. Mr. Arnold became a subjective poet involuntarily, and because the pursuit of truth led him through the furnace of doubt. He has only added one more to the number of those who

> Learn in suffering what they teach in song.

The sensible decrease manifest from this time forth in the flow of his creative impulse, and the increase, *pari passu,* of introspection in its stead, are the first characteristics of this period of transition. The critical bent of his genius now unmistakably asserts itself. Rarely is an impression upon the mental retina simply recorded, but has to be carefully analyzed, sifted, and reduced to a formula. So patiently is the process conducted, that the poet often seems to regard his subject as an entity apart, like a physician who, to watch the effect of an experiment upon himself, undertakes to regulate his own temperature and time his own pulse. In one or two poems, *e.g.,* **"Youth's Agitations"** and **"Growing Old,"** he attains to the ruthless calm of a vivisector. This tone of self-scrutiny is common to both the second and third groups of poems. The distinguishing note of the former is their reflection of the sceptical phase through which the writer was passing. Every thinker worthy of the name has to make such a passage at some time or other, but perhaps it was never undertaken by a larger number of sincere and vigorous minds in company than at the period to which these poems belong. John Sterling, Arthur Clough, Mr. Francis Newman, Mr. Froude, and others of the fellowship, have severally recorded their experience. The incidents doubtless vary in each case, but we remember no more graphic expression of the moral uneasiness and spiritual darkness, often verging on despair, which are among the commonest sequels of such a crisis, than Mr. Arnold has given in his **"Scholar-Gipsy."**

Its imaginative thread is found in a story told by Glanvil of an undergraduate at Oxford, forced by poverty to leave his studies and join a tribe of Gipsies, from whom he acquired a knowledge of their secret lore. Having been recognized and accosted during one of his wanderings by two former fellow-students, he recounted the story of his flight, and of the learning he had gained, declaring his intention at some favourable opportunity of making it known to the world. The peaceful nomadic life, which, by a graceful fiction, he is represented as still leading in the rural neighbourhood of Oxford, and the happy confidence with which he waits for a "heaven-sent moment" to announce his revelation, serve as a pointed contrast to the chaotic unrest of which the University is a typical centre, the self-mistrust and hopelessness of regaining conviction from which the most thoughtful of its members suffer:—

> O life unlike to ours!
> Who fluctuate idly without term or scope,
>   Of whom each strives, nor knows for what he
>   strives,
> And each half lives a hundred different lives;
>   Who wait like thee, but not like thee, in hope.
>
> Thou waitest for the spark from Heaven! and we,
> Light half-believers of our casual creeds,
>   Who never deeply felt, nor clearly will'd,
> Whose insight never has borne fruit in deeds,
>   Whose vague resolves never have been fulfill'd,
> For whom each year we see
> Breeds new beginnings, disappointments new;
>   Who hesitate and falter life away,
> And lose to-morrow the ground won to-day—
>   Ah, do not we, wanderer, await it too?
>
> Yet! we await it, but it still delays,
> And then we suffer! and amongst us one
>   Who most has suffer'd, takes dejectedly
> His seat upon the intellectual throne; . . .
>   This for our wisest! and we others pine,
> And wish the long unhappy dream would end,
> And waive all claim to bliss, and try to bear,
>   With close-lipp'd patience for our only friend—

> Sad patience, too near neighbour to despair;
>   But none has hope like thine!

The tone of sad yearning and bitter dissatisfaction in which this poem is pitched is fortunately not long sustained; but with modified intensity it runs through all the poems belonging to Mr. Arnold's middle period. The **"Stanzas in Memory of Obermann"** (1849) are an expression of deep sympathy with the philosophic Senancour, who, saddened by the spectacle which his age presented, retired to solitary communion with Nature; an example which the poet, perplexed with the "hopeless tangle" of his own time, would fain follow, but for the fate that drives him forth into the world:—

> Thou, sad guide, adieu!
> I go; Fate drives me, but I leave
> Half of my life with you.

In the **"Stanzas from the Grande Chartreuse,"** the sense of his own neutral, transitory attitude, between allegiance to authority that has ceased to control him and acceptance of a system that does not command his reverence, prompts him to sympathy with those adherents of an outworn faith who have the courage to retire from a world that disowns them, and for which they know themselves unfit:—

> Wandering between two worlds, one dead,
>   The other powerless to be born,
> With nowhere yet to rest my head;
>   Like these on earth I wait forlorn.
> Their faith, my tears, the world deride,
> I come to shed them at their side.

In the **"Memorial Verses"** on the death of Wordsworth (1850) his feeling is embodied in a tribute of reverence to the great poetic thinkers who have not been conquered by the problems of their age, but in their several ways have evinced the consciousness of mastery. Byron presented the spectacle of defiant force which, however terrible to witness in its strife "of passion with eternal law," was majestic in virtue of its "fiery life":—

> He taught us little; but our soul
> Had *felt* him like the thunder's roll.

Goethe offered the nobler example of calm æsthetic wisdom:—

> He took the suffering human race,
> He read each wound, each weakness clear,
> And struck his finger on the place,
> And said, '*Thou ailest here, and here!*'
> He looked on Europe's dying hour
> Of fitful dream and feverish power;
> His eye plunged down the weltering strife,
> The turmoil of expiring life;
> He said, '*The end is everywhere!*
> *Art still has truth, take refuge there!*'

Wordsworth, the last of the triad, fulfilled the noblest mission by recalling the soul to sympathy with Nature:—

> He, too, upon a wintry clime
> Had fallen, on this iron time
> Of doubts, despairs, distractions, fears.
> He found us when the age had bound
> Our souls in its benumbing round:
> He spoke, and loosed our hearts in tears.
> He laid us, as we lay at birth,
> On the cool flowery lap of earth;
> Smiles brake from us and we had ease;
> The hills were round us, and the breeze
> Went o'er the sun-lit fields again;
> Our foreheads felt the wind and rain:
> Our youth returned.

With his death, however, the hope of Europe seemed dead:—

> Others will teach us how to dare,
> And against fear our breast to steel;
> Others will strengthen us to bear,
> But who, ah! who will make us feel?
> The cloud of mortal destiny
> Others will front as fearlessly,
> But who, like him, will put it by?

The same jaundiced mood that finds its sombre hues reflected in the world and, though solaced by the memory of the past, discerns no outlook of comfort in the present or the future, recurs in "A Summer-Night;" but here the gracious influence which Wordsworth had worshipped effects a partial cure. Though the poet still carries about with him

> The old unquiet breast,
> Which never deadens into rest,
> Nor ever feels the fiery glow
> That whirls the spirit from itself away;

and questions if there can be any life for man but that of "madman or slave," one who defies his fate or is made captive by it, yet the moonlit, starry heaven suggests that there is a possible alternative:—

> Ye heavens whose pure dark regions have no sign
> Of languor, though so calm, and, though so great,
> Are yet untroubled and unpassionate;
> Who, though so noble, share in the world's toil,
> And, though so tasked, keep free from dust and soil!
> . . . you remain
> A world above man's head, to let him see
> How boundless inight his soul's horizon be,
> How vast, yet of what clear transparency!
> How it were good to live there, and breathe free!
> How fair a lot to fill
> Is left to each man still!

In the lines written beside the grave of Dr. Arnold, in Rugby Chapel (1857) ["**Rugby Chapel**"], this glimmer of hope has brightened. He is remembered as one whose "even cheerfulness" sustained him unwearied through a career of lofty and beneficent exertion, devoted to the service of the Father in whom he trusted and the brothers whom he loved. The son of such a man has assuredly warrant to

> Believe
> In the noble and great who are gone, . . .
> Not like the men of the crowd,
> Who all around me to-day
> Bluster or cringe, and make life
> Hideous, and arid, and vile;
> But souls tempered with fire,
> Fervent, heroic, and good;
> Helpers and friends of mankind.

Nor is the faith wholly vain that such souls may still appear amid their "fainting dispirited race," like angels in the hour of need:—

> Ye alight in our van! at your voice,
> Panic, despair, flee away.
> Ye move through the ranks, recal
> The stragglers, refresh the outworn,
> Praise, re-inspire the brave!
> Order, courage, return;
> Eyes rekindling, and prayers
> Follow your steps as ye go.
> Ye fill up the gaps in our files,
> Strengthen the wavering line,
> Stablish, continue our march
> On, to the bound of the waste,
> On, to the City of God!

Here again Hebraism is plainly struggling to the surface. But the example of one who solves the problem of life by the energetic discharge of a recognized duty is not enough to stimulate a spirit which doubt has paralyzed for action. An example that should suffice for this would be that of a man whose scepticism never let him rest, but urged him unceasingly forward in quest of a satisfactory solution. Such an one Mr. Arnold finds in Arthur Clough, to whose memory his **"Thyrsis"** is dedicated. It forms a companion ode to **"The Scholar-Gipsy,"** but is pitched in a more plaintive key. Since Milton's "Lycidas" and Shelley's "Adonais," no more exquisite monody has been tuned in English to a classic strain. Borrowing the pastoral language of Theocritus, the poet bewails his fellow-shepherd with whom he had so often frequented the Scholar-Gipsy's haunts, especially the neighbourhood of a great elm which they had associated with his wandering existence, and agreed to accept as a token that he still pursued it. Here Thyrsis and his friend had passed the spring of life, rejoicing in "each simple joy the country yields," assaying together their "shepherd-pipes," and cherishing aspirations which Fate and Time had combined to baffle. For Thyrsis "a shadow lowered on the fields," and he could not remain:—

> Some life of men unblest,
> He knew, which made him droop, and filled his head.

> He went; his piping took a troubled sound
> Of storms that rage outside our happy ground;
> He could not wait their passing, he is dead.

Upon his friend also the shadow has fallen:—

> And long the way appears which seemed so short
> To the less practised eye of sanguine youth;
> And high the mountain-tops in cloudy air—
> The mountain-tops where is the throne of Truth;
> Tops in life's morning-sun so bright and bare!
> Unbreachable the fort
> Of the long-battered world uplifts its wall,
> And strange and vain the earthly turmoil grows;
> And near and real the charm of thy repose,
> And night as welcome as a friend would fall.

But accepting as a happy omen that "the tree" still crowns the height, and the Scholar-Gipsy, "by his own heart inspired," still lives his peaceful life and waits for Heaven's opportunity, the poet calls to mind how Thyrsis, animated by the same ambition, followed the same unworldly course:—

> What though the music of thy rustic flute
> Kept not for long its happy country tone:
> Lost it too soon, and learnt a stormy note
> Of men contention-tost, of men who groan,
> Which task'd thy pipe too sore, and tired thy throat:
> It failed, and thou wast mute!
> Yet hadst thou alway visions of our light,
> And long with men of care thou could'st not stay,
> And soon thy foot resumed its wandering way,
> Left human haunt, and on alone till night!

To his friend a like path lies open:—

> Then through the great town's harsh heart-wearying
>   roar,
> Let in thy voice a whisper often come
>   To chase fatigue and fear.
> Why faintest thou? I wandered till I died:
> Roam on! the light we sought is shining still!

In the third group of Mr. Arnold's poems we include those which take the motive here suggested as a point of departure. They indicate a gradual process of recovery from the morbid mental condition in which those belonging to his middle period were written, an approximation to the tone of balanced conviction and healthy hopefulness that characterises his later Essays. Criticism is the form of poetic reflection which these symptoms of convalescence commonly take; the scene and subject of an unhealthy mood being recalled for analysis, and the partial or false view in which it originated corrected by subsequent experience. The poem of "Obermann Once More" thus forms an answer to the "Stanzas in Memory of Obermann," written twenty years before. The spirit of the hermit-philosopher with those despair he had sympathized, and whose solitude he had yearned to embrace, now monishes him to avoid the error of a "frustrate life," and to advance by coura-

geous and cheerful enterprize the attainment of that brighter day which had begun to dawn upon the world:—

> Despair not thou as I despaired,
>   Nor be cold gloom thy prison!
> Forward the gracious hours have fared,
>   And see! the sun is risen.
> He walks the icebergs of the past,
>   A green new earth appears!
> Millions whose life in ice lay fast,
>   Have thoughts and smiles and tears. . . .
>
> But thou, though to the world's new hour,
>   Thou come with aspect marred,
> Shorn of the joy, the bloom, the power,
>   Which best beseem its bard.
> Though more than half thy years be past,
>   And spent thy youthful prime,
> Though round thy firmer manhood cast,
>   Hang weeds of our sad time;
> Whereof thy youth felt all the spell,
>   And traversed all the shade,
> Though late, though dimmed, though weak, yet tell,
>   Hope to a world re-made!

The tone of these verses may be compared with that of a passage in the contemporary Essay, commencing, "And is not the close and bounded intellectual horizon within which we have long lived and moved now lifting up? and are not new lights finding free passage to shine in upon us?" (*Culture and Anarchy,* pp. 9, 10). The active intercourse with the world for which he felt himself unfitted, and undertook only under compulsion, could have given no better proof of its tonic virtue than by thus clearing his perception of the real state of society, and bracing his sense of the obligations of genius in regard to it.

The **"Memorial Verses"** on the death of Wordsworth are in like manner reviewed and answered in **"The Youth of Nature,"** written beside his grave. The "sacred poet" may well be mourned by those to whom he was a priest, but with his death the hope of mankind does not die, for the "loveliness, magic, and grace" of Nature, which he interpreted, transcend and outlast him.

> They are here! they are set in the world!
> They abide! and the finest of souls
> Has not been thrilled by them all,
> Nor the dullest been dead to them quite.
> The poet who sings them may die,
> But they are immortal, and live,
> For they are the life of the world!

The mood in which **"A Summer-Night"** was written is in the same way summoned for comparison with the feelings suggested under similar circumstances at a later period. The wound inflicted on the writer's affections by a recent sorrow, to which the poem of **"A Southern Night"** is consecrated, has made him insensible to the pain of the intellectual trouble that formerly possessed him. The ideal life of man which, as figured in the purity of the starry heavens, once seemed so remote of attainment, now seems nearer to realization, in memory of the "high-souled" "gentle" lives whose loss he is deploring, in presence of the divine beauty of Nature to which they bore affinity:—

> And what but gentleness untired,
>   And what but noble feeling warm,
> Wherever shown, howe'er inspired,
>   Is grace, is charm?
> What else is all these waters are,
>   What else is steeped in lucid sheen,
> What else is bright, what else is fair,
>   What else serene?
> Mild o'er her grave, ye mountains, shine!
>   Gently by his, ye waters, glide!
> To that in you which is divine,
>   They were allied.

The assertion by the affections of their mastery over the intellect in supplying a ground of confidence when its assurance fails, is the theme of **"Dover Beach."** Standing beside the shore from which the tide is ebbing, the "eternal note of sadness" reminds him that—

> The Sea of Faith
> Was once, too, at the full, and round earth's shore
> Lay like the folds of a bright girdle furled;
> But now I only hear
> Its melancholy, long, withdrawing roar,
> Retreating to the breath
> Of the night wind down the vast edges drear
> And naked shingles of the world.

But the reflection brings no longer the old sense that all is lost to him:—

> Ah, love, let us be true
> To one another!

The power of love to reveal man's inner nature to himself, of which his other faculties disclose no glimpse, is the subject of **"A Buried Life"**:—

> Yet still, from time to time, vague and forlorn,
> From the soul's subterranean depth upborne,
> As from an infinitely distant land,
> Come airs, and floating echoes, and convey
> A melancholy into all our day.
> Only, but this is rare!
> When a beloved hand is laid in ours,
> When, jaded with the rush and glare
> Of the interminable hours,
> Our eyes can in another's eyes read clear
> When our world-deafen'd ear
> Is by the tones of a loved voice caress'd:
> A bolt is shot back somewhere in our breast,
> And a lost pulse of feeling stirs again.
> The eye sinks inward, and the heart lies plain,
> And what we mean, we say, and what we would, we
>   know.

> A man becomes aware of his life's flow,
> And hears its winding murmur, and he sees
> The meadows where it glides, the sun, the breeze; . . .
> And then he thinks he knows
> The hills where his life rose,
> And the sea where it goes.

This and such a poem as **"The Future,"** seem inspired by the conviction that our emotional and spiritual instincts, and the harmonies which imagination constructs upon them, impalpable as they are, afford a better guarantee of certitude concerning the mysterious problems of existence than we can obtain elsewhere. To how many of us a vague but tender trust in Love, an *abandon* of imaginative speculation, and sense of room for hope in the infinite possibilities of the universe, are incomparably more satisfying than the dogmatic affirmations of Theology, or the not less dogmatic negations of Science! The poet's voice acquires a fuller and deeper tone than is usual with him as the mystery of the future is thus unfolded to his yearning gaze:—

> Haply the river of Time
> As it grows, as the trees on its marge
> Fling their wavering lights
> On a wider, statelier stream,
> May acquire if not the calm
> Of its early mountainous shore,
> Yet a solemn peace of its own.
> And the width of the waters, the hush
> Of the grey expanse where he floats,
> Freshening its current, and spotted with foam,
> As it draws to the Ocean, may strike
> Peace to the soul of the man on its breast:
> As the pale waste widens around him,
> As the banks fade dimmer away,
> As the stars come out, and the night wind
> Brings up the stream
> Murmurs and scents of the infinite Sea.

The due limitation of the indulgence which should be given to the soul's "aberglaube" is rightly defined in Mr. Arnold's latest criticism. The tendency of such extra-belief "to substitute itself for Science," in cases where Science has something positive to affirm, is undoubtedly, as he points out, a fruitful source of superstition. But he is not less careful to allow that "that which we hope, augur, imagine, is the poetry of life, and has the rights of poetry."[8] It fills up the gap which Science sternly seeks to widen and Theology vainly attempts to bridge over. Herein lies its value, and it is the recognition of this that constitutes the charm of these poems.

The criterion of inward assurance and the experimental sanction of happiness which our spiritual instincts possess, are possessed in a still greater degree by those moral intuitions, reliance on which, as the one verifiable basis of belief, is preached in *Literature and Dogma.* Such poems as **"Self-dependence,"** and **"Palladium"** attest that the talisman which the writer thus commends to the acceptance of all doubtful minds has been long cherished by his own. "Severely clear," he hears a cry from his own heart that answers to the cry of the "self-poised" stars—

> Resolve to be thyself! and know that he
> Who finds himself loses his misery!

Like the Palladium that stood "high 'mid rock and wood" above Troy, which could not fall whilst it was firm—

> Still doth the soul from its lone fastness high,
> Upon our life a ruling effluence send;
> And when it fails, fight as we will, we die,
> And while it lasts we cannot wholly end.

The gradual reassertion by Hebraism of that share of authority which had long been denied to its influence, and the attainment of an equilibrium between it and Hellenism is shown more or less distinctly in **"The Better Part," "Pis-aller," "Progress,"** and **"East London."** To those for whom a creed affords the only stronghold of moral security he has no other gospel to preach: "For God's sake, believe it then!" To those who find in the absence of supernatural control an excuse for lawlessness, he makes an inward appeal:—

> Hath man no second life? *Pitch this one high!*
> Sits there no judge in Heaven our sin to see?
> *More strictly then the inward judge obey!*
> Was Christ a man like us? *Ah! let us try*
> *If we then, too, can be such men as he!*

To those whom zeal for intellectual freedom impels to a rash iconoclasm he points the value of all religious safeguards:—

> Which has not taught weak wills how much they can?
> Which has not fallen on the dry heart like rain?
> Which has not cried to sunk, self-weary man,
> '*Thou must be born again!*'

Every reader of *Culture and Anarchy* will observe the coincidence of its teaching with the drift of the foregoing. The cultivation of a standard of "right reason or best self," so eloquently urged in this Essay, is enjoined as emphatically in **"Morality"** and **"The Second Best."** That

> Tasks in hours of insight willed,
> Can be thro' hours of gloom fulfilled;

that he is the wise man

> Who through all he meets can steer him,
> Can reject what cannot clear him,
> Cling to what can truly cheer him!
>   Who each day more surely learns
> That an impulse, from the distance
> Of his deepest, best existence,
> To the words, 'Hope, Light, Persistence,'
>   Strongly sets and truly burns!

are the rules here prescribed for the healthy conduct of life. The depreciation of our national dignity for want of such a standard of collective right reason, which is the text of the writer's satirical sermon in *Friendship's Garland,* is the subject of a pregnant allusion in the poem of **"Heine's Grave."**

Varied expressions of that intelligent sympathy with the spirit and history of the Christian Church which gives force to Mr. Arnold's conciliatory efforts in *St. Paul and Protestantism,* will be found in two or three of his later sonnets. The simplification of religious ideas to which he has devoted his ultimate efforts is more than once referred to in his poems as a reform that cannot be averted:—

> Alone, self-poised, henceforward man
>   Must labour! must resign
> His all too human creeds, and scan
>   Simply the way Divine.

The moral Pantheism, as one may succinctly describe it, which driven from Personal Theism as an unverifiable hypothesis, finds solid ground in a conception of God as "the Eternal Power, not ourselves, which makes for righteousness," and the Christianity that finds in the method and secret of its founder, inwardness and self-renouncement, the truest philosophy, are not obscurely avowed in such passages as the following:—

> God's wisdom and God's goodness! Ay, but fools
> Misdefine these till God knows them no more.
> Wisdom and Goodness they are God! What schools
> Have yet so much as heard this simple lore?

> * * *

>   When my ill-schooled spirit is aflame,
> Some nobler, ampler stage of life to win,
> I'll stop and say, 'There were no succour here,
> The aids to noble life are all within.'

> * * *

> Calm soul of all things! make it mine
>   To feel amid the city's jar,
> That there abides a peace of thine,
>   Man did not make and cannot mar!

> The will to neither strive nor cry,
>   The power to feel with others, give!
> Calm, calm me more! nor let me die,
>   Before I have begun to live.

The classification thus attempted of Mr. Arnold's chief poems into three groups, representing three stages of mental progress, has been admittedly conjectural, and may be open to correction in detail. If, however, as we believe, it substantially affords the clue to their interpretation, the student who accepts it as a whole can correct the details for himself. It could be wished that in some future edition the author would take the matter out of his critics' hands, and indicate the true order in which his poems should be studied. Their existing arrangement is not unlikely to mislead some readers, and to them these volumes must appear a strange miscellany, a mirror of moods in perpetual flux and reflux. A writer of thoroughly unstable mind is scarcely entitled to take the public into confidence, and can certainly expect no sympathy. One could only criticize to condemn the tendency of such a poem as **"Stanzas from the Grande Chartreuse,"** if it were to be accepted as a definitive expression of conviction. A jeremiad which dismisses the time present as characterized by decayed Faith, and unvivifying Science, and avers that "the kings of modern thought are dumb," waiting for the future, till when it behoves them to follow the example of monastic seclusion, and "die out with these last of the people who believe," could only inspire irritation at the writer's morbid perverseness, or at best such regret as those eccentric utterances of Mr. Ruskin inspire, which seem to proclaim his alienation from the spirit of his age, and his resolution to neutralize the influence he has hitherto exerted upon it. Viewed, however, as one of many phases in an intellectual revolution, the mood here reflected cannot but excite the deepest sympathy, and we welcome its record as a valuable addition to psychological poetry.

The poems that cannot be assigned to one or other of the groups proposed are comparatively few. They do not manifest Mr. Arnold's possession of any qualifications hitherto unnoted; but to two of them, depth of feeling and faithful observation of Nature, they bear fuller testimony. In the series entitled **"Faded Leaves,"** the swift process of a real love-tragedy is recorded with peculiar tenderness. Certain poems which in earlier editions were interspersed with the foregoing, have since been collected into a companion series, entitled **"Switzerland."** The separation is judicious, as the latter mark with much delicacy the gradual awakening of the affections from an illusion not destined to last. Of the delineation of passion Mr. Arnold's poems scarcely afford an example. His **"Modern Sappho,"** a study of a woman's heart, restrained by the height of its love from the low impulses of jealousy, might serve for a type of his own Muse. Her crystalline purity is not to be mistaken for coldness. It is not the flesh that is weak, but the spirit that is stronger.

Perhaps the most touching example of his pathetic vein is the lyric of **"The Forsaken Merman"** to his children, as they relinquish their fruitless quest for the mortal bride and mother who has left them, and returned to earth:—

> Call her once before you go—
> Call once yet!

> In a voice that she will know:
> 'Margaret! Margaret!'
> Children's voices should be dear,
> (Call once more) to a mother's ear;
> Children's voices, wild with pain—
> Surely she will come again!

> Call her once and come away.
> This way, this way!
> 'Mother, dear, we cannot stay!
> The wild white horses foam and fret.
> Margaret! Margaret!'

> Come, dear children, come away down!
> Call no more!
> One last look at the white-wall'd town,
> And the little grey church on the windy shore;
> Then come down!
> She will not come though you call all day,
> Come away, come away!

Mr. Arnold's skill in painting landscape has been shown in the extract given from **"Empedocles on Etna."** Many of the poems to which we have adverted as subjectively gloomy are brightened by occasional glimpses of that objective Nature which was the poet's first love. The touches that thus delineate the change of the seasons afford a relief which cannot be overlooked by the readers of **"The Scholar-Gipsy"** and **"Thyrsis"**:—

> The sweet spring-days
> With whitening hedges and uncrumpling fern,
> And blue-bells trembling by the forest-ways,
> And scent of hay new-mown.

> * * *

> Soon will the high Midsummer pomps come on,
>   Soon will the musk carnations break and swell,
> Soon shall we have gold-dusted snapdragon,
>   Sweetwilliam with his homely cottage-smell,
>   And stocks in fragrant blow.

> * * *

> Through the thick corn the scarlet poppies peep,
> And round green roots and yellowing stalks I see
> Pale blue convolvulus in tendrils creep,
>   And air-swept lindens yield
> Their scent, and rustle down their perfumed showers
> Of bloom on the bent grass where I am laid,
> And bower me from the August sun with shade.

> * * *

> This winter eve is warm,
> Humid the air! leafless yet soft as spring
> The tender purple spray on copse and briars.

If comparatively little stress has been laid upon Mr. Arnold's qualifications as an artist, it is because with him, as in a still greater degree with Mr. Browning, art has been made subordinate to thought. With Mr. Tennyson alone among the poets of our time—taking each at his best—one is sensible of that intimate harmony between spirit and form which not only forbids the separation of one from the other, but makes it inconceivable that the idea could be conveyed in more perfect language. The most quotable of Mr. Arnold's words are not so "married" to music that it would seem profane to divorce them, nor does that music, except in rare moments, keep us under its spell. Art, nevertheless, has been a matter of real concern with him, as is abundantly evident from the careful construction and diction of his principal poems. A few harsh phrases or uneven lines count for nothing, where there is so pervading an impression of order, tune, and polish. Though not specially epigrammatic, he is an eminently luminous writer. How much historic light, for example, is concentrated in this verse on the attitude of Oriental faith during the domination of Rome:—

> The East bowed low before the blast
>   In patient deep disdain:
> She let the legions thunder past,
>   And plunged in thought again.

How truthful in its discernment and wide in its application is this reflection upon life's attrition:—

> This is the curse of life, that not
>   Another, calmer train
> Of wiser thoughts and feelings blot
>   Our passions from our brain;
> But each day brings its petty dust
>   Our soon-choked souls to fill,
> And we forget because we must,
>   And not because we will.

His lyrical scope is limited, but he has treated several forms with success, especially that which for want of a better name must still be called the "regular ode." In several minor lyrics he has justified his adoption of accentual rhythm by proofs of its musical capability that were wanting in the choruses of **Merope.** In his sonnets, though they are not always accurate in form, nor commended to our ear by his division of the octave and sestette into their component parts, the arrangement of the sentences is skilfully adjusted to the conditions imposed. In the management of the eight-syllable couplet, a metre too seldom employed in modern verse, he is extremely successful.

We may conclude with the hope that Mr. Arnold's prolonged absence upon foreign service does not imply (as one of his critics supposes) that he has relinquished the arena in which his first laurels were won. Consummate as is his mastery of English prose, and immediate as may be its efficacy of operation, the gifts which have gained for him the third place in the hierarchy of living poets cannot fail to ensure a more permanent influence. *Pace* Mr. Carlyle's authority, poetic speech is to be preferred to prose speech as a medium of utterance, if for no other reason than this, that it takes firmer hold of the hearer's memory. Music, condensation, grace, point,

emphasis, are elements of eloquence that no teacher can afford to despise, and he can never blend them so perfectly as in poetry. For one apophthegm of our greatest prose writers, Bacon, Hooker, Hobbes, Milton, Taylor, Addison, Gibbon, Burke, that dwells in popular remembrance, Shakespeare, Milton, Dryden, Pope, Goldsmith, Burns, Wordsworth, Byron, Shelley, Tennyson, have uttered a hundred that recur perpetually and most forcibly when the nature is most deeply stirred. Enrolment in their number who have contributed more than any other teachers to supply food which the mind can most readily assimilate—

> Those rare souls
> Whose thoughts enrich the blood o' the world—

is an honour which no one can be indifferent about retaining who has once shown the ambition and the power to secure.

Notes

1. *Under the Microscope* [1872]. By A. C. Swinburne.

2. *Friendship's Garland* is the satirical complement of the serious argument put forth on this head. It denounces with playful but keen ridicule the mechanical idol worship and lack of spontaneous intelligence which constitute our gravest national defects, and have fatally depreciated our international significance.

3. "Rugby Chapel." Poems, (1869), Vol. i. pp. 225-234.

4. *Culture and Anarchy* [1869], p. 23.

5. Ibid., p. 162.

6. "The Shield of Achilles," (Cont. Rev. [*Contemporary Review*], Feb. 1874, p. 335).

7. Preface to *Merope* [1858].

8. *Literature and Dogma,* p. 77.

Richard Holt Hutton (essay date 1887)

SOURCE: Hutton, Richard Holt. "Matthew Arnold." In *Essays on Some of the Modern Guides of English Thought in Matters of Faith*, pp. 99-144. London: Macmillan and Co., 1887.

[*In the following essay, Hutton suggests that Arnold's prose erroneously rejects the idea of a benevolent power, reducing the "secret of Jesus" to mere self-perfection. Hutton argues that Arnold's poetry insightfully captures human experience and sorrow and can inspire its readers to reject the arguments set out in his own prose.*]

The difference between the intellectual and moral atmospheres which seems to have been breathed by Newman and Arnold is so astonishing that one can hardly realise that, for sixty-four years at least, they have been, what they still are, contemporaries. Bunyan, whose *Pilgrim's Progress* was published in 1678, says of his dream: "I espied a little before me a cave, where two giants, Pope and Pagan, dwelt in old time, by whose power and tyranny the men whose bones, blood, ashes, etc., lay there, were cruelly put to death. But by this place Christian went without much danger, whereat I somewhat wondered; but I have learnt since that Pagan has been dead many a day; and as for the other, though he be yet alive, he is, by reason of age, and also of the many shrewd brushes that he met with in his younger days, grown so crazy and stiff in his joints, that he can now do little more than sit in his cave's mouth, grinning at pilgrims as they go by, and biting his nails because he cannot come at them." That appeared 208 years ago; and yet I have just been descanting on one great man who has given in his hearty adhesion to one of these giants after years of meditative hesitation, while the second has been made captive—I will not say by the other giant risen from the grave, for I heartily admit that much of Mr. Arnold's spirit is distinctively Christian, but at least by a successor who has in him more, I think, of Pagan than of Bunyan's Christian lore. What a curious light is this on Mr. Arnold's doctrine of the *Zeitgeist,* the "Time-spirit," which he so much admires. In lecturing in Edinburgh on Butler, he said of the *Analogy*: "The great work on which such immense praise has been lavished is, for all real intents and purposes now, a failure; it does not serve. It seemed once to have a spell and a power; but the *Zeitgeist* breathes upon it, and we rub our eyes, and it has the spell and the power no longer." And in another place he has said: "The Spirit of Time is a personage for whose operations I have the greatest respect; whatever he does is in my opinion of the greatest effect." Well, is it so very great after all? The *Zeitgeist* breathed upon Bunyan and made him believe that Paganism was dead for ever, and that the Papacy was in its dotage. It breathes upon us in the nineteenth century, and while some of its children rub their eyes, and find that Giant Pope is the true sponsor for revelation after all, others rub their eyes, and find that Giant Pagan is still in his youth; that there is indeed no revelation, and that Christianity, so far as it is true at all, is a truth of human nature, not of theology. To my mind the *Zeitgeist* is a will-o'-the-wisp, who misleads us at least as much as he enlightens. In the scene on the Brocken in Goethe's *Faust,* the will-o'-the-wisp, when ordered by Mephistopheles—who also, we may remember, has the greatest admiration for the *Zeitgeist*—to conduct them to the summit, replies—

> So deep my awe, I trust I may succeed
> My fickle nature to repress indeed;
> But zigzag is my usual course, you know.

And that, I think, might very justly be said of Mr. Arnold's Time-spirit. Its usual course is zigzag. It breathes on us, and we can no longer see a truth which was clear yesterday. It breathes again, and like invisible ink held to the fire, the truth comes out again in all its brightness. However, the drift of all this is, that Mr. Arnold, while he sees much which Cardinal Newman has neglected, has certainly neglected more which Cardinal Newman sees, so that they seem to live in worlds as different as their countenances. On the one countenance are scored the indelible signs of what a great Jewish prophet calls "the Lord's controversy"; on the other, whose high benignant brow rises smooth and exulting above a face of serene confidence, there sits the exhilaration which speaks of difficulties surmounted and a world that is either fast coming, or, in the thinker's opinion, must soon come, over to his side. Mr. Arnold is a master of the grand style. He has the port of a great teacher. He derives from his father, the reformer of Rugby, that energy of purpose which makes itself felt in a certain authority of tone. We should never dream of applying to him Wordsworth's fine lines—

> The intellectual power through words and things
> Goes sounding on its dim and perilous way.

Rather would his churches—for in some sense Mr. Arnold may be said to have churches of his own—quote the famous saying—

> Nil desperandum Teucro duce, auspice Teucro.

He has succeeded in almost becoming himself what he has delineated in Goethe—

> For he pursued a lonely road,
>   His eyes on Nature's plan;
> Neither made man too much a God,
>   Nor God too much a man.

Certainly Mr. Arnold has not fallen into the latter error, whether into the former or not. He seems to have no doubts or difficulties in steering his course. He can eviscerate the Bible, and restore its meaning with the supernatural personality excluded. He has shown us how to "evolve" the Decalogue from the two primitive instincts of human nature. He has reconciled Isaiah with the "Time-spirit," and taught even sceptics to read him with exceptional delight. He has shown the Puritans what they might gain from the children of Athens, and the Athenian spirit, wherever it still exists, what it should learn from the Puritans. Take up the volume of his Prose Passages—and I know no book fuller of fascinating reading—and we shall find in it the rebukes which cultivated Germany administers to English Philistines, the rebukes which Conservative good taste addresses to rash Reformers, and the rebukes which brooding self-knowledge delivers to superficial politicians. We may learn there how Ireland would have been dealt with by statesmen who dive beneath the surface; and even how helpless and impotent is popular foreign policy in the hands of a minister guided by middle-class opinion. And when we have learned from his prose how keen and shrewd he is as an observer of the phenomena of his day, we may turn to his poetry, and lose ourselves in wonder at the truth and delicacy of his vision, the purity of his sympathies, the mellow melancholy of his regret, and the irrepressible elation which underlies even that regret itself. I think him so very great a poet that I will keep what I have to say on his poetry to the last; and will begin by referring to his more direct teaching, and especially to that teaching which implicitly accepts from science the exhortation to believe nothing which does not admit of complete verification, and which is intended to find for our age a truly scientific substitute for the theology of which the breath of the *Zeitgeist* has robbed us.

We must remember, then, that though Mr. Arnold proposes to demonstrate for us the truthfulness and power of the Bible, he commences by giving up absolutely the assumption that there is any Divine Being who thinks and loves, revealed in the Bible—a proposition for which he does not consider that there is even "a low degree of probability." One naturally asks, "Well, then, what remains that can be of any use?" Does not the Bible profess, from its opening to its close, to be the revelation of a Being who thinks about man and loves him, and who, because He thinks about man and loves him, converses with him, manifests to him His own nature as well as man's true nature, and insists "thou shalt be holy because I am holy." Mr. Arnold, however, is not at all staggered by this. He holds that "we very properly and naturally make" God a Being who thinks and loves "in the language of feeling"; but this is an utterly unverifiable assumption, without even a low degree of probability. So that why we may "properly and naturally" mislead ourselves by "language of feeling" so very wide of any solid ground of fact, I cannot imagine. We have always reproached the idolaters, as Israel represented them, with worshipping a God who is nothing in the world but the work of men's hands, the cunning workmanship of a carver in wood or stone. But why is it more proper or natural to attribute, in the language of feeling, false attributes to "the stream of tendency, not ourselves, which makes for righteousness," than it is to attribute, in the language of feeling, false attributes to the graven images of an idol-founder? However, this is Mr. Arnold's contention, though at other times he is ready to admit that whenever emotion has been powerfully excited by supposed knowledge, and when that supposed knowledge turns out to be illusion, the emotion will disappear with the disappearance of our belief in the assumptions which we had formerly accepted. I should have thought that this would apply to the Bible, and that if ever we could be convinced that there is not even a low degree of probability for the

conviction that God is a being who thinks and loves, all the emotions excited by the innumerable passages in which He is revealed as such a being would die away and be extinguished. But this is not Mr. Arnold's view. On the contrary, he holds that,

> Starting from what may be verified about God—that He is the Eternal which makes for righteousness—and reading the Bible with this idea to govern us, we have here the elements for a religion more solid, serious, awe-inspiring, and profound, than any which the world has yet seen. True, it will not be just the same religion which prevails now; but who supposes that the religion now current can go on always, or ought to go on? Nay, and even of that much-decried idea of God as the *stream of tendency in which all things seek to fulfil the law of their being,* it may be said with confidence that it has in it the elements of a religion, new indeed, but in the highest degree serious, hopeful, solemn, and profound.

It has always puzzled me very much to make out why Mr. Arnold should think, or say, that it is in any sense "verifiable," in his acceptation of that word, that the power which makes for righteousness is "eternal." But I believe, from a passage in *Literature and Dogma* ([London, 1873] p. 61), that he really means by "eternal" nothing more than "enduring," and by "enduring," enduring in the history of man; so that the verifiable proposition which he takes as the foundation of a new religion is after all nothing more than this, that so far as history gives evidence at all, there has always been hitherto, since man appeared upon the earth, a stream of tendency which made for righteousness. Nevertheless, if the earth came to an end, and there be, as Mr. Arnold apparently inclines to believe, no life for man beyond his life on earth, then the enduring stream of tendency would endure no longer, and "the eternal" would, so far as it was verifiable, sink back into a transitory and extinct phenomenon of the terrestrial past. Well, then, so far as the Bible holds true at all in Mr. Arnold's mind, we must substitute uniformly for the God who there reveals and declares Himself and His love, a being who cannot either declare himself or feel, in our sense, the love which he is said to declare; one who must be discovered by man, instead of discovering himself to man, and who, when discovered, is nothing but a more or less enduring tendency to a certain deeper and truer mode of life, which we call righteous life. No wonder that "the religion in the highest degree serious, hopeful, solemn, and profound," to which Mr. Arnold hopes to convert the world, does not always appear, even to himself, either hopeful or solid. For example, in one of the most beautiful of his poems, **"Stanzas from the Grande Chartreuse,"** he explains, in a very different tone from that of the passage I have just quoted from *Literature and Dogma* (and I think a much more suitable and appropriate tone), how helpless and crippled his religious position really is, and how it came to pass that in visiting the home of one of the austere monastic orders he could feel a certain passion of regret without either much sympathy or much hope:—

> For rigorous teachers seized my youth,
> And purged its faith, and trimmed its fire,
> Showed me the high, white star of Truth,
> There bade me gaze, and there aspire.
> Even now their whispers pierce the gloom:
> *What dost thou in this living tomb?*
>
> Forgive me, masters of the mind!
> At whose behest I long ago
> So much unlearnt, so much resigned—
> I come not here to be your foe!
> I seek these anchorites, not in ruth,
> To curse and to deny your truth;
>
> Not as their friend, or child, I speak!
> But as, on some far northern strand,
> Thinking of his own gods, a Greek,
> In pity and mournful awe, might stand
> Before some fallen Runic stone—
> For both were faiths, and both are gone.
>
> Wandering between two worlds, one dead,
> The other powerless to be born,
> With nowhere yet to rest my head,
> Like these, on earth I wait forlorn.
> Their faith, my tears, the world deride—
> I come to shed them at their side.

In his poetry Mr. Arnold is often frank enough, as he certainly is here. In his prose he will not admit that the Church to which he looks as the Church of the future is "powerless to be born." But powerless to be born it is; a "stream of tendency," more or less enduring, which cannot even reveal itself, is not a power to excite emotion of any depth at all, unless it represents not only a tendency but a purpose. Religion, says Mr. Arnold, is "morality touched with emotion." But surely morality cannot be "touched with emotion" without reason, or at least excuse, for the emotion it is to excite. And yet this is what Mr. Arnold's language seems to point at. In one of his American lectures he appears to say that the emotions will remain even though the objects which properly excite them disappear; and in another passage of the same lecture he nevertheless intimates that even the very same thought may be so expressed as either to excite emotion or not to excite it, the difference between the two modes of expression being, except in its actual effect, quite undiscernible. But if Religion depends on an accident of that kind, Religion is an accident itself. An intention to make for Righteousness rightly excites emotion, but a tendency and an intention are different. Plague, pestilence, and famine, in God's hands, have often made for Righteousness. But without faith in God, plague, pestilence, and famine are more likely to touch immorality with emotion, than to touch morality with it.

How, then, is Mr. Arnold to conjure up the emotion which certainly does not seem to be naturally radiated from this more or less enduring "stream of tendency"? He strives to excite it by disclosing to us the promise of *life,* which is implicit in all conformity to this "stream of tendency"; for life is the word which, in Mr. Arnold's teaching, takes the place of faith. He values Christ's teaching because he says that it discloses the true secret of *life*—because it discloses a new life for the world, even after faith (as we understand it) is dead. This is the promise which he makes his favourite thinker, M. de Senancour, better known as the author of "Obermann," address to him [in **"Stanzas in Memory of the Author of 'Obermann'"**]:—

> Though more than half thy years be past,
> And spent thy youthful prime;
> Though, round thy firmer manhood cast,
> Hang weeds of our sad time
>
> Whereof thy youth felt all the spell,
> And traversed all the shade—
> Though late, though dimm'd, though weak, yet tell
> Hope to a world new-made!
>
> Help it to fill that deep desire,
> The want which rack'd our brain,
> Consumed our heart with thirst like fire,
> Immedicable pain;
>
> Which to the wilderness drove out
> Our life, to Alpine snow,
> And palsied all our word with doubt,
> And all our work with woe—
>
> What still of strength is left, employ
> That end to help attain:
> *One common wave of thought and joy*
> *Lifting mankind again!*

And that is the purpose to which Matthew Arnold has devoted what we may call his quasi-theological writings; in other words, his writings produced to show that we may get all the advantages of theology without the theology—which we can and must do without. This new teaching is that which Tennyson has so tersely and finely expressed in "The Two Voices"—

> 'Tis life, whereof our nerves are scant;
> Oh life, not death, for which we pant;
> More life, and fuller, that I want.

To the same effect Arnold quotes M. de Senancour: "The aim for men is to augment the feeling of joy, to make our expansive energy bear fruit, and to combat in all thinking beings the principle of degradation and misery." And Mr. Arnold's new version of Christianity promises us this life. "The all-ruling effort to live" is identical, he says, with "the desire for happiness," and this craving for life is, he asserts, sanctioned by Christ in the saying, "I am come that men might have *life,* and might have it more abundantly; and ye will not come to me that ye may have life." I had always thought this a promise of life given by a being in whose hands is the power to bestow it. Not so Mr. Arnold. This power of attaining life, and attaining it in greater abundance, is, he declares, a mere natural secret which Christ had discovered, and which any man may rediscover for himself. It is a method of obtaining life, of obtaining "exhilaration." Indeed, exhilaration is, says Mr. Arnold, one of the greatest qualities of the Hebrew prophets. And this exhilaration is attainable by a merely natural process—namely, the renunciation by man of the superficial and temporary self, in favour of the deeper and permanent self. In *Literature and Dogma* Mr. Arnold has explained the "secret of Jesus," the true secret, as he holds, for riding buoyantly upon

> That common wave of thought and joy,
> Lifting mankind again.

We are there told that the essence of Christianity is not the possession of supernatural life flowing from the love or gift of a supernatural being, but is simply the discovery and use of a certain secret of the wise heart. The secret is conveyed in Christ's promise: "He that loveth his life shall lose it, and he that hateth his life in this world shall keep it unto life eternal. Whosoever would come after me, let him renounce himself, and take up his cross daily and follow me." Christ's method, Mr. Arnold says,—

> Directed the disciple's eye inward, and set his consciousness to work; and the first thing his consciousness told him was that he had two selves pulling him different ways. Till we attend, till the method is set at work, it seems as if 'the wishes of the flesh and of the current thoughts' (Eph. [Ephesians] ii. 3) were to be followed as a matter of course; as if an impulse to do a thing means that we should do it. But when we attend we find that an impulse to do a thing is really in itself no reason at all why we should do it, because impulses proceed from two sources quite different, and of quite different degrees of authority. St. Paul contrasts them as the inward man and the man in our members; the mind of the flesh and the spiritual mind. Jesus contrasts them as life properly so named and life in this world. And the moment we seriously attend to conscience, to the suggestions which concern practice and conduct, we can see plainly enough from which source a suggestion comes, and that the suggestions from one source are to overrule suggestions from the other.

> —*Literature and Dogma,* pp. 201-202

The breaking the sway of what is commonly called one's self, ceasing our concern with it, and leaving it to perish, is not, he (*i.e.* Jesus Christ) said, being thwarted or crossed, but *living.* And the proof of this is that it has the character of life in the highest degree—the power of going right, hitting the mark, succeeding.

That is, it has the character of happiness, and happiness is for Israel the same thing as having the Eternal with us—seeing the salvation of God.

> —*Literature and Dogma,* p. 203

Now, surely it is hardly justifiable for Mr. Arnold, in describing the "secret of Jesus," to substitute for the words of Jesus words of his own so very different in tone and meaning from those in which that secret was first disclosed. Where does our Lord ever say that the evidence of spiritual life is in the consciousness it gives us of *hitting the mark,* of *succeeding*? If we are to take our Lord's secret, let us take it in His own language, not in Mr. Arnold's. Turn then to His own language, and what do we find? We find, "Blessed are the pure in heart, for they shall see God." Does that mean the same thing as, "Blessed are the pure in heart, for they shall hit the mark, they shall succeed"? Again, "Blessed are the peacemakers, for they shall be called the children of God." Does that mean the same as, "Blessed are the peacemakers, for they shall attain true success"? "Blessed are ye when men shall revile you and persecute you, and shall say all manner of evil against you falsely for my sake. Rejoice and be exceeding glad, for great is your reward in heaven." Does that promise mean the same as "the more you are persecuted and maligned, the greater is your reward on earth, no matter whether there be any world beyond this or not"? Yet that is what Mr. Arnold tries to make it mean in order to reconcile his interpretation of the "secret of Jesus" with the actual words of Jesus. I believe that Mr. Arnold misreads even the language of the conscience, when he makes it say that as we advance in our development we become aware "of two lives, one permanent and impersonal, the other transient and bound to our contracted self; he becomes aware of two selves, one higher and real, the other inferior and apparent; and that the instinct in him truly to live, the desire for happiness, is served by following the first self and not the second" (*Last Essays on Church and Religion* [1883], pp. 116-117). What we really become aware of is, that behind the loud-voiced, strenuous, well-established self of our lower nature, there is growing up a faint, embryo, struggling, nobler self, without strength, without permanence; but that on the side of that self there pleads another and higher power, offering us, if we listen to the nobler voice, infinite prospects of a new world of communion, a new buoyancy, a new career. It is not the nobler self which is, as Mr. Arnold says, strong and permanent. Nothing can be weaker or more fitful. But the promise is, that if we give ourselves to the weak and fitful but nobler voice, our doing so will bring us into direct communion with one who is really strong, who is really permanent, who is really eternal; not merely what Mr. Arnold means by eternal—namely, *more or less enduring.* I take it that the "secret of Jesus" is wholly misinterpreted if its promise of a communion between the weaker but nobler self and the eternal source of life and light be ignored. It falls in that case from the secret of Jesus to the secret of Matthew Arnold. Now the "secret of Jesus" is life indeed. The secret of Matthew Arnold is only better than death, because it gives its suffrage on the right side, though with the right suffrage it fails to connect the promise and the earnest of joy with which Jesus Christ connected it. I think every reasonable reader of the Bible must perceive that if this promise of permanent joy in an eternal love is not true, the whole chain of Hebrew prophecy is false and misleading, from the time of Abraham to the death of St. Paul.

But then Mr. Arnold will turn upon me with his demand for verification: Can the promise be verified? "Experience proves that whatever for men is true, men can verify." I should answer, certainly it is verifiable in a sense even truer and higher than that in which Mr. Arnold's own *rationale* of the moral secret, which he misnames the secret of Jesus, is verifiable. Even Mr. Arnold admits that his interpretation of the secret of Jesus has not always been verified.

> "People may say," he tells us, "they have not got this sense that their instinct to live is served by loving their neighbours; they may say that they have, in other words, a dull and uninformed conscience. But that does not make the experience less a true thing, the real experience of the race. Neither does it make the sense of this experience to be, any the less, genuine conscience. And it is genuine conscience, because it apprehends what does really serve our instinct to live, or desire for happiness. And when Shaftesbury supposes the case of a man thinking vice and selfishness to be truly as much for his advantage as virtue and benevolence, and concludes that such a case is without remedy, the answer is 'Not at all; let such a man get conscience, get right experience.' And if the man does not, the result is not that he goes on just as well without it; the result is that he is lost."

—*Last Essays on Church and Religion,* pp. 115-116

Well, if that is what Mr. Arnold means by verification, I think that it is easy to show that there is a much more perfect verification for the ordinary and natural interpretation of the "secret of Jesus" than for his mutilated interpretation of it. If it is verification to appeal to the best experience of the best, to the growing experience of those who have most intimately studied the various discipline of life, who can doubt what the reply must be to the question, Does experience testify to the self-sufficiency and adequacy to itself of what Mr. Arnold calls the permanent and higher self, or rather to its growing sense of inadequacy and dependence, and to its constant reference to that higher life in communion with which it lives? I do not hesitate to say that Mr. Arnold's mutilated interpretation of the "secret of Jesus," which omits indeed the very talisman of the whole, will

receive no confirmation at all from the higher experience of the race, which testifies to nothing more persistently than this, that growing humility and the deepest possible sense of the dependence of the nobler self on communion with a righteous being external to it, is the unfailing experience of those in whom the nobler self is most adequately developed. Mr. Arnold's *rationale* of what he erroneously terms the "more permanent" and "stronger" self—but what experience proves to be indeed a very variable and very weak self, leaning on constant communion with another for its strength—is a mutilation of the true experience of man as delivered by the Bible, from Genesis to Revelation. Take the Psalmist: "Whom have I in heaven but thee, and there is none upon earth I desire in comparison with thee. My flesh and my heart faileth, but God is the strength of my heart, and my portion for ever." Take Isaiah: "Woe is me, for I am undone; because I am a man of unclean lips, and I dwell in the midst of a people of unclean lips; for mine eyes have seen the King, the Lord of Hosts." Take St. Paul: "I was with you in weakness, and in fear, and in much trembling. And my speech and my preaching was not with enticing words of man's wisdom, but in demonstration of the Spirit and of power: that your faith should not stand in the wisdom of men, but in the power of God." It is impossible to find in the Bible anything like a reference to the permanent and stronger self which asserts itself in us. The testimony is always to a nobler but weaker self, which leans on the sustaining grace of God. Well, but says Mr. Arnold in opposing Bishop Butler's view that the most we can hope for in this life is to escape from misery and not to obtain happiness,—in this contention Butler goes counter not only to the most intimate, "the most sure, the most irresistible instinct of human nature," but also "to the clear voice of our religion." "Rejoice and give thanks," exhorts the Old Testament. "Rejoice evermore," exhorts the New. That is most true, but what is the ground of these constant exhortations in both Old Testament and New? Surely not the strength and depth of the life, even the higher life, in man, but, on the contrary, the largeness and generosity of the succour granted to the righteous by God. On what, for instance, is grounded the injunction which Mr. Arnold quotes from the Old Testament? On this, that "the Lord hath done marvellous things: his right hand, and his holy arm, hath wrought salvation for him." And again on this, that "the Lord hath made known his salvation: his righteousness hath he openly showed in the sight of the nations." Can Mr. Arnold justify such a ground for rejoicing as that, on the lips of any one who disbelieves altogether in a God who "thinks and loves"? Again, what is the context of the injunction taken from the New Testament? "Rejoice evermore. Pray without ceasing. In everything give thanks: *for this is the will of God in Christ Jesus concerning you.*" The ground of rejoicing is a will—a will which is equally made the ground of prayer; without the ground for praying there could be no ground for rejoicing. Without a *known* will of God there could be neither the one nor the other. And it is the humility which recognises the strength, external to its own, which is the source at once of the joy and the prayer. The life which is so abundantly promised throughout the Bible is indeed not natural life, as Mr. Arnold explains it, but what we are more accustomed to call *grace*—the life poured in from outside.

Nor, indeed, can I understand how Mr. Arnold's explanation can hold at all, without this supernatural source of strength and joy. When Mr. Arnold says that it is the "permanent" and "stronger" self which conquers, and gives us life by the conquest, is it inappropriate to ask, *How* permanent, and *how* strong? Suppose, as has often happened, that the deeper and nobler self suggests a course which involves instant death, where is the permanence? Mr. Arnold will hear nothing of the promise of immortality. That is to him *Aberglaube,* over-belief, belief in excess of the evidence. In some of his most exquisite lines he speaks of death as the

> Stern law of every mortal lot
> Which man, proud man, finds hard to bear,
> And builds himself, I know not what
> Of second life, I know not where.

So that he guarantees us assuredly no *permanence* for the nobler self. And then as to *strength*: Is the nobler self strong enough to endure the hard conditions which are often imposed on us by our best acts—the slander and persecution to which we expose ourselves, the misery which we bring on ourselves? The answer of the Bible is plain enough: No, it is not; but you may rely on the grace promised to the weakest, if you comply with the admonitions of that grace. Mr. Arnold can make no such reply. Unless the nobler self is intrinsically also the stronger self, in his opinion you are lost. It seems to me, then, that the injunction to "rejoice and give thanks," the injunction to "rejoice evermore," cannot be justified except in connection with a trust in One who can give us real succour from without, under the prospect of certain death and the still more certain collapse of human powers in the presence of great trials and temptations.

In a word, the faith taught by revelation is not, as Mr. Arnold himself admits, Mr. Arnold's faith. The former is intended to awaken and discipline a group of genuine *affections,* using the word in the same sense—though in the same sense raised to a higher plane of life—as we use it of the human affections. Read the Psalms, and you will find in them the germs of all the affections generated in His disciples by Christ's own teaching— the shame, the grief, the remorse, the desolation, the hope, the awe, the love in its highest sense, which human beings feel in the presence of a human nature, holier, deeper, richer, stronger, nobler than their own, when they have sinned against it and are conscious of its displeasure, its retributive justice, its joy in human repentance, and its forgiveness. The whole drift of revelation is to excite these affections, to make us feel the divine passion which our human passions elicit, to reach the deepest fountain of our tears, and to fill us with that joy which, however deep, is all humility and all gratitude, because its source is the love of another, and not the strength or buoyancy of our own life. Well, this is not, and could not be, Mr. Arnold's religion. In his expurgated Bible, the affections in this sense have to be omitted. He tells us quite plainly that the facts—or, as he calls them, "the supposed facts"—by which the religious affections have been fostered in us are illusions, that our religion is nothing in the world but the culture of that ideal life which man has happily a tendency to develop. These are his words:

> The future of poetry is immense, because in poetry, where it is worthy of its high destinies, our race, as time goes on, will find an ever surer and surer stay. There is not a creed which is not shaken, not an accredited dogma which is not shown to be questionable, not a received tradition which does not threaten to dissolve. Our religion has materialised itself in the fact—in the supposed fact; it has attached its emotion to the fact, and now the fact is failing it. But for poetry the idea is everything; the rest is a world of illusion—of divine illusion. Poetry attaches its emotion to the idea; the idea *is* the fact.

Well, if that be so, the emotion which Mr. Arnold insists on, in order to transform morality into religion, becomes a very mild and æsthetic kind of emotion indeed,—not one which can penetrate the sinner's heart with anguish, not one which can irradiate the penitent's heart with gratitude. Imagine the changes which you must make in the language of the Psalmist to empty it of what Mr. Arnold calls belief in "the supposed fact," and to conform the emotions to that which is attached to "the idea" alone:—

> Hide thy face from my sins, and blot out all mine iniquities. Create in me a clean heart, O God; and renew a right spirit within me. Cast me not away from thy presence; and take not thy Holy Spirit from me. Restore unto me the joy of thy salvation; and uphold me with thy free Spirit. . . . O Lord, open thou my lips; and my mouth shall show forth thy praise. For thou desirest not sacrifice, else would I give it; thou delightest not in burnt-offering. The sacrifices of God are a broken spirit: a broken and a contrite heart, O God, thou wilt not despise.

Take the divine illusion, as Mr. Arnold calls it, out of this, and how much of "the emotion" requisite for religion would remain? Has he not himself told us?—

> That gracious Child, that thorn-crown'd Man!
> —He lived while we believed.

While we believed, on earth he went,
And open stood his grave.
Men called from chamber, church, and tent;
And Christ was by to save.

Now he is dead! Far hence he lies
In the lorn Syrian town;
And on his grave, with shining eyes
The Syrian stars look down.

In vain men still, with hoping new,
Regard his death-place dumb,
And say the stone is not yet to,
And wait for words to come.

Ah, o'er that silent sacred land,
Of sun, and arid stone,
And crumbling wall, and sultry sand,
Sounds now one word alone!

From David's lips that word did roll,
'Tis true and living yet:
No man can save his brother's soul,
Nor pay his brother's debt.

Alone, self-pois'd, henceforward man
Must labour!—must resign
His all too human creeds, and scan
Simply the way divine.

Well, then, where is the "emotion" with which "morality" must be touched, in order to transform it into religion, to come from? Mr. Arnold makes no answer,—except that it must be emotion excited by ideas alone, and not by supposed facts, which, as he says, will not stand the tests of scientific verification.

But with regard to that asserted demand of science for verification, let me just make one final observation: that in the sense in which Mr. Arnold uses it, to explode all belief in light coming to us from a mind higher than our own, it equally explodes belief in the authority of those suggestions of the deeper self to which what he calls the "secret of Jesus" teaches us to defer. For why are we to obey them? Mr. Arnold replies simply, human *experience* teaches us that it adds to our life, to our happiness, to the vitality of our true and permanent self, to do so. But how are we to get the verification without trying both the wrong way and the right? You cannot found on mere experience *without* the experience. And does, then, the way to virtue lead through sin alone? Mr. Arnold guards himself by saying that some "finely-touched" souls have "the *presentiment*" of how it will be—a presentiment, I suppose, derived by evolution from the experience of ancestors. But is it a duty, then, to found your actions on those obscure intimations which your ancestors' experience may have transmitted to you? Should you not test your ancestors' experience for yourself before adopting it? Should you not sin in order to be sure that sin saps your true life and diminishes your fund of happiness? I fear there is nothing for Mr. Arnold but to admit that this is not sin—that *trying*

evil in order to be sure it *is* evil is not forbidden by any law, if there be no spiritual nature higher than man's, which lays its yoke upon us, and subdues us into the attitude of reverence and awe. The principle which Mr. Arnold calls "verification" is in reality fatal to all purity. It makes experience of evil the ground of good. For myself, I believe that there is enough verification for the purposes of true morality in the recognition, without the test of experience, of the higher character of the nature confronted with our own; and that we may learn the reality of revelation, the reality of a divine influence which should be a law to us, and rebellion against which is, in the deepest sense, sin, without trying the effect of that rebellion, without making proof of both the alternatives before us. The life even of the truest *human* affections is one long protest against the principle that you can know nothing without what is termed experiment and verification in the scientific sense of the word. What creature which has learnt to love tries the effect of piercing the heart of another before it learns to reject that course as treachery? Revelation, as I understand it, is an appeal to the human affections—a divine discipline for them. It no more demands experiment and verification, in the scientific sense which men try to foist so inappropriately into our moral life, than a parent would think of demanding from his child that, in order to be sure that his wishes and commands are wise, the child should make experiments in disobedience, and only conform to his father's injunctions after he had learned by a painful experience that these experiments had ended in pain and discomfiture.

In insisting on the striking, I might almost say the dismaying, contrast between the great Oxford leader, whose whole mind has been occupied with theological convictions from his earliest years of Oxford life to the present day, and the Oxford leader who has avowed himself unable to see even a slender probability that God is a being who thinks and loves, I have said that I hoped to do something to attenuate the paradox before I had done. This is probably the right place to say a few words on the subject, for undoubtedly it is the assumption running through Mr. Arnold's theoretical writings, that no belief is trustworthy which has not what he calls the verification of experience to sustain it, to which we owe his repudiation of all theology. Undoubtedly the twenty years or so by which he is Cardinal Newman's junior made an extraordinary difference in the intellectual atmosphere of Oxford, and of the English world of letters outside Oxford, during the time at which a thoughtful man's mind matures. Mr. Arnold was not too late at Oxford to feel the spell of Dr. Newman, but his mind was hardly one to feel the whole force of that spell, belonging as it does, I think, rather to the stoical than to the religious school—the school which magnifies self-dependence, and regards serene calm, not passionate worship, as the highest type of the moral life. And he was at Oxford too late, I think, for a full understanding of the limits within which alone the scientific conception of life can be said to be true. A little later, men came to see that scientific methods are really quite inapplicable to the sphere of moral truth, that the scientific assumption that whatever is true can be verified is, in the sense of the word "verification" which science applies, a very serious blunder, and that such verification as we can get of moral truth is of a very different, though I will not scruple to say a no less satisfactory, kind from that which we expect to get of scientific truth. Mr. Arnold seems to me to have imbibed the prejudices of the scientific season of blossom, when the uniformity of nature first became a kind of gospel, when the *Vestiges of Creation* was the book in vogue, when Emerson's and Carlyle's imaginative scepticism first took hold of cultivated Englishmen, and when Mr. Froude published the sceptical tales by which his name was first known amongst us. Mr. Arnold betrays the immovable prejudices by which his intellectual life is overridden in a hundred forms; for example, by the persistency with which he remarks that the objection to miracles is that they do not happen, the one criticism which I venture to say no one who had taken pains to study evidence in the best accredited individual cases, not only in ancient but in modern times, would choose to repeat. And again, he betrays it by the pertinacity with which he assumes that you can verify the secret of self-renunciation, the secret of Jesus, in the same sense in which you can verify the law of gravitation, one of the most astounding and, I think, false assumptions of our day. I make bold to say that no one ever verified the secret of self-renunciation yet, or ever even wished to verify it, who had not assumed the moral obligation it involves before even attempting a verification; while with the law of gravitation it is quite different: we believe it solely because it has been verified, or, in the case of the discoverer, because evidence was before him that it might very probably be verified.

But though Mr. Arnold's mind is of the stoical rather than the religious type, and though certain premature scientific assumptions, which were in vogue before the limits of the region in which the uniformity of nature has been verified, had been at all carefully defined, run through all his theoretical writings, it is nevertheless true that his whole intellectual strength has been devoted to sustaining, I cannot say the cause of religion—for I do not think his constant cry for more emotion in dealing with morality has been answered—but the cause of noble conduct, and to exalting the elation of duty, the rapture of righteousness. Allow for his prepossessions—his strangely obstinate prepossessions—and he remains still a figure on which we can look with admiration. We must remember that, with all the scorn which Matthew Arnold pours on the trust we place in God's love, he still holds to the conviction that the tendency

to righteousness is a power on which we may rely even with *rapture*. Israel, he says, took "his religion in rapture, because he found for it an evidence irresistible. But his own words are the best: 'Thou, O Eternal, art the thing that I *long* for, thou art my hope, even from my youth; through thee have I been *holden up* ever since I was born; there is nothing *sweeter* than to take heed unto the commandments of the Eternal. The Eternal is my strength; my heart has trusted in Him, and I am *helped*; therefore my heart *danceth for joy,* and in my song I will *praise* him'" (**Literature and Dogma,** p. 319). And Mr. Arnold justifies that language, though it seems to me clear that with his views he could never have been the first to use it. Still, do not let us forget that he does justify it, that the great Oxonian of the third quarter of this century, though he is separated wide as the poles from Cardinal Newman in faith, yet uses even the most exalted language of the Hebrew seers with all the exultation which even Cardinal Newman could evince for it. I think it is hardly possible to think of such an attitude of mind as the attitude of a common agnostic. The truth is, that his deep poetical idealism saves Mr. Arnold from the depressing and flattening influences of his theoretical views. The poet of modern thought and modern tendencies cannot be, even though he strives to be, a mere agnostic. The insurrection of the agnosticism of the day against faith is no doubt one of its leading features; but the failure of that insurrection to overpower us, the potent resistance it encounters in all our hearts, is a still more remarkable feature. Matthew Arnold reflects both of these characteristics, though the former perhaps more powerfully than the latter.

In passing from the thinker to the poet, I am passing from a writer whose curious earnestness and ability in attempting the impossible will soon; I believe, be a mere curiosity of literature, to one of the most considerable of English poets, whose place will probably be above any poet of the eighteenth century, excepting Burns, and not excepting Dryden, or Pope, or Cowper, or Goldsmith, or Gray; and who, even amongst the great poets of the nineteenth century, may very probably be accorded the sixth or fifth, or even by some the fourth place. He has a power of vision as great as Tennyson's, though its magic depends less on the rich tints of association, and more on the liquid colours of pure natural beauty; a power of criticism and selection as fastidious as Gray's, with infinitely more creative genius; and a power of meditative reflection which, though it never mounts to Wordsworth's higher levels of genuine rapture, never sinks to his wastes and flats of commonplace. Arnold is a great elegiac poet, but there is a buoyancy in his elegy which we rarely find in the best elegy, and which certainly adds greatly to its charm. And though I cannot call him a dramatic poet, his permanent attitude being too reflective for any kind of action, he shows in such poems as the **"Memorial Verses"** on Byron, Goethe, and Wordsworth, in the **"Sick King in Bokhara,"** and **"Tristram and Iseult,"** great precision in the delineation of character, and not a little power even of forcing character to delineate itself. What feeling for the Oriental type of character is there not in the Vizier of the Sick King of Bokhara when he remonstrates with the young king for taking too much to heart the tragic end of the man who had insisted, under the Mahometan law, on being stoned, because in a hasty moment he had cursed his mother!—

> O King, in this I praise thee not!
> Now must I call thy grief not wise.
> Is he thy friend, or of thy blood,
> To find such favour in thine eyes?
>
> Nay, were he thine own mother's son,
> Still, thou art king, and the law stands.
> It were not meet the balance swerved,
> The sword were broken in thy hands.
>
> But being nothing, as he is,
> Why for no cause make sad thy face?—
> Lo, I am old! three kings, ere thee,
> Have I seen reigning in this place.
>
> But who, through all this length of time,
> Could bear the burden of his years,
> If he for strangers pain'd his heart
> Not less than those who merit tears?
>
> Fathers we *must* have, wife and child,
> And grievous is the grief for these;
> This pain alone, which *must* be borne,
> Makes the head white, and bows the knees.
>
> But other loads than this his own
> One man is not well made to bear.
> Besides, to each are his own friends,
> To mourn with him, and show him care.
>
> Look, this is but one single place,
> Though it be great; all the earth round,
> If a man bear to have it so,
> Things which might vex him shall be found.
>
> Upon the Russian frontier, where
> The watchers of two armies stand
> Near one another, many a man,
> Seeking a prey unto his hand,
>
> Hath snatch'd a little fair-hair'd slave;
> They snatch also, towards Mervè,
> The Shiah dogs, who pasture sheep,
> And up from thence to Orgunjè.
>
> And these all, labouring for a lord,
> Eat not the fruit of their own hands;
> Which is the heaviest of all plagues,
> To that man's mind, who understands.
>
> The kaffirs also (whom God curse!)
> Vex one another, night and day;

> There are the lepers, and all sick;
> There are the poor, who faint alway.
>
> All these have sorrow, and keep still,
> Whilst other men make cheer, and sing.
> Wilt thou have pity on all these?
> No, nor on this dead dog, O King!

And again, how deep is the insight into the Oriental character in the splendid contrast between Rome and the East after the Eastern conquests of Rome, in the second of the two poems on the Author of "Obermann" [**"Obermann Once More"**]:—

> In his cool hall, with haggard eyes,
> The Roman noble lay;
> He drove abroad, in furious guise,
> Along the Appian Way.
>
> He made a feast, drank fierce and fast,
> And crown'd his hair with flowers—
> No easier nor no quicker pass'd
> The impracticable hours.
>
> The brooding East with awe beheld
> Her impious younger world.
> The Roman tempest swell'd and swell'd,
> And on her head was hurl'd.
>
> The East bow'd low before the blast
> In patient, deep disdain;
> She let the legions thunder past,
> And plunged in thought again.
>
> So well she mused, a morning broke
> Across her spirit gray;
> A conquering, new-born joy awoke,
> And fill'd her life with day.
>
> 'Poor world,' she cried, 'so deep accurst,
> That runn'st from pole to pole
> To seek a draught to slake thy thirst—
> Go, seek it in thy soul!'

Or take the famous description, in the lines at Heine's grave, of our own country taking up burden after burden, with "deaf ears and labour-dimm'd eyes," as she has just taken up the new burden of Burmah:—

> I chide with thee not, that thy sharp
> Upbraidings often assail'd
> England, my country—for we,
> Heavy and sad, for her sons,
> Long since, deep in our hearts,
> Echo the blame of her foes.
> We, too, sigh that she flags;
> We, too, say that she now—
> Scarce comprehending the voice
> Of her greatest, golden-mouth'd sons
> Of a former age any more—
> Stupidly travels her round
> Of mechanic business, and lets
> Slow die out of her life
> Glory, and genius, and joy.

So thou arraign'st her, her foe;
So we arraign her, her sons.

  Yes, we arraign her! but she,
The weary Titan, with deaf
Ears, and labour-dimm'd eyes,
Regarding neither to right
Nor left, goes passively by,
Staggering on to her goal;
Bearing on shoulders immense,
Atlanteän, the load,
Wellnigh not to be borne,
Of the too vast orb of her fate.

Though not a dramatic poet, it is clear, then, that Matthew Arnold has a deep dramatic insight; but that is only one aspect of what I should call his main characteristic as a poet—the lucid penetration with which he discerns and portrays all that is most expressive in any situation that awakens regret, and the buoyancy with which he either throws off the pain, or else takes refuge in some soothing digression. For Arnold is never quite at his best except when he is delineating a mood of regret, and then his best consists not in yielding to it, but in the resistance he makes to it. He is not, like most elegiac poets, a mere sad muser; he is always one who finds a secret of joy in the midst of pain, who discovers a tonic for the suffering nerve, if only in realising the large power of sensibility which it retains. Take his description of the solitude in which we human beings live—heart yearning after heart, but recognising the eternal gulf between us—a solitude decreed by the power which

  bade betwixt our shores to be
The unplumb'd, salt, estranging sea!

How noble the line, and how it sends a shiver through one! And yet not a shiver of mere regret or mere yearning; rather a shiver of awe at the infinitude of the ocean in which we are all enisled. It is the same with all Arnold's finest elegiac touches. In all of them regret seems to mingle with buoyancy, and buoyancy to have a sort of root in regret. What he calls (miscalls, I think) the "secret of Jesus"—"miscalls," because the secret of Jesus lay in the knowledge of His Father's love, not in the *natural* buoyancy of the renouncing heart—is in reality the secret of his own poetry. Like the East, he bows low before the blast, only to seek strength in his own mind, and to delight in the strength he finds there. He enjoys plumbing the depths of another's melancholy. Thus he says in relation to his favourite *Obermann*—

A fever in these pages burns
Beneath the calm they feign;
A wounded human spirit turns,
Here, on its bed of pain.

Yes, though the virgin mountain-air
Fresh through these pages blows;

Though to these leaves the glaciers spare
The soul of their white snows;

Though here a mountain-murmur swells
Of many a dark-boughed pine,
Though, as you read, you hear the bells
Of the high-pasturing kine—

Yet, through the hum of torrent lone,
And brooding mountain-bee,
There sobs I know not what ground-tone
Of human agony.

But even so, the effect of the verses is not the effect of Shelley's most exquisitely melancholy lyrics. It does not make us almost faint under the poet's own feeling of desolation. On the contrary, even in the very moment in which Arnold cries—

Farewell! Under the sky we part,
In this stern Alpine dell.
O unstrung will! O broken heart!
A last, a last farewell!

we have a conviction that the poet went off with a buoyant step from that unstrung will and broken heart, enjoying the strength he had derived from his communion with that strong spirit of passionate protest against the evil and frivolity of the world. It is just the same with his **"Empedocles on Etna."** He makes the philosopher review at great length the evils of human life, and decide that, as he can render no further aid to men, he must return to the elements. But after he has made his fatal plunge into the crater of the burning mountain, there arises from his friend Callicles, the harp-player on the slopes of the mountain below, the following beautiful strain:—

Through the black, rushing smoke-bursts,
Thick breaks the red flame;
All Etna heaves fiercely
Her forest-clothed frame.

Not here, O Apollo!
Are haunts meet for thee.
But, where Helicon breaks down
In cliff to the sea,

Where the moon-silver'd inlets
Send far their light voice
Up the still vale of Thisbe,
O speed, and rejoice!

On the sward at the cliff-top
Lie strewn the white flocks,
On the cliff-side the pigeons
Roost deep in the rocks.

In the moonlight the shepherds,
Soft lull'd by the rills,
Lie wrapt in their blankets
Asleep on the hills.

—What forms are these coming
So white through the gloom?
What garments out-glistening
The gold-flower'd broom?

What sweet-breathing presence
Out-perfumes the thyme?
What voices enrapture
The night's balmy prime?—

'Tis Apollo comes leading
His choir, the Nine.
—The leader is fairest,
But all are divine.

They are lost in the hollows!
They stream up again!
What seeks on this mountain
The glorified train?—

They bathe on this mountain,
In the spring by their road;
Then on to Olympus,
Their endless abode.

—Whose praise do they mention?
Of what is it told?—
What will be for ever;
What was from of old.

First hymn they the Father
Of all things; and then,
The rest of immortals,
The action of men.

The day in his hotness,
The strife with the palm;
The night in her silence,
The stars in their calm.

And we close the poem with a sense, not of trouble, but of refreshment. So in the tragic story of **"Sohrab and Rustum"**—in which the father, without knowing it, kills his own son, who dies in his arms—the poem ends not in gloom, but in a serene vision of the course of the Oxus as it passes, "brimming and bright and large," towards its mouth in the Sea of Aral, a course which is meant to be typical of the peaceful close of Rustum's stormy and potent and victorious, though tragic, career. It seems to be Matthew Arnold's secret in Art not to minimise the tragedy or sadness of the human lot, but to turn our attention from the sadness or the tragedy to the strength which it illustrates and elicits, and the calm in which even the tumultuous passions of the story eventually subside. Even the sad poem on the Grand Chartreuse closes with a wonderful picture of cloistered serenity, entreating the busy and eager world to leave it unmolested to its meditations—

Pass, banners, pass, and bugles cease;
And leave our desert to its peace.

There is nothing which Matthew Arnold conceives or creates so well, nothing so characteristic of him, as the soothing digressions, as they seem—digressions, however, more germane to his purpose than any epilogue—in which he withdraws our attention from his main subject, to refresh and restore the minds which he has perplexed and bewildered by the painful problems he has placed before them. That most beautiful and graceful poem, for instance, on **"The Scholar-Gipsy,"** the Oxford student who is said to have forsaken academic study in order to learn, if it might be, those potent secrets of Nature, the traditions of which the gipsies are supposed sedulously to guard, ends in a digression of the most vivid beauty, suggested by the exhortation to the supposed lover of Nature to "fly our paths, our feverish contact fly," as fatal to all calm and healing life—

Then fly our greetings, fly our speech and smiles!
    —As some grave Tyrian trader, from the sea,
        Descried at sunrise an emerging prow
    Lifting the cool-hair'd creepers stealthily,
        The fringes of a southward-facing brow
            Among the Ægæan isles;
    And saw the merry Grecian coaster come,
        Freighted with amber grapes, and Chian wine,
        Green, bursting figs, and tunnies steep'd in
brine—
    And knew the intruders on his ancient home,

The young light-hearted masters of the waves—
    And snatch'd his rudder, and shook out more sail;
        And day and night held on indignantly
    O'er the blue Midland waters with the gale,
        Betwixt the Syrtes and soft Sicily,
            To where the Atlantic raves
    Outside the western straits; and unbent sails
        There, where down cloudy cliffs, through sheets
of foam,
        Shy traffickers, the dark Iberians come;
    And on the beach undid his corded bales.

Nothing could illustrate better than this passage Arnold's genius or his art. He wishes to give us a picture of the older type of audacity and freedom as it shakes itself impatiently rid of the paltry skill and timid cunning of the newer age, and plunges into the solitudes into which the finer craft of dexterous knowledge does not dare to follow. His whole drift having been that care and effort and gain and the pressure of the world are sapping human strength, he ends with a picture of the old-world pride and daring which exhibits human strength in its freshness and vigour, and he paints it with all that command of happy poetical detail in which Mr. Arnold so greatly excels. No one knows as he knows how to use detail without overlaying the leading idea which he intends to impress on us. The Tyrian trader, launching out into the deep, in his scorn for the Greek trafficker hugging the shore with his timid talent for small gains, brings home to us how much courage, freedom, and originality we may lose by the aptness for social intercourse which the craft of civilisation brings with it. So he closes his poem on the new scrupulousness and burdensomeness and self-consciousness of human life by recalling vividly the pride and buoyancy of old-world enterprise. I could quote poem after poem which Arnold closes by some such buoyant digression—a buoyant digression intended to shake off the tone of melancholy, and to remind us that the world of imaginative life is still wide open to us. "This problem is insoluble," he seems to say; "but insoluble or not, let us recall the pristine strength of the human spirit, and not forget that we have access to great resources still."

And this is where Arnold's buoyancy differs in kind from Clough's buoyancy, though buoyancy is the characteristic of both these essentially Oxford poets. Clough is buoyant in hope, and sometimes, though perhaps rarely, in faith; Arnold is buoyant in neither, but yet he is buoyant—buoyant in rebound from melancholy reflection, buoyant in throwing off the weight of melancholy reflection. "The outlook," he seems to say, "is as bad as possible. We have lost our old faith, and we cannot get a new one. Life is sapping the noblest energies of the mind. We are not as noble as we used to be. We have lost the commanding air of the great men of old. We cannot speak in the grand style. We can only boldly confront the truth and acknowledge the gloom; and yet, and yet—

Yet on he fares, by his own heart inspired."

Through hope or despair, through faith or doubt, the deep buoyancy of the imaginative life forbids Arnold to rest in any melancholy strain; he only snatches his rudder, shakes out more sail, and day and night holds on indignantly to some new shore which as yet he discovers not. Clough's buoyancy is very different. It is not the buoyancy which shakes off depressing thoughts, but the buoyancy which overcomes them—

Sit, if you will, sit down upon the ground,
Yet not to weep and wail, but calmly look around.
    Whate'er befell
    Earth is not hell;
Now too, as when it first began,
Life is yet life, and man is man.
For all that breathe beneath the heaven's high cope,
Joy with grief mixes, with despondence, hope.
    Hope conquers cowardice, joy grief;
    Or, at least, faith unbelief.
        Though dead, not dead,
        Not gone, though fled,
        Not lost, though vanished,
        In the great gospel and true creed
        He is yet risen indeed,
        Christ is yet risen.

There is Clough's buoyancy of spirit, which goes to the heart of the matter. But Arnold, with equal buoyancy, seems to aim rather at evading than averting the blows of fate. He is somewhat unjust to Wordsworth, I think, in ascribing to Wordsworth, as his characteristic spell,

the power to put aside the "cloud of mortal destiny" instead of confronting it—

Others will teach us how to dare,
And against fear our breast to steel;
Others will strengthen us to bear—
But who, ah! who, will make us feel?
The cloud of mortal destiny,
Others will front it fearlessly—
But who, like him, will put it by?

That, I should have said, is not Wordsworth's position in poetry, but Matthew Arnold's. Wordsworth "strengthened us to bear" by every means by which a poet can convey such strength; but Arnold, exquisite as his poetry is, teaches us first to feel, and then to put by, the cloud of mortal destiny. But he does not teach us, as Wordsworth does, to bear it. We delight in his pictures; we enjoy more and more, the more we study it, the poetry of his exquisite detail; we feel the lyrical cry of his sceptical moods vibrating in our heart of hearts; we feel the reviving air of his buoyant digressions as he escapes from his own spell, and bids us escape too, into the world of imaginative freedom. But he gives us no new strength to bear. He gives us no new light of hope. He gives us no new nerve of faith. He is the greatest of our elegiac poets, for he not only makes his readers thrill with the vision of the faith or strength he has lost, but puts by "the cloud of mortal destiny" with an ease that makes us feel that after all the faith and strength may not be lost, but only hidden from his eyes. Though the poet and the thinker in Matthew Arnold are absolutely at one in their conscious teaching, the poet in him helps us to rebel against the thinker, and to encourage us to believe that the "stream of tendency" which bears him up with such elastic and patient strength is not blind, is not cold, and is not dumb. He tells us—

We, in some unknown Power's employ,
Move on a rigorous line;
Can neither, when we will, enjoy,
Nor, when we will, resign.

But if the "unknown Power" be such that when we will to enjoy, we are taught to resign, and when we will to resign, we are bid, though it may be in some new and deeper sense, to enjoy, surely the "unknown Power" is not an unknowing Power, but is one that knows us better than we know ourselves.

Frederic Harrison (essay date 1896)

SOURCE: Harrison, Frederic. "Matthew Arnold." In *Tennyson, Ruskin, Mill and Other Literary Estimates*, pp. 104-25. New York: The Macmillan Company, 1902.

[*In the following essay, originally published in 1896, Harrison evaluates Arnold as a poet, literary critic, and philosopher. Harrison concludes that Arnold's poetry achieves its success in its marriage of modern thought with the classical ideal; he recognizes Arnold's literary criticism as unparalleled in his day but criticizes his philosophical work for abandoning the adherence to clear principles that defined his criticism.*]

The very name of Matthew Arnold calls up to memory a set of apt phrases and proverbial labels which have passed into our current literature, and are most happily redolent of his own peculiar turn of thought. How could modern criticism be carried on, were it forbidden to speak of 'culture,' of 'urbanity,' of 'Philistinism,' of 'distinction,' of 'the *note* of provinciality,' of 'the great style'? What a convenient shorthand is it to refer to 'Barbarians,' to 'the young lions of the Press,' to 'Bottles,' to 'Arminius,' to 'the Zeit-Geist'—and all the personal and impersonal objects of our great critic's genial contempt!

It is true that our young lions (whose feeding time appears to be our breakfast hour) have roared themselves almost hoarse over some of these sayings and nicknames, and even the 'note of provinciality' has become a little provincial. But how many of these pregnant phrases have been added to the debates of philosophy and even of religion! 'The stream of tendency that makes for righteousness,' 'sweetness and light'—not wholly in Swift's sense, and assuredly not in Swift's temper either of spirit or of brain—'sweet reasonableness,' '*das gemeine,*' the '*Aberglaube,*' are more than mere labels or phrases: they are ideas, gospels—at least, aphorisms. The judicious reader may recall the rest of these epigrams for himself, for to set forth any copious catalogue of them would be to indite a somewhat leonine essay oneself. Lord Beaconsfield, himself so great a master of memorable and prolific phrases, with admirable insight recognised this rare gift of our Arminius, and he very justly said that it was a 'great thing to do—a great achievement.'

Now this gift of sending forth to ring through a whole generation a phrase which immediately passes into a proverb, which stamps a movement or a set of persons with a distinctive cognomen, or condenses a mode of judging them into a portable aphorism—this is a very rare power, and one peculiarly rare amongst Englishmen. Carlyle had it, Disraeli had it, but how few others amongst our contemporaries! Arnold's current phrases still in circulation are more numerous than those of Disraeli, and are more simple and apt than Carlyle's. These ἔπεα πτερόεντα fly through the speech of cultivated men, pass current in the marketplace; they are generative, efficient, and issue into act. They may be right or wrong, but at any rate they do their work: they teach, they guide, possibly may mislead, but they are alive. It was noteworthy, and most significant, how many of these familiar phrases of Arnold's were Greek. He was never tired of recommending to us the charms of

'Hellenism,' of εὐφυΐα, of *epieikeia*, the supremacy of Homer, 'the classical spirit.' He loved to present himself to us as εὐφυής, as ἐπιεικής, as καλοκἀγαθός; he had been sprinkled with some of the Attic salt of Lucian, he was imbued with the classical genius—and never so much so as in his poems.

THE POET

His poetry had the classical spirit in a very peculiar and rare degree, and we can have little doubt now, when so much of Arnold's prose work in criticism has been accepted as standard opinion, and so much of his prose work in controversy has lost its interest and savour, that it is his poetry which will be longest remembered, and there his finest vein was reached. It may be said that no poet in the roll of our literature, unless it be Milton, has been so essentially saturated to the very bone with the classical genius. And I say this without forgetting *Œnone*, or the *Ode on a Grecian Urn*, or the *Prometheus Unbound*, or *Atalanta in Calydon*; for I am thinking of the entire compass of all the productions of these poets who are very often romantic and fantastic. But we can find hardly a single poem of Arnold's that is far from the classical idea.

His poetry, however, is 'classical' only in a general sense, not that all of it is imitative of ancient models, or has any affectation of archaism. It is essentially modern in thought, and has all that fetishistic worship of natural objects which is the true note of our Wordsworthian school. But Arnold is 'classical' in the serene self-command, the harmony of tone, the measured fitness, the sweet reasonableness of his verse. This balance, this lucidity, this Virgilian dignity and grace, may be said to be unfailing. Whatever be its shortcomings and its limitations, Arnold's poetry maintains this unerring urbanity of form. There is no thunder, no rant, no discord, no honey, no intoxication of mysticism or crash of battle in him. Our poet's eye doth glance from heaven to earth, from earth to heaven; but it is never caught 'in a fine frenzy rolling.' It is in this sense that Arnold is classical, that he has, and has uniformly and by instinct, some touch of that 'liquid clearness of an Ionian sky' which he felt in Homer. Not but what he is, in thought and by suggestion, one of the most truly modern, the most frankly contemporary, of all our poets.

It is no doubt owing to this constant appeal of his to modern thought, and in great degree to the best and most serious modern thought, that Arnold's poetry is welcomed by a somewhat special audience. But for that very reason, it is almost certain to gain a wider audience, and to grow in popularity and influence. His own prose has perhaps not a little retarded the acceptance of his verse. The prose is of far greater bulk than his verse: it deals with many burning questions, especially those of current politics and theological controversies; and it

supplies whole menageries of young lions with perennial bones of contention and succulent morsels where-
with to lick their lips. How could the indolent, or even
the industrious reviewer, tear himself from the delight
of sucking in 'the three Lord Shaftesburys'—or it may
be from spitting them forth with indignation—in order
to meditate with Empedocles or Thyrsis in verses which
are at once 'sober, steadfast, and demure.'

The full acceptance of Arnold's poetry has yet to come.
And in order that it may come in our time, we should
be careful not to overpraise him, not to credit him with
qualities that he never had. His peculiar distinction is
his unfailing level of thoughtfulness, of culture, and of
balance. Almost alone amongst our poets since Milton,
Arnold is never incoherent, spasmodic, careless, washy,
or *banal*. He never flies up into a region where the sun
melts his wings; he strikes no discords, and he never
tries a mood for which he has no gift. He has more
general insight into the intellectual world of our age,
and he sees into it more deeply and more surely than
any contemporary poet. He has a trained thirst for nature; but his worship of nature never weakens his reverence of man, and his brooding over man's destiny. On
the other hand, he has little passion, small measure of
dramatic sense, but a moderate gift of movement or of
colour, and—what is perhaps a more serious want—no
sure ear for melody and music.

As poet, Arnold belongs to an order very rare with us,
in which Greece was singularly rich—the order of *gnomic* poets, who condensed in metrical aphorisms their
thoughts on human destiny and the moral problems of
life. The type is found in the extant fragments of Solon,
of Xenophanes, and above all of Theognis. The famous
maxim of Solon—μηδὲν ἄγαν (nothing overdone)—
might serve as a maxim for Arnold. But of all the gnomic poets of Greece, the one with whom Arnold has
most affinity is Theognis. Let us compare the 108 fragments of Theognis, as they are paraphrased by J.
Hookham Frere, with the **Collected Poems** of Arnold,
and the analogy will strike us at once: the stoical resolution, the disdain of vulgarity, the aversion from civic
brawls, the aloofness from the rudeness of the populace
and the coarseness of ostentatious wealth. The seventeenth fragment of Frere might serve as a motto for Arnold's poems and for Arnold's temper—

> I walk by rule and measure, and incline
> To neither side, but take an even line;
> Fix'd in a single purpose and design.
> With learning's happy gifts to celebrate,
> To civilise and dignify the State;
> Not leaguing with the discontented crew,
> Nor with the proud and arbitrary few.

This is the very key-note of so many poems, of *Culture
and Anarchy,* of 'sweetness and light,' of *epieikeia*; it
is the tone of the *euphues,* of the τετράγωνος ἄνευ ψό-
γου, of the 'wise and good.'

This intensely gnomic, meditative, and ethical vein in
Arnold's poetry runs through the whole of his singularly equable work, from the earliest sonnets to the latest domestic elegies. His Muse, as he sings himself, is
ever—

> Radiant, adorn'd outside; a hidden ground
> Of thought and of austerity within.

This deep undertone of thought and of austerity gives a
uniform and somewhat melancholy colour to every line
of his verse, not despairing, not pessimist, not queru-
lous, but with a resolute and pensive insight into the
mystery of life and of things, reminding us of those
lovely tombs in the Cerameicus at Athens, of Hegeso
and the rest, who in immortal calm and grace stand
ever bidding to this fair earth a long and sweet farewell.
Like other gnomic poets, Arnold is ever running into
the tone of elegy; and he is quite at his best in elegy.
Throughout the whole series of his poems it would be
difficult to find any, even the shorter sonnets, which did
not turn upon this pensive philosophy of life, unless we
hold the few Narrative Poems to be without it. His
mental food he tells us was found in Homer, Sophocles,
Epictetus, Marcus Aurelius; and his graver pieces sound
like some echo of the imperial *Meditations,* cast into
the form of a Sophoclean chorus.

Of more than one hundred pieces, short or long, that
Arnold has left, only a few here and there can be classed
as poems of fancy, pure description, or frank surrender
of the spirit to the sense of joy and of beauty. Whether
he is walking in Hyde Park or lounging in Kensington
Gardens, apostrophising a gipsy child, recalling old
times in Rugby Chapel, mourning over a college friend,
or a dead bird, or a pet dog, he always comes back to
the dominant problems of human life. As he buries poor
'Geist,' he speculates on the future life of man; as he
laments 'Matthias' dying in his cage, he moralises on
the limits set to our human sympathy. With all his intense enjoyment of nature, and his acute observation of
nature, it never ends there. One great lesson, he says,
nature is ever teaching, it is blown in every wind—the
harmony of labour and of peace—*ohne Hast, ohne Rast.*
Every natural sight and sound has its moral warning: a
yellow primrose is not a primrose to him, and nothing
more: it reveals the poet of the primrose. The ethical
lesson of nature, which is the uniform burden of Arnold's poetry, has been definitely summed up by him in
the sonnet to a preacher who talked loosely of our 'harmony with nature'—

> Know, man hath all which nature hath, but more,
> And in that *more* lie all his hopes of good.

Not only is Arnold what Aristotle called ἠθικώτατος, a
moralist in verse, but his moral philosophy of life and
man is at once large, wise, and deep. He is abreast of

the best modern thought, and he meets the great problems of destiny and what is now called the 'foundations of belief,' like a philosopher and not like a rhetorician, a sentimentalist, or a theologian. The essential doctrine of his verse is the spirit of his own favourite hero, Marcus Aurelius, having (at least in aspiration if not in performance) the same stoicism, dignity, patience, and gentleness, and no little of the same pensive and ineffectual resignation under insoluble problems. Not to institute any futile comparison of genius, it must be conceded that Arnold in his poetry dwells in a higher philosophic æther than any contemporary poet. He has a wider learning, a cooler brain, and a more masculine logic. It was not in vain that Arnold was so early inspired by echoes of Empedocles, to whom his earliest important poem was devoted, the philosopher-poet of early Greece, whom the Greeks called Homeric, and whose 'austere harmony' they valued so well. Arnold's sonnet on **'The Austerity of Poetry,'** of which two lines have been cited above, is a mere amplification of this type of poetry as an idealised philosophy of nature and of life.

This concentration of poetry on ethics and even metaphysics involves very serious limitations and much loss of charm. The gnomic poets of Greece, though often cited for their maxims, were the least poetic of the Greek singers, and the least endowed with imagination. Aristotle calls Empedocles more 'the natural philosopher than the poet.' Solon indeed, with all his wisdom, can be as tedious as Wordsworth, and Theognis is usually prosaic. Arnold is never prosaic, and almost never tedious: but the didactic poet cannot possibly hold the attention of the groundlings for long. **'Empedocles on Etna,'** published at the age of thirty-one, still remains his most characteristic piece of any length, and it is in some ways his high-water mark of achievement. It has various moods, lyrical, didactic, dramatic—rhyme, blank verse, monologue, and song—it has his philosophy of life, his passion for nature, his enthusiasm for the undying memories of Greece. It is his typical poem: but the average reader finds its twelve hundred lines too long, too austere, too indecisive; and the poet himself withdrew it for years from a sense of its monotony of doubt and sadness.

The high merit of Arnold's verse is the uniform level of fine, if austere, thought, embodied in clear, apt, graceful, measured form. He keeps a firm hand on his Pegasus, and is always lucid, self-possessed, dignified, with a voice perfectly attuned to the feeling and thought within him. He always knew exactly what he wished to say, and he always said it exactly. He is thus one of the most correct, one of the least faulty, of all our poets, as Racine was 'correct' and 'faultless,' as in the supreme degree was the eternal type of all that is correct and faultless in form—Sophocles himself.

As a poet, Arnold was indeed our *Matteo senza errore,* but to be faultless is not to be of the highest rank. And we must confess that in exuberance of fancy, in imagination, in glow and rush of life, in tumultuous passion, in dramatic pathos, Arnold cannot claim any high rank at all. He has given us indeed but little of the kind, and hardly enough to judge him. His charming farewell lines to his dead pets, the dogs, the canary, and the cat, are full of tenderness, quaint playfulness, grace, wit, worthy of Cowper. **'The Forsaken Merman'** and **'Tristram and Iseult'** have passages of delightful fancy and of exquisite pathos. If any one doubt if Arnold had a true imagination, apart from his gnomic moralities, let him consider the conclusion of **'The Church of Brou.'** The gallant Duke of Savoy, killed in a boar hunt, is buried by his young widow in a magnificent tomb in the memorial Church of Brou, and so soon as the work is completed, the broken-hearted Duchess dies and is laid beside him underneath their marble effigies. The poet stands beside the majestic and lonely monument, and he breaks forth—

> So sleep, for ever sleep, O marble Pair!
> Or, if ye wake, let it be then, when fair
> On the carved western front a flood of light
> Streams from the setting sun, and colours bright
> Prophets, transfigured Saints, and Martyrs brave,
> In the vast western window of the nave;
> And on the pavement round the Tomb there glints
> A chequer-work of glowing sapphire-tints,
> And amethyst, and ruby—then unclose
> Your eyelids on the stone where ye repose,
> And from your broider'd pillows lift your heads,
> And rise upon your cold white marble beds;
> And, looking down on the warm rosy tints,
> Which chequer, at your feet, the illumined flints,
> Say: *What is this? we are in bliss—forgiven—*
> *Behold the pavement of the courts of Heaven!*
> Or let it be on autumn nights, when rain
> Doth rustlingly above your heads complain
> On the smooth leaden roof, and on the walls
> Shedding her pensive light at intervals
> The moon through the clere-story window shines,
> And the wind rushes through the mountain pines.
> Then, gazing up 'mid the dim pillars high,
> The foliaged marble forest where ye lie,
> *Hush,* ye will say, *it is eternity!*
> *This is the glimmering verge of Heaven, and there*
> *The columns of the heavenly palaces!*
> And, in the sweeping of the wind, your ear
> The passage of the Angels' wings will hear,
> And on the lichen-crusted leads above
> The rustle of the eternal rain of love.

I have cited this beautiful passage as a specimen of Arnold's poetic gift apart from his gnomic quality of lucid thought. It is not his usual vein, but it serves to test his powers as a mere singer. It has fancy, imagination, metrical grace, along with some penury of rhyme, perfection of tone. Has it the magic of the higher poetry, the ineffable music, the unforgotten phrase? No one has ever analysed the 'liquid diction,' 'the fluid movement' of great poetry so lucidly as Arnold himself. The fluid movement indeed he shows not seldom, especially in his blank verse. **'Sohrab and Rustum,'** a fine poem all through, if just a little academic, has some noble passages, some quite majestic lines and Homero-eid similes. But the magic of music, the unforgotten phrase, is not there. Arnold, who gave us in prose so many a memorable phrase, has left us in poetry hardly any such as fly upon the tongues of men, unless it be—'The weary Titan, staggering on to her goal,' or 'That sweet city with her dreaming spires.' These are fine, but it is not enough.

Undoubtedly Arnold from the first continually broke forth into some really Miltonic lines. Of nature he cries out—

> Still do thy sleepless ministers move on
> Their glorious tasks in silence perfecting.

Or again, he says—

> Whereo'er the chariot wheels of life are roll'd
> In cloudy circles to eternity.

In the **'Scholar-Gipsy,'** he says—

> Go, shepherd, and untie the wattled cotes!
> No longer leave thy wistful flock unfed.

Arnold has at times the fluid movement, but only at moments and on occasions, and he has a pure and highly trained sense of metrical rhythm. But he has not the yet finer and rarer sense of melodious music. We must even say more. He is insensitive to cacophonies that would have made Tennyson or Shelley 'gasp and stare.' No law of Apollo is more sacred than this: that he shall not attain the topmost crag of Parnassus who crams his mouth while singing with a handful of gritty consonants.

It is an ungracious task to point to the ugly features of poems that have unquestionably refined modulation and an exquisite polish. But where nature has withheld the ear for music, no labour and no art can supply the want. And I would ask those who fancy that modulation and polish are equivalent to music to repeat aloud these lines amongst many:—

> The sandy spits, the shore-lock'd lakes.

> * * *

> Kept on after the grave, but not begun.

> * * *

> Couldst thou no better keep, O Abbey old!

> * * *

> The strange scrawl'd rocks, the lonely sky.

> * * *

> From heaths starr'd with broom,
> And high rocks throw mildly
> On the blanch'd sands a gloom.

These last three lines are from **'The Forsaken Merman,'** wherein Arnold perhaps came nearest to the echo of music and to pure fantasy. In the grand lines to Shakespeare he writes—

> Self-school'd, self-scann'd, self-honour'd, self-secure.

Here are seven sibilants, four 'selfs,' three 'sc,' and twenty-nine consonants against twelve vowels in one verse. It was not thus that Shakespeare himself wrote sonnets, as when he said—

> Full many a glorious morning have I seen
> Flatter the mountain-tops with sovereign eye.

It must be remembered that Arnold wrote but little verse, and most of it in early life, that he was not by profession a poet, that he was a hardworked inspector of schools all his days, and that his prose work far exceeds his verse. This separates him from all his contemporary rivals, and partly explains his stiffness in rhyming, his small product, and his lack of melody. Had he been able like Wordsworth, Tennyson, Browning, Swinburne, to regard himself from first to last as a poet, to devote his whole life to poetry, to live the life 'of thought and of austerity within'—which he craved as poet, but did not achieve as a man—then he might have left us poems more varied, more fanciful, more musical, more joyous. By temperament and by training, he, who at birth 'was breathed on by the rural Pan,' was deprived of that fountain of delight that is essential to the highest poetry, the dithyrambic glow—the ἀνήριθμον γέλασμα—

> The countless dimples of the laughing seas.[1]

of perennial poetry. This perhaps, more than his want of passion, of dramatic power, of rapidity of action, limits the audience of Arnold as a poet. But those who thirst for the pure Castalian spring, inspired by sustained and lofty thoughts, who care for that σπουδαιότης—that 'high seriousness,' of which he spoke so much as the very essence of the best poetry,—have long known that they find it in Matthew Arnold more than in any of his even greater contemporaries.

THE CRITIC

About Matthew Arnold as critic of literature it is needless to enlarge, for the simple reason that we have all long ago agreed that he has no superior, indeed no rival. His judgments on our poets have passed into current opinion, and have ceased to be discussed or questioned. It is, perhaps, a grave loss to English literature that Arnold was not able, or perhaps never strove, to devote his whole life to the interpretation of our best poetry and prose, with the same systematic, laborious, concentrated energy which has placed Sainte-Beuve at the head of French critics. With his absorbing professional duties, his far from austere aloofness from the whirlpool of society, his guerilla warfare with journalism, Radicals, theologians, and all devotees of Dagon, it was not fated that Arnold could vie with the vast learning and Herculean industry of Sainte-Beuve. Neither as theologian, philosopher, nor publicist, was Arnold at all adequately equipped by genius or by education for the office of supreme arbiter which he so airily, and perhaps so humorously, assumed to fill. And as poet, it is doubtful whether, with his Aurelian temperament and treacherous ear, he could ever have reached a much higher rank. But as critic of literature, his exquisite taste, his serene sense of equity, and that genial magnanimity which prompted him to give just value for every redeeming quality of those whom he loved the least—this made him a consummate critic of style. Though he has not left us an exhaustive review of our literature, as Sainte-Beuve has done for France, he has given us a group of short, lucid, suggestive canons of judgment, which serve as landmarks to an entire generation of critics.

The function of criticism—though not so high and mighty as Arnold proclaimed it with superb assurance—is not so futile an art as the sixty-two minor poets and the 11,000 minor novelists are now wont to think it. Arnold committed one of the few extravagances of his whole life when he told us that poetry was 'the criticism of life,' that the function of criticism was to see all things as they really are in themselves—the very thing Kant told us we could never do. On the other hand, too much of what is now called criticism is the improvised chatter of a raw lad, portentously ignorant of the matter in hand. It is not the 'indolent reviewer' that we now suffer under, but the 'lightning reviewer,' the young man in a hurry with a Kodak, who finally disposes of a new work on the day of its publication. One of them naïvely complained the other morning of having to cut the pages, as if we ever suspected that he cut the pages of more than the preface and table of contents.

Criticism, according to Arnold's practice, if not according to his theory, had as its duty to lay down decisive canons of cultured judgment, to sift the sound from the vicious, and to maintain the purity of language and of style. To do all this in any masterly degree requires most copious knowledge, an almost encyclopædic training in literature, a natural genius for form and tone, and above all a temper of judicial balance. Johnson in the last century, Hallam, and possibly Southey, in this century, had some such gift: Macaulay and Carlyle had not; for they wanted genius for form and judicial bal-

ance. Now Arnold had this gift in supreme degree, in a degree superior to Johnson or to Hallam. He made far fewer mistakes than they did. He made very few mistakes. The touchstone of the great critic is to make very few mistakes, and never to be carried off his balance by any pet aversion or pet affection of his own, not to be biassed so much as a hair's breadth by any salient merit or any irritating defect, and always to keep an eye well open to the true proportion of any single book in the great world of men and of affairs, and in the mighty realm of general literature.

For this reason we have so very few great critics, for the combination of vast knowledge, keen taste, and serene judgment is rare. It is thus so hard for any young person, for women, to become great in criticism: the young lack the wide experience; women lack the cool judicial temper. It is common enough to find those who are very sensitive to some rare charm, very acute to detect a subtle quality, or justly severe on some seductive failing. The rare power is to be able to apply to a complicated set of qualities the nicely adjusted compensations, to place a work, an author, in the right rank, and to do this for all orders of merit, with a sure, constant, unfailing touch—and without any real or conspicuous mistake.

This is what Arnold did, at any rate for our later poetry. He taught us to do it for ourselves, by using the instruments he brought to bear. He did much to kill a great deal of flashy writing, and much vulgarity of mind that once had a curious vogue. I am accused of being *laudator temporis acti,* and an American newspaper was pleased to speak of me as 'this hopeless old man'; but I am never weary of saying, that at no epoch of our literature has the bulk of minor poetry been so graceful, so refined, so pure; the English language in daily use has never been written in so sound a form by so many writers; and the current taste in prose and verse has never been so just. And this is not a little owing to the criticism of Arnold, and to the ascendency which his judgment exerted over his time.

To estimate that lucidity and magnanimity of judgment which he possessed, we should note how entirely openminded he was to the defects of those whom he most loved, and to the merits of those whom he chiefly condemned. His ideal in poetry is essentially Wordsworthian, yet how sternly and how honestly he marks the *longueurs* of Wordsworth, his flatness, his mass of inferior work. Arnold's ideal of poetry was essentially alien to Byron, whose vulgar, slipshod, rhetorical manner he detested, whilst he recognised Byron's Titanic power: 'our *soul* had felt him like the thunder's roll.' Arnold saw all the blunders made by Dryden, by Johnson, by Macaulay, by Coleridge, by Carlyle—but how heartily he can seize their real merits! Though drawn by all his thoughts and tastes towards such writers as Sénancour,

Amiel, Joubert, Heine, the Guérins, he does not affect to forget the limitations of their influence and the idiosyncrasy of their genius. In these days, when we are constantly assured that the function of criticism is to seize on some subtle and yet undetected quality that happens to have charmed you, and to wonder, in Delphic oracles, if Milton or Shelley ever quite touched that mystic circle, how refreshing it is to find Arnold always cool, always judicial—telling us even that Shakespeare has let drop some random stuff, and calmly reminding us that he had not 'the sureness of a perfect style,' as Milton had. Let us take together Arnold's summing up of all the qualities of Wordsworth, Byron, Keats, Shelley, and we shall see with what a just but loving hand he distributes the alternate meed of praise and blame. *Amant alterna Camœnæ.* But of all the Muses, she of criticism loves most the alternate modulation of *soprano* and *basso.*

Not that Arnold was invariably right, or that all his judgments are unassailable. His canons were always right; but it is not in mortals to apply them unerringly to men and to things. He seems somewhat inclined to undervalue Tennyson, of whom he speaks so little. He has not said enough for Shelley, perhaps not enough for Spenser, nor can we find that he loved with the true ardour the glorious romances of Walter Scott. But this is no place, nor can I pretend to be the man, to criticise our critic. For my own part, I accept his decisions in the main for all English poetry and on general questions of style. Accept them, that is, so far as it is in human nature to accept such high matters—'errors excepted,' *exceptis excipiendis.* The important point on which his judgment is the most likely to be doubted or reversed by the supreme court of the twentieth century, lies in the relative places he has assigned to Wordsworth and to Shelley. He was by nature akin to Wordsworth, alien to Shelley; and the 'personal equation' may have told in this case. For my own part, I feel grateful to Arnold for asserting so well the dæmonic power of Byron, and so justly distinguishing the poet in his hour of inspiration from the peer in his career of affectation and vice. Arnold's piece on the **'Study of Poetry,'** written as an introduction to the collected *English Poets,* should be preserved in our literature as the *norma,* or *canon* of right opinion about poetry, as we preserve the standard coins in the Pyx, or the standard yard measure in the old Jewel-house at Westminster.[2]

THE PHILOSOPHER AND THEOLOGIAN

Matthew Arnold, the philosopher, the politician, the theologian, does not need prolonged notice, inasmuch as he was anxious to disclaim any title to be ranked as any one of the three. But he entered into many a keen debate on philosophy, politics, and religion; and, whilst disavowing for himself any kind of system of belief, he sate in judgment on the beliefs of others, and assured us that the mission of Culture was to be supreme Court of Appeal for all brutalities of the vulgar and all the immaturities of the ignorant. Indeed, since the very definition of Culture was 'to know the best that had ever been done and said,' to be 'a study of perfection,' 'to see things as they really are,' this Delphic priest of Culture was compelled to give us oracles about all the dark problems that harass the souls of philosophers, of politicians, and of theologians. He admitted this sacred duty, and manfully he strove to interpret the inspirations of the God within him. They were often charged with insight and wisdom; they were sometimes entirely mysterious; they frequently became a matter of language rather than of fact. But these responses of the deity have found no successor. Nor does any living mentor now attempt to guide our halting steps into the true path of all that should be done or may be known, with the same sure sense of serene omniscience.

Of Culture—which has so long been a synonym for our dear lost friend—it can hardly be expected that I should speak. I said what I had to say nearly thirty years ago, and I rejoice now to learn from his letters that my little piece gave him such innocent pleasure. He continued to rejoin for years; but, having fully considered all his words, I have nothing to qualify or unsay. We are most of us trying to get what of Culture we can master, to see things as they are, to know the best, to attain to some little measure of Sweetness and Light—and we can only regret that our great master in all these things has carried his secret to the grave. The mystery still remains, *what* is best, *how* are things to be seen really as they are, by *what* means can we attain to perfection? Alas! the oracles are dumb. Apollo from his shrine can no more divine.

What we find so perplexing is, that the master, who, in judging poetry and literature, had most definite principles, clear-cut canons of judgment, and very strict tests of good and bad, doctrines which he was always ready to expound, and always able to teach others, no sooner passes into philosophy, into politics, into theology, than he disclaims any system, principles, or doctrines of any kind. 'Oh!' we hear him cry, 'I am no philosopher, no politician, no theologian. I am merely telling you, in my careless, artless way, what you should think and do in these high matters. Culture whispers it to me, and I tell you; and only the Philistines, Anarchs, and Obscurantists object.' Now, it is obvious that no man can honestly dispose of all that lies *inter apices* of philosophy, politics, and religion, unless he have some scheme of dominant ideas. If he cannot range himself under any of the known schemes, if he be neither intuitionist, experimentalist, or eclectic, if he incline neither to authority, nor to freedom, neither to revelation, nor to scepticism, nor to any of the ways of thinking that lie between any of these extremes—then he must have a brand-new, self-originated, dominant scheme of his own. If he tend towards no known system of ideas, then he tends to his own system; and this is usually the narrowest and most capricious system that can be invented.

Not that Matthew Arnold's judgments in these things were narrow, however personal. It would be easy to show, if this were the place, what were the schools and orders of thought under which he ranged himself. The idea that he was an Ariel, a 'blessed Glendoveer,' or Mahatma of Light, was a charming bit of playfulness that relieved the tedium of debate. Whether as much as he fancied was gained to the cause of Sweetness by presenting the other side in fantastic costumes and airy caricature, by the iteration of nicknames, and the fustigation of dummy opponents, is now rather open to doubt. The public, and he himself, began to feel that he was carrying a joke too far when he brought the Trinity into the pantomime. Some of his playmates, it is said, rather enjoyed seeing themselves on the stage, and positively played up to harlequin and his wand. And it was good fun to all of us to see our friends and acquaintances in motley, capering about to so droll a measure.

With his refined and varied learning, his natural acuteness, and his rare gift of poetic insight, Matthew Arnold made some admirable suggestions in general philosophy. How true, how fruitful are his sayings about Hebraism and Hellenism, about Greece and Israel, about the true strength of Catholicism, about pagan and mediæval religious sentiment, about Spinoza, about Butler, Marcus Aurelius, and Goethe! All of these, and all he says about education, gain much by the pellucid grace and precision with which they are presented. They are presented, it is true, rather as the treasure-trove of instinctive taste than as the laborious conclusions of any profound logic; for Culture, as we have often said, naturally approached even the problems of the universe, not so much from the side of metaphysics as from the side of *Belles-Lettres.* I can remember Matthew Arnold telling us with triumph that he had sought to exclude from a certain library a work of Herbert Spencer, by reading to the committee a passage therefrom which he pronounced to be clumsy in style. He knew as little about Spencer's *Synthetic Philosophy* as he did about Comte's, which he pretended to discuss with an air of laughable superiority, at which no doubt he was himself the first to laugh.

Arnold, indeed, like M. Jourdain, was constantly talking Comte without knowing it, and was quite delighted to find how cleverly he could do it. There is a charming and really grand passage in which he sums up his *conclusion* at the close of his **Culture and Anarchy.** I cannot resist the pleasure of quoting this fine piece of English, every word of which I devoutly believe—

> But for us,—who believe in right reason, in the duty and possibility of extricating and elevating our best self, in the progress of humanity towards perfection,—

for us the framework of society, that theatre on which this august drama has to unroll itself, is sacred; and whoever administers it, and however we may seek to remove them from their tenure of administration, yet while they administer, we steadily and with undivided heart support them in repressing anarchy and disorder; because without order there can be no society, and without society there can be no human perfection.

It so happens that this, the summing up of the mission of Culture, is entirely and exactly the mission of Positivism, and is even expressed in the very language used by Comte in all his writings, and notably in his *Appeal to Conservatives* (1855). How pleasantly we can fancy Culture now meeting the Founder of Positivism in some Elysian Fields, and accosting him in that inimitably genial way: 'Ah, well! I see now that we are not so far apart, but I never had patience to read your rather dry French, you know!'

Of his Theology, or his anti-Theology, even less need be said here. It was most interesting and pregnant, and was certainly the source of his great popularity and vogue. Here indeed he touched to the quick the Hebraism of our middle classes, the thought of our cultured classes, the insurgent instincts of the People. It was a singular mixture—Anglican divinity adjusted to the Pantheism of Spinoza—to parody a famous definition of Huxley's, it was Anglicanism *minus* Christianity, and even Theism. It is difficult for the poor Philistine to grasp the notion that all this devotional sympathy with the Psalmists, Prophets, and Evangelists, this beautiful enthusiasm for 'the secret of Jesus' and the 'profound originality' of Paul, was possible to a man whose intellect rejected the belief that there was even any probable evidence for the personality of God, or for the celestial immortality of the soul, who flatly denied the existence of miracle, and treated the entire fabric of dogmatic theology as a figment. Yet this is the truth: and what is more, this startling, and somewhat paradoxical, transformation scene of the Anglican creeds and formularies sank deep into the reflective minds of many thinking men and women, who could neither abandon the spiritual poetry of the Bible nor resist the demonstrations of science. The combination, amongst many combinations, is one that, in a different form, was taught by Comte, which has earned for Positivism the title of Catholicism *plus* Science. Matthew Arnold, who but for his father's too early death might have been the son of a bishop, and who, in the last century, would himself have been a classical dean, made an analogous and somewhat restricted combination that is properly described as Anglicanism *plus* Pantheism.

Let us think no more of his philosophy—the philosophy of an ardent reader of Plato, Spinoza, and Goethe: of his politics—the politics of an Oxford don who lived much at the Athenæum Club: nor of his theology—the theology of an English clergyman who had resigned his orders on conscientious grounds. We will think only of the subtle poet, the consummate critic, the generous spirit, the radiant intelligence, whose over-ambitious fancies are even now fading into oblivion—whose rare imaginings in stately verse have yet to find a wider and a more discerning audience.

Notes

1. From an unpublished translation of *Prometheus,* by E. H. Pember, Q.C.

2. This does not include mere *obiter dicta* in his familiar *Letters.* A great critic, like the pope, is infallible only when he is speaking *ex cathedra,* on matters of faith.

Henry C. Montgomery (essay date June 1939)

SOURCE: Montgomery, Henry C. "Matthew Arnold, Classicist." *The Classical Journal* 34, no. 9 (June 1939): 532-37.

[*In the following essay, Montgomery explores Arnold's relationship to the classics, chronicling his classical inheritance from his father and stressing his belief that the classics are a critical component of a liberal education.*]

"Matthew Arnold, Classicist," might suggest a number of possible treatments. We might think of him as a poet imbued with the principles of classical poetry; we might collect and discuss his references to the literature and life of antiquity; we might revel in his admirable defense of an education based on the humanities in his reply to Huxley's *Science and Culture*; and we might well reconsider his lectures dealing with the translation of Homer. With none of these is this paper concerned. The approach is much more prosaic, perhaps less worthy, but no less pertinent than the others mentioned. Arnold was interested, deeply, in the teaching of the ancient languages, although he actually engaged in this work for only a brief period. His objectives—familiar term—were very definite in his mind and they are brought to light in certain of his works that considerably postdate his teaching activity. In a recent issue of the *Classical Weekly*[1] Professor W. L. Carr undertakes to suggest that the primary immediate objective of reading Latin may best be attained by the simple method of doing just that and that the time spent on composition is unnecessarily disproportionate, helpful chiefly toward proficiency in composition and nothing else. The remaining pages of this issue of the *Classical Weekly* are devoted to two unfavorable criticisms of his point of view and in the subsequent issue[2] two additional opponents take up the cudgels. Mention is made of this debate because it is recent and convenient. We believe that Professor Carr might have found in Matthew Arnold a kindred spirit and an authority of no insignificant weight.

Arnold's attitude toward the teaching of the classics was in a sense inherited. His father, Thomas Arnold, devoted his entire life to teaching the ancient languages and literature with an influence on English education that is corollary rather than secondary to the influence of his son. The elder Arnold was not a revolutionist but we are told that "he rebelled strongly against the wooden, mechanical, and pedantic fashion in which those languages were often taught, as if the attainment of proficiency in them were an end in itself and not the means to some higher end."[3] Thomas Arnold believed that writers like Aristotle, Plato, Thucydides, Cicero, and Tacitus were inaccurately called "ancient," that their conclusions were just as vital to his own day as to the period in which they were written. It was his aim, then, to use the historical, political, and philosophical values of the ancient authors in the educational scheme of his own times. The "construing," as it was called, of English into Greek and Latin verses was particularly objectionable to him. This type of composition was inflicted upon students of his day with even more vigor than is prose composition today. However, Thomas Arnold conformed to, and tried to make the best of, the method in general practice.

There are surely few men outside the profession of teaching the classics who have been so firmly convinced as Matthew Arnold that in the classics are all the essentials of a liberal education. His position as a school inspector and his skill as an essayist tended to give his opinions an authority and acceptance that those from within the profession may never hope to attain. For these same reasons his views on the teaching objectives of the classics are worthy of consideration. Like his father he felt that through the humanities a man could know himself and his own world, and like his father he was opposed to the conventional methods of approach to the study of the humanities. A few quotations from his works will serve as excellent illustrations of his pedagogical theory. In **The Study of Poetry**[4] we find the following:

> It may be said that the more we know about a classic the better we shall enjoy him; and, if we lived as long as Methuselah and had all of us heads of perfect clearness and wills of perfect steadfastness, this might be true in fact as it is plausible in theory. But the case here is much the same as the case with the Greek and Latin studies of our schoolboys. The elaborate philological groundwork which we require them to lay is in theory an admirable preparation for appreciating the Greek and Latin authors worthily. The more thoroughly we lay the groundwork, the better we shall be able, it may be said, to enjoy the authors. True, if time were not so short, and schoolboys' wits not so soon tired and their power of attention exhausted; only, as it is, the elaborate philological preparation goes on, but the authors are little known and less enjoyed.

It is perhaps a mystery why comments in similar vein should be found in a work by Arnold of which the title and contents have little connection with this line of thought. But found they are and in considerable frequency in his *Higher Schools and Universities in Germany.*[5] It would seem another indication of his keen interest in this phase of the study of languages. In speaking of the necessity for a re-creation of school instruction in letters and in the ancient humanities he says:[6]

> The prolonged philological discipline, which in our present schools guards the access to *Alterthumswissenschaft,* brings to mind the philosophy of Albertus Magnus, the mere introduction to which—the logic—was by itself enough to absorb all a student's time of study.

Arnold was willing to admit that a student like Wolf could combine the philological discipline with the matter to which it was ancillary. But he continues:

> Such students are rare; and nine out of ten, especially in England, where so much time is given to Greek and Latin composition, never get through the philological vestibule at all, never arrive at *Alterthumswissenschaft,* which is a knowledge of the spirit and power of Greek and Roman antiquity learned from its original works.

> But many people have even convinced themselves that the preliminary philological discipline is so extremely valuable as to be an end in itself. . . . No preliminary discipline is to be pressed at the risk of keeping minds from getting at the main matter, a knowledge of themselves and the world. Some minds have . . . a special aptitude for philology, or for pure mathematics—but for one of these there will be ten whose natural access to vital knowledge is through literature, philosophy, history, or some one or more of the natural sciences.[7]

Arnold believed Latin the best of all grammars for the promotion of habits of exactness, but he considered a Latin grammar of thirty pages sufficient and that the number of those who should be given the chance to become intimately acquainted with Latin and Greek as literature was infinitely greater than those whose aptitudes were for composition and scholarship.

Arnold was not entirely opposed to prose composition but thought it should be limited to exercises auxiliary to the sound learning of any language. He had no use for careless and slipshod methods but was convinced that by less emphasis on composition and more on literature the grammatical forms could be learned more exactly and permanently than by ambitious grammatical studies.

In the field of the modern languages, in which the leaders, rightly or wrongly, have followed so closely after the methods and investigations of teachers in the classics, Arnold anticipated the recommendations of the Coleman report and the clear-cut theories of Michael West. To Arnold the aim of teaching a student to speak a modern language was commercial and not liberal—

showy and often useful, but to be regarded as a secondary and subordinate aim. He sums it up in the statement, "It is as literature, and as opening fresh roads into knowledge, that the modern foreign languages, like the ancient, are truly school business."[8]

Arnold's theories on language teaching are still the subject of controversy. Perhaps they always will be; but the opinions of one whose educational theories for the most part have long since been accepted as sound in practice as well as theory should receive thoughtful consideration, especially since they come from such a staunch and expert defender of the humanities as the basis of true education. An inspection of Arnold's essays and certain other works will incline one to accept without reservation the statement that "the argument for classical learning was never more admirably presented than by Matthew Arnold, himself intellectually a product of the classical spirit."[9]

Arnold was neither the first nor the last to suggest that profound grammatical studies are not a reasonable preparation for the reading knowledge of a foreign language. St. Augustine must have had feelings of a similar kind when he said:

> Why do I hate Greek and this harping on such things? For Homer himself . . . was a bitter pill to me as a boy. I believe that Vergil is no less so to Grecian children when they are compelled to learn him. For the difficulty of learning a foreign language was like sprinkling all the pleasures of the fabulous narrations with gall. I didn't understand a word of it, yet they urged me to learn it with all sorts of terrors and punishments.[10]

In more recent years and especially since the publication of the *Classical Investigation* the reading objective seems to have received almost unanimous acceptance, but not so the method of approach. Criticisms of the conventional method have been expressed not only by language teachers but by others as well. In the *Classical Journal*[11] Professor Carr has stated:

> A good many years of experience as a student and teacher of Latin have only strengthened in me a belief that language, even the Latin language, consists much more largely of words than it does of grammatical forms or syntactical principles or any other of those elements which we are accustomed to single out for purposes of study or instruction.

Michael West reaches almost the identical conclusions in the field of the modern languages where the reading objective is generally regarded even more basic than in the ancient languages. West feels that grammar is a medicine, not a form of diet, and should be occasional, intermittent. "But," he says, "so systematic are the schoolmasters that they make the child swallow the whole pharmacopoeia of grammar—whether as a preventive or a panacea, I have never been able to discover."[12] From without the teaching guild we occasionally meet with protests such as these:

There was indeed a glory in Greece and a grandeur in Rome. But this glory and this grandeur have been hidden under a dead weight of Greek and Latin grammar. If we may suppose that some day a method will be found of imparting an agility in the use of these languages, with at the same time a *just* and unsentimental appreciation of the cultures they represent, there will be rejoicing among a certain small class of university students.[13]

Remarks such as the foregoing, while worthy of careful consideration, might perhaps in some quarters be considered as yielding at a time when all yielding is treason. But with Matthew and Thomas Arnold such a criticism would not apply. They lived and taught in a period when the classics were still unchallenged, or only feebly challenged, as the foundation of the educational system. The younger Arnold did indeed live to see the threatened eclipse of the humanities he regarded so highly, but there is no trace of retreat, nothing of the defeatist, in his attitude. Rather it was an objective, self-critical stand at a time when such a stand scarcely seemed necessary.

Notes

1. March 4, 1935, 129-133.
2. March 11, 1935, 137-142.
3. Cf. Sir Joshua Fitch: *Thomas and Matthew Arnold*: New York (1897), 30.
4. *Selections from the Prose Works of Matthew Arnold,* ed. W. S. Johnson: New York (1913), 60 f.
5. London (1874).
6. *Op. cit.,* 177 f.
7. *Op. cit.,* 178-180.
8. *Higher Schools and Universities in Germany,* 191.
9. William Harbutt Dawson, *Matthew Arnold*: New York and London (1904), 130.
10. *Confessions,* "Loeb Classical Library," I, 14.
11. XXIX (February, 1934), 323.
12. *Language in Education,* London (1929), 136.
13. "Small Latin, Less Greek," *The Nation,* CXXXII (1931), 574.

U. C. Knoepflmacher (essay date 1963)

SOURCE: Knoepflmacher, U. C. "Dover Revisited: The Wordsworthian Matrix in the Poetry of Matthew Arnold." In *Matthew Arnold: A Collection of Critical Essays,* edited by David J. DeLaura, pp. 46-53. Englewood Cliffs, N.J.: Prentice-Hall, Inc., 1973.

[*In the following essay, originally published in* Victorian Poetry *in January 1963, Knoepflmacher contends that while Arnold's poetry often draws upon Wordsworthian imagery, phrases, and emotions, it actively subverts much of Wordsworth's poetic philosophy and vision.*]

Much has been written on Matthew Arnold's qualification of Romanticism, on his fluctuating estimates of the English Romantic poets in general and of William Wordsworth in particular. Such studies are generally limited to Arnold's critical opinions.[1] Only occasionally, and then very succinctly, have students of Arnold's poetry dwelled on his creation of what a recent and perceptive critic has called "ironic echoes of Wordsworth": "a version of Wordsworth which is also a criticism and a rejection of Wordsworth's view."[2]

Arnold's poetry is, to a large extent, derivative. It draws on the classics for much of its mythic substance and the stateliness of its rhythm; on Goethe for intellectual content; on sources as remote as the *Bhagavad Gita* for that "wider application" which Arnold felt was "the one thing wanting to make Wordsworth an even greater poet than he is." But the core of Arnold's emotional power is Wordsworthian, and it is so by intent and not by mere coincidence. Arnold's poems avail themselves of situations that are Wordsworthian, images that are Wordsworthian, phrases that are Wordsworthian. This Wordsworthian matrix is enlisted in what essentially amounts to a denial of the vision of Arnold's predecessor, although, at the very same time, it is relied upon to preserve Wordsworth's ability "to make us feel." . . .

I

Arnold's **"Resignation"** is his version, or, more properly, his inversion, of Wordsworth's "Tintern Abbey." The parallelism between the two poems is deliberate. It enables Arnold to employ his predecessor's work as a frame of reference, an ironic "touchstone" essential to his own meaning.[3] **"Resignation"** is almost twice as long as "Tintern Abbey." It abounds in erudite allusions and echoes from sources as varied as Lucretius and Goethe. But the core of the poem is unmistakably Wordsworthian: the setting is the Lake Country of the Romantics; the situation, a return to the earlier associations of the scene by a matured poet and his sister; the import, a creed handed down by the poet to his listener.

In "Tintern Abbey" Wordsworth and Dorothy stand "here upon the banks of this fair river." The poet mourns his lost childhood oneness with Nature but derives joy from the knowledge that his sister still possesses the power that he has lost. The poem ends on a triumphant assertion of his belief in a matured and "sober pleasure" based on the "wild ecstasies" of youth. Memory becomes a source of joy: "Nature never did betray the heart that loved her." The poet, "a worshiper of Nature," can readily become its priest.

In **"Resignation"** the poet and his sister also stand "on this mild bank above the stream," amidst a lush natural landscape which has remained unaltered despite the changes they have suffered. "The loose dark stones" have not moved; "this wild brook" runs on, undisturbed. The scene's permanence sharpens the poet's awareness of his own mutability. He, too, hopes to derive a creed based on his observation of Nature. But while Arnold's yearning for sobering "thoughts" suggested by the surroundings is not unlike Wordsworth's, his interpretation of these surroundings is markedly different. Indeed, the ethical creed that he charts out for his sister and the poetic creed he indirectly prescribes for himself are based on a complete re-definition of a Wordsworthian faith in Nature. To Wordsworth, the communion between Nature and man is in itself an abundant compensation for the mutability of life—it brings about a communion between brother and sister, man and man, and confirms the poet in his role of Nature's high priest. To Arnold, on the other hand, the utter impersonality of the scene before him only accentuates the need for an adequate attitude towards a natural world which can no more provide the "tender joy" that Wordsworth was capable of extracting from it than it can act as a stimulus for the heightened sensations sought by his Faustian sister. He must therefore explain to the Romantic Fausta the limitations suggested by landscape, and, simultaneously, delimit his own functions as new kind of poet, a poet deprived of the "rapt security" inherent in the Romantic vision.

To Arnold the landscape is but an emblem of "the general life," an impersonal power which demands the submission of all men. But rather than becoming a mere object subjected to the capriciousness of "chance," man can achieve the dignity of a rule by "fate" if he understands his own position within the "dizzying eddy" of life. This understanding can come only through detachment. It is achieved instinctively by gypsies plodding in their "hereditary way"; it is achieved consciously by those higher beings who can discern through a special insight "what through experience others learn." In outline, Arnold's schematization is not unlike Wordsworth's. He has identified the landscape before him with an order or plan which he, as a detached observer, is able to perceive; he has maintained that this order can be understood instinctively by some and consciously by others; he has established the need for an acceptance of this plan, "the general life." But, of course, it is the valuation which Arnold places on these elements which is entirely opposed to Wordsworth's. Children unconsciously in touch with the divine have become gypsies instinctively attuned to the buffets of life; the redeeming Dorothy has become the unredeemable Fausta; the isolated poet who converts the "still, sad music of humanity" into a joyful faith has become a detached stoic contemplator, content with a "sad lucidity of soul."[4] For what has changed, above all, is the order perceived by the poet and the manner in which the poet's perception has been achieved.

The divine "presence" perceived by Wordsworth resides in the landscape he sees, as well as in himself. It is:

> a sense sublime
> Of something far more deeply interfused,
> Whose dwelling is the light of setting suns,
> And the round ocean and the living air,
> And the blue sky, and in the mind of man;
> A motion and a spirit, that impels
> All living things, all objects of all thought,
> And rolls through all things.

To Arnold, on the other hand, "the something which infects the world" is not an invisible *primum mobile*. It is the aggregate of all that is visible, an impersonal and tyrannical power which offers "not joy, but peace" to him who apprehends its operations:

> Before him he sees life unroll,
> A placid and continuous whole—
> That general life, which does not cease,
> Whose secret is not joy, but peace;
> That life, whose dumb wish is not miss'd
> If birth proceeds, if things subsist;
> The life of plants, and stones, and rain,
> The life he craves—if not in vain
> Fate gave, what chance shall not control,
> His sad lucidity of soul.

Nature has provided Wordsworth with a "holy love"; it has only confirmed Arnold's saddened intellectual awareness.

"Resignation" and "Tintern Abbey" rely on the modulation of conflicting moods; both poems conclude on the speaker's subjection to a discipline based on Nature. Wordsworth emphasizes the beneficence of this discipline; Arnold emphasizes its grim necessity. In each case, the landscape has acted as a guide. But while for Wordsworth Nature is an active teacher and comforter who readily reveals "a presence that disturbs me with the joy of elevated thoughts," Arnold's "thoughts" are addressed rhetorically to the impassive landscape before him so that it might confirm his own well-rehearsed lesson in the art of "bearing":

> Enough, we live!—and if a life,
> With large results so little rife,
> Though bearable, seem hardly worth
> This pomp of worlds, this pain of birth;
> Yet, Fausta, the mute turf we tread,
> The solemn hills around us spread,
> The stream which falls incessantly,
> The strange-scrawl'd rocks, the lonely sky,
> If I might lend their life a voice,
> Seem to bear rather than rejoice.

The lesson of joy given to Wordsworth is thus subverted. For Arnold's Nature is utterly impervious to the emotional demands of its students. "The meadows and the woods and mountains" speak freely to Wordsworth in the "language of sense." Arnold, however, must scrupulously point out that the language he ascribes to the scene before him is really his own. The turf is "mute," the hills are "solemn," even the rocks are enigmatic and "strange-scrawl'd." The poet thus is forced to superimpose his own order on the scene he sees before him. He can at best attribute an imagined "voice" to the life he sees around him; he can only assume that the landscape would *"seem"* to teach him how to bear.

Wordsworth's vision is transcendent and symbolical: ocean, air, and sky contain the same spirit which dwells "in the mind of man." Arnold's vision is analytical and allegorical: the mind of man can tentatively impose its understanding upon what it apprehends through the senses. Therefore, while Wordsworth's poet is a medium for the divine plan of Nature, Arnold's poet is merely the interpreter of the "dumb" wishes of a neutral universe. Whereas Wordsworth becomes infused and intoxicated by the centrifugal power of Nature, Arnold must stand aside and examine his own relative position in time and space in order to preserve his "lucidity of soul." The scene before him is meaningless in itself. It must be related to Mohammedan pilgrims and Gothic warriors, to Orpheus and to Homer. Intensity is replaced by extensiveness: *"Not deep the poet sees, but wide."* The resolution of Arnold's poem therefore depends entirely on his *a priori* survey of the "general life," a survey brought about by precisely that cultural view which Wordsworth lacked to make "his thought richer and his influence of wider application."

"Resignation" thus represents Arnold's attempt to give a contemporary "application" to Wordsworth's Romantic poem. It is a characteristically Victorian juggling of "heart" and "head": an emotional faith in Nature is qualified by the wider intellectual view afforded by scientific skepticism, historicism, and "Culture." Arnold's qualification also alters Wordsworth's poetic method. The symbolically exalted "green pastoral landscape" becomes an allegorized "green hill-side" arbitrarily invested with qualities corresponding to the human situation. . . .

III

"Resignation" and **"Dover Beach"** are perhaps the most obvious examples of Arnold's use of a Wordsworthian matrix in his poetry. But they are by no means the only ones. Arnold's **"To a Gipsy Child by the Sea-shore"** reverberates with echoes from the "Immortality" ode;[5] his **"East London"** and **"West London"** sonnets are the Victorian counterparts of the London sonnets written by Wordsworth in 1802; the conception of the **"Marguerite"** poems owes much to Wordsworth's use of his "Lucy." There are correspondences in situations and phrases. Images, such as the elm-tree in **"Thyrsis"**

(which recalls the oak of "Michael") or the "sea of life" in **"To Marguerite,"** are invested with Wordsworthian properties.

The introduction of these elements into Arnold's own poetry represents more than a mere negation of Wordsworth's vision. There is a definite effort at conservation on the part of a poet, who, according to Quiller-Couch's witticism, had a notable tendency to regard himself as "Wordsworth's widow."[6] The younger man, whose boyhood "had been spent in the Lake Country and under Wordsworth's affectionate eye,"[7] tried to knit on his own experience to that of his predecessor. For not only Arnold, but a host of other eminent Victorians, regarded Wordsworth with a curious ambivalence. Intellectually, they deplored the simplicity of his natural faith; yet, at the same time, the skeleton of this faith provided them with a vicarious emotional gratification. For Wordsworth was able to do what his successors could no longer achieve. He could convert grief and pain into joyous affirmation; he could draw this affirmation from the element which he called "the still, sad music of humanity," and which Arnold was to re-name "the eternal note of sadness." This is the pattern of some of his greatest poems, "Tintern Abbey," the "Immortality" ode, the opening of *The Prelude*. Even in his "Elegiac Stanzas," written "in bereavement over the tragic death of the poet's dearly beloved brother," was he able to draw hope from suffering and to find soothing emotions by which he could "humanize" his soul. To the Victorians such a feat was definitely worth observing.

Arnold particularly admired this Wordsworthian power of transforming individual grief into a statement of universal affirmation. In his **"Memorial Verses, April 1850,"** he pays homage to his dead predecessor by ranking him above Goethe and Byron. The attitude Arnold takes toward the Laureate is very similar to that which, ninety years later, W. H. Auden was to take towards Yeats. The deceased poet stands for a definite period of history, a simpler world-view which his successor cannot revive. But Wordsworth also stands for something else:

> Ah! since dark days still bring to light
> Man's prudence and man's fiery might,
> Time may restore us in his course
> Goethe's sage mind and Byron's force;
> But where will Europe's latter hour
> Again find Wordsworth's healing power?
> Others will teach us how to dare,
> And against fear our breast to steel;
> Others will strengthen us to bear—
> But who, ah! who, will make us feel?

Others can strengthen us to bear by preaching a "prudent" Goethean renunciation; others can teach us to resist despair through sheer vitality. But Wordsworth's "healing power" is as unretrievable as the shining armor of the Sea of Faith. The question of the hour, therefore, is not only *"who* will make us feel?" but also the implicit *"what* will make us feel?" Arnold never doubts that the power to "make us feel" must be kept alive at all costs; but from where is this feeling to be drawn? Nature no longer offers a religion. The Victorian poet can no longer expect to harmonize the "still, sad music of humanity" into a universal chorus of faith. He must therefore do the second best thing. He must cling to the "eternal note of sadness" itself. He can share it with Wordsworth and lament his own inability to replace this sadness with new feelings of joy, "Wordsworth's healing power." Thus, paradoxically enough, the Victorian poet can engender feeling by bemoaning the loss of feeling. He can preserve Wordsworth's emotional core.

Arnold eventually realized that such a diminished conservation of Wordsworth was not a conservation after all. For, by reiterating an elegiac "note of sadness," Arnold had transgressed against his own rules for "the right Art" by omitting the quality of joy, the joy so deeply felt by Wordsworth but denied to Arnold in **"Resignation"** and **"Dover Beach."** Arnold renounced poetry and turned to the dissemination of Culture. But even in his new role, he remained faithful to his desire to blend Wordsworth's feeling with the intellectualism of his own age. In 1879, nine years before his death, Arnold offered a selection of Wordsworth's poetry to the Victorian reading public. His revision of entire lines and phrases was regarded by some as a sign of editorial irresponsibility. It suggests, however, the extent to which Arnold had taken upon himself the cultural responsibility of preserving Wordsworth as an emotional fount for his age, a task he had already set for himself, long before, in the creation of his own poems.

Notes

1. Among the more recent studies see D. G. James, *Matthew Arnold and the Decline of English Romanticism* (Oxford 1961), and William A. Jamison, *Arnold and the Romantics* (Copenhagen, 1958).

2. W. Stacy Johnson, *The Voices of Matthew Arnold: An Essay in Criticism* (New Haven, 1961), pp. 48, 47. See also Paull F. Baum, *Ten Studies in the Poetry of Matthew Arnold* (Durham, 1958), p. 25ff.: Lionel Trilling, *Matthew Arnold* (New York, 1955), pp. 75ff.; and E. D. H. Johnson, *The Alien Vision of Victorian Poetry* (Princeton, 1952), pp. 152-153.

3. In their otherwise excellent commentary on the poetry of Arnold, C. B. Tinker and H. F. Lowry, though dwelling extensively on the Goethean sources of "Resignation," strangely enough fail to point out that the poem is above all a rebuttal of Wordsworth, who, according to his youthful critic, "should have read more books, among them, no doubt those of the Goethe whom he disparaged without reading him." Only Professor Baum seems to have taken notice of the analogies between "Resignation" and "Tintern Abbey." But he dismisses them cursorily by remarking that the "'exhortations'" of the poets are after all "quite unlike" each other, thus underestimating the importance of this "unlikeness" for a reading of Arnold's poem (*Ten Studies* [*Ten Studies in the Poetry of Matthew Arnold*], pp. 25-26, fn. 3).

4. Arnold's choice of the gypsies as his prime example is extremely significant. His justification of the gypsies to the sister who dismisses them as being "less" than "man" is nothing less than a direct rebuttal of the position taken by Wordsworth in his 1807 poem, "Gipsies." In this little-known poem, Wordsworth regards the gypsies he has met during an excursion as sub-human, almost devilish creatures who are unaffected by the laws of man and Nature. Shunning their fellowmen during the day, totally oblivious of their natural surroundings, Wordsworth's gypsies raise "bolder" fires at night and thus defy the "mighty Moon" and the "very stars" that "reprove" them for their negligence as much as the poet himself. Arnold's gypsies likewise "crouch round the wild flame." But their purpose is simple: they merely want to stay warm in order to "rub through" life. For, unlike Wordsworth's gypsies, they *are* affected by time and change. Their indifference to Nature therefore is not, as with Wordsworth, a reprehensible act of defiance, but, quite to the contrary, represents an expression of their triumph over a natural world which has, in turn, become wholly indifferent towards them. Arnold's gypsies wait stoically "Till death arrive to supersede, / For them, vicissitude and need."

5. Cf. W. Stacy Johnson, pp. 47-51.

6. Quoted by Professor Douglas Bush in "Wordsworth and the Classics," *UTQ* [*University of Toronto Quarterly*], II (April, 1933), 359.

7. Lionel Trilling [*Matthew Arnold*], p. 19.

Selected Bibliography

Baum, Paul F. *Ten Studies in the Poetry of Matthew Arnold.* Durham, N. C.: Duke University Press, 1958.

Johnson, W. Stacy. *The Voices of Matthew Arnold: An Essay in Criticism.* New Haven: Yale University Press, 1961.

Tinker, C. B., and H. F. Lowry. *The Poetry of Matthew Arnold: A Commentary.* London: Oxford University Press, 1940.

Herbert R. Coursen Jr. (essay date autumn 1964)

SOURCE: Coursen, Herbert R., Jr. "'The Moon Lies Fair': The Poetry of Matthew Arnold." *Studies in English Literature, 1500-1900* 4, no. 4 (autumn 1964): 569-81.

[*In the following essay, Coursen studies Arnold's reinterpretation of Wordsworthian scenes, particularly those involving the moon. Coursen submits that Arnold's representation of nature reflects a desire for a "shining unity" between subject and world—a desire that, because of the constraints of the Victorian world, Arnold could not allow himself to believe in.*]

> Raised are the dripping oars,
> Silent the boat! The lake,
> Lovely and soft as a dream,
> Swims in the sheen of the moon.
> The mountains stand at its head
> Clear in the pure June-night,
> But the valleys are flooded with haze.
> Rydal and Fairfield are there;
> In the shadow Wordsworth lies dead.
> So it is, so it will be for aye.
> Nature is fresh as of old,
> Is lovely; a mortal lies dead.

From **"The Youth of Nature"**

Into a serene and moonlit world death has intruded. The death is not merely that of a mortal, not merely that of the poet with whom Arnold felt the most sympathy and kinship. When viewed in terms of Arnold's poetry, Wordsworth's passing becomes symbolic of the disappearance of a calm and majestic world-view which expressed "the joy offered to us in nature."[1] Arnold's poetry can be defined as an attempt to revisit the Wordsworthian scene and to find there the transcendent significance which revealed itself to Wordsworth. The imagery of **"The Youth of Nature"**—the moon, the lake, the mountains—is not accidental; it is Wordsworth's at the height of his power and inspiration—literally, at the top of Mount Snowden:

>   . . . as I looked up,
> The moon hung naked in a firmament
> Of azure without cloud, and at my feet
> Rested a silent sea of hoary mist.
> A hundred hills their dusky backs up-heaved
> All over this still ocean; and beyond,
> Far, far beyond, the solid vapours stretched,
> In headlands, tongues, and promontory shapes,
> Into the main Atlantic . . .
> That vision . . . appeared to me the type
> Of a majestic intellect, its act
> And its possessions, what it has and craves,
> What in itself it is, and would become.
> There I beheld the emblem of a mind
> That feeds upon infinity, that broods
> Over the dark abyss, intent to hear
> Its voices issuing forth to silent light
> In one continuous stream; a mind sustained

> By recognitions of transcendent power,
> In sense conducting to ideal form,
> In soul of more than mortal privilege.

(*The Prelude* XIV.39-47, 64-77)

The landscape in which the moon endows all objects below with beauty is the central setting of Arnold's poetry. He returns to it again and again as if in search of the Wordsworthian revelation. Instead, as we see in **"The Youth of Nature,"** he may encounter death, he may discover that the one who should be standing at the mountain top has sunk into the shadow of the valley, he may find a discrepancy between the natural scene and what occurs within it. What has been suggested of **"The Youth of Nature"** can be applied to much of Arnold's poetry: "Wordsworth's *Prelude,* published shortly before the composition of **'The Youth of Nature,'** may have initiated Arnold's reflections, with their Berkeleyan question as to whether nature lives in itself or in the eye of the beholder."[2] Arnold is unable to adopt the Wordsworthian compromise between perception and creation.[3] Instead, his skepticism prevents him from translating the nature he *wants* to see into convincing poetry; often, what his eye sees is refuted by what his mind knows.

Arnold's characteristic sequence involves an expression of surpassing beauty followed by a heavy qualification:

> So, in its lovely moonlight, lives the soul.
> Mountains surround it, and sweet virgin air;
> Cold plashing, past it, crystal waters roll;
> We visit it by moments, ah, too rare!

(**"Palladium"**[4])

The moonlit scene can be synonymous with man's communion with his soul. As **"Palladium"** implies, however, Arnold rarely captures such a moment; instead, aspiration often dwindles towards disillusionment. The central tension of Arnold's poetry, that between hope and despair, is a constant of his poetic career; from 1852 to 1867 there is little apparent development in his attitude or technique. There are, however, a variety of approaches towards the attainment of a vision which might see "on the face of outward things" the sign of "a majestic intellect." The attempt to recapture the significance of the Wordsworthian scene has three manifestations in Arnold's poetry: 1) the expression of man's disillusionment followed by an attempt at resolution, 2) the disillusionment of man defined in terms of lost love, and 3) the alienation of man from the joys of nature.[5]

The poems which attempt to reconcile man and his world are often unconvincing. In **"A Summer Night,"** a wanderer moves along "The deserted, moon-blanched street" beneath frowning windows. He watches the moon open up "a whole tract of heaven." He remembers "a past night, and a far different scene," where

"Headlands stood out into the moonlit deep / As clearly as at noon." But the memory is not one of those spots of time which illuminates the present with joy; it merely reenforces desolation:

> That night was far more fair—
> But the same restless pacings to and fro,
> And the same vainly throbbing heart was there. . . .

The poem goes on to define two possibilities for man, madness or slavery. The alternatives are to be avoided only if the frantic optimism of the last lines is valid:

> But I would rather say that you remain
> A world above man's head, to let him see
> How boundless might his soul's horizons be,
> How vast, yet of what clear transparency!
> How it were good to abide there, and breathe free;
> How fair a lot to fill
> Is left to each man still!

The ending is a significantly rhetorical prayer for the validity of the Wordsworthian vision.[6] Mere rhetoric, however, can impart no sense of the vision achieved; the hope of the closing lines lies crushed beneath the weight of the poem's pessimism.

"Self-Dependence" involves a similar experience. It opens in despair: "Weary of myself, and sick of asking / What I am and what I ought to be. . . ." The speaker moves out over the sea, crying to the stars and waters,

> Still, still let me, as I gaze upon you,
> Feel my soul becoming vast like you!

Although "with joy the stars perform their shining, / And the sea its long moon-silver'd roll," the poem closes with no sense of the "supremacy / That men, least sensitive, see, hear, perceive, / And cannot choose but feel" (*Prelude* XIV.84-86). Instead, we find rhetoric again:

> Resolve to be thyself; and know that he
> Who finds himself, loses his misery!

Such a ringing affirmation must be of uncertain comfort to one who began "sick of asking / What I am." The final lines illustrate Arnold's dilemma; aphorisms cannot hope to become "recognitions of transcendent power." Not wishing to surrender to pessimism but failing to achieve a vision of refulgent unity, Arnold must resort to rhetoric.

Another example of the poem which attempts resolution is that in which Arnold expresses fully the disillusioning potential of the moonlit scene and then attempts to create through imagery the *feeling* of nature's harmony. With the shift from rhetoric to imagery comes an increment in power. In **"A Southern Night,"** the speaker stands again in the position of Wordsworth:

> The sandy spits, the shore-locked lakes,
>   Melt into open, moonlit sea;
> The soft Mediterranean breaks
>   At my feet, free.

As in **"A Summer Night,"** he remembers a previous evening and its pain:

> Ah! such a night, so soft, so lone,
>   So moonlit, saw me once of yore
> Wander unquiet, and my own
>   Vexed heart deplore.

Now, however, "that trouble is forgot," but only because all other thoughts are crowded out by the death of the speaker's brother:

> Thy memory, thy pain, tonight
> My brother! and thine early lot,
>   Possess me quite.

The poem moves curiously on to discuss the inappropriateness of the grave-sites of the speaker's brother and sister-in-law. The "jaded English" of the "dusty life" should be buried in bustling cities:

> Not by those hoary Indian hills,
>   Not by this gracious Midland sea
> Whose floor to-night sweet moonshine fills,
>   Should our graves be.

Such graves should be inhabited only by figures of romance:

> Some girl, who here from castle-bower,
>   With furtive step and cheek of flame,
> 'Twixt myrtle-hedges all in flower
>   By moonlight came
> To meet her pirate-lover's ship. . . .

After this judgment, however, the speaker is checked by "the midnight breeze," which descends "to the brimmed, moon-charmed main." He thinks of his sister-in-law's "gentle tongue" and of his "high-souled" brother. Finally, he realizes that intrinsic virtues, not romantic trappings, are the important criteria. And so the poem closes harmoniously:

> And what but gentleness untired,
>   And what but noble feeling warm,
> Whatever shown, howe're inspired,
>   Is grace, is charm?
> What else is all these waters are
>   What else is steeped in lucid sheen,
> What else is bright, what else is fair,
>   What else serene?
> Mild o'er her grave, ye mountains, shine!
>   Gently by his, ye waters, glide!
> To that in you which is divine
>   They were allied.

While rhetoric remains, the rhetoric is more successfully blended with imagery than that of **"Self-Dependence."** The fusion of image and conviction helps the poem come closer to capturing the transcendent Wordsworthian mood. That the poem is not more successful is primarily the fault of its concern with the inappropriateness of the grave-sites, which is an ill-timed attack on the Philistines and a transparent contrivance for setting up the resolution of the ending.

"Sohrab and Rustum" offers a similar attempt at resolution. Within the poem we find the moon representing its dual possibilities, presiding over scenes of both love and grief. The effect on Rustum of Sohrab's arrival on the field is described in this Homeric simile:

> Like some young cypress, tall, and dark, and straight,
> Which in a queen's secluded garden throws
> Its slight dark shadow on the moonlit turf,
> By midnight, to a bubbling fountain's sound—
> So slender Sohrab seem'd, so softly rear'd.
> And a deep pity enter'd Rustum's soul
> As he beheld him coming. . . .
>
> (314-320)

When Rustum discovers that it is his son he has killed, the moon appears again:

> And his soul set to grief, as the vast tide
> Of the bright rocking Ocean sets to shore
> At the full moon. . . .
>
> (616-618)

Love has turned to destruction; the moon stands for both. The poem succeeds because it balances skillfully the poignancy of lost love against the warmth of love discovered. Ultimately, the suggestion of spiritual union between father and son outweighs the pain of their separation. The dominant sense of reconciliation justifies the symbolism of the ending:

> But the majestic river floated on,
> Out of the mist and hum of that low land,
> Into the frosty starlight, and there moved,
> Rejoicing, through the hush'd Chorasmian waste,
> Under the solitary moon;—he flowed
> Right for the polar star, past Orgunje,
> Brimming, and bright, and large; then sands begin
> To hem his watery march, and dam his streams,
> And split his currents; that for many a league
> The shorn and parcell'd Oxus strains along
> Through beds of sand and matted rushy isles—
> Oxus, forgetting the bright speed he had
> In his high mountain-cradle in Pamere,
> A foil'd circuitous wanderer—till at last
> The long'd-for dash of waves is heard, and wide
> His luminous home of waters opens, bright
> And tranquil, from whose floor the new-bathed stars
> Emerge, and shine upon the Aral Sea.

In this skillful recapitulation of the narrative, the symbolism suggests search and fulfillment, simultaneous reunion and loss. **"Sohrab and Rustum"** is perhaps Arnold's most successful effort to reinvoke the Wordsworthian emblem of a universal mind which feeds upon infinity.[7]

The poems in which the loss of love predominates embody the characteristic shift from a description of beauty to an expression of loss:

> —Mild shines the cold spring in the moon's clear
>   light:
> God! 'tis *her* face plays in the waters bright.
> "Fair love," she says, "canst thou forget so soon,
> At this soft hour, under this sweet moon?"
>
> **("Tristram and Iseult" 283-286)**

Again, fulfillment is impossible. Tristram's vision is a mocking dream within a nightmare:

> Ah, poor soul! if this be so,
> Only death can balm thy woe.
> The solitudes of the green wood
> Had no medicine for thy mood. . . .
>
> (288-291)

The poem contains, however, a magnificent moonlit scene:

> . . . far beyond the sparkling trees
> Of the castle-park one sees
> The bare heaths spreading, clear as day,
> Moor behind moor, far, far away,
> Into the heart of Brittany.
> And here and there, lock'd by the land,
> Long inlets of smooth glittering sea,
> And many a stretch of watery sand
> All shining in the white moon-beams. . . .
>
> (362-370)

Significantly, this vision would be available only to children and only at the expense of their even fairer dreams (371). The lines form a direct contrast with Tristram's nightmare within a nightmare; the children have dreams more beautiful even than the resplendent scene beyond their windows. This scene contrasts also with the death of love, the fulfillment of Tristram's nightmare:

> You see them clear—the moon shines bright.
> Slow, slow and softly, where she stood,
> She sinks upon the ground;—her hood
> Had fallen back; her arms outspread
> Still hold her lover's hand; her head
> Is bow'd, half-buried, on the bed . . .
> The air of the December-night
> Steals coldly around the chamber bright,
> Where these lifeless lovers be. . . .
>
> (ll. 101-106 and 148-150)

The scene is beautiful, but the moon emphasizes the coldness of death—as if shining down on marble.

As might be expected, the **"Switzerland"** poems, dealing as they do with unfulfilled love, glow with bitter moonlight. In each poem, the moonlight suggests hope and emphasizes subsequent despair. In Number Four, for example, the passion of Luna for Endymion becomes a metaphor for the impossibility of human love. In Number Three, the characteristic movement towards disillusionment suggests a discrepancy between man's aspirations and the limitations which the world imposes:

> How sweet, unreach'd by earthly jars,
> My sister! to maintain with thee
> The hush among the shining stars,
> The calm upon the moonlit sea!
> How sweet to feel, on the boon air,
> All our unquiet pulses cease!
> To feel that nothing can impair
> The gentleness, the thirst for peace—
> The gentleness too rudely hurl'd
> On this wild earth of hate and fear;
> The thirst for peace a raving world
> Would never let us satiate here.

In Number Five, the shift towards despair suggests the sense of profound loss shared by parted lovers in a world this side of Eden:[8]

> But when the moon their hollows lights
> And they are swept by balms of spring,
> And in their glens, on starry nights,
> The nightingales divinely sing;
> And lovely notes, from shore to shore
> Across the sounds and channels pour—
> Oh! then a longing like despair
> Is to their farthest caverns sent;
> For surely once, they feel, we were
> Parts of a single continent!

While moonlight here is subsidiary to the flowing song of the nightingales, it adds a visual unity to the scene and helps to deepen the disillusionment of an imagination rebuffed by the realities of alienation and loss.[9]

The poetry of lost love suggests the ultimate implications of Arnold's theme of disillusionment—man's exclusion from the joys of nature, and, inevitably, the refutation of the Wordsworthian vision. The Scholar Gipsy may

> On some mild pastoral slope
> Emerge, and resting on the moonlit pales
> Freshen thy flowers as in former years
> With dew, or listen with enchanted ears,
> From the dark dingles, to the nightingales.
>
> (216-220)

Man, however, infected with modern life's "strange disease" (203) would only contaminate Eden's freshness:

> But fly our paths, our feverish contact fly!
> For strong the infection of our mental strife,
> Which though it gives no bliss, yet spoils for rest;
> And we should win thee from thy own fair life,
> Like us distracted, and like us unblest.
>
> (221-225)

The situation is that of Luna and Endymion again; mortal man and immortal beauty are incompatible. Nature and man have become alien entities.

The contrast between man and nature is perhaps best illustrated by Empedocles, who enunciates a philosophy of stoic moderation ("Because thou must not dream, thou need'st not then despair," I.426). The irony enforced by Act II, however, is that man cannot stop dreaming, cannot choke his response to beauty. The doctrine which avoids disillusionment ignores beauty—and beauty will not be ignored. Empedocles is trapped between the philosophy which tells him to expect nothing and the beauty which implores him to desire everything. When the world reasserts a beauty for which his philosophy cannot account, Empedocles can view the world only as the hieroglyphic of his deadness:

> . . . the sea of cloud,
> That heaves its white and billowy vapours up
> To moat this isle of ashes from the world,
> Lives; and that other fainter sea, far down,
> O'er whose lit floor a road of moonbeams leads
> To Etna's Liparean sister-fires
> And the long dusky line of Italy—
> That mild and luminous floor of waters lives,
> With held-in joy swelling its heart; I only,
> Whose spring of hope is dried, whose spirit has fail'd
> I, who have not, like these, in solitude
> Maintain'd courage and force, and in myself
> Nursed an immortal vigour—I alone
> Am dead to life and joy, therefore I read
> In all things my own deadness.
>
> (ll. 308-322)

Here on one of the most explicit evocations of the Wordsworthian scene and one of the most emphatic refutations of its significance. **"Empedocles"** [**"Empedocles on Etna"**] is a projection of Arnold's own dilemma—his desire to emulate "Wordsworth's sweet calm"[10] stunted by the "depression and ennui"[11] of his times. Disposing of Empedocles in the crater of Etna did not resolve the dilemma.

That Arnold was not satisfied with the resolution of "Empedocles" is suggested by his exclusion of it from the 1853 edition because it provided no catharsis, only pain. Much of Arnold's best poetry, however, is based on an equally bleak view of man's status in the world. That he could not resolve his dilemma is indicated by **"Dover Beach,"** written some fifteen years after **"Empedocles on Etna."** The years between the poems constitute the span of Arnold's career as a mature poet. The landscape which spreads below the speaker in **"Dover Beach"** is that which Empedocles saw from Etna, that on which Wordsworth gazed from Mount Snowden:

> The sea is calm to-night
> The tide is full, the moon lies fair
> Upon the straits;—on the French coast the light

Gleams and is gone; the cliffs of England stand,
Glimmering and vast, out in the tranquil bay.

But where Wordsworth found in the "roar of waters" a mighty affirmation of the unity implied by the shining scene below him, this man hears in the sound of grating pebbles a note of sadness which denies the transcendent possibilities suggested by the light which gleams down on Dover Beach:

. . . the world, which seems
To lie before us like a land of dreams,
So various, so beautiful, so new,
Hath really neither joy, nor love, nor light,
Nor certitude, nor peace, nor help for pain. . . .

While the poem offers a fragile stay against anarchic darkness ("Ah, love, let us be true . . ."), the desperate hope has been refuted convincingly by many Arnold poems. In **"Dover Beach"** the fact that the moon lies fair only sharpens the recognition that the moon lies.[12]

Arnold's significance as a poet grows from his inability to become a Victorian echo of Wordsworth. He was too honest to surrender to his desire for a shining unity in which he didn't believe. He was too close to the world and its problems to evoke a world which didn't exist.[13] His greatness as a poet lies in the tension between the fierce yearning for the perfection suggested by a resplendent landscape and the tough-minded recognition of the refutation beneath all fair appearances. In that he can be placed "between two traditions," Arnold might be called the representative Victorian poet; he is Romantic in his use of the symbolic landscape, Modern in his finding there only negation. His poetry is an answer to the question he puts to Philomela:

And can this fragrant lawn
With its cool trees, and night,
And the sweet, tranquil Thames,
And moonshine, and the dew,
To thy rack'd heart and brain
Afford no balm?

In Arnold's poetry, as in **"Philomela,"** the moon is the great illusionist, begetting "Eternal passion!" which must be followed inevitably by "Eternal pain!"

Notes

1. Arnold, speaking of Wordsworth in the introduction to Arnold's 1879 selection of Wordsworth.

2. C. B. Tinker and H. F. Lowry, *The Poetry of Matthew Arnold* (London, 1940), p. 188.

3. Cf. ". . . creator and receiver both, / Working but in alliance with the works / Which it beholds." *Prelude* II.258-260. Also II.368 ff., XII.275 ff., XIII.367 ff., XIV.86 ff., etc.

4. As "Palladium" implies, one of Arnold's most frequent images is that of the virtually inaccessible mountain. He employs it from "Continued" (1849) to "Rugby Chapel" (1867). The relevance of the imagery is suggested by these lines from "Thyrsis":

And long the way appears, which seem'd so short
To the less practised eye of sanguine youth;
And high the mountain-tops where is the throne of Truth,
Tops in life's morning-sun so bright and bare!

5. These categories are somewhat arbitrary. They are necessary, however, to demonstrate the various ways in which Arnold expressed a problem which was at once aesthetic and spiritual. Without a system of classification, we would be in danger of being blinded like Tristram (II.71) by the moonlight which floods down on the Arnoldian scene.

6. An explicit prayer for calmness appears at the end of the Wordsworthian "Kensington Gardens."

7. The celebrated "Thyrsis" is, I believe, a far less successful effort. Its artificiality is at least partially the result of Arnold's imposition on his material of the conventions of the pastoral elegy.

8. As if in explicit denial of the unified scene which Wordsworth viewed from Mount Snowden, the central metaphor of Number Five is the island separated from contact with all others. The poem reverberates also, of course, against Donne's famous island-continent passage.

9. In "The Forsaken Merman" (an 1849 poem which could not have been influenced by *The Prelude,* published in 1850) moonlight sharpens the poem's expression of the Merman's loss of love. The poem does not imply, however, the interaction between scene and emotion characteristic of the later poems.

10. "Stanzas: In Memory of the Author of 'Obermann,'" l.79. In "Memorial Verses: April, 1850" Arnold writes of Wordsworth's poetry as if it constituted a return to Eden:

Our youth return'd; for there was shed
On spirits that had long been dead
Spirits dried up and closely furl'd,
The freshness of the early world.

(54-57)

11. The phrase is often employed out of context. In "On the Modern Element in Literature," Arnold is questioning the adequacy of Lucretius's modernity. His conclusion is that Lucretius is "over-strained, gloom-weighted, morbid; and he who is morbid is no adequate interpreter of his age." On these grounds, Arnold eliminated "Empedocles" from the 1853 Edition. He could not, however, eliminate the weight of gloom from subsequent

poetry. It is instructive to note that while Arnold could advocate the exercise of "sweetness and light," he could do so only in prose. In "Empedocles," the lovely songs of Callicles have only a painful effect on Empedocles. Arnold's poetry is pessimistic, his prose inclines towards optimism. Hence—his abandonment of poetry for prose.

12. That there is little development in Arnold's view of the world is suggested again by comparing "Dover Beach" with this section of "Empedocles":

> The world, a rolling flood
> Of newness and delight,
> Draws in the enamour'd gazer to its shining breast . . .
>
> (I.354-356)

13. It is significant that one of the more successful poems which ends with suggestions of Wordsworthian unity, "Sohrab and Rustum," is placed remotely in time, place, and, of course, in style.

William A. Madden (essay date 1967)

SOURCE: Madden, William A. "The Main Movement of Mind." In *Matthew Arnold: A Study of the Aesthetic Temperament in Victorian England,* pp. 49-118. Bloomington: Indiana University Press, 1967.

[*In the following excerpt, Madden examines Arnold's "poems of nostalgia," positing that the main sources of Arnold's nostalgic tendency can be found in his childhood, nature, and history.*]

POEMS OF NOSTALGIA

In what one critic has called the myth of "loss, endurance, and recovery" which governs Arnold's poetry as a whole,[1] the poems of nostalgia represent the initial desolating phase of loss and dislocation during which the dominant emotional impulse is retrospective. As the name implies, the poems of nostalgia give voice to a poetry of memory; looking back to a time of prelapsarian innocence and order, they are haunted by the pathos of innocence and order lost. Arnold's poems in this genre differ from earlier poems dealing with this traditional theme mainly in the intensity and the peculiar quality of their pathos; as a result of the earliness, suddenness, and finality of the loss, they strike a desperate, almost hopeless note. The loss of naiveté which separates the present from the past has entailed intellectual dislocation and a consequent loss of a capacity to focus—in Carlyle's word, to "vent"—emotions on appropriate objects, actions, or values. Arnold's nostalgia arises in his reaction to, and recoil from, the dilemma posed by the discovery that without order the feelings tend to become random and objectless, while without feeling any attainable order becomes mechanical and

stultifying. Indeed, it may be doubted that Arnold experienced for very long a world in which joy and order were harmonized, a world of intellectual naiveté and emotional spontaneity, since even in the earliest poems the persona speaks not of the possession, but of the memory of such a world.[2]

The imagery by which Arnold renders his nostalgia is drawn from three main sources: from memories of his own childhood, from nature, and from the historical past. These vehicles, with their corresponding cluster of subordinate images—though Arnold's repertoire of imagery is not a large one—evoke an imaginative world in which the speaker finds temporary refuge from the confusions and fevers of the present. The persona either judges the present by alluding to a happier past, near or remote, or focuses upon a present world of natural beauty from which he feels himself alienated. Thus the nostalgia is rendered in both temporal and spatial terms. On the one hand, there is the poetic landscape, most frequently the "mild pastoral slope" of **"The Scholar-Gipsy,"** which is an unpopulated terrain that stands opposite the speaker, reminding him of a spontaneous life of unselfconscious integrity which he himself lacks. On the other hand, there is an imaginative evocation of the historical past, which extends the childhood motif into history and enables the speaker to generalize his sense of loss and alienation in an aimless, hectic present which includes the whole of modern society.

An early prize poem, *Cromwell,* is of interest mainly for the way in which it employs the theme of childhood, in Wordsworthian fashion, as the formative period in a childhood-youth-manhood pattern of personal development.[3] Approximately 130 lines, a little less than half of the poem, are given over to the youthful Cromwell, whose childhood dreams are described as not being "idle" since the "man / Still toils to perfect what the child began" (ll. 45-46). After the "first sorrow, which is childhood's grave" (l. 82) has awakened the ambiguous passions of Youth, still—in a variation of the Wordsworthian concept of the child as father to the man—

> . . . Memory's glance the while
> Fell on the cherish'd past with tearful smile;
> And peaceful joys and gentler thoughts swept by,
> Like summer lightnings o'er a darken'd sky.
> The peace of childhood, and the thoughts that roam,
> Like loving shadows, round that childhood's home.
>
> [ll. 69-74]

Peace, joy, gentleness, and innocence, all attach themselves to the memory of childhood, in opposition to the "unrestful lot" (l. 86), the "follies" (l. 79), the "strife" (l. 102) of youthful passions and ambitions. Significantly, however, the mature hero's sense of "the calm, sweet peace—the rest of home" (l. 113) is, in fact, deeper "than childhood ever knew" (l. 116),

Green happy places—like a flowery lea
Between the barren mountains and the stormy sea,

[ll. 117-118]

a country of the mind, therefore, in which the "fleeting thoughts" of the once "heedless child" (ll. 51-52) ripen, after childhood has departed:

With common cares unmingling, and apart,
Haunting the shrouded chambers of his heart.

[ll. 57-58]

Thus the dreams of childhood preserved in the heart long after childhood has been left behind take on a significance which they could not have had during childhood itself; the landscape of childhood is the adult speaker's symbolic projection of the "green happy places" which haunt his heart.

In this early poem Arnold has difficulty reconciling a personally appealing theme with his assigned subject, an ambitious and successful man of the world. Except for the obviously derivative Wordsworthian echoes and occasional near-bathos ("tearful smile"), the long passages on childhood in the first part have an authority of felt experience that is notably lacking in the latter half of the poem, which is devoted to Cromwell's final years and death.

Within the pattern established by **Cromwell,** with its emphasis upon the decisive importance of childhood in forming the man, the treatment of childhood in **"Stanzas in Memory of the Author of 'Obermann'"** illuminates in a particularly useful way Arnold's own childhood experience and the impact of that experience upon his personal development. The poem derives directly from the encounter with that sorrow that is childhood's grave, mentioned in **Cromwell,** but the Obermann stanzas lead to a quite different kind of maturity from that which Arnold imagined for the Puritan hero. Comparing his lot with the lives of three poets of the previous generation who had "attain'd . . . to see their way" (ll. 47-48)—Goethe, Wordsworth, and Sénancour—the speaker in this poem identifies himself with the last, on the grounds that Sénancour's clear head, chilled feeling, and icy despair represent the *maladie* peculiar to a generation which, unlike Wordsworth, cannot avert its eyes "from half of human fate" and, unlike Goethe, was born too late to find a clear course through the mists and storms of a post-Revolutionary age. The speaker attributes this inability to attain either "Wordsworth's sweet calm" or "Goethe's wide / And luminous view" to the special circumstances of his generation's childhood:

But we, brought forth and rear'd in hours
Of change, alarm, surprise—
What shelter to grow ripe is ours?
What leisure to grow wise?

Like children bathing on the shore,
Buried a wave beneath,
The second wave succeeds, before
We have had time to breathe.

[ll. 69-76]

The absence of a leisure in which to "ripen" accounts for the stifled atmosphere, the sense of feeble struggle against overwhelming odds, which characterizes the Arnoldian nostalgia in its more desperate moments. Like Empedocles in a later poem, the persona of the Obermann stanzas cries for air, but he can only pledge himself to preserve the spiritual childhood of those Children of the Second Birth (l. 144) who, like Sénancour (and unlike Cromwell, whose childhood dreams bear ambiguous fruit in mature action), have kept themselves unspotted from the world.

The fruits of worldly success had been contemplated in another early prize-poem, **Alaric at Rome,** in which the actions of maturity are associated, as in **Cromwell,** with childhood dreams. Alaric gazes down from a hill overlooking Rome, reflecting upon the great victory he has just won:

Perchance his wandering heart was far away,
Lost in dim memories of his early home,
And his young dreams of conquest.

[ll. 169-171]

Similarly, Rustum, at the close of his battle with the young Sohrab, "remember'd his own early youth, / And all its bounding rapture" (ll. 619-620), recalling with particular joy his early life with his parents:

. . . all the pleasant life they led,
They three, in that long-distant summer-time—
The castle, and the dewy woods, and hunt
And hound, and morn on those delightful hills
In Ader-baijan.

["Sohrab and Rustum," ll. 627-631]

In a late poem Arnold envisions Heine, too, though engaged in a different kind of warfare, as longing, in the midst of the brilliance of "hot Paris drawing rooms," to remove his spirit

out of the din,
Back to the tranquil, the cool
Far German home of his youth!

["Heine's Grave," ll. 149-151]

There is this difference, however, between the childhood of an Alaric or Rustum or Cromwell (significantly, two of these men of action are the subjects of early poems and Rustum, a later creation, is disillusioned with action) and that of modern spirits like Heine and Arnold himself: the former saw their childhood dreams bear fruit in active lives of heroic scope; the latter look back to childhood as a "sheltered time" uncorrupted by and superior to the feverish, unsatisfactory life of maturity. Arnold consistently employs childhood to evoke an air of innocence, joy, and peace by way of defining the strife, unhappiness, and unrest of an abortive and aimless maturity. Even in the two early poems, the "dreams of wide dominion" attributed to the heroes of the past are haunted by a "Whispering from all around, 'All earthly things must die.'" (**Alaric at Rome,** ll. 175-180)

The theme of childhood is seldom far removed in Arnold's poetry from a feeling for nature which is reminiscent of Wordsworth, although as a reflection of his own sensibility Arnold's treatment may best be described as post-Wordsworthian.[4] The memory of the Wordsworthian harmony of man and nature remained one of Arnold's touchstones of joy and wholeness all his life, but it was a memory, a sense of wholeness irrecoverably lost rather than preserved and transmuted in the exalted philosophic mood of Wordsworth's mature Philosopher. The natural landscape which objectifies Arnold's feeling is therefore correspondingly different. In **"Memorial Verses"** the conjunction of childhood, an instinctive harmony with nature, and a spontaneous happiness serves as the poem's central theme. The speaker feels that the "titanic" force of a Byron and the wisdom of a Goethe may again find worthy spokesmen, but where, he asks, "will Europe's latter hour / Again find Wordsworth's healing power?"

> He too upon a wintry clime
> Had fallen—on this iron time
> Of doubts, disputes, distractions, fears.
> He found us when the age had bound
> Our souls in its benumbing round;
> He spoke, and loosed our hearts in tears.
> He laid us as we lay at birth
> On the cool flowery lap of earth,
> Smiles broke from us and we had ease;
> The hills were round us, and the breeze
> Went o'er the sun-lit fields again;
> Our foreheads felt the wind and rain.
> Our youth return'd; for there was shed
> On spirits that had long been dead,
> Spirits dried up and closely furl'd,
> The freshness of the early world.
>
> [ll. 42-57]

Arnold composed **"Memorial Verses"** as a formal "dirge," and the point of view of the poem, which gives an account of Wordsworth's liberation of English consciousness from the debilitating grip of skepticism, doubt, and social and political unrest, is deliberately historical. The poem is successful, however, because Arnold's own sensibility is in control. The "early world" suggested by the phrase "cool flowery lap" reflects a landscape symbolic of a consciousness premodern in its spontaneity, premoral in its cool unawareness of passion, and presocial in its sheltered seclusion. Here, as

elsewhere in Arnold's poetry, a quiet contemplativeness is suggested by the use of flowers to create a world of frail, innocent, and transient beauty characteristic of childhood itself. It is because this state of "naive" consciousness, of spontaneous simplicity, is consistently portrayed as something to be recovered, something apart and past which can be only temporarily revived by the experience of Wordsworth's poetry and wistfully desired by a generation that has lost the "freshness of the early world," that Arnold's poetic use of nature may be described as post-Wordsworthian. In **"The Buried Life"** Arnold's conversion of Wordsworth's poetic idiom to his own purposes is even more evident:

> But often, in the world's most crowded streets,
> But often, in the din of strife,
> There rises

—not, as for Wordsworth, the transfixing memory of lovely natural objects and sounds, but rather—

> an unspeakable desire
> After the knowledge of our buried life;
> A thirst to spend our fire and restless force
> In tracking out our true, original course.
>
> [ll. 45-50]

Wordsworth's confident, tranquil recollection and renewal of his early experience is replaced by a debilitating doubt and introspection.

The difference in sensibility which separates the two poets as observers of nature is equally apparent in **"Lines Written in Kensington Gardens," "The Youth of Nature,"** and **"The Youth of Man."** The first of these poems arises from an occasion very similar to that which inspired Wordsworth's "Tintern Abbey," and it evolves by exploiting the same dialectic between the peace and loveliness of nature and the "hum" and "jar" of the crowded city. But the ground-note of **"Lines Written in Kensington Gardens"** is plaintive rather than joyful, the voice is that of one earnestly seeking, rather than confidently possessing, spiritual union with the Soul of all things. Upon returning to the scenes of his youth after the feverish excitement of the French Revolution, Wordsworth had explored an undiminished love of "beauteous forms," the memory of which had consoled him during his five-year absence:

> These beauteous forms,
> Through a long absence, have not been to me
> As is a landscape to a blind man's eye:
> But oft in lonely rooms, and 'mid the din
> Of towns and cities, I have owed to them
> In hours of weariness, sensations sweet,
> Felt in the blood and felt along the heart.[5]

The spell of natural forms is as powerful as ever; the joy of their presence remains as fresh as upon the first encounter. Arnold, on the other hand, portrays a speaker

almost apologetic in his yearning to escape the "gir-
dling city's hum," and secondly, someone who is conscious, as Wordsworth seldom is, of other lives, other
responses, other modes of existence.

> In the huge world, which roars hard by,
> Be others happy if they can!
> But in my helpless cradle I
> Was breathed on by the rural Pan.
>
> [ll. 21-24]

The feeling for nature is correspondingly tentative; nature's serenity is not in harmony with the speaker's inner existence but is the measure of what he lacks.

> I, on men's impious uproar hurl'd,
> Think often, as I hear them rave,
> That peace has left the upper world
> And now keeps only in the grave.
> Yet here is peace forever new!
>
> [ll. 25-29]

The discrepancy between the speaker's troubled introspective consciousness and the peace of nature is evident.

> The will to neither strive nor cry,
> The power to feel with others give!
> Calm, calm me more! nor let me die
> Before I have begun to live.
>
> [ll. 41-44]

While the prayer to the "calm soul of all things" with
which the poem concludes recalls Wordsworth's faith in
nature's power to beneficently shape the moral conduct
of man—"His little, nameless, unremembered acts / Of
kindness and of love"—the note of desperation in the
prayer in Arnold's poem, especially in the phrase "helpless cradle," is utterly un-Wordsworthian. A devouring
self-consciousness has distanced nature; Arnold's description of the landscape merely contributes to the
overall impression of alienation.

"The Youth of Nature" opens with yet another elegiac
tribute to Wordsworth, uttered this time against the
background of the Lake Country:

> The gleam of The Evening Star
> Twinkles on Grasmere no more,
> But ruin'd and solemn and grey
> The sheepfold of Michael survives;
> And, far to the south, the heath
> Still blows in the Quantock coombs,
> By the favourite waters of Ruth.
>
> [ll. 18-24]

As in **"Memorial Verses,"** the passing of the Romantic
age and especially of the Wordsworthian sensibility is
recorded:

> He grew old in an age he condemn'd.
> He look'd on the rushing decay
> Of the times which had shelter'd his youth:
> Felt the dissolving throes
> Of a social order he loved;
> Outlived his brethren, his peers,
> And, like the Theban seer,
> Died in his enemies' day.
>
> [ll. 28-35]

The central theme of **"The Youth of Nature"** calls to
mind Wordsworth's famous remarks regarding the likeness of "emotion recollected in tranquility" to real emotion, but a characteristically Arnoldian pathos appears
in the emphasis placed upon the inadequacy of poetry
for expressing the deepest feelings:

> Cold the elation of joy
> In his gladdest, airiest song,
> To that which of old in his youth
> Fill'd him and made him divine.
>
> [ll. 95-98]

Recollected emotion is no longer what it had been for
Wordsworth, "an emotion, kindred to that which was
before the subject of contemplation," but rather a pale
memento of an experience which the poet is unable to
recapture.[6] Nature Herself speaks to the point:

> Weak is the tremor of pain
> That thrills in his mournfullest chord
> To that which once ran through his soul.
>
> [ll. 92-94]

The controlling emotion of **"The Youth of Nature"** is
not simply nostalgia for the Wordsworthian world, but
the oppressive experience of man's transiency set
against the calm, inscrutable, perennial beauty of the
natural world. The effect is close to the Virgilian *lacri-
mae rerum*.

The pantheistic note faintly struck in **"The Youth of
Nature"**—the poet's song is seen as a reflex of those
cosmic forces of life at work in "the unlit gulph" of the
poet—is more explicit in the companion piece, **"The
Youth of Man."** Here, too, the contrast with Wordsworth is notable. As in **"Lines Written in Kensington
Gardens,"** the speaker prays for the restoration of joy
and beauty rather than rejoicing in a Presence whose
light is the light of setting suns.

> Murmur of living,
> Stir of existence,
> Soul of the world!
> Make, oh, make yourselves felt
> To the dying spirit of youth!
>
> [ll. 51-55]

The aging couple's memory of the past as interpreted
by the narrator is dominated by the recollection of a
childhood spent in the sheltered seclusion of a rural retreat.

> . . . the castled house, with its woods,
> Which shelter'd their childhood—the sun
> On its ivied windows; a scent
> From the grey-wall'd gardens, a breath
> Of the fragrant stock and the pink,
> Perfumes the evening air.
> Their children play on the lawns.
> They stand and listen; they hear
> The children's shouts, and at times,
> Faintly, the bark of a dog
> From a distant farm in the hills.
> Nothing besides!
>
> [ll. 64-75]

The bitter-sweet pain of the occasion is elevated, in the conclusion, to the level of a universal nostalgia which includes the speaker:

> Well I know what they feel!
> They gaze, and the evening wind
> Plays on their faces; they gaze—
> Airs from the Eden of youth
> Awake and stir in their soul;
> The past returns—they feel
> What they are, alas! what they were.
>
> [ll. 88-94]

In **"The Future"** the memory of the freshness of an early world and of oneness with nature, associated with Wordsworth in the poems just discussed, is related more generally to a "primitive" age of man, to the "childhood" of the race:

> Who can see the green earth any more
> As she was by the sources of Time?
> Who imagines her fields as they lay
> In the sunshine, unworn by the plough?
> Who thinks as they thought,
> The tribes who then roam'd on her breast,
> Her vigorous, primitive sons?
>
> [ll. 27-33]

Closer to the "snowy mountainous pass" which cradles "the new-born clear-flowing stream" (ll. 9-12), primitive man—the poem here refers specifically to the biblical characters Rebekah and Moses (ll. 36, 45)—could better guard the inner "spring of feeling," could more easily attain the vision "Of God, of the world, of the soul" which flashed on Moses "when he lay in the night by his flock" (ll. 39-46). Wordsworth's achievement, in Arnold's view, lay in his ability to restore through his poetry the fresh and vital spontaneity and therefore the joy of this early world which the moderns had lost. **"The Future"** attempts to sound a note of hope, but like Arnold's other poems, it is most effective in recording the consequences of the disappearance of this early world.

Arnold's projection of the values associated with childhood into an historical past may be seen in three other, quite different, poems, two of them among his major achievements. **"Bacchanalia: or, The New Age"** transposes the contrast between the individual's memory of a sheltered childhood and his sense of the inadequacy of the present—as treated, for example, in **"The Youth of Man"**—into a contrast between Wordsworth's generation and his own. The structure of the poem is organized around an analogy between the quiet nature of Rural Pan (Arnold's own natal deity, Dr. Arnold notwithstanding) and the world of the Past, on the one hand, and between the violent nature of Bacchus and the world of the Present on the other hand. The imaginative landscape of Rural Pan reflects the innocent, premoral, spontaneous existence of quiet contemplation.

> The business of the day is done,
> The last belated gleaner gone.
> And from the thyme upon the height,
> And from the elder-blossom white
> And pale dog-roses in the hedge,
> And from the mint-plant in the sedge,
> In puffs of balm the night-air blows
> The perfume which the day forgoes.
> And on the pure horizon far,
> See, pulsing with the first-born star,
> The liquid sky above the hill!
> The evening comes, the fields are still.
>
> [I, 8-19]

Suddenly, "the wild Maenads" break into the calm "Youth and Iacchus / Maddening their blood":

> Loitering and leaping,
> With saunter, with bounds—
> Flickering and circling
>
>   * * *
>
> Loose o'er their shoulders white
> Showering their hair.
>
> [I, 20-22, 26-27]

Part Two of the poem pursues the analogous contrast between the speaker's memory of the previous generation, with its "now silent warfare" out of which have risen "one of two immortal lights" (II, 20-24)

>   up into the sky
> To shine there everlastingly,
> Like stars over the bounding hill.
> The epoch ends, the world is still
>
> [II, 25-28]

and the turmoil of the present upon which the "stars" gaze down in detachment:

> Thundering and bursting
> In torrents, in waves—
> Carolling and shouting
> Over tombs, amid graves—
> See, on the cumber'd plain
> Clearing a stage,

Scattering the past about,
Comes the new age.

[II, 29-36]

The poem expresses a preference for the past not simply because it was better but primarily because it is past, fixed and orderly in its stillness and unable, like the disorder and action of the Bacchanalian present, to stir and distract the soul.

By combining and organizing these various images of nostalgia in an appropriate myth, Arnold produced in **"The Scholar-Gipsy"** a poem in which innocence, pastoral contemplativeness, and the simple hope of a golden past amplify one another in an imaginative world of perpetual childhood, against which is set "the sick fatigue, the languid doubt" of the present. Inspired by a reading of Glanvil's *The Vanity of Dogmatizing* (and by Keats's stanzaic form) and even more by Arnold's memory of his own Oxford days, the poem succeeds in creating a symbolic figure adequate to the burden of an immense nostalgia.[7] The centrality of the nostalgic impulse is reflected both in the poem's basis in Glanvil and seventeenth-century Oxford, to which Arnold's prefatory note to the poem calls attention, and also in the reference in the opening stanza to "the quest" which the poem itself is about to enact. Moved by the story of the "Oxford scholar poor" who, endowed with "pregnant parts and quick inventive brain," had "tired of knocking at preferment's door" and had abandoned his studies for life among the gipsies (ll. 31-40), the poet-narrator's own inventive brain begins to reconstruct the Gipsy Scholar's new life and in the process creates a figure, landscape, and action that embody the values from which the narrator feels himself being cut off and for which he yearns.

The distinctive mark of the poem's hero is his success in preserving a childlike innocence, the freshness of an early world. He is, above all, a "truant boy" (l. 218).

For early didst thou leave the world, with powers
  Fresh, undiverted to the world without,
    Firm to their mark, not spent on other things;
Free from the sick fatigue, the languid doubt,
Which much to have tried, in much been baffled,
  brings,
O life unlike to ours!

[ll. 161-166]

The inborn powers and the preserved innocence are traced to the Scholar-Gipsy's fortunate birth,

O born in days when wits were fresh and clear,
  And life ran gaily as the sparkling Thames;
    Before this strange disease of modern life,
  With its sick hurry, its divided aims,
    Its heads o'ertax'd, its palsied hearts, was rife

[ll. 201-205]

and to the protagonist's cultivation of his true self in a free, spontaneous, contemplative contact with nature:

Trailing in the cool stream thy fingers wet,
  As the slow punt swings round:
And leaning backward in a pensive dream,
  And fostering in thy lap a heap of flowers

[ll. 75-78]

  Oft thou hast given them store
Of flowers—the frail-leaf'd, white anemony,
Dark bluebells drench'd with dews of summer eves,
And purple orchises with spotted leaves—.

[ll. 86-89]

The Scholar-Gipsy thus inhabits the typical pastoral-childhood landscape of nostalgia in the Arnoldian myth, "watching, all an April day, / The springing pastures and the feeding kine" (ll. 107-108), while the narrator of the poem identifies himself with those who from a distance watch the protagonist "when the stars come out and shine, / Through the long dewy grass move slow away" (ll. 109-110).

In addition to the pleasures of nature enjoyed in studied leisure, the Scholar-Gipsy's existence possesses for the narrator another element, the vital spiritual dimension of hope. "Rapt, twirling in [his] hand a wither'd spray, / And waiting for the spark from heaven to fall" (ll. 119-120), he is set apart not only from his more active seventeenth-century contemporaries but, especially, from the narrator and modern men generally, "Who wait like thee, but not, like thee, in hope" (l. 170). An explicitly religious note appears in the contrast between the Scholar-Gipsy and modern "Vague half-believers of our casual creeds, / Who never deeply felt, nor clearly will'd" (ll. 172-173), among whom the narrator numbers himself. In a passage which reflects Arnold's own inner tensions and his sense of defeat, the speaker in the poem warns the Scholar-Gipsy that he must "fly our paths, our feverish contact fly," lest he too grow distracted "And then thy glad perennial youth would fade / . . . and die like ours" (ll. 222-230). In the concluding tableau, which portrays a "grave Tyrian trader" fleeing the competitive, bustling world of the "merry" and "light-hearted" Greeks and escaping to the simpler life of the "shy traffickers" (ll. 232-250) on the Iberian peninsula, the poem presents an archetype, from an even remoter age, of the uncorrupted, ancient, primeval life of self-dependence, innocence, and hope represented in the poem as a whole by the Scholar-Gipsy himself.[8]

The situations of the Scholar-Gipsy and of the narrator of the poem are thus parallel but distinct. The Scholar-Gipsy flees the life of conventional study and social conformity to a more primitive life among the gipsies in order to await the "spark" that will provide him with insight into the life of men and, according to the poem, give him the power which that insight has to loose the tongue (ll. 45-50). Correspondingly, the narrator escapes to the earlier age—earlier both historically and psychologically—of the Scholar-Gipsy in order to contemplate a way of life free from those "repeated shocks" of the modern world that "Exhaust the energy of strongest souls / And numb the elastic powers" (ll. 144-146). Although it is unnecessary and would be dangerous to press too closely the significance of the "spark from Heaven," it clearly is meant to include a spiritual insight into life as well as artistic skill in utterance. It is significant, on both counts, that although he nurses his "*one* aim, *one* business, *one* desire" (l. 152) with "unclouded joy" (l. 199), the Scholar-Gipsy does not in fact encounter the "spark" without which his life must remain a perpetual quest; he is left, rather, to continue his wanderings "pensive and tongue-tied" (l. 54). Thus there is implicit in **"The Scholar-Gipsy"** a dual sense of longing and frustration. One feels both in the Scholar-Gipsy and in the poet-narrator a frustrated desire to penetrate the ultimate and unattainable meaning of life and to discover the means of expressing it. Unlike his protagonist, however, the speaker has abandoned hope, classing himself with those who "waive all claim to bliss, and try to bear" life in a "close-lipp'd patience" that is "near neighbour to despair" (ll. 191-196). Though muted by the hopeful expectancy, the unclouded joy, of the "truant boy" who occupies the foreground of the poem, the narrator's nostalgia, centering in the loss of that expectancy and joy, extends to a desire for the peace of death: "we others pine, / And wish the long unhappy dream would end" (ll. 191-192). It is the ultimate nostalgia, a longing to return to unconsciousness.

Glanvil's anecdote and the figure of the Scholar-Gipsy provided a spark which loosed Arnold's tongue, enabling him to create a world in which he contemplates, in a language intelligible to his generation, his own and their dilemma. Like the Scholar-Gipsy, Arnold had haunted the Oxford countryside in a lonely quest for the "heaven-sent" skill of the poet—the power to "bind" the minds of other men by skill in language and a special insight into the "workings of men's brains" (l. 46). But for Arnold, as for the Scholar-Gipsy, the spark does not descend, or at least the spark that did descend was not of the kind which the Scholar-Gipsy seems to anticipate. For Arnold the modern poet's intuition and skill bear precisely on the paradoxical discovery that the spark does not fall: that the modern Scholar-Gipsy waits in vain. The current of modern life has so altered, faith has become so attenuated, that as a poet, Arnold can only record the discrepancy between the charm of the early hope and the ennui of the later despair, measuring the one by the other. The persona of the poem identifies himself both with the Scholar-Gipsy and with modern man: he has experienced both the hope of the one and the lassitude of the other. And like the Tyrian trader, he carries his memory of the better world with

him to a new country, there undoing the corded bales of his vision for the benefit of those sensitive and innocent enough to recognize the worth of the content. But as Arnold discovered, the Philistine public of Victorian England was not very interested in the goods of the modern counterpart of the earnest Tyrian who confronted "the shy traffickers" on the Iberian peninsula.

Although **"The Scholar-Gipsy"** is greater—because it is more coherent—than **"Stanzas from the Grande Chartreuse,"** the latter holds the greatest biographical interest of all of Arnold's poems of nostalgia. This poem not only includes the themes of **"The Scholar-Gipsy"** but goes beyond them by bringing into the foreground the predicament of the narrator of the earlier poem as he directly confronts the ultimate spiritual origins of the "sick fatigue" and "languid doubts" of the modern world. The difference between the two poems is most evident in the submersion of the pastoral landscape which occupies such a large place in **"The Scholar-Gipsy"** and dominates the other poems of nostalgia. The consolations of "rural Pan" have been unable to compensate for the poet's deepest loss, at the hands of "rigorous teachers," of his youthful "faith" and "fire." In **"Stanzas from the Grande Chartreuse"** the peculiar Arnoldian feeling for the "mild pastoral slope"—for moonlight, the "pale blue convolvulus," the "warm green-muffled Cumner hills," the "long dewy grass,"— appears very briefly and then only incidentally. Amidst the starkness of the mountain landscape and the general oppressiveness of the monastery, the speaker notices a

> garden, overgrown yet mild,
> See, fragrant herbs are flowering there!
> Strong children of the Alpine wild
> Whose culture is the brethren's care;
> Of human tasks their only one,
> And cheerful works beneath the sun.

[ll. 55-60]

As "children of the Alpine wild," the garden flowers suggest the theme of childhood explored elsewhere in the poem, but the "pastoral" associations with which this theme properly belongs are overlaid and all but obliterated by the speaker's deep religious melancholy. The disappearance of the pastoral landscape, frequently associated in Arnold's poems with the name of Wordsworth, suggests the connection in Arnold's experience between his feeling for nature and his religious history. Both Wordsworth and Christianity had been powerful elements in his formative experience; with his disavowal of the latter as he had been taught it in his youth, the former became, at best, only partially relevant. During Arnold's undergraduate years the most influential English representative of the precarious alliance of Romanticism and Christianity had been John Henry Newman, but already as an undergraduate Arnold had found Newman's solution impossible; he was already composing poetry in which his post-Wordsworthian sensibility was evident. He was never entirely to escape the memory of either Wordsworth or Newman, and **"Stanzas from the Grande Chartreuse"** indicates the deep and important connection between Romanticism and Christianity in Arnold's experience, but it also represents a turning point in Arnold's career, portraying the dire consequences entailed if he should continue to indulge his nostalgia and refuse to confront the world of the present in which he found himself.

The imagery and the action with which the poem opens—as the band of pilgrims ascends

> Through Alpine meadows soft-suffused
> With rain, where thick the crocus blows,
> Past the dark forges long disused,
>
> * * *
>
> Through forest up the mountain-side
>
> [ll. 1-3, 6]

marks the psychological shift from the benign and gentle pastoral world of **"The Scholar-Gipsy"** to a more severe mountain country which is described in images almost Dantesque:

> The autumnal evening darkens round,
>
> * * *
>
> While hark! far down, with strangled sound
> Doth the Dead Guier's stream complain,
> Where that wet smoke, among the woods,
> Over his boiling cauldron broods
>
> [ll. 7, 9-12]

The "spectral vapours white" which soon appear amid the "limestone scars" and "ragged pines" (ll. 13-14), as the pilgrims continue to mount "the stony forest-way" (l. 20), prepare the reader for the "cowl'd forms" that "brush by in gleaming white" (l. 36) in the monastery now in view. Once inside the monastery gate, in the realm of "death in life" (l. 54), the speaker begins his reflections on the central question of the poem, "what am I, that I am here?" (l. 66). The speaker's faith, we learn, has been "prun'd" and his "fire" "quench'd" by stern "masters of the mind" who have shown him "the high white star of Truth" (ll. 67-75).[9] The truth he was urged to seek evidently involves, as a condition for its pursuit, the relinquishing of early hopes and desires which the speaker has found it difficult to abandon, although he can no longer entertain them seriously. The emotional impulse of the poem derives from the speaker's consciousness of having "so much unlearnt, so much resign'd" (l. 75). What he experiences is not the excitement of aspiration but a feeling of loss and desolation, and this feeling controls the imagery and argument alike. While the speaker recognizes his predica-

ment as a personal matter to be solved by himself as best he can, he asks his teachers to recognize that for one with his background to have undergone enlightenment at their hands was bound to be painful. His presence among the monks is not, he argues, a result of emotional capitulation to superstition, but of his failure to find in the austere vision of "Truth" the warmth and fire which will satisfy his ineradicable longings.

The dilemma posed in the juxtaposing of an inescapable but joyless truth and a joyful but "exploded" illusion (l. 98) is evident in the various sets of antithetical images which objectify the tensions in the poem: childhood and maturity, past and present, solitude and society, desire and reason, hope and despair. In this case childhood operates, both literally and symbolically, in opposition to the aridity of maturity which serves as the point of departure for the speaker's reflections. It functions literally—and historically—in the speaker's identification of himself with those "whose bent was taken long ago" (l. 198):

> We are like children rear'd in shade
> Beneath some old-world abbey wall
> Forgotten in a forest-glade,
> And secret from the eyes of all.
>
> [ll. 169-172]

Symbolically childhood embodies a nucleus of values—peace, solitude, innocence, naiveté, happiness—which the "foreign air" of the modern world has destroyed. Moreover, as projected into the past, "childhood" includes the historical world of "our fathers" and beyond them of the "old-world abbey," the Gothic "pointed roofs," and the world of medieval faith generally—the "childhood" of the modern world—symbolized by the Grande Chartreuse. Thus the personal disenchantment of the speaker takes on a larger dimension as representative of a cultural revolution that has overtaken Europe, and beyond this of a cosmic alienation which Arnold refers to when in another poem he speaks of "something that infects the world" (**"Resignation,"** l. 278).

The speaker's account of Carthusian life, however, reveals a new complexity in the persona's feelings toward his childhood and the historical past. On the one hand, the attraction of the cloistered life, the fundamental sympathy which binds those Christians who believe with those Romantics who grieve in joint opposition to the modern world, is conveyed in references to the "shade," the "secluded dells," the "forest-glade," the yellow tapers which shine as "emblems of hope," and the sound of organ music at the end; all these represent one side of the speaker's feeling for the place and for the religious and poetic memories of his youth. On the other hand, and much more impressively, the cloistered life is rendered in images of death—"ghostlike," darkness, coffins, blood, the white forms that "brush by," "white uplifted faces," silence, and quite specifically "death in life." The force of the latter imagery is heightened, moreover, by contrast with a third cluster of images of life in the world: the "passing troops in the sun's beam— / Pennon, and plume, and flashing lance!" whose active life leads men "to life, to cities, and to war" and to the social life of pleasure of the "gay dames" in "sylvan green," whose laughter and cries make the "blood dance" as the "bugle-music on the breeze / arrests with a charm'd surprise" (ll. 188-190). Judged both from the intellectual point of view of his masters and by the instinctive desires of youthful worldly ambitions, the speaker's return to the cloister is a longing for death. Moreover, by juxtaposing the wan and feeble light of the tapers to the flash and color of life outside the cloister, Arnold presents a structure of feeling of greater complexity than the simple opposition of head and heart, present and past, childhood and maturity which characterizes most of the poems of nostalgia. The speaker in the Grande Chartreuse stanzas is caught between three rather than two worlds: the memory of childhood and the past, with their religious "emblems of hope"; a youthful life of pleasure and action in the world; and the lonely, austere ideal of the "high white star of Truth." A paralysis of indecision lies at the center of the poem; the narrator is no longer able to entertain the fruitless dream of Romantic aspiration—"What helps it now that Byron bore," "What boots it Shelley"—which he associates with the past, nor to enter the world and undertake a life of action, nor yet to follow the painful dialogue of the mind with itself which is the way to Truth.

The poem's emotional impulse is therefore not primarily nostalgia for religious faith or romantic inspiration—choice here has in any case been taken out of his hands by his "rigorous teachers"—but a longing for freedom from the intolerable pressure of inner tensions; and since this cannot be secured through choice, the speaker turns instinctively to the peace to be found in death.

> . . . if you cannot give us ease—
> Last of the race of them who grieve
> Here leave us to die out with these
> Last of the people who believe!
>
> [ll. 109-112]

Like the ancient Greek who on some northern strand, "thinking of his own [dead] Gods,"

> In pity and mournful awe might stand
> Before some fallen Runic stone
>
> [ll. 82-83]

the modern man of intellect, standing in the Grande Chartreuse, has no gods of his own to think upon as he contemplates the passing both of Romanticism and of Christianity; he has only the distant, cold star of "Truth." A residual, hopeless desire for *something* has led the narrator to the "living tomb" of the cloister, not in renewed faith but in the vague expectation that in this "desert" of the past he will find the peace that comes with the death of desire.[10]

In rendering the *ne plus ultra* of Arnold's nostalgia, **"Stanzas from the Grande Chartreuse"** leads naturally to a consideration of the poems of dialogue, for once the consolations of the memory of early joys, the peace of nature, or the charm of a lost past were seen as intellectually dishonest as well as harmful to activity, the only alternative was to confront the modern self-consciousness created by the dialogue of the mind with itself. The emotional aridity and general depression which attended this decision is suggested by Arnold's poetic handling of the subtle attractions of death in the **"Stanzas from the Grande Chartreuse."** In an early poem, **"The New Sirens,"** he indicates that he had for a time given, or tried to give, himself to the Romantic muse (ll. 226-232), but with disillusioning results: the emotional and intellectual fluctuations which this pursuit entailed had produced only exhaustion (ll. 195-202). The speaker at one point calls for a return of the sirens (ll. 171-176), but he is already aware that the "slow tide" had set "one way" (l. 220), and he asks to be set free.

> The eye wanders, faith is failing—
> O, loose hands, and let it be!
> Proudly, like a king bewailing,
> O, let fall one tear, and set us free!
>
> [ll. 223-226]

Having made his choice, Arnold resolved to work within the limits imposed by the modern consciousness—the abandonment of the illusions of Christianity and Romanticism. Thus, although the poems mentioned thus far have been classified as poems of nostalgia, there is "movement" within the type; as the past, real or imagined, seems less and less recoverable, the persona comes more and more to confront the fact of a blank and joyless present. **"Stanzas from the Grande Chartreuse,"** in particular, records the moment of transition between the two phases in which the speaker returns, one last time, to a past that is acknowledged to be dead. Even before the memory of the past spent itself in the creative effort of the Grande Chartreuse stanzas Arnold had begun searching for a new "idea," a new ground for joy, a new religion. The beginnings and results of the search are evident in the dialogue poems, some of which were composed and published side by side with the poems of nostalgia in his first volume of poetry.

Notes

1. [A. Dwight] Culler, *Poetry and Criticism of Matthew Arnold*, [Boston, 1961], p. x.

2. The voice of the personae in Arnold's poetry is consistently that of experience looking back on innocence or on disillusioning events, a perspective which Arnold may have got, in part, from Wordsworth, whose poems frequently embody the voice of maturity reflecting on life as already lived. Arnold's tone, however, is that of the young man preternaturally weary rather than that of the sage.

3. Possible religious and political implications have been associated with the selection of Cromwell as the subject of the Newdigate competition for 1842-43. See Tinker and Lowry, *Commentary* [*The Poetry of Matthew Arnold: A Commentary,* (London, 1940)], pp. 323-324, and Kathleen Tillotson, "Matthew Arnold and Carlyle," *Proceedings of the British Academy* XLII (1956), 139.

4. [Lionel] Trilling [*Matthew Arnold* (New York, 1955)], [Louis] Bonnerot [*Matthew Arnold, poète: Essaide biographic Psychologique* (Paris, 1947)], and D. G. James [*Matthew Arnold and the Decline of English Romanticism* (Oxford: 1961)] discuss Arnold's relationship to Wordsworth in the works cited earlier. For recent specialized studies see Leon Gottfried, *Matthew Arnold and the Romantics* (London, 1963), Ch. II, for Arnold's debt to Wordsworth in the areas of morality, politics, and religion; U. C. Knoepflmacher, "Dover Revisited: The Wordsworthian Matrix in the Poetry of Matthew Arnold," *Victorian Poetry,* I (1963), 17-26, on their relationship as poets; and William A. Jamison, *Arnold and the Romantics* (Copenhagen, 1958), pp. 50-53, for Arnold's edition of Wordsworth's poetry.

5. *Poetical Works* [*The Poetical Works of William Wordsworth* ed. Ernest de Selincourt, vol. I-V, 1940-49. Second edition (of Vols. I-III) ed. Helen Darbishire, 1952-54 (Oxford: Clarendon, 1950-54)], II, 260.

6. The following appears among Arnold's notations of possible subjects for poetic treatment: "Thun & vividness of sight & memory compared: sight would be less precious if memory could equally realize for us" (*Commentary,* p. 12).

7. J. P. Curgenven's "'The Scholar-Gipsy': A Study of the Growth, Meaning, and Integration of a Poem," *Litera,* II (1955), 41-58; III (1956), 1-53, seems to me the best reading of the poem.

8. G. Wilson Knight emphasizes the Oriental element in "'The Scholar-Gipsy': An Interpretation," *Review of English Studies,* n. s., VI (1955), 53-62.

9. The impact of the lesson learned from the "teachers" is slightly meliorated in Arnold's later revision of l. 67: "And purged its faith and trimm'd its fire."

10. The concluding line of the original version of the poem, published in *Fraser's* in 1855, reads "forest" instead of "desert." The change reflects, I believe, Arnold's movement of mind in the late fifties: as a "forest" the abbey is a wooded and secluded retreat; as a "desert" it is uninhabitable. If the authors of the *Commentary* are correct in their assumption (pp. 11-12) that the poem represents Arnold's final handling of a topic which he had first proposed to himself in 1849 under the rubric "To Meta—the cloister & life liveable," there seems to have been some ambiguity in Arnold's attitude towards the topic from the beginning. The authors of the *Commentary* read the poem as one of "a series of poems on the various restraints imposed upon the human spirit by the religious sentiment, by the sentiment of love, and by the cloistered or regular life" (p. 338). Were these restraints good or not? Is the phrase "the cloister & life liveable" an equation or a contrast? The former interpretation seems applicable to the verses in the Yale Manuscript to which Tinker and Lowry give the title "To Meta: the Cloister" (*Commentary,* pp. 339-340) as well as to the original version of "Stanzas from the Grande Chartreuse"—at least, decision has been suspended. With the substitution of "desert," an image of death holds the final and decisive place: the cloister has become unliveable.

Geoffrey Tillotson (essay date 1968)

SOURCE: Tillotson, Geoffrey. "Matthew Arnold's Prose: Theory and Practice." In *Matthew Arnold,* edited by Harold Bloom, pp. 37-61. New York: Chelsea House Publishers, 1987.

[*In the following essay, originally published in* The Art of Victorian Prose *in 1968, Tillotson examines Arnold's intense focus on the composition of prose and the usage of words. Citing examples of Arnold's affection for unusual word order, repetition, and striking phrasing, Tillotson probes the effects of these idiosyncrasies on the aesthetic responses of Arnold's readers and postulates that the techniques attest to a desire to unify language and thought.*]

The relation of mind and written words is a topic of long standing, and Arnold's contribution to it must serve as my excuse for making one of my own. In the process I shall draw on Arnold only here and there, reserving my fuller consideration of his theory and practice till the second half of my essay.

Our response to a piece of literature is both intellectual and aesthetic. What is intellectual in it applies itself to the content—to the matter, the way it is being thought about, the conclusions being drawn from it, the purpose it is being made to serve. If we are the best sort of reader, ready to give the author a fair hearing, the intellect starts by being passive, adjusted to watch and acquire. That state, however, cannot last long, because even the fair reader is a critic, and criticism is mental action. We become combative, for we ourselves might have written the piece—we possess a store of matter more or less similar to that being presented to us; we can think for ourselves; we have our own purposes to serve. And so we make a judgment, our judgment being the culmination of a process: as Arnold noted more than once, judgment forms insensibly as reading proceeds.

All this is in the keeping of the intellect. But already our intellectual response has extended to the aesthetic. For everything in the writer's mind exists coloured by his own individuality, the reader's experience of which colouring is an aesthetic experience. This colouring the intellect either approves or disapproves—Pater approved of the "fine atmosphere of mind" he found in Wordsworth's poetry, and George Eliot disapproved of the atmosphere she found in Pater's *Renaissance* as quite "poisonous." The intellectual and the aesthetic also act together because some part of our aesthetic response is prompted by some part of the matter that is engaging our intellect in the first place, and almost all the matter if the piece is mainly descriptive. To matter that has prompted an aesthetic response when encountered in the course of practical living we respond aesthetically all over again at the sight of the words that recall that practical experience—it seems as if we possess an outfit of shadow senses for the purpose. To take a sentence from Sir Thomas Browne as an instance—an instance brief enough to preclude any noticeable response to his strong personality: "But the iniquity of oblivion blindly scattereth her poppy, and deals with the memory of men without distinction to merit of perpetuity." Our aesthetic response to the matter of this is to a composite picture of the scattering of a liquid opiate and the generalised "idea" of a poppy. Moreover, as that same instance shows strikingly, some part of our total aesthetic response to literature is to its words as words.

When we are discussing prose apart from its content we are discussing our aesthetic response *in toto* and what prompts it. Later on I shall have something to say about our aesthetic response (joined with a response on the part of the intellect) to the colouring supplied by Arnold's personality, but neither that sort of response nor the aesthetic response to the sensuous part of the matter invites any discussion. More tricky, however, is the response we make to the words as words.

I have been using the term "literature" so far, but critics have usually restricted the operation of the aesthetic awareness of words as words to the reader of part of literature only—to literature in verse and to literature as

certain sorts of prose. Coleridge so restricted it, specifying "oratory" as a sort of prose that could be ranged with literature in verse. Perhaps others besides myself look back on his remarks as on an era in our education—they illuminated what we had long been fumbling with in twilight. Here is not the place to consider them in detail. All I shall say now is that on maturer thought they throw their light on the whole of literature rather than on a part of it. For the only deep division, as I see it, falls between two sorts of reader—the "literary" readers and the rest—rather than between two sorts of writing. By "literary" readers I mean the readers for whom an author worth the name writes in the first place.

Every literary reader is aware of words on almost all occasions when words are read, and on many when words are spoken. Sometimes he is aware of them as words even when their meaning sharply affects him as a practical person. We have evidence for this in one of Wordsworth's greatest poems, his "Elegiac Verses in Memory of My Brother." In the course of the poem he recalls the arrival of the news, conveyed presumably by letter, of John's death by drowning:

> All vanished in a single word,
> A breath, a sound, and scarcely heard.
> Sea—ship—drowned—shipwreck—so it came,
> The meek, the brave, the good, was gone;
> He who had been our living John
> Was nothing but a name.

Perhaps on occasions like these we gaze at words as a temporary refuge from the things they denote, and perhaps non-literary people gaze in that way as well as literary. However that may be, literary readers make an aesthetic response to words so nearly constant that it is strange to find Coleridge mistaking a difference between degrees of obviousness for a difference of kind. He instanced the prose of Southey as prose composed of words that themselves go unnoticed: "In the very best styles, as Southey's, you read page after page, understanding the author perfectly, without once taking notice of the medium of communication." Surely a literary critic is always aware of words as words. All that varies as he turns from one piece of literature to another is the nature of the particular wording, the qualities of his own response to it, and, later on, his own powers as a worder of that response. To call on the handiest evidence: If I myself read so humble a piece of prose as one conveying instructions, I look at its wording as closely as (I hope) I look at its instructiveness. On an early page in my pocket diary I read the following: "FAINTING. If a person faints, lay him flat on the floor or on a couch. Keep the head low and apply smelling salts or sal volatile on some cotton wool under the patient's nose. Give him a glass of cold water on recovering consciousness." When I read that, I see that I should have preferred to read: "Keep his head low and apply smelling salts or sal volatile on some cotton wool to his nostrils. Give him a glass of cold water when he recovers consciousness." (I retain the order *salts . . . wool* because for practical reasons the sooner salts are mentioned the better. There are several acceptable variants of the last clause including "when he comes round.") If that instruction had been worded so as not to offend my aesthetic sense, I suspect I should have taken in its instructions more deeply (as in any event I should if I were reading it in order to deal with an actual case of fainting on the carpet before me). Even practical instructions are approached in one way by the non-literary reader, and by the literary reader in another. Certainly, I approach Southey's prose with awareness of its words as words, and so must conclude that Coleridge's account of his own experience was mistaken.

To continue these preliminary remarks, let me try to show how thought exists apart from certain aspects of the wording. The end of writing is to produce the intended effect on the mind of the reader by means of the words used. A writer capable of achieving a thought worth expression—that is, a thought of interest to a reader—has achieved a certain amount of its wording along with it. Thought either comes into being along with words—some of them, if not all—or it very soon achieves them. Some part of the final wording, however, cannot but concern the reader's aesthetic sense. For instance, if the thought is made up of a house and Jack, and their interrelation as builder and thing built, the wording could run in various ways:

> The house that Jack built
> The house which Jack built
> The house Jack built
> The house builded by Jack
> The house erected by Jack
> The house Jack erected

and so on, drawing on "domicile" and even "property," and perhaps using the verb "edify" in a rare sense, or the obsolete "edificate." We could not say that the thought had appreciably changed at any point throughout these changes of its expression. But for the purposes of aesthetic response, changes like these are important.

We can see this by examining the corrections in authors' manuscripts, or as edition follows edition. We know, for instance, that Tennyson changed the order of verb and adverb in the line

> Freedom broadens slowly down

so as to avoid the collision of sound represented by the two *s*'s. Or to take an instance from Arnold: the ending of his essay on Marcus Aurelius gave him trouble. Some of the revision represented in the printed texts—the evidence of which is set out in Professor Super's edition

of the prose works—is consequent on an improved clearness of thought. The rest of it was made in the interests of expression. For instance, the text Professor Super has chosen as his copy-text is that of the 1883 edition of *Essays in Criticism,* which received Arnold's last revisions. One of its sentences reads: "And so he remains the especial friend and comforter of all clear-headed and scrupulous, yet pure-hearted and upward striving men, in those ages most especially that walk by sight, not by faith, but yet have no open vision." Both the description of the men and the ages caused Arnold trouble, but I am concerned only with the revisions in the description of the ages. In the *Victoria Magazine,* where the essay was first printed, the last phrase of that description reads: "by faith, that have no open vision." This wording was retained when the essay was included in *Essays in Criticism* (1865), but in the second edition four years later, it became: "by faith, and yet have no open vision." In the new edition of 1880 we find: "by faith, but have, nevertheless, no open vision." A change from "and" to "but" denotes a change in the thinking, but a change from "yet" to "nevertheless" denotes a change in the expression.

Because of this concern with words as words, the critic of prose wording could just as soon be a critic of the wording of poetry. The best qualification for criticising the one is a capacity to criticise the other. The things in the wording of poetry that call for criticism are more striking than those in the wording of prose—more highly coloured, more chimingly musical, more closely packed. They are also more easily recognised and familiar, for there has been much more criticism of the wording of poetry than of prose. But to be a critic of either, one must unite the humble powers that schoolchildren exercise when they triumphantly discover alliteration and the rarer powers of being aware of the whole of the aesthetic response to wording, a whole that exists almost palpably as an object. The critic has to be as much aware of his aesthetic response to wording as Arnold was of his to the shape of a Greek tragedy—in the 1853 Preface to his *Poems* he described it in terms of a group of statuary slowly approached along an avenue until the point comes when it is possessed wholly:

> The terrible old mythic story on which the drama was founded stood, before he entered the theatre, traced in its bare outlines upon the spectator's mind; it stood in his memory, as a group of statuary, faintly seen, at the end of a long and dark vista: then came the Poet, embodying outlines, developing situations, not a word wasted, not a sentiment capriciously thrown in: stroke upon stroke, the drama proceeded: the light deepened upon the group; more and more it revealed itself to the rivetted gaze of the spectator: until at last, when the final words were spoken, it stood before him in broad sunlight, a model of immortal beauty.

Readers differ in the degree to which they make and are aware of this sort of aesthetic response, but some of them make so strong a response and are so much aware of it that they may give it more attention than they are giving to what is being said. For them the wording of Southey's prose, which like Coleridge they will place with the "very best," achieves an elegance that exists as an object before the mental eye, as the walking gait of a racehorse exists before the eyes of the body. Some readers who happen to be what are called atheists can get much pleasure out of reading Newman, even on those occasions when, to their way of thinking, he is talking nonsense. From these instances it follows that in writing of wording as a thing prompting an aesthetic response we have a firm topic.

Before looking at Arnold's practice, there are one or two further distinctions to draw. The critic of the aesthetic response to wording is not concerned with the accuracy of the words as expression. That accuracy is in the keeping of the thought. I have said that when we achieve a thought, it comes to us in some or all of the words suitable for its expression. If the thought is clear, the words will be mainly the right ones. If not, the process of improvement will usually be a process of clarifying the thought. Like many other critics, Arnold did not see this distinction. Look at his characterisation of good prose as having "regularity, uniformity, precision, balance." In that characterisation, which we shall look into more fully later on, the third term is misused. "Precision" applies to all prose as prose is wording and only to certain prose as prose is thinking. When the wording of prose is unsatisfactory, that wording still has precision. It produces a precise aesthetic impression, but a precise impression of vagueness. To exchange it for a precise impression of light, the writer would have to clear up his thought or the mental picture he is wording. Arnold's asking precision from wording is asking for what no wording can fail to provide, however difficult we should find the describing of it. What he meant to ask for was precision of thought or mental picturing.

On another occasion he fails to make a similar distinction. He is recommending an academy on the grounds that it would reduce what he called "provinciality," and is advancing the idea that "not even great powers of mind will keep [a writer's] taste and style perfectly sound and sure, if he is left too much to himself, with no 'sovereign organ of opinions,' in these matters, near him." Here "taste" is ranged alongside "style," but the instances he gives show that it is not the wording he is objecting to but the matter it is expressing, matter that exists just so because of an alleged deficiency in taste. Take his remarks on Ruskin, for instance. He begins by quoting an "exquisite" passage that shows "Mr. Ruskin exercising his genius":

> Go out, in the spring-time, among the meadows that slope from the shores of the Swiss lakes to the roots of their lower mountains. There, mingled with the taller gentians and the white narcissus, the grass grows deep and free; and as you follow the winding mountain paths, beneath arching boughs all veiled and dim with blossom,—paths that for ever droop and rise over the green banks and mounds sweeping down in scented undulation, step to the blue water, studded here and there with new-mown heaps, filling all the air with fainter sweetness,—look up towards the higher hills, where the waves of everlasting green roll silently into their long inlets among the shadows of the pines.

"Exquisite" as the passage is, Arnold—we may note in passing—raises an objection, an objection he brings forward apologetically:

> All the critic could possibly suggest, in the way of objection, would be, perhaps, that Mr. Ruskin is there trying to make prose do more than it can perfectly do; that what he is there attempting he will never, except in poetry, be able to accomplish to his own entire satisfaction: but he accomplishes so much that the critic may well hesitate to suggest even this.

Surely this is an objection raised by a theorist, one who, to use Johnson's terms, judges by "precept" rather than "perception."

In the past, it is true, the sort of matter Ruskin expressed here had usually gone into metre. Nevertheless it would not be too much to say that Ruskin had left off writing verse simply because the matter he now wished to express—matter that included his mature perception of rocks and stones and trees—could not go into metre without being falsified. Arnold should have seen that the meaning Ruskin had achieved demanded expression in prose. To demand verse of him was like asking Bach to put the matter of a recitative into an aria. Both recitative and aria are beautiful, but the one expresses matter which, being narrative, needs to be kept moving along a line, whereas the other expresses matter which, being meditative, needs to be kept circling. The beauty of the recitative is comparatively informal, and that of the aria formal.

If we look again at the passage Arnold quotes, and especially at its striking last phrase, we see pointedly that the touch of a more regular rhythm would have killed it. Arnold, as I say, must have forgotten. That he well knew about matter choosing its form is clear from his own practice. Some of his verse is formal and some comparatively informal, while some of his prose is informal and some comparatively formal. An instance of formal prose is the invocation to Oxford in the Preface to **Essays in Criticism.** According to the precept he turns on Ruskin, that invocation ought not to have been expressed in prose at all. Prose, however, was demanded by its matter, its thought and feeling combined. Even the comparatively informal verse of **"Dover Beach"** would have denied it its rightful rhythm.

It is what Arnold goes on to say, however, that contributes most to our discussion—when he turns to a passage that he has no good word for, a passage in which Ruskin considers the naming of some of the characters in Shakespeare's plays:

> Of Shakespeare's names I will afterwards speak at more length; they are curiously—often barbarously—mixed out of various traditions and languages. Three of the clearest in meaning have been already noticed. Desdemona—"δυσδαιμονία," *miserable fortune*—is also plain enough. Othello is, I believe, "the careful"; all the calamity of the tragedy arising from the single flaw and error in his magnificently collected strength. Ophelia, "serviceableness," the true, lost wife of Hamlet, is marked as having a Greek name by that of her brother, Laertes; and its signification is once exquisitely alluded to in that brother's last word of her, where her gentle preciousness is opposed to the uselessness of the churlish clergy:—"A *ministering* angel shall my sister be, when thou liest howling." Hamlet is, I believe, connected in some way with "homely," the entire event of the tragedy turning on betrayal of home duty. Hermione (ἕρμα), "pillar-like" (ἣ εἶδος ἔχε χρυσέης Ἀφροδίτης); Titania (τιτήνη), "the queen;" Benedick and Beatrice, "blessed and blessing"; Valentine and Proteus, "enduring or strong" (*valens*), and "changeful." Iago and Iachimo have evidently the same root— probably the Spanish Iago, Jacob, "the supplanter."

Arnold comments:

> Now, really, what a piece of extravagance all that is! I will not say that the meaning of Shakespeare's names (I put aside the question as to the correctness of Mr. Ruskin's etymologies) has no effect at all, may be entirely lost sight of; but to give it that degree of prominence is to throw the reins to one's whim, to forget all moderation and proportion, to lose the balance of one's mind altogether. It is to show in one's criticism, to the highest excess, the note of provinciality.

Here it is not the wording he is objecting to, but the matter, and the intellect responsible for it. He is not speaking of prose, but of its content.

Arnold's remark about what is proper matter for prose witnesses to a limitation in his view of the function of prose. He would limit it to the expression of thinking, or, if to more than thinking, then only to the simplest narrative and description—he advised Hardy to narrate in the style Swift had used for *Gulliver's Travels,* overlooking the difference in the degree of complexity between their respective matter. Arnold thought of good prose as being one sort of prose only.

That is how Clough had thought of it in his lecture on Dryden, an excerpt of which had appeared in *Poems and Prose Remains* of 1869. Clough there had written:

> Our language before the Restoration certainly was for the most part bookish, academical, and stiff. You perceive that our writers have first learnt to compose in Latin; and you feel as if they were now doing so in English. Their composition is not an harmonious development of spoken words, but a copy of written words. We are set to study ornate and learned periods; but we are not charmed by finding our ordinary everyday speech rounded into grace and smoothed into polish, chastened to simplicity and brevity without losing its expressiveness, and raised into dignity and force without ceasing to be familiar; saying once for all what we in our rambling talk try over and over in vain to say; and saying it simply and fully, exactly and perfectly.

> This scholastic and constrained manner of men who had read more than they talked, and had (of necessity) read more Latin than English; of men who passed from the study to the pulpit, and from the pulpit back to the study—this elevated and elaborated diction of learned and religious men was doomed at the Restoration. Its learning was pedantry, and its elevation pretence. It was no way suited to the wants of the court, nor the wishes of the people. It was not likely that the courtiers would impede the free motions of their limbs with the folds of the cumbrous theological vesture; and the nation in general was rather weary of being preached to. The royalist party, crowding back from French banishment, brought their French tastes and distastes. James I loved Latin and even Greek, but Charles II liked French better even than English. In one of Dryden's plays is a famous scene, in which he ridicules the fashionable jargon of the day, which seems to have been a sort of slipshod English, continually helped out with the newest French phrases.

> Dryden then has the merit of converting this corruption and dissolution of our old language into a new birth and renovation. And not only must we thank him for making the best of the inevitable circumstances and tendencies of the time, but also praise him absolutely for definitely improving our language. It is true that he sacrificed a great deal of the old beauty of English writing, but that sacrifice was inevitable; he retained all that it was practicable to save, and he added at the same time all the new excellence of which the time was capable.

> You may call it, if you please, a democratic movement in the language. It was easier henceforth both to write and read. To understand written English, it was not necessary first to understand Latin: and yet written English was little less instructive than it had been, or if it was less elevating, it was on the other hand more refining.

> For the first time, you may say, people found themselves reading words easy at once and graceful; fluent, yet dignified; familiar, yet full of meaning. To have organised the dissolving and separating elements of our tongue into a new and living instrument, perfectly adapted to the requirements and more than meeting the desires and aspirations of the age, this is our author's praise. But it is not fully expressed until you add that this same instrument was found, with no very material modification, sufficient for the wants and purposes of the English people for more than a century. The new diction conquered, which the old one had never done, Scotland and Ireland, and called out American England into articulation. Hume and Robertson learnt it; Allan Ramsay and Burns studied it; Grattan spoke it; Franklin wrote it. You will observe that our most popular

works in prose belong to it. So do our greatest orators. A new taste and a new feeling for the classics grew up with it. It translated, to the satisfaction of its time, Homer and Virgil.

The style achieved by Dryden and the eighteenth-century writers generally was the style that Arnold himself wanted to write, after adapting it, of happy necessity, to his own genius. In his Preface to his short edition of *The Six Chief Lives from Johnson's* Lives of the Poets he repeated in his own way what Clough had said:

> It seems as if a simple and natural prose were a thing which we might expect to come easy to communities of men, and to come early to them; but we know from experience that it is not so. Poetry and the poetic form of expression naturally precede prose. We see this in ancient Greece. We see prose forming itself there gradually and with labour; we see it passing through more than one stage before it attains to thorough propriety and lucidity, long after forms of consummate accuracy have already been reached and used in poetry. It is a people's growth in practical life, and its native turn for developing this life and for making progress in it, which awaken the desire for a good prose,—a prose plain, direct, intelligible, serviceable. A dead language, the Latin, for a long time furnished the nations of Europe with an instrument of the kind, superior to any which they had yet discovered in their own tongue. But nations such as England and France, called to a great historic life, and with powerful interests and gifts either social or practical, were sure to feel the need of having a sound prose of their own, and to bring such a prose forth. They brought it forth in the seventeenth century; France first, afterwards England.

> The Restoration marks the real moment of birth of our modern English prose. Men of lucid and direct mental habit there were, such as Chillingworth, in whom before the Restoration the desire and the commencement of a modern prose show themselves. There were men like Barrow, weighty and powerful, whose mental habit the old prose suited, who continued its forms and locutions after the Restoration. But the hour was come for the new prose, and it grew and prevailed. In Johnson's time its victory had long been assured, and the old style seemed barbarous. Johnson himself wrote a prose decidedly modern. The reproach conveyed in the phrase "Johnsonian English" must not mislead us. It is aimed at his words, not at his structure. In Johnson's prose the words are often pompous and long, but the structure is always plain and modern. The prose writers of the eighteenth century have indeed their mannerisms and phrases which are no longer ours. Johnson says of Milton's blame of the Universities for permitting young men designed for orders in the Church to act in plays: "This is sufficiently peevish in a man, who, when he mentions his exile from college, relates, with great luxuriance, the compensation which the pleasures of the theatre afford him. Plays were therefore only criminal when they were acted by academics." We should now-a-days not say *peevish* here, nor *luxuriance,* nor *academics.* Yet the style is ours by its organism, if not by its phrasing. It is by its organism,—an organism opposed to length and involvement, and enabling us to be

clear, plain, and short,—that English style after the Restoration breaks with the style of the times preceding it, finds the true law of prose, and becomes modern; becomes, in spite of superficial differences, the style of our own day.

This desirable style Arnold characterises as having "regularity, uniformity, precision, balance."

I have already suggested that "precision" is a property of the thought rather than of the wording. The other three desiderata amount to no more, I think, than what was expressed by Hopkins in one word when he described his own prose (some of the best written in the nineteenth century) as "evenflowing."

II

Arnold's call for smoothness had topical point. It came more forcefully in view of Carlyle's explosiveness, and a noticeable contemporary cult of an oracular prose consisting of short sentences constructed according to the simplest of patterns. Perhaps this cult recurs periodically in the history of English prose. Thomas Reid had affected it in the mid-eighteenth century. For example: "A man of sense is a man of judgment. Good sense is good judgment. Nonsense is what is evidently contrary to good judgment. Common sense is that degree of judgment which is common to men with whom we can converse and transact business." I have shown elsewhere that a similar syntax was being favoured as the vehicle for description in verse. In prose it was also being favoured in *Ossian* for this and other purposes. More recently there had been the prose of the belletrist R. A. Willmott, who was much read, it seems, and whose *Pleasures, Objects, and Advantages, of Literature. A Discourse* appeared first in 1851 (and last in 1906). From the start he had formed his sentences, as J. A. Froude did, on the subject-verb-object pattern, but at first so disguised the pattern with additions that it was not noticeable; Froude, by those means, made a style that has been much admired. In the *Discourse,* however, Willmott pared his bi- and tri-partite sentences to the minimum. Here is a sample:

> A thoughtful person is struck by the despotic teaching of the modern school. The decisions of the eighteenth century are reversed; the authority of the judges is ignored. Addison's chair is filled by Hazlitt; a German mist intercepts Hurd. Our classical writers daily recede further from the public eye. Milton is visited like a monument. The scholarly hand alone brushes the dust from Dryden. The result is unhappy. Critics and readers, by a sort of necessity, refer every production of the mind to a modern standard. The age weighs itself. One dwarf is measured by another. The fanciful lyrist looks tall, when Pindar is put out of sight.

It is plain that sentences like these, on the barest subject-verb-object pattern, do not provide a staple for extended prose, simply because of the universal law that we soon tire of the repetition of a pattern that is recognisable—the writers who used this oracular style forgot that oracles stop speaking as soon as possible. As I have said, a major writer took up the pattern but made it unrecognisable except to the analyst of wording—there is nothing jerky about Froude's style. One of the greatest, Carlyle, may be said to have made a point of cultivating jerks, but there is no monotony because he multiplied the angles from which they struck the reader.

Like most other nineteenth-century writers, Arnold was fascinated by the strange performance of Carlyle. His brilliant mimicry exists in the letters to Clough, and scraps of it persist till the end—a climax in the late essay on Gray reads as if Carlyle had worded it: "How simply said, and how truly also! Fain would a man like Gray speak out if he could, he 'likes himself better' when he speaks out; if he does not speak out, 'it is because I cannot.'"

Clearly, such prose lacked evenflowingness. The prose Arnold recommended avoided what might be called markedly varying contours, such as characterised oratorical prose. For at least two centuries now the prose written in England had been drawing away from oratory and coming nearer to conversation. In other words, the supposed distance between writer and reader was diminishing. In writing oratorical prose, the writer thinks of himself as dominating his audience from a platform. In writing conversational prose, the writer thinks of himself as on a level with it. And whereas the orator's audience is myriad, the writer of conversational prose has an audience of one. Sterne marked an important point in the history of English written prose when he noted that "Writing, when properly managed (as you may be sure I think mine is) is but a different name for conversation." That remark opens a chapter (book 2, chapter 11) of *Tristram Shandy,* and in the context "conversation" retains some of its older sense of "social intercourse"—Sterne goes on to warn the reader that he is relying on him to draw on his own experience so as to eke out what cannot be written down in all its completeness. But that the word has also much of its newer, narrower meaning is also plain—it comes in the midst of a book that is almost wholly made up of something as near as possible to the prose we talk together. The preference for written conversational prose meant first of all a looser ordering of the matter being expressed, and secondly a more intimate personal colouring, which might show itself as an addition to the matter, but which would very much affect the wording.

The approach made by written prose to conversation had been embarrassed, as Clough implied in the passage I have quoted, by the age-old habit of imitating the syntax of classical Latin. It may be that in the seventeenth century and earlier this imported syntax was as noticeable in cultivated conversation as a syntax flow-ing down from Anglo-Saxon. If so, manners, on which conversation depends, were soon to change. An early, and as it happened fictitious exponent of the newer style showed it at its most brilliant. The conversation of Shakespeare's most voluble personage exhibited a prose strikingly different from most of the prose being written at the time. That Hamlet was of the Court went without saying, but to the courtly he added an at least equal amount of the academical—he was also of the University. The prose he spoke and the familiar letter he wrote to Horatio (that to Ophelia belonged to a different kind) was a prose appropriate for writers who were trying to think about the new matter then coming into man's ken, and whose writings were mainly addressed to the aristocracy. We can imagine Dryden writing it, despite his remark that Shakespeare had imitated the conversation of gentlemen less well than Beaumont and Fletcher—a remark that witnesses to the rate at which manners were changing in the seventeenth century. After Dryden came Addison and Pope. Pope's conversation is represented by Spence, and his written prose by the Preface to the *Works* of 1717, of which I quote a paragraph from near the end:

> If time shall make it the former, may these Poems (as long as they last) remain as a testimony, that their Author never made his talents subservient to the mean and unworthy ends of Party or self-interest; the gratification of publick prejudices, or private passions; the flattery of the undeserving, or the insult of the unfortunate. If I have written well, let it be consider'd that 'tis what no man can do without good sense, a quality that not only renders one capable of being a good writer, but a good man. And if I have made any acquisition in the opinion of any one under the notion of the former, let it be continued to me under no other title than that of the latter.

Addison and Pope gave way to Sterne, who "managed" his conversational prose so as to make it as graceful as theirs while at the same time giving it all the informality possible. Informality, whether maximum or less, might be welcomed in a novel, but not necessarily in prose of thinking, of which there was so much in the nineteenth century. And yet after Sterne's *tour de force* even the most formal prose shed some of its pomp. In Arnold's day even Herbert Spencer yielded up all he could of his native heaviness: at the conclusion of the Preface to his epoch-making *Social Statics* (1850), he referred to certain "relaxations of style" which may "be censured, as beneath the gravity of the subject," and proceeded:

> In defence of them it may be urged, that the measured movement which custom prescribes for philosophical works, is productive of a monotony extremely repulsive to the generality of readers. That no counterbalancing advantages are obtained, the writer does not assert. But, for his own part, he has preferred to sacrifice somewhat of conventional dignity, in the hope of rendering his theme interesting to a larger number.

I might add that the conversational style had its detractors. Perhaps it was his training among the Jesuits that prompted Hopkins to relegate Newman's prose to an inferior category. In a letter to Patmore towards the close of Newman's long life, he wrote:

> Newman does not follow the common tradition—of writing. His tradition is that of cultured, the most highly educated, conversation; it is the flower of the best Oxford life. Perhaps this gives it a charm of unaffected and personal sincerity that nothing else could. Still he shirks the technic of written prose and shuns the tradition of written English. He seems to be thinking "Gibbon is the last great master of traditional English prose; he is its perfection: I do not propose to emulate him; I begin all over again from the language of conversation, of common life."
>
> You too seem to me to be saying to yourself "I am writing prose, not poetry; it is bad taste and a confusion of kinds to employ the style of poetry in prose: the style of prose is to shun the style of poetry and to express one's thoughts with point." But the style of prose is a positive thing and not the absence of verse-forms and pointedly expressed thoughts are single hits and given no continuity of style.

In making this criticism, Hopkins may have been asserting his allegiance not only to the Jesuits but to Pater, his Oxford tutor, who was deliberately writing a prose far from conversational—so far that one critic described it as prose lying in state. In a review of *Dorian Gray,* he recommended writers to write English "more as a learned language," which was to revert to the method of the Elizabethans, and in his late essay, "Style," he recommended the removal of "surplusage." That recommendation had pointed reference to a characteristic of conversational prose, which favoured the sort of expressions I shall note as frequent in Arnold's prose. Meanwhile Oscar Wilde was writing in the conversational style that is still so much with us.

Aesthetic considerations bring strange bedfellows together, and among the disciples of Sterne were Dr. Arnold and Newman. These two take us into the famous Oriel Common Room, to which, in his turn, Matthew Arnold belonged. The prose Dr. Arnold wrote, on occasions at least, is sufficiently indicated by a passage in a letter of Newman's of 1833 in which he sought an opinion about a piece of his own prose from a friend. Having applied the word "flippant" to it (in the older sense of "fluent, talkative, voluble"), he paused to gloss it with "by which I mean what Keble blames in [Dr.] Arnold's writings, conversational." If Newman was uncertain whether or not he had gone too far, it was down a favourite path—he would any day have preferred the flippant to the pompous: there was nothing in him of "stained-glass attitudes," to use Gilbert's brilliant phrase. Froude has left us a picture of Newman's bearing in conversation.

> He, when we met him, spoke to us about subjects of the day, of literature, of public persons and incidents, of everything which was generally interesting. He seemed always to be better informed on common topics of conversation than any one else who was present. He was never condescending with us, never didactic or authoritative; but what he said carried conviction along with it. When we were wrong he knew why we were wrong, and excused our mistakes to ourselves while he set us right. Perhaps his supreme merit as a talker was that he never tried to be witty or to say striking things. Ironical he could be, but not ill-natured. Not a malicious anecdote was ever heard from him. Prosy he could not be. He was lightness itself—the lightness of elastic strength—and he was interesting because he never talked for talking's sake, but because he had something real to say.

Newman's manners are the key to his prose, and to that of Matthew Arnold also. For this purpose we need go no further, in amplification of Froude, than to Clough's oblique description of them in a description of Emerson, who was then on a visit to Oxford:

> Everybody liked him. . . . He is the quietest, plainest, unobtrusivest man possible—will talk but will rarely *discourse* to more than a single person—and wholly declines "roaring." . . . Some people thought him very like Newman. But his manner is much simpler.

Newman managed his elaborate simplicity with deftness. His grace was crisp. But his horror of being "abrupt" was as strong as his horror of being pompous. His walk was as near to a swift gliding as feet and cassock could make it. We know that he never raised his voice, relying on his audience's intent wish to catch what he was saying for his power of reaching them. Over the course of his long life he said much about writing, and all of it penetrates deep. I need quote only two of his remarks.

When J. B. Mozley was embarking on his first article for the *British Critic,* Newman, his former tutor and editor of the magazine, advised him about the sort of prose he ought to write: "In what you write do not be too essayish: i.e., do not begin, 'Of all the virtues which adorn the human breast!'—be somewhat conversational, and take a jump into your subject. But on the other hand avoid abruptness, or pertness. Be *easy* and take the mean—and now you have full directions how to write." (The last remark is jocular—Newman never liked assuming authority, even when he possessed it *ex officio* or by virtue of his genius.) Then there is his description of the notes to his translation of Athanasius: "They are written *pro re natâ,* capriciously, or at least arbitrarily, with matter that the writer happens to have at hand, or knows where to find, and are composed in what may be called an undress, conversational style." The metaphor was academic—on ordinary occasions a Doctor of Theology wore an M.A. gown of black instead of his formal scarlet. Newman's style was often in "undress," if we recall how neat and commodious an

M.A. gown is. He reserved a more formal style for such occasions as forbade the informal—as when he composed his towering "character" of God. Those occasions were few and far between, but only because he chose to make them so. Most of his writing was *"pro re natâ"* because he could rely on the quality of his thinking whenever pen was set to paper. His thinking was a flowing spring which, in view of its source, justified itself in being just that, not needing to organise and formalise itself into "ornamental waters." Froude tells us how well Newman could think in conversation, but he preferred thinking, pen to paper: "I think best when I write. I cannot in the same way think when I speak. Some men are brilliant in conversation, others in public speaking, others find their minds act best when they have a pen in their hands." When he wrote, however, he wrote as he would have spoken in conversation if he had come up to his own high standards for such speech. And if what he first wrote needed much correction—as it always did and which it always got—the changes were as much for the sake of grace of wording as of the revision of the thought.

We can see the appropriateness of a conversational prose for the nineteenth century. That age looked to its writers for help in understanding the universe as it was then being found to be, and for encouragement to do the good deeds that were urgently required if bloody revolution were to be averted by the narrowing of the gap between the Two Nations. In that age of crisis those many who were puzzled and troubled looked to writers for help. They earnestly wanted to hear the opinions of men they honoured, men of genius, "heroes," and to have received them in prose of a formal style would have been chilling if not insulting. They wanted advice by word of mouth. Literature was constantly spoken of at this time as a voice. At the best it was an actual voice, for many of the great writers performed on platforms as lecturers. Even as lecturers they spoke conversational prose, and when their words were available only in printed pamphlet or book, conversational prose was even more welcome. Conversational prose was the nearest thing to the heard human voice.

III

Newman's sister Harriett noted that those who admired him came to write like him. That was Arnold's double fate—we have recently had a thorough examination of the long master-pupil relationship from Professor De-Laura, on the score both of manner and matter (Professor DeLaura goes into the inspiration Arnold found in Newman's ideas not only on culture but, more strangely, on religion). Arnold himself was proud to acknowledge the twofold debt, which, he confessed, people had noticed. What mainly concerns us here is his debt for authorial personality since this had its effect on the wording as well as the matter of Arnold's prose.

Arnold tried to be as like Newman as possible without ceasing to be himself. He came to think that he was more like him than Newman could allow. That he could think so showed how little he understood Newman, who was a churchman first and last and wholly, and who had even doubted if Arnold's father was a Christian. Arnold was spared a sharp reply such as Newman made on occasion, when his urbanity was simply so much polish on the blade. Arnold liked wielding the rapier more than Newman did. There was relish to his reference to "the controversial life we all lead," whereas Newman lamented that the age afforded no time for *"quiet* thought."

And yet Arnold found in Newman's occasional sharpness the inch he extended into an ell. The manner of writing sharply he learned mainly from certain small things of Newman, the chief of which was the series of seven letters printed anonymously in *The Times* during February 1841, and soon collected in pamphlet form as *The Tamworth Reading Room.* They show Newman at the peak of his brilliance—when he found occasion to quote from them in the *Essay in Aid of a Grammar of Assent* thirty years later, he ascribed to them "a freshness and force which I cannot now command." Arnold knew these letters well, as we learn from the quotations from them entered into his notebooks. In them Newman came near to cutting a dash—anonymously, except for those who knew his authorship. Here is the opening of the sixth Letter to serve as a sample of the conversational writing that attracted Arnold: "People say to me, that it is but a dream to suppose that Christianity should regain the organic power in human society which once it possessed. I cannot help that; I never said it could." And which Arnold adopted. This comes towards the close of **"The Function of Criticism at the Present Time"**:

> But stop, some one will say; all this talk is of no practical use to us whatever; this criticism of yours is not what we have in our minds when we speak of criticism; when we speak of critics and criticism, we mean critics and criticism of the current English literature of the day; when you offer to tell criticism its function, it is to this criticism that we expect you to address yourself. I am sorry for it, for I am afraid I must disappoint these expectations.

And so on. The likeness to conversational speech is shown in little by Arnold's preference, which he shared with Newman, for beginning his paragraphs—let alone his sentences—with abrupt monosyllables. In this same essay five begin with "But," three with the conjunctive "For," and one each with "Nay," "Or," "Still," and "Again." In the Academies essay two paragraphs begin with the exclamation "Well," one being a "Well, then," and the other "Well, but." And in the passage about Ruskin I quoted earlier, Arnold's comment, it will be recalled, began with "Now, really."

Arnold designed his authorial personality to be striking, and his prose to match—a thoughtful critic must have pleased him by describing his style in 1883 as "perhaps, more striking than that of almost any other writer at the present time." In his first prose piece Arnold was striking partly by being superior. He aired his intellectual superiority in such runs of wording as these: "What is *not* interesting, is . . . ," and "'The poet', it is said, and by an apparently intelligent critic . . ." (in reprinting, Arnold dropped the insulting "apparently"), which is followed by "Now this view I believe to be completely false" (where the "Now" is an aggravation); a little later comes "And why is this? Simply because . . . ," and "No assuredly, it is not, it never can be so"; and again: "A host of voices will indignantly rejoin . . ."; and still again: "For we must never forget . . ." (he uses "we" but the guiltily forgetful reader knows at whom the finger is pointing). These things are more wholly wording than matter—they exhibit the manner of the egoist living in an age of controversy. That manner exists also in the many conversational intensives that Pater would have reckoned "surplusage"—"very," "signal," "very signal," "quite," "really," "profoundly." Along with these intensives go the vivid slang words, chief among which was "adequate," a term he had learned at Oxford. Near to slang are other informalities Newman had given him the taste for—homely expressions like "got talked of" and homely imagery, such as (to draw on **"The Literary Influence of Academies"**): "that was a dream which will not bear being pulled about too roughly," and "We like to be suffered to lie comfortably in the old straw of our habits, especially of our intellectual habits." I may also note that, like Newman, Arnold prefers that when he strikes out an important phrase it shall be quiet rather than brilliant, as Carlyle's and Ruskin's mainly were—quiet phrases like "the dialogue of the mind with itself" (from the 1853 Preface) and "doing as one likes" (a chapter heading from **Culture and Anarchy**).

Slang, homely and quiet phrases, and homely imagery combine two qualities that Arnold liked to combine— the unassuming and the striking. He liked to blend two opposed aesthetic constituents, which can be variously described. His sentences are both suave and obstructed, smooth and attitudinising, flowing and striking, urbane and barbarous. They have as much of each kind as can coexist in a state of blendedness. They move easily, but among carefully placed obstacles. Newman described the gentleman as one who "never inflicts pain," and who "carefully avoids whatever may cause a jar or a jolt." Arnold's prose has it both ways by alternating long stretches of the gentleman with a flash here and there of the *enfant terrible*. He gives jars and jolts but so deliberately that we accept them as forming part of an individual version of the gentlemanly. To read him is to watch a performance of one who comes near to inflicting pain either without actually doing so, or with

ointment so smartly applied that the sting melts away. Later on I shall qualify this description a little, but it is true in the main. The reader is confident that the writer knows where he is going, whatever bundles of sub-clauses, elaborate adverbs and detachable phrases are thrust into his open arms as he moves ahead. It may have been partly this spikiness of Arnold's that led R. H. Hutton to characterise his prose as "crystal," that of Newman's being "liquid."

Take as a handy instance of all this that note Arnold appended to the first paragraph of **"The Function of Criticism at the Present Time"** when it was collected in his **Essays in Criticism**:

> I cannot help thinking that a practice, common in England during the last century, and still followed in France, of printing a notice of this kind,—a notice by a competent critic,—to serve as an introduction to an eminent author's works, might be revived among us with advantage. To introduce all succeeding editions of Wordsworth, Mr. Shairp's notice might, it seems to me, excellently serve; it is written from the point of view of an admirer, nay, of a disciple, and that is right; but then the disciple must be also, as in this case he is, a critic, a man of letters, not, as too often happens, some relation or friend with no qualification for his task except affection for his author.

Here there are two sentences with eleven interpolations of one sort and another.

That note also serves to illustrate another characteristic of Arnold's wording. Its flowingness is often secured by the use of the lubricating devices I have already mentioned—"I cannot help thinking," "it is permitted that," and the rest. Spikiness exists in the run of the words in "might, it seems to me, excellently serve," where we not only have the severing of auxiliary from verb but the wide severing across a clause and an adverb—an adverb that is itself spiky because of its smart latinity and ticking polysyllables. In the second paragraph of the same essay we get: "should, for greater good of society, voluntarily doom."

The main means of Arnold's strikingness is this sort of unusual word-order. In the first paragraph of the essay I am drawing my instance from we have the striking word-order of "for now many years," but the expected word-order is often rearranged if not to that degree of strikingness:

> Many objections have been made to a proposition which, in some remarks of mine on translating Homer, I ventured to put forth; a proposition about criticism, and its importance at the present day. I said: "Of the literature of France and Germany, as of the intellect of Europe in general, the main effort, for now many years, has been a critical effort; the endeavour, in all branches of knowledge, theology, philosophy, history, art, science, to see the object as in itself it really is." I added,

that owing to the operation in English literature of certain causes, "almost the last thing for which one would come to English literature is just that very thing which now Europe most desires,—criticism"; and that the power and value of English literature was thereby impaired.

Sometimes his inversions become ludicrous—sometimes he does *not* avoid paining us! I have noted elsewhere that

his article **"The Bishop and the Philosopher"** has one paragraph beginning "The little-instructed Spinoza's work could not unsettle . . ." and another beginning "Unction Spinoza's work has not. . . ." If he had been more conversant with Dickens's novels he might have been warned by Mrs. Micawber's example: "'We came,' repeated Mrs. Micawber, 'and saw the Medway. My opinion of the coal trade on that river, is, that it may require talent, but that it certainly requires capital. Talent, Mr. Micawber has; capital, Mr. Micawber has not.'"

And Arnold can pain us by making a sentence carry too many weights—as in this from one of his ecclesiastical essays:

But as it is the truth of its Scriptural Protestantism which in Puritanism's eyes especially proves the truth of its Scriptural church-order which has this Protestantism, and the falsehood of the Anglican church-order which has much less of it, to abate the confidence of the Puritans in their Scriptural Protestantism is the first step towards their union, so much to be desired, with the national Church.

A small instance of his deliberate clumsiness comes at the opening of this same essay: "I daresay this is so; only, remembering Spinoza's maxim that the two great banes of humanity are self-conceit and the laziness coming from self-conceit, I think. . . ." Surely it would have been better to write "coming from it" or "that comes of it," better because we stress the ending of a phrase and so here stress the unimportant word, the repeated "self-conceit." Arnold did not make enough use of our pronouns.

This clumsy but deliberate repetition introduces the most notorious item in Arnold's method of wording— his liking for repeating a word or phrase over and over again. For instance, having designed "regularity, uniformity, precision, balance" as a description of the prose achieved by the eighteenth century, he repeats it six times in the course of one (long) paragraph. Such repetition of invented terms is part of his method, but ill-advisedly so. He goes to ungentlemanly lengths in repeating them—his insistence has something of the *entêté* about it. This was a mistake Newman would not have made. Very occasionally Newman did repeat a word mercilessly, as for instance here:

Again, as to the Ministerial Succession being a form, and adherence to it a form, it can only be called a form because we do not see its effects; did anything *visible*

attend it, we should no longer call it a form. Did a miracle always follow a baptism or a return into the Church, who would any longer call it a form? that is, we call it a form, only so long as we refuse to walk by *faith,* which dispenses with things visible. Faith sees things not to be forms, if commanded, which seem like forms; it realizes consequences. Men ignorant in the sciences would predict no result from chemical and the like experiments; they would count them a form and a pretence. What is prayer but a form? that is, who (to speak generally) sees any thing come of it? But we believe it, and so are blessed. In what sense is adherence to the Church a form in which prayer is not also? The benefit of the one is not seen, nor of the other; the one will not profit the ungodly and careless, nor will the other; the one is commanded in Scripture, so is the other. Therefore, to say that Church-union is a form, is no disparagement of it; forms are the very food of faith.

It is one thing, however, to repeat a monosyllable, and another to repeat a mouthful. Arnold's repeated things are often whole phrases. It may be that his habit was partly encouraged by his love for Homer. He knew the old epics more closely than any other text, except the Bible—in his lectures on translating them he mentions that for two years they were never out of his hands. Homer sometimes repeats a word of great length, and it happens that a note in Pope's translation provides a comment on Arnold's practice. Pope's seventh note on *Iliad* 19 reads:

Verse 197 [of his translation]. The *stern* Aeacides *replies.*] The *Greek* Verse is

Τὸν δ' ἀπαμειξόμενος πζοσέφη πόδας ὠκὺς Ἀχιλλεύς.

Which is repeated very frequently throughout the Iliad. It is a very just Remark of a *French* Critick, that what makes it so much taken notice of, is the rumbling Sound and Length of the Word ἀπαμειξόμενος: [*replies*]: This is so true, that if in a Poem or Romance of the same Length as the Iliad, we should repeat *The Hero answer'd,* full as often, we should never be sensible of that Repetition. And if we are not shock'd at the like Frequency of those Expressions in the Æneid, *sic ore refert, talia voce refert, talia dicta dabat, vix ea fatus erat,* &c. it is only because the Sound of the *Latin* Words does not fill the Ear like that of the Greek ἀπαμειξόμενος.

Pope then proceeds to discuss the modern preference for avoiding the repetition of words, especially of polysyllabic words, and decides that "Either of these Practices is good, but the Excess of either vicious." In Arnold the repetitions are therefore vicious.

There is no offence, however, in what is as common in Arnold as his repeated phrases—his use of long words derived from Greek or Latin, and which if they are repeated, are not noticed as being so. They combine with the other spikinesses to enliven the general flowingness. To draw on a few pages at the beginning of the same essay on Academies we get "prominently," "pre-eminence," "nascent," "instrument," which are sprinkled here and there among the shorter Saxon words that carry the main burden of the thinking. Once Arnold ended an essay with one of these consciously favoured words. In the course of this same essay on Academies he invented a new sense for the epithet "retarding," the sense of slackening the pace of *intellectual* advance, and so can rely on the last word of his essay to come as a climax:

> He will do well constantly to try himself in respect of these, steadily to widen his culture, severely to check in himself the provincial spirit; and he will do this the better the more he keeps in mind that all mere glorification by ourselves of ourselves or our literature, in the strain of what, at the beginning of these remarks, I quoted from Lord Macaulay, is both vulgar, and, besides being vulgar, retarding.

What was desiderated for the conversational style may be described as "lightness." It may come as a surprise to some that the word "light" was one of those greatly favoured in the mid-nineteenth century. Froude, we recall, called Newman "lightness itself," and Arnold begins one of his greatest poems with

> Light flows our war of mocking words.

When his *Essays* [*Essays in Criticism*] came out he hoped that Frederick Locker-Lampson would think its Preface "done with that *light hand* we have both of us such an affection for." They were trying to make the English language more like music composed for that still fairly new instrument, the piano. Gide was to describe French prose as like a piano without pedals. We know how much Arnold admired French prose, but there is something about the English language that prevents its sounding like the amputated instrument of Gide's comparison. Newman and Arnold wanted their prose to be like a piano *with* a sustaining pedal, playing music—shall we say as like the favourite parts of Schubert's as possible, light, airy, flowing, wiry, pale-coloured, preferring to tinkle rather than to pound.

I have said that we make an aesthetic response to the personality shown in writing and that we judge it by the exercise of the intellect. Our aesthetic response to Arnold's authorial personality is one of pleasure tempered by intellectual doubt as to whether or not its pleasantness for the twentieth century was pleasantness for the nineteenth. For some nineteenth-century readers it was decidedly that—Arnold had his numerous admirers. Those admirers, however, were already, we guess, in possession of the sweetness and light he was recommending. To the "elephantine main body" of the bourgeoisie that Arnold was out to transform, he cannot have meant very much. He sometimes used the term that Hazlitt had introduced into the critical vocabu-

lary—"tact." But how little of it he himself exercised! ***Culture and Anarchy*** was met with critics who saw its author as a mere aesthete looking rather out of place in the daily throng of English business: Henry Sidgwick, for instance, ridiculed him as a person "shuddering aloof from the rank exhalations of vulgar enthusiasm, and holding up the pouncet-box of culture betwixt the wind and his nobility." They might have stomached his urbanity if it had been like that of Newman—an, as it were, unconscious urbanity. They could not take the urbanity of one who postured. It seems that he made a big strategical mistake. The writer who had most effect on English culture was William Morris. For him urbanity was fluff and nonsense—unlike Arnold, he was once mistaken for a sea-captain. But if Arnold was bent on being urbane, he ought to have kept his urbanity more like Newman's, which always seemed to exist by right of second nature.

Phillip Raisor (essay date autumn 1973)

SOURCE: Raisor, Phillip. "Matthew Arnold's 'Balder Dead': An Exercise in Objectivity." *Studies in English Literature, 1500-1900* 13, no. 4 (autumn 1973): 653-69.

[*In the following essay, Raisor considers Arnold's poem "Balder Dead" in relation to the poet's 1853 preface to* Poems *and to his professed desire to "settle no questions, give no directives." Raisor suggests that Arnold's ability to identify with multiple characters and multiple possibilities is evidence of this carefully cultivated stance.*]

Whether Matthew Arnold's much neglected **"Balder Dead"** is the poet's triumph over a dying world or his lament for that world has been the dominant problem for critics of the poem. In the only extensive analysis of **"Balder Dead,"** Clyde De L. Ryals argues that "not only does it offer a criticism of life, it also presents a hope for the future; the poet's foot is in the *vera vita* (at least as he sees it), his eye is on the beatific vision."[1] Warren D. Anderson agrees that the poem is a criticism of life, but he would place the poet's foot in the *mala vita* and eye on the *Götterdämmerung*. "Such power as **'Balder Dead'** possesses comes from its elegiac mood, from the sense of sorrow and tenderness, anguished struggle and inevitable defeat that is Arnold's own."[2] Both Ryals and Anderson emphasize the verbal and emotional overtones of the last eighty lines, concluding that either Balder's millennial vision or Hermod's thwarted aspiration is more important. Ryals links Arnold with Balder and his vision of a second Asgard; Anderson links the poet with Hermod and his return to Valhalla. The result, I think, is an oversimplification of Arnold's identification with his characters.

This is not to deny that Arnold did identify with his characters or that personal elements do exist in the poem. Several critics have noted similarities between

Balder and Arnold, the echoes throughout the poem of Arnold's earlier lyrical poetry, his alterations and extensions of the basic Eddic myth, and parallels between his description of Valhalla and his description, in his Letters, of his own epoch.[3] The action, though based on Snorri Sturluson's *Prose Edda,* has forced almost every critic of the poem to feel that Arnold, as C. H. Herford suggests, was "thinking of his own gods."[4] Neither Herford nor Frederick Page (who attempts to connect Balder with "the fortunes of Christianity in history"[5]) can firmly substantiate this probability from internal evidence of the poem. But the constant references to Heaven and Hell, Odin as endemic creator, the satanic Lok, the "ray-crownéd Balder,"[6] and the resurrection theme, strongly suggest that Arnold was neither unaware nor unresponsive to the parallels between pagan myth and modern Christianity.

At issue is not Arnold's presence in the poem, but his treatment of his own experience. This treatment is best seen in connection with Arnold's attempt, first expressed in his letters to A. H. Clough as early as 1847[7] and developed in prefaces and lectures in the 1850's and critical essays in the 1860's, to arrive at a theory of dramatic poetry. The theory, as Sidney M. B. Coulling observes, is Arnold's contribution to the Victorian controversy over the poet's role in his age.[8] In his *Essay on Shelley* (1851) Robert Browning characterized this controversy as the ordinary clash of "opposite tendencies of genius"—the subjective and the objective, and indicated his preference for the latter.[9] A. Dwight Culler notes that a general shift from subjectivity to objectivity was taking place at mid-century: "Wordsworth and Coleridge had made it in the poems which mark the end of their creative years, and Carlyle had made it in *Sartor Resartus.* Newman made it in turning from the private judgment of Anglicanism to the dogmatic principle of the Roman Catholic Church. Ruskin made it in turning from mountains and painting to architecture and society."[10] Arnold made it too, but his change was uneven. Early in his career, says Culler, Arnold was "concerned with developing an aesthetic distance between himself and his subject so that he could contemplate it without being affected by it." But "around 1849 [he] discovered that he also had problems to solve, and, as a result, the volume *Empedocles on Etna* almost totally abandoned" this formalistic view.[11] Arnold recovered this view in his 1853 Preface, insisting that while all experience should be available to the poet, regardless of its private or public nature, he preferred subjects drawn from the past and a perspective on his subjects which permitted him, as Lionel Trilling says, "to settle no questions, give no directives."[12]

* * *

Most critics have assumed that Arnold applied his theory (at least the earliest expressions of it) to **"Balder Dead,"** but they have disagreed on his success. Ken-

neth Allott comments simply that the poem illustrates "the poetic creed of the 1853 Preface."[13] Ryals and Anderson (who agree on this point) contend that the poem contradicts the creed. They argue that in spite of the renunciation of subjectivity in the 1853 Preface, Arnold was unable to re-establish "an aesthetic distance between himself and his subject," and allowed his emotional involvement in the action to determine his position in **"Balder Dead."**[14] However, because both critics arrive at opposite interpretations of the poet's state of mind, I believe it may be maintained that while Arnold delineates a dying world that is as much mid-Victorian England as it is Nordic Valhalla, he remains, throughout the poem, committed to his aim of settling no questions, giving no directives.

* * *

Arnold had the poets of Greek tragedy in mind when, in the 1853 Preface, he wrote the following description of the proper relationship of a poet to his poem and his audience:

> The terrible old mythic story on which the drama was founded stood, before he entered the theatre, traced in its bare
> outlines upon the spectator's mind; it stood in his memory, as
> a group of statuary, faintly seen, at the end of a long and dark
> vista: then came the poet, embodying outlines, developing
> situations, not a word wasted, not a sentiment capriciously
> thrown in: stroke upon stroke, the drama proceeded: the light
> deepened upon the group; more and more it revealed itself to
> the riveted gaze of the spectator: until at last, when the final
> words were spoken, it stood before him in broad sunlight, a
> model of immortal beauty.[15]

It seems to me that Arnold had this description in mind when, less than two months later, he began writing **"Balder Dead."**

The "old mythic story" which Arnold selected from the *Prose Edda* is the climactic tale in "The Beguiling of Gylfi" chapter (sections 49-53).[16] One of the gods, Balder the Good, dreams that he is to be killed. Though protected by the Aesir, his dreams prove prophetic as the jealous Lok deceives the blind Hoder into throwing a fatal mistletoe bough at Balder. Frea, Odin's wife, quiets the grieving gods by sending Hermod to Hell with a request for the beloved Balder's return from the world of the dead. Hela, Lok's daughter, informs Hermod that only if all things, animate and inanimate, weep for Balder will he be returned. Odin sends forth his messengers to all parts of the world to announce the decree and report on its fulfillment. All things do weep for Balder except Lok, disguised as the giantess Thok, who is uncompromising. The angry gods pursue, capture, and bind Lok in a cave where he is to remain until the Twilight of the Gods. On this day the forces of Lok and those of Odin will conclude their conflict in a world battle of mutual annihilation. The day of Ragnarok will be followed by a renewal of heaven and earth and the reappearance of Balder in the new world.

In transforming prose into poetic narrative, Arnold merely reduced the various actions to one, and made it a "terrible old mythic story." The poem begins (*in medias res*) "So on the floor lay Balder dead," and ends before the pursuit and capture of Lok. The slaying of Balder, the incarceration of Lok, and the vision of a new heaven and earth remain within the action, but only as elements of dialogue. In the dialogue, Hela predicts Lok's punishment and Balder anticipates a new universe, but because both projections are undramatized, and because both are only parts of an action, they remain subordinate to the dominant action of the futile quest for Balder's return to Valhalla. Emphasizing the futility of this quest is the narrative structure (the poem is divided into three sections: "Sending," "Journey to the Dead," "Funeral") and the dramatic structure: Balder's death precipitates the action which turns upon the possibility of his resurrection. His resurrection depends upon the outcome of the conflict between Odin and Lok. Lok's victory compounds the original disaster, increasing the degree of calamity. Both arrangements contribute to what Arnold considered, in the 1853 Preface, the necessary conditions for tragic pleasure: "the more tragic the situation, the deeper becomes the enjoyment; and the situation is more tragic in proportions as it becomes more terrible."[17]

Perhaps Arnold was overly optimistic in expecting his audience to be even dimly familiar with the story of Balder. At least, some fifteen years later, he found it necessary to remind a disconcerted reader of his poem (one who did not see the relevance of the ancient tale to himself as a modern reader) that the Nordic legends *should* be in his memory: "We have enough Scandinavianism in our nature and history to make a short *conspectus* of the Scandinavian mythology admissible."[18] In 1853, however, Arnold may have had in mind readers like J. A. Froude who, in a review of Arnold's 1853 volume, suggested that having drawn from Persian history for **"Sohrab and Rustum"** the poet might next turn to Teutonic mythology.[19] Or, perhaps, Arnold had in mind a less sophisticated audience who had at least read Carlyle's brief synopsis of the Balder tale in *Heroes and Hero-Worship* (1841).[20] To make one of these assumptions, at any rate, would allow Arnold to concentrate on what the poet must do with the statuary at the end of a long and dark vista: "then came the poet,

embodying outlines, developing situations [italics mine], not a word wasted, not a sentiment capriciously thrown in."

How is the tragic poet to embody outlines, develop situations? Arnold studied the best authorities, and in his Preface to **Merope** he suggested that the poet follow the Greek pattern of exhibiting "the most agitating matter under the conditions of the severest form."[21] Imitating his predecessors, Arnold in **"Balder Dead"** presented the "most agitating matter" of the victory of death over life.

If the title **"Balder Dead"** suggests the motif of death, the poem itself firmly establishes the gradually emerging triumph of the dead over the gods in Valhalla. Hermod calls Valhalla "the city of Gods / And Heroes, where they live in light and joy" (II.198-199). In recounting for Odin and the other gods the birth of Heaven (which apparently they have forgotten), Frea observes that originally "the paths of night and day" (III.265), of Hell and Heaven, were clearly divided. Heaven was made for joy, compassion, wisdom, invention, and order.

But from the beginning (both of the Creation and the poem) doom hovers over Heaven. Odin (remembering this part of the Creation) has often told the gods that they live only until the day of Ragnarok

> When from the south shall march the fiery band
> And cross the bridge of Heaven, with Lok for guide,
> And Fenris at his heel with broken chain;
> While from the east the giant Rymer steers
> His ship, and the great serpent makes to land;
> And all are marshalled in one flaming square
> Against the gods, upon the plains of Heaven. . . .
>
> (III.475-481)

On this day, Odin says, all the gods will perish:

> For ye, yourselves, ye gods, shall meet your doom,
> All you who hear me, and inhabit Heaven,
> And I too, Odin too, the Lord of all.
>
> (I.28-30)

Believing Odin, the gods find no meaning in life and, in time, develop habits of frivolity, cynicism, hatred, and destruction. At present "Haughty spirits and high wraths are rife / Among the Gods" (III.79-80), Thor says. The daily routine in the tilt-yard is one of "blood, and ringing blows, and violent death" (III.140) followed by feasts of boar and mead. And Oder's "unquiet heart" (III.107) has driven him into distant lands, leaving his wife, Freya, to "vainly seek him through the world" (III.109). Frea puts it this way:

> For not so gladsome is that life in Heaven
> Which gods and heroes lead, in feast and fray,
> Waiting the darkness of the final times.
>
> (I.122-124)

The darkness, before the final times and even before Balder's death, has permeated Heaven.

Balder's death marks a definite stage in the progression toward the final day. It proves, first, that the gods are not immortal. Only the most unimaginative god would fail to see the relationship of this fact to the old rumor. It suggests, secondly, that no defense against the invasion of death is possible:

> For wise he was, and many curious arts,
> Postures of runes, and healing herbs he knew;
> Unhappy! but that art he did not know,
> To keep his own life safe, and see the sun.
>
> (I.210-213)

It indicates, thirdly, a further reduction of harmony in Valhalla. Regner, in his funeral oration, remembers that Balder alone of all the Scalds sung of peace and joy (III.141-143). Thor comments that Balder restrained "The others, labouring to compose their brawls" (III.85-86). Freya reminds the mourners that Balder, of all the gods and mortals, comforted her in the absence of her wandering husband. Only Balder could smooth "all strife in Heaven" (III.88).

Death, clearly, has brought Heaven towards its own environs. The world of the dead is Hell where Hela "with austere control presides" (I.317). Both Christian and classic (Arnold borrowed details from *Paradise Lost* as well as the *Odyssey* and the *Aeneid*),[22] this "Cheerless land / Where idly flit about the feeble shades" (II.181-182) is the domain of mortals whose lives were cowardly and whose deaths were inglorious. For them death is merely a less substantive extension of life. As Balder says, "Their ineffectual feuds and feeble hates / Shadows of hates . . . distress them still" (III.466-467). In this realm of darkness and gloom, the ghosts can neither hope nor change; they must remain underground "Rusting for ever" (III.472). Although honor among the dead is possible, such honor has little value. The path that takes Hermod to Hela's throne, for example, leads him past old warriors who outlived their days of battle and died of disease or old age; "yet, dying, they their armour wore, / And now have chief regard in Hela's realm" (II.168-169). This regard is transferred to Balder when he enters Hell. Being able to comfort the other dead and to relax the "iron frown" (III.463) of Hela, Balder achieves what death allows—the solace of "esteem and function" (III.470), but he remains trapped in gloom and the prisoner of Hela.

The similarity of conditions in Heaven and Hell and the roles that Balder plays in both worlds indicate the diminished quality of existence in Heaven. Even more damaging to Heaven is the preference of many of the gods for Hell. After Balder's death, for example, Frea notes that many gods "Would freely die to purchase

Balder back, / And wend themselves to Hela's gloomy realm" (I.120-121). One of these gods is Hoder, the unwitting slayer of Balder, who "distraught with grief, / Loathing to meet, at dawn, the other gods" (I.249-250), commits suicide. In Hell, Hoder explains to the unsympathetic Hermod that it is just that absence of sympathy which precipitated his act, and asks "And canst thou not, even here, pass pitying by?" (III.400) The absence of compassion in Heaven is also at the center of Balder's acceptance of his imprisonment:

> For I am long since weary of your storm
> Of carnage, and find, Hermod, in your life
> Something too much of war and broils, which make
> Life one perpetual fight, a bath of blood.
>
> (III.503-506)

Through Hoder and Balder, Hermod too learns to deplore this condition. In the final moments of the final interview, Hermod is confronted by Balder's description of life as it is and life as he believes it will be after Ragnarok. The contrast overwhelms him, and watching his friends enter the interior gloom of Hell "fain, / Fain had he followed their receding steps / Though they to death were bound, and he to Heaven . . ." (III.555-557). Preferring Hell to Heaven, Hermod adds his voice to the pervasive criticism of life.

In presenting this "most agitating matter" Arnold was concerned not only with the victory of death over life in the past, but also, as many critics have observed, with that victory in the present.

There is no mistaking the impression that Arnold included the Victorian wasteland in his Nordic desert. Ryals accurately observes that

> Everywhere there is evidence of the depression and ennui which Arnold in his inaugural lecture at Oxford had classified as characteristic of modern times; everywhere there is manifest the sick hurry, the divided aims, the overtaxed heads, and the palsied hearts which are the symptoms of "this strange disease of modern life" diagnosed in **"The Scholar-Gipsy."**[23]

To anyone familiar with Arnold's poetry, it is not difficult to hear precise echoes of these conditions in innumerable lines, characters, and situations of **"Balder Dead."** The battlefields of Valhalla are simultaneously the "darkling plain" of **"Dover Beach."** The "great road" that Oder takes in his restless and "faithful search" is the same road taken by the narrator of **"Stanzas from the Grande Chartreuse"** and the same road that, later, Thyrsis will take in his quest for "A fugitive and gracious light." The final scene of the poem (the interview in Hell between Hermod and Balder) is a reenactment of the dream separation of Arnold and Senancour (a living and a dead poet) in **"Stanzas in Memory of the Author of 'Obermann.'"** Division is always, in the early Arnold, the index to contemporaneity.[24]

My equally distinctive impression is that Arnold included not only symptoms but also causes of the modern disease in this episode. I would go even beyond the intuitions of Herford and Page, and observe that Arnold was thinking of his own world so much that he gave precedence to explanations of a dying world which he later developed in *Culture and Anarchy*. It is not difficult to see that Odin, Frea, and Balder express or embody the ideas which Arnold found in Hebraism, Christianity, and Hellenism. Nor is it difficult to see that the central action of the poem, the attempt to recover Balder from death, is a dramatic consideration of the idea of *resurrection* which was to engage Arnold in his chapter "Porro Unum Est Necessarium" and in greater detail in *St. Paul and Protestantism*. Nor, finally, is it difficult to see that Lok is the manifestation of *sin*, which Arnold in **"Hebraism and Hellenism"** referred to as that "something which thwarts and spoils all our efforts" to achieve perfection.[25] It is clear that while exposing the nature of the Nordic world, Arnold was also revealing the essence of the modern world.

Arnold termed this synthesis a "connexion," and insisted, in his inaugural lecture as Professor of Poetry at Oxford (1857), that it was necessary for an adequate comprehension of a subject: "no single event, no single literature, is adequately comprehended except in its relation to other events, to other literatures."[26] In considering the practice of the great tragic poets, Arnold found the simultaneous representation of past and present worlds central to their vision:

> Aeschylus and Sophocles represent an age as interesting as themselves; the names, indeed, in their dramas are the names of the old heroic world, from which they were far separated; but these names are taken, because the use of them permits to the poet that free and ideal treatment of his characters which the highest tragedy demands; and into these figures of the old world is poured all the fullness of life and of thought which the new world had accumulated.[27]

By "the fulness of life and of thought" Arnold did not mean simply the poet's own life and thought nor merely contemporary views on contemporary problems; he meant "the general intelligence of his age and nation."[28] From the 1853 Preface through **"The Function of Criticism at the Present Time,"** Arnold insisted that the intelligence of his age was unequal to that of the ages of Aeschylus and Shakespeare. Yet his own epoch, he said in his inaugural lecture, contained the contrasts between confusion and clarity, depression and energy, which characterized all epochs. The poet who would adequately interpret his time must work with these contrasts if his view is to have a proper depth and completeness.[29]

Part of this view is voiced by Balder who, in some respects, is the poet of **"A Summer Night"** torn between the demands of the world and those of the self (a typi-

cal Arnoldian dilemma) who is "Never by passion quite possessed / And never quite benumbed by the world's sway." More prominently, he is the poet, like Empedocles, whose greatness is "Railed and hunted from the world." Just as Arnold, spiritually isolated from a deceptive world in **"Dover Beach,"** seeks in personal love the means to endure his seclusion, so Balder, both physically and spiritually isolated from his world, seeks with his wife Nanna, who is with him in Hell, "Some solace in each other's look and speech, / Wandering together through that gloomy world" (I.327-328). An even more important parallel is the step beyond **"Dover Beach"** in which Balder, rejecting mere melancholy endurance, finds, in a broader circumference, the means to hope for a renewal of life:

> For I am long since weary of your storm
> Of Carnage, and find, Hermod, in your life
> Something too much of war and broils, which make
> Life one perpetual fight, a bath of blood.
> Mine eyes are dizzy with the arrowy hail;
> Mine ears are stunned with blows, and sick for calm.
> Inactive therefore let me lie, in gloom,
> Unarmed, inglorious; I attend the course
> Of ages, and my late return to light,
> In times less alien to a spirit mild,
> In new-recovered seats, the happier day.
>
> (III.503-513)

This step, in both detail and spirit, looks forward to the concluding paragraph of **"Porro Unum Est Necessarium"** in which Arnold expresses directly what he had expressed indirectly, through Balder, some fifteen years earlier.

> And now, therefore, when we are accused of preaching up a spirit of cultivated inaction, of provoking the earnest lovers of action, of refusing to lend a hand at uprooting certain definite evils, of despairing to find any lasting truth to minister to the diseased spirit of our time, we shall not be so much confounded and embarrassed what to answer for ourselves. We shall say boldly that we do not at all despair of finding some lasting truth to minister to the diseased spirit of our time; but that we have discovered the best way of finding this to be not so much by lending a hand to our friends and countrymen in their actual operations for the removal of certain definite evils, but rather in getting our friends and countrymen to seek culture, to let their consciousness play freely round their present operations and the stock notions on which they are founded, show what these are like, and how related to the intelligible law of things, and auxiliary to true human perfection.[30]

It is at this point that one might agree with Ryals that "With its closing note of hope for the future **'Balder Dead'** marks a turning point in Arnold's development."[31] Yet I observe that the closing note, the very final note, is not one of hope.

At the end of the poem both Balder and Hermod eye the same goal—a new Heaven. Balder describes to Hermod his vision of a second Asgard:

> Far to the south, beyond the blue, there spreads
> Another Heaven, the boundless—no one yet
> Hath reached it; there hereafter shall arise
> The second Asgard, with another name.
> Thither, when o'er this present earth and Heavens
> The tempest of the latter days hath swept,
> And they from sight have disappeared, and sunk,
> Shall a small remnant of the Gods repair;
> Hoder and I shall join them from the grave.

The creation of the new Heaven will evolve out of the destruction of the first Asgard, and will, by the nature of its evolution, exclude the possibility of conflict:

> There re-assembling we shall see emerge
> From the bright ocean at our feet an earth
> More fresh, more verdant than the last, with fruits
> Self-springing, and a seed of man preserved,
> Who then shall live in peace, as now in war.

> (III.518-531)

Peace and contentment, as opposed to war and anxiety, are here intimately related to the absence of a personal creator, and the natural process by which the new Heaven will emerge allows for no flaw in the creation.

It is apparent that Balder's vision is the *vera vita* and that, accepted in Hela's kingdom, willing to endure the gloom of Hell, accompanied by Nanna and Hoder, satisfied with his rejection of Valhalla, and convinced of the inevitability of the second Asgard, Balder is at last in harmony with the spirit of the universe. It is also apparent that Hermod, watching his friends enter the interior gloom of Hell, is condemned to live, to suffer:

> But Hermod stood beside his drooping horse,
> Mute, gazing after them in tears; and fain,
> Fain had he followed their receding steps,
> Though they to death were bound, and he to Heaven,
> Then; but a power he could not break withheld.
> And as a stork which idle boys have trapped,
> And tied him in a yard, at autumn sees
> Flocks of his kind pass flying o'er his head
> To warmer lands, and coasts that keep the sun;
> He strains to join their flight, and from his shed
> Follows them with a long complaining cry—
> So Hermod gazed, and yearned to join his kin.

> (III.554-565)

Hermod's anguish results, not from his inability to believe in Balder's vision, but from his inability to break the power that separates him from his goal of contentment. He longs to be with the kindred spirits Balder, Hoder, and Nanna in their unthreatened calm, and he would commit suicide if he could, but he is not free to choose the time or means of his death. The echo of Arnold's **"Stanzas in Memory of the Author of 'Obermann'"** is unmistakable:

> We, in some unknown Power's employ,
> Move on a rigorous line;
> Can neither, when we will enjoy,
> Nor, when we will, resign.[32]

Unable to resign from life, Arnold, thus, says farewell to Senancour, his mentor and kindred spirit, who has

> gone away from earth,
> And place with those dost claim,
> The Children of the Second Birth,
> Whom the world could not tame.[33]

The echo suggests the parallel of Arnold with Hermod and Balder with Senancour. This connection makes it possible to argue that the final note of the poem is one of despair—Arnold, like Hermod, finding himself a helpless victim of fate. It is at this point that one might agree with Anderson that although Arnold attempted to write a dramatic poem, his temperament was so fixed that "instinctively" he was "making visible the sombre shapes of his inward vision."[34]

Yet, as I have indicated, Arnold identified not only with Hermod, but also with Balder. This double identification suggests that Arnold accepted two possibilities for the future. If Hermod feels a mysterious power at work which acts frivolously and contrary to his deepest desires, Balder sees the course of ages moving naturally and in harmony with the gods' desires towards perfection. In this respect Arnold has one foot in the *mala vita* and one foot in the *vera vita*. I see nothing in the poem to suggest that Arnold rejected either possibility. In fact, it is precisely the preservation of both possibilities that allows **"Balder Dead"** to fulfill Arnold's own requisites for tragic pleasure.

It is important here to recall, I think, that in the 1853 Preface Arnold tacitly admits that he understood the proper conditions for tragic pleasure (those conditions and that pleasure being defined largely by Aristotle) only after he had published **"Empedocles on Etna."** The problem with **"Empedocles,"** he says, is that it gives primary attention to the mental and emotional states "in which the suffering finds no vent in action; in which a continuous state of mental distress is prolonged, unrelieved by incident, hope, or resistance; in which there is everything to be endured, nothing to be done."[35] This type of situation, Arnold avers, produces pain not pleasure. Yet, he continues, "In presence of the most tragic circumstances, represented in a work of art, the feeling of enjoyment, as is well known, may still subsist; the representation of the most utter calamity, of the liveliest anguish, is not sufficient to destroy it."[36] To properly represent a tragic circumstance, Arnold had to discover how "utter calamity" need not be morbid and could be enjoyable.

As would be expected from his comments on **"Empedocles,"** Arnold concentrated in **"Balder Dead"** on avoiding unrelieved suffering. Balder's death does precipitate grief so intense among the gods that all "Val-halla rang / Up to its golden roof with sobs and cries" (I.11-12). But this anguish is relieved by Frea's proposal that Balder might be returned if Hela's terms are fulfilled. At first

> Through the world was heard a dripping voice
> Of all things weeping to bring Balder back;
> And there fell joy upon the gods to hear.
>
> (III.317-319)

This joy proves to be momentary, however, when Lok refuses to weep. The result is pain proportionate to the degree of delight:

> And as seafaring men, who have long wrought
> In the great deep for gain, at last come home
> And towards evening see the headlands rise
> Of their dear country, and can plain descry
> A fire of withered furze which boys have lit
> Upon the cliffs, or smoke of burning weeds
> Out of a tilled field inland; then the wind
> Catches them, and drives out again to sea;
> And they go long days tossing up and down
> Over the sea-ridges, and the glimpse
> Of port they had makes bitterer far their toil—
> So the Gods' cross was bitterer for their joy.
>
> (III.357-368)

In spite of the sense here of a *lesson taught,* this pattern is repeated when Balder offers to Hermod the hope of a happier day. This vision stimulates Hermod to great excitement, but it proves to be a lever to profound pain when he discovers that he cannot willfully turn dream into reality. Along with Lok and death, suffering prevails, but its progress is not unbroken by expressions of hope and attempts, though disastrous, to act on a belief that something can be done to avert catastrophe.

If Arnold observed that these moments of relief were necessary for tragic pleasure, he also made another discovery, which he explains most clearly in his Preface to **Merope.** If a tragic situation is to please, he says, it must, following the Greek pattern, not only exhibit "the most agitating matter under the conditions of the severest form," it must also restore a proper balance of conflicting forces. He continues,

> Sometimes the agitation becomes overwhelming, and the correspondence is for a time lost, the torrent of feeling flows for a space without check: this disorder amid the general order produces a powerful effect; but the balance is restored before the tragedy closes: the final sentiment in the mind must be one not of trouble, but of acquiescence.[37]

This Aristotelian *catharsis* receives considerable emphasis. As the action moves toward a final calamity

> the thought and emotion swell higher and higher without overflowing their boundaries, to a lofty sense of the mastery of the human spirit over its own stormiest agi-

tations; and this, again, conducts us to a state of feeling which it is the highest aim of tragedy to produce, to *a sentiment of sublime acquiescence in the course of fate, and in the dispensations of human life* [Arnold's italics].[38]

Such a state, he suggests in the 1853 Preface, leaves the audience free of "all feelings of contradiction, and irritation, and impatience."[39]

How did Arnold, having established the victory of death over life, balance at the end of the poem these conflicting forces? A major step in achieving this balance is to indicate that Fate (Arnold's term)—whatever its nature—holds life and death in its control. From Odin's opening statement that Balder's death is not the responsibility of either Hoder or the other gods, but simply the fulfillment of an end long ago predetermined (I.23-35), the poem increasingly emphasizes this theme. It becomes a common denominator that all the gods are agents (or victims) of Fate. Another step is to show that a mastery of the spirit over its own deepest fears is achieved by perception of and submission to a power beyond itself. Balder does dominate his anger and self-pity (when he understands that he cannot be returned to Valhalla) by accepting death and looking forward to the future. Hermod, too, in the final line, overcomes, perhaps, his desire for death and accepts life, returning with a "sigh" to Heaven. Whatever their separate conceptions of Fate, both do submit to their given conditions. A final step in achieving a balance is up to the reader. If he has followed, "stroke upon stroke," the progression of the separate thoughts and feelings of each character, then he is in a position to see, what neither Balder nor Hermod can see, that Lok's victory has not fundamentally changed the possibilities open to the living gods. Death and Life do remain within the order of things.

It may seem odd that one who commends impersonality should write about himself. But there is no paradox here. Arnold attempted to use biographical and contemporary materials in a purely formal manner. Because he used his materials as he thought the Greek tragic poets had used theirs, it seems legitimate to say that Arnold considered himself a part of the classical tradition. To say, as John P. Farrell does,[40] that Arnold's commitment to a particular historical view (rather than his commitment to the ancients) shaped his tragic vision is, I think, unsupported by **"Balder Dead."** To Arnold, says Farrell, "Tragedy ends in a sterile future because the essence of tragedy is historical stalemate."[41] While Farrell emphasizes the expressions of Balder, the centrality of Falkland to the form, and the primacy of history, it seems to me (as I have attempted to show) that Arnold subordinates both expression and character to action, that the "old mythic story" is the governing form, and that history is meaningless in the face of a mysterious cosmic scheme.

Arnold's detachment from and attitude toward the historical process is apparent in his treatment of the problem (which engages all the characters) of how to live in the presence of death. Odin demands that the gods live "With cold dry eyes, and hearts composed and stern" (I.35), their daily life in Heaven; Frea, who contends that "much must still be tried, which shall but fail" (I.130), argues for a self-sacrificial attitude and pattern of behavior in quotidian life; Balder moves from Frea's position to one in which he is willing to simply "endure Death" (III.544-545) until Life is restored. Arnold treats each of these approaches with sympathy. But because he is governed by the dramatic principle that how the gods live has no effect on the future course of events, it is not surprising that he gives no directives on how to live. What Arnold does give is the impression that the consideration of how to live deepens the richness of thought and feeling—and in this he is neither simply personal nor didactic, but in the finest sense dramatic.

Notes

1. "Arnold's 'Balder Dead,'" *Victorian Poetry,* 4 (1966), 81.

2. *Matthew Arnold and the Classical Tradition* (Ann Arbor, 1965), p. 61.

3. See Ryals, pp. 67ff.; Anderson, pp. 58ff.; *The Poems of Matthew Arnold,* ed. Kenneth Allott (New York, 1965), pp. 350-352ff.; C. B. Tinker and H. F. Lowry, *The Poetry of Matthew Arnold: A Commentary* (London, 1950), pp. 91-104.

4. *Norse Myth in English Poetry* (London, 1919), p. 14.

5. "'Balder Dead' (1855)," *Essays and Studies* (English Association), 28 (1942), 61.

6. *The Poems of Matthew Arnold,* ed. Kenneth Allott (New York, 1965), p. 387—hereafter referred to as *Poems.* Also, hereafter, section and line number[s] of "Balder Dead" will be given in the text.

7. See Arnold's letter to Clough written shortly after December 6, 1847, in *The Letters of Matthew Arnold to Arthur Hugh Clough,* ed. H. F. Lowry (London and New York), 1932, p. 63.

8. "Matthew Arnold's 1853 Preface: Its Origin and Aftermath," *Victorian Studies,* 7 (1964), 234.

9. *The Complete Poetic and Dramatic Works of Robert Browning,* portable Cambridge edition (Boston and New York), 1895, p. 1010. See Philip Drew, "Browning's *Essay on Shelley,*" *Victorian Poetry,* 1 (1963), 1-6; also Thomas J. Collins, "Browning's *Essay on Shelley*: In Context," *Victorian Poetry,* 2 (1964), 119-124.

10. *Imaginative Reason: The Poetry of Matthew Arnold* (New Haven, 1966), p. 204.

11. *Ibid.,* p. 200.

12. *Matthew Arnold* (Cleveland and New York), 1955, p. 139.

13. *Poems,* p. 351. See also Hugh Kingsmill, *Matthew Arnold* (London, 1931), pp. 124-125.

14. Ryals, p. 80; Anderson, p. 61.

15. *The Complete Prose works of Matthew Arnold,* ed. R. H. Super (Ann Arbor, 1960), I, 6—hereafter cited as *Prose Works.*

16. For an extended and illuminating discussion of Arnold's use of Bishop Thomas Percy's edition of Mallet's translation of Snorri's *Edda,* see Mary W. Schneider, "The Source of Matthew Arnold's 'Balder Dead,'" *Notes and Queries,* 14 (February, 1967), 56-61.

17. *Prose Works,* p. 2.

18. Letter to F. T. Palgrave in 1869. Quoted by G. W. E. Russell, *Matthew Arnold* (New York, 1904), p. 42.

19. *Westminster Review,* n. s., 5 (1854), 158-159. See *Poems,* p. 351.

20. See *Poems,* p. 351.

21. *Prose Works,* p. 59.

22. See Tinker and Lowry, *A Commentary,* pp. 91-104; also Anderson, pp. 58-60.

23. Ryals, pp. 69-70.

24. In terms of an attitude and frame of mind, Arnold characterized this division as follows: "What those who are familiar only with the great monuments of early Greek genius suppose to be its exclusive characteristics, have disappeared: the calm, the cheerfulness, the disinterested objectivity have disappeared; the dialogue of the mind with itself has commenced." *Prose Works,* p. 1.

25. *Culture and Anarchy,* ed. J. Dover Wilson (Cambridge, 1966), p. 135.

26. *Prose Works,* pp. 20-21.

27. *Prose Works,* p. 31.

28. *Prose Works,* p. 26.

29. *Prose Works,* pp. 21, 35. See also "The Function of Criticism at the Present Time," in *Essays in Criticism, First Series* (London, 1966), pp. 24, 34.

30. *Culture and Anarchy,* pp. 163-164.

31. Ryals, p. 78.

32. *Poems,* p. 136.

33. *Poems,* p. 136.

34. Anderson, p. 61.

35. *Prose Works*, pp. 2-3.

36. *Prose Works*, p. 2.

37. *Prose Works*, p. 59.

38. *Prose Works*, pp. 58-59.

39. *Prose Works*, p. 14.

40. "Matthew Arnold's Tragic Vision," PMLA, 85 (1970), 107.

41. Farrell, p. 117.

Miriam Allott (essay date 1982)

SOURCE: Allott, Miriam. "Matthew Arnold: 'All One and Continuous.'" In *The Victorian Experience: The Poets*, edited by Richard A. Levine, pp. 67-93. Athens: Ohio University Press, 1982.

[*In the following essay, Allott compares Arnold's work to that of George Eliot and several other contemporaries. Touching on both Arnold's wit and his seriousness, Allott concludes that Arnold maintained a consistent (and unequivocally modern) perspective throughout his oeuvre.*]

My familiarity with Matthew Arnold began late in life, in fact not much more than six or seven years ago when I took over some of the work on nineteenth-century poetry in general and Arnold in particular left unfinished at his death by Kenneth Allott. The "experience" has been curious and significant in a number of ways. My own early interests as a university teacher were formed by a sedate academic progress from a master's thesis on E. M. Forster and a doctoral thesis on Henry James to a teaching post on the staff, which led in due time to directing specialist courses on the traditional nineteenth-century novel, with George Eliot figuring prominently and predictably as a high-Victorian sage struggling to forge an honorable answer to the question "how to live" in an age "Of change, alarm, surprise." Arnoldian quotations of this nature came readily even then, the affinity between these eminent agnostic angels being something of which necessarily one had long been aware. But the self-confessed representative of the "main movement of mind" of the age was still seen more or less out of the corner of my eye—"somewhat sideways," as Keats said of certain artistic achievements whose power he sensed but did not properly understand.[1]

Now it is Arnold who has moved to the foreground, though George Eliot, once known, cannot be confined to the peripheral areas of anyone's vision. Her work is a central *massif* linking two vast ranges of English fiction and marked by configurations which belong to both. It obeys the missionary impulse of the early Victorian novelists while yielding, even if unwittingly, to the demand to be heard urged by a pressingly personal and largely sombre vision of things, a demand which her late-Victorian successors, repudiating didacticism and the utilitarian view of literature, responded to as the imaginative writer's real, right and only thing. Similar conflicting impulses shape Arnold's writing career and help to explain why these two figures so readily come together in one's thinking about the peculiarities of their age. It is generally accepted that their shared missionary sense is associated with the early-Victorian and high-Victorian conviction that a writer's duty in that "iron time" was to exhort and encourage others, to "animate," as Arnold has it in a celebrated letter,[2] which meant doing as much as possible on these lines for oneself as well. It is recognized, too, that many writers whose creative gifts were stimulated by feelings of melancholy and loss feared that putting these principles into practice might mean artistic suicide. But it is perhaps less often said that for certain other writers the exercise was not at all out of keeping with their native gifts. George Eliot's finest achievements stem from her novelistic gifts finding at their service a natural bent for lofty, humane, profoundly earnest, "evangelical" proselytizing. This is apparent in the phrasing, the movement, the cadences of even her earliest letters. When as a novelist she permits ingredients from her spiritual autobiography to dominate her exemplary fictional style, her readers can experience more uneasiness than they do even when she is at her most governessy. The anomaly was recognized some time ago by F. R. Leavis when he complained about the damagingly "sentimental" and "immature" elements in the drawing of her heroines (notably the idealistic ardours of Maggie Tulliver and Dorothea Brooke, whom she presents as finely-tuned spirits homeless in an uncomprehending world). The effect is still more pronounced in the religiose passages of *Daniel Deronda*, where she gives head at last to the suppressed religious yearnings of the Dinah Morris in herself, transmogrifying them, so to speak, into Mordecai, with no holds barred.

Fiction is one thing and poetry another, and what works in the former may not work in the other, especially so far as the management of personal feeling is concerned; but a revealing peculiarity in George Eliot, for this reader at any rate, is that alone among Wordsworth's Victorian readers her lifelong admiration for him never faltered, whether his hand was in his breeches pocket or not.[3] She was twenty when she first read his poetry in her recently acquired copy of the six-volume Moxon edition and declared, "I never before met with so many of my own feelings just as I could like them." She must have been thinking chiefly of the poet of the *Lyrical Ballads* (and perhaps Margaret in *The Excursion*) when in 1861 she wrote of *Silas Marner* that no one would be "interested in it but myself (since Wordsworth is dead),"[4] but it is to the "philosophical" Wordsworth whom Arnold deplored that she most consistently turns, especially as he appears in *The Excursion*. It is the case that certain dominating movements in the intellectual and imaginative history of the Victorians can be followed through the complications of their feelings about Wordsworth; and it is important to this history that her fellow devout skeptics from Mill to "Mark Rutherford," whom Arnold liked so much,[5] experienced very mixed feelings about him indeed. Arnold's ambivalences make themselves felt early, as we know from **"Resignation,"** begun about 1843, which looks towards "Tintern Abbey" at the same time that it dissents from it, replacing a Nature which is a constant source of joy and consolation with one that "seems to bear rather than rejoice." The **"Obermann"** poem of 1849 [**"Stanzas in Memory of the Author of 'Obermann'"**] and the two poems written at the time of Wordsworth's death in 1850, **"Memorial Verses"** and **"The Youth of Nature,"** are similarly ambiguous in saluting a poet who brought hope by celebrating the freshness and delight of the natural world in his own

> iron time
> Of doubts, disputes, distractions, fears . . . ,

but was unequal to the needs of the age into which he lived, when

> the complaining millions of men
> Darken in labour and pain . . . ,

so making it hard not to claim, as we read in the Obermann poem, that

> . . . Wordsworth's eyes avert their ken
> From half of human fate . . .

At the other end of his life, in the 1880 introduction to his one-volume edition of selections designed to rescue Wordsworth from the Wordsworthians, Arnold delivered his broadside:

> *The Excursion* abounds with philosophy, and therefore *The Excursion* is to the Wordsworthian what it never can be for the disinterested lover of poetry,—a satisfactory work. 'Duty exists', says Wordsworth in *The Excursion*; and then he proceeds thus—
>
> > . . . Immutably survive
> > For our support, the measures and the forms,
> > Which an abstract intelligence supplies,
> > Whose kingdom is, where time and space are not.
>
> And the Wordsworthian is delighted, and thinks that here is a sweet union of philosophy and poetry. But the disinterested lover of poetry will feel that the lines carry us really not a step further than the proposition which they would interpret; that they are a tissue of elevated but abstract verbiage, alien to the very nature of poetry . . .[6]

The passage moves us in a special way when we recollect that the man writing had for some twenty years abandoned poetry for prose and was now celebrated as his country's foremost critic of its current cultural shortcomings, a critic moreover with his own governessy ways who was displaying some of them now. The reproof found its way to the heart of Wordsworth's other famous admirer, sitting at home in the Priory shortly before moving into Cheyne Walk with her new husband John Cross, and there encountered resistance. A selection of Wordsworth is unsatisfactory "except for travelling and popular distribution," she notes dismissively in her April 1880 letter to Frederic Harrison, because it cannot give "the perfect gems to be found in a single line, or in a dozen lines, which are to be found in the 'dull' poems." She quotes a good passage from Book VIII of *The Prelude* (11.60-8-15) but, an unrepentant "Wordsworthian" still, she offers as "much to your purpose" the pronouncement,

> There is
> One great society alone on earth:
> The noble living and the noble dead . . . ,

and regrets Arnold's omission of the sonnet "I grieved for Buonaparte . . . ," She quotes from the poem "these precious lines," which display the "sweet union of philosophy and poetry" prompting Arnold's amused scorn (the italics are hers):

> 'Tis not in battle that from youth we train
> The governor who must be wise and good,
> And temper with the otherness of the brain
> Thoughts motherly, and meek as womanhood.
> *Wisdom doth live with children round her knees.*[7]

One's affection for Arnold owes a good deal to differences of the kind signalled by these reactions to Wordsworth, and it is clear to me now that the effect produced by his poetry on my own sensibility is governed by a feeling for the whole movement of his creative intelligence. When we speak of "George Eliot" we mean the author of an entire body of writing, and the same goes for Arnold. H. F. Lowry agrees that Arnold's efforts in the two fields of poetry and prose "are *inseparable*":

> . . . the reader who knows only one body if his work can hardly know even that. Voices reverberate back and forth between the verse and the essays; the questions raised in the one are answered in the other . . .[8]

Furthermore, as I was once led to add in another context, "the tone of the one is answered by the tone of the other."[9] The experience of reading Arnold is as much as anything else a matter of responding to a particular temper. Some years ago Douglas Jefferson, in distinguishing Fielding's and Richardson's contrasted styles, singled out the play of humor and the strategic ironic withdrawals of the former and the equally impressive but totally divergent "awful directness" of the latter.[10] It is not far out of the way to see a parallel in Arnold and George Eliot, since she belongs securely in the English Puritan tradition which Professor Jefferson has in mind when discussing Richardson, while Arnold of course engaged in a running battle with the narrowing effects of the tradition in contemporary England. He gathered his forces in the late 1860s for culminating attacks on them in *Culture and Anarchy* and its more polished companion, *Friendship's Garland,* where he bounces them up and down with a fresh access of gaiety and wit. His initial forays in the first series of *Essays in Criticism* show him attempting to draw out some response to European culture from "that powerful but at present somewhat narrow organ the modern Englishman" by introducing him to a number of unfamiliar minor foreign figures—Joubert, Maurice de Guérin, Maurice's still less known sister Eugénie—whose shared "excellence" lay above all in their ownership of, and power to express, a spirit subtly self-scrutizing, honest, imaginative, melancholy and gallant. He felt at home with those writers because he had a good measure of their qualities himself, although in his early Oxford days he might not have wished to acknowledge the affinity. There were reasons in any case why he should have felt the need to dissemble. It is notable that in assuming during his Oxford days his youthful dandyish disguise he drew on other qualities, gaiety and high spirits above all, which he never refers to in any of the people—from Marcus Aurelius to Heine and from Falkland to Senancour—of whom he writes so admiringly and plangently. He was to employ precisely these qualities when seeking "to instruct, elevate, and to amuse" the British public once he had left behind the ten years or so of his poetic career and become "a master of prose and reason" (or at any rate imaginative reason).[11] That phrase referring to the "*utile* and *dulce*" of art is used dismissively by Joyce's cocky Stephen Dedalus, who reminds us of Arnold's supercilious self-protective pose when he announces in *Stephen Hero,* "Everyone . . . who has a character to preserve must have a manner to preserve it with." Art would "never yield its secret to one who is enmeshed with profanities," he declares loftily, and the chief of these is

> the antique principle that the end of art is to instruct, to elevate, and to amuse. I am unable to find even a trace of this Puritanic conception of the aesthetic purpose in the definitions which Aquinas has given of beauty. . . .[12]

Charlotte Brontë, whose peculiar fusion of passionate earnestness and earnest passion gave a new dimension to nineteenth-century English Puritanism, was close to recognizing a reason both for the disguise and the need to make unfrivolous use of the qualities on which it

drew when she met Arnold in 1850 and felt that "the shade of Dr. Arnold seemed to frown on his young representative."[13] This sort of attitude is neatly captured by Max Beerbohm in the sharp inquiry, "Why oh why Uncle Matt will you never be wholly serious?" which he fancifully ascribes in his Matthew Arnold cartoon to the disapproving little girl later to be Mrs. Humphry Ward. It still survives here and there today, especially in quarters where the combination of airy polemics in Arnold's serious essays and the melancholy temper of his poems produces unsettlement and misgiving. There is something in the English—if not also the American—Puritan spirit which can still suspect that to amuse and be amused is a frivolous way of carrying on and certainly incompatible with a proper seriousness of purpose.

And yet the co-existence of wit and serious feeling is increasingly noticeable in English post-modernist literature and it arises for the most part from a brand of stoicism which Arnold would have recognized and understood. At Oxford, as we know from his friend Clough, he was "full of Parisianism" entering a room "with a song of Béranger on his lips," walking with an "air of parading the Rue de Rivoli," letting his hair grow long and regularly "cutting chapel."[14] But from the

> hidden ground
> of thought and austerity within . . . ,

he was at this time composing the poems which surprised everyone when they appeared in his first volume, *The Strayed Reveller* (1849), because of their reflective melancholy and their "knowledge of life and conflict . . . *strangely like experience,*" as his favourite sister Jane put it, underlining the phrase for emphasis.[15] His own crisis of faith, unlike that of many of his contemporaries among the "lost generation" of the 1840s, seems to have taken place off stage but, as with Joyce's artist as a young man, "the episode . . . had resulted in a certain outward self-control which was now found to be very useful."[16] There was additionally an inner "self-control" to which as poet and moralist he also schooled himself. His austere self-commands hint at the hidden turbulence to be brought under discipline. The itinerant preacher, the "restless fool" of the early **"In Harmony with Nature,"** is scorned for exhorting us "To be like Nature strong, like Nature cool," since Nature is "cruel," "stubborn," "fickle," "forgives no debt and fears no grave." But it is the longing to be indeed "strong" and "cool" which lends force to the lines. Echoes of this are felt as far on as 1873 when Arnold's thinking about "Nature" is still governed by misgiving, for the term is "full of pitfalls," as he says in *Literature and Dogma,* and if "we are to give full swing to our inclinations" which self is it in us that we are to follow—"our *apparent* self or a higher real self"?[17] Whether "apparent" or "higher" and "real" the self most urgently present in the early poems is restless, emotional, passionate, lonely and uncertain. Images suggesting longed-for calm arrive together with those suggesting the threatening opposite as in **"In Utrumque Paratus,"** written about 1846, where the Plotinian debate rises in poetic temperature at the end of the third and the start of the fourth stanza:

> The solemn peaks but to the stars are known,
> But to the stars, and the cold lunar beams;
> Alone the sun arises, and alone
>   Spring the great streams.
>
> But if the wild unfather'd mass no birth
>   In divine seats hath known;
> In the blank, echoing solitude if Earth,
> Rocking her obscure body to and fro,
> Ceases not from all time to heave and groan . . .
>
>   (11.18-26)

Calm may perhaps be found on mountain slopes or "some high station," but down in the world are fever, sickness, distress, the distraction from distraction by distraction:

> Not milder is the general lot
> Because our spirits have forgot
> In action's dizzying eddy whirl'd,
> The something that infects the world.
>
>   ("Resignation," 11.275-8)

His need for self-schooling is still more urgently present in the "Switzerland" poems. His temperament is,

> Too strange, too restless, too untamed . . . ,

he owns "a starting feverish heart," forsees "a life alas! / Distracted as a homeless wind . . . ," and fears that there is no help for it but to face,

> This truth—to prove and make thine own:
> Thou hast been, shalt be, art, alone. . . .

The forces ruling his world are as arbitrary as they are implacable, urging wrathfully, "Be counsell'd and retire" and placing eternally between himself and the other—in these poems the figure we know as "Marguerite"—"The unplumb'd salt estranging sea," a line which concentrates, with a peculiarly individual Arnoldian "natural magic," the essence of the sorrowful, hard-fought-for stoicism of the 1849 volume.[18]

Nearly a quarter of a century later, facing as so often before the recognition that though people cannot do without religion neither can they any longer do with it as it is, he offers in place of the arbitrary powers ("A god, a god, their severance ruled") and of "the preternatural, which is now [religion's] popular sanction" but

will have to be given up in the "scientism" of the times, "the mighty forces of love, reverence, gratitude, hope, pity, and awe—all that host of allies which Wordsworth includes under the one name of *imagination*."[19] The gaiety, which in the 1840s was a protective armor for the disturbed self struggling to bring its emotions into creative order, now reappears in fine fettle, this time to safeguard in Wordsworth the poet of "*imagination*" from the poet of "the 'scientific system of thought'" who offers us "at last such poetry as this which the devout Wordsworthians accept" (the passage is from *The Excursion*, Book IX, 11.219-302):

> O for the coming of that glorious time
> When, prizing knowledge as her noblest wealth
> And best protection, this Imperial Realm,
> While she exacts allegiance, shall admit
> An obligation, on her part, to *teach*
> Them who are born to serve her and obey;
> Binding herself by statute to secure,
> For all the children whom her soil maintains,
> The rudiments of letters, and inform
> The mind with moral and religious truth.

He goes on,

> Wordsworth calls Voltaire dull, and surely the production of these un-Voltairian lines must have been imposed on him as a judgment! One can hear them being quoted at a Social Science Congress; one can call up the whole scene. A great room in one of our dismal provincial towns; dusty air and jaded afternoon daylight; benches full of men with bald heads and women in spectacles; an orator lifting up his face from a manuscript written within and without to declaim these lines of Wordsworth; and in the soul of any poor child of nature who may have wandered in thither, an unutterable sense of lamentation, and mourning, and woe![20]

As it happens, the National Association for the Promotion of Social Science (first established in 1856 and featured in 1861 as the Pantopragmatic Society of Peacock's *Gryll Grange*) was dissolved for want of funds six years after this, but these days we have our Further Education courses and our extra-mural seminars in English Literature and some of us may without difficulty "call up the whole scene." We must remember too that George Eliot's spirit was invoked as often as Wordsworth's at meetings of Moral Improvement Societies up and down the country. Her work was similarly culled for "gems," and anthologies of wise sayings were put together from her novels. It is hard now to realise the almost total eclipse of this hugely popular reputation after her death in the 1880s, but from the first beginnings of its revival (a landmark was David Cecil's *Early Victorian Novelists* of 1934), it became a habit to salute her as our first "modern" novelist. But how "modern" is "modern"? The work of our internationally known novelists since the 1950s—Graham Greene, Iris Murdoch, Angus Wilson, Muriel Spark, let us say, along with our university wits, David Lodge and Malcolm Bradbury, who are well known in America—has as its highest common factor a combination of satirical wit with serious, even tragic, feeling, a form of tragi-comedy which, as I have said elsewhere, may well come to be seen as the twentieth-century's dominant literary "kind." It is also present with variations in English contemporary poetry, notably in Philip Larkin's wry verse and the more exuberant but denser, because more deeply sculptured, poems of Seamus Heaney. If this temper is "modern," then George Eliot is certainly not "modern." The claim for her modernity rested on the reach of her psychological insight and her capacity to dramatize inner movements of mind and feeling and at the same time to enliven with her lion's share of the traditional novelist's gift for realistic detail the life of ordinary human beings in an often disappointing everyday world. But with the calling into question of nineteenth-century narrative procedures ("realistic" characterization, plot as a causal sequence consonant with a recognized outward order, the reluctance to bring out into the open bleak feelings of disturbance and conflict), not even her insight into the erosions of a spirit confronting with dismay an increasingly complicated world can make her seem other than resolutely committed to steadying course in that time and place, with as little as possible of disheartening allusion to the "dead world" behind and the alarming world about "to be born."

Arnold's claims to "modernity" are less vulnerable. This is largely because as poet he unflinchingly confronts, while contending with, his own "imagination of disaster," so that his poetry certainly becomes as candid a "dialogue of the mind with itself" as any other in the age. And when the moralist in himself can no longer countenance what he feels to be "morbid" introspection, he directs his critical intelligence to the practical business of safe-guarding values threatened by the order of things which brought the poetry into being in the first place. I must make it clear that I am not using the term "modern" to mean "adequate" in Arnold's evaluative manner, but the fact remains that for new readers—I am thinking especially of my own students—what Arnold writes commands sympathetic response for its authenticity and for its engagement with problems whose far-reaching effects are recognised at every turn of their own road. The response is quickened by their recognition of the interplay between the poet, the critic and the personality of the man who, in his latest years, brought a flavour of his everyday personal self into his engaging and touching dirges for lost household pets (a canary, a cat, a beloved dog). Such readers light up at his remarks about coal in the Elizabethan Age, his mickey-taking in **"The Dissidence of Dissent and the Protestantism of the Protestant Religion,"** his amusement at the lapses in his own "disinterestedness" ("Ruskin was dogmatic and *wrong*"), his failed efforts to emulate the

Barbarians in field sports and his insouciant jokiness—for example at the expense of the unfortunate Mr. Wright, who protested about Arnold's remarks on him as a translator of Homer,

> One cannot always be studying one's own works, and I was really under the impression, till I saw Mr. Wright's complaint, that I had spoken of him with all respect . . . ,

and, as a son and brother, in an affectionate letter home at the time of the Chartist riots in 1848 and the fear of the French invasion,

> Tell Edward I shall be ready to take flight with him the moment the French land, and have engaged a hansom to carry us both from the scene of carnage . . . .[21]

(There is no such kicking up of heels, alas, anywhere in George Eliot or Charlotte Brontë). With a more immediate personal concern, since many will become, or are already, members of the teaching profession, these readers are held by his still all too pertinent views about the English educational system, and, with some wryness, his hard slog as a school inspector. Perhaps the most surprising discoveries are his "democratic" ideas about state government and his struggle to formulate a system of belief capable of meeting spiritual needs without resting on "miracle, mystery and authority," in both of which the effort towards clarity is saluted as well as the limitations in the thinking, most of them stemming from the same traditions of English liberal humanism governing George Eliot's favorite themes and the "outmoded" narrative procedures which accommodate them. But Arnold confronts more explicitly and practically than George Eliot the problem of how to live in an increasingly secular age. His view that poetry must take the place of religion to light up morality is responded to as an anticipation of modern existentialist movements towards the retention of warmth behind our moral perceptions in an age of demythologized religion and increased secularity. (Camus puts this in his own terms in *La Peste* through Tarrou's celebrated inquiry, "Can one be a saint without God?")

This liking for a temper which can be serious without pomposity and amusing without being frivolous has made it easier for new readers to respond sympathetically to Arnold as a poet. In any case, of course, one no longer has the sense of addressing the unconverted when talking about the Victorian poets, though it has taken time for the vast proliferation of nineteenth-century studies during the past twenty years or so to produce its effect. This is partly because scholarship has done everything to uncover information about the social, political and religious background of the age and has devoted itself to minute exegesis of the poetry and the prose, but has done relatively little to illuminate the nature and quality of the literature itself. Things have not been helped, either, by the recent fashion, largely promoted in Britain by television drama and the antiques trade, for what in feeling, stance and style is really "Edwardian" but nevertheless is commonly described as "Victorian." This means that it is all the more imperative to distinguish among the three phases of the period—Early, Middle (or High) and Late—which are as strikingly differentiated in temper and climate as comparable phases in any other period of history. Even so, I think "Victorian" is beginning to be recognized as a term we can reserve for those aspects of the age which have become part of our post-Strachey folklore about it but have little to do with the writers and thinkers who "represent the age's main movement of mind." (The stock ingredients of this lore include among other things sexual prudery, sweated labour, frilled piano legs, antimacassars, poker-work mottoes, Sunday observance, hypocritical relativism, religiose poetry, and a literature consistent with wayside pulpit exhortation).

With much of this débris cleared away, critical response is freer and more flexible (there is a parallel in the case of D. H. Lawrence, who used to be condemned or passionately admired for extra-aesthetic reasons). At the same time, the relative novelty of this "discovery" of the Victorian poets has the effect of heightening appreciation of their curiously wide tonal range. It comes to be accepted, with some critical alertness to the reasons for the inequalities, that for instance, Tennyson is sometimes sentimental and silly, but can be magical; that Browning substitutes bluster for the hard graft of thinking out difficult ideas, but is boldly colloquial, delighted by the drunkenness of things being various and a subtle love poet; and that Clough—well Clough can still be an enormous surprise. Few readers in this largely nonchurchgoing generation have been familiar since childhood with "Say not the struggle nought availeth . . ." (though it is sung in church services yet) but even without these animating Rugbeian lines to afford a comparison it is still an arresting experience to come upon a Victorian "poet of doubt" whose uncertainties stimulate witty inventiveness, as they do in *Amours de Voyage*—whose diffident hero Claude is Clough's version of the nineteenth-century Hamlet figure (found at his most disenchanted in Flaubert and his most alarming in Dostoevsky)—and again in "Dipsychus." probably the most brilliant and original of the manifold "dialogues of the mind with itself" of the age. Then there are the light-hearted *vers-de-société* ("How pleasant it is to have money, heigh ho! . . ."),[22] the animated salute to the lifeforce in "Natura Naturans," and the erotic contributions to the youthful *Ambarvalia* (which upset Mrs. Clough so much). To be able to recognize something of the quality of these varied talents, the unevennesses of which are often traced to a worried engagement between the writer's individual temper and his preoccupa-

tion with his public role, is invaluable equipment in the matter of understanding Arnold's poetic gifts. The absence from these of Tennyson's "natural magic," Browning's dynamism and Clough's wit comes to be seen as the necessary concomitant of a poetry essentially elegiac and melancholy, but not passively so, since it is precisely against nostalgia and inactive melancholy that Arnold's formal and stylistic constraints are posed. When for Clough religious certainties disappeared, the initial sense of desolation and loss was urgent, explicit and plangent, and found expression in what is probably the most powerful of the poems of the "lost generation":

> Christ is not risen!
>
> Christ is not risen, no;
> He lies and moulders low;
> Christ is not risen.
>
> As circulates in some great city crowd
> A rumour changeful, vague, importunate, and loud,
> 　　Or authorship exact,
> 　　Which no man can deny
> 　　Nor verify;
> 　　So spread the wondrous fame;
> 　　　　He all the same
> 　　Lay senseless, mouldering, low,
> 　　　　He was not risen, no,
> 　　　　Christ was not risen!
>
> Ashes to ashes, dust to dust;
> As of the unjust, also of the just—
> 　　Yea, of that Just One too.
> This is the one sad Gospel that is true,
> 　　Christ is not risen.
>
> 　　　　　　　　　("Easter Day," 11.5-8, 48-63)

The reply in the second part of "Easter Day" is still sombre:

> Joy with grief mixes, with despondence hope.
> Hope conquers cowardice, joy grief;
> Or at least, faith unbelief
>
> 　　　　　　　　　("Easter Day" II, 11.32-4)

Arnold's lines in **"Stanzas from the Grande Chartreuse"** on a similar subject are characteristically more reflective, the low-keyed style signalling the taut self-discipline to which the lines themselves refer:

> Wandering between two worlds, one dead,
> The other powerless to be born,
> With nowhere yet to rest my head,
> 　　Like these, on earth I wait forlorn.
> Their faith, my tears, the world deride—
> 　　I come to shed them at their side.
>
> O, hide me in your gloom profound,
> Ye solemn seats of holy pain:
> 　　Take me, cowled forms, and fence me round,
> Till I possess my soul again;

Till free my thoughts before me roll,
Not chafed by hourly false control!

(11.85-96)

The tone of voice is unmistakable and is sustained throughout the ten or so years of Arnold's poetic career. We become accustomed, as not in Clough, to a particular register. This is not to take away from Clough's brilliances in his still smaller handful of poems, but one sees why Arnold grumbled about his friend's fits and starts and told him to settle to his own *assiette*.[23] It has been said that in arranging and classifying Arnold's poetry there are two possible methods.[24] One is to group together the *Weltanschauung* poetry, direct or dramatized, the "pure subject" narrative poems and the love poems, together with the personal elegies. The other is to classify them by style, say the "Keatsian" poems and the "Wordsworthian" poems, the former having more particularity and colour (**"The Scholar Gypsy," "Thyrsis,"** some of **"Tristram and Iseult"**) and the latter more severity and drive in the movement of the argument (**"Mycerinus," "Stanzas from the Grande Chartreuse,"** the **"Obermann"** poems). But the truth is that the work is consistent with itself in a way that resists these ready taxonomic procedures. Even when it is recognized that the stylistic influences are mixed, that they include something of Goethe in the reflective poems and the unrhymed recitations of **"Sohrab and Rustum," "Rugby Chapel," "Howarth Churchyard"** and **"Heine's Grave,"** and something of Tennyson too here and there is passages from **"Mycerinus," "The Forsaken Merman"** and **"The Scholar Gypsy,"** it is still the case that whatever the play of various influences, Arnold forges a personal style, less flowing and hypnotic than Tennyson's, less abrupt and diffuse than Browning's, rarely given to *èlan* and incandescence, but always emotionally honest, in command of tone and temper and sometimes, through the operation of strong feeling under constraint, transcending self-consciousness to produce a fine unimpeded poetic expressiveness. The consistency of this poetic tone and temper sees to it that the melancholy severity of Empedocles's hexameters,

Riches we wish to get,
Yet remain spendthrifts still;
We would have health, and yet
Still use our bodies ill;
Rafflers of our own prayers, from youth to life's last
    scenes . . .

We do not what we ought,
What we ought not, we do,
And lean upon the thought
That chance will bring us through;
But our own acts, for good or ill, are mighty powers. . . .

(I ii 222-6, 237-41)

is still felt in the "Keatsian" poetry of **"The Scholar Gypsy"**:

No, no, thou hast not felt the lapse of hours!
For what wears out the life of mortal men?
    'Tis that from change to change their being rolls;
    'Tis that repeated shocks, again, again,
        Exhaust the energy of strongest souls
        And numb the elastic powers.
Till having used our nerves with bliss and teen,
        And tired upon a thousand schemes our wit
        To the just-pausing Genius we remit
Our worn-out life, and are—what we have been.

(11.141-50)

But then again both the "austere" and the "Keatsian" poems express with particularity and poignancy Arnold's characteristic feeling for the beauty of a natural world which saddens as it delights, for, though separate from man and indifferent, it is subject to the same laws of change and transience. The feeling is not unlike Hardy's and moves the reader as the description of Egdon Heath moves him at the opening of *The Return of the Native*, though Arnold, when all is said, has a more captivating "natural magic." So in **"Resignation,"**

The self-same shadows now, as then,
Play through this grassy upland glen;
The loose dark stones on the green way
Lie strewn, it seems, where then they lay;
On this mild bank above the stream,
(You crush them!) the blue gentians gleam,
Still this wild brook, the rushes cool,
The sailing foam, the shining pool!

(11.98-107)

In spite of the resigned sadness of the poem the "eye is on the object" with the same pleasure that it rests on the natural landscape in Callicles's songs, which set against Empedocles's overtaxed mind the youthful poet's balance of thought and feeling:

The track winds down to the clear stream,
To cross the sparkling shallows; there
The cattle love to gather, on their way
To the high mountain-pastures, and to stay,
Till the rough cow-herds drive them past,
Knee-deep in the cool ford, for 'tis the last
Of all the woody, high, well-water'd dells
On Etna; and the beam
Of noon is broken there by chestnut-boughs
Down its steep verdant sides; the air
Is freshen'd by the leaping stream, which throws
Eternal showers of spray on the moss'd roots
Of trees, and veins of turf, and long dark shoots
Of ivy-plants, and fragrant hanging bells
Of hyacinths, and on late anemonies,
That muffle its wet banks; but glade,
And stream, and sward, and chestnut-trees,
End here; Etna beyond, in the broad glare
Of the hot noon, without a shade,
Slope behind slope, up to the peak, lies bare;
The peak, round which the white clouds play.

(I ii 36-56)

The keenness of the feeling is invariably heightened by the contrast with another order of being, imaged here in "the broad glare / Of the hot noon," as it is with the green, shaded "Keatsian" retreats in **"The Scholar Gypsy,"** where the lines are penetrated with elegiac nostalgia and the "hot noon" is held at a distance while the eye rests on the well-memoried scene.

> Screen'd is this nook o'er the high, half-reap'd field,
>   And here till sundown, shepherd! will I be.
>   Through the thick corn the scarlet poppies peep,
>   And round green roots and yellowing stalks I see
>   Pale pink convolvulus in tendrils creep;
>   And air-swept lindens yield
>   Their scent, and rustle down their perfumed showers
>   Of bloom on the bent grass where I am laid,
>   And bower me from the August sun with shade;
>   And the eye travels down to Oxford's towers.
>
> (11.21-30)

Feeling and the landscape are brought together and associated as in Tennyson, and also as in Tennyson the sense of loss can be made poignantly explicit, though constrained still, and often by formal narrative procedures. Arnold sings of his personal sense of loss through his deserted merman's "lyrical cry"—

> Call her once before you go—
> Call once yet!
> In a voice that she will know:
> Margaret! Margaret!
>
> Children's voices wild with pain—
> Surely she will come again!
> Call her once and come away;
> This way, this way!
> Mother dear, we cannot stay!
> The wild white horses foam and fret!
> Margaret! Margaret!
>
> (11.10-13, 16-22)

—or through the Breton narrator in the third part of **"Tristram and Iseult"** reflecting upon what it is that "wears out the life of mortal men":

> . . . we may suffer deeply, yet retain
> Power to be moved and soothed, for all our pain,
> By what of old pleased us, and will again.
> No, 'tis the gradual furnace of the world,
> In whose hot air our spirits are upcurl'd
> Until they crumble, or else grow like steel—
> Which kills in us the bloom, the youth, the spring—
> Which leaves the fierce necessity to feel,
> But takes away the power—this can avail,
> By drying up our joy in everything,
> To make our former pleasures all seem stale.
> This, or some tyrannous single thought, some fit
> Of passion, which subdues our souls to it,
> Till for its sake alone we live and move—
> Call it ambition, or remorse, or love—
>   This too can change us wholly, and make seem
>   All which we did before, shadow and dream.
>
> (III 116-32)

The setting for the sorrowing Iseult, "dying in a mask of youth," is still beautiful and in its particularized detail even cheerful:

> . . . This cirque of open ground
> Is light and green; the heather, which all round
> Creeps thickly, grows not here; but the pale grass
> Is strewn with rocks, and many a shiver'd mass
> Of vein'd white-gleaming quartz, and here and there
> Dotted with holly-trees and juniper.
> In the smooth centre of the opening stood
> Three hollies side by side, and made a screen,
> Warm with the winter-sun, of burnish'd green
> With scarlet berries gemm'd, the fell-fare's food.
> Under the glittering hollies Iseult stands,
> Watching her children play; their little hands
> Are busy gathering spars of quartz, and streams
> Of staghorn for their hats; anon, with screams
> Of mad delight they drop their spoils, and bound
> Among the holly-clumps and broken ground,
> Racing full speed, and startling in their rush
> The fell-fares and the speckled missel-thrush
> Out of their glossy coverts . . .
>
> (III 13-31)

The salute to the everyday hum of things here and in **"Lines Written in Kensington Gardens"** is regrettably rare in Arnold's poetry. It belongs to the daylight side of his temperament which kept anhedonia at bay in his earlier years and is clearly visible in what we know of his life as an affectionate husband and father. It is the "unburied self" of the family man, the educationist who earned his living as an inspector of schools, the public figure who lectured at Oxford, and the polemicist who took on the hosts of Midian in a zestful campaign against the Philistines. The "buried self" operated on its hidden ground with equal consistency, so that an attempt to group the poems by subject matter and approach is no more successful than the attempt to do so by their prevailing style. There are the poems which might be said on the face of it to support explicitly Arnold's statement that his work represented the main movement of mind in the last quarter of a century—the poems, that is, which reflect not only the issues of the time, but the feelings, mixed and uncertain, which the issues generated. These, I suppose, would always be thought of as including **"Empedocles on Etna,"** the two **"Obermann"** poems, many of the lyrics, including the **"Memorial Verses"** which speak of

> this iron time
> Of doubts, disputes, distractions, fears . . . ,
>
> (11.43-4)

and **"The Scholar Gypsy"** which censures

> This strange disease of modern life
> With its sick hurry, its divided aims
> Its heads o'ertaxed, its palsied hearts . . . ,
>
> (11.203-205)

and the **"Stanzas from the Grande Chartreuse,"** referring to himself as

> Wandering between two worlds, one dead,
> The other powerless to be born . . . .

> (ll.85-6)

the dead world being the old world of settled social relations and religious certainties (before 1832, even before 1789), and the "unborn world" being the age of settlement into new social problems and a religion purged of myths and dogmas. There are also two other kinds of poetry: the love poetry and the long poetic pieces, **"Sohrab and Rustum," "Balder Dead"** and *Merope,* where Arnold, against his own poetic grain, tried to get back to an earlier role of the poet as one who tells stories and teaches implicitly, who "makes something" rather than "thinks aloud." But we have already noted the presence of "public" themes in the **"Marguerite"** love poems—is communication possible? what part can love have in producing the happiness difficult to find with a skeptical consciousness in the modern world?—and the themes link them with the *Weltanschauung* poems. The finest of the love poems, Arnold's most famous lyric **"Dover Beach"**, similarly unites the issues of the time and the theme of love and displays at its best Arnold's gift for expressing the feelings of the transitional times—the indecision, the confusion, the regret. The scene is beautiful, the moonlight and the sea are calm, but the mood once again is one of quiet resigned sadness because the natural world is indifferent to man, beauty is evanescent, and to "see life steadily and see it whole" can only be saddening since the "sea of faith" is ebbing, life is like a night-battle in which confusion reigns and the only consolation is in personal relationships. The poetic temperature rises with the pain and regret of the "melancholy, long, withdrawing roar" and "The vast edges drear / And naked shingles of the world," and the description of the landscape expresses above all loneliness and loss.

In the long narrative poems **"Sohrab and Rustum"** and **"Balder Dead,"** or in the would-be "Sophoclean" *Merope,* Arnold is resolute to stop "tearing himself to pieces" in the effort to speak honestly in "confessional" poems and to devote himself to "the fascination of what's difficult" in solving the exclusively formal problems posed by dealing with given, objective themes. And yet the familiar voice is still heard, especially in the recurrent natural imagery, which is among the most intimately revealing of all poetic resources. The moonlit landscape of **"Dover Beach"** expresses the characteristic Arnoldian combination of delight in and longing for calm and lucidity: it is present in the final lines of **"The Forsaken Merman,"** where desolating pain gives way to resigned acceptance of the way it must be:

> When soft winds blow,
> When clear falls the moonlight,
> When spring-tides are low . . .

> We will gaze, from the sand-hills,
> At the white, sleeping town;
> At the church on the hill-side—
> And then come back down.

> (ll.125-7, 136-9)

The flat finality of the monosyllabic closing line places it a distance from the active unrest of that other closing line, "The unplumbed, salt, estranging sea" (the bitterness constantly on the tongue, no deepest there is none, isolation constantly pressing on the sensibility), which is the state most resolutely fought against because most frequently experienced. A little later in the same period, in **"A Summer Night,"** the "moon-blanched land" is recalled by the "moon-blanched street" where the thought arrives "Of a past night, and a far different scene":

> And the calm moonlight seems to say:
> *Hast thou then still the old unquiet breast,*
> *Which neither deadens into rest,*
> *Nor ever feels the fiery glow*
> *That whirls the spirit from itself away,*
> *But fluctuates to and fro,*
> *Never by passion quite possessed*
> *And never quite benumbed by the world's sway.*

> (ll.26-33)

Unrest, palpable and urgent, consolidates itself in this poem into a physical being, a beleaguered *doppelgänger*, a Flying Dutchman:

> . . . the pale master on his spar-strewn deck
> With anguished face and flying hair
> Grasping the rudder hard,
> Still bent to make some port he knows not where,
> Still standing for some false, impossible shore.
> And sterner comes the roar
> Of sea and wind, and through the deepest gloom
> Fainter and fainter wreck and helmsman loom
> And he too disappears and cares no more.

> (ll.65-73)

Against this wild and dark fated figure is set the conjuration,

> Plainness and clearness, without shadow of stain!
> Clearness divine!

> (ll.76-7)

The moonlight, then, is lucid, plain, clear, and associated with the stars, which carry a similar charge of feeling, unquestionably heightened by sympathetic response to their presence in Keats's poetry. The "same, bright, calm moon" of **"A Summer Night"** is near in more than one sense to "the same bright, patient stars" upon which Hyperion gazes in his trouble. Arnold's stars are always patient and steadfast, like the star in the "Bright star" sonnet, which he frequently and lovingly echoes in poems of the 1840s and early 1850s and wrote out in his copy of Moxon's 1851 selection of Keats's poetry (from which it had been excluded).[25] In **"Quiet Work"** the sonnet beginning "One lesson, Nature, let me learn of thee . . . ," he echoes Keats's "nature's patient, sleepless eremite":

> Still do thy sleepless ministers move on,
> Their glorious tasks in silence perfecting;
> Still working, blaming still our vain turmoil,
> Labourers that shall not fail when man is gone.

The last words in **"Empedocles on Etna"** belong to Callicles's celebration of the harmony and order of the self-dependent universe which ends in quietude:

> The night in her silence,
> The stars in their calm.

Moon, stars and mountains are the constants in this moral universe, the mountains standing for the steep climb to truth, though from the heights, once reached, the traveller gazes downwards, looking out over the earth to see it steadily and whole (and if not "deep" at least "wide"),[26] rather than upwards to find after all no marked lessening of the distance to the remote serenity of moon and stars. The mountain scenery is insistent and seized upon as early as the Lucretius-inspired Rugby Vulgus exercise, **"Juvat ire jugis,"**[27] to suggest the arduous climb towards the "lofty station" and its perspectives. It recurs in poems from the earliest to the latest phases of this poetic career, from **"In Utrumque Paratus,"**

> The solemn peaks but to the stars are known,
> But to the stars and the cold lunar beams . . . ,
>
> (11.18-19)

and the setting in **"Empedocles on Etna"** (1852), where the journey from youth to the disenchantment of middle age is symbolized in the climb from "the wooded region" of Etna to the "melancholy waste" at its summit, to the "mountain-tops" in **"Thyrsis"** (1861),

> . . . high the mountain-tops, in cloudy air,
> The mountain-tops where the throne of Truth,
> Tops in life's morning-sun so bright and bare!
>
> (11.143-6)

Mediating between these self-dependent objects, "too great for haste, too high for rivalry," and the restless, uncertain, diminutive human figure, always wandering, climbing, gazing, longing, there is water. Arnold saw himself as "one who looks on water as the mediator between the incarnate and man," and water when clear is especially loved: "Now I have a perfect passion for

clear water: it is what in a mountain country gives one, I think, most pleasure."[28] But clearness is not its only attribute in the poems. It flows and moves, it may run in hidden channels or on the surface, or again, ceasing to be a river, may widen out into a vast sea, where again it may be stormy or calm. The contrarieties are consistent with themselves for they image the uncertainties producing that desire for calm focussed in the imagery of moon, stars, mountain heights; uncertainties, that is, about our origins and destiny, about how to live and act in a world where the thinking self is, if I may put it so, increasingly "at sea," since now there is "no coherent social faith and order" (the phrase is used by George Eliot in her Prelude to *Middlemarch*). In Arnold the river of life at its calmest flows out to the wide sea of eternity, as Oxus flows into the Aral Sea; or it flows away from its source in the pure origin of things and it is for us to remount the stream of time, as Henry James has it in another context; or else again rivers are hidden currents of the buried self and, divided and unselfknowing as we are, we must attempt to distinguish the kinds and relative authenticities of these different levels of being:

> If what we *say* we feel—below the stream,
> As light, of what we *think* we feel—there flows
> With noiseless current strong, obscure and deep
> The current stream of what we feel indeed.[29]

The complex of feelings generating these images penetrates the "Keats" poems, the *Weltanschauung* poems, the lyrical and personal poems, and finally, breaking through their constraint, the public and "objective" poems, where the aim is to make something instead of thinking aloud. The voice of the youthful Callicles singing of traditional wisdoms and the brightness and harmony of the natural world is heard again in Aepytus whose recollections of youth enliven the painstaking *Merope,*

> We bounded down the swarded slope, we plunged
> Through the dense ilex-thickets to the dogs.
> Far in the wood ahead their music rang;
> And many times that morn we coursed in ring
> The forest round that belt Cyllene's side . . .
>
> (11.790-94)

and, in his mother's lines,

> . . . he, in the glens
> Of Lycaeus afar,
> A gladsome hunter of deer,
> Basks in his morning of youth,
> Spares not a thought to his home.
>
> (11.518-22)

The sense of oppression and longing for calm reappears in **"Balder Dead"** where the willed "animating" lines prophesying the arrival of "The second Asgard," and "an earth / more fresh, more verdant than the last" (III 521, 528-9), are countered by the authentic voice grieving at its own sickness and unrest,

> Mine eyes are dizzy with the arrowy hail;
> Mine ears are stunned with blows, and sick for calm
> . . .

> (III 507-8)

The interplay of these motifs, each heightening the other—youthful vitality and its brevity, longed-for calm and the anxieties which heighten the longing and make it hard to find—gather together in the final part of the first long "public" poem **"Sohrab and Rustum"** (which "in its own way animates" according to its author). The course of an individual life—the course of this particular poetic life we should perhaps rather say—is imaged in the lines reaching to the coda from Sohrab's death-blow at the hands of his father (in Keats's terms a "man of power" rather than a "man of achievement"),

> . . . from his limbs
> Unwillingly the spirit fled away,
> Regretting the warm mansion which it left,
> And youth, and bloom, and this delightful world . . .

> (11.855-8)

The celebrated coda becomes a paradigm for the impending obstacles of age and time as vitality ebbs (**"The Scholar Gipsy,"** we remember, grieves at "The foot less prompt to meet the morning dew, / The heart less bounding at emotion new . . ."), and for the looked-for but perhaps never achievable end:

> The shorn and parcell'd Oxus strains along
> Through beds of sand and matted rushy isles—
> Oxus, forgetting the bright speed he had
> In his high mountain-cradle in Pamere,
> A foil'd circuitous wanderer—till at last
> The long'd-for dash of waves is heard, and wide
> His luminous home of waters opens, bright
> And tranquil, from whose floor the new-bathed stars
> Emerge, and shine upon the Aral Sea.

> (11.10-18)[30]

It is the consistent, authentic, enactment in the whole work of an entire process of being which is so remarkable in Arnold, from the anxious son who wrote **"Myc-erinus,"** thinking that his legacy might include the weakness of heart which killed his father, to the man of morality and character who dedicated himself with his father's purposiveness to the moral and imaginative education of his fellow-countryman. But among the weapons he used for his polemics were those individual "vivacities" which he displayed in his Oxford days and which disquieted his father as they certainly disquieted earnest contemporaries, most keenly, naturally enough, when they came under attack. This son of Thomas Arnold would probably not have approved of "the litera-ture of experience," especially as we have come to know it since Joyce and *A Portrait of the Artist as a Young Man,* a book which lingers under a cloud of disfavour for present-day inheritors of a tradition which requires the firm provision of moral signposts to this and that, but "the literature of experience" is what Matthew Arnold's work as a whole really is. What he did not care to contemplate or act upon—how could he? The *Zeitgeist* was working for and in him but with its lineaments not completely revealed—was the possibility that exploration of the sombre, the dark, the uncertain, might be as fruitful and enriching as the effort towards sweetness and light, that the one indeed hardly has significance without confronting the possibilities of the other. His views about "adequacy" in art illustrate only too well that his public self firmly censored this pressing theme. But his creative self, "flowing / With noiseless current, strong, obscure and deep," knew better and saw to it that the poet would survive long enough for as much as possible of the whole "experience" to find forms of expression which would afford the succeeding age the peculiar delight that accompanies "the shock of recognition."

Notes

1. See Keats's letter to Benjamin Haydon, 8 April 1818 (*Letters,* ed. H. Rollins (1958), i245) and for "the main movement of mind" Arnold's letter of 5 June 1869, "My poems represent, on the whole, the main movement of mind of the last quarter of a century and thus they will probably have their day as people become conscious to themselves—of what that movement of the mind is . . ." (*Letters of Matthew Arnold,* ed. G. W. E. Russell (1895) ii 9). Arnold goes on to compare himself with Tennyson and Browning.

2. "I am glad you like the Gypsy-Scholar—but what does it *do* for you? Homer *animates*—Shakespeare *animates*—the Gypsy-Scholar at its best awakens a pleasing melancholy. But this is not what we want." (Arnold to Clough, 30 November 1853, *Matthew Arnold's Letters to Arthur Hugh Clough,* ed. H. F. Lowry (1932) 146).

3. Keats to J. H. Reynolds, 3 February 1818, "We hate poetry that has a palpable design upon us—and if we do not agree, seems to put its hand in its breeches pocket . . . I will cut all this—I will have no more of Wordsworth" (*Letters* i 244).

4. Letter to Blackwood of 24 February 1861, *The George Eliot Letters* ed. Gordon Haight [1978], and for the earlier reference *Letters* [*George Eliot Letters*] i 34.

5. Recorded in J. W. Gullard's unpublished letter of 24 June 1913, cited Irvin Stock, *William Hale White (Mark Rutherford)* (1956) 3n.

6. "Wordsworth," *The Complete Prose Works of Matthew Arnold,* ed. R. H. Super (1960-77), ix 48-9. The lines quoted are from *The Excursion* iv 73-6.

7. Letter of 19 April 1880, *Letters* [*The George Eliot Letters*] vii 261-2.

8. *Letters to Clough* [*Matthew Arnold's Letters to Arthur Hugh Clough*], 36.

9. *Matthew Arnold: Selected Poems and Prose,* ed. Miriam Allot (1978), xvi.

10. Douglas Jefferson, *Eighteenth-Century Prose 1700-1780, The Pelican Book of English Prose,* ed. Kenneth Allott (1956) III xxii.

11. See "Pagan and Medieval Religious Sentiment," ". . . the imaginative reason . . . the element by which the modern spirit, if it would live right, has chiefly to live" (*Complete Prose Works* [*The Complete Prose Works of Matthew Arnold*] iii 230).

12. James Joyce, *Stephen Hero,* ed. Theodore Spencer (1944) 67, 135.

13. Letter to James Taylor, 15 January 1851, *The Brontes: Their Lives, Friendships and Correspondence* (ed. Wise and Symons, 1932) iii 199.

14. *Letters to Clough,* 25.

15. Quoted in Mr. Humphry Ward's *A Writer's Recollections* (1918) 44. The lines of verse are from Arnold's "Austerity of Poetry" (1867).

16. *Stephen Hero, ed. cit.* 22.

17. *Literature and Dogma* (1873) repr. *Complete Prose Works* ix, vi, 389, 391-2.

18. Quotations from "A Farewell" (11.20, 32, 49-50), "Meeting" (11.29-30, 12), "Isolation. To Marguerite" (1.24).

19. Preface to *God and the Bible* (1875), *Complete Prose Works* vii 377.

20. "Wordsworth," *Complete Prose Works* ix 50.

21. Letter of 24 February 1848, *Letters to Clough* 66. On Mr. Wright, see Preface to *Essays in Criticism, Complete Prose Works* iii 286.

22. *Dipsychus,* Sc. iv, 130-203.

23. Letter of 12 February 1853, *Letters to Clough* 128.

24. Kenneth Allott, unpublished lectures. I owe more than I can say to these for many points made in this part of the paper.

25. I am deeply indebted to Mrs. Mary Moorman who generously made a gift to me of Arnold's copy of this edition, which contains his transcription of "The Bright Star!" sonnet.

26. "Resignation," 1.214.

27. See *Matthew Arnold. The Complete Poems* (ed. Kenneth Allott, 1965), second edition, 1979, Appendix I, pp. 714-16.

28. *Letters to Clough* 34, 92.

29. *Letters of Matthew Arnold,* ed. George Russell (1895) ii, 28; Poems, 1979 edition, 588.

30. For a commentary on these lines, including their expression of "a deep organic need for release from conflict and tension," see *Poems* [*The Poems of Matthew Arnold*], 1979 edition [London: Longman], 354.

James A. Berlin (essay date winter 1983)

SOURCE: Berlin, James A. "Matthew Arnold's Rhetoric: The Method of an Elegant Jeremiah." *Rhetoric Society Quarterly* 13, no. 1 (winter 1983): 29-40.

[*In the following essay, Berlin argues that Arnold's work exhibits rhetorical strategies that draw on both Platonic (in epistemology) and Aristotelian (in style) rhetoric while simultaneously refuting aspects of both models. In the context of this analysis, Berlin presents a reading of the structure and rhetoric of* Culture and Anarchy.]

Despite the wealth of commentary on Arnold's prose, there have been few attempts to consider his method from the perspective of classical rhetoric, particularly the rhetorics of Ancient Greece. Yet Arnold's education, both early and late, was rooted in the Greek tradition. English schools in the nineteenth century underwent a shift in emphasis from Roman to Greek authors, and Arnold's father was at the center of this development—in the public schools through his example at Rugby and at Oxford through his ties with such figures as Edward Copleston and Richard Whately.[1] The elder Arnold's estimate of the value of Aristotle's rhetoric was in fact so high that, in a letter of 1841, he comments: "We have been reading some of the Rhetoric in the Sixth Form this half year, and its immense value struck me again so forcibly that I could not consent to send my son to an University where he would lose it altogether."[2] Mathew Arnold's acquiescence in this Greek revival is obvious throughout his work—most obviously in his marked preference for Greek over Roman models in his pronouncements on art and society.

There are, however, two notable exceptions to this neglect of Arnold's classical orientation in rhetoric. In "Mathew Arnold: The Critic as Rhetorician," Everett Lee Hunt attempts to draw Arnold as a follower of Aristotle in his rhetorical practice. His argument is strained, however, due to his repeated noting of the antithetical Platonic elements in Arnold as a follower of Aristotle in his rhetorical practice, and by his admission at the very start that "(Aristotle's) rhetoric was not in Arnold's mind."[3] A better treatment of Arnold's classical orientation is Walter J. Hipple's "Matthew Arnold, Dialectician," an essay that is not intended to be about Arnold's rhetoric at all but about the systematic nature of his philosophical thought. Hipple sees Arnold as a Platonic dialectician, but not a follower of Plato. He explains: "By declaring Arnold a Platonist, I do not, of course, affirm that he is a disciple of Plato, adopting Plato's principles and subscribing to his doctrine; neither do I imply that Arnold is consciously modelling even his dialectical technique upon that of Plato. I man rather that Arnold is a dialectician, and that, as Plato's is the archetype of dialectical philosophies, Arnold's may be rightly called Platonic."[4] Taken together, Hunt and Hipple present a tantalizing problem. The one sees Arnold's prose as Aristotelian. The other places Arnold within Plato's camp in matters of philosophy, yet argues that Arnold is not a Platonist.

Despite the apparent contradiction, both observers are correct: Arnold is both Aristotelian and Platonic in his method and, simultaneously, opposed to both Aristotle and Plato. The key to the puzzle is to be found in Arnold's synthesis of the rhetorical theories of the two, a synthesis of elements that is itself a prime demonstration of Arnold's rhetorical method. Arnold conceives of his persuasive task in terms of the categories of Aristotelian rhetoric, the system that established the language in which rhetoric has been discussed for 2300 years. Yet this Aristotelian language and technique is used in the service of a Platonic scheme of thought, a scheme based on an epistemology and psychology totally opposed to the Aristotelian world view, including that found in the *Rhetoric*. Before explaining how Arnold carries off this difficult feat, it will be helpful to take a brief look at Aristotelian rhetoric.

Aristotle makes rhetoric's prime objective the discovery of the means for persuasion. The communication situation is seen as the interaction among the elements of what has come to be called the rhetorical triangle—a configuration made up of reality, audience, and speaker or writer. Aristotle assigns each of these a set of persuasive procedures appropriate to it: reality is discussed in terms of the appeal to the emotions—the psychological analysis; and the writer is described in terms of the ethical appeal—the speaker's established through the use of language. Considered from the point of view of philosophy, the elements of the triangle comprise three groups of relationships with the writer at the center of each—forming sets of concerns involving epistemology (writer-reality), psychology (writer-audience), and aesthetics or style (writer-language).[5]

Arnold always conceives of rhetoric within this triad. He substitutes, however, a Platonic epistemology and psychology for an Aristotelian scheme, remaining loyal to Aristotle only in the matter of style, the use of language to establish the writer's ethos. In other words, the surface structure—the style and ethos—of Arnold's prose is Aristotelian, while the deep structure—the epistemology and psychology—is decidedly Platonic. This essay will first set forth the theoretical deep structure of Arnold's rhetoric and then show how it is manifested practically in *Culture and Anarchy*. Doing so will reveal that Arnold's rhetoric describes a way of knowing as well as a way of communicating.

I

The contemporary interpretation of Plato's epistemology most useful in considering Arnold is expressed in Robert Cushman's *Therepeia, Plato's Conception of Philosophy,* and in Stanley Fish's application of it to rhetoric in *Self-Consuming Artifacts, The Aesthetic of the Good Physician.* Strong precedents for these readings are also available in the nineteenth century, especially in Coleridge and in Benjamin Jowett, the latter a tutor during Arnold's residence at Balliol and later a translator of Plato.[6] From this point of view, "the central theme of Platonism regarding knowledge [is that] TRUTH IS NOT BROUGHT TO MAN, BUT MAN TO THE TRUTH." Another way of saying this is that truth can be learned, but not taught. Yet Plato was most decidedly a teacher, so how does he solve the problem of teaching the unteachable? The answer is found in dialectic, the interaction of two speakers engaged in the search for truth. As Plato explains in the *Phaedrus,* dialectic involves Smyth—"the comprehension of scattered particulars in one idea"—and analysis—"the division into species according to the natural formation, where the joint is, not breaking any part as a bad carver might" (Jowett [*The Dialogues of Plato*], II, 144). What is significant about this dialectical process is that it does not discover truth; it leads to truth. The explanation of this important distinction can be found in Plato's discussion of Rhetoric.

In the *Phaedrus,* Plato distinguishes between the rhetorician and the dialectician, a distinction corresponding to the difference between the bad-lover and the good-lover of the same dialogue.[7] The rhetorician—Plato's sophist who in many respects corresponds to the negative view of rhetoric held today—strives to tell the audience what they already hold true and want to have confirmed. He also tries to comfort his audience, pleasing them through flattery, speaking to their most sensual and most base instincts. This kind of text, accordingly, conforms to the established rules of logic of aesthetics, following conventional modes of thought and perception. It claims to contain truth, not to lead to its discovery, and places the source of its authority in the external world, independent of the observer. The product of the rhetorician is not concerned with morality or with questioning the ignorance and corruption of its audience. Thus, established views are encouraged and pride and complacency invited.

The dialectical experience is quite another matter. Dialectic is disruptive because it makes the respondent dissatisfied with his store of opinions. The aim is the recognition and removal of error, a process that is frequently painful since unpleasant personal truths must be faced. The respondent is encouraged to break out of his or her perceptual set, becoming free of the material in order to discover within and for the self what is above and beyond the material. The audience for the dialectician is the best self of the individual, the self obscured by convention. The discourse that arises from dialectic is not logical, orderly, and attractive. Progress towards truth through the discovery of error is uneven and depends on the souls of the interlocutors. Most importantly, dialectic can never express the truth, but can only prepare the soul to discover it, finding it not outside in the material world, but within. As Fish explains, knowledge becomes "the transformation of the mind *into* the object of knowledge" (Fish [*Self-Consuming Artifacts*], p. 19). The discovery is totally within and does not rely on external forms. Finally, dialectic constantly challenges expectations, encouraging dissatisfaction and humility.

Arnold's thinking about truth and the way it is best shared corresponds to this view in surprising ways. The distinction between the rhetorician and dialectician—in Arnold's terms, the rhetorician and the critic or man of culture and intelligence—appears in *Higher Schools and Universities in Germany.* There Arnold paraphrases a section from the *Phaedrus:*

> Nay, as Socrates amusingly said, the man who defers to clap-trap and the man who uses his intelligence are, when they meet in the struggle of active politics, like a doctor and a confectioner competing for the suffrages of a constituency of schoolboys; the confectioner has nearly every point in his favor. The confectioner deals in all that the constituency like. The doctor is the man who hurts them, and makes them leave off what they like and take what is disagreeable. And accordingly the temptation, in dealing with the public and with the trade of active politics, the temptation to be a confectioner is extremely strong, and we see that almost all leading newspapers and leading politicians do in fact yield to it.[8]

The echoes of Plato are striking. The rhetorician panders to the common traits of his audience, while the critic presents what is disruptive because he requires that the ordinary self be left behind. The same contrast is made in the conclusion to *Culture and Anarchy,* where the lasting effect of Plato is compared to the ephemeral impression made by Pericles. And in **"A French Critic on Milton,"** the limitations of the rhetorician are presented in scathing detail. Rhetoric appeals to "readers who seek for praise and blame to suit their own already established likes and dislikes" and is characterized by mere "brilliant writing" (VIII, 166).[9] Against this is placed the authentic critic, the observer who works "to utter real truth about his object" (VIII, 166).[10] And in mentioning truth, we are once again back to the question of epistemology.

For Arnold, truth is discovered through the dialectical interaction of opposing variables. These are most often simply dualities combining to form a synthesis that is more than the parts that go into it. As Hipple explains: "two or three or four of them [variables or polarities] may be employed in a given dialectical situation, and the guise which any one assumes is forever different." The reason for this shifting, explains Hipple, is "a fluid universe, from the stream of which analysis separates for a moment some aspect of things and synthesis relates this fragment to the totality of knowledge and judgment" (Hipple ["Matthew Arnold, Dialectician"], p. 5). Hipple is very close to the target. Arnold's dialectical use of analysis and synthesis is simply a reflection of Plato's explanation of the dialectic in the *Phaedrus.* The method gets a detailed discussion in **"The Function of Criticism at the Present Time,"** where Arnold describes the process of analysis and discovery—the business of the philosopher—and synthesis and exposition—the work of the artist. By the end of the section, the critic is seen to perform both functions himself. In Plato's terms, he is becoming a dialectician. Furthermore, the variables he opposes to each other are frequently more than two because the principle polarities—Hebraism and Hellenism, for example—are simply analyzed into their numerous parts—according to where "the joint is," as Plato would say—before being synthesized into a harmonious whole.

Arnold is always reluctant to say exactly what wholeness in art, society, culture and the like will mean. This the reader must discover alone, and he offers an explanation for his reticence in the Preface to *Essays in Criticism.*

> To try and approach truth on one side after another, not to strive or cry, not to persist in pressing forward, on any one side, with violence and self-will—it is only thus, it seems to me, that mortals may hope to gain any vision of the mysterious Goddess, whom we shall never see except in outline, but only thus even in outline. He who will do nothing but fight impetuously towards her on his own, one favourite, particular line, is inevitably destined to run his head into the folds of the black robe in which she is wrapped.
>
> (III, 286)

In a passage originally following this one but later omitted, Arnold goes on to explain the anti-rational nature of this perception of truth, speaking in a way that places him within the Platonic tradition:

But the truth is, I have never been able to hit it off happily with the logician, and it would be mere affectation in me to give myself airs of doing so. They imagine truth something to be proved, I something to be seen; they something to be manufactured, I as something to be found. I have a profound respect for the elaborate machine-work of my friends the logicians. I have always thought that all machine-work of theirs came from an intuition, to which they gave a grand name of their own. How did they come by this intuition? Ah! if they could tell us that. But no; they set their machine in motion, and build up a fine showy edifice, glittering and unsubstantial like a pyramid of eggs.

(III, 535-536)

Truth is discovered by and within the individual, not formulated and packaged within a discourse. And so the writer must present what led up to this discovery of truth, thereby ridding the reader of error, of false turns in the search. The truth itself can never be stated or logically demonstrated, and attempts to do so lead to the "fine, showy edifice" of rhetoric, "glittering and insubstantial like a pyramid of eggs." It is for this reason, I think, that Arnold continually stresses "delicacy of perception" and the judgment which "comes almost of itself"(III, 283).

II

Examining how this dialectic plays into Arnold's psychology reveals a great deal about its operation. Arnold did not posit a fast and hard set of faculties in the manner of Coleridge or Mill. Instead, he speak of powers: "the power of conduct, the power of intellect and knowledge, the power of beauty, and the power of social life and manners" (VIII, 61-62). Arnold always, however, displays the Platonic preference of the one over the many, so that it is ever his determination that these powers unite together in harmonious wholeness. Arnold explains that "these powers . . . are not isolated, but there is, in the generality of mankind, a perpetual tendency to relate them to one another in diverse ways" (X, 59). The powers must operate together if truth is to be attained, but the exact nature of the truth discovered is never elucidated: once again, it can be learned, but not taught. What Arnold offers instead— what the authentic critic is to offer—is an example of the powers working together in responding to contemporary experience, whether literary, moral, intellectual, or social. The defects of the practical proposals others offer are examined in the light of their failure or success in satisfying all the demands of the powers, and even Arnold's own thinking is measured in this way. Thus, Hebraism is described as appealing too exclusively to conduct and manners, while Hellenism is thought to be too determined by the need to see knowledge and beauty prevail. Either alone is incomplete.[11]

These then are the powers that go into making Arnold's dialogue with the reader. He attempts to appeal to these powers in order to create in the reader an interaction of each power with all, an important departure from Plato in that written language rather than an actual dialogue is involved. Yet Arnold often takes pains to shape his essays in the spirit of the dialogue by carrying on a pretended conversation with an adversary—such as in *Culture and Anarchy*—or by reporting a dialogue—in the manner of *Friendship's Garland*—or by using the conversational style found in both as well as in *Literature and Dogma*. All of these present Arnold displaying the dialectical interplay of the powers in an attempt to achieve wholeness, or showing the failure of the powers to achieve wholeness. Once again, the exact nature of the product of all the faculties acting together is never stated.

Arnold can likewise be observed addressing these powers in his audience, following Plato's suggestion in the *Phaedrus* that the philosopher-rhetorician—if there can be such a thing—must know the nature of the soul so that he can make his message appropriate to his audience. Arnold often discusses this matter of appealing to his audience in his letters to friends and publishers. And anyone who has read at length in his collected works has noticed the difference in tone in *Friendship's Garland* and *Culture and Anarchy,* or the shifts in critical emphasis in his literary essays. These contrasts are largely the result of Arnold altering the message to suit the group being addressed.

What is more to the point, however, is that Arnold's style in these essays often bears a concern for polish and order that is more characteristic of an Aristotelian than a Platonic rhetorician. After all, Aristotle gave the primacy to persuasion in his treatise on rhetoric, not to knowing and communicating truth—although this is not to say that the truth was unimportant to him. Arnold admits to this anti-Platonic inclination in an 1863 letter to his mother: "Partly nature, partly time and study have also by this time taught me thoroughly the precious truth that everything turns upon one's exercising the power of *persuasion,* of *charm*; that without them all fury, energy, reasoning power, acquirement, are thrown away and only render their owner more miserable." In still another letter he admits being apprehensive "that if I cannot charm the wild beast of Philistinism while I am trying to convert him, of being torn to pieces by him."[12] These statements point to the tension in Arnold between the Platonic rhetoric of conversion through challenge and disruption, and the Aristotelian rhetoric of charm and persuasion.

Arnold seems to be responding to a problem at the core of the Platonic notion of dialectic: the dialogue is to have no concern for beauty, yet is to lead to the perception of the true, the good, and the beautiful—again the one including the many. In his own day Arnold had been labelled a "Jeremiah," and in one notable instance, an "elegant Jeremiah" (*Works* [*The Complete Prose*

Works of Matthew Arnold], V. 88). There is a certain appropriateness to this latter appellation since even as Arnold criticizes and questions, he is trying to charm. In more than one place, moreover, he says that beauty is only truth seen from another side, further indicating the need he felt to merge the Platonic rhetoric of disruption with the grace of an Aristotelian product. I must also add that we need only include goodness to have the Platonic merger of the true, the good, and the beautiful—a union which Arnold himself makes in indicating the powers which make up the individual.

III

In the last section of this essay, I would like to apply all that I have said of Arnold's rhetoric to *Culture and Anarchy,* showing not only Arnold's anti-rhetorical Platonic base, but his skill as an Aristotelian rhetorician persuading through charm. Aristotle's logical proofs are, of course, unavailable to Arnold because of his suprarational epistemology, and the pathetic appeal is muted because it threatens the harmonious balance of all the powers. But Arnold does not hesitate to turn to the support for his case provided by the ethical plea, seeking to win the reader's approval while simultaneously attacking the very basis of the reader's vital beliefs and convictions. Arnold's problem is a vexing one: How does one charm while censuring?

The success of *Culture and Anarchy* represents a triumph of structure and tone. The first is the manifestation of Arnold's original use of the Platonic dialectical mode, in his hand a method perfectly suited to grace and precision. The second emerges from Arnold's deft treatment of the ethical appeal, creating a voice which the reader is eventually convinced is trustworthy. Both structure and tone make palatable Arnold's basically harsh message.

The structure of the essay as a whole as well as each section of it proceeds along the lines of successive stages of synthesis and analysis, with Arnold alternating between discussions of the one, and the many making up the one. When *Culture and Anarchy* is viewed as a whole, this movement is apparent in so simple a matter as the titles of the individual essays. The analysis of culture in **"Sweetness and Light"** is followed by **"Doing as One Likes,"** with a play on "one" so that it means both narrow individualism and the unified harmony of culture. Chapter three is called **"Barbarians, Philistines, Populace"** and Chapter four **"Hebraism and Hellenism."** This analysis into parts is once again followed by the repetition of the need for unity, again with the play on "one" in **"Porro Unum Est Necessarium."** Chapter six, **"Our Liberal Practitioners,"** is meant to form the analytical and practical counterpart to the theoretical sweetness and light of unified culture found in the first chapter.

These titles also point to another feature of Arnold's dialectic: the tendency to make paired contraries the center of the discussion. While three items may from time to time appear, as in the classes, these are, at the same time, synthesized into a larger scheme of polar contraries—Hebraism and Hellenism, for example—or are themselves analyzed into sets of polar contraries. Even when Arnold calls upon the Aristotelian tripartite division of virtue—excess, defect and mean—he discusses the *excess* in relation to the mean in one chapter, and the *defect* in relation to the mean in the next. And all of this is more than just a device to order content or to facilitate memory: it is part and parcel of Arnold's view of how truth, or at least the discovery of truth, is structured.

Arnold's characteristic mode of development—alternating analysis and synthesis—can be seen operating in **"Sweetness and Light,"** the first chapter of the piece. In the "Introduction," Arnold has focused on the attacks against his idea of culture made by Bright and by Frederic Harrison, and the first chapter will eventually be seen to be an elaborate and deft answer to this critique, an explanation of the errors in this view. Arnold's initial presentation of the notion of culture is followed by an analysis of it into its components. It is described, in turn, as the pursuit of perfection, an inward perfection, a perfection that prevails throughout society, and a perfection harmonious in the individual and society. This concept is then applied as a measure in examining the worth of Arnold's society, itself divided into component features—faith in machinery, in wealth, and in health and vigour. All are found inadequate to the ideal of culture, now presented as the embodiment of sweetness and light. This dialectical standard is then applied to Nonconformist religion and the lifestyle it encourages. The Nonconformists are, of course, found wanting, and against their view of religion is placed the religious spirit of the Oxford movement, a superior spiritual force. It, however, is defeated by its rival, now seen in political terms as the Liberal cause. This group is presently facing a challenge from a new sphere, the democratic fervor of the lower class. Arnold has at last gotten to Harrison, a spokesman for the new democracy. His system is found to be totally inadequate to the aims it proposes, while culture, the very thing attacked by this system, seems to offer all that Harrison and those he represents want.

This dialectical pattern of successive synthesis and analysis, the presentation of dialectical pairs, and the placing of Arnold's views against those of his opponents appears throughout *Culture and Anarchy.* In subsequent chapters, the concept of culture is expanded as it is analyzed into new parts, parts again synthesized into dialectical pairs, such as Hebraism and Hellenism. And as Holloway points out,[13] Arnold is himself using the method he wishes to recommend as adequate to deal with the problems of the age. Arnold persistently works to approach "truth on one side after another, not to strive or cry, not to persist in pressing forward, on any one side with violence and self-will," in the manner of his opponents. He is himself displaying the free play he advocates, but, it should be noted, a free play which has as its aim the exposing of error. Arnold is not offering truth absolute and eternal. As he says in discussing St. Paul, it is questionable whether "anyman's expression can be a perfect and final expression of truth" (V, 182). What he is recommending instead is a method which involves the development of the whole person so that all the faculties are involved in the discovery of truth. This, of course, is the dialectical method in that all the powers taken together provide truth, not any one exclusively—as seen, for example, in the individual classes. But it is also dialectical in another sense: the errors of political policies, for example, can be recognized by measuring the extent to which they are commensurate with the demands of the whole person, the individual in whom all the powers are acting in harmony.

In **"Liberal Practitioners,"** once again the counterpart to the first chapter, Arnold shows how this standard of harmonious wholeness might be applied by looking at the Nonconformist hostility against Church-establishments, the Real Estate Intestacy Bill, and the proposal for marriage to a deceased wife's sister. His opponents are found mistaken in each case because they take one part of human nature—one of the powers—and make it tyrannize over the others. Thus, a person needs freedom of thought in religion, but he or she also needs a sense of community with others—community provided aplenty by an established church. Similarly, the Real Estate Intestacy Bill is based on the worship of "wealth and station"—what might be considered the need for a certain kind of social life and manners—instead of "intelligence and strenuous virtue." Finally, the marriage of a man to his dead wife's sister should be prevented because, although it is not contrary to the morality of the Old Testament, it violates our sense of the beauty and fitness of things in the relationship of husband and wife.

Throughout *Culture and Anarchy,* Arnold continually plays the role of a Jeremiah, finding reason for regret in the very events celebrated by his contemporaries. In his treatment of the classes, for example, no one escapes his wrath. Yet all of this is ameliorated—is even made elegant—by the tone which Arnold embraces, his diplomatic use of the ethical appeal.[14] In the words of Aristotle, Arnold everywhere gives the "impression of intelligence, character and goodwill"[15] in order to establish confidence with his audience even as he is criticizing it. One way he does this is to place himself within the group that he most forcefully assaults, the Philistines, throughout identifying himself as a Liberal and a member of the middle class, often prefacing his most scathing indictments of his class with this admission. He also appeals to this class by constantly using its language: the terms of the clergy and the Bible. And he takes pains to criticize that which his audience is sure to dislike; Roman Catholicism, for example. His fault finding in treating the classes is further made less provocative by his indicating a virtue that is a counterpart of every fault. All classes can point with pride to their virtues, while their vices, after all, are made less reprehensible since they are only defects or excesses of virtues. In the end Arnold does not seem to have much to gain in all of this because he admits at the start that men of culture, like himself, should not at the present time be entrusted with power; he speaks as a critic, with no practical program to offer.

Finally, in introducing the notion of a "best self" Arnold is instructing his readers how to respond—shaping their responses as he gives them a new way of viewing the self. While each class has its flaws, individuals can rise above the class, can be better than the class-bound ordinary self would dictate. By selecting actual quotations from representatives of each class, statements which show these characters at their worst, Arnold has encouraged his readers to become detached from the speakers who ordinarily represent their points of view. Rather than asking the individual reader to identify with some other class, Arnold creates a fourth group, a stratum that includes all the classes, purged of defects and excesses and brought to perfection through the workings of culture. And all of this is couched in language of certainty, a feature which his audience would have found more acceptable than we do since it was what was wanted and needed in an uncertain time. Furthermore, such assurance in delivery was a commonplace in discussions of church, state, and art.

Finally, I would like to add that critics of Arnold's tone—Leslie Stephen or Geoffrey Tillotson, for example—forget that in his polemical essays, Arnold is engaging in a public performance, a kind of ritualized behavior within a rhetorical tradition. His audience—including those he is attacking—are watching for the effectiveness of his ploys as well as for the truth of his account, delighting at the wit displayed even when they themselves are the victims of it. The closest thing to this behavior today—behavior encouraged in schools and debating societies, formal and informal, in the nineteenth century—is to be found in courts of law. There the most spirited adversaries may be good friends. Arnold in fact enjoyed friendly relations with many of those he takes on in his essays—his cousin Huxley, for example.

What has been demonstrated in Arnold's method in considering society in *Culture and Anarchy* can be seen in his dialectic, the presentation of contrary pairs:

energy and intelligence or literature and dogma, for example. Arnold is also continually concerned with correcting error and showing how an appropriate literary or religious response involves the harmonious operation of all the powers. And despite the polemical nature of most of this prose, it displays a charm that continues to attract readers. Thus, in all his criticism, Arnold is systematic, without surrendering to the temptation to erect a system, a structure that claims to encompass the truth. Instead, he offers a method for arriving at truth, a method unlike the new inductive logic of science or the old deductive logic of Aristotelian philosophy. Meant as an alternative to both, Arnold presents a way of knowing that satisfies all the powers of human nature and unlocks them, enabling them to discover truth in the only way he sees possible—in an act of private apprehension, the best self serving as the agent of vision.

Notes

1. M. L. Clarke, *Classical Education in Britain* (Cambridge: University Press, 1959), pp. 76-80; W. R. Ward, *Victorian Oxford* (London: Frank Cass, 1965), pp. 16-17, 57-59.

2. A. P. Stanley, *Life and Correspondence of Thomas Arnold* (London: B. Fellowes, 1844), II, 260.

3. Everett Lee Hunt, "Matthew Arnold: The Critic as Rhetorician," *The Quarterly Journal of Speech,* XXII (1934), p. 484.

4. Walter J. Hipple, Jr., "Matthew Arnold, Dialectician," *University of Toronto Quarterly,* XXXII (1962), 5.

5. James Kinneavy, *A Theory of Discourse* (New York: W. W. Norton, 1971), pp. 18-19.

6. See James A. Berlin "The Rhetoric of Romanticism: The Case for Coleridge," *Rhetoric Society Quarterly,* X (1980), pp. 62-74; and B. Jowett, trans., *The Dialogues of Plato* (Oxford: Oxford at the Clarendon Press, 1871), pp. 75-102. References to Plato are to the Jowett translation.

7. Robert Cushman, *Therepeia: Plato's Conception of Philosophy* (Chapel Hill: University of North Carolina Press), 1958, p. 213.

8. In discussing the rhetorician and the dialectician, I am summarizing Stanley E. Fish, *Self-Consuming Artifacts, The Aesthetic of the Good Physician* (Berkeley: University of California Press, 1972), pp. 17-20.

9. R. H. Super, ed., *The Complete Prose Works of Matthew Arnold* (Ann Arbor: University of Michigan Press, 1960-1978), VIII, 26.

10. This also explains Arnold's preference in prose for what Lewis E. Gates has called "scenes that are satirically and even maliciously suggestive." See *Three Studies in Literature* (New York: Macmillan, 1899), p. 185.

11. See Gates, pp. 129-139, for a similar position presented from a somewhat different perspective.

12. George W. E. Russell, *Letters of Matthew Arnold 1848-1888* (London: Macmillan, 1901), I, 234, 240.

13. John Holloway, *The Victorian Sage* (London: Macmillan, 1956), pp. 206-207.

14. Holloway, Chap. VII, offers the best treatment of the ethical appeal.

15. *The Rhetoric of Aristotle,* trans. Lane Cooper (New York: D. Appleton, 1932), p. 92.

Emerson R. Marks (essay date 1998)

SOURCE: Marks, Emerson R. "Matthew Arnold." In *Taming the Chaos: English Poetic Diction Theory Since the Renaissance,* pp. 197-215. Detroit: Wayne State University Press, 1998.

[*In the following essay, Marks examines Arnold's belief in the cultural importance of poetry, particularly to the Victorian Age. He defends Arnold's famous use of "touchstones," suggesting that they serve their intended purpose: to improve the public's taste.*]

Despite the temperamental hostility to rational analysis so often deplored in Arnold's literary, social, and religious thought, his pervasive influence on Anglo-American academic literary study faded only with the advent of the New Criticism. As regards poetics, his enduring authority owed much to the impressive ancestry of his persuasion that abstract formulations of how poets use words were fruitless. Earlier versions include the Renaissance "je ne sais quoi," Pope's "nameless graces which no precepts can declare," and the Romantic sense of the ineffability of poetic beauty most arrestingly exemplified in Schlegel's dogma that it could be articulated only in poetry.

Since, however, it is widely assumed that the mysteries of versification are best made less mysterious by reasoned analysis, Arnold's disinclination to apply it may well have contributed to a certain undervaluing of his abiding concern with the subject. This was actuated by a personal sensitivity to "the consummate felicity in diction" of which he deplored the lack in Byron, and which in one of its many varieties he labeled "natural magic." Students of Arnold are surely right to stress in his criticism the cognitive and moral themes which he himself made central; but in doing so they have tended to slight the aesthetic qualities which he considered equally requisite to the weighty cultural mission which he thought poets were uniquely called upon to fulfill. Cardinal Richelieu, he observed in **"The Literary Influence of Academies"** (1864), wisely saw in the French Academy an instrument for strengthening and perpetuating "the *ethical* influences of style in language," influences exerted most powerfully in great verse. In Homer's epics Arnold found nothing more edifying than their style, and in his General Report of 1878 as school inspector he stressed the invaluable formative effect the diction and rhythm of good poetry could have even on readers uncertain of its meaning.[1]

With some impatience toward those less aesthetically percipient, he prided himself on an ability to detect "the ring of false metal" in the tinny rhetoric of Macaulay's *Lays of Ancient Rome,* in which he could hardly read the lines,

> To all men upon this earth
> Death cometh soon or late,

"without a cry of pain." The intemperate tone occasionally evident in the bill of complaint against what struck him as the detestable style of Francis Newman's English *Iliad* measures the depth of its affront to Arnold's sensibilities, just as the matchless language of Homer himself moved him to one of his rare lyrical effusions.

> For Homer's grandeur is not the mixed and turbid grandeur of the great poets of the north, of the authors of *Othello* and *Faust*; it is a perfect, a lovely grandeur. Certainly his poetry has all the energy and power of our ruder climates; but it has, besides, the pure lines of an Ionian horizon, the liquid clearness of an Ionian sky.[2]

An appraisal of Arnold's opinions about poetic language can usefully take as *points d'appui* two dicta from the last decade of his life. The later one maintains the inferiority of prose to verse in "power." More importantly, it commits him to the idea that verse constitutes a distinct category of utterance, a commitment from which Arnold never shrank. Admiring Johnson's *Lives of the English Poets* for its admirable conformity to "the true law of prose," he was careful to discriminate.

> Prose requires a different style from poetry.

> Poetry, no doubt, is more excellent in itself than prose. In poetry man finds the highest and most beautiful expression of that which is in him. . . . Poetry has a different *logic,* as Coleridge said, from prose; poetical style follows another order of evolution than the style of prose.

In Arnold's conception the distinction is generic. Poetic simplicity, "that perfectly simple, limpid style, which is the supreme style of all," is not a rarefied variety of the simplicity of prose. It issues rather from a momentary remission of the emotive intensity which characterizes poetic composition as a whole. In Shakespeare this relaxation yields "the golden, easeful, crowning moments of a manner which is always pitched in another manner from that of prose, a manner changed and heightened."[3]

None of this should be allowed to obscure Arnold's very real sense of the aesthetic virtues of prose, to which he paid tribute in "Maurice de Guérin" (1863). Guérin's *The Centaur,* "a sort of prose poem," he found more instinct with "the magical power of poetry" than the same poet's work in the staple alexandrine meter. Metrical forms, even those which have served as proven vehicles for the monuments of poetic art—such as Greek hexameters, English blank verse, and French alexandrines—can sometimes impose unacceptable restrictions on a poet's freedom of expression. Worst of all in this regard, Arnold thought, was the alexandrine. A poet of genius had better adopt "a more adequate vehicle, metrical or not," for conveying his thoughts.[4] Arnold was not the first champion of metrical utterance to find his faith challenged by the allure of one or another piece of imaginative prose—nor the last.

Yet his sense of a generic gap between prose and verse, however vaguely conceived at times, was always in the forefront of his consciousness, even in casual judgmental remarks. Of a passage of lush natural description by Ruskin he suggests that the author was trying to do in prose what can only be well done in verse. The "key" in which verse is pitched even justified to his mind the traditional poetic locutions on which some critics in the previous century had founded the crucial difference between the two forms. Archaisms like *spake* for *spoke, aye* for *ever, don* for *put on* constitute "the poetic vocabulary, as distinguished from the vocabulary of common speech and of modern prose." Twentieth-century readers inclined to balk at such archaisms as passé might reflect on Hart Crane's recourse to them in his verse and Owen Barfield's theoretical approval of them as features natural to poetic expression.[5]

The earlier of Arnold's two dicta might stand as topic sentence to an account of his entire thought about the poet's use of language. "Now poetry is nothing less than the most perfect speech of man, that in which he comes nearest to being able to utter the truth."[6] Occurring in an essay on Wordsworth, who regarded the poet primarily as one human being addressing others, Arnold's definition is framed appropriately to his immediate subject. Otherwise though, his summary generalization is thrown out without either supporting justification or the badly needed clarification of its terms. In what does "perfection" consist? and what, here, is the precise import of "truth"? In default of clear answers to such questions, we are forced to contrive shaky inferences from the evidence scattered throughout Arnold's critical writings. Of this more below. For the moment it is worth noting that the two clauses of his sentence comprehend the twin aspects of poetry on which Arnold from first to last dwelt with increasing emphasis, and which he came more and more to conceive as interdependent coordinates of its mode of being. These are a unique manipulation of the verbal medium and a cognitive-moral value for which no other kind of discourse provides an adequate substitute. The nature and evaluation of this discourse leads, in Arnold, directly to his "touchstones."

Almost two decades before he introduced *touchstone* into the English critical lexicon, in **"The Study of Poetry"** (1880), Arnold made extensive use of the device itself in a series of lectures delivered during his tenure of the Oxford Professorship of Poetry and printed in 1861 as **On Translating Homer.** He knew no more effective means of conveying to his hearers some sense of the superlative qualities that constituted the "grand style." After quoting two stanzas from Walter Scott's *Marmion,* which he thought below that level of excellence, he offers a defense of his procedure.

> I may discuss what, in the abstract, constitutes the grand style, but that sort of general discussion never much helps our judgment of particular instances. I may say that the presence or absence of the grand style can only be spiritually discerned; and this is true, but to plead this looks like evading the difficulty. My best way is to take eminent specimens of the grand style, and to put them side by side with this of Scott.

He chose four such specimens for the purpose, from the *Iliad,* the *Aeneid,* the *Divine Comedy,* and *Paradise Lost:*

> ἀλλά, φίλος, θάνε καὶ σύ; τί ἦ ὀλοφύρεαι οὕτως;
> κάτθανε καὶ πάτροκλος; ὅ περ σέο πολλὸν ἀμείνων.
>
> [But come, friend, die yourself; why lament in this way? Patroclus
> also died, a far better man than you.]
>
> (*Iliad,* XXI, 106-7)

> Disce, puer, virtutem ex me verumque laborem,
> Fortunam ex aliis.
>
> [Learn valor and true toil from me, my boy; from others learn
> good luck.]
>
> (*Aeneid,* XII, 435-36)

> Lascio lo fele, e vo per dolci pomi
> Promessi a me per lo verace Duca;
> Ma fino al centro pria convien ch' io tomi.

> [I leave the gall and seek after the sweet apples promised me by
> the true Guide; but first I must fall to the very center.]
>
> (*Inferno,* XVI, 61-63)

> His form had not yet lost
> All her original brightness, nor appeared
> Less than archangel ruined, and the excess
> Of glory obscured.
>
> (*Paradise Lost,* Book I, 591-94)

Like the touchstones given in **"The Study of Poetry,"** these fragments all exhibit Arnold's penchant for expressions of heroic resignation, self-denial, and stoic acceptance of tribulation. Except for the *Aeneid,* the works they represent were all to supply additional samples for the later list. The absence of any from Shakespeare, who was to provide two touchstones in 1880, suggests that Arnold had yet to slough off a youthful disdain for his verbal exuberance. The inclusion of Virgil is somewhat surprising, since elsewhere in **On Translating Homer** Arnold treats the long-cherished Virgilian "elegance" as inferior to the Homeric grandeur.[7]

He gives no hint of how grandeur and elegance differ except to insist that grandeur subsists independently of a corresponding dignity of subject matter. In total contradiction of Le Bossu two hundred years earlier, for Arnold the lowliest particulars of the action—eating, drinking, going to bed—occasion no falling off in a nobility of manner which, Arnold never tires of repeating, pervades the entire *Iliad.* He recalls that William Cowper, one of Homer's translators, had complained of how hard it was to render these homely episodes without a lowering of style. In Homer's surmounting that difficulty Arnold sees the main proof of his mastery. Strangely, he makes no reference to Addison's praise of Virgil's ability to describe the manuring of a field with no loss of verbal elegance. Equally strange, since he set such store by the point, is that he never cites a Homeric example. The one doubtful exception is "a passage of the simplest narrative" describing Hector addressing words of encouragement to his allies in battle (*Iliad,* XVII, 216ff.), an instance of "the level regions" of Homer's narrative, which Arnold defends against complaints that they are discords in the heroic strain. The four citations of poetic grandeur deal exclusively with moral elevation, heroic action, or tragic fatality.[8]

Only reluctantly, and still protesting the futility of "verbal definition," did Arnold attempt to formulate his concept, goaded to do so by complaints about the vagueness of his terms *noble* and *grand.* The grand style, he explained, "arises *when a noble nature, poetically gifted, treats with simplicity or with serenity a serious subject.*" This somewhat tautological effort prompted in Arnold's editor W. H. D. Rouse the sobering reflection that no one could improve on Longinus's definition of stylistic grandeur as the expression of a lofty soul. Nonetheless, it becomes clear as he proceeds that he is not merely indulging in the rhetorical gush that sometimes passes muster on the lecture podium. Some of what he says is clear enough. The grand style may never admit the comic. Simplicity and serenity are two of its most important characteristics. Homer is the special master of simple grandeur, while Milton supplies the "best model of the grand style serene." Arnold not only points to examples of each type in Dante, who excels in both, but makes a stab at explaining their peculiar psychological sources. Serenity results from the poet's "saying a thing with a kind of intense compression," as if his mind were burdened with thoughts too numerous and weighty for explicit naming. In one triplet of the *Purgatorio* he finds "a beautiful specimen of the grand style in simplicity, where a noble nature and a poetical gift unite to utter a thing with the most limpid plainness and clarity:

> Tanto dice di farmi sua compagna
> Ch'io sarò là dove fia Beatrice;
> Quivi convien che senza lui rimagna."

> (XXIII, 127-29)

"So long he [Virgil] saith he will bear me company, until I shall be there where Beatrice is: there it behooves that without him I remain"—so Arnold translates, but with the despairing admission that no words of his can convey the "noble simplicity" of Dante's Italian. Then, as though carried away by that consummate example, he declares that the simple style is in fact preferable to the serene, being "the more magical." Arnold cites Pope in support of his own opinion that the *Iliad*'s alliance of consummate expressive simplicity with perfect nobleness is rivaled only in the English Bible. The severe style, he adds somewhat disconcertingly, manifests an intellectual agility that can exist with little or none of the "exquisite faculty" so evident in a simple style: poetic talent.[9]

One might have thought intellectual prowess a prime requisite for the profound application of ideas to life which Arnold exalted in these very lectures and elsewhere as the poets' chief claim to esteem. And yet it was Homer's superb command of the simple variety of stylistic grandeur, he assured his fellow Oxonians, that empowered him in his epics to attain that essential of the poet's moral office with a perfection never since surpassed. All good poetry can stir the heart, but the few masters of the grand style do more: "they refine the raw natural man, they transmute him." Despite the kinks and twists of Arnold's unmethodical presentation, he leaves no doubt that the recipe for his grand style requires a balanced blend of moral, intellectual, and aesthetic ingredients. At no point does he seek to enforce it

by an indiscriminate conflation of the revered epic masterpieces. Though they are equally "grand," the styles of Homer and Milton, he notes, are widely discrepant. The movement of *Paradise Lost* is labored and "self-retarding"; that of the *Iliad,* "flowing, rapid." The opening invocation to the muse in each case alone suffices for illustration, Homer's "ἄειδε, θεά" [sing, goddess] coming in the first line, whereas Milton's "Sing, heavenly muse" is suspended until the sixth. Arnold says little on the role of diction in effecting the grand style, though clearly he thinks it relevant to his thesis. Much of these lectures is given over to a minute destructive analysis of the English vocabulary in which Newman had vainly sought to render the tone and spirit of Homer's Greek. At one point Arnold pronounces Hamlet's image of *grunting* and *sweating* under life's burdens, which Newman adopted in his *Iliad,* to be offensive; at another, he censures George Chapman's "Poor, wretched beasts" as an unsuitable rendition of "ἄ δειλώ," Zeus's apostrophe to Achilles' immortal horses, in a passage to be chosen as a touchstone. The alternative "poor wretches," good enough for a ballad, travesties Homer. (Arnold's own suggestion was "unhappy pair.")[10]

Arnold's recourse to scraps of verse for testing the quality of poetry has had at best a mixed reception. Eliot and Wellek are among those who have objected that lines isolated from their contexts can have little poetic value. Wellek goes so far as to deny that one of Arnold's most prized touchstones, Dante's "E la sua volontate è nostra pace," is even verse.[11]

Though these strictures have merit, they do not justify disparaging the touchstones as an evaluative gimmick. Arnold saw in them an antidote to two fallacious poetic estimates, the historical and the personal. Using the historical estimate, a reader mistakes for intrinsic merit the crucial contribution of a given poet or poem to the development of a nation's poetry. The personal estimate results when a reader overestimates a piece of poetry simply because it happens to appeal to a temperamental idiosyncrasy or stirs memory of an emotionally charged experience. Both estimates impede the sound evaluation which Arnold calls the real one. He claimed that in each of his model passages a tactful reader would find, once it was well lodged in memory, "an infallible touchstone" for ascertaining the worth of any poetry whatsoever. It was probably with Arnold in mind that Arthur Symons, noticing how hard it was for critics to appreciate contemporary poetry, denied that it could be done by "the mere testing of Mr. Yeats or Verlaine by Milton or by Virgil." Though his point is a sound warning against pedantry, one might reply that of two critics otherwise equal in evaluative armament we do well to trust the judgment of the one more thoroughly acquainted with Milton and Virgil, among much else. It is easy to depreciate Arnold's device, with its disquieting suggestion of talismanic powers. It is equally easy to overlook the significant point that by using lines of verse as criteria he grounded his real estimate on the linguistic stuff of which verse is made. His valuation is therefore neither pragmatic, as in the historical estimate, nor unduly affective, as in the personal, and more objective than either.[12]

It is hard to see why John Eels should have concluded that Arnold was insensitive to the aesthetic value of his touchstones, since Eels himself praises their perfection as notable examples of poetic concision and economy, "the best words in the best order" for conveying certain moods. Eels is surely right that the favored excerpts chime with Arnold's pessimistic view of life; right also that as they are taken entirely from tragic drama and epic they reflect the limits of his poetic taste, including his coolness toward the comic. But assuming that their aesthetic quality, with one exception, played no part in Arnold's selection of them, Eels neglects their formal excellence. It is far more likely that Arnold chose them not for their "philosophic" soundness but for their excellence as *poetry,* defined in the essay which introduced them to the public as "thought and art in one"; and that he chose those rather than others of equal poetic merit because they happened to have the additional advantage of embodying what he most deeply felt about human experience. Focusing on this latter motive alone, Eels finds Arnold guilty of his own "personal estimate." But this charge is blunted by the fact that other critics have also praised most of the touchstones, although Arnold may have predisposed a few of them to do so. In a grudging estimate of Arnold's criticism, Eliot, no mean "touchstoner" himself, conceded "the felicity of his quotation: to be able to quote as Arnold did is the best evidence of taste."[13]

The ultimate justification of Arnold's resort to the touchstone method is the pragmatic one validated by his social purpose. He aimed to improve the public's poetic taste, and so dilute the philistinism of the great British middle class to which he himself belonged. What in **"The Scholar Gypsy"** he had deplored as "this strange disease of modern living" required that men and women be taught how to *benefit* from poetry, how to tap the deepest well-springs of its consolatory and sustaining power.[14]

The eleven nuggets of verse Arnold culled in 1880 from Homer, Dante, Shakespeare, and Milton are certainly as remarkable for euphonious diction and movement as for emotive depth or arresting thought. They consist perfectly well, though in varying degrees, with H. F. Lowry's assertion that "with Arnold, as with Carlyle, poetry is musical thought." Yet for Arnold all poetic style, including the grand variety, comprises moral and intellectual content as well. True, he could speak of style as a value-neutral element, a poet's personal cachet, as when he wrote that Wordsworth "has no style," nature seem-

ingly having written his poems for him. But generally, when the subject in any way touches on poetic evaluation, overall excellence and stylistic distinction are synonymous in Arnold.[15]

The citation of Shakespeare among the touchstones is best explained by Arnold's having outgrown his Hellenic fastidiousness of taste. In the Oxford lectures Shakespeare is still of the "so-called" golden age of Elizabethan literature, one "steeped in humours and fantasticality up to its very lips." Much muted in **On the Study of Celtic Literature** (1867), this bias virtually disappears by 1879. Arnold now joins his countrymen in naming Shakespeare and Milton, equally and without reservation, as "our poetical classics," proudly quoting the verdict of a French critic who had recently pronounced the verse of England's greatest dramatic poet to be the most varied and harmonious since the Greeks.[16]

Yet it sometimes appears—the evidence is too inconsistent to be conclusive—that in Arnold's mind two characteristics of the grand style set it off from other poetry of the highest quality, Shakespeare's included. One is a clarity and immediacy of conception conveyed in a limpid nakedness of wording that made him relish Homer's simplicity above Milton's serenity; the other is the capacity to sustain that manner throughout a whole poem, even one of epic length. Coleridge, Eliot, and—notoriously and reductively—Poe denied the possibility or desirability of a lengthy poetic composition being pitched throughout at a high level of intensity. Not so Arnold, who admired the "immortal" lines of Robert Burns's "Farewell to Nancy,"

> Had we never loved sae kindly,
> Had we never loved sae blindly,
> Never met, or never parted,
> We had ne'er been broken-hearted—

only to complain of the author's inability to hold to their level everywhere in his poem. "The rest," he said, "is verbiage." Arnold had no patience with Horace's tolerant concession that Homer himself nods off now and then. On Arnold's reading of him Homer composes "always at his best," is never "quaint and antiquated, as Shakespeare is sometimes." As for grandeur, only in flashes does Shakespeare display the lofty Homeric simplicity, as in Cleopatra's terse invocation of death, "Poor venomous fool, / Be angry and despatch!"[17]

Arnold scorned the judgment of an eminent scholar who found in Tennyson's blank verse the very attributes Arnold had named as the determinants of Homer's greatness, especially *plainness of words and style, simplicity and directness of ideas.* Against what he saw as a typical instance of English blindness to the genuine Greek simplicity, Arnold protested that in Tennyson there is instead an extreme subtlety and curious elaborateness of thought, an extreme subtlety and elaborateness of expression. In the best and most characteristic productions of his genius, these characteristics are most prominent. They are marked characteristics . . . of the Elizabethan poets; they are marked, though not the essential characteristics of Shakespeare himself.

Though distinct from the Shakespearean, it is, he argues, the same fault, manifested in the imagery of such a line as "Now lies the Earth all Danaë to the stars." His main objection is concisely summarized. "In Homer's poetry it is all natural thoughts in natural language; in Mr. Tennyson's poetry it is all distilled thoughts in distilled words." One scents here, as in other Victorian critics, a whiff of Wordsworthian naturalism. But the contrast between Arnold's classically conditioned idea of poetic expression and Wordsworth's is much greater than any shared taste. The two men are separated by the distance between Wordsworth's declared ideal of rustic idiom and what for Arnold constituted the "most perfect speech of man." No one can ever imagine the author of the Prefaces to *Lyrical Ballads* looking with much favor on anything that could be called stylistic grandeur in verse.[18]

Arnold's stress on the simplicity of Homer's stylistic grandeur reflects more than his general disapproval of decorative and ornate verbiage and involuted phrasal structure in poetry. It was also as a poet, concerned with the survival of poetry in the modern world, that he warned against figurative indulgence. This line of argument first appears in the correspondence with his friend Arthur Clough, where it forms part of a youthful dialogue between the two poets on the art in which they hoped to make their marks. At first Arnold pleads for a plain style only because he thought it best suited the maturity of the cultural moment. He flirts here with a historical relativism that would have been hard to reconcile with his later notion of touchstone verses enshrining universally relevant criteria. He is sure that if Shakespeare and Milton had lived in modern England neither would have indulged in "the taking, tourmenté style" then cried up on every hand. Good poetic style is the clearest possible expression of whatever the times demand. This argument reappears a few years later with greater emphasis when he indicts Shelley and Keats for trying to reproduce Elizabethan "exuberance of expression." But now Arnold goes further, to a position that threatens to reduce the dictional component of poetry to the lowly status it had occupied in classical poetic theory. Modern poetry, he thinks, "can only subsist by its contents"; and if it is to become once again the "complete *magister vitae*" that it was in ancient times, it must adopt a style and vocabulary of the most unadorned simplicity. Whether, as Lionel Trilling believed, the expressive baldness of some of Arnold's own poems resulted from this opinion need not concern us here.[19]

A year later these views were absorbed into the critical polemics occasioned by the 1853 edition of his *Poems.* In the preface he invoked both the practice of the Greek poets and the principles Aristotle propounded in his "admirable treatise" to support the view that in a poem it is always some significant human action, its structuring, its over-all *architectonicè,* that matters, not the local attractions of diction, cadence, and image. Modern English poets, he complained, have been led astray in this by the seductive precedent of Shakespeare's verbal profusion. Though Shakespeare had chosen plots admirably adapted to poetic and dramatic treatment, he too was on occasion betrayed by his gift for ornate phrasing, and by a certain "irritability of fancy" that prevented him from allowing his characters to speak plainly even when the dramatic situation called for it.[20]

If these charges seem excessive, they can be excused by the reflection that Arnold was then writing as a critic pressed by the need to vent precepts salubrious to Arnold the poet. Yet even when full allowance is made for the exigencies of Arnold's creative needs, a problem remains. Detractors of the touchstone method may well point to the place in the 1853 preface in which he pours scorn on

> poems which seem to exist only for the sake of single lines and passages; not for the sake of producing any total impression. We have critics who seem to direct their attention merely to detached expressions, to the language about the action, not to the action itself.

Granted, Pope too had condemned among his "partial" critics those who valued poems exclusively for their language. But could there be a more glaring instance of judgment by "detached expressions" than that which advocates the touchstone as criterion? Carefully considered, however, these strictures of Arnold the young poet conflict less with the evaluative method of the mature critic than at first appears. To recall two of the touchstones: not even by the most perverse reading of *Hamlet* or *Paradise Lost* will the complex structure of human action and passion which they represent seem no more than contrivances to provide the troubled prince an opportunity for voicing the lyrical pathos of "Absent thee from felicity awhile," or the epic narrator an occasion for the exquisite phrasing of his reflection on the loss "which cost Ceres all that pain." The Arnold of 1853 was perhaps only offering his personally felt endorsement of the organic interdependence of parts and whole established in Romantic theory. The later Arnold may perhaps be faulted for not making it explicit that in proposing the use of touchstones he was not abandoning that principle. But the thrust of his whole critical output makes it highly probable that nothing in the eleven touchstones recommended them to his choice so much as their symbolic status, each one instinct with the poet's moral vision, which vitalized with varying degrees of intensity almost every strand of his poem's texture. If Arnold was mistaken, if the symbolic charge of the touchstones was a delusion of personal taste, then their validity as evaluative tools is seriously diminished.[21]

Though still reluctant in **"The Study of Poetry"** to inquire "what in the abstract" makes for the finest poetry, he cannot entirely avoid the attempt. Poetic excellence, he explains, is to be found in *both* "matter and substance" and "manner and style." The matter and substance provide the profound truth and high seriousness that distinguishes the greatest poetry, but only to the extent that they are accompanied by a fit style and manner, constituted of the two elements of diction and movement. This complex of paired abstractions comes short of conceptual precision; while the doublets *diction* and *movement* clearly, and *truth* and *seriousness* vaguely, name related qualities, *matter* and *substance,* like *style* and *manner,* seem to be only synonyms. But the imprecision does not lessen his firm grasp of the mutual interdependence of form and content that characterizes the products of metrical mastery. The two "superiorities" subsist in "such steadfast proportion" to each other, he writes, that a deficiency of truth in a poem quite simply forecloses any distinction of diction and movement.[22]

So far so good. Yet there are other statements in Arnold's criticism, a few quite original and richly suggestive, that require a special effort of explication for clearly understanding them. One such, from *Essays in Criticism (First Series)* (1865), expanding on his central doctrine that poetry interprets life, adumbrates his later definition of it as the most perfect possible expression of truth. "I have said that poetry interprets in two ways," he recalls;

> it interprets by expressing with magical felicity the physiognomy and movement of the outward world, and it interprets by expressing, with inspired conviction, the ideas and laws of the inward world of man's moral and spiritual nature. In other words, poetry is interpretative both by having *natural magic* in it, and by having *moral profundity.* In both ways it illuminates man; it gives him a satisfying sense of reality; it reconciles him with himself and the universe.

Arnold could hardly have assigned a loftier mission to poets and poetry than that spelled out in the final clauses of this passage, correspondent with his conviction that modern humanity stood in sore need of such satisfaction and reconciliation.[23]

What remains problematic are the more technical implications of this excerpt. Can either natural magic or moral profundity, though collaborative in all really first-rate poetry, exist separately in mediocre works? So much seems to be implied in his initially assigning them respectively to objective and subjective experi-

ence. In the 1880 critique of Keats, Arnold rated him supreme in "the faculty of naturalistic interpretation." Recalling the dying poet's hope to be among the English poets after death, he remarks with moving concision: "He is; he is with Shakespeare." But to this generous estimate he immediately adds that Keats was never "ripe" for the second mode, the faculty of moral interpretation. And here the serious student of Arnold's poetics encounters an impasse. In the essay on Wordsworth, published in the year immediately preceding that on Keats, he was at pains to explain "the large sense" in which he was using the term *moral,* that is, to comprehend anything dealing with the question of "how to live." Casting about for the relevant touchstone he finds one ready to hand in Milton's

> Nor love thy life, nor hate; but, what thou liv'st,
> Live well; how long or short, permit to heaven.

But Keats too, he adds, just as surely "utters a moral idea" when he consoles the lover depicted on his Grecian urn, eternally denied his kiss, with the words,

> Forever will thou love, and she be fair—

no less surely than does Shakespeare's Prospero musing on "such stuff as dreams are made on."[24]

Arnold's key terms *natural magic* and *moral profundity* are not simple equivalents of the more familiar form and content, or style and matter. As he sometimes speaks of it, natural magic is, to be sure, a stylistic quality, a compelling manner of rendering the natural world. But no critic was ever more insistent than Arnold that good poetic style of any kind was an index of intellectual maturity, all genuine poetic utterance embodying a moral vision, whether the poet sing of a lover's despair or an autumnal scene. Yet this conviction is blurred whenever he alludes to natural magic as a purely autonomous formal grace. Once at least the two views met in direct collision. Shelley, he observed, had natural magic in his rhythm, but possessed neither the intellectual power nor the sanity to compass it in his diction.[25]

Arnold normally implies that in the greatest poetry the magical and moral kinds of interpretation of life are inextricably fused. Yet in Aeschylus he could detect both separately identifiable even in brief phrases. In the *Choephoroi* "δράσαντι παθειν" [let the doer be done by] interprets morally; in *Prometheus Bound* "ἀνήριθμον γέλασμα" [multitudinous laughter (of ocean waves)] renders nature. Presumably the desired fusion obtains in two citations from Shakespeare:

> Full many a glorious morning have I seen
> Flatter the mountain tops with sovereign eye,

and

> There's a divinity that shapes our ends,
> Rough-hew them how we will.

Arnold's syntax would imply that the two quotations, from Sonnet 33 and from *Hamlet*, each embody *both* modes. Their themes, a sunrise and human destiny, might make it seem more likely that the first exemplifies natural magic and the second moral profundity. Yet in the line from the sonnet the morning is so heavily personified as to qualify as moral in Arnold's broad designation of anything pertaining to human existence. But surely the same plea might be made for Aeschylus's image of laughing ocean waves, which, however, Arnold offers as a rendition of nature innocent of moral import.[26]

The weight of evidence favors, barely, the conclusion that the quality for which Arnold could find no more fitting name than natural magic was a stylistic element, not a thematic one. Though little of his poetics is given over to mimesis, he was well aware of its crucial role. In terms which recall Coleridge on the subject, he censured Byron's "copyist" manner of promiscuously adopting for poetic use everything that life offered him, too often forgetting "the mysterious transmutation to be operated on this matter by poetic form." If we take our cue from Arnold himself and pay greater heed to what the touchstones tell us on this issue than to his foggy generalizations about it, we shall be even more convinced that the magic is produced by the linguistic resourcefulness of the poet. He is the magician, not the experiential stuff he labors to "interpret." In *On the Study of Celtic Literature* (1867) Arnold may at first seem to ascribe the faculty not to the poet but to his subject, when he praises the natural magic of Keats's

> White hawthorn and the pastoral eglantine,
> Fast-fading violets cover'd up in leaves.

But we are brought up short by the final exhibit in that book, from *The Merchant of Venice*:

> in such a night
> *Stood Dido with a willow in her hand*
> *Upon the wild sea banks, and waft her love*
> *To come again to Carthage.*

The italics here are Arnold's, who closes his discussion by observing that the lines are "so drenched and intoxicated with the fairy-dew of that natural magic which is our theme, that I cannot do better than end with them." Fair enough. But any reader may add that the main theme of the lines is not the external features of the setting but unrequited love, which in human experience belongs as surely as anything else to the question of "how to live"; and that the magic lies in the poignancy of Shakespeare's moving portrayal of the forsaken Dido's anguish.[27]

Arnold's poetic percipience too obviously outran his capacity for communicating the finer aesthetic subtleties to which he so delicately responded. His own awareness of the frustration involved was revealed in *On Translating Homer*, when he observed that the critic of poetry needed a poise so perfect that the slightest imbalance—of temper, personal crochet, or even erudition—could destroy it. The perception of "poetic truth" is so elusive that even by "pressing too impetuously after it, one runs the risk of losing it." Yet half a dozen years later we find him yielding to a personal inclination toward that very impetuosity. In *Celtic Literature* [*On the Study of Celtic Literature*], readers with an abiding interest in poetic style are alerted by his emphasis on four of the many modes of "handling" nature in verse: the *conventional*, the *faithful*, the *Greek*, and the *magical*. Striking illustrative samples, from Greek, Latin, and English poetry, follow. But only the first of those in English is of any help in defining the mode to which Arnold assigns it. Pope's pompous lunar metaphor, "refulgent lamp of night," makes reasonably clear the manner of the conventional mode. But wherein Keats's

> What little town by river or seashore
> Or mountain-built with peaceful citadel,
>   Is emptied of this folk, this pious morn?

is Greek (apart from setting), "as Greek as a thing from Homer or Theocritus," it is impossible to fathom, even when Arnold points to an accession of radiancy. Even more cryptic is his confidence that readers will be "disposed" to label "Greek" (not "magical"!) the speech from *A Midsummer Night's Dream* beginning

> I know a bank where the wild thyme blows.

There is more of the same—all of it, we should have the humility to admit, perhaps obvious enough to those who share Arnold's schooling in Greek verse. The earnestness of his concern with poetry as an institution vital to cultured living makes it unlikely that he did not himself perceive the stylistic distinctions he names. It is therefore the more regrettable that the terms he adopted to convey them must strike most readers as vague and perversely arbitrary.[28]

Though irretrievably ambiguous, the perfunctory phrase "poetic truth" gains renewed import when used by a critic who believed poetry to be man's most nearly truthful form of utterance. For Arnold the truth in question is truth of a special kind, special and "higher," requiring an idiom suited to a cognitive order alternative to that of science. He thus adopts a major tenet of Romantic poetics, though somewhat reductively defined. Arnold's poetic truth eschews the purely abstract numeration and quantification which, as he thought, contemporary science employed to present the world to human comprehension. His fullest discussion of this idea occurs not in his critical prose but in *Literature and*

Dogma, where he exalts the style of the Bible, which "keeps to the language of poetry," over that of theology, which employs as much as possible the abstract jargon of science. Wordsworth's personification of the earth as "the mighty mother of mankind" thus contrasts with the geographer's "oblate spheroid." The poet conveys something people feel about the planet they inhabit. The literary language of the Bible functions in the same way. It is

> language *thrown out* at an object of consciousness not fully grasped, which inspired emotion. . . . [T]he language of figure and feeling will satisfy us better about it, will cover more of what we seek to express, than the language of literal fact and science. The language of science about it will be *below* what we feel to be the truth.[29]

Arnold here renews a theme that had taken on special urgency since the Enlightenment, the defense of poetry against positivist detraction. In its original form the threat had been idealist, coming at the very outset of recorded criticism in Plato's indictment of poets as deceivers. The best known later apologists, Sidney and Shelley, had responded mainly by making poetry's sensuous attractions, which Plato thought baneful, ancillary to its cognitive utility. But by Arnold's time the stakes had been raised. Ineffectively challenged by the religion of the day, the triumph of scientific "truth" seemed to entail not only the loss of a "world of fine fabling," but the virtual dehumanization and alienation of human beings reduced to "absurd" inhabitants of one of the myriad "oblate spheroids" of an indifferent universe. Though Arnold was by no means the originator of this brand of cosmic pessimism, a motif common in Romantic literature, no one could have felt more personally affected by it than the poet whose most famous lyric envisaged a world having neither "certitude, nor peace, nor help for pain." Moreover, it is Arnold's formulation of this cultural crisis that has been most influential as an intellectual legacy to modern defenders of poetry like John Crowe Ransom and I. A. Richards. Richards credited Arnold with having foreseen that poetry would one day fill the emotional void left by science's "neutralization of nature," and thus save us from the impending chaos. Self-professed Benthamite positivist, Richards cannot admit any such category as *poetic* truth, truth for him being exclusively an affair of science. But he follows Arnold in grounding his analysis of poetic language, in function and form, on an alleged discrepancy from scientific discourse. "In its use of words," as he put it in *Science and Poetry* (1926), "poetry is just the reverse of science." In Richards's thinking, the difference between the two uses becomes so nearly total that poetry is denuded of any cognitive value whatsoever; its salutary working is purely emotive, even neurological. Not so Arnold. For him the emotion attaches first of all to the way the poet thinks, and only because of that does it condition his style. Poetry as much as

science "gives the idea, but gives it touched with beauty, heightened by emotion."[30]

Arnold can nonetheless claim for poetry a kind of truth *above* that of science, one indispensable to its special function of "criticizing," which must always be performed "in conformity to the laws of poetic truth and poetic beauty." He came nearest to clarifying these vague terms in the essay on Wordsworth, by quoting a passage from *The Excursion*:

> One adequate support
> For the calamities of mortal life
> Exists, one only;—an assured belief
> That the procession of our fate, howsoe'er
> Sad or disturbed, is ordered by a Being
> Of infinite benevolence and power;
> Whose everlasting purposes embrace
> All accidents, converting them to good.

Arnold has no quarrel with the faith in divine guidance expressed here. He objects only that the lines have "none of the characters of *poetic* truth, the kind of truth which we require from a poet," and find in abundance elsewhere in Wordsworth.[31] Since he fails to say what aspects of the passage—diction, rhythm, syntax, or nonformal ingredients—make for the deficiency, we are left to guess *what* the linguistic modalities of poetic truth might be. Arnold cited Wordsworth's lines as a negative touchstone, which for him was all that was required to convey a certain lapse from the ideal he named poetic truth. To ask for more would be to ask that the method of the touchstones be replaced by an ontological procedure for which Arnold had neither the taste nor the gift.

Notes

1. Arnold, *Prose Works* [*The Complete Prose Works of Matthew Arnold,* ed. R. H. Super, 11 vols. (Ann Arbor: University of Michigan Press, 1960-77)], IX, 224; III, 234; John Shepard Eels, Jr., *The Touchstones of Matthew Arnold* (New York: Bookman Associates, 1955), pp. 25-26.

2. *Prose Works,* I, 211, 168.

3. Ibid., XI, 331; VIII, 314, 315, 316; III, 362, 363.

4. Ibid., III, 35, 14.

5. Arnold, *Prose Works,* III, 251; I, 180; Barfield, *Poetic Diction* (Middletown, Conn.: Wesleyan University Press, 1973), pp. 152-67.

6. *Prose Works,* IX, 39.

7. Ibid., I, 136-37, 175. Arnold had earlier used the term *grand style* (thus italicized) in the preface to his *Poems* (1853), where he exalts the Greeks as its "unapproachable masters." *Prose Works,* I, 5.

8. Ibid., I, 116-17, 156, 186-87.

9. Ibid., I, 188-90. *On Translating Homer,* ed. W. H. D. Rouse (New York: AMS Press, 1971), p. 197.

10. *Prose Works,* I, 139, 145-46, 155, 129-30, 213.

11. [T. S.] Eliot, *The Use of Poetry* [*The Use of Poetry and the Use of Criticism* (London: Faber and Faber, 1960-77)], p. 146; [René] Wellek [*A History of Modern Criticism: 1750-1950,* 8 vols. (New Haven: Yale University Press, 1955-92)], *History,* pp. 171, 172.

12. Arnold, *Prose Works,* IX, 163-69; Symons, *Studies in Prose and Verse* (New York: E. P. Dutton, 1922. Reprint. New York: AMS Press), p. 195.

13. Eels, *Touchstones of Arnold,* pp. 171, 205; Arnold, *Prose Works,* IX, 162; Eliot, *The Use of Poetry,* p. 118.

14. Arnold, *Poetical Works,* ed. C. B. Tinker and H. F. Lowry (London: Oxford University Press, 1950), p. 195.

15. *The Letters of Matthew Arnold to Arthur Hugh Clough,* ed. Howard Foster Lowry (New York: Oxford University Press, 1932), p. 195; *Prose Works,* IX, 52.

16. *Prose Works,* I, 8-12, 112, 204; IX, 178, 39-40.

17. Ibid., IX, 185; I, 120, 166.

18. Ibid., I, 204, 205.

19. Arnold, *Letters to Arthur Hugh Clough,* pp. 65, 124; Trilling, ed., *The Portable Matthew Arnold* (New York: Viking Press, 1949), p. 39.

20. *Prose Works,* I, 7, 4-11.

21. Ibid., I, 7. Arnold had a very clear idea, quite possibly suggested by Coleridge, of the special quality of symbolic communication. Contrasting the styles of Maurice de Guérin and his sister Eugénie, he wrote that "her words . . . are in general but intellectual signs; they are not like her brother's—symbols equivalent with the thing symbolized. They bring the notion of the thing described to the mind, they do not bring the feeling of it to the imagination." Ibid., III, 86.

22. Ibid., IX, 171, 172.

23. Ibid., III, 33.

24. Ibid., IX, 214, 215, 45.

25. Ibid., III, 34n.

26. Ibid., III, 33.

27. Ibid., IX, 227; III, 378-80. [George] We need not pause over Arnold's persuasion that English poets owe their stylistic natural magic to the Celtic ancestral strain. The overkill of Saintsbury's verdict suffices: "With the bricks of ignorance and the mortar of assumption you can build no critical house." *History of Criticism* [*A History of Criticism and Literary Taste,* 3 vols. (New York: Humanities Press, 1950], III, 527.

28. *Prose Works,* I, 174; III, 377-79.

29. Ibid., VI, 187-90.

30. Richards, *Science and Poetry* (New York: Haskell House, 1974), p. 24; *Essays, Letters, and Reviews by Matthew Arnold* (Cambridge: Harvard University Press, 1960), p. 238.

31. *Prose Works,* IX, 228, 49.

Kate Campbell (essay date 2000)

SOURCE: Campbell, Kate. "Matthew Arnold and Publicity: A Modern Critic as Journalist." In *Journalism, Literature and Modernity: From Hazlitt to Modernism,* pp. 91-120. Edinburgh, Scotland: Edinburgh University Press, 2000.

[*In the following essay, Campbell focuses on the journalistic aspects of Arnold's work, which she believes have been overlooked by scholars of his texts. Using examples from* Culture and Anarchy, *Campbell argues that Arnold's criticism is characteristic of "manipulative publicity," which often eschews reason in favor of impact.*]

Matthew Arnold's criticism in the journals of his day solicited attention in being timely and polemical. A measure of its success, in his lifetime and up until World War One many novels engaged with his ideas directly—among the more well-known, *Daniel Deronda, Jude the Obscure* and *Howard's End.*[1] Arnold's criticism still invites academic attention through raising questions of continuing importance and the cultural capital of its allusions.[2] Since it is also in turns careless, emotive, ironic, mnemonic, rude and a fount of oppositions, it can almost seem programmed for publicity—a model of journalistic flair.

When the Newbolt Report of 1921 misquoted Arnold as writing 'Culture unites classes' instead of using his actual words on culture wanting to do away with classes it was, then, in a sense taking a leaf from his journalistically derived books, its misreading encouraged by his own carelessness and flair.[3] Arnold's persona, ideas and catch-phrases recurred frequently in his day and subsequently. Henry Sidgwick pointed to his publicising ability in 1867 in his 'doing not a little to exasperate and exacerbate' (*CH* [*Matthew Arnold, Prose Writings: The Critical Heritage*], 224) antagonisms despite wishing for, and being capable of, their reconciliation; Richard

Garnett noted in 1901 how 'references to him in contemporary literature are endless, and he is the subject of innumerable critiques'.[4] T. S. Eliot registered the publicist talent in describing him 'a propagandist for criticism rather than a critic'.[5] This chapter challenges established views that neglect Arnold's involvement in publicity by exploring his activity as a journalistic writer.

An index of his extraordinary success as a publicist has been the frequent citation of his reading of the end of Edmund Burke's *Reflections on the Revolution in France*. Here, writing on **'The Function of Criticism'**, he presents disinterested liberal criticism in a powerful image of open-mindedness:

> That return of Burke upon himself is one of the finest things in English literature, or indeed in any literature. That is what I call living by ideas: when one side of a question has long had your earnest support, when all your feelings are engaged, when your party talks this language like a steam-engine and can imagine no other,—still, to be able to think, still to be irresistibly carried, if so it be, by the current of thought to the opposite side of the question . . .
>
> (*SP* [*Matthew Arnold: Selected Prose*], 140)

But as Arnold in fact acknowledges, Burke's final words, declaring the perversity and obstinacy of those 'opposing this mighty current in human affairs', were not referring to his own opposition to the Revolution in France at the close of his book about it (although some extended application is possible), as Arnold broadly makes out. Rather, taking up his question 'What is to be done?', considering 'the best means of combating it' (*SP*, 139), Burke's words look forward to mounting resistance to the spread of sedition: 'this mighty current' appears to be on his side.[6] Arnold's reading is to this extent careless, 'journalistic' in the pejorative sense— his desire father of the famous conservative's trip on thought's current. It was in comparable terms, of Arnold's travesty of John Bright's and Frederic Harrison's understanding of culture to suit his own ends, that the *Morning Star* condemned **'Culture and Its Enemies'** (*CH*, 201-4). Given his academic credentials, it seems Arnold's reading of Burke constitutes an early instance of 'the *temptation of the media*' where intellectuals neglect academic precision in trying to exert pressure through the press.[7] The image of a disinterested Burke entertaining the possibility of his own perversity was nonetheless a publicising *coup*—a kind of 'poetry in history', such a shining image of questioning mind and disinterest as to have been exempt from questioning itself.

In his apparent openness Arnold's Burke could serve as an icon of mid-twentieth-century liberal criticism.[8] Following the development of ideological criticism in the 1980s, Eliot's oxymoron, a 'propagandist for criticism',

more obviously related to Arnold's hegemonic role, 'the propagation of high culture in the service of an organicist nationalism' resting on a disinterested self.[9] Chris Baldick's account of his centrality in academic English was instrumental in this. Here too, though, Arnold's publicising ability seems involved, in the singular importance granted his views. Thus Baldick discusses Arnold's concern with prematurity without reference to the many other political analysts similarly engaged with the phenomenon of political form running in advance of a people's capacity to sustain it and ideas taking hold without being thoroughly comprehended.[10] In general Baldick's Arnold is disconnected from political discourse—his personal authority greatly exaggerated. Despite **Culture and Anarchy**'s subtitle, *An Essay in Social and Political Criticism,* the three 'recognizable phases' Baldick discerns in Arnold's writing exclude the political altogether, comprising 'early, more "classicist", literary-critical writings, the social and theological works of the late 1860's and early 1870's, and the later literary works'.[11] Away from main currents of nineteenth-century political thought, Arnold is demonised, with elitist aspects that were widespread then unduly foregrounded, contrary movements in his thinking eclipsed. In fact, substantially qualifying the high cultural identity, by the mid-1860s Arnold was subject to class discrimination from contemporaries and something of a downmarket familiar—'Matt Arnold' on the news-stand, 'a favourite comedian', an 'elegant Jeremiah', 'Mr. Kid-Glove Cock-Sure' (*CH,* 210).[12]

The labels show a distinct and provocative persona emerging from writing in serious forms. Far from straightforwardly elitist they suggest populist tendencies: something of a hybrid and tease, bringing 'high' culture down, heretically pitched towards readers deemed responsive to entertainment. Hostility to the word 'culture' dates from controversy surrounding Arnold's views, and in a sense the Arnold-bashing of recent years simply perpetuates an antipathy to elite culture that Arnold himself fuelled by contravening its hierarchical norms. Yet academic constructions of a modern in Arnold tend to be elevated, from the sentimental poet haunted by purity who later urged 'control' and distance over modernity's 'vast multitude of facts' (1857) to the critic championing disinterest and Oxford in **Culture and Anarchy** (1869).[13] His criticism of modern journalism (the *Daily Telegraph* especially) feeds into Leavisite criticism, elaborating a foundational myth of the modern in the project of culture holding back seas of anarchy in the form of the modern mass media.[14] These roles variously neglect Sidgwick's 'comedian' 'titillating' his audience with 'airs and graces' (*CH*, 210) and the paradigmatic journalist at whom Fitzjames Stephen scoffed: a 'very clever man, always brilliant', 'with quick sympathies and a great gift of making telling remarks', who 'really does work himself, at any rate for the time being, into an esoteric enthusiasm for the particular point which he enforces'.[15]

The critic now identified with high culture and the elevation of the public sphere could thus be seen as instrumental in their decline. The neo-Kantian Sidgwick inadvertently aligned him with the public sphere's degradation: the movement against anonymous writing had become much the stronger on account of Arnold's writing in 'periodical literature'. Sidgwick's description of Arnold's production turns on the discrepancy between his official eminence and vulgar traits, registered in repetition of the word 'new'. He thus refers to him as 'this new phenomenon', creating 'new and exquisite literary enjoyment' by delivering 'profound truths and subtle observations with all the dogmatic authority and self-confidence of a prophet; at the same time titillating the public by something like the airs and graces, the playful affectations of a favourite comedian' (*CH*, 210). While there may be genuine pleasure here, intimations of a 'choice' experience and shades of patronage qualify it with suggestions of vulgarity. We may object to the archness and anxieties shadowing Sidgwick's validation. But in identifying a hybrid phenomenon overlooked subsequently, challenging 'the centred, dominant cultural norms', he highlights a source of Arnold's capacity to get under the skin of his readers and needle them.[16]

Almost all Arnold's criticism first appeared in print in journal form. Until the mid-1860s many articles were revisions of lectures but even here a periodical readership was in prospect—quite explicitly when giving a lecture on Heine in Oxford it dawned on him that his lectures were aimed at periodical readers rather than the 'dead bones' in front of him.[17] In the *OED* [*Oxford English Dictionary*] journalism refers to 'writing in the public journals'; as mentioned earlier the word's first appearance in English signalled a hybrid phenomenon uniting higher and lower cultural forms. Focusing on Arnold's journalism and publicity leads to both a high cultural tradition of political critique and a modern world of promotion. Both these dimensions of his writing have been neglected.

This chapter examines how his thinking in the 1860s, stressing the value of disinterest and the dissemination of ideas, corresponds to the political thought of the Enlightenment philosopher who prioritised publicity, Immanuel Kant. I suggest how Arnold broadly invokes Kantian political precepts; they even inform his much-quoted criticism of 'a new journalism' in 1887 as 'feather-brained' and lacking objectivity.[18] I argue that Arnold's criticism is also characteristic of a more modern form of publicity involving promotion and flair at reason's expense. Here Enlightenment precepts are undermined and contradicted in unstable journalistic prose, giving it the aspect of 'feather-brained' 'new journalism' itself.

A JOURNALIST AS 'WANDERER BETWEEN TWO WORLDS'?

At the outset though there is the issue of Arnold's move from poetry to journalism from the 1850s. Established generic hierarchies suggest a move from a higher to a lower cultural form. Reviews of Ian Hamilton's recent study *A Gift Imprisoned* demonstrate hierarchy and doubleness in his newspaper press—'poetry/duty', 'worldly clubman and solemn poet', 'poetry/drudgery' and many more.[19] These often make it seem as if he turned from writing altogether in the 1850s, as if no longer producing written words involving craft, inspiration, creativity; as if the conjunction of poet and journalism is exceptional rather than quite common.

There seems, however, much overlap, beyond his understanding of literature as a criticism of life to 'illuminate and rejoice us' (*SP*, 173), straddling all his forms of writing. As glimpsed already, he acceded to a prophetic function that romantic poets had espoused, precisely through journal writing. Psychologically and culturally this entailed a magisterial, upbeat quality. Arnold expressed a desire for this personally and for his 'confused' age but it escaped him in epic poetry, its customary site: 'the mass of men' want 'something to animate and ennoble them not merely to add zest to their melancholy or grace to their dreams.—I believe a feeling of this kind is the basis of my nature—and of my poetics'.[20] Another index of consanguinity and journalism's attraction is his regretting in prose 'the *articulations of the discourse*: one leaps over these in Poetry—places one thought cheek by jowl with another without introducing them and leaves them—but in prose this will not do' (*SL*, 90). While prose in general is here seen as exacting, it seems that in journalism the onus of 'articulations' may be relaxed through its distinctive temporality.

A related index of continuity, impossible to pursue here, is the deployment of a constant geographical arsenal of winds, rivers, streams, currents and the like whereby throughout his career Arnold conceptualised the activity of writing and thinking in terms of inspiration and movement: if the forms of writing change, the activities are seen fairly steadily in this respect. It seems the criticism of no other writer except Jonathan Swift—poet, journal-critic, political observer also—is so imaginatively engaged by language and thought's capacity for carrying their users away. Both positive and negative forms—the hard-earned landing on the opposite side of things for Burke, the glib rhetoric of liberal politicians—are important in Arnold's criticism. His turn to journalism is to a form singularly accommodating of such transports of the self through its informality. Arnold's characterisation of prose especially appreciates the flexibility it offers: 'In prose the character of the vehicle for the composer's thoughts is not determined beforehand; every composer has to make his own choice of vehicle' (*SP*, 159). The increased commercialisation of all levels of journalism after the abolition of the Stamp Duty in 1855, and the beginning of the end of anonymity in the 1860s, each potentially gave contributors much greater opportunity to publish and develop distinctive traits through their 'own choice of vehicle', utilising the expressive potential of the form to elaborate identity through particular serial publications.

The poet who renounced a high literary form that frustratingly tossed him in language and tradition's swell thus elected in critical journalism another implicated in movement. Journalism's etymological root appertains to the daily, and all forms of it tilt towards the quotidian and contingent—if only in resolve to master them. Historically identified with circulation and exchange rather than production, it has prompted numerous analogies between the journalist and the prostitute. These form an undercurrent in Arnold's own critical reception stressing his impropriety and hollowness (as in Sidgwick's reference to his 'titillating'); they culminate in Georg Lukàcs' identification of the two as the apogee of capitalist reification.[21] As 'literature in a hurry' (Arnold's apocryphal definition) journalism comprises both an opportunity for, and a test to, integrity—a sort of pressing invitation to go go, losing or finding oneself in 'expression'. The testing is compounded by the constraints of editorial policy, making it psychologically fraught for aspirants to strict self-possession. Max Weber saw journalism as a scapegoated form, customarily judged by its ethically most reprehensible practitioners; this presumably derives from the sense of something inherently abject in a practice so implicated in the passing moment—an ultimate parasitism confounding humanism.[22]

Writing has of course itself in a logocentric culture always been susceptible to such derivative, inferior status. Its association with prostitution extends beyond the journalist in a tradition dating back to Aristotle. Arnold famously evidences anxieties about criticism's own derivative status in **'The Function of Criticism'** and when young he acknowledged dispossession in utterance itself: 'No man can express more than one side at once . . . but he can have a feeling for the whole if he will not always be labouring after expression and publicity'.[23] More personally, 'I have never yet succeeded in any one great occasion in consciously mastering myself . . . at the critical part I am too apt to hoist up the mainsail to the wind and let her drive' (*SL*, 58). But one crude gauge of the difference between the earlier Arnold and the later is that being carried away fades as

a complaint from within and becomes rather more a criticism made by others against him, as in the earlier quotation from Fitzjames Stephen about Arnold 'working himself . . . into an esoteric enthusiasm'. Or else, as we will see later, a failing Arnold recurrently sees in others.

The change of form, from poetry to journalism, seemingly redirected an attempt at mastery, from the self to intellectual grasp of the world and getting others to shift their viewpoints. Here one must repress a 'modern' melancholy feeling for an 'adequate' grip on the world's multitudinousness—developing one's own nature 'in a number of directions, politically, socially, morally, religiously', so as to reckon with 'the world in its fullness and movement'.[24] The famous 'Arnoldian' ideological gravitation to distance and mastery appear functions of, and in tension with, such 'fullness'—a 'culture of integration' and multiplicity where, as we will see, boundaries are repeatedly crossed. As his private letters demonstrate, Arnold's career became metaphorically dedicated to repeating the achievement of getting his poem *'Empedocles* to the railway bookstall at Derby' (*SL*, 91): crossing boundaries, impinging on his contemporaries.

The bonus of placing the identity of self and world so much in consciousness is that it allows leeway in behaviour, even a personal multitudinousness befitting modern times. For within the framework of the nonidentity of the self with its 'manifestations', all behaviour becomes performance and so ironised—leaving the modern mind to sort out what's what. Arnold's exasperating insouciance signals such 'Indian detachment' hazarding impregnability. The cognitive self can thrive on the plurality confronting it, delighting in his own textual irregularity, instances of 'esoteric enthusiasm' and the windiness of others carried away in language it exposes.

In other words, agonistic quests for originality through seas of poetic tradition could be abandoned for swirling journalistic currents of contemporary criticism. Registering his personal investment in the form makes his erratic prose appear less a function of the form itself than his will. Resigned to contingency, letting himself get 'worked up', he has higher journalism's defence, of 'seeing things as they really are' from within.[25] This warrants setting the present times on the right tracks using any prevailing breeze, in the many discursive models available to him. In short, private subjectivity licenses public plurality in the 'fascinating and exciting' (*SL*, 187) habit of newspaper-writing. Here Hamilton's understanding of the post-poet as having '"renounced renunciation" to become a solid, public-spirited man' rather misses the textual point—an exploitation of renunciation rather, which seems to have public-spirited dimensions but certainly is not solid.[26] Emphasis on the drudgery masks the flair, the franchise of desire and plurality. The goals of lucidity in language and effectivity in the world—with a private, obscure self in the wings, an enabling device for variety and defence against criticism—supplants the earlier, heavier goal of truth to an asocial self.

Demoting language as expressive resource for instrumental usage and performance thus allows more resourceful language. In its range and heterodoxy it reaches out to those outside polite culture in blatant distaste towards Philistines, vulgar expressions like 'stopping their mouths' (*CA* [*Culture and Anarchy*], 50), 'familiar' expressions such as 'a rough time of it' (*CA*, 108). The language of the street connects with a politics antagonistic to 'a condition of splendour, grandeur, and culture, which they [persons without extraordinary gifts or exceptional energy] cannot possibly reach, [and which] has the effect of making them flag in spirit' (*SP*, 105). Through such directness, familiar words and sensory appeals, as explored later, it accommodates unassuming, common modes of expression proscribed in orthodox political thought.

Much of Arnold's 1860s' publication was in the *Cornhill* and *Macmillan's*. These new magazines typified the spread of periodical journalism—with relatively wide middle-class audiences and contribution lists—and the modification of its standards and tone through their relative lightness and entertainment value, mixing fictional and non-fictional prose, for instance. They were among the first to abandon anonymity. Both helped to alter the contours of the public sphere—*Macmillan's* especially including a large proportion of non-university men among its contributors.[27] An *Economist* of 1861 (9 March) saw it as a 'kind of "Chambers Journal" for the higher classes of society'. The *Cornhill* prioritised worldly 'brilliance'. Both magazines sought the extension of existing readerships. Their lack of strong political affiliations made them particularly serviceable for free-playing minds. Arnold also wrote extensively in the *Contemporary Review* and, later, the *Nineteenth Century*, leading 'organs of opinion' known to 'look out for big names, not for good articles'. The latter pioneered the staging of debate in a single issue in the form of a symposium—the formal institutionalisation of the free play of mind within a single journal.[28] The hybridity and contradictoriness in Arnold's prose seem symptomatic of, and more intelligible in the light of, not just his writing journalism but also such historical movements within it.

Arnold thus disregards consistency and boundaries between 'higher' and 'lower' cultural spheres, alternating between desire, duty and reality, and high and low genres and idiom: a certain mutinousness informs his journalism's multitudinousness. Parts of his Homer lectures apparently contravening accepted notions of pro-

fessorial identity prompted Fitzjames Stephen's charge of 'low buffoonery', their being 'not the sort of things which an Oxford Professor ought to deliver officially before the University'.[29] The security of Stephen's public sphere is vested in 'official' delivery; Arnold's breaking ranks threatens loosening things up. The reflexivity and mobility he practises, and his 'irony' in general, are symptomatic of subjectivities and societies turning away from accountability, as elsewhere in modern therapeutic and confessional modalities. Certainly his choice of form enabled extensive revisions—a subject apparently in dialogue and process, ad libbing *ad infinitum*. In this provisional approach apologies proliferate—frequently to individuals, for instance back-handedly to Mr Wright in the Preface to *Essays in Criticism* (*SP*, 126-7), and in other ways too. An apology as to its 'sketchy and generalizing mode of treatment' prefaces the eventual publication of '**The Modern Element in Literature**'.[30] The self-deprecatory posture of 'a man without a philosophy' recurs in **Culture and Anarchy** (*CA*, 98).

Sidgwick registers the lapse from reason's protocols: he judges of 'religious organisations as a dog judges of human beings, chiefly by the scent'. With this most atavistic of the senses went an 'imperturbable cheerfulness' (*CH*, 211) others saw as superciliousness, insouciance—implying some transgression of boundaries and authority. This suggests a self very actively asking for the world's criticism, ostensibly on the strength of knowing the true self it doesn't; but the criticism may be solicited to glean the parameters through which knowledge is produced. The effect of a centre may thus derive from the busy circumference of the public sphere. Both public and private writing show a selfhood pronounced through the world's reflection. This makes a virtue of the prosthetic identity demanded in public—the artificial, proper self needed for 'public' life—by jettisoning its desired sincerity and singularity while exploiting the theatricality (here anticipating Oscar Wilde). Later we will see this in close-up, as Arnold repudiates the 'the drab of the earnest, prosaic, practical, austerely literal' (*SP*, 127), performing a succession of roles in a heady 'self-difference'.[31] The plurality and performance are foregrounded in **Friendship's Garland** (*SP*, 301-39). Here, in a mock correspondence in the *Pall Mall Gazette* running before and after the **Culture and Anarchy** articles in the *Cornhill* satirising the English middle class especially, contradictory tendencies of the self and nations are staged between a sometime Arnoldian-like Prussian commanding 'Get Geist' and a *Daily-Telegraph*-reading Englishman going by the name of Arnold. The virtuosity, satire and slippages as the self and others were uncertainly staged alienated many.

ON ARNOLD'S SOCIO-POLITICAL CRITIQUE AND CULTURE AND ANARCHY

The term 'Arnoldian' widely refers to ideals of 'disinterest', the 'best self' and high culture, assuming an Enlightenment public sphere of political and social progress. Leaving aside its relation to Sainte-Beuve, the emphasis on 'disinterest' and critical reason in *Culture and Anarchy: An Essay in Social and Political Criticism* in particular suggests Kantian values. Disregarding the other thinkers whose presence is evident in his thinking, Arnold's affiliation to a tradition dating back to Immanuel Kant's political writings and theorised by Jürgen Habermas will now be explored through his more politically minded texts of the 1860s, especially *Culture and Anarchy.* My aim here is to heighten awareness of the socio-political identity of Arnold's criticism and its departures from Enlightenment norms as publicity began to assume its current signification and centrality. I argue that in Habermas' terms Arnold embraces both Enlightenment 'critical publicity' and the 'manipulative publicity' of a media society emerging in 'new journalism', advertising and modern party political machinery; relatedly, a movement from a 'Culture-Debating' to a 'Culture-Consuming' Public.[32] The instability, range and versatility that have just been glimpsed in his writing are indicative of such a shift.

'Critical publicity' was the normative mode or principle of the Enlightenment public sphere classically expounded by Kant. Kant in fact usually refers just to publicity in his political writings. There is only glancing notice, in *The Contest of Faculties* (1798), of a specific (spurious form)—'a mendacious form of publicity' (an early sort of public relations exercise) operating in George III's Government (*KPW* [Kant's Political Writings], 186). The principle of publicity, elaborated in Kant's article 'An Answer to the Question, "What is Enlightenment?"' (1784), assumes disinterest in citizens scrutinising the actions of the state through critical reason. The conclusions reached through disinterested reason in the public sphere are by definition right and in this sense there is a principle of publicity. For when in the public sphere citizens putatively abandon their particular interests as private citizens and civil servants. Instead they accede to reason's universal order and protocols: 'by the public use of one's own reason I mean that use which anyone may make of it *as a man of learning* addressing the entire reading public' (*KPW,* 55). Being a 'man of learning' requires conformity with established protocols of reason and language use. The outrageous citizen making 'presumptuous criticism' of 'taxes, where someone is called to pay them', boding 'general insubordination', is in effect rehabilitated through distance from the occasion and 'if, as a learned individual, he publicly voices his thoughts on the impropriety or even injustice of such fiscal measures' (*KPW,* 56).

The abstract, universalising language discretely upheld here by Kant, of 'fiscal measures' (rather than the vulgar need 'to pay' 'taxes') and 'impropriety or even injustice' (suppressing particular instances), offers a

textbook illustration of the linguistic derealisation of the world identified by the French sociologist Pierre Bourdieu in traditional political discourse. Widely 'enabling speakers to speak without thinking what they speak', it 'discredits and destroys the spontaneous political discourse of the dominated';[33] in this respect it promotes 'sweetness and light', shrouding shrill details of complaints and injustices. For Bourdieu in his major work of the 1980s, *Distinction,* the 'essential problem of politics' is precisely the transmutation and distancing required from the assembly of habits, tastes, sensibility, sensations and 'spontaneous discourse' comprising a particular habitus for observance of the conventions of accredited political discourse. Specific interests and the norms of the dominated are both alike censored in the 'sanitised words of official discourse': 'Political analysis presupposes distance, height, the overview of the observer who places himself above the hurly-burly, or the "objectivity" of the historian.'[34] But while much of Bourdieu's socio-political analysis is hostile to disinterest, distance, universalism on account of the dominant interests served through them, on occasion in proper Kantian mode even in *Distinction* he concedes their utility for freedom—the choices and leverage and dignity they bring.[35]

Kant's public sphere is predicated on separation from the private sphere and also the state. And yet its telos is the end of this: reason being integral to mankind's moral nature, public and private will eventually be integrated as morality is realised through it with people subscribing in all their affairs to the freedom that is self-enacted law, so retiring the state. To the end of this realisation the 'public use of one's reason' runs on missionary tracks, disseminating 'the spirit of rational respect for personal value and for the duty of all men to think for themselves' (*KPW,* 55): these are the bases of maturity. The political warrant for free intellectual activity or critical reason is the assurance that its findings *are* intellectual and appertain to the public sphere, not civil society. Indeed, since it means the state is not threatened on any account, freedom of mind is precisely a function of the unfreedom of civil society under Frederick the Great, whose motto might be 'Argue as much as you like and about whatever you like, but obey!' (*KPW,* 59). Ripeness is all; on the road to freedom instrumental uses of reason are clearly proscribed for individuals capable of reason: 'Dogmas and formulas, those mechanical instruments for rational use (or rather misuse) are the ball and chains of his permanent immaturity', 'Men will of their own accord gradually work their way out of barbarism' (*KPW,* 55; 59).

Approximately eighty years later Arnold's critique of contemporary cultural forms focuses particularly on party equivalents of 'dogmas and formulas'. Approaching things rather differently from the philosopher's apparent appeasement of Frederick the Great, he all the same echoes the Kantian proposition in notably Kantian idiom: 'a state which is authoritative and sovereign, a firm and settled course of public order, is requisite if man is to bring to maturity anything precious and lasting now' (*CA,* 204). He is similarly vague in that culture involves subtle and indirect action, 'a frame of mind' (*CA,* 200) like Kant tending to efface the instrumentality of ideas as such beside enlightened subjectivities. Paradoxically—and in human affairs considered 'in the widest sense . . . nearly everything is paradoxical' (*KPW,* 59)—for both writers only the respectful, distant, freedom-permitting pathway of disinterested, objective truth, disdaining practical effects as such so as to preserve individual agency, has the moral authority to effect change: telling 'silently upon the mind of the country', keeping 'up our own communications with the future' (*CA,* 62) is for Arnold what it is about. Increasingly modern literature would be identified with such objectivity, disdaining proximate material ends. Little seems more obviously Kantian than Arnold's concern with 'expansion' and disinterest that phylogenetically connect the history of the individual to that of the polis. The equivalence of Arnold's 'best self' and the state is indicative of this mode of thought.

Habermas proposes that when 'critical publicity' yields to 'manipulative publicity' a series of structuring oppositions upholding the Enlightenment public sphere starts to crumble: public and private, reason and desire, ideas and practice, principle and commerce all become confused. Publicity regresses to a quasi-feudal condition, being represented before a public rather than constituted by it—a masquerade of openness belying prior private agreement. An anarchic ^mélée ensues in the mass media's 'culture of integration', offering a mixed bag of 'human interest' in entertainment and relaxation with the distance, difficulty and reasonableness of the proper public sphere dissolved in appeals to the senses.[36]

Habermas's theorisation is known for avoiding the actual blur of historical processes. Most of Kant's work and other contemporary philosophers' reached a wider audience through discussion in literary reviews that facilitated reading and knowledge.[37] Such mediation necessarily qualifies Habermas' key distinction between the early 'access-increasing' and 'transmitting' functions of journals and the facilitation in a 'culture-consuming' public sphere: typically, then as now, learning of philosophers' work through reviews is easier going. The neglect of Kant's political writings seems in part a function of their appearance in the relatively light-weight form of journals.[38] The neologism 'journalistic' (*OED,* 1829) and James Mill's remarkable critique of the early periodical form (1824) identifying its hegemonic role were themselves indicative of consumer-cradling practices early in the nineteenth century.[39] Regarding Habermas's important distinction between theory and practice, for Edmund Burke, Francis Jeffrey and many others

the founding event of modernity, the French Revolution, was very much related to the power of the press, where theory demonstrated performative capacities officially denied it.[40] This points to a key lacuna in theorisation of a disinterested public sphere, that utterance is not exterior to social relations where it is necessarily implicated in networks of power.[41] However, despite such weaknesses Habermas's engagement with changes identified at the time, taken warily, offers a useful template when considering broad historical shifts.

Kant was seen as 'the philosopher of the French Revolution' (*KPW,* 3), the most arresting event in Arnold's and many others' historical imagination. For Arnold the Revolution taught the ineluctability of political 'expansion' tending to 'mass-democracy' and change as the salient facts of modern life: his office is to alert others to their importance. The range of Arnold's allusions, eclecticism and instability clearly preclude simple association with any one writer; yet examining Kant's political thought, in particular his *Berlin Monthly Journal* article 'An Answer to the Question: "What is Enlightenment?"' (*KPW,* 54-60), establishes significant discursive antecedents of Arnold's thinking, howsoever they had been mediated in other political writings and through more informal processes described by Bourdieu, whereby 'philosophical doxa [are] carried along by intellectual rumour—labels of schools, truncated quotations, functioning as slogans in celebration or polemics'.[42]

Arnold's stated political and cultural values remained fairly constant: progressivism, didacticism, idealism, Europeanism, voluntarism, outreach, dedication to disinterested reason and ideas, preoccupation with prematurity, respect for the existing order, ambivalence to authority, teleological understanding, antipathy to mechanism and formalism, commitment to expansion and free play of the mind, distinction between thought and action, fixation with the French Revolution, attraction to a strong state, concept of 'aliens' and other tenets and lexical indexes such as 'tutelage', 'maturity', the categorical imperative and 'geist' are scattered throughout his 1860s' essays, marking them those of a post-Kantian man. In the general configuration of liberalism and authoritarianism, high moral tone and an extraordinary number of specific instances—echoes, allusions, exact phrasing, specific propositions, qualifications and emphases—they exhibit a Kantian commitment to reason, human autonomy and dignity disdainful of differences augmented by the aesthetic that allows them (associated with Schiller): a Kantian polis seems a crucial reference point in his thinking. This most obviously exceeds the terms of Kantian analysis in its concern with class but even here Arnold's attitude, declining particularity for a universal humanity, has Kantian overtones. By the time of *Culture and Anarchy* the sense of a necessary class dialectic evident in **'On Democracy'** (*SP*, 99-125) had faded to an extraordinarily ahistorical account in which the different classes are almost structurally identical, making them little more than groupings of differing qualities.

Its fierce antipathy to subordination and notion of the English democracy 'throwing off the tutelage of aristocracy' (*SP*, 113) links **'On Democracy'** to 'What is Enlightenment?' A relatively straight, vigorous political account compared with later texts, its acuity and honesty are striking concerning the effects of inegalitarian relationships. Here it seems Arnold is himself daring to know, in conformity with Kant's motto of Enlightenment, '*Sapere aude*! Have courage to use your *own* understanding!' (*KPW*,54). This entails theorising politically, phylogenetically, from the individual to the state, with conviction—seemingly his own experience not masked by irony, shaped in the light of Kantian precepts mediated most obviously by John Stuart Mill:

> Now, can it be denied, that a certain approach to equality, at any rate a certain reduction of signal inequalities, is a natural, instinctive demand of that impulse which drives society as a whole,—no longer individuals and limited classes only, but the mass of a community,—to develop itself with the utmost possible fulness and freedom? Can it be denied, that to be heavily overshadowed, to be profoundly insignificant, has, on the whole, a depressing and benumbing effect on the character?
>
> (*SP*, 104)

A Kantian emphasis on human dignity and autonomy persists in Arnold's criticism alongside a prescriptivism implicated in class interests that tends for many critics to void it.[43] In recent discounting of the egalitarianism Arnold is less seen as a political writer now than in earlier liberal criticism such as Lionel Trilling's. This seems related to an antipathy in poststructuralist thinking to broaching egalitarian sentiment, communal values and, in general, politics as it has been. Yet it is recurrently in this area of critique that Arnold, often so vague, is at his most trenchant. **'My Countrymen'** thus indicts the false-seeming of a nation's touting progress and superiority on the grounds of its actual incapacity for reason and ideas with a keenness at times redolent of Swift and the 'moral desperado' in Carlyle:

> if any one says to you, in your turn: 'The English system of a great landed aristocracy keeps your lower class a lower class for ever, and materialises and vulgarises your whole middle class,' you stare vacantly at the speaker, you cannot even take in his ideas; you can only blurt forth, in reply, some clap-trap . . .
>
> (*SP*, 193)

Here the severity, almost bludgeoning, is somewhat mitigated by 'airs and graces' in the form of literary devices—an ironic footnote respecting Jacobinism; the sustained ironic structure of foreigners' viewpoints. Distancing Arnold from this radical vision, these seem prompted by personal dialectics of empathy and estrangement and anxieties over a 'trenchant authoritative style' (*SP*, 177), with intensity defused in a polite reach for urbanity. The critic who sees **'My Countrymen'** so severely nicely corroborates Carlyle's conception of the press as heir to the pulpit,[44] with the literary devices functioning as emollients and sweeteners.

In subsequent 1860s' texts other Kantian political motifs recur: **'The Function of Criticism'** (*SP*, 130-57) looks back to Kant's 'free teachers of right', forward to *Culture and Anarchy*'s aliens. Its celebration of the French Revolution as demonstrating people's capacity for disinterest echoes Kant's qualified approval on the same ground (*KPW*, 182). In its attack on the Philistines **'My Countrymen'** (*SP*, 175-201) exudes the question of enlightenment: 'What is the modern problem? to make human life, all through, more natural and rational' (*SP*, 189). However, despite this political backdrop, some nudging as to its Prussian credentials in *Friendship's Garland,* and the subtitle announcing *An Essay in Social and Political Criticism*, *Culture and Anarchy* has seldom been regarded as a text of political thought.[45] In Stefan Collini's recent edition of *Culture and Anarchy and Other Writings* in the series, 'Cambridge Texts in the History of Political Thought', political dimensions are appropriately considered but recede before the social since 'we do not turn to him for that kind of intellectual architectonic, based on rigorous analysis of the nature of the state or the logic of political obligation' characterising Western political theory.[46] 'Other Writings' marks the architectonic abyss.

But while formal theoretical analysis is clearly absent, the assumptions just indicated point to a coherent Enlightenment political framework variously taken up by liberals in the nineteenth century, indeed registered by Arnold's critics in accusations of his 'transcendentalism' (for example, *SP*, 175). Inasmuch as Arnold presents 'rather, works of social criticism' concerned to 'cajole, mock, provoke, and persuade', as we will see in the next section, they appear founded on this theoretical structure, hardly lacking in ideas as to political obligations.[47] It seems that the subsequent blurring—an increasing non-specificity—of the historical and political analysis seen in **'On Democracy'** may even be a defensive response to criticisms of an absence of motivation in his political scheme. Frederic Harrison remonstrated 'what am I profited unless I learn how this same fiddlestick, or sauerkraut, or culture (call it as you please), comes to a man?' (*CH*, 229): persuading, cajoling, provoking, mocking, even despising attempt to establish the human connection and take-up of the ideal that Kant's notoriously dry work fails widely to inspire. A strict 'logic of political obligation' is thus neglected as a socio-psychological induction of it is attempted. Absence of motivation inducing men to 'dare to know' and be high-minded is a central criticism of Kant's work; Harrison's criticism suggests Arnold's footnote to **'My Countrymen'** (and other utterances to the same effect), that 'Philosophy has always been bringing me into trouble' (*SP,* 175), is not altogether ironic.

As much as in **'On Democracy'** and **'My Countrymen',** the central problematic in *Culture and Anarchy* is the promotion of reason and order in an expanding body politic—enabling it to *be* enlightened and modern—bequeathed from the Enlightenment. Kant actually circumvents the problem of motivation by conflating reason and morality in human nature; with persons inherently tilted towards the good, motivation is dispensed with on an ideal level. Arnold's cultural criticism in *Culture and Anarchy* in effect comes in at this point of weakness in Kant's theory—both qualifying Kant's voluntarism and displaying 'literary' features which seem, as just noted, politically motivated. The weakness in Enlightenment theory seemed demonstrated in the 1860s' run-up to electoral reform in 1867 when 'critical publicity' seemed feeble given contemporary disturbances; and all the more urgent given the development of party machinery and the political press.

At points echoing Alexis de Tocqueville's analysis and John Stuart Mill's, Arnold's sustained engagement with this changing political landscape has been mostly considered in terms of the contemporary public disturbances and accordingly attenuated. For the alliance between modern newspapers and political parties during the expansion of the newspaper reading public and democracy were crucial features of the English political scene from the 1860s. Together these innovations inaugurated a modern cultural politics, exploited by Gladstone in particular, where the image of leaders, publicity and party organisation are crucial.[48]

Arnold's critique of political leaders, particular measures and press representations relate exactly to these developments, as the enormous specificity of their reference argues. So from his *Essays in Criticism* he repeatedly objects to the 'world of catchwords and party habits' (*SP,* 139) binding those subject to them in a state of immaturity; criticises numerous individuals and developments in public life (a whole article which became a chapter in *Culture and Anarchy* argued with measures favoured by **'Our Liberal Practitioners'**; *CA,* 165-201); and repeatedly criticises newspaper representations for partisanship.[49] Time and again he objects to proposals not based on universal criteria of reason and justice but rather specious private interests of the party machine as in Liberal support for disestablishment of the Irish Church, which he sees as motivated by party political expediency in securing nonconformist support (*CA,* 166-174).

On a notorious occasion he attacks Sir Charles Adderley and Mr Roebuck for pious political rhetoric and Anglo-Saxon triumphalism as they manifest racism, extolling 'the old Anglo-Saxon race . . . [as] the best breed in the whole world'. Again here catchwords and political slogans are undercut on point of their discrepancy with realities of poverty, child murder and brutality in the case of 'a girl named Wragg' taken into custody following her child's murder (*SP,* 144-6). Disinterested, critical reason is required in the electorate and political leaders alike to see through the 'dogmas and formulas' (or the 'sanitised words') of those using a rhetoric of progress that enables 'speakers to speak without thinking what they speak'.

To categorise this and other analysis as 'social' (or 'personal'), more than political, seems to prioritise the interests of organised political bodies and/or theory over the agency of individual subjects: Arnold traces the generalising language back to circumstances that contradict them. Here modern political life appears to start with Enlightenment ideals and the requirement that political subjects exercise 'resolution and courage to use . . . [their understanding] without the guidance of another' (*KPW,* 54), exercising a base-line democratic political function in vigilance towards those in authority.

Arnold's insistent message, focusing recurrently on representations, that political leaders, the electorate and the press generally need to be more critical, becomes less banal than timely given the take-off of a modern media society and politics increasingly conducted through party organisations and cultural forms. Even his confession of his earlier misguided worship of Benjamin Franklin and Jeremy Bentham in **'Sweetness and Light'** (*CA,* 67-8) has a timely edge. For this underlines the outmodedness of Carlylean hero-worship in a modern, disenchanted age, at precisely the point at which politics threatened its revival in the cult of particular leaders. Repeatedly Arnold fastens on 'mendacious' forms of publicity where public figures use universalist Enlightenment terms to promote private interests. His repeated deflation of the rhetoric of political speeches reported in the press—as in the case of Wragg—amounts to exercises in practical criticism and elementary semiotic awareness exposing the politicians' hype through reference to actuality. The grounds of his critique, urging the public sphere's plane of disinterest, free play of mind and critical reason as the test of all, appear consistently and turn on the 'manipulative publicity' outlined by Habermas. In these respects, then, it seems Arnold straightforwardly echoes Enlightenment tenets and applies them reflexively in his analysis of contemporary political phenomena and discourses; in doing so he points to the Enlightenment genealogy of cultural studies.

The 'New Phenomenon': Arnold and 'Manipulative Publicity'

Culture on the one hand and a strong and interventionist state where appropriate were Arnold's quite opposed solutions to the present ills in ***Culture and Anarchy***. Notwithstanding its engagement with contemporary political developments, the call 'to see things as they are' (***CA***, 46), distancing political action, and the aesthetic emphasis on 'sweetness and light' can eclipse the interventionist strand. This, and its many 'literary' features, seem a factor in its invisibility as socio-political discourse. But with a Kantian backdrop ***Culture and Anarchy*** is more remarkable for insisting that culture entails the Hebraic 'passion for doing good' and the related interventionism. While Arnold at times specifically resists the idea that at present 'the world wants fire and strength more than sweetness and light' (***CA***, 205), the intensities of his prose and the role of his state problematise this proposition.

A pressing problem when reading it are the lapses from reason's protocols. Detachment, disinterest, curiosity, urbanity are often absent, most notably in rudeness towards Philistines and intensities where the prose veers towards all-out utterance. An early instance is the gross objectification and sustained sneer at the Philistines beginning, 'Culture says: "Consider these people, then, their way of life, their habits, their manners, the very tones of their voice; look at them attentively"' (***CA***, 52). Later, Arnold defends a non-manipulative public sphere, condemning 'the ordinary popular literature' and those who try 'to give the masses, as they call them, an intellectual food prepared and adapted in the way they think proper for the actual condition of the masses' (***CA***, 69). But soon after he works up a quasi-racist frenzy of righteousness and religious imagery concerning culture and 'the division of light from darkness' (***CA***, 71) that cannot be exonerated from comparable manipulative intent.

Yet the proliferating definitions, joining 'spontaneity of consciousness' and 'strictness of conscience', 'seeing things as they are' and 'the passion for doing good', Hellenic and Hebraic principles in culture, aspire to make this intensity like all departures from equanimity a non-problem. The particular purchase of the Hebraic here seems its justification of a heavy-handedness that departs from the reason and voluntarist ethos of the public sphere. Admitting into it the authoritarianism that Kant (and Arnold too) approves outside it in the state as the very condition of the public sphere's freedom, the Hebraic principle apparently licenses local textual violations of reason to pressure readers into assent. Its extra-textual action is similar, urging state intervention into civil society to the end of ultimately realising perfection. Both textuality and its referent thus see norms of the public sphere contravened with rational protocols and separation of state and civil society suspended. By means of the Hebraic, in short, history's destination may be hastened. Here it seems significant that, much like Bourdieu's understanding of the role of 'intellectual rumour' quoted earlier, Arnold's perception of the public sphere's functioning at times deprecates the importance of books as such and other forms of polite society besides rougher modes boding more expansive and vital communication—'a current of ideas' beyond books making society 'in the fullest measure . . . intelligent and alive' (***SP***, 135).

Hardly fortuitously, then, as the enabling principle of Arnold's textual versatility and contradictions the Hebraic is at one (neglected) point privileged over Hellenic 'sweetness and light': 'culture has one great passion, the passion for sweetness and light. It has one even yet greater! the passion for letting them prevail' (***CA***, 69). Here in this 'touching' self-correction, with Arnold seemingly yielding to some sweet impulse within, readers encounter a paradoxical passion, for letting 'sweetness and light' prevail; or *faux naïveté*. The repetition and punctuation marks insinuate passion in exclamation and self-correction—apparently evidencing the very priority being upheld with the critic 'carried away' into an exclamation mark. At this 'familiar' point perhaps undermining readers' critical faculties, morality interestingly loses its usual imperative cast, becoming a matter of 'letting' sweetness and light prevail, rather than 'making' and 'doing', the customary locutions. Again hardly fortuitously, the moral impulse is relayed as 'passion'—that is, naturalised, so affiliated to the Hellenic.

Such textual manœuvring, especially the sweet spontaneity of the exclamation mark, presumably exemplifies the 'airs' and 'low buffoonery' Sidgwick and Fitzjames Stephen protested. The seeming spontaneity and ingratiating facility evidence a shortfall in reason's norms of distance and difficulty. They try to cajole readers into a mood of acceptance. Often elsewhere Arnold resorts to confessional discourse, writing in the first-person singular, with similar significance attaching to personal display. The public sphere's boundaries required in contrast impersonality and self-collection: 'free teachers of right' 'do not address themselves in familiar tones to the *people* . . . but in respectful tones to the state' (***KPW***, 186).

Soon after the fiercely partisan prophetic voice appears dividing 'light from darkness', looking to 'the revolution of the times; for the old order is passed, and the new arises' (***CA***, 71). Again, as often, highly charged prose seemingly aspires to abolish Kantian critical distance in heavy-gunned Hebraic appeal to tastes and senses which might also be construed as spontaneity of consciousness. Howsoever, it hijacks signifiers of Christianity for its secular substitute, in accordance with the promotional practices of modern journalism and adver- tising: W. T. Stead's investigative journalism 'The Maiden Tribute of Modern Babylon' is an obvious ex- ample of such sensational deployment of religious lan- guage and imagery.[50] Here again the types of the Hel- lenic and Hebraic are not distinct. A rationale appears in a later quotation from the French religious philoso- pher Joubert:

> 'Just what makes worship impressive,' says Joubert, 'is its publicity, its external manifestation, its sound, its splendour, its observance universally and visibly hold- ing its sway . . . the same devotion', as he says in an- other place, 'unites men far more than the same thought and knowledge'.
>
> (*CA,* 171)

Appreciative of the functions of ritual, this passage un- derscores the instrumentalism and appeal to the senso- rium in the overblown passages. It makes Arnold's pur- poseful periodic recycling of religious language seem a kind of necessary softening muzak for the harmonious relations identified with culture: in the method, if sel- dom the precise means, a flagrant publicist of modern times. The emotive prose seemingly presumes people's responsivity to a hard sell—the 'devotion' generated— will enlist them to the cause of culture that ostensibly stands for something else. Arnold was caricatured by Frederic Harrison in terms of 'Culture [sitting] high aloft with a pouncet-box to spare her senses aught unpleasant' (*CH,* 233)—an apotheosis of dandyish fas- tidiousness, preparing the way for Wilde—and the nega- tive response of distaste is a standard feature of his public image. But much of the distinctiveness of *Cul- ture and Anarchy* lies in fulsome orchestration of the senses with appeals to reason.

The Preface of *Culture and Anarchy* entertains some- thing of this internal anarchy in urging the Hellenic be given a top-up of Hebraism's energy that gives 'to man the happiness of doing what he knows' (*CA,* 38). Here, when you do what you know, the boundaries between thought and action and the separate identities of the Hellenic and Hebraic collapse, under the distracting smile of happiness. All in all there seems substantial in- terpenetration of the Hellenic and Hebraic, contrary to the racial dialectic Robert Young elaborates in which each remains distinct.[51] Most obviously, there is 'our race' (*CA,* 38) at their confluence—much as Arnold himself was a product of interracial union of Saxon and Celt.

The instability and permeability of the terms may be part of their attraction for a writer persistently balking at the authority he calls for.[52] They insinuate 'clear' dis- tinctions and their fusion too, graphically: embodiment stretches to what logic cannot reach, granting benefits of identity and non-identity too. What is more (when

apparently speculation as to the resemblance of the En- glish and Jews was common) the racial binary of the Hebraic and Hellenic is somewhat homely and suited to teaching the Puritans a lesson—constituting a sort of al- legory with scant narrative, outdoing them on their own ground.[53] After all, all that 'is said about Hebraism and Hellenism, has for its main result to show how our Pu- ritans, ancient and modern, have not enough added to their care for walking staunchly by the best light they have' (*CA,* 11).

The discursive potency of race has already been glimpsed in the Anglo-Saxon triumphalism Arnold at- tacked through the case of Wragg. The typologisation of class within *Culture and Anarchy* seems to proceed on a similar basis, capitalising on the publicity of the group identities in a particularly flagrant way. For Ar- nold's descriptions and exhortation to disinterest utilise the popular discourse and methods of opponents such as John Bright.[54] Notwithstanding the fact that the call for 'the best self' is philosophically specious, it seems to have had widespread appeal related to its accessibil- ity and, again, a 'homeliness' emanating from 'familiar words'.

I have used them with reference to the first chapter of *Culture and Anarchy* but the Hellenic and Hebraic do not appear until later. This points further to their impor- tance as publicising devices: referring variable assort- ments of mental traits to two racial types offers an easy handle on them. It braces the criticism with quasi- anthropological terms while proceeding as if on the level of a family romance in which different character- istics descending from different family lines are dis- cussed. It is in accord with the practice of personalisa- tion central to modern news discourses and the flight from abstraction Arnold sees the French religious phi- losopher Joubert commending in his *Essays in Criti- cism.* As glimpsed already, the personal—in the form of Arnold's persona, prolific reference to others and gen- eral gravitation to embodiment—figures prominently throughout his work, further marking it off from the im- personal abstract discourse of critical publicity. Other boundaries—most notably between feeling and reason— are repeatedly crossed: as if he demarcates identities, and binary oppositions, for publicist ends, only to refuse them authority also. In this most fundamental respect, it seems Arnold undermines the Enlightenment public sphere through ultimately refusing its binary structure and authority.

One of the most instructive passages in this respect in- volves another key moment of publicity, the virtuoso Preface to the *Essays in Criticism* culminating in a set- piece on Oxford. Disdaining replying to his critics as such as his essays are collected in a book, Arnold in general terms here defends his playfulness in the name of non-violence, humility, righteousness:

To try and approach truth on one side after another, not to strive or cry, nor to persist in pressing forward, on any one side, with violence and self-will—it is only thus, it seems to me, that mortals may hope to gain any vision of the mysterious Goddess, whom we shall never see except in outline, but only thus even in outline. He who will do nothing but fight impetuously towards her on his own, one, favourite, particular line, is inevitably destined to run his head into the folds of the black robe in which she is wrapped.

(*SP,* 126)

The lines tread pre-Raphaelite territory with murky emotions, gender anxieties, a black-robed Goddess, also an ambience of Sunday School tracts about naughty boys—a defence of plurality and freedoms through their exercise. Again hypercharged prose anticipates 'new journalism', in particular the religious and classical imagery saturating 'The Maiden Tribute of Modern Babylon'; and here as often in Arnold's writing there is more than a scent of parody—and/or a wind got up—in the symmetry, emphasis, allusions. Suggestions of parody and extreme theatricality are intensified in the essay's virtuosity as it rushes from the lyrical and neo-chivalric to the neo-classical and *The Dunciad* and then on to a trio of magicians, the Woodford Branch of the Great Eastern Line and the black comedy of a murder. The densely allusive lines celebrate distance and variety over contact and singularity; but the writer who celebrates plurality so energetically comes as close to saying nothing as saying all. His proclivity for performance admits a plural, heterodox self flagrantly at odds with the 'drab of the earnest' and straight ways of the happily named Mr Wright (*SP,* 127).

Further arguing the staginess of the whole, there is a notable redundancy in 'inevitably destined' and a self-refuting insistence in the whole passage that is partly a function of so many pressing monosyllables. So we may ask, exactly whose and what interests are being defended? Why ever does the *head* of the impetuous fighter run 'into the folds'? And why is goddess truth (if she is it) robed in black? The intertextuality of hymn, prayer, poetry—all the chivalric non-fighting echoing Donne, St Ignatius Loyola, Bunyan—seems another attempt to recuperate the energy of the absolute for the cause of plurality; the soft 'folds of the black robe' awaiting that head suggest even the absolute may have abandoned rigidity. In the next paragraph the versatility of the writing argues directly against rectitude and absolutism in the form of that Mr Wright and strict correspondence in a Philistine rule-bound society—'the drab of the earnest, prosaic, practical, austerely literal future' (*SP,* 127).

From such a mixed environment the outlines of Oxford ('the mysterious goddess' transformed, it seems) emerge at the end of the Preface's climb towards it: 'home of lost causes, and forsaken beliefs, and unpopular names,

and impossible loyalties' (*SP,* 130), an ideal centre centred in ex-centricity and plurality. Hardly surprisingly given the paradoxes and opacities on the run-in, the prolongation of the attack on more worldly contemporaries associated with the place—such as Fitzjames Stephen and other *Saturday Review* contributors hostile to Arnold—tends to be overlooked. But 'lost', 'forsaken', 'unpopular', 'impossible' characterise 'this queen of romance' and should not be so entirely deprived of their frequent evaluative load as to have an entirely positive accent. The possibility of barbed criticism and ambivalence is heightened given the preceding comedy: casually we meet three well-known theatrical performers using 'the honourable style of Professor' 'a title I share with so many distinguished men,—Professor Pepper, Professor Andersen, Professor Frickel, and others,—who adorn it, I feel, much more than I do' (*SP,* 127-8). The extent of Arnold's attachment to the university is problematised in the essay; his prose actually implicates 'her' in the 'fierce intellectual life of our century' that he upholds as her antithesis. Readers may be led to take Oxford's refulgence—'her' role as a beacon of culture—unambiguously partly through sensory and intellectual repletion, the 'Preface' comprising a particularly dazzling instance of prophet and comedian in concert.

The mobility journalism's informality seems to have excited in Arnold is particularly apparent in oppositions, definitions and catchphrases whose reference shifts and numerous contradictions. Arnold thus famously deplores animosity ('culture hates hatred', *CA,* 69) excepting his own—approving the passions mentioned above and recurrently lapsing into savagery, as for instance on middle-class religion, 'the very lowest form of intelligential life . . . [offering], for a great treat, a lecture on teetotalism and nunneries'. Even in the act of enunciation, though, this slips the blade of savagery—the bathos of nursery idiom ('a great treat') soliciting its targets on their own ascetic ground to do without and see bigger. The humorous move, appealing to asceticism, weakens the case against it: glimpses of absolutes may even with Philistines be qualified. Indeed it seems disinterest—in the form of a sharing and a sense of commonality where differences are dropped— may be better induced in readers through humour than reason, and the arresting power of virtuosity. Appropriately, given the sliding prose, 'sweetness and light' has the distinction of hardly acceding to the referential at all—a catchphrase that is taken as such, a rallying-cry of taste and disposition, whose usage has become invariably ironic.

George Eliot registers the Philistinism in fact attaching to Arnold's culture in a joke in *Daniel Deronda*. University will give Deronda 'a passport in life', 'a little disinterested culture to make head against cotton and capital, especially in the House'.[55] Here in Eliot's awareness of the Philistine within a critic critiquing the same, and more generally, Arnold's ostensibly 'lucid' oppositions and 'key' categories founder, apparently contributing to his success as a publicist. For if the sense of 'lucidity' or 'clarity' largely derive from the drawing up of succinct formulations, vivid oppositions and types, catchphrases, familiar words, images and strong feeling in what were then termed Arnold's 'vivacities' (as in the animus against the *British Banner, CA,* 111), generating a succession of momentary strong effects above 'the confusion which environs' (*CA,* 202) the reader, they seem to enact the project of culture as a whole in presenting a defence against anarchy. In the face of language's repeated slippages and contradictions the determinate beckons as, say, an idealised Oxford: 'he [Arnold] says a few things in such a way as that *almost inspite of ourselves* we remember them' (*CH,* 149). The 'high standard' or 'authoritative centre' culture broadly implied for Arnold seems locally enacted for Henry James here in words and notions salvaged from time and, apparently, the unconscious, since '*ourselves*' drag against it.

Arnold cherished the general currency his phrases achieved. Writers often deal in 'memorable' phrases, few though—excepting writers of aphorisms, poetry, advertisements—with such virtuosity where what stands out is the standing out, as in 'sweetness and light'. As performance, outdoing ordinary, 'literal' language use, they are a variant of the virtuosity and playfulness already observed in Arnold's criticism. This playfulness is usually taken as relieving the high seriousness and authoritarian tendencies rather than undermining them. But a performative rather than a cognitive or aesthetic office even informs Arnold's famous definition of culture. This invokes routine journalistic functions of taking knowledge out of closets, as it were, and putting it into circulation. Even so, with distinct circularity, 'the best' appears a function of being 'the best that is known and thought in the world'—a feat of publicisation primarily:

> The great men of culture are those who have had a passion for diffusing, for making prevail, for carrying from one end of society to the other, the best knowledge, the best ideas of their time; who have laboured to divest knowledge of all that was harsh, uncouth, difficult, abstract, professional, exclusive; to humanize it, to make it efficient outside the clique of the cultivated and learned, yet still remaining the *best* knowledge and thought of the time.
>
> (*CA,* 70)

The rather plaintive culminating insistence—'yet still remaining the best knowledge'—acknowledges the question the exposition chronically begs: exactly what remains of 'the best' (or of anything?) post such rigorous remodelling? 'The *best* knowledge and thought of the time' appear here, like the 'best self', like culture it-

self, absolutely constituted by the negatives and particularities they escape. Swinging from the margins to the citadels of culture with the divestment of the disconcerting, unprepossessing, complexity, difficulty, abstraction, exclusivity (all particularities or provincialisms of the mind), the retention of identity as 'the best knowledge and thought of the time' after such an overhaul seems an acute instance of consuming resources of singularity and critical challenge and reclaiming their value too, on an impossible 'familiar' basis. Here it seems that identity is forfeited for exchange value and utopianly retained too.

The famous passage suggests Arnold's criticism endorses a journalistic dedication to 'writing for the public' where the best writing stands out by standing out—sufficiently detached for time and space travel, like **'Empedocles on Etna'** on Derby station. This postmodern image enacts hybridity, crossing boundaries and defying authorities, bringing a staging post on the high cultural tour in poetry to the provincial railway passenger; an exotic place-name to bookstalls selling 'familiar words', which it will join. Its excitement exceeds the mixing of aristocrat and likely middle-class reader for in railway technology the vista of mass publicity and the future open up.

'Currency in the world' is upheld against exclusive scholastic usages and difficulty in Arnold's article/essay on **'Joubert'** that anticipates the famous passage above. In part a manual for writers in manipulative publicity, it offers clues to Arnold's publicist abilities. For instance, Arnold includes Joubert's dictum, 'It is by means of familiar words that style takes hold of the reader and gets possession of him'. The essay also suggests a philosophic rationale for Arnold's highly inhabited and topical prose in Joubert's quarrel with metaphysics' preferring abstraction over 'the sensible' world most people relate to: 'Distrust, in books on metaphysics, words which have not been able to get currency in the world.'[56] In this context Arnold's pose of 'plain man' suggests an egalitarian strain and rhetoric: what matters in the world is of it and has purchase within it. He attempts a common appeal through variety, the senses, declaration of preferences, 'familiar words', a teasing persona, cajolery. These features corresponded with changes in contemporary newspaper journalism invoking worldly 'human interest' and egalitarianism. But they share a tendency to buttonhole readers, reducing distance and making dissent more difficult, like the entertainment—the variety act—of a successful comedian. There are obvious calls for, and objections to, associating such strategies with democracy.

This account has drawn on Habermas' study. But since his structuring distinctions were never as clear-cut as he suggests, the question of a historical break in Arnold's criticism is problematised. I have argued that his criticism is politically grounded in Enlightenment theory assuming expansion of the body politic, where reason, the public sphere and journalism are all pivotal. Neglect of this political framework seems to have involved both English hostility to idealism and literary disregard of journalistic form.[57] But Arnold's transgression of the norms of 'critical publicity' needs also to be emphasised, since it situates him—and the 'objective' line of journalism he represents—within the modern practices he denigrates. His journalism thus evidences internally an opposition between two models of journalism customarily located externally, in a bifurcation within journalism at the time he was writing.[58] His own attack on 'a new journalism' in 1887 was indeed instrumental in the currency of the idea of bifurcation by identifying 'a new journalism' which neglected journalism's obligation to 'get at the state of things as they really are'. Yet Arnold ignored this obligation himself, crudely linking 'the democracy' to 'feather-brained' journalism as part of his attack on Irish Home Rule.[59] His 1860s, criticism is unstable and manipulative—emotive, dismissive, careless, personal, confessional: blurring Enlightenment boundaries between public and private, ideas and practice, reason and senses.

His exhibition of typical attitudes among the dominant cultural grouping he belongs to (in scathingly dismissing 'Mr. Wright''s earnestness, for instance) highlights the particular class interests in 'disinterest' and in this respect undermines the project of disinterested reason. Since it supplies critics with plentiful social grounds for objecting to Arnold's critique it points to his partial complicity with attacks on a disinterested sphere. But his high-handed dismissiveness also functions rhetorically by showing fallible humanity. This enhances the vision of a 'best self' and culture through an inoculation of 'human' shortcomings. The many references to Arnold's 'humanity' indicate its centrality to his publicity.

The alternatives show a modern identity charged through performance and publicity: hardly the discrete self of official liberal humanism. The playfulness extends to self-difference and undecidability, so that while it apparently serves serious ends it also tends to their subversion: if Arnold historically represents a new, hybrid kind of critical seriousness in entertaining, mobile prose reaching beyond conventional norms in the public sphere—a sort of seriousness that dare not show as such—he also undermines serious criticism in prose that contradicts key precepts in his criticism and is notably unhinged. My account has argued a fairly orthodox critic of propaganda and journalism, upholding the role of a critical public in modern democracies, but with a keener political edge than 'Arnoldian' usually suggests; also a neglected 'propagandist for criticism', whose own practice resembles 'a new journalism' and subverts Enlightenment norms. Arnold's writing on Joubert not 'trying to fit his ideas into a house' points to journalism's importance here: 'I doubt whether, in an elaborate work on the philosophy of religion, he [Joubert] would have got his ideas to *shine,* to use his own expression, as they shine when he utters them in perfect freedom'.[60] It seems time Arnold's modernity and significance are revised so as to register the interrelationship of ideas and 'expression' and the freedoms and 'shining' journalism enabled in his case, encapsulated in the notion of an unhoused form. Here 'high culture' is qualified in a street act of sorts where critical reason is jostled in 'free' expression.

Notes

See also H. Super (ed.), *The Complete Prose Works of Matthew Arnold,* 11 vols (University of Michigan: Ann Arbor, 1960-77).

1. Late Arnoldian concerns appear in Virginia Woolf, *The Voyage Out* (Penguin: Harmondsworth, 1992 [1915]), for instance 36.

2. On cultural capital see Pierre Bourdieu, *Distinction: A Social Critique of the Judgement of Taste,* tr. Richard Nice (Routledge: London, 1994); Pierre Bourdieu, *The Field of Cultural Production,* ed. Randal Johnson (Polity Press: Cambridge, 1993).

3. On the Newbolt Report and social classes see Chris Baldick, *The Social Mission of English Criticism* (Oxford UP: 1983), 95.

4. 'Arnold, Matthew', *Dictionary of National Biography* (Smith, Elder & Co.: London, 1901), suppl., Vol. 1, 70-5, 75.

5. T. S. Eliot, *The Sacred Wood* (Methuen: London, 1920), 1.

6. Edmund Burke, *Reflections on the Revolution in France* (J. M. Dent: London, 1967), 330.

7. See 'An "Interview" with Jacques Derrida', *Cambridge Review,* Oct. 1992, 131. Arnold's disclaimers (*SP,* 127-8) scarcely detract from his academic authority.

8. It seems more extensive research would establish that Arnold's Burke *was* an icon of this criticism; Keating (*SP,* 11) registers the passage's celebrity.

9. Robert Young, *Colonial Desire: Hybridity in Theory, Culture and Race* (Routledge: London, 1995), 55.

10. Baldick, *Social Mission* [*The Social Mission of English Criticism*], 31-2; acknowledging limitations owing to the exigencies of tracing a 'particular "line"', 16. For early concern with prematurity see Kant, *KPW,* 55.

11. Baldick, *Social Mission,* 26.

12. See Nicholas Murray, *A Life of Matthew Arnold* (Hodder & Stoughton: London, 1996), 229; Sidgwick, *CH*, 210-11.

13. See Perry Meisel, *The Myth of the Modern* (Yale UP: 1987), 39-53; Arnold, 'The Modern Element in Literature', in Miriam Allott (ed.), *Selected Poems and Prose: Matthew Arnold* (J. M. Dent: London, 1993), 135, 130; Tony Pinkney, 'Matthew Arnold and the Subject of Modernity', *Critical Survey*, 4:3 (1992), 226-32.

14. See Meisel, *Myth of the Modern*, 39; on the Arnold-Leavis line see Baldick, *Social Mission*, 193 (final résumé) and *passim*, 162-93.

15. [Fitzjames Stephen], 'Matthew Arnold and His Countrymen', *Saturday Review*, XVIII (3 Dec. 1864), 683. Keating is exceptional in noting 'the humorist' (*SP*, 10) but relates this to literature as distinct from the 'social thought'.

16. On the contestatory force of hybridity see Young, *Colonial Desire*, 22-6.

17. Quoted, Murray, *A Life*, 201.

18. The term 'new journalism' is widely attributed to Arnold with reference to the work of W. T. Stead: see 'Up to Easter', *Nineteenth Century*, May 1887, 638-9; also in Fraser Neiman (ed.), *Matthew Arnold: Essays, Letters and Reviews* (Harvard UP: Cambridge, MA, 1960), 347.

19. Ian Hamilton, *A Gift Imprisoned: The Poetic Life of Matthew Arnold* (Bloomsbury: London, 1998).

20. Quoted, Murray, *A Life*, 141.

21. Georg Lukàcs, *History and Class Consciousness* (Merlin Press: London, 1971), 100.

22. Max Weber, C. Wright Mills and H. H. Gerth (eds), *Essays in Sociology* (Kegan Paul, Trench, Trubner: London, 1947), 96.

23. Letter, August 1849/50?, in S. O. A. Ullmann, *The Yale Manuscript* (University of Michigan Press: Ann Arbor, 1989), 171.

24. See Allott (ed.), *Selected Poems and Prose*, 135, 138. Meisel, *Myth of the Modern*, 39-53, elaborates Arnold's attempts at self-mastery in poetry and continuities in the prose without registering the importance of journalistic form.

25. See Christopher Kent, 'Higher Journalism and the Mid-Victorian Clerisy', *Victorian Studies*, Dec. 1969, 181-98.

26. See Claire Tomalin, 'In His Father's Shadow', *Sunday Times*, 15 Mar. 1998.

27. For Arnold's range see Walter Houghton (ed.), *Wellesley Index to Victorian Periodicals*, 5 vols (Routledge, Kegan Paul: London, 1966-89), Vol. 5, 31-2.

28. Sir John Robinson, *Fifty Years of Fleet Street* (Macmillan: London, 1904), 222.

29. [Fitzjames Stephen], 'Homeric Translators and Critics', *Saturday Review*, XII 27 (July 1861), 95.

30. Allott, *Selected Poems and Prose*, 129.

31. Dependence on others appears in *SL*, 141; the 'prosthetic body' of the public sphere in Michael Warner, 'The Mass Public and the Mass Subject', in Bruce Robbins (ed.), *The Phantom Public Sphere* (University of Minnesota Press: Minneapolis, 1993), 236-43.

32. Jurgen Habermas, *The Structural Transformation of the Public Sphere*, tr. Thomas Burger, asstd. Frederick Lawrence (Polity: Cambridge, 1992), 141-222.

33. Bourdieu, *Distinction*, 462.

34. Ibid., 460; 462; 444.

35. Ibid., for example 446. Bourdieu's allegiance to Enlightenment values is encapsulated in his later expressed goal, 'to universalize the conditions of access to the universal', in Bourdieu, *On Television and Journalism*, tr. Priscilla Parkhurst Ferguson (Pluto: London, 1998), 1.

36. Habermas, *Structural Transformation* [*The Structural Transformation of the Public Sphere*], 175.

37. Giuseppe Micheli and Rene Wellek, *Kant in England 1793-1938* (Routledge: London, 1993), *passim*: see Micheli, 4 ff., on 'trivialisation in the reports' of Kant's writings. My thanks to Gareth Stedman Jones for the Wellek reference.

38. Hans Reiss points towards the significance of different material forms: 'the fact that Kant's great works of critical philosophy are so formidable makes his less exacting political writings appear very much less weighty' (*KPW*, 3).

39. [James Mill], 'Periodical Literature', *Westminster Review*, Jan. 1824, 206-49.

40. Burke, *Reflections* [*Reflections on the Revolution in France*], 294; [Francis Jeffrey], 'Mounier, de l'influence des philosophes', *Edinburgh Review*, I (Oct. 1802), 1 ff.

41. This point can be laboured philosophically in terms of the non-distinctness between constative and performative modes of utterance.

42. Bourdieu, *Cultural Production* [*The Field of Cultural Production*], 32, presents this heterodox intellectual transmission. Extensive reading, mid-century Oxford interest in Kant (see Micheli, and Wellek *Kant in England*, 261 ff.) and friendship with the Kantian John Duke Coleridge all presumably contributed to Arnold's absorption of Kantian tenets.

43. Reiss is not alone in his view that 'the problem of human freedom was at the very core of his [Kant's] thought' (*KPW*, 3).

44. See, for instance, 'The Hero as Man of Letters', in Thomas Carlyle, *On Heroes, Hero-Worship and the Heroic in History* (University of California Press: Berkeley, 1993), 140.

45. Omission of the subtitle in J. Dover Wilson's edition [1932] contributed to this disregard.

46. Stefan Collini (ed.), *Culture and Anarchy and Other Writings* (Cambridge UP: 1993), xxvi.

47. Ibid.

48. See Stephen Koss, *The Rise and Fall of the Political Press in Britain*, 2 vols (Hamish Hamilton: London, 1981) Vol. 1; A. J. Lee, *Origins of the Popular Press*, (Croom Helm: London, 1976); D. A. Hamer, 'Gladstone: The Making of a Political Myth', *Victorian Studies*, 22:1 (1978), 29-50; Patrick Joyce, *Democratic Subjects: The Self and the Social in Nineteenth-Century England* (Cambridge UP: 1994).

49. Walter Houghton, 'Periodical Literature and the Articulate Classes' in Joanne Shattock and Michael Wolff (eds), *The Victorian Periodical Press: Samplings and Soundings* (Leicester UP: 1982), 3-27, broadly contests Arnold's criticisms of the press.

50. See *Pall Mall Gazette*, 4, 6, 7, 8, 10 July 1885; also Judith Walkowitz, *City of Dreadful Delights: Narratives of Sexual Danger in Late-Victorian London* (Virago: London, 1994), 81-120.

51. Young, *Colonial Desire*, 87.

52. Neglected in the writing itself, the irresolution towards authority is otherwise much remarked—for example in Michael J. Levenson, *A Genealogy of Modernism* (Cambridge UP: 1992), 24-7.

53. Young notes ideas of English Jewish resemblance, *Colonial Desire*, 84; and the heterosexuality of hybridity (25-6; inadvertently suggesting more homeliness).

54. See Joyce's controversial *Democratic Subjects*, 124-46.

55. George Eliot, *Daniel Deronda* (Penguin: Harmondsworth, 1983), 217.

56. Arnold, 'Joubert', in his *Essays in Criticism*, first series (Macmillan: London, 1910 [1865]), 281, 283.

57. See here Micheli and Wellek, *Kant in England*, passim.

58. Invoking the 'bifurcation' in the 'journalistic field' in the nineteenth century see, for instance, Bourdieu and the sources he mentions, *On Television and Journalism*, 70, 93-4.

59. Arnold, 'Up to Easter', 639.

60. Arnold, *Essays in Criticism*, 285, 286.

Abbreviations

Page references from Arnold's criticism and letters, contemporary criticism and Kant's political writings appear within the text in brackets, abbreviated as follows:

CA: Matthew Arnold, *Culture and Anarchy*, ed. J. Dover Wilson (Cambridge UP: 1988).

SL: Clinton Machann and Forrest D. Burt (eds), *Selected Letters of Matthew Arnold* (Macmillan: Basingstoke, 1993).

SP: P. J. Keating (ed.), *Matthew Arnold: Selected Prose* (Penguin: Harmondsworth, 1987).

CH: Carl Dawson and John Pfordresher (eds), *Matthew Arnold, Prose Writings: The Critical Heritage* (Routledge & Kegan Paul: London, 1979).

KPW: Hans Reiss (ed.), *Kant's Political Writings*, tr. H. B. Nisbet (Cambridge UP: 1970).

Amanda Anderson (essay date 2001)

SOURCE: Anderson, Amanda. "Disinterestedness as a Vocation: Revisiting Matthew Arnold." In *The Powers of Distance: Cosmopolitanism and the Cultivation of Detachment*, pp. 91-118. Princeton, N.J.: Princeton University Press, 2001.

[*In the following essay, Anderson explores the multiple layers of Arnold's famous disinterestedness and maintains that his intense commitment to objectivity was a response to what he saw as the fundamental challenges of the modern world.*]

The Arnoldian concept of disinterestedness has strongly influenced the development of Anglo-American literary studies, both as an ideal and as an object of ongoing and stringent critique. Matthew Arnold's defense of the distanced viewpoint as a positive achievement of character and culture contrasts with Dickens's elaborate suspicions, yet both writers exemplify a more general cultural anxiety about the moral ramifications of modern objectifying practices. Despite the continuing hold that debates over Arnold exert on our profession, this aspect of Arnold's thought has been under-studied, especially in recent criticism. To Arnold is generally attributed the dubious honor of instituting the discipline of English as a humanistic study of works of literature deemed great and timeless, through a method that appeals to standards of objectivity and reason. While there have been a number of appraisals of Arnold that cogently reconstruct the insistently social and historical dimensions of his work, it nonetheless remains the case that his ideals of criticism as disinterestedness and culture as the pursuit of perfection are often assumed to connect seamlessly to his later touchstone theory of poetic greatness.[1] Such a view, however, misses one of the most important underlying investments of Arnold's thought: its persistent concern with the moral and characterological elements of modern intellectual and aesthetic practices. Acknowledgment of this aspect of Arnold's thought, moreover, is crucial to any comprehensive understanding of his conception of cultivated detachment, whether that be conceived in scientific, aesthetic, or cosmopolitan terms.

The preliminary point to be made about Arnold's ideal of disinterestedness is that, from a philosophical standpoint, it is terminologically and conceptually unsystematic, comprising what are elsewhere in the tradition distinguished as clearly different forms of detachment. Many readers of Arnold assume that the principle of objective realism, the endeavor to "see the object as in itself it really is," is meant to be the primary definition of the critical ideal in **"The Function of Criticism at the Present Time."**[2] Yet also prominent in this 1864 essay is an understanding of criticism as the "free play" of the mind upon conventional or customary ideas. Such flexible judgment is guaranteed, for Arnold, by one's cultivated distance from the practical sphere: criticism must be fully noninstrumental if it is to lay the ground for the fertile growth of future creative epochs. Openly speculative, characterized by constant movement and even a kind of restless negative energy, this form of criticism is celebrated as "a pleasure in itself" (*CPW* [*The Complete Prose Works of Matthew Arnold*] 3:268), a formulation that anticipates the tenets of the Aesthetic Movement and that is situated at an oblique angle to the more serious norm of objective realism that has often been associated with Arnold.[3]

When Arnold speaks of the pleasurable play of the mind upon conventional ideas, he combines what in the Kantian tradition are distinguished as the two separate faculties of aesthetic disinterestedness and critical reason. For Kant, critical reason is the interrogation of custom and the self-conscious authorization of principles, while aesthetic disinterestedness is associated with the free play of the mind and autotelic detachment. Critical reason is of course itself to be distinguished from conceptions of objectivity: the former subjects custom and habit to reflexive interrogation; the latter seeks to identify empirically verifiable facts and laws, relying on a fundamental conception of the objective status of the external world. Arnold's ideals of disinterestedness and criticism unsystematically make appeal to all three cognitive practices: objectivity, critical reason, and aesthetic flexibility. All three appear not only in **"The**

Function of Criticism at the Present Time," but also in the preface to *Culture and Anarchy,* when Arnold writes:

> The whole scope of the essay is to recommend culture as the great help out of our present difficulties: culture being a pursuit of our total perfection by means of getting to know, on all the matters which most concern us, the best which has been thought and said in the world, and, through this knowledge, turning a stream of fresh and free thought upon our stock notions and habits, which we now follow staunchly but mechanically, vainly imagining that there is a virtue in following them staunchly which makes up for the mischief of following them mechanically.
>
> (*CPW* 5:233-34)

In its confident reference to "the best which has been thought and said in the world," a phrase that also occurs repeatedly in **"The Function of Criticism at the Present Time,"** the passage makes an appeal to the objective value of knowledge; in its idea that one should disrupt stock notions and habits, it makes an appeal to reason's interrogation of custom; and in its image of "a stream of fresh and free thought," Arnold's writing obliquely evokes aesthetic free play. Of course, it should be noted that the history of aesthetics beginning with eighteenth-century Enlightenment thinkers in Britain itself manifests different approaches to the question of whether disinterestedness is a distinctively aesthetic mode of apprehension or not. In Addison's writings, for example, the disinterested perception of beauty is opposed to critical reflection, which is construed as overly motivated in its impulse to demonstrate something or to work out a problem. But Shaftesbury, by contrast, directly assigned disinterestedness to the faculty of reason as well as to aesthetic perceptions.[4]

The point here is simply to register the range of forms of detachment to be found in Arnold's work as well as their loose relation to one another. And in addition to the shifting and complex relations among objectivity, critical reason, and aesthetic free play, there is still another form of detachment valued in this essay, a specifically cosmopolitan distance. At key moments, Arnold endorses comparative knowledge and laments English provinciality. Late in the essay, he stresses the need for the English critic to "dwell much on foreign thought" and to "possess one great literature, at least, besides his own; and the more unlike his own, the better" (*CPW* 3:283, 284). Arnold also promotes the idea that commingling of cultures is conducive to an epoch of expansion: indeed, signs of impending expansion are voiced specifically through a metaphor of cosmopolitan openness and imperceptible cultural fusion, made possible by the waning threat of the French Revolution:

> In the first place all danger of a hostile forcible pressure of foreign ideas upon our practice has long disappeared; like the traveller in the fable, therefore, we be-

gin to wear our cloak a little more loosely. Then, with a long peace, the ideas of Europe steal gradually and amicably in, and mingle, though in infinitesimally small quantities at a time, with our own notions.

(*CPW* 3:269)

To be sure, Arnold's self-conscious avoidance of nationalist provinciality in his blanket standard of "the best that is known and thought *in the world*" usually reaches no farther than the boundaries of Western Europe, or, at best, leaps temporally to embrace a more geographically expansive antiquity that includes the East (*CPW* 3:282; my emphasis).[5] But transcendence of provincial narrowness, and specifically transcendence of a constraining *Englishness,* is stressed in various ways throughout Arnold's writing on criticism and culture. An implicit ideal of cosmopolitan cultivation informs his characterization of his fellow countrymen as Philistines and distinctly lacking in light (ideas).[6] The corresponding notion that comparative knowledge or an international perspective will illuminate the tasks of criticism is pursued in many of Arnold's literary essays, most notably **"A French Critic on Milton"** and **"A French Critic on Goethe."**[7] And Arnold identifies as cosmopolitan several of the literary or cultural figures whom he singles out for sustained attention in his writings. It is clearly no accident that Arnold stresses Heinrich Heine's hybrid identity when he introduces him, dramatically, as a hero in the war against Philistinism: "a young man of genius, born at Hamburg, and with all the culture of Germany, but by race a Jew; with warm sympathies for France, whose revolution had given to his race the rights of citizenship."[8] Part of the attraction and relevance of Marcus Aurelius lies in the fact that, as Emperor "in a brilliant centre of civilisation," he maintained a commanding perspective over a highly developed and quintessentially modern empire.[9]

I point to this element of Arnold's thought not because I intend to celebrate him as a champion of cosmopolitanism, thereby answering a well-developed critique of Arnold's ideals as falsely universal and ultimately dangerous. There have certainly been some notable instances of such recuperation, both historically and more recently: conceptions of Arnold as promoting marginality, hybridity, or multiculturalism in *On the Study of Celtic Literature*; or appreciative claims that he is cosmopolitan by method (in his promotion of international vantage points or perspectives) or temperament (in his celebration of diversity and variety).[10] My aim is rather different. Focusing primarily on Arnold's writings of the 1850s and 60s, I want to reconstruct a broader map of Arnoldian detachment, while at the same time arguing that his several conceptions of detachment—disinterestedness, objectivity, cosmopolitanism—all manifest a similar and distinctive pattern of response to the challenge of modernity as Arnold conceived it.[11]

In developing this reading of Arnold, I reframe the question of how we can reconcile, on the one hand, his advocacy of cultivated stances and, on the other, his emphasis on transcendence of the subjective point of view through impersonal or universal entities such as culture, the best self, or the state. The tension between an appeal to subjective stance and an appeal to impersonal entities as the guarantors of value has been criticized in Arnold as a pattern of circular reasoning, whereby each is supposed impossibly to underwrite the other.[12] We can refocus the question if we discover what drives this seeming division. The unifying concern behind Arnold's elaborations of detachment is how to deal with the dual experiences of modernity, whereby the growth of scientific knowledge is both a form of progress and a "fatal event" with regard to traditional sustaining beliefs, and whereby the critical spirit both liberates and disenchants. As is well known, Arnold was profoundly exercised by the problem of value in its broadest sense and persistently concerned that with the loss of religious traditions the moral life—the resources for responding to the crucial question of the relation between knowledge and conduct, or fact and value—was endangered. By closely examining his approach to detachment, we can trace a pattern of response to the challenge of modernity that considerably complicates the view of Arnold as authoritarian in his appeals to absolute standards or foundational values. For while the appeal to noncontingent and nonsubjective value does emerge in the notion that the authority of the state will undergird the best self, or in the idea of the touchstone line, or in the asserted faith that Hellenism and Hebraism will work together toward a single overriding spiritual end, there is another line of thinking in Arnold's work, one that raises up temperament, stance, and character as the site where fact and value might be reconciled, or where the promises of modernity might best be glimpsed. The emphasis here is on the successful subjective enactment or embodiment of forms of universality, as distinguished from other moments where he seems to valorize impersonal or objective standards. Such an approach helps to retrieve one key instance of the nineteenth-century approach to detachment as an ongoing achievement: as something that cannot simply be presumed or asserted but rather must emerge out of concrete practices, guided by shaping aspirations, and intimately linked to the crafting of character and moral selfhood.

The reading of Arnold I will offer might be summed up as a more systematic explanation of David J. DeLaura's observation that "whenever Arnold tries to introduce something that transcends the self, he introduces the self in another guise."[13] The discussion proceeds as follows. First, I examine the ways in which an ideal of scientific objectivity is intricately bound up with Arnold's thinking about race, cultural affiliation, and intercultural relations in the mid-1860s, a time in which Arnold briefly called upon the authority of science in order to elaborate the racial bases for the study, and advancement, of culture. As we shall see, race remains a central category throughout Arnold's writings on science and criticism, serving alternately to thwart and enable the project of cultivated distance. During his romance with science, Arnold tries to reconcile fact and value through an ideal of objective stance construed as continuous with moral vision. Scientific detachment ultimately poses more of a threat than a solution to the challenges of modernity, however, and Arnold relinquishes this particular dream of legitimization, placing his faith in "letters." Yet as I show in the second section of the chapter, the yoking of method and ethos that appears with particularly stark clarity in the embrace of science reappears distinctly throughout all of Arnold's writing on forms of detachment, including those analyses that center on disinterestedness, critical reason, and cosmopolitanism.

In general, this reading of Arnold provides a more comprehensive understanding of the forms of detachment that inform Arnold's ideals of criticism and culture. In so doing, it resituates debates about Arnold and race and revises standard thinking about Arnold's relation to Pater and Wilde. By way of conclusion, I try to assess the success and value of Arnold's attempt to embody ideals through the somewhat paradoxical practice of subjectivizing categories otherwise associated with the impersonal, the objective, or the universal. If Arnold's elaborations of exemplary stance demand a rethinking of the fundamental critiques of Arnold as authoritarian and foundational, as I contend, it is still an open issue whether his concept of enacted universality is itself in need of further critique or refinement. While I favor the project of imagining how universality might be lived or given a concrete characterology, this does not mean, in other words, that any given articulation of embodied universality is itself above critique. As in the previous chapter, and the study as a whole, I therefore engage in a process of immanent critique, first defending Arnold against what I take to be reductive lines of attack, and then subjecting my own defense, and my reconstructed Arnold, to critical scrutiny.

SCIENCE, RACE, AND THE FAILURE OF NATURALISM

Discussion of the categories of race and nationality in Arnold's thought has taken a number of different forms over the years. Trilling, whose 1939 book on Arnold paid admiring attention to the social and historical dimensions of his work, fairly directly confronted the problem of Arnold's "untenable theory of race."[14] He sought to mitigate judgments against Arnold in two ways: by claiming that he was merely reflecting the unexamined intellectual assumptions of his time—preeminently, the tendency to explain national characteristics on the basis of racial nature—and by asserting that Arnold's aim in identifying racial characteristics was to bring people together, not to separate them.[15] Similarly, Frederic E. Faverty's interesting 1951 study, *Matthew Arnold the Ethnologist,* argued that Arnold's aim in his ethnological writings, in contrast to many of his contemporaries, was reconciliation and productive cultural interchange. A prime example adduced is the influential **On the Study of Celtic Literature,** which challenged the prevalent notion that Celtic blood had been expunged from the English peoples; Faverty also cites Arnold's deep belief that it was destructive to allow any single racial element to dominate the life of the individual or nation: the ideals are measure, balance, integration. These defenses begin a tradition whereby Arnold's category of national culture is shown to be importantly complex or revealingly self-undermining. Trilling observes, for example, that it is contradictory to exhort people to give greater prominence to a particular part of their racial nature: "as soon as a people admits an imperative higher than that of its blood—the imperative of reason, for example—the imperative of blood itself is totally negated" (236). Robert Young, who ultimately emphasizes the fact that race underlies Arnold's conception of culture, also points out that Arnold defines "Englishness" not by what it *is* but by what it *lacks* (culture, ideas, light, universal standards). An opposing tradition insists, however, that no matter how far Arnold's theory of race tends to transmute into culture, no matter how willful or mediated the relation between the cultivated individual or group and its racial characteristics, the fact remains that Arnold necessarily relies upon, or always returns to, a bedrock theory of racial difference.[16]

Other aspects of Arnold's treatment of national culture invite the deconstructive approach evident in Trilling and Young, as he unfailingly introduces negative, critical, or trumping elements into what may have initially appeared as a substantive category of race. Insofar as the French element of novelty serves as a catalyst for modern hybrid formations, French national culture becomes not an essence but a force that transforms any pre-existent racial identity it encounters. Similarly, the "hauntings of Celtism" in the English race give rise to an awkward self-consciousness, and thwart spontaneity and naturalness: how can this be simple racial determinism? Beyond these identifications of catalytic or disruptive racial elements, Arnold often attributes individual genius to some form of disjunction with respect to national culture: "And yet just what constitutes special power and genius in a man seems often to be his blending with the basis of his national temperament, some additional gift or grace not proper to that temperament" (*CPW* 3:360, 358). (He then goes on to cite as examples Shakespeare and Goethe.) We are now very close to the cosmopolitanism of exemplary figures like Heine, as well as to the illuminations of exile, represented most strikingly in the case of Spinoza's ex-communication: his persecutors "remained children of Israel, and he became a child of modern Europe."[17]

Such an interpretive strategy aims to uncover, in the course of Arnold's seemingly pervasive race-thinking, either a saving inconsistency or outright reversal. Against the disturbing ideology of Arnold's ethno-logic, it asserts one or more of the following points: (1) the inherent inconsistency of race thinking, (2) Arnold's own and obviously genuine inconsistencies, which somehow mitigate the charge of racialist thinking, or (3) an underrecognized opposing truth in Arnold, something higher than inconsistency but lower than elaborated alternative, the truth of a kind of ennobling relation to cultural identity, brought on by fortuitous hybridity, or the spark of genius, or the cultivated balance that defines harmonious development.

These debates about Arnold's relation to race reflect a genuine division in his thought. It is crucial to acknowledge both sides of his thinking: the reliance on racial nature and the appeal to any number of ways in which consciousness and culture might intensify, channel, or mitigate those racial forces that can never be fully escaped.[18] In his ringing calls for intercultural fusion or individual perfection, racial elements are thus conceived of as malleable to a certain extent, even if fundamental nonetheless. A key passage appears in *On the Study of Celtic Literature*:

> Modes of life, institutions, government, and other such causes, are sufficient, I shall be told, to account for English oratory. Modes of life, institutions, government, climate, and so forth,—let me say it once for all,—will further or hinder the development of an aptitude, but they will not by themselves create the aptitude or explain it. On the other hand, a people's habit and complexion of nature go far to determine its modes of life, institutions, and government, and even to prescribe the limits within which the influences of climate shall tell upon it.

> (*CPW* 3:353)[19]

My primary aim here is to show that the shifting emphases and underlying presupposition of Arnold's writings reflect the privileged place that race and cultural heritage play in Arnold's obsessions with the modern project of achieving psychological, moral, and cultural distance from the "given." Arnold is drawn to and wants to believe in the possibility of transformative and critical relations to what he construes as natural racial forces, but he is also haunted by the fact that such forces are starkly determining. It is in response to this more general apprehension that Arnold's thought produces some of its most distastefully racist moments, as he asserts distinctions among different races and nationalities precisely on the basis of their capacity to respond to the challenges of modernity. (I will discuss in the second half of this chapter the distinctive form his hierarchical thought takes.)

The "modern" was of course a key concept for Arnold throughout his work and foundational in structuring his famous turn from poetry to prose. This is evident in the opening paragraph of the "Preface to the First Edition of *Poems*," in which Arnold explains his decision not to include **"Empedocles on Etna"** in the collection. For Arnold, the Greek figure Empedocles represents a form of consciousness that should no longer be indulged by poets or critics:

> What those who are familiar only with the great monuments of early Greek genius suppose to be its exclusive characteristics, have disappeared: the calm, the cheerfulness, the disinterested objectivity have disappeared; the dialogue of the mind with itself has commenced; modern problems have presented themselves; we hear already the doubts, we witness the discouragement, of Hamlet and of Faust.

> (*CPW* 1:1)

While this passage identifies modernity as something negative that befalls the self, Arnold's inaugural lecture as professor of poetry at Oxford, **"On the Modern Element in Literature,"** views modernity as a constellation of positive conditions: a civil life relatively secure from any intrusions of war or crime, the growth of tolerance, an increase of conveniences, the formation of taste, the capacity for refined pursuits, and above all and supremely, "the intellectual maturity of man himself; the tendency to observe facts with a critical spirit; to search for their law, not to wander among them at random; to judge by the rule of reason, not by the impulse of prejudice or caprice" (*CPW* 1:24).

At issue for Arnold in both the "Preface to *Poems*" and the inaugural lecture as professor of poetry is what precise posture should be adopted toward the distinct conditions and challenges of modernity: **"On the Modern Element in Literature"** describes modernity as "the spectacle of a vast multitude of facts awaiting and inviting [one's] comprehension"; the proper response involves finding "the true point of view from which to contemplate this spectacle" (*CPW* 1:20). It is a question of stance, articulated as a need for some perspective from which one can both contemplate and comprehend; the suggestion is that one must ascend to a point of lofty detachment; indeed, Arnold states that "he who adequately comprehends this spectacle, has *risen* to the comprehension of his age" (*CPW* 1:20: my emphasis). For Arnold, as for a thinker like Hegel, modernity is not so much a historical epoch as a form of consciousness—one that appears throughout human history as a response to momentous cultural transitions. The literature of Periclean Athens represents just such an ennobling response to modern complexities, while the Roman writer Lucretius is modern but *inadequate* because he displays negative versions of contemplation, namely, depression and ennui. (The comments on Lucretius, of course, parallel Arnold's indictment of the brooding and subjective tendencies of Romantic poetry.)

As indicated by Arnold's dramatic emphasis on "the intellectual maturity of man," Arnold follows Kant in identifying modernity largely with the critical spirit, or, to adopt Habermas's terminology, with the postconventional interrogation of prevailing customs, routines, habits, and norms. In the second section of this chapter, I will examine this aspect of Arnold's understanding of modernity. But for Arnold modern also means "scientific," and it is in conjunction with what he sees as the distinct promises and limitations of contemporary science that the issue of race arises most forcefully and dramatically in his work; any full treatment of Arnold's conception of cultural affiliation and detachment, then, must take into account the dimension of his writings that brings science to bear upon the question of racial culture.[20]

It is important to clarify in a preliminary way how Arnold uses the term *science*.[21] Throughout his career, he moves back and forth between a general conception of science as simply disinterested and systematic study, "seeing the object as it really is" in any intellectual domain, and a more narrow conception of the natural sciences. In the first instance, there is no tension between humanistic studies and the sciences, as Arnold states explicitly in the late essay **"Literature and Science"**: "all learning is scientific which is systematically laid out and followed up to its original sources, and . . . a genuine humanism is scientific."[22] But insofar as a privileging of the natural sciences threatens the study of letters, both in the practical sphere of education and as a larger question of culture, then science must not eclipse literature or humanistic studies. To the latter falls the crucial task of relating new scientific knowledge, with its fatal effects on traditional beliefs and ideas, to the supremely important conduct of life, to the moral and spiritual sphere which makes up, to invoke Arnold's famous formulation, three-fourths of life. This is in fact the ultimate argument of **"Literature and Science."** But in the mid-1860s, Arnold briefly called upon the authority of natural science in order to elaborate the racial bases for the study of culture.[23] This was actually a two-pronged effort. On the one hand, Arnold seemed genuinely fascinated by the project of ethnology and was clearly a true believer in the forms of racial generalization that inform his writings on national characteristics and historical trajectories. Such a commitment to ethnological science lies behind the magisterial claim, in **Culture and Anarchy,** that "Science has now made visible to everybody the great and pregnant elements of difference which lie in race" (**CPW** 5:173). On the other hand, Arnold saw the project of ethnology as subordinate to the larger, normative project of ideal culture for the individual, for the nation, and for humanity as a whole. The attempt to build the project of culture upon the findings of ethnology in fact stands at the heart of both **On the Study of Celtic Literature** and **Culture and Anarchy.**

On the Study of Celtic Literature holds out science as the basis for intercultural understanding and reconciliation, particularly with regard to long-standing tensions between the Celt and the Saxon. Indeed, one might say that this work attempts to fuse fact and value through a cosmopolitan science of racial unity. Admittedly, Arnold begins by simply displacing one line of racial demarcation by another, claiming that science has laid the basis for reconciling the Irish and the English by revealing the "native diversity between our European bent and the Semitic bent" (**CPW** 3:301). Later in the text, however, he asserts that science will gradually tend, despite its method of dividing and separating, toward "the idea of the substantial unity of man" (**CPW** 3:330). Although it will be long in coming, ultimate fusion is prefigured insofar as science is continually "showing us affinity where we imagined there was isolation" (**CPW** 3:330).

What is important to recognize here, insofar as it characterizes Arnold's approach to forms of detachment more generally, is that scientific objectivity is conceived of as both constitutive and productive of moral value—largely in response to an underlying anxiety that it is entirely divorced from value.[24] In a way, Arnold attempts in this phase of his intellectual life to give to science the task he later assigns to literature: the task of promoting harmonious unity. As conceived by Arnold, the science of race both renders comprehensible the conditions of racial and cultural makeup and illuminates the unity that lies behind seeming divisions. Science aids comprehension by discerning the hybrid formations that make up contemporary nationalities as well as "the genius of each people" (**CPW** 3:325). For example, science demonstrates English hybridity by showing that the Celtic element has not, contrary to widely held belief, been expunged from the English race. It secures this claim in a broadly scientific way, "by external and by internal evidence," and across a range of domains: "the language and the physical type of our race afford certain data for trying it, and other data are afforded by our literature, genius, and spiritual production generally" (**CPW** 3:337).

A significant portion of **On the Study of Celtic Literature** is thus devoted to uncovering and praising the influence of Celtic sentimentalism on English culture, with the aim of scientifically solving, by essentially rendering moot, a problem of political division.[25] Yet the scientific analysis promoted by Arnold in this text cannot uniformly guarantee the happy results it predominantly and cheerfully offers to us. Indeed, one crucial analysis of the disparate elements that make up the English race yields a dispiriting result:

> The Englishman, in so far as he is German,—and he is mainly German,—proceeds in the steady-going German fashion; if he were all German he would proceed

thus for ever without self-consciousness or embarrassment; but, in so far as he is Celtic, he has snatches of quick instinct which often make him feel he is fumbling, show him visions of an easier, more dexterous behaviour, disconcert him and fill him with misgiving. No people, therefore, are so shy, so self-conscious, so embarrassed as the English, because two natures are mixed in them, and natures which pull them such different ways.

(*CPW* 3:360)

This passage reveals the anxiety that perpetually haunts Arnold's embrace of modernity, his embrace of science specifically and critical detachment more generally. Revealed here is not so much the promise as the threat of science: science contributes to the project of seeing the object as it really is but seems to do so by seeing the object as it *ineluctably* is. That is, science does not so much provide the basis for a reassuring comprehension of the multitude of facts but rather simply uncovers determinations painful to contemplate. In the report of his second official tour of the Continent, written during the same year that he composed the lectures on Celtic literature, Arnold makes the following distinction between letters and science: "The study of letters is the study of the operation of human force, of human freedom and activity; the study of nature is the study of the operation of human limitation and passivity. The contemplation of human force and activity tends naturally to heighten our own force and activity; the contemplation of human limits and passivity tends rather to check it."[26] This is a far cry from the promises of unity and reconciliation that inaugurate the discussion in *On the Study of Celtic Literature*; the passage describing the fumbling Englishman seems precisely to identify human limits and passivity, insofar as the Englishman is literally, physically, manifestly at the mercy of forces that thwart his freedom and activity. Even more: what results from forces of nature in this case is a negative version of the critical spirit, elsewhere heralded as a manifestation of the modern. For the Englishman is modern to the extent that he is self-conscious, but his self-consciousness is limited here to the painful apprehension of his own faltering freedom, which is also, for Arnold, the dire sentence of being unable to maintain a heroic stance precisely because the ideal of equipoise (in the face of forces beyond one's control) is here definitively thwarted by forces beyond one's control. The Englishman as object of scientific study becomes in a sense representative also of the limits of the modern scientific subject, whose strenuous objectivity discloses only the intractability of nature.

Arnold himself does not remain passive in the face of these tragic versions of the modern—a science divorced from value and progress, a self-awareness that does not liberate. As Trilling makes a point of emphasizing, Arnold asserts, in a kind of surprise ending to *On the Study of Celtic Literature,* that natural forces can themselves be subjected to the powers of reason: "So long as we are blindly and ignorantly rolled about by the forces of our nature, their contradiction baffles us and lames us; so soon as we have clearly discerned what they are, and begun to apply to them a law of measure, control, and guidance, they may be made to work for our good and to carry us forward" (*CPW* 3:383). It is interesting that a potent, indeed virtually instrumental, form of self-critical reason (applying a law of measure, control, and guidance) is brought in to guarantee the scientific project. Arnold thereby recasts the stalled and painful self-scrutiny of the Englishman as heroic self-overcoming. We are now baffled and lamed only *before* the project of science and reason has gotten underway, and not, as before, in the quasi-enlightened wake of its ineffectual realizations. Beyond asserting the possibility for the critical channeling of natural forces, Arnold also insists that value resides within the very processes of scientific activity and understanding. Rather than being value-neutral and disturbingly unanswerable in its identification of extrinsic forces, science in this aspect becomes the emblem and generator of moral value. As I have discussed, for Arnold science ideally breaks down the Englishman's alienation from the Irish and thereby fosters a sense of kinship and reconciliation between two groups who exist in antagonism with one another. But, as Arnold himself is keenly aware, this action on the part of science is more fortuitous than guaranteed: reconciliation here issues out of the unknown fact of racial affinity, but elsewhere science could just as easily identify race-based antipathies, as is clear when Arnold tells us that science "[teaches] us which way our natural affinities and repulsions lie" (*CPW* 3:301). To avoid the unsettling consequences of such contingency—the fact that increased sympathy is in this case merely "an indirect practical result" (*CPW* 3:301)—he generates a double argument:

> However, on these indirect benefits of science we must not lay too much stress. Only this must be allowed; it is clear that there are now in operation two influences, both favourable to a more attentive and impartial study of Celtism than it has yet ever received from us. One is the strengthening in us of the feeling of Indo-Europeanism; the other, the strengthening in us of the scientific sense generally. The first breaks down barriers between us and the Celt, relaxes the estrangement between us; the second begets the desire to know his case thoroughly, and to be just to it. This is a very different matter from the political and social Celtisation of which certain enthusiasts dream; but it is not to be despised by any one to whom the Celtic genius is dear; and it is possible, while the other is not.

(*CPW* 3:302-3)

After noting the overcoming of estrangement through the fortuitous discovery of shared origins, that is, Arnold then forwards the noncontingent claim that "the scientific sense generally" is a force for good, because it produces a desire for comprehensive knowledge and fosters forms of objectivity that Arnold equates with justice. Here, the scientific stance is also a moral one: objectivity *is* impartiality, knowledge *is* justice.

In the end, however, Arnold does not maintain his optimism about the moral potentialities of science. Perhaps this is because Arnold cannot shake the sense that science too definitively discloses the ineluctable facticity of racial determinations. Perhaps it is because of the politics of the education systems he inspected, and his need to combat the dominance of science over humanistic studies. We can only speculate as to the relative force of contributing causes, but Arnold's talk of the ultimately unifying aim of science dissipates, and the claim that scientific objectivity produces just appreciations is replaced with a very explicit call to assign questions of morality to the domain of letters. Arnold's early separation between reason and faith, which animated his essays on the dangers of bringing the results of speculative thinking too suddenly to the masses, reappears in a different guise, remapped onto the distinction between Hellenism and Hebraism. But the concern about the contingency of value reappears in Arnold's discussions of the ideals of critical reason and cosmopolitan detachment, which, as I shall argue, more deeply engage the distinctly modern question of whether universal or impersonal value can find subjective embodiment.

COSMOPOLITANISM, RACE, AND ALLEGORIES OF THE MODERN

Arnold's reflections on modernity take the form, in his ethnological or cosmopolitan modes, of emblematic stories about racial and cultural genealogy. The stories that he tells about specific peoples or noteworthy individuals often foreground how racial heritage inflects the challenges of modernity, both the opportunities and struggles associated with living in a disenchanted world. The Englishman carries the burden of a flickering consciousness of thwarted ease: he is self-aware, but only as a stumbler is self-aware. Negative versions of modernity also appear when a particular people is seen as lacking sufficient capacity for science, for critical thinking, for self-control. Thus the situation of the Celt is lamented because, while his capacity for sentiment is laudable and a key component of artistic culture, he has failed to control it: "do not let us wish that the Celt had had less sensibility, but that he had been more master of it" (*CPW* 3:346-47). The English, dominated by Philistinism, are "in a certain sense, of all people the most inaccessible to ideas" (*CPW* 3:113); their failure to establish anything akin to the French Academy bespeaks an inability to perceive that there is "a high, correct standard in intellectual matters" (*CPW* 3:243).

By contrast, some stories tell of a heroic or exemplary relation to modernity enabled by a distinctly disjunctive relation to national culture, one that is ennobling rather than constraining. Heine is a genius because of his cosmopolitanism and his possession of both "the spirit of Greece and the spirit of Judaea"; he is also singled out, dramatically, for his paradoxical ability to detach himself from his own powerful racial determination: "His race he treated with the same freedom with which he treated everything else, but he derived a great force from it, and no one knew this better than himself" (*CPW* 3:127). Heine understands, in the spirit of the modern scientific attitude, what effect his cultural heritage has on him, yet he also has the capacity to subject that heritage to the free play of the critical mind. Thus he delivers on the promise of modernity in his capacity to reflect upon—and transmute through art—that which otherwise operates as unconscious nature or unexamined custom. In more general terms, the French are commended for their devotion to ideas and to the power of reason, and for their high intellectual standards and conscience. Insofar as these are forces that characterize the progressive nature of modernity, the French exemplify and forward the pursuit of culture. Likewise, the Germans are commended for their scientific powers and accomplishments.

Now from one point of view it could appear that Arnold is simply replaying prevalent nineteenth-century assumptions that certain races of Western Europe are more civilized than various other races construed as barbaric. Thus not only the Celt but the Jew and specific Eastern races are seen as lacking in elements that promote intellectual, spiritual, and artistic achievement. Along the same lines, one could indict Arnold's ostensible championing of hybridity or cultural fusion as a distinctly narrow cosmopolitanism, cozily European and Western. Indeed, there was a general assumption within nineteenth-century racial theory that intra-European hybrids were culturally productive while the interbreeding of Europeans with those of geographically distant races was likely to be infertile. A carefully bounded cosmopolitan hybridity, in other words, was fully compatible with a starkly hierarchical racialism.[27] But Arnold is here largely distinguishing races and individuals from one another on the basis of their *relation* to modernity as much as or more than their exemplification of modern achievements. The former requires a certain ingenuity or heroism in the face of modernity's Janus face—it is in no sense simply modernity or civilization triumphant. To that extent it exists at a remove from any simple spectrum of more or less "progressive" races, since ambivalence toward progress, and toward modern forms of detachment themselves, lies at the heart of Arnold's thinking. This in turn produces a parallel ambivalence on Arnold's part toward the characteristics of each national or individual character that he constructs. Heine may be wonderfully hybrid and flexible, but he has an insufficient moral sense; the French devotion to ideas and reason is laudable, but their sensuality and amorality is not; the German may be scientific, but he is also dragged down by the very steady-going nature that ensures his intellectual achievement. Correlatively, as Arnold argues in **Culture and Anarchy,** even though the English suffer from a deficiency of ideas and general intellectual narrowness, they stand out for their honesty and morality; if they can become intelligent, then they will not be undermined by the faults of the French.[28]

The valorized forms of reflective distance that appear in Arnold's emblematic ethnographies pull in two directions. On the one hand, cosmopolitan detachment is presented as a highly particularized practice of taking one's distance from a specified set of conditions, through critical reflection, through discipline and self-control, and through a cultivated posture of contemplation, calm, or aloofness; yet, on the other hand, it is the transcendence of situatedness *tout court.* There is a tension, in other words, between Arnold's valorization of exemplary stances toward the modern and his valorization of a trajectory that escapes contingency into universalism. One could characterize this tension as one between a kind of layered cosmopolitanism and an abstract universalism.[29] In a useful essay, Alan D. McKillop distinguishes between inclusive and exclusive cosmopolitanism: exclusive cosmopolitanism constitutes an abstract universalism, a neutral thinning out of affiliation; inclusive cosmopolitanism embraces multiple affiliation, dialogue, and intercultural experience.[30] I call Arnold's cosmopolitanism "layered" because of the many ways in which it courts multiple affiliation and intercultural perspectives, as for example in the recognition and celebration of hybrid individuals, in the definition of genius as a fortuitous moment of cultural mixing, and in the appreciation of the comparative method in criticism. I refrain from calling it "inclusive," however, because his conception lacks a reciprocal intersubjective dimension, though one could say that there is a highly sublimated form of inclusive cosmopolitanism in Arnold, evident in the dialectical conception of cultural fusion or in the notion of recognizing other races in one's own internal cultural hybridity.

Arnold's abstract universalism, in contrast to his layered cosmopolitanism, removes itself from the embedded context of cultural practice or exchange so as to posit absolute standards. Abstract universalism comes up most notably as counterpoint to forms of provinciality variously construed. In **"The Literary Influence of Academies,"** for example, Arnold holds up the high intellectual standard of the French, contrasting it to the "note of provinciality" that marks the literature of those nations without an academy. Only when a nation has gotten rid of provinciality, moreover, is one brought "on to the platform where alone the best and highest intellectual work can be said fairly to begin. Work done after men have reached this platform is *classical*" (**CPW** 3:245). Similarly, in the preface to **Culture and Anar-**

chy, Arnold opposes the term *provinciality* to the term *totality.* Those who are provincial allow only one side of their humanity to develop—Arnold has in mind here the unmeasured religious zeal of the Nonconformists, their overwhelming Hebraism—whereas those who belong to the ordered and balanced Establishments come nearer to approaching totality, are on the way to perfection.[31] In this instance, Arnold associates sectarianism and pluralism with a loss of guiding standards, standards that must underwrite any pursuit of culture or totality. To allow freedom of religion would only "provincialise us all round" (**CPW** 5:240). Likewise, further in the essay Arnold laments the limitations of class bias, or the ordinary self motivated only by his or her contingent and situated interests. The goal is to foster one's "best self": "By our everyday selves . . . we are separate, personal, at war. . . . But by our *best* self we are united, impersonal, at harmony" (**CPW** 5:134). Culture, the best self, reason and the will of God—all of these ideals are defined against situated bias, which is seen systematically to distort the pursuit of perfection.[32]

How do we place Arnold's abstract universalism in relation to the advocacy of the comparative method, the celebration of illuminating hybridity, and the seductive way that less austere forms of detachment seem recurrently to hold his admiring attention? One could argue that Arnold's particular versions of cosmopolitanism are actually in the service of his abstract universalism. By this reading, those cosmopolitans that he intermittently invokes throughout his prose writings are heroes, or intermittently heroes, not because they embrace diversity, comparatism, or the illuminations of multiple affiliation, but because their particular histories and cultural make-ups promote the establishment of universal standards—in other words, because their particular histories and cultural make-ups paradoxically promote the transcendence of particularity. This would be true not only of exemplary individuals but also of opportune conjunctions in the life of a people or race. So understood, Arnold's approach is everywhere unified by its dialectical approach, where intercultural mixing and contingent historical conditions are ultimately in the service of a higher totality.

Admitting the complexity of Arnold's cosmopolitanism while ultimately underscoring its abstractive ascent toward universalism allows us to account more fully for Arnoldian detachment. It is important to acknowledge, however, that Arnold's thought displays a recurring impulse, even in his appeals to universalism, toward an ideal that is enacted characterologically. What I have been referring to throughout the chapter as enactment and embodiment always matter profoundly to Arnold, and it is crucial to explore more closely what it means for Arnold to conceptualize temperament, stance, and character as the means through which embodied universality can best be represented. This is an argument that requires a rethinking of the tendency to read the revisions of Arnold by Pater and Wilde as expressive of a decisive shift from objective to subjective standards. And it is also an argument that might help us to understand better Arnold's own revisions of himself, particularly his constant protesting that he had been misunderstood and did not advocate a conception of culture as effete aestheticism. For the crucial element in Arnold's emphasis on individual attitude or character lies in the particular way that it reconciles ideals of objectivity and reason with subjective stance and moral value—and it does so in a way very similar to the pattern discerned in his writings on the promises and limits of science.

Arnold's attraction to specific historical and literary figures had to do with two things: his rejection of what he saw as the ignoble subjectivism of the Romantics, which his own turn from poetry to prose was calculated to enforce, and his correlative heroicizing of those who expressed the ideals of detachment that he sought to advance through his own critical writings. But what emerged was an anxiety that the forms of detachment that he valorized were themselves easily detachable from moral substance: this anxiety encompassed not only the realm of science but also the spheres of critical reason and aesthetics (spheres that, as I noted at the outset of the chapter, are frequently undifferentiated in Arnold). This anxiety also prompts his insistence that highly speculative intellectual work, especially modern criticism of the Bible, could have a dangerous effect on the masses and should therefore remain esoteric until its findings had been reconciled to the popular domains of conduct and belief. It also lay behind his need to isolate flaws in those figures who displayed an otherwise admirable detachment: thus the master of irony Heine or the aesthetic, noncommittal Maurice de Guerin are suddenly convicted of amorality after long appreciations of their intellectual and aesthetic modes. The fear that it might be impossible to recover moral substance in the flight from the opposing dangers of subjectivism and traditionalism—both defined against the free play of the creative powers or of disinterested criticism—also lies behind the compensatory insistence that criticism will "naturally and irresistibly" make its benefits felt in the practical sphere, or that culture must be made to prevail, or that Hebraism will provide the moral ballast to Hellenism.

Another key way in which Arnold counteracts this fear—and the one I want to isolate here—is to represent as moral character the very form of detachment he is advocating, to try to make detachment ultimately indistinguishable from moral stance or ethos. This move corresponds to a more general tendency in the culture to articulate the methods of modern intellectual practice as productive not only of new knowledges but of refinements of character among those who practice them with

the proper rigor and self-control. In the introduction, I discussed how recent work by Lorraine Daston and Peter Galison has established this tendency within the natural sciences. Versions of this cultural formation also inhere in other nineteenth-century intellectual and disciplinary spheres. They take on a particularly interesting form when pursued, as they are in Arnold, in the face of elaborate apprehensions about the potential groundlessness of modern life. The force of Arnold's investment is rendered more vivid when we consider that he is insisting on detachment as an achievement of character at the same time that he is condemning certain individuals for lacking moral character precisely because of their detachment. He repeatedly insists that forms of detachment are in the service of perfection, thereby effectively making a virtue of what otherwise appears to him as an alternative to a moral position. At such moments, he will articulate his model of criticism as a blend of impersonal and personal values, through pivot terms that lend flesh to otherwise abstract principles.

A primary example is the famous passage on Goethe from the essay on Heine:

> Goethe's profound, imperturbable naturalism is absolutely fatal to all routine thinking; he puts the standard, once for all, inside every man instead of outside him; when he is told, such a thing must be so, there is immense authority and custom in favor of its being so, it has been held to be so for a thousand years, he answers with Olympian politeness, "But *is* it so? Is it so to *me*?" Nothing could be more really subversive of the foundations on which the old European order rested; and it may be remarked that no persons are so radically detached from this order, no persons so thoroughly modern, as those who have felt Goethe's influence most deeply.
>
> (*CPW* 3:110)

This passage identifies modernity with the capacity for self-authorization of belief that forms the core of the Enlightenment conception of autonomy. It identifies self-authorization as a radical detachment from the preexisting, traditional, or conventional social order. While one might feel a resurgent subjectivism in the passage, a danger that the whims of individual *me*'s might threaten the capacity for any truly justified examination of custom, the passage appears within a context that opposes unthinking custom to rational reflection, and so elevates a principle of reason above the mere whims of the individual. But what is equally prominent in the passage, and also offsets the suggestion of idiosyncrasy, is the notion that Goethe's naturalism is "imperturbable" and that his interrogations are conducted with "Olympian politeness." In both instances, Arnold characterizes Goethe's intellectual stance as an expression equally of manner, a manner that rises above bias, that is in no way reactive or driven by the vicissitudes of impulse or passion. Manner is here utterly continuous with method and principle and gives seamless expression to it.

This example represents a general pattern in Arnold's conception of detachment: it is an ideal that is at once characterological and impersonal. All of its key terms seem to mark the transcendence of subjectivity, yet Arnold repeatedly indicates that it is as much a moral and psychological achievement as a purely intellectual one. We saw this as early as the preface to *Poems,* where he yokes distinctive psychological states—"the calm, the cheerfulness"—to the "disinterested objectivity" that marks Greek genius; similarly, modern "doubt" is also "discouragement." Likewise, in **"The Literary Influence of Academies,"** Arnold stresses that the provincial spirit lacks "graciousness"; that it is betrayed by its "tone," which is marked by violence and "seems to aim rather at an effect upon the blood and senses than upon the spirit and intellect" (*CPW* 3:249). It is commonly noted, of course, that the Arnoldian ideal is an ideal of *Bildung,* and that the achievement of culture involves the cultivation of character. What has been insufficiently explored is the extent to which the ideal of character that Arnold advances involves the attempt to enact, through a distinctly subjective embodiment, the modern promise of universal reason.[33]

At those moments where Arnold directly addressed the need to replace the gap left by the loss of aristocratic nobility, he pointed not to individual temperament but to the state as that which might provide the ballast needed in an increasingly anarchic (i.e., liberal-pluralist) world.[34] He also of course famously yoked reason to the will of God in **Culture and Anarchy,** thus at once highlighting and refusing the question of whether reason can so easily be conflated with a singular conception of the good. It is my argument here that Arnold persistently sought, in less absolutist terms, to give critical reason an ethical dimension, though not exactly a specific content, by casting it as an ideal of temperament or character, whose key attributes bespeak a kind of value-laden value-neutrality: impartiality, tact, moderation, measure, balance, flexibility, detachment, objectivity, composure.[35] These attributes, and the curious conception of an embodied universality to which they give voice, can be summed up by the term pervasive throughout Arnold's writings on culture: perfection. It, like Arnold's Hellenism more generally, points to the transcendence of any rule-governed conception of identity or practice, but nonetheless accords an objective value to what is repeatedly portrayed as not a science but rather an art of reason.[36]

DETACHMENT AS A PRACTICE OF THE SELF

Arnold's ideal of embodied universality is marked throughout by Hellenism and thus yoked to a very specific cultural heritage even as it can seem to transcend all racial and cultural specificity. The term "Olympian" perfectly captures this inherent tension; it carries a Hellenistic reference, but it denotes the capacity to rise above any mortal interest. In its tendency toward a logic of exemplarity, Arnold's universalism here might be compared to the French and European claims of cosmopolitan or universalist exceptionalism criticized by Jacques Derrida in *The Other Heading.*[37] Still, the centrality of the ideal of temperament and stance does establish a line of thinking in Arnold that can be seen as an alternative to his less nuanced appeals to impersonal entities as guarantors of value. Moreover, it partly reconstrues his relation to the later Victorian aesthetes, particularly Pater. Pater is commonly understood to have subjectivized the Arnoldian dictum, especially insofar as the preface to *The Renaissance* famously rewrites Arnold: "in aesthetic criticism the first step towards seeing one's object as it really is, is to know one's own impression as it really is, to discriminate it, to realise it distinctly."[38] Pater and Wilde are seen as holding up stance or temperament as the key to aesthetic experience and criticism, where Arnold believed it was possible to pursue objective standards.[39] Others have certainly pointed to pre-Paterian moments in Arnold, but the point I want to make is that whereas Pater elevates stance itself as a value, Arnold promotes a particular kind of stance, one that can reconcile the objective and the subjective, the universal and the particular. He does so in part so that he may provide an alternative to the aesthetic overvaluing of reflective stance divorced from value (via irony or the protean pursuit of experience), and this desire accounts for his ambivalent critiques of Heine and Maurice de Guerin.

A central question raised by my reading of Arnold is whether his attempt to integrate an ethical dimension into certain practices of detachment is either successful or even credible as an alternative ideal. This is a question that goes beyond the problems raised by Arnold's move toward racial exemplarity. Put simply, can fact and value (in the case of science) or reason and ethos (in the case of the critical spirit) be reconciled in this way, or is this simply a fantasy of reconciliation? In the case of scientific objectivity, I suggest, Arnold's notion of a "scientific sense" that comprises both epistemological and ethical motives (insofar as it "begets the desire to know [the Celt's] case thoroughly, and to be just to it") is simply untenable. Epistemology does not absorb or generate ethics, though knowledge is certainly requisite to the tasks and pleasures of intercultural recognition, and to the larger project of "justice." In the case of criticism or culture—the detachment associated with critical reason rather than science—the question is perhaps more complicated. On the one hand, Arnold's emphasis on stance—and his particular articulation of method as ethos—importantly conceives of cultural ideals as always *enacted,* and not simply pregiven or independent essences. This strain in Arnold, and its link to classical culture, can be assimilated to the "aesthetics of existence" that interested Foucault in his late work, and that served as the basis for a renewed attention to ethics in both his own project and much of the work that has been influenced by the second and third volumes of the *History of Sexuality.* Certainly it is possible to see Arnold's Hellenism, or the ongoing project of perfection, as a technique of the self, one that moreover significantly contrasts with the strongly "code oriented" discipline of Hebraism, though Arnold's classically inflected notion of self-discipline always imported the aversion to physicality that marks Christianity.[40]

On the other hand, many of the specifically ethical problems that attend Foucault's turn to the aesthetics of existence, so resonant for study of Victorian aestheticism and Victorian Hellenism, also can be seen to inhere in Arnold's works. As Thomas McCarthy has argued, one of the central problems with Foucault's late works is the absence of any truly social or intersubjective dimension, the fact that the only zone of liberty resides in the self's action upon the self.[41] Arnold's is an ideal articulated almost exclusively in individualist terms: the only relation is that between the singular subject and those forces and conditions (both intrinsic and extrinsic) that must be controlled, balanced, or heroically faced; missing is any intersubjective or public dialogue. Arnold's aversion to transformative dialogue must be described as crucially different from Foucault's failure to articulate freedom in intersubjective terms: Foucault's avoidance of a dialogical conception of freedom stems from his concerns about the normalizing effects of any social norms; Arnold is worried not about the institution of norms but rather about the disruptive effects of dissent and debate. The point of convergence between the two, however, lies in the inability to imagine reciprocal social relations as a site where one's own principles might be enacted. His protestations about the social dimensions of culture notwithstanding, Arnold seems incapable of construing social interaction in concrete terms. The dialectical model of cultural fusion, wherein Hebraism and Hellenism slowly come into balance, remains a wholly transpersonal form of cultural interaction. Likewise, in *On the Study of Celtic Literature,* recognition and reconciliation are routed through an intellectual project, and genuine politics is dismissed as a "dream."[42]

Arnold's attempt to cast detachment as an *inherently* ethical practice ultimately manifests the limits of his social and political vision. In the new cosmopolitanisms that I discussed in the introduction, enacted universalism stresses the cultivation of phronesis, sensibility, and tact as a response to the inescapably delicate intercultural conditions that obtain in a widening world. Indeed, it is precisely in the rigorous imagining of how universalism might be lived that a more supple, intersubjective, and self-critical characterology comes into play. As I have shown, Arnold does introduce valuable cosmopolitan elements into his articulations of criticism, especially when he considers the value of com-

parative method and the need to cultivate a distanced relation toward one's own heritage. The problem, however, resides in the highly individualized nature of Arnold's ideals—their heroic singularity—as well as in the fact that Arnold does not so much argue for a universalism responding to the demands of difference and cultural specificity as rather suggest that universalism enacted simply *is* tact, that objectivity simply *is* impartiality. Both attracted and troubled by the conditions of freedom that attend disenchantment, Arnold thus risks attributing fixity to the very elements that promise to breathe life into his ideals of modernity.

Notes

1. Among the studies that emphasize the historical and social dimensions of Arnold's work are Lionel Trilling, *Matthew Arnold* (New York: Harcourt Brace Jovanovich, 1954; originally published 1939); Frederic E. Faverty, *Matthew Arnold the Ethnologist* (Evanston: Northwestern University Press, 1951); Morris Dickstein, *Double Agent: The Critic and Society* (New York: Oxford University Press, 1992); Donald Stone, *Communications with the Future: Matthew Arnold in Dialogue* (Ann Arbor: University of Michigan Press, 1997).

2. Matthew Arnold, "The Function of Criticism at the Present Time," in *The Complete Prose Works of Matthew Arnold,* vol. 3: *Lectures and Essays in Criticism,* ed. R. H. Super (Ann Arbor: University of Michigan Press, 1962), 258. Subsequent page number references will be cited parenthetically in the text as *CPW 3.*

3. When I say that criticism is characterized by "even a kind of restless energy," I have in mind the section of "The Function of Criticism at the Present Time" in which Arnold criticizes those who insist we move beyond mere negative critique—in this context Arnold insists that criticism must be "perpetually dissatisfied" (*CPW* 3:280). Also relevant here is the early description of culture, in *Culture and Anarchy,* as "eternally passing on and seeking." See Matthew Arnold, *Culture and Anarchy,* in *The Complete Prose Works of Matthew Arnold,* vol. 5: Culture and Anarchy *with* Friendship's Garland *and Some Literary Essays,* ed. R. H. Super (Ann Arbor: University of Michigan Press, 1965), 111. Subsequent page number references will be cited parenthetically in the text as *CPW 5.*

4. See Jerome Stolnitz, "On the Origins of 'Aesthetic Disinterestedness,'" *Journal of Aesthetics and Art Criticism* 20 (1961-62): 131-43.

5. Arnold states in "The Function of Criticism" that the criticism he is advocating "regards Europe as being, for intellectual and spiritual purposes, one

great confederation, bound to a joint action and working to a common result; and whose members have, for their proper outfit, a knowledge of Greek, Roman, and Eastern antiquity, and of one another" (*CPW* 3:284).

6. Arnold was in fact taken to task repeatedly for his lack of patriotism and even went so far, in the pages of the *Pall Mall Gazette,* to acknowledge the need, as he put it, "to disclaim that positive admiration of things foreign, and that indifference to English freedom, which have often been imputed to me." Quoted in Faverty, *Matthew Arnold the Ethnologist,* 4. Interestingly, Arnold's late lecture "Numbers," delivered in the United States in 1883, acknowledges that he may have underestimated the patriotism of his home audience: "Here, so many miles from home, I begin to reflect with tender contrition, that perhaps I have not,—I will not say flattered the patriotism of my own countrymen enough, but regarded it enough. Perhaps that is one reason why I have produced so very little effect upon them." Matthew Arnold, "Numbers; or The Majority and the Remnant," in *The Complete Prose Works of Matthew Arnold,* vol. 10: *Philistinism in England and America,* ed. R. H. Super (Ann Arbor: University of Michigan Press, 1974), 143-44. Subsequent page number references will be cited parenthetically in the text as *CPW* 10.

7. Both these essays acknowledge without idealizing the aid of extranational distance in the appraisal of literary figures claimed as national treasures by the home country. In the essay on Milton, Arnold writes, "A completely disinterested judgment about a man like Milton is easier to a foreign critic than to an Englishman. From conventional obligation to admire 'our great epic poet' a foreigner is free. Nor has he any bias for or against Milton because he was a Puritan,—in his political and ecclesiastical doctrines to one of our great English parties a delight, to the other a bugbear." Arnold quickly adds, however, that good criticism also requires "a thorough knowledge of the man and his circumstances" and goes on to credit Scherer with extensive knowledge of Milton and his times, and with a general cosmopolitanism of knowledge and character: "He knows thoroughly the language and literature of England, Italy, Germany, as well as of France. Well-informed, intelligent, disinterested, open-minded, sympathetic, M. Scherer has much in common with the admirable critic whom France has lost—Sainte-Beuve." Matthew Arnold, "A French Critic on Milton," in *The Complete Prose Works of Matthew Arnold,* vol. 8: *Essays Religious and Mixed,* ed. R. H. Super (Ann Arbor: University of Michigan Press, 1972), 174, 174-75. Also compare Arnold's articulation of a compara-

tive imperative in "On the Modern Element in Literature": "no single event, no single literature, is adequately comprehended except in its relation to other events, to other literature." *The Complete Prose Works of Matthew Arnold,* vol. 1: *On the Classical Tradition,* ed. R. H. Super (Ann Arbor: University of Michigan Press, 1960), 20-21. Subsequent page number references will be cited parenthetically as *CPW* 1.

8. Matthew Arnold, *Heinrich Heine, CPW* 3:111.

9. Matthew Arnold, "Marcus Aurelius," *CPW* 3:140.

10. See Trilling, *Matthew Arnold*; Faverty, *Matthew Arnold the Ethnologist*; Dickstein, *Double Agent*; Stone, *Communications with the Future.*

11. I restrict the focus of this analysis to the 1850s and 1860s because the pattern of thought that I am identifying takes on a different shape in Arnold's writings on religion in the 1870s, tending toward a kind of mysticism.

12. The most common target of attack is the series of arguments about the ground of culture in *Culture and Anarchy,* in which the state, culture, and individual perfection all depend upon one another for their validation. See Trilling, *Matthew Arnold,* 254; David J. DeLaura, *Hebrew and Hellene in Victorian England: Newman, Arnold, and Pater* (Austin: University of Texas Press, 1969), 77; Steven Marcus, "*Culture and Anarchy* Today," in *Culture and Anarchy,* ed. Samuel Lipman (New Haven: Yale University Press, 1994), 178.

13. Delaura, *Hebrew and Hellene,* 77.

14. Trilling, *Matthew Arnold,* 236. Subsequent page number references will be cited parenthetically in the text.

15. Writing in the 1930s, Trilling was acutely aware of the dangers of race thinking. On balance, he sought to defend Arnold, but he also acknowledged that any use of "the racial hypothesis" conduced to legitimize a volatile and dangerous set of practices: "if some used [the racial hypothesis] for liberalizing purposes, as Arnold himself did, still, by their very assent to an unfounded assumption, they cannot wholly be dissociated from the quaint, curious and dangerous lucubrations of Houston Stewart Chamberlain, Richard Wagner, Woltmann, Treitschke, Rosenberg and the whole of official German thought in the present day" (235).

16. Robert J. C. Young, *Colonial Desire: Hybridity in Theory, Culture and Race* (New York: Routledge, 1995). "Trilling suggests in Arnold's favour that despite his immersion in racial theory, at least Arnold advocated racial mixture. . . . Arnold does not advocate an amalgamation that results in merg-

ing and fusion but rather an apartheid model of dialogic separation: in claiming the continued existence of types, which can still be distinguished by the perceptive ethnologist or literary critic, Arnold keeps to the idea of racial mingling with no loss of distinctness for each racial type, and thus shows his position to be much closer to those on the right such as Edwards, Knox, Nott, and Gliddon" (86-87). This is subsumed as well under a more general set of claims: "Culture has always marked cultural difference by producing the other; it has always been comparative, and racism has always been an integral part of it: the two are inextricably clustered together, feeding off and generating each other. Race has always been culturally constructed. Culture has always been racially constructed" (54).

17. Matthew Arnold, "Spinoza and the Bible," *CPW* 3:158.

18. In his appeal to essential racial nature, Arnold is similar to many but not all of his contemporaries. Criticizing Trilling's attempt to defend Arnold by saying that he is simply a product of his time, Young points out that many of Arnold's contemporaries contested racial thinking; he lists Prichard, Buckle, Huxley, Latham, Lubbock, Mill, Quatrefages, Tylor, and Waitz. See Young, *Colonial Desire,* 63. Trilling, on the other hand, admits the existence of challenges from figures like Mill and Buckle but provides an extensive list of racialists, including Gobineau, Moses Hess, Heine, Ludwig Börne, Stendhal, Meredith, Mme. de Staël, Carlyle, J. A. Froude, Kingsley, J. R. Green, Taine, Renan, and Sainte-Beuve. Trilling goes so far as to say, "Indeed, the list could be made to include nearly every writer of the time who generalized about human affairs" (235).

19. One might contrast this with the following statement by Mill, in *The Principles of Political Economy*: "of all vulgar modes of escaping from the consideration of the effect of social and moral influences on the human mind, the most vulgar is that of attributing diversities of conduct and character to inherent natural differences." Quoted in Trilling, *Matthew Arnold,* 234.

20. I use the term "racial culture" here in part to indicate that for Arnold, as for many nineteenth-century thinkers, "race" was used in a loose way, sometimes with strict reference to physical characteristics, sometimes more expansively, along the lines of what we now call "culture." On this issue, see Young, *Colonial Desire,* 86; George W. Stocking, Jr., *Victorian Anthropology* (New York: The Free Press, 1987), 138-39.

21. The sketch provided in this paragraph is largely drawn from Fred A. Dudley, "Matthew Arnold and Science," *PMLA* 57 (1942): 276-86.

22. Matthew Arnold, "Literature and Science," *CPW* 10:57.

23. "Nowhere else did Arnold make such cordial overtures to science as in the Celtic lectures of 1865 and 1866. Students of ancient Welsh and Irish literature, he believed, should try to be as objective as the philologists and anthropologists, whose contributions toward the understanding of race, led him repeatedly to attribute to science that very power of integration which he found more usually in poetry." Dudley, "Matthew Arnold and Science," 289.

24. In this Arnold manifests the more general tendency among nineteenth-century scientists to "moralize" objectivity. See Lorraine Daston, "The Moral Economy of Science," *Osiris* 10 (1995): 3-24; Lorraine Daston and Peter Galison, "The Image of Objectivity," *Representations* 40 (1992): 81-128; and Lorraine Daston, "Objectivity and the Escape from Perspective," *Social Studies of Science* 22 (1992): 597-618. Also see my introduction for further discussion of the work of Daston and Galison.

25. *On the Study of Celtic Literature* was written in the midst of Fenian violence and anti-Irish reaction. Arnold consistently opposed Home Rule (which he feared would spark a civil war) but did campaign for landlord reform and a federalist system of local provincial government; he also supported concurrent endowment of the Protestant and Catholic churches in Ireland, departing from his usual disestablishmentarian views. See David Lloyd, "Arnold, Ferguson, Schiller: Aesthetic Culture and the Politics of Aesthetics," *Cultural Critique* 2 (1986): 137-69; Thomas S. Snyder, "Matthew Arnold and the Irish Question," *The Arnoldian* 4 (1977): 12-20.

26. Quoted in Dudley, "Matthew Arnold and Science," 290.

27. See Young, *Colonial Desire,* 16.

28. On the issue of Arnold's pervasive ambivalence about specific racial characteristics, see Faverty, *Matthew Arnold the Ethnologist,* 8.

29. This tension between abstract universalism and a more expansive conception of cultural fusion or perspectivalism in many ways replicates the oft-noted tension between Arnold's appeal to objective and timeless standards and his relativist historicism.

30. Alan D. McKillop, "Local Attachment and Cosmopolitanism: The Eighteenth-Century Pattern,"

in *From Sensibility to Romanticism,* ed. Frederick W. Hilles and Harold Bloom (New York: Oxford University Press, 1965), 191-218.

31. In making this argument, Arnold significantly exempts the Jew and the Catholic: because these two religions are, to use Arnold's word, "cosmopolitan," they overcome the deficiencies of other non-Establishment religions (*CPW* 5:238). Cosmopolitanism here, however, is simply expressive of a higher totality, via the religions that transcend provinciality, whereas the Protestant sects in England are both provincial and factionalizing. Both the Establishment and cosmopolitan religions differ from the domestic sects insofar as they exist above and beyond the mere concerns of the local.

32. It is of course interesting that Arnold never attributes insight to the distancing effects of class difference, but only to international or intercultural viewpoints. Young argues that in *Culture and Anarchy* Arnold displaces class conflict by invoking larger racial forces as the determinants of England's cultural history. Young, *Colonial Desire,* 60.

33. In *Matthew Arnold,* Trilling explains that "[c]ulture is reason involving the whole personality" (265), though without exploring the precise forms of reconciliation that I have analyzed here: fact and value, manner and method, reason and tact. Arnold also addresses the issue of character in "Democracy": "It is common to hear remarks on the frequent divorce between culture and character, and to infer from this that culture is a mere varnish, and that character only deserves any serious attention. No error can be more fatal. Culture without character is, no doubt, something frivolous, vain, and weak; but character without culture is, on the other hand, something raw, blind, and dangerous." Matthew Arnold, "Democracy," in *Culture and Anarchy and Other Writings,* ed. Stefan Collini (Cambridge: Cambridge University Press, 1993), 21.

34. I have in mind here *Culture and Anarchy,* but also the essay "Democracy."

35. In some instances, the ideal of temperament animates and informs his description of critical method such that odd personifications—of culture and criticism—appear. I consider these symptomatic distortions—or reversals—of the tendency I am describing. Hence we get formulations such as "culture hates hatred; culture has but one great passion, the passion for sweetness and light" (*CPW* 5:112).

36. This claim needs to be distinguished from those interpretations of Arnold that give centrality to his conception of imaginative reason in "Pagan and Mediaeval Religious Sentiment." Arnold certainly sought to reconcile a series of opposing terms through the concept of "imaginative reason," most centrally reason and faith. And the synthesis offered up by *Culture and Anarchy* is, as DeLaura points out, another version of such a reconciliation, in this case between the moral and the intellectual. I am arguing more generally that the ideal of Hellenism seeks to give an ethical dimension to those stances that Arnold repeatedly feared were divorced from the realm of value.

37. Jacques Derrida, *The Other Heading: Reflections on Today's Europe,* trans. Pascale-Anne Brault and Michael B. Naas (Bloomington: Indiana University Press, 1992), 48.

38. Walter Pater, *The Renaissance: Studies in Art and Poetry,* ed. Donald L. Hill (Berkeley: University of California Press, 1980), xix.

39. See, for example, David Bromwich, "The Genealogy of Disinterestedness," *Raritan* 1 (1982): 62-92.

40. This points to another key limitation to Arnold's conception of embodied universality: its paradoxically aversive relation to the bodily and other forces of nature. Indeed, as we saw in the case of *On the Study of Celtic Literature,* Arnold's conception of stance can take the form, at times, of a stark and repressive relation between the controlling individual and forces of nature—the body, desire, racial nature.

41. Thomas McCarthy, *Ideals and Illusions: On Reconstruction and Deconstruction in Contemporary Critical Theory* (Cambridge: MIT Press, 1991), 72-73.

42. For a related discussion of Arnold's diffusion of political conflict between England and Ireland through a dialectical ideal of assimilation, see Lloyd, "Arnold, Ferguson, Schiller."

Jerry Z. Muller (essay date 2002)

SOURCE: Muller, Jerry Z. "Matthew Arnold: Weaning the Philistines from the Drug of Business." In *The Mind and the Market: Capitalism in Modern European Thought,* pp. 208-28. New York: Alfred A. Knopf, 2002.

[*In the following essay, Muller contends that business was for Arnold what religion was for Karl Marx—a means of deluding the masses. In Muller's view, Arnold's fear that the narrow-minded business world tainted culture and politics was honed during his years as an inspector of middle-class schools and was central to the philosophy espoused in such texts as "The Function of Criticism at the Present Time" and* Culture and Anarchy.]

Like Marx, Matthew Arnold (1822-1888) bridled at the prospect of a world turned "philistine," an epithet that both of them borrowed from Heinrich Heine, the German poet and cultural critic. For Arnold as for Marx, "philistinism" was a pejorative term for the mentality of the commercial and industrial middle classes, which both thinkers saw as increasingly giving the tone to government and society. But while they used the same term to describe the malady, they diverged in their diagnosis of its cause and the prescription for its cure. While Marx thought that religion was the opiate of the masses, diverting their minds from the discontents of capitalism, Arnold thought that business was an opiate, diverting the capitalists from religious and spiritual development. For Marx, the solution was to eliminate capitalism, the economic basis of philistine culture. Arnold, by contrast, regarded the economic achievements of capitalism as real enough, and never imagined that there was a viable economic alternative. What he feared was that the characteristic mentality of the commercial middle class was spilling over into the realms of culture and politics. His antidote was not the elimination of commerce but the improvement of the culture of the nation by intellectuals such as himself, acting through government, the press, and educational institutions. Arnold embodied and helped to shape a social role we might call "the critical but non-alienated intellectual."

Arnold's critique of middle-class philistinism has by now become so familiar that we are apt to underestimate its boldness. For he was writing at the zenith of belief in the cult of progress. The assumption that things were getting better materially was, as already noted, based in reality. At midcentury, Britain's industrial and financial hegemony was unrivaled, and the face of the land was being transformed by industrialization. Half the iron in the world was being produced in Britain. Within a few decades, over five thousand miles of railway had been built, radically reducing travel time between the capital and the provinces, making it possible to go from London to Oxford in an hour—with consequences for both cities.

Signs of economic expansion and social dynamism were everywhere, with none more remarked upon than the Crystal Palace, a vast conservatory of glass and steel built in 1851 to house the Great Exhibition. Nearly a million feet of glass, suspended by a web of 3,300 columns and 2,300 girders, were assembled in a mere seventeen weeks, thanks to the industrial miracle of prefabrication. The exhibition and its Palace of Industry made progress visible and tangible. "The history of the world records no event comparable, in its promotion of human industry, with that of the Great Exhibition of the Works of Industry of all Nations in 1851," boasted Henry Cole, one of its leading sponsors. And in what he thought of as true British fashion, it was not a product of government or of coercion. "A great people invited all civilized nations to a festival, to bring into comparison the works of human skill. It was carried out by its own private means, was self-supporting and independent of taxes and employment of slaves, which great works had exacted in ancient days." The official head of the Great Exhibition was none other than Queen Victoria's consort, Prince Albert, whom Cole praised as "a prince of pre-eminent wisdom, of philosophic mind, sagacity, with power of generalship and great practical ability, [who] placed himself at the head of the enterprise, and led it to triumphant success." As one contemporary noted, the Crystal Palace reflected the age: "It is the aesthetic bloom of its practical character and of the practical tendency of the English nation."[1]

Arnold's vocation was to specify the limits of such practicality. To explain how he came to formulate his critique of philistinism, and his solutions to the problem of spiritual impoverishment amid material plenty that it posed, we must have a look at the milieu from which he sprang and the institutions that converged in his own person.

LIFE AMONG THE PHILISTINES AND HEBRAISTS

Born in 1822, Arnold was four years younger than Marx; he published his most important works of cultural criticism, **Culture and Anarchy,** in 1869, shortly after the publication of the first volume of *Capital.*[2] Matthew's father, Thomas Arnold, was the headmaster of the Rugby School, a novel and remarkably influential educational institution intended to produce gentlemen capable of ruling the country in a Christian spirit. He was also a leading figure of the Broad Church, which sought to retain the established Church of England while making it as inclusive as possible. Matthew Arnold continued his father's commitments but in a more secularized fashion. He looked to men of letters to supply the spiritual guidance and moral encouragement that the priesthood was no longer capable of conveying.

In 1841 Matthew went up to Oxford, having won a scholarship to Balliol College by competitive examination, thus personifying the middle-class ideal of advancement through merit. Thomas Arnold was appointed professor of modern history at the university that same year, but he died shortly after taking up the appointment. The curriculum at Balliol consisted for the most part of the Greek and Latin classics of philosophy and literature, a storehouse from which Arnold (like Marx) would continue to draw. The Balliol connection was to be central not only to Arnold's career but to the larger intellectual project of reforming the ancient universities and enhancing their influence in the government and culture of the nation—in remaking Oxford in the image of Rugby, and remaking the philistine nation in turn.

The system of preferment that had brought the young and impecunious Edmund Burke to the attention of aristocratic politicians almost a century earlier functioned for Arnold as well. At age twenty-four, he became private secretary to a great Whig landowner and senior parliamentarian, Lord Lansdowne, who was just old enough to have heard Burke himself address Parliament. Lansdowne was also head of the Committee of the Council on Education.

Burke first established his reputation as a writer of prose, but it was as a poet that Arnold initially came to public attention. His poetic gifts would eventually lead to a professorship in 1857, when he was elected professor of poetry at Oxford, a position he held for a decade. His professorship only demanded three public lectures each year, commensurate with the pittance it paid. Poetry, even with a professorship attached, was not a profession from which a man could support a family. And so, spurred on by his desire to marry and the need to provide for his prospective offspring, Arnold at age twenty-eight accepted an appointment as one of Her Majesty's inspectors of schools—reluctantly, for fear that it would not allow him time for his own reading and writing. He would hold that job for the next thirty-five years. The work was indeed time-consuming, but Arnold's energy was prodigious. During the next three and a half decades, he produced a stream of essays and books, which when collected amounted to eleven stout volumes of prose, running the gamut from literary criticism to social and political analysis, including two book-length works on educational reform and three more on religious themes.[3]

Unlike Prussia, the England of Arnold's day had no state system of schools, and universal education remained elusive almost a century after Adam Smith had recommended it as an antidote to the negative effects of the market. Creation of a uniform and comprehensive school system on the continental model was stymied by an aristocratic tradition of antipathy toward the power of central government, together with an ongoing suspicion of state schools by non-Anglican Dissenters, who feared that state education would inculcate the tenets of the Church of England. Instead, schools were operated by churches and charities. But beginning in the 1840s, schools became eligible to receive a small government subsidy, in return for which the government sent its inspectors to monitor their quality. To satisfy religious sensibilities, there were separate inspectors for Anglican, Catholic, and Dissenting Protestant schools. Arnold's post took him to schools run by those Protestant groups that had rejected membership in the Church of England, known as Nonconformists or Dissenters.

To a remarkable degree, these Quakers, Presbyterians, Congregationalists, Unitarians, and Baptists formed the backbone of commercial and industrial leadership. The social structure of England was a sandwich, with Anglicans at the top (aristocracy and gentry) and bottom, and with Dissenters in the ever-growing middle. (Methodists, who had begun within the Church of England but were a separate denomination by Arnold's day, formed a layer socially just below the older Dissenting sects.) Excluded by virtue of their religion from government and from aristocratic patronage, from the great universities of Oxford and Cambridge, and from the army and navy, Dissenters went into trade and industry. Their style of life stressed laboring in one's vocation, practical education, sobriety, and high moral conduct.[4] Max Weber was not the first to note that the character traits inculcated by these descendants of the Puritans were conducive to economic advance. Because their experience had made them suspicious of government power, Dissenters formed a leading constituency of middle-class liberalism, and it was from their ranks that prominent liberal leaders, such as John Bright, sprang. Though the very top government posts remained largely in the hands of aristocrats like Lansdowne, by the 1850s this middle class increasingly set the tone of government policy. Below them on the social ladder were the working classes, which remained not only disenfranchised but often barely literate.

Arnold's job as inspector of schools brought him into daily contact with the educational institutions of the middle classes, visiting schools for children aged four to thirteen, primarily in booming industrializing areas of the nation, such as Birmingham. He was often appalled by what he saw. It was from his immersion in these strongholds of the middle classes that Arnold's critique of middle-class culture and politics evolved.

ARNOLD'S CRITIQUE

The inspection of schools launched his first major work of social criticism, an essay entitled **"Democracy,"** which first appeared as the preface to his published report of 1861, ***The Popular Education of France.*** The success of the middle classes in bringing about material advance and political liberty, he lamented, had led to a self-satisfaction that had itself become a barrier to improvement in any larger and higher sense. The middle class believed ardently in industry and in liberty of thought; what it lacked was "culture" and "ideas." "No one esteems them [the middle class] more than I do," he wrote, "but those who esteem them most, and who most believe in their capabilities, can render them no better service than by pointing out in what they underrate their deficiencies, and how their deficiencies, if unremedied, may impair their future."[5] As their influence increased, he feared that the commercial middle classes would "deteriorate" the country by "their low ideals and want of culture." Democracies characteristically define as their highest ideals those of the ordinary man. Echoing Aristotle, Arnold reminded his readers that "the difficulty for democracy is how to find and keep high ideals."[6] As Britain moved toward a broader, more democratic suffrage, Arnold feared that the working class would follow the middle classes in embracing a low and constricted conception of cultural aspiration.

Arnold, like Marx, was repelled by what the latter had called the "*Beschränktheit*" of bourgeois society. And like Marx, Arnold looked to Heine for a polemical term that would capture what Heine called the *ächt britische Beschränktheit* (the "genuine British narrowness"). That epithet was "philistinism," connoting the ethos of "a strong, dogged, unenlightened opponent of the chosen people, of the children of the light." "We have not the expression in English," Arnold noted drolly. "Perhaps we have not the word because we have so much of the thing. At Soli, I imagine, they did not talk of solecisms; and here, at the very headquarters of Goliath, nobody talks of Philistinism.'"[7]

His first public skirmish with the forces of philistinism came in 1862, and it occurred on his home ground, so to speak: schooling. Robert Lowe, a Liberal MP who was Arnold's political superior at the Education Office, had proposed a revision of the method of government funding for schools, based on "payment by results." The scheme was founded on the premise that "the duty of a State in public education is . . . to obtain the greatest possible quantity of reading, writing, and arithmetic for the greatest number."[8] Schools were to be funded based on the performance of their students in the "3 R's." Each school was to be visited annually by a school inspector, who was to quiz every student in English language and arithmetic. For every student who failed to appear or to answer questions successfully, a small sum would be deducted from the school's government funding. Lowe's reform was intended in part to cut costs, but above all to make school funding dependent on measurable results in the most basic and practical of skills, and to bring education into accord with his market-oriented principles by linking payment to performance.[9]

With a dose of bravery or brazenness, Arnold launched a public salvo against his political superior, in **"The Twice-Revised Code,"** an essay that he published in a leading magazine and made certain was distributed to every member of Parliament. He attacked the narrow and mechanical conception of education behind Lowe's plan. The ability to read intelligently, he pointed out, came primarily not from narrowly tailored reading lessons, but from a more general cultivation, imbibed from the family or, failing that, from the school environment, which created the mental desire to read. The goal of the schools, therefore, should be "general intellectual culti-

vation," without which the skills of reading and writing would not develop.[10] The government sought to fund only the most rudimentary of educations instead of responding to "the strong desire of the lower classes to raise themselves."[11] Since many impoverished students would inevitably be absent when the annual test was administered, or would fail the test itself, he predicted that the net effect of the proposed reform would be to reduce the funding of schools for the poor. The education of the people, he concluded, was to be sacrificed to "the friends of economy at any price."[12] Arnold's argument was that market principles were inappropriate in this realm. In the end, Arnold won a partial victory over the philistines: the principle of payment for performance was enshrined in the new legislation, but it accounted for only a part of the government's grant to each school.[13]

Education, for Arnold, was not just the transmission of information or the learning of basic reading and computational skills: it was to be a civilizing agent.[14] Arnold frequently found himself inspecting schools in which students ingested mountains of facts and arithmetic but were bereft of analytic ability and utterly incapable of understanding sophisticated prose or poetry. They were taught not to reason but to cram.[15] Both before and especially after the adoption of "payment for performance," he criticized such education for being "far too little formative and humanizing . . . much in it, which its administrators point to as valuable *results*, is in truth mere machinery," unconcerned with cultivating taste and feeling.[16]

* * *

The "chosen people," to which the philistines were contrasted, were neither the Jews nor the Dissenters, whom Arnold referred to as "Hebraists" because of the strictness of their moral code. For Arnold, the "chosen people" were intellectuals like himself, those who strove for "culture" and practiced "criticism." He used these terms more or less interchangeably. In a widely read 1864 essay, **"The Function of Criticism at the Present Time,"** he defined criticism as "a disinterested endeavor to learn and propagate the best that is known and thought in the world."[17] While Arnold greatly admired Edmund Burke as the man who had done more than any other to bring intellect to bear on British politics, he thought that the British had taken Burke's suspicion of rationalism too much to heart. They had made a stultifying dogma of Burke's perception that rational thought may overstep its bounds in attempting to realize ideals directly, and transformed his gospel of moderation into a generalized suspicion of ideas—and of intellectuals. As a result the British acted as if "practice is everything, a free play of the mind is nothing."[18] The practical, utilitarian mentality, which had been so useful in the creation of material wealth through market activity and industry, had, Arnold thought, become a barrier to any higher or nobler aspiration. The function of contemporary criticism was therefore "to keep man from a self-satisfaction which is retarding and vulgarising, to lead him towards perfection, by making his mind dwell upon what is excellent in itself, and the absolute beauty and fitness of things."[19]

And yet, Arnold suggested, the very accumulation of affluence might set the stage for higher aspiration, and the material comfort being created by capitalism might lead to a demand for intellectual substance:

> In spite of all that is said about the absorbing and brutalising influence of our passionate material progress, it seems to me indisputable that this progress is likely, though not certain, to lead in the end to an apparition [becoming visible] of intellectual life; and that man, after he has made himself perfectly comfortable and has not to determine what to do with himself next, may begin to remember that he has a mind, and that the mind may be made the source of great pleasure. I grant it is mainly the privilege of faith, at present, to discern this end to our railways, our business, and our fortune-making; but we shall see if, here as elsewhere faith is not in the end the true prophet. Our ease, our travelling, and our unbounded liberty to hold just as hard and securely as we please to the practice to which our notions have given birth, all tend to beget an inclination to deal a little more freely with these notions themselves, to canvass them a little, to penetrate a little into their real nature.[20]

With the publication of this essay, Arnold broke through to a larger audience. His books were sold in railway bookstalls, his ideas debated in the pages of newspapers read by bankers and barristers, parliamentarians and businessmen.[21] The essay set off a critical battle in the major magazines of the day.

Arnold's next sally came in **"My Countryman"** (1866), an essay that aroused an even more irate response. Speaking in the voice of a foreign observer of English ways, he raised the question of what would bring about a life satisfying to the modern spirit, and tabulated

> the growth of a love of industry, trade, and wealth; the growth of a love of the things of the mind; and the growth of a love of beautiful things. Of these three factors of modern life, your middle class has no notion of any but one, the first. Their love of industry, trade, and wealth, is certainly prodigious. . . . But what notion have they of anything else? . . . Your middle class is educated, to begin with, in the worst schools of your country. . . . The fineness and capacity of a man's spirit is shown by his enjoyments; your middle class has an enjoyment in its business, we admit, and gets on well in business, and makes money; but beyond that? Drugged with business, your middle class seems to have its sense blunted for any stimulus besides, except religion; it has a religion, narrow, unintelligent, repulsive. . . . Can any life be imagined more hideous, more dismal, more unenviable?[22]

Arnold's book ***Culture and Anarchy: An Essay in Political and Social Criticism*** grew out of a lecture entitled **"Culture and Its Enemies,"** which he delivered at Oxford in June 1867 and published a month later in the *Cornhill Magazine*. It was a plea for attention to what Arnold called "culture" (and its bearers), which he contrasted to the market and to its middle-class devotees.

"Culture" for Arnold represented not so much a distinct body of knowledge as an attitude toward the world and the use of the mind in it. It was "a pursuit of our total perfection by means of getting to know, on all matters which most concern us, the best which has been thought and said in the world; and through this knowledge, turning a stream of fresh and free thought upon our stock notions and habits, which we now follow staunchly but mechanically, vainly imagining that there is a virtue in following them staunchly which makes up for the mischief of following them mechanically." It combined "the scientific passion" to know things as they really are with "the passion of doing good."[23]

It meant attention to one's cultural and mental development, to what Arnold called "inwardness," which he contrasted to "the mechanical and material civilisation we esteem." In a society characterized by the division of labor, culture was contrasted to specialization, "our intense energetic absorption in the particular pursuit we are following." And in a society in which competition loomed so large, culture meant the cultivation of sympathy and of "disinterestedness"—the impartial search for truth. Culture did not mean only self-development; it also had an altruistic element, demanding the pursuit of "*general* perfection, developing all parts of our society."[24] Culture, therefore, was "the endeavor to see things as they are, to draw towards a knowledge of the universal order which seems to be intended and aimed at in the world, and which it is a man's happiness to go along with or his misery to go counter to—to learn, in short, the will of God."[25] And intrinsic to the project of culture, at least as Arnold defined it, was its democratizing thrust, "to make the best that has been thought and known in the world current everywhere."[26]

Time and again, Arnold lamented that the culture of the British middle classes was focused on "machinery," by which he meant far more than mechanical devices.[27] "Machinery" connoted means of any sort. Arnold's complaint was that in a society in which means were increasing, men and women had lost sight of the ends that those means ought to serve. Indeed, they confused the agglomeration of means with the ends of life, and the increase of material wealth with moral improvement. They treated political liberty as a good in itself, instead of asking what purpose that liberty served. And because they identified progress with this "machinery," they were satisfied. (Like Marx, Arnold referred to the worship of means while losing sight of ends as a "fetish."[28]) Culture, by contrast, meant being subject to the self-dissatisfaction that comes from recognizing the gap between what is and what ought to be, a dissatisfaction that was the beginning of personal and collective betterment.

Arnold disparaged neither political freedom nor material affluence. He was grateful for England's political institutions, and nothing he wrote attacked the market as such. What he objected to were the assumptions that liberty was the last word in moral evaluation, and that the principles of free trade, industriousness, and self-interest, which fueled the market, ought to be applied to all other areas of life.

In Arnold's analysis, what too many Britons lacked was the sense that there might be more to collective life than liberty from government, the liberty "to do as one likes." In many ways, his arguments reformulated, in a less ponderous key, Hegel's distinction between choosing arbitrarily and choosing with good reasons. What was being lost in the self-congratulatory rhetoric of English liberty was the very notion that what was important was not just the *possibility* of choice, but what choice was actually made. Lost, too, was the aspiration to lead one's life rationally and reflectively.[29] The habits of mind of those who prided themselves on their dissent from the established church, Arnold argued, left the middle class ill equipped to become the establishment itself. The emphasis on individual freedom, together with the reflexes of dissent, had resulted in a principled antipathy to authority—not only the authority of institutions, but the authority of "right reason," the principle that there are good reasons for living one way rather than another.

Because the English had been taught to value liberty and self-reliance above all, Arnold contended, they gave too little thought and too small a role to the state. The very notion that the state might act in the general interest, rather than in the interest of the particular group that dominated it, was foreign to most Englishmen.[30] The result, Arnold claimed, was both dangerous and tragic.

Dangerous, because the only institution that could ultimately enforce order was losing its legitimacy. Until recently, Arnold maintained, the legitimacy of the government had been based upon deference to the aristocracy and monarchy. But now such deference was fading. Without respect for the state, lawlessness threatened. "As feudalism, with its ideas and habits of subordination dies out," he wrote, "we are in danger of drifting toward anarchy."[31] He cited as an omen a recent incident in which a London crowd, which had assembled in defiance of government order to demand extension of the suffrage to the working class, had torn down the

railings and trampled the flower beds of Hyde Park. Troops were called out to aid the police, but they took no action, and for the next several days thousands of people milled about the park. Despite the rather minor property damage, this train of events evoked the specter of mob violence. To Arnold, it reflected "the deep-seated spiritual anarchy of the English people." He argued that the freedom so valued by liberals, the freedom to be left alone by government to do as one likes (what Americans mean when their response to criticism is "It's a free country"), had become an end in itself, and a barrier to thinking about the need for shared authority. He warned that without the development of a sense of shared authority, embodied in a state that was more than the tool of a particular class, the Hyde Park riots might be a harbinger of greater social disorder.

The underdeveloped British sense of a state capable of pursuing the general interest was tragic because it left unfulfilled the functions that could not be realized by the market or by voluntary activity. Foremost among these was the quantity and quality of education, which were dismal, largely because of suspicion of government and dependence on the market principles of supply and demand. Schooling for the poor was too brief, rarely extending beyond elementary school. Schooling for the middle classes did include secondary schools; the problem there, in Arnold's view, was the limited nature of the subjects taught, and the narrowness of mind such studies reflected and reproduced. Here the law of the market broke down, Arnold suggested:

> The mass of mankind know good butter from bad, and tainted meat from fresh, and the principle of supply and demand may, perhaps, be relied on to give us sound meat and butter. But the mass of mankind do not so well know what distinguishes good teaching and training from bad; they do not here know what they ought to demand, and, therefore, the demand cannot be relied on to give us the right supply. Even if they knew what they ought to demand, they have not sufficient means of testing whether or not this is really supplied to them. Securities, therefore, are needed.

That assurance of quality could be provided by state funding when combined with competent state inspection.[32]

What was needed, according to Arnold, was a stronger state, one based upon the idea of the public interest, and upon the assumption that people might at times act for the sake of the public interest rather than out of self-interest, be it individual self-interest or class self-interest. Yet the very idea of a "best self" that acted upon rational reflection and altruistic motivation was foreign to most of the British population, he asserted.[33]

In laying out his analysis, he divided the population into four groups, each dubbed with a satirical tag: the Barbarians, the Populace, the Philistines, and the Aliens.

The Barbarians were the aristocrats, who possessed a certain style and serenity. But in a modern society, ideas mattered (here, too, a Hegelian echo), and British aristocrats were congenitally averse to ideas; indeed their serenity "appears to come from their never having had any ideas to trouble them."[34] As a result, their era of leadership was passing. The Populace comprised the working classes. Their material want and conditions of life left them excluded from "the best that had been thought and said," and hence prone to think of non-working hours as little more than occasions for drink and "fun." Though in an era of inevitable democracy, power would increasingly flow to them, they were as of yet poorly positioned to exercise that power for the general good. Arnold feared that they would adopt the narrow horizons and mental habits of the middle classes.

The class that actually wielded power (here, too, Arnold agreed with Marx) was the middle class, which had risen as a result of commercialization and industrialization. It was on this class that Arnold concentrated his fire, because, for better or worse, he regarded it as dominant for the historical moment. It was the members of this class that he characterized as Philistines. They were "the people who believe most that our greatness and welfare are proved by our being very rich, and who most give their lives and thought to becoming rich." But, he asked rhetorically, in what did their riches consist?

> Consider these people, then, their way of life, their habits, their manners, the very tones of their voice; look at them attentively; observe the literature they read, the things which give them pleasure, the words which come forth out of their mouths, the thoughts which make the furniture of their minds; would any amount of wealth be worth having with the condition that one was to become just like these people by having it?[35]

Their religion, Arnold conceded, had made them capable of conquering their baser instincts and adhering to a level of personal morality of which they were proud. But by Arnold's lights it had led to an exaggerated level of self-satisfaction.[36] He saw a common denominator behind their religious and economic life, and that was the narrow-mindedness with which they pursued both. Their twin goals were saving their souls and making money. And their "narrow and mechanical" conception of their "religious business"—based on avoiding sin, and a literalist understanding of the Bible and of Heaven and Hell—led in turn to a "narrow and mechanical" conception of their "secular business."[37]

There was, Arnold suggested, an elective affinity between fundamentalism in religion and in economics. Liberals took their economic dogmas and applied them mechanically. They worshiped free trade as a fetish, as an end in itself, rather than asking how it was linked to

personal happiness and national welfare.[38] While their policies had brought about an increase in total population and in wealth, they rarely paused to ask what wealth and population were for, or whether more of each was always desirable. Their belief in the beneficent effects of free trade and the growth of business made any form of government planning and intervention seem heretical.[39] Arnold suggested, by contrast, "that our social progress would be happier if there were not so many of us so very poor, and in busying ourselves with notions of in some way or other adjusting the poor man and business one to the other, and not multiplying the one and the other mechanically and blindly . . . ." "It turns out that our pursuit of free-trade, as of so many other things, has been too mechanical," he wrote. "We fix upon some object, which in this case is the production of wealth, and the increase of manufactures, population, and commerce through free-trade, as a kind of one thing needful, or end in itself; and then we pursue it staunchly and mechanically . . . not to see how it is related to the whole intelligible law of things and to full human perfection, or to treat it as the piece of machinery, of varying value as its relations to the intelligible law of things vary, which it really is."[40]

The unreflective theology of the descendants of the Puritans also got in the way of improving the quality of human life by conscious family planning, Arnold asserted. The growing numbers of urban poor needed to know more than biblical precepts for their ultimate salvation. They needed to be told how to limit their family size "to give their moral life and growth a fair chance!" In place of the "unintelligent Hebraism" that keeps repeating that the man who has a great many children is happy, Arnold resolved to tell the poor that "a man's children are not truly *sent*, any more than the pictures upon his wall, or the horses in his stable are *sent*; and that to bring people into the world, when one cannot afford to keep them and oneself decently and not too precariously, or to bring more of them into the world than one can afford to keep . . . [is] by no means an accomplishment of the divine will or a fulfillment of Nature's simplest laws, but is just as wrong, just as contrary to reason and the will of God, as for a man to have horses, or carriages, or pictures, when he cannot afford them, or to have more of them than he can afford . . . ."[41] Here, Arnold thought, a more calculated weighing of costs and benefits would be conducive to well-being.

If the aristocracy, the middle classes, and the working masses were ill fitted to guide the fortunes of the nation, who then was left? Arnold's answer lay with those he called Aliens. They came from every class, but they were aliens because they had transcended the mental boundaries of their classes of origin. He characterized them as those of every class who by nature have "a curiosity about their best self, with a bent for seeing things as they are, for disentangling themselves from machinery, for simply concerning themselves with reason and the will of God, and doing their best to make these prevail—for the pursuit, in a word, of perfection." The extent to which this "bent" would develop depended upon the encouragement it received. The aim of Aliens such as himself was to spread culture, in order to counter "the unchecked predominance of that class life which is the affirmation of our ordinary self," and to "disconcert mankind in their worship of machinery."[42]

THE ROLES OF THE INTELLECTUAL

Arnold's talk of criticism and of culture sounds airy and disembodied until we recognize that he was speaking on behalf of a group that was in part an existing reality, in part a project that he was working to bring into being. He was, to use an idiom quite foreign to him, an ideologist of the intellectuals, attempting to imbue them with collective self-consciousness and making universal claims on their behalf.

Arnold was part of an intellectual elite that was critical without being alienated from the powers that be. Though they were by no means affluent, they were welcome in the homes of at least some of the business elite. Arnold's whole plan was predicated on the assumption that a portion of the political and economic elites was open to the message he was preaching, and for this he had his own experience as a warrant. Arnold numbered among his friends Louisa de Rothschild, the wife of the head of the London branch of the great banking family, whom he first met in 1858, when he inspected a school on the family's estate. They struck up a friendship that lasted until the end of their days.[43] In his later years, Arnold was befriended by Andrew Carnegie, who had risen from a cottage in Dunfermline, Scotland, to become the steel lord of Pittsburgh and one of the richest men in the world. Carnegie was a true believer in the Arnoldian ideal of the civilizing effects of culture, and devoted much of his fortune to spreading it in the United States, subsidizing libraries throughout the republic. Nor was Arnold alienated from the world of politics: his brother-in-law was a Liberal MP, and Arnold himself knew both Disraeli and Gladstone.

In his easy movement between the worlds of thought and government, Arnold was characteristic of the small group of interlocking families who made up a sort of "intellectual aristocracy."[44] Since they read the same periodicals, belonged to the same clubs (above all, the Athenaeum), and often married one another's relatives, a relatively cohesive group was formed. While critical of the powers that be, they tried to modify what they criticized by working through the institutions of their society.

Unlike the earlier generation of Romantics, who had rejected bourgeois society and sought a historical alternative to it, and unlike the later generation of aesthetes, who sought to carve out a realm outside of bourgeois society, Arnold accepted the market and had a real if restrained appreciation of the virtues of the middle-class merchants, shopkeepers, and entrepreneurs who kept it humming.[45] For Arnold, as for many members of the Victorian intellectual aristocracy, the role of a cultured elite was to aid, elevate, and integrate society. They took their cue from Samuel Taylor Coleridge, who had written of the need to use the Church of England to create a "clerisy," men of culture who were to counter the negative effects of the capitalist ethos and create a shared sense of the authority of the state. Arnold secularized the notion even more.[46]

As we have seen, Hegel had similarly championed the "universal estate" of those imbued with *Bildung* and *Geist*. Arnold knew Hegel's work—some of it firsthand, some of it through Hegel's interpreters in France[47]—and in a satirical self-portrait, Arnold identified himself as a proponent of *"Geist."*[48]

For Arnold, as for Hegel before him and Emile Durkheim after him, the intellectuals were obligated to articulate the rational basis of shared authority in order to provide the social cohesion once offered by common religious belief. Arnold, like Hegel, wanted men of culture to play a larger role in the bureaucracy, to use the state to preserve the commonweal by raising the economic level and security of the working class,[49] but, above all, to raise the cultural and spiritual level of the nation through the nexus of government, schools, universities, and magazines.

The goal of the university reformers of the 1850s and 1860s was to make the ancient institutions of Oxford and Cambridge into nurseries of what Coleridge had called the "clerisy" and Arnold "culture." That meant bringing Oxford and Cambridge into closer contact with the cultural and political currents of the day, and extricating them from their close connection to the Church of England. Until the 1850s, religious tests prevented Dissenters from studying at either university, and teaching at most colleges was restricted to clergymen of the Church of England, mostly men in religious orders bound by vows of celibacy. Because they taught all subjects, few taught any subject well, including theology. Excluded by religion and by vocational interests, the sons of the commercial classes were conspicuous by their absence.[50]

All of this changed in Arnold's day. Both universities developed fellowships open to merit, as determined by competitive examination. Acts of Parliament in 1854 and 1856 opened Oxford and Cambridge to those outside the Church of England. The ranks of the dons were no longer confined to the clergy. The range of subjects taught was expanded, greater specialization of teaching was encouraged, and research became a part of university life. The student body, which before 1870 had been composed for the most part of the sons of landowners and clergymen, came to be dominated by the offspring of the commercial and professional classes thereafter.[51]

The goal of the university reformers, especially at Oxford, was to nurture a spiritual clerisy, which would contribute to the cohesion of a society too dominated by what Thomas Carlyle had called the "cash nexus" (one of Marx and Engels' favorite phrases). The personification of university reform was Benjamin Jowett, who had been Arnold's tutor at Balliol College, and became professor of classics there. Like Coleridge, Jowett developed a spiritual and ideological ideal of the state as a force to counteract the fragmenting effects of commercial society, a view that he had imbibed from Plato and Hegel, and that he shared with Arnold.[52]

As Jowett and his fellow reformers conceived it, the role of college education was twofold. It was to bring about an expansion of horizons and flexibility of mind, by exposing students to what Arnold called "the best that has been thought and said in the world." In that sense, it was defined by its distance from specifically professional education.[53] The universities (or, at least, their colleges) were designed to counter the professional and practical orientation of the business middle class. A diet of classical learning was regarded as particularly well suited to nourishing future statesmen, civil servants, and professional men, and a knowledge of Greek was required for admission to Oxford or Cambridge until the First World War.[54] Those in search of direct preparation for commercial and industrial careers went elsewhere, to the newly founded municipal colleges. Yet the nonprofessional education at Oxbridge was supposed to have very practical value. For the broader horizons it opened and the habits of mind it inculcated were to render its products fit to govern Britain and the empire, and to contest the narrow and unimaginative conceptions of life characteristic of the business-oriented middle classes and the working classes who followed in their wake.

At the same time that he was reshaping Oxford, Jowett was deeply involved in transforming the civil service, opening its ranks, raising its standards, and broadening its purview. That transformation began with the Trevelyan-Northcote Commission of 1853-54, which aimed at reforming the civil service by abolishing patronage and replacing it with a system that based admission upon competitive examinations. The modifications introduced in the decades thereafter weighted the civil service exams to precisely the sort of literary and classical knowledge that Jowett and Arnold favored, and which was increasingly inculcated at the colleges of Oxford and Cambridge.[55] Thus a knowledge of Greek afforded a great advantage to those who took the competitive exams for entry into the civil service and even the royal military academy.[56]

Jowett established a close connection between his college and the civil service in London, beginning with the Education Office. Matthew Arnold was a forerunner and exemplar of that link. When Arnold took up his job as inspector of schools, his superior was his former tutor at Balliol; later, another old friend from Balliol assumed the task. They had found their way from Balliol to the Education Office by patronage, "the recruitment of public servants by private recommendation."[57] Though patronage was soon to be disparaged as conflicting with merit, in Arnold's day it served as a rather efficient sifting mechanism. For Jowett, the civil service in general and the Education Department in particular provided an honorable vocational outlet for the graduates of his college. For London politicians such as Lord Lansdowne and his successors, Balliol provided a source of able men of broadly liberal political opinions and undogmatic religious convictions. In short, it served as an old boy network, of remarkably capable boys, a link that foreshadowed the more formalized entrance by merit later enshrined in the civil service reforms.[58] An impressive number of Arnold's friends and male relatives also pursued careers in the civil service. One brother, Edward Penrose Arnold, was also an inspector of schools; another, Thomas, served in the Colonial Office. Arnold's friend and fellow poet Arthur Hugh Clough served alongside him in the Education Office.

One of the state's most important roles, Arnold believed, was to foster education. Beyond the badly schooled children of the middle class lay the millions of children who received no formal education at all. Their parents would not send them to school unless the government enforced compulsory attendance, a policy that Arnold began to champion in 1853.[59] Arnold's longest book, *Schools and Universities on the Continent,* was intended to cast a fresh light on existing English conditions, in order to deflate his countrymen's assumptions about the adequacy of English education and the purported evils of state regulation of schools, not to mention compulsory education. He held up the German, Swiss, and French systems as models of national systems of education: they provided schooling for all, not only those with the wherewithal to pay, and elevated the education of teachers in order to improve the education of students.[60] He saw opposition to a state-regulated school system as a "pedantic application of certain maxims of political economy in the wrong place."[61] In England, he regretted, government policy was made without taking into account the opinion of those most knowledgeable about education. Here again, France and Germany provided an alternative—and, he thought, preferable—conception of how such matters might be handled.[62] Arnold's campaign for compulsory schooling under state auspices began to bear fruit in his own time. In 1870, the first Comprehensive Act was passed by the

British Parliament. It required local school boards to provide elementary education; attendance was made compulsory a few years later.[63]

The main obstacles toward real progress, Arnold asserted time and time again, was the self-satisfaction engendered by material success, "our high opinion of our own energy and wealth." "This opinion is just," he continued, "but it is possible to rely on it too long, and to strain our energy and our wealth too hard. At any rate, our energy and our wealth will be more fruitful and safer, the more we add intelligence to them. . . ."[64] Intelligence, culture, and criticism: these were the master terms of Arnold's political vision of a democracy, led by a state authority guided by men of culture, recruited from all social classes and motivated by the desire for public service.

In addition to the universities and the civil service, Arnold had at his disposal a third forum for culture and criticism: the commercial journals of opinion.

That there was an interest in culture among the middle classes Arnold knew. To a far greater degree than the aristocracy or the working class, they read—though what they read left much to be desired. Arnold described it as "literature the absolute value of which it is almost impossible to rate too humbly, literature hardly a work of which will reach, or deserves to reach, the future."[65] The challenge was to take that middle class which Arnold admired for its industry and moral seriousness and to imbue it with "culture and intelligence," transforming it into a class "liberalised by an ampler culture, admitted to a wider sphere of thought, living by larger ideas, with its provincialism dissipated, its intolerance cured, its pettinesses purged away."[66]

Another role for the man of culture, as Arnold understood it, was therefore to make "the best that had been thought and said in the world" accessible to a nonprofessional audience. That required the ability to "humanise" knowledge, "to make it efficient outside the clique of the cultivated and learned" by taking the best ideas and laboring "to divest knowledge of all that was harsh, uncouth, difficult, abstract, professional, exclusive," thus bringing it "within the sphere of everyone's interest."[67] The great practitioner of that retailing of ideas was, of course, Voltaire, whom Arnold regarded as a model. One role of the critic, as Arnold understood it, was to open up the horizons of middle-class readers to the cultural and intellectual legacy of the past and to promising developments abroad. No wonder he devoted scores of review essays to acquainting the readers of Victorian journals with the great writers of ancient Greece, the Bible, and the Christian heritage, modern philosophers such as Spinoza, and the literary masters of modern France and Germany. At the same time, he explored issues of public policy and parliamentary contestation in a similarly accessible manner.

The intellectual as public critic seemed especially plausible in Arnold's day, in part because there was a distinct medium and palpable audience for his message. That audience was the readership of the mid-Victorian journals, weekly and monthly, such as *Fraser's Magazine, The Saturday Review, The Fortnightly Review, The Quarterly Review, Macmillan's Magazine, Cornhill Magazine,* and the *Pall Mall Gazette.* Many of the books that we now regard as the classics of Victorian social and political thought first appeared as articles in these magazines, which also carried fiction as well as articles on history, literature, and politics.[68] With a circulation of about 10,000 to 20,000 each, they had an overlapping readership, which made up the circle of "the educated," above all the graduates of the universities and the public schools (i.e., private schools).[69] In an age when the franchise was still limited and before the domination of more specialized journals, writers like Arnold could publish, confident that anyone who really counted in British society would be reached. To be read by an unspecialized audience, in turn, demanded the ability to write with wit and grace, and to avoid the hermetic and the technical.

Unlike Marx, then, Arnold sought not to extirpate the philistines but to convert them. The fact that so many read his essays and bought his books, and now aspired to send their sons to Oxford and Cambridge to be exposed to "the best that had been thought and said in the world," made Arnold's hope plausible.

Arnold's notion of the intellectual as disinterested critic distinguished him from both Marx and Hegel. For Marx, the proper function of the intellectual was to be a partisan on behalf of the proletariat, criticizing bourgeois society for its fundamental, structural oppression. For Hegel, the role of the intellectual was to stand above particular group interests, and to bring to consciousness the ethical basis of modern, capitalist society, in the process creating standards by which to guide politics and culture. Arnold's conception of "aliens" has obvious affinities with this Hegelian image of the intellectual. But "disinterestedness" for Arnold had a rather different meaning. It implied the ability to free oneself from partisanship, to take a distanced enough view to be able to criticize the side of the issue to which one had been committed, as circumstances required. "Living by ideas" he wrote, means that "when one side of a question has long had your earnest support, when all your feelings are engaged, when you hear all round you no language but one, when your party talks this language like a steam-engine and can imagine no other— still to be able to think, still to be irresistibly carried, if so it be, by the current of thought to the opposite side of the question . . ."[70] The role of intellectual, then, was to embody and encourage that quality of mind that

allowed individuals to get some distance from their social, political, and economic milieu, to reflect critically,
and to be carried away by truth.

Arnold's hortatory essays warned his readers of the tendency of the culture of capitalism to promote the expansion of means while losing sight of ultimate ends.
But it was the next generation of German intellectuals
who would make that theme central to their understanding of the culture of capitalism. By the time of the First
World War, a younger generation of intellectuals weaned
on that understanding and despairing of converting the
middle classes would seek far more radical solutions to
those cultural dilemmas.

Notes

1. Asa Briggs, *Victorian People: A Reassessment of Persons and Themes, 1851-1867*, rev. ed. (Chicago, 1970), pp. 16, 35-43, and Asa Briggs, *The Making of Modern England, 1783-1867: The Age of Improvement* (New York, 1965), pp. 395-8.

2. Unless otherwise noted, biographical information on Arnold is drawn from Park Honan, *Matthew Arnold: A Life* (Cambridge, Mass., 1983). Other particularly valuable studies of Arnold include Stefan Collini, *Arnold* (New York, 1988), and Lionel Trilling, *Matthew Arnold* (New York, 1939).

3. R. H. Super (ed.), *The Complete Prose Works of Matthew Arnold* (Ann Arbor, Mich., 1960-1977), a wonderful scholarly edition to which all references apply unless otherwise noted. Henceforth *CPW*.

4. Harold Perkin, *The Origins of Modern English Society, 1780-1880* (Toronto, 1969), pp. 34-6, 71-2, 351-3.

5. Arnold, "Democracy," in *CPW*, vol. 2, pp. 23-4.

6. Aristotle's enduring influence on Arnold is noted by J. Dover Wilson, "Matthew Arnold and the Educationists," in F. J. C. Hearnshaw (ed.), *The Social and Political Ideas of Some Representative Thinkers of the Victorian Age* (New York, 1933), pp. 165-93, at p. 169.

7. Matthew Arnold, *Heinrich Heine, Cornhill Magazine* (August 1863), reprinted in *CPW*, vol. 3, pp. 111-2.

8. Quoted in Matthew Arnold, "The Twice-Revised Code" (1862), in *CPW*, vol. 2, pp. 214-5.

9. Honan, *Matthew Arnold,* pp. 318-9; R. H. Super, notes to "The Twice-Revised Code," in *CPW*, vol. 2, p. 349.

10. Arnold, "The Twice-Revised Code," pp. 223-4.

11. Arnold, "The Twice-Revised Code," p. 226.

12. Arnold, "The Twice-Revised Code," p. 243.

13. Arnold, "The Code Out of Danger" (1862), in *CPW*, vol. 2, pp. 247-51.

14. Chris Baldick, *The Social Mission of English Criticism, 1848-1932* (Oxford, 1983), p. 34.

15. Fred G. Walcott, *The Origins of* Culture and Anarchy*: Matthew Arnold and Popular Education in England* (Toronto, 1970), pp. 7-8.

16. Arnold, "Special Report on Certain Points Connected with Elementary Education in Germany, Switzerland, and France" (1886), in *CPW*, vol. 11, pp. 1, 28.

17. Arnold, "The Function of Criticism at the Present Time," in *CPW*, vol. 3, p. 283.

18. Arnold, "The Function of Criticism at the Present Time," p. 268.

19. Arnold, "The Function of Criticism at the Present Time," p. 271.

20. "The Function of Criticism at the Present Time," p. 269; similarly, *Culture and Anarchy: An Essay in Political and Social Criticism* (henceforth cited as *CA*), *CPW*, vol. 5, pp. 104-5.

21. Honan, *Matthew Arnold*, p. 329.

22. Arnold, "My Countryman," incorporated into *Friendship's Garland* and reprinted in *CPW*, vol. 5, p. 19.

23. *CA*, p. 92.

24. The book was, in that sense, typical of the "culture of altruism" so characteristic of Victorian intellectual life, on which see Stefan Collini, *Public Moralists: Political Thought and Intellectual Life in Britain, 1850-1930* (Oxford, 1991), chapter 2.

25. *CA*, p. 92.

26. *CA*, p. 113.

27. *CA*, p. 96.

28. *CA*, p. 189.

29. *CA*, "Doing As One Likes," passim.

30. *CA*, p. 117.

31. *CA*, p. 118.

32. Arnold, "A French Eton" (1864), in *CPW*, pp. 282-3.

33. *CA*, pp. 134-5.

34. *CA*, p. 125.

35. *CA*, pp. 97-8.

36. *CA*, pp. 101-2.

37. *CA*, pp. 186-7.

38. *CA*, p. 209.

39. *CA*, p. 212.

40. *CA*, pp. 211-3.

41. *CA*, pp. 218-9.

42. *CA*, p. 146.

43. On their relationship, see Ruth apRoberts, *Arnold and God* (Berkeley, 1983), pp. 165-70.

44. N. G. Annan, "The Intellectual Aristocracy," in J. H. Plumb (ed.), *Studies in Social History* (London, 1955), pp. 241-97; T. W. Heyck, *The Transformation of Intellectual Life in Victorian England* (Chicago, 1982), p. 36; and most broadly Collini, *Public Moralists,* chapter 1.

45. Heyck, pp. 190-3, makes a similar point.

46. Ben Knights, *The Idea of the Clerisy in the Nineteenth Century* (Cambridge, 1978), and Stephen Prickett, "'Hebrew' Versus 'Hellene' as a Principle of Literary Criticism," in G. W. Clarke (ed.), *Recovering Hellenism; The Hellenic Inheritance and the English Imagination* (Cambridge, 1988), pp. 137-160.

47. Honan, *Matthew Arnold,* pp. 95-6.

48. See his satirical self-portrait as a proponent of "Geist" in *Friendship's Garland,* a collection of essays written between "The Function of Criticism at the Present Time" and *Culture and Anarchy,* in *CPW,* vol. 5, pp. 37 ff.

49. See Arnold's essay "Democracy" (1861), in *CPW,* vol. 2.

50. Heyck, pp. 157 ff; and Christopher Harvie, "Reform and Expansion, 1854-1871," in M. G. Brock and M. C. Curthoys (eds.), *History of the University of Oxford,* vol. 6, *The Nineteenth Century, Part 1* (Oxford, 1997).

51. R. D. Anderson, *Universities and Elites in Britain Since 1800* (Cambridge, 1995), pp. 48-9; Heyck, op. cit.; Sheldon Rothblatt, *Revolution of the Dons: Cambridge and Society in Victorian England* (New York, 1968); and Christopher Harvie, *The Lights of Liberalism: University Liberals and the Challenge of Democracy, 1860-1886* (London, 1976).

52. Frank M. Turner, *The Greek Heritage in Victorian Britain* (New Haven, Conn., 1981), pp. 427-30.

53. See, for example, John Stuart Mill's 1867 "Inaugural Address at St. Andrews" and the analysis thereof, in Rothblatt, *Revolution of the Dons,* pp. 248 ff.

54. Turner, *Greek Heritage,* p. 5

55. Roy Lowe, "English Elite Education in the Late Nineteenth and Early Twentieth Centuries," in Werner Conze and Jürgen Kocka (eds.), *Bildungsbürgertum im 19. Jahrhundert, Teil I* (Frankfurt, 1985), pp. 147-62, at p. 151; R. D. Anderson, *Universities and Elites,* p. 9; Hans-Eberhard Mueller, *Bureaucracy, Education, and Monopoly: Civil Service Reforms in Prussia and England* (Berkeley, 1984), pp. 191-2.

56. Turner, *Greek Heritage,* p. 5.

57. The quote is from Samuel Finer, quoted in Richard Johnson, "Administrators in Education Before 1870: Patronage, Social Position and Role," in Gillian Sutherland (ed.), *Studies in the Growth of Nineteenth-Century Government* (London, 1972), pp. 110-38, at p. 115.

58. Richard Johnson, "Administrators in Education," pp. 118-21.

59. Walcott, *Origins of* Culture and Anarchy, p. 27.

60. Arnold, "Special Report on Certain Points Connected with Elementary Education in Germany, Switzerland, and France" (1886), in *CPW,* vol. 11.

61. Arnold, "Education and the State," *Pall Mall Gazette,* Dec. 11, 1865; reprinted in *CPW,* vol. 4, pp. 1-4.

62. See especially the 1868 "Preface" to *Schools and Universities on the Continent* in *CPW,* vol. 4, pp. 15-30.

63. Walcott, *Origins of* Culture and Anarchy, p. xiii.

64. Arnold, 1868 "Preface" to *Schools and Universities on the Continent,* p. 30.

65. "A French Eton," *CPW,* vol. 2, p. 316.

66. "A French Eton," p. 322.

67. *CA,* p. 113; "The Bishop and the Philosopher" (1862), *CPW,* vol. 3, p. 41.

68. Collini, *Public Moralists,* pp. 51-4.

69. Heyck, *Transformation,* p. 33; Collini, *Public Moralists,* pp. 52-3.

70. Matthew Arnold, "The Function of Criticism at the Present Time," in *CPW,* vol. 3, p. 267.

Daniel G. Williams (essay date 2006)

SOURCE: Williams, Daniel G. "Matthew Arnold: Culture and Ethnicity." In *Ethnicity and Cultural Authority: From Arnold to Du Bois,* pp. 33-71. Edinburgh, Scotland: Edinburgh University Press, 2006.

[*In the following essay, Williams uses Arnold's lectures on Celtic literature and the United States to probe the relationship between culture and ethnicity at work in*

Arnold's thought. Williams asserts that Arnold's position would ultimately require ethnic minorities to surrender their unique identities in order to be homogenized into the larger culture.]

> The Welsh schools that I have seen are generally on the British system . . . The children in them are generally docile and quick in apprehension, to a greater degree than English children; their drawback, of course, is that they have to acquire the medium of information, as well as the information itself, while the English children possess the medium at the outset. There can, I think, be no question but that the acquirement of the English language should be more and more insisted upon by your Lordships in your relations with these schools as the one main object for which your aid is granted. Whatever encouragement individuals may think it desirable to give the preservation of the Welsh language on grounds of philological or antiquarian interest, it must always be the desire of a Government to render its dominions, as far as possible, homogeneous, and to break down barriers to the freest intercourse between the different parts of them. Sooner or later, the difference of language between Wales and England will probably be effaced, as has happened with the difference of language between Cornwall and the rest of England; as is now happening with the difference of language between Brittany and the rest of France; and they are not the true friends of the Welsh people who, from a romantic interest in their manners and traditions, would impede an event which is socially and politically so desirable for them.

Matthew Arnold, **'HMI [Her Majesty's Inspectors']
Report'** (1852)[1]

'My life', noted Matthew Arnold in 1875, 'is not that of a man of letters but of an Inspector of Schools.'[2] If this is a somewhat surprising statement coming from the figure widely regarded as the Victorian era's leading man of letters, it usefully draws attention to the professional context of Arnold's writings. In discussing Arnold's call, first expressed in his **'Her Majesty's Inspectors' Report of 1852,'** for the eradication of Welsh as a living language, Emyr Humphreys suggests that

> as an agent of the state Arnold realised that he was required to go against his own nature as a poet and play the role of the Philistine, intent on the removal of any obstacles that lay in the road of uniformity, homogeneity and material progress.[3]

The boundary between Arnold the 'poet' and 'agent of the state', or between the 'man of letters' and the HMI, is not as clear-cut as Humphreys suggests, however, for the quotation from the 1852 report above engages with a number of issues that were to reappear throughout Arnold's cultural and critical writings: the role of education in the life of the nation; the role of the government, or state, in establishing social equality; the problem of linguistic and ethnic difference; and the desire to create a 'homogeneous' national culture. Despite his unequivocal call for the eradication of a language

and its culture, it would be too simplistic to follow current trends in dismissing Arnold's **'HMI Report'** as yet another example of his imperial arrogance.[4] It is worth noting, for instance, that Arnold does not represent the children of Wales as backward or immoral, as had been the case five years earlier in the renowned *Report of the Commissioners' Inquiry into the State of Education in Wales.*[5] Indeed, Arnold draws attention to the fact that Welsh children are 'quick in apprehension, to a greater degree than English children'.[6] Thus, within Arnold's **'HMI Report,'** lies a tension between an intolerance of cultural difference and a genuine democratic desire to extend the benefits of an English education, and the values of English culture, throughout Britain. This tension between democratic ideals and cultural intolerance can be perceived in Arnold's writings throughout his life.

Arnold consistently sought to utilise his cultural authority, as both HMI and man of letters, to promote reconciliation: the reconciliation of classes, ethnicities, and religious sects. The vehicle he offers as a means for realising a desired social homogeneity is a 'culture' which transcends historically specific group interests, and which he describes in universalist and abstract terms as being 'disinterested', 'impersonal', and that appeals to, and fosters, the 'best' selves as opposed to the 'ordinary' selves of people.[7] Basing his critical writings on the belief that 'all tendencies of human nature are in themselves vital and profitable; when they are blamed, they are only to be blamed relatively, not absolutely', Arnold's writings are characterised by a general lack of any systematic conceptual rigour.[8] Even a fairly cursory reading of Arnold's most significant works will reveal a series of tensions and paradoxes in his writings. Perhaps the most significant of these tensions derives from two conceptions of culture in his work; on the one hand culture is a normative value, a Utopian ideal, towards which all individuals should aspire while, on the other hand, culture is an active, homogenising and stabilising force in society. The **'HMI Report'** with which I begin represents an early moment in Arnold's writings when an abstract ideal of cultural homogeneity comes face to face with the reality of distinctive linguistic communities on the ground; the ideal of a common, accessible, culture faces the reality of ethnic difference. Arnold's report of 1852 foregrounds what John Burrow has described as 'a dilemma in liberal culture itself':

> How are you to make people aware of the tradition which can both shape their energies into something coherent and by its plurality opens to them new possibilities unless you in some sense first impose it upon them?[9]

The following chapter seeks to explore the relationship between culture and ethnicity in Arnold's writings in the light of Burrow's question. While Arnold's essays ***On the Study of Celtic Literature*** have been the subject of considerable critical commentary in recent years, it has been less widely observed that questions relating to national and ethnic identities were a key preoccupation in Arnold's writings from his earliest **England and the Italian Question** of 1859 through to his final essays on **'Disestablishment in Wales'** and **'Civilisation in the United States'** in 1888.[10] In exploring the relationship between culture and ethnicity in Arnold's writings, I begin by reconstructing his conception of 'culture'.

CULTURE: FROM CLASS TO ETHNICITY

Since Raymond Williams's *Culture and Society*, it has been commonplace to regard Arnold as a key figure in that tradition of Victorian social critics who invoked 'culture' as an alternative source of values to those of a materialist, industrial, society. There is considerable evidence in Arnold's writings to support this characterisation of his work. In the celebrated analysis of **Culture and Anarchy,** for instance, Arnold argues that 'Culture looks beyond machinery, culture hates hatred, culture has one great passion, the passion for sweetness and light'.[11] This passage makes an explicit contrast between 'culture' and 'machinery', and also—in its echoing of St Paul's peroration on charity in his First Epistle to the Corinthians (Chapter 13)—implicitly suggests that Arnold's culture is meant to offer a secular substitute for religious values. While the term 'machinery' refers not only to industrial production but also denotes a broad range of social institutions, the tone and imagery of Arnold's analysis suggest that his idea of culture is a response to the materialist, increasingly secular, values of an industrialised society. Culture, for Arnold, is a 'salutary friend' who exposes 'what an unsound habit of mind it must be which makes us talk of things like coal or iron as constituting the greatness of England'.[12] Culture, he goes on, 'dissipat[es] delusions of this kind' by 'fixing standards that are real'.[13] Thus, in a deliberately striking reversal, Arnold makes culture, understood to be a normative ideal of 'sweetness and light' towards which all individuals should aspire, a more 'real' and material social force than the actual wealth-creating materials of coal and iron. Culture, defined further as 'the best which has been thought and said in the world',[14] 'begets a dissatisfaction which is of the highest possible value in stemming the common tide of men's thoughts in a wealthy and industrial community',[15] and Arnold believes that this function is

> particularly important in our modern world, of which the whole civilisation is . . . mechanical and external, and tends constantly to become more so. But above all in our own country has culture a weighty part to perform, because here that mechanical character, which civilisation tends to take everywhere, is shown in the most eminent degree.[16]

Arnold's culture, then, is 'at variance with the mechanical and material civilisation in esteem with us', and can thus be seen as, in Raymond Williams's words, a 'mitigating and rallying alternative' to the 'derived impetus of a new kind of society'.[17]

It is important to note, however, that Arnold's criticisms are directed not so much at the 'industrial community' itself as at the 'common tide of men's thoughts' within such a community. Arnold states explicitly in **Culture and Anarchy** that culture 'admits the necessity of the movement towards fortune-making and exaggerated industrialism' and 'readily allows that the future may derive benefit from it'.[18] It is within the context of this argument that we may best understand Arnold's conception of the cultural authority assumed by the man of letters in an industrial society, for

> The great men of culture are those who have had a passion for diffusing, for making prevail, for carrying from one end of society to the other, the best knowledge, the best ideas of their time; who have laboured to divest knowledge of all that was harsh, uncouth, difficult, abstract, professional, exclusive; to humanise it, to make it efficient outside the clique of the cultivated and the learned, yet still remaining the best knowledge and thought of the time, and a true source, therefore of sweetness and light.[19]

This passage suggests some of the deeper connections between Arnold's notion of culture and the comments he made on the undesirability of the survival of Welsh as a living language in his **'HMI Report of 1852'**. 'Modern civilisation' for Arnold, while producing society's mechanical character, is also the conduit for the dissemination of culture throughout society. The Welsh language can thus be seen to represent a hindrance to the man of culture's project of diffusing 'the best knowledge . . . from one end of society to the other'.[20] Welsh is 'difficult' and 'abstract' and represents an addition to the other ways of being inaccessible that Arnold wishes to transcend in **Culture and Anarchy.** In his essays **On the Study of Celtic Literature** Arnold reiterates his call for the eradication of Welsh as a living language, and presents his argument in the following terms:

> I must say I quite share the opinion of my brother Saxons as to the practical inconvenience of perpetuating the speaking of Welsh . . . Cornwall is the better for adopting English, for becoming more thoroughly one with the rest of the country. The fusion of all the inhabitants of these islands into one homogeneous, English-speaking whole, the breaking down of barriers between us, the swallowing up of separate provincial nationalities, is a consummation to which the natural course of things irresistibly tends; it is a necessity of what is called modern civilisation, and modern civilisation is a real, legitimate force; the change must come, and its accomplishment is a mere affair of time. The sooner the Welsh language disappears as an instrument of the practical, political, social life of Wales, the better; the better for England, the better for Wales itself.[21]

I will return to discuss the structure and significance of Arnold's Celtic essays, but wish to focus here on the attitude towards 'modern civilisation' contained within this passage. If Arnold often invokes culture as an alternative source of values to industrial society, here he deems 'modern civilisation' to be a 'real, legitimate force' and the source of welcome changes in society. Culture is not opposed to modern civilisation, for the latter creates the context for the dissemination of the former. Arnold's vision, as both cultural critic and HMI, is democratic in the sense that his goal is to construct a shareable, accessible, common culture in Britain that makes the 'best knowledge and thought of the time' relevant to all. That common culture is ultimately based, however, on the belief that society's 'best knowledge' can only be disseminated through the medium of English.

There is, then, a tension in Arnold's writings between an idea of 'culture' as the repository of a set of universal human values that challenge the individualism of modern industrial society, and an idea of culture as dependent upon the 'natural course of . . . modern civilisation' for its broader dissemination.[22] What is common to both positions, however, is the belief that culture functions as an active force within contemporary society. In this respect, commentators such as Terry Eagleton have been incorrect in describing Arnold as invoking a 'traditional culture' in order to 'refine the oafish captains of industry'.[23] Arnold's attitude towards the Welsh and Cornish languages above suggests something of his lack of sentimentalism when it came to 'traditional' cultures, and Arnold's critique of aspects of industrialism is never mounted from the position of a 'traditional' pre-industrial, rural Utopia.[24] While Arnold does invoke ancient Greece as a model of a civilisation imbued by the influence of a human appreciation for nature and the life of the mind, he is primarily concerned with the persistence of an ideal set of Hellenistic values as a cultural force in the present, and, while he elevates Elizabethan England as a period of unsurpassed cultural achievement, it is a past that offers a model for the future, not a Utopia that has been lost for all time.[25] The goal of Arnold's social criticism is not fundamentally to subvert or reverse the direction in which his society is developing but rather to foresee, and offer solutions to, the problems that arise from the nation's industrial development.

In his essay **'Democracy'** Arnold was already offering a clear expression of the crisis that he believed was facing Victorian English society.[26] Originally conceived as a lengthy introduction to his official report on ***The Popular Education of France,*** Arnold is primarily concerned with the emerging problems of England which are discussed in relation to developments in France and, to a lesser extent, the United States. This comparativist approach serves as a guiding principle throughout Arnold's social criticism for, as he noted in 1865, 'a nation is really civilised by acquiring the qualities it by

nature is wanting in'.[27] The central question which the essay seeks to address is presented in the following terms:

> [W]hat action may we rely to replace, for some time at any rate, the action of the aristocracy upon the people of this country, which we have seen exercise an influence in many respects elevating and beneficial, but which is rapidly, and from inevitable causes, ceasing? In other words, and to use a significant modern expression which every one understands, what influence may help us to prevent the English people from becoming, with the growth of democracy, *Americanised*?[28]

Arnold does not explain what the term 'Americanisation' means in this context, but assumes an understanding with his readership. He is referring to the sweeping changes occurring as a result of the social movement towards democracy as manifested in the decline of the aristocracy's influence on the political and cultural life of the nation. This process leaves the middle class to determine the future tone of the national life, a prospect which cannot be welcomed, for the middle class in England is characterised by its narrow, uncultured and 'philistine' conception of what this life should be. Arnold's conceptualisation of class divisions in England are expressed succinctly in a letter he wrote to the Welsh educationalist Hugh Owen:

> We in England have come to that point when the continued advance and greatness of our nation is [*sic*] threatened by one cause, and one cause above all. Far more than by the helplessness of an aristocracy whose day is fast coming to an end, far more than by the rawness of a lower class whose day is only just beginning, we are imperilled by what I call the Philistinism of our middle class.[29]

Arnold famously divided English society into aristocratic 'barbarians', middle class 'philistines', and a working class 'populace'. He recognised that these divisions arose from social inequalities, and argued that 'inequality materialises our upper class, vulgarises our middle class, brutalises our lower'.[30] In light of these new conditions Arnold suggests in **'Democracy'** that social homogeneity may be achieved through action by the state—'the representative acting-power of the nation' and 'the nation in its collective and corporate character'.[31] The creation of a powerful state may now be salutary rather than dangerous, he argues, particularly with regard to the establishment of an elevating system of national education which was already in existence in France and Prussia.

These issues were to carry a greater social and political urgency following the working-class agitations of the 1860s, culminating in the demonstrations in Hyde Park in 1866. These demonstrations had been called by the Reform League following the fall of the Liberal government and with it the first attempts at extending the franchise to working men.[32] If these events underlined the way in which the national culture was dividing along lines of class, this was also the period of renewed Fenian activity in Ireland and North America. Arnold's celebrated analysis of **Culture and Anarchy** sought to address a national culture which he perceived as being threatened by divisive class and ethnic interests. Faced with the twin threats of 'an Irish Fenian and an English rough', Arnold supplemented his call in **'Democracy'** for an empowered state with the suggestion that the current philistinism of the emergent ruling class may be solved through a reliance on a small number of disinterested, classless individuals to direct the national life.[33] He identifies these individuals as 'aliens'—'persons who are mainly led not by their class spirit, but by a general humane spirit'—a minority that transcends the particularistic interests of class and nation and pursues the universal ideals of human culture.[34]

> Natures with this bent emerge in all classes,—among the Barbarians, among the Philistines, among the Populace. And this bent always tends to take them out of their class, and to make their distinguishing characteristic not their Barbarianism or their Philistinism, but their *humanity*. They have, in general, a rough time of it in their lives; but they are sown more abundantly than one might think, they appear where and when one least expects it . . . they hinder the unchecked predominance of that class-life which is the affirmation of our ordinary self, and seasonably disconcert mankind in their worship of machinery.[35]

The classless alien's transcendent 'humanity' allows him to see beyond divisive class interests. The alien's role thus mirrors on a personal level the role of the state on a social level; both seek to foster a cohesive society based on a shared sense of a common human culture.

However, if Arnold argues that 'aliens' exist within all classes, he is primarily concerned with the role of the philistine class in engendering a homogeneous, stable society. 'I myself am properly a Philistine' he notes in **Culture and Anarchy,** and in his essays on Celtic literature he draws attention to the 'soul of goodness' that exists in philistinism itself 'and this soul of goodness I, who am often supposed to be Philistinism's mortal enemy merely because I do not wish it to have things all its own way, cherish as much as anybody'.[36] Behind Arnold's invocation of a 'transcendent' culture, then, lies an argument for the middle class to broaden its outlook in order that its values and aspirations may appeal to the other classes in society. Arnold makes this argument explicit in **The Popular Education of France**:

> It is a serious calamity for a nation that its tone of feeling and grandeur of spirit should be lowered or dulled. But the calamity appears far more serious still when we consider that the middle class, remaining as they are now, with narrow, harsh, unintelligent, and unat-

tractive spirit and culture, will almost certainly fail to mould or assimilate the masses below them, whose sympathies are at the present moment actually wider and more liberal than theirs. They arrive, these masses, eager to enter into possession of the world, to gain a more vivid sense of their own life and activity. In their irrepressible development, their natural educators and initiators are those immediately above them, the middle classes. If these classes cannot win their sympathy or give them their direction, society is in danger of falling into anarchy.[37]

Arnold was, then, a middle-class critic of the middle class. The goal of his criticism was not to question the ultimate desirability of that class adopting the aristocracy's traditional role of political and cultural leadership, but rather to encourage the middle class to face its responsibilities. Arnold sought to expose the widespread philistinism of his class in order to prepare it for its destined position of leadership in the emergent democratic society.

These related arguments for the role of a saving 'alien' element in fostering a social homogeneity, and for the role of the middle class in guiding society by its example, take a different form in the lectures **On the Study of Celtic Literature**.[38] In these essays the English are encouraged to assimilate the Celts in much the same way as the members of the middle class are encouraged to assimilate the 'masses', for the 'alien' antidote to the 'narrowness' of English philistinism lies in the Hellenistic appreciation of nature found among the Celtic peoples; there is 'something Greek in them' states Arnold, 'something humane, something (I am afraid one must add) which in the English common people is not to be found'.[39] An argument for cultural homogeneity developed in terms of class in **Culture and Anarchy** finds its precursor in an argument developed in terms of ethnicity in the essays **On the Study of Celtic Literature**.

CELTICISM AND CONTRIBUTIONISM

As I noted in the introduction, Arnold begins his study of Celtic literature with a somewhat melancholy description of attending an Eisteddfod in Llandudno where, on an 'unfortunate' day of 'storms of wind, clouds of dust and an angry, dirty, sea', he listens to the last representatives of a once proud tradition reciting verse in a language which Arnold admits he does not understand.[40] Upon leaving the festival pavilion he meets

> an acquaintance fresh from London and the parliamentary session. In a moment, the spell of the Celtic genius was forgotten, the Philistinism of our Anglo-Saxon nature made itself felt, and my friend and I walked up and down by the roaring waves, talking not of ovates and bards, and triads and englyns, but of the sewage question, and the glories of our local self government, and the mysterious perfections of the Metropolitan Board of Works.[41]

The English philistine's world of material affairs, of instrumental activity, of the 'machinery' of industrial society, is juxtaposed with the creative, imaginative, poetic world of the Celt. The division in **Culture and Anarchy** between a narrow philistinism and a humanising culture takes the form of a division between Saxons and Celts in the essays on Celtic literature where Arnold's diagnosis is not only directed at English philistines, but at the whole national community:

> Now, then, is the moment for the greater delicacy and spirituality of the Celtic peoples who are blended with us, if it be but wisely directed, to make itself felt, prized and honoured. In a certain measure the children of Taliesin and Ossian have now the opportunity for renewing the famous feat of the Greeks, and conquering their conquerors. No service England can render the Celts . . . can surpass what the Celts can at this moment do for England.[42]

The Celts are invited to participate more fully in the development of the English nation. While the key problem facing Victorian society was expressed in terms of middle-class narrowness in **Culture and Anarchy,** its solution in **On the Study of Celtic Literature** is figured in the language of nationhood and ethnicity; 'Philistinism' is here replaced by 'England', an instrumentalist and materialist 'England' which is to be regenerated by an infusion of poetic Celticism.

This essentially positive reading of Celtic culture has led many critics to overestimate the degree of Arnold's interest in Celtic literatures. Norman Davies notes, for example, that Arnold 'was one of the few prominent Victorians to possess an expert knowledge of Celtic literature. At different times in his career, he was Professor at Oxford of both Poetry and of Celtic Studies.'[43] While Arnold ends his Celtic lectures by calling for the establishment of a 'chair of Celtic at Oxford' as a 'message of peace to Ireland', he never held that chair following its establishment in 1877. Indeed, Arnold, as he disarmingly notes in his essays, had virtually no knowledge of the Celtic languages. In the 'Introduction' to the Celtic essays Arnold admits the 'provisional character' of his remarks and, in the published version of his lectures, he includes footnotes by the Celtic scholar, Lord Strangford, that often point out errors or contradictions in Arnold's statements on philology, ethnology and Celtic culture.[44] Arnold also relied on a wide variety of sources for his examples of Celtic literature. The similarity between Arnold's study and that of his French contemporary Ernest Renan's *La Poesie des Races Celtiques* (1859) has been well established, and Frederick Faverty demonstrates that Arnold borrowed just as extensively from Henri Martin's *Histoire de France* (1855-60) and E. F. Edwards's *Reserches sur les langues celtiques* (1844).[45] To these historical and philological sources can be added the distinction between the Gaelic culture of a feudal Highland society

and the hard-headed commercial ethos of Lowland life popularised in Walter Scott's *Waverley* which itself derived from the visions and fabrications of early romantics such as Gray and Macpherson.[46] Arnold is, then, working within what is by the 1860s a well-established European interest in the exoticised Celtic peripheries, and his admission of ignorance of the Celtic languages, his inclusion of Lord Strangford's corrections, and his reliance on the writings of others for insights and examples, suggest that the lectures were not intended as original contributions to the field of Celtic scholarship. Much has also been made of the racial basis of Arnold's lectures. While the exposure of racial elements in Arnold's thought was both necessary and valuable, there is a tendency, as Douglass Lorimer has recently noted, to portray Victorian intellectuals as 'the racist other in binary opposition to our nonracist self'.[47] There is no doubt that Arnold drew on the period's philological debates regarding Indo-Europeanism, and on the arguments between the monogenists and polygenists (those who argued that humankind came from a single source, and those who argued that there were separate sources for distinctive races) that animated racial discourse during the Victorian era, but his reference to 'the eternal beer, sausages, and bad tobacco' in Germany, for example, suggests that he adopted a fairly light-hearted approach to Victorian racial debates.[48] Arnold, as will become clear in the following analysis, ascribed certain characteristics to specific races but, ultimately, we should look beyond any philological, racial or antiquarian reasons for the motivations that informed Arnold's Celtic lectures. What seemingly begins as a narrow, almost antiquarian, effort to re-evaluate the merits of a particular set of medieval manuscripts—the study of Celtic Literature—becomes, in practice, an extended exercise in defining a national culture. For, despite Arnold's essentially positive reading of Celtic culture, his argument is designed to promote 'the fusion of all the inhabitants of these islands into one homogenous [*sic*], English speaking whole' for 'the swallowing up of separate provincial nationalities, is a consummation to which the natural course of things inevitably tends'.[49] Beneath Arnold's reappraisals of Celtic literature and of English national identity, lies a meditation upon the status of the Celts within a process of English expansion.

In order to understand Arnold's conception of nationhood in relation to this process of English expansion, we need to turn to his first published pamphlet on **England and the Italian Question** (1859).[50] In this essay Arnold makes the case for the validity of Italy's nationalist aspirations which, in 1859, led to a war against Austria with the goal of achieving Italian unification. 'Is it true that the principle of nationality, in virtue of which the Italians claim their independence, is chimerical?' asks Arnold, a question which 'depends on the merits of the particular case in which the principle of nationality is invoked'.[51] He is concerned with defending the status of Italy as a great nation, deserving of national unity, and, typically, develops the argument comparatively with reference to England and France, 'who respectively represent the two greatest nationalities of modern Europe'.[52]

> Let an Englishman or a Frenchman . . . ask himself what it is that makes him take pride in his nationality, what it is which would make it intolerable to his feelings to pass, or to see any part of his country, pass under foreign dominion. He will find that it is the sense of self-esteem generated by knowing the figure which his nation makes in history; by considering the achievements of his nation in war, government, arts, literature, or industry. It is the sense that his people, which has done such great things, merits to exist in freedom and dignity, and to enjoy the luxury of self respect . . . Except England and France, no country can have this feeling of self-esteem in so high a degree as Italy.[53]

Italy deserves to exist in a state of national independence because of her cultural, political, industrial and military successes. Here, then, is an example of a justified nationalism. Having established Italy's right to self-determination, Arnold warns that the 'principle of nationality' should not always be acted upon, for

> It would have prevented the amalgamation of Cornwall and Wales with England, of Brittany with France. Small nationalities inevitably gravitate towards the larger nationalities in their immediate neighbourhood. Their ultimate fusion is so natural and irresistible that even the sentiment of the absorbed race ceases, with time, to struggle against it; the Cornishman and the Breton become at last, in feeling as well as in political fact, an Englishman and a Frenchman. Great nationalities refuse to be thus absorbed; their resilience from fusion is as natural and inevitable as is the gravitation of petty nationalities towards it.[54]

The argument could not be clearer. While France, England and Italy deserve to exist 'in freedom and dignity', the lesser nations of Europe are to undergo an inevitable process of 'amalgamation'. In having a great past Italy is like England, and unlike Poland and Ireland:

> A Pole does not descend by becoming a Russian, or an Irishman by becoming an Englishman. But an Englishman, with his country's history behind him, descends and deteriorates by becoming anything but an Englishman; a Frenchman, by becoming anything but a Frenchman; an Italian, by becoming anything but an Italian.[55]

The Italians are, at the time of writing, an amalgamated people like the Poles and the Irish. Yet, because of their history, the Italians rightfully aspire to national unity and self-determination. Arnold constructs a narrative of the Italian past that leads inevitably to nationhood. Ireland and Poland, on the other hand, cannot hope for national independence for they have no narrative that

could plausibly lead to it. It seems that what informs Arnold's argument here are two distinct concepts of nationhood; the one historical and active, the other racial and passive.

Edward Said offers an useful means of theorising these two divergent conceptions of nationhood towards the end of *Orientalism*. Said's study, as I noted in the introduction, has been widely criticised for its conflation of the various modes of cultural representation through which the non-Western world has been constructed. He does (as Bart Moore-Gilbert has noted) allow 'for some variations between the fields of knowledge which constitute Orientalism', however, in particular the following distinction between what he describes as 'vision' and 'narrative'.

> Against this static system of 'synchronic essentialism' I have called vision because it presumes that the whole Orient can be seen panoptically, there is constant pressure. The source of pressure is narrative, in that if any Oriental detail can be shown to move, or to develop, diachrony is introduced into the system. What seemed stable—and the Orient is synonymous with stability and unchanging eternality—now appears unstable . . . Narrative, in short, introduces an opposing point of view, perspective, consciousness to the unitary web of vision; it violates the serene Apollonian fictions asserted by vision.[56]

Said does not develop the argument further, perhaps because the implication that 'vision' exists prior to, and independent of, its mediations, makes the distinction unsustainable in practice. While Said traces the tendencies to visualise and narrativise within Orientalist discourse, I would like to adopt the two terms, as a means of characterising Arnold's two conceptions of nationhood as 'visualised' and 'narrativised'. The English and the Italians possess the latter kind of nationality; it is a product of history, diachronic and subject to further change. The nationhood of the Poles, the Welsh, and the Irish is conceived of in visualised terms, demonstrating certain eternal racial characteristics, synchronic, atemporal and static.

The argument is slightly modified in the essays on Celtic literature, for now visualised racial traits are to be compared with narrativised political nations. Thus, Arnold produces a Celt characterised by certain enduring visible traits. 'The Celtic genius' he notes has 'sentiment as its main basis, with love of beauty, charm spirituality for its excellence . . . ineffectualness and self-will for its deficit.'[57] The Celt is 'always ready to react against despotism of fact' is 'sensual' and is 'particularly disposed to feel the spell of the feminine idiosyncrasy; he has an affinity to it; he is not far from its secret'.[58] This inevitably, and crucially, makes the Celt 'ineffectual in politics',[59] a notion which is developed further:

. . . I know my brother Saxons, I know their strength, and I know that the Celtic genius will make nothing of trying to set up barriers against them in the world of fact and brute force, of trying to hold its own against them as a political and social counter-power, as the soul of a hostile nationality. To me there is something mournful . . . in hearing a Welshman or an Irishman make pretensions,—natural pretensions, I admit, but how hopelessly in vain!—to such a rival self-establishment . . . The bent of our time is towards science, towards knowing things as they are; so the Celt's claims towards having his genius and its works fairly treated, as objects of scientific investigation, the Saxon can hardly reject, when these claims are urged simply on their own merits, and are not mixed up with extraneous pretensions which jeopardise them. What the French call the *science des origines,* the science of origins . . . is very incomplete without a thorough critical account of the Celts, and their genius, language and literature.[60]

The desire to observe the Celts scientifically while denying them any hope of national self-determination is made explicit. The Saxons are the agents of history, who have the power to 'reject' or accept the Celts' claims to genius as they like. The relatively benevolent Arnold is prepared to accept that claim, as long as it is not part of a wider political agenda.[61] He thus goes on to produce a contributionist argument in which the Celts are flattered into accepting a subsidiary position for themselves in relation to the historically emergent English.

This aspect of Arnold's argument poses a challenge to Benedict Anderson's theory that modes of racial definition have no direct relationship with modes of defining nationality:

The fact of the matter is, that nationalism thinks in terms of historical destinies, while racism dreams of eternal contaminations, transmitted from the origins of time through an endless sequence of loathsome copulations: outside history.[62]

The two versions of nationhood—visualised and narrativised—existing within Arnold's writings suggest, however, that racism and nationalism are not mutually exclusive for, even as he invokes the historical destiny of nations, Arnold does so against the 'eternal' characteristics of races.[63] Nevertheless, the word 'contaminations' in Anderson's analysis carries negative resonances that do not appear in Arnold's work—indeed, Arnold sees the 'loathsome contaminations' as essentially positive in a process of biological and cultural amalgamation. Arnold notes, for instance, that the purpose of his essay is to 'lead towards solid ground where the Celt may with legitimate satisfaction point to traces of the gifts and workings of his race' within the life of Victorian England.[64] He thus argues that, while the remaining residual members of the Celtic races are expected to aban-

don all political aspirations and linguistic distinctions in order to contribute fully to the expansion of the English nation, this process of racial intermingling has, in fact, been occurring for centuries. Arnold notes that, within the English people, not only are there some whose ancestors are Celtic, and some whose ancestors are Saxon, but the two lines have become literally joined through intermarriage. The character of English literature is thus not only the product of cultural fusion but it has also been produced by the joining of the essences of two races:

[H]ere in our country, in historic times, long after the Celtic embryo had crystallised into the Celt proper, long after the Germanic embryo had crystallised into the German proper, there was an important contact between the two peoples; the Saxons invaded the Britons and settled themselves in the Britons' country. Well, then, here was a contact which one might expect would leave its traces; if the Saxons got the upper hand, as we all know they did, and made our country be England and us be English, there must yet, one would think, be some trace of the Saxon having met the Briton; there must be some Celtic vein or other running through us.[65]

In order to offer a complete account of the elements involved in the construction of the English racial hybrid, Arnold also has to account for the presence of Norman blood in his brew of racial essences:

I have got a rough, but, I hope, clear notion of these three forces, the Germanic genius, the Celtic genius, the Norman genius. The Germanic genius has steadiness as its main basis, with commonness and humdrum for its defect, fidelity to nature for its excellence. The Celtic genius, sentiment as its main basis, with love of beauty, charm and spirituality for its excellence, ineffectualness and self will for its defect. The Norman genius, talent for affairs as its main basis, with strenuousness and clear rapidity for its excellence, hardness and insolence for its defect, and now to try and trace these in the composite English genius.[66]

Maintaining that the true strength of the English is derived from their blending in one race the positive aspects of Teuton and Celt, he argues that the potential of such a hybrid cannot be achieved without self-knowledge.

So long as this mixed constitution of our nature possesses us . . . we are blindly and ignorantly rolled about by the forces of our nature; . . . so soon as we have clearly discerned what they are and begun to apply to them a law of measure, control and guidance they may be made to work for our good and to carry us forward . . . Then we may use the German faithfulness to Nature to give us science, and to free us from insolence and self-will; we may use the Celtic quickness of perception to give us delicacy and to free us from hardness and Philistinism; we may use the Latin decisiveness to give us strenuous clear method, and to free us from fumbling and idling.[67]

The attempt here is to control the components of one's racial heredity. Arnold accordingly attempts to trace the historical racial and linguistic origins of the English—Saxon, Celt and Norman—to their cultural manifestations in language, and proceeds by contrasting English prose as exemplified in the news pages of the *London Times* to the German prose of the *Cologne Gazette*. 'At noon a long line of carriages extended from Pall Mall to the Peer's entrance of the Palace of Westminster', writes the correspondent of *The Times,* while the *Gazette* has 'Nachdem die Vorbereitungen zu dem auf dem Gürzenich-Saale zu Ehren der Abgeordneten statt finden sollenden Bankette bereits vollständig getroffen worden waren, fand heute vormittag auf polizeiliche Anordnung die Schliessung sämmtlicher Zugänge zum Gürzenich statt'.[68] Arnold concludes: 'surely the mental habit of a people who express their thoughts in so very different a manner, the one rapid, the other slow, the one plain, the other embarrassed, the one trailing, the other striding, cannot be essentially the same'.[69] It follows that there must be something other than common Teutonic stock, which Germans and Saxons share, that accounts for the difference. Philology is then used to reinforce the racial argument that the English people are a hybrid of Teutonism and Celticism.

The Celts, in this argument, are deemed to be less an actually existing people than a historic people whose ideals persist as a cultural force within the English composite self. Stefan Collini has noted that there is an ambiguity in Arnold's use of terms such as 'Puritanism', 'Hebraism' and 'Hellenism', for it is often not clear whether these terms are 'intended to stand for some ideal-typical set of qualities' or whether they refer to a 'particular historical embodiment of those qualities'.[70] This ambiguity also characterises Arnold's use of the term 'Celticism' and, in this respect, his representation of the Celt shares a number of features with the representation of the Jew in his writings. Arnold makes a connection between Celts and Jews in his first Celtic lecture where he recalls that as a child 'I was taught to think of Celt as separated by an impassable gulf from Teuton; my father, in particular, was never weary of contrasting them'[71], and goes on to note that:

> Certainly the Jew,—the Jew of ancient times, at least,—then seemed a thousand degrees nearer than the Celt to us. Puritanism had so assimilated Bible ideas and phraseology; names like Ebenezer, and notions like that of hewing Agag in pieces, came so natural to us, that the sense of affinity between the Teutonic and the Hebrew nature was quite strong; a steady, middle-class Anglo-Saxon much more imagined himself Ehud's cousin than Ossian's.[72]

Arnold contrasts this belief of his childhood with the discoveries of Victorian ethnologists. Science, notes Arnold, 'the science of origins' has established the 'true natural grouping of the human race' and has demonstrated that 'a Semitic unity' is 'separated by profound distinguishing marks from the Indo-European unity' that is shared by both Teuton and Celt.[73] Arnold's strategy here, then, is to elevate the position of the Celts in the estimation of his Victorian readers by demonstrating that they, unlike the Jews, share a racial affinity with the English. Whereas the Celts may be assimilated into a dominant Englishness

> the modern spirit tends more and more to establish a sense of native diversity between our European bent and the Semitic bent, and to eliminate, even in our religion, certain elements as purely and excessively Semitic, and therefore, in right, not combinable with our European nature, not assimilable by it.[74]

Racial science is invoked as a means of establishing the distance between European and Jewish peoples. This argument of 1867 certainly throws a somewhat unflattering light on Arnold's case in *Culture and Anarchy* a few years later for the 'Hellenization' of philistine attitudes that are based on a 'Hebraic' religious moralism, and, indeed, much has been made in recent criticism of the racial basis of Arnold's cultural thought.[75] It is worth noting, however, that Arnold's 'Hebraism' in *Culture and Anarchy* is not dependent on any innate racial components—he makes no references, for instance, to the mental capacity or anatomy of Jews—but is rather a term used to refer to moral values that are traced back to Jewish laws and are sustained in the modern period by Christianity.[76] In *Literature and Dogma* Arnold argues that the Bible should remain a central text within English culture and notes that 'as long as the world lasts, all who want to make progress in righteousness will come to Israel for inspiration, as to the people who have the sense for righteousness most glowing and strongest'.[77] This argument, however, leads Arnold into making 'an extraordinary distinction' with regard to the 'Hebrew people':

> In spite of all which in them and in their character is unattractive, nay, repellent,—in spite of their shortcomings even in righteousness itself and their insignificance in everything else,—this petty, unsuccessful, unnameable people, without politics, without science, without art, without charm, deserve their great place in the world's regard, and are likely to have it more, as the world goes on, rather than less.[78]

Arnold, it seems, has little respect for actually existing Jews in the present but admires the 'devout energy' of Hebraism's historical form in the past.[79] Even as a child it is towards 'the Jews of ancient times', not contemporary Jews, that he felt an affinity.[80] Arnold's notion of 'Hebraism' thus seems to entail stripping contemporary Jewish culture of all content—'without politics, without science, without art'—so that (to use the terms of my earlier analysis) the visualised, static, characteristics and values of an ancient and valuable Jewish culture of the past, become a contributory historical force within the narrativised, developmental, universal culture of the present.

The structure of Arnold's argument regarding the Jews is replicated in his treatment of the Celts. Arnold, as I've already noted, firmly believed that Wales should divest itself of its language, and this is an argument that he also applies to Ireland where he deems the Irish language to be 'the badge of the beaten race, the property of the vanquished'.[81] His views regarding the Celtic languages are particularly significant in the light of his stated belief that it is 'by the forms of its language' that 'a nation expresses its very self', and that 'what a people . . . says in its language, its literature, is the great key'.[82] Thus, to argue that 'the Welshman' should 'speak English, and if he is an author let him write English', is to deny the Welsh any vestiges of nationhood.[83] If language, for Arnold, offers a means of accessing a people's history, to deny them their language is to deny them a future as Welshmen. Thus, if Arnold was to depict modern-day Jews as lacking in any cultural attributes while the values of an historic Hebraic culture represented one necessary constituent in the creation of a unifying cultural realm, he also expected the Celts to be divested of their cultural distinctions in order that 'Celticism', like 'Hebraism', could function as an historic force contributing to a cultural 'perfection'. Celticism, like Hebraism, is always essentially repressed within Arnold's idea of culture; it was once alive in the past but is now sublimated in the present as part of a hybrid English culture.

In Arnold's *On the Study of Celtic Literature* solutions for the problems engendered by a process of increasing democratisation—identified as 'Americanisation' in **'Democracy'**—are sought in the ethnic hybridity that Arnold believes characterises the 'English' nation. His concept of the 'alien', introduced in *Culture and Anarchy,* carries suggestive connotations in this context, for the agents in the creation of a less philistine England were not only to be the 'disinterested' and classless 'aliens' but also the 'sensual', 'feminine' and alien Celts. If the task facing the philistines is to transform themselves in assimilating the 'masses', thus creating a homogeneous, classless society, the role for England among the nations is similarly to incorporate the potentially disruptive Celtic peoples into its national boundaries. The contributionist argument of *On the Study of Celtic Literature,* where the founding of a Celtic chair at Oxford is designed to send 'a message of peace to Ireland', is part of this homogenising programme.[84] The drive in Arnold's criticism is always towards reconciliation; towards creating a common cultural sphere that unites the individual religious, ethnic and class interests within society. To realise this essentially liberal vision,

however, minorities within the state are expected to divest themselves of any cultural distinctions so that they may participate fully in an allegedly universalist culture. This conception of the relationship between culture and ethnicity was to form the basis for Arnold's later writings on America.

CULTURE, CLASS AND ETHNICITY IN AMERICA

By the 1880s Arnold was widely recognised as England's leading man of letters, a position that allowed him to embark on two lecture tours of the United States in 1884 and 1886. Following a long preoccupation with questions of religion in the 1870s, these visits to the United States coincided with a renewed commitment to tackling political and social issues in his writings. While Arnold, in **'Democracy'**, had encouraged the English to follow the French model of statehood and democracy, by the 1880s he no longer believed that France—whose idea moved masses were now absorbed in worshipping the 'great goddess Lubricity'—could provide a satisfactory alternative.[85] In his essay **'Numbers'**, written especially for the first American lecture tour, Arnold deploys the racial argument, developed in the lectures on Celtic literature, to explain why France could no longer be considered a suitable model for England's social and cultural development:

> By taking the Frenchman who is commonly in view,— the usual type of speaking, doing, vocal, visible, Frenchman—we may say, and he will probably be not at all displeased at our saying, that the German in him has nearly died out, and the Gallo-Latin has quite got the upper hand. For us, however, this means that the chief source of seriousness and of moral ideas is failing and drying up in him, and that what remains are the sources of Gaulish salt, and quickness, and sentiment, and sociability, and sensuality, and rationality. And, of course, the play and working of these qualities is [*sic*] altered by their being no longer in combination with a dose of German seriousness, but left to work themselves. Left to work by themselves, they give us what we call the *homme sensuel moyen,* the average sensual man.[86]

As France degenerated into its celebration of 'the average sensual man', America forced itself upon Arnold's attention with a new immediacy. As he noted in his essay on *Civilization in the United States*:

> To us . . . the future of the United States is of uncalculable importance. Already we feel their influence much, and we shall feel it more. We have a good deal to learn from them; we shall find in them, also, many things to beware of, many points in which it is to be hoped our democracy may not be like theirs.[87]

In the last decade of his life, Arnold drew on his characteristically comparativist mode of analysis to bring the key political and cultural issues of the 1880s—

disestablishment of the Church, Irish Home Rule, the failures of Liberalism—up against American sources of inquiry.

If Arnold's homogenising vision had functioned to deny the Jews and Celts any cultural distinctions in the 1860s, his writings on American civilisation were significantly based on the assumption that 'the people of the United States' are 'the English on the other side of the Atlantic'.[88] 'The first thing to remember' notes Arnold in **'A Word More About America'**, 'is that the people over there is at bottom the same people as ourselves', a view that he reiterates in his essay on **'Emerson'**:[89]

> You are fifty millions mainly sprung, as we in England are mainly sprung, from that German stock which has faults indeed,—faults which have diminished the extent of its influence, diminished its power of attraction and the interest of its history, and which seems moreover just now, from all I can see and hear, to be passing through a not very happy moment, morally, in Germany proper. Yet of the German stock it is, I think, true, as my father said more than fifty years ago, that it has been a stock, 'of the most moral races of men that the world has yet seen, with the soundest laws, the least violent passions, the fairest domestic and civil virtues'. You come, therefore, of about the best parentage which a modern nation can have.[90]

Despite his earlier admiration for France, and in spite of his belief that the dull Saxon should be enlivened by the vital Celtic strain, there is considerable evidence in Arnold's later writings to support Frederic Faverty's observation that

> . . . he placed his deepest trust in the 'serious German races'. Theirs were the sterling virtues, theirs the solid, if also unhappily the stolid, qualities which the world must fall back on at last. It is because he knows them to be strong that he speaks chiefly of their weaknesses. By pointing out their defects, he will enable them to become stronger still.[91]

While Arnold suggests that the Americans may take considerable pride in the racial heritage which they share with the English, by underlining the common ancestry of the two nations he is ultimately denying Americans any sense of cultural exceptionalism.

Whereas Arnold celebrated the mixed, hybrid nature of the English race in his lectures *On the Study of Celtic Literature,* his argument for the common racial background of the English and American peoples ignored the considerable ethnic diversity that characterised the United States by the time of his visits in the 1880s. As I noted in the introduction, America by this period was emerging as one of the leading nations of the capitalist world. The nation's industrial expansion attracted the wave of 'new immigrants'—the southern and eastern Europeans—who entered the United States in unprecedented numbers in the decades after the Civil War. Be-

fore 1860 most immigrants had come from Britain, Ireland, Germany and Scandinavia: five million had arrived in the forty years between 1820 and 1860. The next forty years, however, saw fourteen million new arrivals to the United States, the vast majority of whom came from Italy and Poland, Russia, Austria, Turkey, Greece and Syria.[92] The Roman Catholic or Jewish and non-English-speaking majority settled primarily in the cities of the north-east and Midwest, where they frequently took the least skilled industrial jobs and were viewed by the native-born and by earlier arrivals with apprehension and distrust. Their sheer numbers radically altered the ethnic composition of the nation, and their different manners and customs, modes of dress and religious observances were seen as threatening and disruptive to the dominance of Anglo-Saxon norms.[93]

Arnold's argument that the United States was essentially an Anglo-Saxon nation carries considerable significance within this context of ethnic diversity, for his beliefs functioned to reinforce the threatened cultural dominance of the Anglo-Saxon race. Arnold was not blind to this ethnic diversity, however. In **'A Word About America'**, his first piece on the United States written before his visits, he quotes James Russell Lowell in noting that from 'sturdy father to sturdy son, we have been making this continent habitable for the weaker Old World breed that has swarmed to it during the last half century'.[94] 'This may be quite true' notes Arnold, and in his later **'A Word More About America'** he notes that American domestic service 'is done for them by Irish, German, Swedes, negroes'.[95] This ethnic diversity is not a problem, however, for '. . . when the immigrant from Europe strikes root in his new home, he becomes an American'.[96] John Henry Raleigh is right to list 'the idea that the races must be conciliated to enrich one another' as one of the 'mutual congenialities' between Arnold and America, and it would seem that the American ideal of what became known as the 'melting pot'—in which ethnic and racial differences would be dissolved into a common identity—relates closely to the contributionism that informed Arnold's lectures on Celtic literature.[97] In terms of the theory of national identity that I developed earlier, the static, visual characteristics of the 'Irish, German, Swedes, negroes', are seen to contribute to the dominant narrative of the essentially Anglo-Saxon American nation.

These contributionist beliefs inform Arnold's writings on the Southern States. He begins his essay on General Grant by regretting the lack of attention given to the Northern General's memoirs in England, and explains this fact by noting that

> General Grant, the central figure of these *Memoirs,* is not to the English imagination the hero of the American Civil War; the hero is Lee, and of Lee the *Memoirs* tell us little.[98]

Arnold's biographers have noted his affinity to the more 'English' South which he, like many other leading members of the English intelligentsia, had hoped would win the Civil War so as to humble Yankee pride.[99] Arnold was no white supremacist, however. While in Richmond, Virginia, he surprised his hosts by requesting to see one of the all-black schools in the area, where he

> saw children who I took for granted were whites, and said—'So the races are educated together'. 'No', said the superintendent, 'there is a law against it throughout the South: the children you see have a strain of negro blood in them and are so returned by their parents.' I had to make a little speech to them, and in return they sang for me 'Dare to be Daniel' with negro energy.[100]

While Arnold's reference to 'negro energy' suggests an acceptance of racial difference, his experience at the school leads him to state unequivocally in a letter to his sister that he is 'astonished' by the 'line of demarcation between the white and the negro in the south still'.[101] Arnold's racial theory is utilised in order to describe, and is always secondary to, the cultural characteristics of nations and peoples. It is never offered as the basis for racial segregation. It is therefore logical that the existence of African Americans would not shake Arnold's belief in the essentially Anglo-Saxon character of the United States. Indeed, by educating all races together, they would be offered access to, and potentially contribute to, the great tradition of English and European knowledge. As in his description of the amalgamation of the Celts into the bloodstream and cultural stream of the English nation, the various ethnicities of the United States would become amalgamated into an American populace defined culturally as 'the English race in the United States'.[102] Ethnicity, for Arnold, is ultimately determined by culture, not blood. If, at times, Arnold emphasises the pervasive influence of race and heredity, this strain in his thought is always tempered by his belief that a 'community of practice is more telling than a community of origin'.[103]

Thus, while the racial theories developed in the Celtic essays resurface in Arnold's essays on America, the kinship on which he insists between the United States and England is primarily formulated in cultural terms. This formulation allows Arnold to ridicule the notion of an independent literary tradition in the United States and he, significantly, invokes the Celtic periphery in order to make his point.

> Therefore in literature we have 'the American Walter Scott', 'the American Wordsworth'; nay, I see advertised *The Primer of American Literature*. Imagine the face of Philip or Alexander at hearing of a Primer of Macedonian Literature! Are we to have a Primer of Canadian Literature too, and a Primer of Australian? We are all contributories to one great literature—English Literature. The contribution of Scotland to this literature is far more serious and important than that of America has yet had time to be; yet a 'Primer of Scotch Literature' would be an absurdity.[104]

In **'Civilisation in the United States',** Arnold couples his rejection of literary distinctiveness with a rejection of the linguistic distinctiveness that nineteenth-century Americans often claimed for themselves.[105] Scotland is again invoked to underline the absurdity of American claims to cultural independence.

> For every English writer they have an American writer to match. And him good Americans read; the Western States are at this moment being nourished and formed, we hear, on the novels of a native author called Roe, instead of Scott and Dickens . . . Far from admitting that in literature they have as yet produced little that is important, they play at treating American literature as if it were a great independent power; they reform the spelling of the English language by the insight of their average man . . . It reminds me of a thing in Smollett's dinner-party of authors. Seated by 'the philosopher who is writing a most orthodox refutation of Bolingbroke, but in the meantime has just been presented to the Grand Jury as a public nuisance for having blasphemed in an alehouse on the Lord's day'—seated by this philosopher is 'the Scotchman who is giving lectures on the pronunciation of the English language'.[106]

Culturally, then, America has no greater right to autonomy than the amalgamated Celtic periphery and, while all England's cultural dependants contribute to that 'one great literature—English Literature', there is no question as to whom should set the norms of language and canon formation.

If Arnold considers Roe a secondary author, he does, at various moments, register his admiration for William Dean Howells, Henry James and most significantly, Ralph Waldo Emerson.[107] In his lecture on Emerson, written and presented during his first visit to the United States, Arnold notes that his subject was not a great poet, not a great writer, or a great philosopher. Having 'cleared the ground' he goes on to note that Emerson's significance lies in his status as 'the friend and aider of those who live in the spirit'.[108] In this respect, Emerson 'has lessons for both branches of our race', and thus functions as an exemplar of the underlying racial and cultural affinities between England and America.

> I figure him to my mind as visible upon earth still, as still standing here by Boston Bay, or at his own Concord, in his habit as he lived, but of heightened stature and shining feature, with one hand stretched out towards the East, to our laden and labouring England; the other towards the ever-growing West, to his own dearly-loved America,—'great, intelligent, sensual, avaricious America'. To us he shows for guidance his lucid freedom, his cheerfulness and hope; to you his dignity, delicacy, serenity, elevation.[109]

In these final lines of the lecture Arnold progresses from the particular of Emerson's Concord to his significance in the wider world of English culture. The American author stands as a Colossus bridging two nations, a powerful representative of the essential cultural unity that exists between the 'two branches' of the English race.

This view of the essential unity between America and England breaks down, however, when Arnold turns to the political realm, which is the subject of much of his writing on the United States. America, Arnold admits, is characterised by a unique class structure and a political formation quite different from, and superior to, that in England. While he locates the roots of that political distinctiveness in the American Revolution (1775-83), Arnold also wishes to play down the revolutionary impetus and political divisiveness of that event.

> Let us concede . . . that chance and circumstance, as much as deliberate foresight and design, have brought the United States into their present condition, that moreover the British rule which they threw off was not the rule of oppressors and tyrants which declaimers suppose, and that the merit of the Americans was not that of oppressed men rising against tyrants, but rather of sensible young people getting rid of stupid and overweening guardians who misunderstood and mismanaged them.[110]

The relationship between England and America is here expressed in terms of 'guardians' and 'young people'. Arnold underlines the fundamental connection between the two countries even in describing the event which arguably destroyed that connection. While Americans may have been lucky, notes Arnold, not to have had a well-established class structure when they gained their political independence, they are to be congratulated 'to have forborne all attempts' at inventing one. American uniqueness lies most significantly for Arnold in its class structure, which is described as follows:

> I have said somewhere or other that, whereas our society in England distributes itself into Barbarians, Philistines and Populace, America is just ourselves, with the Barbarians quite left out, and the Populace nearly. This would leave the Philistines for the great bulk of the nation; a livelier sort of Philistine than ours, and with the pressure and the false ideal of our Barbarians taken away, but left all the more to himself, and to have his full swing.[111]

In the American context, then, class and nation become virtually synonymous terms; 'That which in England we call the middle class is in America virtually the nation.'[112] This domination of the national space by the philistine class leads to two somewhat contradictory results in Arnold's opinion. On the one hand, it gives rise to a banal culture which lacks the beauty and distinction necessary for an interesting civilisation. On the other hand, philistine domination gives rise to an admirably homogeneous, and politically stable, society. I shall discuss these observations in turn.

As early as 1848 Arnold was already arguing that the greatest threat to the educated world was the 'intolerable *laideur* of the well-fed American masses'.[113] His final published essay, **'Civilisation in the United States'**,

takes this threat as its subject and is a meditation upon the nature of civilisation itself. Civilisation, for Arnold, 'is the humanisation of man in society', the fulfilment of 'the law of perfection' that exists within human nature.[114]

> And perhaps what human nature demands in civilisation, over and above all those obvious things which first occur to our thoughts—what human nature, I say, demands in civilisation, if it is to stand as a high and satisfying civilisation, is best described by the word *interesting*. Here is the extraordinary charm of the old Greek civilisation—that it is so *interesting*. Do not tell me only, says human nature, of the magnitude of your industry and commerce; of the beneficence of your institutions, your freedom, your equality; of the great and growing number of your churches and schools, libraries and newspapers; tell me also if your civilisation—which is the grand name you give to all this development—tell me if your civilisation is *interesting*.[115]

This evocative passage, where Arnold adopts the voice of 'human nature' in questioning the reader's assumed preoccupation with material progress, introduces the key category of 'interest'. In the light of this passage it is clear that Arnold was making a significant critique of American civilisation when, in writing to Grant Duff from Massachusetts in the summer of 1886, he noted that 'compared with life in England' America is 'so uninteresting, so without savour and without depth'.[116] The great sources of interest, for Arnold, are 'distinction' and 'beauty', the absence of which in America is betrayed by its restless and rootless citizenry, its art and architecture, its political leaders, and its sensationalist newspapers. This lack of 'distinction' and 'beauty' is explained by invoking race, class, and the lack of history.

> Then the Americans come originally, for the most part, from that great class in English society amongst whom the sense for conduct and business is much more strongly developed than the sense for beauty. If we in England were without the cathedrals, parish churches and castles of the Catholic and feudal age, and without the houses of the Elizabethan age, but had only the towns and buildings which the rise of our middle class has created in the modern age, we should be in much the same case as the Americans.[117]

If America is to be the emergent model of democracy, then **'Civilisation in the United States'** suggests that the beauty and distinction which are wholly necessary in attaining 'a renovated and perfected human society on earth' are wholly lacking in American civilisation. The essay **'Numbers'** (1884), which Arnold read most often on his first American tour, seeks to offer some solutions for the problems he believed were facing American culture.

'Numbers' develops and elaborates on several of the positions that Arnold had initially adopted in the 1860s. Its purpose was to convince its American readers that, in any society, ancient or modern, the majority of people are unreliable and that only the few, the 'remnant', can be expected to give sound judgement and wisdom. This is particularly the case in America, for

> . . . in a democratic community like this, with its new-ness, its magnitude, its strength, its life of business, its sheer freedom and equality, the danger is in the absence of the discipline of respect; in hardness and materialism, exaggeration and boastfulness; in a false smartness, a false audacity, a want of soul and delicacy.[118]

Arnold justified his rudeness in telling his readers that the majority of them lacked taste and judgement by assuring them that he had been just as blunt with his own countrymen, which indeed he had. As we saw earlier in both **'Democracy'** and *Culture and Anarchy* Arnold had dismissed each of the modern English classes as a potential source of leadership, and placed his hopes for the future in a small number of classless 'aliens'. In **'Numbers'** the word 'aliens', which may have invoked the spectre of the new immigrants in an American context, was replaced by the word 'remnant', which was perhaps more likely to invoke the persistence of an Anglo-Saxon stock. Thus, while the lecture is not directly concerned with issues of ethnicity, there may have been deeper reasons than linguistic currency, or biblical resonance, behind Arnold's transformation of 'aliens' into 'remnant'. The word 'numbers' refers not only to the sum total of people that make up a democratic society, but also more specifically to the 'remnant' of cultivated leaders, for if 'the majority is and must be in general unsound everywhere', then 'to enable the remnant to succeed, a large strengthening of its numbers is everything'. America offered Arnold the tantalising prospect of a society of such immensity that the remnant could potentially increase its numbers so that it might become 'incomparable, all-transforming'.[119]

If the domination of the philistine class had lead to a civilisation devoid of beauty and distinction, a civilisation which depended on a classless and cultured remnant to solve its cultural problems, then the domination of the middle class in America had also lead to a social homogeneity which was wholly positive with regard to political organisation. The Americans, Arnold enthused, are 'impregnably strong' against invasion from without and their lack of class distinctions within means that they live in a society that 'is not in danger from revolution'.[120]

> Not only have they not the distinction between noble and bourgeois, between aristocracy and the middle class; they have not even the distinction between bourgeois and peasant or artisan, between middle and lower class. They have nothing to create it and compel recognition of it.[121]

Given this lack of class distinctions the Americans are

> A people homogeneous, a people which had to constitute itself in a modern age, an epoch of expansion, and which has given to itself institutions entirely fitted for such an age and epoch, and which suit it perfectly—a people not in danger of war from without, not in danger of revolution from within—such is the people of the United States. The political and social problem, then, we must surely allow that they solve successfully.[122]

While this positive view of American political institutions is sustained throughout Arnold's writings on America, it is particularly emphasised in his initial response to his first American visit, **'A Word More About America'**. As with the essays on Celtic literature, however, the positive view of America ultimately functions to highlight what is lacking in English social and political institutions: 'More than half one's interest in watching the English people of the United States comes, of course, from the bearing of what one finds there upon things at home, among us English people ourselves in these islands.'[123] Again, a common racial heritage connecting the English and Americans is emphasised as the basis for comparison in other spheres. Ultimately **'A Word About America'** is less concerned with conditions in the United States than it is with those in another country—Ireland. America offered Arnold another context within which to discuss the divisive ethnic identities of the United Kingdom.

The dominant theme of **'A Word More About America'** is that the 'political sense' in America is 'sounder' than that in England. Whereas Americans have successfully solved the political and social problem, and whereas Americans see things 'straight' and 'clear', the English are still searching for the political path that they should take. Nowhere is this English uncertainty more evident than in their policy towards Ireland, about which there is no 'clear vision of the great, the profound changes still to be wrought before a stable and prosperous society' could be established there.[124] Arnold had shown his interest in the Irish question in his essays on Celtic literature, by editing the papers of Burke in 1881, and in several articles during the 1870s, most notably **'Irish Catholicism and British Liberalism'** and **'The Incompatibles'**.[125] It was, however, Gladstone's announcement late in 1885, under pressure from the Parnellites, that he planned to offer a measure of home rule that aroused the 'apprehensions' which made Ireland the chief concern of Arnold's final years. Arnold's solution to the problem of Ireland's potential secession from Britain is based on an analogy with the American division of state and federal powers:

> Is not the cure . . . found in a course like that followed in America, in having a much less numerous House of Commons, and in making over a large part of its business to local assemblies, elected, as the House of Commons itself will henceforth be elected, by household suffrage? . . . Wholes neither too large nor too

small, not necessarily of equal population by any means, but with characters rendering them in themselves fairly homogeneous and coherent, are the fit units for choosing these local assemblies. Such units occur immediately to one's mind in the provinces of Ireland, the Highland and Lowlands of Scotland, Wales north and south, groups of English counties such as present themselves in the circuits of the judges or under the names of East Anglia or the Midlands.[126]

The creation of provincial legislatures to control local affairs is thus seen as a means of addressing Irish grievances without creating an independent Irish state that would endanger 'the unity of the Empire'.[127]

Arnold's views on Ireland may be regarded, in terms of culture and politics, as a mirror image of his views on America. In the case of America, he recognises the nation's political independence while denying it any sense of an independent cultural or literary tradition. In the case of Ireland he is prepared to accept the existence of an independent Celtic literary tradition in the past, while simultaneously denying the Celtic nations the potential for political independence in the present or future. In 1886 the 'political crisis' which he foresaw and wished to avoid was that of the breakup of Britain.

> Ireland has been a nation, a most unhappy one. Wales, too, and Scotland, have been nations. But politically they are now nations no longer, any one of them. This country could not have risen to its present greatness if they had been. Give them separate Parliaments, and you begin, no doubt, to make them again nations politically. But you begin also to undo what has made this country great.[128]

Central to Arnold's advocacy of regional assemblies across Britain lies a desire to break up the potential national geographies of the Celtic periphery into regions; the *provinces* of Ireland, *north* and *south* Wales, the *highlands* and *lowlands* of Scotland. Again, the model is the United States, with the status of Ireland within Britain compared with that of the Southern states within America.

> Ireland could address no stronger mandate to Parliament to give Home Rule than the Southern States addressed to the North to give them a separate Congress and a separate executive . . . If it would have been dangerous to grant a Southern Congress and a Southern executive, then it would be dangerous to grant an Irish parliament, and an executive responsible to it.[129]

While Arnold believes the United Sates in the post-Civil War period to have achieved a peaceful, homogeneous society, this remains an unattained goal for Britain, a goal that can be achieved only by alleviating Irish grievances thus uniting the region closer into the institutions of the British state. When Gladstone introduced his Home Rule Bill on 8 April 1886, Arnold described the action as the 'nadir' of liberalism, fulfilling his direst predictions about the direction in which the Liberal party was heading, and revealing Gladstone as a 'dangerous' minister.[130]

Arnold's goal of incorporating the Irish ever closer into the structures of the British state can be considered a part of his wider cultural agenda; his desire to create a truly homogeneous, democratic culture within the islands of Great Britain. In this respect his wish to create a polity without national divisions is fundamentally related to his desire for constructing a society without class divisions. Class and national identity are intertwined throughout Arnold's contributionist writings in this respect. 'Inequality is our bane' he notes, while the American 'source of strength . . . in political and social concerns' lies in the 'homogeneous character of American society'.[131] In his discourses on America, as in the earlier social analyses of *Culture and Anarchy* and *On the Study of Celtic Literature,* Arnold's potentially democratic desire to achieve a common culture ultimately reaffirms the cultural, and political, authority of the dominant society. In the American context, the role of an emergent multi-ethnic and thriving working-class culture is largely ignored in the reaffirmation of the hegemonic dominance of Anglo-Saxon traditions. In 'England'—it is rarely Britain—the regional ethnic solidarities of the Celtic periphery are discounted in the attempted reconceptualisation of a homogeneous national culture.

CONCLUSION

If I have argued that Arnold's conception of 'culture' was developed in response to the divisive class and ethnic interests that were fermenting within British industrial society, I am also aware of the dangers of overemphasising the extent of Arnold's sense of alienation from that society. Arnold does not stand in such an adversarial relation to his culture as his direct criticisms of Victorian society may lead us to believe. Even at his most critical, he is appealing to a body of beliefs and values that he shares with his readers. Arnold is not a critic who attempts to subvert the social values of English society, nor to reverse the direction of its development. His goal is to reinforce and encourage the role of a broadly defined culture, and the authority of the man of letters, within the life of the nation. It would also be a mistake, however, to overemphasise Arnold's typicality for he is profoundly uncharacteristic of his age in myriad ways: his cosmopolitan Europeanism; his desire to alleviate class and ethnic grievances through education; his attention to the literature of the Celtic peoples; his promotion of a cultural humanism as opposed to the scientific positivism of his time. Much recent writing on Arnold has not addressed the oppositional nature of his works, but has rather used him as an exemplar of all that was wrong in Victorian society.[132]

It seems that the very act of identifying malfunction becomes in Arnold's writings an appeal for cohesion. Thus, to utilise the presumed homogeneity of American society as a means of denouncing the divisive methods used by the English in governing Ireland, functions as political critique while simultaneously reinforcing the English right to govern the island. To criticise the philistinism of the middle classes of England and America is also to underline the future role of this class as the leaders of democratic society. To place the cultured 'alien', or culturally sensitive 'remnant', in a position outside society from which it can critique and possibly transform current trends in the national life, is to perform a strategic manoeuvre that makes the marginal position of the alienated intellectual the very centre of that society being critiqued. Arnold's criticism is always geared towards reconciliation, towards the creation of a common cultural sphere that unites the individual religious, ethnic and class interests within society. To realise this vision, however, ethnic minorities within the 'English' nation state are expected to abandon their cultural distinctions. While Arnold was certainly atypical in making the case for the centrality of the Celtic races in the historical narrative of the English nation, there is ultimately no space for languages or literatures other than English within his conception of its culture.

Notes

1. Arnold, 'Report from 1852' in Sutherland (ed.), *Arnold on Education*, p. 23.

2. Arnold, 'Porro Unum Est Necessarium' (1878), *CPW* [*The Complete Prose Works of Matthew Arnold*], VIII, p. 374.

3. Humphreys, *Taliesin Tradition*, p. 179. I would like to thank the late W. Gareth Evans for his generous assistance in locating materials on Arnold as HMI. On Arnold in Wales see W. G. Evans, 'The Bilingual Difficulty'.

4. Robert Young makes Arnold's cultural thought complicit with colonial practice when he notes that the 'compulsory national education' advocated by Arnold shared much of its rationale with 'the spirit of colonialism'. *Colonial Desire*, p. 51. Edward Said notes, with no evidence to support his case, that Arnold supported General Edward Eyre's brutal suppression of the Jamaican uprising in 1866. *Culture and Imperialism*, p. 157. Arnold in fact expresses his opposition to Eyre's actions in 'A Courteous Explanation' (1866), *CPW* V, p. 35. These critiques are symptomatic of a wider tendency to treat Arnold as the embodiment of conservative Victorian values. For a lucid discussion of this phenomenon see Stefan Collini's 'Afterword' to the Clarendon Paperback Edition of *Matthew Arnold*, pp. 125-38.

5. The report of the Education Commission of 1847 was promptly dubbed 'Brad y Llyfrau Gleision'/ 'The Treason of the Blue Books', after the Treason of the Long Knives of the Saxons in the days of Vortigern. Accurate enough in its exposure of educational deficiencies in Wales, the Report moved on to attack Nonconformity, the morals of Welsh people (especially the women), and the Welsh language itself. For a brief account in English see P. Morgan, 'From a Death to a View', pp. 92-8. For a more detailed analysis see G. T. Roberts, *Language of the Blue Books*.

6. Arnold, 'Report from 1852', p. 23.

7. These terms come from Arnold's celebrated essays on *Culture and Anarchy* (1869), *CPW*, V, pp. 113, 145-6.

8. Arnold, *On the Study of Celtic Literature* (1867), in *CPW* III, p. 348.

9. Burrow, 'Introduction' to *Limits of State Action*, p. xxxiv.

10. Arnold, *England and the Italian Question* (1859), in *CPW* I, pp. 65-96. 'Disestablishment in Wales' (1888) and 'Civilisation in the United States' (1888) in *CPW* XI, pp. 334-9, 350-69.

11. Arnold, *Culture and Anarchy* (1869), *CPW* V, p. 112.

12. Arnold, *CPW* V, p. 97.

13. Ibid. p. 97.

14. Arnold, 'Preface' to *Culture and Anarchy* (1869), *CPW* V, p. 233.

15. Arnold, *CPW* V, p. 98.

16. Ibid. p. 95.

17. Ibid. p. 95. Williams, *Culture and Society*, p. xviii.

18. Arnold, *CPW* V, p. 105.

19. Ibid. p. 113.

20. Ibid. p. 113.

21. Arnold, *On the Study of Celtic Literature* (1867), *CPW* III, pp. 296-7.

22. Ibid. pp. 296-7.

23. Eagleton, *Heathcliff* [*Heathcliff and the Great Hunger*], p. 302.

24. It is interesting in this context to note that, while Arnold plays a pivotal role in Williams's *Culture and Society*, he does not appear in *The Country and the City*. The reason, no doubt, is that the distinction between the country and city does not play a significant part in Arnold's cultural criticism.

25. On Arnold's invocations of Greece see Coulling, *Matthew Arnold and his Critics*, pp. 62-99, and of Elizabethan England see Collini, *Matthew Arnold*, p. 78.

26. Arnold, 'Democracy' (1861), which forms an introduction to his *The Popular Education of France* in *CPW* II, pp. 3-29.

27. Arnold, *Letters of Matthew Arnold Volume 2*, p. 431.

28. Arnold, 'Democracy' (1861), *CPW* II, pp. 15-16.

29. Arnold quotes the letter in his 'Introduction' to *On the Study of Celtic Literature* (1867), *CPW* III, p. 390. On Owen, see B. Davies, *Hugh Owen*.

30. This useful synopsis of the position that Arnold had held from the 1860s onwards comes from 'Equality' (1878) in *CPW* VIII, p. 302.

31. Arnold, 'Democracy', *CPW* II, pp. 26-7.

32. See Williams, *Culture and Society*, pp. 126-9.

33. Arnold, *Culture and Anarchy* (1869), in *CPW* V, p. 121.

34. Ibid. p. 146.

35. Ibid. pp. 145-6.

36. Ibid. p. 144. Arnold, *On the Study of Celtic Literature*, *CPW* III, p. 348.

37. Arnold, 'Democracy', *CPW* II, p. 26.

38. Arnold delivered his lectures on Celtic literature at Oxford on the following dates: 6/7/1865, 7/7/65, 24/2/66, 26/5/66, and they appeared in *The Cornhill Magazine* between March and July 1866. They were eventually published in book form by Smith, Elder and Co. in 1867. See Murray, *Life of Matthew Arnold*, pp. 226-31, and Super's notes on the lectures in *CPW* III, pp. 539-40.

39. Arnold, *On the Study of Celtic Literature*, in *CPW* III, p. 345.

40. Ibid. pp. 294-5.

41. Ibid. pp. 295-6.

42. Ibid. p. 390.

43. Davies, *The Isles*, p. 784.

44. Arnold, *On the Study of Celtic Literature, CPW* III, p. 387.

45. Faverty, *Arnold the Ethnologist*. On the influence of Renan see Bromwich, *Matthew Arnold* [*Matthew Arnold and Celtic Literature*], and on Renan and Edwards see Young, *Colonial Desire*.

46. For a discussion of Arnold's Celtic lectures within a Scottish context see Chapman, *Gaelic Vision*.

47. Lorimer, 'Reconstructing Victorian Racial Discourse', p. 187.

48. Arnold, *On the Study of Celtic Literature, CPW* III, 342. On Victorian racial thought see Stepan, *Idea of Race* [*The Idea of Race in Science*]. On Arnold and race see Young, *Colonial Desire,* and on philology see N. Thomas, 'Renan, Arnold and Unamuno'. Young draws attention to Arnold's admiration for Joseph Arthur Comte de Gobineau, whose *Essay on the Inequality of Races* (1853-5) is 'regarded as a precursor for fascist racial theory' (Young, *Colonial Desire*, p. 85.) Even in the rare cases where Arnold does draw extensively on Gobineau, such as his essay on 'A Persian Passion Play'(1871), there is little evidence of his being influenced by racial thought (See Faverty, *Arnold the Ethnologist*, pp. 43, 228.) Indeed, Arnold notes explicitly 'that if the interest of the Persian passion-plays had seemed to me to lie solely in the curious evidence they afford of the workings of patriotic feeling in a conquered people, I should hardly have occupied myself with them at this length', *CPW* VII, p. 34.

49. Arnold, *On the Study of Celtic Literature, CPW* III, p. 296.

50. Arnold, *England and the Italian Question* (1859), *CPW* I, pp. 65-96.

51. Ibid, p. 70.

52. Ibid, p. 71.

53. Ibid. pp. 71-2.

54. Ibid. p. 71.

55. Ibid. p. 73.

56. Said, *Orientalism*, p. 240.

57. Arnold, *On the Study of Celtic Literature, CPW* III, p. 311.

58. Ibid. pp. 344, 345, 347.

59. Ibid. p. 346.

60. Ibid. p. 299.

61. It is worth stressing the originality of Arnold's analysis within the context of the period's anti-Celticism. A sense of the English view of the Celts in the 1860s can be gleaned from the reviews of Arnold's lectures that appeared in *The Times* and *The Daily Telegraph*. According to *The Times*,

> The Welsh language is the curse of Wales . . . An Eisteddfod is one of the most mischievous and selfish pieces of sentimentalism which could possibly be perpetrated. It is simply foolish interference with the natural progress of civilisation and prosperity . . . Not only the energy and

power, but the intelligence and music of Europe have come mainly from Teutonic sources, and this glorification of everything Celtic, if it were not pedantry, would be sheer ignorance. The sooner all Welsh specialities disappear from the face of the earth the better.

Quoted in Dawson and Pfordresher (eds), *Arnold*: [*The Critical Heritage—Vol. 1*:] *Prose Writings,* pp. 159-66. See also L. P. Curtis, *Anglo-Saxons and Celts.*

62. Anderson, *Imagined Communities,* p. 136.

63. In a revisionist account of mid-nineteenth-century British culture, Peter Mandler suggests that a 'civilisational' rather than 'racial' perspective characterised the thought of the period. The problem of his analysis is that he concentrates almost wholly on how the English conceived of England and Englishness. Arnold's writings suggest that a civilisational view of England could happily coexist, and was even predicated upon, a racial view of the Celts. See Mandler, '"Race" and "Nation"'.

64. Arnold, *On the Study of Celtic Literature, CPW* III, p. 389.

65. Ibid. p. 336.

66. Ibid. p. 351.

67. Ibid. p. 383.

68. Ibid. p. 351.

69. Ibid. pp. 351-2.

70. Collini, *Matthew Arnold,* p. 79.

71. Arnold, *On the Study of Celtic Literature, CPW* III, 300.

72. Ibid. p. 300.

73. Ibid. pp. 300, 301.

74. Ibid. p. 301.

75. On the influence of Victorian racial thought on Arnold see Young, *Colonial Desire,* Appiah and Gutman, *Color Conscious,* Cheyette, *Constructions of 'the Jew'.*

76. See, for example, Arnold, *Culture and Anarchy, CPW* V, pp. 165, 172.

77. Arnold, *Literature and Dogma,* (1873) in *CPW* VI, pp. 199.

78. Ibid. p. 199.

79. Arnold, *Culture and Anarchy, CPW* V, p. 255.

80. Arnold, *On the Study of Celtic Literature, CPW* III, p. 300.

81. Ibid. p. 293.

82. Ibid. pp. 334, 335.

83. Ibid. p. 297.

84. Ibid. p. 386.

85. Arnold, 'Numbers' (1884), in *CPW* X, p. 158.

86. Ibid. p. 157.

87. Arnold, 'Civilisation in the United States' (1888), *CPW* XI, p. 368.

88. Arnold, 'A Word About America' (1882), *CPW* X, p. 2.

89. Arnold, 'A Word More About America' (1882), *CPW* X, p. 198.

90. Arnold, 'Emerson' (1883), *CPW* X, p. 163.

91. Faverty, *Arnold the Ethnologist,* p. 76.

92. See Daniels, 'The Immigrant Experience'.

93. See Trachtenberg, *Incorporation of America,* pp. 87-8.

94. Arnold, 'A Word About America', *CPW* X, p. 12.

95. Arnold, 'A Word More About America', *CPW* X, 200.

96. Ibid. 200.

97. Raleigh, *Arnold and American Culture,* p. 250. This view of racial and cultural assimilation became known as the 'melting pot' theory. The term was not generally used in nineteenth-century America. It was popularised in 1908 in a play of that name by an English Jew, Israel Zangwill. See Sollors, *Beyond Ethnicity,* pp. 66-101.

98. Arnold, 'General Grant' (1887), *CPW* XI, p. 144.

99. See Honan, *Matthew Arnold,* p. 402, and Trilling, *Matthew Arnold,* p. 402.

100. Arnold, *Letters of Matthew Arnold Vol. 5,* p. 362.

101. Ibid. p. 362.

102. Arnold, 'A Word More About America', *CPW* X, p. 203.

103. Arnold, 'A French Critic on Goethe' (1878), *CPW* VIII, p. 256.

104. Arnold, 'General Grant' (1887), *CPW* XI, p. 177.

105. On debates regarding the distinctiveness of American English, see Nettels, *Language, Race, and Social Class,* pp. 41-61. On language debates in the United States more generally see Shell, 'Babel in America'.

106. Arnold, 'Civilisation in the United States' (1888), *CPW* XI, pp. 364-5.

107. For Arnold on Howells see 'Emerson'(1883), *CPW* X, p. 180, on James, 'A Word About America', *CPW* X, p. 7.

108. Arnold, 'Emerson', *CPW* X, p. 177.

109. Ibid. p. 186.

110. Arnold, 'A Word More About America', *CPW* X, p. 197.

111. Arnold, 'A Word About America', *CPW* X, p. 7.

112. Ibid. p. 10.

113. Arnold, *Letters of Matthew Arnold Volume 1,* p. 95.

114. Arnold, 'Civilisation in the United States', *CPW* XI, pp. 356, 357.

115. Ibid. p. 357.

116. Arnold, *Letters of Matthew Arnold Volume 6,* p. 183. Arnold expresses this view in noting the limitations of Andrew Carnegie's book on 'the material progress of this country', *Triumphant Democracy.*

117. Arnold, 'Civilisation in the United States', *CPW* XI, p. 359.

118. Arnold, 'Numbers' (1884), *CPW* X, p. 162.

119. Ibid. p. 164.

120. Arnold, 'A Word More About America', *CPW* X, pp. 198, 199.

121. Ibid. pp. 199-200.

122. Ibid. p. 202.

123. Ibid. p. 203.

124. Ibid. p. 206.

125. 'Irish Catholicism and British Liberalism' (1878) in *CPW* VIII, pp. 321-47, and 'The Incompatibles' (1881) collected in *CPW* IX, pp. 238-85.

126. Arnold, 'A Word More About America', *CPW* X, p. 210.

127. Ibid. p. 210.

128. Arnold, 'The Political Crisis' (1886), *CPW* XI, p. 79.

129. Arnold, 'The Zenith of Conservatism' (1886), *CPW* XI, pp. 132-3.

130. Arnold, 'The Nadir of Liberalism' (1886), *CPW* XI, and 'The Zenith of Conservatism', *CPW* XI, pp. 124, 135.

131. Arnold, 'A Word More About America', *CPW* X, pp. 213, 209.

132. See Arac, *Critical Genealogies.* Said, *Culture and Imperialism.*

Bibliography

Anderson, Benedict, *Imagined Communities: Reflections on the Origins and Spread of Nationalism* (London: Verso, 1983).

Appiah, Kwame Anthony and Amy Gutmann, *Color Conscious: The Political Morality of Race* (Princeton, NJ: Princeton University Press, 1996).

Arac, Jonathan, *Critical Genealogies: Historical Situations for Postmodern Studies* (New York: Columbia University Press, 1987).

Arnold, Matthew, *The Complete Prose Works of Matthew Arnold,* ed. R. H. Super, 11 vols (Ann Arbor: University of Michigan Press, 1960-77):

i: *On the Classical Tradition* (1960).

ii: *Democratic Education* (1962).

iii: *Lectures and Essays in Criticism* (1962).

iv: *Schools and Universities on the Continent* (1964).

v: *Culture and Anarchy* (1965).

vi: *Dissent and Dogma* (1968).

vii: *God and the Bible* (1970).

viii: *Essays Religious and Mixed* (1962).

ix: *English Literature and Irish Politics* (1973).

x: *Philistinism in England and America* (1974).

xi: *The Last Word* (1977).

Arnold, Matthew, *The Letters of Matthew Arnold, Vol. 1: 1829-1859,* ed. Cecil Y. Lang (Charlottesville and London: The University of Virginia Press, 1996).

Arnold, Matthew, *The Letters of Matthew Arnold, Vol. 2: 1860-1865,* ed. Cecil Y. Lang (Charlottesville and London: The University of Virginia Press, 1997).

Arnold, Matthew, *The Letters of Matthew Arnold, Vol. 5: 1879-1884,* ed. Cecil Y. Lang (Charlottesville and London: The University of Virginia Press, 2001).

Arnold, Matthew, *The Letters of Matthew Arnold, Vol. 6: 1885-1888,* ed. Cecil Y. Lang (Charlottesville and London: The University of Virginia Press, 2001).

Arnold, Matthew, 'Report from 1852', in Gillian Sutherland (ed.), *Matthew Arnold on Education* (Harmondsworth: Penguin Education, 1973), pp. 23-4.

Bromwich, Rachel, *Matthew Arnold and Celtic Literature: A Retrospect 1865-1965* (Oxford: Clarendon Press, 1965).

Burrow, J. W., 'Introduction' to Wilhelm von Humboldt, *The Limits of State Action,* ed. and trans. J. W. Burrow (Cambridge: Cambridge University Press, 1969).

Chapman, Malcolm, *The Gaelic Vision in Scottish Culture* (London: Croom Helm, 1978).

Cheyette, Brian, *Constructions of 'the Jew' in English Literature and Society: Racial Representations, 1875-1945* (Cambridge: Cambridge University Press, 1993).

Collini, Stefan, *Matthew Arnold: A Critical Portrait* ([1988] Oxford: Clarendon Press, 1994).

Coulling, Sidney, *Matthew Arnold and his Critics: A Study of Arnold's Controversies* (Athens, OH: Ohio University Press, 1974).

Curtis Jr, L. P., *Anglo-Saxons and Celts: A Study of Anti-Irish Prejudice in Victorian England* (Bridgeport, CT: New York University Press, 1968).

Daniels, Roger, 'The Immigrant Experience in the Gilded Age', in Charles W. Calhoun (ed.), *The Gilded Age: Essays on the Origins of Modern America* (Wilmington, DE: SR Books, 1996), pp. 63-89.

Davies, B. L., *Hugh Owen, 1804-1881* (Cardiff: University of Wales Press, 1977).

Davies, Norman, *The Isles: A History* (London: Macmillan, 1999).

Dawson, Carl and John Pfordresher (eds), *Matthew Arnold: The Critical Heritage—Vol. 1: Prose Writings* ([1979] London: Routledge, 1995).

Eagleton, Terry, *Heathcliff and the Great Hunger: Studies in Irish Culture* (London: Verso, 1995).

Evans, Gareth W., 'The "Bilingual Difficulty": HMI and the Welsh Language in the Victorian Age', *The Welsh History Review/Cylchgrawn Hanes Cymru* 16:4 (1993), pp. 494-513.

Faverty, Frederic E., *Matthew Arnold, the Ethnologist* (Evanston, IL: Northwestern University Press, 1951).

Honan, Park, *Matthew Arnold: A Life* (London: Weidenfeld and Nicolson, 1981).

Humphreys, Emyr, *The Taliesin Tradition: A Quest for the Welsh Identity* ([1983] Bridgend: Seren Books, 1989).

Lorimer, Douglass, 'Reconstructing Victorian Racial Discourse', in Gretchen Gerzina (ed.), *Black Victorians, Black Victoriana* (New Brunswick: Rutgers University Press, 2003), pp. 187-207.

Mandler, Peter, '"Race" and "Nation" in Mid-Victorian Thought', in Stefan Collini, Richard Whatmore and Brian Young (eds), *History, Religion and Culture: British Intellectual History, 1750-1950* (Cambridge: Cambridge University Press, 2000), pp. 224-44.

Morgan, Prys, 'From a Death to a View: The Hunt for a Welsh Past in the Romantic Period', in Hobsbawm and Ranger (eds), *The Invention of Tradition* (Cambridge: Cambridge University Press, 1983), pp. 43-100.

Murray, Nicholas, *A Life of Matthew Arnold* (London: Hodder and Stoughton, 1995).

Nettels, Elsa, *Language, Race, and Social Class in Howells's America* (Lexington: University of Kentucky Press, 1988).

Raleigh, John Henry, *Matthew Arnold and American Culture* (Berkeley: University of California Press, 1961).

Roberts, Gwyneth Tyson, *The Language of the Blue Books: The Perfect Instrument of Empire* (Cardiff: University of Wales Press, 1998).

Said, Edward, *Orientalism: Western Conceptions of the Orient* ([1978] London: Penguin, 1995).

Shell, Marc, 'Babel in America: The Politics of Linguistic Diversity in the United States', *Critical Inquiry* 20:1 (Fall 1993), pp. 103-28.

Sollors, Werner, *Beyond Ethnicity: Consent and Descent in American Culture* (New York: Oxford University Press, 1986).

Stepan, Nancy, *The Idea of Race in Science: Great Britain, 1800-1960* (London: Macmillan, 1982).

Thomas, Ned, 'Renan, Arnold, Unamuno: Philology and the Minority Languages', *Bedford Occasional Papers: Essays in Language Literature and Area Studies* 6 (1984), pp. 1-14.

Trachtenberg, Alan, *The Incorporation of America: Culture and Society in the Gilded Age* (New York: Hill and Wang, 1982).

Trilling, Lionel, *Matthew Arnold* ([1939] New York: Columbia University Press, 1949).

Williams, Raymond, *Culture and Society: Coleridge to Orwell* ([1958] London: Hogarth Press, 1990).

Young, Robert J. C., *Colonial Desire: Hybridity in Theory Culture and Race* (London: Routledge, 1995).

Kirstie Blair (essay date 2006)

SOURCE: Blair, Kirstie. "'The Old Unquiet Breast': Matthew Arnold, Heartsickness, and the Culture of Doubt." In *Victorian Poetry and the Culture of the Heart,* pp. 145-80. Oxford, England: Clarendon Press, 2006.

[*In the following essay, Blair connects Arnold's worries about the health of his own heart with his frequent use of heart imagery in his poetry. According to Blair, the cold or erratic heart in Arnold's work conveys a concern with poetry's failure as a source of sympathy and moral strength in an unfeeling world, as well as expressing Arnold's preoccupation with the inadequacy of religion in modern times.*]

Of all the poets in this study, Matthew Arnold was probably the one most anxious about the state of his 'starting, feverish' heart. His father died of angina pectoris, and the account of his sudden death as recorded by Latham became the classic case study of this disease, frequently cited in medical textbooks. Angina was a disease which was represented as both organic and sympathetic, which meant that it was potentially hereditary but could also be induced (or heightened) by nervous problems or emotional upset. It was the heart disease which required the sufferer to take the most care with regard to his or her heart, in terms of avoiding feelings and situations which might induce an attack. Since it involved the heart acting without warning or control, it was also classified as a 'spasmodic' disease. Henry Clutterbuck, in 1840, ascribes it definitely to 'a sudden spasm of the heart', while Charles Williams, more cautiously, blames it on 'exalted sensibility of the nerves of the heart', an odd phrase, since 'exalted' usually implies religious ecstasy or high emotion.[1] Matthew Arnold, as a poet and the son of a victim (who was also of course a literary man), was doubly susceptible. The younger Thomas Arnold remarked in an obituary of his brother that in 1846, when Matthew was 24, 'he knew that he was in a certain sense doomed—an eminent physician having told him that the action of his heart was not regular, and that he must take great care of himself'.[2] When Arnold's own son was born, he wrote to his mother:

> I had my own doubts about his dear little heart having constantly remarked its singular agitations at times. But I should not be the least surprised if Brodie or whoever sees him pronounces it only to be an infantine irregularity, and that there is no structural defect.[3]

The picture of Arnold leaning over his son's cradle anxiously watching his heartbeat suggests the extent of his worry about inherited cardiac problems. The reassurance here is not entirely confident: Arnold has already called in an expert on the heart to examine his baby son. He writes to his sister in 1856 that the sympathetic alarm occasioned by his son's illness has also 'nearly developed in me the complaint he is said to have' because it caused 'a fuller beating of the heart than I like'.[4]

In the light of these fears, the emphasis in Arnold's poems on the 'vainly throbbing', 'teased, o'erlaboured' heart and the 'feverish blood' may have specifically personal as well as cultural and poetic implications.[5] Arnold is preoccupied with the idea that the heart, the

source of feeling, is inaccessible and unresponsive. While one reason for this is found in his focus on the weaknesses of the individual heart, he also uses the alienated heart as a general image to represent the failure of affect, the sense that poetry has ceased to convey healthful sympathy, morality, and reassurance and is instead transmitting disease and uncertainty—inasmuch as it succeeds in transmitting anything at all. The isolation which is a central motif in many of Arnold's poems is presented as a lack of heart-to-heart communication. His interest in the state of his own heart doubtless informs some of this imagery, but he equally tends to evade the personal and describe heartsickness as endemic, a condition of the age and of modern poetry. Arnold's major poems of the 1850s ('**Empedocles on Etna**' in particular) share many of the concerns of spasmodic writing and of the poems by Barrett Browning and Tennyson examined elsewhere. But Arnold came from a slightly younger generation than Tennyson and the Brownings, whose poetic careers were more or less firmly established by 1850, and was separated by class, education, and religion from the spasmodic poets who were his near contemporaries. His poetic experimentation is intriguing in the light of developments around mid-century because he effectively rejected these developments by cutting '**Empedocles on Etna**' from his 1853 collection, criticizing Clough's experiments in form (in *The Bothie of Tober-na-Vuolich* and *Amours de voyage*), refusing to read Alexander Smith, and expressing distaste for *Maud* and for Barrett Browning, whom he described in 1858 as 'hopelessly confirmed in her aberration from health, nature, beauty and truth'.[6] Arnold came from a different poetic background. His family linked him to Wordsworth and to John Keble, his education to Rugby, where ideals of Christian manliness were being formed under the influence of his father, and to Oxford, which he attended at the height of the conflict over Tractarianism. The culture of the heart which he experienced and assessed in his poetry, drawn from these backgrounds, was in many respects distinct from that encountered by other poets in this study.

While earlier chapters located the heart in relation to medicine, poetics, and gender, this chapter places Arnold's poetry in the context of the religious heart, and more precisely in relation to High Anglican values. Arnold stands at the meeting point of three traditions in Victorian Christianity: his father's Broad Church faith, which had some points in common with Evangelicalism and involved a liberal toleration for other creeds and denominations; the High Church religion of Tractarian Oxford, represented by his godfather John Keble; and the doubt and loss of faith which became an increasing topic of discussion after mid-century, and which affected many of his contemporaries and friends, including Clough. Arnold's poetry is hesitant about subscribing to any one doctrine, but it draws its agonizing over feeling and affect from a combination of the high valuation of emotion—located and experienced in the heart—found in each of these traditions, and the fear that such emotion is now lost. His poetry asks questions about faith, feeling, and faith in feeling which contemporary religious thinkers were debating. Should faith be based on an emotional heartfelt apprehension rather than intellectual assent? Where do our emotions and feelings come from and can we trust them? If faith is reliant upon feeling, how can it be expressed and conveyed to others, or is it necessarily personal and incommunicable?

The heart has of course always been a significant religious symbol, representing the location of God and of faith within the human body, and during the nineteenth century these traditional connotations became increasingly important as the rational and intellectual framework of Christian belief crumbled. The heart (if it could be trusted) seemed to offer a bulwark against doubt by providing comprehensible proof of faith on an individual level. The individual's felt experience of God's presence in his or her heart could not be easily challenged. Evangelicalism gave added impetus to the religious and biblical tradition of the feeling heart by emphasizing it as the site of a regenerate faith and the medium for a personal relationship with Christ. William James, in his classic work on religious faith, used a case study of Stephen Bradley's Evangelical conversion from 1829 to illustrate the role of emotional excitement in religious belief:

> At first, I began to feel my heart beat very quick all on a sudden, which made me at first think that perhaps something is going to ail me, though I was not alarmed for I felt no pain. My heart increased in its beating, which soon convinced me that it was the Holy Spirit from the effect it had on me.[7]

Palpitation is initially taken here as a potential symptom of sickness, before the reading shifts to a religious interpretation. Physical responses, which seem to take place in the heart independently of the rest of the body and the mind, are a signal of God's presence; for this speaker, it seems self-explanatory that such heartfelt effects must be spiritual in origin. Isaac Taylor, brother of the popular Evangelical children's poets Jane and Anne Taylor and himself a widely read Evangelical writer, argued in his *Natural History of Enthusiasm* (also from 1829) that 'Divine energy' manifested itself in two ways, corresponding to mind and body, and that:

> As the one kind of Divine energy does not display its presence by convulsive or capricious irregularities, but by the unnoticed vigour and promptitude of the functions of life, so the other energy cannot, without irreverence, be thought of as making itself felt by extra-natural impulses, or sensitive shocks upon the intellectual system; but must rather be imagined as an equable pulse of life, throbbing from within and diffusing softness, sensibility and force throughout the soul.[8]

The first kind of energy, felt in the body, corresponds to the healthy motions of heart and lungs, processes which ensure the continuation of life and operate without conscious thought. Taylor's book contrasts with Bradley's account in that it sets out to counteract the valorization of excessive emotion and sensibility as symptoms or products of faith, in a deliberate response to the trend towards 'enthusiasm' in the early nineteenth century. His metaphor of faith as a steady and calming pulse is common in devotional writings and hymns of the period. 'Speak to my warring passions: Peace! I Say to my trembling heart: Be still!', wrote Charles Wesley in the late eighteenth century.[9] William Cowper, on the other hand, begs for an access of feeling:

> O make this heart rejoice, or ache;
>   Decide this doubt for me;
> And if it be not broken, break,
>   And heal it, if it be.[10]

Wesley and Cowper follow a standard Biblical trope whereby feelings of doubt and fear are displaced onto the heart, which is then accused of hindering the whole man. The heart is the aspect of the body, or self, on which God acts directly. Cowper's 'doubt' is ambiguous: either doubt of God's presence, which would be resolved by any sense of Him in the heart, doubt as to whether the speaker's heart deserves to be made to rejoice or to ache, or perhaps doubt as to whether the heart itself is capable of feeling. Such 'introspective, physically intimate' language, describing the relationship between Christ and the speaker in terms of body and blood, became gradually unacceptable in mainstream churches as the century progressed, if still popular outside them.[11] Christopher Wordsworth, brother of the poet and a High Church Anglican, later summed up this attitude when he described Evangelical language such as 'Let me to thy bosom fly' as 'inexpressibly shocking', a comment which suggests that his shock is related to the implication that God or Christ possesses a physical body, a 'bosom', and could be embraced.[12]

If nineteenth-century Evangelicalism introduced the discourse of the feeling heart from the 'low' branch of the Church, from the other extreme came an increased concentration on the heart in Roman Catholicism. The Society of the Sacred Heart was officially founded in 1800 and granted a mandate from the Pope in 1826. In 1856 the Feast of the Sacred Heart was extended to the whole Church.[13] The subsequent emphasis on Christ's wounded, fleshly heart doubtless contributed to Anglican writers' anxiety about dwelling on the heart in their own writings. Henry Manning, who had moved from Evangelicalism to Tractarianism before converting, wrote in 1873 that '[T]he heart of Jesus is a heart of flesh—a heart taken from the substance of His Blessed Mother—a symbol, indeed, because it best symbolizes and manifests the eternal love of God; but it is more than this, it is also a reality'.[14] The heart is a means of summing up Christ's humanity, and so its flesh and blood materiality needs to be stressed. Hopkins, another Tractarian convert, was more anxious to play down the naked physicality of Christ's heart, defensively arguing that:

> The heart, I say, is agreed to be one of the noble or honourable members of the body. There would no doubt be something revolting in seeing the heart alone, all naked and bleeding, torn from the breast; but that is not in question here: Christ's heart is lodged within his sacred frame, and there alone is worshipped. And considered as within the breast, who is there however truly or delicately, however even falsely or affectedly modest who ever thought it shame to speak of the human heart?[15]

Hopkins uses the heart's status as a literary and cultural symbol to argue that it is more than a physical organ and hence can be discussed without a shameful focus on the body itself. 'Revolting' introduces a sense of distaste for the physical heart even as Hopkins attempts to deny it. There is an air here of protesting too much, as he apparently implies that discussing the heart *could* be immodest.

The heart's all-purpose currency as a religious image also meant that it could be used by those who were not necessarily Christian, in Establishment terms, to express a more secular and generalized faith. 'Feel it in thy heart, and then say whether it is of God! This is Belief, all else is Opinion,' wrote Carlyle at a climactic moment of *Sartor Resartus* (1833-4).[16] In a note from his time at Cambridge, possibly addressed to Tennyson, Arthur Hallam commented: 'With respect to prayer, you ask how am I to distinguish the operations of God in me from motions in my own heart? Why should you distinguish them, or how do you know there is any distinction?'[17] Susan Shatto and Marion Shaw note that in the original manuscript draft of the *Memoir* [*Alfred Lord Tennyson: A Memoir* (1901)] there are quotation marks around 'from motions in my own heart', suggesting that these might have been Tennyson's own words, and therefore implying that he had expressed doubt about the link between God and the heart which Hallam supports here.[18] Hallam's response and Carlyle's contemporary assertion both give feeling and emotion, located in the heart, the status of religious acts. These extracts give the impression that the writer is testing the motions of their heart to see whether they are sufficiently Christian. But this assumes that he or she is capable of making such a distinction. Hallam's comment once again implies that God could be present in the physical self, not simply metaphorically located in the heart as a spiritual site. He may then be guilty of the transgression warned of by the philosophical and medical writer William Newnham, in his discussion of the responsive heart:

> It can scarcely be necessary to caution the unwary or the captious reader against the *abuse* which may be made of this physical agency, so as to *mis*-represent the operations of the Holy Spirit of God . . . as blended with, or equivalent to, the mere impulses of *animal feeling*.[19]

Casual correlations of God and 'my own heart', Newman suggests, might be dangerous, in associating spirituality with a fallible, undependable human organ and thus privileging individual feeling over external authority.

The heart was the basis of appeal when rational proof of Christianity seemed lost. 'All my conviction is but faith, and it proceeds from the heart, and not from the understanding', wrote the influential German philosopher and alleged atheist Johann Fichte.[20] The heart underpins Ludwig Feuerbach's controversial *The Essence of Christianity* (1841), in which he argues for sympathy, a religion of love, and identification with Christ as human; just as it also serves as an important image in the secular humanism of George Eliot, his translator. Feuerbach's imagery again suggests that he is considering the actual physical heart as well as the heart as spiritual symbol:

> As the action of the arteries drives the blood into the extremities, and the action of the veins brings it back again, as life in general consists of a perpetual systole and diastole; so is it in religion. In the religious systole man propels his own nature from himself, he throws himself outward; in the religious diastole he receives the rejected nature into his heart again.[21]

The pulsation of the heart and movements of the circulation provide a parallel for religious feeling. As in studies of poetic rhythm, this links physical, human processes to the Divine. Feuerbach sums up his argument about the significance of human feeling and emotion in religion by stating, 'The truly religious man unhesitatingly assigns his own feelings to God.'[22] This again implies that religion is purely a matter of personal feeling; there can be no external check on whether God is inspiring the individual or not. Following these continental thinkers, Francis Newman (John Henry Newman's brother) wrote in *Phases of Faith* (1850), his defence of rationalism and historical criticism of the Bible, that the prerequisite for faith was '*the heart's belief in the sympathy of God with individual man*'.[23] Personal feelings and perceptions of sympathetic warmth, located in the heart, could not be disproved—which produces a dichotomy wherein the heart is simultaneously an unassailable and an unstable basis on which to rest religious belief.

Such use of the heart to defend what would have appeared to members of the Anglican Establishment as infidelity and near-heretical questioning of tradition and authority provides some reason why High Church poets and theologians, including those writers who influenced Arnold most strongly in his youth, were deeply suspicious of discussing the heart and of appearing to rely on it as a guide, in either poetry or religion. For the leading poets and theologians of the Oxford Movement—Keble, John Henry Newman, Edward Pusey, and Isaac Williams—the heart remains essential to faith, but only if it is shaped and disciplined by God and the Church rather than dictating faith itself. While recognizing their own debts to Evangelicalism (the childhood faith of many Tractarians) it was precisely the kind of interpretation of and reliance upon physical and emotional experience offered by Cowper's hymns and in accounts such as Stephen Bradley's that these writers deplored. Edward Pusey complained in 1838, in a letter on Dr Arnold, that the false ingredient in Arnold's liberal Broad Church theories was the Evangelical tendency to look to the feelings 'as something in themselves, something to be analysed, used as a criterion of the spiritual state'.[24] Newman expanded on this in his comments on Evangelicalism:

> There is a widely, though irregularly spread School of doctrine among us, within and without the Church, which aims at and professes peculiar piety as directing its attention to the heart itself, not to anything external to us, whether creed, actions or ritual. I do not hesitate to assert that this doctrine is based upon error, that it is really a specious form of trusting man rather than God.[25]

Rather than allowing 'heart' to encompass a vague and nebulous realm of feeling, Newman emphasizes that the heart is intrinsically human ('the heart *itself*') and is therefore, in his terms, unreliable. While 'certain dispositions of the heart', as Isaac Williams put it, are necessary for the reception of faith, these dispositions are formed by church duties, which create an appropriate framework for experiencing and understanding feelings, rather than being naturally part of the heart, whether the latter is considered as a physical or spiritual site.[26]

Clough, writing to a friend in 1838 about being at Oxford at the height of the Tractarian movement, remarked:

> And it is no harm but rather good to give oneself up a little to hearing Oxford people, and admiring their good points, which lie, I suppose, principally in all they hold in opposition to the Evangelical portion of society—the benefit and beauty and necessity of forms—the ugliness of feelings put on unnaturally soon and consequently kept up by artificial means, ever strained and never sober.[27]

Clough accurately defines the oppositional stance of Tractarianism, its attempt to stem the flood of 'feelings' in religion. As he notes, Tractarians saw this appeal to feeling as 'strained', false, even embarrassing, an unpardonable giving way to sentiment. 'Check every rising feeling at once,' Pusey bluntly advised a correspon-

dent in 1844.[28] The use of 'forms' restrains feeling by incorporating it into a traditional structure, just as poetic form contains in this sense the emotions of a poem. Clough and his correspondent, J. P. Gell, were debating at this point whether the exposure of feeling in poetry could ever be justified. Gell asserts, defensively, that poets have 'a certain manliness, which takes away from their public display all that unpleasant appearance of sophistication'. 'Sophistication' might well be equivalent to keeping up feelings 'by artificial means'. The question of whether (male) poets should write from and of personal feeling is, Gell writes, 'linked to that of "relating experience" in religious affairs'.[29] He associates the writing of poetry with religious self-expression, and implies that both might be incompatible with manly Christian reserve. Excessive religious feeling or enthusiasm was (as we have seen with other forms of intense feeling) tainted with effeminacy, creating another potential source of anxiety or embarrassment about heartfelt revelation.

Charlotte Yonge's anecdote about Keble's correction to her novel *Heartsease* is well known: 'The chief alteration I remember was that a sentence was erased as "coarse", in which Theodora said she really had a heart, though some people thought it was only a machine for pumping blood.'[30] Keble might have objected to the description of the heart as mechanism, but it seems more probable that he was alarmed by a female character referring directly to her physical heart. The smallest association of the heart with physicality is still assumed to verge on indecency. Over-hasty discussion of the heart's feelings, Keble's censorship suggests, could shock the reader, besides exposing the writer to the shame of having shared what should be private. To insist on the heart's emotion is impolite and unfeminine. Keble's correction to Yonge's work also fits with the key Tractarian doctrine of 'Reserve', associated both with Keble's theories and with his personal actions and habits. Reserve, a concept codified by Isaac Williams in his two tracts on the subject, initially referred to the process by which religious revelation is withheld until the individual is prepared to receive it. As a general idea, however, it came to be interpreted in terms of the need for self-control and caution in personal expression. The difficulties of expression, plus the possibility that emotional self-revealings could become out of control, were such that it was preferable to exercise reserve in describing feeling, particularly though not exclusively when that feeling related to religion.

Reserve was frequently imagined in terms of preventing the heart from eluding the control of mind and will. As Pusey wrote in a sermon on the vacillations of faith: 'The heart may, and must, rise and sink; we can, by God's grace, control it, hold it down, keep it outwardly still, hinder it from having any wrong vent; we cannot hush its beatings.'[31] 'Still' here does not mean 'motionless'—the heart cannot be still except in death—but is used in the archaic sense of 'soft, subdued', like the 'still small voice' speaking through the storm in 1 Kings 19: 12. 'Outwardly' is also important. Pusey does not imply that strong emotion can be avoided but that it should be repressed lest it become visible to others. This extract beautifully sums up a widespread Tractarian attitude. It is not that the heart should not play a part in faith—this is impossible, if man 'cannot hush' it—but that this part must be controlled. Pusey continues by assuring his listeners that once the heart is under God's command: 'Thy heart will still rise and sink; but it will rise and sink, not restlessly, nor waywardly, not in violent gusts of passion; but, whether rising or sinking . . . resting in stillness on the ocean of the Love of God.'[32] The heart is a wilful organ needing to be disciplined by God, lest it become prey to dangerous passions. Keble's immensely popular book of religious verse *The Christian Year* (1827) similarly uses repeated imagery of the wayward heart being calmed or comforted by God's will. The 'untuned heart' the poet brings to God in his opening 'Dedication' is gradually tuned in the course of *The Christian Year*, as the speaker subjects himself to God and asks Him to provide peace for body and mind: 'The languid pulses Thou canst tell, | The nerveless spirit tune.'[33] Keble shares Pusey's view that the excitable, throbbing heart is something to be avoided rather than sought. Addressing the heart in 'Seventh Sunday after Trinity', he writes:

> Sweetly thy sickening throbs are ey'd
> By the kind Saviour at thy side;
> For healing and for balm e'en now thine hour is come.
>
> (16-18)

'Sickening' potentially disturbs the metrical pattern if it is not elided. Such throbbing is 'sickening' because it might create heartsickness, Keble suggests, but there is also a sense that observing or feeling the heart's palpitation is distasteful. Anything other than a sobering and steady pulsation is regarded with misgiving. Later in the poem, Keble writes of 'The curse of lawless hearts, the joy of self-control' (56). As I have argued elsewhere, the process of regulating the heart in time with God's will in Keble's writing takes place through rhythm as well as content, as each poem underlines its conservative sentiments by returning to a reassuringly controlled beat.[34] Clough, who, like Arnold, was very familiar with Keble's poetry, echoes this outlook and that of Pusey in an unpublished poem: 'But thou, O human heart of mine, | Be still, contain thyself, and bear' ('In a London Square', 7-8). It also recurs throughout the poetry of Christina Rossetti, in which the heart is repeatedly admonished and instructed in calmness and self-discipline. Diane D'Amico, for instance, has noted that in Rossetti's copy of *The Christian Year* she chose to underline many of Keble's references to the heart and its sufferings, suggesting that she felt these had some personal relevance to her, as a High Church advocate, a poet, and perhaps particularly as a female poet.[35]

To examine how the principle of exercising reserve with regard to the heart operated in poetry, I want to turn to two contrasting sonnets, one by Richard Trench, written in 1838 after he had adopted High Church principles, and one by Frederick Faber, an Oxford Movement poet who later converted to Roman Catholicism, from his 1840 collection. Trench's sonnet strongly expresses the need for caution in revealing the heart:

> A wretched thing it were, to have our heart
> Like a broad highway or a populous street,
> Where every idle thought has leave to meet,
> Pause, or pass on as in an open mart;
> Or like some road-side pool, which no nice art
> Has guarded that the cattle may not beat
> And foul it with a multitude of feet,
> Till of the heavens it can give back no part.
> But keep thou thine a holy solitude,
> For he who would walk there, would walk alone;
> He who would drink there, must be first endued
> With single right to call that stream his own;[36]

Making the heart, the most private and intimate organ, into a marketplace has connotations of prostitution, besides those of simple buying and selling, as does the image of a pool fouled by animals. The heart's blood is soiled and muddied, perhaps, because vice could (as humoral theory attested) alter the constitution of the blood. Trench's sonnet ends with an exhortation to the reader:

> Keep thou thine heart, close-fastened, unrevealed,
> A fenced garden and a fountain sealed.
>
> (13-14)

This imagery, drawn from the lover in the Song of Solomon, suggests parallels between virginity or celibacy and the preservation of the heart's privacy. The heart should be withdrawn from the world, guarded. In this sonnet it is the set form itself, the 'nice art' of the sonnet, which does the guarding, fencing the heart in. The act of keeping the heart 'close-fastened', however, might also create tension in the writing of poetry. Keble argued in his influential lectures as Oxford Professor of Poetry that poetry provided a 'safety-valve' for feelings that might otherwise be mentally and physically dangerous, including religious feeling:

> [N]othing takes such entire possession of the human heart, and, in a way concentrates its feeling, as the thought of God and an eternity to come: . . . nothing so powerfully impels it, sadly and anxiously, to look round on all sides for remedy and relief. As a result of this, Religion freely and gladly avails itself of every comfort and assistance which Poetry might afford.[37]

For Keble, the heart inevitably seeks release from oppressive feeling, and it is in the regulated form of poetry that this release is best found. Poetry can reassure the poet (and implicitly the reader) of the secure prom-ise of Christianity, removing doubt and fear. While it stems from the heart, however, it must still, as Trench's poem advises, maintain a stance of dignity and self-control: it is both expressive and carefully managed.

Written only two years after Trench's poem, Faber's sonnet 'The Confessional' exposes the difficulties of this position and the tensions between reserve and ex-pression in Tractarian poetics. The poet agonizes about his revelation of his heart to an intimate male friend:

> Now thou hast seen my heart. Was it too near?
> Didst thou recoil from the o'erpowering sight;
> That vision of a scarred and seamed soul?
> Ah! yes: thy gentle eyes were filled with fear
> When looks and thoughts broke out from my control,
> Bursting themselves a road with fiercest might—
> Wide-opening secret cells of foulest sin,
> And all that lurks in that dark place within!
> Well, be it so, dear friend! It was but right
> That thou shouldst learn where blossoms yet may
>   bless,
> And where for ever now there must be blight
> Riven with burning passion's torrent course,
> Shattered and splintered all with sin's mad force—
> Thou saw'st my heart, and did not love me less.[38]

'Heart' is used here as synonymous to 'soul', but the imagery of 'cells', rushing 'torrents', and the dark places within has physiological resonance, suggesting the depths of the body. The hint of something sinister lurking at the heart is similar to Coleridge's comment in *Aids to Reflection* (and Trench's early letter on that subject), although Faber takes this rhetoric to exhaus-tive extremes.[39] There are, as in Trench's poem, clear implications that the release of the heart's forces is con-nected with the exposure of passion—passion which, in this imagery, looks suspiciously sexual. Faber, an ex-treme partisan of Catholic Anglicanism who converted to Roman Catholicism in 1845, was unsurprisingly re-garded with some hesitation by its more restrained lead-ers, and himself demonstrated fears that his poems to his young male friends would be misinterpreted when he revised and cut them from later collections.[40] 'The Confessional' manages to abandon reserve entirely while agonizing over it. The speaker claims to fear self-revelation, and expects that it will induce distaste, even while being incapable of restraining himself from it. But the poem does react to Tractarian ideals of con-straint, order, and self-repression despite its excesses in that it is 'ruled' to some degree by its formal qualities, the regular rhyme scheme and metre. It flirts with the idea of containment through the sonnet structure and the iambic pentameter, yet uses a rhyme scheme (*abcacbddbebffe*) that does not fit into any established sonnet form. In the irruption of a rhyming couplet which does not rhyme with any other line ('Riven with burn-

ing passion's torrent course | Shattered and splintered all with sin's mad force') into the final quatrain, for in-stance, this sonnet is partially 'splintered', forced out of shape.

Faber's emphasis on the 'blight' at his heart might also have some bodily correlation in his own anxieties about his health. In 1842, he wrote to a close friend: 'I have had some frightening work at my heart, but medical exam. seems to have ascertained that there is no disease (structural) but that it was a confinement of mind caused by nervous excitement and overwork.'[41] Like Mark Pat-tison, Faber perceives himself as falling prey to the 'nervous excitement' caused by the fervid religious at-mosphere of Oxford controversies. Note also how he recognizes the difference between 'structural' and sym-pathetic disease: further evidence that the distinction was commonly known and discussed. Such comments feed into Faber's statements about his wayward heart and its lack of appropriate behaviour. Always concerned about his over-emotional disposition and propensity to-wards violent feeling, he commented after his conver-sion that the strictness of Roman Catholicism might help to tame the heart: 'The red cross on my rough habit must keep that little beater down, and bid it beat, not less ardently, but for Jesus only.'[42] As both Trench's and Faber's poems show, the focus on heartfelt emotion in Anglican-inflected religious discourse led to intense interest in it, and ambiguous responses whereby the revelation of emotion clashes with its containment. Whether Faber's poem 'gives healing relief to secret mental emotion, yet without detriment to modest re-serve: and while giving scope to enthusiasm, yet rules it with order and due control', as Keble prescribed, is un-certain, to say the least.[43] The heart has implicitly defied these prescriptions.

* * *

In an unpublished poem, 'Whence are ye, vague desires', Clough sums up the ambiguities surrounding the conjunction of the spiritual heart with the physical, material organ by asking whether these desires are:

> A message from the blest
>   Or bodily unrest;
> A call to heavenly good
>   Or fever in the blood.
>
> (20-4)

As in Hallam's comment or Newnham's warning this suggests the difficulty of separating religious impulses from the pathological. Clough's poem is both light and serious, for the different possibilities of interpreting these 'vague desires' would lead to very different ends. By the 1840s, the decade when Clough and Arnold at-tended Oxford and published their first poems, the in-fluence of the Oxford Movement was fading, with a large number of high-profile conversions to Roman Catholicism (Newman and Faber among them), and the rise of doubt as an 'observable and much-discussed cultural phenomenon', perhaps best exemplified by the publication of J. A. Froude's *The Nemesis of Faith* in 1849 and its subsequent burning in Oxford.[44] A poem from the same year by Clough, implicitly addressed to God, asks: 'Be thou but there,—in soul and heart, | I will not ask to feel thou art' ('υμνος αυμνος' ('A hymn, yet not a hymn'), 39-40). Although this initially seems to indicate confidence in God's presence, there is some ambiguity about the speaker's motives, one of which might be the fear that if he did make this request, he would be unable to feel, too hardened to recognize the sensation of faith. By not requiring a response from God, moreover, the speaker hints at his anxiety that there might be no answer to his demands. If God's presence is not felt, experienced as a reality, what is the difference between faith and doubt? And even if God's presence is felt, Clough's poems suggest, we might not be able to trust our own sensations.

Both Clough and Arnold's poems written during and after their Oxford years circle around these issues, featuring heroes who are afraid to trust their emotional responses or bemoan their inability to feel, whether in relation to faith or romance. Arnold's poems in particular stage a series of laments for the loss of feeling in his age, a loss which he associates with the inaccessibility and insensibility of the heart and its potential sickness. The 'fierce necessity to feel' (**'Iseult of Brittany'**, 124), Arnold's poems argue, painfully remains, while the power which would enable feeling—a power strongly associated with poetry itself—has been taken. In **'Memorial Verses'**, written on Wordsworth's burial in 1850, Arnold recalls a time when poets were physicians to the human condition: Goethe diagnosed its ills and Wordsworth's poetry soothed and 'loosed the heart' (47), in the cathartic relief identified by the poetics of Keble and others. This time, however, is past and no new poet has arisen with the same capacities: 'Others will strengthen us to bear— | But who, ah! who, will make us feel?' (66-7). As he remarks in a notebook entry:

> The misery of the present age is not in the intensity of men's suffering—but in their incapacity to suffer, joy, feel at all, wholly & profoundly—in their having their susceptibility eternally agac´εe by a continual dance of ever-changing objects.[45]

Throughout the notebooks and the poetry Arnold discusses 'feeling' obsessively but with great ambiguity, as something his poems both long for and shrink away from. In **'The New Sirens'**, for example, he writes:

> 'Come', you say, 'the brain is seeking,
> While the sovran heart is dead;

> Yet this gleaned, when Gods were speaking,
> Rarer secrets than the toiling head.

> 'Come', you say, 'opinion trembles,
> Judgment shifts, convictions go;
> Life dries up, the heart dissembles—
> Only, what we feel, we know.'

> (77-84)

The dichotomy between brain and heart, seen in many Victorian poems, is frequently stated in this way in Arnold's poetry. That is, he writes that the heart would be and has in the past been the preferred guide, but is now dead or at least impotent and has therefore given way to the head. Allott supplies the note: 'Arnold never subscribed to the extreme Romantic view of the "new sirens" that "Only, what we feel, we know" (l. 84), but he believed with many Victorians that it was a mistake to exalt "head" over "heart".'[46] 'Only, what we feel, we know', however, is potentially ironic, for if the heart 'dissembles' how can we trust in the truth of feeling? Arnold attempts to draw together affect and intellect, but if the heart is dead or lying there is no obvious location for affect. Moreover, the comma after 'Only' suggests a possible reading of 'we' as exclusive rather than inclusive, referring to the Sirens, 'what *we* feel, *we* know'. The succeeding lines, 'Hath your wisdom felt emotions? | Will it weep our burning tears?' (85-6), would then tempt (or taunt) the speaker of the poem by remarking on the inability of modern man to experience the emotional charge that the New Sirens offer, perhaps because he has become too intellectual. 'Your wisdom' and 'it' (rather than 'you') is distancing, and the combination of 'wisdom' and 'emotion' (concepts usually placed in opposition) itself seems to mock the physical/spiritual uncertainties and ambiguities of the rhetoric of feeling. 'Feeling' is the temptation held out to poets by these dubious representatives of passion and Romanticism, but the suggestion in **'The New Sirens'** is that to accept it would mean alienating oneself from the modern world, where feeling is not tenable—a tantalizing impossibility.

Arnold's poetry of the 1850s takes the heart as the organ of feeling and then laments the subject's inability to access, trust, or rely upon it. He seems to seek the security and reserve offered by Tractarian poetics, but is also fascinated by the poetry of sensation and affect, of spasms and palpitations, advocated by Hallam and practised by Keats, Shelley, Tennyson, and the spasmodic poets, among others. As a child, Arnold was taught to repeat lyrics from *The Christian Year,* and the influence of Keble's poetry, in which adherence to set principles and a steady beat is paramount, is clear in his own.[47] Arnold's conception of metre, as expressed in the Preface to **Merope** (1858), maintains the need for metre as a restraining force:

Powerful thought and emotion, flowing in strongly marked channels, make a stronger impression: this is the main reason why a metrical form is a more effective vehicle for them than prose: in prose there is more freedom, but, in the metrical form, the very limit gives a sense [of] precision and emphasis. The sense of emphatic distinctness in our impressions rises, as the thought and emotion swell higher and higher without overflowing their boundaries.[48]

The function of metre here is apparently not to damp down emotions but to enhance them, something like Wordsworth and Coleridge's accounts. A greater impact is made by the contrast between form and freedom than by freedom itself. Form is the passage or channel through which liquid feelings and thoughts can flow and by which they are controlled. This imagery might be related to Arnold's constant description of the hidden interior life as a river or stream, partly reminiscent of the circulation of blood in the body. The confidence with which Arnold states this theory in the late 1850s, however, is not quite borne out by his earlier poetry. Limits, in many of his poems, are both sought and rejected, form is simultaneously unsteady and carefully controlled, and the containment of emotion leads to its dissipation as often as its strength. An unfinished poem from his notebooks, in which the speaker considers retiring from the world, asks:

> Say, my father, does the tired
> Restless heart in this retreat
> Learn to know what it desired,
> Knowing, clasp it and securely beat?
>
> ('**To Meta: The Cloister**', 29-32)

The trochaic measure, falling to a graceful conclusion in the final extra foot of the last line, and the confident rhymes, indicate the safety which the heart is offered. Yet the metre is not regular tetrameter—each line ends on a stressed syllable, meaning that either the final beat is missing, left implicit, or the lines awkwardly consist of two or three trochees and an amphibrach. The beat here is not quite secure. The 'father' addressed is a monk, and this passage acts as a homage to Arnold's poetic and religious fathers: Keble, his godfather, and Newman, whom he described as one of the greatest influences on his life. But Arnold cannot quite share the Christian conviction that makes the renunciation of the world and of emotion in exchange for confidence and security worthwhile. The poem questions (in rhythm as well as content) rather than accepts. In '**The Second Best**', he writes:

> Moderate tasks and moderate leisure,
> Quiet living, strict-kept measure
> Both in suffering and in pleasure—
>   'Tis for this thy nature yearns.
>
> (1-4)

Measure here is indeed more strictly kept, as, assuming an elision on 'moderate', the first three lines follow a trochaic tetrameter pattern. The poem continues by advocating that man reject thinking and reading in favour of obedience to an 'impulse, from the distance | Of his deepest, best existence' (21-2). 'Impulse' hovers between suggesting a physiological basis, a 'pulse' of feeling, and a religious or moral drive, perhaps stimulated by God. In 1873, Arnold argued in *Literature and Dogma* that 'native, instantaneous, mechanical impulses' should be controlled and regulated by 'Conduct'. Describing an impulse as both 'native' (presumably in the sense of 'natural') and 'mechanical' recalls language used to discuss the heartbeat. Arnold attempts to combine the mechanical and organic concepts of bodily impulses in one. Given that he associates the control exercised by 'Conduct' with the very 'object of religion', then the aim of religion becomes to some extent the regulation of impulses.[49] Yet his earlier poetry is again deeply divided over whether this is something to be sought or rejected. The pointed title of '**The Second Best**' leaves it open to debate whether the 'second best' option is the 'moderate' life which the poet feels he should espouse, or more generally the compromise the modern world demands from him, in that he yearns for a world of passion and sensation while recognizing the impossibility and undesirability of achieving it.

Many of Arnold's best-known poems represent this by simultaneously celebrating and rejecting a surrender to 'impulse'. In '**Isolation: To Marguerite**' the speaker laments his heart's lapse into feeling:

> Farewell!—and thou, thou lonely heart,
> Which never yet without remorse
> Even for a moment didst depart
> From thy remote and sphered course
> To haunt the place where passions reign—
> Back to thy solitude again!
>
> (13-18)

The 'remote' course is equivalent to the distanced perspective Arnold advises for the poet in '**Resignation**', where his vision of the poet suggests withdrawal from earthly affairs:

> The poet, to whose mighty heart
> Heaven doth a quicker pulse impart,
> Subdues that energy to scan
> Not his own course, but that of man.
>
> (144-7)

Arnold here follows the common notion that the poet's heart is more sensitive, but no sooner has he introduced this idea than he turns, at the line-ending, to the definite assertion that this pulse is 'subdued'. The poet's energies are thus turned outwards rather than inwards, possessing a wider scope than individual feeling. In order to fulfil the correct conditions of poetic creation, this suggests, the speaker of **'Isolation'** would necessarily have to return to his 'solitude'. But while he commands and berates the 'lonely heart' and its 'conscious thrill of shame' (19) at stooping to this level, there is also a sense of loss and regret in **'Isolation'**, as the heart's failure to find a reciprocated love confirms the speaker's solitude. Human sympathy is fallible and in this poem at least there is no alternative source of sympathy in God.

Even while Arnold repeatedly rejects the 'quicker pulse' and 'passions' of human feeling, the fact that his poems constantly return to such imagery and emphasize the speaker's failure to subdue his heart might suggest that he recognizes this struggle is itself 'poetic'. Several of his poems hint at a cautious adherence to the idea that great poetry necessarily stems from the heart, from passionate, restless feeling. In **'A Summer Night'** the poet is asked (or asks himself):

> Hast thou then still the old unquiet breast,
> Which neither deadens into rest,
> Nor ever feels the fiery glow
> That whirls the spirit from itself away,
> But fluctuates to and fro,
> Never by passion quite possessed
> And never quite benumbed by the world's sway?
>
> (27-33)

These lines are uneasy in their distribution of stresses, shifting between tetrameter and pentameter lines, and the rhythm becomes seriously unsteady in the truncated line 'But fluctuates to and fro', where 'fluctuates' disturbs the beat because it adds the possibility of an extra syllable. These lines are also unsettled because of the recurrence of two unstressed beats at different points within the line, e.g. 'Néver bў pássioň', 'bў thě wórld's swáy'. Such fluctuation is the reverse of the calm mind and body of the ideal Anglican religious poet. 'You are too content to *fluctuate,*' wrote Arnold to Clough in 1853, perhaps accusing him of a failing which he himself feared.[50] The lines vacillate because, it seems, Arnold is again unsure of the answer which is being sought—should the poet seek to have an 'unquiet breast', or reject it? Which is preferable, passion or numbness? The middle ground which Arnold seeks in such poems as **'Resignation'**, where the poet can calmly withdraw from individual passions to a clear vantage point, no longer exists. As in many of Arnold's poems, the poet's passion here is described from a spectator position, in the second person, not as if it inhabited the speaker's body. Arnold's 'fiery glow', 'spirit', and so forth are not obviously physical. Whereas Barrett Browning's ability to surprise (and sometimes scandalize) the reader comes from the lurking possibil-

ity that her images can be read literally and in physical terms, Arnold's imagery eschews a literal reading. The passage thereby seems more detached. It is as though Arnold introduces this passage into the poem to assure the reader that he is suffering the agonies and ecstasies of the poet, while avoiding the necessity to express them or own them himself. The description of the 'unquiet breast' is contained because it is voiced by an external force, and in the final line, it turns out to be more controlled than is apparent. 'Possessed' looks back to 'rest', and the world's 'sway' is a pun: while it seems to fit with 'fluctuates', 'sway' equally suggests stern command. What seemed wavering suddenly appears, in another light, rigidly fixed.

In common with many of the poets discussed earlier, Arnold's poems gesture towards symptoms of heart disease in that the heart as represented here inevitably veers between oversensitive palpitation and acute sensation and coldness and hardness—all potentially signs of either organic or sympathetic disease. He is uncertain, however, whether viewing a disturbed heart as a valuable poetic gift is possible, and invariably discusses the heart in a curiously remote tone of mingled desire, anxiety, and envy. A. Dwight Culler notes a comment in a letter to Clough, in which Arnold paraphrases Hamlet: 'but thou'dst not think, Horatio, how ill it is here—'.[51] 'Again the dash', Culler comments, 'to indicate that, if the reader wishes to supply the words "about the heart" he may, but the writer himself would be embarrassed by so direct a reference to that palpitating organ.'[52] Culler is right to identify embarrassment as a force here. Arnold is, almost coyly, shying away from overt self-revelation, evincing the kind of reticence shown by Keble's editing of Yonge's novel, as opposed to the self-dramatization of a poet like Byron, whom Arnold describes as displaying 'the pageant of his bleeding heart' throughout Europe (**'Stanzas from the Grande Chartreuse'**, 136). But Arnold's hesitation to mention the heart also dramatizes his stance of distance from it: the quotation trails off before it can definitely indicate the heart's problems. Of course, this serves to draw attention to the heart's absence and so gives it an important imaginative presence.

Critics have considered the 'buried life', a concept which Arnold repeatedly returns to in his poems of the 1850s, as something without a specific location or frame of reference, an ambiguous 'hidden ground within' or an empty linguistic construct, a reference to concealed desire.[53] Arnold is writing in a tradition, however, where the void within the breast is an established literary trope connected to heartsickness and the inability to feel, and his recurring imagery of the hidden interior self is closer to this tradition than has been noted. It seems clear from his poems that the buried life not only has a definite imaginative location in the heart, but is itself analogous to it. At first, for example, **'The Buried Life'** avoids using the word 'heart':

> But there's a something in this breast,
> To which thy light words bring no rest,
> And thy gay smiles no anodyne.
>
> (6-8)

In the same way as Arnold's reference to Hamlet, the odd phrase '*a* something' highlights this avoidance, because the indefinite article points towards one object, something material. The phrasing might hint that the poet's heart is so far removed that he can no longer even confidently identify it as such, or state that he possesses a heart at all. Meanwhile, the iambic tetrameter pulses steadily behind his words. 'Anodyne' is a term Arnold also uses of Tennyson's *In Memoriam* in **'The Scholar-Gipsy'** (190), and which he associates with the (futile) attempt to produce affective poetry. **'The Buried Life'** continues:

> Alas! is even love too weak
> To unlock the heart, and let it speak?
> Are even lovers powerless to reveal
> To one another what indeed they feel?
>
> (12-15)

The slight jar to the metre caused by the extra syllable in 'unlock', requiring readers to perform their own elision ('T'unlock'), could signal the resistance of the heart to being opened. The addition of an extra foot in the last two lines here, with the qualifiers 'even' and 'indeed', moves away from the four-beat rhythm and into a more varied measure, as the line lengths of the poem and the iambic pulse begin to waver and stumble. Arnold denies the commonplace that lovers understand each other's hearts, a denial that means that all men and women, no matter how intimate, are banned from comprehension of another and self-revelation. Poetry, as Keble argued, should provide an outlet. Yet in **'The Buried Life'** the lack of communication seems to refer to the act of writing the poem itself. Arnold as poet cannot convey what he feels, he can only discuss the general impossibility of feeling. For Keble and Newman, in addition, God's sympathy for and understanding of men's feelings serves as a replacement for human comprehension and a higher good; whereas for Arnold the lack of human sympathy equals the removal of the only possible outlet for feeling. David DeLaura convincingly argues that Arnold secularizes Newman's idea of 'inwardness', faith dwelling in the heart, which means that religion is no longer available, in this poem, as an external frame of reference into which the inward life can be absorbed.[54]

The four references to the heart (plus that 'something') in the first twenty-eight lines of **'The Buried Life'** naturally suggest the possibility that the 'unregarded river of our life' (39) that runs 'through the deep recesses of our breast' (38) is akin to the blood and the circulation. The dual movements of 'eddying' and 'driving' on in this poem could relate to the pulsation of the heart as well as the motion of the stream. Physiological texts commonly use similar imagery. The medical writer H. M. Hughes, for example, deploys an extended metaphor of streams and rivers throughout his lengthy discussion of the circulation.[55] Arnold equates tracking man's 'true, original course' with:

> A longing to inquire
> Into the mystery of this heart which beats
> So wild, so deep in us—to know
> Whence our lives come and where they go.
> And many a man in his own breast then delves,
> But deep enough, alas! none ever mines.
>
> (51-6)

The solution to all life is to be found in the beating heart, but again it recedes from knowledge. This seems slightly stilted and generalized, 'us' and 'his' rather than 'me' and 'mine'. The rhythm of these lines eddies, indicating restless enquiry rather than conclusion. Discovering the heart corresponds to finding the origins of the self and discovering the potential of truthful self-expression, the power not only to feel but to make words correspond with feelings:

> A bolt is shot back somewhere in our breast,
> And a lost pulse of feeling stirs again.
> The eye sinks inward, and the heart lies plain,
> And what we mean, we say, and what we would, we
>   know.
>
> (84-7)

Line 84 recalls the literal 'doors' or valves of the heart (which, in a diseased heart, threaten to become corroded and stop the circulation). The passive tense ('is shot back') gives no sense of how (or by whose agency) this release happens. The metre here becomes more regular, although the variation from iambic measure on 'Ănd ă lŏst pŭlse' suggests a slight disorder in pulsation, and line 87, longer by an extra foot and slowed down by the pauses created by the punctuation, is left uncertainly hanging on without a rhyme.

Arnold's use of rhythm echoes the uneasiness he feels about the heart. William Oram suggests, on **'The Scholar-Gipsy'**: 'What sets it off from most Romantic myths of self-division is its insistence that the loss of contact with one's deepest self is a means of protection', an insight which suggests that Arnold's denial of the buried life—of contact with the heart—may be a deliberate strategy.[56] In the light of his own fears about cardiac disease, for instance, dissociating the self from the heart's actions might be sensible. Trotter writes that 'Arnold hopes that the "buried life" of men could pace itself, could find respite from the insistent, jarring rhythms of the modern world.'[57] But Arnold's refusal to 'pace' his own lines steadily, in the rhythmical cross-currents of **'A Buried Life'**, indicates a partial rejection of this hope. It could also show that for Arnold it is less a hope than a fear, in that a rhythmically steady interior life would be devoid of the shocks and starts which form the poetic impulse. Assuming that he chooses his measures carefully, there is something almost defiant in his refusal to keep to a steady beat, his resistance to harmonious conclusions.

This is particularly evident in **'Empedocles on Etna'**, Arnold's long poem of 1852, which he later cut from the 1853 volume. His decision to do so was doubtless in part based on his worry that **'Empedocles'** would be read as a 'spasmodic' poem. It certainly shares many of the characteristics of Smith and Dobell's work, featuring a godlike speaker suffering from passion and near-insanity who laments his alienation from the world, a mixture of genres and forms, and a tendency to use or describe irregular measures. The 'jarring rhythms' of Empedocles' long speech to Pausanius are a good example:

> And we feel, day and night,
> The burden of ourselves—
> Well, then, the wiser wight
> In his own bosom delves,
> And asks what ails him so, and gets what cure he can.
>
> (I. ii. 127-31)

Or:

> Once read thy own breast right,
> And thou hast done with fears;
> Man gets no other light,
> Search he a thousand years.
> Sink in thyself! there ask what ails thee, at that shrine!
>
> (I. ii. 142-6)

The short quatrains seem self-contained and measured, reasoning, before the final line of each stanza disrupts the pattern. These long lines pivot back on themselves, requiring the reader to search the previous stanza for a rhyme. They create a sense of expansion, urgency in the alliteration and haste of phrases such as 'gets what cure he can', which is immediately succeeded by constraint as the lines are held back, checked. The trimeter of the quatrain and hexameter of the long lines reject both common measure and the straightforward iambic pentameter. Empedocles uses the rhetoric of the heart with scorn and bitterness, mocking the idea of heart as 'shrine' and as cure. His imagery of 'delving' in the bosom recalls **'The Buried Life'**, an allusion which ironizes Empedocles' reference by suggesting that there is little cure to be found, because 'deep enough, alas!

none ever mines'. Both poems imagine the 'breast' as a subterraneous region ('sink in thyself') of caverns, rivers, and veins of ore, dark and dangerous.

Empedocles used to be a healer, as Pausanius sadly remarks:

> He could stay swift diseases in old days,
> Chain madmen by the music of his lyre,
> Cleanse to sweet airs the breath of poisonous streams,
>
> (I. i. 115-17)

The affective healing power of Empedocles' music also makes him a model for the poet. Pausanius, himself a physician, links Empedocles' malady with the evil state of his times, but more so with 'some root of suffering in himself, | Some secret and unfollowed vein of woe' (I. i. 151-2). From having the power to cure, Empedocles has become trapped in an impotent interior life. He 'hears nothing but the cry of the torrents, | And the beating of his own heart' (II. 213-14). Over-attention to the heart's sounds and motions is, of course, a symptom if not a cause of disease, and even these 'torrents' could be an externalized representation of rushing blood. Empedocles' disordered circulation, 'the veins swell, | The temples tighten and throb there—' (II. 215-16), and pleas for more air have been compared to Arnold's own fears of heart disease. One medical writer notes that in angina pectoris, 'any exertion at once produces so anxious a desire for more air as can be expressed by no fitter term than the *air-hunger* of the Germans'.[58] Arnold wrote to Clough: '*congestion of the brain* is what we suffer from—I always feel it and say it—and cry for air like my own Empedocles.'[59] 'Congestion' is (as we have seen) an illness stemming from a rush of blood to the affected part, comparable to 'determination'. It is perhaps significant, too, that the historical Empedocles, who wrote on physiology as well as philosophy, argued that respiration and circulation were intimately linked, and that the heartbeat caused the motions of the lungs in breathing.[60]

Empedocles is thus sick at heart both actually and metaphorically. He traces man's progress in terms of the heart's decay, from the happiness of 'youthful blood' (I. ii. 352) to 'Our shivering heart is mined by secret discontent' (I. ii. 366), to:

> We pause; we hush our heart,
> And thus address the Gods:
> 'The world hath failed to impart
> The joy our youth forebodes,
> Failed to fill up the void which in our breasts we bear.'
>
> (I. ii. 372-6)

'Our heart' makes it seem that men share one communal heart, unless Empedocles is regally referring to himself in the third person, avoiding personal reference to his own heart. The speaking or clamouring heart in the first line is replaced by a void in line 376. 'Bear' can mean either to carry, or to suffer. 'Mining' the heart will only produce evidence of a prior loss and emptiness: while man sought to 'delve' into its riches, it has already been undermined. 'Once read thy own breast right | And thou hast done with fears' is in this sense ironic. What man discovers in his breast is a lack, an incapacity to feel and so an inability to fear—the kind of inability that leads to suicide. Empedocles' leap into the volcano is a surrender to this void, and hence to the passions inside himself, given that the volcano's flames and eruptions are themselves an established image of feelings warring within the self.

In Empedocles' account of man's ailments and attempted cures, one of the causes of sickness is, crucially, the frustration of being unable to choose one's own rhythm:

> Born into life!—we bring
> A bias with us here,
> And, when here, each new thing
>   Affects us we come near;
> To tunes we did not call our being must keep chime.
>
>   (I. ii. 192-6)

'Affect', Empedocles states, is outside man's control; we have no choice about how we are influenced. Two apparently contradictory responses to the world—instinctive and controlled—are juxtaposed here in a manner which once more recalls poetic debates about organic versus mechanical rhythm. But they turn out not to be contradictions, in that man is affected against his will, forced to react in certain ways, so that native impulses and even affect itself are part of a wider regulatory scheme, whether this is natural (physiological) or supernatural. While man seeks to impose his will on the world, 'Limits we did not set | Condition all we do' (I. ii. 184-5). The question that Empedocles cannot answer is, who did set these limits? Does their apparent existence prove the presence of the gods, or God?

Arnold wrote in his list of projects for 1849: 'Empedocles—refusal of limitation by the religious sentiment.'[61] One aspect of this refusal is the rejection of harmonious rhythm, the desire not to be contained by the measure of a possibly non-existent deity. Empedocles holds out the seductive possibility of accepting defeat: 'Man's measures cannot mete the immeasurable All' (I. ii. 341). Assuming an elision on 'th'imm-', this is one of the more harmonious long lines of this section. But he immediately counteracts, contemptuously, 'Fools!' (I. ii. 347). As there is no firm evidence that the gods exist, man's measure does not have a sure reference point or analogy and hence cannot be steady or peaceful, but is instead reflected in pointless physiologi-cal spasms and fluctuations. 'Nor does being weary prove he has where to rest' (I. ii. 351), Empedocles concludes, in a line which awkwardly rejects the iambic measure, demonstrating its own lack of restfulness. As in **'The Buried Life,'** the possibility of a respite from broken, hesitant rhythms is claimed as a comforting illusion, which the modern poet has perforce to reject. The end of **'Empedocles on Etna',** however, does not even allow the reader to have confidence in this rejection, because after Empedocles' agonized suicide the final lines of Callicles' hymn are perfectly rhymed and exactly equivalent in metre:

> The day in his hotness,
> The strife with the palm;
> The night in her silence,
> The stars in their calm.
>
>   (II. 465-8)

Does this harmony, continuing without Empedocles' disruptions, simply show the limitations of Callicles' outlook on the world, or might it indicate that Empedocles was wrong to reject the gods, that something persists below or around the broken rhythms of man? This is the question that Arnold's poems often seem to circle round, never quite providing a final answer.

Arnold's rejection of **'Empedocles on Etna'** as 'morbid', offering no hope or comfort, seems to suggest that he saw this vision of heartsickness and suicide as overly extreme. His preface famously argues that the purpose of poetry is to create pleasure, and through this morality.[62] This and his later criticism gives poetry a vital role in culture and civilization, but, as has often been remarked, there is a strong divide between the principles stated in the prose and those embodied in the earlier poems, with their repeated failures of sympathetic communication. His poetry of the 1850s strongly suggests that poetic affect and sympathy are fruitless and that the incapacity to feel anything healthy or good, any sense of connection to others—represented in the distant and diseased heart—is an inescapable component of modern life. The decay of religious belief means that Christianity cannot quite offer the desired security for the heart, and even if it did, this security might be stultifying rather than inspiring. Form as well as content contributes to the resulting oscillation between passionate involvement and extreme detachment in Arnold's poems. When in **'Stanzas from the Grande Chartreuse'** he recalls the passions of Shelley and Byron, he suggests that these have faded without trace and that time has not proven their worth. 'Have restless hearts one throb the less?' (144) because Shelley lived and sung? Arnold seems to invite a negative answer. His poems are the most expressive of all Victorian poetry in their descriptions of the poetic crisis which so many believed in, a crisis of endemic heartsickness, in which a culture of feeling seemed destroyed and the loss of faith provided no trustworthy external authority.

Notes

1. Henry Clutterbuck, *On the Proper Administration of Blood-Letting for the Prevention and Cure of Disease* (London: S. Highley, 1840), 56. Charles Williams, *The Pathology and Diagnosis of Diseases of the Chest,* 4th edn. (London: John Churchill, 1840), 233.

2. *Manchester Guardian,* 18 May 1888. Cited by A. Dwight Culler in *Imaginative Reason: The Poetry of Matthew Arnold* (New Haven: Yale University Press, 1966), 61.

3. To Mary Arnold, 25 Nov. [1852], Lang [Arnold, *The Letters of Matthew Arnold,* ed. Ceal Y. Lang, 6 vols. (Charlottesville, University Press of Virginia, 1996-2001)], i. 248.

4. To Jane Forster, 6 Dec. 1856, ibid. i. 348.

5. 'A Summer Night', 24; 'The River', 17; 'Stanzas in Memory of the Author of "Obermann"', 94.

6. To Frances du Quaire, 9 Feb. 1858, Lang, i. 383.

7. William James, citing Bradley, in *The Varieties of Religious Experience,* introd. Reinhold Niebuhr (New York: Simon & Schuster, 1997), 161.

8. Isaac Taylor, *Natural History of Enthusiasm* (London: Holdsworth & Ball, 1829), 63. Tennyson (and Hallam) were also familiar with Taylor's works. Eleanor Mattes discusses Taylor's influence on Tennyson in *In Memoriam: The Way of a Soul* (New York: Exposition Press, 1951), 40-3.

9. *A Rapture of Praise: Hymns of John and Charles Wesley,* selected by A. M. Allchin and H. A. Hodges (London: Hodder and Stoughton, 1966), 111.

10. W. Cowper and J. Newton, *Olney Hymns* (London: [n.p.], 1779), 81.

11. Susan Tamke, *Make a Joyful Noise unto the Lord: Hymns as a Reflection of Victorian Social Attitudes* (Athens: Ohio University Press, 1978), 140.

12. Christopher Wordsworth, *Thoughts on English Hymnody: or, Preface to 'The Holy Year'* (London: Rivington, 1865), p. xxxi.

13. See Margaret Williams, *The Society of the Sacred Heart: History of a Spirit 1800-1975* (London: Darton, Longman and Todd, 1978).

14. Henry Manning, *The Divine Glory of the Sacred Heart* (London: Burns and Oates, 1873), 12-13.

15. *Sermons* [*The Sermons and Devotional Writings of Gerard Manley Hopkins,* ed. Christopher Dev-

lin (London: Oxford University Press, 1959)], 102. On Hopkins's anxiety about the unity of body and soul in Christ, see the Conclusion, 303-4.

16. Thomas Carlyle, *Sartor Resartus* (London: Chapman and Hall, 1896), 155.

17. Cited in [Hallam Tennyson] *Memoir* [*Alfred Lord Tennyson: A Memoir,* 2 vols. (London: George Bell, 1901], i. 44.

18. [Tennyson] *In Memoriam,* ed. Susan Shatto and Marion Shaw (Oxford: Clarendon Press, 1982), 284.

19. William Newnham, *The Reciprocal Influence of Body and Mind Considered* (London: J. Hatchard, 1842), 578.

20. Johann Fichte, *The Destination of Man,* trans. Mrs Percy Sinnett (London: Chapman, Brothers, 1846), 74. This book expresses Fichte's liberal opinion that faith cannot be objectively assessed or defined. He was accused of atheism in Germany in the 1790s.

21. Ludwig Feuerbach, *The Essence of Christianity,* trans. George Eliot (1841), introd. Karl Barth (New York: Harper and Row, 1957), 31.

22. Feuerbach, 55.

23. Francis Newman, *Phases of Faith,* introd. U. C. Knoepflmacher (Leicester: Leicester University Press, 1970), 133.

24. E. B. Pusey, 20 Aug. 1838, in *Spiritual Letters of E. B. Pusey,* ed. J. O. Johnston and W. C. E. Newbolt (London: Longmans, Green, 1898), 41.

25. J. H. Newman, 'On the Introduction of Rationalistic Principles into Revealed Religion', in *Essays: Critical and Historical,* 2 vols. (London: Basil Montagu Pickering, 1872), i. 30-101 (p. 95).

26. 'Religious doctrines and articles of faith can only be received according to certain dispositions of the heart; these dispositions can only be formed by a repetition of certain actions.' Williams, 'On Reserve in Communicating Religious Knowledge' (Part 2), Tract 87, *Tracts for the Times 1838-1840* (London: J. G. & F. Rivington, 1840), v. 58.

27. To J. P. Gell, 8 May [1838], *The Correspondence of Arthur Hugh Clough,* ed. F. L. Mulhauser, 2 vols. (Oxford: Clarendon Press, 1957), i. 71.

28. Pusey (1898) [*Spiritual Letters of E. B. Pusey,* ed. J. O. Johnston and W. C. E. Newbolt (London: Longmans, Green, 1898)], 25.

29. J. P. Gell to Clough, 13 July 1838, Clough, ed. Mulhauser (1957), i. 77.

30. Charlotte M. Yonge, *Musings over the 'Christian Year' and 'Lyra Innocentium'* (Oxford: James Parker, 1871), p. xxxvi.

31. E. B. Pusey, *Parochial Sermons,* 2 vols. (Oxford: John Henry Parker, 1853), i. 96.

32. Ibid. 96.

33. John Keble, 'Dedication', line 7 and 'Second Sunday after Epiphany', lines 51-2, *The Christian Year, Lyra Innocentium and Other Poems* (Oxford: Oxford University Press, 1914). All further references given in the text.

34. Kirstie Blair, 'John Keble and the Rhythm of Faith', *Essays in Criticism,* 53 (2003), 129-51.

35. Diane D'Amico, 'Christina Rossetti's *Christian Year*: Comfort for the "Weary Heart"', *Victorian Newsletter,* 72 (1987), 36-42 (p. 39).

36. Richard Chenevix Trench, 'Sonnet', in *Poems, Collected and Arranged* (London: Macmillan, 1865), 37. Trench served as curate to Hugh James Rose, one of the original leaders of what came to be known as the Oxford Movement.

37. *Keble's Lectures on Poetry, 1832-1841,* trans. E. K. Francis, 2 vols. (Oxford: Clarendon Press, 1912), i. 55, ii. 480.

38. Frederick William Faber, 'The Confessional', in *The Cherwell Water-Lily and Other Poems* (London: J., G., F. and J. Rivington, 1840), 68.

39. See below, p. 182.

40. For details of these revisions and a longer study of 'The Confessional', see Kirstie Blair, 'Breaking Loose: Frederick Faber and the Failure of Reserve', in *Victorian Poetry,* 44 (2006).

41. To J. B. Morris, 27 Sept. 1842. Unpublished letter, London Oratory Archives.

42. Cited in John Edward Bowden, *The Life and Letters of Frederick William Faber* (London: Thomas Richardson, 1869), 303.

43. Keble (1912) [*Keble's Lectures on Poetry*], i. 22.

44. Frank Turner, 'The Victorian Crisis of Faith and the Faith that was Lost', in Richard Helmstadter and Bernard Lightman (eds.), *Victorian Faith in Crisis* (Houndmills: Macmillan, 1990), 9-38 (p. 10).

45. *Matthew Arnold: The Yale Manuscript,* ed. S. O. A. Ullmann (Ann Arbor: University of Michigan Press, 1989), 145.

46. Allott and Super [Arnold, *Matthew Arnold: A Critical Edition of the Major Works,* ed. Miriam

Allot and R. H. Super (Oxford: Oxford University Press, 1986)], 52 n.

47. Park Honan, *Matthew Arnold: A Life* (London: Weidenfeld & Nicolson, 1981), 12. Honan suggests that 'The Buried Life' is the poem closest to Tractarian poetics (p. 227). On Keble's influence, see Daniel Kline, '"For rigorous teacher seized my youth": Thomas Arnold, John Keble and the Juvenilia of Arthur Hugh Clough and Matthew Arnold', in Kirstie Blair (ed.), *John Keble in Context* (London: Anthem, 2004), 143-58.

48. Allott and Super, 682-701 (p. 697).

49. *The Complete Prose Works of Matthew Arnold,* ed. R. H. Super, 11 vols. (Ann Arbor: University of Michigan Press, 1960-77), vi. 179, 174-5.

50. To Clough, 30 Nov. 1853, Lang, i. 28.

51. [*c.*15 Dec. 1849], ibid. i. 167.

52. Culler [*Imaginative Reason*], 57.

53. See David Trotter, 'Hidden Ground Within: Matthew Arnold's Lyric and Elegiac Poetry', *ELH* 44 (1977), 526-53. Trotter briefly discusses Keble's interest in the buried life in relation to Arnold's (pp. 546-7).

54. David DeLaura, *Hebrew and Hellene in Victorian England: Newman, Arnold, and Pater* (Austin: University of Texas, 1969), p. xi.

55. H. M. Hughes, *A Clinical Introduction to the Practice of Auscultation* (London: Longman, Brown, Green and Longmans, 1845), 204-6.

56. William A. Oram, 'Arnold's "Scholar-Gipsy" and the Crisis of the 1852 *Poems*', *Modern Language Quarterly,* 45 (1984), 144-62 (p. 149).

57. Trotter (1977) ['Hidden Ground Within'], 526.

58. George W. Balfour, 'Clinical Lectures on Diseases of the Heart', *Edinburgh Medical Journal,* 19 (1873-4), 1058.

59. 12 Feb. 1853, Lang, i. 254.

60. Gweneth Whitteridge summarizes Empedocles' views in William Harvey, *An Anatomical Disputation Concerning the Movement of the Heart and the Blood in Living Creatures,* trans. and introd. Gweneth Whitteridge (Oxford: Blackwell, 1976), 23 n. Arnold could have known of Empedocles' medical fame from his reading of several lives of Empedocles and Simon Karsten's *Philosophen Graecorum Veterum Operum Reliquiae* (1830), a copy of which he owned. See C. B. Tinker and H. F. Lowry, *The Poetry of Matthew Arnold: A Commentary* (London: Oxford University Press, 1940), 289.

61. Arnold [*Matthew Arnold: The Yale Manuscript*], ed. Ullmann, 114.

62. 'Preface to *Poems* (1854)', in Allott and Super, 589-609. See especially pp. 591-2.

FURTHER READING

Bibliographies

Machann, Clinton. *The Essential Matthew Arnold: An Annotated Bibliography of Major Modern Studies.* New York: Maxwell Macmillan International, 1993, 177 p.

Provides an annotated bibliography of Arnold criticism published between 1900 and 1991.

Tollers, Vincent L. *A Bibliography of Matthew Arnold.* University Park: Pennsylvania State University Press, 1974, 172 p.

Documents a period of intense critical disputes over Arnold's legacy as a poet and critic and includes a full bibliography of his works.

Biographies

Gates, Lewis E. Introduction to *Selections from the Prose Writings of Matthew Arnold,* pp. 9-90. London: Henry Holt and Company, 1898.

Offers a comprehensive introduction to Arnold's biography, cultural theories, criticism, and literary style and includes a chronological list of major and minor works.

Hamilton, Ian. *A Gift Imprisoned: The Poetic Life of Matthew Arnold.* New York: Basic Books, 1999, 241 p.

Describes Arnold's educational and professional careers.

Criticism

Dixon, James Main. "A Nineteenth Century Sadducee." In *Modern Poets and Christian Teaching: Matthew Arnold,* pp. 123-47. New York: Eaton and Mains, 1906.

Argues that, despite his "open-minded rationalism," Arnold had a deeply conservative respect for the Bible and religious tradition.

Farrel, John P. "Matthew Arnold's Tragic Vision" *PMLA* 85, no. 1 (January 1970): 107-17.

Differentiates Arnold's nineteenth-century sense of tragedy from Greek and Shakespearean tragedy, claiming it fails in that it results in a "historical stalemate."

Fitch, Sir Joshua Girling. *Thomas and Matthew Arnold and Their Influence on English Education.* London: W. Heinemann, 1904, 277 p.

Explores the theories of education of both Matthew Arnold and his father, Thomas, and their application to modern education.

Letwin, Shirley Robin. "Matthew Arnold: Enemy of Tradition." *Political Theory* 10, no. 3 (August 1982): 333-51.

Takes issue with the notion that Arnold championed tradition and state authority, claiming that Arnold's view of both authority and anarchy has commonly been misconstrued.

Levine, George. "Matthew Arnold: The Artist in the Wilderness." *Critical Inquiry* 9, no. 3 (March 1983): 469-82.

Contends that Arnold's criticism was itself a creative and artistic act.

Logan, Peter Melville. "Fetishism and Freedom in Matthew Arnold's Cultural Theory." *Victorian Literature and Culture* 31, no. 2 (2003): 555-74.

Examines the fetishistic aspects of contemporary Arnold scholarship and its roots in Arnold's own criticism.

Longenbach, James. "Matthew Arnold and the Modern Apocalypse." *PMLA* 104, no. 5 (October 1989): 844-55.

Evaluates Arnold's apocalyptic rhetoric in "Empedocles on Etna" in relation to that of T. S. Eliot in "The Waste Land."

Pratt, Linda Ray. *Revisiting Matthew Arnold.* New York: Twayne Publishers, 2000, 174 p.

Traces Arnold's poetic and biographical development, attempting to apply Arnoldian concepts to postmodern experience.

Roper, Alan. "Mount Etna." In *Arnold's Poetic Landscapes,* pp. 183-208. Baltimore: The Johns Hopkins Press, 1969.

Presents an extended reading of the poem "Empedocles on Etna" and offers the opinion that the unity created between the poem's setting and the philosophical reflections of its central character render the work unique in Arnold's corpus.

Schneider, Mary W. "The Activity of Poetry." In *Poetry in the Age of Democracy: The Literary Criticism of Matthew Arnold,* pp. 135-72. Lawrence: University Press of Kansas, 1989.

Catalogs Arnold's search for universal poetical values in his critical essays.

Stone, Donald. *Communications with the Future: Matthew Arnold in Dialogue: Henry James, Charles-Augustin Sainte-Beuve, Ernest Renan, Michel Foucault, Friedrich Nietzsche, Hans-George Gadamer, William James, Richard Rorty, John Dewey.* Ann Arbor: University of Michigan Press, 1997, 218 p.

Compares Arnold's literary and cultural theories with those of various nineteenth- and twentieth-century thinkers.

————. "Matthew Arnold and the Pragmatics of Hebraism and Hellenism." *Poetics Today* 19, no. 2 (summer 1998): 179-98.

Discusses the famous distinction between Hebraism (associated with character, conduct, and obedience) and Hellenism (associated with culture and the critical ability to see things as they truly are) that Arnold outlined in *Culture and Anarchy* and traces the influence of other thinkers, notably the German poet Heinrich Heine, on Arnold's essay, warning against the common oversimplification of Arnold's position as a complete dismissal of Hebraism or a wholehearted validation of Hellenism.

Walcott, Fred G. *The Origins of* Culture and Anarchy: *Matthew Arnold and Popular Education in England.* Toronto: University of Toronto Press, 1970, 161 p.

Appraises the influence of Arnold's position as an educator on his criticism and cultural theory.

White, Helen C. "Matthew Arnold and Goethe." *PMLA* 36 (1921): 436-53.

Investigates Arnold's immense critical debt to Goethe.

Jules Michelet
1798-1874

French historian, nonfiction writer, essayist, and biographer.

The following entry presents an overview of Michelet's life and works. For additional discussion of Michelet's career, see *NCLC*, Volume 31.

INTRODUCTION

Jules Michelet was known in his day as a great national historian; he was also esteemed as a prominent social thinker and a sophisticated prose stylist. Viewing history as not simply the recording of facts, he refused to be bound by the traditional belief in an objective, scientific, and detached approach, a position that infuriated other historians of the day. Instead, he imposed a personal perspective on historical events, treating his work as the composition of the life of a people. Michelet inspired the youth of his day both with his polemical public lectures, delivered in the months before the Revolutions of 1848, and in such popular works as *Le peuple* (1846; *The People*). Best known for his 17-volume *Histoire de France* (1833-67), he celebrated French national identity as having its basis in the land and in those who worked it. For this reason, Michelet became strongly associated with the Romantic movement.

BIOGRAPHICAL INFORMATION

Michelet was born on August 21, 1798, to a lower-middle-class Parisian couple. His father, Furcy Michelet, operated a printing press throughout the turbulent years of the French Revolution and may have been responsible for printing some revolutionary manifestos. Young Jules was later employed in the print shop as an assistant to his father. The business declined under Napoleon's censorship and finally closed in 1812. The family suffered extreme poverty, but Furcy still managed to enroll his son in the College de Charlemagne, where Michelet graduated at the top of his class. As his academic career was just getting under way, his mother, Angélique, became ill; she died in February 1815. His early experience of political repression, impoverishment, and tragedy enabled Michelet to identify with the lower strata of society and to sympathize with the liberal ideals embodied in the French Revolution—the major event that inspired much of his writing.

As Michelet remarked in later life, education provided a way out of his dreary family situation. After winning first prize in French oration and Latin translation at the general competition held at the Institut de France in 1816, Michelet went on to achieve a secondary-school diploma in 1817 and a bachelor of arts degree in 1818, completing his formal education in 1821 with the successful defense of his doctoral dissertation. Michelet followed his early successes by earning a professorship in philosophy and history at the École Normale Supérieure in 1827 and, in the same year, publishing *Principes de la philosophie de l'histoire, traduits de la* Scienza nuova *de J. B. Vico*. A translation of Italian philosopher Giambattista Vico's *Scienza nuova,* Michelet's book was an immediate success; reviewers were impressed with his sophisticated rendering of what was at the time a somewhat obscure work.

In the aftermath of the July Revolution of 1830, Michelet commenced work on a number of historical projects that reflected his interest in universal liberty and France's revolutionary heritage. The first of these works, *Introduction à l'histoire universelle,* was published in 1831. The following year, at the behest of historian François Guizot, Michelet was appointed head of the historical section of the National Archives, a position that enabled him to access original documents hitherto ignored by historians. At this time Michelet maintained a close association with the Catholic Church, and he identified the universal progression of liberty in Western history as a Christian form of self-sacrifice. The first volume of his great *Histoire de France* offers an almost breathless paean to the tradition of asceticism practiced in the Christianity of the Middle Ages. As scholar Pieter Geyl observed [see Further Reading], Michelet initially viewed Catholicism and the monarchy as the two forces responsible for French unity, a belief reinforced by France's greatest martyr, Jeanne d'Arc. Michelet began to realize, however, that the July Revolution was more a victory for the monarchy than for *the people,* a reality brought home by the massive unemployment crisis of 1837. Appointed as a professor at the Collége de France in 1838, Michelet used his prestigious academic position to criticize the government and to push for democratic reforms.

Most contemporary critics identify 1843, the year that marked the reversal of Michelet's attitude toward the church, as the beginning of the second phase of his career. Previously conservative Catholics, Michelet and colleague Edgar Quinet reacted strongly to the Church's interference in the affairs of the French people, particularly to the Jesuits' challenge to state control of education. Michelet and Quinet expressed these views frankly in a series of lectures delivered at the Collége de France in 1843 and subsequently published under the title *Des Jésuites* (1843; *The Jesuits*). In his nonfiction work *Du prêtre, de la femme, de la famille* (1845; *Priests, Women, and Families*), Michelet also presented an anticlerical position. His next work, *The People,* considered one of his greatest achievements, represented the historian's first explicit self-identification with the working class.

The culmination of Michelet's exploration of liberal democracy was his seven-volume *Histoire de la Révolution Française* (1847-53; *History of the French Revolution*). It was in this work that Michelet established the personal and passionate voice that so enraged his contemporaries, who felt that history should be written objectively. Michelet's personal involvement in the politics of his day came with a price, however. In 1847 he was suspended from his teaching duties because of disturbances that appeared to have been inspired by his public lectures; four years later he was forced out a second and final time for continuing to celebrate revolutionary ideals in his lectures. Finally, in 1852 he was also dismissed from his archival duties for refusing to swear allegiance to Louis Napoleon, the emperor of the Second Empire. To support himself in subsequent years, Michelet composed books on popular subjects, such as natural history and women in European society. After at last completing the final volume of his mammoth *Histoire de France* in 1867, Michelet began work on *Histoire du XIXème siècle* (1872-75). He had completed three volumes of the new opus when he died in Hyères on February 9, 1874.

MAJOR WORKS

Dispensing with traditional forms of historiography that relied on facts and statistics, Michelet made it his chief goal to enliven his books with the socioeconomic details that made up a given society. To the chagrin of his contemporaries, he addressed his subject matter intimately, as though in conversation. *The People,* for example, begins, "Do we wish to know the fixed idea, the ruling passion of the French peasant; we have only to take a country walk of a Sunday, and follow him. There he is, yonder before us. It is two o'clock; his wife is at vespers; he is in his Sunday's best. I warrant you he is going to see his mistress." Moreover, in many of his popular historical works, including *L'oiseau* (1856; *The Bird*), *L'insecte* (1857; *The Insect*), *L'amour* (1858; *Love*), and *La femme* (1860; *Woman*), Michelet's writing style is lyrical and emotional, qualities not usually

associated with historical writing. An anonymous reviewer of *Love* remarked in 1859, "He is absolutely, and in every sense of the word, an 'artist'" (*North American Review* 89, no. 184). In fact, critic David Carroll argued in a 1998 article that Michelet's major works were inspired by what the historian himself identified as the "art of the people." Commentators have noted that his view of historical life was influenced by the writings of Vico; in "Michelet and His *History of the French Revolution*" (*Debates with Historians,* 1955), Geyl asserts, "It was in Vico that [Michelet] had found proclaimed the triumph of imagination over analysis and the feeling for the fullness that is true to life."

Michelet's *History of the French Revolution* in particular presents the French people as the heroes of the Revolution. As Geyl noted, the writing is filled with Michelet's "vehement comments, his moans and his cries of joy." He felt that the brutal violence of the Revolution was essential to historical progress and that Robespierre and the rest of the National Convention that ruled France from 1792 until 1795 (during the Reign of Terror) were simply "gripped in the tongs of necessity." Commentators have been quick to point out that despite Michelet's enthusiasm for the Revolution, he identified with a moderate course, one exemplified, in Michelet's thinking, in the actions of revolutionary leader Georges Danton, whose notion of "universal love" was ultimately silenced when he was sent to the guillotine in 1794. Moreover, Michelet was not, as some critics have maintained, an apologist for excessive violence. He believed that such events as the storming of the Bastille in 1789 and the formation of the National Assembly in 1790 represented the apex of his country's political unity. This ideal fueled the arguments for fair working conditions and more humane treatment of the people expressed in his remaining volumes.

Michelet wrote his history of the French Revolution out of his own involvement in the new revolutionary struggles and in the hopes of making an impact on current events in France. He composed the first, optimistic volumes (which covered the years 1789-90) in 1847, when a contemporary rebellion was imminent. In "Michelet's Purpose," scholar Oscar Haac [see Further Reading] contended that "What [Michelet] wanted to resurrect was not so much the event as it occurred as the purpose of those who brought it about, particularly if their objective could elucidate contemporary aims." The historian himself claimed that the Revolution became his "all-powerful interpreter" of French history, so it is perhaps not surprising that he delayed the writing of most of France's pre-Revolutionary history until after he had published his volumes on the Revolution itself. Upset by both the ultimate failure of the French Revolution and the failure of the 1848 Revolution in his own day, however, Michelet found the portrayal of the post-1790 period troubling and even traumatic. In what is now recognized as a characteristic feature of his career, Michelet voiced his exhaustion after completing the first section on the revolutionary period: Geyl quotes him as having said, "I leave behind me an unrepeatable moment of my life" and "Impoverished and diminished, I take my leave."

CRITICAL RECEPTION

Many of Michelet's contemporaries disparaged his subjective form of historiography, criticizing both his manner of inserting personal reflections in his books and his role as a political provocateur in his public lectures. French literary historian Charles Augustin Sainte-Beuve, for example, felt that Michelet's performance in one of his 1840s lectures was ridiculous, while German poet Heinrich Heine ridiculed Michelet's unabashed Romanticism. Michelet's staunch patriotism became the primary bone of contention for subsequent historians, historiographers, and cultural critics during the next hundred years.

One of the most substantial twentieth-century critiques of Michelet's nationalist perspective came from Pieter Geyl, whose *Debates with Historians* includes a chapter on Michelet's coverage of the French Revolution. After discussing some of the roots of Michelet's ideological leanings, Geyl describes what he sees as unremitting prejudice in the author's portrayal of France's glorious history. "An out and out revolutionary imperialist, was Michelet," Geyl writes, concluding that Michelet was responsible for disseminating the "cult of the Revolutionary tradition, which has had such disastrous consequences for his beloved France." Other critics see Michelet as a fervent liberal idealist rather than a rabid patriot. Writing at about the same time as Geyl, Oscar Haac maintained that Michelet's enthusiastic celebration of his country was based in feelings that France was the ideal of universal liberty; his love of France provided a "link between democratic hope and patriotic fervor." Despite the apparent flaws in his method, Haac concluded, Michelet's great contribution to French historiography was in his manner of tracing past historical events leading up to the Revolution. Michelet's faith in the progress of liberty throughout French history, Haac added, became a faith in the French people of his own day, who were in a position to realize the revolutionary ideals.

While nineteenth- and twentieth-century critics have identified Michelet's reverence for the French peasantry as no more than a symptom of his Romanticism, Arthur Mitzman modified this interpretation in his 1996 article, "Michelet and Social Romanticism: Religion, Revolution, Nature," suggesting that Michelet's anticlerical turn in the 1840s reflected a "social romantic" perspec-

tive on French history. Mitzman elaborates, "Social romanticism was the semi-religious quest for harmony in social existence, in nature, and in the cosmos of dissenting writers and ideologists during the 1840s." The movement, Mitzman maintains, was part of the efforts of the "humanitarian Left"—which included, among others, Pierre Leroux, George Sand, Jean Reynaud, Victor Hugo, Eugéne Sue, Edgard Quinet, and Pierre-Jean de Béranger—"to write the common people into society, politics, religion, and history." Michelet and his dissenting allies objected to Old Regime notions about the "uneducated populace." Mitzman argues that *The People*, in which Michelet first identifies himself with the common people, is his "social romantic manifesto."

PRINCIPAL WORKS

De percipienda infinitate secundum Lockium (essay) 1819

Tableau chronologique de l'histoire moderne (history) 1825

Tableaux synchroniques de l'histoire moderne (history) 1826

Précis de l'histoire moderne (history) 1827

Principes de la philosophie de l'histoire, traduits de la Scienza nuova de J. B. Vico [translator] (nonfiction) 1827

Histoire de la République Romaine [*History of the Roman Republic*]. 2 vols. (history) 1831

Introduction à l'histoire universelle (history) 1831

Précis de l'histoire de France jusqu'à la Révolution Française (history) 1833

Histoire de France. 17 vols. (history) 1833-67

Mémoires de Luther, écrits par luimême [*The Life of Luther, Gathered from His Own Writings, by M. Michelet*] (biography) 1835

Origines du droit français (nonfiction) 1837

Des Jésuites [*The Jesuits*] (nonfiction) 1843

Du prêtre, de la femme, de la famille [*Priests, Women, and Families*] (nonfiction) 1845

Le peuple [*The People*] (nonfiction) 1846

Cours professé au Collège de France (nonfiction) 1847-48; also published as *L'étudiant*, 1877

Histoire de la Révolution Française [*History of the French Revolution*]. 7 vols. (history) 1847-53

Les femmes de la Révolution [*The Women of the French Revolution*] (nonfiction) 1854

Légendes démocratiques du Nord (nonfiction) 1854

L'oiseau [*The Bird*] (nonfiction) 1856

L'insecte [*The Insect*] (nonfiction) 1857

L'amour [*Love*] (nonfiction) 1858

La femme [*Woman*] (nonfiction) 1860

La mer [*The Sea*] (nonfiction) 1861

La sorcière [*La sorcière: The Witch of the Middle Ages*] (nonfiction) 1862

Bible de l'humanité [*The Bible of Humanity*] (nonfiction) 1864

La montagne [*The Mountain*] (nonfiction) 1868

Nos fils (nonfiction) 1869

La France devant l'Europe [*France Before Europe*] (nonfiction) 1871

Histoire du XIXème siècle. 3 vols. (history) 1872-75

Oeuvres complètes. 46 vols. (history and nonfiction) 1898-1903

Journal. 4 vols. (memoirs) 1976

CRITICISM

Alexander Herzen (letter date 1851)

SOURCE: Herzen, Alexander. "The Russian People and Socialism: An Open Letter to Jules Michelet." In *From the Other Shore and The Russian People and Socialism*, translated by Moura Budberg and Richard Wollheim, pp. 163-208. London: Weidenfeld and Nicolson, 1956.

[*In the following letter, originally written in 1851 and published in Paris in 1852, Herzen responds to the first few pamphlets of Michelet's 1854 nonfiction work* Legendes democratiques du Nord, *which, Herzen claims, present a disparaging view of the Russian people.*]

Sir,

You occupy so high a place in the general esteem, everything that you write is received by European Democracy with that unbounded confidence which your noble pen has won for you as a right, that I cannot refrain from replying to you on a matter which touches upon my most deep-seated convictions: on, that is, the description of the Russian people that appears in your noble work on Kosciusko [*Poland and Russia: A Legend on Kosciusko*].[1]

A reply is all the more necessary, since it is time that Europe was made to realize that nowadays speaking about Russia is no longer a matter of speaking about a country that is absent, distant, mute.

For we are present, we who have left our country only so that free Russian speech may be heard in Europe. And we hold it our duty to speak out when a man, who quite rightly enjoys such immense authority, tells us that 'he knows—that he swears to it—that he can prove that Russia doesn't exist, that the Russians are not human, that they are devoid of all moral sense.'

Do you mean by this official Russia, the Empire of façades, the Byzantine-German government? If so, you are right. We agree in advance with everything you say. We feel no need to rush into the breach. The Russian government has enough agents in the Paris press to provide a permanent stream of eloquent justifications of its doings.

But it is not only official society that you deal with in your book. You have taken the problem and have gone to its very roots. You have written about the People.

The poor Russian people has no one of its own to raise a voice in its defence. I ask you, then—can we, in such circumstances, without gross cowardice, stay silent?

The Russian people, Sir, does exist. It lives. It is not even very old. It is very young. Sometimes (it is true) one dies young, before one has had time to live. It can happen, but not in the ordinary run of events.

For the Russian people the past is dark: the present is terrible: but for all that, it lays some claim to the future, it *has no belief* in its present condition. It has the audacity to hope: and it hopes all the more, since it possesses so little.

The most difficult period for the Russian people is drawing to a close. A terrible struggle lies ahead of it. And this is the moment for which its enemies have been preparing for a hundred years.

The great question, Russia's 'to be or not to be', will soon be resolved. But before the battle, one has no right to despair of the outcome.

The Russian question is assuming grave and disturbing proportions. People of all parties feel concern about it. But it seems that in doing so, they concern themselves too much with the official Russia, the Russia of the Tsar, and too little with the unknown Russia, the Russia of the people.

But even if you insist on looking at Russia solely from the point of view of its government, do you not think that it would be as well to have a rather better knowledge of this uncomfortable neighbour who has mastered the art of infiltrating into every corner of Europe, here with spies, there with bayonets? The Russian government reaches out to the Mediterranean as protector of the Ottoman Porte, to the Rhine as protector of its German uncles and connexions, to the Atlantic as the protector of ORDER in France.

It would be as well, I say, to form a true estimate of this universal protector, and to discover whether this mysterious empire has in fact any other justification for its existence than that of fulfilling the repulsive vocation that the St Petersburg Government has assumed: that of being a barrier cast across the high road of human progress.

Europe is approaching a terrible cataclysm. The world of the Middle Ages has come to an end. The world of feudalism is expiring. The religious and political revolutions are petering out under the weight of their own complete impotence. They have great achievements to their credit, but they have failed to complete their tasks. They have stripped Throne and Altar of the prestige they once enjoyed, but they have not established the era of freedom. They have lit new desires in the hearts of men but they have not provided ways of satisfying them. Parliamentarianism, Protestantism—these are mere prevarications, temporary measures, attempts to stave off the flood, which can arrest only for a short while the process of death and rebirth. The time for them has passed. Since 1848 it has become apparent that no amount of delving into Roman law, of barren casuistry, of thin philosophic deism, of sterile religious rationalism can hold back society from fulfilling its destiny.

The storm draws near. There can no longer be doubt about it; on this point revolutionaries and reactionaries agree. Men's minds are unbalanced: a serious question, a question of life and death, lies heavy on their hearts. Men grow worried, disturbed. They ask themselves, is it still possible for Europe, that hoary Proteus, that decaying organism, to find within itself the strength to bring about its own recovery? And having asked the question, they dread the answer. They tremble with suspense.

It *is* a grave question.

Will old Europe find the means to rid itself of its sluggish blood, so that it may plunge headlong into the limitless future—the future, that passionate, fatal creature who draws us all towards her with irresistible force, towards whom we fling ourselves with utter recklessness, not caring whether our path is driven across the ruins of our ancestral homes, whether we have to squander the treasure of ancient civilizations and the material wealth of modern culture?

On both sides the position is fully understood. Europe has slipped back into the grim, unbroken darkness that must come before the dawn of the final struggle It is not life but mere suspense, anxiety. Everything is upside down. There is no regard for law, no justice, not even a semblance of liberty. A secular and irreligious inquisition reigns supreme: civil rights have been suspended, and in their stead martial law and a state of siege proclaimed. There is only one moral force that still has any authority over men, that still demands and receives their obedience: and that is Fear, which is universal. All other issues have to give way before the over-riding interest of Reaction. Governments that to all appearances are sharply divided on questions of principle, come together affectionately to form a single oecumenical police force. The Emperor of Russia, without troubling to conceal his loathing for the French, rewards the Prefect of the Paris police: the King of Naples confers a decoration on the President of the Republic with his own hand—the hand of a turnkey: the King of Prussia muffles himself up in his Russian uniform and hurries off to Warsaw to embrace his old enemy the Emperor of Austria and receive the blessing of Nicholas—Nicholas, the heretical Emperor, who, to complete the picture, lends out his soldiers to protect the Roman Pontiff. On this witches' Sabbath, on this Walpurgis night of reaction, all personal security vanishes: safeguards that exist even in the most backward societies, in China, in Persia, are no longer respected in the capitals of what was once the civilized world.

We can no longer believe our eyes. Is this really the Europe that we once knew and loved?

Indeed if there were no longer an England, free and proud, if that diamond set in the silver sea,[2] as Shakespeare called it, no longer shone bright: if Switzerland were to deny its principles time and time again, like St Peter in fear of Caesar: if Piedmont, the one free, strong element in Italy, the last refuge of civilization which, expelled from the North, shelters south of the Alps but without daring to cross the Appennines, were suddenly to grow insensible to all human feelings—if in a word, these three countries were to fall victims to that pestilential air which blows from Paris and Vienna, then we should have to say that the dissolution of the old world was complete, that the parricidal hands of the conservatives had done their worst and that barbarism was already upon us in France and Germany.

Turning away from this chaos, from the writhings of insanity and the tears and pains of childbirth, turning away from this world as it falls into rotting pieces by the cradle's side, men's eyes turn involuntarily to the East.

There, like some dark mountain emerging from the mists, may be discerned the unfriendly, menacing contours of an empire: it seems to advance upon one like an avalanche—or like an impatient heir anxious to hurry on the last protracted moments of his dying benefactor.

This empire, totally unknown two centuries ago, has suddenly burst in upon the world, as if by sheer force, and with no invitation, with no real right, has taken its place at the council table of the sovereigns of Europe, and has peremptorily demanded its share of the booty, although this was won without its assistance.

No one has yet dared oppose its claims to interfere in the affairs of Europe.

Charles XII tried to do so; his sword, till then invincible, shivered in the attempt. Frederick II wanted to oppose the encroachments of the Petersburg Court; Königsberg and Berlin fell before the might of the Northern foe. The Emperor Napoleon penetrated to the very heart of this giant, at the head of half a million men—and escaped as best he could, alone, on a broken down common sledge. Europe looked on with amazement at Napoleon's flight, at the Cossack hosts hot on his trail, at the Russian armies marching towards Paris, bestowing national independence on Germany as though they were scattering alms by the wayside. Like a monstrous vampire, Russia seems to exist only in order to fasten on the mistakes of nations and their kings. Yesterday we saw her all but destroy Austria by way of helping her against Hungary: to-day we may see her proclaim the Mark of Brandenburg a province of the Russian Empire while professing to be the protector of the King of Prussia.

And yet on the very eve of the great struggle, how little we know about this new adversary—this arrogant nation, armed to the teeth, ready to march across the frontier at the slightest gesture from its confederates in reaction. We scarcely know what arms it carries, or the colour of its flag—and we rest content with official statements, with vague, current notions, barely noticing how much the various accounts we hear contradict one another.

From some we hear only of the omnipotence of the Tsar, of the arrogance of the government, of the cringing servility of the people: while others tell us that the despotism of St Petersburg is not a part of the national life, that the people, bent double under the twin yoke of the Emperor and the aristocracy, endure oppression without accepting it, suffer but are not broken—and all the while provide the cement that keeps together the vast Colossus that bestrides them. Some there are who say that the Russian people are a disgusting rabble of drunkards and helots, and there are others who say that Russia is the home of an intelligent and gifted race.

There is to me something tragic about the senile, hopeless fashion in which the old world runs together all these various views about its enemy.

In this whole vast farrago of incompatible opinions, there is so much evidence of tragic frivolity, of deeply embedded prejudice, of real failure to adapt oneself, that if we look for a parallel in history, our thoughts, whether we like it or not, inevitably turn to the decadence of Rome.

For it was in just this way that people in those days, on the very eve of the Christian revolution, on the very eve of the victory of barbarism, used to speak of Rome as immortal, and of the Nazarene sect as a negligible lunatic element, and ridiculed the dangers to which the unrest in the barbarian world should have made them alive.

* * *

Sir, you have the distinction of being the first person in France to have spoken of the Russian people. You put your hand on the very heart, on the very source of life. And it seemed as if the truth was about to be disclosed to you, had you not, in a sudden access of rage, pulled back the hand you had stretched out in friendship, and straightway the source seemed to run clouded and muddy.

With real distress I read your words of anger. It was with a heavy heart that I looked through them—and looked in vain—for the historian, for the philosopher, above all for that man of goodwill so familiar to us all. Let me hasten to add that I fully understand the cause of your indignation: it was sympathy for the misfortunes of Poland that prompted you to speak as you did. For sympathy with our Polish brothers is a feeling that we also know well, save that with us it is an occasion not merely for compassion but for remorse and shame. You talk about loving Poland? Surely we all love her, but can we not do so without having to persecute some other country no less wretched in its fate—and persecute it merely because it was press-ganged into serving its tyrannical government in a career of crime? Let us be generous. Let us not forget that only recently we were offered the spectacle of a country that boasts of universal suffrage and a citizen army, none the less prepared to help in the maintenance of ORDER from Warsaw to Rome. . . . Look at what has been going on under your very eyes . . . and yet we don't say that the French are no longer human. We are more patient.

It is time to forget this unhappy fratricidal strife. Neither side can emerge from it victorious. Both Russia and Poland go down before a common enemy. The martyrs, the victims themselves, turn their back upon the past finding it no less painful than we do. Your distinguished friend whom you quote, the great poet Mickiewicz, is proof of this.

I beg you, Sir, not to speak of the views of this Polish poet as displaying 'clemency, the faults of the saints.' No: they are rather the fruits of long and careful thought, of a deep insight into the destiny of the Slav world. It is noble to forgive one's enemies, but there is something still worthier of mankind: and that is to understand them, because to understand is necessarily to forgive, to justify, to reconcile.

The Slav world is moving towards unity: a tendency which became evident immediately after the Napoleonic period. The idea of a Slav federation is already explicit in the revolutionary plans of Pestel and Mouraviev.[3] Several Poles actually took part in the Russian conspiracy.

When the revolution of 1830 broke out in Warsaw, the Russian people showed no animosity whatever towards those who had rebelled against the Tsar. The young were heart and soul with the Polish cause. I can remember the enthusiasm with which we seized upon the news from Warsaw: we wept like children as we read about the famous memorial service celebrated in the Polish capital in commemoration of our Petersburg martyrs.[4] Any sympathy expressed for the Poles ran us the risk of the most appalling punishments, and so we had to conceal it in our hearts and remain silent.

It is possible that at the time of the war of 1830 the dominant sentiments in Poland were still a violent hatred—a sentiment entirely justified—and an exclusive form of nationalism. Since then, Mickiewicz, the various philological and historical studies produced by Slav writers, a deeper acquaintance with other European people acquired in the course of long wanderings in exile, have worked together to give a very different turn to Polish thought. The Poles have come to feel that the battle is not between them and the Russian people: they have learnt that they cannot fight otherwise than FOR THEIR FREEDOM AND OURS—to quote the solemn words inscribed on their revolutionary flag.

The heroic emissary Konarski, who was tortured and shot in Vilna in 1839, ignored all differences of nationality when he called on Russians and Poles alike to rise in revolt. Russia showed her gratitude in a way that was at once tragic and yet typical of everything that she has done since that day when she first came under the heel of the German jackboot.

An enthusiastic, passionate, fanatical young man, by the name of Koravaev, a Russian officer in the regiment garrisoning the fortress, decided to rescue Konarski. The day when he would be on duty came round. All the arrangements necessary for an escape had been made, when he was betrayed by one of those who had been accused at the same time as the Polish martyr, and the whole plan had to be abandoned. The young man was arrested: he was put in chains and sent to the mines of Siberia, there to expiate his crime, the crime of having obeyed a call higher than military orders. Nothing has been heard of him since.

I spent five years in exile in the remote provinces of the Russian Empire. There I had the opportunity of meeting a considerable number of Polish exiles, for in every district town one comes across them, either surrounded by their complete families or else leading wretched, solitary lives. I should very much like to call them as witnesses in my cause. Several of them have in the meanwhile returned to their homes. They would all—I am quite sure—speak of the abundant sympathy that they received from the local inhabitants. I am not, of course, talking here of the police or of the upper military hierarchy. This latter class is nowhere remarkable for its love of liberty, and least of all in Russia. Or again I could quote for your benefit those Polish students who every year are sent off to universities in Russia in order to keep them well away from Polish schools. I should like them to describe for themselves the welcome that they everywhere received from their new colleagues. They used to leave us with tears in their eyes.

You may remember, Sir, that in Paris in 1847 when the Polish émigrés were celebrating the anniversary of their revolution, a Russian appeared on the platform to appeal for friendship and beg that the past should be forgotten. That was our unhappy friend Michael Bakunin. But I do not want to quote only the example of one of my fellow countrymen. I want to appeal to one of those who are thought to be our enemies, a man whom you yourself mentioned in your fine epic about Kosciusko. Ask the Nestor of Polish democracy what he thinks on this subject, ask M. Biernacki, one of the ministers of revolutionary Poland, for his views. I will abide by the verdict of this noble intellect, although long periods of unhappiness might well have embittered him against anything connected with the name of Russia. He will not belie me.

The solidarity that binds Poland and Russia to one another and thence to the whole Slav world, cannot be denied: it stands out so clearly. I can go further: without Russia the Slav world has no future: without Russia, it will wither away, it will miscarry, it will be swallowed up by the German element, it will become Austria, it will fail to be itself. But I cannot believe that this in fact is to be its mission, its fate.

* * *

I must confess, Sir, that in studying the exposition of your ideas, I find I am quite unable to accept the argument whereby you try to prove that Europe as a whole is one living person, of which each nation is an indispensable organ.

It seems to me that all the Romano-German nations are necessary to the European world because they exist: but it would be difficult to prove that they exist because they are necessary. Aristotle made the distinction between pre-existing necessity and *a posteriori* necessity. Nature accepts the inevitability of existent facts: but, for all that, there is a great deal of change and variety within what is as yet unrealized and is still to be. It is then only on this principle that the Slav world can claim its unity—a claim strengthened by the fact that it consists entirely of one race.

Centralization is contrary to the Slav genius; federalism, on the other hand, is its natural form of expression. Once the Slav world has become unified, and knit together into an association of free autonomous peoples, it will at last be able to enter on its true historical existence. Its past can be seen only as a period of preparation, of growth, of purification. The historic forms of the State have never answered to the national ideal of the Slavs, an ideal which is vague, instinctive if you like, yet by the same token gives promise for the future of a truly remarkable vitality. In all their actions, the Slavs have always revealed a strange sort of detachment, a curious kind of apathy. So for instance we have the case of Russia changing as a whole from idolatry to Christianity, without any repercussion, without any revolution, simply out of passive obedience to the Grand Prince Vladimir and out of deference to Kiev. Without any regrets, people flung their old idols into the Volkhov and submitted to the new God as though it were a new idol.

Five hundred years later, a part of Russia accepted in just the same manner a civilization that had been ordered from abroad and bore upon it a German trademark.

The Slav world is like a woman who has never loved and so seems indifferent to all that goes on around her: listless, detached, remote. But we cannot tell what will happen in the future: the woman is young, and even now something seems to be stirring within her, making her heart beat faster.

If what is at stake is the richness of the national genius, we only need point to Poland—the only Slav country so far to enjoy freedom and power at the same moment.

The Slav world is not the heterogeneous affair it seems to be. Underneath the veneer of aristocratic, liberal, catholic, Poland, of monarchic, oppressed, Byzantine Russia, underneath the democratic system of the Serb Voyevod and the Austrian bureaucracy that oppresses Illyria, Dalmatia and the Banat, underneath the patriarchal régime of the Osmanlis and the holy rule of the Archbishop of Montenegro, there is one single race, physiologically and ethnographically homogeneous.

The majority of the Slav peoples have never been subjugated by a conquering race. For them submission has, on the whole, been confined to the recognition of an overlord and to the payment of some form of tribute. Such, for instance, was the Mongol rule in Russia. As a result, the Slavs have managed to preserve for some hundreds of years their nationality, their way of life and their language.

The great question then is this: Is it reasonable to expect that Russia will be the nucleus of this crystallization, the centre towards which the Slav world will gravitate? a question we should ask realizing that so far she is the only section of that great race to be even provisionally organized into a State; and that there she stands, powerful, independent, armed with two swords, the one pointed against Germany, the other threatening Turkey. There could be no doubt at all about the answer to this question, if the Petersburg government had the faintest inkling of its national vocation, if any humane idea of any sort whatever could even once penetrate that gloomy and dull-witted despotism. But, as things are, how can anyone of any integrity or decency dare suggest to the western Slavs that they should ally themselves with an empire which lives in a permanent state of siege and where the sceptre is wielded like a truncheon in the hands of a flogging corporal.

The idea of a union based on the principles of freedom must not be confused with Imperial Panslavism, as it has been expounded in the past by misguided or corrupted men.

At this point, logic compels us to raise what is really the most serious, the most genuine question of all:

If we suppose that the Slav world has prospects of some more developed form of life in the future, then, which of all its somewhat embryonic elements is the most advanced, which gives the best ground for such hopes? If the Slavs are right in believing that their hour has come, then this element must necessarily be that which is in line with revolutionary ideas in Europe.

You have suggested which this element might be, you have touched upon it, but then you let it elude your grasp while you brushed away a tear of compassion for the fate of Poland.

You maintain that 'the basis of the life of the Russian people is COMMUNISM': you assert that 'its strength is founded on a form of agrarian law, on perpetual subdivision of the land.'

What a terrible MENE TEKEL have you pronounced. . . . Communism as a basis of life! Subdivision of the land as a source of strength! How is it, Sir, that you were not frightened by your own words?

Should we not pause here for reflection, and not leave the question until we have convinced you whether this is in fact the truth or whether it is pure fantasy?

As though there were any other real subjects of inquiry, any other serious questions for the nineteenth century than this question of communism and land division!

Carried away by indignation, you proceed: 'What they (the Russians) lack is that essential human attribute, the moral faculty, the sense of right and wrong. Truth and justice mean nothing to them. Mention these words to them—and they are mute, they smile at you, they don't understand what you are talking about.' Who are these Russians with whom you have spoken? And what notions of Justice and Truth are they that the Russians cannot understand? For in a genuinely revolutionary age, it is not enough simply to mention the words *truth* and *justice*. For these words no longer need have a meaning that is fixed and unambiguous for all of us alike.

The Justice and Truth of the old Europe are the injustice and falsehood of the Europe that is being born.

Nations are products of Nature: History is merely a progressive continuation of animal development. We shall get no nearer the truth as long as we consider Nature from the point of view of praise or blame. She has no time either for a Montyon prize or for our condemnations. Such moral categories do not apply to her: they are too subjective. It seems to me that a whole nation as such cannot be either completely good or totally bad: a nation is always true: there is no such thing as a nation that is a lie. All that Nature can do is to bring into existence that which is practically possible under certain given conditions: and then once it exists, to foster its growth by means of that divine ferment, that creative restlessness, that insatiable thirst, that need for self-fulfilment—the endless desire that exists in all living creatures.

Some peoples contrive to have a pre-historic, others an unhistoric, existence: but *once they have entered* the great stream of History, which is one and indivisible, all alike belong to humanity and, conversely, the whole of humanity's past belongs to them. In universal history—which is in fact humanity viewed in its progressive and active aspect—an aristocracy based on facial features, an aristocracy based on skin gradually become extinct. Anything that is not human has no part to play in history and consequently we never find there either a whole people entirely on the level of the herd or a whole people entirely elect.

No one nowadays could be so blind or so ungrateful as not to recognize the enormously important rôle that France plays in the fate of Europe: but, Sir, I must confess that I find it impossible to say, as you do, that France is a necessary condition, is a *sine qua non* of the march of history.

Nature never stakes her all on a single card. Rome, the Eternal City, which at one time could make a fair claim to be the ruler of the world, sank into decline, disintegrated, became extinct, and Humanity in its inhumanity moved on.

On the other hand, short of accusing Nature of absurdity and madness, I should find it difficult to see nothing but an outcast race, a lie, a mere conglomeration of creatures lower than mankind but with all the vices of mankind, in a nation which has a thousand formative years to its credit, which has with a rare obstinacy preserved its national integrity, which has welded itself into an empire, and which has affected the course of history—more so perhaps than it should have.

And such a view becomes even more unplausible when one realizes that this country, on its enemies' own admission, is anything but static. It is not a country, like China, that having attained some form of social organization more or less suited to its requirements, has sunk into a heavy sleep, into a condition of *semper idem*: even less is it a country, like that of the Hindus, that has outlived its strength and is now dying of senile decay. On the contrary, Russia is an Empire still in its youth; a building that still has about it the smell of fresh plaster, where everything is experimental and in a state of transition, where nothing is final, where people are always making changes, many of which are for the worse but all of which are at least changes. Such, in brief, is the people that, according to you, is based on Communism, that draws its strength from the subdivision of land.

After all, Sir, why do you reproach the Russian people? What is the real substance of your accusation?

'The Russian', you say, 'is a liar and a thief: he is a habitual liar and a habitual thief: and is so innocently, for it is in his nature to be so.'

Sir, I will not here comment on the excessive generality of this observation, but I should like to put to you, if I may, this simple question: Who in such cases is the victim, whom does the Russian lie to, and whom does he steal from? And the answer surely is that it is the landowner, the official, the civil servant, the judge, the police officer—in other words, the sworn enemies of the peasant, men whom he has come to look upon as Germanized apostates and traitors. Deprived of all means of self-protection, he tries to trick his oppressors, to deceive them, and, in doing so, is surely right. Cunning, a great thinker has said, is the irony of brute force.[5]

The Russian peasant who has, as you have rightly observed, a strong aversion to every form of landed property, who is improvident and indolent by temperament, has gradually and imperceptibly found himself caught up in the tentacles of the German bureaucracy and the feudal power. He has submitted to this degrading yoke with, I agree, the passivity of despair, but he has never believed either in the authority of his lord, or in the justice of the courts, or in the equity of the administration. For almost two hundred years, his whole life has been one long, dumb, passive opposition to the existing order of things: he has endured oppression, he has groaned under it: but he has never accepted anything that goes on outside the life of the rural commune.

The idea of the Tsar still enjoys some considerable prestige in the mind of the peasant. But it is not the actual Tsar Nicholas whom he adores, it is rather an abstract idea, a myth, a kind of Providence, an Avenger of evils, an embodiment of justice in the popular imagination.

Apart from the Tsar, only the Clergy are capable of having any moral influence on Orthodox Russia. The higher clergy are the sole representatives of ancient Russia within the administration. The clergy have never shaved off their beards, and through this very fact have remained on the side of the people. The people have complete faith in anything they are told by a monk. However, the monks and the higher clergy, for all their talk about being dedicated to matters not of this world, are almost entirely indifferent to the people. The village priest has lost all influence on account of his greed, his drunkenness, and his close association with the police. Here again, it is not the man but the idea that the people respect.

As for the Dissenters, they hate both the Tsar and the village priest, both the man and the idea.

Apart from the Tsar and the Clergy, all the other elements within society and the administration are utterly alien and ultimately hostile to the people. The peasant is, quite literally, outside the law: the law contrives to offer him absolutely no protection whatsoever, and his only share in the existing order of things is confined to the payment of the double tribute which grinds him down: the tribute of blood and the tribute of sweat. So, spurned on all sides, he comes to feel that the government is not for him but against him, that the single aim of the administration and the nobility is to extort from him as much work and as much money as possible. Realizing this and blessed with a certain shrewd, cunning intelligence he manages to deceive all of them all the time. Nor could he very well do anything else, because if he told them the truth, that would be an admission, an acceptance on his part of their power: if he didn't steal from them (and notice that he is accused of stealing when he conceals any part of the produce of his own labour), if he didn't steal from them, then this would be a recognition on his part—and a quite fatal one—of the propriety of these exactions, of the rights of the landowners and of the fairness of his judges.

In order to appreciate the real position of the Russian peasant, you need to see him before one of these courts of law: you have only to see for yourself the sad, frightened eyes, the sullen set of the jaw, the anxious searching look he turns on all around him, to realize that his position is no better than that of a captured rebel brought before a court martial, or that of a traveller facing a gang of brigands. From the first glance, it is quite clear that the victim has no trust in these cruel, hostile, implacable creatures who interrogate him and torture him and finally mulct him dry. He knows that if he has any money, then he will be acquitted, and if he hasn't, he will be condemned without mercy.

When he speaks, he uses a somewhat antiquated Russian: whereas the judge and his clerks use the modern bureaucratic language which is so garbled an affair as to be barely intelligible. First they fill whole folios with their ungrammatical solecisms, and then they reel it off at the peasant in a high nasal twang as fast as they can go. What he hears is an undifferentiated flux of noise, of which he must, if he is to preserve his skin, make such sense as he can. He is fully aware of what is at issue, and is on his guard. He is sparing in his use of words, tries hard to cover up his nervousness, and the result is that he stands there with an asinine look on his face, like a great booby, like someone who has lost the power of speech.

He leaves the court in the same wretched state whether he has been condemned or whether he has been acquitted. The difference between the two verdicts seems to him a matter of mere chance or luck.

In much the same way, when he is summoned as a witness, he insists on perjuring himself, on knowing nothing, on denying everything, even when the evidence on the other side is overwhelming. In the eyes of the Russian people, there is no stigma attached to a man merely because he has been found guilty in a court of law. Convicts and those who are sentenced to transportation are in popular parlance called '*unfortunates*'.

The Russian peasant has no real knowledge of any form of life but that of the village commune: he understands about rights and duties only when these are tied to the commune and its members. Outside the commune, there are no obligations for him—there is simply violence. The fatal element in his character is that he submits to the violence, not that, in his own way, he denies it and tries to protect himself by guile. It is far more honest to lie before a judge whom one doesn't acknowledge, than to make some show of respect for a jury packed by the police, whose monstrous corruption is as clear as daylight. The peasant respects his institutions only in so far as he finds embodied there his own notions of Right and Justice.

There is one fact that has never been denied by anyone who has any real first-hand knowledge of the Russian people. And that is that they very rarely cheat one another. An almost boundless good faith prevails amongst them: contracts and written agreements are quite unheard of.

Problems connected with surveying are necessarily extremely complicated on account of the perpetual subdivision of the land according to the number of people working on it.⁶ And yet the peace of the Russian countryside is never disturbed by any complaints or litigation. The government and the landowners ask for nothing better than some pretext for interference, but none is ever afforded them. The petty differences that arise are quickly settled either by the elders or by the commune: everyone abides by such decisions without reservation. The same thing happens in the nomadic communes of artisans (the *artel*). There are a number of such *artels*—builders, carpenters and other sorts of artisans—each consisting of several hundred people drawn from different communes, who come together for a given period of time, for a year for instance, and so form a group. When the year is up, the workers share out the produce on the basis of the work they have done, in each case abiding by the general decision. The police have not so far had the satisfaction of being able to interfere in these arrangements. The association, I must emphasize, generally holds itself responsible for all the workers who comprise it.

The bonds between peasants of the same commune are much closer when the commune is not Orthodox but Dissenter. From time to time the government organizes a savage raid on one of these Dissenting communes. The whole population is imprisoned and then deported, without any preconceived plan, without any repercussions, without any provocation, without any necessity, merely in compliance with the instructions of the clergy or the depositions of the police. It is in the course of these persecutions of Dissenters, that one can see the Russian peasant as he really is and observe the solidarity that ties him to his fellows. One can see him on such occasions tricking the police, rescuing his fellow believers, hiding the holy books and vessels, undergoing the most appalling tortures without uttering a word. I challenge anyone to produce a single example of a Dissenting commune that has been betrayed by a peasant, even an Orthodox.

This trait in the ordinary Russian makes all police inquiries extremely difficult to carry out. And I heartily congratulate him on it. The Russian peasant has no other morality than that which flows quite instinctively and naturally from his communal life: it is profoundly national in character and the little that he knows about the Gospels fortifies him in it: the shocking corruption of the government and of the landlords binds him ever more closely to his traditional customs and to his commune.⁷ The commune has preserved the Russian people from Mongol barbarism, from Imperial civilization, from the Europeanized landowners and from the German bureaucracy: the organic life of the commune has persisted despite all the attempts made on it by authority, badly mauled though it has been at times. By good fortune it has survived right into the period that witnesses the rise of Socialism in Europe.

For Russia this has been a most happy providence.

The Russian aristocracy is entering on a new phase of its existence. Born of an anti-national revolution, it has accomplished its appointed task. It has brought into being a vast empire, a large army, and a centralized government. Devoid of all principles and traditions, it has nothing further to do. It has, it is true, arrogated to itself another task, that of importing Western civilization into Russia, and it had some measure of success in doing this so long as it played the part of being a civilized governing class.

This part it has now abandoned.

The government which originally cut itself off from the people in the name of civilization, has now, a hundred years later, hurriedly cut itself off from civilization in the name of absolutism.

This happened as soon as it detected the tricolour of liberalism dimly visible, like a spectre, through the tendencies of civilization. It then tried to fall back on the idea of nationalism and on the people. But this was impossible: there was by now no common ground between the people and the government—the people had grown completely away from the government, and the government in turn seemed to see in the masses something even more terrifying than anything it knew—the Red Spectre. All things considered, liberalism seemed to be less dangerous than the prospect of a new Pugachev.⁸ But the horror and the disgust in which all liberal ideas were held had now become such that the government could no longer make its peace with civilization.

From then onwards, the sole aim of Tsarism has been Tsarism, ruling for ruling's sake. Immense new forces have been called into being, each one of them at once supplementing and neutralizing all the others, so that in this way a quite artificial stability has been attained.

But autocracy for autocracy's sake is ultimately an impossibility: it is too pointless, too sterile.

This has now been realized, and so some sort of outlet has been looked for in Europe. Russian diplomacy is feverishly active: there is a constant despatch of notes, agents, suggestions, threats, promises, spies. The Emperor sees himself as the natural protector of all German princes. He dabbles in every petty intrigue in every petty court. He settles all their little differences, bestowing on one a reprimand, on another a Grand Duchess. But even this doesn't exhaust his energy. He has become the policeman of the whole world, the prop of all forms of reaction and all forms of barbarism. He sets himself up as the supreme representative of the monarchical principle in Europe, giving himself the airs of an aristocrat, as though he were a Bourbon or a Tudor and had for his courtiers Devonshires, or, at the very lowest, Montmorencys.

The sad part of this is that there really is nothing in common between feudal monarchy with its avowed principles, its roots in the past, its social and religious ideology, and the Napoleonic despotism of St Petersburg, which has no principles behind it, and is based entirely on grim historic necessity and some passing need that it satisfies.

And gradually the Winter Palace, like a mountain peak at the end of the warm season, becomes covered over with layer upon layer of snow and ice. The sap, which was artificially induced to rise into these elevated social reaches, now slowly recedes from them, so that all they can now command is a certain brute strength, a mere physical hardness like that of a rock good for a while longer against the waves of revolution which break idly at its base.

Surrounded by his generals and his ministers and his officers and his bureaucrats, Nicholas defies his isolation, but visibly he grows gloomier: he becomes morose, preoccupied. He realizes that no one has any affection for him, he senses the gloomy silence that surrounds him, through which he can hear only too well the distant rumblings that seem to draw closer. The Tsar tries to forget all this, and announces to the world that his sole concern is the aggrandizement of the Imperial power.

Such declarations are nothing new: for the last twenty-five years he has toiled unremittingly, without respite, for this cause and this alone: in pursuit of it he has spared nothing, neither tears nor blood.

Everything that he has undertaken has prospered: he has crushed Polish nationalism, and in Russia he has extinguished liberalism.

What more can he want? Why is he so depressed?

The Emperor knows that Poland is not really dead. And in place of the liberalism that he has persecuted with such gratuitous savagery for that exotic flower could never have taken root in Russian soil, being quite alien to the national character—he now sees another problem lowering like a storm cloud.

The people are beginning to murmur and grow restless under the yoke of the nobility: small revolts break out all the time: you yourself, Sir, have referred to one terrible instance of this.

The party of movement, of progress, demands the emancipation of the peasants; and its members are ready to set an example by sacrificing their own rights. The Tsar is in a state of permanent indecision, and has lost the power of all real thought: he wants emancipation, and yet does all he can to prevent it.

He has come to see that the emancipation of the peasant is tantamount to the emancipation of the land: and that the emancipation of the land would in turn usher in a social revolution and would make rural communism sacrosanct. To evade this question of emancipation is certainly impossible: to postpone it until the reign of his successor would be easier but cowardly, and the time gained would really be no better than time spent in a wretched posting-station waiting for fresh horses.

From all this you can see what a blessing it is for Russia that the rural commune has never been broken up, that private ownership has never replaced the property of the commune: how fortunate it is for the Russian people that they have remained outside all political movements, and, for that matter, outside European civilization, which would undoubtedly have sapped the life of the commune, and which to-day in Socialism has achieved its own negation.

Europe, as I have pointed out elsewhere, has never solved the antinomy of the State and the individual, but it has stated the problem. Russia approaches the same problem from a quite different direction, but it has had no greater success in finding a solution to it. It is then in the shadow of this problem that we find the source of our equality.

Europe, now on the point of taking the first step forward in a social revolution, is confronted by a country that can provide an actual instance of an attempt—a crude, barbaric attempt perhaps, but still an attempt of a sort—in the direction of the division of the land amongst those who work it. And observe that this lesson is provided not by civilized Russia but by the people themselves in their daily lives. We Russians who have absorbed European civilization cannot hope to be more than a means to an end—the yeast in the leavening—a bridge between the Russian people and revolutionary Europe. The future of Russia lies with the *moujik,* just as the regeneration of France lies with the worker.

But if this is so, then surely the Russian people have some claim on your indulgence? Surely, Sir, this is so.

Poor peasant! So intelligent, so simple in his habits, so easily satisfied, he has been seized on as the butt of every vicious attack. The Emperor decimates his number by conscription: the landowner steals every third day of his working week: the *tchinovnik*[9] worms out of him his last rouble. The peasant suffers all in silence, but without despair. He holds hard to his commune. If someone tears a limb off it, it heals over, it comes together all the more. The fate of the poor peasant surely deserves pity, and yet he receives none: instead of commiseration, he is showered with abuse.

You, Sir, deny the last refuge that is open to him, the one place left where he can still feel himself to be a man, where he can know love and not fear. For you say that 'his commune is not really a commune, his family is not really a family, his wife is not really his wife: before she belongs to him, she belongs to his lord; his children are not really his children, and who knows who is their father?'

In this style you hold up this unfortunate people not to scientific scrutiny but to the scorn of the whole world, which will read and accept and admire all these fine stories that you give them.

It is then my duty to say something on the subject.

The family is something very highly developed amongst all the Slav races: it is possibly here that we have the source of their conservatism, the limit of their negative tendency.

The prototype of the commune is the family owning all things in common.

Amongst these rural families, there is no desire to split up into different households, and so one often finds three or four generations living together under one roof and ruled over in a patriarchal manner either by the grandfather or by a great-uncle. Women, for the most part, lead a rather oppressed life, as is generally the case in an agricultural community, but in Russia they are treated with respect when their sons come of age and even more so if they are the widows of family chiefs.

It is by no means uncommon to find the conduct of affairs entirely in the hands of a grey-haired grandmother. Can it, then, really be said that the family doesn't exist in Russia?

Now let us turn to the relations that exist between the landowner and his serf families.

But if we are to have a clear picture of the situation, we must first distinguish between the law and the abuses of the law, between what is permitted and what is criminal.

The *droit du seigneur* has never existed among the Slav peoples.

The landowner has no legal right to demand either the first joys of marriage or any subsequent infidelity. If the law were properly enforced in Russia, then the seduction of a serf would be punished in exactly the same way as an offence against a free woman: that is to say, it would make the offender liable either to penal servitude or to exile in Siberia according to the gravity of the actual offence. So much for the law: now let us look at the facts.

It is undeniable that with the social position that the aristocracy are allowed by the Government, it is very easy for them to seduce the wives and daughters of their serfs. The landowner, with his powers of confiscation and punishment, can always find husbands willing to hand over their wives, and fathers ready to dispose of their daughters—rather like that splendid French nobleman in the middle of the eighteenth century who, according to Peuchot's *Mémoires,* begged for the special privilege of being allowed to install his daughter in the Parc-aux-Cerfs.

It is scarcely surprising that honest fathers and husbands can obtain no redress against the nobility, thanks to the excellent judiciary in Russia. They find themselves in a position much like that of Monsieur Tiercelin whose daughter of eleven was abducted by Berryer with the connivance of Louis XV. I do not deny that such disgusting abuses are perfectly possible—indeed one has only to think of the crude and depraved habits of one section of the Russian nobility to realize it. But this does not mean that the peasants are indifferent spectators of their masters' debauchery: far from it.

Let me produce some evidence for this.

Half the landowners who are murdered by their peasants and statistics show that the total is between sixty and seventy a year) are killed in revenge for their erotic exploits. The peasant very seldom brings an action against his master because he knows that the court will completely disregard his grievances. But he has his axe, in the use of which he is a real master, and he knows it.

So much for the peasantry: and now, Sir, I beg you to bear with me for a little in what I have to say about civilized Russia.

Our intellectual movement has fared no better at your hands than our national character: with a single stroke of the pen you dismissed everything that we have ever done, all the work of our fettered hands.

One of Shakespeare's characters, at a loss for some way to humiliate an opponent he despises, exclaims: 'I even doubt your existence.' You have gone further, Sir: you don't doubt the non-existence of Russian literature.

I quote your very words:

> I cannot attach any real importance to the efforts of a few clever people in St Petersburg, who have experimented a little with the Russian language rather as if it were a learned language and have deceived Europe with a wan travesty of a national literature. If it were not for my deep respect for Mickiewicz and his saintly aberrations, I really should blame him for the charity, one might almost say the indulgence, with which he speaks of this frippery.

I am quite unable, Sir, to find any reason for the scornful way in which you receive the first agonized cry of a people awakening in its prison-house, a movement which the gaoler tries to stifle at birth.

Why have you been so unwilling to listen to the heart-rending accents of our sad poetry, of our songs which are merely tears given tongue? What is it that has warped your understanding of the nervous, hysterical laughter in our literature, of the unfailing irony which conceals the deep wound in our heart, and which is, in the last analysis, the terrible confession of our utter impotence?

How I wish I could translate for you adequately some of the lyrical poems of Pushkin, or Lermontov, or some of Koltsov's ballads! Then you would welcome us with open arms, you would be the very first to beg us to forget everything you had said before.

Apart from the communal life of the *moujik,* there is nothing so characteristic of Russia, nothing that bodes so well for her future as her literary movement.

Between the peasant and literature there looms up the ghastly figure of official Russia, of 'the Russian lie, of the Russian cholera'—as you have so well named it.

This Russia starts with the Emperor and you can follow it right down from soldier to soldier, from clerk to clerk, until you come to the humblest official in a police-station in the farthest district of the Empire. In this way it ramifies indefinitely and at every stage—like the '*bolgi*' of Dante—it gains a new power for evil, it becomes even more depraved and tyrannical. So we have this living pyramid of crimes, abuses, impositions, floggings, the work of inhuman German officials everlastingly on the make, of illiterate judges everlastingly drunk, of aristocrats everlastingly toadying: the whole thing welded together by ties of common gain and common guilt, and in the last resort upheld by six hundred thousand automata armed with bayonets.

The peasant never defiles himself by any contact with the world of cynical officialdom: he suffers—that is the extent of his guilt.

The opposition to official Russia consists of a handful of desperate men who spend their lives in denouncing it, attacking it, unmasking it, sapping its strength.

From time to time one of these lone champions is dragged off to prison, tortured, deported to Siberia, but his place does not stay empty for long: fresh champions step into the breach. Such is our tradition, our inalienable inheritance.

The ghastly consequences that attend the spoken word in Russia inevitably increase its effectiveness. The voice of the free man is listened to with love and veneration, because in our country, it is raised only when there is something serious to say. The decision to put one's thoughts on paper is one not lightly made when at the foot of every page there looms up the prospect of a policeman, a *troika,* a *kibitka,* and in the distance Tobolsk or Irkoutsk.

In my last pamphlet, I wrote enough about Russian literature: here I shall only add a few general observations.

Sadness, scepticism, irony—these are the three strings of the Russian lyre.

When Pushkin begins one of his finest poems with these restrained, melancholy words:

> There is no justice on earth—nor any above us either.
> That is as clear to me as a simple musical scale.[10]

doesn't this chill your heart, don't you seem to see behind the apparent tranquillity a broken life, don't you detect a man who has become inured to suffering?

Lermontov, barely 30 years of age, filled with disgust at the society in which he finds himself, addresses one of his contemporaries in these words:

> I look on my generation with grief: its future is blank and grim: it will grow old in inaction, it will sink under the weight of doubt and barren science.
>
> Life exhausts us like a journey without a destination.
>
> We are like those ratheripes which are sometimes found, strange orphans amongst the blossom: they delight neither the eye nor the palate: they fall as they ripen. . . .
>
> We hurry towards the tomb, without happiness, without glory, and before we die we cast a look of bitter scorn over our past.
>
> We shall pass through this world unnoticed, a pensive, silent, soon forgotten company.
>
> We shall leave nothing to our descendants, no fruitful idea, no work of genius, and they will insult our remains with some contemptuous verse or with the sarcasm a destitute son might use to his spendthrift father.

I know of only one other modern poet who has sounded the sombre notes of the human heart with the same intensity. He, too, was a poet born in slavery, and he likewise died before the rebirth of his native country. I mean that apologist of death, the famous Leopardi, he who saw the world as a vast league of criminals ruthlessly warring against a few virtuous madmen.

Russia has produced only one painter who is widely known: Brullov.[11] Where did this artist look for his inspiration? What is the subject of his masterpiece which won him something of a reputation in Italy?

Look at this strange work.

Across an enormous canvas you see groups of terrified and bewildered people. Despite their efforts to escape, many are dying, the victims of an earthquake, of a volcanic eruption, of a truly cataclysmic storm. They are overwhelmed by some savage, senseless, evil force against which all struggle is unavailing. Such is the kind of inspiration that can be drawn from the atmosphere of Petersburg.

The Russian novel is entirely a study in pathological anatomy. It is one long diagnosis of the evil that consumes us, one sustained work of self-accusation, a pitiless, inexorable accusation. What we never hear is that gentle voice which comes down from Heaven, the voice that announced to Faust the forgiveness of the young, sinful girl. We must not look here for consolation, the only voices to be heard are those of doubt and damnation. And yet if Russia is to achieve salvation, it will be on account of this profound awareness that we have of our predicament, and the scant trouble we take to conceal it from the world.

He who frankly admits his failings, feels that he has something within him that will survive and overcome any disaster: he knows that he can redeem the past, and not only hold his head high but that, as in Byron's tragedy, he can turn from being 'Sardanapalus the profligate to Sardanapalus the hero.'

The Russian people do not read. Nor, of course, were Voltaire and Diderot read by villagers; they were read by the aristocracy and the Third Estate. In Russia the enlightened section of the Third Estate is part of the aristocracy, for the aristocracy nowadays includes everyone who is above the level of the people: it even includes an aristocratic proletariat which at one end merges into the people, and it includes a proletariat of freed men who work their way up the social scale and then become noble. This process of movement, this continual flux, gives the Russian aristocracy a character which you find nowhere else amongst the privileged classes of Europe. In short, all Russian history since Peter I is entirely the history of the aristocracy, and of the influence of European civilization upon it. Here I must mention that the size of the aristocracy in Russia is at least half that of the total number of electors in France, since the law of May 31st.[12]

During the eighteenth century, the most important theme in neo-Russian literature was the development of that rich, sonorous and magnificent language that we use today: a language which is at once supple and powerful, capable of expressing the most abstract notions of German metaphysics, and also the light, witty, sparkling phrases of French conversation. This literature, called into being by the genius of Peter the Great, bears, it is true, a sort of governmental imprint—but in those days being on the side of government meant being on the side of reform, almost on the side of revolution.

The Imperial throne was, right up to the great revolution of '89, majestically draped in the grandest robes of European civilization and philosophy. It was fitting that Catherine II should be entertained with villages[13] made out of cardboard and with wooden palaces with the distemper still fresh upon them: no one knew better than she the art of *mise-en-scène*. At the Hermitage Voltaire and Montesquieu and Beccaria vied with one another in displaying their talents. You know, Sir, the reverse of the medal.

Meanwhile, a strange, unexpected note began to break in on the triumphal choruses of Pindaric odes to which the Court was given over. It was a note in which sarcastic irony, a tendency towards criticism and scepticism were apparent, and it was, I must say, the one truly national note to be heard, the only note sounded that had any real vitality in it, that gave any promise for the future. The others, transitory and exotic affairs, were doomed to perish.

The true character of Russian thought, whether in poetry or in speculation, emerges only in a fully developed, vital form after the accession of Nicholas. The distinctive traits of this movement, are a new and tragic sense of right and wrong, an implacable spirit of negation, a bitter irony, a tortured self-questioning. Sometimes a note of wild laughter accompanies it, but it is laughter without gaiety.

Living under these truly oppressive conditions, the Russian, who possesses an unclouded intelligence and a ruthlessly logical mind, soon emancipated himself from religion and traditional morality.

The emancipated Russian is the most independent creature in the world. And what indeed could there be to restrain him? A sense of the past? . . . But then isn't the starting point of modern Russia just the denial of tradition and national sentiment?

Or a sense of the past indefinite, the Petersburg period? But that surely lays no obligation on us: 'this fifth act of a blood-stained drama, set in a brothel'[14] freed us from our old beliefs, but committed us to no new ones.

Your history, on the other hand, the history of the West, provides us with certain lessons, but no more: we do not consider ourselves the legal executors of your past.

We can share your scepticism—it is your faith that leaves us cold. You are too religious for us. We can share your animosities—it is your attachment to the legacy of the past that is incomprehensible to us. We are too oppressed, too wretched to make do with a mere half-liberty. You have your commitments to consider, your scruples to restrain you—but we have none of this, no commitments and no scruples—it is merely that for the moment we are powerless.

Here, Sir, is the source of that irony, of that rage that drives us to desperate measures, that takes possession of us and forces us on and on until it brings us to Siberia and the rack, to exile and early death. We have dedicated ourselves to a cause but without hope, in disgust and boredom. There is something truly irrational about our lives, but nothing that is either banal or stagnant or bourgeois.

Do not accuse us of being immoral merely because we do not respect the things that you respect. Would you condemn a foundling for having no respect for his parents? We are free agents, because we are self-made. The only element of tradition that we accept is that involved in our organic, our national way of life: and that is inherent in our very being: it is in our blood, it acts upon us more like an instinct than like some external authority to which we feel we must bend our wills. We are independent, because we possess nothing. There are literally no demands upon our affections. All our memories are tinged with bitterness and resentment. The fruits of civilization and learning were offered us at the end of the knout.

What obligation, then, have we, the younger sons, the castaways of the family, to acknowledge any of your traditional duties? And how could we in all honesty accept this threadbare morality of yours, a morality which is neither humane nor Christian, which has no existence outside a few rhetorical exercises and speeches for the prosecution? How can you expect us to have any respect for the praetorium in which you administer your Barbaro-Roman justice, for those gloomy, oppressive vaults, where no light or air ever penetrates, rebuilt in the Middle Ages and then patched up by the enfranchised Third Estate? What goes on in them is possibly better than the robbery that goes on in the Russian courts, but could anyone maintain that it had anything to do with justice?

It is quite clear that any difference there may be between your laws and our Ukases lies almost entirely in the wording of their preambles. Ukases start with a painful truth—'The Tsar commands . . .'—whereas your laws start with an insulting lie, the triple Republican motto, the ironical invocation in the name of the French people. The *Code Nicholas* is intended to be unreservedly against mankind and in favour of authority. The *Code Napoléon* seems really no different. There are already enough impositions that we are forced to endure, without our making the position worse by imposing new ones on ourselves of our own free will. In this respect our situation is exactly like that of the peasantry. We bow to brute force: we are slaves because we have no way of freeing ourselves: but whatever happens, we shall accept nothing from the enemy camp.

Russia will never be Protestant.

Russia will never be *juste-milieu*.

Russia will never stage a revolution with the sole aim of ridding herself of Tsar Nicholas only to replace him by a multitude of other Tsars—Tsar-deputies, Tsar-tribunals, Tsar-policemen, Tsar-laws.

Possibly we ask too much, and shall achieve nothing. That may be so, but we shall not despair. Before 1848, Russia neither should nor could have embarked on a career of revolution. At that time she had still much to learn—and she is learning it. Even the Tsar himself sees this: and this is the reason why he has made himself the scourge of the universities, of all speculation, of all learning. He is struggling hard to isolate Russia from the rest of the world and to stamp out all civilization: He is true to his profession—*il fait son métier*.

Will he succeed?

I have said elsewhere one must not put blind faith in the future; every foetus has the right to develop, but for all that not every foetus does develop. The future of Russia does not depend on herself alone: it is bound up with the future of Europe as a whole. Who can foretell what lies in store for the Slav world, should Reaction and Absolutism triumph over the European Revolution?

Perhaps it will perish—who knows?

But then Europe also will perish. . . .

And history will continue in America. . . .

* * *

I had written as far as this, Sir, when I received the last two pamphlets composing your epic. My first impulse on reading them was to throw what I had written on the fire. A man with your noble and generous heart did not need to wait for someone else to protest before according justice to a despised country. With your sympathy and kindness of heart, you couldn't keep up for long the rôle of the inexorable judge, of the avenger of a martyred race. You contradict yourself, but such contradictions are sublime.

However, when I reread my letter, it occurred to me that you might find there some observations about Russia and the Slav world that were new to you: so I decided to send it. I have complete confidence that you will pardon me for those passages where I allowed myself to be carried away by barbarian fury. It is not for nothing that Cossack blood flows in one's veins. I so longed to be able to change your opinions about the Russian people: it was so sad, so painful for me to see you treat us with such ruthlessness: I couldn't altogether suppress the grief that I felt and I let my pen run away with me. Now I see that you do not despair of us: I see that under the Russian peasant's coarse kaftan, you discover a human being, and now, for my part, I must confess to you that we perfectly understand what sort of picture the mere name of Russia conjures up in the mind of every free person. We have so often cursed our unhappy country ourselves. You know that well, Sir, else you would not have written those remarkable words—'Everything that we have said about the moral nullity of Russia is feeble in comparison with what Russians themselves have said about it.'

But, like you, we now feel that the time for these funeral orations on Russia is over and with you we say 'sous la tombe est une étincelle'[15]—'in the tomb—a spark of life'. You suspected it, guided by the insight of love: but we have seen it, we have experienced it. The spark of life has not been quenched, neither in the torrents of blood that have flowed, nor in the snows of Siberia, nor in the depths of mines and prisons. May it continue to smoulder under the ashes—for the cruel, bitter, icy wind that blows from Europe is strong enough to put it out. Russia finds herself hemmed in between two Siberias: the one white with snow, the other 'white' in its opinions.

For us the hour of action has not yet come. France can still rightly boast of having the honour of the van: all the difficulties of decision are still hers—and will be so even in 1852. It is obvious that Europe must take the lead—whether it be into the tomb or into a new life—and we shall follow her not just because Europe is older than us but because there is this intimate link—as I have tried to bring home to you—between social revolution on the one hand and the fate of the Slav world on the other. The day of action may still be far off: the day of conscience, of thought, of speech has already dawned. We have lived long enough in sleep and silence: it is now time to tell of our dreams, to impart the fruit of our meditations.

Indeed, whose fault is it that the world had to wait until 1843, for the day 'when a German (Haxthausen) discovered'—that is the very word you use—'the Russia of the peasantry, of which until then people knew no more than they did of America before Christopher Columbus.'

It is our fault. It is the fault, I freely admit it, of our dumbness, of our cowardice, of the way we have allowed our tongues to be paralysed with fear, our imagination blighted by terror. Outside our frontiers we are even terrified of admitting how terrified we are of our chains. Born convicts, condemned to wear fetters until the day of our death, we feel insulted when people refer to us as willing slaves, as the negroes of the north, and yet we never think of openly disabusing them.

We must make up our minds whether we intend to endure these accusations, or whether we intend to put a stop to them and let free Russian speech be heard once again. It is far better to die under suspicion of being human than to bear the brand of slavery on one's forehead for ever, to live under the shameful reproach of being a slave by desire.

Unfortunately, in Russia, free speech is found shocking, terrifying. I tried to lift a small corner of the thick veil that hides us from the gaze of Europe: I confined myself to certain general intellectual tendencies, certain long-term aspirations, certain organic developments that the future holds in store: and yet, for all that, my pamphlet—about which you were kind enough to express yourself in such flattering terms—made a painful impression in Russia. Friends, people whom I respect, raised their voices in condemnation. People accused it of being an admission of guilt. An admission . . . of what sort of crime? Of the crime of unhappiness, of suffering, of a desire to escape from our hateful position. . . . Poor, dear friends, forgive me this fault—for now I am falling into it again!

Ah, Sir, it is a hard and terrible thing to endure the yoke of slavery without being able to strike a blow, without any immediate hope of release. In the end it crushes even the best, the noblest, the most enthusiastic of men. Where is the hero who will not ultimately give way to weariness and despair, and exchange all these dreams for a little peace before he dies?

No, I will not be silent. My words shall avenge these unhappy creatures, broken under the dead weight of Russian absolutism, of this infernal régime which brings men to the brink of moral collapse, to a state of dreamlike apathy.

We must speak out—otherwise no one will ever suspect how much that is both beautiful and sublime lies locked in the breasts of these brave men and will be buried with them when they die, under the snows of exile, in tombs that may not even bear their dishonoured names—their sacred names, rather, which their friends will preserve in their hearts but never dare breathe aloud.

We have only to open our mouths, only to murmur a few words about what we want or what we hope for, when at once they clamp down on us, and try to turn the cradle of free speech into its grave. How can we live like this?

At a certain moment the human intellect comes of age and when it does, it can no longer be kept in bondage, not in the chains of censorship nor in the leading-strings of prudence. When this happens, propaganda becomes one of nature's needs. For how can it be enough to whisper in our neighbour's ear, when even the knell of the tocsin may well fail to rouse him from his stupor?

From the revolt of the Streltsy[16] to the conspiracy of December the 14th, there was no serious political rising in Russia. The explanation is simple enough. Among the people at large there was no really coherent revolutionary movement. In some matters they found themselves in agreement with the Government, and on many others they took their opinions from the Government. Only the peasants, cut off from all the benefits of the Imperial régime and more oppressed than ever before, attempted a revolution. The whole of Russia from the Urals to Penza, Simbirsk and Kazan, was, for several months, under the sway of Pugachev. The Imperial army was forced to fall back before these Cossack onslaughts and General Bibikov who had been sent out from Petersburg to take over command, wrote back from Nijni Novgorod if I am not mistaken: 'Things are going very badly: the most frightening thing is not the armed hordes of the rebels, but the state of mind of the people which is bad, very bad.'

Finally, after the most incredible efforts, the insurrection was crushed. From that time onwards the people sank into a state of total apathy, dumbness, indifference.

But while the mass of the people slumbered the aristocracy showed signs of progress. Civilization slowly began to penetrate their consciousness, and, if we need real living proof of their political maturity, of their moral progress, which ultimately committed them to some form of action, we have those wonderful men, those heroes, of whom you have so well remarked that 'they, alone, in the very jaws of the dragon, attempted the bold blow of December the 14th.'

Their defeat and the terrorism of the present reign have succeeded in smothering all progressive ideas and putting a stop to any more of these premature attempts. Issues of a rather different sort have come to the fore: people are no longer prepared to risk their lives for a constitution, now that they know that any Charter granted in Petersburg can always be neutralized by some chicanery on the part of the Tsar: the fate of the Polish constitution exists as a permanent warning.

For ten years, people struggled on at purely intellectual tasks, without ever risking a word, until eventually they found themselves in such a state of anxiety and depression that 'they threw away their lives for the pleasure of a moment's freedom', for the mere possibility of expressing something of what was in their minds.

Some, with that frivolity, that recklessness which is to be found only amongst Poles and Russians, gave up everything that they had and went abroad to try and find some distraction for their depression: others, unable to overcome the horror that they felt for the St Petersburg régime, buried themselves in the depths of their estates. The younger generation became immersed either in Panslavism or in German philosophy or in history or in economics: in a word, no one in Russia who felt any natural bent for intellectual matters either would or could remain idle and tranquil.

The recent case of Petrashevsky who was sentenced to the mines for life, and his friends who were deported in 1849, for organizing revolutionary clubs a stone's throw from the Winter Palace, adequately reveals, both in the bold recklessness of the victims, and in the obvious hopelessness of the undertaking, that the period of rational calculation is over, that the desire for action can no longer be thwarted, that people prefer running the certain risk of some punishment or other to remaining dumb, impassive witnesses of the Petersburg tyranny. There is a popular Russian fable that tells of a Tsar who, suspecting his wife of unfaithfulness, ordered her to be placed in a barrel with her son. The Tsar then had the barrel sealed and cast into the sea.

For many years the barrel floated on the waters. Meanwhile the young prince grew and grew, until he could touch the ends of the barrel with his head and his feet. Every day the lack of space proved more and more irksome to him. One day he said to his mother, 'O royal mother, allow me to stretch myself to my full length.'

'Tsarevitch, my son,' replied his mother, 'beware of doing what you say: for the barrel will burst and you will perish in the salt waves.' For a moment the Tsarevitch was silent, and then, having thought the matter over very carefully, he said: 'Royal mother, I will stretch myself. Better to stretch oneself in freedom once and then perish.'

There, Sir, you have our history.

It will be a black day for Russia when she can no longer find men who are willing to dare everything, whatever the risk, simply for the pleasure of stretching themselves in freedom once.

But there is no immediate danger of this. . . .

Involuntarily the name of Michael Bakunin comes before the mind. Bakunin has provided Europe with proof that a Russian can possess revolutionary ability.

I was deeply moved, Sir, by the noble words you used about him: unhappily these words will never reach him.

International crime has surpassed itself—Saxony handed the victim over to Austria: the Hapsburg despatched him to Nicholas. I am informed by friends in Petersburg that he is now in Russian hands. He is in Schlüsselburg, in that fortress of evil memory, once the prison of the young prince Ivan, the grandson of the Tsar Alexis, who was kept cooped up there like a wild animal, until he was murdered by Catherine the Second: she ordered his death herself, while her own hands were still stained with her husband's blood, and then had the wretched officer who had faithfully carried out her orders executed.

In that damp dungeon lapped by the icy waters of Lake Ladoga, Bakunin has already been tortured. The authorities know quite well that he will never speak—nor is there anything that they need to know from him—and yet they torture him[17]. . . . This is no place for dreams or hopes.

Let him then sleep his last sleep, let him die, for there is no way of rescuing him. A martyr betrayed by two treacherous Governments, each of which still holds in its bloody hands some morsels of his flesh. . . .

May his name be sacred, and avenged . . . but by whom? . . .

For all of us shall perish by the wayside; it will then fall to you, in your grave, sombre, majestic accents, to remind our children that they have a debt to discharge. . . .

I will conclude on this note, on the thought of this martyr. It is in his name and in mine that I warmly press your hand.

Alexandre Herzen

Nice Maritime

September 1851

Notes

1. *Poland & Russia: a Legend of Kosciusko* [1851].

2. 'Diamant enchâssé dans l'argent de la mer.'

3. Leaders of the abortive Decembrist revolt in 1825. Both were executed by Nicholas I in 1826.

4. i.e. the Decembrists.

5. *Biography of Hegel* by Rosenkranz ([1844; Hegel's] Posthumous works).—A.H. [Alexander Herzen]

6. And not according to the number of children.—A.H.

7. The peasants on one of the communes belonging to Prince Kozlovsky, bought their freedom at a price agreed upon with the landowner. The land was then divided up between the peasants in accordance with the amount of money that each had contributed to the fund that had bought them their liberty. This arrangement seemed to be one that was as fair as it was natural. However, the peasants found it so awkward and so little in accord with their ordinary way of life, that they decided to make themselves jointly responsible for the purchase money and regard it simply as a debt incurred by the commune as a whole, and to proceed with the division of the land on what was for them the normal system. The authority for this is Haxthausen who recounts it in his *Études sur la vie populaire en Russie* [1847]. The author visited the commune in question personally.

M. Tengoborski, a member of the Russian Council of State, in a book recently published in Paris and bearing a dedication to the Emperor Nicholas, says that the system of land-division seems to him unfavourable to agricultural development (as though agriculture had to be favourable to agricultural development!), but he adds: 'It would be very difficult to obviate these disadvantages, because the system of land division is bound up with the organization of the communes which *it would be dangerous to touch*: it rests on the fundamental notion of the unity of the commune and the equal right of every member of it to a share in the communal land. In this way, it reinforces and strengthens the communal spirit which is one of the stablest elements in the social organization. It is at the same time one of the best bulwarks against the increase of the proletariat and communist ideas.' (It is easy to realize that a people already enjoying the practice of the commune has nothing to fear from communist ideas.) 'What is remarkable is the good sense and the efficiency with which the peasants, generally without any external assistance, modify the inconvenient features of the system to suit local conditions, and the readiness with which they make adjustments to offset any inequality of distribution arising out of the quality of the soil itself, and the confidence with which they submit to adjudication by the elders of the commune. One might easily imagine that these land allocations, which have to be frequently revised, would give rise to innumerable disputes, and yet the parties involved seldom appeal to established authority. This fact, which is surprising in itself, can admit of only one explanation, and that is that the system, for all its potential defects, has become so much identified with the way of life and habits of the people that they put up with its drawbacks without a murmur.'

'The notion of association'—says the same author—'is as natural to the Russian peasant and as integral to all aspects of his life, as the notion of corporation, the municipal idea, which is central to the bourgeoisie of the West, is in conflict with his habits and outlook.' *Études sur les forces productives de la Russie* [1852-54], by M. Tengoborski, vol. I, p. 331 and p. 142.—A.H.

8. Leader of a cossack peasant revolt in the 18th century.

9. i.e. the government official.

10. *Mozart and Salieri*. The poem has been quite perfectly translated into German, by M. Bornstaedt, in a little volume of translations from Pushkin and Lermontov.—A.H.

11. Karl Brullov (1799-1852), the first Russian painter to win an international reputation, was born in Italy, of Huguenot extraction and came to Russia as a child. He studied in Rome, and his reputation was made entirely on the strength of *The Destruction of Pompeii* (1828-30). This picture was inspired by a visit to the ruins and influenced by Pliny's descriptions and Pacini's opera *L'ultimo giorno di Pompei* (1825). The enormous vogue that it enjoyed was due partly to its vast scale, partly to its eclectic combination of melodramatic lighting and reminiscences of Italian masters. Sir Walter Scott is said to have stood in front of it for an hour and declared it to be not a picture but an epic. It directly inspired Bulwer Lytton's novel. On his return to Russia, Brullov never repeated his early success, although some of his portraits are interesting studies. *The Destruction of Pompeii* now hangs in the Russian Museum, Leningrad.

12. French electoral law of May 31st, 1850, abolishing universal male suffrage and reducing register of voters from 10 million to 7 million.

13. Herzen is here referring to the famous Tauric expedition of Catherine II, January-June 1787, when the Empress made a ceremonial progress down the Dnieper to the Crimea: en route she was joined by Joseph II. Potemkin is said to have decorated the river banks with cardboard villages.

14. As it has been admirably described by a writer in *Il Progresso*, in the course of an article on Russia, August 1st, 1851.—A.H.

15. cf.

   . . . Si ta tombe est fermée
   Laisse-moi, dans ta cendre un instant ranimée,
   Trouver une étincelle. . . .

   A. de Musset: *Une Soirée Perdue*

16. The mutiny of the Streltsy regiments in 1698.

17. 'The author was misinformed. Bakunin remained, even now remains, in a casemate in Petersburg; and he was not tortured. Nicholas is reported to have said, after speaking with him: "He is a noble but dangerous madman. Such maniacs must not be permitted in the streets."'—Note to the translation of 1855.

In fact both Herzen and his original translator were misinformed. Bakunin was not tortured, he did not meet Nicholas, and he spoke. He sent the Tsar a 'confession' in which he professed to repent of his mutinous activities. This remarkable document was unknown and unpublished until after the revolution of 1917. Bakunin was sent to Siberia whence he escaped in 1859.

North American Review (review date July 1859)

SOURCE: "Contemporary French Literature." *North American Review* 89, no. 184 (July 1859): 209-231.

[*In the following excerpt, the anonymous author exposes the negative portrayal of women in Michelet's 1858 nonfiction book* L'amour *(Love).*]

Every instinct of propriety has been offended [by Michelet's **L'Amour**], and, let us hasten to say, we do not mean in the ordinary acceptation of the word only, but in the artistic sense also. Here is a writer, whose trade has been history, seeking suddenly his inspiration where novelists mostly seek theirs; here is a man of between sixty and seventy, choosing for his theme that of which youths and maidens of eighteen or twenty usually conceive themselves to be the authorized professors. There could be no one possible *convenance*, to use the French term, observed in a dissertation upon *Love*, the author of which should be the "erudite artist" (as he styles himself), Michelet,—nor is any *convenance* observed. "'T is a mad" book, "my masters," is the only phrase thoroughly applicable to this extraordinary rhapsody. If, however, it were nothing but an extraordinary rhapsody, it would be a waste of time to speak of it. It is more than that, inasmuch as it contains, here and there, some of those curious and inspired pages, which perhaps no one but Michelet is capable of writing. In this respect he has judged his own faculties remarkably well, when he calls himself an "erudite artist." Michelet, as we have more than once taken occasion to say, is not merely an historical writer,—not, indeed, an historian of the same species as any other; for the quality that predominates in him is the quality that is least required by the mere historian,—imagination. Yet this faculty is not in him so absolute that it can suffice for the purposes of production, as it does, for instance, with Sir Walter Scott. No! Michelet's imagination requires to be provoked by some fact. He does not invent dramatic situations or characters; but when he meets them in history, he takes fire at once, and poetizes them. He is one of the most singular exemplifications of the possibility of "imagining what is known." When any passage of history has become so thoroughly fixed in his memory that it is, as it were, part of himself, he then employs a process of re-creation, and the forms that in reality are evoked by his knowledge have entirely the air of being evoked by his imagination. In a purely psychological point of view, Michelet is one of the most interesting organizations which it is possible to study. He is absolutely, and in every sense of the word, an "artist"; but an artist who does not provide the stuff on which he operates, but must have the raw material furnished ready to his hand. He is erudite beyond belief, and if he had not his artistic qualities, he might have been a Benedictine,—just as, if he had not his erudition, he might, perhaps, have been a Victor Hugo, or a Beethoven, had the ray of his thought happened to pass through the prism of music.

Into the reasons which have, all at once, determined Michelet to "imagine" the hackneyed subject of Love, we need not enter. *L'Amour* is, of course, a book which every man and woman in France (and indeed throughout the European continent) will read, and which will most likely go through an unlimited number of editions. Yet we are much mistaken if any Continental reader is otherwise than strangely disappointed with the volume, and, above all, if those for whom it is ostensibly written do not throw it aside in indignant disdain. The book purports to be written in order to vindicate the rights of Continental wives to be better treated by their husbands; yet so strangely is this undertaking carried out, that the woman would (according to Anglo-Saxon notions of female dignity) cover herself with shame, who should accept the kind of "protectorate" M. Michelet demands for her.

The book is so exclusively, so extravagantly French, that it is next to impossible to describe it for the readers of any other country; still, although mistaken in the manner in which he has executed his work, M. Michelet had an honest intention in writing it, and this we cannot avoid taking into account. We will give the words in which the author himself announces what he intends his book shall be. Addressing himself to the young men of all classes in Paris, he says:—

> Think well over all this, my dear friend, whatever you are, whether a student in the schools, or an artisan,—your position is of no consequence. Begin already, in your days and hours of recreation, to reflect, to prepare, to settle what is to be the future portion of your life. Profit by these hours, and if this book reaches you by chance, read over some of its pages, and think of them. The book (amongst other defects) is a short one. Others will take up the subject and enlarge upon it, and say,

better than I have done, what is to be said. When he who writes this volume shall be under the earth, and enjoying rest from all his labors, a cleverer man than he is will take the idea of his imperfect sketch, and write, perhaps, a great and immortal work. But as, after all, the element whereof it would be formed is the same in you and in me, and is simply the human heart and its affections, you may yourself, all alone, and upon my unconnected notes, compose beforehand the chronicle of your life. Think it all over on Sundays, when the Bacchanalian round of your giddy comrades pouring down the staircase halts a moment at your door, and says: "What are you doing?—we wait for you,—we are off to the *Chaumière,* with Amanda and Jeanneton!" Answer them, "I will come later,—I have still something to do."

> If you reply to them these words, I will answer for the performance of a miracle; I will answer for it, that between the two pale flowers that are planted before your window, struggling against the Parisian atmosphere, a third will spring to life,—a flower, and yet a woman,—the dim, sweet semblance of a future affianced bride!

Now this justice we must render to M. Michelet. What he has done voluntarily and *de parti pris,* in this strange production, is full of morality; what is immoral, indecent, in every sense revolting and absolutely insane, is involuntary. His aim is to introduce into the conjugal practices of France somewhat of those habits and feelings that make marriage so blessed a tie in Anglo-Saxon countries. He is shocked at what he sees around him, and he feels that between husband and wife there ought to exist some bond more tender, more worthy, than that of mere pecuniary interest. He acknowledges to himself, that two beings who are to go through life, perhaps to encounter misfortune together, should be "matched" in other respects than in their "dot" alone. But the way in which he sets to work to remedy the evil is wrong, and increases a thousand-fold the debasement of the wife. His very system is founded on the inferiority, we might almost say, the degradation, of woman; for he represents her as so weak in health and organization, that all notion of her serving as a *helpmate* becomes impossible; and he apparently holds her virtue and good conduct as things so fragile, that he fancies, unless by lynx-like vigilance, no husband can ever make sure of his domestic honor and happiness. The worst of all this is, that a tolerably large portion of the feminine population of France will agree with M. Michelet, and actually be disposed to think that he treats women as they should be treated, and that his book is written in their favor. The thousand minute and—as they would seem to a woman of Anglo-Saxon race—humiliating attentions that M. Michelet's "model husband" pays to his wife, force upon you the conviction that the latter is physically and morally infirm; and up to a certain point, so are a large proportion of Parisian women,—the sickly hot-house products of the falsest civilization upon the face of the whole earth. In order to see how much truth there is in this, and how unhealthy a race of women M.

Michelet has habitually had under the range of his ob-servation, it would suffice to read the chapters of his work that are consecrated to the health of his heroine, the pages which he entitles "L'Hygiène." It is enough to make one take a dislike to all Frenchwomen for ever-more, for you cannot avoid seeing what miserable, *un-fortified* creatures—bodily and mentally—they are. Study well what M. Michelet reckons the perfection of *régime* for a young woman, and you will see what the result must be. This chapter is interesting; for it ex-plains a good deal of what French women are, and *why* they are so. Nothing is done to *strengthen* them. There is no good fat meat, no beef and mutton, no cold water, no out-of-door exercise, no fine racing gallops upon a generous horse and over broad, breezy downs, no mus-cular development aiding the development of that grand source of the superiority of English and American women, self-reliance, no true courage, no true sense of honor, no honesty, none of the higher qualities whereby his *wife* is a man's best friend, his companion, and his equal. M. Michelet's heroine, his "model wife," is inca-pable of assuming responsibility,—she is, we repeat it, *infirm*; yet let it not be forgotten, she is the type of at least half the Frenchwomen whom Frenchmen would call "charming."

Richard R. Chase Jr. (essay date spring 1992)

SOURCE: Chase, Richard R., Jr. "Jules Michelet and the Nineteenth-Century Concept of Insanity: A Roman-tic's Reinterpretation." *French Historical Studies* 17, no. 3 (spring 1992): 725-46.

[*In the following essay, Chase considers the relation-ship between Michelet's consistent engagement with medical theories of contagion and his notion that "healthy ideas could be transmitted among the people, despite the countervailing influence of the monarchy and the clergy."*]

Despite the historical attention that Jules Michelet con-tinues to receive, there has been no adequate explana-tion of his defense of democracy within the context of his century, when conservatives, and frequently liberals, held that the masses were insane and needed guidance from a ruling class and a paternalistic government.[1] Michel Foucault first emphasized the use of psychology to categorize the people as incompetent and dangerous, which in turn has led to a common conclusion, summa-rized by Jan Goldstein, that nineteenth-century psychol-ogy was "antidemocratic."[2] Edmund Burke, Thomas Carlyle, and François Guizot were among those who helped to create this attack on democracy by defining the French Revolution and the resulting Terror as an in-sanity that led the masses to excess.[3] This conclusion received widespread medical support, especially from the alienist Jean-Etienne Esquirol and his pupils, trained at Charenton, who explained that monomania was con-tagious; if not controlled by the government, a desire such as that for equality, arising from the French Revo-lution, would spread until it consumed the nation with its infection.[4] My article is indebted to Foucault but also to those historians, such as Michael Ignatieff and Daniel Pick, who insist that the rhetorical use of nineteenth-century concepts of psychology was complex and thus not limited to antidemocratic polemic.[5]

Michelet's argument is a case in point. His histories can only be understood as a defense of the people, a de-fense that, in three ways, can be broadly defined as medical. Firstly, he accepted the science of his time. From psychology he borrowed the widely held convic-tion that passions were contagious and from physiology he argued that ideas themselves, and not mere predispo-sitions, would be transmitted from one generation to the next. These so-called biological laws made it appear certain that Jeanne d'Arc's heroic example would spread throughout society and then to succeeding generations; France's salvation would be assured. The birth of a na-tion, as with an individual, seemed to depend on these medical laws. In a letter to Pierre-Joseph Proudhon, Michelet explained, "[In history], what I look for . . . is the demonstration of this grand Being [the nation], the laws of her life, the forms of her reason, in a word, *her psychology.*"[6]

Michelet relied on medicine because it could validate a nineteenth-century political argument. Psychology and physiology assured that healthy ideas could be transmit-ted among the people, despite the countervailing influ-ence of the monarchy and the clergy, who transmitted only mindless submission to succeeding generations by inculcating acceptance of hereditary rule and original sin and who maintained that the contagious nature of obsessions would only lead to dissolution and eventu-ally to suicide for the individual and the nation. In con-trast, Michelet argued that the natural act of the repro-ductive process insured that the government could adopt a laissez-faire attitude because there existed a law that, in biology as in economics, insured progress and thus should not be contravened. No outside class or govern-ment need interfere with the progress that biology and history assured. As he explained, "Our legislative doc-tors treat each symptom that appears here or there as an isolated and distinct case." Instead, "before trying every external and local remedy, it would be useful to inquire into the inner evil that produces all these symptoms."[7] In anticipation of Foucault, Michelet criticized those who neither understood nor correctly applied the true laws of medicine: "Too many people notice only out-ward causes. . . . Our philanthropists have this fine idea, and so they think they can preserve or cure man only by building him tombs."[8]

Secondly, Michelet's defense of democracy required the transvaluation of those who had been labeled as incompetent. Consequently, he created the myth of Jeanne d'Arc in order to transform both the commoner and women: instead of a curse, they represented France's salvation. The mythologizing of the Maiden was important because in myth values can be changed into their opposite.[9] Michelet transformed the weak into the strong, the ill into those who bring health to the nation. His rhetorical tour de force, which placed the masses at the forefront of historical progress, depended on a redefinition of insanity itself: the people were indeed mad, but—standing this argument on its head—the people's monomaniacal desire for freedom represented the very passion that would bring unity to France. The people's insanity represented determination, just as a woman's monthly illness, to use the century's parlance, was responsible for mankind's cure. Michelet was not a misogynist, as some historians implied.[10] Female suffering, physical and mental, was transformed into strength, because women were ultimately responsible for transmitting the ideas of freedom and sacrifice to their children. They gave birth to the nation itself.

Thirdly, Michelet's histories were based on a complex process of identification whereby he associated himself with the people, France with the hospital, and Jeanne d'Arc with the physician whose lasting example would initiate a cure. They were also based on his own adolescence, when he suffered, in his words, from "la fièvre mentale."[11] Through the rehabilitation of the people he transvalued his own illness; he identified his pain with that of the people and their tortured past. History, he explained, represented a "violent psychological chemistry, where my individual passions, where my people become me, and where my *moi* returns to animate the people."[12] At the beginning of **The People,** he confessed, "I have found it [the book] above all in the recollections of my youth. To know the life of the people and their toils and sufferings, I had only to question my memory."[13] He had seen his own pain reflected first in the inmates at the asylums that he frequented as a youth and then in the historical sufferings of the people. He began to make these associations when his family lived at a *maison de santé*, where his father worked from 1815-18,[14] and then at Bicêtre and the Salpêtrière, where his first and best friend, Paul Poinsot, interned until his premature death in 1820. "I have very often traversed Bicêtre and the Salpêtrière. I went there to see an intern, a friend whom I have lost. There, I saw how the young doctor could learn, in all things psychological, if he took the time. I have seen at the Salpêtrière what no person could ever fathom: the wound of France."[15] The true healer was Poinsot, who helped Michelet overcome his own emotional turmoil.[16] Jeanne d'Arc would play a similar historical role as France's physician. The people's enemies became Poinsot's antithesis; they were the false healers in the form of priest and clerical con-

fessor and in the guise of monarchy and then empire. Michelet lent power to his histories by transferring his own feelings to his historical subjects. Personal experience allowed him to remain a romantic, despite his debt to science, because he studied the people not from the perspective of a physician, the detached observer, but from within the emotional pain itself.

However, Michelet was not satisfied with basing his works on subjective experience, emotion, and faith. In his mind, Christian histories demanded a blind acceptance of a legendary past that contradicted reason. According to François Furet, Michelet sought to create "the credo of the new age, the modern religion," which would support "the revolutionary foundation as absolute, rooted in something beyond the human."[17] Science, based on biological principles, would serve as the bedrock with which to create history anew. These principles must be explained more fully before Michelet's histories can be appreciated as a scientifically based rebuttal to antidemocratic criticism.

THE MEDICAL LEGACY

Michelet shared a fascination with science, and particularly medicine, that was common to the nineteenth century. During the French Revolution, Philippe Pinel had begun to unlock the mysteries of the mind when he began to treat insanity, a disease previously held to be largely incurable. Pinel and his pupils, including Esquirol, appeared to be the Newtons of their age; they were discovering the laws of mental behavior. Contagion seemed to be as centrally important to psychology as gravity was to physics. Passions were infectious. A single obsession was particularly dangerous, because a monomaniac witnessed long and seemingly rational periods when detection of the disease was nearly impossible, giving time for unhealthy ideas to spread among a gullible populace. Psychology, however, was not unrivaled in this fascination with science. Physiologists also emphasized the influence of the body on the mental process. A philosophical debate resulted where alienists, most frequently as defenders of idealism and man's free will, associated physiology with materialistic determinism.[18] Heated rhetoric often ensued, but compromise was possible because man, being both mind and body, was logically influenced by both. Neither pure idealism nor doctrinaire materialism could be maintained. Physiologists often sought to prove that ideas were transmitted in a material fashion through the hereditary process, for logic seemed to dictate that ideas, which after all were contagious among strangers, would assuredly be passed from mother to child, particularly during times of passionate turmoil. Such critical moments included menstruation and conception; the ideas that obsessed the mother at these times would be transmitted to the fetus and then to posterity. Nineteenth-century fascination with the female reproductive cycle becomes understandable in this context. Novelists might emphasize the destructive guilt, transmitted by an adulteress, which led to the destruction of her family, but Michelet chose to concentrate upon the more prevalent emotion of maternal sacrifice, which, when transmitted, led to fraternity and the birth of the nation.

Michelet singled out two alienists, Philippe Pinel and Ulysse Trélat, and two physiologists, Bruno Jacques Béraud and Prosper Lucas, as particularly influential.[19] Agreeing with Pinel, Michelet concluded: "The passions are contagious," a concept that Michelet had already learned to appreciate by the time he had read Trélat's book, *La Folie lucide*: "In a beautiful recent book, *La Folie lucide,* one sees what a fixed idea is,"[20] what Pinel's famous student, Esquirol, might call monomania. By definition, a "fixed idea" was contagious and, as Trélat went on to explain, could be transmitted by hereditary influence not only to the individual but also to "a learned civilization, because if bad is transmittable, good is equally so; one inherits healthy faculties as one inherits unhealthy faculties."[21] Michelet had come to this conclusion by a two-step process for which the key dates of 1840-42 and then 1856-59 can be documented. His belief in the infectious and beneficial nature of love, which helped to alter his attitude towards nature and womankind, began in 1840. Arthur Mitzman explains that Michelet's new, more positive conception of "natural fecundity and maternity as the source of human brotherhood" developed after the death of Pauline, Michelet's first wife, in 1839 and during a period from 1840-42, when the historian fell in love with François-Adèle Dumesnil.[22] Love, which Michelet experienced so intensely, was contagious; it would spread until fraternity had triumphed.

This general idea was translated into specific scientific theory by a series of treatises that were written, according to Michelet, from "1827 to 1847."[23] He became particularly impressed by these works in a period from 1856 to 1859, when the names of physiologists began to appear in his *Journal [Jules Michelet: Journal]*.[24] This period coincides with the time when he began to write his natural histories and to accelerate his studies on womanhood.[25] These books have traditionally been either criticized or discounted, but when analyzed in conjunction with his *Histoire de France,* which he resumed in 1854, they should be seen as the culmination of Michelet's thought.[26] His earlier belief in the contagious nature of ideas became tangible in both a personal and scientific manner that seemingly confirmed each other. On an intimate level his *Journal* is filled with descriptions of the monthly cycles of his second wife, Athénaïs, whom he had married in 1849.[27] The mysteries of female biology were, in Michelet's mind, revealed by the theories of the physiologists who, his *Journal* indicates, had also become his friends.

Michelet had observed numerous dissections of the brain and had "studied a great number of both sexes of all ages" under the supervision of Dr. Béraud.[28] This scientist and confidant had shown, according to Michelet, that the generational transmission of ideas did not merely account for illness and degeneracy but also for the creation of exceptional people who then helped to further civilization.[29] Heredity, as so conceived, altered first the individual and then the species, not only anatomically but also emotionally and intellectually.[30] Moral characteristics were likewise transmitted. Heredity determined the process whereby people acquired "their aptitudes, their tastes," and which, according to Béraud, lead to the formulation of the "loi de perfectionnement." The results of this process could be either good or bad. When bad passions were transmitted, mankind descended to a "condition of abrutissement, that is to say, the gradual return to a state further and further removed from the state of social perfection"; when good passions were transmitted, individual and social progress was assured.[31]

Béraud admitted that many of his ideas came from Lucas, who, in turn, built on the work of Jean Jacques Coste and Charles Négrier. Coste and Négrier had begun the study, in Michelet's terminology, of "ovology,"[32] or the science of reproduction. These theories became so well known that Emile Zola explained that his novel, *Madelaine Férat,* was based on "this thesis [of the generational transmission of ideas] from Michelet and doctor Lucas."[33] Michelet himself credited Lucas for culminating earlier findings in order to develop the laws of generational transmission of ideas from both parents to their offspring. The female role remained paramount, leading Michelet to conclude that "the object of love, woman, in her essential mystery, longtime ignored, misunderstood, has been revealed by a series of discoveries."[34]

Physiologists focused upon the crucial question: when did impregnation occur? Agreeing with the earlier conclusions of Négrier and Coste, Béraud formulated what was taken to be the most scientific—but is, in retrospect, the most surprising—answer: women became pregnant during menstruation! Lucas disagreed with what was, according to him, the majority opinion, but only to argue that a woman was as likely to become pregnant during any time of the month.[35] This debate seemed crucial because these physiologists agreed on a larger issue: the generational transmission of both physical and psychological traits appeared certain and, in Lucas's words, depended on the "states of health or illness of the father and of the mother, at the moment of coitus." Sexual relations should be timed to correspond with the physical and psychological health of both parents and with times when passions were under control, which would exclude intercourse during menstruation, because the female would be physically exhausted as well as emotionally distraught. Lucas also counseled that relations with people suffering from a variety of illnesses, both mental and physical, should be avoided.[36] Other physicians, such as Trélat, argued that moral persuasion would not be sufficient and that the government should pass laws that prohibited unhealthy unions.[37]

Michelet, however, emphasized the positive; namely, that it was the unique historical and biological role of women which determined that healthy ideas would be passed on to the children of France. He concluded that women, formerly considered "impure," were in reality the vehicles of mankind's progress.[38] Jeanne d'Arc had begun this process, and her rebellion then had become contagious during the fifteenth century. Frenchmen had to be cured by a process that Pinel and other alienists called the moral treatment, whereby unhealthy obsessions would be replaced by healthy ideas, such as those offered by the Maiden's example.[39] Her suffering became contagious and was transmitted to each subsequent generation through women's willingness to accept the sacrifice inherent in childbirth and motherhood. This willingness for sacrifice then became the dominant passion that was transmitted to each child. Each birth represented an act of fraternity that would grow in every generation until a united France had been achieved.[40]

According to Michelet, Lucas had developed a scientific law of progress because "the generative act does not give a unique result but . . . has multiple and lasting effects that often continue into the future." Therefore, "the first impregnation has influenced the future for many years."[41] He marveled at this biological chain where an idea proceeded from mother to fetus to society: "Our physiological way, so prodigiously complicated, goes its way without demanding counsel. It has been thus for the perpetuation of the human species, operated by love and marriage, by the constitution of the family."[42] Such conclusions, according to Michelet, were supported between 1840 and 1850 by the Académie des sciences and the Collège de France to the point where the laws governing the hereditary transmission of ideas became "accepted as an article of human faith."[43]

MICHELET'S REDEFINITION OF INSANITY

Michelet was convinced that biological discoveries could be applied directly to the study of the past. He exclaimed, "No time is out of the pale of science; the future itself belongs to . . . [sciences] that are sufficiently advanced to enable one to predict the return of phenomena, as can be done in the physical sciences and will be one day (in a conjectural manner) in the historical sciences."[44] He believed in a medical law of progress that worked according to a psychological dialectic, like a struggle between passions, which should not be suppressed, as was commonly counseled. All progress de-

pended upon this battle between the passions—one harmonizing, the other alienating—to which Michelet referred as the *moi* versus the *non-moi*. Such terminology is often difficult to analyze because it seems to be more poetic than scientific. Yet, similar and equally vague language appeared in the medical literature of the period. For example, the ideas of Jacques-Joseph Moreau de Tours, an alienist most remembered for his study on the psychological effects of hashish, can help elucidate Michelet's thought by keeping the discussion within a nineteenth-century framework.[45] Moreau explained that the *moi* by itself was "*infertile, sterile*" unless it interacted with society. Through this contact, Moreau stated in prose reminiscent of Michelet's Romantic style: The isolated *moi* is transfigured, it becomes "the human *moi*; it is the individual transformed into humanity, it is humanity transformed into the individual."[46] In his histories, Michelet explained the manner whereby Frenchmen, trapped within themselves, could not progress; the *moi* could only grow through contact with others, a confrontation that was initially viewed as a struggle with the other, or the *non-moi*. Pain resulted at first, but this emotional confrontation was a prerequisite for individual and social progress. In France's case, historical progress resulted because mankind would not accept the submissive role relegated by the church and the monarchy.[47] These two institutions were the *non-moi*, ironically necessary because their injustices forced man to revolt against his pain and alienation. Rebellion was initially psychological and sacrificial, and in this matter revolution mirrored the values inherent in childbirth. The people, forced to confront the other, the *non-moi*, revolted; their heroism was transmitted through the generations, leading inexorably to national unity.

The complexity of Michelet's vision of a psychology based on the will to sacrifice and its attendant hope, a vision in which the process of historical revolution conflated with biological childbirth, belies the generalization that insanity was a simple label, used in the nineteenth century to censure and control. For Michelet, insanity represented the psychologically enslaved condition whereby the people became alienated from each other, but it also represented an act of defiance, as the people revolted against the potential tyranny of passionate and political domination. He insisted, however, "The beautiful, great heroic insanities are enlightened by passions; . . . the most foolhardy has the effect of wisdom."[48] This heroic revolt achieved progress on a political level as a rebellion against the people's oppressors and on a psychological and more fundamental level as a refusal to accept mankind's own disease. History became the slow, spiral-like struggle whereby man was repressed and made ill, then revolted and made well, until finally true, although temporary, freedom had been achieved during the French Revolution. Hereditary transmission of this heroic idea of revolt would lead to genuine nationalism: passionate discord would end and insanity would disappear when the final confrontation of the *moi* versus the *non-moi* had been played out.

AN ANALYSIS OF MICHELET'S HISTORIES

In a necessarily brief examination of Michelet's historical work, four periods can be singled out as crucial stages in the generational transmission of this idea of fraternity: the Hundred Years' War, the Wars of Religion, the Regency during the minority of Louis XV, and the French Revolution. Each represented a painful era of division but also an important stage when nationalism was transmitted, a time of cure, when the people became increasingly aware of their insanity as well as the means to conquer it through fraternity—a final harmonization of the passions. In each period the internal psychological war between an insanity that was destructive and the revolt against the pain that this insanity engendered was mirrored in the confrontation of either leading individuals or institutions. The *non-moi*, the destructive madness of Charles VI, Charles IX, the daughter of the Regent Philippe d'Orléans, and the Bastille, was confronted and eventually overcome by the *moi*, the heroic madness of the masses led by Jeanne d'Arc, by witches, and by John Law, until eventually the people conquered it on their own. Their rebellion was insane; it was undertaken against all odds to fight against all the injustice that king, priest, and the people's own psychological torment had imposed throughout the centuries. Insanities during the French Revolution, so discredited by antidemocratic writers, according to Michelet, represented instead the people's most glorious struggle to become free at last.

In his **Histoire de France,** Michelet concluded that Frenchmen had first become aware of their nationality during the Hundred Years' War, an idea that would be transmitted until it culminated in the fraternal revolt of 1789. He explained the first positive effects of this psychological confrontation, brought about by facing the English, a foreign adversary, the *non-moi.* Here Michelet gave credit to the English, as Karl Marx would to the Industrial Revolution: enemies forced the people into such misery that a revolt, leading to historical progress, became inevitable. "The struggle against England," Michelet explained, "rendered France an immense service. Forced to unite against the enemy, the provinces found among themselves a people. It was in seeing themselves next to the English that they felt they were in France. It is with nations as with the individual who knows and distinguishes his personality by the resistance from what is not his: he notices the *moi* by the *non-moi.*"[49]

Progress is paradoxical, because, as Michelet asserts, "it is necessary that humanity suffer and be patient, that it merit its [progress's] arrival."[50] The English invasion

brought additional misery to the people by spreading political discord and creating civil war. Everywhere people were forced to face their own divisions and submission. This realization brought about revolt, a psychological confrontation where the *moi* faced the *non-moi.* The people "avoided becoming idiots only by becoming madmen," he wrote, "An access of somber insanity struck in this [fourteenth] century."[51] Madness, therefore, was a revolt against such brutalizing authorities. The people learned to know their own feelings through their confrontation with insanity and thereby recognized that they desired national unity and its individual counterpart, emotional harmony.[52] "If wisdom consists in knowing one's self and in pacifying it," he observed, "no epoch was more naturally insane."[53]

This period of insanity was mirrored in the mad king, Charles VI, just as the general feeling of unity became symbolized by Jeanne d'Arc.[54] The Maiden and the mad king represented the emotional confrontation within the average Frenchman. In Michelet's words, "The individual history explains the general history. The insanity of the king was not of the king alone: the realm had its part in it."[55] Man's progress resulted precisely because of this painful confrontation of the *moi,* represented by the healthy will of Jeanne, versus the *non-moi,* symbolized by the diseased will of Charles VI, the English, the nobility, and the church.

During the Hundred Years' War, the most important confrontation took place not on the battlefield but within the mental struggles of Frenchmen. According to Michelet, "Life is a combat . . . but one should not complain about it; rather it is tragic when the combat ends. The interior war of *l'homo duplex* [the confrontation of the *moi* versus the *mon-moi*] is exactly what sustains us. Contemplate it, this war, raging not only in the king, but in the realm, and in the Paris of that time, which represented this war so well."[56] The people of France, of Paris, represented the *homo duplex,* the divided man struggling through insanity and thereby learning to become one. The initial result of these insanities, however, was even greater political division. Charles VI's madness led to countless crimes, culminating in the murder of Louis d'Orléans in 1407. Two factions resulted: Armagnacs killed Burgundians, but France herself became the real victim.[57] Michelet compared the failure to reunite France by physical force to the inadequacies of the period's medicine: "There was already, as today, materialistic medicine, which bled the body without caring for the soul, which wanted to cure the physical illness [*le mal physique*] without examining the psychological illness [*le mal moral*]."[58]

The real cure for France came from a combination of psychological and physical treatment initiated by Jeanne d'Arc. "The modern heroes," Michelet explained, "*they are the heroes of action.*" They instituted "the justice of

God, which acts, which combats, which saves and heals." Of Jeanne d'Arc's advice to Charles VII to proceed to Reims and there claim the crown, he writes, "The Maiden alone had this advice, and this heroic insanity was wisdom itself."[59] Insanity had pointed to its own cure, to its own path toward unity, which was symbolized by the reestablishment of Valois control under the rightful heir, Charles VII. Michelet described the period of Charles VII's reign as one of cure, to be contrasted to the English feudal divisions mirrored in their own mad king, Henry VI.[60] Such language led to the conclusion, reported in the newspaper, *La Boussole*, that Michelet had described the Maiden as insane. The alienist, Louis Florentin Calmeil, later labeled her a *théomaniac*, a monomaniac obsessed with religious visions.[61] In his **Journal**, Michelet emphasized that he had rejected such charges so vehemently that *La Boussole* had apologized and retracted the original statement.[62]

Michelet explained that Jeanne was an exception; she was the child-woman who represented perfect national unity. "This prolongation of childhood," he wrote, "was a singularity of Jeanne d'Arc, who remained a small girl and was never a woman."[63] She was subject neither to passionate divisions, which were considered to begin mainly at adolescence, nor to the physiological trials occasioned by the onset of menstruation.[64] Jeanne represented both individual and national fraternity, a psychological unity that she typified as the people's true healer and as Charles VII's true confessor. Like Poinsot, she was no longer divided by passions; she foreshadowed the unity that both individual and nation were to become. On the other hand, the English and the church, who tortured Jeanne to death, remained the implacable enemies of the nation itself. Michelet knew that Jeanne's and the people's attachment toward nationalism would continue, despite the delays created by monarchy and the Gallican church, because nationalism was transmitted at the moment of conception through the contagious nature of fixed ideas.

In the sixteenth century, the people's emotional conflict again created a nationalistic revolt during the Wars of Religion. The suffering of the masses once more became mirrored in the monarchy. As Michelet stated, "A madman was born, Charles IX, the furious inspirer of Saint-Bartholomew's Day."[65] This tragic event again resulted in partisan rivalries, which through contagion led to further madness.[66] "The dreams and insanities of Francis I in 1515 [during the Italian Wars], when France was strong, were the follies of a young man," he explained; "those of the Guises and of Diane, in 1547, with a ruined France, were an insanity of the mentally ill [*une démence d'aliénés*]." As earlier, a foreign enemy, this time the Spanish, helped spread the disease. With this infection, however, an increasing number of Frenchmen became aware of their nationality. "It is

time," Michelet admonished, "to look at the great psychological facts of the epoch, [which are] more important than any political fact. They are all in three words: *sorcery, convents, casuistry*."[67]

Catherine B. Clément has already noted the heroic role the sorceress played for Michelet. She "is insane; she possesses 'the illuminism of lucid insanity.'"[68] Michelet described her repeatedly as a *demi-fou*, a monomaniac of "*half-sane, half-insane* madness."[69] Her psychological pain mirrored the agony of the people whom she had doctored for a thousand years. Internal conflict led to the realization that she must revolt against the Christian acceptance of pain and disease as the just punishments from God.[70] "Foreshadowing of the modern Prometheus are to be seen in her," Michelet explained, "a beginning of industry, above all of the sovereign industry that heals and revivifies men."[71] She spread this rebellion in the Black Mass, which Michelet described as "the frenzied outbreaks of a maddened brain, lifting impiety to the level of popular indignation."[72] She represented "the general insanity of the time," which led to clandestine *sabbats*, a "brutal unity, confused and mad [*vertige*],"[73] and which marked the beginning of fraternity and the nation. Jeanne d'Arc's example once again spread to others, who in turn became persecuted as witches; yet, their insanity insured the continuation of fraternity and the nation's progress.

The church was particularly responsible for crushing this revolt throughout French history. In **La Sorcière** Michelet concentrated upon one Charlotte Cadière, who from 1729 through 1731 suffered unbearably at the hands of her confessor. She had written, in words that could apply to any age, about her own progression beyond monomania: "I became more than half mad. I felt such a craving for pain!" Thus, for Michelet, "The mighty cry of pain . . . is the true inward meaning of the Witches' Sabbath. . . . It expresses not only material sufferings, . . . but a very abyss of agony." Therefore, "she [the sorceress in general and Cadière in particular] is left horror-stricken, half wild with remorse and passionate revolt."[74] Rebellion came from the pain of mental torment. Heroic passions arose from the individual's confrontation with the *non-moi*, which externally was the false confessor but internally was the growing awareness of one's own submissive insanity. The individual was ultimately faced with either revolt or suicide.

Progress was assured because mankind would never accept its own demise; the spirit of revolt spread from Jeanne to women to succeeding generations until the next period of rebellion, which erupted during the Regency of Louis XV. Commentators of Michelet have wondered why he devoted one of eighteen volumes of his **Histoire de France** to this short and neglected segment of French history. This period, however, was similar to the Hundred Years' War and the Wars of Religion; all were insane revolts that led toward national unity. The Regency crisis was also prepared by the preceding miseries of the people, this time due to Louis XIV's wars, increased taxation, and the famine of 1707. The pain caused by these events was again mirrored in a public figure, probably the duchesse du Berry, the daughter of the Regent, Philippe d'Orléans.[75] Michelet called her "half mad [*demi-fou*]," a monomaniac whom he compared to the mad kings, Charles VI and Charles IX. These monarchs had been fundamentally important to their periods, but there was no comparable historical significance to the duchesse de Berry, who died in 1719 at the age of twenty-four. She served as a literary device, as a foil to the emotional turmoil of her period.[76] "She had all the chaos of the [eighteenth] century," Michelet wrote. He examined her madness further, referring at this point to Trélat: "In a beautiful recent book, *La Folie lucide*, one sees what a fixed idea is. No chimera and no crime where such an idea cannot lead. One sees there, moreover, that these *demi-fous* are crafty, very apt at intrigue. They are excellent instruments for those who know how to make use of them."[77] This description provided a convenient way to explain the intrigue caused by the Regent's daughter.

On a second level, monomania characterized a Regency where monetary gain was the fixed idea of every member of government, each of whom, therefore, could be manipulated by the financier, John Law. On a third level, because the Regent's daughter symbolized the eighteenth century as a whole, monomania stood for an Enlightenment age that was preoccupied and finally tricked by the notion of man's infallible reason. On the fourth and most significant level, Michelet explained, the positive effect of this insanity manifested itself: the people became preoccupied with obsessions of equality and unity, and this monomania led progressively and inexorably to the French Revolution.

The Regency period was dominated by John Law, who was the heroic counterpart to the Regent's daughter. "An insanity . . . seized it [the period] at this moment," Michelet wrote, "the discovery of a prodigious mine of gold: the marvelous System that changed all paper into gold." His analogy was obvious: he was comparing medieval alchemy to Law's proposal to print paper money, a scheme that had been shunned as mad but had suddenly become accepted. In Michelet's words, "The fruit flourished, a true rose, a voluptuous beauty— Insanity. For the first time, Insanity was dressed decently, richly, and, one could say, like a queen; Insanity, fresh and fat, . . . as was the daughter of the Regent."[78] Man's awareness and acceptance of madness became crucial. During the Enlightenment the insanities of crown, church, and nobility were increasingly criticized. More importantly, the people no longer had to hide their insanity, as sorceress and alchemist had been

so cruelly forced to do in earlier periods. The people's *idée fixe* of revolt, silently passed through generations, could come out into the open and culminate in 1789. Michelet, therefore, explained the importance of Law's system in the broadest terms: "There was never a more general movement. It was not, as one seems to believe, a simple affair of finance, but a social revolution; it existed already in the minds. The *System* was the effect much more than the cause. An immense fermentation had preceded it."[79]

Michelet claimed that the people became as heroically determined to change their oppressed situation as Law had been to convert paper into gold. Both dreamed of overturning the hierarchy of society and nature that church and government had accepted as permanent. Michelet wrote, "Law was evidently mad with the vertigo of utopia."[80] This dizzying insanity led to his disgrace, just as passionate excess would later discredit the Great Revolution. Michelet concluded that neither Law nor the people were guilty, but like all monomaniacs, they could easily be tricked and led astray.

Michelet equated the people's desire for fraternity with love, which he defined as that emotion which "is so strong that it believes the contrary to what it sees. The more the thing [love] is illogical, insane, absurd, . . . the more it is a matter of faith."[81] The people's efforts would thus be insane. Like Law's actions, they were based on a conviction of love and the faith that they could accomplish so much, when all around them were proofs to the contrary. This faith was the wisdom of the people's insanity, and it was what led to the Revolution.[82]

The French Revolution represented the culmination of the people's awakening, a cure that had begun during the Hundred Years' War. The counterparts to the people's internal emotional struggles were thus no longer major political figures. During the Revolution, psychological confrontation became mirrored in key events: the storming of the Bastille, the Fête de la Fédération of 1790, and their opposite, the two Terrors. In his book on the Revolution Michelet explained this historic change. Under Louis XV, "humanity, still feeble, placed its unity in a sign, a visible living sign, a man, an individual. Henceforth, unity, more pure, and free from this material condition, will consist in the union of the hearts, the community, [and] the mind, the passion of sentiments and ideas arising from identity of opinions."[83] This growing sense of fraternity resulted in the Revolution, which in turn represented the culminating act of insanity: "The lunacy of the Revolution was here wisdom."[84] The insanity had spread from the revolt of the few, who had been ridiculed by society, to all the people. "How long," Michelet asked, "is insanity's progress confined to children and fools, to poets and madmen? And yet one day that madness proves to be the common sense of all!"[85]

The most significant event of the Revolution was the storming of the Bastille, when the people "attained what is morally the highest degree of order—unanimity of feeling." Michelet described the time before its capture as an evening that "had been stormy, agitated by a whirlwind of ungovernable frenzy. With daylight, one idea dawned upon Paris." Seized by monomania, the people struck at their oppressors. Michelet went on to describe the fall of the prison: "Correctly speaking, the Bastille was not taken; it surrendered. Troubled by a bad conscience, it went mad and lost all presence of mind."[86] Insanity confronted itself again; the people madly revolted against an insane injustice.

July 14 became the microcosm of the Revolution as well as France's entire history. As such, the symbol of the Bastille's insanity was fourfold. Firstly, the Bastille represented the insane old regime which had taught the people to remain passive. The people were, therefore, justified in attacking it. Secondly, the prison symbolized ill treatment and false cures offered by society's leaders before 1789.[87] Thirdly, the storming of the Bastille represented a moment of great heroic insanity, when the people sought to cure themselves by acting as one. Fourthly, as Michelet described the atrocities that occurred after its fall, the image of insanity removed the people's guilt. This use of the insanity defense transferred the blame to the nobles and the church, who for centuries had ruled by keeping the people insane.[88]

The people's unity culminated in the Fête de la Fédération of 1790, when passions became harmonized and the people united. The Fédération was the instance of the true fraternity that Jeanne d'Arc had anticipated; yet, it was also a moment that could not last. Because all historical movements originated from psychological confrontation, there remained not only the chance but the necessity of divisive passions that would give rise to the next *non-moi*. During the Revolution the people would suffer, but only to prepare France for the more permanent unity that the Maiden and then the Fête de la Fédération had prefigured and that biological law assured. The loss of women's support doomed the Revolution, which was based on fraternity and on the sacrifice made by mothers, each of whom was responsible for the generational transmission of ideas. "What was lacking," claimed Michelet, "was sacrifice, the immolation of passion."[89] The enemies of the people knew precisely where to strike, for the greatest blow to Revolutionary fraternity was dealt when priests subverted the women. Through the contagion of divisive passions, this tragedy turned families and then entire areas, such as the Vendée, against the Revolution.[90] Priests, as false confessors, had driven the people against themselves, just as earlier clerics had persecuted the sorceress, typified by Charlotte Cadière.

This destructive insanity spread among the people, resulting in the September massacres: "The massacres had succeeded to a state of madness, of horrible fascination, and of hydrophobic fury."[91] This attack reached its cruelest heights, according to Michelet, when Parisians attacked the poor, the ill, and the insane at Bicêtre. Michelet's greatest biographer, Paul Viallaneix, states that there was no true looting of the hospital of Bicêtre itself; in fact, the raid differed in nature from the other massacres.[92] Michelet's intent, however, was more poetic than strictly factual, because the attack on the hospital symbolized the antithesis of the people's rescue of those interned at the Bastille. The assault of the inmates at Bicêtre, an image of the insane people attacking the insane, symbolized the horrible internal conflicts to which the people had once again been reduced. In just over three years the people's insanity had become egoistic and cruel in imitation of the Old Regime that they were attempting to defeat.

This passionate excess, which doomed the Revolution, then spread to factions within the Convention. Unreasonable fears of ubiquitous plots replaced the former faith in unity. Michelet summarized that development as "this terrible scaffolding of insanities." As fear built upon fear, the Great Terror resulted. "What would happen," Michelet asked, "if in this sick France, the horrible epidemic were to strike, more contagious than any other, this frightful longing for death."[93] In short, an unhealthy monomania had replaced a healthy obsession; the people had not been given the time for a cure. "In order to return to the source of the disaster," Michelet observed, "one very tragic thing, before 1800, was the madness, a kind of mental alienation. The nightmare of the Terror and of the general war had upset the spirits, putting them outside all reason and totally out of balance."[94]

According to Michelet, history, as the Revolution demonstrated, never progressed in a straight line. Man's complex emotional makeup led to successive periods of crisis. Each era witnessed a higher level of man's development; each stage prepared for mankind's next heroic effort. The death of the Revolution could lead only to greater future unity, an idea that Michelet expressed poetically. Referring to the Revolution's enemies, he wrote, "The sword they plunged into her heart works miracles and heals."[95]

Any analysis of Michelet's histories can be checked against his natural histories, which, by his own admission, were allegories of France's past: "All natural history I had begun to regard as a branch of the political."[96] In *La Mer,* for instance, the ocean represented France's stormy past. He compared the tempests to the Revolution's excesses, which attracted the attention of the casual observer. As if attempting to instruct a conservative such as Edmund Burke, Michelet argued, "These [storms] are the accidents that pass at the surface and do not at all reveal the true mysterious personality of the sea." The waves, he continued, "gave me the impression of a frightful *mob,* a horrible populace, not of men, but of barking dogs—a million, a billion bulldogs, enraged, or rather, mad." Below these waves, there existed "an unknown ocean, that of the sufferings of the people."[97] The true history, then, which Michelet explained in terms of a polyp's molting, like each crisis in France's history, represented pain and vulnerability. Each molting was a psychological trial, a "beautiful insanity," which created "the effort and all the progress in the world."[98] This struggle was not as obvious as the madness of the waves that most observers noticed. The real historical drama was played out below the surface in the unseen and insane striving of the individual will to progress against all odds.[99] By writing *La Mer,* Michelet had fulfilled a promise made in 1821: "I had in mind to write the *History of a drop of water,* and I believe that I am going to do this insane thing."[100] The drop of water was the individual, alienated by destructive insanities transmitted by the people's enemies to keep the masses separate and submissive. The French people's heroic, yet insane, effort represented a common desire to form a nation, a single ocean. He compared this ocean to mother's milk, which united all living things. The sea's depths, like the people's history, had its understandable rhythms, its natural laws of psychology and physiology that regulated movement and insured progress.

Notes

1. Notable works on Michelet include, Georges Cogniot, "Qu'est-ce que le peuple pour Michelet et pour nous?," *Europe: Revue littéraire mensuelle* 535-536 (Nov.-Dec. 1973): 43-51; Jeanlouis Cornuz, *Jules Michelet: Un Aspect de la pensée religieuse au XIXe siècle* (Geneva, 1955); Jean Guéhenno, *L'Evangile éternel, étude sur Michelet* (Paris, 1970); Oscar A. Haac, *Jules Michelet* (Boston, 1982); Edward K. Kaplan, *Michelet's Poetic Vision: A Romantic Philosophy of Nature, Man, & Woman* (Amherst, Mass., 1977); Stephen A. Kippur, *Jules Michelet: A Study of Mind and Sensibility* (Albany, N. Y., 1981); Arthur Mitzman, *Michelet, Historian: Rebirth and Romanticism in Nineteenth-Century France* (New Haven, Conn., 1990); Linda Orr, *Jules Michelet: Nature, History, and Language* (Ithaca, N. Y., 1976); Charles Rearick, "Symbol, Legend, and History: Michelet as Folklorist-Historian," *French Historical Studies* 7 (Spring 1971): 72-92; Paul Viallaneix, *La Voie royale: Essai sur l'idée de peuple dans l'oeuvre de Michelet,* new ed. (Paris, 1971).

2. See especially, Michel Foucault, *Histoire de la folie à l'âge classique* (Paris, 1961); idem, *Les Mots et les choses: Une Archéologie des sciences humaines* (Paris, 1966); idem, *Naissance de la clinique: Une Archéologie du regard médical,* 2nd ed. (Paris, 1972); idem. *Surveiller et punir: Naissance de la prison* (Paris, 1975); Jan Goldstein, "'Moral Contagion': A Professional Ideology of Medicine and Psychiatry in Eighteenth- and Nineteenth-Century France," in *Professions and the French State, 1700-1900,* ed. Gerald Geison (Philadelphia, 1984), 215; idem, *Console and Classify: The French Psychiatric Profession in the Nineteenth Century* (Cambridge, 1987), including pp. 2-4 for her discussion of "anti-psychiatry"; especially Robert Castel, *L'Ordre psychiatrique: L'Age d'or de l'aliénisme* (Paris, 1976); and Marcel Gauchet and Gladys Swain, *La Pratique de l'esprit humain: L'Institution asilaire et la révolution démocratique* (Paris, 1980).

3. Edmund Burke, *Reflections on the Revolution in France* (Indianapolis, 1955); Thomas Carlyle, *The French Revolution: A History* (New York, 1934); Richard Chase, Jr., "The Influence of Psychology on Guizot and Orleanist Policies," *French History* 3 (Spring 1989): 177-93.

4. Jean-Etienne Esquirol, *Des maladies mentales considérées sous les rapports médical, hygiénique et médico-légal,* 3 vols. in 2 (Paris, 1838), 1:52-53, 588, 669. For a summary of Esquirol's anti-democratic argument, see the account of Esquirol in René Semelaigne, *Les Grands Aliénistes français: Philippe Pinel, Esquirol, Ferrus, Jean-Pierre Falret, Félix Voisin, Georget* (Paris, 1894).

5. Michael Ignatieff, "State, Civil Society, and Total Institutions: A Critique of Recent Social Histories of Punishment," in *Crime and Justice: An Annual Review of Research,* eds. M. Tonry and N. Morris (Chicago, 1981) 3:156-57, 168, 179-80; Daniel Pick, *Faces of Degeneration: A European Disorder, c. 1848-c. 1918* (Cambridge, 1989), 235-36.

6. Jules Michelet, *Histoire de la Révolution française,* ed. G. Walter, 2 vols. (Paris, 1952), 2:1001. Also see B. F. Bart, "Michelet and Proudhon: A Comparison of Methods," *French Studies* 4 (April 1950): 128-41.

7. Jules Michelet, *The People,* trans. J. P. McKay (Urbana, Il., 1973), 108-9.

8. Ibid., 49.

9. G. S. Kirk, *Myth: Its Meaning and Functions in Ancient and Other Cultures* (Cambridge, 1974), 83.

10. Jeanne Calo, *La Création de la femme chez Michelet* (Paris, 1975); Cynthia E. Russett, *Sexual Science: The Victorian Construction of Womanhood* (Cambridge, Mass., 1989), 30.

11. Jules Michelet, *Jules Michelet: Ecrits de Jeunesse, journal (1820-1823)—Mémorial journal des idées,* ed. P. Viallaneix, 5th ed. (Paris, 1959), 13.

12. Jules Michelet, *Jules Michelet: Journal,* eds. P. Viallaneix and C. Digeon, 4 vols. (Paris, 1959-76), 1:362.

13. Michelet, *The People,* 3.

14. Jules Michelet, *Ma jeunesse* (Paris, 1884), 152-55. These pages include Michelet's description of the first nude woman whom he ever saw. She was insane, having been seduced, impregnated, and abandoned at sixteen. She was the opposite of Michelet's myth of Jeanne d'Arc.

15. Gaëton Picon, *L'Etudiant: Précédé Michelet et la parole historienne* (Paris, 1970), 73-74.

16. Michelet, *Ma jeunesse,* 214.

17. François Furet, "Michelet," in *A Critical Dictionary of the French Revolution,* eds. F. Furet and M. Ozouf, trans. A. Goldhammer (Cambridge, Mass., 1989), 982, 986.

18. Many of these philosophical debates are summarized by George Boas, *French Philosophies of the Romantic Period* (New York, 1964).

19. Jules Michelet, *L'Amour,* 4th ed. (Paris, 1859), 30, 444-45; Jules Michelet, *The Women of the French Revolution,* trans. M. R. Pennington (Philadelphia, Pa., 1855), 117.

20. Jules Michelet, *Histoire de France,* 18 vols. (n.p., n.d.), 16:223.

21. Ulysse Trélat, *La Folie lucide: Etudiée et considérée au point de vue de la famille et de la société* (Paris, 1861), 320.

22. Mitzman, *Michelet, Historian,* 26-29. Madame Dumesnil was the mother of Alfred, Michelet's son-in-law.

23. Michelet, *L'Amour,* 7.

24. In particular, see Michelet, *Journal* [*Jules Michelet: Journal*], 2:300, 333-34, 459-66; 3:49-50, 424.

25. Michelet's natural histories include *L'Oiseau,* 6th ed. (Paris, 1859), *L'Insecte* (Paris, 1858), *La Mer,* 2nd ed. (Paris, 1861), *La Montagne* (Paris, 1868). His most revealing studies on women are *L'Amour* and *La Femme* (Paris, 1860).

26. Mitzman concurs that Michelet's natural histories have largely been ignored. See Mitzman, *Michelet, Historian,* 284. Mitzman, who ends his study in 1854, does not treat two notable exceptions: Kaplan, *Michelet's Poetic Vision,* and Orr, *Jules Michelet.*

27. The sexual problems that partially account for these observations are summarized in Mitzman, *Michelet, Historian,* 201-3.

28. Michelet, *La Femme,* 34, 54-56.

29. Bruno Jacques Béraud, *Elements de physiologie de l'homme et des principaux vertébrés, répondant à toutes les questions physiologiques du programme des examens de fin d'année,* 2nd ed., 2 vols. (Paris, 1856-57), 2:750-59.

30. Ibid., 824-25. For a similar opinion, see Prosper Lucas, *Traité philosophique et physiologique de l'hérédité naturelle dans les états de santé et de maladie du système nerveux avec l'application méthodique des lois de la procréation au traitement général des affections dont elle est le principe,* 2 vols. (Paris, 1847-50), 1:8.

31. B. Béraud, *Elements de physiologie de l'homme,* 2:824. For a similar conclusion that there was a "hereditary law [which] exists in nations and renders perfection gradually to the human species," see A. Pierre Béraud, *De la phrénologie humaine appliquée à la philosophie, aux moeurs, et au socialisme* (Paris, 1848), 356.

32. Jean Jacques Coste, *Histoire générale et particulière du développement des corps organisés, publiée sous les auspices de M. Villemain, ministre de l'instruction publique,* 2 vols. in 1 (Paris, 1847-59); Charles Négrier, *Recherches anatomiques et physiologiques sur les ovaires dans l'espèce humaine, considérés spécialement sous le rapport de leur influence dans la menstruation* (Paris, 1840).

33. See Michelet, *Journal,* 4:76, and the note on 401.

34. Michelet, *L'Amour,* 7.

35. Béraud, *Elements de physiologie de l'homme,* 2:398-99; Lucas, *Traité philosophique et physiologique,* 2:916-17.

36. Lucas, *Traité philosophique et physiologique,* 2:906-22. At the time epilepsy was seen as a severe form of mental illness.

37. Trélat, *La Folie lucide,* 321-28.

38. Michelet, *L'Amour,* 8.

39. Philippe Pinel, *Traité médico-philosophique sur l'aliénation mentale,* 2nd ed. (Paris, 1809). The moral treatment was equivalent to the psychological treatment, in contrast to physical treatments such as bleeding and purging.

40. Jules Michelet, *Lettres inédites addressés à Mlle Mialaret (Mme Michelet)* (Paris, 1899), 152. Also see Edward K. Kaplan, "Les Deux Sexes de l'esprit: Michelet phénoménologue de la pensée créatrice et morale," *Europe: Revue littéraire mensuelle* 535-536 (Nov.-Dec. 1973), 103.

41. Michelet, *L'Amour,* 449.

42. Michelet, *La Femme,* 270. For similar conclusions see Lucas, *Traité philosophique et physiologique,* 1:2.

43. Michelet, *La Femme,* 271-72.

44. Jules Michelet and Edgar Quinet, *The Jesuits,* trans. from the French, ed. L. Edwards (New York, 1845), 66-67.

45. Jacques-Joseph Moreau de Tours, *Etudes psychiques sur la folie* (Paris, 1840).

46. Ibid., 6-7 (emphasis added).

47. Jules Michelet, *The Bible of Humanity,* trans. V. Calfa (New York, 1877), 151. Michelet distinguished between the "active passion," which led to progress, and the "passive passion," which resulted in decline. He argued that the passive passion was first introduced by Alexander the Great, who by combining the role of king and priest used government and religion to control the people.

48. Michelet, *Histoire de France,* 15:345.

49. Ibid., 2:69 (emphasis added).

50. Ibid., 78.

51. Ibid., 8:235.

52. Ibid., 4:302.

53. Ibid., 5:15.

54. Ibid., 1:32-33.

55. Ibid., 5:16.

56. Ibid., 47.

57. Ibid., 81.

58. Ibid., 59. "*Le mal moral*" would have been treated better by the moral treatment prescribed by Pinel and his pupils.

59. Ibid., 1:31-32, 6:136.

60. Ibid., 6:249.

61. Louis Florentin Calmeil, *De la folie considérée sous le point de vue pathologique, philosophique, historique et judiciaire,* 2 vols. (Paris, 1845; reprint ed., New York, 1976), 1:127-35.

62. Michelet, *Journal,* 1:606.

63. Michelet, *Histoire de la Révolution française,* 2:497. Also see Michelet, *The Women of the French Revolution,* 234-35.

64. Michelet, *Histoire de la Révolution française,* 2:497; Michelet, *The People,* 119.

65. Michelet, *Histoire de France,* 10:304.

66. Ibid., 12:64.

67. Ibid., 11:12, 13:109.

68. Catherine B. Clément, "Michelet et Freud: De la sorcière à l'hystèrique," *Europe: Revue littéraire mensuelle* 535-536 (Nov.-Dec. 1973): 114.

69. Jules Michelet, *Satanism and Witchcraft: A Study in Medieval Superstition,* trans. of *La Sorcière* by A. R. Allison (New York, 1971), xv.

70. Clément, "Michelet et Freud," 115; Michelet, *Satanism and Witchcraft,* xviii.

71. Michelet, *Satanism and Witchcraft,* ix-x.

72. Ibid., 106.

73. Michelet, *Histoire de France,* 8:107, 13:122. I have translated "vertige" as "mad." Michelet often used many synonyms for madness or insanity. Examples include Michelet's description of the Great Terror: "Avant 1800, une chose fort tragique, c'est le vertige, une sorte d'aliénation mentale." He depicted the exploration of the Basques as follows: "L'Elan basque et la folie lucide qui se guida si bien autour du monde." According to Trélat, "La Folie lucide" was a form of monomania, which allowed Michelet to refer to the Basques as "les héros du vertige." See Jules Michelet, *Histoire du XIXe siècle,* new ed., 3 vols. (Paris, 1880), 1:xv; Michelet, *La Mer,* 274, 270; Trélat, *La Folie lucide.*

74. Michelet, *Satanism and Witchcraft,* 274, 317-18, 322. Michelet also emphasized the capability of priests to drive women mad in Jules Michelet, *Priests, Women, and Families,* trans. from the French, third ed. by C. Cocks, 2nd English ed. (London, 1846), especially 126, 264.

75. Michelet, *Histoire de France,* 11:12.

76. Michelet does not mention the name of the regent's daughter but the most obvious choice is the duchesse de Berry, described in J. H. Shennan, *Philippe, Duke of Orléans: Regent of France, 1715-1723* (London, 1979), 128. An alternative explanation is that the daughter was in fact *l'homo-duplex* as represented in Alexandre Dumas, *Oeuvres de Alexandre Dumas: Une Fille du régent* (Paris, 1931). Dumas contrasted the worldly duchesse de Berry with her cloistered sister, Louise-Adélaide d'Orléans. The daughter, by remaining unnamed by Michelet, may have symbolized the struggle between these two sisters, the *moi* versus the *non-moi.*

77. Michelet, *Histoire de France,* 16:220, 223.

78. Ibid., 230.

79. Ibid., 289.

80. Ibid., 336.

81. Ibid., 18:160.

82. Ibid., 225.

83. Jules Michelet, *History of the French Revolution,* ed. with an intro. by G. Wright, trans. C. Cocks (Chicago, 1967), 53.

84. Quotation from Michelet in Pieter Geyl, *Debates with Historians* (Groningen, Netherlands, 1955), 78. Geyl does not give his source.

85. Michelet, *History of the French Revolution,* 39.

86. Ibid., 161, 176.

87. Michelet had discussed the false treatments of Friedrich Anton Mesmer in medicine and Charles Alexandre de Calonne in finance as anticipations of the storming of the Bastille, which symbolized all the false cures offered by the Old Regime. See Michelet, *Histoire de France,* 18:275.

88. Michelet, *History of the French Revolution,* 204-5. For an analysis of the insanity defense, see Raymond de Saussure, "The Influence of the Concept of Monomania on French Medico-Legal Psychiatry (from 1825 to 1840)," *Bulletin of the History of Medicine and Allied Sciences* 1 (July 1946): 365-97.

89. Michelet, *Histoire de la Révolution française,* 1:533.

90. Ibid., 1145-70.

91. Ibid., 1090.

92. Ibid., 149, 1088-89. For another criticism of Michelet's account of the attack on the hospital, see Paul Bru, *Histoire de Bicêtre, (hospice-prison-asile) d'après des documents historiques* (Paris, 1890), 80.

93. Michelet, *Histoire de la Révolution: française,* 1:1196, 2:160.

94. Michelet, *Histoire du XIXe siècle,* 1:xv.

95. Michelet, *The People,* 199.

96. Jules Michelet, *The Bird,* trans. W.-H. D. Adams, new ed. (London, 1872), 52.

97. Jules Michelet, *La Mer,* 60, 85; Michelet, *Histoire de la Révolution française,* 1:536, 431.

98. Michelet, *La Mer,* 169-68.

99. Michelet's choice of language is crucial to understanding his histories. He selected the word "mue," that had been used to describe the polyp's molting, in order to symbolize the people's rebellion to achieve freedom. The insane but really healthy revolt, the *moi,* was contrasted to a debilitating insanity, the *non-moi,* made contagious by English incendiary pamphlets. British leaders were also overcome with "une sorte de rage mue," as were French nobles and clergy who became "amueté" or maddened.

100. Michelet, *Ecrits de Jeunesse,* 225.

Arthur Mitzman (essay date October 1996)

SOURCE: Mitzman, Arthur. "Michelet and Social Romanticism: Religion, Revolution, Nature." *Journal of the History of Ideas* 57, no. 4 (October 1996): 659-82.

[*In the following essay, Mitzman explores Michelet's rejection of Catholicism in favor of a "semi-religious" belief in social harmony.*]

In 1851, shortly before his second and definitive suspension from his teaching at the Collège de France, Jules Michelet told a young friend of his dissatisfaction with the meager political impact of the Republican professors of the time: "Our present propaganda . . . has resembled strongly that which might be made by a man enclosed in a crystal glass. He finds his voice to be resounding and very strong: that's because it breaks against the inner surface. But those who are outside, the men of the people, hear nothing."[1]

Michelet had become painfully aware of how little his voice had been heard outside the crystal in June 1848, when barricade-builders outside his house on the Rue des Postes responded to his son-in-law's appeal not to expose the dwelling of the great historian to artillery fire by asking, "Who is Michelet?"[2] This occurred two years after the publication of *Le Peuple* and only months after the appearance of his celebration of the commoners' festivals of federation in 1790, both texts being landmarks in the social romantic anticipation of 1848. In fact it was the 1848 Revolution itself that had diminished the resonance of Michelet's ideas, by polarizing the country in a way that made it impervious to his message of social harmony.

Before 1848, Michelet was a central figure in the intellectual disaffection that delegitimized the July Monarchy. His work in the 1840s had shifted from the historical erudition of his many-volumed *Histoire de France* to contemporary polemics against the clergy and the government: attacks on the Jesuits and the Church[3] swiftly broadened to a conflict with the intellectual and political establishment of the period. In *Le Peuple* (1846), Michelet combined an analysis of the profound social divisions within the French nation with a remarkable sketch of the relation between civilization and nature, a Rousseauian appeal to the natural qualities of the common people and an invocation of the genius of the future, who would be gifted with "the two sexes of the spirit."

Le Peuple was the first of a series of works on nature, women, and the common people, those three "others" of nineteenth-century high culture, that have throughout this century fascinated cultural historians. In the historiographical tradition, its author has been celebrated by those who viewed him as their predecessor in the broadening of history-writing to include culture and mentalities, such as Lucien Febvre and Jacques Le Goff, and denigrated by those, like Pieter Geyl, who have been outraged by his nationalistic pathos and his blatant subjectivity.[4] I shall suggest in this essay that all of these aspects of Michelet's work are rooted in his significance in the 1840s as a social romantic, the contemporary and friend of George Sand, Lamennais, Pierre Leroux, and others.

For apart from what Michelet has come to mean, as totem or as scarecrow, to the scholarship of the twentieth century, he was enmeshed in the ideological conflicts of his own time. Without an understanding of those conflicts, an important perspective on his place in the history of ideas will be missing, a perspective which, moreover, may shed some light on the broader historical significance of the social romanticism he represented. For example, the "ideological" Michelet was best known in his own time as an anticlerical.[5] Indeed, his version of the Romantic *évangile éternel,* which he developed in the 1840s, takes a privileged place among the efforts of intellectuals in the first half of the nineteenth century to work out new religious conceptions to replace a moribund Catholicism.[6] Yet the principal framework of his polemical activity was not the Church but the liberal academic establishment, with which he was at war from his 1843 lectures on the Jesuits to his dismissal from his official functions at the beginning of the Second Empire.

MICHELET AND THE JULY MONARCHY: FROM LIBERALISM TO SOCIAL ROMANTICISM

Seen from the standpoint of the early years of his career, roughly 1825 to 1835, Michelet would seem an improbable candidate for any kind of romanticism. Given his impoverished, artisan background as well as his intellectual formation, identification with the group of well-heeled dreamers around Victor Hugo, even after their conversion to *Le Globe*'s liberalism, was altogether unlikely. His teacher in the Lycée Charlemagne, Abel François Villemain, and his mentor during the mid-twenties, Cousin, were part of the group of liberal intellectuals who stood apart both from the restoration of aristocratic power and from the Catholic romanticism which, until the late twenties, was the lapdog of that power. In fact, before 1830 the conservative liberal François Guizot considered Michelet reliable enough to recommend him as the tutor of Charles X's granddaughter and, after the *trois glorieuses,* as his replacement at the Sorbonne and as head of the historical section of

the Archives Nationales. Louis Philippe followed the judgment of his predecessor and appointed Michelet tutor of his daughter, and Adolphe Thiers chose to preface a reedition of his history of the revolution with Michelet's book-length *Précis de l'histoire de France.*[7]

Accordingly, Michelet's first history of philosophy was a self-conscious echo of the liberalism that triumphed in the July Revolution.[8] Staking out a position independent of Victor Cousin's eclecticism, which he saw as overly deterministic, Michelet viewed history as the eternal struggle of human freedom against material and social "fatality."[9] The victory of French liberals in 1830 was for him a high point in that struggle. Far from appreciating the dark sensuality and heroic egoism of the romantic poets and playwrights of the period, Michelet placed the highest value in the struggle for human freedom on ascetic idealism: the rejection of material satisfactions and self-sacrifice. If there were questions about Michelet's liberalism in the 1830s, they were less about possible romantic or social inclinations than about his conservative Catholic tendencies: the part of his *Histoire de France* that dealt with the great cathedrals of the High Middle Ages seemed a strange homage to the spirit of Christian asceticism for someone who was reputed to be the disciple of Cousin and the ally of Thiers.

In 1843, a decade after this homage, Michelet appeared to have reversed ground. In the lectures he gave with Quinet at the Collège de France on the Jesuits, he began a war with the Church over its challenge to state control of education. Four years later, in the preface and introduction to his own history of the revolution, he pronounced the principles of Christianity and of the French Revolution to be utterly incompatible; indeed, the Revolution itself contained the basic religious principle of the modern age—Justice—which was fundamentally opposed to the Christian principle of Grace. Moreover, throughout his seven-volume study, Michelet sought to transcend the Voltairean liberalism which he identified with his own political origins as well as the first phase of the Revolution, to locate in the Paris of the first Commune and in Danton the germ of the social and religious revolution of the nineteenth century. He was not the only such seeker. The first volumes of Michelet's *French Revolution* appeared in the same year as Louis Blanc's initial volume on the subject, Lamartine's eight-part *Histoire des Girondins,* and Alphonse Esquiros's *Histoire des Montagnards.* The July Monarchy was nearing its end in crisis, polarization, scandal, and massive disaffection; and Michelet, like the others, was preparing his compatriots for a new 1789. In fact, more than the others, he had the obligation as well as the right to do so. For in the *Götterdämmerung* of the *juste milieu* during the late forties, the evolution of Michelet was both cause and symptom of the regime's vanishing base.

Despite its surface appearance of bourgeois stability, the July Monarchy had never been able to legitimize itself on the essential terrain of the capital. The revolution of July 1830 had been won by a combination of liberals, republicans, and revolutionary artisans. The first group wanted the Charter and a king who would live up to it; the second, a vastly expanded suffrage and a republic; the artisans, on the whole Bonapartist, were more concerned with the right to organize their trades than with politics. The liberals, with the political expertise of a Thiers, a Guizot, and a Casimir Perier, quickly installed Louis-Philippe and spent the next four years using the army and the judiciary to settle their differences with insurrectionary Republicans and rioting artisans. Only between 1835 and 1840 were the streets of Paris free, apart from the occasional conspiratorial fiasco, of the tumult that had repeatedly jeopardized the regime during its first years. The republicans were then imprisoned or intimidated; the artisans saw the basis of their economic struggle undermined by massive unemployment in the crisis of 1837.

The years of calm ended in 1840. A new artisan strike wave and a foreign policy disaster in the Middle East reawakened republican hopes and kindled the militancy of a disparate group of socialists and romantics.[10] Cabet's *Voyage en Icarie*, Proudhon's *Qu'est-ce que la propriété?*, Louis Blanc's *Organisation du Travail*, and Pierre Leroux's *De l'humanité* all appeared in the same year as George Sand's *Le Compagnon du tour de France*. The first important workers' paper, the Saint-Simonian *La Ruche Populaire*, founded in December 1839, was followed in 1840 by the Christian Socialist *L'Atelier*, and in 1841 by Cabet's *Le Populaire*, and the dissident Cabetist *La Fraternité*. In the same year Sand, Leroux, and Louis Viardot launched *La Revue Indépendante*, which quickly became the principal organ for the social romantic tendency that represented this new militancy on the cultural front.

Two things require explanation here. One is the nature and the source of the social romantic option. The other is how Michelet came to be involved with it and what, specifically, he did to advance its cause.

THE POLITICAL ROOTS OF SOCIAL ROMANTICISM

Social romanticism was the semi-religious quest for harmony in social existence, in nature, and in the cosmos of dissenting writers and ideologists during the 1840s. As such, it pulled together diverse efforts of what Paul Bénichou has called the humanitarian Left to write the common people into society, politics, religion, and history. These efforts were the work of ex-Saint-Simonians like Leroux and Jean Reynaud, of Christian Socialists like Lamennais, of popular romantic novelists such as George Sand, Victor Hugo, and Eugène Sue, of left liberal men of letters like Michelet, Quinet, and the

popular poet Béranger.[11] They expressed the urgency of the moment in the idiom of the age. The urgency was for the broadest possible coalition against the prevailing system, an alliance of disenfranchised popular elements with critical intellectuals and with those left-liberal and republican elements excluded by the various governments of the Party of Resistance. The prevailing romantic idiom lent itself easily to the need for oppositional consensus: in the poetry of Lamartine and Chateaubriand, it was an idiom of cosmic harmony; in Hugo's *Notre Dame de Paris* and in the various romantic borrowings from the theater of farce and melodrama, it reflected the popular culture; and in the feuilletons of Sand and Sue, it took on the radical contours of early socialism. Lamennais, in *Paroles d'un croyant* of 1834 and *Le Livre du Peuple* of 1837 had already set a broad Christian Socialist framework for the social romantics of the 1840s, to which Michelet's **Le Peuple** of 1846 gave an unmistakable left-nationalist echo.

All of these intellectual forces represented a challenge not only to the ideological presuppositions of the July Monarchy about the necessary relation between ruler and ruled but to broader assumptions about the hierarchical relations between high and low, be they between mankind and nature, spirit and matter, the king and his subjects, men and women, fathers and children, masters and workmen, or elite culture and popular culture—assumptions that linked the governing bourgeois elites of the nineteenth century to old regime attitudes. For in contrast to the quest of radical forces for a levelling of political barriers between high and low and, concomitantly, for the integration of the popular into the elite culture, the attitudes of the governing elites continued the mixture of fear, contempt, and moralizing pedagogy toward the common people which, before 1789, had characterized the "civilizing offensive" of church and state.[12]

In fact, even the revolutionary lawyers and journalists of the Third Estate, like most of the late eighteenth-century elite culture, were inspired by the values of the Old Regime, which included the assumption that the uneducated populace was lazy, mendacious, and superstitious and, where not hopelessly criminal, urgently in need of the moral guidance of their superiors. Nonetheless they quickly realized that their only hope of breaking the intransigence of the *ancien régime* was precisely by alliance with the burly popular classes: the tennis court oath could hardly have brought the monarchy to its knees without the storming of the Bastille. The result was the revolutionary fraternity of 1789-90, source and model of the social romantic coalition. Not only the social barrier between high and low but also the economic one between traditional producers and modern free trade advocates gave way to the political imperative. Given the initial consensus among disgruntled masters, exploited journeymen and modernizing legists about the necessity for dismantling the Old Regime's corporate structure, this alliance became the basis for the enormous political momentum the Revolution built up in its first years. In fact the primacy of the political was such that even after the Le Chapelier legislation of 1791, when the artisanry began to realize the danger to its existence posed by the new liberal order, the form taken by its new militancy was the essentially political organization of the sans-culottes, in which small capitalists played a leading role.

It was not only the revolutionary moment of 1789 that created the basis for overcoming the manifest social differences between bourgeois and plebs. Despite the disdain in which the educated bourgeois held the common people, the predominantly artisanal industrial economy and the enormous splintering of the world of petty commerce—features of the French economy that survived until the twentieth century—created a society in which the *menu peuple* were rarely very far away from their bourgeois superiors and were in principle susceptible to the appeals of property and propriety.

Thus, though the Terror and the anti-parliamentary militancy of the sans-culottes divided revolutionary ranks from 1793 on, the moment of revolutionary unity between bourgeois and plebs remained a latent possibility, embedded in the social relations and political needs of the age and reincarnated briefly in 1830 and more palpably in the pre-1848 mentality of social romanticism. One might speak of a structural basis for the democratic and republican movements that created the first three French Republics, whatever the latent tensions between the partners.[13] Something of this openness to the common people was reflected within the July Monarchy's liberal establishment in the loose coalition known as *le mouvement,* which soon lost out to the conservative *résistance* but with which both Thiers and Cousin, Michelet's patrons, had been vaguely associated in 1830-31.

At a purely cultural level, the social romantic celebration of the common people, made possible by the political and social force field, involved more than Hugo's and Dumas's borrowings from popular melodrama.[14] The traditional popular culture, repressed by clerical and bourgeois morality before the Revolution and by revolutionary ideologues after 1789, had experienced a major revival during the Empire and influenced all areas of life in the first half of the nineteenth century. Particularly important was the impact on the urban elite culture. Carnival and other popular festivities in Paris were shared by high and low as at no time since the sixteenth century.[15] Emblematic of the revival of carnival's grotesque humor was the enormous popularity among the Romantics of both Rabelais and Shakespeare, whose earlier fusions of elite and popular culture were intuitively felt to be addressing the cultural situation of the nineteenth century.[16] At a less elevated level,

the farce melodrama of Frédérick Lemaître, the *commedia dell'arte* mime work of a Debureau,[17] united the king's subjects in a republic of laughter, while Philipon's *Le Charivari* used the concept of a traditional ritual of humiliation to satirize the *juste milieu* for the educated.

There is more. The July Revolution of 1830 had catalyzed profound layers of revolt in the bourgeois youth of Paris.[18] The intuitive grasp of the popular culture was part of a broader cultural resistance to the productivist values of the new bourgeois hegemony, values that in some ways intensified the civilizing offensive of the Old Regime.[19] The first circles of Bohemian poets and artists were applying the individualism of the age to areas the liberal economists found frightening: to the exploration of their emotional, aesthetic and sexual capacities.[20] In the romantic literature of the period, starving poets ranted against the materialist middle class, apocalyptic visions and dark themes of androgyny and incest challenged philistine complacency. Street corner prophets of class, personal, and sexual liberation abounded: it was the age in which the "Mapah" ostentatiously proclaimed to Parisians his double sexuality.[21]

All of this cultural ferment occurred at a time when the post-revolutionary elites were renewing themselves with new blood from below. Though most of the leading figures in the first generation of romantic writers—Lamartine, Vigny, Musset, Hugo, Dumas, Sand—descended from the aristocratic or Napoleonic elites, many others from their and subsequent generations of intellectuals and artists were of humble, frequently artisan, origin. Apart from Michelet, Pierre Leroux, Daumier, Courbet, and Proudhon were brought up in, or in proximity to, the popular culture. Even George Sand, whose father and grandmother were related to the Bourbons, never forgot her seamstress mother.

PERSONALITY, VALUES, IDEOLOGY: THE BIOGRAPHICAL COMPONENT

Michelet's transformation, then, from apolitical liberal in the thirties to social romantic in the forties was rooted both in July Monarchy liberalism and in his own social background. A living bridge between cultures, Michelet was able to comprehend both the Parisian popular strata he was raised in and the elite of the free professions to which he had ascended. Yet, until he was over forty, Michelet made little reference to and seemed to have little feeling for his personal origins. Only in **Le Peuple,** written in 1845, did he identify himself as a man of the people, and one can trace the change in his values that led to **Le Peuple** at most back to the early 1840s. Apart from the altered intellectual and political climate around 1840, what induced the new vision that brought Michelet into conflict with the Church from 1843 on and with the political and cultural establishment of the July Monarchy a couple of years later?

I have discussed this elsewhere.[22] In brief, Michelet's career revealed a flight from his lower middle-class origins that carried him, in a little more than a decade, from secondary school teaching to the most prestigious academic institution in France, the Collège de France, established in the Renaissance by Francis I as a counterweight to the clerically dominated Sorbonne. This social escape from his personal origins might be construed in psychological terms as simultaneously the internalization of the ascetic spirit of his mother and a flight from her emotional significance for him, conceived as threatening. In fact both Michelet's early liberalism and his subsequent leap to the social romantic option were made possible not only by the politics and ideologies of the time but by his own psychological development as well.

In 1839 Michelet's wife died of tuberculosis, and he was overcome by a guilty awareness that he had neglected her and his family ties generally for the sake of his career. Shortly after, between 1840 and 1842, he was profoundly influenced by a liaison with Madame Dumesnil, mother of one of his Collège de France auditors. Madame Dumesnil first approached him in connection with her son's health, and she quickly became a model of the caring parent which he now regretted he had not been. Though she died of cancer in 1842, the relationship triggered a latent reverence for motherhood and nature that had been buried in him for decades under a crust of anti-feminist asceticism.

Scholars have pointed out Michelet's earlier, more complex evaluations of nature and popular culture, evident in his fascination for Creuzer's work on mythology and in the interest in folk culture inspired Vico, and by his contact with Jacob Grimm (concretized in his **Origines du droit français** of 1838).[23] No doubt these earlier evaluations provided an intellectual foundation for subsequent changes in values and ideology. Between 1840 and 1843, however, Michelet altered not only his ideas concerning nature and motherhood but also those about religion, freedom, and history. During the last months of Madame Dumesnil's life, the deeply shaken scholar read and reread the writings of the dissident Saint-Simonians Pierre Leroux and Jean Reynaud on reincarnation and the immortality of the soul. He also came under the influence of the Lyon mystic Jean-Pierre Ballanche and of the physiologist Etienne Geoffroy Saint-Hilaire, a friend of Leroux,[24] who argued the continuity in the world of living things, from the highest and most complicated forms of life to the most elementary.

To put the change in Michelet's ideas in its simplest terms, from a basic belief in the linear progress of freedom through conflict with and liberation from the natural world, he came to accept a cyclical view of nature and spiritual existence built on the principle of harmony, in which the key human values were nurturance

and sociability, summed up in the concept of *fraternité*. The maternal spirit that he associated with Madame Dumesnil infused not only the material universe, in which he saw God as a nurturent mother, but also human history, which it was the historian's task to create as well as to retell: "Of what is history made, if not of me? Of what would history be remade and retold, if not of me?" A key concept infusing all these ideas was that of *accouchement*, which was used by Ballanche and Hugo as well, and signified not only birth but the entire natural cycle of birth, death, and rebirth. Invoking the spirit of Joachim of Fiore, Michelet called his new religious and philosophical ideas an *évangile éternel*, a concept he shared at the time with Pierre Leroux and George Sand.[25]

The various sources of Michelet's new cosmology were not just tied together ideologically; he knew the authors of several of them personally as well. He had a long talk with the son of Geoffroy Saint-Hilaire, who continued his father's work, a few days before Madame Dumesnil's death. A year later, when Michelet's assault on the Jesuits made his new radicalism public, Leroux's and Sand's *Revue indépendante* rushed to support him and asked for contributions from him.[26] One of them was a brief homage to his mother, signalling the changed personal attitude that Madame Dumesnil's influence had brought about. When Michelet visited his friend Quinet in the summer of 1847, he found him in a vacation colony that included Jean Reynaud, who had earlier been the ideological companion of Leroux, and Geoffroy Saint-Hilaire's son, who was continuing the work of his deceased father. Ballanche, Leroux, and Reynaud, apart from their impact on Michelet, influenced George Sand—I have mentioned Leroux's and Sand's partnership in editing the *Revue Indépendante*—as well as Alphonse Esquiros and Eugène Sue, all social romantics with whom Michelet developed ties in the forties and fifties.

Michelet's value reversal occurred, then, in the broader context of his ideological choices and friendships. In particular, his relations with two figures whose intellectual and institutional positions constituted a polar antithesis in the cultural politics of the July Monarchy are paradigmatic for those choices: Félicité de Lamennais, the outsider, his friend, and Victor Cousin, the insider, his enemy.

LAMENNAIS VERSUS COUSIN: INTELLECTUALS AND POLITICS IN THE 1840s

Lamennais, by the example of his principled opposition to the powers of both church and state after 1830, became the most prominent symbol of social romanticism, an inspiration for Sand, Esquiros, Sue, and others. Expelled from the Church, his Christianity radicalized to the point that he became the leading Christian socialist of the age, seeing in the common people the true martyrdom of Christ. He opposed war, violence, and the death penalty, preached a humanitarian Christ and the union of man with God, believed in brotherhood, *la patrie,* and individual property as the basis of liberty, and in human progress—if necessary by revolution.[27] In the tense climate of 1840 Louis-Philippe's judiciary claimed that Lamennais's vituperative attack on the government (in *Le Pays et le gouvernement*) had inspired an attempt on the king's life and sent him to the prison of Sainte-Pélagie for the year 1841.[28]

As Michelet became ever more critical of the government in the 1840s, he found in Lamennais a friend and supporter. He had been impressed by Lamennais's conservative Catholic *Essai sur l'indifférence* in the twenties and sympathetically inclined to him in the early thirties as well—one source has him attending the private lectures Lamennais gave in 1831. But in the period of Lamennais's conflict with Rome (and of his radicalization), there are no references to him in Michelet's *Journal*: the historian, busy making his own career with the help of *juste milieu* liberals, may have seen association with the firebrand priest as compromising to his chances. The first such reference, after ten years of silence, was in 1844: "A l'institut pour m. de Lamennais, contre Cousin."[29] The juxtaposition is characteristic for Michelet's institutional position in the decade to come. Michelet had already identified Cousin as his principal enemy within the establishment and Lamennais as an ally in his campaign against Cousin.

Lamennais and Cousin had not always been at loggerheads. In the mid-twenties, when Lamennais was simply known as a conservative—if intelligent and independent—theologian, and Cousin, in his Carbonari phase, was a victim of *Ultra* disfavor, they valued one another.[30] But from the early thirties, their career trajectories crossed and their relations were envenomed. In the years that Lamennais's liberalism led to his expulsion by the clerical hierarchy, Cousin became a stalwart of the liberal *juste milieu,* inclined by his philosophical position to use Catholic institutions to keep the masses quiet; in return, of course, the Church was to accept Cousin's control over the philosophical formation of the elites in the lycées and the Ecole Normale.[31] He was one of the sharpest advocates of repression in the early thirties, and his vehement support in 1835 for the death penalty against a revolutionary accused of attempted regicide won him from Lamennais the sobriquet of *le Platon de la guillotine.*[32]

Michelet probably had not heard of this, but he did know Cousin well. He had been Cousin's disciple in 1824, then his colleague and rival at the reestablished Ecole Normale from 1827 on. His *Introduction à l'histoire universelle* of 1831 had been directed against his *maître*'s Hegelian historical determinism. Moreover,

Michelet knew quite well how powerful Cousin was in directing the educational policies of the July Monarchy and in insuring that the secondary school staff was periodically purged of radical anti-clericals.[33] In fact, Cousin's eclecticism was the unofficial philosophy of the July Monarchy. The best-known polemic against Cousin was in Pierre Leroux's *Réfutation de l'eclecticisme* of 1839 in which Michelet, if he had occasion to forget the many key positions of his former *patron,* could consult the list on page 84: "Chambre des pairs . . . Conseil royal de l'université . . . Faculté . . . Ecole normale . . . Académie . . . Journal des savants . . . la Commission littéraire." The following year Michelet could have added "Minister of Education." But it would probably have been a few years more before Michelet would have agreed with Leroux's acid criticism of Cousin: "There are two powers in particular, two very ancient powers, against which modern philosophy had always been at war: the kings and the priests. Monsieur Cousin has made himself the courtisan [*sic*] of the kings and the priests."[34]

In fact, Cousin's strength did not derive from his very temporary position as minister in 1840, but from his control, as one of the permanent members of the *conseil royal* that advised the minister, over secondary school appointments in the teaching of philosophy. The draft bill of 1841 on secondary education that stirred the Catholics to militant opposition was not directly his handiwork but that of his successor Villemain, Michelet's old history teacher from the Lycée Charlemagne. The essential question was the position of Catholic teachers under a university statute that gave the state, in principle, complete control over secondary education. The position of the many Catholic schools had never been clearly established under this statute and it was Villemain's unhappy task to do so. His proposal to place the teaching credentials of teachers at Catholic schools and seminaries under state control raised a hornet's nest of clerical opposition, which the prudent withdrawal of the bill did not pacify. After ten years of caution, triggered by the militant and massive anti-clericalism that followed the July Revolution and was sustained by the division of the Church into a liberal wing led by Montalembert and *L'Avenir* and a reactionary one led by Veuillot and *L'Univers,* churchmen overcame their differences to unite behind an intransigent opposition to the *monopole universitaire.* What made this opposition particularly intolerable to the anti-clerical republicans, and moreover gave them an argument against Orleanist liberals in power, was the fact that the clerical campaign was sparked by various pseudonymous writers of the reactionary Jesuit Order, which was supposed to have been banned from France during the Restoration but was clearly being tolerated by the government. Using the rhetoric of romantic vitalism, Michelet attacked the Jesuits for their machine-like power, which he saw as inherently counter-revolutionary, the very death of the liberty they were claiming for the Church.[35]

When Michelet launched, with Edgar Quinet, his assault on the Jesuits, he knew that Cousin, though himself under fire in the Catholic press, could not stand behind any overt attack on the Church. At the beginning he probably did not realize how much Cousin was mortified by the polemic. The powerful philosopher of Eclecticism was a key figure in the Orleanist establishment, which, based on the votes of a small minority of the population, necessarily had to avoid issues which would arouse either its conservative or its reformist opponents. The clerical issue, in polarizing the country around the education question, incited Catholics and Republicans to attack the government as well as each other. The issue had to be neutralized; the liberals' cautious and long-term strategy had to be given another chance to outmaneuver the Church. In 1845 Guizot sent Rossi, a native-born Italian who also taught in the Collège de France, to negotiate a settlement with the Pope.[36] After months of laborious negotiation the papacy agreed to close—at least in name—the various Jesuit colleges that were not supposed to exist, in return for a muzzling of the outspoken professors. Shortly after, Quinet was suspended from his chair in the Collège de France for going beyond the narrow description of his teaching responsibility. Two years later, it was Michelet's turn. Less than two months before the February Revolution, he too was suspended from his teaching, because of "disturbances" preceding his lectures.

Michelet's suspension proved to be counter-productive. His lectures, which dealt with the students as a potentially revolutionary force, a link between bourgeois and common people, and which he then published in the form of a weekly pamphlet, gained more notoriety than they would have if confined to the lecture hall of the Collège de France.[37] Moreover, student militants seized on Michelet's suspension as a cause célèbre to organize the youth of the Latin Quarter in demonstrations that shortly after merged with those for the banned reformist banquet of February, the immediate spark for the Revolution of 1848.[38]

In March 1848, under the education ministry of the provisional government, Michelet and Quinet were triumphantly reinstated in their chairs. Even before this happened, Michelet had proposed to the new Minister of Education, the former Saint-Simonian Hippolyte Carnot, to enlarge Cousin's stronghold, the *Académie des Sciences Morales et Politiques,* from 30 to 40 members, an obvious attempt to pack it with anti-Cousinians. Michelet's proposal has the character of a Social Romantic power play: virtually all of his candidates were hostile to Cousin and Eclecticism and most of them were part of the core group of Social Romantic men of letters. They included Lamennais, Quinet, Mickiewicz, the poet Béranger, and the philosopher Félix Ravaisson—all close personal friends—as well as Pierre Leroux, Jean Reynaud, George Sand, Lamartine, Louis Blanc, and Michelet's sympathetic colleague Arago. The hostility toward Cousin of Mickiewicz, the mystical Polish poet who, as a sign of the total rejection by the intellectual establishment of his messianic nationalism, had been purged from the Collège de France even before Michelet and Quinet, was as predictable as Lamennais's. Béranger was an intimate of Lamennais as well as of Michelet; and the dissident Saint-Simonian Pierre Leroux, author, as we have seen, of a *Refutation de l'éclecticisme,* was co-editor with Sand of the *Revue Indépendante,* and had long worked together with his friend Reynaud in publishing the *Nouvelle Encyclopédie.* About Félix Ravaisson, a former secretary of his, Michelet wrote: "le premier métaphysicien du temps, jusqu'ici écarté de L'Institut par l'éclecticisme."[39]

Hidden in this description is a suggestion that the difference between Cousin and Michelet went beyond tactical questions, beyond the evident differences of position and temperament between insiders and outsiders, and even beyond the theoretical differences mentioned above. Ravaisson, like many others first helped by Cousin and then blocked in his philosophical career because of differences with the master, was indeed an important philosopher, eulogized at his death by no less than Henri Bergson. In examining Ravaisson's critique of Cousin,[40] we discover that the hostility between Cousin and Michelet reflects the opposition of two ideological modes of thought: one which implements and supports the civilizing offensive of the nineteenth century French bourgeoisie and one which, at least by implication, opposes it in the name of social romantic ideals of harmony.

For Cousin's Eclecticism not only distinguished sharply—as had most eighteenth-century philosophes—between the high-minded spirit of the educated elite, accessible to the esoteric wisdom of the philosophers, and the animal-like character of the common people, it buttressed this pedagogical distinction by a metaphysical one between the world of natural sensation and perception and the world of "the good, the true and the beautiful," the world of disembodied mind and of philosophical reflection. In doing so, the Eclectics refuted the "ideologues" of the Napoleonic era, as had the "doctrinaires" before them; the Idéologues, faithful to the materialist tradition of Condillac, traced all knowledge and morality back to physical sensations.[41] Cousin based his sharp dichotomy between physical sensation and philosophical reflection, alone capable of generating moral, aesthetic, or scientific ideas, on Plato, on Descartes, on the Scotch philosophers of the late eighteenth century, and on Maine de Biran.[42]

Now none of the philosophical tendencies opposed to Eclecticism in the 1840s wanted to revive the materialism of the Idéologues, but what most of them did have in common—I am thinking of the social romantics Leroux, Quinet, Reynaud, and Michelet as well as of their friend Félix Ravaisson—was a rejection of the split between nature and mind.[43] Ravaisson, better trained in the history of philosophy than the others, opposed Cousin's intellectual genealogy of the unbridgeable gulf between sensation and reflection with a genealogy of their connectedness, running from Aristotle to Leibniz to himself. But for all of them, the higher moral faculties were linked inseparably to the world of nature and accordingly to the social representations of that world: the common people and their culture, and they bitterly opposed the separation between high and low postulated by the "official" Eclectic philosophy.[44]

I have suggested above that such a link was a corollary to their social, political, and religious quest for harmony between high and low. Nowhere was this clearer than in Michelet's *Le Peuple,* in many respects a social romantic manifesto.[45]

MICHELET'S SOCIAL RELIGION: HUMAN NATURE AND THE ROMANTIC REVOLUTION

Michelet's social vision in *Le Peuple* may have been precipitated by his relationship with Madame Dumesnil,[46] but it is hardly conceivable without the alluring presence of the social romantic mentality. The historian's breakthrough in the early 1840s to his own repressed and feared nature made him receptive to the social romantic quest for harmony in all other domains. *Le Peuple* is in the first place a plea for the unity of the French people in the revolutionary ideals of fraternity and social justice, for the destruction of the barriers separating peasant from townsman, educated from non-educated, industrial worker from factory owner, artisan from master, the poor from the idle rich, and the embattled shopkeeper from everyone else. Its initial section, *Servage et haine,* discusses in these terms the alienation and oppression of virtually all these groups in the contemporary society; its second, *De l'affranchissement par l'amour—la nature,* outlines the instinctual, natural basis for liberation from societal estrangement; its third, *De l'affranchissement par l'amour—la patrie,* discusses the social and political bases of this liberation: the social community of the nation.

Thus, a theory of human nature underlies the new community; it is summarized toward the end of the second part, where Michelet argues that the truth of the common people, its "plus haute puissance," its "grande âme," lies in "l'homme de génie" (186). This creative genius, incarnation of the popular spirit, is androgyne, embodying the "two sexes of the spirit," popular in-

stinct and cultivated reflection. He adds that it is female as well as male, child-like as well as adult, savage as well as civilized, popular as well as aristocratic.

It is from the standpoint of this union of natural instinct and reflection that Michelet condemns most of the institutions of western civilization—religious, philosophical, political, and economic—for their rejection of the natural, for their machine-like and anti-popular character. In 1843 "machinism" had been his principal accusation against the Jesuits. Here the charge is expanded. The Church, though its doctrine of election seems democratic, is actually aristocratic by the complexity of its doctrines and the small number of men capable of understanding them. Worst of all, the Church condemned natural instinct since the Fall as in principle corrupt and postulated as the condition for salvation the abstract formulas of a metaphysical science (172).

Michelet's main attack on machinism appears in the concluding chapter to part I of *Le Peuple.* His point of departure is the insight that, in addition to all the moral and material torments of the modern world order, there is a psychological one: mankind has become extremely sensitive to the deprivations imposed by nature and society. And it is just now, he argues, that collective, mechanical, vastly impersonal systems roll on in their enormity: immense, majestic, indifferent, without any awareness that its little wheels, moving so painfully, are living men (143).

The historian traces the prehistory of this machinism back to the military and administrative machines of the age of absolutism; these, he says, were an attempt to compensate for the fundamental weakness of the Christian Middle Ages, which preached love but only succeeded in consecrating hatred, inequality, and injustice. Absolutism, however, had not yet produced machinism, since its machines depended entirely on human participation. Real machinism occurs only in the modern world, which creates machines independent of humanity, such as the new textile factories, "workers of iron" with "a hundred thousand arms and a hundred thousand teeth." This industrial machinism leads, he argues, to "the infinite multiplication of monotonous products . . . by the art of a single day, they dispense us from being artists every day." Machinism also takes the form, for Michelet, of "political machines to make our social acts uniformly automatic, to make patriotism unnecessary." This, however, is not the worst. In an open attack on the establishment philosophy of Victor Cousin (unnamed, but all knowledgeable Frenchmen associated him with "philosophie d'état") Michelet writes:

> Machinism nonetheless wants more; man is not yet mechanised enough. He retains his solitary reflection, his philosophical meditation, the pure idea of the True. There one cannot reach him, unless a borrowed scho-

lasticism pulls him out of himself to enmesh him in its formulas. Once he has put his foot on this wheel that turns vacuously, the thinking machine, engaged in the political machine, will roll on triumphantly and will be called "philosophy of the state."

(144)

Supplementing this philippic against machinism (in Part II, chapter vi) is a thumbnail history of the relation between human thought—philosophy and religion—and the realm of animal nature, from ancient India to modern times. Michelet reverses his earlier abhorrence of Indian culture's celebration of nature; India is here represented, because of its belief that animals contain sleeping or enchanted human souls, as the hearth of the tradition of universal fraternity, exemplified in its gifts of pity and its infinite fertility. Contrariwise, Greek and Roman antiquity was doomed by its prideful contempt for nature, its exclusive and self-centered concern for art:

> This proud antiquity, which wanted nothing that was not noble, succeeded only too well in suppressing all the rest. Everything that appeared base and ignoble disappeared from sight; the animals perished as well as the slaves. Relieved of both, the Roman Empire entered the majesty of the desert. Always expending and never replenishing itself, the earth became, among so many monuments that covered it, a garden of marble. There were still cities but no more fields; circuses, arches of triumph, but no more huts, no more plowmen. Magnificent roads still awaited voyagers who no longer used them; sumptuous aqueducts continued to carry rivers to silent cities, and quenched the thirst of no one.

Christianity, though in principle warmer toward the human race than ancient Rome had been, nonetheless maintained against nature what Michelet called *un préjugé judaïque*; it put an enormous distance between man and his animal nature, which it abominated and identified with Satan. Though serious study of popular culture is a recent phenomenon, Michelet had been concerned with it in his *Origines du droit français*; he knew that the devil was a very real part of the medieval mental world, since popes, emperors, bishops, and monks all swore they had seen him and the churches sculpted him into their facades as a horned beast, and he fantasized what peasant attitudes toward nature must have been in the Christian Middle Ages—fearful. Nonetheless, he was aware of the discrepancy between what the Christianized peasantry was supposed to think about nature and what they expressed in their festival rituals and folklore, such as the legend of Geneviève de Brabant, saved in the forest by a wild doe: he hypothesized that the peasants, perhaps inspired by their children's openness to the domestic animals, resisted Christianity's contempt for nature. What he called *le génie populaire* carried out, he thought, a timid "rehabilitation of nature . . . and the earth regained its fertility." In

Church festivals open to the popular culture, like those of the Christmas season, the donkey took a privileged position.[47]

At the end of this remarkable chapter on values toward nature, Michelet recurs to the contemporary scene and to the scholarly war in which he and his friends were engaged with the *philosophie d'état*. Despite the warmth of the popular culture toward the animal kingdom, "the Councils closed the Church to it [and] the philosophers, who matched the theologians in pride and coldness, decided it had no soul." Against the official philosophers, Michelet advances a contemporary philosopher with "a human heart." The naturalist Etienne Geoffroy Saint-Hilaire, whose interests overlapped the human and the animal worlds, had studied the human foetus and discovered in its transformations a recapitulation of animal metamorphoses: "Thus in woman's womb, in the true sanctuary of nature, is revealed the mystery of universal fraternity. . . ."

It should be evident from all this that Michelet's attack on Cousin's semiofficial eclecticism in *Le Peuple,* like most social romantic positions, had powerful religious overtones. In fact the socialism of the period, from the Saint-Simonians of 1830 to the democratic socialists of 1848, usually considered itself a replacement of Christianity; moreover, the Saint-Simonians had anticipated Michelet's desire to rehabilitate the body scorned by Christianity at a moment when Michelet himself was preaching the subjugation of the body.[48] The desire to replace Christianity by the exalted creed of the modern Revolution is the motive inspiring Michelet's *Histoire de la Révolution Française,* which he started in 1846 and completed two years after the demise of the republic, in 1853. If Michelet initially focussed on the "classical" side of this creed (*la justice*), he quickly added to it a social aspect, which he integrated to the "religious" revolution through the concept of fraternity.

THE FRENCH REVOLUTION AS SOCIAL THEOLOGY: FROM FRATERNAL EPIPHANY TO DIES IRAE

For Michelet the roots of religious and political questions were so intertwined that for all practical purposes they could be considered as one, both in past and present. While the Old Regime monarchy shared with the Catholic Church that represented its moral order the principle of arbitrary grace, the Revolution which overthrew it relied ethically on the contrary principle of Justice, which made it in Michelet's eyes necessarily anti-Christian; it was nonetheless as profoundly religious as the system it replaced. In fact, anyone reading hurriedly the first ten pages of Michelet's introduction to his book on the Revolution might think he had stumbled by mistake into a theological treatise: there seem to be as many references to grace and damnation as to justice and revolution, and the only names he will read are those of Adam, Jesus Christ, God, Saint Paul, and Papinian. This is somewhat misleading, since Michelet was by then a convinced anti-Christian. The fact remains that Michelet's view of the Revolution was profoundly influenced by the religious overtones of French social romanticism and the 1848 Revolution.

I have discussed elsewhere the interrelation of Michelet's work on the Revolution with his personal biography and with the politics of the period.[49] In brief: after a visionary description of the significance of the rural "festivals of federation" in 1790, which emphasized the quest by popular forces of a matriarchally-tinted, socially harmonious "Jerusalem of hearts," he became increasingly critical, as his book progressed, of most of the revolutionaries. Partly this was because so many of them, educated under the Old Regime, appeared unclear about the fundamental difference opposing their cause to that of the Christian faith, and compromised themselves and the Revolution in seeking some kind of rapprochement with Catholicism. Partly, however, it was also because in the course of his six years of work on the Revolution, a new revolution had broken out; and Michelet, after the bitterness caused by the civil war between rich and poor in June 1848, became radicalized.

This is not to say that he was transformed into an advocate of violent revolution, but rather that his social romantic idealism became more militant. A sudden new love in November 1848, for an expatriated and returned private tutor, Athenaïs Mialaret, led to marriage in March 1849, and the immediate result was a rejuvenation of Michelet's quest for social harmony.[50] Moreover, he continued to infuse his lectures with the values of revolutionary fraternity: as the conservative Party of Order obtained ever more authority over the frightened middle classes, his amphitheater became a rallying point for idealistic students still devoted to the Revolution. By March 1851 the Cousinian head of the Collège de France, Barthélemy Saint-Hilaire, on instructions from the ministry, could organize a majority of Michelet's colleagues to vote for his suspension. A year later, after the Bonapartist seizure of power, Michelet was dismissed from his teaching as well as his archival functions.

The last quarter of his history of the Revolution, dealing with the Terror and the popular movements of the year before Thermidor, reflect this change in the personal and political context of his work. They reveal a shift in focus away from what he came to call the classic or the political revolution, to what he viewed as an embryonic religious and social revolution, which he believed was embodied in the Cordeliers Club, in the social legislation of the Convention and in the Paris Commune. Early in his history, Michelet had identified the

Cordeliers Club with the rebirth of the Joachimite *évangile éternel* and with the spirit of the federations of 1790. Here he saw it as the herald of "the social and religious age of the Revolution." In sweeping terms he contrasted "the classical revolution of Rousseau and Robespierre" to "the other, the romantic revolution, which roars, confused, outside the walls, like a voice of the ocean." Cut off from the "romantic revolution," the "classical" one had no chance.[51]

His reference to the ocean was not casual. In his disillusion with the course of politics, Michelet was painfully conscious of the sardonic echoes between past and present: if the coup of 2 December was not exactly Thermidor, it was as much the death blow of the Second Republic and of social romanticism as the Terror and Thermidor were that of the first revolutionary vision of fraternity, a vision he believed in so profoundly that he became breathless and physically ill as he described its demise. The ocean was a key metaphor in his reflections on the symmetry of the natural and political worlds as he was about to begin his apocalyptic description of the Terror. Clinging to a stubborn belief in the regenerative power of nature, a residue of the romantic revolution that, surviving its execution, was to guide him and other Republicans through the dark years of the Second Empire, Michelet wrote:

> I plunge with my subject into night and winter. The stubborn storm winds that have pounded my windows for the last two months on these hills of Nantes, accompany with their voice, sometimes serious, sometimes harrowing, my Dies Irae of '93. . . . Many things that remained misunderstood have appeared clearly in the revelation of these voices of the ocean. . . . That these winter threats, all these semblances of death, were in no way death but to the contrary life, the profound renewal. From the destructive powers, from the violent metamorphoses in which you thought it crushed, emerges the eternal irony of nature, buoyant and smiling.[52]

CONCLUSION: ON THE SIGNIFICANCE OF SOCIAL ROMANTICISM

European Romanticism, appearing at the end of the absolutist Old Regime, heralded and questioned the twin modern revolutions that define the nineteenth and twentieth centuries: nationalism and capitalist industrial production. The English romantics protested simultaneously against the scarring of the natural and cultural landscapes by the Industrial Revolution, and against the desiccated utilitarianism that accompanied it; the German ones, against the bureaucratic *Kleinstaaterei* held in place by the Napoleonic invasion and against the unimaginative rationalism that characterized both the old and the new oppressors; the French ones against the utilitarian, materialist values, the atomization, and the social injustices of the new bourgeois society.

In all of these cases the obvious obsolescence of the Old Regime and the fragility and lack of authority of the new one unleashed aspirations in the artist and intellectual—aspirations alternately egoistic and altruistic—for another order of things. Sometimes these aspirations were cast in the ideological mold of a patriotic idealism (associated with the heroism of the Revolution), sometimes in that of a demonic exaltation of the self, sometimes in that of a mystical community of humanity with nature, and sometimes one of these was mixed with another. Common to all of them was a dialectical conflict between two underlying mentalities, both of them provoked by the cataclysmic social and political changes of the period: on the one hand, a utopian yearning rooted in the antinomian impulse of transgression, the rejection of the laws and principles of both the old and the new moral orders, and, on the other, a nostalgic yearning for a rapidly disappearing, pre-modern world. This last could be that of the decentralized pre-absolutist elite culture, particularly that of the aristocracy, proud, individualistic, and, in France and elsewhere, devoted to luxury and the ethic of conspicuous consumption. Or it could be that of the popular culture, epitomized in Rabelais, the carnivalesque and the charivari. But in either case, this nostalgia coexisted uneasily with the transgressional impulse, sometimes integrating with it, sometimes rejecting it.

The social romantic group that Michelet aligned with in the eighteen forties—Sand, Leroux, Sue, etc.—represented clearly a fusion of the value on heroic idealism associated with the national revolution and the notion of mystical community with nature.[53] In the years leading up to 1848 Michelet's thinking was guided by patriotic idealism as well as by a version of the ideology of mystical community, his *évangile éternel*. The latter was based on a transfigured notion of nature as divine, harmonious, beneficent, and nurturant; and it was this "romantic heresy," to use Bénichou's term, that had become the indispensable foundation of his political engagement.

Although religious conviction suffused Michelet's world-view in this period, we should not fall into the trap of contrasting his visionary ideas with a presumed hard-nosed scientific logic of his liberal opponents. The ontological distinctions between spirit and matter made by the liberal philosophers of the July Monarchy, the Eclectics and Doctrinaires around Cousin, Guizot, and Jouffroy, also corresponded to a value bias—that of the new bourgeois elite—and had an equally religious and social motivation. Moreover, the Eclectics and Doctrinaires were opposed not merely by the literati of social romanticism but by materialist- or pantheist-oriented members of the scientific establishment of the time: within the *Académie des Sciences Morales et Politiques*, by medical "physiologues" such as Edwards and Broussais, and outside of it, by natural scientists like Geoffroy Saint-Hilaire and by philosophers like Ravaisson, all of these being friends of Michelet whose ideas he

used to buttress his *évangile*. The reason Michelet and his social romantic friends had such wide influence in the years before 1848 is that their publications were received sympathetically by a major wing of the intellectual elite and the youth.

Cousin, Guizot, and their associates, however, were centrally embedded in the power structure of the July Monarchy, which viewed itself, in the historiographical vision of Augustin Thierry, as the end of history.[54] In the tradition of Absolutism's *offensive moralisatrice* against peasant immorality, the establishment thinkers drew sharp boundaries between mind and body, male and female, the high culture of the elites and the popular culture of the masses, the capacities of the wealthy, educated few and those of the impoverished and illiterate common people. Since they were convinced they had found the solution to the break-up of the ancien regime, they viewed all who opposed them, whether on the issue of church-state relations or on that of political and social justice, as muddleheaded troublemakers. But for those who remained unconvinced by their position, the antinomian, transgressional romantic option—which in science, in history, in culture generally, sought harmony between all the high/low antitheses assumed by the liberal civilizers—remained open.

It is worth recalling that Michelet was not always a social romantic, having begun his career in the liberal ambience of the future powerholders of the July Monarchy. In fact the similarities between the historical interests and perceptions of Augustin Thierry and Michelet, underlined by Lionel Gossman, reveal the difficulty (though not the impossibility) of sharply opposing July Monarchy Liberals and Romantics. Nonetheless around 1840, impelled both by his personal dissatisfaction about what he had become and by the resurgent tide of social romantic criticism, Michelet fundamentally altered his concepts of nature, society, and history and joined his critical voice to that of Lamennais, Sand, Leroux, Hugo,[55] and others.

We have recently heard powerful echoes of Thierry's annunciation of the end of history, but that is not the only similarity between the contemporary scene and the ideological self-celebration of the July Monarchy. After several decades of post-war welfare states, Europe east and west has slipped into a neo-liberalism and an egoistic individualism rather similar to that against which the social romantics of the July Monarchy protested in the name of human fraternity. These similarities, however, are accompanied by vast differences. Post-Revolutionary France witnessed the restructuring of society based on the rationalist and productivist values of the national and industrial revolutions of 1750-1870; our own era, with its stagnating multi-national economies, its mounting structural unemployment and its looming ecological disasters probably signifies the decomposition of that restructured society. Indeed, the need to break out of the exclusive concern with linear material progress and rationalization to a renewed understanding of the cyclical character of much of our world and of the links between the social and the natural orders has been repeatedly stressed even by the leaders of the present world industrial society. The youth revolt of the 1960s may be interpreted as the first, chaotic effort to reorient modern mentalities in this direction.

If the rebellion of the '60s proved ephemeral, the problems it addressed remain. In this context a new look at the social romantic critique of nineteenth-century liberalism and at the anti-Cartesian philosophical sources on which it drew might help to save us from what seems increasingly to be the post-modern destiny: confronting mega-problems with mini-ideas. For at a certain point the magnitude of social and ecological pain will produce a fevered reaction: the antinomian angel of cosmic harmony, now apparently dormant in the dust of history, is not likely to remain there forever. Should we not be able to face that angel with a sympathetic and enlightened understanding, it could do as much harm as good.

Notes

1. Emile Ollivier, *Journal I, 1846-1860,* eds. Theodore Zeldin and Anne Troisier de Diaz (Paris, 1961), 79 (Olivier's summary of Michelet's position).

2. Eugène Noel, *J. Michelet et ses enfants* (Paris, 1878), 229f.

3. Michelet, *Les Jésuites* (Paris, 1843); *Le Prêtre, la femme et la famille* (Paris, 1845).

4. Lucien Febvre, *Michelet* (Geneva, 1946), and *Michelet et la Renaissance* (Paris, 1993); Jacques Le Goff, "The Several Middle Ages of Jules Michelet," in *Time, Work, & Culture in the Middle Ages* (Chicago, 1980), 3-28, and "L'Histoire au-dela d'elle-même," *L'arc,* 52 (1972); Pieter Geyl, *Geschiedenis als Medespeler* (Utrecht, 1958), 61, 68.

5. In addition to the books cited in note 3: *Nos fils* (Paris, 1869).

6. Henri de Lubac S.J., *La Postérité spirituelle de Joachim de Flore,* tome II: *De Saint-Simon à nos jours* (Paris, 1981), 189-221 (chap. 14, "Michelet et Quinet"); D. G. Charlton, *Secular Religions in France, 1815-1870* (London, 1963); Frank Bowman, "Illuminism, etc." in Charlton (ed.), *The French Romantics* (London, 1984), vol. 1; Paul Bénichou, *Le Temps des prophètes: Doctrines de l'âge romantique* (Paris, 1977); Edward Kaplan, *Michelet's Poetic Vision: A Romantic Philosophy of Nature, Man, Woman* (Amherst, Mass., 1977).

7. Viallaneix, *La Voie Royale Essai sur l'idée du peuple dans l'oeuvre de Michelet* (Paris, 1971), 29f; A. Thiers, *Histoire de la Révolution Française précédée d'un précis de l'histoire de France, par M. Michelet,* (2 vols.; Bruxelles, 1840)

8. See Jules Michelet, *Introduction à l'histoire universelle* (Paris, 1831) repr. in Michelet, *Oeuvres complètes,* ed. by Paul Viallaneix (Paris, 1971), II.

9. Monod (*La vie et la pensée de Jules Michelet [1798-1852]* [Paris, 1923], I, 187-95) shows conclusively that Michelet's "Introduction" was reacting in Vichian voluntarist terms not only to Thierry's liberal racism and to the Saint-Simonian pantheism of the period, but above all to the historical determinism of Cousin in the latter's lectures of 1828, published as *Introduction à l'Histoire de la Philosophie* (Paris, 1861).

10. See William H. Sewell Jr., *Work and Revolution in France: The Language of Labor from the Old Regime to 1848* (Cambridge, 1980), 219-22; Manet van Montfrans, "Le Rhin," *Yearbook of European Studies* (Borders and Territories), 6 (Amsterdam, 1993), 134f. Paul Thureau-Dangin, *Histoire de la Monarchie de Juillet, Livre IV: La crise de la Politique Extérieure (mai 1839-juillet 1841)* (Paris, 1908); and A. Jardin and A. J. Tudesq, *La France des notables 1815-1848* (Paris, 1973), II, 215; I, 231.

11. Roger Picard, *Le Romantisme social* (New York, 1944); David Owen Evans, *Le Socialisme romantique: Pierre Leroux et ses contemporains,* (Paris, 1948); David Owen Evans, *Social Romanticism in France 1830-1848* (Oxford, 1951); Fr. & J. Fourastié, *Les Ecrivains témoins du peuple* (Paris, 1964); *L'Esprit Républicain: Colloque d'Orléans, 4 et 5 septembre 1970, présenté par Jacques Viard* (Paris, 1972) (contributions on the social romantics by Viallaneix, Lacassagne, Salomon, Savidan and Sabiani); *Romantisme,* no. 9 (1975), *Le Peuple;* Alexandrian, *Le socialisme romantique* (Paris, 1979); Société d'histoire de la Révolution de 1848 et des Révolutions du XIXe siècle, *1848, les utopisme sociaux: Utopie et action à la veille des journées de février* (Paris, 1981); Geneviève Bollème, *Le peuple par écrit* (Paris, 1986); Gérard Fritz, *L'Idée de peuple en France du XVIIe au XIXe siècle* (Paris, 1988); Alain Pessin, *Le Mythe du peuple et la société français du XIXe siècle* (Paris, 1992).

12. A. Mitzman, "The Civilizing Offensive: Mentalities, High Culture and Individual Psyches," *Journal of Social History,* 20 (1987), 663-87. See H.-A. Frégier, *Des Classes dangereuses de la population dans les grandes villes et des moyens de les rendre meilleures* (Brussels, 1840); the title page

notes that the author was *chef de bureau à la préfecture de la Seine,* and that his monograph was *récompensé en 1838 par l'Institut de France (Académie des Sciences Morales et Politiques),* in other words, by the official intellectual establishment of the July Monarchy. Frégier's title was echoed in 1958 by Louis Chevalier, *Classes laborieuses et classes dangereuses à Paris pendant la première moitié du XIXe siècle* (Paris, 1958, 1978). Unfortunately, Chevalier's work has convinced an entire generation of scholars that there was no important difference between the establishment's top down view of the common people and that of its social romantic opponents, an argument opposed in this study.

13. See, among others, Maurice Agulhon, *La République au village* (Paris, 1970); Ted Mardagant, *French Peasants In Revolt: The Insurrection of 1851* (Princeton, 1975); William Sewell, *op. cit.*; and Louis Girard, *Etude comparée des mouvements révolutionnaires en France en 1830, 1848 et 1870-71, Fasc. I, Cours de la Sorbonne* (Paris, n.d. [±1970]).

14. W. D. Howarth, *Sublime and Grotesque: A Study of French Romantic Drama* (London 1975), 123, 201-24, 241-44 (on Hugo and Dumas); Anne Übersfeld, *Le Roi et le bouffon: Étude sur le théâtre de Hugo de 1830 à 1839* (Paris, 1974), 77-89, 226f, 390, 547-49. See Julia Przybos, *L'Entreprise mélodramatique* (Paris, 1987); A. Übersfeld, "Les Bons et les méchants," *Revue des sciences humaines,* 162 (1976), 193-203.

15. A. Faure, *Paris Carème-Prenant, Du Carnaval à Paris au XIXe siècle* (Paris, 1978).

16. On Shakespeare: Stendhal, *Racine et Shakespeare* (Paris, 1823), and Hugo, *William Shakespeare* (Paris, 1863). Hugo's theory of the sublime and the grotesque was presented in his preface to *Cromwell* in 1827. On Rabelais, Michelet's Introduction to the Renaissance in his *Histoire de France* (Paris, 1855); and the book on Rabelais [*Rabelais*] of Michelet's friend Eugène Noel (Paris, 1850). Balzac's *Contes drolatiques* (Paris, 1833), in sixteenth-century French, is clearly modeled on Rabelais and even devotes a chapter to the *curé de Meudon.* Mikhail Bakhtin's *Rabelais and his World* (Cambridge, Mass., 1968) highlights the significance of Rabelais as mediator between popular and high culture, and Anne Übersfeld discusses Hugo in relation to Bakhtin's theories on Rabelais, the grotesque and carnival, *op. cit.* 461-506.

17. Lemaître and Debureau are treated in Robert Baldick, *The Life and Times of Fréderick Lemaître* (London, 1959) and have been immortalized in Marcel Carné's film of 1944, *Les Enfants du paradis.*

18. Pierre Barbéris, "*Mal du siécle ou d'un romantisme de droite à un romantisme de gauche*" in *Romantisme et Politique 1815-1851: Colloque de l'Ecole Normale Supérieure de Saint-Cloud (1966)* (Paris, 1969), 164-82; Jean-Claude Caron, *Générations romantiques: Les étudiants de Paris & le quartier Latin (1814-1851)* (Paris 1991), 295-315.

19. *Ibid.,* 151-67. Writing of the period 1814-51 as a whole, Caron describes the world of the students as "un monde de solidarités masculines quasi claniques, de ruptures violentes mais temporaires avec ses origines, enclin à braver les interdits politiques or sociaux, défiant la société établie sous sa forme civile ou militaire, parfois débauché." Caron adds that the notables were never as afraid of the students as they were of the working classes. See also A. Mitzman, "Roads, Vulgarity, Rebellion and Pure Art: The Inner Space in Flaubert and French Culture," *Journal of Modern History,* 51 (1979), 504-24.

20. See Jerrold Seigel, *Bohemian Paris* (New York, 1986).

21. Bénichou, *op. cit.,* 429-35.

22. Mitzman, *Michelet, Historian: Rebirth and Romanticism in 19th Century France* (New Haven, 1990), 16-76.

23. See Donald R. Kelley, *Historians and the Law in Postrevolutionary France* (Princeton, 1984), 101-12; Charles Rearick, *Beyond the Enlightenment: Historians and Folklore in Nineteenth Century France* (Bloomington, 1974), 82-102; Michelet, *Correspondance générale* (Paris, 1994), I, showing fulsome praise for Creuzer.

24. Viard "George Sand et Michelet Disciples de Pierre Leroux" in *Revue d'Histoire Littéraire de la France,* 75 (1975), 758.

25. See Marjorie Reeves and Warwick Gould, *Joachim of Fiore and the Myth of the Eternal Evangel in the Nineteenth Century* (Oxford, 1987), 65-114; Jacques Viard, *op. cit.,* 749-73, esp. 764.

26. Viard, *op. cit.,* 764.

27. Cf. F. Duine, *Lamennais, sa vie, ses idées, ses ouvrages etc.* (Paris, 1922), 213-92; and Bénichou, *op. cit.* 121-74.

28. Duine, *op. cit.,* 217.

29. Michelet, *Journal, I* (Paris, 1959), 13 janvier 1844.

30. Jean René Derré, *Lamennais, ses amis et le mouvement des idées à l'époque romantique 1824-1834* (Paris, 1962), 180n.

31. Monod, *op. cit.,* II, 151.

32. Derré, *op. cit.,* 181n.

33. Monod, *op. cit.,* 150. Apparently, Cousin saw no necessary opposition between the "principles" of Catholicism and his own Eclecticism.

34. Pierre Leroux, *Réfutation de l'éclecticisme* (Paris, 1839), 85.

35. Laurens van der Heijden's dissertation-in-progress at the University of Amsterdam deals with this controversy. See also Michel Leroy, *Le mythe Jésuite de Béranger à Michelet* (Paris 1992), 75-91.

36. Thureau-Dangin, *op. cit.,* V, 563.

37. *Cours professé au Collège de France* (Paris, 1848, repr. 1877, *L'Etudiant*).

38. Caron, *op. cit.* 369-73.

39. Cited in Eric Fauquet, *Michelet, ou la gloire du professeur d'histoire* (Paris, 1990), 325. The entry in Michelet's journal for 6 January 1844: "Pour Ravaisson à l'Institut," comes just one week before the similar entry, "A l'Institut pour M. de Lamennais, contre Cousin," which referred to Lamennais's exclusion from the *Académie des Sciences Morales et Politique*.

40. Félix Ravaisson, *La Philosophie en France au dix-neuvième siècle* (Paris, 1983), 18-34. Ravaisson further discusses the ideas of Lamennais, Leroux, and Reynaud.

41. P.-J.-G. Cabanis, *Rapports du physiques et du moral de l'homme* (Paris, 1980 [1844, first ed., 1802]); Prosper Alfaric, *Laromiguière et son école: Étude biographique* (Paris, 1929); André Jardin, *Histoire du Libéralisme politique de la crise de l'absolutisme à la constitution de 1875* (Paris, 1985), 136-61, 186-88 and 250-62; Pierre Rosenvallon, *Le Moment Guizot* (Paris, 1985); Felix Ravaisson, *La Philosophie en France au dix-neuvième siècle* [Paris, 1984 (1868)]; and Hippolyte Taine, *Les philosophes Français du dix-neuvième siècle* (Paris, 1860 [deuxième édition]; also Sophie Leterrier, *Les Sciences Morales et Politiques à l'Institut de France 1795-1850* (unpublished thèse de doctorat, Paris 1993).

42. See *Oeuvres choisies de Maine de Biran, avec introduction par Henri Gouhier* (Paris, 1942).

43. S. F. Baekers, "Clara contra de man zonder eigenschappen: Schelling en Musil," *De Gids* ([Amsterdam] July 1991), discusses a similar rejection of the body-mind split as central to the early German romantic philosophy of Hegel, Schelling, and Hölderlin.

44. The first open break with Eclecticism in Michelet's circle was that of Edgar Quinet, in the second lecture (11 February) of his course of 1845, published as *Le Christianisme et la Révolution Française* (Paris, 1984). Quinet treated Eclecticism as the obsolete philosophy of the Restoration, crippled by its association with the government of the July Monarchy; he condemned it for its refusal to confront the Church, for its abandonment to Catholicism of the common people and announced its replacement by "the philosophy of the Revolution" (45). In his concluding lecture in June, Quinet invoked the *Evangile éternel* of "*la Justice*" as an absolute religion (274). Quinet's lecture attacking Eclecticism was provoked by a violently critical review of Michelet's *Du Prêtre, de la femme, de la Famille* (1845) by Émile Saisset, a Cousinian; the situation is well documented in Viallaneix's notes to Michelet's *Journal*, I (884-86). Quinet's attack on the Cousinians was noted in Michelet's journal and is mentioned briefly in François Furet's *La Gauche et la révolution au milieu du dix-neuvième siècle, Edgar Quinet et la question du Jacobinisme 1865-1870* (Paris, 1986). It is discussed in Elizabeth Brisson, "L'Enseignement de Quinet au College de France," in *Edgar Quinet ce Juif errant, Actes du Colloque international de Clermont-Ferrand,* ed. by Simone Berand-Griffiths and Paul Viallaneix (Clermont-Ferrand, 1978), 100-103, and in Richard Howard Powers, *Edgar Quinet: A Study in French Patriotism* (Dallas, 1957), 121f.

45. I use the Viallaneix edition of 1974.

46. Mitzman, *Michelet, Historian.*

47. In *La Sorcière* (1862), Michelet went much further and argued that, because of the Christian relegation of nature to the domain of Satan, the popular religion of the Middle Ages developed, through witchcraft, a means of retaining the older view of the relation between man and the natural world. Max Milner has argued that other romantics—Sand, Esquiros, Leroux, Hugo—preceded Michelet in connecting the myth of Satan to the defense by the popular culture of its traditional values: "La Signification politique de Satan" (*Romantisme et Politique 1815-1851, Colloque e l'École Normale Supèrieure de Saint-Cloud [1966]* (Paris, 1969), 160; also Milner, *Le Diable dans la littérature française de Cazotte à Baudelaire 1771-1861* (2 vols.; Paris, 1960).

48. *Doctrine de Saint-Simon: Exposition—2e anneé, 7e séance* (Paris, 1830), 92-93. (Reference supplied by Sophie Leterrier.)

49. Mitzman *Michelet, Historian,* 117-261.

50. See the course summary he wrote for his fiancée in his journal on 21 January 1849, quoted in Mitzman, *Michelet, Historian,* 204.

51. Michelet, *Histoire de la Révolution Française,* II, 408.

52. *Hist. de la Rév. Fr.* [*Histoire de la Révolution Française*] II, 696. Michelet indicates in the auto-biographical introduction to *L'oiseau,* written in September 1855, the itinerary that led him from the celebration of nature, and in particular of the link between man and the animal world in *Le Peuple,* to his works on natural history. Michelet, *L'Oiseau,* édition critique par Edward Kaplan in *Oeuvres complètes,* tome XVII (Paris, 1986), 62.

53. Compare the titles of the second and third parts of *Le Peuple*: "DE L'AFFRANCHISSEMENT PAR L'AMOUR. La Nature," and "DE L'AFFRANCHISSEMENT PAR L'AMOUR. La Patrie." (I reproduce the typography of the *Table* of the 1846 edition, approved by Michelet.)

54. Lionel Gossman, "Thierry and Liberal Historiography" in *Between History and Literature* (Cambridge, Mass., 1990), 145.

55. The evolution of Hugo toward social romanticism is discussed by Robert Sayre and Michael Löwy in *L'insurrection des Misérables: Romantisme et révolution en Juin 1832* (Paris, 1992), 39-44, and by Alain Pessin, *op. cit.,* 55-98.

David Carroll (essay date spring 1998)

SOURCE: Carroll, David. "The Art of the People: Aesthetic Transcendence and National Identity in Jules Michelet." *boundary 2, Special Issue: Thinking Through Art: Aesthetic Agency and Global Modernity* 25, no. 1 (spring 1998): 111-37.

[*In the following essay, Carroll assesses Michelet's fictional construction of the French "people" in his historical writing.*]

Invent or perish.

—Jules Michelet, *Le Peuple*

Nationalities, which we accept as already made frames, who made them?

—Jules Michelet, Course at the Collège de France

A history is a work of art as well as science.

—Jules Michelet, *Histoire de la Révolution française*

When revolution is hypostatized to the point where it far outweighs its specific objectives, one is bound to ask whether revolutionary politics does not have more to do with religion or aesthetics than with ethics, more to do with poetry than with history.

—Lionel Gossman, *Between History and Literature*

Literary critics and historians have always had a difficult time classifying the nineteenth-century romantic French historian Jules Michelet, continually disagreeing over whether to treat him primarily as an imaginative poet or as an innovative historian. In a phrase that not only acknowledges both the literary and historical aspects of his work but also emphasizes the way in which the poetic dimensions of his writing are at the core of his historical innovations, Jacques Rancière has recently claimed that Michelet is responsible for nothing less than "a revolution in the poetic structures of knowledge."[1]

Given Michelet's interest in such factors as climate, geography, population changes, and diet as formative forces in history and his desire to write the history of those who did not have a history and who had not been allowed to speak in history, his name has often been evoked by a variety of *Annales* historians as one of their most important precursors.[2] It could also be argued that he provided the model for a form of French nationalist history that even historians critical of Michelet's romantic idealization of the Revolution and what some would call his excessively literary style and practice continue to follow.

For example, in the opening lines of his introduction to *The Identity of France,* the multivolume work he left unfinished at his death, the noted *Annales* historian Fernand Braudel evokes the similarity between his feelings for France and those of Michelet to testify to the depth and complexity of his own nationalist sentiments. Braudel acknowledges, however, that the major problem he faced in writing his study of French national identity was how to keep these sentiments, mainly "the demanding and complicated passion" he, like Michelet, felt for France, from overwhelming his neutrality and objectivity as a historian:

> That passion will rarely intrude upon the pages of this book. . . . For I am determined to talk about France as if it were an other country, an other fatherland, an other nation: "to observe France," as Charles Péguy said, "as if one were not part of it." The historian's craft, as it has developed, in any case condemns us to coldness, to the exclusion of the heart. . . . Let us purge ourselves of our passions, whether they are dictated by our nature, our social position, our personal experience, our fits of rage or enthusiasm . . . or the many pervasive influences of our age.[3]

Coldness of heart and the purging of personal and historically determined passions are thus necessary requirements for the modern historian who has the obligation to analyze and treat all subjects and problems objectively—even, or especially, the problem of the identity of his own nation.[4]

But if this is so, why evoke his own love for France, and why refer to Michelet in the first place? The answer is that having made claims to coldness and objectivity, it is not at all clear that Braudel really thinks that "France" could or should ever be exclusively an object of the science of history. For he also acknowledges that there are advantages to studying the country he identifies as his own that have nothing to do with scientific knowledge and everything to do with a deeper form of "instinctive knowledge" of the home and the homeland: "I have come rather late in the day to my home ground, though with a pleasure I will not deny: for the historian can really be on an equal footing only with the history of his own country; he understands almost instinctively its twists and turns, its complexities, its originalities, and its weaknesses. Never can he enjoy the same advantages, however learned he might be, when he resides in someone else's house" (*IF* [*The Identity of France*], 1:15; translation modified). Instinct and the natural affinity historians allegedly have with their own country thus reveal what the foreigner can never know and what historians themselves never know when they reside outside their own home, even if such emotional attachments and identificatory mechanisms still risk blinding historians to other, more objective facts. But scientific objectivity in turn assumes that the neutralization of affect is, in fact, not just desirable but also possible and that identity is a historical object like any other.

The problem being raised by Braudel's contradictory comments about the relation of affect and objectivity is how historians can possibly be at home and not at home in their own home at the same time, how they can *feel* with the heart of the nationalist and at the same time *analyze* with the mind and cold objectivity of the foreigner, how they can be simultaneously intimate with and distant from the nation they love and that they are required by their craft to treat with disinterest. That is, how they can treat the nation at once as a historical-political *concept* and as an affective, imaginary projection, or *fictional construct*.[5] Whatever the strategy chosen for resolving or working around this problem, at the very least it is clear that both analytical and imaginative faculties are necessary for historians of national identity to accomplish their task, even if these faculties seem to oppose and contradict each other rather than to work harmoniously together toward a common goal.

Near the end of his introduction, Braudel distances himself from Michelet, whom he considers his model for love of country but not for historical methodology or narrative practice, by asserting that for him, "a nation in the process of creating or re-creating itself is not a simple character, a 'person' as Michelet *poetically* put it" (*IF,* 1:18; my emphasis). Braudel argues instead that the French nation is constituted by a "multitude of realities and living beings which are poorly captured by the thread of a day-by-day, week-by-week, year-by-year historical chronology" (*IF,* 1:18). As such, the nation fails to meet the restrictive, objective definition of a person. Personifying France is thus a poetic act that may move the reader to identify with and even "love" France but that cannot be defended on objective historical grounds. At the same time, however, if France should never be treated "poetically" as a human subject or person, if personification is ruled out from the start, it is difficult to see how France could still be thought to have any sort of identity at all.

As if to give France a more profound identity than that provided by poetic personification, Braudel acknowledges that he considers both the prehistory of France and its history proper to be "one and the same process"—because, as he says, "*our* villages were . . . taking root in *our* soil in the third millennium before Christ" (*IF,* 1:20; my emphasis). A *French* ancestor, therefore, apparently had been tilling the land and building villages for a very long time, thus giving, in the form of "an obscure history, running along under the surface, refusing to die" (*IF,* 1:20), a more profound continuity to a process that day-by-day historical chronologies distort when they present history exclusively in terms of a narrative of discrete events. The soil and the villages of the geographic area that would much later be identified as France were thus already French long before they were in fact called French.

For the nationalist historian speaking primarily to a national audience, they are always already "ours," because underlying the surface continuity or discontinuity of events lies the deeper continuity provided first by the land and then by the people and the nation. Identity and the possibility of identification are thus deeply rooted in history and given a material support in the land itself. It could be argued, therefore, that Braudel rejects a form of personification for being too subjective and poetic to replace it with an allegedly less poetic and more objective form. Braudel, like Michelet, does, in fact, describe France as an active "human" subject, "shaping [itself] by its own hand" (*IF,* 1:23) in a process of development that is originally geological and geographic before being cultural and political. This means that in Braudel, what could be called a geographic or geological poetics replaces Michelet's more explicitly romantic-populist poetics of identification. The differences between the two poetics and the two forms of personification and identification are, however, much less drastic than Braudel assumes.[6]

According to the logic of the *longue durée,* therefore, "France" does constitute a unified subject or person after all, but one defined primarily by material determinates of long duration, not discrete, discontinuous events. The French, although they are a people with multiple origins and histories, are still ultimately, on the deepest level of their material existence, fashioned by a single process from the earliest of times. And as Braudel has written elsewhere and repeats at the end of the second volume of his history of the identity of France, this singular process makes men what they are: "For men do not make history, rather it is history above all that makes men" (*IF,* 2:679). In the same vein, it could be said that for Braudel, the people do not make the nation; rather, the nation or the homeland makes the people.

Of course, many historians would not accept the terms of Braudel's description of his complicated relation to his own nation and its identity.[7] An increasing number of historians have for some time, in fact, questioned "the national myth" that has dominated the work of major historians and writers from at least the time of Michelet to the present. Raoul Giradet describes the myth as "a kind of geographic predestination of the French nation."[8] Suzanne Citron puts it even more polemically, when she asserts that historical texts and school textbooks that recount the history of an eternal France already existing before it is born, with its people destined from the earliest times to be the people of freedom, represent nothing less than "the catechism of a religion of France."[9]

Critiques such as these of the mythical, religious characteristics of nationalist historiography and of its political uses at the very least reveal that "France" is always more than a strictly political or historical concept. All nationalist "religions of France" demand a belief in, an identification with, and a commitment to an ideal of the nation. They are supported by processes of identification that cannot be explained exclusively in terms of objective, historical criteria. The "complicated passions" one feels for one's homeland and the "poetic" devices found in the work of nationalist historians and writers that serve to induce, form, and perform these passions thus can be said to play a crucial role in the construction of the identity of France and its people.

It is the nature of Michelet's version of this "catechism of a religion of France" that interests me in this essay, especially the contradictory status and nature of his richly poetic figure or fiction of the French people and its relation to both the question of race and the ideal of universal freedom. In his attempt to defend the ideal of the republic and not simply to give the French Revolution an inaugural place in French history[10] but also to raise it up to a purely spiritual level as the telos of all of human history, Michelet treats history as a process of redemption. History is for him the new secular religion, with the Revolution presented as being nothing less than the negation and transcendence of Christianity, its successor in redemptiveness.[11]

At the same time, history is not a religion in the strictly religious sense, for revolutionary spirituality is of a different and more complex kind—at the same time more elevated and more material—than that of its Christian predecessor. Not only do the spiritual dimensions of history not need any church, any priesthood (or pope), any dogma, or any cult to sustain them, but also and more important, postrevolutionary history opposes and negates at each step all religious claims to spiritual superiority. And given that Michelet lacks a specific religious (or political) doctrine to support his redemptive history, he puts in its place an idealized fiction of the French people as the symbol of his nation's spiritual transcendence of necessity, materiality, and even history itself.

In the notice to his short early work *Introduction à l'histoire universelle* (1831), Michelet makes the following "modest proposal," which is perhaps one of the basic assumptions of all nationalist histories: that everything in universal history leads to and sets the stage for the history of the nation. "This little book could just as well have been entitled *Introduction à l'histoire de France*; it is to France that it leads. . . . Through logical and historical deduction, its author came to the same conclusion: that his glorious country is from this time on the pilot and vessel of humanity."[12] All historical roads for Michelet thus lead not to Rome but to France, because France was chosen in and by history to represent all humanity and lead it to its redemption. In the eternal war against nature and fatalism—"with the world began a war that must finish with the world and not before" (*OC* [*Oeuvres complètes de Jules Michelet*], 2:229)—France (the West) is the predestined victor.

All roads lead to France because all roads in the romantic-nationalist imagination—which in this case is also the republican imagination—lead from the East to the West and thus away from the fatalism of nature, climate, geography, and race. These material determinants originally gave birth to the human genre, but if they are not repeatedly negated and transcended, they will impede and eventually destroy its growth and self-realization:

> Follow from the Orient to the Occident . . . the migrations of the human genre; observe it in this long voyage from Asia to Europe, from India to France, and you will see at each stop the fatal power of nature diminish and the influence of race and climate become less tyrannical. At the point of departure, in India, in the cradle of races and religions, *the womb of the world* [in English in the original text], man is bent over, prostrate under the omnipotence of nature. He is a poor child at the breast of his mother, a feeble and dependent creature.
>
> (*OC,* 2:229)

The "first birth" and childhood of the human genre thus occur in the Orient. The "poor child," who will, through a long process of migration and development, become an adult, begins his journey far from France, tied to and dominated by a nature that is both nurturing and tyrannical.

In an important sense, however, the child is already French. He simply needs to mature, to free himself from nature (his "mother"), his land, and his race, and to become his own *man*—for it is not surprising that the people is personified as a young man who makes this journey west away from his nurturing/tyrannical mother. Those who do not or cannot make this journey are destined to remain subject to the tyranny of race and climate and to remain in this sense outside of redemptive history. Their identity is predetermined once and for all and is passed on from generation to generation. Identification with their land and with their race is an allegedly immediate, natural process, but one that negates their freedom to be other than what they already are and have always been destined to be. Insomuch as they are determined by the process, they have no control over it.

This particular version of a primal origin in nature (personified, of course, as the East) and the voyage toward liberation and the West it necessitates underlie all of Michelet's early speculations on the French nation and people as the nation and people of freedom. This version of a universal history of humanity, of course, conforms to, if not establishes, a model for what is now called the metanarrative of Eurocentrism. We should not forget, however, that the ideal and driving force of Michelet's partisanly nationalist Eurocentrism is universal human freedom, which here, as elsewhere, cannot easily be separated from its nationalist context and freed of its particular historical and cultural limitations. At the same time, French nationalism is given a glorious alibi by being associated with the ideal of universal human freedom.

This raises the question of why the freedom of the West, the freedom allegedly established by the French Revolution, needs to be staged by this particular (pre)history. Why does the birth of the French as a people in and through the Revolution require this long gestation period, this mythical past that consists of a denial and a destruction of a primitive, maternal other, a distancing of self from the fiction of an Orient defined and dominated by nature, that is, by climate, geography, and, above all, race? Whatever the various answers to such questions might be, it is significant that in Michelet, not just French nationalism but also the freedom it personifies rest on and are supported by such a prehistory, a history even the most republican forms of nationalism cannot simply leave behind.

A free people is born predominantly to be repeatedly born again, and each of its births serves to reenact other births and to recall its profound unity and deep identity—an identity before identity, the identity of "la France profonde." At the same time, each birth recalls the continued proximity of the people to its "material" origins and limitations, which it both needs as support

for its identity and which it must repeatedly negate and overcome as impediments to its full realization. This is also to say that the people who is always already born is never really completely born, that each of its births is partial or breached, that it must continually await and anticipate its next and, perhaps this time, successful, total birth. National identity and the processes of identification are thus never fixed once and for all. No stable model for the national ego exists—even in the racist ideologies that claim the contrary—and this means that the identity of the nation and its people are imaginary constructs or fictions that can and must always be reformed and re-performed. A people that is racially determined is quite simply not a people; a nation that is racially defined is not a nation.

When humanity finally reaches the West on its journey to freedom, the war against the East continues, but now within the West as well as outside it. If Greece, for example, occupies "an intermediary point . . . where, freeing itself from fatal nature, the flower of freedom has just blossomed," it is also true that "the world of Greece was pure combat; combat against Asia and combat in Greece itself, the struggle of Ionians and Dorians, of Sparta and Athens" (*OC*, 2:233). Greece struggles to define itself against the East and to keep it outside, and at the same time forces allegedly originating in and metaphorically associated with the East reappear in the struggles within Greece that once again pit freedom and material determinism against each other, but now in a different, Greek form.

Each step forward thus paradoxically carries with it the conflict between the forces of enslavement and freedom that history had allegedly already resolved and from which it had distanced itself. The struggle against its other, the East, is a part of the prehistory of the West, of its distant past, and a dominant and recurring force of renewal within its present, a recurring element of the repeated (re)birth(s) of the West. In Rome, "we"—free, Western man, "we" the French—are born (once again/ not yet) in the renewed conflict between East and West, which Rome stages in the Colosseum as the struggle between Christianity and "Barbarism": "The Christian and the Barbarian, the representatives of freedom for the Occident and for the Orient, met in the arena of the Colosseum. We are born of their union, both we and the entire future [of the world]" (*OC*, 2:236). Combat leads not to the total defeat and elimination of one of the participants but to their union through the assimilation of one combatant into the other. Resulting from the combat is the birth of a new, freer humanity, of a "we" of the future, not of the past, of an Occidental "we" that has incorporated the Oriental "we" into itself—but not completely or definitively.[13]

Michelet argues that Rome not only staged such combats but also triumphed over and moved away from the insularity of the Greek world and the city-state, thus opening up the Western world both inwardly and outwardly. Such "openness" and the process of assimilation it supports, which are described as the "inhaling" and "exhaling" of various peoples, constitute for Michelet the essence of progress.[14] Rome's mistake (and step backward) was not assimilation—which is as necessary for life as breathing—but rather believing that "this magnificent adoption of peoples" was the sign that the Roman people "had accomplished the work of humanity" (*OC*, 2:234). Michelet, in this instance, criticizes such arrogance, for this supreme accomplishment would, of course, be reserved for the French at a later moment in history. "Rome was mistaken as Alexander had been; the barbarians, the Christians, and the slaves protested, each one in his own way, that Rome was not the city of the world, and broke in diverse ways with this deceitful unity" (*OC*, 2:234).

It is thus possible for the "birth of humanity" to occur too soon and, if it does, to produce inevitably divided forms or misshapen identities or fictions of a people. In all but exceptional (revolutionary) moments, birth does, in fact, occur too soon, and a deceitful unity and universality reimpose a form of enslavement on all peoples who cannot be included or represented in or by such fictions. Unity and assimilation are thus necessary, but not sufficient, conditions for universality and freedom; it all depends on what kind of unity is produced (imagined, staged) and on what kind of birth occurs.[15] In any case, authentic unity for Michelet can never be forced; it must emerge on its own out of internal necessity and not be imposed from the outside for political reasons. The birth (creation) of a people is modeled after the free, organic unity of the work of art and not after what Michelet characterizes as the superficial and most often repressive material unification constituted by the state or imposed by political parties and institutions of both the Left and the Right.

When "the East" (fatality) explicitly appears not just at but also well inside the borders of Europe, as Michelet argues is the case for Italy and especially for Germany, it is because race and climate in various European countries or regions still dominate freedom: "Thus within Europe itself, which seemed to reserve freedom for itself, fatality pursues us. We found it in the world of the tribe and that of the city, in Germany and in Italy. In one place as in the other, moral freedom is prevented, oppressed by local influences of race and climate. . . . The country is reflected [in man]; one would say as in a mirror. Germany is totally in the figure of the German" (*OC*, 2:246-47). To be exclusively the product of one's land or race, that is—in this case, to be completely "German"—is not to be free. When a people displays too prominently in its physical being the marks of race and climate, when it is so under the influence of local forces immediately identified with its land, then a people is so much its land or race that it cannot be it-

self. It is so much a determined, visible, material identity that it fails to achieve or it loses its spiritual identity.

At this point, the narrative recounting universal history as the war between East and West explicitly takes the form of a struggle within Europe of the West against itself and, more specifically, of France against all other European countries, and especially against England. This struggle is primarily against racial determinism:

> In such countries [Germany, Italy, England, and Spain], there will be the juxtaposition of diverse races, never their intimate fusion. The mixing of races, the mixture of opposed civilizations, is nevertheless the most powerful auxiliary of freedom. The diverse fatalities civilizations bring to this mixture are annulled and neutralized in it, one by the other. . . . Races and ideas are combined and complicated in advancing toward the Occident. Their mixture, so imperfect in Italy and Germany, unequal in Spain and England, is in France equal and perfect. What is the least simple, the least natural, the most artificial, that is to say, the least fatal, the most human, and the most free part of the world is Europe; the most European of all countries is my country, France.

> (*OC*, 2:247)

The supreme privilege given to France (and the ideal of Europe represented by France) is thus that of a country and a people who have allegedly overcome geographic and racial determinism and achieved a perfect fusion of peoples, civilizations, and ideas—which is, for Michelet, the very definition of freedom itself. The most mixed and artificial, that is, the least determined of peoples, is also the most fully human and the freest of peoples.

The French are a people in the strongest sense of the term—in fact, they are the chosen people of history—because they are not racially determined but *self-constructed*. The French thus represent the model of a pure and free artifact or "fiction" of a people, with fiction having the sense of the active creating or fashioning of self.[16] If the most human trait of a free people is the ability to assimilate others into itself and in this way constantly re-create itself as an identity, France is also exemplary in this regard: "This intimate fusion of races constitutes the identity of our nation, its personality," the complex identity of "this multiple unity, of this gigantic person composed of thirty million men" (*OC*, 2:248). True freedom thus has two sides: It is both a freedom from natural (geographic, racial) determination and a freedom to assimilate others and create or fashion oneself as a "gigantic person" or persona out of or as this fusion of various peoples. Freedom, for Michelet, is always the freedom to create unity out of diversity, to make one out of many.

Michelet acknowledges in his 1869 preface to his monumental *Histoire de France* that he took from Vico, whom he calls his only master, the "principle of living force, of humanity creating itself" (*OC,* 4:14), and applied it to all of history and specifically to the problem of the formation of peoples. In an earlier work, he elaborated at greater length on what it means to be the creator of self: "The Creator made man similar to himself, that is to say, a creator. Man also creates in his own image. . . . Man carries in himself a tireless artist who works at the same time outside and inside. This force both drains him and sustains him. It is his *causa vivendi.* By means of it, he makes himself and recognizes himself better each day. He incessantly fashions his own mold, and he is to himself his own Prometheus" (*Origines du droit français cherchées dans les symboles et formules du droit universel* [1837], *OC,* 3:626-27). French history is for Michelet essentially the narrative of how "the work of France on itself" formed France, how the French people as the supreme artists of history incessantly molded themselves and came "more each day" to recognize themselves in that mold (*OC,* 3:634).

This is why, to be free, a people must be repeatedly born, for each birth is a new creation of self. Michelet shows how, in the Revolution, the French people is fully born, and from the perspective of that total birth, previous "partial" births can be uncovered and a French people already existing before its full birth to itself can be revealed. For example, Michelet claims that in 1356, the French people is already born with the emergence of Jeanne d'Arc: "It is not without something like a religious emotion that we will try to characterize the solemn moment when a thing without a name is born, at first nothing but soon everything: the people. To whoever asks the date of our birth, let us boldly reply: 1356. It is that year when the child that France in labor had been announcing for half a century was produced in the world" (**"Cours de 1834-35,"** *OC,* 5:11). With Jeanne d'Arc, France gives birth to itself, to the child it already is/will gradually become, the child that will be recognized by the postrevolutionary French as their own ancestor.

The year 1356 is also the moment when the brutes of the Jacquerie change into the saviors of the country, when Jacques is transformed into Jeanne, when the unruly, disruptive male peasant is replaced by the more feminine and yet more militant, spiritual symbol of the people. Jeanne is, for Michelet, the unique embodiment of all of France, a young woman who represents all French *men*:[17]

> Under the rude education of wars, under the rod of the English, the brute will be transformed into a man. . . . Jacques will become Jeanne, Jeanne the Virgin, the Maid. The popular expression, *a good Frenchman,* dates from that period. . . . From that time on, we have a country. These are Frenchmen, these peasants, don't blush, they are already the French people. It is you, O France. . . . Soiled, disfigured, we will bring

this people to the light of day of justice and history so that we finally will be able to say to this ancient people of the fourteenth century: "You are my father, you are my mother. You conceived me in tears. You have cut through sweat and blood to make France for me. May you be blessed in your grave!"

> (*Histoire de France, OC,* 5:236)

What it takes to be French and a true descendant of these "first" French men and women is the act of recognition itself by which one sees in the peasants of the fourteenth century and in Jeanne d'Arc herself one's own spiritual "father" and "mother." Roots deep enough in France to have had one's actual ancestors descend from that period are not the issue. It is not a question of blood or historical lineage but of historical imagination and the love of and identification with one's homeland and its history and myths.

To be oneself is not to be an other. For the French, it means above all not to be English, and the wars against the English have an important role to play in both making the French and making them recognize who they are. Michelet claims that "it is England that teaches France to know itself. England is France's merciless guide in this painful initiation. At the very moment injustice is consummated when an Englishman makes himself king, France feels itself to be France" (*Précis de l'histoire de France* [1833], *OC,* 3:107). As Michelet says in his **"Discours d'Ouverture"** at the Faculté des Lettres (9 January 1834), "The French owe the English a great debt," for in the struggles against the English, the French became themselves and identified themselves with an image of themselves and with France (*OC,* 3:222).

As important as the struggle to become and remain French through constant battles with the English and all those who would attempt to conquer the French (to subjugate or assimilate them) is the assimilation of other peoples into the French people. Michelet acknowledges, however, that the assimilation of others, which, as we have seen, constitutes for him the strength and superiority of the French over others, is also intimately linked to conquest and rarely, if ever, occurs without violence: "The Frenchman wants above all to imprint his personality on the conquered, not as his own but as the model of the good and the beautiful. That is his naïve belief. He believes that there is nothing more profitable he can do for the world than to give it his ideas, his customs, and his tastes. He converts other peoples, sword in hand, and after the combat, . . . he shows them everything they will gain in becoming French" (*Introduction à l'histoire universelle, OC,* 2:249). The French cannot become more fully themselves without either distancing themselves from others—primarily the English—or making others less themselves and more French. Thus, Michelet's progressive, liberal ideal of the universal fusion of peoples and races also explicitly carries along in it the necessity of conquest and cultural domination in the name of both freedom and national identity.

The incorporation/colonization of the other must be considered an essential part of Michelet's fiction of the French people, even if the French form of conquest is allegedly not "the egotistical and material politics" of either Rome or England (*OC,* 2:249) and not a manifestation of "the inflexible pride of England [which] constructed an eternal obstacle to the fusion of races" (*OC,* 2:252). It is thus a more spiritual than physical form of conquest, "the assimilation of different forms of intelligence [and] the conquest of wills" (*OC,* 2:249). One of the dilemmas of republican nationalism has always been the contradiction that in the name of freedom and assimilation, others are conquered, oppressed, enslaved, colonized, or deported. This contradiction does not necessarily transform the Western notion of freedom into a hypocritical defense of Western hegemony or undermine all the emancipatory claims of republican forms of nationalism. It does, however, reveal the tensions within all forms of nationalism—even the "good" republican forms—between free assimilation and conquest, between the ideal of universal freedom and the realities of material necessity, national interest, and political and cultural hegemony.

The ideal guiding the course of history for Michelet and best embodied by the French is thus the organic unification of all peoples. Such unification demands the total spiritualization of politics and history rather than political (material) unity, which actually has divisive effects on a people: "Matter wants dispersion, spirit wants unity. Essentially divisible matter aspires to disunion, discord. Material unity is nonsense. In politics, it is tyranny. Spirit alone has the right to unify, alone it includes" (*OC,* 4:328). The question remains, however, as to exactly what Michelet means by "spiritual unity."

In principle, the most spiritual of peoples would apparently also have to be the people who had distanced itself the most from all material determinants, from not just racial but also geographic determination. As we have seen, Michelet's romantic metanarrative of universal freedom charts such a course. The situation is more complex than this, however, given that the freest, most unified, and therefore most spiritual of peoples—the French—have also remained the most intimately and passionately linked to the land. Their attachment to the land, however, is one of love, not necessity, and the land to which they are attached is more a spiritual than a material entity: "[In France,] man and the land hold on to each other, and they do not leave each other; there is between them a legitimate marriage, for life and until death. The Frenchman has married France."[18] No other people shares the same relation with the land and the nation, a relation that is fundamentally free and affectionate (even passionate) and that constitutes a life-long marriage contract. After seemingly being left behind in the East in Michelet's narrative, the land thus comes back to play a central role in the process of the self-creation and realization of the people as the very support for the freedom necessary for a people to make itself, to be itself, and to identify with itself.

Michelet insists, however, that in France the land on its own does not originally or directly make the people. Rather, the people makes the land what it is, and thus what in turn the people itself is: "Yes, man makes the land. . . . Don't ever forget that if you want to understand how much he loves it and with what passion. . . . This land, where man has for so long deposited what is best in man, his vitality and his substance, his effort, his virtue, he clearly senses that it is a human land, and he loves it as a person" (*P* [*Le Peuple*], 84). What the peasant loves in the land he cultivates is an idealized reflection of himself, of what he and his ancestors before him have put in it, the (human) form he and they have given it. More artist than laborer, the peasant loves the "person" he has created out of the land, just as the romantic artist might see himself as giving human form to, investing himself in, and identifying with his own creation. The peasant (re-)creates himself as a free individual in and through his creative labor and identifies with the land that he has transformed into a reflection of himself. Agriculture is thus, in Michelet's terms, the original form of culture and primarily a spiritual rather than a physical or economic activity; it is the most basic form of self-formation and even the model for the self-creation of the people in general.[19]

This is why Michelet argues that France's destiny depends on the fate of the peasantry, with the peasantry considered not as a specific social class or group but as the universal subject of (self-)creation. If the peasantry were to be destroyed through its economic dependency on the middle class, and the peasant "expropriated from his life itself" (*P,* 91), what would occur would not just be "the fall of a class of men but that of the *patrie*" as a whole (*P,* 90). It would entail the destruction of the land as a spiritual entity and of all the progressive values that Michelet roots in the primary identification of man with the land and through the land with himself. One can exploit and live off the peasant and the land for only so long before each is weakened and then destroyed. Such destruction is ultimately the threat Michelet sees in modernity, technology, capitalism, and their "foreign" agents.[20]

In *Le Peuple,* Michelet describes the various social classes in terms of how much (or rather how little) of the peasant, how much of his love for the land and the love of the land for him, how much of his freedom, creativity, and sociability, they retain. The further removed from the land a group or class is, the less French, the less imaginative and creative, and the less human it is. He gives an extreme image of the antipeasant (the anti-Frenchman, the antihuman) in the workers tied to their machine in the factory, becoming less alive, less human every day, *men-machines*: "A miserable little people of men-machines who are only half-alive, who produce marvelous things and who do not reproduce themselves, who engender only for death and perpetuate themselves only by absorbing into themselves other populations" (*P,* 98).[21] Mass production is the opposite of creation, just as engendering for death is the opposite of engendering for life, and the absorption of other populations to replace those who cannot reproduce and replace themselves is the opposite of assimilation and self-creation.

But, as serious as, if not more serious than, the physical destruction of the workers is the transformation of their hearts and minds by the monotony of the tasks assigned to them. Certain factories are "veritable hell[s] of boredom" with a "metallic, indifferent, pitiless heart" formed in the workers in order to survive (*P,* 99). The worker next to his or her machine can feel nothing, and, even worse, can no longer even dream: "The machine allows for no dreaming, no distraction. . . . Here, it is necessary that man conform to his trade, that the being of flesh and blood . . . submit to the invariability of this being of steel" (*P,* 99). The worker thus gradually loses the capacity to imagine another state, another life; he or she loses the capacity to imagine at all. Without imagination, there is no creativity, no identification with others, and no love. Without imagination, there is no people, there is nothing. This is the result of "work that demands neither force nor dexterity, which never demands thought. Nothing, nothing, and always nothing!" (*P,* 103). Resistance to this reduction of the mind and thus of the person to nothing represents for Michelet the primary task of the people in modernity. It is a question of life or death.

The worker chained to his machine represents a more general problem for Michelet, namely, the machinization of society in general, which is the antipoetic principle of industrialized modernity against which Michelet fights in the name of the creativity of man. Generalized machinization is what threatens everyone, not just the worker chained to his or her machine but all those who are chained to the administrative and political machines of modernity: "The greatest achievement of Machinism would be to do without men. . . . Political machines to make our social acts uniformly automatic, to exempt us from patriotism; industrial machines which, once created, multiply an unlimited number of monotonous products, and which, by one day's art, exempt us from being artists every day. . . . No more men, therefore, in literary work, no more passion, no more capriciousness" (*P,* 144-45). What would be left after a generalized machinization would be only the

remnants of the nation, of art, of philosophy, and of the people itself: "the State minus the homeland; industry and literature minus art; philosophy minus critical investigation; humanity minus man" (*P,* 145). Against the machine, Michelet constantly holds up the ideal of an aesthetics of life and politics, of the capacity of a people to imagine, create, and re-create the world and itself.

Michelet argues that a total transformation of all aspects of life is necessary and will occur with the restoration of the integrity of the heart: "The disease is in the heart. Let the cure also be in the heart!" (*P,* 147). The redemptive task is thus more aesthetic-metaphysical than political, a task that the historian-artist can better fulfill than the political militant: the task of aiding the people to restore its symbolic affinity with the land and thus to restore and re-create itself. The fundamental spiritual problem for the people, as Michelet presents it, is thus how to reverse the process leading the people away from its poetic essence: "The people has less poetry in itself, and it finds less in the society that surrounds it" (*P,* 158). If "the core subsists" (*P,* 159), however, even in the most unfree and unpoetic of situations—the two are equivalents—it means that no situation is ever definitive when it comes to the French. This is what makes the French once again "the opposite of the English" (*P,* 160), who, lacking this poetic essence, seem irreversibly on a path to destruction. Instinctive, energetic dreamers, the French, by definition, somehow have been able to hold on to the inner poetic spirituality that sustains them.

Michelet is not, however, proposing a nostalgic return to original man or even to the land and the simplicity of the life of the peasant qua poet. Rather, he is concerned with finding a model for overcoming material determination and division *in history* in a way that would not ignore the movement of time and negate what he feels is the undeniable progress of history toward freedom and the spiritual unification of all humanity. The peasant, no matter how much of an "artist" he is in his work on the land, in fact constitutes only a partial model of the unification of the people and its identification with itself. The model is incomplete without the intellectual (bourgeois) counterpart to the peasant, a figure who Michelet claims is identical to the peasant but at the same time his opposite. This figure is equal to the peasant in imagination and creativity but also possesses the gift of expressing in words and forms what the peasant silently feels and experiences. Michelet uses the highly charged romantic term *genius* to refer to this figure who represents nothing less than the collective Subject itself. The genius is *the Subject* of art—both producing and a product of art. The genius is also thus *the Subject* of history, the producer and product of history.

The genius retains the essence of the simple man and raises this essence to a higher, self-reflexive level: "He is the simple man par excellence, the child of all children, he is the people more than the people themselves. . . . The simplicity of the genius is the true form of simplicity. . . . The genius has the gift of childhood in a way the child never has. . . . The genius retains in himself native instinct in all its grandeur" (*P,* 185). The genius raises the idea of the people to the highest level of truth by giving it form and by making the intuitive, instinctual, and emotional bases of the people explicit, visible, and thus fully historical. The genius in this way also makes the silent voice of the people be heard: "The most elevated idea of the people is found with difficulty in the people. . . . The people is found in its truth, in its highest potential, only in the man of genius; in him resides the great soul. . . . Why be astonished by this? His voice is that of the people; mute in itself, the people speaks in this man" (*P,* 186). The highest idea and most complete figure of the people paradoxically *cannot* be found in the people. Only the genius possesses the truth of the people and is capable of creating a figure of the people equal to that ideal. Only in and through the genius can the silent voice of the people finally be heard. This also reveals once again how in all its different dimensions and expressions the people is *created,* a fiction with which the national collectivity is asked to identify. The people has a voice *it* never actually uses but, when it is (re)produced by the genius in its name, is asked to recognize as its own.[22]

Michelet's *Le Peuple* is thus not only one of the most dramatic and moving portraits of the people ever written. It is also one of the most forceful defenses of the privileged place held by the genius—the writer-artist-historian—in the self-realization of the people. The genius is a man who is both "man" and "woman," both "harmonic and fertile," the perfect synthesis of all sexual, generational, cultural, and class opposites: of "man and woman, child and adult, barbarian and civilized, people and aristocracy" (*P,* 187). The project of the people, for Michelet, is to be equal to the genius, to be the *chef d'oeuvre* the true artist makes it and himself to be, to be the ultimate form of the harmonic, productive, and self-created work of art. The people realizes and spontaneously and fully expresses its identity only at exceptional moments of its history. It comes to full awareness of that realization—even, or especially, at moments of decline, impoverishment, division, and conflict—in the work of the genius.

The genius represents nothing less than the possibility of an aesthetic re-creation of self and thus the transcendence of material restrictions and divisions even in the most desperate historical and political situations. For the genius is able to represent dramatically and retain in the present the experience of those historical moments of transcendence that gave birth to the people and that continue to make the people what it is. Revolution and the re-creation of a collective self by itself are, in Michelet, inextricably entwined.

In his 1847 preface to his *Histoire de la Révolution française,* Michelet describes the Revolution as the key to all history, containing both the secrets of the past and the foundation for the future: "[The spirit of the Revolution] contains the secret of all previous times. In it alone France was conscious of itself. In every moment of weakness, when we seem to forget ourselves, it is there that we should look for ourselves, capture ourselves" (*HRF* [*Histoire de la Révolution française*], 1:1).[23] A people who forgets itself perishes. A people who sees itself as a people and has recognized and continues to recognize itself in such moments of self-creation and self-recognition cannot perish. For Michelet, it is the responsibility of both literature and history to prevent a people from forgetting itself, from forgetting the Revolution in which it was born and in which it realized itself fully, and from ignoring the creative powers it possesses and its capacity to give birth to itself and re-create itself again and again.

Michelet characterizes the French Revolution as the total transcendence of history, for in a single moment, all material limitations, even space and time themselves, were negated and a new creation produced, a new spiritual people born: "Where are the ancient differences of place and race, those geographic oppositions which are so strong, so decisive? Everything disappeared, geography is killed. No more mountains, no more rivers, no more obstacles between men. . . . The two material conditions to which life is subjected, time and space, perished. . . . A strange *vita nuova* begins for France, one that is eminently spiritual and that makes its Revolution a kind of dream, at times delightful, at times terrible" (*HRF,* 1:406). The Revolution in one moment accomplishes spectacularly the end of all of history, even if that moment cannot be sustained in or as history. Revolution thus has the characteristics of an intense aesthetic experience of immanence; it is a kind of dream that is at the same time beautiful and frightening in its power and scope. As the intensification, dramatization, and universalization of the processes of self-creation, unification, and identification, the Revolution presents the people as a fully realized spiritual entity, a total, sublime work of art.[24]

In **"L'Héroisme de l'Esprit"** (1854, 1868-1869), Michelet argues that freedom is the origin and basis for both art and history and that the freedom to create is the most basic and universal of all freedoms: "Freedom, the vibrant force, is the universal instrument for making, for creating through art, remaking, re-creating through history. In order to make use of it, you have to have it in yourself. The vigor of the artist depends on it" (*OC,* 4:40). As there is no art without the interior gift of freedom, there is no writing of history, either, for the historian's task is not simply to record or narrate faithfully the past but to re-create it, to "resurrect the past," as Michelet repeats many times throughout his work.[25]

But there is no history without freedom in another sense as well, because without the creative force of freedom, the people, *the Subject of history,* does not and cannot exist and thus does not make itself or make history in the first place. A people that is already made—completely fashioned as a finished product—and that has one and only one birth, would no longer need to create itself again. It would have no use for a freedom it in fact would no longer have within it, and there would be no art and no history for it to make or remake—or to make or remake it.

In the logic of what I would call Michelet's aesthetics of the nation, an already fashioned people is one that has become a material entity, even if it is not directly produced by climate, geography, or race. If this is so, culture, religion, politics, and even history itself, when they are posited as the defining forces in the formation of a people, could be considered to function as material determinants in the same way race does. No matter how contradictory the narratives of the birth(s) of the nation created by nationalist historians, no matter how diversified and conflictual they might argue the formation of the people is, no matter how many ingredients they claim have been added to the melting pot constituted by the nation, whenever they posit or assume that the making of the people has been accomplished, its unity and identity established, at that moment, the fiction of the people they construct can be said to function exactly like the "fictive ethnicity" of race,[26] even if they have strenuously opposed or rejected the specific category of race itself. The question that remains to be answered is whether Michelet's fiction of the French people constitutes a fictive ethnicity.

The problem cannot be resolved by assuming that in all instances the term *people* is in fact diametrically opposed to and has nothing in common with race, that history and biology are always uncommunicating opposites. For as Gérard Noiriel polemically puts it, a form of national identity that functions like race can be said to be the product of history rather than biology: "What biology refused France, history gave it as a gift. Thanks to the millennial rootedness of the inhabitants of the soil, time was able in the long term to accomplish its assimilating work and to fuse diverse races together into a new race."[27] Particularly at moments when further immigration is seen as a threat to the well-being of a people, the very diversity acknowledged to constitute a people can be used to argue against further or a different form of diversification; the creative process of the making of a people can become the basis for an argument against any further complication or remaking of the people. Any republican form of nationalism that gives in to the temptation to try to protect its identity and culture against foreign influences negates or at least limits the very freedom it would also claim constitutes it. And a nationalism that did not in any way give in to such temptations would probably not still be considered a nationalism at all.

A critical approach to the question of national identity, however, would itself not be effective if it were simply oppositional, given the hybrid nature of all nationalisms. Etienne Balibar has argued that it is difficult, if not impossible, to separate the good from the bad forms of nationalism, "the one which tends to construct a state or a community and the one which tends to subjugate; the one which refers to right and the one which refers to might; . . . the one which derives from love . . . and the one which derives from hate."[28] If this is so, then at the very least, identification with the homeland—with even the best of homelands—should be seen as being much more contradictory and less instinctive or natural than all nationalisms assume or dogmatically proclaim. If identification is never the simple, natural, instinctive process it is most often presented as being, then national identity is never really secure, either before or after the aesthetic processes forming and supporting identification have produced their contradictory effects.[29]

In analyzing in Michelet "the ambivalence of effects" (and affects) that "forms part of the very history of all nationalisms,"[30] I have especially emphasized how Michelet's aesthetic transcendence of race determines a particularly powerful and seductive fiction of the French people. It is above all the fiction of a people who is free, self-created, and open to internal diversification through the continual assimilation of and transformation of and by other peoples and cultures. It is the fiction of a people that remains itself in or by being other. The French are thus, for Michelet, clearly and unambiguously the opposite of a predetermined race.

Michelet thus attempts to relegate once and for all the question of race to the Dark Ages of national history by treating the French as *the people* of freedom, as an idealized species that has overcome its material and biological roots. The fictive ethnicity that Michelet attributes to the French, which is the product of a long historical process in which race has been negated and transcended as a determining force, should thus never be confused with either the racial concepts of the people he constantly attacked or the racist theories that would be more fully developed and that would take on a nefarious political form in the late nineteenth and early twentieth centuries. At the same time, the fact that ethnicity—no matter how spiritual or aesthetic its form—is still a central component of Michelet's fiction of the people points to one of the principal limitations of all forms of nationalism, even of nationalisms that identify with the Revolution and universalistic, antiracist values. Michelet's work reveals that the art of the people, no matter how progressive and republican the nationalism to which it is linked, is, in fact, a highly contradictory art.

Notes

Unless otherwise noted, all translations from the French are my own.

1. Evoking "the burdensome" nature of "this ancestor" of the *Annales* school in the eyes of "well-trained historians who have trouble seeing what the rigors and cautions of method owe to the romantic historian's passions, phantasms, and effects of language," Jacques Rancière nevertheless argues that "Michelet's 'phantasms' and effects of style really define the conditions of the scientific speaking of the *Annales,* that they are the operators for what has recently been termed an epistemological break," or of what he prefers to call "a revolution in the poetic structures of knowledge" (*The Names of History: On the Poetics of Knowledge,* trans. Hassan Melehy [Minneapolis: University of Minnesota Press, 1994], 42).

2. Lucien Febvre, one of the founders of the *Annales* school, claims that Michelet had "foreseen, anticipated everything" (*La Terre et l'évolution humaine* [Paris: La Renaissance du Livre, 1922], 64). Pierre Nora, one of many contemporary *Annales* historians to continue to give Michelet a central place in his work, speaks of Michelet as the central presence of the entire collective enterprise of *Les Lieux de mémoire*: "Michelet is located nowhere specifically in this book because he is everywhere. Michelet transcends every possible place of memory because among all the other figures he is . . . the common denominator, the soul of these *Lieux de mémoire*" ("La nation-mémoire," in *Les Lieux de mémoire, II: La Nation,* ed. Pierre Nora, vol. 3 [Paris: Gallimard, 1986], 649).

3. Fernand Braudel, *The Identity of France,* 2 vols., trans. Siân Reynolds (London: Collins, 1988, 1990), 1:15-16, translation modified. Hereafter, this work is cited parenthetically as *IF.*

4. It is interesting that Braudel quotes Péguy in this context, for Péguy was, in fact, a severe critic of the dry, objective positivism that dominated academic history at the turn of the century and a staunch defender of the mysticism and spiritualism of the very few people he considered true nationalists, those who were led by their heart and not their head. He was, therefore, an enthusiastic fan of Michelet, whom he polemically evoked as a model for his attacks against positivist historians, republican politicians, and modernity in general: "No occasion should be lost . . . to proclaim again that Michelet is the very genius of history, first of all, because it is true, and, second, because it bothers so many people and because it is such a huge ordeal for our great friends, the moderns" ("Clio: Dialogue de l'Histoire et de l'âme païenne," in *Oeuvres en prose complètes,* 3 vols., ed. Robert Burac [Paris: Gallimard, Bibliothèque de la Pléiade, 1987, 1988, 1992], 3:1028).

5. See Benedict Anderson, *Imagined Communities: Reflections of the Origin and Spread of National-ism* (London: Verso, 1991). Anderson defines the nation as "an imagined political community," because "the members of even the smallest nation will never know most of their fellow-members, . . . yet in the minds of each lives the image of their communion." This means for him that "communities are to be distinguished, not by their falsity/genuineness, but by the style in which they are imagined" (6).

6. Philippe Carrard, in *The Poetics of the New History: French Historical Discourse from Braudel to Chartier* (Baltimore, Md.: Johns Hopkins University Press, 1992), calls attention to Braudel's highly motivated use of geological metaphors: "Braudel, then, sketches the central question of the 'identity' of France with geological metaphors: . . . this identity is the result of what the past has left in 'successive layers,' just as the 'powerful strata' of the earth's crust originate in the deposits of 'marine sediments.' If France has an identity, it should thus be regarded as a 'residue,' an 'amalgam,' the outcome of 'additions' and 'mixtures'" (202). In spite of Braudel's distrust of poetically formulated expressions of "personhood," Carrard calls Braudel "the uncontested master of personification" among *Annales* historians, "something which is not devoid of irony given the fact that Braudel . . . has explicitly come out against using the figure in historiography" (205). Carrard claims that "nearly every page [of *The Identity of France*] accommodates some form of personification" (205) and that this provides Braudel with a "powerful rhetorical shortcut" for resolving the problem of how geographic, national, and social formations can be said to have or provide an identity for a people (209). Carrard concludes that Braudel's reference to Michelet's love of France "pays tribute to Michelet's rhetoric as well as to his patriotic feelings" (217).

7. See especially Gérard Noiriel, *Le Creuset français: Histoire de l'immigration, XIXe-XXe siècle* (Paris: Seuil, 1988), for a provocative criticism of Braudel's *Identity of France,* which Noiriel argues is "prisoner of a holistic conception" of the nation (59) and "impregnated with a 'philosophy' of rootedness" (62). Noiriel opposes Braudel's (and Michelet's) notion of national identity with a history of immigration, which would entail "a deconstruction of the Nation as a collective entity" (61). In the opening lines of a chapter entitled "Uprooted" (in English in the original), Noiriel ironically asks Michelet, Braudel, and "all the historians who have so successfully celebrated the virtues of rootedness in the soil" to pardon him for the book he has written: "The ancestors who are being convened here are the uprooted of the history of France," all those who, although they are remembered by "millions of inhabitants of this

country, have no place in our history books and have never been invited to the festivities of our national commemorations" (127).

8. Raoul Giradet, *Mythes et mythologies politiques* (Paris: Seuil, 1970), 156.

9. Suzanne Citron, *Le Mythe national: L'Histoire de France en question* (Paris: Les Editions Ouvrières, 1991), 25.

10. See François Furet, *Penser la Révolution française* (Paris: Gallimard, 1978), for a polemical critique of "this obsession with origins, with which all national history is woven" and in which "1789 is the date of birth, the zero year of the new world founded in equality" (14). In opposition to Michelet's *Histoire de la Révolution française,* which he considers "the most penetrating of the histories of the Revolution that was written in the mode of identity," Furet places Tocqueville's history, the "only one to have imagined the same history in the inverse mode of sociological interpretation" (28).

11. For example, in his 1847 introduction to the *Histoire de la Révolution française,* ed. Gérard Walter, 2 vols. (Paris: Gallimard, Bibliothèque de la Pléiade, 1952), Michelet asserts that "the Revolution continues Christianity and contradicts it. It is at the same time its heir and its adversary. . . . The Revolution founds fraternity on the love of man for man, on mutual obligation, on Law and Justice. This base is fundamental and needs no other" (1:25). Hereafter, this work is cited parenthetically as *HRF.*

Later in the same work, Michelet claims that "in Brittany and elsewhere, the Revolution took the side of man against the fief. A holy, human, decision that was as charitable as it was reasonable according to both God and the Spirit. The world should . . . recognize the truly religious character of the Revolution. . . . Attacked as being impious, the Revolution was ultra-Christian; it did the things Christianity should have done" (*HRF,* 1:1142). For an analysis of the religious dimensions of Michelet's portrayal of the Revolution, see Lionel Gossman, "Michelet's Gospel of Revolution," in *Between History and Literature* (Cambridge, Mass.: Harvard University Press, 1990). This volume also includes another important essay on Michelet, "Jules Michelet and Romantic Historiography." Gossman argues that "history was Michelet's religion, the Revolution was its Revelation, and his own *History of the Revolution* was intended as nothing less than the Gospel of a new religion of humanity. . . . [It was] a *sacred* history, . . . and it aimed to inspire its readers and promote an *imitatio,* an identification and dedication equivalent to those inspired by the Gospels" (203-4).

12. *Oeuvres complètes de Jules Michelet,* ed. Paul Viallaneix, 20 vols. (Paris: Flammarion, 1971-1987), 2:227. Hereafter, this work is cited parenthetically as *OC.*

13. Lionel Gossman highlights the dialectical complexity of Michelet's geographic distinctions in "The Go-Between: Jules Michelet, 1789-1874," *MLN* 89 (1974): "In relation to India, for instance, Persia is the occident of the orient; and in relation to Egypt, Judea is the West of the Middle East. Germany . . . is 'l'Inde de l'Europe,' Italy is its occident" (505). Gossman argues that the oppositions are "increasingly internalized" as Michelet narrates history's journey west, so that in imperial Rome, "the orientalized occident finally encounters the occidentalized orient" (506).

14. "Rome increases and decreases with the regularity of a living organism; it inhales, I dare to say, Latin, Sabine, Etruscan peoples, and having become Roman, it exhales them outside into its colonies. In this way it assimilates everyone" (*OC,* 2:234).

15. Such false births occur frequently in history, for Charlemagne later repeated the mistake of Rome, creating a "material and deceitful unity [that] lasted the life of one man" (*OC,* 2:237). It is also at least partially true of the unity realized during the French Revolution itself, whose "tragic moments" were, for Michelet, due to the revolutionaries' impatience at not realizing the complete unity of the people immediately rather than letting it be born and mature on its own: "What characterizes these times is that in their impatience to realize their desires, they [the revolutionaries] imagined that unity was going to come to them already made, to fall on them like a miracle. . . . Unity, while the law decrees it from on high, must flourish from below, from the depth of human wills" (*HRF,* 1:203).

16. I am using "fiction" here in Philippe Lacoue-Labarthe's sense of "the fiction of the political." See especially *Heidegger, Art and Politics: The Fiction of the Political,* trans. Chris Turner (Cambridge, Mass.: Basil Blackwell, 1990), in which Lacoue-Labarthe discusses the centrality of this notion to the history of political theory: "The political (the City) belongs to a form of *plastic art,* formation and information, *fiction* in the strict sense. This deep theme which derives from Plato's politico-pedagogic writings . . . and reappears in the guise of such concepts as *Gestaltung* (configuration, fashioning) or *Bildung,* a term with a revealingly polysemic character (formation, constitution, organization, education, culture, etc.)" (66).

17. Michelet insists on what could be called the symbolic bisexuality of Jeanne as well as on her hy-

brid nature as both a saint and a soldier, a spiritual and a material being: "No one should be surprised that the people appears here as a woman, if from patience and the twelve virtues a woman moves on to virile virtue, to the virtue of war, if the saint becomes soldier" (*Histoire de France, OC*, 6:48).

18. Jules Michelet, *Le Peuple*, ed. Paul Viallaneix (Paris: Flammarion, 1974), 80. Hereafter, this work is cited parenthetically as *P.* Michelet's peasant is "a man," and the land he loves is characterized first as his mistress and then as his wife.

19. In the same vein, Michelet opposes the artisan, the true artist of production, to both the manufacturer and the merchant, whom he describes in the following terms: "*The merchant does not create at all;* he does not have the considerable happiness, worthy of man, of giving birth to something, of seeing advance in his hands a work which takes form, which becomes harmonious, which through his progress corresponds to its creator" (*P,* 123).

20. These foreign agents are the property owners, bankers, and usurers who live off the peasants' labor. For Michelet, they are primarily the English, the French bourgeoisie, and "the Jews": "The peasant, becoming the serf of the usurer, would not only be miserable, he would also have less heart. A sad, troubled, trembling debtor who is afraid to meet his lender and who hides, do you believe that this man still has much courage? What would become of a race raised in this way, under the terror of the Jews?" (*P,* 88). Paul Viallaneix, Michelet specialist and editor of the paperback edition of *Le Peuple* as well as his *Oeuvres complètes,* unsuccessfully tries to explain away Michelet's anti-Semitic remark by arguing in a note on the same page that "the term 'Jew' is taken in its most common sense, such as Toussenel defined it in his pamphlet, *Les Juifs, rois de l'époque,* which was read by Michelet on August 15, 1845: 'I warn the reader that this word is generally being taken in its popular acceptance: *Jew, banker, money changer*'" (*P,* 88). Obviously, such a justification raises more questions than it answers, for the association of Jews with economic exploitation and England, the primary enemy not just of France but also of freedom and spirituality in general, is far from a unique occurrence in Michelet's work. In his *Histoire de France,* for example, Michelet attacks English literature in the following way: "No nation is further from grace. . . . From Shakespeare to Milton, from Milton to Byron, their beautiful and somber literature is skeptic, Judaic, and satanic, in one word, anti-Christian" (*OC,* 6:111). Suffice it to say here that the source of the misery of the people, for Michelet, is always located outside the people. It comes from those "foreign bodies" that cannot be assimilated into the people and

against which the people must vigilantly defend itself. In spite of remarks such as those just quoted, anti-Semitism cannot be considered central to Michelet's notion of the French people and is not for him a biologically determined concept. Lionel Gossman is certainly right, therefore, to suggest that in Michelet's 1869 preface to his *Histoire de la Révolution française* "it is possible that he also wanted to signal his opposition to racial (or racist) theories in the strict sense of the term, because around 1869, such theories had already become more frequent. Michelet, for example, could have confronted them in the writings of Gobineau or Renan" ("Jules Michelet: Histoire nationale, biographie, autobiographie," *Littérature* 102 [May 1996]:46 n. 32).

21. In spite of the gravity of the situation in France, Michelet reassures his readers in a note that he has confidence that France will be restored to itself and that the worst of all possible fates—becoming another England—will not occur: "The extension of *machinism* (to designate this system with a name) is it to be feared? Must the machine invade everything? France, will it become in its relation to the machine another England? To these serious questions, I answer without hesitation: No" (*P,* 96).

22. Michelet, near the end of his life, had to admit with great regret, however, as he looked back on his writing, that he had failed precisely to capture the true voice of the people: "I was born people, I had the people in my heart. . . . But its language, its language, it was not accessible to me. I wasn't able to make the people speak" ("Nos Fils" [1869], *OC,* 20:498). In admitting such a failure, Michelet is also indirectly acknowledging the failure of his entire redemptive historical enterprise.

23. François Furet, a severe critic of all historians who treat the Revolution as the founding moment of French history, acknowledges that Michelet has an important role to play in the creation of the myth of the revolutionary origin of the French nation. He finds reasons, however, to pardon him, at least in part: "[Of the group of historians of the Revolution comprised of Tocqueville, Guizot, and Michelet,] Michelet is the one who interiorized revolutionary ideology the most. But he takes up the history of the Revolution after having covered the entire history of France. This passion of the past for the past, combined with the extraordinary diversification of his analysis of revolutionary history, frees him from teleology" (*Penser la Révolution française,* 117). It is, we would have to admit, a strange defense, given that Michelet's interest in "the entire history of France" certainly cannot be separated from his interiorization of revolutionary ideology, if by that Furet means the

belief in the myth of the birth of the French people in the Revolution and the accompanying myth of the universal destiny of this chosen people. And yet, Furet's comments are not completely off the mark, because Michelet is never completely satisfied with any of the births he attributes to the people or with the different "lives" of the nation he narrates or projects. This does not free Michelet from teleology, but it does complicate his relation to it.

24. Lionel Gossman warns of some of the possible consequences of what I would call Michelet's aestheticization of the Revolution at the end of "Michelet's Gospel of Revolution": "The experience of transcending the bounds of the everyday, as we now know, may be completely indifferent to ethical considerations, and glorification of the *moment . . .* leads easily to a political Walpurgisnacht, in which all the cows are black" (*Between History and Literature,* 223).

25. For example, in his long dedication to his friend Edgar Quinet, which serves as a preface to *Le Peuple,* Michelet distinguishes himself from other historians for having "named [history] with a name that no one had ever used. Thierry saw history as a *narration,* and Mr. Guizot as *an analysis.* I named it *resurrection,* and this is the name it will keep" (*P,* 73).

26. I am referring to Etienne Balibar's use of this term in his essay, "The Nation Form: History and Ideology," in Etienne Balibar and Immanuel Wallerstein, *Race, Nation, Class: Ambiguous Identities* (London: Verso, 1991): "I apply the term 'fictive ethnicity' to the community instituted by the nation-state. This is an intentionally complex expression in which the term fiction . . . should not be taken in the sense of a pure and simple illusion without historical effects, but must, on the contrary, be understood by analogy with the *persona ficta* of the juridical tradition in the sense of an institutional effect, a 'fabrication.' No nation possesses an ethnic base naturally, but as social formations are nationalized, the populations included within them, divided up among them or dominated by them are ethnicized—that is, represented in the past or in the future *as if* they formed a natural community, possessing of itself an identity of origins, culture and interests which transcends individuals and social conditions" (96). In another essay from the same collection, "Racism and Nationalism," Balibar argues that "racist theories necessarily contain an aspect of sublimation, an idealization of the species, the privileged figure of which is aesthetic" (58).

27. Gérard Noiriel, *Population, immigration et identité nationale en France, XIXe-XXe siècle* (Paris: Hachette, 1992), 30.

28. Balibar, "Racism and Nationalism," 47.

29. See Jacques Derrida, *Le Monolinguisme de l'autre* (Paris: Galilée, 1996), especially concerning the questions of national identity and the "mother tongue." Derrida says this about national identity: "Our question is still identity. What is identity, this concept whose transparent identity to itself is still dogmatically presupposed by so many debates on monoculturalism or multiculturalism, on nationality, citizenship, belonging in general? . . . To be Franco-Maghrebin 'like me,' is . . . certainly not to have an excess or a wealth of identities, attributes, or names. It would rather and above all betray a *confusion of identity* [un *trouble de l'identité*]" (31-32).

30. Balibar, "Racism and Nationalism," 48.

FURTHER READING

Biographies

Kippur, Stephen A. *Jules Michelet: A Study of Mind and Sensibility.* Albany: State University of New York Press, 1981, 269 p.

    Covers the major events and influences in Michelet's life, as well as including a reading of his works and a survey of available criticism.

Mitzman, Arthur. *Michelet, Historian: Rebirth and Romanticism in Nineteenth-Century France.* New Haven: Yale University Press, 1990, 339 p.

    Offers a psychobiographical study of Michelet's intellectual and cultural influences, emphasizing the tumultuous years between 1840 and 1855.

Criticism

Blix, Göran. "The Prison-House of Revolutionary Memory: The Politics of Oblivion in Michelet, Hugo, and Dumas." *French Forum* 32, no. 3 (fall 2007): 39-64.

    Explores the insights of Michelet, Victor Hugo, and Alexandre Dumas into the removal of prisoners from the historical record and from society.

Edelstein, Dan. "Between Myth and History: Michelet, Lévi-Strauss, Barthes, and the Structural Analysis of Myth." *Clio* 32, no. 4 (summer 2003): 397-414.

    Presents an account of Michelet's treatment of various myths and his influence on structuralist historians Claude Lévi-Strauss and Roland Barthes.

Geffen, Arthur. "Whitman and Jules Michelet—One More Time." *American Literature* 45, no. 1 (March 1973): 107-14.

Compares "The Communion of Love," a chapter in Michelet's book *La femme,* to Walt Whitman's poem "Passage to India."

Geyl, Pieter. "Michelet and His *History of the French Revolution.*" In *Debates with Historians,* pp. 56-90. Groningen: J. B. Wolters and The Hague: Martinus Nijhoff, 1955.
> Criticizes Michelet's position in *Histoire de la Révolution Française* (*History of the French Revolution*) as blatantly nationalist and imperialist.

Haac, Oscar A. "Michelet's Purpose." *Proceedings of the American Philosophical Society* 94, no. 5 (October 1950): 494-501.
> Argues that Michelet's works are meant to be read as a continuous exposition of the democratic idealism first disseminated during the French Revolution.

Hooper, John. "Changing Perceptions of Jules Michelet as Historian: History Between Literature and Science, 1831-1874." *Journal of European Studies* 23, no. 3 (September 1993): 283-99.
> Discusses the various positions on the study of history—whether it is an art or a science—of Michelet and his critics.

Kogan, Vivian. *Self-Fashioning and National Consciousness in Jules Michelet.* Chapel Hill: University of North Carolina Press, 2006, 322 p.
> Considers the construction of Michelet's narrative persona and its influence on his nationalistic ideals.

Le Goff, Jacques. "The Several Middle Ages of Jules Michelet." In *Time, Work, and Culture in the Middle Ages,* translated by Arthur Goldhammer, pp. 3-28. Chicago: University of Chicago Press, 1980.
> Attempts to revive Michelet's reputation among medievalists by comparing his techniques to both contemporary and modern approaches to history.

Murphy, J. P. "Proust and Michelet: Intertextuality as Aegis." *French Studies* 53, no. 4 (October 1999): 417-29.
> Examines the influence of Michelet's journalistic persona and descriptive style on the writings of Marcel Proust.

Orr, Linda. *Jules Michelet: Nature, History, Language.* Ithaca, N.Y.: Cornell University Press, 1976, 215 p.
> Studies the effects of Michelet's use of natural and mythological imagery in conjunction with certain linguistic flourishes.

Rearick, Charles. "Symbol, Legend, and History: Michelet as Folklorist-Historian." *French Historical Studies* 7, no. 1 (spring 1971): 72-92.
> Describes Michelet's treatment of French folklore and the influence of folklore on history and society.

Tollebeek, Jo. "'Renaissance' and 'Fossilization': Michelet, Burckhardt, and Huizinga." *Renaissance Studies* 15, no. 3 (September 2001): 354-66.
> Characterizes the thoughts of Michelet and other historians on the state of nineteenth-century societies in relation to the Renaissance.

Vinken, Barbara. "Wounds of Love: Modern Devotion According to Michelet." *Clio* 36, no. 2 (spring 2007): 155-75.
> Contrasts Michelet's "new lay religion of Republic, People and Fatherland" with traditional French Catholicism.

Williams, John R. *Jules Michelet: Historian as a Critic of French Literature.* Birmingham, Ala.: Summa Publications, 1987, 105 p.
> Analyzes Michelet's treatment of various works of French literature, ultimately concluding that Michelet cannot be considered a literary critic.

Additional coverage of Michelet's life and career is contained in the following sources published by Gale: *European Writers,* **Vol. 5;** *Guide to French Literature, 1789 to the Present;* *Literature Resource Center;* **and** *Nineteenth-Century Literature Criticism,* **Vol. 31.**

How to Use This Index

The main references

> **Calvino, Italo**
> 1923-1985 .... CLC 5, 8, 11, 22, 33, 39,
> 73; SSC 3, 48

list all author entries in the following Gale Literary Criticism series:

AAL = *Asian American Literature*
BG = *The Beat Generation: A Gale Critical Companion*
BLC = *Black Literature Criticism*
BLCS = *Black Literature Criticism Supplement*
CLC = *Contemporary Literary Criticism*
CLR = *Children's Literature Review*
CMLC = *Classical and Medieval Literature Criticism*
DC = *Drama Criticism*
FL = *Feminism in Literature: A Gale Critical Companion*
GL = *Gothic Literature: A Gale Critical Companion*
HLC = *Hispanic Literature Criticism*
HLCS = *Hispanic Literature Criticism Supplement*
HR = *Harlem Renaissance: A Gale Critical Companion*
LC = *Literature Criticism from 1400 to 1800*
NCLC = *Nineteenth-Century Literature Criticism*
NNAL = *Native North American Literature*
PC = *Poetry Criticism*
SSC = *Short Story Criticism*
TCLC = *Twentieth-Century Literary Criticism*
WLC = *World Literature Criticism, 1500 to the Present*
WLCS = *World Literature Criticism Supplement*

The cross-references

> See also CA 85-88, 116; CANR 23, 61;
> DAM NOV; DLB 196; EW 13; MTCW 1, 2;
> RGSF 2; RGWL 2; SFW 4; SSFS 12

list all author entries in the following Gale biographical and literary sources:

AAYA = *Authors & Artists for Young Adults*
AFAW = *African American Writers*
AFW = *African Writers*
AITN = *Authors in the News*
AMW = *American Writers*
AMWR = *American Writers Retrospective Supplement*
AMWS = *American Writers Supplement*
ANW = *American Nature Writers*
AW = *Ancient Writers*
BEST = *Bestsellers*
BPFB = *Beacham's Encyclopedia of Popular Fiction: Biography and Resources*
BRW = *British Writers*
BRWS = *British Writers Supplement*
BW = *Black Writers*
BYA = *Beacham's Guide to Literature for Young Adults*
CA = *Contemporary Authors*
CAAS = *Contemporary Authors Autobiography Series*
CABS = *Contemporary Authors Bibliographical Series*
CAD = *Contemporary American Dramatists*
CANR = *Contemporary Authors New Revision Series*
CAP = *Contemporary Authors Permanent Series*
CBD = *Contemporary British Dramatists*
CCA = *Contemporary Canadian Authors*
CD = *Contemporary Dramatists*
CDALB = *Concise Dictionary of American Literary Biography*

CDALBS = Concise Dictionary of American Literary Biography Supplement
CDBLB = Concise Dictionary of British Literary Biography
CMW = St. James Guide to Crime & Mystery Writers
CN = Contemporary Novelists
CP = Contemporary Poets
CPW = Contemporary Popular Writers
CSW = Contemporary Southern Writers
CWD = Contemporary Women Dramatists
CWP = Contemporary Women Poets
CWRI = St. James Guide to Children's Writers
CWW = Contemporary World Writers
DA = DISCovering Authors
DA3 = DISCovering Authors 3.0
DAB = DISCovering Authors: British Edition
DAC = DISCovering Authors: Canadian Edition
DAM = DISCovering Authors: Modules
   DRAM: Dramatists Module; **MST:** Most-studied Authors Module;
   MULT: Multicultural Authors Module; **NOV:** Novelists Module;
   POET: Poets Module; **POP:** Popular Fiction and Genre Authors Module
DFS = Drama for Students
DLB = Dictionary of Literary Biography
DLBD = Dictionary of Literary Biography Documentary Series
DLBY = Dictionary of Literary Biography Yearbook
DNFS = Literature of Developing Nations for Students
EFS = Epics for Students
EW = European Writers
EWL = Encyclopedia of World Literature in the 20th Century
EXPN = Exploring Novels
EXPP = Exploring Poetry
EXPS = Exploring Short Stories
FANT = St. James Guide to Fantasy Writers
FW = Feminist Writers
GFL = Guide to French Literature, Beginnings to 1789, 1798 to the Present
GLL = Gay and Lesbian Literature
HGG = St. James Guide to Horror, Ghost & Gothic Writers
HW = Hispanic Writers
IDFW = International Dictionary of Films and Filmmakers: Writers and Production Artists
IDTP = International Dictionary of Theatre: Playwrights
LAIT = Literature and Its Times
LAW = Latin American Writers
JRDA = Junior DISCovering Authors
MAICYA = Major Authors and Illustrators for Children and Young Adults
MAICYAS = Major Authors and Illustrators for Children and Young Adults Supplement
MAWW = Modern American Women Writers
MJW = Modern Japanese Writers
MTCW = Major 20th-Century Writers
NCFS = Nonfiction Classics for Students
NFS = Novels for Students
PAB = Poets: American and British
PFS = Poetry for Students
RGAL = Reference Guide to American Literature
RGEL = Reference Guide to English Literature
RGSF = Reference Guide to Short Fiction
RGWL = Reference Guide to World Literature
RHW = Twentieth-Century Romance and Historical Writers
SAAS = Something about the Author Autobiography Series
SATA = Something about the Author
SFW = St. James Guide to Science Fiction Writers
SSFS = Short Stories for Students
TCWW = Twentieth-Century Western Writers
WLIT = World Literature and Its Times
WP = World Poets
YABC = Yesterday's Authors of Books for Children
YAW = St. James Guide to Young Adult Writers

Literary Criticism Series
Cumulative Author Index

Apollonius of Rhodes
See Apollonius Rhodius
Apollonius Rhodius c. 300B.C.-c.
220B.C. .... **CMLC 28**
See also AW 1; DLB 176; RGWL 2, 3
Appelfeld, Aharon 1932- ... **CLC 23, 47; SSC
42**
See also CA 112; 133; CANR 86, 160;
CWW 2; DLB 299; EWL 3; RGHL;
RGSF 2; WLIT 6
Appelfeld, Aron
See Appelfeld, Aharon
Apple, Max (Isaac) 1941- .... **CLC 9, 33; SSC
50**
See also AMWS 17; CA 81-84; CANR 19,
54; DLB 130
Appleman, Philip (Dean) 1926- .... **CLC 51**
See also CA 13-16R; CAAS 18; CANR 6,
29, 56
Appleton, Lawrence
See Lovecraft, H. P.
Apteryx
See Eliot, T(homas) S(tearns)
Apuleius, (Lucius Madaurensis) c. 125-c.
164 .... **CMLC 1, 84**
See also AW 2; CDWLB 1; DLB 211;
RGWL 2, 3; SUFW; WLIT 8
Aquin, Hubert 1929-1977 .... **CLC 15**
See also CA 105; DLB 53; EWL 3
Aquinas, Thomas 1224(?)-1274 ..... **CMLC 33**
See also DLB 115; EW 1; TWA
Aragon, Louis 1897-1982 .... **CLC 3, 22;
TCLC 123**
See also CA 69-72; 108; CANR 28, 71;
DAM NOV, POET; DLB 72, 258; EW 11;
EWL 3; GFL 1789 to the Present; GLL 2;
LMFS 2; MTCW 1, 2; RGWL 2, 3
Arany, Janos 1817-1882 .... **NCLC 34**
Aranyos, Kakay 1847-1910
See Mikszath, Kalman
Aratus of Soli c. 315B.C.-c.
240B.C. .... **CMLC 64, 114**
See also DLB 176
Arbuthnot, John 1667-1735 .... **LC 1**
See also DLB 101
Archer, Herbert Winslow
See Mencken, H. L.
Archer, Jeffrey 1940- .... **CLC 28**
See also AAYA 16; BEST 89:3; BPFB 1;
CA 77-80; CANR 22, 52, 95, 136; CPW;
DA3; DAM POP; INT CANR-22; MTFW
2005
Archer, Jeffrey Howard
See Archer, Jeffrey
Archer, Jules 1915- .... **CLC 12**
See also CA 9-12R; CANR 6, 69; SAAS 5;
SATA 4, 85
Archer, Lee
See Ellison, Harlan
Archilochus c. 7th cent. B.C.- .... **CMLC 44**
See also DLB 176
Ard, William
See Jakes, John
Arden, John 1930- .... **CLC 6, 13, 15**
See also BRWS 2; CA 13-16R; CAAS 4;
CANR 31, 65, 67, 124; CBD; CD 5, 6;
DAM DRAM; DFS 9; DLB 13, 245;
EWL 3; MTCW 1
Arenas, Reinaldo 1943-1990 .. **CLC 41; HLC
1; TCLC 191**
See also CA 124; 128; 133; CANR 73, 106;
DAM MULT; DLB 145; EWL 3; GLL 2;
HW 1; LAW; LAWS 1; MTCW 2; MTFW
2005; RGSF 2; RGWL 3; WLIT 1
Arendt, Hannah 1906-1975 .... **CLC 66, 98;
TCLC 193**
See also CA 17-20R; 61-64; CANR 26, 60,
172; DLB 242; MTCW 1, 2

Aretino, Pietro 1492-1556 .... **LC 12, 165**
See also RGWL 2, 3
Arghezi, Tudor
See Theodorescu, Ion N.
Arguedas, Jose Maria 1911-1969 .... **CLC 10,
18; HLCS 1; TCLC 147**
See also CA 89-92; CANR 73; DLB 113;
EWL 3; HW 1; LAW; RGWL 2, 3; WLIT
1
Argueta, Manlio 1936- .... **CLC 31**
See also CA 131; CANR 73; CWW 2; DLB
145; EWL 3; HW 1; RGWL 3
Arias, Ron 1941- .... **HLC 1**
See also CA 131; CANR 81, 136; DAM
MULT; DLB 82; HW 1, 2; MTCW 2
Ariosto, Lodovico
See Ariosto, Ludovico
Ariosto, Ludovico 1474-1533 ... **LC 6, 87; PC
42**
See also EW 2; RGWL 2, 3; WLIT 7
Aristides
See Epstein, Joseph
Aristophanes 450B.C.-385B.C. .... **CMLC 4,
51; DC 2; WLCS**
See also AW 1; CDWLB 1; DA; DA3;
DAB; DAC; DAM DRAM, MST; DFS
10; DLB 176; LMFS 1; RGWL 2, 3;
TWA; WLIT 8
Aristotle 384B.C.-322B.C. .... **CMLC 31;
WLCS**
See also AW 1; CDWLB 1; DA; DA3;
DAB; DAC; DAM MST; DLB 176;
RGWL 2, 3; TWA; WLIT 8
Arlt, Roberto (Godofredo Christophersen)
1900-1942 .... **HLC 1; TCLC 29**
See also CA 123; 131; CANR 67; DAM
MULT; DLB 305; EWL 3; HW 1, 2;
IDTP; LAW
Armah, Ayi Kwei 1939- . **BLC 1:1, 2:1; CLC
5, 33, 136**
See also AFW; BRWS 10; BW 1; CA 61-
64; CANR 21, 64; CDWLB 3; CN 1, 2,
3, 4, 5, 6, 7; DAM MULT, POET; DLB
117; EWL 3; MTCW 1; WLIT 2
Armatrading, Joan 1950- .... **CLC 17**
See also CA 114; 186
Armin, Robert 1568(?)-1615(?) .... **LC 120**
Armitage, Frank
See Carpenter, John (Howard)
Armstrong, Jeannette (C.) 1948- .... **NNAL**
See also CA 149; CCA 1; CN 6, 7; DAC;
DLB 334; SATA 102
Arnauld, Antoine 1612-1694 .... **LC 169**
See also DLB 268
Arnette, Robert
See Silverberg, Robert
**Arnim, Achim von (Ludwig Joachim von
Arnim)** 1781-1831 .. **NCLC 5, 159; SSC
29**
See also DLB 90
Arnim, Bettina von 1785-1859 ...... **NCLC 38,
123**
See also DLB 90; RGWL 2, 3
Arnold, Matthew 1822-1888 ..... **NCLC 6, 29,
89, 126, 218; PC 5, 94; WLC 1**
See also BRW 5; CDBLB 1832-1890; DA;
DAB; DAC; DAM MST, POET; DLB 32,
57; EXPP; PAB; PFS 2; TEA; WP
Arnold, Thomas 1795-1842 .... **NCLC 18**
See also DLB 55
Arnow, Harriette (Louisa) Simpson
1908-1986 ...... **CLC 2, 7, 18; TCLC 196**
See also BPFB 1; CA 9-12R; 118; CANR
14; CN 2, 3, 4; DLB 6; FW; MTCW 1, 2;
RHW; SATA 42; SATA-Obit 47
Arouet, Francois-Marie
See Voltaire

Arp, Hans
See Arp, Jean
Arp, Jean 1887-1966 .... **CLC 5; TCLC 115**
See also CA 81-84; 25-28R; CANR 42, 77;
EW 10
Arrabal
See Arrabal, Fernando
Arrabal, Fernando 1932- .. **CLC 2, 9, 18, 58;
DC 35**
See also CA 9-12R; CANR 15; CWW 2;
DLB 321; EWL 3; LMFS 2
Arrabal Teran, Fernando
See Arrabal, Fernando
Arreola, Juan Jose 1918-2001 .... **CLC 147;
HLC 1; SSC 38**
See also CA 113; 131; 200; CANR 81;
CWW 2; DAM MULT; DLB 113; DNFS
2; EWL 3; HW 1, 2; LAW; RGSF 2
Arrian c. 89(?)-c. 155(?) .... **CMLC 43**
See also DLB 176
Arrick, Fran
See Angell, Judie
Arrley, Richmond
See Delany, Samuel R., Jr.
Artaud, Antonin (Marie Joseph)
1896-1948 .... **DC 14; TCLC 3, 36**
See also CA 104; 149; DA3; DAM DRAM;
DFS 22; DLB 258; EW 11; EWL 3;
GFL 1789 to the Present; MTCW 2;
MTFW 2005; RGWL 2, 3
Arthur, Ruth M(abel) 1905-1979 ..... **CLC 12**
See also CA 9-12R; 85-88; CANR 4; CWRI
5; SATA 7, 26
Artsybashev, Mikhail (Petrovich)
1878-1927 .... **TCLC 31**
See also CA 170; DLB 295
Arundel, Honor (Morfydd)
1919-1973 .... **CLC 17**
See also CA 21-22; 41-44R; CAP 2; CLR
35; CWRI 5; SATA 4; SATA-Obit 24
Arzner, Dorothy 1900-1979 .... **CLC 98**
Asch, Sholem 1880-1957 .... **TCLC 3**
See also CA 105; DLB 333; EWL 3; GLL
2; RGHL
Ascham, Roger 1516(?)-1568 .... **LC 101**
See also DLB 236
Ash, Shalom
See Asch, Sholem
Ashbery, John 1927- ... **CLC 2, 3, 4, 6, 9, 13,
15, 25, 41, 77, 125, 221; PC 26**
See also AMWS 3; CA 5-8R; CANR 9, 37,
66, 102, 132, 170; CP 1, 2, 3, 4, 5, 6, 7;
DA3; DAM POET; DLB 5, 165; DLBY
1981; EWL 3; GLL 1; INT CANR-9;
MAL 5; MTCW 1, 2; MTFW 2005; PAB;
PFS 11, 28; RGAL 4; TCLE 1:1; WP
Ashbery, John Lawrence
See Ashbery, John
Ashbridge, Elizabeth 1713-1755 .... **LC 147**
See also DLB 200
Ashdown, Clifford
See Freeman, R(ichard) Austin
Ashe, Gordon
See Creasey, John
Ashton-Warner, Sylvia (Constance)
1908-1984 .... **CLC 19**
See also CA 69-72; 112; CANR 29; CN 1,
2, 3; MTCW 1, 2
Asimov, Isaac 1920-1992 ..... **CLC 1, 3, 9, 19,
26, 76, 92**
See also AAYA 13; BEST 90:2; BPFB 1;
BYA 4, 6, 7, 9; CA 1-4R; 137; CANR 2,
19, 36, 60, 125; CLR 12, 79; CMW 4;
CN 1, 2, 3, 4, 5; CPW; DA3; DAM POP;
DLB 8; DLBY 1992; INT CANR-19;
JRDA; LAIT 5; LMFS 2; MAICYA 1, 2;
MAL 5; MTCW 1, 2; MTFW 2005; NFS
29; RGAL 4; SATA 1, 26, 74; SCFW 1,
2; SFW 4; SSFS 17; TUS; YAW

Askew, Anne 1521(?)-1546 .... **LC 81**
See also DLB 136

Assis, Joaquim Maria Machado de
See Machado de Assis, Joaquim Maria

Astell, Mary 1666-1731 .... **LC 68**
See also DLB 252, 336; FW

Astley, Thea (Beatrice May)
1925-2004 .... **CLC 41**
See also CA 65-68; 229; CANR 11, 43, 78;
CN 1, 2, 3, 4, 5, 6, 7; DLB 289; EWL 3

Astley, William 1855-1911 .... **TCLC 45**
See also DLB 230; RGEL 2

Aston, James
See White, T(erence) H(anbury)

Asturias, Miguel Angel 1899-1974 .... **CLC 3,
8, 13; HLC 1; TCLC 184**
See also CA 25-28; 49-52; CANR 32; CAP
2; CDWLB 3; DA3; DAM MULT; NOV;
DLB 113, 290, 329; EWL 3; HW 1; LAW;
LMFS 2; MTCW 1, 2; RGWL 2, 3; WLIT
1

Atares, Carlos Saura
See Saura (Atares), Carlos

Athanasius c. 295-c. 373 .... **CMLC 48**

Atheling, William
See Pound, Ezra (Weston Loomis)

Atheling, William, Jr.
See Blish, James (Benjamin)

Atherton, Gertrude (Franklin Horn)
1857-1948 .... **TCLC 2**
See also CA 104; 155; DLB 9, 78, 186;
HGG; RGAL 4; SUFW 1; TCWW 1, 2

Atherton, Lucius
See Masters, Edgar Lee

Atkins, Jack
See Harris, Mark

Atkinson, Kate 1951- .... **CLC 99**
See also CA 166; CANR 101, 153; DLB
267

Attaway, William (Alexander)
1911-1986 .... **BLC 1:1; CLC 92**
See also BW 2, 3; CA 143; CANR 82;
DAM MULT; DLB 76; MAL 5

Atticus
See Fleming, Ian; Wilson, (Thomas) Woodrow

Atwood, Margaret 1939- . **CLC 2, 3, 4, 8, 13,
15, 25, 44, 84, 135, 232, 239, 246; PC 8;
SSC 2, 46; WLC 1**
See also AAYA 12, 47; AMWS 13; BEST
89:2; BPFB 1; CA 49-52; CANR 3, 24,
33, 59, 95, 133; CN 2, 3, 4, 5, 6, 7; CP 1,
2, 3, 4, 5, 6, 7; CPW; CWP; DA; DA3;
DAB; DAC; DAM MST, NOV, POET;
DLB 53, 251, 326; EWL 3; EXPN; FL
1:5; FW; GL 2; INT CANR-24; LAIT 5;
MTCW 1, 2; MTFW 2005; NFS 4, 12,
13, 14, 19; PFS 7; RGSF 2; SATA 50,
170; SSFS 3, 13; TCLE 1:1; TWA; WWE
1; YAW

Atwood, Margaret Eleanor
See Atwood, Margaret

Aubigny, Pierre d'
See Mencken, H. L.

Aubin, Penelope 1685-1731(?) .... **LC 9**
See also DLB 39

Auchincloss, Louis 1917- ..... **CLC 4, 6, 9, 18,
45; SSC 22**
See also AMWS 4; CA 1-4R; CANR 6, 29,
55, 87, 130, 168; CN 1, 2, 3, 4, 5, 6, 7;
DAM NOV; DLB 2, 244; DLBY 1980;
EWL 3; INT CANR-29; MAL 5; MTCW
1; RGAL 4

Auchincloss, Louis Stanton
See Auchincloss, Louis

Auden, W(ystan) H(ugh) 1907-1973 . **CLC 1,
2, 3, 4, 6, 9, 11, 14, 43, 123; PC 1, 92;
TCLC 223; WLC 1**
See also AAYA 18; AMWS 2; BRW 7;
BRWR 1; CA 9-12R; 45-48; CANR 5, 61,
105; CDBLB 1914-1945; CP 1, 2; DA;
DA3; DAB; DAC; DAM DRAM, MST,
POET; DLB 10, 20; EWL 3; EXPP; MAL
5; MTCW 1, 2; MTFW 2005; PAB; PFS
1, 3, 4, 10, 27; TUS; WP

Audiberti, Jacques 1899-1965 .... **CLC 38**
See also CA 252; 25-28R; DAM DRAM;
DLB 321; EWL 3

Audubon, John James 1785-1851 . **NCLC 47**
See also AAYA 76; AMWS 16; ANW; DLB
248

Auel, Jean M(arie) 1936- .... **CLC 31, 107**
See also AAYA 7, 51; BEST 90:4; BPFB 1;
CA 103; CANR 21, 64, 115; CPW; DA3;
DAM POP; INT CANR-21; NFS 11;
RHW; SATA 91

Auerbach, Berthold 1812-1882 .... **NCLC 171**
See also DLB 133

Auerbach, Erich 1892-1957 .... **TCLC 43**
See also CA 118; 155; EWL 3

Augier, Emile 1820-1889 .... **NCLC 31**
See also DLB 192; GFL 1789 to the Present

August, John
See De Voto, Bernard (Augustine)

Augustine, St. 354-430 .... **CMLC 6, 95;
WLCS**
See also DA; DA3; DAB; DAC; DAM
MST; DLB 115; EW 1; RGWL 2, 3;
WLIT 8

Aunt Belinda
See Braddon, Mary Elizabeth

Aunt Weedy
See Alcott, Louisa May

Aurelius
See Bourne, Randolph S(illiman)

Aurelius, Marcus 121-180 .... **CMLC 45**
See also AW 2; RGWL 2, 3

Aurobindo, Sri
See Ghose, Aurabinda

Aurobindo Ghose
See Ghose, Aurabinda

Ausonius, Decimus Magnus c. 310-c.
394 .... **CMLC 88**
See also RGWL 2, 3

Austen, Jane 1775-1817 ...... **NCLC 1, 13, 19,
33, 51, 81, 95, 119, 150, 207, 210; WLC
1**
See also AAYA 19; BRW 4; BRWC 1;
BRWR 2; BYA 3; CDBLB 1789-1832;
DA; DA3; DAB; DAC; DAM MST, NOV;
DLB 116; EXPN; FL 1:2; GL 2; LAIT 2;
LATS 1:1; LMFS 1; NFS 1, 14, 18, 20,
21, 28, 29; TEA; WLIT 3; WYAS 1

Auster, Paul 1947- .... **CLC 47, 131, 227**
See also AMWS 12; CA 69-72; CANR 23,
52, 75, 129, 165; CMW 4; CN 5, 6, 7;
DA3; DLB 227; MAL 5; MTCW 2;
MTFW 2005; SUFW 2; TCLE 1:1

Austin, Frank
See Faust, Frederick

Austin, Mary (Hunter) 1868-1934 . **SSC 104;
TCLC 25**
See also ANW; CA 109; 178; DLB 9, 78,
206, 221, 275; FW; TCWW 1, 2

Averroes 1126-1198 .... **CMLC 7, 104**
See also DLB 115

Avicenna 980-1037 .... **CMLC 16, 110**
See also DLB 115

Avison, Margaret 1918-2007 .... **CLC 2, 4, 97**
See also CA 17-20R; CANR 134; CP 1, 2,
3, 4, 5, 6, 7; DAC; DAM POET; DLB 53;
MTCW 1

Avison, Margaret Kirkland
See Avison, Margaret

Axton, David
See Koontz, Dean R.

Ayala, Francisco (de Paula y Garcia Duarte)
1906- .... **SSC 119**
See also CA 208; CWW 2; DLB 322; EWL
3; RGSF 2

Ayckbourn, Alan 1939- ...... **CLC 5, 8, 18, 33,
74; DC 13**
See also BRWS 5; CA 21-24R; CANR 31,
59, 118; CBD; CD 5, 6; DAB; DAM
DRAM; DFS 7; DLB 13, 245; EWL 3;
MTCW 1, 2; MTFW 2005

Aydy, Catherine
See Tennant, Emma

Ayme, Marcel (Andre) 1902-1967 ... **CLC 11;
SSC 41**
See also CA 89-92; CANR 67, 137; CLR
25; DLB 72; EW 12; EWL 3; GFL 1789
to the Present; RGSF 2; RGWL 2, 3;
SATA 91

Ayrton, Michael 1921-1975 .... **CLC 7**
See also CA 5-8R; 61-64; CANR 9, 21

Aytmatov, Chingiz
See Aitmatov, Chingiz

Azorin
See Martinez Ruiz, Jose

Azuela, Mariano 1873-1952 .. **HLC 1; TCLC
3, 145, 217**
See also CA 104; 131; CANR 81; DAM
MULT; EWL 3; HW 1, 2; LAW; MTCW
1, 2; MTFW 2005

Ba, Mariama 1929-1981 ...... **BLC 2:1; BLCS**
See also AFW; BW 2; CA 141; CANR 87;
DNFS 2; WLIT 2

Baastad, Babbis Friis
See Friis-Baastad, Babbis Ellinor

Bab
See Gilbert, W(illiam) S(chwenck)

Babbis, Eleanor
See Friis-Baastad, Babbis Ellinor

Babel, Isaac
See Babel, Isaak (Emmanuilovich)

Babel, Isaak (Emmanuilovich)
1894-1941(?) . **SSC 16, 78; TCLC 2, 13,
171**
See also CA 104; 155; CANR 113; DLB
272; EW 11; EWL 3; MTCW 2; MTFW
2005; RGSF 2; RGWL 2, 3; SSFS 10;
TWA

Babits, Mihaly 1883-1941 .... **TCLC 14**
See also CA 114; CDWLB 4; DLB 215;
EWL 3

Babur 1483-1530 .... **LC 18**

Babylas 1898-1962
See Ghelderode, Michel de

Baca, Jimmy Santiago 1952- . **HLC 1; PC 41**
See also CA 131; CANR 81, 90, 146; CP 6,
7; DAM MULT; DLB 122; HW 1, 2;
LLW; MAL 5

Baca, Jose Santiago
See Baca, Jimmy Santiago

Bacchelli, Riccardo 1891-1985 .... **CLC 19**
See also CA 29-32R; 117; DLB 264; EWL
3

Bach, Richard 1936- .... **CLC 14**
See also AITN 2; BEST 89:2; BPFB 1; BYA
5; CA 9-12R; CANR 18, 93, 151; CPW;
DAM NOV, POP; FANT; MTCW 1;
SATA 13

Bach, Richard David
See Bach, Richard

Bache, Benjamin Franklin
1769-1798 .... **LC 74**
See also DLB 43

Bachelard, Gaston 1884-1962 ...... **TCLC 128**
See also CA 97-100; 89-92; DLB 296; GFL
1789 to the Present

Bachman, Richard
See King, Stephen

Bembo, Pietro 1470-1547 .... **LC 79**
See also RGWL 2, 3
Benary, Margot
See Benary-Isbert, Margot
Benary-Isbert, Margot 1889-1979 .... **CLC 12**
See also CA 5-8R; 89-92; CANR 4, 72;
CLR 12; MAICYA 1, 2; SATA 2; SATA-
Obit 21
Benavente (y Martinez), Jacinto
1866-1954 .... **DC 26; HLCS 1; TCLC 3**
See also CA 106; 131; CANR 81; DAM
DRAM, MULT; DLB 329; EWL 3; GLL
2; HW 1, 2; MTCW 1, 2
Benchley, Peter 1940-2006 .... **CLC 4, 8**
See also AAYA 14; AITN 2; BPFB 1; CA
17-20R; 248; CANR 12, 35, 66, 115;
CPW; DAM NOV, POP; HGG; MTCW 1,
2; MTFW 2005; SATA 3, 89, 164
Benchley, Peter Bradford
See Benchley, Peter
Benchley, Robert (Charles)
1889-1945 .... **TCLC 1, 55**
See also CA 105; 153; DLB 11; MAL 5;
RGAL 4
Benda, Julien 1867-1956 .... **TCLC 60**
See also CA 120; 154; GFL 1789 to the
Present
Benedict, Ruth 1887-1948 .... **TCLC 60**
See also CA 158; CANR 146; DLB 246
Benedict, Ruth Fulton
See Benedict, Ruth
Benedikt, Michael 1935- .... **CLC 4, 14**
See also CA 13-16R; CANR 7; CP 1, 2, 3,
4, 5, 6, 7; DLB 5
Benet, Juan 1927-1993 .... **CLC 28**
See also CA 143; EWL 3
Benet, Stephen Vincent 1898-1943 ..... **PC 64;
SSC 10, 86; TCLC 7**
See also AMWS 11; CA 104; 152; DA3;
DAM POET; DLB 4, 48, 102, 249, 284;
DLBY 1997; EWL 3; HGG; MAL 5;
MTCW 2; MTFW 2005; RGAL 4; RGSF
2; SSFS 22; SUFW; WP; YABC 1
Benet, William Rose 1886-1950 ..... **TCLC 28**
See also CA 118; 152; DAM POET; DLB
45; RGAL 4
Benford, Gregory 1941- .... **CLC 52**
See also BPFB 1; CA 69-72, 175, 268;
CAAE 175, 268; CAAS 27; CANR 12,
24, 49, 95, 134; CN 7; CSW; DLBY 1982;
MTFW 2005; SCFW 2; SFW 4
Benford, Gregory Albert
See Benford, Gregory
Bengtsson, Frans (Gunnar)
1894-1954 .... **TCLC 48**
See also CA 170; EWL 3
Benjamin, David
See Slavitt, David R.
Benjamin, Lois
See Gould, Lois
Benjamin, Walter 1892-1940 .... **TCLC 39**
See also CA 164; CANR 181; DLB 242;
EW 11; EWL 3
Ben Jelloun, Tahar 1944- .... **CLC 180**
See also CA 135, 162; CANR 100, 166;
CWW 2; EWL 3; RGWL 3; WLIT 2
Benn, Gottfried 1886-1956 .. **PC 35; TCLC 3**
See also CA 106; 153; DLB 56; EWL 3;
RGWL 2, 3
Bennett, Alan 1934- .... **CLC 45, 77**
See also BRWS 8; CA 103; CANR 35, 55,
106, 157; CBD; CD 5, 6; DAB; DAM
MST; DLB 310; MTCW 1, 2; MTFW
2005
Bennett, (Enoch) Arnold
1867-1931 .... **TCLC 5, 20, 197**
See also BRW 6; CA 106; 155; CDBLB
1890-1914; DLB 10, 34, 98, 135; EWL 3;
MTCW 2

Bennett, Elizabeth
See Mitchell, Margaret (Munnerlyn)
Bennett, George Harold 1930- .... **CLC 5**
See also BW 1; CA 97-100; CAAS 13;
CANR 87; DLB 33
Bennett, Gwendolyn B. 1902-1981 .... **HR 1:2**
See also BW 1; CA 125; DLB 51; WP
Bennett, Hal
See Bennett, George Harold
Bennett, Jay 1912- .... **CLC 35**
See also AAYA 10, 73; CA 69-72; CANR
11, 42, 79; JRDA; SAAS 4; SATA 41, 87;
SATA-Brief 27; WYA; YAW
Bennett, Louise 1919-2006 .... **BLC 1:1; CLC
28**
See also BW 2, 3; CA 151; 252; CDWLB
3; CP 1, 2, 3, 4, 5, 6, 7; DAM MULT;
DLB 117; EWL 3
Bennett, Louise Simone
See Bennett, Louise
Bennett-Coverley, Louise
See Bennett, Louise
Benoit de Sainte-Maure fl. 12th cent.
- .... **CMLC 90**
Benson, A. C. 1862-1925 .... **TCLC 123**
See also DLB 98
Benson, E(dward) F(rederic)
1867-1940 .... **TCLC 27**
See also CA 114; 157; DLB 135, 153;
HGG; SUFW 1
Benson, Jackson J. 1930- .... **CLC 34**
See also CA 25-28R; DLB 111
Benson, Sally 1900-1972 .... **CLC 17**
See also CA 19-20; 37-40R; CAP 1; SATA
1, 35; SATA-Obit 27
Benson, Stella 1892-1933 .... **TCLC 17**
See also CA 117; 154, 155; DLB 36, 162;
FANT; TEA
Bentham, Jeremy 1748-1832 .... **NCLC 38**
See also DLB 107, 158, 252
Bentley, E(dmund) C(lerihew)
1875-1956 .... **TCLC 12**
See also CA 108; 232; DLB 70; MSW
Bentley, Eric 1916- .... **CLC 24**
See also CA 5-8R; CAD; CANR 6, 67;
CBD; CD 5, 6; INT CANR-6
Bentley, Eric Russell
See Bentley, Eric
ben Uzair, Salem
See Horne, Richard Henry Hengist
Beolco, Angelo 1496-1542 .... **LC 139**
Beranger, Pierre Jean de
1780-1857 .... **NCLC 34**
Berdyaev, Nicolas
See Berdyaev, Nikolai (Aleksandrovich)
Berdyaev, Nikolai (Aleksandrovich)
1874-1948 .... **TCLC 67**
See also CA 120; 157
Berdyayev, Nikolai (Aleksandrovich)
See Berdyaev, Nikolai (Aleksandrovich)
Berendt, John 1939- .... **CLC 86**
See also CA 146; CANR 75, 83, 151
Berendt, John Lawrence
See Berendt, John
Beresford, J(ohn) D(avys)
1873-1947 .... **TCLC 81**
See also CA 112; 155; DLB 162, 178, 197;
SFW 4; SUFW 1
Bergelson, David (Rafailovich)
1884-1952 .... **TCLC 81**
See also CA 220; DLB 333; EWL 3
Bergelson, Dovid
See Bergelson, David (Rafailovich)
Berger, Colonel
See Malraux, (Georges-)Andre

Berger, John 1926- .... **CLC 2, 19**
See also BRWS 4; CA 81-84; CANR 51,
78, 117, 163; CN 1, 2, 3, 4, 5, 6, 7; DLB
14, 207, 319, 326
Berger, John Peter
See Berger, John
Berger, Melvin H. 1927- .... **CLC 12**
See also CA 5-8R; CANR 4, 142; CLR 32;
SAAS 2; SATA 5, 88, 158; SATA-Essay
124
Berger, Thomas 1924- .... **CLC 3, 5, 8, 11, 18,
38, 259**
See also BPFB 1; CA 1-4R; CANR 5, 28,
51, 128; CN 1, 2, 3, 4, 5, 6, 7; DAM
NOV; DLB 2; DLBY 1980; EWL 3;
FANT; INT CANR-28; MAL 5; MTCW
1, 2; MTFW 2005; RHW; TCLE 1:1;
TCWW 1, 2
Bergman, Ernst Ingmar
See Bergman, Ingmar
Bergman, Ingmar 1918-2007 ..... **CLC 16, 72,
210**
See also AAYA 61; CA 81-84; 262; CANR
33, 70; CWW 2; DLB 257; MTCW 2;
MTFW 2005
Bergson, Henri(-Louis) 1859-1941 . **TCLC 32**
See also CA 164; DLB 329; EW 8; EWL 3;
GFL 1789 to the Present
Bergstein, Eleanor 1938- .... **CLC 4**
See also CA 53-56; CANR 5
Berkeley, George 1685-1753 .... **LC 65**
See also DLB 31, 101, 252
Berkoff, Steven 1937- .... **CLC 56**
See also CA 104; CANR 72; CBD; CD 5, 6
Berlin, Isaiah 1909-1997 .... **TCLC 105**
See also CA 85-88; 162
Bermant, Chaim (Icyk) 1929-1998 ... **CLC 40**
See also CA 57-60; CANR 6, 31, 57, 105;
CN 2, 3, 4, 5, 6
Bern, Victoria
See Fisher, M(ary) F(rances) K(ennedy)
Bernanos, (Paul Louis) Georges
1888-1948 .... **TCLC 3**
See also CA 104; 130; CANR 94; DLB 72;
EWL 3; GFL 1789 to the Present; RGWL
2, 3
Bernard, April 1956- .... **CLC 59**
See also CA 131; CANR 144
Bernard, Mary Ann
See Soderbergh, Steven
Bernard of Clairvaux 1090-1153 .. **CMLC 71**
See also DLB 208
Bernard Silvestris fl. c. 1130-fl. c.
1160 .... **CMLC 87**
See also DLB 208
Bernart de Ventadorn c. 1130-c.
1190 .... **CMLC 98**
Berne, Victoria
See Fisher, M(ary) F(rances) K(ennedy)
Bernhard, Thomas 1931-1989 ..... **CLC 3, 32,
61; DC 14; TCLC 165**
See also CA 85-88; 127; CANR 32, 57; CD-
WLB 2; DLB 85, 124; EWL 3; MTCW 1;
RGHL; RGWL 2, 3
Bernhardt, Sarah (Henriette Rosine)
1844-1923 .... **TCLC 75**
See also CA 157
Bernstein, Charles 1950- .... **CLC 142**,
See also CA 129; CAAS 24; CANR 90; CP
4, 5, 6, 7; DLB 169
Bernstein, Ingrid
See Kirsch, Sarah
Beroul fl. c. 12th cent. - .... **CMLC 75**
Berriault, Gina 1926-1999 .... **CLC 54, 109;
SSC 30**
See also CA 116; 129; 185; CANR 66; DLB
130; SSFS 7,11

Bonham, Frank 1914-1989 .... **CLC 12**
See also AAYA 1, 70; BYA 1, 3; CA 9-12R;
CANR 4, 36; JRDA; MAICYA 1, 2;
SAAS 3; SATA 1, 49; SATA-Obit 62;
TCWW 1, 2; YAW

Bonnefoy, Yves 1923- .... **CLC 9, 15, 58; PC 58**
See also CA 85-88; CANR 33, 75, 97, 136;
CWW 2; DAM MST, POET; DLB 258;
EWL 3; GFL 1789 to the Present; MTCW
1, 2; MTFW 2005

Bonner, Marita
See Occomy, Marita (Odette) Bonner

Bonnin, Gertrude 1876-1938 .... **NNAL**
See also CA 150; DAM MULT; DLB 175

Bontemps, Arna(ud Wendell)
1902-1973 ..... **BLC 1:1; CLC 1, 18; HR
1:2**
See also BW 1; CA 1-4R; 41-44R; CANR
4, 35; CLR 6; CP 1; CWRI 5; DA3; DAM
MULT, NOV, POET; DLB 48, 51; JRDA;
MAICYA 1, 2; MAL 5; MTCW 1, 2;
SATA 2, 44; SATA-Obit 24; WCH; WP

Boot, William
See Stoppard, Tom

Booth, Irwin
See Hoch, Edward D.

Booth, Martin 1944-2004 .... **CLC 13**
See also CA 93-96, 188; 223; CAAE 188;
CAAS 2; CANR 92; CP 1, 2, 3, 4

Booth, Philip 1925-2007 .... **CLC 23**
See also CA 5-8R; 262; CANR 5, 88; CP 1,
2, 3, 4, 5, 6, 7; DLBY 1982

Booth, Philip Edmund
See Booth, Philip

Booth, Wayne C. 1921-2005 .... **CLC 24**
See also CA 1-4R; 244; CAAS 5; CANR 3,
43, 117; DLB 67

Booth, Wayne Clayson
See Booth, Wayne C.

Borchert, Wolfgang 1921-1947 .... **TCLC 5**
See also CA 104; 188; DLB 69, 124; EWL
3

Borel, Petrus 1809-1859 .... **NCLC 41**
See also DLB 119; GFL 1789 to the Present

Borges, Jorge Luis 1899-1986 ... **CLC 1, 2, 3,
4, 6, 8, 9, 10, 13, 19, 44, 48, 83; HLC 1;
PC 22, 32; SSC 4, 41, 100; TCLC 109;
WLC 1**
See also AAYA 26; BPFB 1; CA 21-24R;
CANR 19, 33, 75, 105, 133; CDWLB 3;
DA; DA3; DAB; DAC; DAM MST,
MULT; DLB 113, 283; DLBY 1986;
DNFS 1, 2; EWL 3; HW 1, 2; LAW;
LMFS 2; MSW; MTCW 1, 2; MTFW
2005; PFS 27; RGHL; RGSF 2; RGWL
2, 3; SFW 4; SSFS 17; TWA; WLIT 1

Borne, Ludwig 1786-1837 .... **NCLC 193**
See also DLB 90

Borowski, Tadeusz 1922-1951 .... **SSC 48;
TCLC 9**
See also CA 106; 154; CDWLB 4; DLB
215; EWL 3; RGHL; RGSF 2; RGWL 3;
SSFS 13

Borrow, George (Henry)
1803-1881 .... **NCLC 9**
See also BRWS 12; DLB 21, 55, 166

Bosch (Gavino), Juan 1909-2001 ..... **HLCS 1**
See also CA 151; 204; DAM MST, MULT;
DLB 145; HW 1, 2

Bosman, Herman Charles
1905-1951 .... **TCLC 49**
See also CA 160; DLB 225; RGSF 2

Bosschere, Jean de 1878(?)-1953 ... **TCLC 19**
See also CA 115; 186

Boswell, James 1740-1795 ... **LC 4, 50; WLC
1**
See also BRW 3; CDBLB 1660-1789; DA;
DAB; DAC; DAM MST; DLB 104, 142;
TEA; WLIT 3

Boto, Eza
See Biyidi, Alexandre

Bottomley, Gordon 1874-1948 ..... **TCLC 107**
See also CA 120; 192; DLB 10

Bottoms, David 1949- .... **CLC 53**
See also CA 105; CANR 22; CSW; DLB
120; DLBY 1983

Boucicault, Dion 1820-1890 .... **NCLC 41**
See also DLB 344

Boucolon, Maryse
See Conde, Maryse

Bourcicault, Dion
See Boucicault, Dion

Bourdieu, Pierre 1930-2002 .... **CLC 198**
See also CA 130; 204

Bourget, Paul (Charles Joseph)
1852-1935 .... **TCLC 12**
See also CA 107; 196; DLB 123; GFL 1789
to the Present

Bourjaily, Vance (Nye) 1922- ...... **CLC 8, 62**
See also CA 1-4R; CAAS 1; CANR 2, 72;
CN 1, 2, 3, 4, 5, 6, 7; DLB 2, 143; MAL
5

Bourne, Randolph S(illiman)
1886-1918 .... **TCLC 16**
See also AMW; CA 117; 155; DLB 63;
MAL 5

Boursiquot, Dionysius
See Boucicault, Dion

Bova, Ben 1932- .... **CLC 45**
See also AAYA 16; CA 5-8R; CAAS 18;
CANR 11, 56, 94, 111, 157; CLR 3, 96;
DLBY 1981; INT CANR-11; MAICYA 1,
2; MTCW 1; SATA 6, 68, 133; SFW 4

Bova, Benjamin William
See Bova, Ben

Bowen, Elizabeth (Dorothea Cole)
1899-1973 . **CLC 1, 3, 6, 11, 15, 22, 118;
SSC 3, 28, 66; TCLC 148**
See also BRWS 2; CA 17-18; 41-44R;
CANR 35, 105; CAP 2; CDBLB 1945-
1960; CN 1; DA3; DAM NOV; DLB 15,
162; EWL 3; EXPS; FW; HGG; MTCW
1, 2; MTFW 2005; NFS 13; RGSF 2;
SSFS 5, 22; SUFW 1; TEA; WLIT 4

Bowering, George 1935- .... **CLC 15, 47**
See also CA 21-24R; CAAS 16; CANR 10;
CN 7; CP 1, 2, 3, 4, 5, 6, 7; DLB 53

Bowering, Marilyn R(uthe) 1949- .... **CLC 32**
See also CA 101; CANR 49; CP 4, 5, 6, 7;
CWP; DLB 334

Bowers, Edgar 1924-2000 .... **CLC 9**
See also CA 5-8R; 188; CANR 24; CP 1, 2,
3, 4, 5, 6, 7; CSW; DLB 5

Bowers, Mrs. J. Milton 1842-1914
See Bierce, Ambrose (Gwinett)

Bowie, David
See Jones, David Robert

Bowles, Jane (Sydney) 1917-1973 ..... **CLC 3,
68**
See also CA 19-20; 41-44R; CAP 2; CN 1;
EWL 3; MAL 5

Bowles, Jane Auer
See Bowles, Jane (Sydney)

Bowles, Paul 1910-1999 ..... **CLC 1, 2, 19, 53;
SSC 3, 98; TCLC 209**
See also AMWS 4; CA 1-4R; 186; CAAS
1; CANR 1, 19, 50, 75; CN 1, 2, 3, 4, 5,
6; DA3; DLB 5, 6, 218; EWL 3; MAL 5;
MTCW 1, 2; MTFW 2005; RGAL 4;
SSFS 17

Bowles, William Lisle 1762-1850 . **NCLC 103**
See also DLB 93

Box, Edgar
See Vidal, Gore

Boyd, James 1888-1944 .... **TCLC 115**
See also CA 186; DLB 9; DLBD 16; RGAL
4; RHW

Boyd, Nancy
See Millay, Edna St. Vincent

Boyd, Thomas (Alexander)
1898-1935 .... **TCLC 111**
See also CA 111; 183; DLB 9; DLBD 16,
316

Boyd, William 1952- .... **CLC 28, 53, 70**
See also CA 114; 120; CANR 51, 71, 131,
174; CN 4, 5, 6, 7; DLB 231

Boyesen, Hjalmar Hjorth
1848-1895 .... **NCLC 135**
See also DLB 12, 71; DLBD 13; RGAL 4

Boyle, Kay 1902-1992 .... **CLC 1, 5, 19, 58,
121; SSC 5, 102**
See also CA 13-16R; 140; CAAS 1; CANR
29, 61, 110; CN 1, 2, 3, 4, 5; CP 1, 2, 3,
4, 5; DLB 4, 9, 48, 86; DLBY 1993; EWL
3; MAL 5; MTCW 1, 2; MTFW 2005;
RGAL 4; RGSF 2; SSFS 10, 13, 14

Boyle, Mark
See Kienzle, William X.

Boyle, Patrick 1905-1982 .... **CLC 19**
See also CA 127

Boyle, T. C.
See Boyle, T. Coraghessan

Boyle, T. Coraghessan 1948- ..... **CLC 36, 55,
90; SSC 16**
See also AAYA 47; AMWS 8; BEST 90:4;
BPFB 1; CA 120; CANR 44, 76, 89, 132;
CN 6, 7; CPW; DA3; DAM POP; DLB
218, 278; DLBY 1986; EWL 3; MAL 5;
MTCW 2; MTFW 2005; SSFS 13, 19

Boz
See Dickens, Charles (John Huffam)

Brackenridge, Hugh Henry
1748-1816 .... **NCLC 7**
See also DLB 11, 37; RGAL 4

Bradbury, Edward P.
See Moorcock, Michael

Bradbury, Malcolm (Stanley)
1932-2000 .... **CLC 32, 61**
See also CA 1-4R; CANR 1, 33, 91, 98,
137; CN 1, 2, 3, 4, 5, 6, 7; CP 1; DA3;
DAM NOV; DLB 14, 207; EWL 3;
MTCW 1, 2; MTFW 2005

Bradbury, Ray 1920- ... **CLC 1, 3, 10, 15, 42,
98, 235; SSC 29, 53; WLC 1**
See also AAYA 15; AITN 1, 2; AMWS 4;
BPFB 1; BYA 4, 5, 11; CA 1-4R; CANR
2, 30, 75, 125, 186; CDALB 1968-1988;
CN 1, 2, 3, 4, 5, 6, 7; CPW; DA; DA3;
DAB; DAC; DAM MST, NOV, POP;
DLB 2, 8; EXPN; EXPS; HGG; LAIT 3,
5; LATS 1:2; LMFS 2; MAL 5; MTCW
1, 2; MTFW 2005; NFS 1, 22, 29; RGAL
4; RGSF 2; SATA 11, 64, 123; SCFW 1,
2; SFW 4; SSFS 1, 20; SUFW 1, 2; TUS;
YAW

Bradbury, Ray Douglas
See Bradbury, Ray

Braddon, Mary Elizabeth
1837-1915 .... **TCLC 111**
See also BRWS 8; CA 108; 179; CMW 4;
DLB 18, 70, 156; HGG

Bradfield, Scott 1955- .... **SSC 65**
See also CA 147; CANR 90; HGG; SUFW
2

Bradfield, Scott Michael
See Bradfield, Scott

Bradford, Gamaliel 1863-1932 .... **TCLC 36**
See also CA 160; DLB 17

Bradford, William 1590-1657 .... **LC 64**
See also DLB 24, 30; RGAL 4

Bradley, David, Jr. 1950- ...... **BLC 1:1; CLC
23, 118**
See also BW 1, 3; CA 104; CANR 26, 81;
CN 4, 5, 6, 7; DAM MULT; DLB 33

Bradley, David Henry, Jr.
See Bradley, David, Jr.

Bradley, John Ed 1958- .... **CLC 55**
See also CA 139; CANR 99; CN 6, 7; CSW
Bradley, John Edmund, Jr.
See Bradley, John Ed
Bradley, Marion Zimmer
1930-1999 .... **CLC 30**
See also AAYA 40; BPFB 1; CA 57-60; 185;
CAAS 10; CANR 7, 31, 51, 75, 107;
CPW; DA3; DAM POP; DLB 8; FANT;
FW; GLL 1; MTCW 1, 2; MTFW 2005;
SATA 90, 139; SATA-Obit 116; SFW 4;
SUFW 2; YAW
Bradshaw, John 1933- .... **CLC 70**
See also CA 138; CANR 61
Bradstreet, Anne 1612(?)-1672 .... **LC 4, 30,
130; PC 10**
See also AMWS 1; CDALB 1640-1865;
DA; DA3; DAC; DAM MST, POET; DLB
24; EXPP; FW; PFS 6; RGAL 4; TUS;
WP
Brady, Joan 1939- .... **CLC 86**
See also CA 141
Bragg, Melvyn 1939- .... **CLC 10**
See also BEST 89:3; CA 57-60; CANR 10,
48, 89, 158; CN 1, 2, 3, 4, 5, 6, 7; DLB
14, 271; RHW
Brahe, Tycho 1546-1601 .... **LC 45**
See also DLB 300
Braine, John (Gerard) 1922-1986 . **CLC 1, 3,
41**
See also CA 1-4R; 120; CANR 1, 33; CD-
BLB 1945-1960; CN 1, 2, 3, 4; DLB 15;
DLBY 1986; EWL 3; MTCW 1
Braithwaite, William Stanley (Beaumont)
1878-1962 ...... **BLC 1:1; HR 1:2; PC 52**
See also BW 1; CA 125; DAM MULT; DLB
50, 54; MAL 5
Bramah, Ernest 1868-1942 .... **TCLC 72**
See also CA 156; CMW 4; DLB 70; FANT
Brammer, Billy Lee
See Brammer, William
Brammer, William 1929-1978 .... **CLC 31**
See also CA 235; 77-80
Brancati, Vitaliano 1907-1954 .... **TCLC 12**
See also CA 109; DLB 264; EWL 3
Brancato, Robin F(idler) 1936- .... **CLC 35**
See also AAYA 9, 68; BYA 6; CA 69-72;
CANR 11, 45; CLR 32; JRDA; MAICYA
2; MAICYAS 1; SAAS 9; SATA 97;
WYA; YAW
Brand, Dionne 1953- .... **CLC 192**
See also BW 2; CA 143; CANR 143; CWP;
DLB 334
Brand, Max
See Faust, Frederick
Brand, Millen 1906-1980 .... **CLC 7**
See also CA 21-24R; 97-100; CANR 72
Branden, Barbara 1929- .... **CLC 44**
See also CA 148
Brandes, Georg (Morris Cohen)
1842-1927 .... **TCLC 10**
See also CA 105; 189; DLB 300
Brandys, Kazimierz 1916-2000 .... **CLC 62**
See also CA 239; EWL 3
Branley, Franklyn M(ansfield)
1915-2002 .... **CLC 21**
See also CA 33-36R; 207; CANR 14, 39;
CLR 13; MAICYA 1, 2; SAAS 16; SATA
4, 68, 136
Brant, Beth (E.) 1941- .... **NNAL**
See also CA 144; FW
Brant, Sebastian 1457-1521 .... **LC 112**
See also DLB 179; RGWL 2, 3
Brathwaite, Edward Kamau
1930- ..... **BLC 2:1; BLCS; CLC 11; PC
56**
See also BRWS 12; BW 2, 3; CA 25-28R;
CANR 11, 26, 47, 107; CDWLB 3; CP 1,
2, 3, 4, 5, 6, 7; DAM POET; DLB 125;
EWL 3

Brathwaite, Kamau
See Brathwaite, Edward Kamau
Brautigan, Richard (Gary)
1935-1984 .... **CLC 1, 3, 5, 9, 12, 34, 42;
PC 94; TCLC 133**
See also BPFB 1; CA 53-56; 113; CANR
34; CN 1, 2, 3; CP 1, 2, 3, 4; DA3; DAM
NOV; DLB 2, 5, 206; DLBY 1980, 1984;
FANT; MAL 5; MTCW 1; RGAL 4;
SATA 56
Brave Bird, Mary
See Crow Dog, Mary
Braverman, Kate 1950- .... **CLC 67**
See also CA 89-92; CANR 141; DLB 335
Brecht, (Eugen) Bertolt (Friedrich)
1898-1956 ..... **DC 3; TCLC 1, 6, 13, 35,
169; WLC 1**
See also CA 104; 133; CANR 62; CDWLB
2; DA; DA3; DAB; DAC; DAM DRAM,
MST; DFS 4, 5, 9; DLB 56, 124; EW 11;
EWL 3; IDTP; MTCW 1, 2; MTFW 2005;
RGHL; RGWL 2, 3; TWA
Brecht, Eugen Berthold Friedrich
See Brecht, (Eugen) Bertolt (Friedrich)
Bremer, Fredrika 1801-1865 .... **NCLC 11**
See also DLB 254
Brennan, Christopher John
1870-1932 .... **TCLC 17**
See also CA 117; 188; DLB 230; EWL 3
Brennan, Maeve 1917-1993 ... **CLC 5; TCLC
124**
See also CA 81-84; CANR 72, 100
Brenner, Jozef 1887-1919 .... **TCLC 13**
See also CA 111; 240
Brent, Linda
See Jacobs, Harriet A(nn)
Brentano, Clemens (Maria)
1778-1842 .... **NCLC 1, 191; SSC 115**
See also DLB 90; RGWL 2, 3
Brent of Bin Bin
See Franklin, (Stella Maria Sarah) Miles
(Lampe)
Brenton, Howard 1942- .... **CLC 31**
See also CA 69-72; CANR 33, 67; CBD;
CD 5, 6; DLB 13; MTCW 1
Breslin, James
See Breslin, Jimmy
Breslin, Jimmy 1930- .... **CLC 4, 43**
See also CA 73-76; CANR 31, 75, 139, 187;
DAM NOV; DLB 185; MTCW 2; MTFW
2005
Bresson, Robert 1901(?)-1999 .... **CLC 16**
See also CA 110; 187; CANR 49
Breton, Andre 1896-1966 .. **CLC 2, 9, 15, 54;
PC 15**
See also CA 19-20; 25-28R; CANR 40, 60;
CAP 2; DLB 65, 258; EW 11; EWL 3;
GFL 1789 to the Present; LMFS 2;
MTCW 1, 2; MTFW 2005; RGWL 2, 3;
TWA; WP
Breton, Nicholas c. 1554-c. 1626 .... **LC 133**
See also DLB 136
Breytenbach, Breyten 1939(?)- .. **CLC 23, 37,
126**
See also CA 113; 129; CANR 61, 122;
CWW 2; DAM POET; DLB 225; EWL 3
Bridgers, Sue Ellen 1942- .... **CLC 26**
See also AAYA 8, 49; BYA 7, 8; CA 65-68;
CANR 11, 36; CLR 18; DLB 52; JRDA;
MAICYA 1, 2; SAAS 1; SATA 22, 90;
SATA-Essay 109; WYA; YAW
Bridges, Robert (Seymour)
1844-1930 .... **PC 28; TCLC 1**
See also BRW 6; CA 104; 152; CDBLB
1890-1914; DAM POET; DLB 19, 98
Bridie, James
See Mavor, Osborne Henry

Brin, David 1950- .... **CLC 34**
See also AAYA 21; CA 102; CANR 24, 70,
125, 127; INT CANR-24; SATA 65;
SCFW 2; SFW 4
Brink, Andre 1935- .... **CLC 18, 36, 106**
See also AFW; BRWS 6; CA 104; CANR
39, 62, 109, 133, 182; CN 4, 5, 6, 7; DLB
225; EWL 3; INT CA-103; LATS 1:2;
MTCW 1, 2; MTFW 2005; WLIT 2
Brinsmead, H. F(ay)
See Brinsmead, H(esba) F(ay)
Brinsmead, H. F.
See Brinsmead, H(esba) F(ay)
Brinsmead, H(esba) F(ay) 1922- ...... **CLC 21**
See also CA 21-24R; CANR 10; CLR 47;
CWRI 5; MAICYA 1, 2; SAAS 5; SATA
18, 78
Brittain, Vera (Mary) 1893(?)-1970 . **CLC 23**
See also BRWS 10; CA 13-16; 25-28R;
CANR 58; CAP 1; DLB 191; FW; MTCW
1, 2
Broch, Hermann 1886-1951 ... **TCLC 20, 204**
See also CA 117; 211; CDWLB 2; DLB 85,
124; EW 10; EWL 3; RGWL 2, 3
Brock, Rose
See Hansen, Joseph
Brod, Max 1884-1968 .... **TCLC 115**
See also CA 5-8R; 25-28R; CANR 7; DLB
81; EWL 3
Brodkey, Harold (Roy) 1930-1996 .. **CLC 56;
TCLC 123**
See also CA 111; 151; CANR 71; CN 4, 5,
6; DLB 130
Brodsky, Iosif Alexandrovich 1940-1996
See Brodsky, Joseph
See also AAYA 71; AITN 1; AMWS 8; CA
41-44R; 151; CANR 37, 106; CWW 2;
DA3; DAM POET; DLB 285, 329; EWL
3; MTCW 1, 2; MTFW 2005; RGWL 2, 3
Brodsky, Joseph . **CLC 4, 6, 13, 36, 100; PC
9; TCLC 219**
See Brodsky, Iosif Alexandrovich
Brodsky, Michael 1948- .... **CLC 19**
See also CA 102; CANR 18, 41, 58, 147;
DLB 244
Brodsky, Michael Mark
See Brodsky, Michael
Brodzki, Bella .... **CLC 65**
Brome, Richard 1590(?)-1652 .... **LC 61**
See also BRWS 10; DLB 58
Bromell, Henry 1947- .... **CLC 5**
See also CA 53-56; CANR 9, 115, 116
Bromfield, Louis (Brucker)
1896-1956 .... **TCLC 11**
See also CA 107; 155; DLB 4, 9, 86; RGAL
4; RHW
Broner, E(sther) M(asserman)
1930- .... **CLC 19**
See also CA 17-20R; CANR 8, 25, 72; CN
4, 5, 6; DLB 28
Bronk, William (M.) 1918-1999 .... **CLC 10**
See also CA 89-92; 177; CANR 23; CP 3,
4, 5, 6, 7; DLB 165
Bronstein, Lev Davidovich
See Trotsky, Leon
Bronte, Anne
See Bronte, Anne
Bronte, Anne 1820-1849 ..... **NCLC 4, 71, 102**
See also BRW 5; BRWR 1; DA3; DLB 21,
199, 340; NFS 26; TEA
Bronte, (Patrick) Branwell
1817-1848 .... **NCLC 109**
See also DLB 340
Bronte, Charlotte
See Bronte, Charlotte

2; MTCW 1, 2; MTFW 2005; RGSF 2; SATA 66; SATA-Obit 70; SFW 4; SSFS 4, 12; SUFW 2; WLIT 4

Carter, Angela Olive
See Carter, Angela

Carter, Martin (Wylde) 1927- .... **BLC 2:1**
See also BW 2; CA 102; CANR 42; CD-WLB 3; CP 1, 2, 3, 4, 5, 6; DLB 117; EWL 3

Carter, Nick
See Smith, Martin Cruz

Carter, Nick
See Smith, Martin Cruz

Carver, Raymond 1938-1988 ..... **CLC 22, 36, 53, 55, 126; PC 54; SSC 8, 51, 104**
See also AAYA 44; AMWS 3; BPFB 1; CA 33-36R; 126; CANR 17, 34, 61, 103; CN 4; CPW; DA3; DAM NOV; DLB 130; DLBY 1984, 1988; EWL 3; MAL 5; MTCW 1, 2; MTFW 2005; PFS 17; RGAL 4; RGSF 2; SSFS 3, 6, 12, 13, 23; TCLE 1:1; TCWW 2; TUS

Cary, Elizabeth, Lady Falkland
1585-1639 .... **LC 30, 141**

Cary, (Arthur) Joyce (Lunel)
1888-1957 .... **TCLC 1, 29, 196**
See also BRW 7; CA 104; 164; CDBLB 1914-1945; DLB 15, 100; EWL 3; MTCW 2; RGEL 2; TEA

Casal, Julian del 1863-1893 .... **NCLC 131**
See also DLB 283; LAW

Casanova, Giacomo
See Casanova de Seingalt, Giovanni Jacopo

Casanova, Giovanni Giacomo
See Casanova de Seingalt, Giovanni Jacopo

Casanova de Seingalt, Giovanni Jacopo
1725-1798 .... **LC 13, 151**
See also WLIT 7

Casares, Adolfo Bioy
See Bioy Casares, Adolfo

Casas, Bartolome de las 1474-1566
See Las Casas, Bartolome de

Case, John
See Hougan, Carolyn

Casely-Hayford, J(oseph) E(phraim)
1866-1903 .... **BLC 1:1; TCLC 24**
See also BW 2; CA 123; 152; DAM MULT

Casey, John (Dudley) 1939- .... **CLC 59**
See also BEST 90:2; CA 69-72; CANR 23, 100

Casey, Michael 1947- .... **CLC 2**
See also CA 65-68; CANR 109; CP 2, 3; DLB 5

Casey, Patrick
See Thurman, Wallace (Henry)

Casey, Warren (Peter) 1935-1988 .... **CLC 12**
See also CA 101; 127; INT CA-101

Casona, Alejandro
See Alvarez, Alejandro Rodriguez

Cassavetes, John 1929-1989 .... **CLC 20**
See also CA 85-88; 127; CANR 82

Cassian, Nina 1924- .... **PC 17**
See also CWP; CWW 2

Cassill, R(onald) V(erlin)
1919-2002 .... **CLC 4, 23**
See also CA 9-12R; 208; CAAS 1; CANR 7, 45; CN 1, 2, 3, 4, 5, 6, 7; DLB 6, 218; DLBY 2002

Cassiodorus, Flavius Magnus c. 490(?)-c. 583(?) .... **CMLC 43**

Cassirer, Ernst 1874-1945 .... **TCLC 61**
See also CA 157

Cassity, (Allen) Turner 1929- .... **CLC 6, 42**
See also CA 17-20R; 223; CAAE 223; CAAS 8; CANR 11; CSW; DLB 105

Cassius Dio c. 155-c. 229 .... **CMLC 99**
See also DLB 176

Castaneda, Carlos (Cesar Aranha)
1931(?)-1998 .... **CLC 12, 119**
See also CA 25-28R; CANR 32, 66, 105; DNFS 1; HW 1; MTCW 1

Castedo, Elena 1937- .... **CLC 65**
See also CA 132

Castedo-Ellerman, Elena
See Castedo, Elena

Castellanos, Rosario 1925-1974 .... **CLC 66; HLC 1; SSC 39, 68**
See also CA 131; 53-56; CANR 58; CD-WLB 3; DAM MULT; DLB 113, 290; EWL 3; FW; HW 1; LAW; MTCW 2; MTFW 2005; RGSF 2; RGWL 2, 3

Castelvetro, Lodovico 1505-1571 .... **LC 12**

Castiglione, Baldassare 1478-1529 ..... **LC 12, 165**
See also EW 2; LMFS 1; RGWL 2, 3; WLIT 7

Castiglione, Baldesar
See Castiglione, Baldassare

Castillo, Ana 1953- .... **CLC 151, 279**
See also AAYA 42; CA 131; CANR 51, 86, 128, 172; CWP; DLB 122, 227; DNFS 2; FW; HW 1; LLW; PFS 21

Castillo, Ana Hernandez Del
See Castillo, Ana

Castle, Robert
See Hamilton, Edmond

Castro (Ruz), Fidel 1926(?)- .... **HLC 1**
See also CA 110; 129; CANR 81; DAM MULT; HW 2

Castro, Guillen de 1569-1631 .... **LC 19**

Castro, Rosalia de 1837-1885 ... **NCLC 3, 78; PC 41**
See also DAM MULT

Castro Alves, Antonio de
1847-1871 .... **NCLC 205**
See also DLB 307; LAW

Cather, Willa (Sibert) 1873-1947 . **SSC 2, 50, 114; TCLC 1, 11, 31, 99, 132, 152; WLC 1**
See also AAYA 24; AMW; AMWC 1; AMWR 1; BPFB 1; CA 104; 128; CDALB 1865-1917; CLR 98; DA; DA3; DAB; DAC; DAM MST, NOV; DLB 9, 54, 78, 256; DLBD 1; EWL 3; EXPN; EXPS; FL 1:5; LAIT 3; LATS 1:1; MAL 5; MBL; MTCW 1, 2; MTFW 2005; NFS 2, 19; RGAL 4; RGSF 2; RHW; SATA 30; SSFS 2, 7, 16, 27; TCWW 1, 2; TUS

Catherine II
See Catherine the Great

Catherine, Saint 1347-1380 .... **CMLC 27**

Catherine the Great 1729-1796 .... **LC 69**
See also DLB 150

Cato, Marcus Porcius
234B.C.-149B.C. .... **CMLC 21**
See also DLB 211

Cato, Marcus Porcius, the Elder
See Cato, Marcus Porcius

Cato the Elder
See Cato, Marcus Porcius

Catton, (Charles) Bruce 1899-1978 . **CLC 35**
See also AITN 1; CA 5-8R; 81-84; CANR 7, 74; DLB 17; MTCW 2; MTFW 2005; SATA 2; SATA-Obit 24

Catullus c. 84B.C.-54B.C. .... **CMLC 18**
See also AW 2; CDWLB 1; DLB 211; RGWL 2, 3; WLIT 8

Cauldwell, Frank
See King, Francis (Henry)

Caunitz, William J. 1933-1996 .... **CLC 34**
See also BEST 89:3; CA 125; 130; 152; CANR 73; INT CA-130

Causley, Charles (Stanley)
1917-2003 .... **CLC 7**
See also CA 9-12R; 223; CANR 5, 35, 94; CLR 30; CP 1, 2, 3, 4, 5; CWRI 5; DLB 27; MTCW 1; SATA 3, 66; SATA-Obit 149

Caute, (John) David 1936- .... **CLC 29**
See also CA 1-4R; CAAS 4; CANR 1, 33, 64, 120; CBD; CD 5, 6; CN 1, 2, 3, 4, 5, 6, 7; DAM NOV; DLB 14, 231

Cavafy, C. P.
See Kavafis, Konstantinos Petrou

Cavafy, Constantine Peter
See Kavafis, Konstantinos Petrou

Cavalcanti, Guido c. 1250-c. 1300 .... **CMLC 54**
See also RGWL 2, 3; WLIT 7

Cavallo, Evelyn
See Spark, Muriel

Cavanna, Betty
See Harrison, Elizabeth (Allen) Cavanna

Cavanna, Elizabeth
See Harrison, Elizabeth (Allen) Cavanna

Cavanna, Elizabeth Allen
See Harrison, Elizabeth (Allen) Cavanna

Cavendish, Margaret Lucas
1623-1673 .... **LC 30, 132**
See also DLB 131, 252, 281; RGEL 2

Caxton, William 1421(?)-1491(?) .... **LC 17**
See also DLB 170

Cayer, D. M.
See Duffy, Maureen (Patricia)

Cayrol, Jean 1911-2005 .... **CLC 11**
See also CA 89-92; 236; DLB 83; EWL 3

Cela (y Trulock), Camilo Jose
See Cela, Camilo Jose

Cela, Camilo Jose 1916-2002 .... **CLC 4, 13, 59, 122; HLC 1; SSC 71**
See also BEST 90:2; CA 21-24R; 206; CAAS 10; CANR 21, 32, 76, 139; CWW 2; DAM MULT; DLB 322; DLBY 1989; EW 13; EWL 3; HW 1; MTCW 1, 2; MTFW 2005; RGSF 2; RGWL 2, 3

Celan, Paul
See Antschel, Paul

Celine, Louis-Ferdinand
See Destouches, Louis-Ferdinand

Cellini, Benvenuto 1500-1571 .... **LC 7**
See also WLIT 7

Cendrars, Blaise
See Sauser-Hall, Frederic

Centlivre, Susanna 1669(?)-1723 .... **DC 25; LC 65**
See also DLB 84; RGEL 2

Cernuda (y Bidon), Luis
1902-1963 .... **CLC 54; PC 62**
See also CA 131; 89-92; DAM POET; DLB 134; EWL 3; GLL 1; HW 1; RGWL 2, 3

Cervantes, Lorna Dee 1954- ..... **HLCS 1; PC 35**
See also CA 131; CANR 80; CP 7; CWP; DLB 82; EXPP; HW 1; LLW; PFS 30

Cervantes (Saavedra), Miguel de
1547-1616 .... **HLCS; LC 6, 23, 93; SSC 12, 108; WLC 1**
See also AAYA 56; BYA 1, 14; DA; DAB; DAC; DAM MST, NOV; EW 2; LAIT 1; LATS 1:1; LMFS 1; NFS 8; RGSF 2; RGWL 2, 3; TWA

Cesaire, Aime
See Cesaire, Aime

Cesaire, Aime 1913-2008 .... **BLC 1:1; CLC 19, 32, 112, 280; DC 22; PC 25**
See also BW 2, 3; CA 65-68; 271; CANR 24, 43, 81; CWW 2; DA3; DAM MULT, POET; DLB 321; EWL 3; GFL 1789 to the Present; MTCW 1, 2; MTFW 2005; WP

Daly, Mary 1928- .... **CLC 173**
See also CA 25-28R; CANR 30, 62, 166;
FW; GLL 1; MTCW 1

Daly, Maureen 1921-2006 .... **CLC 17**
See also AAYA 5, 58; BYA 6; CA 253;
CANR 37, 83, 108; CLR 96; JRDA; MAI-
CYA 1, 2; SAAS 1; SATA 2, 129; SATA-
Obit 176; WYA; YAW

Damas, Leon-Gontran 1912-1978 ... **CLC 84;**
TCLC 204
See also BW 1; CA 125; 73-76; EWL 3

Dana, Richard Henry Sr.
1787-1879 .... **NCLC 53**

Dangarembga, Tsitsi 1959- .... **BLC 2:1**
See also BW 3; CA 163; NFS 28; WLIT 2

Daniel, Samuel 1562(?)-1619 .... **LC 24, 171**
See also DLB 62; RGEL 2

Daniels, Brett
See Adler, Renata

Dannay, Frederic 1905-1982 .... **CLC 3, 11**
See also BPFB 3; CA 1-4R; 107; CANR 1,
39; CMW 4; DAM POP; DLB 137; MSW;
MTCW 1; RGAL 4

D'Annunzio, Gabriele 1863-1938 ... **TCLC 6,**
40, 215
See also CA 104; 155; EW 8; EWL 3;
RGWL 2, 3; TWA; WLIT 7

Danois, N. le
See Gourmont, Remy(-Marie-Charles) de

Dante 1265-1321 .... **CMLC 3, 18, 39, 70; PC**
21; WLCS
See also DA; DA3; DAB; DAC; DAM
MST, POET; EFS 1; EW 1; LAIT 1;
RGWL 2, 3; TWA; WLIT 7; WP

d'Antibes, Germain
See Simenon, Georges (Jacques Christian)

Danticat, Edwidge 1969- . **BLC 2:1; CLC 94,**
139, 228; SSC 100
See also AAYA 29; CA 152, 192; CAAE
192; CANR 73, 129, 179; CN 7; DLB
350; DNFS 1; EXPS; LATS 1:2; MTCW
2; MTFW 2005; NFS 28; SSFS 1, 25;
YAW

Danvers, Dennis 1947- .... **CLC 70**

Danziger, Paula 1944-2004 .... **CLC 21**
See also AAYA 4, 36; BYA 6, 7, 14; CA
112; 115; 229; CANR 37, 132; CLR 20;
JRDA; MAICYA 1, 2; MTFW 2005;
SATA 36, 63, 102, 149; SATA-Brief 30;
SATA-Obit 155; WYA; YAW

Da Ponte, Lorenzo 1749-1838 .... **NCLC 50**

d'Aragona, Tullia 1510(?)-1556 .... **LC 121**

Dario, Ruben 1867-1916 .... **HLC 1; PC 15;**
TCLC 4
See also CA 131; CANR 81; DAM MULT;
DLB 290; EWL 3; HW 1, 2; LAW;
MTCW 1, 2; MTFW 2005; RGWL 2, 3

Darko, Amma 1956- .... **BLC 2:1**

Darley, George 1795-1846 .... **NCLC 2**
See also DLB 96; RGEL 2

Darrow, Clarence (Seward)
1857-1938 .... **TCLC 81**
See also CA 164; DLB 303

Darwin, Charles 1809-1882 .... **NCLC 57**
See also BRWS 7; DLB 57, 166; LATS 1:1;
RGEL 2; TEA; WLIT 4

Darwin, Erasmus 1731-1802 .... **NCLC 106**
See also DLB 93; RGEL 2

Darwish, Mahmoud 1941-2008 .... **PC 86**
See also CA 164; CANR 133; CWW 2;
EWL 3; MTCW 2; MTFW 2005

Darwish, Mahmud -2008
See Darwish, Mahmoud

Daryush, Elizabeth 1887-1977 ...... **CLC 6, 19**
See also CA 49-52; CANR 3, 81; DLB 20

Das, Kamala 1934-2009 ..... **CLC 191; PC 43**
See also CA 101; CANR 27, 59; CP 1, 2, 3,
4, 5, 6, 7; CWP; DLB 323; FW

Dasgupta, Surendranath
1887-1952 .... **TCLC 81**
See also CA 157

Dashwood, Edmee Elizabeth Monica de la
Pasture 1890-1943 .... **TCLC 61**
See also CA 119; 154; DLB 34; RHW

da Silva, Antonio Jose
1705-1739 .... **NCLC 114**

Daudet, (Louis Marie) Alphonse
1840-1897 .... **NCLC 1**
See also DLB 123; GFL 1789 to the Present;
RGSF 2

Daudet, Alphonse Marie Leon
1867-1942 .... **SSC 94**
See also CA 217

d'Aulnoy, Marie-Catherine c.
1650-1705 .... **LC 100**

Daumal, Rene 1908-1944 .... **TCLC 14**
See also CA 114; 247; EWL 3

Davenant, William 1606-1668 .... **LC 13, 166;**
PC 99
See also DLB 58, 126; RGEL 2

Davenport, Guy (Mattison, Jr.)
1927-2005 . **CLC 6, 14, 38, 241; SSC 16**
See also CA 33-36R; 235; CANR 23, 73;
CN 3, 4, 5, 6; CSW; DLB 130

David, Robert
See Nezval, Vitezslav

Davidson, Donald (Grady)
1893-1968 .... **CLC 2, 13, 19**
See also CA 5-8R; 25-28R; CANR 4, 84;
DLB 45

Davidson, Hugh
See Hamilton, Edmond

Davidson, John 1857-1909 .... **TCLC 24**
See also CA 118; 217; DLB 19; RGEL 2

Davidson, Sara 1943- .... **CLC 9**
See also CA 81-84; CANR 44, 68; DLB
185

Davie, Donald (Alfred) 1922-1995 .... **CLC 5,**
8, 10, 31; PC 29
See also BRWS 6; CA 1-4R; 149; CAAS 3;
CANR 1, 44; CP 1, 2, 3, 4, 5, 6; DLB 27;
MTCW 1; RGEL 2

Davie, Elspeth 1918-1995 .... **SSC 52**
See also CA 120; 126; 150; CANR 141;
DLB 139

Davies, Ray(mond Douglas) 1944- ... **CLC 21**
See also CA 116; 146; CANR 92

Davies, Rhys 1901-1978 .... **CLC 23**
See also CA 9-12R; 81-84; CANR 4; CN 1,
2; DLB 139, 191

Davies, Robertson 1913-1995 .. **CLC 2, 7, 13,**
25, 42, 75, 91; WLC 2
See also BEST 89:2; BPFB 1; CA 1, 33-
36R; 150; CANR 17, 42, 103; CN 1, 2, 3,
4, 5, 6; CPW; DA; DA3; DAB; DAC;
DAM MST, NOV, POP; DLB 68; EWL 3;
HGG; INT CANR-17; MTCW 1, 2;
MTFW 2005; RGEL 2; TWA

Davies, Sir John 1569-1626 .... **LC 85**
See also DLB 172

Davies, Walter C.
See Kornbluth, C(yril) M.

Davies, William Henry 1871-1940 ... **TCLC 5**
See also BRWS 11; CA 104; 179; DLB 19,
174; EWL 3; RGEL 2

Davies, William Robertson
See Davies, Robertson

Da Vinci, Leonardo 1452-1519 ..... **LC 12, 57,**
60
See also AAYA 40

Daviot, Gordon
See Mackintosh, Elizabeth

Davis, Angela (Yvonne) 1944- .... **CLC 77**
See also BW 2, 3; CA 57-60; CANR 10,
81; CSW; DA3; DAM MULT; FW

Davis, B. Lynch
See Bioy Casares, Adolfo; Borges, Jorge
Luis

Davis, Frank Marshall 1905-1987 ... **BLC 1:1**
See also BW 2, 3; CA 125; 123; CANR 42,
80; DAM MULT; DLB 51

Davis, Gordon
See Hunt, E. Howard

Davis, H(arold) L(enoir) 1896-1960 . **CLC 49**
See also ANW; CA 178; 89-92; DLB 9,
206; SATA 114; TCWW 1, 2

Davis, Hart
See Poniatowska, Elena

Davis, Natalie Zemon 1928- .... **CLC 204**
See also CA 53-56; CANR 58, 100, 174

Davis, Rebecca (Blaine) Harding
1831-1910 .... **SSC 38, 109; TCLC 6**
See also AMWS 16; CA 104; 179; DLB 74,
239; FW; NFS 14; RGAL 4; SSFS 26;
TUS

Davis, Richard Harding
1864-1916 .... **TCLC 24**
See also CA 114; 179; DLB 12, 23, 78, 79,
189; DLBD 13; RGAL 4

Davison, Frank Dalby 1893-1970 ..... **CLC 15**
See also CA 217; 116; DLB 260

Davison, Lawrence H.
See Lawrence, D. H.

Davison, Peter (Hubert) 1928-2004 . **CLC 28**
See also CA 9-12R; 234; CAAS 4; CANR
3, 43, 84; CP 1, 2, 3, 4, 5, 6, 7; DLB 5

Davys, Mary 1674-1732 .... **LC 1, 46**
See also DLB 39

Dawson, (Guy) Fielding (Lewis)
1930-2002 .... **CLC 6**
See also CA 85-88; 202; CANR 108; DLB
130; DLBY 2002

Day, Clarence (Shepard, Jr.)
1874-1935 .... **TCLC 25**
See also CA 108; 199; DLB 11

Day, John 1574(?)-1640(?) .... **LC 70**
See also DLB 62, 170; RGEL 2

Day, Thomas 1748-1789 .... **LC 1**
See also DLB 39; YABC 1

Day Lewis, C. 1904-1972 .. **CLC 1, 6, 10; PC**
11
See also BRWS 3; CA 13-16; 33-36R;
CANR 34; CAP 1; CN 1; CP 1; CWRI 5;
DAM POET; DLB 77; EWL 3; MSW;
MTCW 1, 2; RGEL 2

Day Lewis, Cecil
See Day Lewis, C.

de Andrade, Carlos Drummond
See Drummond de Andrade, Carlos

de Andrade, Mario 1892(?)-1945 ... **TCLC 43**
See also CA 178; DLB 307; EWL 3; HW 2;
LAW; RGWL 2, 3

Deane, Norman
See Creasey, John

Deane, Seamus (Francis) 1940- ...... **CLC 122**
See also CA 118; CANR 42

de Athayde, Alvaro Coelho
See Pessoa, Fernando

de Beauvoir, Simone
See Beauvoir, Simone de

de Beer, P.
See Bosman, Herman Charles

De Botton, Alain 1969- .... **CLC 203**
See also CA 159; CANR 96

de Brissac, Malcolm
See Dickinson, Peter (Malcolm de Brissac)

de Campos, Alvaro
See Pessoa, Fernando

de Chardin, Pierre Teilhard
See Teilhard de Chardin, (Marie Joseph)
Pierre

de Conte, Sieur Louis
See Twain, Mark

Ferdowsi, Hakim Abolghasem
See Ferdowsi, Abu'l Qasem
Ferguson, Helen
See Kavan, Anna
Ferguson, Niall 1964- .... **CLC 134, 250**
See also CA 190; CANR 154
Ferguson, Niall Campbell
See Ferguson, Niall
Ferguson, Samuel 1810-1886 .... **NCLC 33**
See also DLB 32; RGEL 2
Fergusson, Robert 1750-1774 .... **LC 29**
See also DLB 109; RGEL 2
Ferling, Lawrence
See Ferlinghetti, Lawrence
Ferlinghetti, Lawrence 1919(?)- .... **CLC 2, 6, 10, 27, 111; PC 1**
See also AAYA 74; BG 1:2; CA 5-8R; CAD; CANR 3, 41, 73, 125, 172; CDALB 1941-1968; CP 1, 2, 3, 4, 5, 6, 7; DA3; DAM POET; DLB 5, 16; MAL 5; MTCW 1, 2; MTFW 2005; PFS 28; RGAL 4; WP
Ferlinghetti, Lawrence Monsanto
See Ferlinghetti, Lawrence
Fern, Fanny
See Parton, Sara Payson Willis
Fernandez, Vicente Garcia Huidobro
See Huidobro Fernandez, Vicente Garcia
Fernandez-Armesto, Felipe 1950- .... **CLC 70**
See also CA 142; CANR 93, 153, 189
Fernandez-Armesto, Felipe Fermin Ricardo
See Fernandez-Armesto, Felipe
Fernandez de Lizardi, Jose Joaquin
See Lizardi, Jose Joaquin Fernandez de
Ferre, Rosario 1938- ...... **CLC 139; HLCS 1; SSC 36, 106**
See also CA 131; CANR 55, 81, 134; CWW 2; DLB 145; EWL 3; HW 1, 2; LAWS 1; MTCW 2; MTFW 2005; WLIT 1
Ferrer, Gabriel (Francisco Victor) Miro
See Miro (Ferrer), Gabriel (Francisco Victor)
Ferrier, Susan (Edmonstone)
1782-1854 .... **NCLC 8**
See also DLB 116; RGEL 2
Ferrigno, Robert 1947- .... **CLC 65**
See also CA 140; CANR 125, 161
Ferris, Joshua 1974- .... **CLC 280**
See also CA 262
Ferron, Jacques 1921-1985 .... **CLC 94**
See also CA 117; 129; CCA 1; DAC; DLB 60; EWL 3
Feuchtwanger, Lion 1884-1958 .... **TCLC 3**
See also CA 104; 187; DLB 66; EWL 3; RGHL
Feuerbach, Ludwig 1804-1872 ..... **NCLC 139**
See also DLB 133
Feuillet, Octave 1821-1890 .... **NCLC 45**
See also DLB 192
Feydeau, Georges (Leon Jules Marie)
1862-1921 .... **TCLC 22**
See also CA 113; 152; CANR 84; DAM DRAM; DLB 192; EWL 3; GFL 1789 to the Present; RGWL 2, 3
Fichte, Johann Gottlieb
1762-1814 .... **NCLC 62**
See also DLB 90
Ficino, Marsilio 1433-1499 .... **LC 12, 152**
See also LMFS 1
Fiedeler, Hans
See Doeblin, Alfred
Fiedler, Leslie A(aron) 1917-2003 ..... **CLC 4, 13, 24**
See also AMWS 13; CA 9-12R; 212; CANR 7, 63; CN 1, 2, 3, 4, 5, 6; DLB 28, 67; EWL 3; MAL 5; MTCW 1, 2; RGAL 4; TUS
Field, Andrew 1938- .... **CLC 44**
See also CA 97-100; CANR 25

Field, Eugene 1850-1895 .... **NCLC 3**
See also DLB 23, 42, 140; DLBD 13; MAICYA 1, 2; RGAL 4; SATA 16
Field, Gans T.
See Wellman, Manly Wade
Field, Michael 1915-1971 .... **TCLC 43**
See also CA 29-32R
Fielding, Helen 1958- .... **CLC 146, 217**
See also AAYA 65; CA 172; CANR 127; DLB 231; MTFW 2005
Fielding, Henry 1707-1754 .... **LC 1, 46, 85, 151, 154; WLC 2**
See also BRW 3; BRWR 1; CDBLB 1660-1789; DA; DA3; DAB; DAC; DAM DRAM, MST, NOV; DLB 39, 84, 101; NFS 18; RGEL 2; TEA; WLIT 3
Fielding, Sarah 1710-1768 .... **LC 1, 44**
See also DLB 39; RGEL 2; TEA
Fields, W. C. 1880-1946 .... **TCLC 80**
See also DLB 44
Fierstein, Harvey (Forbes) 1954- ..... **CLC 33**
See also CA 123; 129; CAD; CD 5, 6; CPW; DA3; DAM DRAM, POP; DFS 6; DLB 266; GLL; MAL 5
Figes, Eva 1932- .... **CLC 31**
See also CA 53-56; CANR 4, 44, 83; CN 2, 3, 4, 5, 6, 7; DLB 14, 271; FW; RGHL
Filippo, Eduardo de
See de Filippo, Eduardo
Finch, Anne 1661-1720 ..... **LC 3, 137; PC 21**
See also BRWS 9; DLB 95; PFS 30
Finch, Robert (Duer Claydon)
1900-1995 .... **CLC 18**
See also CA 57-60; CANR 9, 24, 49; CP 1, 2, 3, 4, 5, 6; DLB 88
Findley, Timothy (Irving Frederick)
1930-2002 .... **CLC 27, 102**
See also CA 25-28R; 206; CANR 12, 42, 69, 109; CCA 1; CN 4, 5, 6, 7; DAC; DAM MST; DLB 53; FANT; RHW
Fink, William
See Mencken, H. L.
Firbank, Louis 1942- .... **CLC 21**
See also CA 117
Firbank, (Arthur Annesley) Ronald
1886-1926 .... **TCLC 1**
See also BRWS 2; CA 104; 177; DLB 36; EWL 3; RGEL 2
Firdaosi
See Ferdowsi, Abu'l Qasem
Firdausi
See Ferdowsi, Abu'l Qasem
Firdavsi, Abulqosimi
See Ferdowsi, Abu'l Qasem
Firdavsii, Abulqosim
See Ferdowsi, Abu'l Qasem
Firdawsi, Abu al-Qasim
See Ferdowsi, Abu'l Qasem
Firdosi
See Ferdowsi, Abu'l Qasem
Firdousi
See Ferdowsi, Abu'l Qasem
Firdousi, Abu'l-Qasim
See Ferdowsi, Abu'l Qasem
Firdovsi, A.
See Ferdowsi, Abu'l Qasem
Firdovsi, Abulgasim
See Ferdowsi, Abu'l Qasem
Firdusi
See Ferdowsi, Abu'l Qasem
Fish, Stanley
See Fish, Stanley Eugene
Fish, Stanley E.
See Fish, Stanley Eugene
Fish, Stanley Eugene 1938- .... **CLC 142**
See also CA 112; 132; CANR 90; DLB 67

Fisher, Dorothy (Frances) Canfield
1879-1958 .... **TCLC 87**
See also CA 114; 136; CANR 80; CLR 71; CWRI 5; DLB 9, 102, 284; MAICYA 1, 2; MAL 5; YABC 1
Fisher, M(ary) F(rances) K(ennedy)
1908-1992 .... **CLC 76, 87**
See also AMWS 17; CA 77-80; 138; CANR 44; MTCW 2
Fisher, Roy 1930- .... **CLC 25**
See also CA 81-84; CAAS 10; CANR 16; CP 1, 2, 3, 4, 5, 6, 7; DLB 40
Fisher, Rudolph 1897-1934 ...... **BLC 1:2; HR 1:2; SSC 25; TCLC 11**
See also BW 1, 3; CA 107; 124; CANR 80; DAM MULT; DLB 51, 102
Fisher, Vardis (Alvero) 1895-1968 .... **CLC 7; TCLC 140**
See also CA 5-8R; 25-28R; CANR 68; DLB 9, 206; MAL 5; RGAL 4; TCWW 1, 2
Fiske, Tarleton
See Bloch, Robert (Albert)
Fitch, Clarke
See Sinclair, Upton
Fitch, John IV
See Cormier, Robert
Fitzgerald, Captain Hugh
See Baum, L(yman) Frank
FitzGerald, Edward 1809-1883 ...... **NCLC 9, 153; PC 79**
See also BRW 4; DLB 32; RGEL 2
Fitzgerald, F(rancis) Scott (Key)
1896-1940 ... **SSC 6, 31, 75; TCLC 1, 6, 14, 28, 55, 157; WLC 2**
See also AAYA 24; AITN 1; AMW; AMWC 2; AMWR 1; BPFB 1; CA 110; 123; CDALB 1917-1929; DA; DA3; DAB; DAC; DAM MST, NOV; DLB 4, 9, 86, 219, 273; DLBD 1, 15, 16; DLBY 1981, 1996; EWL 3; EXPN; EXPS; LAIT 3; MAL 5; MTCW 1, 2; MTFW 2005; NFS 2, 19, 20; RGAL 4; RGSF 2; SSFS 4, 15, 21, 25; TUS
Fitzgerald, Penelope 1916-2000 . **CLC 19, 51, 61, 143**
See also BRWS 5; CA 85-88; 190; CAAS 10; CANR 56, 86, 131; CN 3, 4, 5, 6, 7; DLB 14, 194, 326; EWL 3; MTCW 2; MTFW 2005
Fitzgerald, Robert (Stuart)
1910-1985 .... **CLC 39**
See also CA 1-4R; 114; CANR 1; CP 1, 2, 3, 4; DLBY 1980; MAL 5
FitzGerald, Robert D(avid)
1902-1987 .... **CLC 19**
See also CA 17-20R; CP 1, 2, 3, 4; DLB 260; RGEL 2
Fitzgerald, Zelda (Sayre)
1900-1948 .... **TCLC 52**
See also AMWS 9; CA 117; 126; DLBY 1984
Flanagan, Thomas (James Bonner)
1923-2002 .... **CLC 25, 52**
See also CA 108; 206; CANR 55; CN 3, 4, 5, 6, 7; DLBY 1980; INT CA-108; MTCW 1; RHW; TCLE 1:1
Flaubert, Gustave 1821-1880 .... **NCLC 2, 10, 19, 62, 66, 135, 179, 185; SSC 11, 60; WLC 2**
See also DA; DA3; DAB; DAC; DAM MST, NOV; DLB 119, 301; EW 7; EXPS; GFL 1789 to the Present; LAIT 2; LMFS 1; NFS 14; RGSF 2; RGWL 2, 3; SSFS 6; TWA
Flavius Josephus
See Josephus, Flavius
Flecker, Herman Elroy
See Flecker, (Herman) James Elroy

Greene, Bette 1934- .... **CLC 30**
   See also AAYA 7, 69; BYA 3; CA 53-56;
   CANR 4, 146; CLR 2, 140; CWRI 5;
   JRDA; LAIT 4; MAICYA 1, 2; NFS 10;
   SAAS 16; SATA 8, 102, 161; WYA; YAW

Greene, Gael .... **CLC 8**
   See also CA 13-16R; CANR 10, 166

Greene, Graham 1904-1991 .. **CLC 1, 3, 6, 9,
   14, 18, 27, 37, 70, 72, 125; SSC 29, 121;
   WLC 3**
   See also AAYA 61; AITN 2; BPFB 2;
   BRWR 2; BRWS 1; BYA 3; CA 13-16R;
   133; CANR 35, 61, 131; CBD; CDBLB
   1945-1960; CMW 4; CN 1, 2, 3, 4; DA;
   DA3; DAB; DAC; DAM MST, NOV;
   DLB 13, 15, 77, 100, 162, 201, 204;
   DLBY 1991; EWL 3; MSW; MTCW 1, 2;
   MTFW 2005; NFS 16; RGEL 2; SATA
   20; SSFS 14; TEA; WLIT 4

Greene, Robert 1558-1592 .... **LC 41**
   See also BRWS 8; DLB 62, 167; IDTP;
   RGEL 2; TEA

Greer, Germaine 1939- .... **CLC 131**
   See also AITN 1; CA 81-84; CANR 33, 70,
   115, 133, 190; FW; MTCW 1, 2; MTFW
   2005

Greer, Richard
   See Silverberg, Robert

Gregor, Arthur 1923- .... **CLC 9**
   See also CA 25-28R; CAAS 10; CANR 11;
   CP 1, 2, 3, 4, 5, 6, 7; SATA 36

Gregor, Lee
   See Pohl, Frederik

Gregory, Lady Isabella Augusta (Persse)
   1852-1932 .... **TCLC 1, 176**
   See also BRW 6; CA 104; 184; DLB 10;
   IDTP; RGEL 2

Gregory, J. Dennis
   See Williams, John A(lfred)

Gregory of Nazianzus, St.
   329-389 .... **CMLC 82**

Gregory of Rimini 1300(?)-1358 . **CMLC 109**
   See also DLB 115

Grekova, I.
   See Ventsel, Elena Sergeevna

Grekova, Irina
   See Ventsel, Elena Sergeevna

Grendon, Stephen
   See Derleth, August (William)

Grenville, Kate 1950- .... **CLC 61**
   See also CA 118; CANR 53, 93, 156; CN
   7; DLB 325

Grenville, Pelham
   See Wodehouse, P(elham) G(renville)

Greve, Felix Paul (Berthold Friedrich)
   1879-1948 .... **TCLC 4**
   See also CA 104; 141, 175; CANR 79;
   DAC; DAM MST; DLB 92; RGEL 2;
   TCWW 1, 2

Greville, Fulke 1554-1628 .... **LC 79**
   See also BRWS 11; DLB 62, 172; RGEL 2

Grey, Lady Jane 1537-1554 .... **LC 93**
   See also DLB 132

Grey, Zane 1872-1939 .... **TCLC 6**
   See also BPFB 2; CA 104; 132; DA3; DAM
   POP; DLB 9, 212; MTCW 1, 2; MTFW
   2005; RGAL 4; TCWW 1, 2; TUS

Griboedov, Aleksandr Sergeevich
   1795(?)-1829 .... **NCLC 129**
   See also DLB 205; RGWL 2, 3

Grieg, (Johan) Nordahl (Brun)
   1902-1943 .... **TCLC 10**
   See also CA 107; 189; EWL 3

Grieve, C. M. 1892-1978 ... **CLC 2, 4, 11, 19,
   63; PC 9**
   See also BRWS 12; CA 5-8R; 85-88; CANR
   33, 107; CDBLB 1945-1960; CP 1, 2;
   DAM POET; DLB 20; EWL 3; MTCW 1;
   RGEL 2

Grieve, Christopher Murray
   See Grieve, C. M.

Griffin, Gerald 1803-1840 .... **NCLC 7**
   See also DLB 159; RGEL 2

Griffin, John Howard 1920-1980 ..... **CLC 68**
   See also AITN 1; CA 1-4R; 101; CANR 2

Griffin, Peter 1942- .... **CLC 39**
   See also CA 136

Griffith, David Lewelyn Wark
   See Griffith, D.W.

Griffith, D.W. 1875(?)-1948 .... **TCLC 68**
   See also AAYA 78; CA 119; 150; CANR 80

Griffith, Lawrence
   See Griffith, D.W.

Griffiths, Trevor 1935- .... **CLC 13, 52**
   See also CA 97-100; CANR 45; CBD; CD
   5, 6; DLB 13, 245

Griggs, Sutton (Elbert)
   1872-1930 .... **TCLC 77**
   See also CA 123; 186; DLB 50

Grigson, Geoffrey (Edward Harvey)
   1905-1985 .... **CLC 7, 39**
   See also CA 25-28R; 118; CANR 20, 33;
   CP 1, 2, 3, 4; DLB 27; MTCW 1, 2

Grile, Dod
   See Bierce, Ambrose (Gwinett)

Grillparzer, Franz 1791-1872 .... **DC 14;
   NCLC 1, 102; SSC 37**
   See also CDWLB 2; DLB 133; EW 5;
   RGWL 2, 3; TWA

Grimble, Reverend Charles James
   See Eliot, T(homas) S(tearns)

Grimke, Angelina Weld 1880-1958 ... **HR 1:2**
   See also BW 1; CA 124; DAM POET; DLB
   50, 54; FW

Grimke, Charlotte L. Forten
   1837(?)-1914 .... **BLC 1:2; TCLC 16**
   See also BW 1; CA 117; 124; DAM MULT,
   POET; DLB 50, 239

Grimke, Charlotte Lottie Forten
   See Grimke, Charlotte L. Forten

Grimm, Jacob Ludwig Karl
   1785-1863 .... **NCLC 3, 77; SSC 36, 88**
   See also CLR 112; DLB 90; MAICYA 1, 2;
   RGSF 2; RGWL 2, 3; SATA 22; WCH

Grimm, Wilhelm Karl 1786-1859 .. **NCLC 3,
   77; SSC 36**
   See also CDWLB 2; CLR 112; DLB 90;
   MAICYA 1, 2; RGSF 2; RGWL 2, 3;
   SATA 22; WCH

Grimm and Grim
   See Grimm, Jacob Ludwig Karl; Grimm,
   Wilhelm Karl

Grimm Brothers
   See Grimm, Jacob Ludwig Karl; Grimm,
   Wilhelm Karl

Grimmelshausen, Hans Jakob Christoffel
   von
   See Grimmelshausen, Johann Jakob Christoffel von

Grimmelshausen, Johann Jakob Christoffel
   von 1621-1676 .... **LC 6**
   See also CDWLB 2; DLB 168; RGWL 2, 3

Grindel, Eugene 1895-1952 .... **PC 38; TCLC
   7, 41**
   See also CA 104; 193; EWL 3; GFL 1789
   to the Present; LMFS 2; RGWL 2, 3

Grisham, John 1955- .... **CLC 84, 273**
   See also AAYA 14, 47; BPFB 2; CA 138;
   CANR 47, 69, 114, 133; CMW 4; CN 6,
   7; CPW; CSW; DA3; DAM POP; MSW;
   MTCW 2; MTFW 2005

Grosseteste, Robert 1175(?)-1253 . **CMLC 62**
   See also DLB 115

Grossman, David 1954- .... **CLC 67, 231**
   See also CA 138; CANR 114, 175; CWW
   2; DLB 299; EWL 3; RGHL; WLIT 6

Grossman, Vasilii Semenovich
   See Grossman, Vasily (Semenovich)

Grossman, Vasily (Semenovich)
   1905-1964 .... **CLC 41**
   See also CA 124; 130; DLB 272; MTCW 1;
   RGHL

Grove, Frederick Philip
   See Greve, Felix Paul (Berthold Friedrich)

Grubb
   See Crumb, R.

Grumbach, Doris 1918- .... **CLC 13, 22, 64**
   See also CA 5-8R; CAAS 2; CANR 9, 42,
   70, 127; CN 6, 7; INT CANR-9; MTCW
   2; MTFW 2005

Grundtvig, Nikolai Frederik Severin
   1783-1872 .... **NCLC 1, 158**
   See also DLB 300

Grunge
   See Crumb, R.

Grunwald, Lisa 1959- .... **CLC 44**
   See also CA 120; CANR 148

Gryphius, Andreas 1616-1664 .... **LC 89**
   See also CDWLB 2; DLB 164; RGWL 2, 3

Guare, John 1938- .... **CLC 8, 14, 29, 67; DC
   20**
   See also CA 73-76; CAD; CANR 21, 69,
   118; CD 5, 6; DAM DRAM; DFS 8, 13;
   DLB 7, 249; EWL 3; MAL 5; MTCW 1,
   2; RGAL 4

Guarini, Battista 1538-1612 .... **LC 102**
   See also DLB 339

Gubar, Susan 1944- .... **CLC 145**
   See also CA 108; CANR 45, 70, 139, 179;
   FW; MTCW 1; RGAL 4

Gubar, Susan David
   See Gubar, Susan

Gudjonsson, Halldor Kiljan
   1902-1998 .... **CLC 25**
   See also CA 103; 164; CWW 2; DLB 293,
   331; EW 12; EWL 3; RGWL 2, 3

Guedes, Vincente
   See Pessoa, Fernando

Guenter, Erich
   See Eich, Gunter

Guest, Barbara 1920-2006 ... **CLC 34; PC 55**
   See also BG 1:2; CA 25-28R; 248; CANR
   11, 44, 84; CP 1, 2, 3, 4, 5, 6, 7; CWP;
   DLB 5, 193

Guest, Edgar A(lbert) 1881-1959 ... **TCLC 95**
   See also CA 112; 168

Guest, Judith 1936- .... **CLC 8, 30**
   See also AAYA 7, 66; CA 77-80; CANR
   15, 75, 138; DA3; DAM NOV, POP;
   EXPN; INT CANR-15; LAIT 5; MTCW
   1, 2; MTFW 2005; NFS 1

Guevara, Che
   See Guevara (Serna), Ernesto

Guevara (Serna), Ernesto
   1928-1967 .... **CLC 87; HLC 1**
   See also CA 127; 111; CANR 56; DAM
   MULT; HW 1

Guicciardini, Francesco 1483-1540 ..... **LC 49**

Guido delle Colonne c. 1215-c.
   1290 .... **CMLC 90**

Guild, Nicholas M. 1944- .... **CLC 33**
   See also CA 93-96

Guillemin, Jacques
   See Sartre, Jean-Paul

Guillen, Jorge 1893-1984 . **CLC 11; HLCS 1;
   PC 35**
   See also CA 89-92; 112; DAM MULT,
   POET; DLB 108; EWL 3; HW 1; RGWL
   2, 3

Guillen, Nicolas (Cristobal)
   1902-1989 .... **BLC 1:2; CLC 48, 79;
   HLC 1; PC 23**
   See also BW 2; CA 116; 125; 129; CANR
   84; DAM MST, MULT, POET; DLB 283;
   EWL 3; HW 1; LAW; RGWL 2, 3; WP

Guillen y Alvarez, Jorge
   See Guillen, Jorge

James, Montague (Rhodes)
   1862-1936 .... **SSC 16, 93; TCLC 6**
   See also CA 104; 203; DLB 156, 201;
   HGG; RGEL 2; RGSF 2; SUFW 1

James, P. D.
   See White, Phyllis Dorothy James

James, Philip
   See Moorcock, Michael

James, Samuel
   See Stephens, James

James, Seumas
   See Stephens, James

James, Stephen
   See Stephens, James

James, T.F.
   See Fleming, Thomas

James, William 1842-1910 .... **TCLC 15, 32**
   See also AMW; CA 109; 193; DLB 270,
   284; MAL 5; NCFS 5; RGAL 4

Jameson, Anna 1794-1860 .... **NCLC 43**
   See also DLB 99, 166

Jameson, Fredric 1934- .... **CLC 142**
   See also CA 196; CANR 169; DLB 67;
   LMFS 2

Jameson, Fredric R.
   See Jameson, Fredric

James VI of Scotland 1566-1625 .... **LC 109**
   See also DLB 151, 172

Jami, Nur al-Din 'Abd al-Rahman
   1414-1492 .... **LC 9**

Jammes, Francis 1868-1938 .... **TCLC 75**
   See also CA 198; EWL 3; GFL 1789 to the
   Present

Jandl, Ernst 1925-2000 .... **CLC 34**
   See also CA 200; EWL 3

Janowitz, Tama 1957- .... **CLC 43, 145**
   See also CA 106; CANR 52, 89, 129; CN
   5, 6, 7; CPW; DAM POP; DLB 292;
   MTFW 2005

Jansson, Tove (Marika) 1914-2001 ... **SSC 96**
   See also CA 17-20R; 196; CANR 38, 118;
   CLR 2, 125; CWW 2; DLB 257; EWL 3;
   MAICYA 1, 2; RGSF 2; SATA 3, 41

Japrisot, Sebastien 1931-
   See Rossi, Jean-Baptiste

Jarrell, Randall 1914-1965 .... **CLC 1, 2, 6, 9,
   13, 49; PC 41; TCLC 177**
   See also AMW; BYA 5; CA 5-8R; 25-28R;
   CABS 2; CANR 6, 34; CDALB 1941-
   1968; CLR 6, 111; CWRI 5; DAM POET;
   DLB 48, 52; EWL 3; EXPP; MAICYA 1,
   2; MAL 5; MTCW 1, 2; PAB; PFS 2, 31;
   RGAL 4; SATA 7

Jarry, Alfred 1873-1907 .... **SSC 20; TCLC 2,
   14, 147**
   See also CA 104; 153; DA3; DAM DRAM;
   DFS 8; DLB 192, 258; EW 9; EWL 3;
   GFL 1789 to the Present; RGWL 2, 3;
   TWA

Jarvis, E.K.
   See Ellison, Harlan; Silverberg, Robert

Jawien, Andrzej
   See John Paul II, Pope

Jaynes, Roderick
   See Coen, Ethan

Jeake, Samuel, Jr.
   See Aiken, Conrad (Potter)

Jean-Louis
   See Kerouac, Jack

Jean Paul 1763-1825 .... **NCLC 7**

Jefferies, (John) Richard
   1848-1887 .... **NCLC 47**
   See also DLB 98, 141; RGEL 2; SATA 16;
   SFW 4

Jeffers, John Robinson
   See Jeffers, Robinson

Jeffers, Robinson 1887-1962 .... **CLC 2, 3, 11,
   15, 54; PC 17; WLC 3**
   See also AMWS 2; CA 85-88; CANR 35;
   CDALB 1917-1929; DA; DAC; DAM
   MST, POET; DLB 45, 212, 342; EWL 3;
   MAL 5; MTCW 1, 2; MTFW 2005; PAB;
   PFS 3, 4; RGAL 4

Jefferson, Janet
   See Mencken, H. L.

Jefferson, Thomas 1743-1826 . **NCLC 11, 103**
   See also AAYA 54; ANW; CDALB 1640-
   1865; DA3; DLB 31, 183; LAIT 1; RGAL
   4

Jeffrey, Francis 1773-1850 .... **NCLC 33**
   See also DLB 107

Jelakowitch, Ivan
   See Heijermans, Herman

Jelinek, Elfriede 1946- .... **CLC 169**
   See also AAYA 68; CA 154; CANR 169;
   DLB 85, 330; FW

Jellicoe, (Patricia) Ann 1927- .... **CLC 27**
   See also CA 85-88; CBD; CD 5, 6; CWD;
   CWRI 5; DLB 13, 233; FW

Jelloun, Tahar ben
   See Ben Jelloun, Tahar

Jemyma
   See Holley, Marietta

Jen, Gish
   See Jen, Lillian

Jen, Lillian 1955- .... **AAL; CLC 70, 198, 260**
   See also AMWC 2; CA 135; CANR 89,
   130; CN 7; DLB 312; NFS 30

Jenkins, (John) Robin 1912- .... **CLC 52**
   See also CA 1-4R; CANR 1, 135; CN 1, 2,
   3, 4, 5, 6, 7; DLB 14, 271

Jennings, Elizabeth (Joan)
   1926-2001 .... **CLC 5, 14, 131**
   See also BRWS 5; CA 61-64; 200; CAAS
   5; CANR 8, 39, 66, 127; CP 1, 2, 3, 4, 5,
   6, 7; CWP; DLB 27; EWL 3; MTCW 1;
   SATA 66

Jennings, Waylon 1937-2002 .... **CLC 21**

Jensen, Johannes V(ilhelm)
   1873-1950 .... **TCLC 41**
   See also CA 170; DLB 214, 330; EWL 3;
   RGWL 3

Jensen, Laura (Linnea) 1948- .... **CLC 37**
   See also CA 103

Jerome, Saint 345-420 .... **CMLC 30**
   See also RGWL 3

Jerome, Jerome K(lapka)
   1859-1927 .... **TCLC 23**
   See also CA 119; 177; DLB 10, 34, 135;
   RGEL 2

Jerrold, Douglas William
   1803-1857 .... **NCLC 2**
   See also DLB 158, 159, 344; RGEL 2

Jewett, (Theodora) Sarah Orne
   1849-1909 . **SSC 6, 44, 110; TCLC 1, 22**
   See also AAYA 76; AMW; AMWC 2;
   AMWR 2; CA 108; 127; CANR 71; DLB
   12, 74, 221; EXPS; FL 1:3; FW; MAL 5;
   MBL; NFS 15; RGAL 4; RGSF 2; SATA
   15; SSFS 4

Jewsbury, Geraldine (Endsor)
   1812-1880 .... **NCLC 22**
   See also DLB 21

Jhabvala, Ruth Prawer 1927- . **CLC 4, 8, 29,
   94, 138; SSC 91**
   See also BRWS 5; CA 1-4R; CANR 2, 29,
   51, 74, 91, 128; CN 1, 2, 3, 4, 5, 6, 7;
   DAB; DAM NOV; DLB 139, 194, 323,
   326; EWL 3; IDFW 3, 4; INT CANR-29;
   MTCW 1, 2; MTFW 2005; RGSF 2;
   RGWL 2; RHW; TEA

Jibran, Kahlil
   See Gibran, Kahlil

Jibran, Khalil
   See Gibran, Kahlil

Jiles, Paulette 1943- .... **CLC 13, 58**
   See also CA 101; CANR 70, 124, 170; CP
   5; CWP

Jimenez (Mantecon), Juan Ramon
   1881-1958 .... **HLC 1; PC 7; TCLC 4,
   183**
   See also CA 104; 131; CANR 74; DAM
   MULT, POET; DLB 134, 330; EW 9;
   EWL 3; HW 1; MTCW 1, 2; MTFW
   2005; RGWL 2, 3

Jimenez, Ramon
   See Jimenez (Mantecon), Juan Ramon

Jimenez Mantecon, Juan
   See Jimenez (Mantecon), Juan Ramon

Jin, Ba 1904-2005 .... **CLC 18**
   See Cantu, Robert Clark
   See also CA 244; CWW 2; DLB 328; EWL
   3

Jin, Xuefei 1956- .... **CLC 109, 262**
   See also CA 152; CANR 91, 130, 184; DLB
   244, 292; MTFW 2005; NFS 25; SSFS 17

Jin Ha
   See Jin, Xuefei

Jodelle, Etienne 1532-1573 .... **LC 119**
   See also DLB 327; GFL Beginnings to 1789

Joel, Billy
   See Joel, William Martin

Joel, William Martin 1949- .... **CLC 26**
   See also CA 108

John, St.
   See John of Damascus, St.

John of Damascus, St. c.
   675-749 .... **CMLC 27, 95**

John of Salisbury c. 1115-1180 ..... **CMLC 63**

John of the Cross, St. 1542-1591 .... **LC 18,
   146**
   See also RGWL 2, 3

John Paul II, Pope 1920-2005 .... **CLC 128**
   See also CA 106; 133; 238

Johnson, B(ryan) S(tanley William)
   1933-1973 .... **CLC 6, 9**
   See also CA 9-12R; 53-56; CANR 9; CN 1;
   CP 1, 2; DLB 14, 40; EWL 3; RGEL 2

Johnson, Benjamin F., of Boone
   See Riley, James Whitcomb

Johnson, Charles (Richard) 1948- . **BLC 1:2,
   2:2; CLC 7, 51, 65, 163**
   See also AFAW 2; AMWS 6; BW 2, 3; CA
   116; CAAS 18; CANR 42, 66, 82, 129;
   CN 5, 6, 7; DAM MULT; DLB 33, 278;
   MAL 5; MTCW 2; MTFW 2005; RGAL
   4; SSFS 16

Johnson, Charles S(purgeon)
   1893-1956 .... **HR 1:3**
   See also BW 1, 3; CA 125; CANR 82; DLB
   51, 91

Johnson, Denis 1949- . **CLC 52, 160; SSC 56**
   See also CA 117; 121; CANR 71, 99, 178;
   CN 4, 5, 6, 7; DLB 120

Johnson, Diane 1934- ...... **CLC 5, 13, 48, 244**
   See also BPFB 2; CA 41-44R; CANR 17,
   40, 62, 95, 155; CN 4, 5, 6, 7; DLB 350;
   DLBY 1980; INT CANR-17; MTCW 1

Johnson, E(mily) Pauline 1861-1913 . **NNAL**
   See also CA 150; CCA 1; DAC; DAM
   MULT; DLB 92, 175; TCWW 2

Johnson, Eyvind (Olof Verner)
   1900-1976 .... **CLC 14**
   See also CA 73-76; 69-72; CANR 34, 101;
   DLB 259, 330; EW 12; EWL 3

Johnson, Fenton 1888-1958 .... **BLC 1:2**
   See also BW 1; CA 118; 124; DAM MULT;
   DLB 45, 50

Johnson, Georgia Douglas (Camp)
   1880-1966 .... **HR 1:3**
   See also BW 1; CA 125; DLB 51, 249; WP

Johnson, Helene 1907-1995 .... **HR 1:3**
   See also CA 181; DLB 51; WP

Lang, Fritz 1890-1976 .... **CLC 20, 103**
See also AAYA 65; CA 77-80; 69-72;
CANR 30

Lange, John
See Crichton, Michael

Langer, Elinor 1939- .... **CLC 34**
See also CA 121

Langland, William 1332(?)-1400(?) .... **LC 19,
120**
See also BRW 1; DA; DAB; DAC; DAM
MST, POET; DLB 146; RGEL 2; TEA;
WLIT 3

Langstaff, Launcelot
See Irving, Washington

Lanier, Sidney 1842-1881 . **NCLC 6, 118; PC
50**
See also AMWS 1; DAM POET; DLB 64;
DLBD 13; EXPP; MAICYA 1; PFS 14;
RGAL 4; SATA 18

Lanyer, Aemilia 1569-1645 .... **LC 10, 30, 83;
PC 60**
See also DLB 121

Lao Tzu c. 6th cent. B.C.-3rd cent.
B.C. .... **CMLC 7**

Lao-Tzu
See Lao Tzu

Lapine, James (Elliot) 1949- .... **CLC 39**
See also CA 123; 130; CANR 54, 128; DFS
25; DLB 341; INT CA-130

Larbaud, Valery (Nicolas)
1881-1957 .... **TCLC 9**
See also CA 106; 152; EWL 3; GFL 1789
to the Present

Larcom, Lucy 1824-1893 .... **NCLC 179**
See also AMWS 13; DLB 221, 243

Lardner, Ring
See Lardner, Ring(gold) W(ilmer)

Lardner, Ring W., Jr.
See Lardner, Ring(gold) W(ilmer)

Lardner, Ring(gold) W(ilmer)
1885-1933 ..... **SSC 32, 118; TCLC 2, 14**
See also AMW; BPFB 2; CA 104; 131;
CDALB 1917-1929; DLB 11, 25, 86, 171;
DLBD 16; MAL 5; MTCW 1, 2; MTFW
2005; RGAL 4; RGSF 2; TUS

Laredo, Betty
See Codrescu, Andrei

Larkin, Maia
See Wojciechowska, Maia (Teresa)

Larkin, Philip (Arthur) 1922-1985 ... **CLC 3,
5, 8, 9, 13, 18, 33, 39, 64; PC 21**
See also BRWS 1; CA 5-8R; 117; CANR
24, 62; CDBLB 1960 to Present; CP 1, 2,
3, 4; DA3; DAB; DAM MST, POET;
DLB 27; EWL 3; MTCW 1, 2; MTFW
2005; PFS 3, 4, 12; RGEL 2

La Roche, Sophie von
1730-1807 .... **NCLC 121**
See also DLB 94

La Rochefoucauld, Francois
1613-1680 .... **LC 108**
See also DLB 268; EW 3; GFL Beginnings
to 1789; RGWL 2, 3

**Larra (y Sanchez de Castro), Mariano Jose
de** 1809-1837 .... **NCLC 17, 130**

Larsen, Eric 1941- .... **CLC 55**
See also CA 132

Larsen, Nella 1893(?)-1963 ... **BLC 1:2; CLC
37; HR 1:3; TCLC 200**
See also AFAW 1, 2; AMWS 18; BW 1;
CA 125; CANR 83; DAM MULT; DLB
51; FW; LATS 1:1; LMFS 2

Larson, Charles R(aymond) 1938- ... **CLC 31**
See also CA 53-56; CANR 4, 121

Larson, Jonathan 1960-1996 .... **CLC 99**
See also AAYA 28; CA 156; DFS 23;
MTFW 2005

La Sale, Antoine de c. 1386-1460(?) . **LC 104**
See also DLB 208

Las Casas, Bartolome de
1474-1566 .... **HLCS; LC 31**
See also DLB 318; LAW; WLIT 1

Lasch, Christopher 1932-1994 .... **CLC 102**
See also CA 73-76; 144; CANR 25, 118;
DLB 246; MTCW 1, 2; MTFW 2005

Lasker-Schueler, Else 1869-1945 ... **TCLC 57**
See also CA 183; DLB 66, 124; EWL 3

Lasker-Schuler, Else
See Lasker-Schueler, Else

Laski, Harold J(oseph) 1893-1950 . **TCLC 79**
See also CA 188

Latham, Jean Lee 1902-1995 .... **CLC 12**
See also AITN 1; BYA 1; CA 5-8R; CANR
7, 84; CLR 50; MAICYA 1, 2; SATA 2,
68; YAW

Latham, Mavis
See Clark, Mavis Thorpe

Lathen, Emma
See Hennissart, Martha

Lathrop, Francis
See Leiber, Fritz (Reuter, Jr.)

Lattany, Kristin
See Lattany, Kristin Hunter

Lattany, Kristin Elaine Eggleston Hunter
See Lattany, Kristin Hunter

Lattany, Kristin Hunter 1931- .... **CLC 35**
See also AITN 1; BW 1; BYA 3; CA 13-
16R; CANR 13, 108; CLR 3; CN 1, 2, 3,
4, 5, 6; DLB 33; INT CANR-13; MAI-
CYA 1, 2; SAAS 10; SATA 12, 132; YAW

Lattimore, Richmond (Alexander)
1906-1984 .... **CLC 3**
See also CA 1-4R; 112; CANR 1; CP 1, 2,
3; MAL 5

Laughlin, James 1914-1997 .... **CLC 49**
See also CA 21-24R; 162; CAAS 22; CANR
9, 47; CP 1, 2, 3, 4, 5, 6; DLB 48; DLBY
1996, 1997

Laurence, Jean Margaret Wemyss
See Laurence, Margaret

Laurence, Margaret 1926-1987 ..... **CLC 3, 6,
13, 50, 62; SSC 7**
See also BYA 13; CA 5-8R; 121; CANR
33; CN 1, 2, 3, 4; DAC; DAM MST; DLB
53; EWL 3; FW; MTCW 1, 2; MTFW
2005; NFS 11; RGEL 2; RGSF 2; SATA-
Obit 50; TCWW 2

Laurent, Antoine 1952- .... **CLC 50**

Lauscher, Hermann
See Hesse, Hermann

Lautreamont 1846-1870 .... **NCLC 12, 194;
SSC 14**
See also DLB 217; GFL 1789 to the Present;
RGWL 2, 3

Lautreamont, Isidore Lucien Ducasse
See Lautreamont

Lavater, Johann Kaspar
1741-1801 .... **NCLC 142**
See also DLB 97

Laverty, Donald
See Blish, James (Benjamin)

Lavin, Mary 1912-1996 . **CLC 4, 18, 99; SSC
4, 67**
See also CA 9-12R; 151; CANR 33; CN 1,
2, 3, 4, 5, 6; DLB 15, 319; FW; MTCW
1; RGEL 2; RGSF 2; SSFS 23

Lavond, Paul Dennis
See Kornbluth, C(yril) M.; Pohl, Frederik

Lawes, Henry 1596-1662 .... **LC 113**
See also DLB 126

Lawler, Ray
See Lawler, Raymond Evenor

Lawler, Raymond Evenor 1922- .... **CLC 58**
See also CA 103; CD 5, 6; DLB 289; RGEL
2

Lawrence, D. H. 1885-1930 ... **PC 54; SSC 4,
19, 73; TCLC 2, 9, 16, 33, 48, 61, 93;
WLC 3**
See also BPFB 2; BRW 7; BRWR 2; CA
104; 121; CANR 131; CDBLB 1914-
1945; DA; DA3; DAB; DAC; DAM MST,
NOV, POET; DLB 10, 19, 36, 98, 162,
195; EWL 3; EXPP; EXPS; GLL 1; LAIT
2, 3; MTCW 1, 2; MTFW 2005; NFS 18,
26; PFS 6; RGEL 2; RGSF 2; SSFS 2, 6;
TEA; WLIT 4; WP

Lawrence, David Herbert Richards
See Lawrence, D. H.

Lawrence, T. E. 1888-1935 ..... **TCLC 18, 204**
See also BRWS 2; CA 115; 167; DLB 195

Lawrence, Thomas Edward
See Lawrence, T. E.

Lawrence of Arabia
See Lawrence, T. E.

Lawson, Henry (Archibald Hertzberg)
1867-1922 .... **SSC 18; TCLC 27**
See also CA 120; 181; DLB 230; RGEL 2;
RGSF 2

Lawton, Dennis
See Faust, Frederick

Laxness, Halldor (Kiljan)
See Gudjonsson, Halldor Kiljan

Layamon fl. c. 1200- .... **CMLC 10, 105**
See also DLB 146; RGEL 2

Laye, Camara 1928-1980 .. **BLC 1:2; CLC 4,
38**
See also AFW; BW 1; CA 85-88; 97-100;
CANR 25; DAM MULT; EWL 3; MTCW
1, 2; WLIT 2

Layton, Irving 1912-2006 ..... **CLC 2, 15, 164**
See also CA 1-4R; 247; CANR 2, 33, 43,
66, 129; CP 1, 2, 3, 4, 5, 6, 7; DAC; DAM
MST, POET; DLB 88; EWL 3; MTCW 1,
2; PFS 12; RGEL 2

Layton, Irving Peter
See Layton, Irving

Lazarus, Emma 1849-1887 ...... **NCLC 8, 109**

Lazarus, Felix
See Cable, George Washington

Lazarus, Henry
See Slavitt, David R.

Lea, Joan
See Neufeld, John (Arthur)

Leacock, Stephen (Butler)
1869-1944 .... **SSC 39; TCLC 2**
See also CA 104; 141; CANR 80; DAC;
DAM MST; DLB 92; EWL 3; MTCW 2;
MTFW 2005; RGEL 2; RGSF 2

Lead, Jane Ward 1623-1704 .... **LC 72**
See also DLB 131

Leapor, Mary 1722-1746 .... **LC 80; PC 85**
See also DLB 109

Lear, Edward 1812-1888 ..... **NCLC 3; PC 65**
See also AAYA 48; BRW 5; CLR 1, 75;
DLB 32, 163, 166; MAICYA 1, 2; RGEL
2; SATA 18, 100; WCH; WP

Lear, Norman (Milton) 1922- .... **CLC 12**
See also CA 73-76

Least Heat-Moon, William
See Trogdon, William

Leautaud, Paul 1872-1956 .... **TCLC 83**
See also CA 203; DLB 65; GFL 1789 to the
Present

Leavis, F(rank) R(aymond)
1895-1978 .... **CLC 24**
See also BRW 7; CA 21-24R; 77-80; CANR
44; DLB 242; EWL 3; MTCW 1, 2;
RGEL 2

Leavitt, David 1961- .... **CLC 34**
See also CA 116; 122; CANR 50, 62, 101,
134, 177; CPW; DA3; DAM POP; DLB
130, 350; GLL 1; INT CA-122; MAL 5;
MTCW 2; MTFW 2005

Madhubuti, Haki R. 1942- .... **BLC 1:2; CLC 2; PC 5**
See also BW 2, 3; CA 73-76; CANR 24, 51, 73, 139; CP 2, 3, 4, 5, 6, 7; CSW; DAM MULT, POET; DLB 5, 41; DLBD 8; EWL 3; MAL 5; MTCW 2; MTFW 2005; RGAL 4

Madison, James 1751-1836 .... **NCLC 126**
See also DLB 37

Maepenn, Hugh
See Kuttner, Henry

Maepenn, K. H.
See Kuttner, Henry

Maeterlinck, Maurice 1862-1949 .... **DC 32; TCLC 3**
See also CA 104; 136; CANR 80; DAM DRAM; DLB 192, 331; EW 8; EWL 3; GFL 1789 to the Present; LMFS 2; RGWL 2, 3; SATA 66; TWA

Maginn, William 1794-1842 .... **NCLC 8**
See also DLB 110, 159

Mahapatra, Jayanta 1928- .... **CLC 33**
See also CA 73-76; CAAS 9; CANR 15, 33, 66, 87; CP 4, 5, 6, 7; DAM MULT; DLB 323

Mahfouz, Nagib
See Mahfouz, Naguib

Mahfouz, Naguib 1911(?)-2006 . **CLC 52, 55, 153; SSC 66**
See also AAYA 49; AFW; BEST 89:2; CA 128; 253; CANR 55, 101; DA3; DAM NOV; DLB 346; DLBY 1988; MTCW 1, 2; MTFW 2005; RGSF 2; RGWL 2, 3; SSFS 9; WLIT 2

Mahfouz, Naguib Abdel Aziz Al-Sabilgi
See Mahfouz, Naguib

Mahfouz, Najib
See Mahfouz, Naguib

Mahfuz, Najib
See Mahfouz, Naguib

Mahon, Derek 1941- .... **CLC 27; PC 60**
See also BRWS 6; CA 113; 128; CANR 88; CP 1, 2, 3, 4, 5, 6, 7; DLB 40; EWL 3

Maiakovskii, Vladimir
See Mayakovski, Vladimir (Vladimirovich)

Mailer, Norman 1923-2007 ... **CLC 1, 2, 3, 4, 5, 8, 11, 14, 28, 39, 74, 111, 234**
See also AAYA 31; AITN 2; AMW; AMWC 2; AMWR 2; BPFB 2; CA 9-12R; 266; CABS 1; CANR 28, 74, 77, 130; CDALB 1968-1988; CN 1, 2, 3, 4, 5, 6, 7; CPW; DA; DA3; DAB; DAC; DAM MST, NOV, POP; DLB 2, 16, 28, 185, 278; DLBD 3; DLBY 1980, 1983; EWL 3; MAL 5; MTCW 1, 2; MTFW 2005; NFS 10; RGAL 4; TUS

Mailer, Norman Kingsley
See Mailer, Norman

Maillet, Antonine 1929- .... **CLC 54, 118**
See also CA 115; 120; CANR 46, 74, 77, 134; CCA 1; CWW 2; DAC; DLB 60; INT CA-120; MTCW 2; MTFW 2005

Maimonides, Moses 1135-1204 ..... **CMLC 76**
See also DLB 115

Mais, Roger 1905-1955 .... **TCLC 8**
See also BW 1, 3; CA 105; 124; CANR 82; CDWLB 3; DLB 125; EWL 3; MTCW 1; RGEL 2

Maistre, Joseph 1753-1821 .... **NCLC 37**
See also GFL 1789 to the Present

Maitland, Frederic William 1850-1906 .... **TCLC 65**

Maitland, Sara (Louise) 1950- .... **CLC 49**
See also BRWS 11; CA 69-72; CANR 13, 59; DLB 271; FW

Major, Clarence 1936- ...... **BLC 1:2; CLC 3, 19, 48**
See also AFAW 2; BW 2, 3; CA 21-24R; CAAS 6; CANR 13, 25, 53, 82; CN 3, 4, 5, 6, 7; CP 2, 3, 4, 5, 6, 7; CSW; DAM MULT; DLB 33; EWL 3; MAL 5; MSW

Major, Kevin (Gerald) 1949- .... **CLC 26**
See also AAYA 16; CA 97-100; CANR 21, 38, 112; CLR 11; DAC; DLB 60; INT CANR-21; JRDA; MAICYA 1, 2; MAIC-YAS 1; SATA 32, 82, 134; WYA; YAW

Maki, James
See Ozu, Yasujiro

Makin, Bathsua 1600-1675(?) .... **LC 137**

Makine, Andrei 1957-
See Makine, Andrei

Makine, Andrei 1957- .... **CLC 198**
See also CA 176; CANR 103, 162; MTFW 2005

Malabaila, Damiano
See Levi, Primo

Malamud, Bernard 1914-1986 .. **CLC 1, 2, 3, 5, 8, 9, 11, 18, 27, 44, 78, 85; SSC 15; TCLC 129, 184; WLC 4**
See also AAYA 16; AMWS 1; BPFB 2; BYA 15; CA 5-8R; 118; CABS 1; CANR 28, 62, 114; CDALB 1941-1968; CN 1, 2, 3, 4; CPW; DA; DA3; DAB; DAC; DAM MST, NOV, POP; DLB 2, 28, 152; DLBY 1980, 1986; EWL 3; EXPS; LAIT 4; LATS 1:1; MAL 5; MTCW 1, 2; MTFW 2005; NFS 27; RGAL 4; RGHL; RGSF 2; SSFS 8, 13, 16; TUS

Malan, Herman
See Bosman, Herman Charles; Bosman, Herman Charles

Malaparte, Curzio 1898-1957 .... **TCLC 52**
See also DLB 264

Malcolm, Dan
See Silverberg, Robert

Malcolm, Janet 1934- .... **CLC 201**
See also CA 123; CANR 89; NCFS 1

Malcolm X
See Little, Malcolm

Malebranche, Nicolas 1638-1715 .... **LC 133**
See also GFL Beginnings to 1789

Malherbe, Francois de 1555-1628 .... **LC 5**
See also DLB 327; GFL Beginnings to 1789

Mallarme, Stephane 1842-1898 ...... **NCLC 4, 41, 210; PC 4**
See also DAM POET; DLB 217; EW 7; GFL 1789 to the Present; LMFS 2; RGWL 2, 3; TWA

Mallet-Joris, Francoise 1930- .... **CLC 11**
See also CA 65-68; CANR 17; CWW 2; DLB 83; EWL 3; GFL 1789 to the Present

Malley, Ern
See McAuley, James Phillip

Mallon, Thomas 1951- .... **CLC 172**
See also CA 110; CANR 29, 57, 92; DLB 350

Mallowan, Agatha Christie
See Christie, Agatha (Mary Clarissa)

Maloff, Saul 1922- .... **CLC 5**
See also CA 33-36R

Malone, Louis
See MacNeice, (Frederick) Louis

Malone, Michael (Christopher) 1942- .... **CLC 43**
See also CA 77-80; CANR 14, 32, 57, 114

Malory, Sir Thomas 1410(?)-1471(?) . **LC 11, 88; WLCS**
See also BRW 1; BRWR 2; CDBLB Before 1660; DA; DAB; DAC; DAM MST; DLB 146; EFS 2; RGEL 2; SATA 59; SATA-Brief 33; TEA; WLIT 3

Malouf, David 1934- .... **CLC 28, 86, 245**
See also BRWS 12; CA 124; CANR 50, 76, 180; CN 3, 4, 5, 6, 7; CP 1, 3, 4, 5, 6, 7; DLB 289; EWL 3; MTCW 2; MTFW 2005; SSFS 24

Malouf, George Joseph David
See Malouf, David

Malraux, (Georges-)Andre 1901-1976 .... **CLC 1, 4, 9, 13, 15, 57; TCLC 209**
See also BPFB 2; CA 21-22; 69-72; CANR 34, 58; CAP 2; DA3; DAM NOV; DLB 72; EW 12; EWL 3; GFL 1789 to the Present; MTCW 1, 2; MTFW 2005; RGWL 2, 3; TWA

Malthus, Thomas Robert 1766-1834 .... **NCLC 145**
See also DLB 107, 158; RGEL 2

Malzberg, Barry N(athaniel) 1939- ... **CLC 7**
See also CA 61-64; CAAS 4; CANR 16; CMW 4; DLB 8; SFW 4

Mamet, David 1947- .. **CLC 9, 15, 34, 46, 91, 166; DC 4, 24**
See also AAYA 3, 60; AMWS 14; CA 81-84; CABS 3; CAD; CANR 15, 41, 67, 72, 129, 172; CD 5, 6; DA3; DAM DRAM; DFS 2, 3, 6, 12, 15; DLB 7; EWL 3; IDFW 4; MAL 5; MTCW 1, 2; MTFW 2005; RGAL 4

Mamet, David Alan
See Mamet, David

Mamoulian, Rouben (Zachary) 1897-1987 .... **CLC 16**
See also CA 25-28R; 124; CANR 85

Mandelshtam, Osip
See Mandelstam, Osip (Emilievich)
See also DLB 295

Mandelstam, Osip (Emilievich) 1891(?)-1943(?) .... **PC 14; TCLC 2, 6**
See Mandelshtam, Osip
See also CA 104; 150; EW 10; EWL 3; MTCW 2; RGWL 2, 3; TWA

Mander, (Mary) Jane 1877-1949 ... **TCLC 31**
See also CA 162; RGEL 2

Mandeville, Bernard 1670-1733 .... **LC 82**
See also DLB 101

Mandeville, Sir John fl. 1350- ...... **CMLC 19**
See also DLB 146

Mandiargues, Andre Pieyre de
See Pieyre de Mandiargues, Andre

Mandrake, Ethel Belle
See Thurman, Wallace (Henry)

Mangan, James Clarence 1803-1849 .... **NCLC 27**
See also BRWS 13; RGEL 2

Maniere, J.-E.
See Giraudoux, Jean(-Hippolyte)

Mankiewicz, Herman (Jacob) 1897-1953 .... **TCLC 85**
See also CA 120; 169; DLB 26; IDFW 3, 4

Manley, (Mary) Delariviere 1672(?)-1724 .... **LC 1, 42**
See also DLB 39, 80; RGEL 2

Mann, Abel
See Creasey, John

Mann, Emily 1952- .... **DC 7**
See also CA 130; CAD; CANR 55; CD 5, 6; CWD; DLB 266

Mann, (Luiz) Heinrich 1871-1950 ... **TCLC 9**
See also CA 106; 164, 181; DLB 66, 118; EW 8; EWL 3; RGWL 2, 3

Mann, (Paul) Thomas 1875-1955 . **SSC 5, 80, 82; TCLC 2, 8, 14, 21, 35, 44, 60, 168; WLC 4**
See also BPFB 2; CA 104; 128; CANR 133; CDWLB 2; DA; DA3; DAB; DAC; DAM MST, NOV; DLB 66, 331; EW 9; EWL 3;

GLL 1; LATS 1:1; LMFS 1; MTCW 1, 2;
MTFW 2005; NFS 17; RGSF 2; RGWL
2, 3; SSFS 4, 9; TWA
Mannheim, Karl 1893-1947 .... **TCLC 65**
See also CA 204
Manning, David
See Faust, Frederick
Manning, Frederic 1882-1935 .... **TCLC 25**
See also CA 124; 216; DLB 260
Manning, Olivia 1915-1980 .... **CLC 5, 19**
See also CA 5-8R; 101; CANR 29; CN 1,
2; EWL 3; FW; MTCW 1; RGEL 2
Mannyng, Robert c. 1264-c.
1340 .... **CMLC 83**
See also DLB 146
Mano, D. Keith 1942- .... **CLC 2, 10**
See also CA 25-28R; CAAS 6; CANR 26,
57; DLB 6
Mansfield, Katherine
See Beauchamp, Kathleen Mansfield
Manso, Peter 1940- .... **CLC 39**
See also CA 29-32R; CANR 44, 156
Mantecon, Juan Jimenez
See Jimenez (Mantecon), Juan Ramon
Mantel, Hilary 1952- .... **CLC 144**
See also CA 125; CANR 54, 101, 161; CN
5, 6, 7; DLB 271; RHW
Mantel, Hilary Mary
See Mantel, Hilary
Manton, Peter
See Creasey, John
Man Without a Spleen, A
See Chekhov, Anton (Pavlovich)
Manzano, Juan Franciso
1797(?)-1854 .... **NCLC 155**
Manzoni, Alessandro 1785-1873 ... **NCLC 29, 98**
See also EW 5; RGWL 2, 3; TWA; WLIT 7
Map, Walter 1140-1209 .... **CMLC 32**
Mapu, Abraham (ben Jekutiel)
1808-1867 .... **NCLC 18**
Mara, Sally
See Queneau, Raymond
Maracle, Lee 1950- .... **NNAL**
See also CA 149
Marat, Jean Paul 1743-1793 .... **LC 10**
Marcel, Gabriel Honore 1889-1973 . **CLC 15**
See also CA 102; 45-48; EWL 3; MTCW 1, 2
March, William
See Campbell, William Edward March
Marchbanks, Samuel
See Davies, Robertson
Marchi, Giacomo
See Bassani, Giorgio
Marcus Aurelius
See Aurelius, Marcus
Marcuse, Herbert 1898-1979 .... **TCLC 207**
See also CA 188; 89-92; DLB 242
Marguerite
See de Navarre, Marguerite
Marguerite d'Angouleme
See de Navarre, Marguerite
Marguerite de Navarre
See de Navarre, Marguerite
Margulies, Donald 1954- .... **CLC 76**
See also AAYA 57; CA 200; CD 6; DFS 13;
DLB 228
Marias, Javier 1951- .... **CLC 239**
See also CA 167; CANR 109, 139; DLB
322; HW 2; MTFW 2005
Marie de France c. 12th cent. - ...... **CMLC 8, 111; PC 22**
See also DLB 208; FW; RGWL 2, 3
Marie de l'Incarnation 1599-1672 ..... **LC 10, 168**
Marier, Captain Victor
See Griffith, D.W.

Mariner, Scott
See Pohl, Frederik
Marinetti, Filippo Tommaso
1876-1944 .... **TCLC 10**
See also CA 107; DLB 114, 264; EW 9;
EWL 3; WLIT 7
Marivaux, Pierre Carlet de Chamblain de
1688-1763 .... **DC 7; LC 4, 123**
See also DLB 314; GFL Beginnings to
1789; RGWL 2, 3; TWA
Markandaya, Kamala
See Taylor, Kamala
Markfield, Wallace (Arthur)
1926-2002 .... **CLC 8**
See also CA 69-72; 208; CAAS 3; CN 1, 2,
3, 4, 5, 6, 7; DLB 2, 28; DLBY 2002
Markham, Edwin 1852-1940 .... **TCLC 47**
See also CA 160; DLB 54, 186; MAL 5;
RGAL 4
Markham, Robert
See Amis, Kingsley
Marks, J.
See Highwater, Jamake (Mamake)
Marks-Highwater, J.
See Highwater, Jamake (Mamake)
Markson, David M. 1927- .... **CLC 67**
See also AMWS 17; CA 49-52; CANR 1,
91, 158; CN 5, 6
Markson, David Merrill
See Markson, David M.
Marlatt, Daphne (Buckle) 1942- .... **CLC 168**
See also CA 25-28R; CANR 17, 39; CN 6,
7; CP 4, 5, 6, 7; CWP; DLB 60; FW
Marley, Bob
See Marley, Robert Nesta
Marley, Robert Nesta 1945-1981 ...... **CLC 17**
See also CA 107; 103
Marlowe, Christopher 1564-1593 . **DC 1; LC 22, 47, 117; PC 57; WLC 4**
See also BRW 1; BRWR 1; CDBLB Before
1660; DA; DA3; DAB; DAC; DAM
DRAM, MST; DFS 1, 5, 13, 21; DLB 62;
EXPP; LMFS 1; PFS 22; RGEL 2; TEA;
WLIT 3
Marlowe, Stephen 1928-2008 .... **CLC 70**
See also CA 13-16R; 269; CANR 6, 55;
CMW 4; SFW 4
Marmion, Shakerley 1603-1639 .... **LC 89**
See also DLB 58; RGEL 2
Marmontel, Jean-Francois 1723-1799 .. **LC 2**
See also DLB 314
Maron, Monika 1941- .... **CLC 165**
See also CA 201
Marot, Clement c. 1496-1544 .... **LC 133**
See also DLB 327; GFL Beginnings to 1789
Marquand, John P(hillips)
1893-1960 .... **CLC 2, 10**
See also AMW; BPFB 2; CA 85-88; CANR
73; CMW 4; DLB 9, 102; EWL 3; MAL
5; MTCW 2; RGAL 4
Marques, Rene 1919-1979 .. **CLC 96; HLC 2**
See also CA 97-100; 85-88; CANR 78;
DAM MULT; DLB 305; EWL 3; HW 1,
2; LAW; RGSF 2
Marquez, Gabriel Garcia
See Garcia Marquez, Gabriel
Marquis, Don(ald Robert Perry)
1878-1937 .... **TCLC 7**
See also CA 104; 166; DLB 11, 25; MAL
5; RGAL 4
Marquis de Sade
See Sade, Donatien Alphonse Francois
Marric, J. J.
See Creasey, John
Marryat, Frederick 1792-1848 .... **NCLC 3**
See also DLB 21, 163; RGEL 2; WCH
Marsden, James
See Creasey, John
Marsh, Edward 1872-1953 .... **TCLC 99**

Marsh, (Edith) Ngaio 1895-1982 .. **CLC 7, 53**
See also CA 9-12R; CANR 6, 58; CMW 4;
CN 1, 2, 3; CPW; DAM POP; DLB 77;
MSW; MTCW 1, 2; RGEL 2; TEA
Marshall, Alan
See Westlake, Donald E.
Marshall, Allen
See Westlake, Donald E.
Marshall, Garry 1934- .... **CLC 17**
See also AAYA 3; CA 111; SATA 60
Marshall, Paule 1929- .... **BLC 1:3, 2:3; CLC 27, 72, 253; SSC 3**
See also AFAW 1, 2; AMWS 11; BPFB 2;
BW 2, 3; CA 77-80; CANR 25, 73, 129;
CN 1, 2, 3, 4, 5, 6, 7; DA3; DAM MULT;
DLB 33, 157, 227; EWL 3; LATS 1:2;
MAL 5; MTCW 1, 2; MTFW 2005;
RGAL 4; SSFS 15
Marshallik
See Zangwill, Israel
Marsilius of Inghen c.
1340-1396 .... **CMLC 106**
Marsten, Richard
See Hunter, Evan
Marston, John 1576-1634 .... **LC 33**
See also BRW 2; DAM DRAM; DLB 58,
172; RGEL 2
Martel, Yann 1963- .... **CLC 192**
See also AAYA 67; CA 146; CANR 114;
DLB 326, 334; MTFW 2005; NFS 27
Martens, Adolphe-Adhemar
See Ghelderode, Michel de
Martha, Henry
See Harris, Mark
Marti, Jose 1853-1895 ..... **HLC 2; NCLC 63; PC 76**
See also DAM MULT; DLB 290; HW 2;
LAW; RGWL 2, 3; WLIT 1
Martial c. 40-c. 104 .... **CMLC 35; PC 10**
See also AW 2; CDWLB 1; DLB 211;
RGWL 2, 3
Martin, Ken
See Hubbard, L. Ron
Martin, Richard
See Creasey, John
Martin, Steve 1945- .... **CLC 30, 217**
See also AAYA 53; CA 97-100; CANR 30,
100, 140; DFS 19; MTCW 1; MTFW
2005
Martin, Valerie 1948- .... **CLC 89**
See also BEST 90:2; CA 85-88; CANR 49,
89, 165
Martin, Violet Florence 1862-1915 .. **SSC 56; TCLC 51**
Martin, Webber
See Silverberg, Robert
Martindale, Patrick Victor
See White, Patrick (Victor Martindale)
Martin du Gard, Roger
1881-1958 .... **TCLC 24**
See also CA 118; CANR 94; DLB 65, 331;
EWL 3; GFL 1789 to the Present; RGWL
2, 3
Martineau, Harriet 1802-1876 ...... **NCLC 26, 137**
See also DLB 21, 55, 159, 163, 166, 190;
FW; RGEL 2; YABC 2
Martines, Julia
See O'Faolain, Julia
Martinez, Enrique Gonzalez
See Gonzalez Martinez, Enrique
Martinez, Jacinto Benavente y
See Benavente (y Martinez), Jacinto
Martinez de la Rosa, Francisco de Paula
1787-1862 .... **NCLC 102**
See also TWA
Martinez Ruiz, Jose 1873-1967 .... **CLC 11**
See also CA 93-96; DLB 322; EW 3; EWL
3; HW 1

Martinez Sierra, Gregorio
See Martinez Sierra, Maria

Martinez Sierra, Gregorio
1881-1947 .... **TCLC 6**
See also CA 115; EWL 3

Martinez Sierra, Maria 1874-1974 .. **TCLC 6**
See also CA 250; 115; EWL 3

Martinsen, Martin
See Follett, Ken

Martinson, Harry (Edmund)
1904-1978 .... **CLC 14**
See also CA 77-80; CANR 34, 130; DLB
259, 331; EWL 3

Marti y Perez, Jose Julian
See Marti, Jose

Martyn, Edward 1859-1923 .... **TCLC 131**
See also CA 179; DLB 10; RGEL 2

Marut, Ret
See Traven, B.

Marut, Robert
See Traven, B.

Marvell, Andrew 1621-1678 .... **LC 4, 43; PC
10, 86; WLC 4**
See also BRW 2; BRWR 2; CDBLB 1660-
1789; DA; DAB; DAC; DAM MST,
POET; DLB 131; EXPP; PFS 5; RGEL 2;
TEA; WP

Marx, Karl (Heinrich)
1818-1883 .... **NCLC 17, 114**
See also DLB 129; LATS 1:1; TWA

Masaoka, Shiki -1902
See Masaoka, Tsunenori

Masaoka, Tsunenori 1867-1902 ..... **TCLC 18**
See also CA 117; 191; EWL 3; RGWL 3;
TWA

Masaoka Shiki
See Masaoka, Tsunenori

Masefield, John (Edward)
1878-1967 .... **CLC 11, 47; PC 78**
See also CA 19-20; 25-28R; CANR 33;
CAP 2; CDBLB 1890-1914; DAM POET;
DLB 10, 19, 153, 160; EWL 3; EXPP;
FANT; MTCW 1, 2; PFS 5; RGEL 2;
SATA 19

Maso, Carole 1955(?)- .... **CLC 44**
See also CA 170; CANR 148; CN 7; GLL
2; RGAL 4

Mason, Bobbie Ann 1940- ... **CLC 28, 43, 82,
154; SSC 4, 101**
See also AAYA 5, 42; AMWS 8; BPFB 2;
CA 53-56; CANR 11, 31, 58, 83, 125,
169; CDALBS; CN 5, 6, 7; CSW; DA3;
DLB 173; DLBY 1987; EWL 3; EXPS;
INT CANR-31; MAL 5; MTCW 1, 2;
MTFW 2005; NFS 4; RGAL 4; RGSF 2;
SSFS 3, 8, 20; TCLE 1:2; YAW

Mason, Ernst
See Pohl, Frederik

Mason, Hunni B.
See Sternheim, (William Adolf) Carl

Mason, Lee W.
See Malzberg, Barry N(athaniel)

Mason, Nick 1945- .... **CLC 35**

Mason, Tally
See Derleth, August (William)

Mass, Anna .... **CLC 59**

Mass, William
See Gibson, William

Massinger, Philip 1583-1640 .... **LC 70**
See also BRWS 11; DLB 58; RGEL 2

Master Lao
See Lao Tzu

Masters, Edgar Lee 1868-1950 ...... **PC 1, 36;
TCLC 2, 25; WLCS**
See also AMWS 1; CA 104; 133; CDALB
1865-1917; DA; DAC; DAM MST,
POET; DLB 54; EWL 3; EXPP; MAL 5;
MTCW 1, 2; MTFW 2005; RGAL 4;
TUS; WP

Masters, Hilary 1928- .... **CLC 48**
See also CA 25-28R, 217; CAAE 217;
CANR 13, 47, 97, 171; CN 6, 7; DLB
244

Masters, Hilary Thomas
See Masters, Hilary

Mastrosimone, William 1947- .... **CLC 36**
See also CA 186; CAD; CD 5, 6

Mathe, Albert
See Camus, Albert

Mather, Cotton 1663-1728 .... **LC 38**
See also AMWS 2; CDALB 1640-1865;
DLB 24, 30, 140; RGAL 4; TUS

Mather, Increase 1639-1723 .... **LC 38, 161**
See also DLB 24

Mathers, Marshall
See Eminem

Mathers, Marshall Bruce
See Eminem

Matheson, Richard 1926- .... **CLC 37, 267**
See also AAYA 31; CA 97-100; CANR 88,
99; DLB 8, 44; HGG; INT CA-97-100;
SCFW 1, 2; SFW 4; SUFW 2

Matheson, Richard Burton
See Matheson, Richard

Mathews, Harry 1930- .... **CLC 6, 52**
See also CA 21-24R; CAAS 6; CANR 18,
40, 98, 160; CN 5, 6, 7

Mathews, John Joseph 1894-1979 .. **CLC 84;
NNAL**
See also CA 19-20; 142; CANR 45; CAP 2;
DAM MULT; DLB 175; TCWW 1, 2

Mathias, Roland 1915-2007 .... **CLC 45**
See also CA 97-100; 263; CANR 19, 41;
CP 1, 2, 3, 4, 5, 6, 7; DLB 27

Mathias, Roland Glyn
See Mathias, Roland

Matsuo Basho 1644(?)-1694 ...... **LC 62; PC 3**
See also DAM POET; PFS 2, 7, 18; RGWL
2, 3; WP

Mattheson, Rodney
See Creasey, John

Matthew of Vendome c. 1130-c.
1200 .... **CMLC 99**
See also DLB 208

Matthews, (James) Brander
1852-1929 .... **TCLC 95**
See also CA 181; DLB 71, 78; DLBD 13

Matthews, Greg 1949- .... **CLC 45**
See also CA 135

Matthews, William (Procter III)
1942-1997 .... **CLC 40**
See also AMWS 9; CA 29-32R; 162; CAAS
18; CANR 12, 57; CP 2, 3, 4, 5, 6; DLB
5

Matthias, John (Edward) 1941- .... **CLC 9**
See also CA 33-36R; CANR 56; CP 4, 5, 6,
7

Matthiessen, F(rancis) O(tto)
1902-1950 .... **TCLC 100**
See also CA 185; DLB 63; MAL 5

Matthiessen, Peter 1927- ... **CLC 5, 7, 11, 32,
64, 245**
See also AAYA 6, 40; AMWS 5; ANW;
BEST 90:4; BPFB 2; CA 9-12R; CANR
21, 50, 73, 100, 138; CN 1, 2, 3, 4, 5, 6,
7; DA3; DAM NOV; DLB 6, 173, 275;
MAL 5; MTCW 1, 2; MTFW 2005; SATA
27

Maturin, Charles Robert
1780(?)-1824 .... **NCLC 6, 169**
See also BRWS 8; DLB 178; GL 3; HGG;
LMFS 1; RGEL 2; SUFW

Matute (Ausejo), Ana Maria 1925- .. **CLC 11**
See also CA 89-92; CANR 129; CWW 2;
DLB 322; EWL 3; MTCW 1; RGSF 2

Maugham, W. S.
See Maugham, W(illiam) Somerset

Maugham, W(illiam) Somerset
1874-1965 .. **CLC 1, 11, 15, 67, 93; SSC
8, 94; TCLC 208; WLC 4**
See also AAYA 55; BPFB 2; BRW 6; CA
5-8R; 25-28R; CANR 40, 127; CDBLB
1914-1945; CMW 4; DA; DA3; DAB;
DAC; DAM DRAM, MST, NOV; DFS
22; DLB 10, 36, 77, 100, 162, 195; EWL
3; LAIT 3; MTCW 1, 2; MTFW 2005;
NFS 23; RGEL 2; RGSF 2; SATA 54;
SSFS 17

Maugham, William Somerset
See Maugham, W(illiam) Somerset

Maupassant, (Henri Rene Albert) Guy de
1850-1893 . **NCLC 1, 42, 83; SSC 1, 64;
WLC 4**
See also BYA 14; DA; DA3; DAB; DAC;
DAM MST; DLB 123; EW 7; EXPS; GFL
1789 to the Present; LAIT 2; LMFS 1;
RGSF 2; RGWL 2, 3; SSFS 4, 21; SUFW;
TWA

Maupin, Armistead 1944- .... **CLC 95**
See also CA 125; 130; CANR 58, 101, 183;
CPW; DA3; DAM POP; DLB 278; GLL
1; INT CA-130; MTCW 2; MTFW 2005

Maupin, Armistead Jones, Jr.
See Maupin, Armistead

Maurhut, Richard
See Traven, B.

Mauriac, Claude 1914-1996 .... **CLC 9**
See also CA 89-92; 152; CWW 2; DLB 83;
EWL 3; GFL 1789 to the Present

Mauriac, Francois (Charles)
1885-1970 .... **CLC 4, 9, 56; SSC 24**
See also CA 25-28; CAP 2; DLB 65, 331;
EW 10; EWL 3; GFL 1789 to the Present;
MTCW 1, 2; MTFW 2005; RGWL 2, 3;
TWA

Mavor, Osborne Henry 1888-1951 .. **TCLC 3**
See also CA 104; DLB 10; EWL 3

Maxwell, Glyn 1962- .... **CLC 238**
See also CA 154; CANR 88, 183; CP 6, 7;
PFS 23

Maxwell, William (Keepers, Jr.)
1908-2000 .... **CLC 19**
See also AMWS 8; CA 93-96; 189; CANR
54, 95; CN 1, 2, 3, 4, 5, 6, 7; DLB 218,
278; DLBY 1980; INT CA-93-96; MAL
5; SATA-Obit 128

May, Elaine 1932- .... **CLC 16**
See also CA 124; 142; CAD; CWD; DLB
44

Mayakovski, Vladimir (Vladimirovich)
1893-1930 .... **TCLC 4, 18**
See also CA 104; 158; EW 11; EWL 3;
IDTP; MTCW 2; MTFW 2005; RGWL 2,
3; SFW 4; TWA; WP

Mayakovsky, Vladimir
See Mayakovski, Vladimir (Vladimirovich)

Mayhew, Henry 1812-1887 .... **NCLC 31**
See also DLB 18, 55, 190

Mayle, Peter 1939(?)- .... **CLC 89**
See also CA 139; CANR 64, 109, 168

Maynard, Joyce 1953- .... **CLC 23**
See also CA 111; 129; CANR 64, 169

Mayne, William (James Carter)
1928- .... **CLC 12**
See also AAYA 20; CA 9-12R; CANR 37,
80, 100; CLR 25, 123; FANT; JRDA;
MAICYA 1, 2; MAICYAS 1; SAAS 11;
SATA 6, 68, 122; SUFW 2; YAW

Mayo, Jim
See L'Amour, Louis

Maysles, Albert 1926- .... **CLC 16**
See also CA 29-32R

Maysles, David 1932-1987 .... **CLC 16**
See also CA 191**

DLB 45; DLBD 7; EWL 3; EXPP; FL 1:6;
MAL 5; MBL; MTCW 1, 2; MTFW 2005;
PAB; PFS 14, 17; RGAL 4; SATA 20;
TUS; WP

Moore, Marie Lorena 1957- ...... **CLC 39, 45, 68, 165**
See also AMWS 10; CA 116; CANR 39, 83, 139; CN 5, 6, 7; DLB 234; MTFW 2005; SSFS 19

Moore, Michael 1954- .... **CLC 218**
See also AAYA 53; CA 166; CANR 150

Moore, Thomas 1779-1852 .... **NCLC 6, 110**
See also DLB 96, 144; RGEL 2

Moorhouse, Frank 1938- .... **SSC 40**
See also CA 118; CANR 92; CN 3, 4, 5, 6, 7; DLB 289; RGSF 2

Mora, Pat 1942- .... **HLC 2**
See also AMWS 13; CA 129; CANR 57, 81, 112, 171; CLR 58; DAM MULT; DLB 209; HW 1, 2; LLW; MAICYA 2; MTFW 2005; SATA 92, 134, 186

Moraga, Cherríe 1952- ... **CLC 126, 250; DC 22**
See also CA 131; CANR 66, 154; DAM MULT; DLB 82, 249; FW; GLL 1; HW 1, 2; LLW

Moran, J.L.
See Whitaker, Rod

Morand, Paul 1888-1976 .... **CLC 41; SSC 22**
See also CA 184; 69-72; DLB 65; EWL 3

Morante, Elsa 1918-1985 .... **CLC 8, 47**
See also CA 85-88; 117; CANR 35; DLB 177; EWL 3; MTCW 1, 2; MTFW 2005; RGHL; RGWL 2, 3; WLIT 7

Moravia, Alberto
See Pincherle, Alberto

Morck, Paul
See Rolvaag, O.E.

More, Hannah 1745-1833 ...... **NCLC 27, 141**
See also DLB 107, 109, 116, 158; RGEL 2

More, Henry 1614-1687 .... **LC 9**
See also DLB 126, 252

More, Sir Thomas 1478(?)-1535 ... **LC 10, 32, 140**
See also BRWC 1; BRWS 7; DLB 136, 281; LMFS 1; NFS 29; RGEL 2; TEA

Moreas, Jean
See Papadiamantopoulos, Johannes

Moreton, Andrew Esq.
See Defoe, Daniel

Moreton, Lee
See Boucicault, Dion

Morgan, Berry 1919-2002 .... **CLC 6**
See also CA 49-52; 208; DLB 6

Morgan, Claire
See Highsmith, Patricia

Morgan, Edwin 1920- .... **CLC 31**
See also BRWS 9; CA 5-8R; CANR 3, 43, 90; CP 1, 2, 3, 4, 5, 6, 7; DLB 27

Morgan, Edwin George
See Morgan, Edwin

Morgan, (George) Frederick
1922-2004 .... **CLC 23**
See also CA 17-20R; 224; CANR 21, 144; CP 2, 3, 4, 5, 6, 7

Morgan, Harriet
See Mencken, H. L.

Morgan, Jane
See Cooper, James Fenimore

Morgan, Janet 1945- .... **CLC 39**
See also CA 65-68

Morgan, Lady 1776(?)-1859 .... **NCLC 29**
See also DLB 116, 158; RGEL 2

Morgan, Robin (Evonne) 1941- .... **CLC 2**
See also CA 69-72; CANR 29, 68; FW; GLL 2; MTCW 1; SATA 80

Morgan, Scott
See Kuttner, Henry

Morgan, Seth 1949(?)-1990 .... **CLC 65**
See also CA 185; 132

Morgenstern, Christian (Otto Josef Wolfgang) 1871-1914 .... **TCLC 8**
See also CA 105; 191; EWL 3

Morgenstern, S.
See Goldman, William

Mori, Rintaro
See Mori Ogai

Mori, Toshio 1910-1980 ... **AAL; SSC 83, 123**
See also CA 116; 244; DLB 312; RGSF 2

Moricz, Zsigmond 1879-1942 .... **TCLC 33**
See also CA 165; DLB 215; EWL 3

Morike, Eduard (Friedrich)
1804-1875 .... **NCLC 10, 201**
See also DLB 133; RGWL 2, 3

Morin, Jean-Paul
See Whitaker, Rod

Mori Ogai 1862-1922 .... **TCLC 14**
See also CA 110; 164; DLB 180; EWL 3; MJW; RGWL 3; TWA

Moritz, Karl Philipp 1756-1793 .... **LC 2, 162**
See also DLB 94

Morland, Peter Henry
See Faust, Frederick

Morley, Christopher (Darlington)
1890-1957 .... **TCLC 87**
See also CA 112; 213; DLB 9; MAL 5; RGAL 4

Morren, Theophil
See Hofmannsthal, Hugo von

Morris, Bill 1952- .... **CLC 76**
See also CA 225

Morris, Julian
See West, Morris L(anglo)

Morris, Steveland Judkins (?)-
See Wonder, Stevie

Morris, William 1834-1896 . **NCLC 4; PC 55**
See also BRW 5; CDBLB 1832-1890; DLB 18, 35, 57, 156, 178, 184; FANT; RGEL 2; SFW 4; SUFW

Morris, Wright (Marion) 1910-1998 . **CLC 1, 3, 7, 18, 37; TCLC 107**
See also AMW; CA 9-12R; 167; CANR 21, 81; CN 1, 2, 3, 4, 5, 6; DLB 2, 206, 218; DLBY 1981; EWL 3; MAL 5; MTCW 1, 2; MTFW 2005; RGAL 4; TCWW 1, 2

Morrison, Arthur 1863-1945 .... **SSC 40; TCLC 72**
See also CA 120; 157; CMW 4; DLB 70, 135, 197; RGEL 2

Morrison, Chloe Anthony Wofford
See Morrison, Toni

Morrison, James Douglas
1943-1971 .... **CLC 17**
See also CA 73-76; CANR 40

Morrison, Jim
See Morrison, James Douglas

Morrison, John Gordon 1904-1998 ... **SSC 93**
See also CA 103; CANR 92; DLB 260

Morrison, Toni 1931- . **BLC 1:3, 2:3; CLC 4, 10, 22, 55, 81, 87, 173, 194; SSC 126; WLC 4**
See also AAYA 1, 22, 61; AFAW 1, 2; AMWC 1; AMWS 3; BPFB 2; BW 2, 3; CA 29-32R; CANR 27, 42, 67, 113, 124; CDALB 1968-1988; CLR 99; CN 3, 4, 5, 6, 7; CPW; DA; DA3; DAB; DAC; DAM MST, MULT, NOV, POP; DLB 6, 33, 143, 331; DLBY 1981; EWL 3; EXPN; FL 1:6; FW; GL 3; LAIT 2, 4; LATS 1:2; LMFS 2; MAL 5; MBL; MTCW 1, 2; MTFW 2005; NFS 1, 6, 8, 14; RGAL 4; RHW; SATA 57, 144; SSFS 5; TCLE 1:2; TUS; YAW

Morrison, Van 1945- .... **CLC 21**
See also CA 116; 168

Morrissy, Mary 1957- .... **CLC 99**
See also CA 205; DLB 267

Mortimer, John 1923-2009 .... **CLC 28, 43**
See Morton, Kate
See also CA 13-16R; 282; CANR 21, 69, 109, 172; CBD; CD 5, 6; CDBLB 1960 to Present; CMW 4; CN 5, 6, 7; CPW; DA3; DAM DRAM, POP; DLB 13, 245, 271; INT CANR-21; MSW; MTCW 1, 2; MTFW 2005; RGEL 2

Mortimer, John C.
See Mortimer, John

Mortimer, John Clifford
See Mortimer, John

Mortimer, Penelope (Ruth)
1918-1999 .... **CLC 5**
See also CA 57-60; 187; CANR 45, 88; CN 1, 2, 3, 4, 5, 6

Mortimer, Sir John
See Mortimer, John

Morton, Anthony
See Creasey, John

Morton, Thomas 1579(?)-1647(?) .... **LC 72**
See also DLB 24; RGEL 2

Mosca, Gaetano 1858-1941 .... **TCLC 75**

Moses, Daniel David 1952- .... **NNAL**
See also CA 186; CANR 160; DLB 334

Mosher, Howard Frank 1943- .... **CLC 62**
See also CA 139; CANR 65, 115, 181

Mosley, Nicholas 1923- .... **CLC 43, 70**
See also CA 69-72; CANR 41, 60, 108, 158; CN 1, 2, 3, 4, 5, 6, 7; DLB 14, 207

Mosley, Walter 1952- ... **BLCS; CLC 97, 184, 278**
See also AAYA 57; AMWS 13; BPFB 2; BW 2; CA 142; CANR 57, 92, 136, 172; CMW 4; CN 7; CPW; DA3; DAM MULT; POP; DLB 306; MSW; MTCW 2; MTFW 2005

Moss, Howard 1922-1987 . **CLC 7, 14, 45, 50**
See also CA 1-4R; 123; CANR 1, 44; CP 1, 2, 3, 4; DAM POET; DLB 5

Mossgiel, Rab
See Burns, Robert

Motion, Andrew 1952- .... **CLC 47**
See also BRWS 7; CA 146; CANR 90, 142; CP 4, 5, 6, 7; DLB 40; MTFW 2005

Motion, Andrew Peter
See Motion, Andrew

Motley, Willard (Francis)
1909-1965 .... **CLC 18**
See also AMWS 17; BW 1; CA 117; 106; CANR 88; DLB 76, 143

Motoori, Norinaga 1730-1801 .... **NCLC 45**

Mott, Michael (Charles Alston)
1930- .... **CLC 15, 34**
See also CA 5-8R; CAAS 7; CANR 7, 29

Moulsworth, Martha 1577-1646 .... **LC 168**

Mountain Wolf Woman 1884-1960 . **CLC 92; NNAL**
See also CA 144; CANR 90

Moure, Erin 1955- .... **CLC 88**
See also CA 113; CP 5, 6, 7; CWP; DLB 60

Mourning Dove 1885(?)-1936 .... **NNAL**
See also CA 144; CANR 90; DAM MULT; DLB 175, 221

Mowat, Farley 1921- .... **CLC 26**
See also AAYA 1, 50; BYA 2; CA 1-4R; CANR 4, 24, 42, 68, 108; CLR 20; CPW; DAC; DAM MST; DLB 68; INT CANR-24; JRDA; MAICYA 1, 2; MTCW 1, 2; MTFW 2005; SATA 3, 55; YAW

Mowat, Farley McGill
See Mowat, Farley

Mowatt, Anna Cora 1819-1870 ..... **NCLC 74**
See also RGAL 4

Moye, Guan
See Yan, Mo

Mo Yen
See Yan, Mo

na Gopaleen, Myles
See O Nuallain, Brian
Nagy, Laszlo 1925-1978 .... **CLC 7**
See also CA 129; 112
Naidu, Sarojini 1879-1949 .... **TCLC 80**
See also EWL 3; RGEL 2
Naipaul, Shiva 1945-1985 .... **CLC 32, 39; TCLC 153**
See also CA 110; 112; 116; CANR 33; CN 2, 3; DA3; DAM NOV; DLB 157; DLBY 1985; EWL 3; MTCW 1, 2; MTFW 2005
Naipaul, Shivadhar Srinivasa
See Naipaul, Shiva
Naipaul, V. S. 1932- . **CLC 4, 7, 9, 13, 18, 37, 105, 199; SSC 38, 121**
See also BPFB 2; BRWS 1; CA 1-4R; CANR 1, 33, 51, 91, 126, 191; CDBLB 1960 to Present; CDWLB 3; CN 1, 2, 3, 4, 5, 6, 7; DA3; DAB; DAC; DAM MST, NOV; DLB 125, 204, 207, 326, 331; DLBY 1985, 2001; EWL 3; LATS 1:2; MTCW 1, 2; MTFW 2005; RGEL 2; RGSF 2; TWA; WLIT 4; WWE 1
Naipaul, Vidiahar Surajprasad
See Naipaul, V. S.
Nakos, Lilika 1903(?)-1989 .... **CLC 29**
Napoleon
See Yamamoto, Hisaye
Narayan, R.K. 1906-2001 ...... **CLC 7, 28, 47, 121, 211; SSC 25**
See also BPFB 2; CA 81-84; 196; CANR 33, 61, 112; CN 1, 2, 3, 4, 5, 6, 7; DA3; DAM NOV; DLB 323; DNFS 1; EWL 3; MTCW 1, 2; MTFW 2005; RGEL 2; RGSF 2; SATA 62; SSFS 5; WWE 1
Nash, Fredric Ogden
See Nash, Ogden
Nash, Ogden 1902-1971 ...... **CLC 23; PC 21; TCLC 109**
See also CA 13-14; 29-32R; CANR 34, 61, 185; CAP 1; CP 1; DAM POET; DLB 11; MAICYA 1, 2; MAL 5; MTCW 1, 2; PFS 31; RGAL 4; SATA 2, 46; WP
Nashe, Thomas 1567-1601(?) . **LC 41, 89; PC 82**
See also DLB 167; RGEL 2
Nathan, Daniel
See Dannay, Frederic
Nathan, George Jean 1882-1958 .... **TCLC 18**
See also CA 114; 169; DLB 137; MAL 5
Natsume, Kinnosuke
See Natsume, Soseki
Natsume, Soseki 1867-1916 .... **TCLC 2, 10**
See also CA 104; 195; DLB 180; EWL 3; MJW; RGWL 2, 3; TWA
Natsume Soseki
See Natsume, Soseki
Natti, Lee 1919- .... **CLC 17**
See also CA 5-8R; CANR 2; CWRI 5; SAAS 3; SATA 1, 67
Natti, Mary Lee
See Natti, Lee
Navarre, Marguerite de
See de Navarre, Marguerite
Naylor, Gloria 1950- . **BLC 1:3; CLC 28, 52, 156, 261; WLCS**
See also AAYA 6, 39; AFAW 1, 2; AMWS 8; BW 2, 3; CA 107; CANR 27, 51, 74, 130; CN 4, 5, 6, 7; CPW; DA; DA3; DAC; DAM MST, MULT, NOV, POP; DLB 173; EWL 3; FW; MAL 5; MTCW 1, 2; MTFW 2005; NFS 4, 7; RGAL 4; TCLE 1:2; TUS
Neal, John 1793-1876 .... **NCLC 161**
See also DLB 1, 59, 243; FW; RGAL 4
Neff, Debra .... **CLC 59**

Neihardt, John Gneisenau
1881-1973 .... **CLC 32**
See also CA 13-14; CANR 65; CAP 1; DLB 9, 54, 256; LAIT 2; TCWW 1, 2
Nekrasov, Nikolai Alekseevich
1821-1878 .... **NCLC 11**
See also DLB 277
Nelligan, Emile 1879-1941 .... **TCLC 14**
See also CA 114; 204; DLB 92; EWL 3
Nelson, Alice Ruth Moore Dunbar
1875-1935 .... **HR 1:2**
See also BW 1, 3; CA 122; 124; CANR 82; DLB 50; FW; MTCW 1
Nelson, Willie 1933- .... **CLC 17**
See also CA 107; CANR 114, 178
Nemerov, Howard 1920-1991 .... **CLC 2, 6, 9, 36; PC 24; TCLC 124**
See also AMW; CA 1-4R; 134; CABS 2; CANR 1, 27, 53; CN 1, 2, 3; CP 1, 2, 3, 4, 5; DAM POET; DLB 5, 6; DLBY 1983; EWL 3; INT CANR-27; MAL 5; MTCW 1, 2; MTFW 2005; PFS 10, 14; RGAL 4
Nepos, Cornelius c. 99B.C.-c.
24B.C. .... **CMLC 89**
See also DLB 211
Neruda, Pablo 1904-1973 .. **CLC 1, 2, 5, 7, 9, 28, 62; HLC 2; PC 4, 64; WLC 4**
See also CA 19-20; 45-48; CANR 131; CAP 2; DA; DA3; DAB; DAC; DAM MST, MULT, POET; DLB 283, 331; DNFS 2; EWL 3; HW 1; LAW; MTCW 1, 2; MTFW 2005; PFS 11, 28; RGWL 2, 3; TWA; WLIT 1; WP
Nerval, Gerard de 1808-1855 ... **NCLC 1, 67; PC 13; SSC 18**
See also DLB 217; EW 6; GFL 1789 to the Present; RGSF 2; RGWL 2, 3
Nervo, (Jose) Amado (Ruiz de)
1870-1919 .... **HLCS 2; TCLC 11**
See also CA 109; 131; DLB 290; EWL 3; HW 1; LAW
Nesbit, Malcolm
See Chester, Alfred
Nessi, Pio Baroja y
See Baroja, Pio
Nestroy, Johann 1801-1862 .... **NCLC 42**
See also DLB 133; RGWL 2, 3
Netterville, Luke
See O'Grady, Standish (James)
Neufeld, John (Arthur) 1938- .... **CLC 17**
See also AAYA 11; CA 25-28R; CANR 11, 37, 56; CLR 52; MAICYA 1, 2; SAAS 3; SATA 6, 81, 131; SATA-Essay 131; YAW
Neumann, Alfred 1895-1952 .... **TCLC 100**
See also CA 183; DLB 56
Neumann, Ferenc
See Molnar, Ferenc
Neville, Emily Cheney 1919- .... **CLC 12**
See also BYA 2; CA 5-8R; CANR 3, 37, 85; JRDA; MAICYA 1, 2; SAAS 2; SATA 1; YAW
Newbound, Bernard Slade 1930- .... **CLC 11, 46**
See also CA 81-84; CAAS 9; CANR 49; CCA 1; CD 5, 6; DAM DRAM; DLB 53
Newby, P(ercy) H(oward)
1918-1997 .... **CLC 2, 13**
See also CA 5-8R; 161; CANR 32, 67; CN 1, 2, 3, 4, 5, 6; DAM NOV; DLB 15, 326; MTCW 1; RGEL 2
Newcastle
See Cavendish, Margaret Lucas
Newlove, Donald 1928- .... **CLC 6**
See also CA 29-32R; CANR 25
Newlove, John (Herbert) 1938- .... **CLC 14**
See also CA 21-24R; CANR 9, 25; CP 1, 2, 3, 4, 5, 6, 7

Newman, Charles 1938-2006 .... **CLC 2, 8**
See also CA 21-24R; 249; CANR 84; CN 3, 4, 5, 6
Newman, Charles Hamilton
See Newman, Charles
Newman, Edwin (Harold) 1919- ...... **CLC 14**
See also AITN 1; CA 69-72; CANR 5
Newman, John Henry 1801-1890 . **NCLC 38, 99**
See also BRWS 7; DLB 18, 32, 55; RGEL 2
Newton, (Sir) Isaac 1642-1727 ..... **LC 35, 53**
See also DLB 252
Newton, Suzanne 1936- .... **CLC 35**
See also BYA 7; CA 41-44R; CANR 14; JRDA; SATA 5, 77
New York Dept. of Ed. .... **CLC 70**
Nexo, Martin Andersen
1869-1954 .... **TCLC 43**
See also CA 202; DLB 214; EWL 3
Nezval, Vitezslav 1900-1958 .... **TCLC 44**
See also CA 123; CDWLB 4; DLB 215; EWL 3
Ng, Fae Myenne 1956- .... **CLC 81**
See also BYA 11; CA 146; CANR 191
Ngcobo, Lauretta 1931- .... **BLC 2:3**
See also CA 165
Ngema, Mbongeni 1955- .... **CLC 57**
See also BW 2; CA 143; CANR 84; CD 5, 6
Ng, Fae Myenne *(see above)*
Ngugi, James T.
See Ngugi wa Thiong'o
Ngugi, James Thiong'o
See Ngugi wa Thiong'o
Ngugi wa Thiong'o 1938- .... **BLC 1:3; 2:3; CLC 3, 7, 13, 36, 182, 275**
See also AFW; BRWS 8; BW 2; CA 81-84; CANR 27, 58, 164; CD 3, 4, 5, 6, 7; CD-WLB 3; CN 1, 2; DAM MULT, NOV; DLB 125; DNFS 2; EWL 3; MTCW 1, 2; MTFW 2005; RGEL 2; WWE 1
Niatum, Duane 1938- .... **NNAL**
See also CA 41-44R; CANR 21, 45, 83; DLB 175
Nichol, B(arrie) P(hillip) 1944-1988 . **CLC 18**
See also CA 53-56; CP 1, 2, 3, 4; DLB 53; SATA 66
Nicholas of Autrecourt c.
1298-1369 .... **CMLC 108**
Nicholas of Cusa 1401-1464 .... **LC 80**
See also DLB 115
Nichols, John 1940- .... **CLC 38**
See also AMWS 13; CA 9-12R, 190; CAAE 190; CAAS 2; CANR 6, 70, 121, 185; DLBY 1982; LATS 1:2; MTFW 2005; TCWW 1, 2
Nichols, Leigh
See Koontz, Dean R.
Nichols, Peter (Richard) 1927- .... **CLC 5, 36, 65**
See also CA 104; CANR 33, 86; CBD; CD 5, 6; DLB 13, 245; MTCW 1
Nicholson, Linda .... **CLC 65**
Ni Chuilleanain, Eilean 1942- ...... **PC 34**
See also CA 126; CANR 53, 83; CP 5, 6, 7; CWP; DLB 40
Nicolas, F. R. E.
See Freeling, Nicolas
Niedecker, Lorine 1903-1970 ..... **CLC 10, 42; PC 42**
See also CA 25-28; CAP 2; DAM POET; DLB 48
Nietzsche, Friedrich (Wilhelm)
1844-1900 .... **TCLC 10, 18, 55**
See also CA 107; 121; CDWLB 2; DLB 129; EW 7; RGWL 2, 3; TWA
Nievo, Ippolito 1831-1861 .... **NCLC 22**
Nightingale, Anne Redmon 1943- .... **CLC 22**
See also CA 103; DLBY 1986

O'Connor, Edwin (Greene)
    1918-1968 .... **CLC 14**
    See also CA 93-96; 25-28R; MAL 5
O'Connor, (Mary) Flannery
    1925-1964 .... **CLC 1, 2, 3, 6, 10, 13, 15,
        21, 66, 104; SSC 1, 23, 61, 82, 111;
        TCLC 132; WLC 4**
    See also AAYA 7; AMW; AMWR 2; BPFB
        3; BYA 16; CA 1-4R; CANR 3, 41;
        CDALB 1941-1968; DA; DA3; DAB;
        DAC; DAM MST, NOV; DLB 2, 152;
        DLBD 12; DLBY 1980; EWL 3; EXPS;
        LAIT 5; MAL 5; MBL; MTCW 1, 2;
        MTFW 2005; NFS 3, 21; RGAL 4; RGSF
        2; SSFS 2, 7, 10, 19; TUS
O'Connor, Frank 1903-1966
    See O'Donovan, Michael Francis
O'Dell, Scott 1898-1989 .... **CLC 30**
    See also AAYA 3, 44; BPFB 3; BYA 1, 2,
        3, 5; CA 61-64; 129; CANR 12, 30, 112;
        CLR 1, 16, 126; DLB 52; JRDA; MAI-
        CYA 1, 2; SATA 12, 60, 134; WYA; YAW
Odets, Clifford 1906-1963 ..... **CLC 2, 28, 98;
        DC 6**
    See also AMWS 2; CA 85-88; CAD; CANR
        62; DAM DRAM; DFS 3, 17, 20; DLB 7,
        26, 341; EWL 3; MAL 5; MTCW 1, 2;
        MTFW 2005; RGAL 4; TUS
O'Doherty, Brian 1928- .... **CLC 76**
    See also CA 105; CANR 108
O'Donnell, K. M.
    See Malzberg, Barry N(athaniel)
O'Donnell, Lawrence
    See Kuttner, Henry
O'Donovan, Michael Francis
    1903-1966 .... **CLC 14, 23; SSC 5, 109**
    See also BRWS 14; CA 93-96; CANR 84;
        DLB 162; EWL 3; RGSF 2; SSFS 5
Oe, Kenzaburo 1935- .. **CLC 10, 36, 86, 187;
        SSC 20**
    See also CA 97-100; CANR 36, 50, 74, 126;
        CWW 2; DA3; DAM NOV; DLB 182,
        331; DLBY 1994; EWL 3; LATS 1:2;
        MJW; MTCW 1, 2; MTFW 2005; RGSF
        2; RGWL 2, 3
Oe Kenzaburo
    See Oe, Kenzaburo
O'Faolain, Julia 1932- .... **CLC 6, 19, 47, 108**
    See also CA 81-84; CAAS 2; CANR 12,
        61; CN 2, 3, 4, 5, 6, 7; DLB 14, 231, 319;
        FW; MTCW 1; RHW
O'Faolain, Sean 1900-1991 ...... **CLC 1, 7, 14,
        32, 70; SSC 13; TCLC 143**
    See also CA 61-64; 134; CANR 12, 66; CN
        1, 2, 3, 4; DLB 15, 162; MTCW 1, 2;
        MTFW 2005; RGEL 2; RGSF 2
O'Flaherty, Liam 1896-1984 .... **CLC 5, 34;
        SSC 6, 116**
    See also CA 101; 113; CANR 35; CN 1, 2,
        3; DLB 36, 162; DLBY 1984; MTCW 1,
        2; MTFW 2005; RGEL 2; RGSF 2; SSFS
        5, 20
Ogai
    See Mori Ogai
Ogilvy, Gavin
    See Barrie, J(ames) M(atthew)
O'Grady, Standish (James)
    1846-1928 .... **TCLC 5**
    See also CA 104; 157
O'Grady, Timothy 1951- .... **CLC 59**
    See also CA 138
O'Hara, Frank 1926-1966 .... **CLC 2, 5, 13,
        78; PC 45**
    See also CA 9-12R; 25-28R; CANR 33;
        DA3; DAM POET; DLB 5, 16, 193; EWL
        3; MAL 5; MTCW 1, 2; MTFW 2005;
        PFS 8, 12; RGAL 4; WP

O'Hara, John (Henry) 1905-1970 . **CLC 1, 2,
        3, 6, 11, 42; SSC 15**
    See also AMW; BPFB 3; CA 5-8R; 25-28R;
        CANR 31, 60; CDALB 1929-1941; DAM
        NOV; DLB 9, 86, 324; DLBD 2; EWL 3;
        MAL 5; MTCW 1, 2; MTFW 2005; NFS
        11; RGAL 4; RGSF 2
O'Hehir, Diana 1929- .... **CLC 41**
    See also CA 245; CANR 177
O'Hehir, Diana F.
    See O'Hehir, Diana
Ohiyesa
    See Eastman, Charles A(lexander)
Okada, John 1923-1971 .... **AAL**
    See also BYA 14; CA 212; DLB 312; NFS
        25
Okigbo, Christopher 1930-1967 ..... **BLC 1:3;
        CLC 25, 84; PC 7; TCLC 171**
    See also AFW; BW 1, 3; CA 77-80; CANR
        74; CDWLB 3; DAM MULT, POET; DLB
        125; EWL 3; MTCW 1, 2; MTFW 2005;
        RGEL 2
Okigbo, Christopher Ifenayichukwu
    See Okigbo, Christopher
Okri, Ben 1959- .... **BLC 2:3; CLC 87, 223**
    See also AFW; BRWS 5; BW 2, 3; CA 130;
        138; CANR 65, 128; CN 5, 6, 7; DLB
        157, 231, 319, 326; EWL 3; INT CA-138;
        MTCW 2; MTFW 2005; RGSF 2; SSFS
        20; WLIT 2; WWE 1
Old Boy
    See Hughes, Thomas
Olds, Sharon 1942- .. **CLC 32, 39, 85; PC 22**
    See also AMWS 10; CA 101; CANR 18,
        41, 66, 98, 135; CP 5, 6, 7; CPW; CWP;
        DAM POET; DLB 120; MAL 5; MTCW
        2; MTFW 2005; PFS 17
Oldstyle, Jonathan
    See Irving, Washington
Olesha, Iurii
    See Olesha, Yuri (Karlovich)
Olesha, Iurii Karlovich
    See Olesha, Yuri (Karlovich)
Olesha, Yuri (Karlovich) 1899-1960 . **CLC 8;
        SSC 69; TCLC 136**
    See also CA 85-88; DLB 272; EW 11; EWL
        3; RGWL 2, 3
Olesha, Yury Karlovich
    See Olesha, Yuri (Karlovich)
Oliphant, Mrs.
    See Oliphant, Margaret (Oliphant Wilson)
Oliphant, Laurence 1829(?)-1888 .. **NCLC 47**
    See also DLB 18, 166
Oliphant, Margaret (Oliphant Wilson)
    1828-1897 .... **NCLC 11, 61; SSC 25**
    See also BRWS 10; DLB 18, 159, 190;
        HGG; RGEL 2; RGSF 2; SUFW
Oliver, Mary 1935- ... **CLC 19, 34, 98; PC 75**
    See also AMWS 7; CA 21-24R; CANR 9,
        43, 84, 92, 138; CP 4, 5, 6, 7; CWP; DLB
        5, 193, 342; EWL 3; MTFW 2005; PFS
        15, 31
Olivi, Peter 1248-1298 .... **CMLC 114**
Olivier, Laurence (Kerr) 1907-1989 . **CLC 20**
    See also CA 111; 150; 129
O.L.S.
    See Russell, George William
Olsen, Tillie 1912-2007 .... **CLC 4, 13, 114;
        SSC 11, 103**
    See also AAYA 51; AMWS 13; BYA 11;
        CA 1-4R; 256; CANR 1, 43, 74, 132;
        CDALBS; CN 2, 3, 4, 5, 6, 7; DA; DA3;
        DAB; DAC; DAM MST; DLB 28, 206;
        DLBY 1980; EWL 3; EXPS; FW; MAL
        5; MTCW 1, 2; MTFW 2005; RGAL 4;
        RGSF 2; SSFS 1; TCLE 1:2; TCWW 2;
        TUS

Olson, Charles (John) 1910-1970 .. **CLC 1, 2,
        5, 6, 9, 11, 29; PC 19**
    See also AMWS 2; CA 13-16; 25-28R;
        CABS 2; CANR 35, 61; CAP 1; CP 1;
        DAM POET; DLB 5, 16, 193; EWL 3;
        MAL 5; MTCW 1, 2; RGAL 4; WP
Olson, Merle Theodore
    See Olson, Toby
Olson, Toby 1937- .... **CLC 28**
    See also CA 65-68; CAAS 11; CANR 9,
        31, 84, 175; CP 3, 4, 5, 6, 7
Olyesha, Yuri
    See Olesha, Yuri (Karlovich)
Olympiodorus of Thebes c. 375-c.
    430 .... **CMLC 59**
Omar Khayyam
    See Khayyam, Omar
Ondaatje, Michael 1943- ..... **CLC 14, 29, 51,
        76, 180, 258; PC 28**
    See also AAYA 66; CA 77-80; CANR 42,
        74, 109, 133, 172; CN 5, 6, 7; CP 1, 2, 3,
        4, 5, 6, 7; DA3; DAB; DAC; DAM MST;
        DLB 60, 323, 326; EWL 3; LATS 1:2;
        LMFS 2; MTCW 2; MTFW 2005; NFS
        23; PFS 8, 19; TCLE 1:2; TWA; WWE 1
Ondaatje, Philip Michael
    See Ondaatje, Michael
Oneal, Elizabeth 1934- .... **CLC 30**
    See also AAYA 5, 41; BYA 13; CA 106;
        CANR 28, 84; CLR 13; JRDA; MAICYA
        1, 2; SATA 30, 82; WYA; YAW
Oneal, Zibby
    See Oneal, Elizabeth
O'Neill, Eugene (Gladstone)
    1888-1953 ... **DC 20; TCLC 1, 6, 27, 49;
        WLC 4**
    See also AAYA 54; AITN 1; AMW; AMWC
        1; CA 110; 132; CAD; CANR 131;
        CDALB 1929-1941; DA; DA3; DAB;
        DAC; DAM DRAM, MST; DFS 2, 4, 5,
        6, 9, 11, 12, 16, 20, 26; DLB 7, 331; EWL
        3; LAIT 3; LMFS 2; MAL 5; MTCW 1,
        2; MTFW 2005; RGAL 4; TUS
Onetti, Juan Carlos 1909-1994 ...... **CLC 7, 10;
        HLCS 2; SSC 23; TCLC 131**
    See also CA 85-88; 145; CANR 32, 63; CD-
        WLB 3; CWW 2; DAM MULT, NOV;
        DLB 113; EWL 3; HW 1, 2; LAW;
        MTCW 1, 2; MTFW 2005; RGSF 2
O'Nolan, Brian
    See O Nuallain, Brian
O Nuallain, Brian 1911-1966 .... **CLC 1, 4, 5,
        7, 10, 47**
    See also BRWS 2; CA 21-22; 25-28R; CAP
        2; DLB 231; EWL 3; FANT; RGEL 2;
        TEA
Ophuls, Max
    See Ophuls, Max
Ophuls, Max 1902-1957 .... **TCLC 79**
    See also CA 113
Opie, Amelia 1769-1853 .... **NCLC 65**
    See also DLB 116, 159; RGEL 2
Oppen, George 1908-1984 .... **CLC 7, 13, 34;
        PC 35; TCLC 107**
    See also CA 13-16R; 113; CANR 8, 82; CP
        1, 2, 3; DLB 5, 165
Oppenheim, E(dward) Phillips
    1866-1946 .... **TCLC 45**
    See also CA 111; 202; CMW 4; DLB 70
Oppenheimer, Max
    See Ophuls, Max
Opuls, Max
    See Ophuls, Max
Orage, A(lfred) R(ichard)
    1873-1934 .... **TCLC 157**
    See also CA 122
Origen c. 185-c. 254 .... **CMLC 19**

Payne, Alan
See Jakes, John
Payne, Rachel Ann
See Jakes, John
Paz, Gil
See Lugones, Leopoldo
Paz, Octavio 1914-1998 . **CLC 3, 4, 6, 10, 19, 51, 65, 119; HLC 2; PC 1, 48; TCLC 211; WLC 4**
See also AAYA 50; CA 73-76; 165; CANR 32, 65, 104; CWW 2; DA; DA3; DAB; DAC; DAM MST, MULT, POET; DLB 290, 331; DLBY 1990, 1998; DNFS 1; EWL 3; HW 1, 2; LAW; LAWS 1; MTCW 1, 2; MTFW 2005; PFS 18, 30; RGWL 2, 3; SSFS 13; TWA; WLIT 1
p'Bitek, Okot 1931-1982 . **BLC 1:3; CLC 96; TCLC 149**
See also AFW; BW 2, 3; CA 124; 107; CANR 82; CP 1, 2, 3; DAM MULT; DLB 125; EWL 3; MTCW 1, 2; MTFW 2005; RGEL 2; WLIT 2
Peabody, Elizabeth Palmer 1804-1894 .... **NCLC 169**
See also DLB 1, 223
Peacham, Henry 1578-1644(?) .... **LC 119**
See also DLB 151
Peacock, Molly 1947- .... **CLC 60**
See also CA 103, 262; CAAE 262; CAAS 21; CANR 52, 84; CP 5, 6, 7; CWP; DLB 120, 282
Peacock, Thomas Love 1785-1866 .... **NCLC 22; PC 87**
See also BRW 4; DLB 96, 116; RGEL 2; RGSF 2
Peake, Mervyn 1911-1968 .... **CLC 7, 54**
See also CA 5-8R; 25-28R; CANR 3; DLB 15, 160, 255; FANT; MTCW 1; RGEL 2; SATA 23; SFW 4
Pearce, Ann Philippa
See Pearce, Philippa
Pearce, Philippa 1920-2006 .... **CLC 21**
See also BYA 5; CA 5-8R; 255; CANR 4, 109; CLR 9; CWRI 5; DLB 161; FANT; MAICYA 1; SATA 1, 67, 129; SATA-Obit 179
Pearl, Eric
See Elman, Richard (Martin)
Pearson, Jean Mary
See Gardam, Jane
Pearson, Thomas Reid
See Pearson, T.R.
Pearson, T.R. 1956- .... **CLC 39**
See also CA 120; 130; CANR 97, 147, 185; CSW; INT CA-130
Peck, Dale 1967- .... **CLC 81**
See also CA 146; CANR 72, 127, 180; GLL 2
Peck, John (Frederick) 1941- .... **CLC 3**
See also CA 49-52; CANR 3, 100; CP 4, 5, 6, 7
Peck, Richard 1934- .... **CLC 21**
See also AAYA 1, 24; BYA 1, 6, 8, 11; CA 85-88; CANR 19, 38, 129, 178; CLR 15, 142; INT CANR-19; JRDA; MAICYA 1, 2; SAAS 2; SATA 18, 55, 97, 110, 158, 190; SATA-Essay 110; WYA; YAW
Peck, Richard Wayne
See Peck, Richard
Peck, Robert Newton 1928- .... **CLC 17**
See also AAYA 3, 43; BYA 1, 6; CA 81-84, 182; CAAE 182; CANR 31, 63, 127; CLR 45; DA; DAC; DAM MST; JRDA; LAIT 3; MAICYA 1, 2; NFS 29; SAAS 1; SATA 21, 62, 111, 156; SATA-Essay 108; WYA; YAW
Peckinpah, David Samuel
See Peckinpah, Sam

Peckinpah, Sam 1925-1984 .... **CLC 20**
See also CA 109; 114; CANR 82
Pedersen, Knut 1859-1952 .. **TCLC 2, 14, 49, 151, 203**
See also AAYA 79; CA 104; 119; CANR 63; DLB 297, 330; EW 8; EWL 8; MTCW 1, 2; RGWL 2, 3
Peele, George 1556-1596 .... **DC 27; LC 115**
See also BRW 1; DLB 62, 167; RGEL 2
Peeslake, Gaffer
See Durrell, Lawrence (George)
Peguy, Charles (Pierre) 1873-1914 .... **TCLC 10**
See also CA 107; 193; DLB 258; EWL 3; GFL 1789 to the Present
Peirce, Charles Sanders 1839-1914 .... **TCLC 81**
See also CA 194; DLB 270
Pelagius c. 350-c. 418 .... **CMLC 112**
Pelecanos, George P. 1957- .... **CLC 236**
See also CA 138; CANR 122, 165; DLB 306
Pelevin, Victor 1962- .... **CLC 238**
See also CA 154; CANR 88, 159; DLB 285
Pelevin, Viktor Olegovich
See Pelevin, Victor
Pellicer, Carlos 1897(?)-1977 .... **HLCS 2**
See also CA 153; 69-72; DLB 290; EWL 3; HW 1
Pena, Ramon del Valle y
See Valle-Inclan, Ramon (Maria) del
Pendennis, Arthur Esquir
See Thackeray, William Makepeace
Penn, Arthur
See Matthews, (James) Brander
Penn, William 1644-1718 .... **LC 25**
See also DLB 24
PEPECE
See Prado (Calvo), Pedro
Pepys, Samuel 1633-1703 ... **LC 11, 58; WLC 4**
See also BRW 2; CDBLB 1660-1789; DA; DA3; DAB; DAC; DAM MST; DLB 101, 213; NCFS 4; RGEL 2; TEA; WLIT 3
Percy, Thomas 1729-1811 .... **NCLC 95**
See also DLB 104
Percy, Walker 1916-1990 .... **CLC 2, 3, 6, 8, 14, 18, 47, 65**
See also AMWS 3; BPFB 3; CA 1-4R; 131; CANR 1, 23, 64; CN 1, 2, 3, 4; CPW; CSW; DA3; DAM NOV, POP; DLB 2; DLBY 1980, 1990; EWL 3; MAL 5; MTCW 1, 2; MTFW 2005; RGAL 4; TUS
Percy, William Alexander 1885-1942 .... **TCLC 84**
See also CA 163; MTCW 2
Perdurabo, Frater
See Crowley, Edward Alexander
Perec, Georges 1936-1982 .... **CLC 56, 116**
See also CA 141; DLB 83, 299; EWL 3; GFL 1789 to the Present; RGHL; RGWL 3
Pereda (y Sanchez de Porrua), Jose Maria de 1833-1906 .... **TCLC 16**
See also CA 117
Pereda y Porrua, Jose Maria de
See Pereda (y Sanchez de Porrua), Jose Maria de
Peregoy, George Weems
See Mencken, H. L.
Perelman, S(idney) J(oseph) 1904-1979 .. **CLC 3, 5, 9, 15, 23, 44, 49; SSC 32**
See also AAYA 79; AITN 1, 2; BPFB 3; CA 73-76; 89-92; CANR 18; DAM DRAM; DLB 11, 44; MTCW 1, 2; MTFW 2005; RGAL 4

Peret, Benjamin 1899-1959 .... **PC 33; TCLC 20**
See also CA 117; 186; GFL 1789 to the Present
Perets, Yitskhok Leybush
See Peretz, Isaac Loeb
Peretz, Isaac Leib (?)-
See Peretz, Isaac Loeb
Peretz, Isaac Loeb 1851-1915 .... **SSC 26; TCLC 16**
See Peretz, Isaac Leib
See also CA 109; 201; DLB 333
Peretz, Yitzhok Leibush
See Peretz, Isaac Loeb
Perez Galdos, Benito 1843-1920 ..... **HLCS 2; TCLC 27**
See also CA 125; 153; EW 7; EWL 3; HW 1; RGWL 2, 3
Peri Rossi, Cristina 1941- .. **CLC 156; HLCS 2**
See also CA 131; CANR 59, 81; CWW 2; DLB 145, 290; EWL 3; HW 1, 2
Perlata
See Peret, Benjamin
Perloff, Marjorie G(abrielle) 1931- .... **CLC 137**
See also CA 57-60; CANR 7, 22, 49, 104
Perrault, Charles 1628-1703 .... **LC 2, 56**
See also BYA 4; CLR 79, 134; DLB 268; GFL Beginnings to 1789; MAICYA 1, 2; RGWL 2, 3; SATA 25; WCH
Perrotta, Tom 1961- .... **CLC 266**
See also CA 162; CANR 99, 155
Perry, Anne 1938- .... **CLC 126**
See also CA 101; CANR 22, 50, 84, 150, 177; CMW 4; CN 6, 7; CPW; DLB 276
Perry, Brighton
See Sherwood, Robert E(mmet)
Perse, St.-John
See Leger, Alexis Saint-Leger
Perse, Saint-John
See Leger, Alexis Saint-Leger
Persius 34-62 .... **CMLC 74**
See also AW 2; DLB 211; RGWL 2, 3
Perutz, Leo(pold) 1882-1957 .... **TCLC 60**
See also CA 147; DLB 81
Peseenz, Tulio F.
See Lopez y Fuentes, Gregorio
Pesetsky, Bette 1932- .... **CLC 28**
See also CA 133; DLB 130
Peshkov, Alexei Maximovich 1868-1936 .... **SSC 28; TCLC 8; WLC 3**
See also CA 105; 141; CANR 83; DA; DAB; DAC; DAM DRAM, MST, NOV; DFS 9; DLB 295; EW 8; EWL 3; MTCW 2; MTFW 2005; RGSF 2; RGWL 2, 3; TWA
Pessoa, Fernando 1888-1935 .... **HLC 2; PC 20; TCLC 27**
See also CA 125; 183; CANR 182; DAM MULT; DLB 287; EW 10; EWL 3; RGWL 2, 3; WP
Pessoa, Fernando Antonio Nogueira
See Pessoa, Fernando
Peterkin, Julia Mood 1880-1961 ...... **CLC 31**
See also CA 102; DLB 9
Peters, Joan K(aren) 1945- .... **CLC 39**
See also CA 158; CANR 109
Peters, Robert L(ouis) 1924- .... **CLC 7**
See also CA 13-16R; CAAS 8; CP 1, 5, 6, 7; DLB 105
Peters, S. H.
See Henry, O.
Petofi, Sandor 1823-1849 .... **NCLC 21**
See also RGWL 2, 3
Petrakis, Harry Mark 1923- .... **CLC 3**
See also CA 9-12R; CANR 4, 30, 85, 155; CN 1, 2, 3, 4, 5, 6, 7

Powers, J(ames) F(arl) 1917-1999 ..... **CLC 1, 4, 8, 57; SSC 4**
See also CA 1-4R; 181; CANR 2, 61; CN 1, 2, 3, 4, 5, 6; DLB 130; MTCW 1; RGAL 4; RGSF 2

Powers, John
See Powers, John R.

Powers, John R. 1945- .... **CLC 66**
See also CA 69-72

Powers, Richard 1957- .... **CLC 93**
See also AMWS 9; BPFB 3; CA 148; CANR 80, 180; CN 6, 7; DLB 350; MTFW 2005; TCLE 1:2

Powers, Richard S.
See Powers, Richard

Pownall, David 1938- .... **CLC 10**
See also CA 89-92, 180; CAAS 18; CANR 49, 101; CBD; CD 5, 6; CN 4, 5, 6, 7; DLB 14

Powys, John Cowper 1872-1963 ... **CLC 7, 9, 15, 46, 125**
See also CA 85-88; CANR 106; DLB 15, 255; EWL 3; FANT; MTCW 1, 2; MTFW 2005; RGEL 2; SUFW

Powys, T(heodore) F(rancis) 1875-1953 .... **TCLC 9**
See also BRWS 8; CA 106; 189; DLB 36, 162; EWL 3; FANT; RGEL 2; SUFW

Pozzo, Modesta
See Fonte, Moderata

Prado (Calvo), Pedro 1886-1952 ... **TCLC 75**
See also CA 131; DLB 283; HW 1; LAW

Prager, Emily 1952- .... **CLC 56**
See also CA 204

Pratchett, Terence David John
See Pratchett, Terry

Pratchett, Terry 1948- .... **CLC 197**
See also AAYA 19, 54; BPFB 3; CA 143; CANR 87, 126, 170; CLR 64; CN 6, 7; CPW; CWRI 5; FANT; MTFW 2005; SATA 82, 139, 185; SFW 4; SUFW 2

Pratolini, Vasco 1913-1991 .... **TCLC 124**
See also CA 211; DLB 177; EWL 3; RGWL 2, 3

Pratt, E(dwin) J(ohn) 1883(?)-1964 . **CLC 19**
See also CA 141; 93-96; CANR 77; DAC; DAM POET; DLB 92; EWL 3; RGEL 2; TWA

Premacanda
See Srivastava, Dhanpat Rai

Premchand
See Srivastava, Dhanpat Rai

Prem Chand, Munshi
See Srivastava, Dhanpat Rai

Premchand, Munshi
See Srivastava, Dhanpat Rai

Prescott, William Hickling 1796-1859 .... **NCLC 163**
See also DLB 1, 30, 59, 235

Preseren, France 1800-1849 .... **NCLC 127**
See also CDWLB 4; DLB 147

Preussler, Otfried 1923- .... **CLC 17**
See also CA 77-80; SATA 24

Prevert, Jacques (Henri Marie) 1900-1977 .... **CLC 15**
See also CA 77-80; 69-72; CANR 29, 61; DLB 258; EWL 3; GFL 1789 to the Present; IDFW 3, 4; MTCW 1; RGWL 2, 3; SATA-Obit 30

Prevost, (Antoine Francois) 1697-1763 .... **LC 1**
See also DLB 314; EW 4; GFL Beginnings to 1789; RGWL 2, 3

Price, Edward Reynolds
See Price, Reynolds

Price, Reynolds 1933- .. **CLC 3, 6, 13, 43, 50, 63, 212; SSC 22**
See also AMWS 6; CA 1-4R; CANR 1, 37, 57, 87, 128, 177; CN 1, 2, 3, 4, 5, 6, 7; CSW; DAM NOV; DLB 2, 218, 278; EWL 3; INT CANR-37; MAL 5; MTFW 2005; NFS 18

Price, Richard 1949- .... **CLC 6, 12**
See also CA 49-52; CANR 3, 147, 190; CN 7; DLBY 1981

Prichard, Katharine Susannah 1883-1969 .... **CLC 46**
See also CA 11-12; CANR 33; CAP 1; DLB 260; MTCW 1; RGEL 2; RGSF 2; SATA 66

Priestley, J(ohn) B(oynton) 1894-1984 .... **CLC 2, 5, 9, 34**
See also BRW 7; CA 9-12R; 113; CANR 33; CDBLB 1914-1945; CN 1, 2, 3; DA3; DAM DRAM, NOV; DLB 10, 34, 77, 100, 139; DLBY 1984; EWL 3; MTCW 1, 2; MTFW 2005; RGEL 2; SFW 4

Prince 1958- .... **CLC 35**
See also CA 213

Prince, F(rank) T(empleton) 1912-2003 .... **CLC 22**
See also CA 101; 219; CANR 43, 79; CP 1, 2, 3, 4, 5, 6, 7; DLB 20

Prince Kropotkin
See Kropotkin, Peter

Prior, Matthew 1664-1721 .... **LC 4**
See also DLB 95; RGEL 2

Prishvin, Mikhail 1873-1954 .... **TCLC 75**
See also DLB 272; EWL 3 !**

Prishvin, Mikhail Mikhailovich
See Prishvin, Mikhail

Pritchard, William H(arrison) 1932- .... **CLC 34**
See also CA 65-68; CANR 23, 95; DLB 111

Pritchett, V(ictor) S(awdon) 1900-1997 .. **CLC 5, 13, 15, 41; SSC 14, 126**
See also BPFB 3; BRWS 3; CA 61-64; 157; CANR 31, 63; CN 1, 2, 3, 4, 5, 6; DA3; DAM NOV; DLB 15, 139; EWL 3; MTCW 1, 2; MTFW 2005; RGEL 2; RGSF 2; TEA

Private 19022
See Manning, Frederic

Probst, Mark 1925- .... **CLC 59**
See also CA 130

Procaccino, Michael
See Cristofer, Michael

Proclus c. 412-c. 485 .... **CMLC 81**

Prokosch, Frederic 1908-1989 ...... **CLC 4, 48**
See also CA 73-76; 128; CANR 82; CN 1, 2, 3, 4; CP 1, 2, 3, 4; DLB 48; MTCW 2

Propertius, Sextus c. 50B.C.-c. 16B.C. .... **CMLC 32**
See also AW 2; CDWLB 1; DLB 211; RGWL 2, 3; WLIT 8

Prophet, The
See Dreiser, Theodore

Prose, Francine 1947- .... **CLC 45, 231**
See also AMWS 16; CA 109; 112; CANR 46, 95, 132, 175; DLB 234; MTFW 2005; SATA 101, 149, 198

Protagoras c. 490B.C.-420B.C. ...... **CMLC 85**
See also DLB 176

Proudhon
See Cunha, Euclides (Rodrigues Pimenta) da

Proulx, Annie
See Proulx, E. Annie

Proulx, E. Annie 1935- ...... **CLC 81, 158, 250**
See also AMWS 7; BPFB 3; CA 145; CANR 65, 110; CN 6, 7; CPW 1; DA3; DAM POP; DLB 335, 350; MAL 5; MTCW 2; MTFW 2005; SSFS 18, 23

Proulx, Edna Annie
See Proulx, E. Annie

Proust, (Valentin-Louis-George-Eugene) Marcel 1871-1922 ..... **SSC 75; TCLC 7, 13, 33, 220; WLC 5**
See also AAYA 58; BPFB 3; CA 104; 120; CANR 110; DA; DA3; DAB; DAC; DAM MST, NOV; DLB 65; EW 8; EWL 3; GFL 1789 to the Present; MTCW 1, 2; MTFW 2005; RGWL 2, 3; TWA

Prowler, Harley
See Masters, Edgar Lee

Prudentius, Aurelius Clemens 348-c. 405 .... **CMLC 78**
See also EW 1; RGWL 2, 3

Prudhomme, Rene Francois Armand
See Sully Prudhomme, Rene-Francois-Armand

Prus, Boleslaw 1845-1912 .... **TCLC 48**
See also RGWL 2, 3

Prynne, William 1600-1669 .... **LC 148**

Prynne, Xavier
See Hardwick, Elizabeth

Pryor, Aaron Richard
See Pryor, Richard

Pryor, Richard 1940-2005 .... **CLC 26**
See also CA 122; 152; 246

Pryor, Richard Franklin Lenox Thomas
See Pryor, Richard

Przybyszewski, Stanislaw 1868-1927 .... **TCLC 36**
See also CA 160; DLB 66; EWL 3

Pseudo-Dionysius the Areopagite fl. c. 5th cent. - .... **CMLC 89**
See also DLB 115

Pteleon
See Grieve, C. M.

Puckett, Lute
See Masters, Edgar Lee

Puig, Manuel 1932-1990 .... **CLC 3, 5, 10, 28, 65, 133; HLC 2**
See also BPFB 3; CA 45-48; CANR 2, 32, 63; CDWLB 3; DA3; DAM MULT; DLB 113; DNFS 1; EWL 3; GLL 1; HW 1, 2; LAW; MTCW 1, 2; MTFW 2005; RGWL 2, 3; TWA; WLIT 1

Pulitzer, Joseph 1847-1911 .... **TCLC 76**
See also CA 114; DLB 23

Pullman, Philip 1946- .... **CLC 245**
See also AAYA 15, 41; BRWS 13; BYA 8, 13; CA 127; CANR 50, 77, 105, 134, 190; CLR 20, 62, 84; JRDA; MAICYA 1, 2; MAICYAS 1; MTFW 2005; SAAS 17; SATA 65, 103, 150, 198; SUFW 2; WYAS 1; YAW

Purchas, Samuel 1577(?)-1626 .... **LC 70**
See also DLB 151

Purdy, A(lfred) W(ellington) 1918-2000 .... **CLC 3, 6, 14, 50**
See also CA 81-84; 189; CAAS 17; CANR 42, 66; CP 1, 2, 3, 4, 5, 6, 7; DAC; DAM MST, POET; DLB 88; PFS 5; RGEL 2

Purdy, James 1914-2009 .... **CLC 2, 4, 10, 28, 52**
See also AMWS 7; CA 33-36R; 284; CAAS 1; CANR 19, 51, 132; CN 1, 2, 3, 4, 5, 6, 7; DLB 2, 218; EWL 3; INT CANR-19; MAL 5; MTCW 1; RGAL 4

Purdy, James Amos
See Purdy, James

Purdy, James Otis
See Purdy, James

Pure, Simon
See Swinnerton, Frank Arthur

Pushkin, Aleksandr Sergeevich
See Pushkin, Alexander

Pushkin, Alexander 1799-1837 . **NCLC 3, 27, 83; PC 10; SSC 27, 55, 99; WLC 5**
See also DA; DA3; DAB; DAC; DAM DRAM, MST, POET; DLB 205; EW 5; EXPS; PFS 28; RGSF 2; RGWL 2, 3; SATA 61; SSFS 9; TWA

Pushkin, Alexander Sergeyevich
See Pushkin, Alexander

P'u Sung-ling 1640-1715 .... **LC 49; SSC 31**

Putnam, Arthur Lee
See Alger, Horatio, Jr.

Puttenham, George 1529(?)-1590 ...... **LC 116**
See also DLB 281

Puzo, Mario 1920-1999 .... **CLC 1, 2, 6, 36, 107**
See also BPFB 3; CA 65-68; 185; CANR 4, 42, 65, 99, 131; CN 1, 2, 3, 4, 5, 6; CPW; DA3; DAM NOV, POP; DLB 6; MTCW 1, 2; MTFW 2005; NFS 16; RGAL 4

Pygge, Edward
See Barnes, Julian

Pyle, Ernest Taylor 1900-1945 .... **TCLC 75**
See also CA 115; 160; DLB 29; MTCW 2

Pyle, Ernie
See Pyle, Ernest Taylor

Pyle, Howard 1853-1911 .... **TCLC 81**
See also AAYA 57; BYA 2, 4; CA 109; 137; CLR 22, 117; DLB 42, 188; DLBD 13; LAIT 1; MAICYA 1, 2; SATA 16, 100; WCH; YAW

Pym, Barbara (Mary Crampton) 1913-1980 .... **CLC 13, 19, 37, 111**
See also BPFB 3; BRWS 2; CA 13-14; 97-100; CANR 13, 34; CAP 1; DLB 14, 207; DLBY 1987; EWL 3; MTCW 1, 2; MTFW 2005; RGEL 2; TEA

Pynchon, Thomas 1937- .. **CLC 2, 3, 6, 9, 11, 18, 33, 62, 72, 123, 192, 213; SSC 14, 84; WLC 5**
See also AMWS 2; BEST 90:2; BPFB 3; CA 17-20R; CANR 22, 46, 73, 142; CN 1, 2, 3, 4, 5, 6, 7; CPW 1; DA; DA3; DAB; DAC; DAM MST, NOV, POP; DLB 2, 173; EWL 3; MAL 5; MTCW 1, 2; MTFW 2005; NFS 23; RGAL 4; SFW 4; TCLE 1:2; TUS

Pythagoras c. 582B.C.-c. 507B.C. . **CMLC 22**
See also DLB 176

Q
See Quiller-Couch, Sir Arthur (Thomas)

Qian, Chongzhu
See Ch'ien, Chung-shu

Qian, Sima 145B.C.-c. 89B.C. .... **CMLC 72**

Qian Zhongshu
See Ch'ien, Chung-shu

Qroll
See Dagerman, Stig (Halvard)

Quarles, Francis 1592-1644 .... **LC 117**
See also DLB 126; RGEL 2

Quarrington, Paul 1953- .... **CLC 65**
See also CA 129; CANR 62, 95

Quarrington, Paul Lewis
See Quarrington, Paul

Quasimodo, Salvatore 1901-1968 .... **CLC 10; PC 47**
See also CA 13-16; 25-28R; CAP 1; DLB 114, 332; EW 12; EWL 3; MTCW 1; RGWL 2, 3

Quatermass, Martin
See Carpenter, John (Howard)

Quay, Stephen 1947- .... **CLC 95**
See also CA 189

Quay, Timothy 1947- .... **CLC 95**
See also CA 189

Queen, Ellery
See Dannay, Frederic; Hoch, Edward D.; Lee, Manfred B.; Marlowe, Stephen; Sturgeon, Theodore (Hamilton); Vance, Jack

Queneau, Raymond 1903-1976 ..... **CLC 2, 5, 10, 42**
See also CA 77-80; 69-72; CANR 32; DLB 72, 258; EW 12; EWL 3; GFL 1789 to the Present; MTCW 1, 2; RGWL 2, 3

Quevedo, Francisco de 1580-1645 ...... **LC 23, 160**

Quiller-Couch, Sir Arthur (Thomas) 1863-1944 .... **TCLC 53**
See also CA 118; 166; DLB 135, 153, 190; HGG; RGEL 2; SUFW 1

Quin, Ann 1936-1973 .... **CLC 6**
See also CA 9-12R; 45-48; CANR 148; CN 1; DLB 14, 231

Quin, Ann Marie
See Quin, Ann

Quincey, Thomas de
See De Quincey, Thomas

Quindlen, Anna 1953- .... **CLC 191**
See also AAYA 35; AMWS 17; CA 138; CANR 73, 126; DA3; DLB 292; MTCW 2; MTFW 2005

Quinn, Martin
See Smith, Martin Cruz

Quinn, Peter 1947- .... **CLC 91**
See also CA 197; CANR 147

Quinn, Peter A.
See Quinn, Peter

Quinn, Simon
See Smith, Martin Cruz

Quintana, Leroy V. 1944- ...... **HLC 2; PC 36**
See also CA 131; CANR 65, 139; DAM MULT; DLB 82; HW 1, 2

Quintilian c. 40-c. 100 .... **CMLC 77**
See also AW 2; DLB 211; RGWL 2, 3

Quiroga, Horacio (Sylvestre) 1878-1937 ... **HLC 2; SSC 89; TCLC 20**
See also CA 117; 131; DAM MULT; EWL 3; HW 1; LAW; MTCW 1; RGSF 2; WLIT 1

Quoirez, Francoise 1935-2004 ... **CLC 3, 6, 9, 17, 36**
See also CA 49-52; 231; CANR 6, 39, 73; CWW 2; DLB 83; EWL 3; GFL 1789 to the Present; MTCW 1, 2; MTFW 2005; TWA

Raabe, Wilhelm (Karl) 1831-1910 . **TCLC 45**
See also CA 167; DLB 129

Rabe, David (William) 1940- .. **CLC 4, 8, 33, 200; DC 16**
See also CA 85-88; CABS 3; CAD; CANR 59, 129; CD 5, 6; DAM DRAM; DFS 3, 8, 13; DLB 7, 228; EWL 3; MAL 5

Rabelais, Francois 1494-1553 .... **LC 5, 60; WLC 5**
See also DA; DAB; DAC; DAM MST; DLB 327; EW 2; GFL Beginnings to 1789; LMFS 1; RGWL 2, 3; TWA

Rabi'a al-'Adawiyya c. 717-c. 801 .... **CMLC 83**
See also DLB 311

Rabinovitch, Sholem 1859-1916 .... **SSC 33, 125; TCLC 1, 35**
See also CA 104; DLB 333; TWA

Rabinovitsh, Sholem Yankev
See Rabinovitch, Sholem

Rabinowitz, Sholem Yakov
See Rabinovitch, Sholem

Rabinowitz, Solomon
See Rabinovitch, Sholem

Rabinyan, Dorit 1972- .... **CLC 119**
See also CA 170; CANR 147

Rachilde
See Vallette, Marguerite Eymery; Vallette, Marguerite Eymery

Racine, Jean 1639-1699 .. **DC 32; LC 28, 113**
See also DA3; DAB; DAM MST; DLB 268; EW 3; GFL Beginnings to 1789; LMFS 1; RGWL 2, 3; TWA

Radcliffe, Ann (Ward) 1764-1823 ... **NCLC 6, 55, 106**
See also DLB 39, 178; GL 3; HGG; LMFS 1; RGEL 2; SUFW; WLIT 3

Radclyffe-Hall, Marguerite
See Hall, Radclyffe

Radiguet, Raymond 1903-1923 ...... **TCLC 29**
See also CA 162; DLB 65; EWL 3; GFL 1789 to the Present; RGWL 2, 3

Radishchev, Aleksandr Nikolaevich 1749-1802 .... **NCLC 190**
See also DLB 150

Radishchev, Alexander
See Radishchev, Aleksandr Nikolaevich

Radnoti, Miklos 1909-1944 .... **TCLC 16**
See also CA 118; 212; CDWLB 4; DLB 215; EWL 3; RGHL; RGWL 2, 3

Rado, James 1939- .... **CLC 17**
See also CA 105

Radvanyi, Netty 1900-1983 .... **CLC 7**
See also CA 85-88; 110; CANR 82; CDWLB 2; DLB 69; EWL 3

Rae, Ben
See Griffiths, Trevor

Raeburn, John (Hay) 1941- .... **CLC 34**
See also CA 57-60

Ragni, Gerome 1942-1991 .... **CLC 17**
See also CA 105; 134

Rahv, Philip
See Greenberg, Ivan

Rai, Navab
See Srivastava, Dhanpat Rai

Raimund, Ferdinand Jakob 1790-1836 .... **NCLC 69**
See also DLB 90

Raine, Craig 1944- .... **CLC 32, 103**
See also BRWS 13; CA 108; CANR 29, 51, 103, 171; CP 3, 4, 5, 6, 7; DLB 40; PFS 7

Raine, Craig Anthony
See Raine, Craig

Raine, Kathleen (Jessie) 1908-2003 .. **CLC 7, 45**
See also CA 85-88; 218; CANR 46, 109; CP 1, 2, 3, 4, 5, 6, 7; DLB 20; EWL 3; MTCW 1; RGEL 2

Rainis, Janis 1865-1929 .... **TCLC 29**
See also CA 170; CDWLB 4; DLB 220; EWL 3

Rakosi, Carl
See Rawley, Callman

Ralegh, Sir Walter
See Raleigh, Sir Walter

Raleigh, Richard
See Lovecraft, H. P.

Raleigh, Sir Walter 1554(?)-1618 .... **LC 31, 39; PC 31**
See also BRW 1; CDBLB Before 1660; DLB 172; EXPP; PFS 14; RGEL 2; TEA; WP

Rallentando, H. P.
See Sayers, Dorothy L(eigh)

Ramal, Walter
See de la Mare, Walter (John)

Ramana Maharshi 1879-1950 .... **TCLC 84**

Ramoacn y Cajal, Santiago 1852-1934 .... **TCLC 93**

Ramon, Juan
See Jimenez (Mantecon), Juan Ramon

Ramos, Graciliano 1892-1953 .... **TCLC 32**
See also CA 167; DLB 307; EWL 3; HW 2; LAW; WLIT 1

Rampersad, Arnold 1941- .... **CLC 44**
See also BW 2, 3; CA 127; 133; CANR 81; DLB 111; INT CA-133

Rampling, Anne
See Rice, Anne

Ramsay, Allan 1686(?)-1758 .... **LC 29**
See also DLB 95; RGEL 2

Ramsay, Jay
See Campbell, Ramsey

Ramuz, Charles-Ferdinand
1878-1947 .... **TCLC 33**
See also CA 165; EWL 3

Rand, Ayn 1905-1982 ...... **CLC 3, 30, 44, 79;
SSC 116; WLC 5**
See also AAYA 10; AMWS 4; BPFB 3;
BYA 12; CA 13-16R; 105; CANR 27, 73;
CDALBS; CN 1, 2, 3; CPW; DA; DA3;
DAC; DAM MST, NOV, POP; DLB 227,
279; MTCW 1, 2; MTFW 2005; NFS 10,
16, 29; RGAL 4; SFW 4; TUS; YAW

Randall, Dudley (Felker)
1914-2000 .... **BLC 1:3; CLC 1, 135; PC
86**
See also BW 1, 3; CA 25-28R; 189; CANR
23, 82; CP 1, 2, 3, 4, 5; DAM MULT;
DLB 41; PFS 5

Randall, Robert
See Silverberg, Robert

Ranger, Ken
See Creasey, John

Rank, Otto 1884-1939 .... **TCLC 115**

Rankin, Ian 1960- .... **CLC 257**
See also BRWS 10; CA 148; CANR 81,
137, 171; DLB 267; MTFW 2005

Rankin, Ian James
See Rankin, Ian

Ransom, John Crowe 1888-1974 .. **CLC 2, 4,
5, 11, 24; PC 61**
See also AMW; CA 5-8R; 49-52; CANR 6,
34; CDALBS; CP 1, 2; DA3; DAM POET;
DLB 45, 63; EWL 3; EXPP; MAL 5;
MTCW 1, 2; MTFW 2005; RGAL 4; TUS

Rao, Raja 1908-2006 . **CLC 25, 56, 255; SSC
99**
See also CA 73-76; 252; CANR 51; CN 1,
2, 3, 4, 5, 6; DAM NOV; DLB 323; EWL
3; MTCW 1, 2; MTFW 2005; RGEL 2;
RGSF 2

Raphael, Frederic (Michael) 1931- ... **CLC 2,
14**
See also CA 1-4R; CANR 1, 86; CN 1, 2,
3, 4, 5, 6, 7; DLB 14, 319; TCLE 1:2

Raphael, Lev 1954- .... **CLC 232**
See also CA 134; CANR 72, 145; GLL 1

Ratcliffe, James P.
See Mencken, H. L.

Rathbone, Julian 1935-2008 .... **CLC 41**
See also CA 101; 269; CANR 34, 73, 152

Rathbone, Julian Christopher
See Rathbone, Julian

Rattigan, Terence (Mervyn)
1911-1977 .... **CLC 7; DC 18**
See also BRWS 7; CA 85-88; 73-76; CBD;
CDBLB 1945-1960; DAM DRAM; DFS
8; DLB 13; IDFW 3, 4; MTCW 1, 2;
MTFW 2005; RGEL 2

Ratushinskaya, Irina 1954- .... **CLC 54**
See also CA 129; CANR 68; CWW 2

Raven, Simon (Arthur Noel)
1927-2001 .... **CLC 14**
See also CA 81-84; 197; CANR 86; CN 1,
2, 3, 4, 5, 6; DLB 271

Ravenna, Michael
See Welty, Eudora

Rawley, Callman 1903-2004 .... **CLC 47**
See also CA 21-24R; 228; CAAS 5; CANR
12, 32, 91; CP 1, 2, 3, 4, 5, 6, 7; DLB
193

Rawlings, Marjorie Kinnan
1896-1953 .... **TCLC 4**
See also AAYA 20; AMWS 10; ANW;
BPFB 3; BYA 3; CA 104; 137; CANR 74;
CLR 63; DLB 9, 22, 102; DLBD 17;
JRDA; MAICYA 1, 2; MAL 5; MTCW 2;
MTFW 2005; RGAL 4; SATA 100; WCH;
YABC 1; YAW

Ray, Satyajit 1921-1992 .... **CLC 16, 76**
See also CA 114; 137; DAM MULT

Read, Herbert Edward 1893-1968 ..... **CLC 4**
See also BRW 6; CA 85-88; 25-28R; DLB
20, 149; EWL 3; PAB; RGEL 2

Read, Piers Paul 1941- .... **CLC 4, 10, 25**
See also CA 21-24R; CANR 38, 86, 150;
CN 2, 3, 4, 5, 6, 7; DLB 14; SATA 21

Reade, Charles 1814-1884 .... **NCLC 2, 74**
See also DLB 21; RGEL 2

Reade, Hamish
See Gray, Simon

Reading, Peter 1946- .... **CLC 47**
See also BRWS 8; CA 103; CANR 46, 96;
CP 5, 6, 7; DLB 40

Reaney, James 1926-2008 .... **CLC 13**
See also CA 41-44R; CAAS 15; CANR 42;
CD 5, 6; CP 1, 2, 3, 4, 5, 6, 7; DAC;
DAM MST; DLB 68; RGEL 2; SATA 43

Reaney, James Crerar
See Reaney, James

Rebreanu, Liviu 1885-1944 .... **TCLC 28**
See also CA 165; DLB 220; EWL 3

Rechy, John 1934- ..... **CLC 1, 7, 14, 18, 107;
HLC 2**
See also CA 5-8R, 195; CAAE 195; CAAS
4; CANR 6, 32, 64, 152, 188; CN 1, 2, 3,
4, 5, 6, 7; DAM MULT; DLB 122, 278;
DLBY 1982; HW 1, 2; INT CANR-6;
LLW; MAL 5; RGAL 4

Rechy, John Francisco
See Rechy, John

Redcam, Tom 1870-1933 .... **TCLC 25**

Reddin, Keith 1956- .... **CLC 67**
See also CAD; CD 6

Redgrove, Peter (William)
1932-2003 .... **CLC 6, 41**
See also BRWS 6; CA 1-4R; 217; CANR 3,
39, 77; CP 1, 2, 3, 4, 5, 6, 7; DLB 40;
TCLE 1:2

Redmon, Anne
See Nightingale, Anne Redmon

Reed, Eliot
See Ambler, Eric

Reed, Ishmael 1938- . **BLC 1:3; CLC 2, 3, 5,
6, 13, 32, 60, 174; PC 68**
See also AFAW 1, 2; AMWS 10; BPFB 3;
BW 2, 3; CA 21-24R; CANR 25, 48, 74,
128; CN 1, 2, 3, 4, 5, 6, 7; CP 1, 2, 3, 4,
5, 6, 7; CSW; DA3; DAM MULT; DLB
2, 5, 33, 169, 227; DLBD 8; EWL 3;
LMFS 2; MAL 5; MSW; MTCW 1, 2;
MTFW 2005; PFS 6; RGAL 4; TCWW 2

Reed, John (Silas) 1887-1920 .... **TCLC 9**
See also CA 106; 195; MAL 5; TUS

Reed, Lou
See Firbank, Louis

Reese, Lizette Woodworth
1856-1935 .... **PC 29; TCLC 181**
See also CA 180; DLB 54

Reeve, Clara 1729-1807 .... **NCLC 19**
See also DLB 39; RGEL 2

Reich, Wilhelm 1897-1957 .... **TCLC 57**
See also CA 199

Reid, Christopher (John) 1949- .... **CLC 33**
See also CA 140; CANR 89; CP 4, 5, 6, 7;
DLB 40; EWL 3

Reid, Desmond
See Moorcock, Michael

Reid Banks, Lynne 1929- .... **CLC 23**
See also AAYA 49; BYA 7; CA 1-4R; CANR
6, 22, 38, 87; CLR 24, 86; CN 4, 5, 6;
JRDA; MAICYA 1, 2; SATA 22, 75, 111,
165; YAW

Reilly, William K.
See Creasey, John

Reiner, Max
See Caldwell, (Janet Miriam) Taylor
(Holland)

Reis, Ricardo
See Pessoa, Fernando

Reizenstein, Elmer Leopold
See Rice, Elmer (Leopold)

Remarque, Erich Maria 1898-1970 . **CLC 21**
See also AAYA 27; BPFB 3; CA 77-80; 29-
32R; CDWLB 2; DA; DA3; DAB; DAC;
DAM MST, NOV; DLB 56; EWL 3;
EXPN; LAIT 3; MTCW 1, 2; MTFW
2005; NFS 4; RGHL; RGWL 2, 3

Remington, Frederic S(ackrider)
1861-1909 .... **TCLC 89**
See also CA 108; 169; DLB 12, 186, 188;
SATA 41; TCWW 2

Remizov, A.
See Remizov, Aleksei (Mikhailovich)

Remizov, A. M.
See Remizov, Aleksei (Mikhailovich)

Remizov, Aleksei (Mikhailovich)
1877-1957 .... **TCLC 27**
See also CA 125; 133; DLB 295; EWL 3

Remizov, Alexey Mikhaylovich
See Remizov, Aleksei (Mikhailovich)

Renan, Joseph Ernest 1823-1892 . **NCLC 26,
145**
See also GFL 1789 to the Present

Renard, Jules(-Pierre) 1864-1910 .. **TCLC 17**
See also CA 117; 202; GFL 1789 to the
Present

Renart, Jean fl. 13th cent. - .... **CMLC 83**

Renault, Mary
See Challans, Mary

Rendell, Ruth
See Rendell, Ruth

Rendell, Ruth 1930- .... **CLC 28, 48, 50**
See also BEST 90:4; BPFB 3; BRWS 9;
CA 109; CANR 32, 52, 74, 127, 162, 190;
CN 5, 6, 7; CPW; DAM POP; DLB 87,
276; INT CANR-32; MSW; MTCW 1, 2;
MTFW 2005

Rendell, Ruth Barbara
See Rendell, Ruth

Renoir, Jean 1894-1979 .... **CLC 20**
See also CA 129; 85-88

Rensie, Willis
See Eisner, Will

Resnais, Alain 1922- .... **CLC 16**

Revard, Carter 1931- .... **NNAL**
See also CA 144; CANR 81, 153; PFS 5

Reverdy, Pierre 1889-1960 .... **CLC 53**
See also CA 97-100; 89-92; DLB 258; EWL
3; GFL 1789 to the Present

Reverend Mandju
See Su, Chien

Rexroth, Kenneth 1905-1982 .... **CLC 1, 2, 6,
11, 22, 49, 112; PC 20, 95**
See also BG 1:3; CA 5-8R; 107; CANR 14,
34, 63; CDALB 1941-1968; CP 1, 2, 3;
DAM POET; DLB 16, 48, 165, 212;
DLBY 1982; EWL 3; INT CANR-14;
MAL 5; MTCW 1, 2; MTFW 2005;
RGAL 4

Reyes, Alfonso 1889-1959 .... **HLCS 2; TCLC
33**
See also CA 131; EWL 3; HW 1; LAW

Reyes y Basoalto, Ricardo Eliecer Neftali
See Neruda, Pablo

Reymont, Wladyslaw (Stanislaw)
1868(?)-1925 .... **TCLC 5**
See also CA 104; DLB 332; EWL 3

Reynolds, John Hamilton
1794-1852 .... **NCLC 146**
See also DLB 96

Reynolds, Jonathan 1942- .... **CLC 6, 38**
See also CA 65-68; CANR 28, 176

Reynolds, Joshua 1723-1792 .... **LC 15**
See also DLB 104

Reynolds, Michael S(hane)
1937-2000 .... **CLC 44**
See also CA 65-68; 189; CANR 9, 89, 97

Reza, Yasmina 1959- .... **DC 34**
See also AAYA 69; CA 171; CANR 145;
DFS 19; DLB 321

Reznikoff, Charles 1894-1976 .... **CLC 9**
See also AMWS 14; CA 33-36; 61-64; CAP
2; CP 1, 2; DLB 28, 45; RGHL; WP

Rezzori, Gregor von
See Rezzori d'Arezzo, Gregor von

Rezzori d'Arezzo, Gregor von
1914-1998 .... **CLC 25**
See also CA 122; 136; 167

Rhine, Richard
See Silverstein, Alvin; Silverstein, Virginia
B(arbara Opshelor)

Rhodes, Eugene Manlove
1869-1934 .... **TCLC 53**
See also CA 198; DLB 256; TCWW 1, 2

R'hoone, Lord
See Balzac, Honore de

Rhys, Jean 1890-1979 .... **CLC 2, 4, 6, 14, 19,
51, 124; SSC 21, 76**
See also BRWS 2; CA 25-28R; 85-88;
CANR 35, 62; CDBLB 1945-1960; CD-
WLB 3; CN 1, 2; DA3; DAM NOV; DLB
36, 117, 162; DNFS 2; EWL 3; LATS 1:1;
MTCW 1, 2; MTFW 2005; NFS 19;
RGEL 2; RGSF 2; RHW; TEA; WWE 1

Ribeiro, Darcy 1922-1997 .... **CLC 34**
See also CA 33-36R; 156; EWL 3

Ribeiro, Joao Ubaldo (Osorio Pimentel)
1941- .... **CLC 10, 67**
See also CA 81-84; CWW 2; EWL 3

Ribman, Ronald (Burt) 1932- .... **CLC 7**
See also CA 21-24R; CAD; CANR 46, 80;
CD 5, 6

Ricci, Nino 1959- .... **CLC 70**
See also CA 137; CANR 130; CCA 1

Ricci, Nino Pio
See Ricci, Nino

Rice, Anne 1941- .... **CLC 41, 128**
See also AAYA 9, 53; AMWS 7; BEST
89:2; BPFB 3; CA 65-68; CANR 12, 36,
53, 74, 100, 133, 190; CN 6, 7; CPW;
CSW; DA3; DAM POP; DLB 292; GL 3;
GLL 2; HGG; MTCW 2; MTFW 2005;
SUFW 2; YAW

Rice, Elmer (Leopold) 1892-1967 ...... **CLC 7,
49; TCLC 221**
See also CA 21-22; 25-28R; CAP 2; DAM
DRAM; DFS 12; DLB 4, 7; EWL 3;
IDTP; MAL 5; MTCW 1, 2; RGAL 4

Rice, Tim(othy Miles Bindon)
1944- .... **CLC 21**
See also CA 103; CANR 46; DFS 7

Rich, Adrienne 1929- ..... **CLC 3, 6, 7, 11, 18,
36, 73, 76, 125; PC 5**
See also AAYA 69; AMWR 2; AMWS 1;
CA 9-12R; CANR 20, 53, 74, 128;
CDALBS; CP 1, 2, 3, 4, 5, 6, 7; CSW;
CWP; DA3; DAM POET; DLB 5, 67;
EWL 3; EXPP; FL 1:6; FW; MAL 5;
MBL; MTCW 1, 2; MTFW 2005; PAB;
PFS 15, 29; RGAL 4; RGHL; WP

Rich, Barbara
See Graves, Robert

Rich, Robert
See Trumbo, Dalton

Richard, Keith
See Richards, Keith

Richards, David Adams 1950- .... **CLC 59**
See also CA 93-96; CANR 60, 110, 156;
CN 7; DAC; DLB 53; TCLE 1:2

Richards, I(vor) A(rmstrong)
1893-1979 .... **CLC 14, 24**
See also BRWS 2; CA 41-44R; 89-92;
CANR 34, 74; CP 1, 2; DLB 27; EWL 3;
MTCW 2; RGEL 2

Richards, Keith 1943- .... **CLC 17**
See also CA 107; CANR 77

Richardson, Anne
See Roiphe, Anne

Richardson, Dorothy Miller
1873-1957 .... **TCLC 3, 203**
See also BRWS 13; CA 104; 192; DLB 36;
EWL 3; FW; RGEL 2

Richardson, Ethel Florence Lindesay
1870-1946 .... **TCLC 4**
See also CA 105; 190; DLB 197, 230; EWL
3; RGEL 2; RGSF 2; RHW

Richardson, Henrietta
See Richardson, Ethel Florence Lindesay

Richardson, Henry Handel
See Richardson, Ethel Florence Lindesay

Richardson, John 1796-1852 .... **NCLC 55**
See also CCA 1; DAC; DLB 99

Richardson, Samuel 1689-1761 ...... **LC 1, 44,
138; WLC 5**
See also BRW 3; CDBLB 1660-1789; DA;
DAB; DAC; DAM MST, NOV; DLB 39;
RGEL 2; TEA; WLIT 3

Richardson, Willis 1889-1977 .... **HR 1:3**
See also BW 1; CA 124; DLB 51; SATA 60

**Richardson Robertson, Ethel Florence
Lindesay**
See Richardson, Ethel Florence Lindesay

Richler, Mordecai 1931-2001 .... **CLC 3, 5, 9,
13, 18, 46, 70, 185, 271**
See also AITN 1; CA 65-68; 201; CANR
31, 62, 111; CCA 1; CLR 17; CN 1, 2, 3,
4, 5, 7; CWRI 5; DAC; DAM MST, NOV;
DLB 53; EWL 3; MAICYA 1, 2; MTCW
1, 2; MTFW 2005; RGEL 2; RGHL;
SATA 44, 98; SATA-Brief 27; TWA

Richter, Conrad (Michael)
1890-1968 .... **CLC 30**
See also AAYA 21; AMWS 18; BYA 2; CA
5-8R; 25-28R; CANR 23; DLB 9, 212;
LAIT 1; MAL 5; MTCW 1, 2; MTFW
2005; RGAL 4; SATA 3; TCWW 1, 2;
TUS; YAW

Ricostranza, Tom
See Ellis, Trey

Riddell, Charlotte 1832-1906 .... **TCLC 40**
See also CA 165; DLB 156; HGG; SUFW

Riddell, Mrs. J. H.
See Riddell, Charlotte

Ridge, John Rollin 1827-1867 ...... **NCLC 82;
NNAL**
See also CA 144; DAM MULT; DLB 175

Ridgeway, Jason
See Marlowe, Stephen

Ridgway, Keith 1965- .... **CLC 119**
See also CA 172; CANR 144

Riding, Laura
See Jackson, Laura

Riefenstahl, Berta Helene Amalia
1902-2003 .... **CLC 16, 190**
See also CA 108; 220

Riefenstahl, Leni
See Riefenstahl, Berta Helene Amalia

Riffe, Ernest
See Bergman, Ingmar

Riffe, Ernest Ingmar
See Bergman, Ingmar

Riggs, (Rolla) Lynn
1899-1954 .... **NNAL; TCLC 56**
See also CA 144; DAM MULT; DLB 175

Riis, Jacob A(ugust) 1849-1914 ..... **TCLC 80**
See also CA 113; 168; DLB 23

Rikki
See Ducornet, Erica

Riley, James Whitcomb 1849-1916 .... **PC 48;
TCLC 51**
See also CA 118; 137; DAM POET; MAI-
CYA 1, 2; RGAL 4; SATA 17

Riley, Tex
See Creasey, John

Rilke, Rainer Maria 1875-1926 .... **PC 2;
TCLC 1, 6, 19, 195**
See also CA 104; 132; CANR 62, 99; CD-
WLB 2; DA3; DAM POET; DLB 81; EW
9; EWL 3; MTCW 1, 2; MTFW 2005;
PFS 19, 27; RGWL 2, 3; TWA; WP

Rimbaud, (Jean Nicolas) Arthur
1854-1891 ... **NCLC 4, 35, 82; PC 3, 57;
WLC 5**
See also DA; DA3; DAB; DAC; DAM
MST, POET; DLB 217; EW 7; GFL 1789
to the Present; LMFS 2; PFS 28; RGWL
2, 3; TWA; WP

Rinehart, Mary Roberts
1876-1958 .... **TCLC 52**
See also BPFB 3; CA 108; 166; RGAL 4;
RHW

Ringmaster, The
See Mencken, H. L.

Ringwood, Gwen(dolyn Margaret) Pharis
1910-1984 .... **CLC 48**
See also CA 148; 112; DLB 88

Rio, Michel 1945(?)- .... **CLC 43**
See also CA 201

Rios, Alberto 1952- .... **PC 57**
See also AAYA 66; AMWS 4; CA 113;
CANR 34, 79, 137; CP 6; DLB 122;
HW 2; MTFW 2005; PFS 11

Ritsos, Giannes
See Ritsos, Yannis

Ritsos, Yannis 1909-1990 .... **CLC 6, 13, 31**
See also CA 77-80; 133; CANR 39, 61; EW
12; EWL 3; MTCW 1; RGWL 2, 3

Ritter, Erika 1948(?)- .... **CLC 52**
See also CD 5, 6; CWD

Rivera, Jose Eustasio 1889-1928 ... **TCLC 35**
See also CA 162; EWL 3; HW 1, 2; LAW

Rivera, Tomas 1935-1984 .... **HLCS 2**
See also CA 49-52; CANR 32; DLB 82;
HW 1; LLW; RGAL 4; SSFS 15; TCWW
2; WLIT 1

Rivers, Conrad Kent 1933-1968 .... **CLC 1**
See also BW 1; CA 85-88; DLB 41

Rivers, Elfrida
See Bradley, Marion Zimmer

Riverside, John
See Heinlein, Robert A.

Rizal, Jose 1861-1896 .... **NCLC 27**
See also DLB 348

Roa Bastos, Augusto 1917-2005 ...... **CLC 45;
HLC 2**
See also CA 131; 238; CWW 2; DAM
MULT; DLB 113; EWL 3; HW 1; LAW;
RGSF 2; WLIT 1

Roa Bastos, Augusto Jose Antonio
See Roa Bastos, Augusto

Robbe-Grillet, Alain 1922-2008 ..... **CLC 1, 2,
4, 6, 8, 10, 14, 43, 128**
See also BPFB 3; CA 9-12R; 269; CANR
33, 65, 115; CWW 2; DLB 83; EW 13;
EWL 3; GFL 1789 to the Present; IDFW
3, 4; MTCW 1, 2; MTFW 2005; RGWL
2, 3; SSFS 15

Robbins, Harold 1916-1997 .... **CLC 5**
See also BPFB 3; CA 73-76; 162; CANR 26, 54, 112, 156; DA3; DAM NOV; MTCW 1, 2

Robbins, Thomas Eugene 1936- . **CLC 9, 32, 64**
See also AAYA 32; AMWS 10; BEST 90:3; BPFB 3; CA 81-84; CANR 29, 59, 95, 139; CN 3, 4, 5, 6, 7; CPW; CSW; DA3; DAM NOV, POP; DLBY 1980; MTCW 1, 2; MTFW 2005

Robbins, Tom
See Robbins, Thomas Eugene

Robbins, Trina 1938- .... **CLC 21**
See also AAYA 61; CA 128; CANR 152

Robert de Boron fl. 12th cent. - .... **CMLC 94**

Roberts, Charles G(eorge) D(ouglas)
1860-1943 .... **SSC 91; TCLC 8**
See also CA 105; 188; CLR 33; CWRI 5; DLB 92; RGEL 2; RGSF 2; SATA 88; SATA-Brief 29

Roberts, Elizabeth Madox
1886-1941 .... **TCLC 68**
See also CA 111; 166; CLR 100; CWRI 5; DLB 9, 54, 102; RGAL 4; RHW; SATA 33; SATA-Brief 27; TCWW 2; WCH

Roberts, Kate 1891-1985 .... **CLC 15**
See also CA 107; 116; DLB 319

Roberts, Keith (John Kingston)
1935-2000 .... **CLC 14**
See also BRWS 10; CA 25-28R; CANR 46; DLB 261; SFW 4

Roberts, Kenneth (Lewis)
1885-1957 .... **TCLC 23**
See also CA 109; 199; DLB 9; MAL 5; RGAL 4; RHW

Roberts, Michele 1949- .... **CLC 48, 178**
See also CA 115; CANR 58, 120, 164; CN 6, 7; DLB 231; FW

Roberts, Michele Brigitte
See Roberts, Michele

Robertson, Ellis
See Ellison, Harlan; Silverberg, Robert

Robertson, Thomas William
1829-1871 .... **NCLC 35**
See also DAM DRAM; DLB 344; RGEL 2

Robertson, Tom
See Robertson, Thomas William

Robeson, Kenneth
See Dent, Lester

Robinson, Edwin Arlington
1869-1935 .... **PC 1, 35; TCLC 5, 101**
See also AAYA 72; AMW; CA 104; 133; CDALB 1865-1917; DA; DAC; DAM MST, POET; DLB 54; EWL 3; EXPP; MAL 5; MTCW 1, 2; MTFW 2005; PAB; PFS 4; RGAL 4; WP

Robinson, Henry Crabb
1775-1867 .... **NCLC 15**
See also DLB 107

Robinson, Jill 1936- .... **CLC 10**
See also CA 102; CANR 120; INT CA-102

Robinson, Kim Stanley 1952- ... **CLC 34, 248**
See also AAYA 26; CA 126; CANR 113, 139, 173; CN 6, 7; MTFW 2005; SATA 109; SCFW 2; SFW 4

Robinson, Lloyd
See Silverberg, Robert

Robinson, Marilynne 1943- ..... **CLC 25, 180, 276**
See also AAYA 69; CA 116; CANR 80, 140, 192; CN 4, 5, 6, 7; DLB 206, 350; MTFW 2005; NFS 24

Robinson, Mary 1758-1800 .... **NCLC 142**
See also BRWS 13; DLB 158; FW

Robinson, Smokey
See Robinson, William, Jr.

Robinson, William, Jr. 1940- .... **CLC 21**
See also CA 116

Robison, Mary 1949- .... **CLC 42, 98**
See also CA 113; 116; CANR 87; CN 4, 5, 6, 7; DLB 130; INT CA-116; RGSF 2

Roches, Catherine des 1542-1587 ...... **LC 117**
See also DLB 327

Rochester
See Wilmot, John

Rod, Edouard 1857-1910 .... **TCLC 52**

Roddenberry, Eugene Wesley
1921-1991 .... **CLC 17**
See also AAYA 5; CA 110; 135; CANR 37; SATA 45; SATA-Obit 69

Roddenberry, Gene
See Roddenberry, Eugene Wesley

Rodgers, Mary 1931- .... **CLC 12**
See also BYA 5; CA 49-52; CANR 8, 55, 90; CLR 20; CWRI 5; INT CANR-8; JRDA; MAICYA 1, 2; SATA 8, 130

Rodgers, W(illiam) R(obert)
1909-1969 .... **CLC 7**
See also CA 85-88; DLB 20; RGEL 2

Rodman, Eric
See Silverberg, Robert

Rodman, Howard 1920(?)-1985 .... **CLC 65**
See also CA 118

Rodman, Maia
See Wojciechowska, Maia (Teresa)

Rodo, Jose Enrique 1871(?)-1917 .... **HLCS 2**
See also CA 178; EWL 3; HW 2; LAW

Rodolph, Utto
See Ouologuem, Yambo

Rodriguez, Claudio 1934-1999 .... **CLC 10**
See also CA 188; DLB 134

Rodriguez, Richard 1944- .... **CLC 155; HLC 2**
See also AMWS 14; CA 110; CANR 66, 116; DAM MULT; DLB 82, 256; HW 1, 2; LAIT 5; LLW; MTFW 2005; NCFS 3; WLIT 1

Roethke, Theodore 1908-1963 ... **CLC 1, 3, 8, 11, 19, 46, 101; PC 15**
See also AMW; CA 81-84; CABS 2; CDALB 1941-1968; DA3; DAM POET; DLB 5, 206; EWL 3; EXPP; MAL 5; MTCW 1, 2; PAB; PFS 3; RGAL 4; WP

Roethke, Theodore Huebner
See Roethke, Theodore

Rogers, Carl R(ansom)
1902-1987 .... **TCLC 125**
See also CA 1-4R; 121; CANR 1, 18; MTCW 1

Rogers, Samuel 1763-1855 .... **NCLC 69**
See also DLB 93; RGEL 2

Rogers, Thomas 1927-2007 .... **CLC 57**
See also CA 89-92; 259; CANR 163; INT CA-89-92

Rogers, Thomas Hunton
See Rogers, Thomas

Rogers, Will(iam Penn Adair)
1879-1935 .... **NNAL; TCLC 8, 71**
See also CA 105; 144; DA3; DAM MULT; DLB 11; MTCW 2

Rogin, Gilbert 1929- .... **CLC 18**
See also CA 65-68; CANR 15

Rohan, Koda
See Koda Shigeyuki

Rohlfs, Anna Katharine Green
See Green, Anna Katharine

Rohmer, Eric
See Scherer, Jean-Marie Maurice

Rohmer, Sax
See Ward, Arthur Henry Sarsfield

Roiphe, Anne 1935- .... **CLC 3, 9**
See also CA 89-92; CANR 45, 73, 138, 170; DLBY 1980; INT CA-89-92

Roiphe, Anne Richardson
See Roiphe, Anne

Rojas, Fernando de 1475-1541 ... **HLCS 1, 2; LC 23, 169**
See also DLB 286; RGWL 2, 3

Rojas, Gonzalo 1917- .... **HLCS 2**
See also CA 178; HW 2; LAWS 1

Rolaag, Ole Edvart
See Rolvaag, O.E.

Roland (de la Platiere), Marie-Jeanne
1754-1793 .... **LC 98**
See also DLB 314

Rolfe, Frederick (William Serafino Austin Lewis Mary) 1860-1913 .... **TCLC 12**
See also CA 107; 210; DLB 34, 156; GLL 1; RGEL 2

Rolland, Romain 1866-1944 .... **TCLC 23**
See also CA 118; 197; DLB 65, 284, 332; EWL 3; GFL 1789 to the Present; RGWL 2, 3

Rolle, Richard c. 1300-c. 1349 ...... **CMLC 21**
See also DLB 146; LMFS 1; RGEL 2

Rolvaag, O.E.
See Rolvaag, O.E.

Rolvaag, O.E.
See Rolvaag, O.E.

Rolvaag, O.E. 1876-1931 .... **TCLC 17, 207**
See also AAYA 75; CA 117; 171; DLB 9, 212; MAL 5; NFS 5; RGAL 4; TCWW 1, 2

Romain Arnaud, Saint
See Aragon, Louis

Romains, Jules 1885-1972 .... **CLC 7**
See also CA 85-88; CANR 34; DLB 65, 321; EWL 3; GFL 1789 to the Present; MTCW 1

Romero, Jose Ruben 1890-1952 .... **TCLC 14**
See also CA 114; 131; EWL 3; HW 1; LAW

Ronsard, Pierre de 1524-1585 . **LC 6, 54; PC 11**
See also DLB 327; EW 2; GFL Beginnings to 1789; RGWL 2, 3; TWA

Rooke, Leon 1934- .... **CLC 25, 34**
See also CA 25-28R; CANR 23, 53; CCA 1; CPW; DAM POP

Roosevelt, Franklin Delano
1882-1945 .... **TCLC 93**
See also CA 116; 173; LAIT 3

Roosevelt, Theodore 1858-1919 ..... **TCLC 69**
See also CA 115; 170; DLB 47, 186, 275

Roper, Margaret c. 1505-1544 .... **LC 147**

Roper, William 1498-1578 .... **LC 10**

Roquelaure, A. N.
See Rice, Anne

Rosa, Joao Guimaraes 1908-1967
See Guimaraes Rosa, Joao

Rose, Wendy 1948- . **CLC 85; NNAL; PC 13**
See also CA 53-56; CANR 5, 51; CWP; DAM MULT; DLB 175; PFS 13; RGAL 4; SATA 12

Rosen, R.D. 1949- .... **CLC 39**
See also CA 77-80; CANR 62, 120, 175; CMW 4; INT CANR-30

Rosen, Richard
See Rosen, R.D.

Rosen, Richard Dean
See Rosen, R.D.

Rosenberg, Isaac 1890-1918 .... **TCLC 12**
See also BRW 6; CA 107; 188; DLB 20, 216; EWL 3; PAB; RGEL 2

Rosenblatt, Joe
See Rosenblatt, Joseph

Rosenblatt, Joseph 1933- .... **CLC 15**
See also CA 89-92; CP 3, 4, 5, 6, 7; INT CA-89-92

Rosenfeld, Samuel
See Tzara, Tristan

Rosenstock, Sami
See Tzara, Tristan

Schelling, Friedrich Wilhelm Joseph von
1775-1854 .... **NCLC 30**
See also DLB 90

Scherer, Jean-Marie Maurice
1920- .... **CLC 16**
See also CA 110

Schevill, James (Erwin) 1920- .... **CLC 7**
See also CA 5-8R; CAAS 12; CAD; CD 5,
6; CP 1, 2, 3, 4, 5

Schiller, Friedrich von 1759-1805 ...... **DC 12;
NCLC 39, 69, 166**
See also CDWLB 2; DAM DRAM; DLB
94; EW 5; RGWL 2, 3; TWA

Schisgal, Murray (Joseph) 1926- .... **CLC 6**
See also CA 21-24R; CAD; CANR 48, 86;
CD 5, 6; MAL 5

Schlee, Ann 1934- .... **CLC 35**
See also CA 101; CANR 29, 88; SATA 44;
SATA-Brief 36

Schlegel, August Wilhelm von
1767-1845 .... **NCLC 15, 142**
See also DLB 94; RGWL 2, 3

Schlegel, Friedrich 1772-1829 .... **NCLC 45**
See also DLB 90; EW 5; RGWL 2, 3; TWA

Schlegel, Johann Elias (von)
1719(?)-1749 .... **LC 5**

Schleiermacher, Friedrich
1768-1834 .... **NCLC 107**
See also DLB 90

Schlesinger, Arthur M., Jr.
1917-2007 .... **CLC 84**
See Schlesinger, Arthur Meier
See also AITN 1; CA 1-4R; 257; CANR 1,
28, 58, 105, 187; DLB 17; INT CANR-
28; MTCW 1, 2; SATA 61; SATA-Obit
181

Schlink, Bernhard 1944- .... **CLC 174**
See also CA 163; CANR 116, 175; RGHL

Schmidt, Arno (Otto) 1914-1979 ...... **CLC 56**
See also CA 128; 109; DLB 69; EWL 3

Schmitz, Aron Hector 1861-1928 ..... **SSC 25;
TCLC 2, 35**
See also CA 104; 122; DLB 264; EW 8;
EWL 3; MTCW 1; RGWL 2, 3; WLIT 7

Schnackenberg, Gjertrud 1953- ...... **CLC 40;
PC 45**
See also AMWS 15; CA 116; CANR 100;
CP 5, 6, 7; CWP; DLB 120, 282; PFS 13,
25

Schnackenberg, Gjertrud Cecelia
See Schnackenberg, Gjertrud

Schneider, Leonard Alfred
1925-1966 .... **CLC 21**
See also CA 89-92

Schnitzler, Arthur 1862-1931 ..... **DC 17; SSC
15, 61; TCLC 4**
See also CA 104; CDWLB 2; DLB 81, 118;
EW 8; EWL 3; RGSF 2; RGWL 2, 3

Schoenberg, Arnold Franz Walter
1874-1951 .... **TCLC 75**
See also CA 109; 188

Schonberg, Arnold
See Schoenberg, Arnold Franz Walter

Schopenhauer, Arthur 1788-1860 . **NCLC 51,
157**
See also DLB 90; EW 5

Schor, Sandra (M.) 1932(?)-1990 ..... **CLC 65**
See also CA 132

Schorer, Mark 1908-1977 .... **CLC 9**
See also CA 5-8R; 73-76; CANR 7; CN 1,
2; DLB 103

Schrader, Paul (Joseph) 1946- . **CLC 26, 212**
See also CA 37-40R; CANR 41; DLB 44

Schreber, Daniel 1842-1911 .... **TCLC 123**

Schreiner, Olive (Emilie Albertina)
1855-1920 .... **TCLC 9**
See also AFW; BRWS 2; CA 105; 154;
DLB 18, 156, 190, 225; EWL 3; FW;
RGEL 2; TWA; WLIT 2; WWE 1

Schulberg, Budd 1914- .... **CLC 7, 48**
See also AMWS 18; BPFB 3; CA 25-28R;
CANR 19, 87, 178; CN 1, 2, 3, 4, 5, 6, 7;
DLB 6, 26, 28; DLBY 1981, 2001; MAL
5

Schulberg, Budd Wilson
See Schulberg, Budd

Schulman, Arnold
See Trumbo, Dalton

Schulz, Bruno 1892-1942 .. **SSC 13; TCLC 5,
51**
See also CA 115; 123; CANR 86; CDWLB
4; DLB 215; EWL 3; MTCW 2; MTFW
2005; RGSF 2; RGWL 2, 3

Schulz, Charles M. 1922-2000 .... **CLC 12**
See also AAYA 39; CA 9-12R; 187; CANR
6, 132; INT CANR-6; MTFW 2005;
SATA 10; SATA-Obit 118

Schulz, Charles Monroe
See Schulz, Charles M.

Schumacher, E(rnst) F(riedrich)
1911-1977 .... **CLC 80**
See also CA 81-84; 73-76; CANR 34, 85

Schumann, Robert 1810-1856 ...... **NCLC 143**

Schuyler, George Samuel 1895-1977 . **HR 1:3**
See also BW 2; CA 81-84; 73-76; CANR
42; DLB 29, 51

Schuyler, James Marcus 1923-1991 .. **CLC 5,
23; PC 88**
See also CA 101; 134; CP 1, 2, 3, 4, 5;
DAM POET; DLB 5, 169; EWL 3; INT
CA-101; MAL 5; WP

Schwartz, Delmore (David)
1913-1966 . **CLC 2, 4, 10, 45, 87; PC 8;
SSC 105**
See also AMWS 2; CA 17-18; 25-28R;
CANR 35; CAP 2; DLB 28, 48; EWL 3;
MAL 5; MTCW 1, 2; MTFW 2005; PAB;
RGAL 4; TUS

Schwartz, Ernst
See Ozu, Yasujiro

Schwartz, John Burnham 1965- .... **CLC 59**
See also CA 132; CANR 116, 188

Schwartz, Lynne Sharon 1939- .... **CLC 31**
See also CA 103; CANR 44, 89, 160; DLB
218; MTCW 2; MTFW 2005

Schwartz, Muriel A.
See Eliot, T(homas) S(tearns)

Schwarz-Bart, Andre 1928-2006 .... **CLC 2, 4**
See also CA 89-92; 253; CANR 109; DLB
299; RGHL

Schwarz-Bart, Simone 1938- . **BLCS; CLC 7**
See also BW 2; CA 97-100; CANR 117;
EWL 3

Schwerner, Armand 1927-1999 .... **PC 42**
See also CA 9-12R; 179; CANR 50, 85; CP
2, 3, 4, 5, 6; DLB 165

**Schwitters, Kurt (Hermann Edward Karl
Julius)** 1887-1948 .... **TCLC 95**
See also CA 158

Schwob, Marcel (Mayer Andre)
1867-1905 .... **TCLC 20**
See also CA 117; 168; DLB 123; GFL 1789
to the Present

Sciascia, Leonardo 1921-1989 .. **CLC 8, 9, 41**
See also CA 85-88; 130; CANR 35; DLB
177; EWL 3; MTCW 1; RGWL 2, 3

Scoppettone, Sandra 1936- .... **CLC 26**
See also AAYA 11, 65; BYA 8; CA 5-8R;
CANR 41, 73, 157; GLL 1; MAICYA 2;
MAICYAS 1; SATA 9, 92; WYA; YAW

Scorsese, Martin 1942- .... **CLC 20, 89, 207**
See also AAYA 38; CA 110; 114; CANR
46, 85

Scotland, Jay
See Jakes, John

Scott, Duncan Campbell
1862-1947 .... **TCLC 6**
See also CA 104; 153; DAC; DLB 92;
RGEL 2

Scott, Evelyn 1893-1963 .... **CLC 43**
See also CA 104; 112; CANR 64; DLB 9,
48; RHW

Scott, F(rancis) R(eginald)
1899-1985 .... **CLC 22**
See also CA 101; 114; CANR 87; CP 1, 2,
3, 4; DLB 88; INT CA-101; RGEL 2

Scott, Frank
See Scott, F(rancis) R(eginald)

Scott, Joan .... **CLC 65**

Scott, Joanna 1960- .... **CLC 50**
See also AMWS 17; CA 126; CANR 53,
92, 168

Scott, Joanna Jeanne
See Scott, Joanna

Scott, Paul (Mark) 1920-1978 ...... **CLC 9, 60**
See also BRWS 1; CA 81-84; 77-80; CANR
33; CN 1, 2; DLB 14, 207, 326; EWL 3;
MTCW 1; RGEL 2; RHW; WWE 1

Scott, Ridley 1937- .... **CLC 183**
See also AAYA 13, 43

Scott, Sarah 1723-1795 .... **LC 44**
See also DLB 39

Scott, Sir Walter 1771-1832 .... **NCLC 15, 69,
110, 209; PC 13; SSC 32; WLC 5**
See also AAYA 22; BRW 4; BYA 2; CD-
BLB 1789-1832; DA; DAB; DAC; DAM
MST, NOV, POET; DLB 93, 107, 116,
144, 159; GL 3; HGG; LAIT 1; RGEL 2;
RGSF 2; SSFS 10; SUFW 1; TEA; WLIT
3; YABC 2

Scribe, (Augustin) Eugene 1791-1861 . **DC 5;
NCLC 16**
See also DAM DRAM; DLB 192; GFL
1789 to the Present; RGWL 2, 3

Scrum, R.
See Crumb, R.

Scudery, Georges de 1601-1667 .... **LC 75**
See also GFL Beginnings to 1789

Scudery, Madeleine de 1607-1701 .. **LC 2, 58**
See also DLB 268; GFL Beginnings to 1789

Scum
See Crumb, R.

Scumbag, Little Bobby
See Crumb, R.

Seabrook, John
See Hubbard, L. Ron

Seacole, Mary Jane Grant
1805-1881 .... **NCLC 147**
See also DLB 166

Sealy, I(rwin) Allan 1951- .... **CLC 55**
See also CA 136; CN 6, 7

Search, Alexander
See Pessoa, Fernando

Seare, Nicholas
See Whitaker, Rod

Sebald, W(infried) G(eorg)
1944-2001 .... **CLC 194**
See also BRWS 8; CA 159; 202; CANR 98;
MTFW 2005; RGHL

Sebastian, Lee
See Silverberg, Robert

Sebastian Owl
See Thompson, Hunter S.

Sebestyen, Igen
See Sebestyen, Ouida

Sebestyen, Ouida 1924- .... **CLC 30**
See also AAYA 8; BYA 7; CA 107; CANR
40, 114; CLR 17; JRDA; MAICYA 1, 2;
SAAS 10; SATA 39, 140; WYA; YAW

Sebold, Alice 1963- .... **CLC 193**
See also AAYA 56; CA 203; CANR 181;
MTFW 2005

Second Duke of Buckingham
See Villiers, George

Srivastava, Dhanpat Rai
1880(?)-1936 .... **TCLC 21**
See also CA 118; 197; EWL 3
Ssu-ma Ch'ien c. 145B.C.-c.
86B.C. .... **CMLC 96**
Ssu-ma T'an (?)-c. 110B.C. .... **CMLC 96**
Stacy, Donald
See Pohl, Frederik
Stael
See Stael-Holstein, Anne Louise Germaine
Necker
Stael, Germaine de
See Stael-Holstein, Anne Louise Germaine
Necker
Stael-Holstein, Anne Louise Germaine
Necker 1766-1817 .... **NCLC 3, 91**
See also DLB 119, 192; EW 5; FL 1:3; FW;
GFL 1789 to the Present; RGWL 2, 3;
TWA
Stafford, Jean 1915-1979 .. **CLC 4, 7, 19, 68;
SSC 26, 86**
See also CA 1-4R; 85-88; CANR 3, 65; CN
1, 2; DLB 2, 173; MAL 5; MTCW 1, 2;
MTFW 2005; RGAL 4; RGSF 2; SATA-
Obit 22; SSFS 21; TCWW 1, 2; TUS
Stafford, William (Edgar)
1914-1993 .... **CLC 4, 7, 29; PC 71**
See also AMWS 11; CA 5-8R; 142; CAAS
3; CANR 5, 22; CP 1, 2, 3, 4, 5; DAM
POET; DLB 5, 206; EXPP; INT CANR-
22; MAL 5; PFS 2, 8, 16; RGAL 4; WP
Stagnelius, Eric Johan 1793-1823 . **NCLC 61**
Staines, Trevor
See Brunner, John (Kilian Houston)
Stairs, Gordon
See Austin, Mary (Hunter)
Stalin, Joseph 1879-1953 .... **TCLC 92**
Stampa, Gaspara c. 1524-1554 .. **LC 114; PC
43**
See also RGWL 2, 3; WLIT 7
Stampflinger, K.A.
See Benjamin, Walter
Stancykowna
See Szymborska, Wislawa
Standing Bear, Luther
1868(?)-1939(?) .... **NNAL**
See also CA 113; 144; DAM MULT
Stanislavsky, Constantin
1863(?)-1938 .... **TCLC 167**
See also CA 118
Stanislavsky, Konstantin
See Stanislavsky, Constantin
Stanislavsky, Konstantin Sergeievich
See Stanislavsky, Constantin
Stanislavsky, Konstantin Sergeivich
See Stanislavsky, Constantin
Stanislavsky, Konstantin Sergeyevich
See Stanislavsky, Constantin
Stannard, Martin 1947- .... **CLC 44**
See also CA 142; DLB 155
Stanton, Elizabeth Cady
1815-1902 .... **TCLC 73**
See also CA 171; DLB 79; FL 1:3; FW
Stanton, Maura 1946- .... **CLC 9**
See also CA 89-92; CANR 15, 123; DLB
120
Stanton, Schuyler
See Baum, L(yman) Frank
Stapledon, (William) Olaf
1886-1950 .... **TCLC 22**
See also CA 111; 162; DLB 15, 255; SCFW
1, 2; SFW 4
Starbuck, George (Edwin)
1931-1996 .... **CLC 53**
See also CA 21-24R; 153; CANR 23; CP 1,
2, 3, 4, 5, 6; DAM POET
Stark, Richard
See Westlake, Donald E.

Statius c. 45-c. 96 .... **CMLC 91**
See also AW 2; DLB 211.
Staunton, Schuyler
See Baum, L(yman) Frank
Stead, Christina (Ellen) 1902-1983 ... **CLC 2,
5, 8, 32, 80**
See also BRWS 4; CA 13-16R; 109; CANR
33, 40; CN 1, 2, 3; DLB 260; EWL 3;
FW; MTCW 1, 2; MTFW 2005; NFS 27;
RGEL 2; RGSF 2; WWE 1
Stead, William Thomas
1849-1912 .... **TCLC 48**
See also BRWS 13; CA 167
Stebnitsky, M.
See Leskov, Nikolai (Semyonovich)
Steele, Richard 1672-1729 ... **LC 18, 156, 159**
See also BRW 3; CDBLB 1660-1789; DLB
84, 101; RGEL 2; WLIT 3
Steele, Timothy (Reid) 1948- .... **CLC 45**
See also CA 93-96; CANR 16, 50, 92; CP
5, 6, 7; DLB 120, 282
Steffens, (Joseph) Lincoln
1866-1936 .... **TCLC 20**
See also CA 117; 198; DLB 303; MAL 5
Stegner, Wallace (Earle) 1909-1993 .. **CLC 9,
49, 81; SSC 27**
See also AITN 1; AMWS 4; ANW; BEST
90:3; BPFB 3; CA 1-4R; 141; CAAS 9;
CANR 1, 21, 46; CN 1, 2, 3, 4, 5; DAM
NOV; DLB 9, 206, 275; DLBY 1993;
EWL 3; MAL 5; MTCW 1, 2; MTFW
2005; RGAL 4; TCWW 1, 2; TUS
Stein, Gertrude 1874-1946 .... **DC 19; PC 18;
SSC 42, 105; TCLC 1, 6, 28, 48; WLC
5**
See also AAYA 64; AMW; AMWC 2; CA
104; 132; CANR 108; CDALB 1917-
1929; DA; DA3; DAB; DAC; DAM MST,
NOV, POET; DLB 4, 54, 86, 228; DLBD
15; EWL 3; EXPS; FL 1:6; GLL 1; MAL
5; MBL; MTCW 1, 2; MTFW 2005;
NCFS 2; NFS 27; RGAL 4; RGSF 2;
SSFS 5; TUS; WP
Steinbeck, John (Ernst) 1902-1968 ... **CLC 1,
5, 9, 13, 21, 34, 45, 75, 124; SSC 11, 37,
77; TCLC 135; WLC 5**
See also AAYA 12; AMW; BPFB 3; BYA 2,
3, 13; CA 1-4R; 25-28R; CANR 1, 35;
CDALB 1929-1941; DA; DA3; DAB;
DAC; DAM DRAM, MST, NOV; DLB 7,
9, 212, 275, 309, 332; DLBD 2; EWL 3;
EXPS; LAIT 3; MAL 5; MTCW 1, 2;
MTFW 2005; NFS 1, 5, 7, 17, 19, 28;
RGAL 4; RGSF 2; RHW; SATA 9; SSFS
3, 6, 22; TCWW 1, 2; TUS; WYA; YAW
Steinem, Gloria 1934- .... **CLC 63**
See also CA 53-56; CANR 28, 51, 139;
DLB 246; FL 1:1; FW; MTCW 1, 2;
MTFW 2005
Steiner, George 1929- .... **CLC 24, 221**
See also CA 73-76; CANR 31, 67, 108;
DAM NOV; DLB 67, 299; EWL 3;
MTCW 1, 2; MTFW 2005; RGHL; SATA
62
Steiner, K. Leslie
See Delany, Samuel R., Jr.
Steiner, Rudolf 1861-1925 .... **TCLC 13**
See also CA 107
Stendhal 1783-1842 .... **NCLC 23, 46, 178;
SSC 27; WLC 5**
See also DA; DA3; DAB; DAC; DAM
MST, NOV; DLB 119; EW 5; GFL 1789
to the Present; RGWL 2, 3; TWA
Stephen, Adeline Virginia
See Woolf, (Adeline) Virginia
Stephen, Sir Leslie 1832-1904 .... **TCLC 23**
See also BRW 5; CA 123; DLB 57, 144,
190
Stephen, Sir Leslie
See Stephen, Sir Leslie

Stephen, Virginia
See Woolf, (Adeline) Virginia
Stephens, James 1882(?)-1950 .... **SSC 50;
TCLC 4**
See also CA 104; 192; DLB 19, 153, 162;
EWL 3; FANT; RGEL 2; SUFW
Stephens, Reed
See Donaldson, Stephen R.
Stephenson, Neal 1959- .... **CLC 220**
See also AAYA 38; CA 122; CANR 88, 138;
CN 7; MTFW 2005; SFW 4
Steptoe, Lydia
See Barnes, Djuna
Sterchi, Beat 1949- .... **CLC 65**
See also CA 203
Sterling, Brett
See Bradbury, Ray; Hamilton, Edmond
Sterling, Bruce 1954- .... **CLC 72**
See also AAYA 78; CA 119; CANR 44, 135,
184; CN 7; MTFW 2005; SCFW 2; SFW
4
Sterling, George 1869-1926 .... **TCLC 20**
See also CA 117; 165; DLB 54
Stern, Gerald 1925- .... **CLC 40, 100**
See also AMWS 9; CA 81-84; CANR 28,
94; CP 3, 4, 5, 6, 7; DLB 105; PFS 26;
RGAL 4
Stern, Richard (Gustave) 1928- ... **CLC 4, 39**
See also CA 1-4R; CANR 1, 25, 52, 120;
CN 1, 2, 3, 4, 5, 6, 7; DLB 218; DLBY
1987; INT CANR-25
Sternberg, Josef von 1894-1969 .... **CLC 20**
See also CA 81-84
Sterne, Laurence 1713-1768 .. **LC 2, 48, 156;
WLC 5**
See also BRW 3; BRWC 1; CDBLB 1660-
1789; DA; DAB; DAC; DAM MST, NOV;
DLB 39; RGEL 2; TEA
Sternheim, (William Adolf) Carl
1878-1942 .... **TCLC 8, 223**
See also CA 105; 193; DLB 56, 118; EWL
3; IDTP; RGWL 2, 3
Stevens, Margaret Dean
See Aldrich, Bess Streeter
Stevens, Mark 1951- .... **CLC 34**
See also CA 122
Stevens, R. L.
See Hoch, Edward D.
Stevens, Wallace 1879-1955 . **PC 6; TCLC 3,
12, 45; WLC 5**
See also AMW; AMWR 1; CA 104; 124;
CANR 181; CDALB 1929-1941; DA;
DA3; DAB; DAC; DAM MST, POET;
DLB 54, 342; EWL 3; EXPP; MAL 5;
MTCW 1, 2; PAB; PFS 13, 16; RGAL 4;
TUS; WP
Stevenson, Anne (Katharine) 1933- .. **CLC 7,
33**
See also BRWS 6; CA 17-20R; CAAS 9;
CANR 9, 33, 123; CP 3, 4, 5, 6, 7; CWP;
DLB 40; MTCW 1; RHW
Stevenson, Robert Louis (Balfour)
1850-1894 ... **NCLC 5, 14, 63, 193; PC
84; SSC 11, 51, 126; WLC 5**
See also AAYA 24; BPFB 3; BRW 5;
BRWC 1; BRWR 1; BYA 1, 2, 4, 13; CD-
BLB 1890-1914; CLR 10, 11, 107; DA;
DA3; DAB; DAC; DAM MST, NOV;
DLB 18, 57, 141, 156, 174; DLBD 13;
GL 3; HGG; JRDA; LAIT 1, 3; MAICYA
1, 2; NFS 11, 20; RGEL 2; RGSF 2;
SATA 100; SUFW; TEA; WCH; WLIT 4;
WYA; YABC 2; YAW
Stewart, J(ohn) I(nnes) M(ackintosh)
1906-1994 .... **CLC 7, 14, 32**
See also CA 85-88; 147; CAAS 3; CANR
47; CMW 4; CN 1, 2, 3, 4, 5; DLB 276;
MSW; MTCW 1, 2

Author Index

Warner, Marina 1946- .... **CLC 59, 231**
    See also CA 65-68; CANR 21, 55, 118; CN
    5, 6, 7; DLB 194; MTFW 2005
Warner, Rex (Ernest) 1905-1986 ...... **CLC 45**
    See also CA 89-92; 119; CN 1, 2, 3, 4; CP
    1, 2, 3, 4; DLB 15; RGEL 2; RHW
Warner, Susan (Bogert)
    1819-1885 .... **NCLC 31, 146**
    See also AMWS 18; DLB 3, 42, 239, 250,
    254
Warner, Sylvia (Constance) Ashton
    See Ashton-Warner, Sylvia (Constance)
Warner, Sylvia Townsend
    1893-1978 .. **CLC 7, 19; SSC 23; TCLC**
    131
    See also BRWS 7; CA 61-64; 77-80; CANR
    16, 60, 104; CN 1, 2; DLB 34, 139; EWL
    3; FANT; FW; MTCW 1, 2; RGEL 2;
    RGSF 2; RHW
Warren, Mercy Otis 1728-1814 ..... **NCLC 13**
    See also DLB 31, 200; RGAL 4; TUS
Warren, Robert Penn 1905-1989 .. **CLC 1, 4,**
    6, 8, 10, 13, 18, 39, 53, 59; PC 37; SSC
    4, 58, 126; WLC 6
    See also AITN 1; AMW; AMWC 2; BPFB
    3; BYA 1; CA 13-16R; 129; CANR 10,
    47; CDALB 1968-1988; CN 1, 2, 3, 4;
    CP 1, 2, 3, 4; DA; DA3; DAB; DAC;
    DAM MST, NOV, POET; DLB 2, 48, 152,
    320; DLBY 1980, 1989; EWL 3; INT
    CANR-10; MAL 5; MTCW 1, 2; MTFW
    2005; NFS 13; RGAL 4; RGSF 2; RHW;
    SATA 46; SATA-Obit 63; SSFS 8; TUS
Warrigal, Jack
    See Furphy, Joseph
Warshofsky, Isaac
    See Singer, Isaac Bashevis
Warton, Joseph 1722-1800 ... **LC 128; NCLC**
    118
    See also DLB 104, 109; RGEL 2
Warton, Thomas 1728-1790 .... **LC 15, 82**
    See also DAM POET; DLB 104, 109, 336;
    RGEL 2
Waruk, Kona
    See Harris, (Theodore) Wilson
Warung, Price
    See Astley, William
Warwick, Jarvis
    See Garner, Hugh
Washington, Alex
    See Harris, Mark
Washington, Booker T(aliaferro)
    1856-1915 .... **BLC 1:3; TCLC 10**
    See also BW 1; CA 114; 125; DA3; DAM
    MULT; DLB 345; LAIT 2; RGAL 4;
    SATA 28
Washington, George 1732-1799 .... **LC 25**
    See also DLB 31
Wassermann, (Karl) Jakob
    1873-1934 .... **TCLC 6**
    See also CA 104; 163; DLB 66; EWL 3
Wasserstein, Wendy 1950-2006 . **CLC 32, 59,**
    90, 183; DC 4
    See also AAYA 73; AMWS 15; CA 121;
    129; 247; CABS 3; CAD; CANR 53, 75,
    128; CD 5, 6; CWD; DA3; DAM DRAM;
    DFS 5, 17; DLB 228; EWL 3; FW; INT
    CA-129; MAL 5; MTCW 2; MTFW 2005;
    SATA 94; SATA-Obit 174
Waterhouse, Keith (Spencer) 1929- . **CLC 47**
    See also BRWS 13; CA 5-8R; CANR 38,
    67, 109; CBD; CD 6; CN 1, 2, 3, 4, 5, 6,
    7; DLB 13, 15; MTCW 1, 2; MTFW 2005
Waters, Frank (Joseph) 1902-1995 .. **CLC 88**
    See also CA 5-8R; 149; CAAS 13; CANR
    3, 18, 63, 121; DLB 212; DLBY 1986;
    RGAL 4; TCWW 1, 2
Waters, Mary C. .... **CLC 70**
Waters, Roger 1944- .... **CLC 35**

Watkins, Frances Ellen
    See Harper, Frances Ellen Watkins
Watkins, Gerrold
    See Malzberg, Barry N(athaniel)
Watkins, Gloria Jean
    See hooks, bell
Watkins, Paul 1964- .... **CLC 55**
    See also CA 132; CANR 62, 98
Watkins, Vernon Phillips
    1906-1967 .... **CLC 43**
    See also CA 9-10; 25-28R; CAP 1; DLB
    20; EWL 3; RGEL 2
Watson, Irving S.
    See Mencken, H. L.
Watson, John H.
    See Farmer, Philip Jose
Watson, Richard F.
    See Silverberg, Robert
Watts, Ephraim
    See Horne, Richard Henry Hengist
Watts, Isaac 1674-1748 .... **LC 98**
    See also DLB 95; RGEL 2; SATA 52
Waugh, Auberon (Alexander)
    1939-2001 .... **CLC 7**
    See also CA 45-48; 192; CANR 6, 22, 92;
    CN 1, 2, 3; DLB 14, 194
Waugh, Evelyn 1903-1966 ... **CLC 1, 3, 8, 13,**
    19, 27, 44, 107; SSC 41; WLC 6
    See also AAYA 78; BPFB 3; BRW 7; CA
    85-88; 25-28R; CANR 22; CDBLB 1914-
    1945; DA; DA3; DAB; DAC; DAM MST,
    NOV, POP; DLB 15, 162, 195; EWL 3;
    MTCW 1, 2; MTFW 2005; NFS 13, 17;
    RGEL 2; RGSF 2; TEA; WLIT 4
Waugh, Evelyn Arthur St. John
    See Waugh, Evelyn
Waugh, Harriet 1944- .... **CLC 6**
    See also CA 85-88; CANR 22
Ways, C.R.
    See Blount, Roy, Jr.
Waystaff, Simon
    See Swift, Jonathan
Webb, Beatrice (Martha Potter)
    1858-1943 .... **TCLC 22**
    See also CA 117; 162; DLB 190; FW
Webb, Charles 1939- .... **CLC 7**
    See also CA 25-28R; CANR 114, 188
Webb, Charles Richard
    See Webb, Charles
Webb, Frank J. .... **NCLC 143**
    See also DLB 50
Webb, James, Jr.
    See Webb, James
Webb, James 1946- .... **CLC 22**
    See also CA 81-84; CANR 156
Webb, James H.
    See Webb, James
Webb, James Henry
    See Webb, James
Webb, Mary Gladys (Meredith)
    1881-1927 .... **TCLC 24**
    See also CA 182; 123; DLB 34; FW; RGEL
    2
Webb, Mrs. Sidney
    See Webb, Beatrice (Martha Potter)
Webb, Phyllis 1927- .... **CLC 18**
    See also CA 104; CANR 23; CCA 1; CP 1,
    2, 3, 4, 5, 6, 7; CWP; DLB 53
Webb, Sidney (James) 1859-1947 .. **TCLC 22**
    See also CA 117; 163; DLB 190
Webber, Andrew Lloyd
    See Lloyd Webber, Andrew
Weber, Lenora Mattingly
    1895-1971 .... **CLC 12**
    See also CA 19-20; 29-32R; CAP 1; SATA
    2; SATA-Obit 26
Weber, Max 1864-1920 .... **TCLC 69**
    See also CA 109; 189; DLB 296

Webster, John 1580(?)-1634(?) ...... **DC 2; LC**
    33, 84, 124; WLC 6
    See also BRW 2; CDBLB Before 1660; DA;
    DAB; DAC; DAM DRAM, MST; DFS
    17, 19; DLB 58; IDTP; RGEL 2; WLIT 3
Webster, Noah 1758-1843 .... **NCLC 30**
    See also DLB 1, 37, 42, 43, 73, 243
Wedekind, Benjamin Franklin
    See Wedekind, Frank
Wedekind, Frank 1864-1918 .... **TCLC 7**
    See also CA 104; 153; CANR 121, 122;
    CDWLB 2; DAM DRAM; DLB 118; EW
    8; EWL 3; LMFS 2; RGWL 2, 3
Wehr, Demaris .... **CLC 65**
Weidman, Jerome 1913-1998 .... **CLC 7**
    See also AITN 2; CA 1-4R; 171; CAD;
    CANR 1; CD 1, 2, 3, 4, 5; DLB 28
Weil, Simone (Adolphine)
    1909-1943 .... **TCLC 23**
    See also CA 117; 159; EW 12; EWL 3; FW;
    GFL 1789 to the Present; MTCW 2
Weininger, Otto 1880-1903 .... **TCLC 84**
Weinstein, Nathan
    See West, Nathanael
Weinstein, Nathan von Wallenstein
    See West, Nathanael
Weir, Peter (Lindsay) 1944- .... **CLC 20**
    See also CA 113; 123
Weiss, Peter (Ulrich) 1916-1982 .. **CLC 3, 15,**
    51; DC 36; TCLC 152
    See also CA 45-48; 106; CANR 3; DAM
    DRAM; DFS 3; DLB 69, 124; EWL 3;
    RGHL; RGWL 2, 3
Weiss, Theodore (Russell)
    1916-2003 .... **CLC 3, 8, 14**
    See also CA 9-12R; 189; 216; CAAE 189;
    CAAS 2; CANR 46, 94; CP 1, 2, 3, 4, 5,
    6, 7; DLB 5; TCLE 1:2
Welch, (Maurice) Denton
    1915-1948 .... **TCLC 22**
    See also BRWS 8, 9; CA 121; 148; RGEL
    2
Welch, James (Phillip) 1940-2003 ..... **CLC 6,**
    14, 52, 249; NNAL; PC 62
    See also CA 85-88; 219; CANR 42, 66, 107;
    CN 5, 6, 7; CP 2, 3, 4, 5, 6, 7; CPW;
    DAM MULT, POP; DLB 175, 256; LATS
    1:1; NFS 23; RGAL 4; TCWW 1, 2
Weldon, Fay 1931- . **CLC 6, 9, 11, 19, 36, 59,**
    122
    See also BRWS 4; CA 21-24R; CANR 16,
    46, 63, 97, 137; CDBLB 1960 to Present;
    CN 3, 4, 5, 6, 7; CPW; DAM POP; DLB
    14, 194, 319; EWL 3; FW; HGG; INT
    CANR-16; MTCW 1, 2; MTFW 2005;
    RGEL 2; RGSF 2
Wellek, Rene 1903-1995 .... **CLC 28**
    See also CA 5-8R; 150; CAAS 7; CANR 8;
    DLB 63; EWL 3; INT CANR-8
Weller, Michael 1942- .... **CLC 10, 53**
    See also CA 85-88; CAD; CD 5, 6
Weller, Paul 1958- .... **CLC 26**
Wellershoff, Dieter 1925- .... **CLC 46**
    See also CA 89-92; CANR 16, 37
Welles, (George) Orson 1915-1985 .. **CLC 20,**
    80
    See also AAYA 40; CA 93-96; 117
Wellman, John McDowell 1945- ...... **CLC 65**
    See also CA 166; CAD; CD 5, 6; RGAL 4
Wellman, Mac
    See Wellman, John McDowell; Wellman,
    John McDowell
Wellman, Manly Wade 1903-1986 ... **CLC 49**
    See also CA 1-4R; 118; CANR 6, 16, 44;
    FANT; SATA 6; SATA-Obit 47; SFW 4;
    SUFW
Wells, Carolyn 1869(?)-1942 .... **TCLC 35**
    See also CA 113; 185; CMW 4; DLB 11

Literary Criticism Series
Cumulative Topic Index

This index lists all topic entries in Gale's *Children's Literature Review* (CLR), *Classical and Medieval Literature Criticism* (CMLC), *Contemporary Literary Criticism* (CLC), *Drama Criticism* (DC), *Literature Criticism from 1400 to 1800* (LC), *Nineteenth-Century Literature Criticism* (NCLC), *Short Story Criticism* (SSC), and *Twentieth-Century Literary Criticism* (TCLC). The index also lists topic entries in the Gale Critical Companion Collection, which includes the following publications: *The Beat Generation* (BG), *Feminism in Literature* (FL), *Gothic Literature* (GL), and *Harlem Renaissance* (HR).

NCLC Cumulative Nationality Index

DUTCH

Multatuli (Eduard Douwes Dekker) **165**

ENGLISH

Ainsworth, William Harrison **13**
Arnold, Matthew **6, 29, 89, 126, 218**
Arnold, Thomas **18**
Austen, Jane **1, 13, 19, 33, 51, 81, 95, 119, 150, 207, 210**
Bage, Robert **182**
Bagehot, Walter **10**
Barbauld, Anna Laetitia **50, 185**
Barham, Richard Harris **77**
Barnes, William **75**
Beardsley, Aubrey **6**
Beckford, William **16, 214**
Beddoes, Thomas Lovell **3, 154**
Bentham, Jeremy **38**
Blake, William **13, 37, 57, 127, 173, 190, 201**
Blind, Mathilde **202**
Bloomfield, Robert **145**
Borrow, George (Henry) **9**
Bowles, William Lisle **103**
Brontë, Anne **4, 71, 102**
Brontë, Charlotte **3, 8, 33, 58, 105, 155, 217**
Brontë, Emily (Jane) **16, 35, 165**
Brontë, (Patrick) Branwell **109**
Browning, Elizabeth Barrett **1, 16, 61, 66, 170**
Browning, Robert **19, 79**
Bulwer-Lytton, Edward (George Earle Lytton) **1, 45**
Burney, Fanny **12, 54, 107**
Burton, Richard F(rancis) **42**
Byron, George Gordon (Noel) **2, 12, 109, 149**
Carlyle, Jane Welsh **181**
Carlyle, Thomas **22, 70**
Carroll, Lewis **2, 53, 139**
Clare, John **9, 86**
Clough, Arthur Hugh **27, 163**
Cobbett, William **49**
Coleridge, Hartley **90**
Coleridge, Samuel Taylor **9, 54, 99, 111, 177, 197**
Coleridge, Sara **31**
Collins, (William) Wilkie **1, 18, 93**
Cowper, William **8, 94**
Crabbe, George **26, 121**
Craik, Dinah Maria (Mulock) **38**
Cumberland, Richard **167**
Dacre, Charlotte **151**
Darwin, Charles **57**
Darwin, Erasmus **106**
De Quincey, Thomas **4, 87, 198**
Dickens, Charles (John Huffam) **3, 8, 18, 26, 37, 50, 86, 105, 113, 161, 187, 203, 206, 211, 217**
Disraeli, Benjamin **2, 39, 79**
D'Israeli, Isaac **217**
Dobell, Sydney Thompson **43**
Du Maurier, George **86**
Dyer, George **129**
Eden, Emily **10**
Eliot, George **4, 13, 23, 41, 49, 89, 118, 183, 199, 209**
FitzGerald, Edward **9, 153**
Forster, John **11**
Froude, James Anthony **43**
Gaskell, Elizabeth Cleghorn **5, 70, 97, 137, 214**
Gilpin, William **30**
Gladstone, William Ewart **213**
Godwin, William **14, 130**
Gore, Catherine **65**
Hallam, Arthur Henry **110**
Hamilton, Elizabeth **153**
Haydon, Benjamin Robert **146**
Hays, Mary **114**
Hazlitt, William **29, 82**
Hemans, Felicia **29, 71**
Holcroft, Thomas **85**
Hood, Thomas **16**

Hopkins, Gerard Manley **17, 189**
Horne, Richard Hengist **127**
Horne Tooke, John **195**
Hughes, Thomas **207**
Hunt, (James Henry) Leigh **1, 70**
Huxley, T(homas) H(enry) **67**
Inchbald, Elizabeth **62**
Ingelow, Jean **39, 107**
Jefferies, (John) Richard **47**
Jerrold, Douglas William **2**
Jewsbury, Geraldine (Endsor) **22**
Keats, John **8, 73, 121**
Keble, John **87**
Kemble, Fanny **18**
Kingsley, Charles **35**
Kingsley, Henry **107**
Lamb, Charles **10, 113**
Lamb, Lady Caroline **38**
Lamb, Mary **125**
Landon, Letitia Elizabeth **15**
Landor, Walter Savage **14**
Lear, Edward **3**
Lee, Sophia **191**
Lennox, Charlotte Ramsay **23, 134**
Levy, Amy **59, 203**
Lewes, George Henry **25, 215**
Lewis, Matthew Gregory **11, 62**
Linton, Eliza Lynn **41**
Macaulay, Thomas Babington **42**
Malthus, Thomas Robert **145**
Marryat, Frederick **3**
Martineau, Harriet **26, 137**
Mayhew, Henry **31**
Mill, Harriet (Hardy) Taylor **102**
Mill, John Stuart **11, 58, 179**
Mitford, Mary Russell **4**
Montagu, Elizabeth **117**
More, Hannah **27, 141**
Morris, William **4**
Newman, John Henry **38, 99**
Norton, Caroline **47, 205**
Oliphant, Laurence **47**
Opie, Amelia **65**
Paine, Thomas **62**
Pater, Walter (Horatio) **7, 90, 159**
Patmore, Coventry Kersey Dighton **9**
Peacock, Thomas Love **22**
Percy, Thomas **95**
Piozzi, Hester Lynch (Thrale) **57**
Planché, James Robinson **42**
Polidori, John William **51**
Radcliffe, Ann (Ward) **6, 55, 106**
Reade, Charles **2, 74**
Reeve, Clara **19**
Reynolds, John Hamilton **146**
Robertson, Thomas William **35**
Robinson, Henry Crabb **15**
Robinson, Mary **142**
Rogers, Samuel **69**
Rossetti, Christina (Georgina) **2, 50, 66, 186**
Rossetti, Dante Gabriel **4, 77**
Sala, George Augustus **46**
Shelley, Mary Wollstonecraft (Godwin) **14, 59, 103, 170**
Shelley, Percy Bysshe **18, 93, 143, 175**
Smith, Charlotte (Turner) **23, 115**
Southey, Robert **8, 97**
Surtees, Robert Smith **14**
Symonds, John Addington **34**
Tennyson, Alfred **30, 65, 115, 202**
Thackeray, William Makepeace **5, 14, 22, 43, 169, 213**
Thelwall, John **162**
Tonna, Charlotte Elizabeth **135**
Trelawny, Edward John **85**
Trollope, Anthony **6, 33, 101, 215**
Trollope, Frances **30**
Warton, Joseph **118**
Williams, Helen Maria **135**
Wood, Mrs. Henry **178**
Wordsworth, Dorothy **25, 138**
Wordsworth, William **12, 38, 111, 166, 206**
Yearsley, Ann **174**

FILIPINO

Rizal, José **27**

FINNISH

Kivi, Aleksis **30**
Lonnrot, Elias **53**
Runeberg, Johan **41**

FRENCH

Augier, Emile **31**
Balzac, Honoré de **5, 35, 53, 153**
Banville, Théodore (Faullain) de **9**
Barbey d'Aurevilly, Jules-Amédée **1, 213**
Baudelaire, Charles **6, 29, 55, 155**
Becque, Henri **3**
Beranger, Pierre Jean de **34**
Bertrand, Aloysius **31**
Borel, Pétrus **41**
Chamisso, Adelbert von **82**
Chateaubriand, François René de **3, 134**
Comte, Auguste **54**
Constant (de Rebecque), (Henri) Benjamin **6, 182**
Corbière, Tristan **43**
Crèvecoeur, Michel Guillaume Jean de **105**
Daudet, (Louis Marie) Alphonse **1**
Delacroix, Eugene **133**
Desbordes-Valmore, Marceline **97**
Dumas, Alexandre (fils) **9**
Dumas, Alexandre (pere) **11, 71**
Duras, Claire de **154**
Feuillet, Octave **45**
Flaubert, Gustave **2, 10, 19, 62, 66, 135, 179, 185**
Fourier, Charles **51**
Fromentin, Eugène (Samuel Auguste) **10, 125**
Gaboriau, Émile **14**
Gautier, Théophile **1, 59**
Genlis, Stéphanie-Félicité de **166**
Gobineau, Joseph-Arthur **17**
Goncourt, Edmond (Louis Antoine Huot) de **7**
Goncourt, Jules (Alfred Huot) de **7**
Hugo, Victor (Marie) **3, 10, 21, 161, 189**
Joubert, Joseph **9**
Kock, Charles Paul de **16**
Laclos, Pierre Ambroise François **4, 87**
Laforgue, Jules **5, 53**
Lamartine, Alphonse (Marie Louis Prat) de **11, 190**
Lautréamont **12, 194**
Leconte de Lisle, Charles-Marie-René **29**
Maistre, Joseph **37**
Mallarmé, Stéphane **4, 41, 210**
Maupassant, (Henri René Albert) Guy de **1, 42, 83**
Mérimée, Prosper **6, 65**
Michelet, Jules **31, 218**
Musset, (Louis Charles) Alfred de **7, 150**
Nerval, Gérard de **1, 67**
Nodier, (Jean) Charles (Emmanuel) **19**
Pixérécourt, (René Charles) Guilbert de **39**
Renan, Joseph Ernest **26, 145**
Rimbaud, (Jean Nicolas) Arthur **4, 35, 82**
Sade, Donatien Alphonse François **3, 47**
Sainte-Beuve, Charles Augustin **5**
Sand, George **2, 42, 57, 174**
Scribe, (Augustin) Eugène **16**
Senancour, Etienne Pivert de **16**
Staël-Holstein, Anne Louise Germaine Necker **3**
Stendhal **23, 46, 178**
Sue, Eugene **1**
Taine, Hippolyte Adolphe **15**
Tocqueville, Alexis (Charles Henri Maurice Clérel Comte) de **7, 63**
Vallès, Jules **71**
Verlaine, Paul (Marie) **2, 51**
Vigny, Alfred (Victor) de **7, 102**
Villiers de l'Isle Adam, Jean Marie Mathias Philippe Auguste **3**

GERMAN

Arnim, Achim von (Ludwig Joachim von Arnim) **5, 159**
Arnim, Bettina von **38, 123**
Auerbach, Berthold **171**
Bonaventura **35**
Börne, Ludwig **193**
Büchner, (Karl) Georg **26, 146**
Chamisso, Adelbert von **82**
Claudius, Matthias **75**
Droste-Hülshoff, Annette Freiin von **3, 133**
Eichendorff, Joseph **8**
Engels, Friedrich **85, 114**
Feuerbach, Ludwig **139**
Fichte, Johann Gottlieb **62**
Fontane, Theodor **26, 163**
Fouqué, Friedrich (Heinrich Karl) de la Motte **2**
Freytag, Gustav **109**
Goethe, Johann Wolfgang von **4, 22, 34, 90, 154**
Grabbe, Christian Dietrich **2**
Grimm, Jacob Ludwig Karl **3, 77**
Grimm, Wilhelm Karl **3, 77**
Hauff, Wilhelm **185**
Hebbel, Friedrich **43**
Hegel, Georg Wilhelm Friedrich **46, 151**
Heine, Heinrich **4, 54, 147**
Herder, Johann Gottfried von **8, 186**
Hoffmann, E(rnst) T(heodor) A(madeus) **2, 183**
Hölderlin, (Johann Christian) Friedrich **16, 187**
Humboldt, Alexander von **170**
Humboldt, Wilhelm von **134**
Immermann, Karl (Lebrecht) **4, 49**
Jean Paul **7**
Kant, Immanuel **27, 67**
Kleist, Heinrich von **2, 37**
Klinger, Friedrich Maximilian von **1**
Klopstock, Friedrich Gottlieb **11**
Kotzebue, August (Friedrich Ferdinand) von **25**
La Roche, Sophie von **121**
Ludwig, Otto **4**
Marx, Karl (Heinrich) **17, 114**
Mörike, Eduard (Friedrich) **10, 201**
Novalis **13, 178**
Schelling, Friedrich Wilhelm Joseph von **30**
Schiller, Friedrich von **39, 69, 166**
Schlegel, August Wilhelm von **15, 142**
Schlegel, Friedrich **45**
Schleiermacher, Friedrich **107**
Schopenhauer, Arthur **51, 157**
Schumann, Robert **143**
Storm, (Hans) Theodor (Woldsen) **1, 195**
Tieck, (Johann) Ludwig **5, 46**
Varnhagen, Rahel **130**
Wagner, Richard **9, 119**
Werner, Friedrich Ludwig Zacharias **189**
Wieland, Christoph Martin **17, 177**

GREEK

Foscolo, Ugo **8, 97**
Solomos, Dionysios **15**

HUNGARIAN

Arany, Janos **34**
Liszt, Franz **199**
Madach, Imre **19**
Petofi, Sándor **21**

INDIAN

Chatterji, Bankim Chandra **19**
Dutt, Michael Madhusudan **118**
Dutt, Toru **29**

IRISH

Allingham, William **25**
Banim, John **13**
Banim, Michael **13**
Boucicault, Dion **41**
Carleton, William **3, 199**
Croker, John Wilson **10**
Darley, George **2**
Edgeworth, Maria **1, 51, 158**
Ferguson, Samuel **33**
Griffin, Gerald **7**
Jameson, Anna **43**
Le Fanu, Joseph Sheridan **9, 58**
Lever, Charles (James) **23**
Maginn, William **8**
Mangan, James Clarence **27**
Maturin, Charles Robert **6, 169**
Merriman, Brian **70**
Moore, Thomas **6, 110**
Morgan, Lady **29**
O'Brien, Fitz-James **21**
Sheridan, Richard Brinsley **5, 91**

ITALIAN

Alfieri, Vittorio **101**
Collodi, Carlo **54**
Da Ponte, Lorenzo **50**
Foscolo, Ugo **8, 97**
Gozzi, (Conte) Carlo **23**
Leopardi, Giacomo **22, 129**
Manzoni, Alessandro **29, 98**
Mazzini, Guiseppe **34**
Nievo, Ippolito **22**

JAMAICAN

Seacole, Mary Jane Grant **147**

JAPANESE

Akinari, Ueda **131**
Ichiyō, Higuchi **49**
Motoori, Norinaga **45**

LITHUANIAN

Mapu, Abraham (ben Jekutiel) **18**

MEXICAN

Lizardi, Jose Joaquin Fernandez de **30**
Najera, Manuel Gutierrez **133**

NORWEGIAN

Collett, (Jacobine) Camilla (Wergeland) **22**
Wergeland, Henrik Arnold **5**

POLISH

Fredro, Aleksander **8**
Krasicki, Ignacy **8**
Krasiński, Zygmunt **4**
Mickiewicz, Adam **3, 101**
Norwid, Cyprian Kamil **17**
Slowacki, Juliusz **15**

ROMANIAN

Eminescu, Mihail **33, 131**

RUSSIAN

Aksakov, Sergei Timofeevich **2, 181**
Bakunin, Mikhail (Alexandrovich) **25, 58**
Baratynsky, Evgenii Abramovich **103**
Bashkirtseff, Marie **27**
Belinski, Vissarion Grigoryevich **5**
Bestuzhev, Aleksandr Aleksandrovich **131**
Chaadaev, Petr Iakovlevich **197**
Chernyshevsky, Nikolay Gavrilovich **1**
Derzhavin, Gavriil Romanovich **215**
Dobrolyubov, Nikolai Alexandrovich **5**
Dostoevsky, Fyodor Mikhailovich **2, 7, 21, 33, 43, 119, 167, 202**
Gogol, Nikolai (Vasilyevich) **5, 15, 31, 162**
Goncharov, Ivan Alexandrovich **1, 63**
Granovsky, Timofei Nikolaevich **75**
Griboedov, Aleksandr Sergeevich **129**

Herzen, Aleksandr Ivanovich **10, 61**
Karamzin, Nikolai Mikhailovich **3, 173**
Krylov, Ivan Andreevich **1**
Lermontov, Mikhail Yuryevich **5, 47, 126**
Leskov, Nikolai (Semyonovich) **25, 174**
Nekrasov, Nikolai Alekseevich **11**
Ostrovsky, Alexander **30, 57**
Pavlova, Karolina Karlovna **138**
Pisarev, Dmitry Ivanovich **25**
Pushkin, Alexander (Sergeyevich) **3, 27, 83**
Radishchev, Alexander **190**
Saltykov, Mikhail Evgrafovich **16**
Smolenskin, Peretz **30**
Turgenev, Ivan **21, 37, 122**
Tyutchev, Fyodor **34**
Zhukovsky, Vasily (Andreevich) **35**

SCOTTISH

Baillie, Joanna **2, 151**
Beattie, James **25**
Blair, Hugh **75**
Campbell, Thomas **19**
Carlyle, Thomas **22, 70**
Ferrier, Susan (Edmonstone) **8**
Galt, John **1, 110**
Hogg, James **4, 109**
Jeffrey, Francis **33**
Lockhart, John Gibson **6**
Mackenzie, Henry **41**
Miller, Hugh **143**
Oliphant, Margaret (Oliphant Wilson) **11, 61**
Scott, Walter **15, 69, 110, 209**
Smith, Alexander **59**
Stevenson, Robert Louis (Balfour) **5, 14, 63, 193**
Thomson, James **18**
Wilson, John **5**
Wright, Frances **74**

SERBIAN

Karadžić, Vuk Stefanović **115**

SLOVENIAN

Kopitar, Jernej **117**
Prešeren, Francè **127**

SPANISH

Alarcon, Pedro Antonio de **1**
Bécquer, Gustavo Adolfo **106**
Caballero, Fernan **10**
Castro, Rosalia de **3, 78**
Espronceda, Jose de **39**
Larra (y Sanchez de Castro), Mariano Jose de **17, 130**
Martínez de la Rosa, Francisco de Paula **102**
Tamayo y Baus, Manuel **1**
Zorrilla y Moral, Jose **6**

SWEDISH

Almqvist, Carl Jonas Love **42**
Bremer, Fredrika **11**
Stagnelius, Eric Johan **61**
Tegner, Esaias **2**

SWISS

Amiel, Henri Frederic **4**
Burckhardt, Jacob (Christoph) **49**
Charriere, Isabelle de **66**
Gotthelf, Jeremias **117**
Keller, Gottfried **2**
Lavater, Johann Kaspar **142**
Meyer, Conrad Ferdinand **81**
Wyss, Johann David Von **10**

UKRAINIAN

Shevchenko, Taras **54**

VENEZUELAN

Bello, Andrés **131**

NCLC-218 Title Index

ISBN-13: 978-1-4144-3852-8
ISBN-10: 1-4144-3852-4

90000

9 781414 438528

For Reference

Not to be taken from this room